Transcending Signs

Semiotics, Communication and Cognition

Edited by
Paul Cobley and Kalevi Kull

Volume 35

Transcending Signs

Essays in Existential Semiotics

Edited by
Eero Tarasti

Assistant editors
Sayantan Dasgupta, Paul Forsell and Aleksi Haukka

DE GRUYTER
MOUTON

ISBN 978-3-11-162712-0
e-ISBN (PDF) 978-3-11-078916-4
e-ISBN (EPUB) 978-3-11-078920-1
ISSN 1867-0873

Library of Congress Control Number: 2022941715

Bibliographic information published by the Deutsche Nationalbibliothek
The Deutsche Nationalbibliothek lists this publication in the Deutsche Nationalbibliografie; detailed bibliographic data are available on the internet at http://dnb.dnb.de.

© 2024 Walter de Gruyter GmbH, Berlin/Boston
This volume is text- and page-identical with the hardback published in 2023.
Cover design based on a design by Martin Zech, Bremen
Typesetting: Integra Software Services Pvt. Ltd.

www.degruyter.com

Eero Tarasti
Preface to the anthology *Transcending Signs*
As an Introduction

I am afraid I have to speak a little about myself in order to make this rather extensive collective work comprehensible. This book is, of course, all about existential semiotics. What is existential semiotics, though? That question was asked of me as early as in 1990 by John Gallman of Indiana University Press in Bloomington when he published my first monograph in this project, *Existential Semiotics*, in the series edited by Thomas A. Sebeok. To tell it briefly: existential semiotics is a combination of two issues: existential philosophy and classical semiotics. To return to my own researcher's position: I had a background in both.

As a quite young school student at Normal Lyceum in Helsinki I was interested in German speculative philosophy and started to translate into Finnish, first, Heidegger's *Sein und Zeit* and then Hegel's *Wissenschaft der Logik*. In both I reached the half way point of those heavy books, but then stopped because no one in Finland, at that time, was interested in these scholars. Finnish philosophy was and still is strongly dominated by the so-called Anglo-analytic school and great names such as Georg Henrik von Wright and Jaakko Hintikka. Yet, to tell the truth, I also translated a major part of Rudolph Carnap's *Der logische Aufbau der Welt*, noticing only now that some of its ideas seem to appear in this new doctrine of existential semiotics. However, I am sure that John Gallman understood by 'existential' something like the American transcendentalists, such as Ralph Waldo Emerson, Henry Thoreau etc.

Nevertheless, then came my studies at the University and at Sibelius Academy and I recognized new 'masters'. I discovered the structuralism of Claude Lévi-Strauss, my great idol, whom I subsequently met in Paris and whose lectures and even paths to Brazil I followed. Moreover, in Paris, I became a student of Algirdas Julien Greimas. So, over decades, semiotics was, for me, synonymous with the Paris School. The Greimassian 'system' was so coherent and convincing; indeed, he said to his pupils that if they only faithfully followed *parcours génératif* he could himself sign all the works and analyses of his students and followers. Ultimately, the correct result was guaranteed by the axiomatic method. As early as then I secretly thought and doubted that then there would no longer be any progress in science; all had been already established. *Das Wahre war schon längst gefunden. . . das alte Wahre, fass es an!* said Goethe: The truth was discovered long time ago. . . the old truth, grasp it again!

So I believed I would have the courage to try something on my own and combine those two sources of my scholarly life so far into one synthesis. Thus emerged the first essays in existential semiotics as a new paradigm of semiotics.

By no means did it mean any return to existentialism, albeit I was inspired by such writers as Kierkegaard, Heidegger, Jaspers, Arendt, Sartre, de Beauvoir, Marcel, Wahl etc. I tried to launch new concepts in semiotic vocabulary, terms which one could certainly not find in any published encyclopedia of semiotics, like transcendence, *Dasein,* zemic etc. My first model, in fact, was concerned with *Dasein* (the term which I always left untranslated whether writing in English, French, Italian or Finnish), the world in which we live, surrounded and attacked perpetually by signs. Yet, there was the space beyond *Dasein* which I called in my model transcendence. That is a philosophical, strongly loaded notion; yet, let me give here the easiest definition for it: transcendence is anything which is absent in the world, yet present in our minds. The movement of the subject in transcendence I nominated a transcendental act, leading the subject to either nothingness (the Sartrean *Néant*) via logical operation of 'negation' – or to plenitude or the *pleroma* of the Gnostic philsosophers, via an act of 'affirmation'. These movements led to new categories of signs whereby I by no means wanted to challenge Peirce's categories; accordingly, they were act-signs, pre-signs, post-signs, as-if-signs, genosigns, phenosigns, endosigns, exosigns etc. Moreover, the notion of transcendence is approached by many in the current collection referring naturally also to Kant and his ideas of transcendent and transcendental.

Yet, my model was developed further by reference to other categories of Hegel: *an-sich-sein* and *für-sich-sein*. This was then further elaborated into four categories of being-in-oneself, being-for-oneself plus being-in-myself and being-for- myself. This was possible as a result of borrowing the distinction *Moi* and *Soi* from the French semiotician Jacques Fontanille and the philosopher Paul Ricoeur. Those four cases were put into a semiotic square and so one arrives at entities like $Moi1$ = body, $Moi2$ = person, $Soi2$ =social practice, and $Soi1$ = values and norms. In fact, the model was nothing less than a theory to portray the human mind: in order to define it one needed always minimally these four categories: body, person, practice, and value. Body and person were on the side of the concrete, the *sensible* of Lévi-Strauss, while practice and value were on the side of the abstract, his *intelligible*. *Moi* was the same as Me and *Soi* the society. If one were to follow Theodor Adorno, there would always prevail a conflict between these two categories.

An important step further was that the four modes of being were in a constant flow and change. So they were connected by 'Z', e.g. either moving from concrete to abstract i.e. as sublimation or, *vice versa*, as embodiment. Moreover, I started to call the whole model Zemic by combining the 'Z', the dynamic movement and the 'emic' category invented by the American linguist Kenneth Pike to indicate that the whole process was seen, felt, and experienced from *inside,* as interoceptive, to use Greimas's term. Its opposition would have been etic. i.e. interpretation of the world by external or exteroceptive categories.

A further movement of proper semiotic nature entered when the zemic manifested as particular signs and texts. These could be called sig-zemics. Yet, the relation was not automatically organic – as in Greimas or even in Heidegger – but appeared via multiple varieties of **representation.** There was the movement of 'transduction' from one sig-zemic to another sig-zemic, to use Aleksi Haukka's concept.

Morover, the movement within the zemic was not always the one going from *M1* to *M2* and then to *S2* and *S1,* but it could occur in whatsoever order and, furthermore, with conflicts among these modes. Most recently, a new notion of 'mirror-zemic' has been launched by Sayantan Dasgupta as an interpretation of Sartre's theory of emotions, portraying the emotional reaction to the encounter of an unexpected, other zemic world. That could also be called by *Befindlichkeit* or *Stimmung,* the atmosphere of Heidegger . . . or even the pathetic fallacy of John Ruskin. For Greimas, such an emotional reaction would have been a 'meaning effect', *effet de sens.*

The idea of transcendence underwent yet more subtle development in the supra-zemic (i.e. cognitive) level where we reflect upon the zemic's creation of concepts suitable to it – something like searching for the essence; *Wesen,* as Hegel would say; and therefrom further to what I have called 'radical transcendence' of which we ultimately cannot say anything directly and of which we can speak only by metaphors, as Solomon Marcus proposed. The two epistemological movements were possible: either from 'up to down' via the announcement of transcendence – the case of theology – or from 'down to up', when we believe that transcendence is our mental construction, as Sartre suggests, in order to create a universe which is more complete than our deficient *Dasein.*

This is the point where existential semiotics has reached in 2022. But no one knows what its further growth will be, since, according to Peircean Fallibilism, theories live and change all the time. What, then, would be the position of existential semiotics in relation to already existing schools of thought? For the first, if we adopt the definition of semiotics by Umberto Eco as a two-part issue of signification plus communication, we can see immediately how, in fact, the whole of semiotics is a transcendental art. Signification is where the sign is something which refers to something absent, i.e. transcendental. *Aliquid stat pro aliquo.* Communication: when Mr. A says something to Mr. B, in the well-known model of dialogue proposed by Saussure, he can never be sure whether he is understood – and this is because Mr. B is to him an alien-psychic, i.e. transcendental creature.

Nevertheless, Greimassians might think that once the master has found the truth we need only to study and reflect upon it. Heideggerians may ponder why we should change anything in his teachings. However, many also believe that both continental philosophy and semiotics are in constant progress and renovation. Existential theory may be a response to the challenge of the epistemes of our time. Many applications of the empirical cases in this collection show that new existential methods of analysing cultural phenomena are possible and that they open hitherto unknown avenues. Likewise, in this manner, practical consequences as a kind of social or individual therapy are possible (in the form of post-colonial analysis and ways of resistance; this was already the dream of Greimas himself as early as his *Structural Semantics*). Possibly, the existential approach may finally prove to be that 'surrounding' (*englobant*) theory in which the Paris School once believed but which is now, together with other schools, included and embedded in this new paradigm as its 'surrounded' (*englobé*).

Contents

Eero Tarasti
Preface to the anthology *Transcending Signs* —— V

Figure list —— XV

Jaan Valsiner
Finnish Baroque of existential semiotics: Eero Tarasti's musical synthesis of the voluptuous dance of signs —— 1

Vilmos Voigt
Above and beneath of existential semiotics? —— 7

Solomon Marcus
Exact sciences and the semiotics of existence —— 15

Susan Petrilli and Augusto Ponzio
Voice as transcendence and otherness —— 35

Sami Pihlström
The Transcendental and the Transcendent —— 47

Eero Tarasti
The metaphysical system of existential semiotics —— 77

Kristian Bankov
Being, resistance and post-truth —— 99

Aurel Codoban
From semiotic pragmatism to existential semiotics —— 119

Eric Landowski
Structural, yet existential —— 131

Daniel Charles
Prolegomena on the semiotics of silence (from Jankélévitch to Tarasti) —— 157

Daniel Charles
Myth, music and postmodernity —— 167

Ramūnas Motiekaitis
XX century philosophical paradigms of Japan and the West: A view from Greimassian perspective —— 181

Elżbieta Magdalena Wąsik
Thought and consciousness in language as prerequisites for the existential-identity perception of the human self —— 199

Zdzisław Wąsik
***Umwelt*, *Lebenswelt*, *Dasein* & *monde vécu* – (de)constructing the semiotic cosmology of human existentiality** —— 225

Roberto Mastroianni
Aesthetics and human praxis. Notes on the existential semiotics of Eero Tarasti —— 249

Juha Ojala
Eero Tarasti, existential semiotics, music, and mind. On the existential and cognitive notions of situation —— 259

Otto Lehto
Cosmologies of life after Peirce, Heidegger and Darwin —— 273

Merja Bauters
Existential semiotics, semiosis and emotions —— 289

Sayantan Dasgupta
***The Plane of Dasein*. Existential Semiotics and the problem of the medium** —— 313

Morten Tønnessen
Existential universals. Biosemiosis and existential semiosis —— 327

Francesco Spampinato
Memories of the body and pre-signity in music: Points of contact between Existential Semiotics and Globality of Languages —— 343

Sari Helkala-Koivisto
The existential question between musical and linguistic signification —— 353

Guido Ipsen
Growth and entropy in semiosis: Signs coming full circle —— 373

Daniel Röhe
Creativity in existential semiotics and psychoanalysis —— 389

Pertti Ahonen
Ethnomethodological, symbolic interactionist, semiotic and existential micro-foundations of research on institutions —— 405

Dario Martinelli
"Disturbing quiet people" – on the hyper-bureaucratization and corporatization of universities —— 429

Terri Kupiainen
The modes of being inside (or outside) the value fragment: The application of Tarasti's theory of subject, transcendence and modalities of self to the consumer research —— 459

Jean-Marie Jacono
Existential semiotics and sociology of music —— 481

Reijo Mälkiä
Destruction of cultural heritages: The case of Jerusalem in the Light of Jeremiah's prophecies —— 491

Ricardo Nogueira de Castro Monteiro
From identity to transcendence: A semiotic approach to the survival of the Carolingian cycle in the Brazilian cultural heritage —— 501

Cleisson Melo
Saudade: A semiotic study of the cultural episteme of Brazilian existence —— 521

Rahilya Geybullayeva
Semiolinguistic look on mythology, cultural history and meanings of places in Azerbaijan —— 539

Mattia Thibault
Ludo Ergo Sum: Play, existentialism and the ludification of culture —— 567

Altti Kuusamo
Uncertain signifiers: 'An Affective Phantasy' in Jacopo Pontormo's *Joseph in Egypt* —— 579

Onur, Zeynep and Onur, Ayşe
Existential being of an artist —— 599

Hamid Reza Shairi
An essay on the Persian calligraphy in the light of the theory of existential semiotics by Eero Tarasti —— 607

Vesa Matteo Piludu
Transcending violence: Artistic interpretations of the myths of Kullervo from the Kalevala to Tero Saarinen —— 623

Tristian Evans
Existential soundtracks: Analysing semiotic meanings in minimalist and post-minimal music —— 659

Antonio Santangelo
Existential choices of existential signs. *Love stories, structuralism, and existential semiotics* —— 685

Xiaofang Yan and Yan Liu
Exploration on the construction of existential semiotic theory of film criticism —— 699

Massimo Leone
The transcendent arithmetic of Jesus: An exercise in semiotic reading —— 711

Aleksi Haukka
Descriptions of death in the Book of Job —— 725

Katriina Kajannes
Memory in Eero Tarasti's novel Europe/Perhaps —— 741

Leena Muotio
Varieties of masculine subjectivity in the Finnish modern literature according to Eero Tarasti's Zemic-model —— 757

Massimo Berruti
H.P. Lovecraft's subjectivity: an existential semiotic perspective —— 773

Márta Grabócz
Structure and meaning in music. A dialogue with Greimas —— 801

Bernard Vecchione
Existential semiotics and musical hermeneutics: On musical sense advention —— 819

Mathias Rousselot
Lohengrin by Wagner. Existential narrative-analysis of the Prelude to act I —— 847

Paolo Rosato
The emergence of individual subjects in Western music —— 863

Július Fujak
Existential semiotics and correla(c)tivity of (non-conventional) music (Personal retrospection) —— 883

Lina Navickaitė-Martinelli
When a few Me-Tones meet: Beethoven *à la russe* —— 897

Rodrigo Felicissmo
In the quest of compositional matrices for music themes concerning landscape: Exploring senses as a means for creative processes. Villa-Lobos and his existential signs —— 919

Malgorzata Grajter
Musical arrangement and literary translation as signs: Preserving and renewing cultural heritages —— 941

Joan Grimalt
Gustav Mahler's Wunderhorn orchestral songs: A topical analysis and a semiotic square —— 957

Małgorzata Gamrat
Beyond the signs: Art and an artist's life in Hector Berlioz's Opus 14 —— 983

Aurèlia Pessarrodona
The singing body in a zemic approach: The case of Miguel Garrido —— 999

Notes on contributors —— 1021

Person index —— 1039

Subject index —— 1049

Figure list

Vilmos Voigt

Figure 1   Z-graph —— 9

Kristian Bankov

Figure 1   Model of semiosis and resistance —— 109

Ramūnas Motiekaitis

Figure 1   Metaterms —— 194

Juha Ojala

Figure 1   The communicational and significational structure of narrative music. Adapted from Tarasti (1998: 47; 1996b: 434) —— 265
Figure 2   Network of alternative chains of event, and the actual chain of events. Adapted from Tarasti 1998: 51 —— 268

Otto Lehto

Figure 1   Peirce in ideal-archetypal categories —— 277
Figure 2   Bio-existential semiosis grounded on a space-time phenomenological reality —— 282

Merja Bauters

Figure 1   Two organisms are interacting through the *Soi*. According to Tarasti, only through the *Soi*, the *Ich – Ton* and the *Dich – Ton* can have a connection to each other. It is since only between the *Sois*, the communication proper is possible (Tarasti 2004: 96–97) —— 300
Figure 2   If the interaction is taken as semiosis then *Ich – Ton* and *Dich – Ton*, that is the semiotic selves, are also overlapping with the other organism and also with the *Umwelt* —— 300
Figure 3   Peirce's description of the intensity of ideas from the past to present and from the present towards the future (Peirce 1935: 104 in Valsiner 1998: 243) —— 303
Figure 4   The spiral of semiosis rising from the pull or tension —— 305
Figure 5   The chain of semiosis and the "continuous becoming" —— 306

Francesco Spampinato

Figure 1	Semiotic and pre-semiotic triangle —— 347	
Figure 2	Double pre-signity of bodily memories —— 348	

Daniel Röhe

Figure 1	Imagination and endo-dialogue (introjection) —— 391
Figure 2	endo and exo-dialogue (projection) —— 392
Figure 3	Zemic model as a diagnostic tool in Wozzeck's and Macbeth's —— 397
Figure 4	Spectrum of creativity —— 399

Terri Kupiainen

Figure 1	The categories of subject are being in *Dasein* (Tarasti 2010b, 2009: 1765–1767) —— 464
Figure 2	The value ethics and ontology of subject's *Dasein* from a fragmentation perspective. An application of Tarasti's (2009) theory of subject. Two most important modes and modalities are marked with an oval circle —— 474

Jean-Marie Jacono

Figure 1	M. Musorgsky. *Pictures at an Exhibition*. 'Catacombae', m. 1–7. St. Petersburg: Bessel, 1874 —— 486
Figure 2	Existential semiotic model of *Dasein* and two "transcendental" acts: negation and affirmation (Tarasti 2012: 73) —— 488

Reijo Mälkiä

Figure 1	Theoretical framework —— 492
Figure 2	Zemic in time —— 493
Figure 3	Holy Jerusalem —— 494
Figure 4	*Dasein* and representation of Jerusalem —— 495
Figure 5	Representations and suprazemic —— 499

Ricardo Nogueira de Castro Monteiro

Figure 1	Mario de Andrade's transcription of a *Chegança* he witnessed in 1928 in Natal, RN —— 508
Figure 2	Transcription of a *Chegança* witnessed in 2002 in Pilar, AL —— 509
Figure 3	Photo by the author of Master Bumba's *Chegança*: Captain battling the Moorish King —— 515

| Figure 4 | Reduction of the first phrase resulting in the C – B – A – G line —— 515 |
| Figure 5 | Reduction of the second phrase resulting in the G – F – E – D line —— 516 |

Cleisson Melo

Figure 1	Semiotic Square and Z-Model – Existential Semiotics by Eero Tarasti —— 528
Figure 2	Saudade: Z-Model —— 529
Figure 3	Chega de Saudade – m. 09–24 —— 532
Figure 4	Chega de Saudade – m. 35–50 —— 532
Figure 5	Saudade (1899) by Almeida Junior (197cm x 101cm) —— 534
Figure 6	Saudade (1899) by Almeida Junior – Tears detail —— 535

Altti Kuusamo

Figure 1	Jacopo Pontormo: *Joseph in Egypt*. 1515–1518. Oil on wood. 96,5 x 109,5 cm. National Gallery, London. Photo: By permission of National Gallery, London —— 580
Figure 2	Jacopo Pontormo: *Joseph sold to Potiphar*. 1515. Oil on wood. 61 x 51,6 cm. National Gallery, London. Photo: By permission of National Gallery, London —— 584
Figure 3	Andrea del Sarto: *Joseph in Egypt*. 1515. Oil on wood, 98 x 135 cm. Galleria Palatina, Florence. Photo: Wikimedia Commons —— 590
Figure 4	The basic semic dimensions. The division between euphoria and dysphoria —— 592

Hamid Reza Shairi

Figure 1	Masoud Mohammdzadeh Chamazkoti, Veresk Design Studio, Iran, 2021 —— 613
Figure 2	Masoud Mohammdzadeh Chamazkoti, Veresk Design Studio, Iran, 2021 —— 614
Figure 3	Marzieh Aghili, Art school and Gallery, Iran, 2021 —— 620

Vesa Matteo Piludu

| Figure 1 | Carl Eneas Sjöstrand, *Kullervo Addressing his Sword* (*Kullervo puhuu miekalleen*). 1868, 260 cm, plaster. Finnish National Gallery / The Ateneum Art Museum, Helsinki. Photo: Finnish National Gallery / Hannu Aaltonen —— 629 |
| Figure 2 | Akseli Gallen-Kallela, *Kullervo Cursing* (*Kullervon kirous*), 1899, 184 × 102,5 cm, oil on canvas. Collection: Antell Collections. Finnish National Gallery / The Ateneum Art Museum, Helsinki. Photo: Finnish National Gallery / Pirje Mykkänen and Jouko Könönen —— 636 |

Figure 3	Akseli Gallen-Kallela, *Kullervo Departs for the War* (*Kullervon sotaanlähtö*), 1901, 89 × 128 cm, tempera on canvas. Finnish National Gallery / The Ateneum Art Museum. Helsinki. Photo: Finnish National Gallery / Hannu Pakarinen —— **636**
Figure 4	Akseli Gallen-Kallela, *Kullervo Herding his Wild Flocks* (*Kullervo petokarjoineen*), 1917, 70 × 68 cm, watercolour. Finnish National Gallery / The Ateneum Art Museum. Helsinki. Photo: Finnish National Gallery / Pirje Mykkänen —— **637**
Figure 5	Kullervo (Samuli Poutanen) falling on his knees, doing the descending part of the movement "Kullervo's hand". Tero Saarinen's choreography *Kullervo*, 2015. Photo: Sakari Viika, Finnish National Opera and Ballet and Tero Saarinen Company —— **648**
Figure 6	Kullervo (Samuli Poutanen) and his sister (Terhi Räsänen) doing the ascending part of the movement "Kullervo's hand". Tero Saarinen's choreography *Kullervo*, 2015. Photo: Sakari Viika, Finnish National Opera and Ballet and Tero Saarinen Company —— **648**
Figure 7	Kullervo (Pekka Louhio) and his sister (Johanna Nuutinen) doing the descending part of the movement "Kullervo's hand". Tero Saarinen's choreography *Kullervo*, 2015. Photo: Mikki Kunttu, Finnish National Opera and Ballet and Tero Saarinen Company —— **649**
Figure 8	Kimmo (David Scaratino) and Kullervo (Samuli Poutanen). Tero Saarinen's choreography *Kullervo*, 2015. Photo: Sakari Viika, Finnish National Opera and Ballet & Tero Saarinen Company —— **649**
Figure 9	The death of Kullervo (Samuli Poutanen). Tero Saarinen's choreography *Kullervo*, 2015. Photo: Sakari Viika, Finnish National Opera and Ballet and Tero Saarinen Company —— **650**

Tristian Evans

Figure 1	Reproduction of Tarasti's "paths of existential semiotics" model —— **664**

Xiaofang Yan and Yan Liu

Figure 1	Zemic model (Tarasti 2015:26) —— **704**
Figure 2	Zemic model (Tarasti 2015: 27) —— **704**

Massimo Leone

Figure 1	Cover of *The Childhood of Jesus* by J.M. Coetzee. Penguin books —— **715**

Aleksi Haukka

Figure 1	Negation of Job's *Dasein* —— **733**

Figure list — **XIX**

Leena Muotio

Figure 1 Eero Tarasti's Z-model —— **761**
Figure 2 Comparison of Tarasti's and Bakhtin's models —— **769**

Márta Grabócz

Figure 1 The five archetypal forms proposed by V. Karbusický (1990: 195) —— **805**
Figure 2 General diagram of the articulation of the semes (or affects, topics) in the Andante of Mozart's "Prague" Symphony K. 504 (the numbers on the lines correspond to the evolution and the stages in the unfolding of the sonata form) —— **811**
Figure 3 Diagram of the evolution of the signifieds in the first movement of Beethoven's Waldstein Sonata op.53 divided into four narrative programmes (Grabócz 2009: 188) —— **812**
Figure 4 Diagram by M. Grabócz, after Eero Tarasti's analysis of Chopin's Polonaise-Fantaisie (Op. 61) divided into 10 narrative programmes (Tarasti 1987/1996). This chart was completed by M. Grabócz with regard to the marks of dysphoria or euphoria, thus pointing out the pathemic evolutions of the piece (+ or − signs) —— **813**

Bernard Vecchione

Figure 1 From a OB philosophy to a BO philosophy —— **828**
Figure 2 BO philosophy of enunciating / annunciating —— **830**

Mathias Rousselot

Figure 1 Grail theme. bars 5 to 12, violin 5 —— **848**
Figure 2 Prelude's «shape» —— **850**
Figure 3 Plot «shape» —— **851**
Figure 4 Initial state, bars 1 à 4 —— **851**
Figure 5 Bar 13 —— **852**
Figure 6 Crescendo of the whole orchestra, bars 50–51 —— **852**
Figure 7 Arpeggio of D major, bar 53 —— **852**
Figure 8 Slow dramatic descent bars 57–67 —— **853**
Figure 9 Final state, *stasis* in A major, mesure 68–72 —— **853**
Figure 10 Bars 46–49 —— **856**
Figure 11 Bar 65, reduction of the orchestral score —— **859**

Paolo Rosato

Figure 1 Ich-ton and Otherness —— **865**
Figure 2 *Moi* as the Difference, *Soi* as the Identity —— **867**

Figure 3	Otherness as individuals and/or abstract objects —— 868
Figure 4	Co-operation between *Moi* and *Soi* in filtering external Otherness —— 868
Figure 5	Being-in-itself and the actual subject —— 869
Figure 6	Inner intentionality —— 870
Figure 7	Inner intentionality at the beginning of Plainchant —— 875
Figure 8	Scheme of relationships —— 875
Figure 9	Relationships between categories —— 876
Figure 10	Musical and linguistic *Soi* —— 877
Figure 11	Musical *Moi* and *Soi* —— 879
Figure 12	*Moi* becomes conscious of its own musical individuality —— 880
Figure 13	Modalities with respect to *Soi* and *Moi* —— 881

Július Fujak

| Figure 1 | Alternative model of the musical semiosis —— 893 |

Lina Navickaitė-Martinelli

| Figure 1 | Individuality and standards in the art of a performer (after Eero Tarasti's theory of subjectivity) —— 909 |

Rodrigo Felicissmo

Figure 1	The "Melody of the Mountains" composition technique. The photo by Elisa Bracher represents a music transcription by Rodrigo Felicissimo's artistic sketch work from *Condoriri La derecha* at Andes mountains in Bolivia. The "Mirror of the Mountains Project" – **Bienalsur**, 2016 —— 920
Figure 2	In Elisa Bracher's exhibition, *Field of Bells (dedicated in memory of the educator Sonia Maria Sawaya Botelho Bracher) was* a musical poem installation that traces musical correspondence with the photograph taken by the artist in the Arctic. The piece was created using the method developed by Heitor Villa-Lobos, to musically transpose the sinuosity of the mountains. *Luctus Lutum Exhibition*, **Gallery Raquel Arnaud**, 2015. Field of Bells – an artistic expedition toward landscape, sketches, and music composition: exploring geographical landmarks for creative purposes —— 921
Figure 3	Elisa Bracher, from the "Mirror of the Mountains" series, 2017. Painting on rice paper, 61 x 80 cm —— 923
Figure 4	The "God's Finger" Mountain Range, from *Serra dos Órgãos, Teresópolis, Rio de Janeiro*, Brazil. Photograph by Eric Hess, extracted from (ALMEIDA, [no date]: p.153). Library collection of the Institute of Brazilian Studies from University of São Paulo. Discussion presented at the symposium Sources of Creativity: from Local to Universal. International symposium around Eero Tarasti's work in the eve of his 70th birthday at the Academy of Cultural Heritages and the Semiotic Society of Finland. Mikkeli, 8 – 10 August 2018 —— 927

Figure 5	Silk paper, Villa-Lobos drawing graphic. Note the design of the melodic drawings written by the composer with detail the use of the chromatic scale, located to the left of the drawing. (VILLA-LOBOS, [no date], MVL-HVL millimeter scale 13- FE 833). Collection Villa-Lobos Museum —— 928
Figure 6	The "God's finger" melodic theme. Extracted from the *Cruzeiro* magazine (Pires, 1940) Collection Villa-Lobos Museum —— 929
Figure 7	Transcription of the melody portrayed in the magazine *O Cruzeiro* (Pires, 1940). Villa-Lobos wrote this melody under a drawing of the rock formation of the *Serra dos Órgãos* mountain range —— 929
Figure 8	The solo played by the clarinet cites the theme of the *Serra dos Órgãos* mountains range. Villa-Lobos, *Symphony No. 6* (measures 35–58). Handwritten copy by H. Villa-Lobos, p. 40 —— 930
Figure 9	The introduction of the second solo played by the viola, then the third solo is presented by the horns III, IV. Collection of Villa-Lobos Museum —— 931
Figure 10	The chart above was carried out by fixing the points according to the melody notes obtained by Villa-Lobos. Our version is a retrograded version of the composer process —— 932
Figure 11	Graphic made from the melody notes obtained by Villa-Lobos manuscript of the *Serra dos Órgãos*. Our version shows the resulting design of the simple association of the notes —— 932
Figure 12	The *"zemic model"* into Villa-Lobos compositional technique —— 934

Malgorzata Grajter

Figure 1	An object-oriented model of interactions between sign, interpretant and object (Stecconi 1999: 255; cf. Tarasti 2000: 33) —— 944
Figure 2	Triadic concept of a sign in reference to translation and its adaptation to musical arrangement —— 944
Figure 3	Domestication and foreignization as basic translational strategies described by Friedrich Schleiermacher and Lawrence Venuti —— 946
Figure 4	Invariant core: Stanisław Moniuszko – *Znasz-li ten kraj* op. 73 nr 2, mm. 3–6 [1–4], extracted from transcriptions by: Bernhard Wolff, Henryk Melcer-Szczawiński, Władysław Krogulski, Jan Adam Maklakiewicz, Feliks Grąbczewski and Ignacy Rzepecki (editors), and jazz version by Włodek Pawlik. Author's elaboration —— 948

Joan Grimalt

Figure 1	A semiotic square to classify musical meaning —— 966
Figure 2	Semiotic Square with four isotopies in Mahler's *Wunderhorn* music —— 972

Aurèlia Pessarrodona Pérez

Figure 1 Tarasti's Zemic model (source: Tarasti 2012: 135–138) —— **1002**
Figure 2 Comparision between the portrait of Miguel Garrido and that of José Espejo (source: supplement by Cruz 1777) —— **1004**

Jaan Valsiner
Finnish Baroque of existential semiotics: Eero Tarasti's musical synthesis of the voluptuous dance of signs

Abstract: I wrote this book review in deep appreciation of the lifetime work of Eero Tarasti-- a real artist in science and scientist in art. The tour-de-force through important ideas that the book included was mindboggling and continues to be very stimulating. Eero Tarasti is one of the very best scholars who has grown up on the Finnish granite grounds, while thriving on music and existential ideas of which the present anthology is a good example. He is a fossil in the human sciences who keeps reminding us all about our limits while using the piano instead of powerpoint to make crucial points for our understandings.

Keywords: piano, existentialism, baroque, semiosis

Reading Tarasti is not easy.[1] The author's enormous erudition shows on every page of the book, and his capability of weaving together various ideas into nice new improvisations seems well supported by his unique reliance on music as the inspiration for new ideas. Like the movement of a melody, the text in this book could be considered to approximate *Der Ring des Nibelungen* in its dramatic elaboration of the earlier version of existential semiotics into a transcendental one. Tarasti – much like Wagner – takes the reader through various dramatic expositions of the semiotic square of Algirdas Greimas, arriving at the basic scheme that takes on the form of letter Z (p. 31, and especially in chapter 10 where a new theory of performing arts is offered) of the relating of the personal and the social in the process of semiosis. That scheme – *de facto* a non-linear continuum between different structures of *Moi* and *Soi* – is subsequently applied to various phenomena of cultural construction – music, film, etc.

Tarasti's book is delicious to read, yet for contemporary readers who are used to all kinds of dieting programs – both culinary and intellectual – it includes a thick layer of philosophical and historical accumulations of knowledge. This book is a treat to the philosophically sophisticated reader, while a layperson is likely to find it too complex for easy reading. The author's style of writing lives up

---

[1] Published originally: 2015. Tarasti E. Sein und Schein: Explorations in existential semiotics. *Culture & Psychology* 21 1: 137–141. The Author(s) 2015 Reprints and permissions: sagepub.co.uk/ journalsPermissions.nav. DOI: 10.1177/1354067X15570487

https://doi.org/10.1515/9783110789164-001

to that of a complex musical composition – deep existential philosophical ideas emerge in the middle of chatting about all key figures of semiotics of today and of the past. The personal stories that are interspersed with semiotic analyses are refreshing to the reader.

1 Being-in-myself < > being-for-myself

Tarasti's focus on linking *Moi* ("being-in-myself") and *Soi* ("being-for-myself") constitutes the core of his existential semiotics. In Tarasti's own words,

> My intention was to specify the category of Being by providing this basic modality with new aspects drawn from Kant and Hegel, and to follow the phases of this concept further, from Kierkegaard to Sartre and Fontanelle... Being-in-itself and Being-for-myself were turned into Being-in-and-for-myself in existential semiotics. (p. 29)

This kind of intellectual tradition is deeply grounded in European cultural traditions, and might not resonate very easily with the philosophical traditions of the Anglo-Saxon world. Yet it links well with cultural psychology today, starting from the domain of dialogical self (Hermans & Gieser: 2012), and ending with the dynamic semiosis side of the field (Valsiner: 2014). Tarasti's focus on the *Moi*< >*Soi* tensions and dynamics is a welcome innovation to a field where categorizations often dominate over the study of processes that generate new subjective moments in our lives.

2 Dynamics of signs

Tarasti's important innovation is in turning the traditionally static focus of semiotics into a dynamic theoretical system. This gives promise – for connection with psychology – yet it also brings challenges. The label *existential* is in some sense a misnomer, since the dynamics of sign mediation includes both the exploration of the inner meaning systems of the person, as well as that of a society. What unifies all levels is the focus on dynamics:

> Existential semiotics explores the life of signs from within. Unlike most previous semiotics, which investigated only the conditions of particular meanings, existential semiotics studies phenomena in their uniqueness. It studies signs in movement and thus in flux, that is, as signs becoming signs, and defined as pre-signs, act-signs, and post-signs... Completely new sign categories emerge in the tension between reality, as *Dasein*, and whatever lies

beyond it. We have to make a new list of categories in the side of that once done by Peirce. Such new signs so far discovered are, among others, trans-signs, endo- and exo-signs, quasi-signs (or as-if-signs), and pheno/geno-signs. (p. 8)

There is much new in Tarasti's book. Still most of the novelties have the character of little inventions while the author is chasing answers to basic questions. The latter include the need to make sense of communication.

3 New models of communication

New semiotics needs new theory of communication. Tarasti provides it (pp. 137–139), overcoming the centrality of the message and the person, in favour of the context. The examples he provides (p. 138) are three models, all of which involve directional relation between signs. The relations can change in time, creating new configurations. Furthermore, there is a coordinated relation between the message and the context, both of which are constructed:

> an artist or a politician, when launching new ideas, at the same time creates the environment that is appropriate for them. Wagner creates Bayreuth, functionalists Bauhaus, semioticians Imatra,[2] and so on. . . . It is hard to pay equal attention to both message and context. If the context is underlied, then no attention is given to the message which then acts as a side-effect. . . . Any element can cease to be pertinent if attention is focused on other elements that surround it. (pp. 137–138)

There is much support to Tarasti's effort to re-think communication theory. The focus on coordination in the making of the message and its context – or, in other terms, creating the frame – is a key issue in all our communication processes. The attempted power of mass media testifies for that. Yet it also leads to semiotic crisis (semiocrisis):

> In general semiocrisis means that the visible, observable signs of social life do not correspond to its immanent structures. Signs have lost their isotopies, their connections to their true meanings. Benevolent media try to improve the situation, returning to the stable good times before the semiocrisis. (p. 153)

If Charles Sanders Peirce were to comment on that situation, he would point out that it is precisely the openness of signs for new situations that includes rendering themselves useless. By making the person free from here-and-now, signs

---

[2] Tarasti himself has been the key figure in this history of semiotics summer schools, well documented in the book.

make themselves alienated from their immediate relations with phenomena. Semiocrisis can be aggravated by the pollution of the semiosphere (p. 148). How is "pollution control" possible? Tarasti's answer is – through resistance.

4 Semiotics of resistance

A whole chapter (chapter 9) is dedicated to semiotic of resistance. This is appropriate. In social contexts involving active meaning-makers it is the role of signs to correct the avalanche of social suggestions encoded in a multiplicity of sign forms. We live in a cloud of semiotic dust that all sources of communication throw at us as more or less explicit social suggestions. We resist the suggestions – encoded through signs – by other signs. The process of communication is not that of a "communion" but that of a duel – fought by signs and counter-signs. The loser is to "participate in the society" that the winner has defined. The existential becomes consumeristic (Brinkmann: 2008), and the genre of entertainment becomes a basic need. Semiotics is existential also in the sense of the survival of the signifying powers, not just of the human beings.

Resistance makes negation possible. This idea is hidden in Tarasti's coverage – the 13 types of negation appear long before (p. 11) in the book than the coverage of resistance (chapter 9). Furthermore, negation of the negation which is the cornerstone of any systematically dialectical perspective that is to explain the emergence of novelty, is not systematically covered. Tarasti's teacher – Algridas Greimas – did not focus on novelty, that was left to Tarasti's existential semiotics of year 2000 which now, 14 years later, becomes transcendental. In that move, resistance – and negation based on it – are crucial theoretical ideas, yet the synthesis through the second negation is not elaborated.[3] It is implied, though. Tarasti's transcendental semiotics recognizes the movement in time from what is to what is not (yet), but it does not chart out any trajectory of development. Developmental semiotics may need to come after its transcendental relative, perhaps.

---

[3] For instance, none of the 13 negation types on p. 11 are set up to work upon one another. They could – parody of destruction (both listed as negation types) can create a basis for new construction of idea. We see many examples of parody in efforts to overcome social fetishes and stupidities, in art, literature, and theatre.

5 The music of food

Semioticians like to eat well. This is evident in Tarasti's coverage of semiotics of food and eating. The important feature of food-related actions is the construction of elaborate meaningful foods with the ultimate goal of their destruction. All the sophisticated preparations of fancy foods of deep symbolic meanings – the gourmet at its best – end up devoured by the receiving human beings who, despite using the sophisticated cutlery and dishes for eating, demolish the gentle foods in most barbarous ways. Culture of foods ends at the act of mastication:

> The undeniable sad truth is that the semiotic sign of food is at its inception doomed to destruction, and that this species of signs does not have the same stability as, say, those of painting, literature or architecture. Gastronomy should thus be equated with the performing arts of music, theatre, dance, and the like, whose signs are always bound with time that is understood not only as fleeting and fragile moments but as the very physical basis on which they subsist (p. 247)

Yet before the food reaches the mouth it is an arena of cultural construction in many ways. Semioticians would always have their daily bread if they deal with semiotics of foods. Adding to it the possible analyses of the ways foods become to signify something else – patriotism, feeling at home, or negotiation of one's beauty – and we have a full research program for future semioticians to consume.

Tarasti points to the similarity of eating and musical performance (p. 246), and this analogy is valid. A musician works with scores – written version of music – and needs to recreate the musical piece in practice, with one's own interpretation. Similarly, a person who cooks may use a recipe, yet the precise creation of the food involves improvisation. Going to a restaurant is similar to an evening at a concert, and devouring a hamburger in a street corner fast-food place is the analogue of a use of one's MP3 player.

Yet the analogy continues – following Marcel Proust, Tarasti adds the activity of receiving guests into the same category (p. 256). Here I have doubts – for sure such activity is transient, but the destructive component (as is present in the case of foods) might not be similar at all.

6 Signs as transient relations

Signs are transient – they change from floating to stable. The roots of this modification of otherwise static semiotic schemes go back to the disputes between Schelling and Hegel in early 19th century (p. 269), with further support from our contemporary John Deely (p. 272). The critical innovation comes on p. 274 –

changing the significant and signifie relation, a static borrowing from de Saussure, into a membrane:

Signifiant
x x ↑ x x ↑ x x
Signifié

Yet the arrows are oriented only in one direction. And what is missing is a set of conditions – catalytic circumstances (Cabell & Valsiner: 2014) perhaps – that could reverse the direction of these arrows.

Nevertheless, the new focus on relationship allows Tarasti to integrate Jakob von Uexküll's biosemiotic model of semiosis into his programme of existential semiotics. Biological terms are seductive – Tarasti elaborates on the notion of semiogerm (pp. 278–279), but fails to take the implications of that notion to its full potentials. He also fails to understand the full meaning of Theodor Lipps' notion of *Einfühlung* (p. 279) considering it "enlivening by acquaintance", and focusing on *Ausfühlung* instead. If one remains committed to von Uexküll's Funtionskreis idea, the feeling into the world feeds further into new signs that emerge from that feeling.

In sum, Eero Tarasti has created his Magnum Opus. He has benefitted from his deep knowledge of music, and has used that knowledge at every junction of his theory building. The book is similar to a complex orchestra performance in which different groups of instruments are given less or more voice at different phases of the unfolding of the story by the conductor who is constantly ready to improvise. The result is a remarkable contribution to the sphere of understanding of the complexity of the human mind. The author allows no cheap shortcut to the superficial interests of the unprepared crowds. And that is a major contribution in the 21st century to any science of the human beings.

References

Brinkmann, Svend. 2008. Changing psychologies in the transition from industrial society to consumer society. *History of the Human Sciences* 21(2). 85–110.
Cabell, Kenneth R. & Jaan Valsiner. 2014. *The catalyzing mind*. New York, NY: Springer.
Hermans, Hubert J.M. & Thorsten Gieser. 2012. *Handbook of the dialogical self theory*. Cambridge, UK: Cambridge University Press.
Valsiner, Jaan. 2014. *Invitation to cultural psychology*. London, UK: Sage.

Vilmos Voigt
Above and beneath of existential semiotics?

Abstract: By about 2000 Eero Tarasti outlined the semiotic of music. He was following the mainstream semiotics, first of all the French schools of semiotics. By about 2010 he turned towards the semiotic theory. He was using existential philosophy in the proper sense of existentialism (from Kierkegaard to Sartre). Tarasti constructed a complex semiotics, declaring the Z-graph as the base of sign process. At the same time (from 2000 to 2010) international semiotics has developed into different directions. Some chapters, as zoosemiotics changed into semiotics of living signs (see the actual school of Tartu semiotics). and the Lotman school of literary texts gave place to general semiotics of culture. There are some completely new attempts of semiotic theory (as e.g, by Alain Badiou).

The existential semiotics of Tarasti can be seen as continuation of modern semiotics and as beginning of a new trend. It is necessary to place it into the general panorama of semiotics: "above" and "beneath".

Keywords: philosophy, phenomenology, history of ideas, semiotic square

It was a surprising fact that only about ten years ago there was a Finnish musicologist, Eero Tarasti (2000) who has started to build up a "philosophy of semiotics". If we take into account only the years of the actual, international semiotics there could have been other candidates for the same task. The American Charles Sanders Peirce and, to a lesser degree, Charles Morris were trained in philosophy (mostly in pragmatism). Among the founding fathers of the 20th-century European linguistic semiotics, Ferdinand de Saussure was not interested in philosophy, but the Danish linguist, Louis Hjelmslev, as well as his French follower, Roland Barthes had a "philosophic vein". In Paris, there was always a firm tendency to connect social sciences with philosophy. Leading scholars, like Claude Lévi-Strauss, who was not a philosopher at all, sometimes acted as such, and their critics accepted that view too. Among the *coryphaei* of semiotics, A. J. Greimas or Julia Kristeva, in their summarizing essays, came close to general statements – but not trespassing into domains of philosophy. As for the actual French philosophy, Paul Ricoeur and Jacques Derrida are often driving quasi-philosophical discourse of postmodernism, and the references to them (by e.g. Richard Rorty, Paul de Man, Arthur C. Danto and others, who are more or less professional philosophers) do not refrain from philosophical argumentation – still they did not suggest any proper theory of semiotics. Famous protagonists of contemporary international semiotics (as e.g. Thomas A. Sebeok or Yury Lotman) were born and sworn empiricists, far away from any speculative statements. German hermeneuticians of yesterday (first of all, Hans-Georg Gadamer) were influential philosophers, but they did not want to draw a theory for semiotics.

Among prominent contemporary semioticians (in the proper sense of the word), there are few philosophers (e.g. Lucia Santaella, John Deely or Augusto Ponzio), who combine the study of signs with philosophy – but hitherto without suggesting a strict philosophical theory of semiotics.

Nevertheless, French philosophers of today and yesterday (as e.g. Emmanuel Lévinas, Maurice Merleau-Ponty or Alain Badiou) have been quoted recently by few semioticians, again, without constructing a theory of semiotics, which is more curious a fact, because Merleau-Ponty or Badiou have elaborated a very wide panorama of epistemology, behaviour, gnoseology etc., and they expressed some straightforward remarks on signs.

Thus was the situation, when Eero Tarasti started to write his theoretical essays (published jointly later in his book *Existential Semiotics*). At that time, he stood alone on the street leading towards a philosophical theory of semiotics. The references in his book (Tarasti 2000) clearly show that the term "existential" was borrowed from Kierkegaard, Heidegger and Sartre. On the theoretical level, it was Heidegger's *opus magnum* (*Sein und Zeit*) and Sartre's phenomenological ontology (*L'être et le néant*) from which the basic terms (*Dasein, negation* etc.) were learned. From the very first moment, Tarasti saw in "sign-processes" a dynamic phenomenon, which exists when the abstract *Being (Sein)* will be an actual (present) one: *Dasein*.

The dynamism in using the signs is as old a suggested method of interpretation as is the semiotics itself. It is a well-known fact that even the famous *aliquid pro aliquo* formula (however, only indirectly!) goes back to Augustine, who interprets the sign as something "bringing the invisible close to the actual interpreter". Throughout the manifold development of Peirce's notions for "sign", the "dynamic interpretation" remained the starting point. When the "late" Peirce (in letters to Lady Welby) lists various existing forms of signs, including vision, copy, trace, omen, oracle, prophecy, prayer, revelation etc., none of those can be understood without a "dynamic" use of the sign. It is another question, how all of those "social phenomena" could be forced into one single model of signs and sign processes.

When Tarasti elaborated his system using the so-called "*Z-graph*", he definitely calculated upon the dynamism of sign processes.

Here the "Ego/Self" (*Moi*) is contrasted with the "It/World" (*Soi*), and the interpreter (*Moi*) depicts the world (*Soi*) in a dynamic way: starting from *Moi1* arriving finally to *Soi1*.

Recently, when Tarasti (2010: 4–5) was also listing a broad set of social and cultural phenomena directed into the four corners of that famous "semiotic square",

```
Moi 1---/Moi 2
(Soi 4)  /  (Soi 3)
        /
Soi 2 /---- Soi 1
(Moi 3)     (Moi 4)
```

Figure 1: Z-graph.

he rendered "primary, kinetic energy, wish" etc. to the upper left corner – "identity, personality, truth, stability" etc. to the upper right corner – "social roles, institutions, use" etc. to the lower-left corner – "norms, values, general codes" to the lower right corner (Figure 1). This list is more than a strictly semiotic systematisation, moreover, it is the panorama of items for coming semiotic investigations.

Tarasti's new viewpoint emanates clearly from the recent survey of his previous statements, pointing out not less than 32 further research topics. Tarasti shows a cascade of references to communication, music, behaviour, social institutions, philosophical and ethical problems etc. Still, I have found in Tarasti's existential semiotics two important topics, which are not present there: animals and gods. I think leaving them outfrom the system is not accidental.

As the "rise and fall" of zoosemiotics in recent sign systems' studies show, there has always been a dilemma in the very heart of the "animal signs" phenomenon. On one hand, everybody is noticing the signs of the appearance of animals. But, on the other hand, we do not know, whether the animals deal with them as signs. And if yes – exactly how? The crucial problem of zoosemiotics is that of the role of the interpreter.

Thomas Sebeok, who started to use the term "zoosemiotics" first in about 1965, described in dozens of interesting papers the "nature and culture" components of signs. Using striking examples (as the "dance of the bees", or lies among the animals, "personal names" in animal communication, etc.), he has always warned the readers from oversimplifying the similarities between human and animal "signs". (See his collected papers: 1991). When Sebeok chose as the model for zoosemiotics the idea of *Umwelt* (by the genial but curious scientist-enthusiast, Jacob von Uexküll), it was only temporary relief from criticism, which later came back to zoosemiotics in a mighties wave. But it is obvious that in human-animal interaction, we find the same use of signs as in "true" human use of signs. To study it, it could be a legitimate chapter of any existential semiotics too.

As for the God/s/~god/s/ -- there was no serious attempt hitherto to describe the semiotics of religion. Handbooks of semiotics testify the strange omission. There exist papers on the semiotics of religious practice, but on "God" there is no good semiotic treatment written. I hold for typical that in the best handbook of international semiotics (Nöth 2000), there is a short chapter on magic, but there is no chapter on religion, and the sporadic references in the handbook to the religion usually speak about theology (and not of g/God/s). Similarly to the case of zoosemiotics, if we do not have a semiotics understanding of g/God/s, it is no obstacle for finding semiotics in the discourses about religion. Thomas Aquinas or John Poinsot wrote hundreds of pages about the classification of signs, connected with theology and logic. But it does not substitute a semiotic understanding of g/God/s. It is easy to show that Nöth's position is not an occasional one. In the otherwise transparent and bulky (751 pages!) recent Russian dictionary of "semiotics of culture" (Makhlina 2009), there is no entry on religion (or on zoosemiotics).

Omitting g/God/s from semiotics at least it is typical in modern times. Augustine, Thomas Aquinas, John Poinsot and others wrote breakthrough works on signs and communication in general, but just for "divine" semiotics, they did not say too much (see the interesting summary by Deely 2009). This is an interesting but complicated topic, so I am not going here into detailed reasoning.

To give an apodictic and very short answer to the question, why g/God/s and animals are absent in the existential semiotics: I think for the animals, there exists the *Soi* and does not exist the *Moi*, and for the g/God/s there exists the *Moi* and does not exist the *Soi*.

Of course, when we, human beings, speak about signs of animals or of g/Gods – we follow the general *Z-graph* without difficulty. In fact, we use there the anthropomorphisation of animal or divine signs: according to its "language", birds expose "bridal" plumage, Buddha has a "thousand arms", all with distinct "gestures". Physicians and veterinarians can equally use the same technique of diagnosis for animal and men. Theologians can speak easily on the attributes of the "Heaven and Hell" or the "seven deadly sins". In a figurative speech, we may say that horses "understand" the wishes of their owners. The "eye" of Almighty God "sees" everything. But in both cases, there are serious logical difficulties concerning such statements. (1) Paul the famous octopus "could" "predict" the results of the 2010 World Cup football matches – for the press. But not for himself. (2) If God "sees" something, he is not a God any more, but a common being of nature. G/god/s must "look" in a different way than we do: they must "read the wishes of the heart" and not the visible signs or the texts. G/god/s used to speak in cryptic and dubious sentences, like the Delphi oracle, knowing more than normal knowledge. When they "speak" our language, they are not G/god/s any more.

Just from a truly "existential" point of view, sign-systems do not work all the time. Dogs and horses do not obey always, they do not understand always. Lost cats and dogs learn "another" names for themselves. Many animals ate their own children – a good example of confusing *Moi/Soi*. Gods do not listen to all prayers. They destroy pious and infamous persons with the same stroke – as it was so often discussed in the history of philosophy. The signs often do not "exist" properly for them.

All the above said remarks are not criticising Tarasti's Z-graph solution. Just the opposite is true. Existential semiotics by its foundation is human semiotics. Its boundaries are the human boundaries. I may know that some rocks are smaller, others are larger. Some are grey, others are of red colour. Natural phenomena can be prominently different – even without the existence of any human observer or interpretant. Human observers or interpretants give name to them, accept their qualities as signs. But rocks are not signs in themselves. They do not "exist", they do not stand for existential semiotics. Eero Tarasti's semiotics is a typical case of social semiotics, in which we – after a long dynamic process – understand and express something. When referring to various fields of human culture, Tarasti enriches the understanding of *Moi* and *Soi*. Today *Soi* is growing so rich, and the *Moi* reflects more and more of it. Today, the signs, sign systems, sign processes are more abundant than ever before. Tarasti's recent studies adequately describe that richness.

When Tarasti sculptured his theory of existential semiotics, he looked back to some of the antecedents of existentialism, first of all, the German phenomenology of Husserl and Dilthey. In German philosophy, as a continuation, we may not claim only for Heidegger. E.g. Gadamer and the new hermeneutics was another continuation of the phenomenology. Tarasti did not follow that road (despite some references). Another possibility for "following up" the actual philosophy opened in the post-war French philosophy, first of all by Maurice Merleau-Ponty. Here I could not go into the analysis of his rich legacy, but I suggest not to forget his "early" views on behaviour (1942) with final remarks on signification, on perception (1945, the English translation much later: 1962) presenting the "World as Being" topic. His paradigmatic essays were collected into a volume (1948) called "Sign and Non-Sign". He published also a short introduction about the "signs" (1960). Today he is world-famous and the interpretations start from his "late" works, e.g. on "visible and invisible" (written between 1959–1961, published posthumously 1964, English translation 1968). When Tarasti introduced his theory of sign-acquisition, the phenomenology of Merleau-Ponty has helped. But now, when the full circle of "world view" and "social institutions" are incorporated into Tarasti's system – an actual re-reading of Merleau-Ponty's works will surprise the reader: how close are to each other the two descriptions of sign processes!

Just in the latest papers of Tarasti (2009), we find another turn in his way towards a theory of semiotics. After a (previous) phase of his endeavour in phenomenological philosophy, he turned back to social phenomena (like Umberto Eco did it in his post-epistemological phase). Frankly, before the last years, instead of that, I was waiting from Tarasti for a more close approach to the excellent late phenomenological French philosophy, both to Merleau-Ponty and Badiou.

It would be a tempting topic to combine or contrast Tarasti's actual view of existential semiotics with their ideas and their developments, but it falls out of the tasks of my recent paper. I just have to show, how productive and how complicated would be that kind of comparison.

One of the early major works of Alain Badiou was his book on "Being and Event". (In French 1988, the late English translation is only from 2006a). The book was written against the mere linguistic understanding of epistemology. (Badiou's earlier work on the subject (1982) was milder against the structuralism). Instead of structural and semiotic methods, he turned towards mathematic models and set theory in order to have a better understanding of the "being". Later (2006b) Badiou extended his model to describe the "world", i.e. the culture and its manifestations. Not only the topics, but his arguments often resemble Tarasti's way of thinking. However, Badiou describes the world – and does not intend to shape a theory of signs. Because his works are well known also in Finland, I hope a special study on Badiou's "semiotics" will be soon elaborated there.

In my paper, I could not give full references to the problems and persons I just have briefly mentioned above. To continue that laconic way of speaking, I have to present the fact of my paper only in one sentence: Tarasti's actual theory of semiotics is good for French phenomenology and it is useless both for "above" and "beneath" of existential philosophy; it does not fit neither for g/God/s/ = "above", nor for the animals, or, more generally, the nature = beneath of existential semiotics. I think the fact is not a loss but a gain to semiotics.

There are several schools of philosophy, and works, which are excellent for one trend, and might be useless for the other. If "existential" semiotics is a good step forward for some schools, the same arguments may be out of context for other approaches. But it is the case in every particular "trend" in sciences. It is beyond any doubt that Tarasti's "existential semiotics" revitalized the philosophical enquiry into semiotics. If we borrow an Old Norse metaphor for qualifying it, we should name it as the *Midgard*-semiotics, *i.e.* a "central" semiotics. But there are other semiotic worlds as well: "above" and "beneath", "before" and "after" of it.

References

Badiou, Alain. 1982. *Théorie du sujet*. Paris: Seuil
Badiou, Alain. 1988. *L'Être et l'Événement*. Paris: Seuil.
Badiou, Alain. 2006a. *Being and Event*. New York: Continuum.
Badiou, Alain. 2006b. *Logiques des mondes*. Tome 2 of L'Être et l'Événement. Paris: Seuil.
Deely, John. 2009. *Augustine & Poinsot. The Protosemiotic Development*. Volume I in the *Postmodernity in Philosophy. A Poinsot Trilogy*. Scranton, PA & London: University of Scranton Press.

Makhlina, Svetlana. 2009. *Slovar' po semiotike kul'tury* [Dictionary of Culture Semiotics]. Sankt-Peterburg: "Iskusstvo – SPB"
Merleau-Ponty, Maurice. 1942. *La structure de comportement*. Paris: Presses Universitaires de France.
Merleau-Ponty, Maurice. 1945. *Phénomenologie de la perception*. Paris: Gallimard.
Merleau-Ponty, Maurice. 1948. *Sens et Non-sens*. Paris: Nagel.
Merleau-Ponty, Maurice. 1960. *Signes*. Paris: Gallimard.
Merleau-Ponty, Maurice. 1962. *Phenomenology of Perception*. London: Routledge and Kegan Paul.
Merleau-Ponty, Maurice. 1964. *Le visible et l'invisible*. Paris: Gallimard.
Merleau-Ponty, Maurice. 1968. *The Visible and the Invisible*. Evanston, Illinois: Northwestern University Press.
Nöth, Winfried. 2000. *Handbuch der Semiotik*. (2., vollständig neu bearbeitete und erweiterte Auflage). Stuttgart/Weimar: Verlag J. B. Metzler.
Sebeok, Thomas A. 1990. *Essays in Zoosemiotics*. (Toronto Semiotic Circle Monographs 5). Toronto: Toronto Semiotic Circle.
Tarasti, Eero. 2000. *Existential Semiotics*. Bloomington: Indiana University Press.
Tarasti, Eero. 2009. *Fondéments de la sémiotique existentielle*. Paris: Harmattan.
Tarasti, Eero. 2010. Olemisen ja subjektin moodit eli 32 teesiä [Modalities of Being and Subject or 32 Theses]. *Synteesi* 29(2). 2–25.

Solomon Marcus
Exact sciences and the semiotics of existence

Abstract: We have to ask first why exact and natural sciences have so modest place in Tarasti's theories. The answer is in the role of subject and subjectivity. At first sight it may seem to be ignored in scientific discourse, but in fact it is strongly present. One may list fields of subject to be studied: nature of scientific creativity, emergence of meaning in exact sciences, scientific approach to the problem of existence and infinity, presence of transcendence. All these involve semiotic problems. Yet, since Galilei and Newton, scholars are used to separate subject and object. In fact, Niels Bohr, Werner Heisenberg and Martin Heidegger all worked in the 1920s and were able to distinguish subject and object, often one obscure and the other clear. Like Gilbert Durand says about conscious and unconscious.

In speech act theory sign becomes itself an object. Self-referential approaches take place when communication of the world (primary communication) turns into communication of communication (higher order communication). Meaning emerges often via metaphors which have a creative power. Jacques Hadamard saw similarity between psychology of mathematics and how Mozart represents musical creativity in his letters. In Tarasti's theory the moment of illumination is crucial and so it is as well in mathematics like Henri Poincaré said. There is also the issue of irrationality: how signs emerge after all. By transcendence ultimately we encounter high spirituality, high complexity and high surprise. We can prepare a list of types of existence and the semiotic one among them.

Keywords: transcendence, mathematics, epistemology

1 Are exact sciences concerned by a semiotics of existence?

Eero Tarasti's existential semiotics has its roots in music, semiotics and philosophy; his fields of excellence.[1] This fact explains why his approach is, on the one hand, one of an artist, on the other hand, one of a philosopher and semiotician.

---

[1] Imatra, June 2006

Social aspects also have a rich presence in his book on existential semiotics, mainly in the second part (Tarasti 2000). However, his main interest is to understand the semiotic nature of existence, of human existence. This is a total topic and no type of human creativity could be eliminated. If we accept this idea, then we may ask, for instance, why exact and natural sciences have such a modest place in Tarasti's approach. Obviously, one can explain this fact by the type of his intellectual training. But the main reason is the predominant mentality according to which in exact and natural sciences the role of the subjective factors and trans-factors is very poor. Our aim in the following is to reject this claim and show that there is an alternative itinerary of existential semiotics, starting from mathematics, logic, physics, chemistry, biology and computer science. As a matter of fact, the itinerary we are proposing is not so much alternative but cooperative, it is directed towards some universal patterns and paradigms, which belong to all types of human creativity.

2 Key words and main ideas in existential semiotics

Existential semiotics involves some key words and ideas related to the process of emergence of signs, to existence, to subject (versus object) and self, to transcendence, to negation, anguish and distress, to affirmation, illumination and plenitude. Are they the exclusive privilege of arts and humanities? We will argue for a negative answer to this question. There is a gap between the internal life of science, the very nature of scientific creativity, on the one hand, and the dry way science is exposed at all levels, from general school till university, with accent on procedure and operations, rather than on ideas and imagination, on the other hand. The true life of the so-called heavy sciences remains hidden to the general public. We will take one by one some basic ideas of existential semiotics and show their real face in the field of heavy sciences. We will begin with the role of the subject (in its relation to the object), then we will discuss the nature of scientific creativity (vs the artistic creativity), the emergence of meaning in heavy sciences, the way science raises the problem of existence and infinity, the essential presence of transcendence, of the negation-affirmation interplay. As we will see, all these problems involve semiotic processes.

3 Bohr, Heisenberg and Heidegger challenge the subject-object distinction

Classical science, as it was launched by Galilei and Newton, was based on the tacit but firm presupposition of the existence of a sharp distinction between subject and object and on the assumption that the subject has no significant impact on the object of investigation. In other words, the latter is never significantly modified by the former or by the tools he is using in the investigation process. Generations after generations repeated the claim that science is objective, while poetry and art are subjective. Step by step, and from various directions, this representation of the subject-object relation had to be replaced by another one, revealing an increasing role of the subject and the increasing difficulty to establish a border between subject and object. The most spectacular results in this respect were Niels Bohr's complementarity principle and Werner Heisenberg's uncertainty principle, both stated in the same year 1927, when Martin Heidegger's *Sein und Zeit* is published. All these three authors throw a shadow over our capacity to distinguish the subject from the object. Heidegger considers that, as observers, we are a part of the world we are trying to describe. To some extent, when we begin to describe it, we introduce a separation from our practical life. A large part of what we are communicating and thinking is not deliberate; through it, it is our biological evolution and our cultural history that acquire meaning. According to Bohr, "classical exact sciences were looking for a univoque mode of description, able to eliminate any possible influence of the observer, of the subject". "The description of nature was based on the determination of a line of separation between the object and the subject, so the role of the observer was negligible". This no longer happens in quantum physics. Bohr stated that one cannot measure at the same time the particle features (position, speed) and the wave features (wavelength, frequency, amplitude) of an electron. Any experiment is obliged to select one of these two aspects. Heisenberg is also concerned with quantum objects. He stated that one cannot measure with unlimited accuracy both the position and the speed of a quantum object: measuring one of them is always at the expense of the accuracy in measuring the other one. This impossibility is factual, so it is not a result of the insufficient knowledge of the quantum object. In both cases (Bohr and Heisenberg), we are faced with some conjugate pairs, i.e., with some pairs of requirements, each of them very natural, but getting in conflict when they are considered together. So, the compromise is unavoidable: each of them can be satisfied only at the expense of the other. So, complementarity does not mean collaboration, "It always involves mutual exclusiveness among the considered terms" (Bohr 1961: 71).

4 Gamow on the crisis of observation at the atomic level

At the quantum level, the instruments we are using modify the behaviour of the quantum object, events at this scale cannot be observed and registered with certainty. In this respect, George Gamow (1958: 3) proposes some interesting analogies.

In the world of everyday experience, we can observe a phenomenon and register its behaviour, without significant interference in its development. But if we try to take the temperature of a cup of coffee with the same thermometer we use to take the temperature of the water in a big recipient, then obviously the thermometer will absorb so much heat that the temperature of the coffee will change significantly. We can avoid this difficulty by using a small chemical thermometer, whose influence on the coffee temperature will be negligible. One can even take the temperature of an object having the dimensions of a living cell if we use a miniature instrument, whose caloric capacity is almost negligible. But at the atomic scale, we can never observe the modification determined by the introduction of a measurement instrument. The impossibility to determine both the cinematic and the dynamic properties of quantum objects show that at this level of reality no clear separation is possible between the action of the observer and the phenomena observed.

For Bohr, what we call 'phenomenon' in quantum physics is no longer something that happens in an 'objective reality', but "a totality of effects that can be observed in some given experimental conditions" (Bohr 1961: 85).

5 From quantum to computational and from physics to psychoanalysis

Quantum complementarity was supplemented by a principle of computational complementarity (Svozil 1994): If the author of an experiment is part of a system S, then any measurement of some aspect of S makes impossible the measurement of another, complementary aspect. If the physical world is conceived as the result of universal computation, then complementarity becomes unavoidable in its operational perception.

According to Gilbert Durand (disciple of Gaston Bachelard), the author of "Structures anthropologiques de l'imaginaire", Heisenberg's uncertainty principle has a correspondent in the field of humanities: the impossibility to make precise both terms of a couple of entities which are naturally associated. The germ of this situation appears already with Freud and Jung: inside a phenomenon, we may have two contradictory things, such that when one of them is made explicit by observation or explanation, the other remains in obscurity. For Durand, the conscious and the unconscious are exactly in this situation. If one of them can be the object of a psychologic investigation, then the other is no longer available psychologically, it becomes only a reservoir of socio-cultural and historical effects and resonances (Durand 1987: 149–161).

6 Objective information, a chimera; from thermodynamics and biology to semiotics

The study of information emerged in the second half of the XIXth century from two sources: thermodynamics, for information as a quantitative entity, and Darwinian biology for information as form, i.e., as a qualitative entity. Only the second itinerary agrees with the Latin etymology of 'information'. The first itinerary lead in the XXth century to Shannon's information theory born from the idea to separate information from meaning. Messages are reduced to signals and the information can be measured. But the price we have to pay in order to measure the information is to renounce its meaning aspect. Measured information is objective but poor. On the other hand, information as form knows in the XXth century a spectacular itinerary. F. de Saussure, E. Cassirer, B. Russell – A.N. Whitehead, G. Lukacs, D'Arcy Thompson, D. Hiabelt, Russian formalism, Max Scheler, A. Jolles, V. Propp, M. Ghyka, L. Hjelmslev, R. Huyghe, R. Thom, R. Spencer-Brown, G. Bateson, U. Maturana – F. Varela, B. Mandelbrot, D. Hofstadter have, as a common denominator, the attention paid to various aspects of form. But information and meaning remained with the status of a conjugate pair. The field of objective information is very restricted; most information is of a mixed subjective-objective nature, as we have shown in S. Marcus' 'Media and self-reference' (1997a:15–46).

After many attempts, the marriage between information and meaning proved to be impossible. All kinds of compromises were adopted. Biology is still looking for an adequate notion of information. Let us recall that already towards the end of the XIXth century, the German biologist Augustus Weissmann observes that it seems that in the field of heredity there are phenomena that cannot be explained only in terms of matter and energy; we need something more, and Weissmann called it 'information'. After the appearance of Shannon's information theory, many authors in biology adopted his view. They did not observe that Shannon is dealing with global aspects of information, while in the field of heredity we need a local idea of information, able to make meaningful the information of a DNA string, for instance. Ultimately, the help came from the so-called cybernetics of second-order, including the observer; the start in this respect belongs to G. Bateson (*Steps to an ecology of mind*, 1973), who also proposes a new notion of information: it is a difference that makes a difference. In order to make clearer the mixed subjective-objective nature of this way to understand information, Jesper Hoffmeyer and Claus Emmeche ('Code duality and the semiotics of nature', 1991) put Bateson's definition in the following form: it is a difference that it is perceived by somebody as a difference. In this way, the dependence of information from a subject for whom it makes sense is made explicit.

7 The competition between information and sign

Søren Brier (CD-ROM, article 99169) formulates the problem whether the Wiener-Schrodinger quantitative paradigm of information could successfully cope with the problems of meaning and communication in living systems, language systems and social systems. In this respect, the information paradigm was in competition with the semiotic paradigm as it was developed by Ch. S. Peirce and, in the XXth century, by Thomas Sebeok, the initiator of biosemiotics. Schrodinger, with his book *What is life?* (1946), and G. Bateson, with his book about the ecology of mind (1973), are considered by Brier as expressing an analogy between information, on the one hand, and neg-entropy and evolutionary order, as an accumulation of thermo-dynamic negentropy, on the other hand. A link is suggested in this way, observes Brier, between matter and mind and, consequently, the possibility of artificial intelligence, followed by the possibility to transfer human mind on internet, under the form of self-organizing programs. Making a clear distinction between the Shannon variant and the Wiener variant of information theory, Brier associates to Schrodinger and Wiener not only the name of Bateson but also those of Tom Stonier (1997) and L. von Bertalanffy, the founder of system theory via biology. Brier sees in this line of thought a way to bridge information and consciousness, life and qualia. Making a synthesis of this approach, Brier claims that people, machines, animals and organizations process information in the same way. But this is true only if we ignore intuitions and emotions and we take into consideration only the conscious and logical thinking, while understanding is reduced to the analytical one. The subject is seen only in its cognitive aspect and, in this respect, we tend to see it as a computer. Brier is suggesting in this way the compromise making information able to simulate human existence. Some improvements came from thermodynamics far from equilibrium, non-linear dynamics, deterministic chaos, and fractals. But despite all these additions, the information paradigm remains powerless with respect to meaning and sense.

8 Other failures in separating the subject from the object: Induction, linguistic relativism and constructivism

The reasoning by induction was traditionally considered as a way to acquire knowledge about the objective world. At a careful examination, however, we realize that induction is not a move from particular to general, it is a circular itinerary between them. Indeed, let us consider an experiment leading to a finite number of points in the plane, telling us that at various moments t we had a specific position of coordinates t, s(t). If we want now to dress a curve passing by all these points, we have to make a choice among infinitely many possibilities and this choice is determined by a previous idea we have about the respective phenomenon or by a purely psychological aesthetic need. So, subject and object become actors in the same game and it is impossible to separate their actions.

Another example of subject-object interference is the so-called linguistic relativism analyzed by E. Sapir (1921) and B. L. Whorf (1956) and according to which our very perception of the physical world is programmed by the language we speak. For instance, it was proved that the perception of colours is strongly influenced by the way in which colour terminology is structured. On the other hand, authors such as Max Black (1962), J. Fishman (1960) and P. Herriot (1977), accepting the interest of Sapir-Whorf's hypothesis, try to restrict its domain of validity. Computer programming languages confirm to some extent the linguistic relativism.

In the last decades, a new doctrine emerged, called (linguistic) constructivism, whose main claim is that each speaker is building on its own the meanings of its language. The process of learning a language is a personal constructor, a creative one, while the competence to perform this construction comes from our innate resources (N. Chomsky 1975; Siegfried Schmidt and his journal SPIEL; Grace 1987).

9 Predictions and speech acts under the sign of self-reference

The field of predictions is another example of subject-object circularity. Not all predictions are in this situation. Prediction of solar or lunar eclipses is based on a clear separation between the subject making the prediction and the object of prediction. Man has no influence on the movement of planets around the sun. It is not the same situation in the case of meteorological predictions. Man's influence on the state of the atmosphere is no longer negligible, as it was until the XIXth century. Various modifications of the man-nature relations, as a result of the scientific, technological and social evolution, may have a considerable impact on the ecological system of our planet and the warnings coming from authors such as Barry Commoner and Arnold Toynbee are symptomatic in this respect. Some changes observed in the last decades in the climate of our planet are the result of human action. A sharp, rigorous separation between the subject making the meteorological prediction and the climate forming the object of the prediction no longer exists, although the precise nature of this influence exercised by human action on the atmosphere around us is not yet well known.

The circular nature of predictions becomes clearer and more significant when they are applied to the economic-social life. The subject making a social prediction belongs to the human society that is just the object of his prediction; at the same time, the society (in contrast with the atmosphere, in the case of meteorological predictions) may become aware of the predictions concerning its future development and change its behaviour, in order to invalidate the prediction. Opinion polls before various types of elections are typical in this respect, they have sometimes a decisive influence and this is the reason why they are under interdiction in the immediate days preceding elections. Another interesting situation is that of a prediction made by an economist, concerning some events whose realization essentially depends on the decision factors in economy, while the prediction was required just by the same decision factors, in order to know what decision to take.

Very relevant is the so-called speech act theory (Austin 1962; Searle 1969), whose basic assumption is expressed just by the title of Austin's book (*How to Do Things with Words*): the possibility to do things with words. Speech acts can simultaneously assert and perform (establish) the fact they are asserting. The sign becomes its own object. Promising or requiring something is a speech act because in this case language is not referring to something exterior to it, it is referring to a situation created just by it. Once-more, self-reference is present.

10 From communication about the world to communication about communication

Communication is another process with strong self-referential tendencies. Marshall McLuhan's slogan "the medium is the message" (see McLuhan 1962), later the title of another book, by Sergio Lepri (*Medium e messaggio* 1986, 2000), calls attention on a typical self-referential process in contemporary communication: the initial message about the world is step by step abandoned in favour of another one, about itself. The medium, initially a simple window to permit us to convey a message, becomes itself a message, claiming to be the main message we have to convey. The subject-object distinction is again in question. As subjects, we communicate, we change messages either about the world around us or about our own person. At this stage, we may assume that the subjects which communicate may be firmly different from the object of the communication process. In other words, we start by communicating about the world. This first step, let us call it communication of first order, is followed by a second one, where the object of communication is just the communication of the first order. Continuing in this way, we reach, for any positive integer n, a communication process of order n. So, at least theoretically, the communication of the first order, let us call it primary communication, because it is directly about the world, is replaced step by step by communication about communication (more precisely, communication of order n about the communication of order n-1). Is this a purely speculative way to approach communication? Not at all! Look in any newspaper and you shall find out that most news is communication of higher-order, only a few of them belong to the primary communication.

Now, it is clear that any new intermediate level in the escalation of the communication process will work also as a new source of deterioration of the initial message. For n enough large, the risk to get at the n-th step of the process a very distorted message in respect to the initial one is increasing. But the big danger is that, in most cases, we can no longer reconstitute the initial message and sometimes even its existence is doubtful. Take for instance the huge enterprise called "Science Citation Index", where we find, for any published paper, who cited it, when and where. A big rooted tree is born in this way, but in most cases, we do not know exactly the root, because it is very far in the past, and we do not know its further evolution, so it is only a fragment of a tree. Such trees account for that adventure of human being we call science. Communication turns to itself and it generates a new universe, the universe of communication, challenging the proper universe and sometimes replacing it abusively.

11 Models and metaphors; bridging the subject and the object

Tarasti considers (p. 11 of his book) that the subject becomes an existential being that creates the meaning across two acts, the first of which happens within the framework of objective signs. The emergence of meaning in science is placed within this framework but, as we have shown in S. Marcus' 'Metaphors as dictatorship' (1997b), signs occurring in this process are not just objective, they cannot avoid the subject-object circularity. Let us recall that a model B for a phenomenon A aims to study A by a method incompatible with the nature of A or with its degree of complexity, but compatible with B. We need this strategy in those cases in which methods compatible with A prove to be insufficient for the understanding of A. For instance, if A is an empirical phenomenon, it cannot be directly approached by a mathematical method; we imagine then a formal construction B, by means of which we try to simulate the phenomenon A. Similarly, if A' is an entity that cannot be sufficiently understood in terms of directly referring to A', we imagine another entity B, by means of which we could express better some properties of A'. For instance, if we want to say that somebody is courageous, beautiful, powerful, proud, noble, we better use a metaphor B' such as 'lion' and we say 'he is a lion'; in this way, by a single, very expressive word, we express better what we wanted to say. A model B of A accounts only partially for A, because their analogy is only in some respect true. Moreover, B has to fulfil two opposite requirements: on the one hand, B should be enough similar to A, in order to have a chance that what is valid and relevant for B is valid and relevant also for A; on the other hand, B should be enough different from A, in order to have a chance to find a method applicable to B, but not to A. So, B is only an approximation of A and this approximation can always be improved. There exists no final model of A, there is only a potentially infinite sequence of cognitive models 'converging' to A. Something similar happens with the metaphor. There is a permanent tension between frame and focus, to use the terminology of Black (1962), in analogy with the tension existing between an object and its model. The focus is both similar to and different from the frame; similar, to show that it refers to the frame; different, in order to be able to bring something new, i.e., different in respect to the given frame (in "he is a lion", 'he' is the frame, while 'lion' is the focus). It appears that both models and metaphors have a conflictual structure because they have to fulfil opposite requirements, like in the double bind situation known from psychiatry. For a more detailed comparative analysis of models and metaphors, see Marcus (1997b) already mentioned.

12 The creative power of models and metaphors; their circular structure

Now we have to show how models and metaphors acquire a cognitive and creative function, how do they make possible the emergence of meaning in science. Let us consider the example of the emergence of the idea of irrationality, so important for the Greek antiquity and playing a basic role in Tarasti's approach, for whom the existential thinking should be in its essence irrational. For those who fear that we give to this word a meaning different from what Tarasti has in view, we will come back on this question later. Pythagoras discovered the impossibility to find a number corresponding to the length of the diagonal of a unit square; for that time, only numbers which are of the form p/q, with p and q positive integers and q different from zero were known. The problem was how to enlarge the idea of a number, in such a way that the respective diagonal could be measured. The difficulty was determined by the fact that no number of the form p/q exists whose square is equal to 2. To put it in the form of a question, we will formulate it as follows: imagine an extension of the idea of a number, according to which, in the new framework, there exists a number x which is, in respect to 2 in a relation similar to that of n in respect to the square of n (n being a positive integer). If we succeed to solve this problem and because n is said to be the square root of the square of n, we will call x the square root of 2. As a matter of fact, it took about two thousand years to solve the respective problem; it happened in the second half of the XIXth century when the general notion of a real number was introduced. However, much earlier a special sign for the square root of 2 was introduced, even though this picture for x was meaningless. But here a remark is necessary: it was meaningless conceptually, but it was not at all meaningless metaphorically. Indeed, x is introduced by means of an analogy and the abbreviation of this analogy is just the metaphor: x is the square root of 2. In what is different this metaphor from the usual metaphors such as the Aristotle metaphor "Oldness is the evening of life"? Aristotle's metaphor is the result of the analogy: "oldness is in respect to life what evening is in respect to the day". All entities involved here, oldness, life, evening and day, have an already existing clear status. On the contrary, in the Pythagoras situation, only three vertices of the square have an already established conceptual status: 2, n and square of n; the fourth vertex x is conceptually meaningless and the role of the metaphor is just to help the emergence of a new concept. We could say that in Aristotle's situation the metaphor has an assertory structure, while in the case of Pythagoras the metaphor has an interrogative structure. The Aristotle metaphor is in respect to an already existing entity, while Pythagoras metaphor is in respect to an entity which is not pre-existent to the metaphorical process: the notion of a real number. Clearly, in the second case, we have a circular, self-referential situation, a subjective-objective process. According to terminology introduced by Earl R. Mac Cormac (1976) we call Aristotle's metaphor epiphoric, while Pythagoras metaphor was during two thousand years diaphoric and became epiphoric only in the XIXth century. Let us observe that there are creative metaphors eternally diaphoric, for instance, the metaphors of the Divinity. There are also creative metaphors today diaphoric, but that can become epiphoric in a near or distant future.

13 The psychological identity of scientific and artistic creativity

One of the most interesting analyses of the psychological nature of scientific creativity is the book *Essai sur la psychologie de l'invention mathematique* by Jacques Hadamard, one the greatest mathematicians in the first half of the XXth century. The English edition *The psychology of invention in the mathematical field* was published in 1954. Hadamard sees the process of scientific invention in three steps. There is first a <u>preparation</u> that can be very long (accumulation of data, some of which are selected for further specific combinations), a second step is <u>incubation</u> (a period in which some ideas are reconsidered, by a process that cannot be kept under control); then comes the third step, <u>illumination</u>, including the unexpected appearance of a new, seductive combination, which in many cases may disappoint. The last step, conscious and rational, is of <u>verification and accuracy of details</u>.

After this description of the psychology of invention/discovery in mathematics, Hadamard makes reference to a letter sent by Mozart to his sister (he mentions that this letter is reproduced at p. 177 of *Essai sur le genie dans l'art*, by Gabriel Seailles (1852–1922)). Here is the letter:

> When I am in a good mood or when I am walking after a good meal, or during the night, when I cannot sleep, I am overwhelmed by all kinds of thoughts. How do they appear? I don't know and I am not interested in this. I keep those that I like and sometimes I begin to hum them; or at least other people told me that I proceed in this way. As soon as I find out a theme, another melody appears, joining the previous one, in agreement with the global requirements of the composition: the counterpoint, the part of each instrument. All these melodic fragments yield the whole work. If nothing diverts my attention, my soul is in the fire of inspiration. The work grows; I extend it, I see it clearer and clearer, until I have in my head the whole composition. My mind seizes it at once, in the same way in which, my eye captures by only one look a beautiful painting or a good-looking boy. The work does not appear to me in successive steps, with each part in details, as it will later happen, it is offered to my imagination as a whole.

> How does it happen that, when I am working, my compositions get the Mozartian form and style? Exactly as it happens that my big and aquiline nose is only mine. I don't look for originality and it would be difficult for me to define my style.

Hadamard (1954) observes the striking similarity between his representation of the psychology of mathematical creativity and Mozart's representation of the psychology of musical creativity: both are organized according to the scenario "preparation – incubation – illumination – verification and accuracy of details". The culminating step in this scenario is the third one, the illumination, associated by excellence to creativity; it is the explosion that in semiotics is usually associated with the abductive moment dominating the inductive and the deductive components, but impossible in absence of them.

14 Illumination as a culminating moment of creativity is bridging illumination as a symptom of transcendence

Now, going back to Tarasti's approach, we will observe how important is for him the illumination moment. In the second chapter of his book, "Signs and Transcendence", the symptom of transcendence is an unexpected (surprising) illumination. At p. 21, Tarasti points out how a usual experience may change step by step in a transcendent one, taking the form of a new illumination of a sign, of an object, of a text from the field of *Dasein*. Giving several examples from the field of music, Tarasti observes (p. 29) that, examining the message of an artist, the semiotician reaches the illumination of existence, as an expression of the individual subject. So, illumination as a symptom of transcendence reaches the illumination as the culminating moment of creativity, be it scientific or artistic.

The importance of the illumination moment is asserted also by writers such as Lamartine and Paul Valéry and by scientists such as Henri Poincaré, Helmholtz, Charles Hermite, K. Weierstrass and Joseph Bertrand. This fact is organically associated with the importance of the unconscious factors (dreams, other activities during sleeping), intuitive and emotional factors in all types of human creativity.

15 Creativity as articulation of choices and combinations

Paul Valéry asserts that any act of intelligence involves two types of operations: choices and combinations; but genius is mainly related to happy choices. Poincaré has similar opinions, but he believes that possible rules in making choices are implicit rather than explicit, unconscious rather than conscious. He also stresses the basic role of affective-emotional life and aesthetic factors in making good choices. Already Helmholtz, referring to his own experience, underlined the role of the unconscious in making happy choices; he claimed that he never got a successful idea when he was at his working table.

A synthesis of the ideas concerning the representation of creativity as an alternation of choices and combinations was proposed by Jacques Hadamard (1954). More recently, Yves Bouligand (1985: 83–91) focuses on the same idea (in conflict with the common belief) that discovery and invention in mathematics are not rational acts. Like in other fields, creativity in mathematics involves intuitions, abductive inferences, imagination and revelation.

We could dress a typology of creators, according to their dominant feature. For instance, K. Weierstrass, B. Riemann, Ch. Hermite, J. Bertrand and B. Russell are all mathematicians, but the first of them is predominantly analytic, the second one is predominantly intuitive, the third one is predominantly logic, while the fourth one is predominantly spatial and geometric. There is also a typology in respect to choices and combinations, according to which Riemann and Poincaré were great in choices, while Paul Erdös, in the second half of the XXth century, was very inspired in combinatorial operations.

The contrast between the explicit, public appearance of science in terms of axiomatic deductive logic and the hidden life of science, dominated by questions, attempts, failures, intuition, emotion, abductive inferences, unconscious and aesthetic factors, is one of the main sources of the misunderstanding having among its victims the apparent impossibility to bridge heavy sciences and existential semiotics.

16 Irrationality

"The very concept of sign may be fundamentally irrational. The sign emerges from emptiness, from Nothingness, it is a happy fortuitousness" (Tarasti 2000: 173). This is a way to state an open problem: "How do the signs emerge?" This question seems to be of the same difficulty as "How life emerged?" or "How did the Universe start?".

According to Peirce, signs emerge from signs and generate signs, there is no initial or final sign and any question concerning the move from non-semiosis to semiosis is ignored. Theoretically, semiosis is essentially a mediation process, in contrast with hermeneutics, which is direct, i.e., non-mediated. Professor Tarasti perhaps remembers the 1983 decade at Cérisy-la-Salle, focused on a debate between semiotics (A. J. Greimas) and hermeneutics (Paul Ricoeur). The difficulty to approach the delicate problem of how signs emerge is the fact that we are part of the world of signs, so we are both observers and observed in this respect. Things are similar to the difficulty to understand the time, with respect to which, again, we are both observers and observed. Tarasti is right in considering non-semiosis as an empty space, because it is not available to us and, in this case, the emergence of signs from non-signs is 'irrational'. In mathematics, irrational numbers are those whose representation is essentially infinite, so they are available only partially, via some finite approximations; in this sense, the label 'irrational' is motivated. We reach irrational numbers only transcending the world of mathematical processes with a finite number of steps. The old Greek civilization of Pythagoras was shocked by the impossibility to measure the diagonal of the unit square and we can imagine the feeling of Nothingness associated with the respective historical moment. This first step, essentially negative, was followed by another one, positive, of plenitude, related to the creation of the concept of a real number and to the possibility to consider, for each real number, its square root. But these two moments were separated by two thousand years.

17 Transgression, as a way to acquire meaning

When a problem is in front of us, in a given framework, a general procedure to approach it is to transgress the respective framework and to move into another one, with a more powerful explanatory capacity. For instance, art is proposing a fictional universe that may have in respect to the real one a higher capacity to mean and to explain. In his general relativity, Einstein, in order to better understand Newton's law of gravitation acting in the three-dimensional Euclidean space, considers a broader framework, a four-dimensional space-time, and he shows that gravitation in the three-dimensional space is the effect of the curvature of the space-time. From the elementary mathematics, we remember that the successive extensions of the numerical framework were motivated by the need to make it meaningful in the general case some natural operations; so we moved from natural numbers to integers, from integers to rational numbers and from rational to real numbers. Solving algebraic equations required, in its turn, the extension of the framework of real numbers to a broader one, of complex (imaginary) numbers. Things do not stop here.

Leibniz introduced the idea of an infinitely small, as a quantity which is fixed, but smaller than any number of the form $1/n$, where n is an arbitrary strictly positive integer. During about three centuries, nobody was able to give a coherent interpretation of Leibniz's idea. In the second half of the past century, A. Robinson succeeded to consider a framework more comprehensive than that of the real numbers, called the non-standard universe, where the idea of an infinitely small becomes meaningful, but not as a real number; it is, however, an element of the non-standard universe. This idea was applied to the study of exchange economy, in order to explain the behaviour of the participants in a market economy, when the number of participants is increasing. The method consisted in replacing the standard universe by a non-standard one, leading so to what is called a non-standard exchange economy. The author of this work, Gérard Debreu, won the Nobel prize in economics.

Very often, we transgress the initial framework not in the direction of a more comprehensive one, but in the direction of a framework being in a relation of analogy or of contiguity with the initial one. Metaphorical and metonymic processes are transgressions of this type.

The universe of the infinitely small (the quantum universe, for instance) takes profit from the examination of the macroscopic universe because in the latter we can use our intuitions, and our language, while in the former our capacities are to a large extent powerless. We get a better understanding of our own country by transgressing its borders and knowing other countries. We understand better the Euclidean geometry by moving to the more comprehensive framework of absolute geometry, where the axiom of parallels is ignored; so, both Euclidean and non-Euclidean geometries are parts of the new framework. Similar procedures are used in practically all fields of knowledge.

18 Transcendence: High spirituality, high complexity, high surprise

As a high form of spirituality, transcendence is a common denominator of all forms of intellectual creativity, their climax moment. But does science have a spiritual dimension? A negative answer to this question is often suggested, rarely expressed explicitly. We meet frequently slogans of the type: "science deals only with the concrete, material world", "modern science dehumanizes man", "science provides us with information, but brings about no spiritual gain". Such slogans are simply false, they denote ignorance or/and misunderstanding. At the Imatra 2005 session of semiotics, we have lectured about the spiritual dimension of mathematics. Some meetings are organized under the slogan "Bridging science and spirituality". It is suggested in this way that science and spirituality are away from each other to such an extent that we need to build a bridge between them, in order to diminish their discrepancy. The reality is just the opposite. Science has a very rich internal spiritual life and this fact explains why it is able to interact with other spiritual fields.

In our Western culture, we refer to old Greek traditions, where chronologically myths appeared first, then appeared literature (see Homer) and a few centuries later emerged mathematics, with Thales and Pythagoras. Poetry and mathematics are usually described in contrastive terms; however, they share some important features, inherited from myths: they all propose some fictional worlds; they all use symbolization; they all need to transgress the everyday logic and to adopt, more or less explicitly, what we call today a non-classical logic; as a consequence, they all are impregnated of syntactic, semantic and pragmatic paradoxes. So, the way is open to conflicts with the intuitive perception and expectations and to discrepancies between the intelligible and the visible. Myths, poetry and mathematics are all based on a principle of semiotic optimization: maximum of meaning in the shortest possible expression. They also share the assumption of a holographic principle: the local may account sometimes for the global, the instantaneous may account for the eternal, the anthropos for the cosmos, the individual for the general, the finite for the infinite. Recall William Blake's famous verses: "To see the world in a grain of sound/and the heaven in a wild flower./Hold infinity in the palm of your hand/and eternity in an hour". Infinity is one of the most important forms of transcendence, involving a whole hierarchy: the finite accounting for the infinite, the countable infinite accounting for the infinite of the power of the continuum, the infinite of a given cardinality accounting for the infinite of a higher cardinality.

A symptom of the high complexity associated with transcendence is the essential role of imprecision in all kinds of spiritual creativity. This fact is well-known in the case of poetry and art, but less known in the case of science. However, at a careful examination, we observe that most mathematical results involve approximation, randomness, fuzziness, generality, negligibility, ambiguity or other forms of imprecision. As a matter of fact, the distinctive feature of imprecision is just its high complexity: the number of parameters that should be evaluated is too large to be performed.

From high spirituality and complexity, there is only one step to high surprise. Let us take the Greek wonder faced with the existence of the phenomenon of irrationality. The surprise was so high that its effect was decisive for Greek mathematics. We could dress a hierarchy of facts in respect to their degree of surprise: trivial; obvious, but not trivial; expected, but not obvious; neuter (neither expected, nor unexpected); unexpected, but not surprising; surprising, but within the limits of human imagination; beyond what can be imagined at a certain historical moment. The last type could be associated with a kind of craziness, in its positive sense (in contrast with its negative, pathological meaning). Marston Morse writes somewhere that mathematics is sometimes crazy. Perhaps, he had in view moments such as Abel's discovery of the impossibility to solve by radicals algebraic equations of degree higher than 4 and Galois' theorem giving the deep purely qualitative reason of this fact. We may also think of Gödel's incompleteness theorem asserting the impossibility to have, for some types of formal systems, both consistency and completeness. Robinson's non-standard analysis could also be included in these types of scientific results, we could call them crazy, meaning by this that they pushed far away the limits of human imagination. "Transcendence" is associated with "beyond"; with results of the mentioned type, human spirituality is moving beyond some already accepted limits. By Gödel's incompleteness theorem, for instance, we learn that to prove the consistency of some types of formal systems we need to leave the respective systems and reach a more comprehensive universe, whose consistency will require a new, broader universe etc. Going beyond an existing framework is thus a human need telling us how essential is the 'trans' operator having transcendence as its prototype.

19 Existence and its typology

The main idea of our approach to existential semiotics is to use a way valid for any type of human spiritual creativity. Our stress on exact sciences is motivated by the fact that they are considered a field of the object rather than one of the subject. We argued however in favour of a strong involvement of the subject in the so-called exact sciences too and we used ideas belonging to all fields of spiritual creativity. So, the way is open to a unified approach to the semiotics of existence. We stressed the psychological identity of scientific and artistic creativity, the similar role of illumination, of irrationality and of transcendence in science and art. There exists however a whole typology of existence, according to its nature and degree of effectiveness. For instance, if we refer to the existence of the human body, we have first its material existence (related to the verb 'to have') consisting of some atoms. The most visible, material existence is also the most inconsistent because during five years all our atoms have changed. More stable is its structural existence (related to the verb 'to be'), consisting of the patterns, the arrangements of the atoms. The genetic existence (associated with the verb 'to inherit') consists of the features transferred from our parents and ancestors. The reproductive and sexual existence (associated with the verb 'to transfer to descendants') consists of the capacity to have children; the managerial existence (associated with the verb 'to control' or 'to coordinate') is of three types, according to the nature of prostheses under control: muscular, sensorial and cerebral. The most important cerebral prosthesis is the electronic computer, leading to the computational existence (associated with the verb 'to do something effectively'), consisting of the capacity to make our products as constructive as possible. Here, we should distinguish the complexity (cost) of doing something. Very important is the interactive existence (associated with the verb 'to interact'), consisting of the interactions of our body with the external world. Here we should include the ecological existence and the communicational existence, as parts of our interactive (dynamical) existence. Then comes the semiotic existence (associated with the verb 'to mean', 'to signify'), consisting of the capacity to mean in various ways; this existence is one of the second-order because it consists of the capacity to signify the other, already considered types of existence. The procedures to mean may be of various types, for instance, they may be symbolic, iconic (metaphorical) or indexical (metonymic). There is a whole history of the metaphorical use of the human body in the Greek antiquity, during the Roman empire, in the Middle Age, until our time.

No claim to have given a complete account of the types of the existence of the human body. Our desire was only to suggest the complexity of the problem. But even from this incomplete account, we learn to what extent the existence of the human body cannot be understood in absence of reference to what is beyond it. From this apparently elementary problem, there is a long way until we reach the idea of the existence (identity) of a person, with its mind, soul and spirit. Leibniz, with his famous mind/body problem, is challenging us still today and we realize the high complexity of the idea of self, of 'ego' and of 'human existence'. We are indebted to Eero Tarasti for the way he stimulated us in this respect.

References

Austin, John Langshaw. 1962. *How to do things with words*. Oxford: Clarendon Press.
Bateson, Gregory. 1973. *Steps to an ecology of mind*. St Albans: Granada.
Black, Max. 1962. *Models and metaphors*. Ithaca, N.Y.: Cornell Univ.ersity Press.
Bohr, Niels. 1961. *Physique atomique et connaissance humaine*. Paris: Gallimard.
Bouligand, Yves. 1985. Invention et innovation. In *Encyclopaedia Universalis*. Paris.
Chomsky, Noam. 1975. *Reflections on language*. New York: Pantheon.
Durand, Gilbert. 1987. *La science, face aux confns de la connaissance*. Paris: Felin.
Fishman, J. 1960. A systematization of the Whorfian hypothesis. *Behavioral Science* 5(4). 323–339.
Gamow, George. 1958. The principle of uncertainty. *Scientific American* 198(1). 51–57.
Grace, George W. 1987. *The linguistic construction of reality*. London: Croom Helm.
Hadamard, Jacques. 1954. *The Psychology of Invention in the Mathematical Field*. New York: Dover Publications.
Herriot, Peter. 1977 [1970]. *Introduction to the psychology of language*.
Hoffmeyer, Jesper & Claus Emmeche. 1991. Code-duality and the semiotics of nature. In Myrdene Anderson & Floyd Merrell (eds.), *On Semiotic Modeling*, 117–166. Berlin & New York: Mouton de Gruyter.

Lepri, Sergio. 2000. *Medium e messagg*. Torino: Gutenberg.
MacCormac, Earl R. 1976. *Metaphor and myth in science and religion*. Durham, NC: Duke.
Marcus, Solomon. 1997a. Media and self-reference. In Winfried Nöth (ed.), *Semiotics of the Media*, 15–48. Berlin: Mouton de Gruyter.
Marcus, Solomon. 1997b. Metaphor as dictatorship. In Jeff Bernard (ed.), *World of signs-World of things*. Vienna.
McLuhan, Marshall. 1962. *Gutenberg Galaxy*. Toronto: University of Toronto Press.
Sapir, Edward 1921. *Language: an introduction to the study of speech*. New York: Harcourt, Brace and World.
Searle, John R. 1969. *Speech acts*. London & New York: Cambridge University Press.
Stonier, Tom. 1997. *Information and meaning; an evolutionary perspective*. Berlin: Springer.
Tarasti, Eero. 2000. *Existential Semiotics*. Bloomington: Indiana University Press.
Whorf, Benjamin Lee. 1956. *Language, Thought and Reality*. Cambridge, Mass.: MIT Press.

Susan Petrilli and Augusto Ponzio
Voice as transcendence and otherness

Abstract: Semiotics and philosophy are closely interconnected in a relation that constitutes the very condition for their scientificness and critical capacity. Philosophy explores the external margins of the "semiotic field", the excess with respect to semiotics, the "science," "theory" or "doctrine of signs". Eero Tarasti's existential semiotics responds to this philosophical excess and presents itself as critique as it examines fundamental problems of our times, the reality of today's world with a focus on the relation between signs and transcendence. Transcendence is connected with otherness, the desire of otherness by contrast to the Same, the Subject, Identity, by contrast to alternatives offered by realistic acceptance of the world as it is. Existential semiotics recognizes the centrality of dialogue for semiosis. Here "dialogue" is not only understood as exchange of rejoinders among interlocutors, but also among utterances, texts, among interpreted and interpretant signs, to evoke Barthes among signs *scriptible* and *lisible*. Dialogue also evokes the voice, literally but also nonliterally, voice connected to the existential semiotics of the other, voice as trace, expression in its singularity, as sense transcendent with respect to meaning, unique and unrepeatable, voice as utterance, oral utterance, but also in *writing*, writing beyond the letter, writing *avant la lettre*. In this perspective, dialectics is developed in terms of utterances and texts, and signs are valorized in terms of dialogism and of their capacity to flourish and reflect beyond the conventional limits of identity and being. Existing is a difficult task for the subject, a lifelong demand and a challenge.

Keywords: dialogue, otherness, transcendence, voice, writing

In *Existential Semiotics*[1] (2000) Eero Tarasti addresses the question of the relation between signs and transcendence. A demand of our time, transcendence has different expressions which all share a common characteristic: the need to overcome dominant worldview, a realistic worldview, and reach beyond resigned accept-

---

[1] *Existential Semiotics* by Eero Tarasti was published in Italian translation, in an enlarged and revised edition, under the title *Introduzione alla semiotica esistenziale*, in the book series, 'Nel segno,' directed by Augusto Ponzio and myself (It. trans. Massimo Berruti, Bari, Laterza, 2008). By comparison with the English original, the Italian translation consists of five parts (instead of three), reorganized into a homogeneous and systematic whole. These two books, the original English and its Italian counterpart, share a common goal which is to relate semiotics to fundamental problems of our time, hence to the reality of today's world.

https://doi.org/10.1515/9783110789164-004

ance of the world as it is. Transcendence is connected with the logic of alterity. In such a light it is possible to question the Same, the Subject, Identity (Ponzio 1994, 1996, 2006c, 2019). Transcendence implies desire of the other, which is to say of the other beyond any alternatives offered by realistic acceptance of the world as it is (Petrilli 2013; Petrilli and Ponzio 2003a, 2019a).

Themes proposed by Tarasti in *Existential Semiotics* include: reality as 'energy fields'; the categories of 'being out' or 'being in,' the connection between external/internal; the classical distinction between objective/subjective; the problem of 'states' before the formation of signs; signs considered in sign situations; signs as they are detached from the world of *Dasein*; and the transcending subject that in its act of existing puts signs in motion; finally, the question: Given that the real manifests itself in resistance, where is this resistance placed: in the sphere of transcendence, or in the world of *Dasein*? (Tarasti 2000: 13). Reality consists of 'energy fields' where particular connections prevail according to laws that can only be described or conceptualized with great difficulty. However, it is only possible to recognize these connections if one is there, that is, on the basis of participating observation, and not of external observation. The categories of 'being out' or 'being in' (*In-sein/Ausser-sein*) cannot be separated from the classical distinction between objective and subjective. In fact, these terms do not indicate two separate spheres, but two different approaches to the same world of *Dasein*.

An essential element of *Dasein* as human existence is the voice because in it there appears the most important force and energy of the semiotic universe: the voice manifests our desire and will to express something. In his essay "Voice and Identity" (in Petrilli 2008: 287–301), Tarasti focuses on the voice as movement from the immanent to the transcendent, from the same to the other, from identity to alterity. In the voice the *langue* becomes *parole*, *meaning* becomes *sense*, intention, intentionality (Petrilli 2009; Petrilli and Ponzio 2016, 2019b). The voice strives to break through the borders of a solipsistic *Dasein*; it reaches out to another *Dasein*. In the voice virtuality becomes reality as desire finds its possibility of expression.

What characterizes the human voice? Petrus Hispanus in *Summule logicales* (see Peter of Spain 1972) distinguishes between *vocum significativa* (significant voice) and *vocum non-significativa* (non-significant voice) (for Peter of Spain our reference is to the 2010 bilingual Medieval Latin/Italian edition of *Summule logicales*, edited by Augusto Ponzio). Unlike the non-verbal voice, the naturally significant voice (*vocum significativa naturaliter*) –, the significant verbal voice is articulate (Aristotele: *kata suntheken*, in terms of composition, combination, syntax; mistaken translation by Ammonius and Boetius: *ad placitum*):

> Vox significativa naturaliter est illa que apud omnes idem representat, ut gemitus infirmorum, latratus canum.

> Vox significativa ad placitum est illa que ad voluntatem instituentis aliquid representat.
> (Peter of Spain 1972, quotation from the bilingual Medieval Latin/ Italian edition, 2010: 4)

"Vox significativa non naturaliter" but "ad placitum" is an articulate voice with a social character, in other words it signifies by convention. The main part of social life is filled with sound, particularly human sounds. This is true (in the case of human silent communication as well) both in "interior dialogue" and in communication by non-verbal signs, as in certain monasteries where in spite of their vows of silence the monks and nuns – as Tarasti observes citing Thomas Sebeok and Jean Umiker-Sebeok from *Monastic Sign Languages*, 1987 – are able to communicate with each other.

Tarasti observes that voice is a tool of expression as well as a spontaneous act; in both cases voice is oriented towards another, emerging as an essential element of the intersubjective relationship. In the first case, as a tool of expression it can be affective or what Roman Jakobson calls "phatic"; in the second case, as a spontaneous act it can be "conative" (cf. L. Ponzio 2015). Voice is inevitably intonated and intonation always differs when an utterance in the concrete context of live communication is reiterated. Obviously, articulate voice is connected to the body, voice is incarnate voice, but at the same time the voice transcends the organic, material dimension, the articulate voice is not reducible to the biology of the body. As sense, planning, intentionality the articulate voice is the instrument through which the human being reaches out to the world, "se projette vers le monde", as says Maurice Merleau-Ponty, cited by Tarasti in "Voice and identity" (2008: 288) from Merleau-Ponty's *Phénoménologie de la perception* (1945), specifically from the chapter titled, "Le corps comme expression et la parole". Echoing the statement made by Ferdinand de Saussure in his own phenomenological language on the relationship between *langue* and *parole*, Merleau-Ponty maintains that the essential thing is not the physiological-anatomical act of speaking, but rather

> the tensions of the throat, pressing the air through tongue and teeth, a certain manner of playing with our body suddenly creates a certain figurative sense and signification which goes beyond our body. In order for this miracle to happen it is indispensable for the phonetic gesture to employ the already acquired alphabets of signification, for the verbal gesture to materialize in a certain panorama common to speakers, since to understand others presupposes a given common world. (Merleau-Ponty 1945: 226)

Tarasti cites Merleau-Ponty again in "Voice and Identity," in a section titled "Education," and further clarifies this point:

> Merleau-Ponty states that voice and speech *transcend* our anatomical body: to ourselves, our body is not an object, since we *are* our body. Such a statement supports the general view of singing as the only musical genre in which we are our own instrument. Merleau-Ponty continues: "The way man uses his body transcends his body as a simply biological entity" (1945: 221). It is impossible to consider man's primary level as somehow "natural", on which more cultural and spiritual levels are added. Our behaviours yield significations that transcend anatomical preconditions.
> (Tarasti 2008: 296–297)

Even though, as Tarasti points out, Roland Barthes' perspective on the phenomenon of voice is different from Merleau-Ponty's approach, there is a certain analogy between them. In his essay, "The Grain of the Voice", Barthes makes a distinction between *genosong* and *phenosong*. Genosong refers to the physiological aspect of singing, the corporeal vocal technique that engages the whole body. Phenosong relies on the primacy of language, text and civilisation, the sublimation of the physical level to that of high culture (Barthes 1981: 295).

To focus on the voice implies to take an approach to language (in linguistics and in semiotics or philosophy of language) that privileges the utterance, the living cell of discourse, the *parole*, as the main verbal unit, and not the sentence, the dead cell of *langue*. The sentence is not endowed with intonation or accentuation, it is not related to speech, it does not have an interlocutor, a receiver, nor a context, the sentence has no tacit, implicit, understood meaning, it is devoid of a point of view, therefore the sentence has no voice. Voice conveys meaning and signifies sense, meaning, significance, the voice is bearer and signifier of meaning, the articulate voice is endowed with sense, which is the condition for meaning as responsive understanding (Petrilli 2012a, 2014b).

Not sentences, but utterances constitute the semiotic material of communication not only in orality, but also in writing. And in writing, where the voice is obviously absent, nonetheless its presence is felt through the written word's "intonation," so to say, its "accentuation". Indeed, a translation is not effectively a translation if it does not convey the original's particular accentuation in the target language. To translate is to reaccentuate. To render a text well in another language is to express the original accentuation appropriately. A good translation is one that conveys the correct intonation.

All such aspects must be taken into consideration by a linguistic theory with claims to adequacy. On this account, a limit in Chomskyan linguistics is his search for the "deep structures" of language, whether a question of the oral utterance or the written. As in the case of the Prefect in Edgard Allan Poe's short story, *The Purloined Letter* (1978 [1845]), who insisted on carrying out a *deep* investigation in his search for the robbed letter and failed to trace it because it was hidden on the surface, under everybody's very eyes, as generally occurs – and Auguste Dupin was well aware of the dynamics, for he knew that searching in the depths could lead to ignoring phenomena closer to the surface. The double meaning of "letter", understood, that is, both in the sense of an "epistle" and of a "letter in the alphabet," tells us that understanding in the word, in the utterance, also consists in surfaces because the voice is there to be perceived, even if not in the guise of intonation as occurs in orality, but as accentuation which can always be traced in writing as well. And in fact a major limit in Chomskyian linguistics consists in its electing as the object of analysis the abstract sentences of abstract speech.

Voice is a characteristic that distinguishes and individualizes sound, it is connected to various practices that aim to obtain consent, the voice is an element of charisma. Moreover, the voice is connected to sacred practices and to different levels of consciousness. Again in "Voice and Identity," precisely in the section titled "Transcendence," Tarasti claims that: "Prenatal experiences show that man's sensations (exteroceptive signs) both begin and end with voices. Even a person in a deep coma can be reached by the voice. Hence the voice unites the visible and the invisible" (2008: 290–291).

The voice is connected to orality in two forms: primary voice which prevails in face-to-face communication; and secondary voice which is recorded and mechanically reproduced by telephones, on TV, mobile phones.

In various passages in his essays on the voice, Tarasti dwells on the relation between voice and music. Voice as sound is an important element in music and its presence in different ways contributes to characterising the different periods and trends in the history of music.

But we will consider another aspect of the voice that is not connected with sound, with the grain of the voice in a literal sense. Barthes uses this expression and like Julia Kristeva (1982) not just in the literal sense, In fact, after Barthes's death, to the question "what remains of Barthes?," Kristeva responds: "the grain of the voice," because Barthes, as she explains, is not a man who leaves messages (Kristeva 1982).

> [. . .] j'ai l'impression que cet écrivain nous donne d'abord et essentiellement *une voix* [. . .]. C'est (peu) dire qu'il n'est pas un homme de message. Certains ont dû être déçus de voir délivrer, du haut des institutions les plus prestigieuses, un enseignement si pleinement vocal, si peu initiatique, si peu platonicien en somme, si peu pater-filialiste. Je l'entends encore se dire *ennuyé* – un mot qui stoppait chez lui la rancune, rendait impossible le ressentiment, éliminait la haine – de leur aigreur. Et jubiler discrètement dans le "grain de la voix" d'avoir su déjouer ainsi le piège suprême de l'institution et/ou du sens en leur lieu même. La voix comme lieu de l'affect? Comme traversée du sens? Comme antidote de la haine? (Kristeva 1982: 120)

This nonliteral meaning of voice is connected to the existential semiotics of the other. Voice thus understood is trace, singular expression, *saying* versus *said* (according to Levinas), an act understood as a unique and unrepeatable event.

Voice in this sense is the utterance, not only the oral utterance, but also the utterance in *writing*, writing versus transcription, writing as understood by Roland Barthes, Jacques Derrida, Julia Kristeva.

Mikhail M. Bakhtin too uses voice in this sense, to indicate a singular perspective, a particular point of view, to stay in a position without the possibility of substitution, of replacement. Described in such terms, voice is connected to responsibility without alibis, to responsibility intended not in a technical sense, as special responsibility, responsibility relative to a particular role, profession, competence, but as responsibility that Bakhtin calls "moral responsibility". On a linguistic level, voice in this sense is a characteristic of the utterance, both oral and written, understood as a singular, unique act, with its unrepeatable intonation, accentuation. "Voice" is understood in this sense when Bakhtin talks about Dostoevsky's "polyphonic novel". According to Bakhtin dialogism is encounter and interweaving of voices (Bachtin e il suo Circolo 2014; Petrilli 2012b; Ponzio 1994, 1998, 2015).

The voice is always oriented towards another voice. In this sense it is transcendent, "transgredient". One's own utterance, both oral and written, alludes always and in spite of itself, whether it knows it or not, to the utterance of others. No judgment-utterance, no living proposition can be separated from an orientation, a standpoint; the utterance of live discourse necessarily takes a stand towards the other. This means that the utterance is never oriented directly towards its theme. There is always a process of refraction in the word, for the word is always mediated by the relation to others, which is a relation of both the cognitive and affective orders. Judgment-utterances are at once allocution-utterances, therefore utterances that enter into dialogic contact with other utterances. Consciousness of self is reached and perceived against the background of the consciousness that another has of it; "I-for-myself" against the background of "I-for-the-other". Therefore dialogism also presents itself in the single voice, in the single utterance, as interference among contradictory voices present in every "atom" of this utterance, in the most subtle structural elements of discourse, thus of consciousness.

Dialogism is inseparable from voice understood in this nonliteral sense. Otherwise, it becomes abstract and void dialectics. Dialogue takes place among *voices* – not monologic and integral voices, but internally dialogic and divided voices – and *voices* allude to the ideological position *embodied* in the world (Ponzio 1993). Bakhtin highlights the problematic of the voice's embodiment. He states that Dostoevsky's hero is *voice* and that the author does not show it to us as though it were an object, but has us listen to it (Petrilli 2019; Ponzio 2006b). In Bakhtin's view, (monologic) dialogues are neither dialectical nor synthetic given that no contradictions arise from *disembodied ideas*. In Dostoevsky's polyphonic novel the idea is not conceived as a monologic conclusion, but rather as the event of interacting voices.

The logic of Dostoevsky's polyphonic novel is presented in terms of dia-logic. This is possible because *ideas are embodied in different voices that are unindifferent to each other* (Petrilli and Ponzio 2000; Ponzio 1990). As much occurs in spite of, or even because of, the effort to ignore each other, therefore, in spite of the delusory effort to elude the mix up of voices in which differences flourish. Dialogism constitutes the real life of word and thought with respect to which monologic dialogue is an abstraction, a representation relieved of the condition of responsibility without alibis. On the contrary, dialogism as we are describing it implies interconnectedness with every other body in the living world, therefore unlimited responsibility/answerability, the original modality of being in the world of each and every one of us, whose embodiment is expressed through the voice, in a relation to being whose body in its singularity occupies a position that cannot be exchanged with any other (Ponzio 1997, 2007, 2009a, 2009b). And when, in "From Notes Made in 1970–71" (presented in English translation in the 1986 collection *Speech Genres and Other Late Essays*), Bakhtin describes the process that leads from concrete dia-logics without synthesis to abstract monologic dialectics, he indicates the voice as a fundamental element in the distinction between dia-logics and dialectics:

> Take a dialogue and remove the voices (the partitioning of voices), remove the intonations (emotional and individualizing ones), carve out abstract concepts and judgments from living words and responses, cram everything into one abstract consciousness – and that's how you get dialectics. (Bakhtin 1986: 147)

In Bakhtin's view, the voice, its embodiment, the body differentiate dialogue as conceived by Dostoevsky from dialogue in Plato where (as much as dialogue is not completely monologized, pedagogical) the multiplicity of voices is cancelled in the idea. Plato is interested in the disembodied ideal, the idea as being and not as a dialogic event, the event itself of dialogue. In Plato, participation in the idea is not participation in dialogue, but in the being of the idea. Consequently, different and unindifferent voices are annulled in the unity of belonging to a common entity. Moreover, in Bakhtin's view another element which distinguishes the two types of dialogue is that dialogue in Dostoevsky by comparison to Plato, is neither cognitive nor philosophical. Bakhtin prefers to relate dialogue in Dostoevsky to biblical and evangelical dialogue, as in Job for example, because of its internally infinite structure that has no possibility of synthesis and is external to the sphere of knowledge. All the same, Bakhtin warns us that not even biblical dialogue provides the more substantial characteristics of dialogue traceable, instead, in Dostoevsky's writings.

The text – formed out of the semiotic material of the dialogical word, the dialogical utterance – lives in encounter among voices. In one of his final papers, "Methodology for the Human Sciences" (1974) (included in his 1979 collection and it too translated into English in the 1986 collection cited above), Bakhtin claims that

> The text lives only by coming into contact with another text (with context). [. . .] We emphasize that this contact is a dialogic contact between texts (utterances) and not a mechanical contact of "opposition," [. . .] among abstract elements [. . .]. Behind this contact is a contact of personalities and not of things. (1979, Eng. trans. in Bakhtin 1986: 162)

The specific logic of the text takes the form of dia-logic, dialectics among texts. However, dialogue does not only involve a relationship among texts and discourses, but also among utterances. Dialogic relationships are not only possible among (relatively) whole utterances, but also inside any signifying part of an utterance, indeed it is possible to hear somebody else's voice even in the individual word:

> Thus dialogic relationships can permeate inside the utterance, even inside the individual word, as long as two voices collide within it dialogically [. . .].
> (Bakhtin 1963, Eng. trans.: 184)

Text, utterance and word are dialogic. But they address

> [. . .] the word not in a system of language and not in a "text" excised from dialogic interaction, but precisely within the sphere of dialogic interaction itself, that is, in that sphere where discourse lives an authentic life. For the word is not a material thing but rather the eternally mobile, eternally fickle medium of dialogic interaction. It never gravitates toward a single consciousness or a single voice. The life of the word is contained in its transfer from one mouth to another, from one context to another context, from one social collective to another, from one generation to another generation. In this process the word does not forget its own path and cannot completely free itself from the power of these concrete contexts into which it has entered. (Bakhtin 1963, Eng. trans.: 202)

Furthermore, dialogic relationships are also possible between language styles, social dialects, etc., insofar as they are perceived as voices, as evaluative positions, as linguistic expressions of different worldviews. Dialogism in the utterance as a whole, or in its separate parts or in its individual words is also the effect of inner reservation, of a certain distance taken from them by the author. And the forms of this dialogic relationship between the author and his or her own utterances – irony, parody, detachment, critique – depends on the relationship between the author and his or her interlocutors whether they be present or absent, imaginary or real (cf. Bakhtin 1963, Eng. trans.: 184).

In the final part of *Marxism and Philosophy of Language*, Voloshinov (1929, Eng. trans. 1973: 156–159) focuses on the relation between the voice as a unique dialogic position and perspective and the voice in the literal sense, that is, as sound. The question concerns the possibility of phonic embodiment – that is, of embodiment in the voice as sound – of reported speech manifest in the context of the author's discourse. Recitation is obviously possible in the case of a theatrical text, a text designed for acting, but a perfect, absolute recitation is impossible in the case of the novel, specially the polyphonic novel as well as certain poems – as, for example, in Puškin's "Departure," examined by Bakhtin in his early essay "Toward a Philosophy of the Act" (1920–1924, in Bachtin e il suo Circolo 2014: 33–168). The difficulty of evaluative, expressive intonation consists here in a constant shifting movement from the evaluative purview of the author to that of the character, of the hero, and back again. "The absolute acting out of reported speech, where a work of fiction is read aloud, is admissible only in the rarest cases" (Bakhtin 2014: 157–159). In artistic prose, a perfect translation from voice as evaluation and point of view to voice as sound is generally impossible. In the encounter among voices, literary writing can achieve what in oral language is difficult or nearly impossible (Petrilli and Ponzio 2003b; Ponzio 2010a, 2010b). It ensues that literary writing is capable of evidencing the effective signifying potential, the infinite play of surfaces and capacity for transcendence characteristic of texts and utterances.

References

Bachtin Michail e il suo Circolo. 2014. *Opere 1919–1930*, bilingual Russian/Italian edition, trans. (with Luciano Ponzio), ed., intr. (xi–xxxii) and comment by Augusto Ponzio, series "Il Pensiero Occidentale", director-in-chief Giovanni Reale. Milan: Bompiani. [The book includes the following works in Russian and in Italian: by Mikhail Bakhtin, "Art and responsibility" (1919), "For a Philosophy of the Responsible Act" (1920–24 and "Fragment of Chapter I of *Author and hero in aesthetic activity* (1920–24), and *Problems of Dostoevsky's Artwork*, 1929; by Ivan I, Kanev, "Contemporary Vitalism" (1926); by Pavel Medvedev, *The Formal Method in the Science of Literature* (1928); by Valentin Voloshinov, "Discourse in life and in poetry" (1926), *Freudism* (1927), *Marxism and the Philosophy of Language* (1929), "Stylistics of artistic discourse" (1930), and "On the margins between poetics and linguistics" (1930)].

Bakhtin, Mikhail. 1929. *Problemy tvorchestva Dostoevskogo*. Leningrad: Priboj; bilingual Russian/Italian edition in Bachtin e il suo Circolo 2014, 1053–1423.

Bakhtin, Mikhail. 1963. *Problemy poetiki Dostoevskogo*, 2nd revised and enlarged edition of Bakhtin 1929. Moscow: Sovetskij pisatel'. (Eng trans. *Problems of Dostoevsky's Poetics* by C. Emerson, W. C. Booth (Introduction). Manchester: Manchester University Press, 1984.)

Bakhtin, Mikhail. 1965. *Rabelais and His World*. Eng. trans. and ed. by K. Pomorska. Cambridge: Massachusetts Institute of Technology, 1968. (New trans. by H. Iswolsky. Bloomington: Indiana University Press, 1984.)

Bakhtin, Mikhail. 1979. *Estetica slovesnogo tvorčestva* [Aesthetics of verbal art]. Moscow: Iskusstovo; *L'autore e l'eroe. Teoria letteraria e scienze umane*, Clara Strada, Janovič (trans.). Turin: Einaudi, 1988.

Bakhtin, Mikhail. 1981. *The Dialogic Imagination: Four Essays*, ed. C. Emerson & M. Holquist. Austin: University of Texas Press.

Bakhtin, Mikhail. 1986. *Speech Genres & Other Late Essay*, ed. C. Emerson & M. Holquist. Austin: University of Texas Press.

Bakhtin, Mikhail. 1990. *Art and Answerability*, ed. M. Holquist & V. Liapunov. Austin: University of Texas Press.

Barthes, Roland. 1977. *Image, Music, Text*. New York: Hill and Wang.

Barthes, Roland. 1981. *Le grain de la voix*. Paris: Seuil.

Kristeva, Julia 1982. La voix de Barthes. *Communications. Roland Barthes* 36. 119–123. Paris: Seuil.

Levinas, Emmanuel. 1961. *Totalité et Infini*. The Hague: Martinus Nijhoff. (1968, 1971; *Totality and Infinity*, Eng. trans. and intro. by A. Lingis & J. Wild. Dordrecht-Boston-London: Kluwer Academic Publishers, 1991.)

Levinas, Emmanuel. 1974. *Autrement qu'être ou au-dela de l'essence*. The Hague: Nijhoff. (Eng. trans. *Otherwise than Being or Beyond Essence*, by A. Lingis. Pittsburgh: Duquesne University Press, 2000.)

Merleau-Ponty, Maurice. 1945. *Phénoménologie de la perception*. Paris: Gallimard.

Peter of Spain (Petrus Hispanus). 1972 [c. 1230]. *Tractatus*, called afterward *Summule logicales*. First critical edition from the manuscript with an introduction by L. M. De Rijk. Assen, Netherlands: Van Gorcum. It. trans. from Latin, intro. & ed. by A. Ponzio, *Tractatus. Summule logicales*, bilingual Medieval Latin/Italian edition. Milan: Bompiani, 2003, new and revised edition, 2010.

Petrilli, Susan (ed. and intr.). 2008. *Approaches to Communication. Trends in Global Communication Studies* [includes chapters by M. Danesi, F. Merrell, T. L. Short, A. Ponzio, G. Vaughan, B. Godard, P. Cobley, T. A. Sebeok, J. Deely, J. Bernard, Eero and Eila Tarasti, J. Cutler-Shaw, G. Withalm]. Madison, WI: Atwood.

Petrilli, Susan. 2009. *Signifying and Understanding. Reading the Works of Victoria Welby and the Significs Movement*. Semiotics, Communication and Cognition. Berlin: De Gruyter Mouton.

Petrilli, Susan. 2010. *Sign Crossroads in Global Perspective. Semioethics and Responsibility*, ed. J. Deely. New Brunswick (U.S.A.) and London (U.K.): Transaction Publishers.

Petrilli, Susan. 2012a. *Expression and Interpretation in Language*, Pref. Vincent Colapietro, xv–xviii. New Brunswick: Transaction.

Petrilli, Susan. 2012b. *Altrove e altrimenti. Filosofia del linguaggio, critica letteraria e teoria della traduzione in, con e a partire da Bachtin*. Milan: Mimesis.

Petrilli, Susan. 2013. *The Self as a Sign, the World, and the Other. Living Semiotics*, Foreword by Augusto Ponzio, xiii–xvi. New Brunswick: Transaction Publishers.

Petrilli, Susan. 2014a. *Sign Studies and Semioethics*. Boston-Berlin: De Gruyter Mouton.

Petrilli, Susan (ed.). 2014b. *Semioetica e comunicazione globale*. (Athanor, XXIV, 17). Milan: Mimesis.

Petrilli, Susan (ed.). 2015. *Scienze dei linguaggi e linguaggi delle scienze*. Athanor XXV, 18. Milan: Mimesis.
Petrilli, Susan. 2016. *The Global World and Its Manifold Faces*. Bern-New York: Peter Lang.
Petrilli, Susan (ed.). 2017a. *Challenges to Living Together*. Milan: Mimesis International.
Petrilli, Susan (ed.). 2017b. *Pace, pacificazione, pacifismo e i loro linguaggi*. Athanor XXVI, 20. Milan: Mimesis.
Petrilli, Susan. (ed.). 2017c. *Digressioni nella storia. Dal tempo del sogno al tempo della globalizzazione*. Milan: Mimesis.
Petrilli, Susan. 2019a. *Significare, interpretare e intendere*. Lecce: Pensa Multimedia.
Petrilli, Susan. 2019b. *Signs, Language and Listening. Semioethic Perspectives*. Ottawa: Legas.
Petrilli, Susan (ed.). 2019c. *Diritti umani e diritti altrui*. Athanor XXX, 23. Milan: Mimesis.
Petrilli, Susan; Ponzio, Augusto. 2000. *Philosophy of Language, Art and Answerability in Mikhail Bakhtin*. New York, Toronto, Ottawa: Legas.
Petrilli, Susan. 2003a. *Semioetica*. Rome: Meltemi.
Petrilli, Susan. 2003b. *Views in Literary Semiotics*. Toronto: Legas.
Petrilli, Susan. 2005. *Semiotics Unbounded. Interpretive Routes in the Open Network of Signs*. Toronto: Toronto University Press.
Petrilli, Susan. 2016. *Lineamenti di semiotica e di filosofia del6linguaggio*. Perugia: Guerra edizioni.
Petrilli, Susan. 2019. *Identità e alterità. Per una semioetica della comunicazione*, Athanor XXIX, 22. Milan: Mimesis.
Petrilli, Susan. 2019. *Dizionario, Enciclopedia, Traduzione fra César Durmarsais e Umberto Eco*. Alberobello, Bari: AGA; Paris: Itali; Parigi, L'Harmattan.
Poe, Edgar Allan. 1978. *The Purloined Letter* (1845). In *The Complete Poems and Stories of Edgar Allan Poe*, eds. A. H. Quinn and E. H. O'Neill, vol. 2, 593–607. New York: Alfred A Knopf.
Ponzio, Augusto. 1990. *Man as a Sign. Essays on the Philosophy of Language*, ed., trans. intro. and Appendixes by S. Petrilli. Berlin: Mouton de Gruyter.
Ponzio, Augusto. 1992. *Dialogo e narrazione*. Lecce: Milella.
Ponzio, Augusto. 1993. *Signs, Dialogue and Ideology*, ed. S. Petrilli. Amsterdam: John Benjamins.
Ponzio, Augusto. 1994. *Scrittura, dialogo, alterità. Tra Bachtin e Lévinas*. Florence: La Nuova Italia; new. ed. Palomar, Bari, 2008.
Ponzio, Augusto.1996. *Subjectivité et alterité dans la philosophie de Emmanuel Lévinas*. Paris: L'Harmattan.
Ponzio, Augusto.1998. *La revolución bajtiniana. El pensamiento de Bajtin y la ideologia contemporanea*, trans. by M. Arriaga Florez. Madrid: Catedra.
Ponzio, Augusto.1997. *Elogio dell'infunzionale. Critica dell'ideologia della produttività*. Rome: Castelvecchi, 2nd reviewed and amplified edn. Milan: Mimesis, 2004.
Ponzio, Augusto.2006a. *The Dialogic Nature of Sign*. Ottawa: Legas.
Ponzio, Augusto.2006b. *La cifrematica e l'ascolto*. Bari: Graphis.
Ponzio, Augusto.2006. The I questioned. Emmanuel Levinas and the critique of occidental reason. *Subject Matters. A Journal of Communication Studies and the Self*, Special Edition 3(1). 1–42. London Metropolitan University 2006. (This volume contains contributions commenting Augusto Ponzio's essay on Levinas, authored by Adam Zachary Newton, Michael B. Smith, Robert Bernasconi, Graham Ward, Roger Burggraeve, Bettina Bergo, William Paul Simmons, Annette Aronowiz).

Ponzio, Augusto. 2007. *Fuori luogo. L'esorbitante nella riproduzione dell'identico*. Rome: Meltemi; 2nd ed. Milan: Mimesis, 2013.
Ponzio, Augusto. 2009a. *L'écoute de l'autre*. Paris: L'Harmattan.
Ponzio, Augusto. 2009b. *Emmanuel Levinas, Globalisation, and Preventive Peace*, Eng. trans. by S. Petrilli. New York, Ottawa, Toronto: Legas.
Ponzio, Augusto. 2010a. *Rencontre de paroles. L'autre dans le discours*, coll. "Les Voix du Livre", dirigée par Giovanni Dotoli. Paris: Alain Baudry et Cie.
Ponzio, Augusto. 2010b. *Procurando uma palavra outra*. San Carlo (Brasile): Pedro e João Editores.
Ponzio, Augusto (ed.). 2011. *Incontri di parole*. Athanor. Semiotica, Filosofia, Arte, Letteratura, XXI, 14. Milan: Mimesis.
Ponzio, Augusto. 2015 [1992]. *Tra semiotica e letteratura. Introduzione a Michail Bachtin*. Milan: Bompiani.
Ponzio, Augusto. 2019a. *Con Emmanuel Levinas. Alterità e identità*. Filosofie, n. 618. Milan: Mimesis.
Ponzio, Augusto. 2019b. *Encontros de Palavras*. O outro no discurso, 2nd edn. San Carlo: Pedro&João.
Ponzio, Augusto. 2019c. *A ligeireza da palavra. Em dialogo com Valdemir Miotello*. San Carlos: Pedro&João.
Ponzio, Luciano. 2015. *Roman Jakobson e i fondamenti della semiotica*. Milan: Mimesis.
Tarasti Eero. 2000. *Existential Semiotics*. Bloomington: Indiana University Press; Enlarged Italian edition, *Introduzione alla semiotica esistenziale*. It. trans by M. Berruti, intr. by A. Ponzio & S. Petrilli, 7–16. (In book series Nel Segno, ed. by Susan Petrilli & Augusto Ponzio.) Bari: Giuseppe Laterza, 2008.
Tarasti Eero. 2008. "Voice and identity." In Susan Petrilli (ed.) *Approaches to Communication. Trends in Global Communication Studies*, 287–301. Madison, WI: Atwood.
Umiker-Sebeok, Jean & Thomas A. Sebeok. 1987. *Monastic Sign Languages*. Berlin, New York, Amsterdam: Mouton de Gruyter.
Voloshinov, Valentin N. 1929. *Marxism and Philosophy of Language*. Eng. trans. New York: Seminar Press, 1983. (Russian original and Italian translation in *Bachtin e il suo Circolo* 2014, 1461–1840.)

Sami Pihlström
The Transcendental and the Transcendent

Abstract: It is one of the key ideas of Kantian transcendental philosophy that the concepts of the transcendental and the transcendent are kept distinct. Roughly, the transcendental denotes the conditions and limits of humanly possible experience, while the transcendent is something that goes beyond those limits. However, in some cases no adequate understanding of certain specific transcendental conditions is possible without reference to what is seen as transcending the limits set by those conditions. This paper discusses cases in which a commitment to something that is taken as transcendent from the perspective of a certain kind of experience, or form of life, is a transcendental requirement for the intelligibility of that kind of experience or form of life. In Kantian terms, the question is whether the legitimate employment, or perhaps regulative employment, of a transcendent idea or principle can be transcendentally defended or vindicated. Accordingly, the paper draws attention to a puzzling but philosophically interesting interplay of the transcendental and the transcendent that has relevance to the historical interpretation of transcendental philosophy as well as to the philosophy of religion in particular.

Keywords: transcendental philosophy, transcendental conditions, transcendence, limits, Kant, I., Wittgenstein, L.

1 Introduction: The Kantian background

It is, as is well known, a feature of utmost importance to Immanuel Kant's transcendental philosophy that the concepts of the *transcendental* and the *transcendent* are strictly kept separate.[1] The latter refers to something that lies beyond human experience and knowledge (such as things in themselves, or the unknowable objects of the "ideas of pure reason" critically analyzed in Kant's Transcendental Dialectic, i.e., the soul, freedom, and God), whereas the former denotes the limits and/or conditions of experience and knowledge, particularly the necessary conditions for the possibility of cognitive experience that Kant examines in his

---

[1] This paper focuses on the concepts of the transcendental and the transcendent only in post-Kantian philosophy. Thus, I shall set aside the medieval discussions of *transcendentalia*, that is, such concepts as Being, One, True, or Good, which were thought to apply to all beings.

Transcendental Aesthetic (i.e., space and time as *Anschauungsformen*) and Transcendental Analytic (i.e., the pure concepts of understanding, or the categories).[2] One of Kant's most emphatic formulations of the distinction is the following:

> Wir wollen die Grundsätze, deren Anwendung sich ganz und gar in den Schranken möglicher Erfahrung hält, *immanente*, diejenigen aber, welche diese Grenzen überfliegen sollen, *transzendente* Grundsätze nennen. Ich verstehe unter diesen nicht den *transzendentalen* Gebrauch oder Missbrauch der Kategorien, welcher ein blosser Fehler der nicht gehörig durch Kritik gezügelten Urteilskraft ist, die auf die Grenze des Bodens, worauf allein dem reine Verstande sein Spiel erlaubt ist, nicht genug achtat; sondern wirkliche Grundsätze, die uns zumuten, alle jene Grenzpfähle niederzureissen und sich einen ganz neuen Boden, der überall keine Demarkation erkennt, anzumassen. Daher sind *transzendental* und *transzendent* nicht einerlei. Die Grundsätze des reinen Verstandes, die wir oben [i.e., in the Transcendental Analytic] vortrugen, sollen bloss von empirischem und nicht von transzendentalem, d.i. über die Erfahrungsgrenze hinausreichendem Gebrauche sein. Ein Grundsatz aber, der diese Schranken wegnimmt, *ja gar sie zu überschreiten gebietet*, heisst *transzendent*.[3]

From the Kantian point of view, then, a transcendent principle more radically transgresses the boundaries of human experience than a transcendental one (or one transcendentally and non-empirically employed); it not only (tries to) step outside the limits set for the empirical employment of the principles of understanding (or categories) but removes the very limitation itself, or at least seeks to do so. There are several other passages in the first *Critique* in which Kant tries to spell out what he means by the "transcendent". For example, we are told that there is no adequate empirical employment for transcendent principles.[4] Kant himself, however, may be claimed to, at least occasionally, obscure his terminology. The "pure concepts of reason" examined in the Dialectic are "transcendental ideas" (*transzendentale Ideen*), while their employment is, typically, "tran-

---

[2] See Immanuel Kant, *Kritik der reinen Vernunft*, ed. Raymund Schmidt (Hamburg: Felix Meiner, 1990) (A = 1st ed., 1781; B = 2nd ed., 1787). I have also used the Norman Kemp Smith translation, *Critique of Pure Reason* (London: Macmillan, 1929). The famous Kemp Smith translation, unlike the more recent (and more reliable) one by Paul Guyer and Allan Wood (Kant, *Critique of Pure Reason*, Cambridge: Cambridge University Press, 1998), can also be found as a searchable electronic edition prepared by Stephen Palmquist: see http://humanum.arts.cuhk.edu.hk/Philosophy/Kant/cpr/.
[3] Kant, *Kritik der reinen Vernunft*, A295–296/B352–353. The passage is from the introduction to the Transcendental Dialectic.
[4] Kant, *Kritik der reinen Vernunft*, A308/B365. For explicit uses of the term "transcendent" (*transzendent*) in relation to traditional metaphysics, see B427, A771/B799 on rational psychology (employing the transcendent concept of the soul), and A420/B447–448, A456/B484 on rational cosmology (employing the concept of the world, or transcendental ideas as *Weltbegriffe*).

scendent".⁵ Another passage, from the conclusion of the Antinomies, makes things somewhat clearer:

> Solange wir mit unseren Vernunftbegriffen bloss die Totalität der Bedingungen in der Sinnenwelt, und was in Ansehung ihrer der Vernunft zu Diensten geschehen kann, zum Gegenstande haben; so sind unsere Ideen zwar transzendental, aber doch *kosmologisch*. Sobald wir aber das Unbedingte (um das es doch eigentlich zu tun ist) in demjenigen setzen, was ganz ausserhalb der Sinnenwelt, mithin ausser aller möglichen Erfahrung ist, so werden die Ideen *transzendent*; sie dienen nicht bloss zur Vollendung des empirischen Vernunftgebrauchs (der immer eine nie auszuführende, aber dennoch zu befolgende Idee bleibt), sondern sie trennen sich davon gänzlich, und machen sich selbst Gegenstände, deren Stoff nicht aus Erfahrung genommen, deren objektive Realität auch nicht auf der Vollendung der empirischen Reihe, sondern auf reinen Begriffen a priori beruht. Dergleichen transzendente Ideen haben einen bloss intelligiblen Gegenstand, welchen als ein transzendentales Objekt, von dem man übrigens nichts weiss, zuzulassen, allerdings erlaubt ist, wozu aber, um es als ein durch seine unterscheidenden und inneren Prädikate bestimmbares Ding zu denken, wir weder Gründe der Möglichkeit (als unabhängig von allen Erfahrungsbegriffen), noch die mindeste Rechtfertigung, einen solchen Gegenstand anzunehmen, auf unserer Seite haben, und welches daher ein blosses Gedankending ist.⁶

The objects of transcendent ideas, or of ideas and principles whose employment is transcendent, thus remain "mere intelligible objects", "mere thought-things" (*Gedankendinge*), comparable to Kant's famous *noumena*. Roughly, Kant's picture is that the transcendental ideas of soul, freedom, and God can be employed either immanently or, if they are taken to be concepts of real entities (if "sie für Begriffe von wirklichen Dingen genommen werden"), in a transcendent manner: "Denn nicht die Idee an sich selbst, sondern bloss ihr Gebrauch kann, entweder in Ansehung der gesamten möglichen Erfahrung *überfliegend* (transzendent), oder *einheimisch* (immanent) sein [. . .]."⁷ The transcendental ideas of the Dialectic may,

---

5 Kant, *Kritik der reinen Vernunft*, A327/B383.
6 Kant, *Kritik der reinen Vernunft*, A565–566/B593–594.
7 Kant, *Kritik der reinen Vernunft*, A643/B671. In the *Methodenlehre*, Kant speaks about the "censorship" (*Zensur*) of reason which should lead to doubting the transcendent use of principles (A760–761/B788–789). Close to the conclusion of the entire *Critique*, in the section on the Architectonic of Pure Reason (a later section of the Doctrine of Method), Kant distinguishes between transcendental philosophy (also labelled "ontology") and the "physiology of pure reason" as subdisciplines of metaphysics, describing the latter as a rational study of nature. He further elaborates on the divisions within this physiology: "Nun ist aber der Gebrauch der Vernunft in dieser rationalen Naturbetrachtung entweder physisch, oder hyperphysisch, oder besser, entweder *immanent* oder *transzendent*. Der erstere geht auf die Natur, so weit als ihre Erkenntnis in der Erfahrung (*in concreto*) kann angewandt werden, der zweite auf diejenige Verknüpfung der Gegenstände der Erfahrung, welche alle Erfahrung übersteigt. Diese *transzendente* Physiologie hat daher entweder eine *innere* Verknüpfung, oder *äussere*, die aber beide über mögliche Er-

moreover, have legitimate *regulative* employment, but they can have no *constitutive* employment in the way in which the transcendental conditions of experience to be found in sensibility and understanding do; that is, they cannot be used to constitute a transcendent rationalist system of knowledge.[8]

I have quoted Kant extensively in order to provide some context for the reflections that follow, but my purpose in this essay is not to settle the historical question of what Kant meant by the two notions I am examining. The relation between the transcendental and the transcendent does deserve philosophical scrutiny even in our own time, however. Indeed, this distinction is all too often overlooked today. We easily find otherwise insightful and careful thinkers somewhat carelessly using these two terms more or less interchangeably, or at least without making clear what their meanings are. We also find philosophers deliberately blurring the distinction: for instance, A.W. Moore passes over Kant's distinction "for the sake of simplicity", while inaccurately claiming that transcendental idealism postulates a *transcendent* (non-empirical) dependence of "some aspects of the form of that to which our representations answer" on "some aspects of the representations."[9]

In many cases, including perhaps Moore's, using the word "transcendental" would suffice; the talk about transcendent entities or transcendence often leads to trouble.[10] It would, however, be too simple just to drop the transcendent and stick to the transcendental, because in some cases no adequate understanding of

---

fahrung hinausgehen, zu ihrem Gegenstande; jene ist die Physiologie der gesamten Natur, d.i. die *transzendentale Welterkenntnis*, diese des Zusammenhanges der gesamten Natur mit einem Wesen über Natur, d.i. die transzendentale *Gotteserkenntnis*." (A845–846/B873–874.) See also A799/B827. We will in what follows be mostly interested in transcendent appeals to a world-external being, or God, thus on the "external" (*äussere*) part of transcendent (*hyperphysisch*) use of reason.

8 Cf. especially the closing of the Transcendental Dialectic. Kant, *Kritik der reinen Vernunft*, A702–703/B730–731.

9 A.W. Moore, *Points of View* (Oxford: Clarendon Press, 1997), pp. 116, 122n8. See also Moore, "Human Finitude, Ineffability, Idealism, Contingency", *Nous* 26 (1992), 427–446.

10 This criticism, of course, is not directed against those who carefully use the concepts of the transcendental and the transcendent in a manner related, but not identical, to Kant's. An example of such a usage is provided by Edmund Husserl's phenomenology, in which the "transcendence" of external objects is part of the transcendental structure of the meaning-bestowing transcendental self, ego, or consciousness, to whom those transcendent objects are given in experience. Consciousness, for Husserl, is transcendental precisely because of its intentional relation to transcendent objects – and the same seems to hold for, e.g., Jean-Paul Sartre's reflections on the "transcendence of the ego". On Husserl's place in the "transcendental tradition" starting with Kant, see especially David Carr, *The Paradox of Subjectivity: The Self in the Transcendental Tradition* (Oxford and New York: Oxford University Press, 1999). See also, e.g., John D. Caputo,

certain *specific* transcendental conditions is possible without reference to what is seen as transcending the limits set by those conditions. I shall, in the following, discuss cases in which a commitment to something that is taken as transcendent from the perspective of certain kind of experience, or form of life,[11] is a transcendental requirement for the intelligibility of that kind of experience or form of life. In Kantian terms, the question is whether the legitimate employment or perhaps regulative employment, of a certain transcendent idea or principle, can be transcendentally defended or vindicated. We will, thus, notice a puzzling but philosophically interesting interplay of the transcendental and the transcendent.

It should be noted that I am no semiotician; yet, given the interest in "transcendence" in recent "existential semiotics",[12] my purely philosophical reflections may (I hope) be helpful in this context. In any event, it should be clear that the issue I shall be examining concerns the conditions and limits of human representational capacities. Insofar as the nature of representation is relevant to semiotics, the distinction between the transcendent and the transcendental, as well as their "interplay", should also be.[13]

2 Arguing transcendentally for transcendence?

As an obvious source of relevant examples of transcendental reasoning about the transcendent, I shall consider a particular language-game, or a group of language-games, namely, the religious one(s),[14] and briefly examine two specific

---

"Transcendence and the Transcendental in Husserl's Phenomenology", *Philosophy Today* 23 (1979), 205–216.
11 I am deliberately using this Wittgensteinian expression. For some discussions of whether, and how, Wittgenstein's (later) philosophy should be interpreted as a form of transcendental inquiry, see Sami Pihlström, *Naturalizing the Transcendental: A Pragmatic View* (Amherst, NY: Prometheus/Humanity Books, 2003), ch. 2, and Pihlström, "Recent Reinterpretations of the Transcendental", *Inquiry* 47 (2004), 289–314.
12 I am particularly indebted to Eero Tarasti's work here. See especially his book in Finnish, *Arvot ja merkit* ["Values and Signs"] (Helsinki: Gaudeamus, 2004), as well as his earlier *Existential Semiotics: Advances in Semiotics* (Bloomington and Indianapolis: Indiana University Press, 2000).
13 Whenever I speak about language, language-games, language-use, etc., in the following, my semiotically-minded readers may construe my claims broadly as being, *mutatis mutandis*, about any human employment of signs.
14 Speaking about "the religious language-game" is highly problematic, of course, and I make no claims about Wittgenstein's own views in the philosophy of religion.

problems pertaining to religious language-use, namely, the problem of the existence of God (section 2.1) and the problem of evil (section 2.2).

I have chosen to focus (in section 2.1) on a transcendental argument for theism drawn from Charles Taylor's work, instead of, say, the more explicitly transcendental "Martin – Frame Debate" on TAG (the transcendental argument for the existence of God) vs. TANG (the transcendental argument for the non-existence of God).[15] The latter exchange of arguments is an exchange between a somewhat fundamentalist believer (John N. Frame) and a stubborn atheist (Michael Martin) about whether God's existence is a necessary presupposition for logic, science, and morality (as Frame believes) or whether, rather, God's non-existence can be seen as such a presupposition. Martin argues that God's existence would make logic dependent on God's will and thus contingent (which is absurd), would violate basic scientific principles (because science can admit no miracles) and would destroy objective morality (because the morally right, pretty much like the logically necessary, would be dependent on God's arbitrary judgment). Needless to say, a Christian believer like Frame contests these claims and argues, apologetically, that no logical or even meaningful thought, let alone science or morality, is possible in the absence of God. The exchange does contain interesting discussion of, e.g., the concept of a miracle and the concept of God's necessary existence, but it throws little light on the relation between the transcendental and the transcendent. Frame can be read as a thinker postulating a transcendent being as a transcendental condition of something we take for granted (logic, science, morality), but his argument is hardly sophisticated enough to deserve detailed philosophical attention from people not so strongly committed – either to Christian theism or to atheism *à la* Martin. In short, both Frame and Martin operate on a level of generality that hides rather than illuminates the key issues. Neither TAG nor TANG is helpful as an evaluation of a genuine religious believer's thinking. A more pragmatic and contextualized strategy, such as Taylor's, is worth exploring.[16]

---

[15] This debate between Michael Martin and John N. Frame, with numerous responses by both authors (1996–1997), can be found at the "Internet Infidels" website, http://www.infidels.org/library/modern/michael_martin/martin-frame/, with links to Frame's statements at http://www.reformed.org/apologetics/martin/frame_contra_martin.html.

[16] There are many more examples that might be considered but that I must leave aside here. For example, for an account of Paul Tillich's epistemology of religious belief as an attempt to legitimate the transcendent by appealing to the transcendental, see Dirk-Martin Grube, "A Critical Reconstruction of Paul Tillich's Epistemology", *Religious Studies* 33 (1997), 67–80.

2.1 Is there a transcendental argument for theism?

As an example of a truly transcendental – and truly interesting – argument for theism, i.e., for the existence of God (and, specifically, God's grace) as an indispensable presupposition of our moral lives, we may take a look at Taylor's argument, as analyzed in a recent essay by D.P. Baker.[17] First, however, some terminological issues must be settled. The notion of a transcendental *argument* (not only the modern notion of the "transcendental" as such) goes back to Kant, whose Transcendental Deduction of the categories is usually taken to be a model of transcendental arguments. In such arguments, something (such as the categories) is shown to be a necessary precondition for the possibility of something that we take as given or unproblematic (such as the cognitive experience of objects). While these arguments, in Kant and more recent writers, are often interpreted as intending to refute skepticism, e.g., Humean skepticism about causality, they do not stand or fall with this anti-skeptical project. They can be construed more broadly as arguments investigating *how* we are committed, in our lives and practices, to certain concepts, such as the concepts of causality (Kant) or rule-following (Wittgenstein), which may be seen as conditions for the possibility of cognitive experience or meaningful language, respectively. Thus, a *pragmatic* reinterpretation of the transcendental strategy of argumentation is available, although mainstream discussions of these matters today still understand transcendental arguments as inherently epistemological and anti-skeptical.[18]

One more historical note is needed at this point before we take a closer look at Taylor's (and Baker's) Kantian-like transcendental argument. While we may say

---

[17] See D. P. Baker, "Charles Taylor's *Sources of the Self*: A Transcendental Apologetic?", *International Journal for Philosophy of Religion* 47 (2000), 155–174. Baker specifically discusses Taylor's highly influential work *Sources of the Self: The Making of the Modern Identity* (Cambridge: Cambridge University Press, 1989). For an analysis of Taylor as a philosopher engaging in transcendental argumentation, see also Pihlström, *Naturalizing the Transcendental*, ch. 6, as well as Sami Pihlström, "Pragmatic and Transcendental Arguments for Theism: A Critical Examination", *International Journal for Philosophy of Religion* 51 (2002), 195–213. Taylor's attitude to religion is also discussed in Michael L. Morgan, "Religion, History and Moral Discourse", in James Tully (ed.), *Philosophy in an Age of Pluralism: The Philosophy of Charles Taylor in Question* (Cambridge: Cambridge University Press, 1994), pp. 49–66. It should not be forgotten that while Taylor endorses theism, he believes that secularism is the "only available mode" for a modern democracy: see Charles Taylor, "Modes of Secularism", in Rajeev Bhargava (ed.), *Secularism and Its Critics* (Delhi: Oxford University Press, 1998), pp. 31–53.

[18] See, e.g., Robert Stern (ed.), *Transcendental Arguments: Problems and Prospects* (Oxford and New York: Oxford University Press, 1999), and Robert Stern, *Transcendental Arguments and Scepticism: Answering the Question of Justification* (Oxford: Clarendon Press, 2000); for a pragmatic criticism of this approach, cf. Pihlström, *Naturalizing the Transcendental*.

that Kant invented transcendental arguments, he did not apply such arguments in theology.[19] For Kant, transcendental arguments, such as the famous Deduction or the Refutation of Idealism, were designed to show how certain things are required as preconditions of humanly possible experience. God, if he exists, falls outside humanly possible experience. No argument, transcendental or otherwise, can entitle our belief in God in the way in which we are entitled to believe in causality, for instance, or in the forms of pure intuition, viz., space and time. According to Kant, we simply cannot know, either *a priori* or *a posteriori*, that God exists; God is neither an object of possible experience nor a transcendental presupposition of the possibility of experience. Yet, Kant famously wanted to restrict the scope of knowledge in order to make room for faith,[20] and regarded God's existence as a "postulate of practical reason" required in his moral philosophy.[21] As Kant argues in his second *Critique*, morality requires that we aim at the Highest Good, or *summum bonum*, and thus pursue the happiness of those who obey the moral law – even though happiness itself can by no means be an ethical motive for our actions. Since such happiness and thus the Highest Good itself are not guaranteed for ethical persons in the empirical world of appearances, we need to "postulate" God's existence (along with freedom and the immortality of the soul) in order to account for our moral pursuit. God will, we are entitled to *hope*,

---

19 It may actually be historically incorrect to claim that Kant invented the transcendental form of argumentation because a "hidden" transcendental argument for the existence of God has been found in Descartes (especially in his *Discourse*, part IV): see Rowland Stout, "Descartes's Hidden Argument for the Existence of God", *British Journal for the History of Philosophy* 6 (1998), 155–168. As Stout puts it, this argument "works by going backwards round the famous Cartesian Circle. It turns out when the method of doubt is applied that there are some propositions that survive the most radical sceptical doubts, namely, that I think and that I exist. However, no propositions, not even these, are certain beyond doubt unless there is a non-deceiving transcendent being – God – guaranteeing the truth of clear and distinct ideas. So God exists." (Stout 1998: 156.) If successful, such an argument would transcendentally secure the existence of a transcendent God. The existence of God provides a "transcendental guarantee" for the general rule that every proposition clearly and distinctly perceived by the intellect is certainly true (158–159). Stout identifies several problems in Descartes's argumentation, among them the fact that it does not prove the existence of a benign God, i.e., a God with moral properties (166). The argument we find in Taylor, as examined by Baker, is clearly different in this regard, although it may share the same transcendental structure. (For some reflections on why argumentative structure alone is not sufficient for demarcating transcendental arguments from other kinds of argument, see Pihlström, "Recent Reinterpretations of the Transcendental".)
20 Kant, *Kritik der reinen Vernunft*, Bxxx.
21 Immanuel Kant, *Kritik der praktischen Vernunft* (ed. by Wilhelm Weischedel, in *Immanuel Kant: Werke*, vol. 6, Darmstadt: Wissenschaftliche Buchgesellschaft, 1983; A=1788), A223.

ultimately reward those who act purely on the grounds of their respect for the moral law.

This might be labelled a transcendental argument, although in Kant's own terms it is not one. While God's existence is, in Kant's view, a condition for the possibility of the moral life as we experience it, we cannot *know* that God exists. The argument for God's existence as a postulate of practical reason does not yield knowledge; its epistemic status is different from the conclusions of the transcendental arguments offered in Kant's theoretical philosophy, which are taken to be indubitable. As was pointed out in the introduction, Kant criticized the transcendent use of reason involved in all attempts to claim knowledge about God (or about the world as a totality). It is also worth noting that Kant explicitly urges us *not* to resort to transcendental arguments in theology. Now, it has been widely believed that Kant himself never used the term "transcendental argument" – and that it is a much more recent coinage, introduced in the twentieth century, gaining wider usage in the literature only since P.F. Strawson's seminal work, *Individuals*[22] – but this is not true. There is one passage in the first *Critique* in which the term does occur,[23] and the context is interesting from the perspective of the philosophy of religion. In his attack on what he calls the "physico-theological" proof of God's existence – that is, what is today labelled the "argument from design" – Kant says that the purposiveness and harmony of nature can only prove the contingency of the *form* of the world, not of the substance or *matter* of the world (and thus the need for a transcendent creator); in order to prove the latter, we would have to prove "that the things in the world would not of themselves be capable of such order and harmony, in accordance with universal laws, if they were not *in their substance* the product of supreme wisdom". But we can at most prove that there has been an "architect", not that there has been a creator. This is insufficient for proving "an all-sufficient primordial being". He concludes: "To prove the contingency of matter itself, we should have to resort to a transcendental argument, and this is precisely what we have here set out to avoid."[24]

---

[22] P. F. Strawson, *Individuals: An Essay in Descriptive Metaphysics* (London and New York: Routledge, 1959/1993).
[23] As Paul Franks and Barry Stroud note in their contributions to Stern (ed.), *Transcendental Arguments*, this has been observed by David Bell.
[24] Kant, *Critique of Pure Reason*, Kemp Smith translation, A627/B655. The German original reads as follows: "Wollten wir die Zufälligkeit der Materie selbst beweisen, so müssten wir zu einem transzendentalen Argumente unsere Zuflucht nehmen, welches aber hier eben hat vermieden werden sollen." So this clearly refutes the widespread belief that Kant himself never used the term "transcendental argument", although it must be acknowledged that his usage is somewhat different from the modern one. He is, in effect, saying that transcendental arguments are *not* a solid part of transcendental philosophy. Perhaps he should here have used the term "transcend-

The "transcendental argument" for the existence of God that Baker finds in Taylor's defence of moral realism in *Sources of the Self* is, then, not strictly speaking Kantian, because for Kant such arguments are impossible in the theological case, but it does bear resemblance to the general model of transcendental argumentation we can adopt from Kant. Of course, Taylor is not arguing that God's existence is a necessary presupposition for the possibility of cognitive experience; just like Kant's, his theistic argument is restricted to the sphere of morality. In Kant's terms, he does not *prove* God's existence. This is hardly surprising: no one should today dream of the possibility of giving a deductive philosophical proof for theism in such a manner that atheists would become convinced and turn into believers. Kant's and, before him, Hume's arguments against ontological, cosmological and design proofs are so powerful that the prospects of infallibly demonstrating the existence of God look hopeless. Taylor's argument, while transcendental, does not lead to an indubitable conclusion about God's necessary existence. But it is, clearly, an argument trying to demonstrate our need to postulate God in order to account for our moral experience. Thus, it provides a case study of a transcendental argument which is not logically conclusive but may nevertheless illuminate important interconnections between some central concepts we use to structure our lives or "lifeworld", including in particular concepts seeking to represent the transcendent.[25]

In Baker's formulation, Taylor's argument can be reconstructed as follows:
1. We are essentially subjects.
2. It is essential to our manner of being as subjects that we perceive the world in moral terms.

---

ent", referring to arguments that purport to show something about what falls beyond the reach of human experience and understanding. See, however, also Kant's discussion of the methodological requirements of "transcendental proofs" (*Beweise*) at A782/B810 ff.

25 In Stern's terms (see his *Transcendental Arguments and Scepticism*, ch. 1), we may say that we are here dealing with a concept- or belief-directed (and thus relatively modest) transcendental argument, instead of a truth-directed (and thus immodest) one. However, Stern's distinction, also employed by several contributors to his edited volume, *Transcendental Arguments*, trivializes the core of Kantian transcendental philosophy, because one of Kant's key points is that the transcendental conditions for the possibility of experience are *ipso facto* conditions for the possibility of the *objects* of experience. It is this "transcendental idealism" that most recent authors pursuing transcendental arguments, like Stern, find mysterious and unacceptable. From the point of view of pragmatism (my favourite overall philosophical framework both in this essay and elsewhere), Kantian idealism can, however, receive a more naturalized interpretation which nevertheless leaves intact its central idea, the entanglement of our inescapable beliefs and concepts, on the one hand, and the structure of the world for us, on the other. I shall try to employ this strategy below, although no general reinterpretation of transcendental idealism in pragmatic terms is possible here.

3. It is essential to a moral outlook that it takes a "hypergood perspective".
4. It is the nature of a hypergood that it orders and shapes other goods into a framework.
5. We are therefore beings whose experience is defined by a moral framework which is dominated by a hypergood.[26]

In brief, then, Taylor (in Baker's view) argues that insofar as we are subjects or agents, which is something that we must take as given, we are inevitably committed to a moral framework in which one or another "hypergood" is operative. Such a commitment is, humanly speaking, inescapable. That this view is (though largely implicitly) based on a transcendental argument can clearly be seen, for instance, from the following statement by Taylor: "[D]oing without frameworks is utterly impossible for us; [. . .] the horizons within which we live our lives and which make sense of them have to include these strong qualitative discriminations. [. . .] [L]iving within such strongly qualified horizons is constitutive of human agency, [. . .] stepping outside these limits would be tantamount to stepping outside what we would recognize as integral, that is, undamaged human personhood."[27] In brief, no humanly *meaningful* life – that is, life-oriented toward certain goals or values found worth striving for – is possible without an overarching framework defined by one or another dominating "hypergood".

Baker suggests that this *general* transcendental argument must, according to Taylor, be further supported by a *specific* transcendental argument. Here we finally end up with the theistic proposal. For Taylor, according to Baker, theism provides the "best account" of the goods we find indispensable to our moral experience.[28] The general transcendental argument according to which a moral framework dominated by a "hypergood" is an inescapable feature of our moral experience relies on the following more specific argument:
1. It is indispensable to our moral framework that it includes certain specific goods, which can be orientated to and described in differing ways (for example, 'grace' [. . .]).

---

[26] Baker, "Charles Taylor's *Sources of the Self*", 163.
[27] Taylor, *Sources of the Self*, 27. For Taylor's account of the nature of transcendental arguments – including the indubitability of their conclusions, given that their premises are correct – see his paper, "The Validity of Transcendental Arguments" (1979), reprinted in Charles Taylor, *Philosophical Arguments* (Cambridge, MA and London: Harvard University Press, 1995), ch. 2.
[28] Baker, "Charles Taylor's *Sources of the Self*", 166. I am not trying to determine whether this is correct as an interpretation of Taylor. I am interested in the argument itself.

2. It is the Best Account of these goods that they be understood as part of a theistic account. That is, once the [...] goods are clearly articulated, it is indispensable to a Best Account of those goods that they be described in theistic terms.²⁹

Thus, Taylor's "hypergood" is most naturally interpreted in a transcendent or transcendence-invoking manner. An overarching, dominating good structuring all the lower-level goods strongly valued in human life can only be grounded in, or can only result from, God and his grace.

However, Baker finds Taylor's argument wanting because transcendental arguments ought to be *indubitable* and there is undeniably still room for doubt in the theistic indispensability claim. Taylor does not, it seems, provide us with a sufficient rational reason for believing in God, and hence his argument is not apodictically certain. The transcendental reasoning Taylor engages in simply fails to show that the existence of a hypergood (such as God's grace) is indispensable to our moral experience. At best, Baker seems to be saying, Taylor may succeed in showing that we need to believe in God in order to account for the phenomenology of our moral experience; he cannot show that our belief must be true. It is obviously one thing to claim that we cannot help believing that *p* and another thing to claim that our belief that *p* accurately represents the facts or the way the world is independently of our beliefs.³⁰

However, this inevitable circularity of transcendental argumentation need not worry us, if we construe these arguments in a *pragmatic* fashion, running together transcendental and *abductive* (pragmatically explanatory or elucidatory) arguments, as well as the *ontological* and *epistemic* status of transcendental arguments.³¹ In fact, transcendental arguments can only get going if we follow Kant in rejecting the split between the ontological and epistemic conclusions to be drawn from such arguments, or the corresponding split between arguments designed to establish the *truth* of their conclusion and those merely designed to establish our inescapable *need to believe* the conclusion. This is a truly pragmatist move: if it is humanly inescapable, say, as a precondition of moral experience or meaningfulness in life, to believe in God, then that belief is *ipso facto* pragmat-

---

29 Baker, "Charles Taylor's *Sources of the Self*", 167.
30 Baker, "Charles Taylor's *Sources of the Self*", 170–171. Thus, Baker assumes – as Taylor himself seems to do, too, in "The Validity of Transcendental Arguments" – that a valid transcendental argument ought to be truth-directed in Stern's above-described sense. But perhaps a belief-directed or concept-directed argument *is* sufficient, or at least all we can legitimately hope for, in such a problematic case as theism.
31 For such a suggestion in a different context, see Pihlström, *Naturalizing the Transcendental*, ch. 3.

ically true for us.³² The notion of truth is, in pragmatism, "humanized": there is no higher perspective available for us regarding the truth or falsity of any belief than a perspective lying within the commitments of our best – most critical and self-reflective – practice.

Consequently, *if* Taylor succeeds in showing that we really *have to* believe in God's existence in order to account for the source of the "hypergoods" we find inevitable in our self-image as moral agents, then, if we are also prepared to follow pragmatists like William James, we cannot but regard God's existence as a pragmatically true postulate for us.³³ Endorsing this conditional claim is of course quite different from proving God's existence demonstratively, but Taylor's argument is hardly meant to be demonstrative in the sense in which the classical theistic proofs were. On the contrary, it is much closer to Kant's above-discussed way of deriving theism, as a postulate of practical reason, from the rationally binding nature of the moral imperative (rather than the other way around).

Indeed, if we synthesize pragmatic and transcendental arguments, as I am suggesting we should do, then Kant's pragmatic argument, which turns theism into a presuppositional necessity from the point of view of morality (which we treat as given and undeniable unless we are moral nihilists or skeptics),³⁴ will turn out to be a transcendental argument in this more flexibly construed sense. *Pace*

---

32 This kind of a connection between William James's "will to believe" doctrine and his pragmatist theory of truth is discussed in Sami Pihlström, *Pragmatism and Philosophical Anthropology: Understanding Our Human Life in a Human World* (New York: Peter Lang, 1998), chs. 5–6. For James's famous (or notorious) discussions of truth, see especially his *Pragmatism: A New Name for Some Old Ways of Thinking* (ed. by Frederick H. Burkhardt, Fredson Bowers, and Ignas K. Skrupskelis, Cambridge, MA and London: Harvard University Press, 1975; first published 1907), lecture VI. Even distinguished James scholars fail to pay attention to the Jamesian pragmatist's *deliberate* blurring of the distinction between what is pragmatically needed and what is epistemically justified: see, e.g., Richard M. Gale, *The Philosophy of William James: An Introduction* (Cambridge: Cambridge University Press, 2005).
33 On the tensions in James's pragmatist philosophy of religion, see, e.g., the following recent contributions to James scholarship: Richard M. Gale, *The Divided Self of William James* (Cambridge: Cambridge University Press, 1999); Gale, *The Philosophy of William James*; Wayne Proudfoot (ed.), *William James and the Science of Religion: Re-experiencing the Varieties of Religious Experience* (New York: Columbia University Press, 2004). It is also worth noting that Taylor has over the past few years worked on James's philosophy of religion: see Charles Taylor, *Varieties of Religion Today: William James Revisited* (Cambridge, MA and London: Harvard University Press, 2002), as well as my review of Taylor's book in the *Transactions of the Charles S. Peirce Society* 39:2 (2003).
34 See Sami Pihlström, *Pragmatic Moral Realism: In Search for Ethical Seriousness* (Amsterdam and New York: Rodopi, 2005) for a statement of why we definitely should not be moral nihilists or skeptics.

Kant himself, transcendental arguments thus defined may have a legitimate use in theology, more specifically moral theology – following Kant's own example. But this redefinition of the notion of a transcendental argument requires that we soften the requirement of the indubitability of the conclusions of such arguments. The transcendental principles that can be established through transcendental reasoning are certain, indubitable, or apodictic only *contextually*, only, say, in a certain historical and cultural setting in which people find certain beliefs or the use of certain concepts inevitable. This amounts to something like a "relativized *a priori*", which has been a major topic in post-Kantian discussions of the nature of *a priori* principles, especially in the twentieth century.

It is important to see that pragmatically reconstructed and contextualized transcendental arguments are *not* intended as refutations of skepticism, either in the theistic case or more generally. As Baker's criticism of Taylor's transcendental argumentation shows, it is impossible to conclusively refute the skeptic in the theistic case. Transcendental arguments – Taylor's or indeed Kant's own – proceeding to the theistic conclusion *via* considerations of morality leave their conclusion inadequately supported from the point of view of the skeptic, who can, of course, *also* adopt moral skepticism, refusing to treat our moral orientation as inescapable and constitutive of our agency in the way in which Kant and Taylor treat it as such.[35] One may even point out that it is hopeless to overcome either moral or religious skepticism by means of a transcendental, or any, argument, because morality, pretty much like religion, requires something like faith and is thus essentially fragile and vulnerable – something one can lose, though not usually as a result of an argument.[36]

In this sense, transcendental arguments are *internal* to the practices the moral agent or the religious believer is already engaging in, i.e., internal to practices within which the skeptical threat does not arise at all. These arguments, non-skeptically rather than anti-skeptically reinterpreted, can only secure our need to maintain certain beliefs or to employ certain concepts (representing the transcendent) insofar as we go on engaging in the practices we actually do engage in, practices from which the arguments themselves begin and gain their signifi-

---

[35] Here we should remember that *moral realism*, the view that there is something like objective rightness or wrongness when it comes to ethical evaluation, and that morality is not just a matter of personal (or cultural) taste, style, or arbitrary preference, is the goal of Taylor's general transcendental argument, as analyzed by Baker. For a more detailed investigation of the possibility of defending moral realism transcendentally, see Pihlström, *Naturalizing the Transcendental*, ch. 7, and *Pragmatic Moral Realism*, especially chs. 1–2.
[36] Cf., e.g., David Wisdo, *The Life of Irony and the Ethics of Belief* (Albany: SUNY Press, 1993).

cance, practices within which the kind of transcendence the arguments defend is naturally assumed.[37]

I see, then, *some* hope for pragmatic-cum-transcendental arguments for a theistic world-view construed as a presupposition of our moral lives in a pragmatist (primarily Jamesian) or Kantian-Taylorian manner, but such arguments must, as we have seen, be considered fallible and only contextually binding, as all pragmatic arguments must. There is, then, no point in trying to prove God's existence from a philosophical point of view lying outside religious life itself. Elaborating on this insight is where "Wittgensteinian" philosophers of religion, among others, have done a great job.[38] But if we end up endorsing their (e.g., Phillips's) views, do we have to subscribe to *fideism*, the thesis that religious belief needs no evidential (or, more generally, rational) defence or justification at all? Such questions will remain open here. We have at any rate come very close to the thesis that theism cannot be rationally demonstrated or even defended to an unbeliever or skeptic at all. Insofar as *any* arguments can be given here, their relevant audience will already have to be committed to theism. Thus, Baker is in a sense right. Taylor cannot succeed in proving God's existence by means of a transcendental argument drawn on the requirements of moral realism; nor can any other transcendental inquirer, even Kant himself. But I have pointed out that, in a more flexible, contextualized, and historically sensitive sense, transcendental arguments (for the transcendent or for any philosophical thesis) are not irrelevant, and contemporary philosophers of religion, as well as semioticians, ignore them at their own peril. Within a practice, a field of commitments, or form of life, they may have an important role to play in the elucidation of the relations between the concepts employed and the commitments made, even concepts referring to the transcendent. For a certain kind of moral outlook, theism *may* turn out to be a necessary pragmatic precondition. This *may* even be the case with our, modern Westerners', moral outlook – but it may not. Transcendental arguments, when pragmatized, must, in any case, be relativized to the practice-laden context in which they are

---

[37] What we have arrived at, I think, is a case study that shows the limitations of the purely epistemological, anti-skeptical treatments of transcendental arguments, to be found, e.g., in the two volumes by Robert Stern cited above. Alternatively, we may say that skepticism about God's existence is one *prima facie* legitimate area of application for transcendental arguments if those arguments are taken to be inherently anti-skeptical, but since there will always be room for skepticism here, those arguments, thus construed, can (as we have seen Baker argue) achieve very little in that area. Fortunately, a broader construal is available – for pragmatists, at least.

[38] I am thinking about D. Z. Phillips's work, in particular, here, although I am not going to analyze in any detail the views of any particular Wittgensteinian philosopher. For an introductory text in the philosophy of religion with Wittgensteinian emphases, see B.R. Tilghman, *An Introduction to the Philosophy of Religion* (Oxford and Cambridge, MA: Blackwell, 1994).

understood as effective and relevant to the human experience. Otherwise, there is for them no practical work to do, neither in the postulation of transcendence nor in more mundane matters.

2.2 The problem of evil and the limits of language

I shall now move on to my second, more specific example, also drawn from religious language(-games). While Taylor's argument, analyzed above, emphasizes the "hypergoods" dominating our ethical agency, it may be interesting to take up another religiously relevant notion, evil. The contrast to Taylor's views is clear, but similar transcendental issues about our ability to represent the transcendent arise.

The *problem of evil* is often presented as a simple argument which is supposed to be fatal to theism:
1. A benevolent, omniscient and omnipotent (etc.) God, the creator of the world, exists. (Theistic presupposition.)
2. If such a being exists, then s/he prevents all unnecessary evil. (Apparent necessary truth.)
3. However, there is plenty of unnecessary evil in the world, i.e., evil that an omnipotent being apparently could prevent or remove. (Empirical matter of fact.)
4. Therefore, God (as described in the first premise) cannot exist.

According to this argument, theism collapses, at least in its traditional forms, as the indisputable existence of evil is presented as a challenge to the believer. If God is good but cannot prevent or remove unnecessary evil, then s/he cannot be omnipotent. If there is some evil s/he does not know about, then s/he cannot be omniscient. And if God is both omniscient and omnipotent but does not remove the unnecessary evil there is, then s/he is not wholly good. The theist will have to give up one or another of the traditional attributes of God, or else s/he will have to give up theism altogether. Presented in this manner, the problem of evil has been used as an *atheological* argument, to demonstrate that the theist is confused in believing both in the existence of God and in the (empirical) reality of evil.

The problem of evil – like, presumably, any philosophical argument – can, however, never be neutrally formulated in a situation in which no world-views or *weltanschaulichen* commitments (e.g., religious or non-religious ones) are at work. On the contrary, its very formulation presupposes all kinds of things, and here a transcendental analysis may help us to view the situation accurately. Very simply, the problem of evil must be presented in language, or, at least, in signs or symbols of some kind; now, if we follow the Wittgensteinian line of thought (transcendentally interpreted) according to which there can be no meaning without there being habitual *use* of expressions within public human ways of acting, language-games, we should admit that the meanings of our linguistic expressions, including "evil" and "God", are inextricably entangled with their use in language-games and thus in our practices (or forms of life).[39] Arguably, for a genuine believer who speaks about God in a religious way, belief in God's existence is the background of any conceivable discursive treatment of evil. The plausibility of the premises of *any* argument, including the supposedly atheological problem of evil, will be evaluated against this background. One of the three premises might then be denied, or alternatively, the religious person might contest human beings' ability to argumentatively evaluate or reason about God's volitions and actions, which, after all, must remain a great mystery for humans. This attitude may be both religiously and conceptually inevitable for someone playing a religious language-game. The believer may point out that it is *nonsensical* for a human being even to try to evaluate God's works or to argue about them. God is, simply, sovereign; we humans are tiny, unimportant creatures.[40] *We* cannot ask whether God's will or the world-order s/he has created is just or unjust. God is sovereignly beyond human understanding and standards of justice.

What does all this have to do with the transcendental and the transcendent? The crucial link is the question about the limits of language. One comes close to breaking the limits of meaningful discourse in examining the problem of evil atheologically. From the point of view of the religious person (within her/his language-game), the atheological arguer simply fails to use the word "God" religiously; the atheologian presents an abstract argument that breaks the rules of the religious language-game, or belongs to an entirely different language-game whose statements are only of limited relevance to religious life.[41] If, following

---

39 Cf., again, Pihlström, *Naturalizing the Transcendental*, ch. 2, and Pihlström, "Recent Reinterpretations of the Transcendental".
40 At this point, the believer I have imagined might, for instance, appeal to the Book of Job. For a philosophically-informed treatment, see John T. Wilcox, *The Bitterness of Job: A Philosophical Reading* (Ann Arbor: University of Michigan Press, 1989).
41 It is natural to think that this argument would be presented by a Wittgensteinian philosopher of religion (e.g., again, D. Z. Phillips), although I am not here attributing it to anyone in particular. For an exchange between Phillips and other well-known philosophers of religion (Richard Swinburne, John Hick) on the problem of evil, see Stuart C. Brown (ed.), *Reason and Religion* (Ithaca, NY: Cornell University Press, 1977), chs. 4–6. For other Wittgenstein-inspired treatments of the problem of evil, rejecting the supposed atheological force of this problem, see Wisdo, *The Life of Irony and the Ethics of Belief*, 92–101; Stephen Mulhall, *Faith and Reason* (London: Duckworth, 1994); Tilghman, *An Introduction to the Philosophy of Religion*, ch. 5.

Wittgenstein, we hold that the meaning of our linguistic expressions is grounded in their use in language-games, we are forced to admit that the meanings of words such as "God" and "evil" – like the meanings of other religiously relevant expressions (such as "mercy" and "sin") – may vary among language-games. In particular, the meanings of these terms may vary as one moves from religious discourse to secular (atheist) discourse, or *vice versa*, from a certain kind of habitual employment of concepts and/or symbols to another.

If this analysis is correct, then the problem of evil cannot function as an atheological argument, because the one who presents the argument uses language differently from the (imagined) believer whose view is the object of the argument. It is right here that we encounter a limit of language, of what can and cannot be meaningfully said in a language-game. Conversely, a believer who tries to overcome the problem of evil through a "theodicy" likewise breaks the limits of religious language. What the Wittgensteinian considerations offered here to refute, then, is not only atheological criticism of the theist's conception of God but also the traditional theist's attempt to provide a theodicy.[42] Both the atheological charge of God's injustice and the theodicist's defence of God against such charges are, from the point of view of genuinely religious trust in God, equally blasphemous and conceptually muddled. Accordingly, the truly religious person sees the problem of evil as a practical problem of how to live religiously in a world in which evil is an undeniable reality.[43]

The religious discourse on evil is of special significance here, because what the religious language-user takes to be ineffable (i.e., the transcendent, or what transcends the bounds of sense) partly determines what can be meaningfully

---

[42] We cannot say, of course, that the argumentation presented here would, in any way, harm atheism as such, because the atheist can refuse to "play" religious language-games. One simply need not engage in religious language-use at all. What the Wittgensteinian transcendental argumentation focusing on the limits of religious language may be said to refute, or at least seriously problematize, is "theodicism", whether theist or atheist. Theodicism is a view according to which a theodicy is required as a response to the problem of evil; if the theist fails to provide one, her/his position has been defeated.

[43] See Mulhall, *Faith and Reason*, pp. 19, 67–68; Tilghman, *An Introduction to the Philosophy of Religion*, p. 194; as well as Phillips, "The Problem of Evil", in Brown (ed.), *Reason and Religion*, p. 119. This issue is discussed from the perspective of William James's pragmatism, with comparisons to the Wittgensteinian-cum-transcendental approach, in Sami Pihlström, "On the Reality of Evil: A Jamesian Investigation", *Streams of William James* 4:2 (2002), 12–21. Phillips notes, in a transcendental tone of voice (though without invoking such a vocabulary), that the theodicist (such as Richard Swinburne) "distorts what we know or goes beyond the limits of what we are prepared to think"; indeed, "to ask of what use are the screams of the innocent [. . .] is to embark on a speculation we should not even contemplate. We have our reasons, final human reasons, for putting a moral full stop at many places." ("The Problem of Evil", pp. 103, 115.)

said in religious language. That something *is* viewed as transcendent functions as a transcendental precondition of the meaningfulness of expressions used within religious life. As Jeff Malpas correctly notes, Kant himself "seems occasionally to designate something as '*transcendental*', even though it involves the positing of something '*transcendent*', in virtue of the fact that the positing is itself a requirement of the structure of the possibility of knowledge".[44] A conception of what lies *beyond* the expressive power of a language(-game), as codified in the (possibly changing) rules of the game, crucially affects what lies *within* the limits, i.e., what can be said and done in the language-game. In this case, a conception of God's sovereignty as something that cannot be intelligibly expressed in language but is only possible, say, as an object of mystical admiration, along with the corresponding acknowledgement of the mysterious or even unconceptualizable reality of extreme evil, may decisively influence what can be said about evil (or, say, justice) in, or by means of, religious language. We cannot step outside the language-games in which our lives are most deeply based – this, if anything, is the fundamental idea of Wittgensteinian transcendental examination of the limits of language. But we can, "from within", stare at the bounds of sense, just as the believer stares at the transcendence s/he believes to exist while remaining bound to her/his earthly existence (from which evil can never be eliminated). The one who observes, from within a religious use of language, that there are (theodicist) "speculations we should not even contemplate",[45] limits of ethically responsible human thought and language-use is firmly rooted in a this-worldly, human, way of experiencing the world, but it is her/his somewhat other-worldly conception of transcendence that enables her/him to draw the limits of (ethically acceptable) language-use that s/he draws through her/his life and faith.

There is, of course, the possible reply – analogous to Hegel's famous critique of Kant – that, in order to draw a limit, one will have to go beyond it, to already occupy a place "on the other side". But the conception of transcendental philosophy put forward here is designed to meet this challenge by insisting on the possibility of examining transcendental limits (of experience, meaningfulness, and so on) "from within". Hence the metaphor of "staring at" the limits, as contrasted to the one of drawing some definite limits which could only be drawn from a point of view lying beyond them. A pragmatically oriented transcendental philosophy

---

[44] Jeff Malpas, "Introduction", in Malpas (ed.), *From Kant to Davidson: Philosophy and the Idea of the Transcendental* (London and New York: Routledge, 2003), p. 2.
[45] Cf. Phillips's paper cited above.

admits that human ways of setting limits are never permanent but remain fallible and can always be contested.[46]

In sum, we may say that the relevance of the problem of evil to the philosophy of language (and to transcendental philosophy and semiotics more inclusively) is at least twofold. First, we may ask whether (and in what sense) one can represent evil itself and what one actually represents when addressing this topic. Secondly, one may ask what representing evil entails, especially, what it requires from our use of other symbolic expressions, e.g., our employment of the notion of God. The problem framework of evil offers interesting material to illuminate the ways in which the meanings of our concepts become deformed if one fails to recognize the specific features of the language-games (or, more generally, sign systems or symbolic frames of reference) one employs, scientific and religious ones included. In this case, there is a great difference between taking God's existence (or the statement, "God exists") to be a hypothesis to be tested in the light of evidence (in which case the empirically undeniable existence of evil would amount to counter-evidence) and taking it to be a genuinely religious statement. Arguably, for a truly religious person, *nothing* can count as evidence against God's existence. For such a person, faith is simply not a matter of testing a hypothesis. Religious concepts and the statements one formulates by employing them simply play crucially different roles in the language-games of the believer and the atheologian. For a Wittgensteinian who ties meaning to use, the meanings of these concepts and statements are, then, widely different in these two cases.

Accordingly, acknowledging (transcendentally) the bounds of sense, the limits of language, can orientate one's participation in a particular language-game – what one does or can do within the bounds of sense defining that particular language-game – in a significant way. This is what I have meant by claiming that a conception of something as transcendent from the point of view of a particular language-game can, on a transcendental level, function as a precondition of the meaningfulness of what is or can be said and done within the game, thus constituting the boundaries that the transcendent feature itself (*qua* transcendent) inevitably transgresses. One of the peculiarities of human language-use is, then, that the possibility of transgressing the limits of meaningful use of concepts is, in some cases at least, built into the very practice of language-use at issue.

---

[46] To deal with this challenge adequately, I would have to discuss Hegel's relation to Kant and present-day Hegelians' views on transcendental arguments. This task cannot be taken up here.

The case we have considered is also one that throws some light on the relation between transcendental philosophy as a *methodology* and as a *metaphysics*.[47] In the case of the problem of evil, a metaphysical commitment to transcendence affects the legitimate methodology of examining the meaning of concepts and the justification of beliefs within the given (religious) language-game. A number of difficult philosophical issues will, undeniably, remain unsettled here, the gravest one among them being presumably the problem of *relativism*.[48] This, however, is a problem we must learn to live with (rather than imagining that it could be solved for good), at least, insofar as we are willing to let our pragmatic basic convictions, the (possibly historically changing) certainties "in action" that provide the non-foundational "foundation" for whatever we are able to say or think in our language, affect our abilities to consider philosophical arguments sound or unsound, or relevant or irrelevant. There is no royal road to an overcoming of relativism, as long as the pragmatic contextuality of any form of humanly intelligible sign-use is taken seriously.

3 Ethics and value: The limits of language reconsidered

The discussion of religious language in the previous section was partly, though not explicitly, based on Wittgenstein's (and some of his followers') ideas. It is worthwhile to say a few more words on the relation between religious and ethical language, as conceived by Wittgenstein. This again leads us to the problem of the relation between the transcendental and the transcendent. Perhaps we can say that *both* are present in Wittgenstein's views on ethics: the ethical thinker's commitment to *transcendent*, ineffable moral values (e.g., "*the* right way") is a *transcendental* condition for the possibility of serious ethical life and thinking. One might argue, again with a Wittgensteinian tone of voice, that unless the ethical value is something transcendent and absolute, in comparison to our always rel-

---

47 See my discussion of this issue in Sami Pihlström, "Methodology without Metaphysics? A Pragmatic Critique", *Philosophy Today* 48 (2004), 188–215; also cf. Pihlström, "Recent Reinterpretations of the Transcendental".
48 It is a standard charge against Wittgensteinian philosophers of religion that they end up with some sort of relativism or fideism, declaring that ultimately the religious person just plays a religious language-game whose meanings and normative commitments are not vulnerable to external critique. I cannot further discuss this problem here, although it is intimately related to the metaphilosophical questions surrounding transcendental philosophy.

ative and transitionary human projects, it is not ethical in any deep sense. This, however, needs some elaboration.

In a couple of famous remarks toward the end of the *Tractatus*,[49] Wittgenstein tells us that ethics and aesthetics are one, that they are based on the will of the subject ("my will"), and that they are, like logic, "transcendental".[50] The 1929 "Lecture on Ethics" continues along similar lines. Having described ethics as an inquiry into what is valuable or really important or into the meaning of life or what makes life worth living, Wittgenstein says that these expressions can be used in a trivial and relative sense or an absolute and ethical sense.[51] The value judgments of ethics are absolute, not relative, and therefore they lie beyond what can be stated in language. The absolutely good or the absolutely valuable has no more literal sense than the experience of being "*absolutely* safe" has; thus, in ethics, we necessarily misuse language.[52] Ethical value, in short, is not on a par with worldly facts (which include relative values, means for certain ends). People who try to write about ethics or religion "run against the boundaries of language".[53] As the *Tractatus* puts it, there can be no ethical propositions (or sentences, *Sätze*), because nothing "higher" can be expressed in propositions or sentences; ethical value, or the "meaning" (*Sinn*) of the world, must lie "outside the world".[54] Ethics, then, is something sublime, otherworldly – transcendent. Or is it?

Dale Jacquette reads Wittgenstein as subscribing to the thesis that ethics "transcends the natural world".[55] This is so, because, according to Wittgenstein (in the *Tractatus*), the "metaphysical subject" is a necessary condition for any ethical value and this subject transcends the natural world.[56] The subject itself, as transcendent, is thus the source of the transcendence of ethics. The result is that ethics belongs to that which must be passed over into silence according to the famous final prop-

---

[49] Ludwig Wittgenstein, *Tractatus Logico-Philosophicus* (1921), trans. by David Pears and Brian McGuinness (London: Routledge and Kegan Paul), 1973, 6.373 and especially 6.4 ff.
[50] "Ethics is transcendental." (Wittgenstein 1921: 6.421).
[51] Ludwig Wittgenstein, "A Lecture on Ethics", in Wittgenstein, *Philosophical Occasions 1912–1951*, eds. James C. Klagge and Alfred Nordmann (Indianapolis and Cambridge: Hackett, 1993), 37–44 (here p. 38). The lecture was originally published in *The Philosophical Review* 74 (1965), 3–12.
[52] Wittgenstein, "A Lecture on Ethics", 41.
[53] Wittgenstein, "A Lecture on Ethics", 44.
[54] Wittgenstein, *Tractatus*, 6.42 and 6.41. Note also the reference to the "metaphysical, transcendent" feature of happy and harmonious life in Ludwig Wittgenstein, *Notebooks 1914–1916*, eds. G.H. von Wright and G.E.M. Anscombe (Oxford: Blackwell, 1961; 2nd ed. 1979), entry on July 30, 1916 (cf. *Tractatus*, 6.43).
[55] Dale Jacquette, "Wittgenstein on the Transcendence of Ethics", *Australasian Journal of Philosophy* 75 (1997), 304–332 (here 306–307).
[56] Jacquette, "Wittgenstein on the Transcendence of Ethics", 313.

osition of the *Tractatus*. There can be no (deep, interesting, or non-vulgar) talk about ethics or values at all – but only trivial, shallow, relativized value-talk. As Jacquette puts it, "there is only the transcendence of ethical attitude and practice that colours the world of objective fact with ethical-aesthetic value in subjective experience grounded by the world-transcendent metaphysical subject".[57]

Jacquette's (and many other interpreters') way of speaking about the transcendence of ethics and about the subject as transcendent may, however, be subjected to critical scrutiny. Wittgenstein's statement that ethics (as well as aesthetics) is *transcendental* should be taken seriously;[58] given his Kantian-Schopenhauerian background and the generally extremely carefully constructed text of the *Tractatus*, it seems implausible to suppose that Wittgenstein would simply have ignored the Kantian distinction or have made a slip of pen here. Despite Wittgenstein's undeniably mystical bias, there is, arguably, a sense in which ethics does *not*, according to him, lie "outside" or "above" the world (and human life) in any literal sense of these words. It lies, rather, at the *limit* of the world, for ethics, like religion and aesthetics, provides for Wittgenstein a view to the world as a (limited) whole, as something valuable in a higher sense. In short, given Wittgenstein's discussion of the metaphysical subject as a "limit of the world" in the *Tractatus*,[59] one may say that ethics is essentially about the subject's perspective or attitude to the world and life, a perspective constituting a condition for the possibility of the world. This position is compatible with, or may even require, the "transcendental solipsism" one finds Wittgenstein developing in the *Tractatus*: the subject (as the limit of the world) sees her/his world as a whole under the aspect of ethical or aesthetic value, *sub specie aeternitatis*. There is no (at least not clearly) "transcendence" here – but only transcendentality.[60]

---

[57] Jacquette, "Wittgenstein on the Transcendence of Ethics", 320. Jacquette is careful to remind us that this by no means implies ethical nihilism but only a non-theoretical attitude to ethics and aesthetics, "Wittgenstein on the Transcendence of Ethics", 322–323.
[58] Cf. also Heinrich Watzka, *Sagen und Zeigen: Die Verschränkung von Metaphysik und Sprachkritik beim frühen und beim späten Wittgenstein* (Stuttgart: Kohlhammer, 2000), 100–101.
[59] Wittgenstein, *Tractatus*, 5.632.
[60] The reading of Wittgenstein's transcendental solipsism, upon which these thoughts are based, is developed in Sami Pihlström, *Why Solipsism Matters* (London and New York: Bloomsbury, 2020). In that book, I develop the connection between solipsism and ethics in ch. 5. (See Wittgenstein's *Tractatus*, 5.6–5.641, for the extremely condensed line of thought culminating in the qualified endorsement of solipsism.) I have here learned a lot from Richard J. Brockhaus's reading, according to which, no otherworldliness (viz., transcendence in the standard sense) should be read into Wittgenstein's views, ethical or any other views: see Brockhaus, *Pulling Up the Ladder: The Metaphysical Roots of Wittgenstein's Tractatus Logico-Philosophicus* (La Salle, IL: Open Court, 1991). For a very different overall reading of Wittgenstein but for a similar rejection

I am not sure, however, whether this transcendental yet non-transcendent interpretation of ethical value and of the ethical (metaphysical) subject as conceived of by Wittgenstein can really be carried through. The above-cited formulations in the "Lecture on Ethics", in particular, seem to affirm a picture according to which ethics is a (desperate) attempt to speak about something that lies beyond the boundaries of language, steps over the legitimate limits within which meaning is found. One option might be to interpret Wittgenstein as offering a transcendental argument in favour of certain transcendent assumptions – analogously to the treatment of the problem of evil analyzed in section 2.2 above.

Perhaps the detailed recent interpretation of Wittgenstein's early views on ethics and ontology by Martin Stokhof may help us here.[61] Referring to the discussion of the will in the *Tractatus*, Stokhof does speak about the "ineffability of value"[62] and about the "transcendent nature of the will with regard to the world and the concomitant transcendent nature of ethics".[63] He immediately adds, however, that this transcendence is logical, not ontological: "All our acting takes place in the world and hence our will, our ethical attitudes, are immanent at the same time."[64] Values, although they do transcend the world, should not be sought in an "ontologically transcendent realm", because the world is primarily a linguistic notion, rather than an ontological one.[65] True, the (ethically) good "in an absolute sense" can – or should, according to Wittgenstein – be seen as "an attribute of God's Will", but even here the transcendence involved is *not* absolute but is "tied to the world", given Wittgenstein's identification of God with "how

---

of transcendent otherworldliness (without rejecting the term "transcendental"), see Cora Diamond, "Ethics, Imagination and the Method of Wittgenstein's *Tractatus*" (1991), in Alice Crary and Rupert Read (eds.), *The New Wittgenstein* (London and New York: Routledge, 2000), 149–173. Even more misleadingly than Jacquette, Linhe Han assumes that Wittgenstein places ethics and the metaphysical subject in a transcendent, otherworldly "domain": cf. his paper, "Philosophy as Experience, as Elucidation and as Profession: An Attempt to Reconstruct Early Wittgenstein's Philosophy", *Grazer Philosophische Studien* 51 (1996), 23–46; see here pp. 26, 40–42.

61 See Martin Stokhof, *World and Life as One: Ethics and Ontology in Wittgenstein's Early Thought* (Stanford, CA: Stanford University Press, 2002), especially ch. 4. It may be worth pointing out that Stokhof generally reads Wittgenstein in a Kantian context, as examining, transcendentally, the question of how meaning is possible. (Unfortunately, Stokhof does not comment on Jacquette's 1997 paper, cited earlier in this section.)

62 Stokhof, *World and Life as One: Ethics and Ontology in Wittgenstein's Early Thought*, 210–212.

63 Stokhof, *World and Life as One: Ethics and Ontology in Wittgenstein's Early Thought*, 208. The crucial passage referred to is *Tractatus* 6.43: "If good or bad willing changes the world, it can only change the limits of the world, not the facts; not that which can be expressed by language." (I am here quoting Stokhof's own translation, which is slightly emended.)

64 Stokhof, *World and Life as One: Ethics and Ontology in Wittgenstein's Early Thought*, 209.

65 Stokhof, *World and Life as One: Ethics and Ontology in Wittgenstein's Early Thought*, 238.

things stand".⁶⁶ Stokhof thus argues that the distinction between the individual, psychological subject and the metaphysical (willing, ethical) subject – a distinction between two different perspectives from which the world can be viewed – is not a distinction between two separate ontological realms, that is, between empirical reality and otherworldly transcendence.⁶⁷ Through Wittgenstein's linguistic turn of the "Kantian program", the notion of transcendence is transformed, rearticulated as an essentially linguistic (or, as one also might suggest, semiotic) notion:

> So, ethics is transcendental not because values are outside the world, in some otherworldly, platonic realm, nor because they cannot be grasped in thought, but because ethics "cannot be said." There are values and they are in the world, but not in the same way as contingent objects and situations are. And they are accessible, also for the individual subject, albeit not by means of its discursive powers of language and thought. [. . .] By placing ethics outside the realm of the meaningful, Wittgenstein tries to safeguard it from argumentation and disputes, dogmatism and feuds. There is an absolute value, but it is not accessible for the discursive mind and the corresponding linguistic ways of interacting with the world.⁶⁸

According to Stokhof, Wittgenstein is saying that we can view the world from the point of view of logic and ontology, "from the midst of things", but also *sub specie aeterni*, "as a limited whole, of which the limits are determined by the ethical will". These, again, are not two different ontological spheres but two ways of viewing the same thing or two ways of interacting with the world.⁶⁹ As Stokhof further explains his conception of the peculiar sense of transcendence involved in Wittgenstein's position:

> Ethical value is in the world. It is an intrinsic aspect of our actions and our actions are clearly part of the world. In this sense the world has an ethical dimension and value is immanent. But these intrinsic ethical properties cannot be expressed in language and hence in the world as it appears in our language, and hence in our thought, value is not to be found. In that sense value is transcendent. Immanence and transcendence are logical and not onto-

---

66 Stokhof, *World and Life as One: Ethics and Ontology in Wittgenstein's Early Thought*, 215–216. (See Wittgenstein, *Notebooks*, entry on August 1, 1916. Another notebook entry, on July 8, 1916, identifies God with "fate" and with "the world" as independent of our will.)
67 Stokhof, *World and Life as One: Ethics and Ontology in Wittgenstein's Early Thought*, 235, see also 245.
68 Stokhof, *World and Life as One: Ethics and Ontology in Wittgenstein's Early Thought*, 236.
69 Stokhof, *World and Life as One: Ethics and Ontology in Wittgenstein's Early Thought*, 237. Stokhof's "one-world" reading of the *Tractatus* could be compared to analogous one-world treatments of Kant's distinction between appearances and the thing in itself, e.g., in Henry E. Allison, *Kant's Transcendental Idealism: An Interpretation and Defense* (New Haven, CT and London: Yale University Press, 1983). I discuss Allison's project, and related ones, in Pihlström, *Naturalizing the Transcendental*, as well as in Pihlström, "Methodology without Metaphysics?".

logical categories, since the world and its limits is a logical and not an ontological notion. Only in this way can the *Tractatus* be read as a coherent whole.[70]

Stokhof believes that his reading of Wittgenstein, with the qualified sense of ineffability and transcendence involved, may save a "down-to-earth", practical way of dealing with moral problems, and that the value of the *Tractatus* may even lie in its invitation to lead a fundamentally ethically concerned everyday life.[71] I am not sure whether his interpretation can secure such a result – although I do see major similarities between Wittgensteinian moral philosophy and (neo)pragmatism in ethics.[72] Be that as it may, it seems to me clear that Stokhof's reading is superior to Jacquette's, which leaves the crucial concepts of the transcendental and the transcendent largely unexplained. Stokhof, thoroughly familiar with the Kantian context of transcendental philosophy from which Wittgenstein's inquiries take their departure, succeeds in showing how Wittgenstein's remarks on ethical value and the ethical (metaphysical) subject actually yield a rearticulated notion of the transcendent. Insofar as God is involved in Wittgenstein's project as "fate" or the way the world really is (as seen *sub specie aeterni*), a crucial link between the concerns of the philosophy of religion (section 2 above) and moral philosophy (the present section) has been established. In both, a re-articulation of the traditional Kantian distinction between transcendentality and transcendence is urgently needed.

The question remains whether, say, Taylor's ethical argument for theism – for a transcendent source of the "hypergoods" structuring our normative orientation in the world – could be interpreted in a way analogous to Stokhof's non-ontological treatment of Wittgenstein. I must leave this issue for another time. I doubt that Taylor himself, a Catholic believer, would be excited about this option, though.

4 Concluding remarks: A transcendentally constituted transcendence?

We have, through a study of a few closely related cases of religious and ethical language-use, ended up with the need to acknowledge, in addition to the transcendental limits of meaningful language, the transcendental role played (at least on some occasions) by the transcendent. We have reached this conclusion

---

70 Stokhof, *World and Life as One: Ethics and Ontology in Wittgenstein's Early Thought*, 238.
71 Stokhof, *World and Life as One: Ethics and Ontology in Wittgenstein's Early Thought*, 245, 249.
72 This is a comparison I undertake in Pihlström, *Pragmatic Moral Realism*.

through relatively simple examples; yet, even these cases are sufficient to make the claim that a commitment to the transcendent *may* play a transcendental role in our linguistic practices. On the other hand, no alarming commitment to any pre-critical (non-Kantian) form of metaphysical idealism follows, because the transcendent, according to our pragmatic and Wittgensteinian view, is relativized to the transcendental limits of the particular language-game in question, such as the religious discourse on evil or the ethical discourse on values. In such a given language-game, conversely, the transcendental limits are partly set (through our changing practices) by something's being acknowledged, by the relevant participants in the practice, as transcendent. This is a circle, of course, but hardly any more disturbing than the reflexive circularity inherent in virtually any employment of a transcendental method.

We might, at this point, draw a distinction between *absolute* and *relative* notions of transcendence, suggesting that the former lies beyond *any* human limits (of sense, of cognition, etc.), while the latter remains relativized to some particular language-game and might not be transcendent from the point of view of some other language-game. This distinction becomes elusive, however, as soon as we note that it is only against the background of, or relative to, some particular practice or language-game that anything (even, say, divinity) can be said to transcend all human limits. Thus, the "absolutely transcendent" can be conceived as such only from the perspective of one or another relativizing practice. This is perhaps to say that a genuinely transcendental approach has no use for the notion of absolute transcendence, though it is able to – or indeed must, as I have suggested – accommodate relativized forms of transcendence.

If our commitments to the transcendent are, then, inevitably, humanly relativized and (as we might say) "perspectival" ones, the final question arises whether we, because of our (supposedly) transcendental need to postulate the transcendent, actually *construct* the transcendent. Does the transcendent, if real, depend *on us* for its reality – on our human, especially ethical or ethico-religious perspectives, interests, needs, and perspectives? Could any humanly intelligible notion of transcendence be reinterpreted in such a relativized fashion, or is only an absolute transcendence transcendent enough?[73]

I must admit that, through the discussion of my chosen examples, I have hardly found any final or general answers to the questions I have raised in this essay. But I hope that a pragmatic view of the role played by transcendental conditions in

---

[73] Cf. here the discussion of William James's pragmatist philosophy of religion as a view committed to a kind of ontological constructivism in Pihlström, *Pragmatism and Philosophical Anthropology*, as well as several papers on James in Proudfoot (ed.), *William James and the Science of Religion*. Taylor's defence of theism can be claimed to face similar problems.

various areas of our lives, even by transcendentally established commitments to transcendence, may offer some help in highlighting the specific nature of such conditions and commitments. Thus, pragmatist philosophy, whose very aim is to render abstract philosophizing relevant to human life, is not an enemy of, but actually needs, the concepts of the transcendental and the transcendent.[74]

References

Allison, Henry E. 1983. *Kant's Transcendental Idealism: An Interpretation and Defense.* New Haven, CT and London: Yale University Press.
Baker, D. P. 2000. Charles Taylor's *Sources of the Self*: A Transcendental Apologetic? *International Journal for Philosophy of Religion* 47. 155–174.
Brockhaus, Richard J. 1991. *Pulling Up the Ladder: The Metaphysical Roots of Wittgenstein's Tractatus Logico-Philosophicus.* La Salle, IL: Open Court.
Brown, Stuart C. (ed.). 1977. *Reason and Religion.* Ithaca, NY: Cornell University Press.
Caputo, John D. 1979. Transcendence and the Transcendental in Husserl's Phenomenology. *Philosophy Today* 23. 205–216.
Carr, David. 1999. *The Paradox of Subjectivity: The Self in the Transcendental Tradition.* Oxford and New York: Oxford University Press.
Diamond, Cora. 2000 [1991]. Ethics, Imagination and the Method of Wittgenstein's *Tractatus*. In Alice Crary & Rupert Read (eds.), *The New Wittgenstein*, 149–173. London and New York: Routledge.
Gale, Richard M. 1999. *The Divided Self of William James.* Cambridge: Cambridge University Press.
Gale, Richard M. 2005. *The Philosophy of William James: An Introduction.* Cambridge: Cambridge University Press.

---

[74] I am grateful to Hanne Appelqvist, Heikki Kannisto, Ted Schatzki, and Eero Tarasti for discussions of the relation between the transcendental and the transcendent that led to the idea of writing this paper. Some of the discussion in this article slightly overlaps with two earlier papers of mine: section 2.1 partly draws on "Pragmatic and Transcendental Arguments for Theism", while section 2.2 elaborates on and extends a few brief passages originally included in "Recent Reinterpretations of the Transcendental".

[Note added in 2021: The first version of this essay was written in 2004. As the book for which it was originally drafted has been in the making for a relatively long time, the discussion has moved forward in many ways. I have not been able to update the references, but I believe the basic issues are still worth exploring. Over the years, I have discussed the topic of the paper in a number of publications: e.g., Sami Pihlström, *Transcendental Guilt: Reflections on Ethical Finitude* (Lanham, MD: Lexington Books, 2011), *Pragmatic Pluralism and the Problem of God* (New York: Fordham University Press, 2013), *Death and Finitude: Toward a Pragmatic Transcendental Anthropology of Human Limits and Mortality* (Lanham, MD: Lexington Books, 2016), and *Why Solipsism Matters* (London: Bloomsbury, 2020); as well as Sari Kivistö and Sami Pihlström, *Kantian Antitheodicy: Philosophical and Literary Varieties* (Basingstoke: Palgrave Macmillan, 2016).]

Grube, Dirk-Martin. 1997. A Critical Reconstruction of Paul Tillich's Epistemology. *Religious Studies* 33. 67–80.
Han, Linhe. 1996. Philosophy as Experience, as Elucidation and as Profession: An Attempt to Reconstruct Early Wittgenstein's Philosophy. *Grazer Philosophische Studien* 51. 23–46.
Jacquette, Dale. 1997. Wittgenstein on the Transcendence of Ethics. *Australasian Journal of Philosophy* 75. 304–324.
James, William. 1975 [1907]. *Pragmatism: A New Name for Some Old Ways of Thinking*, eds. Frederick H. Burkhardt, Fredson Bowers & Ignas K. Skrupskelis. Cambridge, MA and London: Harvard University Press.
Kant, Immanuel. 1990 [1781/1787]. *Kritik der reinen Vernunft,* (A = 1st ed., 1781; B = 2nd ed., 1787), ed. Raymund Schmidt. Hamburg: Felix Meiner. (*Critique of Pure Reason*, Eng. trans. by Norman Kemp Smith London: Macmillan, 1929).
Kant, Immanuel. 1983. *Kritik der praktischen Vernunft*, ed. Wilhelm Weischedel. In *Immanuel Kant: Werke*, vol. 6, Darmstadt: Wissenschaftliche Buchgesellschaft; A=1788.
Malpas, Jeff (ed.). 2003. *From Kant to Davidson: Philosophy and the Idea of the Transcendental*. London and New York: Routledge.
Moore, A. W. 1992. Human Finitude, Ineffability, idealism, Contingency. *Nous* 26. 427–446.
Moore, A. W. 1997. *Points of View*. Oxford: Clarendon Press.
Mulhall, Stephen. 1994. *Faith and Reason*. London: Duckworth.
Pihlström, Sami. 1998. *Pragmatism and Philosophical Anthropology: Understanding Our Human Life in a Human World*. New York: Peter Lang.
Pihlström, Sami. 2002. On the Reality of Evil: A Jamesian Investigation". *Streams of William James* 4(2). 12–21.
Pihlström, Sami. 2002. Pragmatic and Transcendental Arguments for Theism: A Critical Examination. *International Journal for Philosophy of Religion* 51. 195–213.
Pihlström, Sami. 2003. *Naturalizing the Transcendental: A Pragmatic View*. Amherst, NY: Prometheus/Humanity Books.
Pihlström, Sami. 2003. [Review on Charles Taylor's *Varieties of Religion Today: William James Revisited*]. *Transactions of the Charles S. Peirce Society* 39(2). 342–347.
Pihlström, Sami. 2004. Methodology without Metaphysics? A Pragmatic Critique. *Philosophy Today* 48. 188–215.
Pihlström, Sami. 2004. *Solipsism: History, Critique, and Relevance*. Tampere: Tampere University Press.
Pihlström, Sami. 2004. Recent Reinterpretations of the Transcendental. *Inquiry* 47. 289–314.
Pihlström, Sami. 2005. *Pragmatic Moral Realism: In Search for Ethical Seriousness*. Amsterdam and New York: Rodopi.
Proudfoot, Wayne (ed.). 2004. *William James and the Science of Religions: Re-experiencing the Varieties of Religious Experience*. New York: Columbia University Press.
Stern, Robert (ed.). 1999. *Transcendental Arguments: Problems and Prospects*. Oxford & New York: Oxford University Press.
Stern, Robert 2000. *Transcendental Arguments and Scepticism: Answering the Question of Justification*. Oxford: Clarendon Press.
Stokhof, Martin. 2002. *World and Life as One: Ethics and Ontology in Wittgenstein's Early Thought*. Stanford, CA: Stanford University Press.
Stout, Robert. 1998. Descartes's Hidden Argument for the Existence of God. *British Journal for the History of Philosophy* 6. 155–168.

Strawson, P. F. 1993 [1959]. *Individuals: An Essay in Descriptive Metaphysics*. London and New York: Routledge.
Tarasti, Eero. 2000. *Existential Semiotics: Advances in Semiotics*. Bloomington: Indiana University Press.
Tarasti, Eero. 2004. *Arvot ja merkit*. Helsinki: Gaudeamus.
Taylor, Charles. 1989. *Sources of the Self: The Making of the Modern Identity*. Cambridge: Cambridge University Press
Taylor, Charles. 1994. Religion, History and Moral Discourse. In James Tully (ed.), *Philosophy in an Age of Pluralism: The Philosophy of Charles Taylor in Question*, 49–66. Cambridge: Cambridge University Press.
Taylor, Charles. 1995 [1979]. The Validity of Transcendental Arguments, reprinted in Charles Taylor, *Philosophical Arguments*. Cambridge, MA and London: Harvard University Press.
Taylor, Charles. 1998. Modes of Secularism. In Rajeev Bhargava (ed.), *Secularism and Its Critics*, 31–53. Delhi: Oxford University Press.
Taylor, Chares. 2002. *Varieties of Religion Today: William James Revisited*. Cambridge, MA and London: Harvard University Press.
Tilghman, B. R. 1994. *An Introduction to the Philosophy of Religion*. Oxford and Cambridge, MA: Blackwell.
Watzke, Heinrich. 2000. *Sagen und Zeigen: Die Verschränkung von Metaphysik und Sprachkritik beim frühen und beim späten Wittgenstein*. Stuttgart: Kohlhammer.
Wilcox, John T. 1989. *The Bitterness of Job: A Philosophical Reading*. Ann Arbor: University of Michigan Press.
Wisdo, David. 1993. *The Life of Irony and the Ethics of Belief*. Albany: SUNY Press.
Wittgenstein, Ludwig. 1973 [1921]. *Tractatus Logico-Philosophicus*. Eng. trans by David Pears & Brian McGuinness. London: Routledge and Kegan Paul.
Wittgenstein, Ludwig. 1993 [1965]. A Lecture on Ethics. In Wittgenstein, *Philosophical Occasions 1912–1951*, eds. James C. Klagge & Alfred Nordmann, 37–44. Indianapolis and Cambridge: Hackett; originally published in *The Philosophical Review* 74 (1965), 3–12.
Wittgenstein, Ludwig. 1979 [1961]. *Notebooks 1914–1916*, G.H. von Wright and G.E.M. Anscombe (eds.). Oxford: Blackwell.

Eero Tarasti
The metaphysical system of existential semiotics

Abstract: Existential semiotics is an effort to combine two issues which at first sight seem to be irreconcilable, namely the classical semiotics – say, in its European Saussure-based form like in the Paris School of A.J. Greimas – and the continental philosophy having its roots in the German-French tradition from Kant and Hegel to Heidegger and Jaspers, and moreover to Jean Wahl, Gabriel Marcel and Jean-Paul Sartre. This new paradigm of semiotics has constituted its own metalanguage and concepts from *Dasein*, modalities, zemic, suprazemic, trans-zemic, transcendental, *Moi* and *Soi*.

Yet, in order to develop this theory further we may see how well it fits as the framework of interpretation of other philosophical systems. Such a comparison at the same time illuminates the epistemic foundations of itself and attempts to make its basic issues operational conceptual tools for the examination of diverse philosophies. Thus such classical issues as substance, truth, language, existence etc are analyzed using the zemic model and its variants like sig-zemic i.e. representations of the zemic modes, and log-zemic i.e. the logical operations inherent in the semiosis, such as sublimation, embodiment, trans-ascendence, trans-descendence, dialogue, similarity/difference, teleological relations as the tools of such enterprise. Philosophers from Aristotle to Leibniz, Spinoza, Schelling – and McTaggart and Wittgenstein can find their common denominators when their theories are interpreted in the context of existential semiotics.

Keywords: continental philosophy, classical semiotics, transcendence, zemic, Moi/Soi, existentiality, Wittgenstein, McTaggart

motto: "*Ich bin Ich*" (F.W.J.Schelling)

I have always been fascinated by difficult and incomprehensible texts, books and theories. When I arrived in Paris in 1973 to study semiotics – or structuralism – at the seminar of A.J. Greimas, I did not first – to say it honestly – understand almost anything of what was said there. His two hundred Italian, South-American, and French pupils spoke fast French and used expressions which were to me strange. This forced me to get the basic work of the school at hand, Greimas's *Sémantique structurale,* which, true, had appeared as early as in 1967 and to translate it into Finnish (then it came out in 1982). I was comforted to read recently in the memories of Georg Henrik v. Wright about his experiences in Cambridge in the 1930s when he met Wittgenstein: "I listened enchanted without understanding much but still sufficiently in order to note in my diary in the same day that it had been the most peculiar impression I had ever got from any person" (v. Wright 2001: 81) and elsewhere: "Accordingly I visited Wittgenstein's lectures in the Easter term. . . ..of lectures I did not catch very much".

I have never been discouraged at myself by such situation, but have taken it as a challenge. This has happened with the works of two philosophers, Wittgenstein and McTaggart. The magnum opus by the latter, *The Nature of Existence I-II* (1927/1988), I have borrowed from library numerous times, kept on my shelve and always had to abandon it. Yet, now in the summer of 2020, situation changed: I suddenly started to interpret him with my own existential semiotics and its socalled 'zemic' model and at once his philosophy began to open. The same occurred with the *Tractatus* by Wittgenstein (1922/2001). And thereafter a.o. the work *Remarks on the Philosophy of Psychology* and the notations by G.E. Moore on Wittgenstein's Cambridge lectures 1930–1933 (2016). This opening was a somehow similar experience as in literature, like Ulysses by Joyce, which I had also tried to read, heavens, hundred times but now I received its two Finnish translations, by Pentti Saarikoski and Leevi Lehto. Unexpectedly I could understand his greatness. A.o. I discovered a radically new way to portray music verbally. When I compared it to Marcel Proust and his music scenes, the difference was striking; one could say that Joyce is a paradigmatic interpreter whereas Proust is syntagmatic, to put it in semiotic terms (of this I shall write more). Yet, there is in the background of both Joyce and Wittgenstein the fact they both were very musical. Hence one could argue that this was *Geburt der Philosophie. . . ..oder Literatur . . . aus dem Geiste der Musik.*

As to Wittgenstein, there was also the occasion that I had the joy to learn to know v. Wright as a young student. He told me several times that I should read what Wittgenstein wrote about music and study it. But then, in the 1970s and 1980s, I did not understand to follow his advice. However, I tried to bring together my teachers Greimas and v. Wright for a dialogue in some of my congresses but it did not work. Greimas would of course have spoken only French and v. Wright English. Moreover the conception of v. Wright about Frenchmen was, as he said to me, that "French are truly nice but they always get angry at the end!" Still, Greimas highly respected v. Wright, namely as the elaborator of modal logics to which even his own semiotic system had ended up in the 1980s. When I entered Greimas's seminar he introduced me: "*Monsieur Tarasti, compatriote de v. Wright*".

In any case, when developing my own theory I have conceived that I had to connect it more substantially to the European philosophical tradition. One starting point of my zemic-model was naturally the Hegelian logics but there are likewise other metaphysicians in the history of philosophy, which seemed to be possibilities to deepen my theory. Accordingly, I started to study Wittgenstein and McTaggart with my zemic model – and I got the same feeling Greimas had once as a guest of Paul Perron in Toronto:he said to his host: "I wonder if you understand that my theory is *englobant* (surrounding) and you are *englobé* (surrounded)!" I felt now also that my zemic model was *englobant* – to which I could embed whatsoever philosophical systems, even so cryptic as the one by McTaggart. His faithful pupil had been C.D.Broad . . .the supervisor of v. Wright in Cambridge. . . .. Who had published broad (!) explanatory works on his master. Yet, I considered it best to read McTaggart directly. He was Hegelian, bu still not despised in the British academic world. Bertrand Russell, the logical empirist, tells in his memories:

> Hegel supposed that universe was a unity holding keenly together, his world was like pudding in the sense that if you touched whatsoever part of it, the whole vibrated; but it was another thing like a pudding in the sense that it could not be cut into slices. The belief that the universe seemed to consist of parts was erroneous to his mind. The only reality was the Absolute and this was the name he gave to God. Hegel's philosophy satisfied me for a while. When it was propagated to me by its adherents and particularly McTaggart, who was then one of my close friends, it looked both charming and legitimate. McTaggart was about six years older than me and all his life had he been a devote pupil of Hegel. He had a remarkable impact on his contemporaries, and I also got for some time under his guidance. It was weirdly pleasant to make one believe that time and space were unreal, and matter an illusion and that the world consisted only of spirit. Nevertheless, on one day at a moment of dissent I turned away from pupil to the Maser himself and I discovered in Hegel a mess of misunderstanding and such issues which did not look much better than puns. Therefore I gave up with his philosophy.   (Russell 1957:25)

Although v. Wright was pupil of the Hegelian C.D. Broad he does not speak in his memories about McTaggart. However in the University of Helsinki, S. Albert Kivinen gave a lecture series on McTaggart in the 1980s and his concept of ontic communism.

Before I ponder in the light of zemic theory, Wittgenstein and McTaggart, I make an overview on the history of philosophy; this is reasonable since many notions of McTaggart are stemming from old sources and not in the least from such classic as the Metaphysics by Aristotle. It is strange that I seriously read this work only now. . . albeit it is from this all should have been started! One does not need to read long time in order to realize that this is congenial, totally central, completely fresh and actual thought. It is no wonder that the Persian Avicenna read it 40 times and learned it by heart.

1 Aristotle

Aristotle says right at the beginning: "Being and substance have not been explained clearly, but they are not the moment where motion starts since they are rather reason of immobility and rest" (Aristotle 2012). One may immediately tell that here one goes to the core of our zemic model, namely to the question: what is the force which puts zemic to move, to those two drections which are embodiment and sublimation, therefore heaviness and lightness? In the background looms the assumption that we identify substance with zemic. "Only substances can have ideas...therefore ideas are substances! (Aristotle 2012: I, 9, 990b25, p. 27): We could thus say that they are parts of substance or its category of *Soi1*." One should ponder what effects the ideas have upon observable entities, either eternal or vanishing, since they are not reasons of their movement or change taking place therein! This again would seem to refute our hypothesis that ideas are a part of substance or zemic and put in motion the process from the spiritual to material, or from *Soi* to *Moi*, i.e. to embodiment. Let us read more.

It has been said in *Phaidon* by Plato that ideas are causes of both being and birth... when we want to reduce substances to their principles... or categories of log-zemic as we could say (see later definition of log-zemic) and of which we have discovered seven altogether.

Insofar as movement is concerned, both big and small, it is clear that ideas move (I, 9, 992b5, p. 30). Yet, if this is not true, where the movement is stemming from?

If there are elements, they can be possessed only by substances, or if there are $Moi1$, $Moi2$, $Soi2$, and $Soi1$, they belong to the substance as its elements. It is clear that we cannot suppose to have any previous knowledge of them. Therefore, if there is a science which is all-encompassing, the student of it would not have anterior knowledge of it. Comment: would this science be the same as semiotics?

Aristotle deals with the problem of change in the framework of 'zemic' as we could interpret him (II, 2, 994a20, p. 33): "It is not possible to go down from some higher principle...one emerges from the other in two ways. Either so that boy becomes a man or like water becomes air. As we said that boy becomes a man, what is involved is becoming of something which has come, or it is coming of the complete from incomplete..." Accordingly, $M1$ transforms into a person $M2$ and so to say gets complete. A student is a learned *in spe*. This is meant when we say that a student becomes learned or $Moi2$ becomes $Soi2$, learned. Yet, the contrary is not possible: man cannot become any longer boy. But what is the first cause, Aristotle thinks whether $M1$ has some inner force . . ...*élan vital* as we could say like Henri Bergson (or 'intellectual effort' as explained by the Bulgarian Bergson scholar Kristian Bankov)... which would put it to motion from some inner force.

This is the problem of all so-called growth and education. The solution of Rousseau in *Emile*.

Aristotle reflects then which science should study the sameness, the otherness, similarity, difference, contrariety, the primary things (we would say what is forgrounded, which has the attraction point), secondary things and all other what the dialecticians try to examine. They were in our zemic model categories of log-zemic. Has anyone only one contrary opposition? (III, 1, 995b20, p. 37); this is the core problem of the entire Paris school. Aristotle asks: are principles and elements species or parts of which every being consists of?

The concrete being or entity is defined by Aristotle as substrate. Is there something in addition to a concrete entity? For instance is there in addition to zemic a level of what we call 'suprazemic' or essence? Are the principles of the perishable and unperishable same or are they all unperishable? One or being is not regarding the entities some other but the substance of the beings, as Plato or Pythagoreans thought, or not, when the substrate were some other as what Empedocles says the **friendship** to be. Are principles universals or particular things, are they actually or potentially and are they that in some other way and in relation to movement? (III, 1, 996a10, p. 37) We are here again in the core of the issue: does the inner movement of zemic emerge from these principles of log-zemic: embodiment, sublimation, *pousser/tirer* (these terms refers to my new theory of performing arts as two principal movements of playing, see Tarasti 2021 (forthcoming), heavy/light, tranascendence/transdescendence (as a gesture obs!) dialogicity, sameness/difference or fragmentaric nature, teleological goal or resistance? (see definitions of all these a little later here).

How the principle of movement and the nature of the goodness could appear in immobile entities (III, 2, 996a25, p. 38)? Every issue has to be either denied or affirmed (III, 2, 996b26, p. 39). Is there for all these substances only one science or different sciences? Answer to our mind: semiotics studies substrate, and existential semiotics substance. Or does the science of zemic do it for substrate and the science of suprazemic the substance as a conceptual science? Essence cannot be proved (III, 2, 997a30, p. 40). What is that which scrutinizes qualities of substance? The answer is extremely difficult says Aristotle, but why?

He inquires: do the substances perceivable by sense exist? Nothing would be more strange than to claim that in the visible universe there would be still others such that they were same as perceivable entities except that the latter ones were eternal, and the former ones perishable. Comment: shift towards transcendence denies this and on suprazemic level we are outside the universe or *Dasein* and even more when we reach the trans-zemic level. We absolutize the properties of zemic and call them universals. Yet, Aristotle is very empirical!

Are the principles of the perishable... i.e. zemic... and unperishable i.e. suprazemic and transzemic... the same or not? If they are same how others can be perishable and others unperishable? (III, 4, 1000a5, p. 45) Empedokles proposes that the reason of perishing is the **quarrel.** Unless the quarrel were not an ingredient of everything, all would be one. To him quarrel is the cause of being and vanishment of the good. Friendship... remember here Nietzsche's *Hymnus an die Freundschaft*, his composition he thought to be unperishable. One could infer in our theory: zemic vanishes but its logical categories or log-zemics do not!

Aristotle ponders the problem of One and the being (III, 4, 1001a5, p. 48). The substance of the beings must be one and being. If one is not a substance and even if we had the idea of one, however, the same problem would emerge. Namely how there could appear in the side of one another one? It should be not-one (see later Schelling and his principle of *Ich/nicht-Ich*, me/not-me). Yet, all being is either one or many, of which each one is one.

Therefore: in the side of zemic1 there can be another zemic2 and third zemic3 etc. Endlessly. This is the problem of the multiplicity, which then was so central to Deleuze and which explains the existence of the social. Namely – if we anticipate a little our reasoning – the 'determining correspondence' by McTaggart means precisely the connections among diverse zemics and their correspondences!

Almost all think that the being and substance consist of contrasts (IV, 2, 1004b30) – this idea was then directly herited by structuralists. There is a limitless amount of socalled accidental properties, and so we cannot here list them (IV, 4, 1007a13, p. 61). This idea would be expressed by the present language: there is innumerous amount of **data.** It cannot be all listed for instance as an answer to the question what is man. If all the properties are accidental, then there would be no living being determined essentially as man; in other words, existentially or zemically. If there is something like a man, it would mean something which is one or substance of something..... or in our system a zemic!

Here one has sketched already many elements also for existential semiotics, like what causes its movement and how in the level of sigzemic, like in a musical work, for instance, in a concerto, themes influence each other and what in general constitutes the discursive logics of music, i.e what can follow from which theme. Suprazemic and zemic can also be seen as the realisation of potential and actual. Essence is always only potential ,and it has to become actual in zemic. In any case, in Aristotle, the basic concepts of metaphysics have been clearly determined, later philosophies are to a great extent only reactions to these fundamental distinctions.

2 Leibniz

If we skip over Aristotle to Leibniz and embed it in turn to our zemic philosophy we get one step further. At the end is looming, as a goal, the existential analysis of whatsoever cultural phenomenon, not in the least of music.

Gottfried Wilhelm Leibniz (1597–1652) is naturally one of those spiritual giants of the baroque age, who dealt with all possible problems on earth and beyond. He dreamed of an encyclopedic general science – accordingly a kind of semiotics already (perhaps Umberto Eco got his idea of 'encyclopedia of knowledge' from him) – which was included in a huge project in the work *Demonstrationes catholicae*, which was never completed. About it Simo Knuuttila writes, in his preface to Leibniz's selected studies, that "following the baroque idea the enterprise was since the beginning above standards" (Leibniz 2011: 11). He also occupied stately functions in the service of dukes; he was a mathematician, who planned a counting machine, waged a polemics with Newton about a totally futile issue, namely which one had invented something before the other. He elaborated arithmetic unequivocal symbol system, which also included, in the side of scientific terms, written signs which we unambiguously use like in the arithmetics (Leibniz 2011: 12). How analogic this is to our own zemic system and symbols of log-zemic, a kind notation of existential semiotic analysis.

The name of Leibniz is naturally connected to monadology, which is the metaphysical system developed by him and in which the aforementioned Aristotelian notions are brought to a new conceptual field and enlightening. His essay from 1714 begins: "Monad whereof it is spoken here is nothing but a simple substance, which is contained in combinations". If in the above, while dealing with Aristotle, we juxtaposed substance and zemic, here we identify monad and zemic. A general view on monad is that it is a limited self-enclosed unit. Leibniz's monad thus seems to be a very static entity, but he immediately starts to talk about its changes: "Every creature is under change. Yet, the changes of monads are due to their inner principle, since the external cause is not able to influence them internally. In the side of a change there must be richness of details what cause the variety of its parts." In the changing zemic i.e. inside it there are its modes M1M2S2S1. Leibniz states that the inner principle which may effectuate change of shift from one state – or zemic – to another is desire. But do *M1M2S2S1* desire each other or do they rather oppose and resist each other? On the other hand, the principle of desire, *désir*, is carrying force of all narration since Propp and consquently if the zemic modes are arranged into a narration, the force supporting it is certainly desire. And if we in general make the fundamental question which power is behind the two main movement of zemic, sublimation and embodiment, it were thus desire, and in such a case our theory would preserve its contact with the Paris School of semiotics and the Greimas system a.o.

Leibniz says: Every one who admits that soul is a simple substance has to accept also the multiplicity of this monad.

Yet, now I have gone ahead of things. Let us still continue a little about Leibnizian monads. Leibniz thinks that the elements and structure of the world could be enlarged so that one could enter there as if into a mill. Or he makes a similar experiment like Plato with his sphere, inside which we already conceived whole our zemic in a previous essay. Such a visitor could only find parts which push each other, hence M1, M2, S2 etc; but what is involved are the inner functions of simple substances, which we have identified as log-zemics with their own signs (diagram 1):

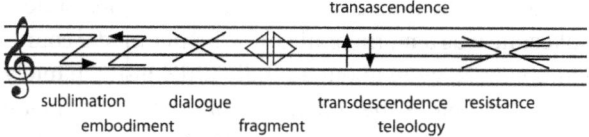

Diagram 1: Functions of various log-zemic categories.

Now, Leibniz calls his simple substance – which is after all not so simple! – *entelekias*, they are perfect and selfsufficient. They are incorporeal automates – perhaps computers of our time?

Then Leibniz announces that all simple substances or created monads could be called **souls**. Soul is identified with monad in a state in which we do not remember anything, like when we faint or when we are occupied by a deap sleepless sleep (p. 335). Yet, on the other hand, all is linked with affects and unless our perception would not contain anything more particular and higher and more strongly felt we were always in that unconsciousness. Or Leibniz refers to the existence of modalities, which colour the monads.

Although each created monad or zemic represents the whole universe, it represents more exactly the body to which it is connected – or *Moi1* in zemic and whose *entelekeia* or soul it is; for monad or zemic belongs to a body and monad is the entelekeia of the body or soul. From this emerges what we can call a living being.

Among substances prevails pre-established harmony, and substances fit together since they are representations of the same universe (or they follow the breath of *Brahma*, what is in my theory the 'new' metaphysical principle, to this I shall still return; Leibniz hardly knew oriental philosophy).

Moreover, there is a harmony between the physical realm of nature and the moral realm of **grace**. The essences of the suprazemic constitute 'a divine city' since Leibniz argues: there is harmony between the God, the architect of the machine of the universe, and the God, the monarch of the divine city of the spirits (suprazemics). I would say here: excellent that the notion of grace appeared here so logically formulated. Of course Thomas Aquinas had already postulated it as the principle without which the universe would not exist a moment. Altogether this has brought us forward with the concept of transcendence in our own theory.

3 Spinoza

We know that Leibniz visited Hague to meet Spinoza in 1676, one year before his death. There is little information about this visit; albeit Leibniz himself argued differently that Spinoza made an impact upon him. He writes to Justel that what is involved is a dangerous book. According to Leibniz, for Christianity, risky were the following theses: God and substance are the same; created entities are variations of God himself or moduses and that God does not have understanding nor will and that all has been subordinated to a fatal necessity. . .and that in the eternal life soul does not have any sensations, memory or will.

Yet, from the viewpoint of our zemic theory, Spinoza helps us greatly to determine the whole notion of transcendence. The zemics . . . . those psychophysical creatures were moduses of transcendence – *alles vergängliche* (so: zemic!) *ist ein Gleichnis*, was said at the end of *Faust II*. Hence all the vanishing zemics are metaphors of transcendence. God and substance are the same – i.e. transcendence is present in the substances of zemics, – as it was postulated, a.o. as transcendental gestures sublimation/embodiment, but also as an escape to the transzemic world, as the negation and affirmation of the zemic world, as was said in our very first existential model of *Dasein* (Tarasti 2000). In the eternal life, there is, according to Spinoza, no sensation, memory etc. We have also pondered this already, see a.o. reference to Brahms' *Ein deutsches Requiem: Und ihre Thaten folgen ihnen nach. . ..i.e.* the transzemic units what they may be, have memory, they remember what they have done previously in the zemic world.

However, let us look directly at what Spinoza presents in his *Ethics*. In the opening chapter on God i.e. transcendence, we could remark that he immediately declares: "By substance I undertand what is in itself and is conceived via itself, in other words its notion does not need notion of any other entity, from which it should be constituted." So it is and this is compatible with Leibnizian monad-zemic theory.

"V. By modus I understand states of substance or what is in other and is conceived via this other." If Spinoza's 'Other' means *Soi*, this fits very well.

As known Spinoza wants to dress his theory into an axiomatic form. So next come several axiomas:

I. "All that which is, is either in itself or in the other" . This can be read: in *Moi* or in *Soi*. "What cannot be understood by another, must be comprehended by itself". Or: if the Soi i.e. praxis and values do not explain the phenomenon we have to turn to *Moi*.

"Those who do not have anything common with each other cannot be either understood via others," Or: if we have two zemics, who do not have any common mode of M1M2S2S1, i.e. their qualifications are different i.e. their states and positions in the zemic movement following the Z figures, arrows, dialogicity, transcendences etc.

Then Spinoza postulates radically that no subsance can exist or be conceived outside God. In other words, all is transcendence, radiation of the grace descending from above.

All that which is, is in God and nothing can be nor conceived without God. Therefore: all depends on transcendence! Moduses do not exist to Spinoza's mind and they cannot be comprehended without substance. Or the moduses *M1M2S2S1* do not exist as such but only as parts of zemic and its position in the Z structure.

In addition, Spinoza defines our transcendence: God is the internal cause of all beings, not external. In other words, transcendence, so to say, 'lives' inside the zemic.

P. 74: It depends totally on the decision and will of God what each creature is. I.e. there is a transcendental metamodality of will. Metamodalities are therefore not at all some kind of weakened modalities,but contrarily stronger than them. But if they have emerged in the zemic world from quite concrete ad empirical modes, how they can then appear in transcendence as a kind of transfigured variables? If will, can, know, and must can be determined apriori in the transzemic world, then we cannot avoid the situation in which we are able to describe them verbally only as metaphors. Is there will, can, know etc as such, *an sich*?

I finish the examination of Spinoza here. We have received a lot of impulses to our zemic model and can say that it has served as the context for interpreting Spinoza or the theory surrounding it; *Englobant*. Particularly our view on transcendence has got specification. Even if not the final solution in any way.

Before I come to those two philosophers who are especially rewarding for our zemic theory, McTaggart and Wittgenstein, I still throw a glimpse in the field of German philosophy to Schelling who has remained there a little aside. In his time, Schelling was a competitor of Hegel but was underestimated. Yet, for our zemic theory, we discover a lot of essential formulation of the concept of subject itself, of which Schelling uses the term 'Ich' , I.

4 Schelling

He starts with the statement: If you want to know something, then you also want that your knowledge would have reality. Knowledge without reality, *Realität*, is no knowledge. This evokes to us the words by Erda from the *Nibelungen Ring* of Richard Wagner: *Mein Schlafen ist Träumen, mein Träumen ist Sinnen, mein Sinnen ist Walten des Wissen*. In other words, only such knowledege which is stemming from the unconscious dream is real knowledge, which also has power and force in the *Dasein*.

The absolute I is determined in the first place by that which cannot in any way become an object. The fact that there exists an absolute I cannot be proved objectively (here is a similar thought as in Kierkegaard). I, if it has to exist absolutely, must be out of any sphere of objective demonstrability. Schelling comes to his motto: *Ich bin weil ich bin!*

I am! My ego contains being which preceeds, anticipates any thought or phantasy. I am because I am! This may be upsetting everyone suddenly. The fact that I am because it is, is not easy to grasp immediately; because I is defined only by itself and absolute, it can never become another being, object. We cannot say: all that which thinks is because by it the thinking subject would be determined as an object: I think therefore I am, (or reference to Descartes).

I is thus given only by itself absolutely. When I has been defined absolutely in the human knowledge, all the contents of our knowledge have to appear only via me. And as a contrast to me. In other words, we would say in our theory: all knowledge has to be related to zemic. If this I is absolute, then all that which is not me, has to be as a contrast to it not-me (p. 24).

Finally all our knowledge does not have any value unless it is realized by its own force, and this is the same as the real through the freedom. The beginning and end of all philosophy is.....freedom! In our theory, the freedom again is possible only by the notion of transcendence which liberates it from the chains of zemic and stops its inner movement i.e. the horizontal one by a vertical one, which can appear metaphorically also inside the zemic (sublimation and embodiment).

The essence of the ego is freedom, declares Schelling (p. 33). This freedom is positive since we do not want any thing as such, *das Ding an sich*, but purely set or postulated by itself, only contemporary, excluding any not-I, which we call freedom. Ego cannot appear as a concet (p. 35) or as suprazemic we would say. Ego can be defined only in intuition, *Anschauung*. I is I only because it can never become an object. But it cannot exist in any sense perception, but only in the intellectual. Where is an object, there is a sense perception. Yet, is then the absolute ego the same as the ego of the suprazemic?

5 McTaggart

Now I move to the next philosophical system which perhaps more illuminates the nature of zemic, i.e. to McTaggart. As a background, one does not know any other thing than that he is one of those British, Hegelian Cambridge philosopher, whose system is truly difficult... but it opens, hopefully, via existential semiotics as its one possible interpretation and variant.

McTaggart announces right at the beginning of *The Nature of Existence I-II* (1927/1988) what he is aiming for: "In this work I propose to consider what can be determined as to the characteristics which belong to all that exists, or, again, which belong to Existence as a whole" (p. 3). And the Existent is for him "...a species of the Real". All that exists must be universally admitted, be real, while the position has been maintained, that there is reality which does not exist. The first question then is what is meant by reality or Being – the two words, as generally used, are equivalents. Yet, one may here immediately comment that if the term 'exist' is assumed in the sense of Kierkegaard, it is not that simple. Kierkegaard has noted (in his *Ending unscientific postscript*) that it is in fact serious and demanding assignment or in this sense all mere being is not yet existing.

In existential semiotics again existing is reserved just to the modes of being in the zemic model or existing is possible only through those four determinants: body, person, praxis, and values.

McTaggart then ponders which kind of true beliefs there are about existing; the question changes to the form, which kind of true statements there are about it, i.e. to a linguistic problem. Yet, in the chapter, "Method", he states immediately that the problem of existence is not solved inductively. It cannot be applied to the problem which kind of properties belong to all that exists and to the existence as a whole. We are not only particularly aware of the cases of yellow but about yellow in general, i.e. universally yellow, but what is awareness or consciousness? Consciousness of substances is different from consciousness of particulars. No substance is simple. This McTaggart considers empirical but apriori truth (cf. Kant's synthetic judgements apriori). Could we ask, one can find there at least two parts (p. 42) or *Moi* and *Soi*? This can be called ultimate empirical belief. It is properly called ultimate since although it is based on something – the perception – it is not based on any other belief. There is an important difference between ultimate beliefs which are apriori and those which are empirical.

The section "Substance" starts with the chapter Existence. We reserve the term to 'exist' to zemic which is the same as to be zemically. Yet McTaggart has to pose the same question as Leibniz. Does anything exist? Hence we are interested in the problem whether something exists. Here essential is the expression 'something is'.

However, that which exists must have some Quality and that is something he considers undefinable. All that which is true about something must have a quality. Yet, qualities can be further analyzed and find in them parts whose entirety is a compound quality. At once, quality seems to be a phenomenological concept and refer to existence such as we perceive it. Whatsoever that exists has qualities and limitlessly, but finally there is something which exists without being itself a quality and that is what McTaggart calls a substance.

It is true that the nature of all is unity as well as multitude. It has been argued that substance is nothing separate from qualities and therefore the very notion of substance is impossible. This is a mistake. Quality can exist only as a quality of something else, which exists (p.699). The qualities of existant are impossible without substance just like there is no substance without qualities.

Therefore substance does exist. Yet, then we have to ask whether substances are many or only one? Is then a substance, for instance, a person differentiated? Regarding our own theory we could already infer that this differentiation just means the differentiation of the substance into four modes $M1M2S2S1$.

However, next question deals with relation. If there is plurality of substances, we must have interrelations among substances. Substances which are to each other in relationship of similarity of difference are similar or different. The relationship, just like quality, is undefinable. We can show this by some examples. When we say that A is larger than B or that A is B's father or that A is to the right of B and A loves B or A does not know B, we postulate relations in which A stands for B. Then McTaggart lists various cases of relationships: identity, difference, similarity etc. dealing with substances. We have already at our zemic model come to at least seven different relations which dwell inside differentiated substance or zemic: sublimation, embodiment, transascendence, transdescendence, similarity/dissimilarity (fragmentary), dialogicity, teleologicity and resistance...and portrayed them by own symbols (see above p. 84).

Moreover, McTaggart ponders primary qualities and recurrent qualities – when primary ones are broader by their meaning than the original quality. When chacarcteristics is not simple, but it has parts or elements, we do not know their meaning unless we know meaning of the parts. If humanity means quality to be rational and animal, we do not know the meaning of humanity unless we know meaning of the animal. This fits well with our zemic: we cannot say that our subject is entirely body or *Moi1* because it belongs to the definition of zemic and it is, at the same time, in relation with three other parts or properties i.e. person, praxis, and values.

Intrinsic determination is universal or always when there is one quality also other quality occurs. Intrinsic determination exists between two qualities in two substances or: if in zemic1 *M1M2S2S1* its *M1'* is same as the corresponding *M1"* in zemic2 then what is involved is such an inner determination.

Here we have now accordingly moved to determine the origin of the social or situation in which several substances have to fit together, adapt to each other, take into account each others' characteristics in order to function and exist in the world.

In the chapter XVII (p. 145) McTaggart extends the sphere of groups to concern the whole universe. Universe is its own substance. There is a substance which contains all contents and of which every other substance is a part.

Universal determination then concerns whole universes as substances where we above spoke about external determination between two substances (zemics) and the qualities therein (for instance M1' ad M1" in zemic1 and zemic2).

Organic unity is an essential problem, the term 'organic' and its use concerning the character of substance. Is substance – or zemic – an organic entity? If some substance A has a part B whose nature consists of qualites XYZ then A has as its quality to possess the property whose qualities are XYZ. From this follows a relation between A and B themselves. A substance which is a whole may be considered as compounded of its parts. But it can be also taken as a manifestation of the nature of A, the existence of the part may be taken as dependent on the existence of the whole. Instead of considering the parts as constituting the whole we may take the whole as issuing its parts. So the parts are manifestations of the whole regarding zemics, and therefore if zemic A contains zemic B as its part they together constitute one whole.

In the chapter Infinite divisibility of substance, there is an excellent formulation regarding our theory (p. 177) : "It would be universally admitted that each of us perceives some sense-data and also by introspection various events which take place within himself. I think that in addition to this it is possible for a man to perceive himself and that most men do so frequently though not always. . .if a man perceives himself he does not by doing so perceive anything which is simple. Each self has many parts which are simultaneous. At many moments if not at all moments, the field of consciusness is differentiated. If the perceptions, judgments and volitions of a self are parts of that self this would prove that self was not simple." This fits well as a proof of the inner division of zemic into those four modes.

McTaggart's theory of *determining correspondence* is an important opening to the social dimension and ethics. The parts of the substances A B, C, and D are connected through inner correspondences, when he indicates for instance B! C to mean that part of B which corresponds to C and B1, C1, D that part of B which corresponds to C and that to D. This chain he calls determining correspondence. Since, by the sufficient portrayal of B and C, we conclude the sufficient portrayal of B1 C1.

This situation is easily changeable into a zemic model by a diagram in which the arrows connect A and B zemic to their modes (diagram 2):

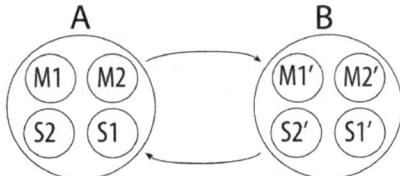

Diagram 2: Interaction among modes of two zemic units.

Or M1 and M1' are in such a corresponding relationship. This completely explains the phenomenon of the 'social'. Only the fact that these modes in two zemic are similar – or different – enable the interaction between them, This can be applied directly to music: let us take two sonata themes or two Wagner's leitmotifs or subject and countersubject in a Bach fugue.

Yet, this is linked with the problem: does it signify that M1 and M1' are in this determining correspondence which accordingly M1 *dominates*, orders and rules over M1'? Or shall we come here to my model of postcolonial analysis, in which work, the agents or zemics called dominant and dominated? What is involved is therefore also a relation of power; master and slave.

Here we can stop to think of our own zemic system. There I have distinguished the level of log-zemic which consists of 7 logical relations or categories or how you want to call them, namely inside substances or between them i.e. inside the zemics in modes or between different zemics. As already, by following McTaggart, we have concluded that the relations of zemic to each other are dertermined just on the level of primary parts of those modes M1M2S2S1 which influence **over** the borders of zemic among each other. What is involved is of course whether these laws are valid among the modes of log-zemic for instance so that *M1* of zemic1 causally influence *M2* or *S1* of zemic2? For instance, such a musical work as Chausson piano quartet in which there are four parts, represents a zemic and it has certain relations among those parts. The main motif of Zemic1 M2 is originating from a previous zemic namely Wagner's clock motif in *Parsifal*.

In McTaggart, the selves constitute their own community. He sees the term self in a very similar sense as substance. He says directly (p. 271) that ". . .the unity of the universe and the individuality of the primary parts are so related that a high degree of the one is compatible with a high degree of other. . . ...Unity of the universe is due to the fact that its primary parts are connected by a relation which is possible only between terms which are highly developed individuals." (P. 271). Or we might add here: subjects i.e. zemics.

McTaggart comes to the statement in book II chapter, "Considerations on selves", as follows:

> We have come to the conclusion that all that exists is spiritual, that the primary parts in the system of determining correspondence are selves, and that the secondary parts of all grades are perceptions. The selves then occupy a unique position in the universe. They and they alone are primary parts.

In any case, I leave now here the system of McTaggart by the conclusion that it can be in its entirety interpreted as one variable of the zemic theory, whose concepts can be reinterpreted without doing injustice to them in the zemic world.

6 Wittgenstein

From the great philosophers of the 20th century, we still have Wittgenstein, whom we have already discussed a little. I do not know what Wittgenstein thought of McTaggart, but the opinion of Bertrand Russell we already know. As I said Wittgenstein belongs to those thinkers whom I have not earlier understood at all. Yet, I have taken it as a challenge and always tried again. As told earlier, I was in this issue encouraged by v. Wright, a pupil of Wittgenstein and close friend. It feels something unbelievable that almost through my whole academic career I have been sitting at the Department of Musicology at Vironkatu 1, in the adress where on the other side of the street there was Dep. of Theoretical philosophy; there all Wittgenstein manuscripts were preserved and edited for publishing. I never went to see them – unlike the manuscripts of Charles Sanders Peirce in Indianapolis. For me, it has always been an enigma how two so different 'existential' characters and 'zemics' like Wittgenstein and v. Wright could do with each other. Wittgenstein, a demoniac personality and v. Wright, the model of British calmness and common sense (albeit he was from a Finnish-Swedish noble family). V. Wright finally invited Wittgenstein to his house in Cambridge when he got ill and took care of him until the end. The sister of Wittgenstein then invited the v. Wrights for a visit to her castle in Austria. Accordingly v. Wright encouraged me often to get familiar with the music philosophy of Wittgenstein – or rather his disparate thoughts about music in many connections. Wittgenstein doubtless belongs to those musical philosophers whose work if anyone emerged *aus dem Geiste der Musik* like in Nietzsche. In my project, *Musical signification*, the Austrian philosopher Josephine Papst studied Wittgenstein. The French musicologist Antonia Soulez published a book about Wittgenstein and music: *Au fil du motif. Autour de*

Wittgenstein et la musique (2012). In Wittgenstein's output lives the whole repertoire of romantc art music, but also the Viennese school and the music he did not like. To that category belonged a.o. Mahler. Yet, he also said formally: "Tell me an English artist and I can with a certainty say it is humbug.". The performance of music was important to him and his philosophy of music was based on gesture and physionomy; he could show at a performance of chamber music how one had to play one part by imagining a stick of a conductor in his hand."If you want to speak about music, you have to be able to do it (Soulez 2012: 23). Yet, unlike Adorno, Soulez remarks Wittgenstein does not reveal to us technically how he analysed music. To understand a phrase was for him analogous to understanding of a melody (Soulez 2012: 21). In understanding a melody, one had not to go behind it to ponder what else is conveyed except itself.

It is known that the philosopher played clarinet well (like Peirce did, too!) and he was able to whistle whole movements of symphonies. His brother Paul was pianist, the one who lost his right hand in the 1st world war and to whom then Ravel wrote his concerto for left hand. In any case he was hypersensitive for music. Yet, at least this was not the factor which united him with v. Wright who was not particularly musical (although played piano).

Why his philosophy is so difficult to access? One reason is that he was dyslexic. I was told this by Jaakko Hintikka once on a journey to a symposium of European Academy in Roskilde, Denmark. Since he was not able to read phrases in a logical order from paper his lectures were always improvised and freely spoken. This caused a kind of aphoristic form and fragmentary presentation. If his manner to produce discourse is juxtaposed with some McTaggart or C.D. Broad, he is a paradigmatic thinker, whereas the others are syntagmatic, proceeding linearly, like also Heidegger (on him v. Wright once said that in his philosophy every phrase refers to all that has been said and will be said).

However, let us once again open his *Logisch-Philosophische Abhandlung. Tractatus Logico-Philosophicus* which he wrote during the 1st world war and after and which appeared as its early version in 1922 and made him famous at once.

It begins impressively:

> *Die Welt ist alles was der Fall ist. Die Welt ist die Gesamteit der Tatsachen nicht der Dinge.*
> World is all that which is a case. World is the whole fact, not of things.

If we start right now our zemic interpretation, it would be tempting to understand the concept of *Tatsache* expressly as a zemic – as the substance of Aristotle, Leibniz, Spinoza, Schelling, and McTaggart. But will this work? What does *Fall* mean? Case. It is a quite deictic expression i.e. it refers to some moment or place. World is determined by facts and that it is the same as all facts (all zemics!). The facts in a logical state are the world. World dissolves into facts. . . what is a case is a fact, which is the maintenance of facts. Now appeared a new term *Sachverhalten*, states of affairs.Then comes the concept of *Gegenstand*. A spatial entity, *Gegenstand* must be in an infinite space. Colour has its color space. Tone must have its pitch. The thing of a touch is hardness etc.

Substance is the one which exists independent of what is the case. It is form and content. Comment: we get here close to earlier metaphysics. Space, time, and color are for a thing. Only because there are things, world has a fixed form. Stable, durable things are same. . .. The configuration of things makes a state of affairs. In a state of affairs, the things hang contained in each other, like members in a chain. . . Comment again: this is just like direct application of zemic. The chain of things is the chain of the modes of zemic or *M1M2S2S1*!

Then (p. 12) argument 2.1 We make images of facts. . . in other words, we represent them and make signs of them in our sig-zemic. Image is a model of reality. So, zemic is also model of reality, zemic or rather sig-zemic is the measure of reality, which expression Wittgenstein used about his notion of image or picture.

In what follows Wittgenstein's *Abbildung* is the same as the representation in semiotics whereby zemic leads to sig-zemic. If then *Bild*, image is sig-zemic then the Z model correctly portrays its form; it is true what Wittgenstein says, namely that every image is also logical. Logical image or picture can describe the world. Just so goes the Z movement in our zemic model. The image represents a possible state of affairs in a logical space. Image corresponds the reality or not. Image presents the reality independently its being true or false, by the form of portrayal and here we can only say: these forms of representation are just those categories of log-zemic!

Thereafter Wittgenstein reflects upon phrases. Phrase is not any mixture of words (*Wie das musikalische Thema kein Gemisch von Tönen*). Phrase is articulated. Also music is like a phrase, a sig-zemic, which refers to *Tatsache* or zemic or substance if one wants. Yet, this reference is difficult! Jose Ortega y Gasset already spoke about how art gets detached from the human. . .or zemic! Music cannot be reduced directly to reality, otherwise we fall from the absolute music to socialist realism.

The things of thought are equal to elements of phrase sign. These elements are simple signs and phrase is then 'completely analysed'; in other words, simple signs are sigzemics M1' M2' etc. And the phrase: a completely analyzed zemic. Relation M1' and M2' (in circle). The name M1' means the being M1 when M1 is the meaning of the sign M1' in circle). *Bedeutung*. . .but not its *Sinn*, I would add here.

The name *M1* (in circle) = *Urzeichen* or Wittgenstein says: *Der Name ist durch keine Definition weiter zu zergliedern: er ist ein Urzeichen*. The meaning of signs, *Bedeutung* must be already known M1, M2, only the phrase has a sense, *Sinn*. Phrase itself is expression, *Ausdruck* and *Ausdruck* is all that is essential to a phrase, what phrases have in common.

Sinn = Satz

Diagram 3: Meaning within four different phrases.

Ausdruck is a constant, anything else is variable. Or constants are zemic's phrases and again variables all the elements which do not have there their immediate place. Hence there are signs which do not belong or find place among constants of zemic and they are consequently variables in the diagram 4:

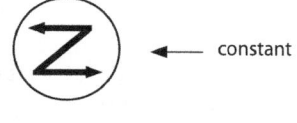
← constant

XXXX ← variables

Diagram 4: Inside of zemic, i.e. 'constant', and outside of zemic, i.e. 'variables'.

Are we here already talking about transcendence? Variable is the external element of constant, a transcendent; in this sense we can talk about it only by symbols.

(P. 84) Wittgenstein speaks about truth function: *Der Elementarsatz ist eine Wahrheitsfunktion seiner Selbst*.

He says: Truth functions are no material relations or functions; yet, when Wittgenstein states: they do not tell as such anything. *Alle Sätze der Logik sagen dasselbe. Nichts.*

Is truth operation a) the relationship of sig-zemic to zemic?, b) or the inner form sig-zemic or zemic? c) or interpretation of variable in zemic? For instance, when we note: to this *Tatsache* corresponds this Elementary phrase x,y,z = M1M2S2. . ., d) or each operation in the level of suprazemic? What is -*M1* or -*M2* i.e. the negation of zemic? Is it existential, I have to ask.

When we think of Frege's distinction of *Sinn* and *Bedeutung*, he already stated that every well-formed phrase must have a sense. If then some phrase does not have in spite of all sense it is due to the fact that its parts do not have a meaning or *Bedeutung*. In other words: *Sinn* = *Satz* (diagram 3) and *Bedeutung* = *Elementarsatz* and *Elementarsatz* in turn refers to *Tatsache* in zemic.

Important: *Sinn* = phrases together; *Bedeutung* = references to elementary phrases.

P. 136 *Ich bin meine Welt*

Das denkende, vorstellende Subject gibt es nicht. I am my world. There is no thinking, conceiving subject.

P. 156 *Die Logik ist transcendental.*

P. 174 *Der Tod ist keine Ereignis des Lebens. Den Tod erlebt man nicht* (Death is no event of life. Death is not experienced)

When we do not understand by eternity any temporal duration but the intemporality, then the one lives eternally who lives in the present.

Das Gefühl der Welt als begrenztes Ganzes ist das mystische.

These are thoughts by Wittgenstein already interpreted with our zemic; at least to myself the fairly mystic doctrine opened in a different manner. Another thing is what Wittgenstein specialists think thereof.

References

Aristotle. 2012. *Metafysiikka* [Metaphysics], Finnish trans. by Tuija Jatakari, Kati Näätsaari & Petri Pohjanlehto; comments by Simo Knuuttila. Helsinki: Gaudeamus.
Broad, Charlie Dunbar. 1976. *Examination of McTaggart's Philosophy I-II*. New York: Octagon Books.
Greimas, Algirdas Julien & Joseph Courtés. 1979. *Sémiotique. Dictionnaire raisonné.* Paris:Hachette.
Herman, A.L. 1976. *An Introduction to Indian Thought.* New Jersey: Prentice Hall
Hobbes, Thomas. 1999. *Leviathan,* Finnish trans. by Tuomo Aho. Tampere: Vastapaino.
Jolley, Nicholas (ed.). 1995. *The Cambridge Companion to Leibniz.* Cambridge: Cambridge University Press.
Joyce, James. 1982 [1916]. *A Portrait of the Artist as a Young Man*; *Taiteilijan omakuva nuoruuden vuosilta,* Finnish trans. by Alex Matson. Helsinki: Tammi
Klostermaier, Klaus K. 1994. *A Survey of Hinduism.* New York: State University of New York Press
Leibniz, Gottfried Wilhelm. 2011. *Filosofisia tutkielmia* [Philosophical Investigations], eds. Tuomo Aho ja Markku Roinila. Helsinki: Gaudeamus
McTaggart, John & Ellis. 1964. *A Commentary on Hegel's Logic.* New York: Russell & Russell.
McTaggart, John. 1988. *The Nature of Existence I-II.* Cambridge: Cambridge University Press
Pankhurst, Tom. 2008. *Schenkerguide.* A Brief Handbook and Website for Schenkerian Analysis. New York: Routledge.
Russell, Bertrand. 1957. *Muotokuvia muistista ja muita esseitä* [Portraits from memory and other essays], Finnish trans. by J. A. Hollo. Porvoo, Helsinki: WSOY

Schelling, Friedrich Wilhelm Josef. 1971. *Frühschriften. Vom Ich als Prinzip der Philosophie oder über das Unbedingte im menschlichen Wissen*. Intr. & ed. Helmut Seidel & Lothar Kleine. Berlin: Akademie-Verlag.

Soulez, Antonia. 2012. *Au fil du motif. Autour de Wittgenstein et la musique*. Paris: Editions Delatour France.

Spinoza, Benedictu de. 1994. *Etiikka* [Ethics]. Finnish trans. & comments by Vesa Oittinen. Helsinki: Gaudeamus

Stenius, Erik. 1960. *Wittgenstein's Tractatus. A Critical exposition of its main lines of thought*. Oxford: Basil Blackwell.

Tarasti, Eero. 2012. *Semiotics of Classical Music. How Mozart, Brahms and Wagner Talk To Us*. Berlin: Mouton de Gruyter.

Tarasti, Eero. 2015. *Sein und Schein. Explorations in existential semiotics*. Berlin: Mouton de Gruyter.

Tarasti, Eero. 2021. Existential Semiotics and Its Application to Music: The Zemic Theory and Its Birth from the Spirit of Music. In Paulo Chagas (ed.), *Sounds from Within. Phenomenology and Practice*, 29–57. (Numanities – Arts and Humanities in Progress 18,). Springer, Cham. https://doi.org/10.1007/978-3-030-72507-5_2

Wagner, Richard. 1975. Das Braune Buch. Tagebuchaufzeichnungen *1865 bis 1882*. Zürich: Atlantis Verlag.

Wittgenstein, Ludwig. 1980. *Remarks on the Philosophy of Psychology*. Vol. 1. ed. G.E.M. Anscombe & G.H. von Wright, English trans. by G.E.M. Anscombe. Oxford: Basil Plackwell

Wittgenstein, Ludwig. 1989. *Logisch-philosophische Abhandlung. Tractatus logico-philosophicus*. Kritische Edition, ed. Brian McGuinness & Joachim Schulte. Frankfurt am Main: Suhrkamp.

Wittgenstein, Ludwig. 1997. *Denkbewegungen*. Tagebücher 1930–1932/1936–1937., ed. Ilse Somavilla. Innsbruck: Haymon.

Wittgenstein, Ludwig. 2008. *Philosophical Investigations*. Eng. trans. by G.E.M. Anscombe. Oxford: Blackwell Publishing.

Wittgenstein, Ludwig. 2016. *Lectures. Cambridge 1930–1933*. From the Notes of G.E. Moore, ed. David G. Stern, Brian Rogers & Gabriel Citron. Cambridge: Cambridge University Press

Wright, Georg Henrik von. 2001. *Elämäni niin kuin sen muistan* [My Life as I remember it] . Helsinki: Otava.

Kristian Bankov
Being, resistance and post-truth

Abstract: In this chapter I am confronting the idea of resistance as it has been elaborated by Eero Tarasti and myself within existential semiotics with the same notion in Umberto Eco (supported by Heidegger, Dilthey and Peirce) when the Italian thinker reflects on the semiotic foundation of being. If we agree with Eco that Being is what can be talked of in many ways, then it should be necessarily also *what resists in many ways* to our discursive attempts, aimed at its fixation in writing. Follows an articulation of three different typologies of resistance, depending on whether the aim of discourse is the physical world, language/ socially constructed reality or the mind. Such articulation prevents from certain epistemological misunderstandings and helps us understand important distortions in the perceptions of truth in the age of social media and digital culture in general. The consequences of such distortions are illustrated with examples from how the COVID-19 crisis is handled by policy makers and public opinion and how the scientific discourse is overshadowed by alternative discourses, far less resistant to subjective opinions, commercial interests and contingencies.

Keywords: semiosis, resistance, reality, mind, post-truth

1 Existential semiotics and resistance

Eero Tarasti's *existential semiotics* became the most important semiotic doctrine in the early phase of my scientific career. When I met the eminent Finnish semiotician, I had just graduated from the University of Bologna with a thesis fitting Bergson's philosophy into the problems of semiotics. Existential semiotics gave a huge boost to these interests of mine, and thanks to Professor Tarasti, they materialized in a doctorate, defended with honors at the University of Helsinki (Bankov 2000). The topic of resistance was implicit in both existential semiotics and my research before our meeting, but the reason for this article is the development it received after that.

During the years of my postdoctoral research, I had the opportunity to participate regularly in the seminars of Eero Tarasti and it was there that the main ideas were formed, as well as the basis for my first article, entirely devoted to the topic of resistance (Bankov 2004). Subsequently, it provoked a kind of scientific dialogue and the paper was quoted in detail in the famous article of the Finnish semiotician, also devoted entirely to the topic of resistance (Tarasti 2009). This text is a deepening of this key topic for existential semiotics, designed for one of the main problems of modern digital society – the devaluation of truth in public debate, which has moved almost entirely to the arena of social media. But the main part of the text is giving credit to another giant of semiotics – Umberto Eco.

The Italian semiotician was in Sofia for a special conference dedicated to his book *Kant and the Platypus* ([1997] 2000) and I had the great privilege of presenting to him a paper entitled "Being and Resistance", receiving invaluable feedback "directly from the source". Interestingly, during the conference, even before my presentation, there was an intense debate between Eco and Gianni Vattimo, another star of the event, on the topic of resistances of textual interpretation. Here, for the first time, I present in the form of a scientific article this confrontation, in an international edition, on the topic of existential semiotics with the theoretical framework that Eco opens in *Kant and the Platypus* on the notion of the *resistances of being* (Eco 2000: 50 ff).

2 The frame of Eco's semiotics

With *A Theory of Semiotics* ([1975] 1976), Eco rises to the position of the only contemporary author who is able to create a coherent and consistent theory, not failing to include any significant author or idea that has contributed to the establishment of the discipline. In addition, he outlines a global vision for the development of semiotics, which is not polemical but constructive and whose foresight we have become increasingly convinced of over the past decade. For instance, the Internet is literally the embodiment of the encyclopedic model of culture with which Eco summarizes his theoretical views in *A Theory of Semiotics* (Bankov 2017).

Eco retains the same style until his last theoretic work – *Kant and the Platypus* ([1997] 2000). There, the global vision of semiotics is enriched by the contribution of the cognitive sciences, but without in the least distancing it from its philosophical premises. I have directed my research precisely to this work of Eco, and to the first chapter, in which he directly confronts the most global of the philosophical problems – that of Being. Eco explains that this choice "It's not a matter of delusions of grandeur but of professional duty" (Eco 2000: 4). And it seems that everything said so far makes this phrase sound less ironic than if taken simply as a witty remark.

It was a pleasant surprise to me that Eco's report, which opened the conference in the crowded hall of the Sheraton Hotel, was based almost entirely on this chapter from *Kant and the Platypus*, although the announced title created very different expectations. However, good surprises did not stop there. One of the first disputes during the discussions broke out between Eco and Gianni Vattimo on the topic of "resistance of being", which was literally my topic. This controversy continued on the second day, and when the time came to present this paper, I enjoyed an extremely favourable "high start".

3 "Resistance" in *Kant and the Platypus*

So, what does Eco mean by the expression "resistance of being"?

After *A Theory of Semiotics* ([1975] 1976), Eco devoted two of his most important books, *The Role of the Reader* ([1979] 1994) and *Limits of Interpretation* (1990), as well as many articles and essays, to the problem of open texts. According to him, certain types of texts, especially literature and other creative genres, naturally suggest the possibility of being interpreted in many different ways, but there is no instance to determine any of these interpretations as the only correct one. Such a production to some extent reflects the then "spirit of the time" and largely overlaps with the literary "deconstruction". But Eco's theoretical goal was exactly the opposite, and in fact, his efforts are devoted to giving some criteria for the validity of these interpretations, which would entitle some of them, but deny arbitrary "interpretive walks." It is obvious to him that it is wrong to say exactly what the message of a novel is, but at the same time it is no less obvious that there are things that a novel could not want to say under any circumstances. This is the *limit of interpretation* – negatively constituted by the multitude of inadmissible interpretations. Beyond this limit, according to Eco, the reader does not interpret but uses the text for his own purposes.

In *Kant and the Platypus*, in the chapter "On Being", Eco develops the theme of the limits of interpretation at the ontological level. Eco's semiotic ontology is synthesized in a phrase he borrows from Aristotle: being is what can be talked of in many ways (43). The existing becomes being when for someone, under some aspect, it appears as a semantically articulated reality. The existing is the cause, the engine of semiosis (the process of signification), but its existence depends on its interpretive realizations in a human social or individual environment. The question posed by Eco is: do these interpretive realizations have a limit? The answer is yes: "I speak of Being only inasmuch as I feel that what is sets limits on our freedom of speech". In other words, being renders resistance to human interpretive endeavours, disciplines them, and sanctions, so to speak, their success. The interaction with the resistance of being is postponed involuntarily in the social conventions that carry its meaning, namely the languages and other sign systems that make up the culture. According to Eco, there are lines of resistance in existence, which predetermine a similar semantic articulation of the world around us in very different cultures. Here are some eloquent quotes:

> We learn by experience that nature seems to manifest stable tendencies. It is not necessary to think of obscure and complex laws, like those of universal gravitation, but of simpler, more immediate experiences, such as the rising and setting of the sun, gravity, the objective existence of the species. The universals may well be a figment and infirmity of thought, but once dog and cat have been identified as species, we learn immediately that if we mate a dog with a dog, another dog is born of it, but if we mate a dog with a cat, nothing is born of it – and even if something were born, it would not be able to reproduce itself. This still does not mean that there is a certain (I would like to say "Darwinian") reality of the genera and species. It is only intended to suggest that even though speaking in *generalia* may be an effect of our *penuria nominum*; nonetheless, *something* resistant [. . .]What does it mean to say there is "purport" before any sensate articulation effected by human cognition? I would prefer to translate Hjelmslev's *meaning* as "sense," a term that can suggest both meaning (but there is no meaning or content before a given language has segmented and organized the *continuum*) and *direction* or *tendency*. As if to say that in the magma of the continuum there are lines of resistance and possibilities of flow, as in the grain of wood or marble, which make it easier to cut in one direction than in another. (51–53)

As can be seen, Eco attributes great importance to the concept of resistance and seems to naturally "close" the semiotic ontology, starting from the position that "being is what can be talked of in many ways" (43). The topic of resistance is present implicitly and explicitly throughout the book and, in my opinion, makes possible one of the most reliable coherent readings of an otherwise quite diverse collection of essays interpreting central semiotic problems. On the other hand, as can be seen from the quotations, Eco did not find it necessary to systematically present his views on resistance, and this to some extent obscures the philosophical potential of this intuition. Therefore, the purpose of this paragraph is to systematize what Eco has said about the resistance of being and also to outline several possible directions in which this topic could bridge the gap between the doctrine of signs and important philosophical issues, of course without forgetting that, although in an unsystematic way, the supporting columns of these bridges are the work of Eco himself.

However, before making purely theoretical suggestions, I shall say a few words about the use of the concept of resistance in the authors, which Eco quotes in the aforementioned chapter of *Kant and the Platypus*.

4 "Resistance" in Dilthey, Heidegger and Peirce

When speaking explicitly about resistance, Eco quotes mainly four authors – Vattimo, Hjelmslev, Heidegger and Peirce. Vattimo is often associated with a position that largely ignores the resistance of being. Perhaps one of the reasons for Eco to write a chapter on being was to include in it one of his essays from the collection *Weak Thought* ([1983] 2012), compiled by Vattimo and Pier Aldo Rovati. This collection provokes many contradictory reviews, including the fact that the authors in it sent the being "on vacation" (Eco 2000: xii). Although in the controversy held at the Sofia conference between the two philosophers, Vattimo often distinguished between the resistance of the outside world and that of the texts, as if in his major works he was more concerned with denying it than defining it. That is why Eco rightly claims that he was incorrectly ranked among the representatives of weak thought, although by many other criteria his essay successfully fits into the idea of the collection of the same name.

Hjelmslev is among the authors who have strongly influenced Eco and is certainly the only structuralist among them. As can be seen from the quotation above, Hjelmslev's contribution is mostly about the connection between arbitrary sign systems and the resistance that the outside world exerts to its semantic segmentation. In Hjelmslev, we are talking about "directions/meanings" and "lines of tendency", which predetermine the "portions of reality", conventionally associated with sign systems. But Hjelmslev, like Vattimo, does not isolate the subject and does not use the term "resistance."

Among the authors quoted by Eco, only Heidegger and Peirce make this move. For both, resistance is a constitutive factor of reality. But interestingly, Eco does not cite the places where Heidegger and Peirce speak explicitly about resistance, but deductively justifies his choice using other passages. In any case, the overall result is accurate, as the passages I found do not contradict what Eco has interpretively attributed to the cited authors, but only enrich it. Even in the commentary after my report, he said he was surprised that Peirce had written so directly on the subject and then gave examples of how he explained Peirce's categories of "firstness" and "secondness" to his students, commenting on the quote I shall attach below. It turned out that there were similar examples in *Kant and the Platypus*, but apparently, at that time, Eco had not thought of them (see 2.8 and 2.8.3).

In the chapter "On Being", Heidegger's formulation of the ontological problem serves as a leading thread of Eco's analysis. The first example of the resistance of being is one of the central themes in Heidegger's philosophy:

> One can only agree with Heidegger: the problem of being is posed only to those thrown into Being-there, into the *Dasein*, of which our disposition both to notice that something is there and to talk about it is a part. And in our Being-there we have the fundamental experience of a Limit that language can say in advance (and therefore only predict), in one way only, beyond which it fades into silence: it is the experience of Death. (50–51)

We, for our part, cannot but agree with Eco that the subject must be opened with the most insurmountable of all resistances –that of the finitude of the human life, that has provoked unimaginable amounts of discourse in the history of mankind and which will surely stimulate the imagination for peoples' mitigating religious narratives. But looking more closely at *Being and Time*, we come across paragraph 43, "*Dasein*, Worldhood, and reality," in which Heidegger comments much more theoretically on the problem of resistance, using this very concept, the German "Widerstand". In his analysis, with a rather heavy terminological apparatus, Heidegger argues that *reality appears as resistance*, but that such a statement is valid only if it is based on *Dasein's* ontological interpretation, namely that the constituent elements can only be thought of as given in an always already open world, and not as instances that determine the psychological characteristics of "life". The main criticism is directed at Dilthey, who seems to be the original source of the idea of resistance in German philosophy. The most important part of Heidegger's analysis, however, concerns the connection of the theme of resistance with *Dasein's* temporal structure – *Care*: "Only entities with this kind of Being [whose way of being is Care] can come up against something resistant as something within-the-world" (254). As we will see, it is the temporal dimension of resistance that makes it an anthroposemiotic phenomenon, thus avoiding all apparent analogies with the stimulus-response logic that unites all species.

Dilthey's contribution is important to the present study, not only because he seems to have been the first to put the term into circulation (Peirce used it before him, but did not publish it), but also because he has one of the most enduring and valid distinctions between the natural sciences and the sciences of the spirit, for which I shall use the typology of resistance below. Although seemingly nowhere does Dilthey mix the two themes, there are enough reasons for him to do so. The article through which Dilthey introduces the concept of resistance has the complex title "Contributions to the Solution of the Problem of Our Belief in the Reality of the External World and Its Right". Here is how he summarizes his position:

> As a child presses his hand against a chair in order to move it, he measures his power against the resistance; his own life and the object are experienced together. But now let the child be locked up. It is in vain that he rattles against the door; now his entire excited will becomes aware of the compulsion of an overwhelming powerful external world that hinders and

restricts, and compresses, as it were, his own self-willed life. The desire to escape from the displeasure and to gratify his impulses is followed by the consciousness of obstruction, displeasure and dissatisfaction. What the child thus experiences follows him through his entire adult life. The resistance becomes pressure. We seem to be everywhere surrounded by walls of actual facts through which we cannot break. The impressions remain, no matter how much we would like to change them; they vanish although we strive to cling to them; impulses of motion directed by the idea of avoiding something that causes pain are, under certain circumstances, always followed by emotions that hold us within the realm of pain. Thus, the reality of the external world grows, so to speak, progressively more dense around us.

(Dilthey 1890: 105)

When Eco mentions Peirce in his chapter about the resistance of being, he does so in a rather roundabout way. Eco summarizes the position of Habermas, who in turn analyzes the way Peirce rejects Kant's "thing in itself." This leads to the quote we saw at the beginning.

A closer reading, however, shows that Peirce repeatedly uses the term "resistance", especially when explaining the category of "secondness." Of the many suitable passages, I chose this one because it contains the same closed-door figure that Dilthey uses (probably written in 1880):

> The actuality of the event seems to lie in its relations to the universe of existents. A court may issue injunctions and judgments against me and I not care a snap of my finger for them. I may think them idle vapor. But when I feel the sheriff's hand on my shoulder, I shall begin to have a sense of actuality. Actuality is something brute. There is no reason in it. I instance putting your shoulder against a door and trying to force it open against an unseen, silent, and unknown *resistance*. We have a two-sided consciousness of effort and *resistance*, which seems to me to come tolerably near to a pure sense of actuality. On the whole, I think we have here a mode of being of one thing which consists of how a second object is. I call that Secondness.
> (CP 1.24, my italics)

As we well know about Peirce, the three categories are inseparable elements of the semiosic process, which makes resistance an integral part of the constitution of the human type of experience. Therefore, his model of the sign process will serve as the basis of our model of resistance.

5 Triadic model of resistance

"Being is what can be talked of in many ways," Eco repeatedly insisted, quoting Aristotle. From what has been said so far, however, we could draw another complementary hypothesis: *Being is what resists in many ways*.

In most of the examples quoted so far, it seems that resistance has been identified with the objective course of external reality, which does not easily obey our desires and intentions. Vattimo, however, contrasted this kind of resistance with the text's resistance. Eco's theory of the limits of interpretation can also be seen as a theory of the resistance of texts to their arbitrary interpretation. In his book on translation, Eco (2003) literally uses the term "resistance" when commenting on his experience as a translator. In *Kant and the Platypus*, he uses as well the concept of resistance when he speaks of the conventionality of the meaning of concepts, or as he calls them – *cognitive types*. According to him, some traits are more resistant than others (see 4.4). I would also expand the phenomenon of resistance to cases of intersubjective interaction. For example, the type of resistance is that of the team I work for when my suggestions are rejected. We generally encounter resistance when we want our interaction with other people to proceed in one way, and it takes a completely different direction. But resistance can also be experienced on an individual level, without contact with others or the material environment – for example, when we do mathematical calculations in mind. Not to mention the complex resistances theorized by psychoanalysis that psychotherapists struggle with.

Both Peirce and Eco contrast the phenomenon of resistance with the work of the imagination. Peirce calls it *play of musement* (see CP 6.458–462). Eco gives examples of poetic construction of possible worlds (78). At first glance, the opposition seems logical, but a closer look at the experience shows that resistance is universal. Anyone who has tried to write poetry knows very well that mere fantasy is not enough and that the main effort is to give a conventional form to many unstable impressions and images. Here, too, it is not a question of a psychological phenomenon, but of a confrontation with a so-called "hardened" intersubjective (social) reality, such as the culturally established sign systems. The same, of course, applies to other forms of creativity, where, according to Eco himself, the author always implicitly inscribes a reader model, which means that the creative act is fixed in writing that the author chooses according to his own ideas about the encyclopedic competence of potential interpreters of the text. The form always resists the creative impulses.

Perhaps only dreams and unshared fantasies are a kind of semiosis that does not meet resistance. And if dreams are a much more complex phenomenon than the simple mentioning presupposes, then we could say that daydreams meet as much resistance as they become "real", and that it is normal for them to gradually develop into shared plans for the future which already carry the full burden of different types of resistance.

The examples could go on for a long time. From now on, our goal is to try to propose a model that introduces some typology into this infinitely diverse phenomenon. The effectiveness of the model will depend on whether we can use it to analyze (or position) different forms of discourse or prediscursive forms of semiosis, which is ultimately the modality of the existence of being, since, as we have already said, being is what is talked of and accordingly resisting, in many ways.

Of great help in justifying my choice of approach was part of Prof. Eco's lecture, in which he spoke about "A model of knowledge of the world" (Chapter 1.8 in *Kant and the Platypus*). In the lecture, he had illustrated the model with diagrams that are not present in the book. The triadic nature of the model was even clearer in these schemes, which is also my initial hypothesis. What the two models have in common is Peirce's concept of semiosis, which deserves a brief recollection.

The simplified version of the semiotic triangle is wrongly attributed to Peirce, in which three completely independent instances are given – object, sign and interpretant. For Peirce, the important thing is the triadic connection on which the sign function is based. None of the three elements can be considered independently of the other two. The object, or the thing in itself (Peirce calls it a *Dynamic Object*), is never given directly in its entirety, but always only some aspect of it "presents" it to the consciousness in the form of an *interpretant*. Peirce calls this aspect of the dynamic object an immediate object, representamen, or sign. So the sign would not make sense as something in itself, because its essence is precisely in the relationship between the object and the interpreter, in the mediation of experience. The dynamic object, in turn, is a logical construction, since everything that has become the object of naming is already an immediate object. The dynamic object can be considered only as the thing that makes us take it into account, the reason for the semiosis, which, however, takes place through the immediate object and the interpretant. The dynamic object is the impetus, which, however, we learn from the other two elements of semiosis that carry it out. The situation is similar with the interpretant. (See Eco 2000: Ch. 1)

Following the principle of the interconnectedness of the elements of semiosis, I posed the question from a slightly different angle. What are the minimum conditions for producing discourse?

I chose the term discourse because it seems, to me, more adequate than a sign when we talk about the real processes of signification through which consciousness is constantly realized. Perhaps the concept of modelling would be even more accurate if it were separated from its technocratic aura. Therefore, the answer to the question would be interesting: what models consciousness? The answer is: it constantly models variants of itself. This is semiosis.

At least that is what it looks like if we take Bergson's analysis of the duration of consciousness and Heidegger's analysis of *Dasein's* temporal structure. Consciousness is always projected to the future, it always implicitly carries in itself a vision of the world, because awareness is possible only in an always meaningfully open world. The more experience we gain, the more our implicit world grows and accordingly makes more hypotheses about the forthcoming, more potential models of ourselves. So consciousness is projected to the future, and, at the same time, it draws from past experience. As Heidegger says, this is an *ecstatical unity* (coexistence) on which the temporal structure of *Dasein* is based (see Heidegger 1962: § 65, 377–379). Bergson uses the term *thickness of duration*, which characterizes each moment of consciousness, depending on the span of past and forthcoming (future) of the life project in which it is involved.

One of the original proposals of this study is the connection of two seemingly distant philosophical issues – *semiosis and time*. It follows from the above that the mediation that sign processes guarantee to experience (its detachment from the stimulus-response logic), its semantically articulated storage in memory and its use to construct models for a possible course of events projected in the future *is the condition of possibility for the temporal structure of consciousness*. The semantic articulation of the experience stored in the memory means that an arbitrary, so to say, "free will" access is provided to it, which makes the past an autonomous instance of consciousness. The opposite is true when all the experience gained has the structure of the stimulus-response and, accordingly, access to this type of sensorimotor memory is dependent on the sensory stimuli of the present. This is a problem faced by numerous trainers and scientists who have tried to teach primates and other animals to use language or other arbitrary sign systems. The non-human animal can be trained to perform an infinitely complex "program", including the release of a series of sounds that is clearly an accumulated experience, but access to that experience needs a specific sensory stimulus to enact it automatically. Thus, the past is always a function of the stimuli of the present, which eliminates it as an autonomous instance of the temporal structure of consciousness and thus deprives it of deep semiosis (although apparently, the reaction of stimuli seems like an "interpretation" of a sign). Similar considerations can be made for the projections of the future. Although I cannot be sure at all what exactly is going on in the "black boxes" of non-human animals, I can be sure what is not going on there, and that is the symbolic temporal manipulation of experience that would be the case with the socio-cultural way of being where non-hereditary cultural information is employed (see Bergson 1988:77 ff).

This "biosemiotic" digression was necessary to highlight exactly which aspects of the seemingly pervasive phenomenon of semiosis were singled out as essential to the resistance model. So what are the minimum conditions for producing discourse? (see Figure 1)
1) We need human consciousness, as we have seen, temporally structured. Although "consciousness" is the term that the quoted philosophers use, more exact is what in the English-speaking world is called "mind" or "sujet" in French.

2) A *dynamic object*, or what Eco calls the "thing", the reality external to the mind, in the independent existence of which no semiotic paradigm is in doubt, although for some "textualist" currents it has no substantial impact for semiosis.
3) We need a *language and a community* that shares it, or at least another human being with whom to communicate and share experiences. Only a human being can introduce another human being into a semiotically articulated world. This can be done with the help of language or another "artificial" sign system. The language is not innate. There is an innate predisposition to learn a language and various other sign systems and a huge amount of information. If the child does not have contact with another human-speaking being, his or her language ability is impaired and cannot be restored.

The presence of a mind as a prerequisite for semiosis should not suggest any dualism. As has already been emphasized enough, the model of the sign and, accordingly, the concept of the above three prerequisites lie on the premise of the indivisibility of the three elements. Semiotic consciousness is always consciousness of something. As Eco himself insists when interpreting Heidegger, language (signs) is the condition for some of the existing things (people) to realize (comprehend) the very phenomenon of existence. As we have seen, however, the signs are not an autonomous instance as well, but they depend on the terms of the relation they are actualizing and so on.

Semiosis is an ecstatical unity (to use Heidegger's expression) of three irreducible instances – object, mind and society/language.

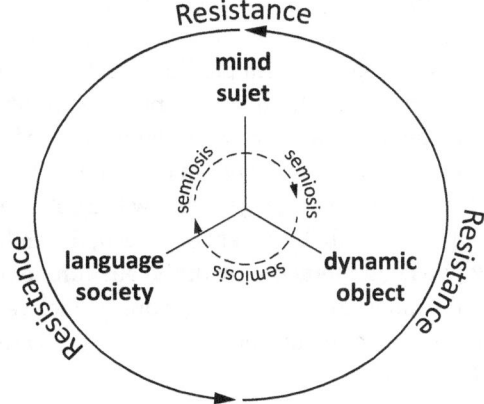

Figure 1: Model of semiosis and resistance.

Therefore, in the analysis of resistance, we cannot abstract from the indicated characteristics of semiosis. Resistance to semiosis, which produces discourse or modelled projects of action, is also composite. In other words, all three instances of semiosis are a source of different, irreducible to each other types of resistance. Resistance has a complex structure, but we can make assumptions about the deriving characteristics of the discourse with which we describe the world.

From what has been said so far, it seems that clarifying the constituent nature of resistance could lead to original views on many controversies in the philosophy of science, in the methodology of the human sciences, and other particular theoretical fields. An extensive study with such a focus is the distant horizon of realization of these ideas, while here I shall try to give just a few examples.

The resistance that the surrounding world exerts in our interaction with it is the foundation of our primordial confidence in its existence, regardless of our desires and fantasies. However, resistance becomes more and more dynamic with the increase of the accumulated experience, which we can "project outwards". From this point of view, the accumulation of experience can be seen as attained resistance, or more precisely attained persistence. This means that everyone's worldview is made up of many stable elements that always respond in an identical way when we interact with them. This process of assimilation begins long before the appearance of the semiotic abilities in humans and is based on the acquisition of sensorimotor coordination and sense of balance of the body, the physical manipulative skills of the limbs, etc.

Before the "cultural" processes begin, the human being has already acquired many motor schemes, which mainly affect those aspects of the environment that "respond" in an identical way in interaction with them, that is, what is "acquired" when someone has physically adapted to the environment. For example, this is the only way to teach children to walk. In this phase, cognitive processes are the embodiment in the (pre)consciousness of countless simple but effective "prescriptions" of the stimulus-reaction type, which form in the nervous system something like a "map" of the external persistence of the material environment in which the child grows. In this phase, the differences between the child and the more evolved mammals are small (throughout the passage, I follow the observations of Lev Vygotsky, especially [1930] 1994). With the advent of speech, the child gradually enters a qualitatively new phase of interaction with the environment, in which he gradually begins to mentally model his upcoming actions, while even in the most developed primates the implementation of elementary tasks is always a function of concrete, mostly visual perception.

But the important thing to note is that the acquired resistance/persistence continues to be the foundation for cognitive processes in the advanced stages of cognitive development. Language introduces the human being into the temporal dimension of existence, transforms the ego into identity; consciousness, as noticed above, acquires the ecstatical structure of unity of past and future, but this only intensifies and, so to speak, complicates the need for persistence, for embodied stability in the relation with the external world. Bergson calls this feature of living organisms the principle of *Primum vivere*. The human consciousness becomes able to model itself in different ways and to regulate its "behavior" as a result of a free choice and therefore consistent with the consequences of that free choice.

But all these models (or projects, scenarios, eventualities, etc.) would not have value in themselves if they did not lie on a broad basis of "steadiness" coming from cognitively acquired persistence, which Peirce would call "habit". We often find ourselves in a situation of complete uncertainty. Imagine a situation when our car stops for no apparent reason. However unclear we may be about what to do, our action plans always include secure elements (affordances) such as the fact that we can rely on the hardness of the pavement or the slope (respectively on the permanent action of gravity), the strength of the tow rope, the function of the screw jack, of the electric light, etc. In general, a person "carries" within her cognitive inventory a huge "array" of acquired persistence, something like a sensorimotor habitus, which gives the feeling of "the natural order of things".

Viewed from this point of view, the Enlightenment project for science is to discover all "persistences" in nature, to describe them as laws and to "implant" them in social life in the name of progress and well-being of societies. The language in which this is possible, according to the same project, is mathematics. As Galileo puts it, the book of nature is written in the language of mathematics, which implicitly gives an idealized status to resistance, and therefore to the process of transforming it into *assimilated persistence*, that is, the corpus of experimental science with its universal laws. Through technology, the assimilated persistence creates habits on a mass level in society. However, as it becomes clear from a moment on, the ideal of unified science turned out to be a Chimera, the enlightenment project lost the battle with the resistance of the physical world around us. The scientific community in the 20th century became fragmented, the scientific discourse became fragmented, logically incompatible theories begin to coexist, for which the criteria of truth increasingly lean towards the practical applicability and the number of representatives of the scientific community who "believe" in them (Bankov 2008).

One of the reactions against the failure of the Enlightenment project for a unified science goes in the direction of the other term of resistance – language. However, logical positivists do not perceive it as an autonomous area of resistance, but rather see the problem in its logical imperfection. The idea is that there is a possibility to find such a language that will neutralize all the "parasitic" elements in scientific productivity and put the scientific community back in the situation of its members (scientists, teams) to contribute to a single project of universal description (assimilation) of the reality around us. As we know, this project did not take place in the way it was intended, although the progress of the scientific methodology as a result of the attempts of its implementation is indisputable.

As another reaction to the failure of the Enlightenment project, but with the opposite sign, phenomenology, and therefore hermeneutics, can be considered. Despite the complex and well-balanced analysis for the purpose of the present study, which in the *Crisis*, Husserl makes on the relationship between the "mathematized reality of the natural sciences" and the specific "lifeworld" of individuals, this philosophical direction focuses decisively on the study of language-mind relation at the expense of attention to the resistances of the "dynamic object". This means that in existential phenomenology and hermeneutics for the constitution of the human world much more value is given to historically established sign systems and symbolic forms, to social interaction and interpretive activity, than to the "regular" and objective persistence of the material world, which we are constantly confronted with. Hence the problematic notion of truth, which starts from a firm position against the scientific-positivist ideal of the universality of the method. Here again, however, a careful analysis (as we have already said, to be carried out in a future extensive study) would show that ignoring resistance, insofar as it is a derivative of the ecstatic unity of the three instances of semiosis, leads to the underestimation of important areas of knowledge that cannot be reduced to forms of discursive practice.

In the scheme presented here, the representatives of the so-called "post-positivism" are very well positioned, who, although from the "kitchen of science", find ways to integrate various insights from the sciences of man and society into their models, thus uniting the two opposing reactions to the failure of the Enlightenment project. Thus, the history and social role of science, the personal qualities of scientists and the "free market" of ideas become factors influencing scientific activity and its theoretical results. In other words, these authors expand the "front" of the resistances with which the scientist struggles, without denying, however, the central role of the objective persistence of the material world, which is the main subject of the natural sciences.

Therefore, in our model of semiosis, we can isolate the objective resistance/persistence as immanent to the dynamic object. This means that a certain type of discourse aimed at describing the material world can be guided by the ideal of objective description, which establishes observable and verifiable persistences. This does not mean that there is the possibility of describing once and for all the true nature of things (our model of semiosis denies this possibility in principle), but that the truth of the discourse thus achieved has an unlimited "shelf life", at least until another description gave better coherence to a larger number of observable facts. But even then the truth of many described persistences survives – for example, that bodies fall with the same acceleration, regardless of their mass, is true even after the theory of relativity.

In other words, this abstract schematization "proves" the fundamental impossibility of discursive descriptions of the functioning of society, language or mind to have the universal and lasting truth of the descriptions of objects that do not contain these elements. Such discursive descriptions are made with language, which is a unifying characteristic of a community and are undertaken by individuals (minds), which leads to the following situation – as society, language and mind are the results of social discursive activity in the broadest sense of the concept (all are derivatives of culture, unlike material reality, which in its natural form has developed independently of human civilization), it, and each new discourse, basically continues the same work, that is, develops these instances, which, at the same time, tries to fix as objective persistences. Something more. The very fact that the methodology of research in humanities is of the same discursive nature as their object of study is a guarantee of the impossible independence between the two. The very act of defining the object of study is already an intervention on its structure, a presupposition of its future coherence. On the contrary, in the natural sciences, it is the absolute "otherness" of the object in relation to its discursive description that is a guarantee of authentic or objective resistance. Therefore, the types of truth in the humanities bear the mark of this mixing, although there are numerous attempts to win back a status identical to that of the natural sciences.

Let us take the most extreme example. This model shows us that in many cases "a lie repeated 1,000 times becomes true." It is not difficult to imagine that this "principle" of Nazi propaganda could succeed in many cases. For example, if in a community, it is repeated that the Aryan race is superior to the others, if this continues for generations and if there is no possibility in the public space to launch other views on the issue, then, at some point, this will be established as the most natural thing in the world. But this would also happen with the statement that people are equal, that everyone should work as hard as they can and get as much as they need, as communist ideology claims. A mad dictator fixated with philosophy may use propaganda to impose as an irrefutable truth some philosophical idea, for example, "space and time are the universal and necessary forms in which all things are perceived" and, for that, he will probably need fewer efforts than in previous two cases. In all three examples, the propaganda machine will be needed to overcome a certain kind of resistance of discursive nature. But no propaganda can help if someone tries to impose the opinion, for example, that bodies fall on Earth with an acceleration of 3.8 m/s^2. Precisely because the nature of the resistance that such a statement must overcome is qualitatively different from its discursive ones. What could happen is to give the notation "3.8 m/s^2" to the persistent and independent of this notation observable fact, which the overall discursive coherence of science requires to be 9.8 m/s^2. But then propaganda will have to deny science as a historically established whole that everyone knows and believes in, without it being clear what it will replace it with.

Theories in the field of society, language or mind bear the burden of this principle, specifying that in normal cases one does not start from lies to arrive at forcibly imposed truths, but rather the authors start from a discursively constructed framework, within which both the problems and the parameters for their solution are set at the same time. The theory interacts with the object because they are partially or completely homogeneous instances. Like these opinion polls, whose "objective" results are determined by the way the questions are asked. In the natural sciences, too, the results are predetermined by the theoretical framework of describing the problem, and under no circumstances can they be independent of it. But the resistance that the facts exert is a completely independent instance (the "interviewer" cannot influence their course with his/her questions) and therefore a reason for another kind of "inquiry". Here we are not talking about "discovering the truth" about things, but about a discursive (mental) invention of a model that reveals persistence in a certain, defined by scientists, portion of a dynamic object (reality). There is nothing to prevent another scientist or team from constructing a model for another configuration of persistences, partially including the first, to reveal new aspects of the same observable phenomena and therefore to amend the status of the first model without cancelling it. But in any case, one thing is certain – somewhere out there we have something that resists and persists in a way that guarantees the criteria for the validity of the models and is a condition for truth that lasts in an identical way over time.

On the contrary, the authors of discourses (theories) in the fields of language, society and mind deal with a truth that is rather rhetorical and very similar to the *work of a lawyer* (the idea is of Rorty, see 1982: 211–230). The reality they deal with is interpretive because it is partially or entirely socially constructed and, accordingly, does not guarantee objective resistance. The philosophers in question, like the lawyer, reconstruct portions of reality, for which it is clear in advance what they aim to prove. From there, the difference between good and bad theories becomes a derivative of many factors, which are of the nature of coherent interpretation of facts, reliable citation of authors and handling of tradition, effective communication, narrative skills and many more. But it is certainly always possible to agree on the value of these discourses because they, too, encounter resistance which, although of a different configuration, sanctions their validity.

6 The resistances of the post-truth situation

"Post-truth" is a diagnosis of present-day digital society reflecting the way in which the functions of truth and trust in the socio-cultural cohesion have changed. The cited authors, on the basis of whose ideas I built the typology of resistance, have referred to different cultural situations to each other, but all based on the high prestige of the professional discursive practice, led by the pursuit of truth. Even Rorty's insightful considerations about the role of the philosopher and the strange status of truth in that field suggest that professionals, i.e. authors, who have undergone years of academic research training and scientifically informed argumentation, must work on the knowledge front to produce guidelines for the political agenda strategies. In the age of social media, these standards have been sharply lowered. Extremely popular platforms such as *Facebook*, *Twitter*, *Instagram*, etc. have provided an opportunity for long-lasting fixed by writing participation in the formation of the socio-political agenda of billions of people, the vast majority of whom are completely deprived of discursive methodology and research training. In other words, the struggle against the resistance of being, i.e. the capture of the persistences of the dynamic object, led by scientists and professionals in research discourse, completely dismantled into the broad public debate, which eventually began to directly influence policymakers.

As stated in Bankov (2021), the Web 2.0 platforms opened the industry of the self-expression – the "I-pistemology", as one of the most insightful authors, depicts the situation (van Zoonen 2012: 60): "Where epistemology is concerned with the nature, sources and methods of knowledge, then *I*-pistemology answers these questions from the basis of *I* (as in me, myself) and *I*dentity, with the *I*nternet as the great facilitator." *I-pistemology* would mean that today the options of self-expression make most of us authors rather than addressees of the public discourse, thus the scarcity of deep attention and research is double: not only we dedicate less time for the discourse of single others, but we need more and more attention from them.

I-pistemology is about the impossibility to involve the others in the public space with deep, scientific arguments. It is about a shift on a mass level from a culture dominated by the discourse of real trained experts to a culture dominated by influencers, who catch the moods and the attention of their targets in a most superficial way. It is about the collapse of trust in the traditional institutions of the social fabric and substituting it with a trust in personal opinions, forged in the echo-chambers of social media (van Zoonen 2012: 57). Such opinions usually reflect the most favourable views for the ego-trade (Bankov 2021). *I-pistemology* is the transformation of our digitally mediated social interaction into a profitable data mining where corporations and policymakers skip the necessity of real research and long term commitment and get access to social trends, ready to be capitalized and politically abused.

The phenomenon of the *echo-chamber* in social media is another shortcut of digital culture to allow its representatives to reduce the existential resistances. The echo-chamber is a result of profit-oriented algorithms in social media which regulate our social activity there and thus create a distorted perception of the offline reality. In order to provide more relevant content, social media make users see only what other users, with the same values and attitudes, are doing, increasing in this way the satisfaction and the time spent in the platforms. The long term effect is that our discursive activity there meets less resistance than if the audience was average for the whole society, but since this is implicit, the impression of the user is that his/her rightness reflects the mainstream opinions. In such way were legitimized and thus encouraged in public space, racist, xenophobic and many other incorrect attitudes, which would not have emerged if the public sanction on them was the real one and not the distorted one in the echo-chambers. According to many, this effect boosted the rise of populist movements like Brexit, Trump, Salvini in Italy, etc., the consequences of which shook institutions of the Western democracies, remained stable for centuries before that. Phenomena of crowd psychology emerged where the crowd effect consists in reduction of the ethical standards of behaviour, but, for the first time, this was not in the city squares, but among people alone in front of their computers (Bankov 2020).

Probably the most explicit occurrence of the distorted structure of the resistances of being in digital culture came with the COVID-19 pandemic. Nothing similar had happened before since the advent of social media. The core of the problem was somewhere in the dynamic object, completely independent of our opinions. Understanding it and finding a cure was a scientific challenge, opposing strong resistance and rejecting a huge number of scientific conjectures, generated by analogy with known viruses. Social media propelled the initial scientific hesitation, generating an unprecedented number of narratives in the multiplicity of echo-chambers, which afterwards were resistant to any scientific proof. Those narratives covered opinions from the most apocalyptic scenarios to complete rejection of the existence of coronavirus. Thus, for instance, when finally was accepted by the majority of experts that the mask is useful, the authorities in most countries could not create public acceptance and consensual implementation of such measure. In other words, when finally the scientists, i.e. the minds in the frontline of the struggle with the resistance of the dynamic object, started to obtain results and to be able to prescribe valid measures, the link with society, i.e. the public opinion/policy-making was intercepted by the success of methodologically non-valid narratives, whose rhetoric superiority and emotional benefits for the targets, legitimized by the echo-chambers, granted them more success. This brought to the paradoxical situation when finally the vaccine is available, the majority of people reject it, and even among such experts as doctors and medical staff in Bulgaria, there is only 11% who declared ready to be vaccinated!

It would have been easy for me to say that doctors are wrong in that, but actually, I am immersed in the same post-truth situation and when it will come to concrete actions of vaccination, I shall be far from the certainty with which, in theory, I describe this reality. The existential decision-making today is hardened by a compromised ontological commitment with the dynamic object, even for those who advocate for science, because even the scientific community is affected by the effects of the market pressure and the short term objective of policymakers.

References

Bankov, Kristian. 2000. *Intellectual Effort and Linguistic Work: Semiotic and Hermeneutic Aspects of the Philosophy of H. Bergson*. Acta Semiotica Fennica IX. Helsinki & Imatra: International Semiotics Institute at Imatra.

Bankov, Kristian. 2004. Infinite Semiosis and Resistance. In Eero Tarasti (ed.) *From Nature to Psyche*, 175–181. (Acta Semiotica Fennica XX). Helsinki & Imatra: Internatioal Semiotics Institute at Imatra, Semiotic Society of Finland.

Bankov, Kristian. 2017. Eco and the Google Search Innovations. In Torkild Thellefsen & Bent Sørensen (eds.) *Umberto Eco in His Own Words*, 119–126. Berlin: De Gruyter Mouton.

Bankov, Kristian. 2020. Cyberbullying and hate speech in the debate around the ratification of the Istanbul convention in Bulgaria: a semiotic analysis of the communication dynamics. *Social Semiotics*, 30(3). 344–364.

Bankov, Kristian. 2021. Flags, Identity, Memory: from nationalisms to the post-truth uses of collective symbols. In Anne Wagner, & Sarah Marusek (eds.), *Flags, Color, and the Legal Narrative*. London, New York: Springer.

Bergson, Henri. 1988 [1896]. *Matter and Memory*. Tr. by N. M. Paul & W. S. Palmer. New York: ZoneBooks.

Dilthey, Wilhelm. 1890. Contributions to the Solution of the Problem of Our Belief in the Reality of the External World and Its Right; Sitzungsberichte der Kgl. Preuss. Akademie der Wissenschaften zu Berlin. Berlin.

Eco, Umberto. 1975. *Trattato di semiotica generale*. Milano: Bompiani.

Eco, Umberto. 1976. *A Theory of Semiotics*. Bloomington (IN): Indiana University Press.

Eco, Umberto. 1979. *Lector in fabula*. Milano: Bompiani.

Eco, Umberto. 1994 [1990]. *The Limits of Interpretation*. Bloomington (IN): Indiana University Press.

Eco, Umberto. 1994. *The Role of the Reader: Explorations in the Semiotics of Texts Advances in Semiotics*. Bloomington (IN): Indiana University Press.

Eco, Umberto. 1984. *Semiotica e filosofia del linguaggio*. Torino: Einaudi.

Eco, Umberto. 1986. *Semiotics and the Philosophy of Language*. Bloomington (IN): Indiana University Press.

Eco, Umberto. 2000 [1997]. *Kant and the Platypus*. London: Vintage.
Eco, Umberto. 2003. *Dire quasi la stessa cosa*. Milano: Bompiani.
Heidegger, M. 1962. *Being and Time*. London: Blackwell.
Peirce, Charles. 1934–1948. *Collected Papers*. Cambridge, MA: Harvard University Press.
Rorty, Richard. 1982. *Consequences of Pragmatism*. Minneapolis, MI: University of Minnesota press.
Tarasti, Eero. 2009 "Semiotics of resistance: Being, memory, history – the counter-current of signs". *Semiotica* 173. 41–71.
Van Zoonen, Liesbet. 2012. I-Pistemology: Changing truth claims in popular and political culture. *European Journal of Communication* 27(1). 56–67.
Vattimo, Gianni & Pier Aldo Rovatti (eds.). 2012. *Weak Thought*. New York: Suny Press.
Vygotsky, L. 1994. *Vygotsky Reader*., ed. René van der Veer & Jaan Valsiner. London: Blackwell.

Aurel Codoban
From semiotic pragmatism to existential semiotics

Abstract: What gave to French semiotics, which has dominated most of the second half of the 20th century, its epistemological strength, has, nonetheless, represented its foremost deficiency: beginning with the three possible directions of sign analysis, semantics, syntax and pragmatics, the project of structural semiotics has abridged semantics to syntax and programmatically ignored pragmatics. Eero Tarasti's program is that of putting together a semiotics that would take into account what has been called semiotic pragmatism, which means man's bond with signs, both as creator of signs, and as their interpreter, but all this in the registry of existential expressivity. To achieve this program, Eero Tarasti does resort to phenomenology, hermeneutics and existentialism, unexpectedly because in the thematic domain of recent continental philosophy, semiotic and existential are, to some extent, disjunctive concepts. Along with Heidegger and Sartre's philosophy and along with the Heideggerian and Gadamerian hermeneutics emerges a subject different from that of Kant, an existential subject in the proximity of the Christian idea of person through the conscious and anxious assimilation of freedom. Thus, Eero Tarasti's programmatic and explicit option is not that much for a semiotic-pragmatic manifest, but for a semiotics that can integrate and, consequently, which suffers all the consequences of assuming an existential subject. That is to say Eero Tarasti regards the artist and his creation as semiotic subject and semiosis so as to entail a critique of communication stemming from signification, which is the reverse of the structuralist position that reduces signification to communication.

Keywords: Eero Tarasti, semiotics, existential, pragmatics, subject, structuralism, existentialism, communication

In the thematic domain of recent continental philosophy, semiotic and existential are, to some extent, disjunctive concepts. Only to some extent, as the strict opposition is, in fact, between semiotics (semiology) and hermeneutics. The concept of existence, given its Heideggerian and Sartrean background, implies understanding, which, in turn, implies hermeneutics. Oppositions like these have already made their presence felt in the problematic realm of Occidental philosophy. As an example: Parmenide's idea of being (immobility of being) goes against Heraclit's becoming idea (evolution of being). Plato has dealt with this opposition by agreeing with both Heraclites and Parmenides but asymmetrically; that is by appreciating the Parmenidean heavens of pure, immobile ideas more than the Heraclitean world of becoming, in which we are situated. Once the being has become relative to what we know, as Berkeley's dictum goes ("to be is to be perceived"), the quarrel between empiricists and rationalists emerged. The one to make a synthesis between these two positions was Kant who, exactly like his predecessor – Plato – agreed with both parties but again in a structured and asymmetrical approach, i.e. more with the rationalists than the empiricists.

At present, as the main philosophical theme of our time is communication: being and what we know are now relative to what we communicate. But do we communicate based on a language structure or, rather, due to the Heideggerian adverse reciprocity between Being and Man? Moreover, does the intellection of signs pertain to a semiotic reading or to a hermeneutic interpretation? Which is right – structuralist semiology or hermeneutics? As we all know, a great synthesis such as those of Kant and Plato is absent. But, taking into consideration certain circumstances, such a synthesis is to be expected. These circumstances refer to the fact that, as the third generation of structuralist semiologists, the postmodernists, have warned us, the age of the great legitimating narratives, the age of the great philosophical, speculative structures, seems to have definitely passed. Thus, we should expect not so much a great theory but a different and better practice of communication. Dimly, it has made its presence felt in Vattimo and his followers' (1983) "weak thought" or in Derrida's (1967) deconstructivism. But these formulas have offered so far only fragmentary solutions and not the great practice of communication, twin with both semiotics and hermeneutics.

Structural semiotics has dominated most of the second half of the 20th century What gave this semiotics its epistemological strength, what set the grounds for its methodological imperialism, has, nonetheless, represented its foremost deficiency: beginning with the three possible directions of sign analysis, as pointed out by Morris (1971), following Peirce's ideas, semantics (the association of signs with their meaning), syntax (the association between signs) and pragmatics (the association between signs and humans), the project of structural semiotics has abridged semantics to syntax and programmatically ignored pragmatics. Undoubtedly, this theoretical attitude originates in Saussure. For Saussure (1969), who was a linguist, the privileged sign was that of verbal communication, the word. Also right from the beginning, the act of signifying was firmly bound to the language system (*langue*), to what makes communication possible, and not to the process of speaking (*parole*), i.e. to the utterance. Due to this exclusive interest in communicating rather than expressing, the act of signifying came to be associated exclusively with the relation between signs. That is, the interest in linguistic signs has been conceived too abstractly to be of importance to actual pragmatics.

Simultaneously, the sphere of signs in which Peirce (1998: 289–99) was interested was too broad. This is why he associated meaning with cognoscibility rather than with communication. It is true that this option also raised issues: if signs pertain to knowledge, and not to communication, they are not as unambiguous as Saussure, in his structural semiotics, has seen them. Likewise, afterwards, one of his adherents, Morris, preferred to relate meaning to behavior. Along this line of thinking emerged what Eero Tarasti calls the American semiotics, interested in non-verbal communication and sustained by the science of nature and behavioral science.[1] Assuming behavior as the origin of the acts of signifying may be quite essential if we realize the fact that motivation, distinctive especially for some non-linguistic signs such as clues, signals, symptoms and images, overtakes the arbitrariness of the linguistic sign, i.e. the analogical surpasses the digital, how Watzlavick puts it, in the establishment of the sign's paradigm. Indeed, such an extensive paradigm of the sign had triumphed in the last quarter of the 20th century firstly due to the ongoing importance of images in communication, and afterwards because of other non-verbal aspects of semiotics: sounds, gestures, odors (like perfumes).

But this is not the dimension of semiotics' evolution that Eero Tarasti pursues in *Existential Semiotics* (2000). The most important mutation for Tarasti is the insertion of the dimension of time. Indeed, as in the Parmenidean eleatism, or as in modern rationalism, classic semiotics has not proved itself appropriate for process or movement analysis. But the existential semiotics of Eero Tarasti sets on analyzing precisely "processes, temporality, signs in flux, and particularly in the states before fixation into a sign, or what I call 'pre-signs'" (Tarasti 2000: 7). "A semiotic act occurs as the production of an act-sign by means of the help of a pre-sign or enunciant / utterant; or the act takes place as the interpretation of the act-sign by means of the help of the post-sign or interpretant" (Tarasti 2000: 33). Certainly, from a semiotic point of view, the most interesting moment of signs is that occurring before and after their constitution, when they are neither indefinite nor limited by principle, whilst the life of signs, not infinite but still having limits of principle, does not come to an end when reified.[2]

---

[1] Let us remember, nonetheless, that in the domain of French structuralist semiology, too, a similar current had developed, one that, as well together and against the dominant linguistic semiology, bound signification to behavior: Lucien Goldman (1970) and Pierre Francastel (1967), inspired by Jean Piaget's genetic psychology.

[2] Obviously, the distinction between the pre-sign and the trans-sign does not blend with the one between interior-exterior, i.e. endo-sign and exo-sign: the issue here is not that of the interior or exterior surface of signs. According to Eero Tarasti, each of the two surfaces of the sign, the sig-

Inasmuch as semiotics, dominated by structuralism, ignored the pragmatic aspect of pre-signs with humans, as their creators, it also ignored the other side of the pragmatic process, the moment of understanding. The type of semiotic reading proposed by structuralists consisted solely in applying the appropriate code. They were interested in the conditions necessary for the possibility of understanding, not in the moment or process of understanding. But without the understanding of signs, there is no sense: the mere reading of signs may as well belong to machines. According to the thesis of existential philosophy, more Sartrean than Heideggerian, signs are always situated; they find themselves in a given position, a spatially and temporally concrete position, in a given context. Every sign is relative to the situation in which it occurs: it denies or verifies it. If the strength of a sign stems from the situation, which is a sort of semantic isotropy, subsequently the sign is a weak sign. Structuralism has attached more importance to the structures that sustain signs, thus to strong signs in connection to situations, than to the situations in which they occur, thus to the strength of the sign. Conversely, hermeneutics has preferred to contextualize signs, to weaken them so that they would submit to interpretation and understanding, rather than to semiotic reading.

Surely, there has been a time when semiotics and hermeneutics were cohesive and when reading and interpretation were one and the same. The early rhetoric-philological hermeneutics started from explicitness, through interpretation, towards understanding, by means of a movement that resembles the one of semiotic reading. But hermeneutics has always had an adversary, an opposed figure as far as interpretation is concerned: at first, hermetism, during late modernity, the negative hermeneutics practiced by the masters of suspicion invoked by Ricoeur (1969) – Marx, Freud and Nietzsche – and, at present, in late modernity and postmodernism, semiology. As opposed to the Heideggerian and Gadamerian hermeneutics, which considered itself to be a project against method, semiotics, especially the structuralist one, sought or tagged itself as being scientific, i.e. methodic in the manner of hard sciences. That is why Eero Tarasti believes that it had no interest, up until recently, in the processes of signs, but in what can be quantified and generalized, which goes well with what Husserl called the understanding of meaning. Examining from this perspective the 15 possible understanding definitions (see Tarasti 2000: 65–69), Eero Tarasti identifies them with different semiotic operations. This has become possible for the reason that, considering the perspective of the end of the 20th century and the subsequent

---

nificant and the significate, can be equally seen both from the outside, as from the inside. Endo- and exo-signs are act-signs that pre-signs precede and trans-signs transcend. (Tarasti 2000: 55)

evolution and convergence, semiotics nowadays accepts the idea that semiosis is communication plus signification, that sign and meaning are not covered as essential concepts of semiotics through describing the process of communication as a connection from the emitter to the receiver, nor that the elucidation of the sign's structure, without investigating its context, isotropy, or socio-sphere exhaust semiotic act (Tarasti 2000: 17).

Communication's course of action not only implies the dynamic of signifying, but also entails, as it is not a natural but an artificial process, with finality, a subject seeking his own expression through this process. Starting from this manner to conceive signification, as opposed to the positions of structuralist pragmatics, even European semiotics has grown an interest in pragmatics, in man's bond with signs and in this semiotic subject's quality. But if, after 1990, semiotics conceived man as a semiotic subject, it had more interest in neural networks or the narrative's actors than the actual quality of man as a semiotic subject, i.e. in the way man uses signs so as to express himself. This is why Eero Tarasti's program is that of putting together a semiotics that would take into account what has been called semiotic pragmatism, which means man's bond with signs, both as creator of signs, and as their interpreter, but all this in the registry of existential expressivity.

To achieve this program, Eero Tarasti does not resort to Saussurean linguistics and not even to the psychological and social sciences of behavior, but, unexpectedly, to phenomenology, hermeneutics and existentialism, actually implying a broader area of thinking methods, from Hegel and Kierkegaard to Heidegger and Sartre. Certainly, this in not the way to revive pragmatics, as both hermeneutics and pragmatics in fact exclude the interest in signs' relationship with man: in contrast to structural semiology, it reduces syntax and pragmatics to semantics. At the same time, again in contrast to structural semiotics, it implies a subject that, in modern psychological-historical hermeneutics, was an elaborate type of the Kantian-Hegelian one, which became, through the Heideggerian and Gadamerian philosophical hermeneutics, especially through Heidegger and Sartre, an existential subject. Evidently, as with all Occidental thinking, the situation here is slightly more complicated. The project of man as a person was a fundamentally Christian one. However, through Kantian philosophy, Modernity could only conceive it – due to its perspective on necessity and liberty – either as the subject of knowledge, as it is approached in the *Critique of Pure Reason*, either as the subject of morals, as it is approached in the *Critique of Practical Reason*. Along with Heidegger and Sartre's philosophy and along with the Heideggerian and Gadamerian hermeneutics emerges a subject different from that of Kant, an existential subject in the proximity of the Christian idea of person through the conscious and anxious assimilation of freedom. This is the subject that Eero

Tarasti intends to recover in his semiotic project. Of course, his thought does not tackle solely with this subject. Against the classic unity of the subject, present in the case of existentialism and against the monologue-interpretation, he adopts the postmodern idea of the plural subject, or of the plural person: the fact that man changes his roles helps him see the world from different points of view and is one of the appropriate explications of the possibility of understanding (Tarasti 2000: 73).

Thus, Eero Tarasti's programmatic and explicit option is not that much for a semiotic-pragmatic manifest, but for a semiotics that can integrate and, consequently, which suffers all the consequences of assuming an existential subject. What Eero Tarasti intends to do with his theory on the sign's course of action – the denial of the world of objective signs, alongside with its grammars and laws, the return to a world which is empty of sense and the corroboration of the world's soul significant plenitude – is to invoke the human subject that places signs into movement in his act of existing (Tarasti 2000: 12). Transcendence is actually transcending – as in Herman Hesse's (1969) *Steppenwolf*, so as to imitate the style of *Existential Semiotics*' footnotes –, it too creates the required dialectic both for the correction of existentialists' negativist subjectivism, and the positive plenitude of signs from the structuralist semiology. This is the point in which Eero Tarasti distances himself from the semioticians that generally correlate semiotics with communication and that, turned towards the world, study objects and texts as signs. He sets up rather to illuminate existence, by means of a method of translumination opposing the science that scrutinizes details, looks for constants and obtains the truth by breaking apart from the presence of the subject presence. On the contrary, the Tarastian semiotics searches the phenomena's individuality and particularity, their soul, that opens only in the presence of the subject. It operates from abstract to concrete, from the official biography to the daily emotions and inner experiences that guide peoples' choices.

If we adopt this method, which is similar to that of the great artists, then the physical reality of signs radically changes: signs are nothing more than a surface on which the subject, the soul, moves. It is not the structuralist semiotician, but the artist that becomes the sign's lecture and manufacturing norm. But the existential subject's introduction in semiotics does not mean a copy of the existentialist one, Sartrean or Heideggerian. And this is not as much or not only because, as opposed to existentialist individualism, he refuses from the beginning the solipsism in the name of an implied community of creators. If, at first level, Eero Tarasti counterposes plenitude to the sole type of transcendence admitted by Sartre, denial, plenitude, at the second level he seems to counterpoise on one hand simple anxiety on the other "the mere anxiety's denial to her positive side", close not only to Zen, but to Quietism as well. For Eero Tarasti, the existential subject's sign of existence is anxiety. But the capacity to resist anxiety reveals itself to be the capacity required to create (Tarasti 2000: 92). That is to say Eero Tarasti regards the artist and his creation as semiotic subject and semiosis so as to entail a critique of communication stemming from signification, which is the reverse of the structuralist position that reduces signification to communication. The subject of Tarasti's semiotics is a creator of signs (Semeiourg) or an interpreter, a creator of signs who is ethically responsible, in search of authenticity, which corresponds to the artist's human condition. Existential semiotics can be straightforwardly defined as the anxious and authentic subject's semiotics, in his anxious search for the authentic.

It was one of modernity's characteristics to build up man from bottom to top, beginning from interest, desire or fear. Late modernity and postmodernity however, emphasized especially desire, which is the case with the Greimasian narrative grammar. The subject of desire is less human, he is much closer to how machines function; hence Eero Tarasti's refusal to constitute man following the path of desire. Anxiety, in change, is an existential sentiment closely related to the creatural, Avraamic one. It is a type of restoration, a much weaker one, of course, of the aged manner of constituting man from top to bottom, from his essence to his digressions, towards falling or sin. However, Tarasti makes use of the existential subject's anxiety semiotically so as to point out an incongruence between the signifier and the signified, a disarray between the expression and the content, a conflict between two semiotic systems: the internal semiotic structure of the subject and that of the external world and especially so that he can to assert that utterance precedes language (Tarasti 2000: 81–82).

Eero Tarasti's existential pragmatics thus becomes a third attempt, after Vattimo and his followers' "weak thought" and Derrida's "deconstruction", to unravel the issue of semiotics and hermeneutics' synthesis, of reading signs and interpreting them. Analyzing the cultural metamorphoses of the categorial and stylistic existential/structural couple, Eero Tarasti understands that it materializes in many alternatives and combinations. From this perspective, in Eero Tarasti's thought the peculiar combination of structural semiotics and existential hermeneutics would take the aspect of a (structural) semiotics with an existential (hermeneutic) subject.

After postmodernism however, this existential semiotics cannot – as none of the other two attempts could – take the form of a great, more or less, speculative theory. In its "intuitive" and "fragmentary" form, it must articulate the already given solutions in the problematic field of philosophy. Certainly, more or less explicitly, as in the great synthesis of Plato, concerning eleatism, or Kant, concerning rationalism, Eero Tarasti leans in favor of semiotics rather than hermeneutics, since he considers the former more capable to extend its analysis to daily communication than the latter. At the same time, his semiotics is different from structuralist semiology because it includes, following the American tradition, the domain of non-verbal signs, including images, both visual and acoustic.

But what light does this semiotics with an existential subject cast upon everyday communication? Does it impose, as we alleged at the beginning that postmodernism's expectations tried to, a different practice of communication? An important part of Tarasti's book is focused on the actual analysis of concrete, everyday communication. Nevertheless, the project of existential semiotics outlined by Eero Tarasti, owing to its existential characteristic, goes from the beginning to the end hand in hand with a critique of present communication. The immediate observation that imposes itself upon us is that, in our civilization, the representation of the world as text and, generally speaking, the preeminence of text, have become lifeless. Indeed, we have irrevocably entered into a civilization of image. The problem is that we have done it without getting nearer to the represented reality.

The images offered by mass-media have the indicial aura of traditional images, but are the product of an electronic, a digital construction (Flusser 1997) rather than of a technical reproduction (Benjamin 1955). In mass communication, sign-images send to one another and validate each other. Our senses do not enter in direct contact with the object anymore. Between the primordial experience and virtual reality emerged another one characterized by the conflicts invoked by McLuhan (1962), who warned us against the alienation of senses and direct experience. We are thus deprived of our bonds to referential reality by means of direct analogical icons and effect-indicators, to the advantage of some indirect indicators produced and maneuvered as languages – perfumes, additives in food, etc. – or some images turned into mass-media language.

What actually allows indicators and images to turn into language in the new mass-media is the representation mechanism of representation. Evidently, the fact that man is a creator of tools by means of which he creates other tools characterizes, as already outlined, both his humanity and his double linguistic articulation. However, the problem is that, unlike art, which is a sort of representation, a simulation of reality, television, the video recorder, computers produce a media world that is, in its whole, a *simulacrum*. The difference lies in the fact that artistic representation only allows the elaboration of a restrictive reality representation, whilst in the mass-media universe reality is abandoned before the representation's limitations (Tarasti 2000: 210). Thus, if the double articulated nature of tools allows a more efficient intervention into the world, the representation of representation estranges us from reality.

Our civilization is about to leave reality and dwell into a new environment, in a world whose reality becomes a virtual one. But the strength of the actual civilization resides, as did the strength of all the past ones, in the capacity to build and justify its own environment. It is true that in some other times, as in our own, we had been warned against such dangers that proved to be not quite effective. Nevertheless, nowadays the environment built by our civilization seems to separate us from reality more than other medias built by past civilizations during the course of history. The symbol of this situation is represented by virtual reality alongside its so much appreciated characteristics: interactivity and immersion. But, at a more careful analysis, interactivity proves itself to be an *intra*-activity, because the subject does not encounter another type of reality. And immersion does not mean sinking into another reality than his own self (Tarasti 2000: 212).

Of course, the semiotic critique is not that naïve to invoke an absolute reality such as the Kantian thing in its self (*Ding an sich*). For Tarastian semiotics, which is an existential one, the problem of reality is actually the problem of authenticity. But authenticity means being here and now. And the existential subject of Tarastian subject programmatically sets out to be here and now. The *Semiotic First* (Peirce 1993: 469) is the reality, the zero degree, even if enriched by the signs of human history, in which I, the subject, in order to be authentic, must be here and now, without relocations and *uncommitted*. The characteristic of reality, as Tarastian existential semiotics conceives it, is the fact that it opposes the subject, that it manifests a resistance, similar to how, in the process of communication, the Other manifests his presence through a defining and necessary resistance. In misunderstanding – often developed in a conflict – lies the possibility of the authentic meeting with the other! In this warning against all fusional mystic the presence of Christianity in the Tarastian existential thinking is felt.

But the actual praxis of mass communication, despite its declared attention to the other, either dissolves it by fusion or ignores it plain and simply. Virtual reality is based on the category of similitude, and its perspective on the world is eternal solipsism, autism. This is why computer games do not reveal to us, such as their devotees and some too optimist theoreticians hope, the life of sign from inside. The player is caught in an eternal synchronicity; he is far from Bergson's creative interval. Even playing with a traditional game device remains more complex than moving the mouse. The Tarastian existential semiotics rediscovers the Hegelian-Heideggerian-Existentialist scheme of objectivity as alienation in the process of actual media communication: the more intelligence we invest in our exterior, the more objective we make it by means of various semiotic products, machines, computers, the less intelligence remains for our selves, for our own humanity.

Actual communication is a tautological and autistic one, i.e. tautistic (Sfez 1992). It has become too autonomic, too imperialistic in what regards reality, on the one hand, and, on the other, too much of a parasite in what regards existential signification. The mass-media "specialists" forget that information – a species of "to know" – is inter-relational with "to want", "to be able to" (technical abilities), "to have to" (rules), system of belief, affects (Tarasti 2000: 210). In turn, the existentialist semiotician that takes all this into account may discover and draw a map of the area between what audience thinks it desires (often manipulated by mass media officials) and what it thinks it does not wish for (Tarasti 2000: 211). Semiotics is almost the only analytical thinking that encompasses/identifies/exposes the semiotic nature of mass-media without forgetting human values. (Tarasti 2000: 212). Therefore, Eero Tarasti's existential semiotics proves to be the actual theoretical critique of present communication practice, tautological and autistic, and the existential project of an authentic communication. Not only the interest shifts from the sign to the manner in which people make use of the semiotic resources, in order to communicate and interpret communication – that also becomes a type of semiotic production –, but it is also a praxis centered on observation and analysis, so as to render this utilization as authentic as possible. We could, in a Wittgensteinian manner, say that, by introducing the existential subject in the centre of the semiotic course of action, Tarastian semiotics sets out to fight against the bewitching of our intellect's means by our media and technology-driven means of communication.

References

Benjamin, Walter. 1955. *Illuminationen. Ausgewälte Schriften*. Frankfurt am Main: Suhrkamp Verlag.
Derrida, Jacques. 1967. *De la grammatologie*, Les Éditions de Minuit.
Francastel, Pierre. 1967. *La Figure et le lieu: l'ordre visuel du Quattrocento*. Paris: Gallimard.
Flusser, Vilém. 1997. *Für eine Philosophie der Photographie*. Göttingen: European Photography.
Goldman, Lucien. 1970. *Structures mentales et création culturelle*. Paris: 10/18
Greimas, Algirdas Julien. 1966. *Sémantique structurale: recherche et méthode*. Paris: Larousse.
Hesse, Herman. 1969. *Steppenwolf*, tr. Basil Creighton. New York: Bantam Book.
McLuhan, Marshal. 1962. *The Gutenberg Galaxy: The Making of Typographic Man*. Toronto: University of Toronto Press.
Morris, Charles W. 1971. *Writings on the general theory of signs*. The Hague: Mouton.
Ricoeur, Paul. 1969. *Le conflit des interprétations. Essais d'herméneutique I*. Paris: Le Seuil.
Peirce, Charles Sanders. 1993. *Writings of Charles S. Peirce, A Chronological Edition, Volume 5 (1884–1886)* ed. by Fisch Kloesel et al. Bloomington, Indianapolis: Indiana University Press.

Peirce, Charles Sanders. 1998. *The Essential Peirce. Selected Philosophical Writings,* Volume 2 (1893–1913). Bloomington, Indianapolis: Indiana University Press.
Saussure, Ferdinand de. 1969. *Cours linguistique générale.* Paris: Payot.
Sfez, Lucien. 1992. *Critique de la Communication.* Paris: Le Seuil.
Tarasti, Eero. 2000. *Existential Semiotics.* Bloomington, Indianapolis: Indiana University Press.
Vattimo, Gianni & Pier Aldo Rovatti (eds.). 1983. *Il pensiero debole.* Milano: Feltrinelli.

Eric Landowski
Structural, yet existential

Abstract: For most structuralist semioticians, scientificity commands to restrict the field of the discipline to the boundaries of texts while the existential dimension of lived experience is considered out of reach. Yet, Greimas's interest was initially not just in text analysis but in meaning in general or, as he put it, the "meaning of life". In *Structural Semantics* he adopted the widest possible conceptual framework : "the situation of man", surrounded "from the cradle to the grave" with a world of signs. What was at stake at that stage was indeed our existential condition as semiotic beings. But a methodological shift soon led from such a reflection concerning sense as experienced to the construction of a grammar of meaning as "manifested" in texts viewed as the lieu *par excellence* of tangible semiotic data. It amounted to letting life aside, so to speak. Our purpose is to return (not as a philosopher but as a semiotician) to the original interrogation and show that the existential experience of sense can be semiotically conceptualised and rigorously studied. In the first place, this requires to extend the horizon of meaning far beyond textually readable significations. Hence our proposal for a sociosemiotic model based on the articulation between dictinct *regimes of meaning* themselves stemming from a set of interdefined syntactic *regimes of interaction*. Our claim is that the enlarged structural approach thus conceived is fit for integrating the existential dimension of meaning into the field of reflection and analysis of our discipline.

Keywords: existential, experience, interaction, meaning, regime (of meaning and interaction)

1 From experience to texts and the way back

In Spring 2000, Eero Tarasti published his Existential Semiotics, followed, in 2009, by a largely reshuffled French version, *Fondements de la sémiotique existentielle*. During the same period[1], I had got used to employing, without knowing, the same expression, as appears especially in the conclusion of *Passions sans nom*, the third of my Essays in sociosemiotics: "Vers une sémiotique existentielle" (Tarasti

---

[1] The following text is an entirely reshuffled version, translated by the author, of "¿Habría que rehacer la semiótica?", *Contratexto*, 20, 2012 and "Une sémiotique à refaire?", *Galáxia*, 26, 2013.

https://doi.org/10.1515/9783110789164-009

2000 and 2009; Landowski 2004: 293–305). My purpose was to underline the need for and even to herald the advent of an existential semiotics, although from a much less philosophically based perspective. Be it a mere coincidence or not, both lines of thinking did point in the same direction, a direction which earlier had been, in my view, at the root of the semiotic project as a whole, at least as initially understood by Greimas.

Such a claim will probably both surprise the outsiders of the Greimasian semiotic circle and go against the grain of some of its insiders' beliefs. For most of the orthodox structural semioticians, the "scientificity" of their procedures imposes to limit the practice of their skill to the boundaries of texts. They will consider it risky or even pointless to venture beyond these remits. As a consequence, such terms as, in particular, "existence", "experience", "vécu" or "presence" are not to be found under the pens of most "French school" semioticians apart from a few exceptions (Greimas 1987; Geninasca 1997a; Landowski 1997; Parret 2001). But the main reason for resisting such notions, rather than just methodological, is epistemological. The problem arises from the complex approach to meaning that an "existential" questioning implies: without invalidating the assets of textual analysis, it orients the reflexion towards another, a complementary conception of what is meaning, or sense. This said, it is true that if at the start Greimas had not temporarily but deliberately – "strategically" was his word – restricted his attention to a level which excluded such concerns, most of the analytical concepts and models we now dispose of would probably not have been developed. The counterpart for this stance was the disconnect between structural semiotics and other branches, especially the Peircian line of thinking. Indeed, C.S. Peirce and his successors have always advocated for a broader scope and a more general basis.

Yet, in Greimas's mind, the initial question was also about meaning in general. Not only the meaning of texts, but also of human behaviours, of history and, as he would often put it, the "meaning of life" (Greimas 1966: 5; Greimas and Courtés 1979: 245). In *Structural Semantics*, his first book, written in order to refound semantics with a view to transcend the limits of the then dominating lexical, linguistic or logic approaches, he put aside the most elementary epistemological precautions and adopted the widest possible frame of thinking: no more, no less, "the situation of man (. . .) from the cradle to the grave surrounded with and assaulted by all sorts of meanings trying to grasp our attention from everywhere" (p. 8, our translation). In other words, at that preliminary stage, what was at stake was our very existential condition as semiotic beings.

But at the same time, in accordance with the subtitle of the same founding book, "Methodological research", he was aware of the fact that the "scientific vocation" of his project demanded to be acutely wary about possible deviations towards impressionism or other possible derailings into psychologising considerations. The other pitfall to avoid was the risk of giving oneself up to mere speculative thinking, bound to end up in some vague philosophy of language. Therefore, because semiotics aspired to become a theory worthy of the name, with its own operating methods, it had to circumscribe its object – meaning – as an object of "science" in its own right. Hence the transition that early took place from a broad reflexion concerning meaning as "experienced" to procedures of analysis of meaning as "manifested" – a move which led to the already mentioned focalisation on texts, viewed as the lieu par excellence of positive and tangible semiotic manifestations. This amounted to letting, so to say, "life" apart. Thereafter, structural semiotics became doubtless a method (if not a science yet) but disconnected from its initial quest.

What we propose is to return to the original interrogation. Although it may sound more philosophical than what the majority of semioticians pursue, we purport to justify its relevance and treat it as a semiotician and not as a philosopher. We postulate that the split between "life" and "science", one supposedly excluding the other, which seems to be implicitly agreed here, is not irreducible. On the contrary, the existential experience of sense can be semiotically conceptualised and, hence, rigorously studied. Moreover, the theoretical developments that this demands are essential to what we consider to be the justification of the semiotic endeavour. Without awaiting from semiotics any answer to metaphysical questions, what would be the point of theorising the processes by which meaning is produced if it was not also to contribute to making oneself more lucid about the ways how, in one's own mind, life comes (or not) to make sense? More technically, our project of reopening the scope of structural semiotics stems directly from the practice of the existing models and from the critical gaze that the simple fact of practising them inevitably brings about. This will not lead to neglecting what textual analyses have allowed to achieve, nor to invalidate the basic principles of the discipline, to which we fully adhere. Our goal at proposing a certain amount of revisions and complements is to revitalise their practice and to enlarge the field of their application.

2 State of the art

The problem with Greimas's founding position whereby he put at the start our very existential condition – the "situation of man" – is that by nature this situation includes in its boundaries the semiotician himself, as enunciating and, in principle, knowing subject. Can a discipline be founded on such grounds? If the semantic universe is the world in which we find ourselves "definitely locked up"

(Greimas 1966: 117), and if on the other hand a semantic theory may only be conceived as a metalinguistic description of an object that should be hierarchically distinct from it, then it is impossible for the analyst to say anything semantically relevant about the surrounding world that he has chosen as the object of his scrutiny but at the same time in which he acknowledges to find himself encompassed. Contrary to what the prefix in the word *meta*-language invites us to, we cannot claim to be able to grasp the world from the outside or from above, since we are included in it. Faced with this fundamental issue, Greimas invents a solution of grand style.

2.1 Promises of an invention

In front of the unsurpassable nature of our "situation" – our belonging to the world of meaning supposed to be analysed – Greimas proposes: "The best that we can do is at least to become aware of the worldview that finds itself involved in it, both as a meaning per se and a condition of the advent of this meaning" (Greimas 1966: 117, our translation). In other words, since an objectification of the world proves impossible from the outside and from a distance, the sole remaining possibility is to look at it "from the inside" and elicit what "finds itself involved in it": namely, a certain "worldview".

What he meant by "worldview" is not a collection of particular contents that we would project onto the outer world to give it a certain colour, for example, romantic or apocalyptic. This worldview is a structural organisational principle in the form of a grid through which the world is cut out into units which, in turn, are assembled to give it a form that eventually has a meaning for us. Greimas adds that this grid in the light of which the world turns into a "meaningful universe" has a peculiar *theatrical* nature: the way it works is to make us behold "a small show" (*un petit spectacle*), a performance that is susceptible of being reproduced in "millions of copies". On this scene where the world carries meanings as it is turned into language (or, better, into discourse, otherwise the show would rather look like a still picture), "the content of the actions keeps continuously changing, the actors vary, but the *performance-utterance* remains the same" (Greimas 1966: 173).

From then on, structural semiotics developed its most original feature: the fallback of the question of meaning into a theory of *narrativity*. The invariant element that such a structural approach supposes – what will remain the same under the surface of ever-varying utterances – is an interactantial syntax whose units, "a process, a few actors, a more or less circumstantial situation" (Greimas 1966: 117), and the rules that they abide by, were progressively elicited by the narrative grammar. After the examination of widely varied textual corpora, this grammar was completed in the course of the 1970s (Greimas and Courtés 1979). It now constitutes the core of the Greimasian theory. It was widespread under the name of *a standard model* and is still applied today in analyses in which the teachings that were given at that time can yet be found, often to the letter.

Predictably enough, what was initially a groundbreaking innovation progressively got frozen. This happened all the more easily as the efficacy of the model allowed a routine, strictly programmed descriptive procedure which left no room for questioning the foundations of the theory, its ideological presuppositions or its anthropological implications. Along the same line, the very notion of narrativity, however promising it remains, was soon to be enclosed within the limits of the so-called "narrative schema", a rigid grid soon coined *canonical*, as though it was of utmost importance to declare, for educational purposes, that the model was unsurpassable. This was putting aside the intention of its author who viewed it as a partial and temporary step, susceptible to stimulate rather than freeze thinking, and therefore bound to be outdated one day (Greimas and Courtés 1979: 247, "Narrative schema"). Yet, research continued, at least among some of the collaborators next to Greimas, who, in private, happened himself to say that semiotics was "to be redone" (Geninasca 1997b: 42; Landowski 2012).

All it took to think it was possible to reignite the intellectual momentum of its beginnings, and simultaneously revive its primal link with the existential dimension, was to read Greimas again and to review our own practice and analyses with a critical eye. In doing so, what appeared is that most of the objections expressed vis-à-vis the works of the Greimasian circle were legitimate, but at the same time surmountable (Geninasca, 1997b; Bucher, 1997; Landowski 1997b; Kersyte, 2009). This is why we have been striving to overcome the deadlocks that have for a long time limited the potential of the discipline and hampered its development as a reflection on the plurality of possible regimes of meaning and their relationship with the diversity of actual "forms of life".

2.2 Text, context, situation

"Outside the text there is no salvation". This phrase, one day let out by Greimas during the '70s in a workshop gathering a few literary specialists in Brazil, was the first obstacle. It has been the source of a persistent misunderstanding ever since. The visitor's purpose was merely to invite his audience to be logical with themselves and to work on the texts properly speaking, rather than to speculate (which was fashionable at the time) on the external parameters having presided over their writing, such as their authors' social environment, their psychology and so on. But although the circumstances in which this motto was uttered were very specific, it rapidly became a creed of universal reach, followed to the letter. It was interpreted as an edict drawing an impassable borderline between two heterogeneous zones: the texts (any verbal discourse, preferably written) considered as the stronghold of the semiotician, and all around this fiefdom a supposedly forbidden zone, the "context", made of nothing less than society, history, reality, "life"!

This misinterpretation proceeds from an epistemological confusion between empirical objects and the object of knowledge. If indeed texts are empirical objects of high interest to the semiotician (as to everybody), the object of semiotic knowledge, as for it, is not the text but the meaning. And unlike the treasure in Ali Baba's cave, meaning is not something to be found ready-made, hidden underneath the surface of a text, as though it had been previously deposited there and was waiting to be seized. Be it textual or otherwise, meaning is always a construction and as such it is highly dependent on the intertext that the interpreter will take into account to achieve this construction, as well as on the "context" in which the said construction is made.

However, the notion of context is inappropriate – it is theoretically misleading. In more adequate words, any verbally or non verbally enunciated discourse makes sense according to the way in which the partners of the communication process construct, at the same time and inseparably, both the meaning of their communicative exchange and that of the *situation* in which it takes place (Landowski 1997a, ch. 6; 2004, ch. 1). A "situation" is in itself meaningful. Unlike the context, which is a referential state of being, it is a semiotic construct – just as the text itself. Instead of exterior and supposedly causative variable, it is an inner part of the global semiotic setting that the interactants are facing. The parameters of a situation thus conceived comprehend, among other elements, the respective images that the interlocutors project on one another in their capacity of interacting subjects, thereby outlining their respective actantial and actorial statuses. Discursive semiotics describes these simulacra in terms of thematic roles and modal determinations. But the notion of situation allows for more than that. It implies that among the infinitely numerous spatial, temporal and actorial elements of the environment, the analysis should recognise and integrate within its scope all those (and only those) which appear as hypothetically relevant variables for attributing a meaning to the communication or the interaction, as viewed by the participants. In other words, there is not, at the centre, "the text", considered as *the* semiotic object, and around it a non-semiotic "context", but one unique semiotic reality, just one object of analysis which is the *discourse in situation*, since both the discourse and the situation produce together, as semiotic constructs, a single meaning.

Therefore, a semiotician's task cannot be limited to deciding on what a text may mean according to its sole immanent structures. The hjemslevian principle of immanence is fully maintained, but applied at a higher level: not anymore at the level of the text per se but at that of a *semiotically constructed object* including discourse and situation. By definition, this object is never empirically given. Both the participants of the communication or the interaction, and the analyst, have to construct it, each at his respective level and with his own instruments – and both at their own risks.

But beyond the modal, actantial and thematic components of the interactants' simulacra, which address the cognitive competence of the agents, other variables also come into play, which appertain to the sensitive dimension and also contribute to giving sense to a determined situation. They summon our almost innate capacity to sense, to "feel", the effects of meaning that emanate from such patterns as the plastic or rhythmic – that is to say æsthesic – characteristics of any object (including texts). This is where another deadlock appears.

3 Narration or experience?

On the pretext that the sensitive dimension of objects cannot be reduced to a set of categorical oppositions between easily named units and that it is not clear how it could fit into the syntactic models of the narrative grammar, many semioticians deem it as wiser to ignore it. Unlike the positivity of the syntactico-semantic concatenations of a text, the kind of meaning that emerges from sensitive experience would belong to the ineffable.

This is a paradox. Could there be anything more concrete, more incarnate and more minutely structured – less ineffable – than the arrangements of plastic and rhythmic qualities that allow us to make sense of such manifestations as a piece of music, the changing expressions of a face or someone's demeanour in the course of a conversation? The signification we grasp from what is seen, heard or felt has obviously little to do with the meaning attached to a word, a sentence or a text. What we perceive in these instances is a variety of forms that directly affect us, without the mediation of verbal discourse. The fact that the æsthesic dimension of sensemaking encompasses, in particular, the *æsthetic* experience of art goes without saying. But outside this domain, it is in play almost in all our activities, even in domains that one might like to be immune to unpredictable reactions due to sensitivity. It is especially true of the political arena.

3.1 Discourse *versus* presence

As one of the most obvious activities of politicians is speaking (and accessorily writing), it has become only natural to analyse their discourses. Analysts traditionally interrogate their ideological, doctrinal or programmatic contents, as well as their rhetoric devices, the argumentative procedures and the persuasive or manipulative strategies at work. More recently, realising that this type of discourse is directed to both the intellect and the affect, the analyses have tried to report also on the emotions and passions that it is supposed to trigger. But this "pathemic" dimension, which is semiotically describable in terms of modal syntax, leaves apart a deeper dimension, precisely that of the "sensitive", which can be semiotically approached only in terms of *æsthesia*.

Politicians have nowadays become so familiar to us through the media that the boundaries between the way in which we look at them and the way we judge our relatives tend to blur. If we have a high opinion of some of them, if others "get on our nerves", the reasons why are not limited to the stances that they adopt vis-à-vis such and such issue that we deem as important. This is also the result of the æsthesic effects which emanate from their complexions, the tones and rhythms of their voices – their *hexis* – thereby reflecting a specific mode of "being-in-the-world".[2] This trend towards the sensitive dimension, although not entirely new, nowadays increasingly affects the status, the forms and even the very *lieu* of the political scene. In older times, in the eyes of an average citizen, politics belonged to some abstract space which was constructed by the analyses and the narratives of a limited number of authoritative voices in charge of interpreting history, explaining the present time and paving the way to a plausible future, so that the collective life seemed to unfold in the manner of an ample and intelligible story. Today, another way to practice politics seems to impose itself: it is no more considered mainly as an objectivable level of reality surfacing in the form of small epics or grand utopian dreams; instead, it tends to become a space of intersubjective relationships, experienced as an almost intimate interpersonal connection, as though face to face, *in præsentia*.

This shift, which may largely explain the present success of populist leaders over the world, can be conceptualised with the distinction between two semiotic *regimes of significance*. Yesterday, for almost everyone, politics *had a meaning* conveyed by *narration*. Today, it rather *makes sense* through direct *experience*. While, according to opinion polls, its meaning as a narration tends dramatically to vanish, it recovers its power to marshal people the moment it is envisaged as a lived æsthesic experience.

---

[2] Translating literally Maurice Merleau-Ponty's notion of *être-au-monde* (Merleau-Ponty, 1945).

3.2 The discourse of experience

But politics is only one among many other semiotic constructs. The two regimes of significance that we have brought to light about it – experience as making sense and narration as having a meaning – have a much broader reach.

Narration (in general terms) and specific narratives (in actual communication) are what brings some meaning (and some value) into our lives, even though the actual experience may sometimes tend to be just the opposite (either insignificant routine through humdrum monotony, or nonsensical chaos by dint of unpredictable accidents). But independently from this form of significance conveyed by our own or others' narrative discourses, we often happen – in front of a work of art, a landscape, a person, etc. – to be "assaulted" (recalling the first pages of *Sémantique structurale*) by another kind of significance that immediately (that is to say without the mediation of language) *makes sense* although it emanates from no articulated discourse or structured narrative. This second form, no narrative could relate or tell it (as one "tells" a story). In order to do so, it would have to be reduced to objectified, textualised, legible elements. But even so, these elements of signification "in paper" (another of Greimas's words) would only imperfectly reflect the experience of our directly grasping what did make sense æsthesically in our lived relationship with the object.

The fact that such an immediate experience cannot be told does not entail that it is inexpressible. On the contrary, from Proust to Sarraute, from Kafka to Musil, from Sterne to Woolf, from Leopardi to Svevo, from Dostoïevski to Tsvetaïeva, many authors have striven to express it – to *say* (if not to tell) it. United in the particular way they have gazed the world with a somehow pre-phenomenological eye, they have invented forms of writing that constitute what we can call the *discourse of experience* (Landowski, 2007a). This discourse is acknowledgedly distinct from the experience itself, but it has the capacity to capture its movement, to discursively reflect the dynamics of the relationship to things, people or oneself upon which the experience of an immediate sense-making is founded. So much so, that in front of this type of texts, we readers feel like participating in the advent of this meaning ourselves. Moreover, the borderline between such a literary reconstruction of experience and a more "scientific" approach is difficult to nail down. Where is it exactly located between what Proust and Merleau-Ponty respectively wrote? In the same vein, one might hardly identify any clear disconnect between *Nausea* and the final chapters of *Being and Nothingness*, where Sartre conducts an analysis of the immediate experience of viscousness, slipperiness, etc., that ends up in a project of "existential psychoanalysis".

In order to build an existential semiotics, capable of reporting on this experienced sense, the necessary tools could be found neither in the standard narrative grammar nor in its extensions towards passions or tensivity (Greimas and Fontanille 1991; Fontanille and Zilberberg 1998). The semiotics of passions limits itself to applying the modal grammar, initially designed to describe the "doings" of the actants of a narrative, to the syntax of their "states of feelings". And if the so-called tensive semiotics offers a useful perspective to analyse the variations of intensity that may occur along a process, it says nothing about the qualitative parameters presiding over the immediate sense effects grasped by the subjects (Landowski 2004: 44–49). As for us, from these limitations of the theoretical and methodological assets, we never drew the conclusion that the existential question is semiotically irrelevant or that the status of the sense that is grasped through experience can be but extra-semiotic. The true issue lied in the incompleteness of the existing models. We have therefore attempted to complete them and tried to make them more powerful.

4 The socio-semiotic perspective

The proposed shifts from textual analysis to situational and then experiential issues led to extending the relevance of the discipline to broader fields than those covered so far. At the same time, this extension can be described as a long journey towards the subjects' interiority. Starting from the *text* in its objective status of "uttered utterance" – what is most external – it aimed at what is most internal – the *experience* of sense as one lives it – via an intermediary level, the *situation*, defined as an intersubjective meaningful configuration. This necessitated the construction of a set of new concepts such as *union, contagion, adjustment, assent, self-fulfilment*, among others (Landowski 2005 and 2009). Rather than entering into their systematic presentation, we shall try to show how the resulting model permits to get in closer contact with lived experience without giving up any of the conceptual rigour required by a semiotic approach. Our work consisted mainly in rejigging the two basic components – narrativity and figurativity – upon which the classic semiotic theory of discourse is based, and reappraising the way how they are logically linked to one another.

4.1 *Junction* versus *union*

The overarching principle of the standard narrative grammar posits that all the fluctuations that affect our material as well as our moral condition as subjects are dependent on operations of "junction" – either "conjunctions", which make us possess "value objects" that we are supposed to aspire to, or "disjunctions" that deprive us of them. Such a model is perfectly adequate when applied to an enclosed space of interaction – typically the space of the folktale – inside which what one of the protagonists receives is necessarily lost by another. And one of its advantages is that it allows a simple and easy formalisation. But its main drawback is to be ideologically biased. Everything, from the most concrete artifact to the most abstract knowledge, is viewed as susceptible to be traded in the form of values, some meant for consumption, others purely modal (such as power), that are destined to transit among owners obeying to a universal syntax of *exchange*, in very much the same way as any merchandise awaiting to be sold and bought (Landowski 2004: 73–76; 2019). Society appearing thus as a vast market, such a grammar of intersubjectivity, insofar as it leads to describing life as a mere succession of gains and losses whatever their specific nature, reflects a very restricted, essentially economical vision of human affairs.

In the early 1990s, when Greimas's last book, *On Imperfection*, was published and simultaneously when awoke among some semioticians a growing interest in the works of such philosophers as Merleau-Ponty and Sartre, what was rediscovered is that there are interactions – also to be semiotically accounted for – that are quite independent of any transfer of objects among subjects. Taking on one of Sartre's phrases, independently of the relations of possession that subjects establish with what belongs to the realm of *having*, they also experience, amid one another and their environment, certain "links of *being*" (Sartre 1947: 325). According to a terminology borrowed from Merleau-Ponty, prior to being decomposed into discrete units offered to our desire or our appropriation, the world is present to us as a *meaningful totality*. In other words, what in itself and immediately ensures that there is (or may be) some meaning in our relationships to others and to the reality surrounding us is merely our *being-in-the-world*, independently of any mediation via socially categorised and valued objects (Merleau-Ponty, 1945, *passim*).

Semiotically speaking, this leads to conclude that, in addition to a regime of meaning focusing on the category of "junction", we have to recognise another regime of significance, founded on the sensitive co-presence of the actants. Within this framework, the objects are not any longer reduced to the status of interchangeable elements, the values of which would be, as formerly, appraised in regard to predetermined programmes of acquisition. Instead, they now *make sense* on the basis of the immanent organisation of their æsthesic qualities as perceived by subjects who are endowed with something that they lacked under the former regime: a body, as the locus of a general *sensitivity* which not only will allow for somatic sensations but also for forms of affect like "empathy", intuitive "sympathy" or semiotic contagion understood as the capability to feel the feeling of other beings, not necessarily human (Landowski 2004: ch. 6). From there on, as long as an actant is able to æsthesically sensing the other, and reciprocally, the door opens to relations that do not abide anymore by the sole laws of junction, but possibly by what we call the logic of *union*. Union is not a state of being, nor a kind of fusion. It is a *mode of interaction*. The relations it involves do not annihilate the interactants' identities. On the contrary, the syntax here in play tends to highlight and exalt them inasmuch as it is on the basis of the participants' respective and in principle mutually respected sensitivities that they coordinate their doings. In the best of cases, by way of mutual adjustments (as, for instance, in dancing (Sparti 2015)), it may lead to the constitution of a complex new entity in which each of the interactants finds a form of his (or its, or her) own self-fulfilment, as conditioned by the other's accomplishment. Union then appears as a creative mode of sense co-construction, in the interaction (Landowski 2004: ch. 3.1; 2005: ch. 4).

This duality of regimes applies also to the metasubjects we are, we semioticians as analysts, especially in the perspective of an existential semiotics which, in our view, by nature implies a dialectical relationship with what we analyze: at the same time, in accordance with a regime of sensitive relationships, and in a position of objectifying exteriority. In the past, the corresponding tasks have usually been distributed among distinct researchers, as if they were incompatible. On the contrary, we assume the necessity of integrating them both in a single approach: to "sense" as deeply as possible from inside the way how our objects of analysis æsthesically make sense (according to the logic of union), without giving up on the requirements of the discipline's general theoretical and methodological principles, thereby staying within the limits of the epistemology which founded the semiotics of junction.

4.2 Regimes of meaning in the interaction

Once the limits of the logic of junction have been passed, new possibilities open for a really general theory of the construction and apprehension of meaning in the interaction. In everyday life, whatever may be the project to be realised, the problem to be solved or the affair to settle, it is an empirically observable fact that in function of one's culture or of some personal idiosyncrasy each one is inclined to privilege a determined style of action, a preferred strategy rather than others equally possible. Many, who do not feel safe but in an ordered and mastered surrounding, would dream to *program* the behaviour of people as well as the course of things in such a manner as to ascertain to the most minute details their control on whatever operation in which they find themselves involved. Others will see everywhere but machinations and intrigues and think they may reach their goals only by themselves *manipulating* those they have to deal with. Others still would prefer to trust in their intuition and on-the-spot reactions, in their capacity to feel a situation and the intimate dispositions of those with whom they interact, so as to best *adjust* their own behaviour in the right moment. Others again would preferably discard any idea of a plan, manoeuvre or attunement, believing that it is safer to simply confide in chance and therefore to cross the fingers waiting for some happy (or unhappy) *accident* which providence may have decided for them and to which they possibly give, in advance, their assent.

Programming, manipulating, adjusting or consenting to what is inevitable, each of these alternative forms of doing translates at the same time a specific way of conceiving the sense of life, and results in a specific style of behaviour when it comes to interacting with somebody else or with whatever object. These variants might be considered as simply corresponding to a series of psychologically possible traits of personality, in which case, we semioticians would have to do no more than recording their existence. However, what makes them relevant from our point of view is the fact that each of them is articulated according to the syntax of one specific regime of meaning and interaction in such a way that although apparently contingent and heterogeneous these attitudes structurally interdefine one another and, considered as a whole, shape a system of structural transformations which owes nothing to psychology.

Strangely enough, among these configurations which intuitively are so familiar to us, the standard narrative grammar had recognized only two: the "manipulation", among subjects, and the "programming" of operations realised upon or with non-subjects. Whereas the latter would remain hardly sketched until quite recently,[3] the former, on the contrary, focused all the attention. It immediately appeared as the "canonical" form of narrativity as such, practically its unique and necessary grammatical modelling – the reason why at that time it could not be viewed as what we now call a "regime", one interactional regime among others. Our first task consisted anyway in reconsidering the classical definitions of these two syntactic and actantial constructions and in making explicit their respective theoretical basis.

As it became then clear, the latter is based upon a general principle of *regularity* manifested by the immutability of the so-called "thematic roles" assigned to the protagonists of the interaction. Under its rule, things and beings obey necessary and constant laws. And insofar as these laws (be they natural, social, psychological, etc.) are accessible to human understanding, their knowledge makes the behaviour of the agents they regulate predictable and thereby minimises the

---

[3] See, however (Greimas 1979).

risks of misunderstandings and failure when interacting with them. Thus based on the recognition of the regularities which somehow "program" and up to a certain point explain the course of actions, this regime is that of *programming*. But recognising the regularity of a given behaviour does not amount to giving it a meaning. On the contrary. As long as under this regime one has to do only with actors, be they human or not, whose behaviour is reduced to the execution of immutable algorithms deriving from their submission to one or another form of determinism, their lack of a proper will and of whatever degree of autonomy, in other words, their quality of non-subjects excludes by definition, on their part, any form of the reflexivity which is presupposed by the very notion of a "meaningful" behaviour (Petitimbert 2017). As a result, programming will be associated with meaninglessness.

The former syntax, that of *manipulation*, has its ground in a principle of *intentionality*, defined as a mix of volition and cognition (not necessarily implying clear "conscience"). A "manipulator" is definable as someone who aims at making others accept to do what they would not do unless feeling impelled or tempted to do so by the former's manoeuvres (such as threats, promises, etc.). Therefore, far from following a predefined algorithm, doing consists here, in the first place, in deciding to do. This entails that the intersubjective relationships will take the shape of a syntax of reciprocal persuasion among willing subjects-of-reason. In turn, this supposes that although each agent pursues his own objectives, all of them ought to share to some extent a common set of values permitting them to negotiate in order to achieve their respective goals by means of agreements. Such a logic begs the question of the origin of the subjects' "will" which appears as necessarily subtending their moves. Although an individual or collective self-determination is not excluded (at least at the most superficial level of observation), the key element in this respect consists in the recognition, by those whose "intentions" it rules, of some transcendent agency – the so-called "sender" – be it named as "God", the "Providence", the "Reason", the "Party", the "master" or the "father" (among other culturally widespread figures liable to feature this meta-actant). It is ultimately that hierarchically superior agency that defines, for the sake of the community, the good and the evil, the right and the wrong, etc., thereby providing its members with a common system of reference and evaluation, and founding the common sentiment of meaningfulness for "life".

Hence the figures of the manipulator and of the programmer. In contrast, two complementary figures lacked in the framework of the standard grammar: on one side, that of the subject confident in his capacity to feel *in vivo* the potentialities of a situation, to turn to his favour the tendency of things or the desire of people, to grasp and exploit improvisedly the "kairos" – in a word, the *opportunist*; on the other side, the figure of the *fatalist* who lets chance decide for him. Apart from the fact that these two figures may be formally derived, by logical transformations, from the syntactic definitions of the two previous ones, empirical experience obliged us to take them both into consideration and thereby enrich the model. That is why alongside the standard regimes already mentioned – which at losing their monopoly do not lose anything of their relevance – we introduced two complementary regimes based respectively upon the principle of *sensitivity* and that of *alea*: the regime of adjustment to the other interactant and that of assent to the accidents of life.

One of the main defining features of the regime of *adjustment* is the absence of any transcendent level of reference. In its context, what might rule the interaction and ensure its meaningfulness stems from the interactive process itself. The principle which founds this possibility consists in the postulated mutual sensitivity which enables the interactants to feel one another's feelings, combined with an innate availability in front of circumstances, a disposition to welcome opportunities that the present state of affairs unexpectedly may offer. In such conditions, an interaction may ideally take the form of a kind of dance in which the moves of each acting subject are inspired by the others' moves, in such a way that through reciprocal coordination the very process of interaction continuously invents and transforms its own functioning conditions and recreates its immanent meaning. With the works of Marcel Détienne and Jean-Pierre Vernant or François Jullien, as well as those of Victor Turner, Paul Rabinow, Tim Ingold or James Clifford, among others, anthropology provides a rich material to deepen the understanding of such an interactional syntax and in particular the idea of immanent productivity of meaning and value attached to interaction as such (Detienne and Vernant 1974; Jullien 2000; Rabinow 1977; Ingold 2000; Turner 1986; Clifford 2013).

The last regime is that of *accident* and nonsense, a semiotic vacuum founded on a principle of *irregularity*. Indeed, focusing on the irregularity of phenomena and the unpredictability that it entails represents another important option which is at the root of another series of culturally attested manners of answering – although negatively – the question of the meaning of life. Fatalism appears as one of its most common forms: "So it happens, there is no reason for it." Such an attitude, which ignores or denies the existence of laws that might make what happens minimally predictable and what exists a little more understandable falls into what we call the *assent* to the accidental. It encapsulates all kinds of conceptions according to which reality is either the absurd produce of pure chance or ruled by factors that escape all power or influence, or by actors whose designs lay beyond human cognitive grasp, as alluded to in the phrase "*credo quia absurdum*" (Landowski 2012a). This regime thus implements a complementary form of negativity as regards signification: whereas in programming the *meaninglessness* of the observable regularities tends to be perceived as an insufficiency – the lack of a meaning that one would have searched for – under the regime of accident, negativity is due to an excess, that of the frightening, blinding, paralysing presence of *nonsense*.

Regime of interaction based upon *regularity*: *programming* (strategies of the "programmer"). Regime of significance: *meaninglessnes*.	Regime of interaction based upon *alea*: *accident*(and possibly assent) (strategies of the "fatalist"). Regime of significance: *nonsense*.

Regime of interaction based upon *intentionality*: *manipulation* (strategies of the "manipulator"). Regime of significance: to "*have a meaning*".	Regime of interaction based upon *sensitivity:* *adjustment* (strategies of the "opportunist") Regime of significance: to "*make sense*".

Diagram 1: Regimes of meaning.

Forming a system and admitting various forms of combination or superposition between regimes, the overall syntax of this model allows accounting for the widest variety of interactional practices. Nevertheless, the construction of such a broadened grammar of narrativity was not sufficient. The status, the forms and the role of *figurativity*, and, most importantly, its articulation with the narrative component, had to be reexamined as well.

5 Forms of being in the world

According to the circumstances, in function of the contexts and of the nature of the relations that we search to establish with what surrounds us, we oscillate permanently between two very different ways of looking at the world and try to make it significant. A semiotic problematic claiming to be relevant as regards lived experience is bound to take both into consideration.

5.1 To read – to grasp

Most often we look at the world almost as if it were a surface like a page of a book, covered with signs which we have learned to read. Our understanding then consists in the interpretation of manifest forms which, verbal or not, constitute the equivalent of texts supposedly "wanting to say" something and "*having a meaning*". But it also occurs that for some reason we stop regarding (or do not yet regard) the world as a network of signs to be decrypted. In such moments, there is nothing to be interpreted or deciphered, nothing to be read, no text at all – and yet there may still (or already) have some sense that we do grasp in a different manner. Indeed, occasionally, instead of searching almost obsessively marks of intelligible discourses supposedly addressed to us, we take the risk of letting ourselves be impregnated by the inherent plastic or rhythmic qualities of whatever may appear in front of us. Our gaze upon the world then passes from the mode of *reading* (*la lecture*) applied unto pre-categorised significations, to that of a *grasping* (*la saisie*) focused on the æesthesic features of a world that "*makes sense*" to us. Admittedly, we may often have a sentiment that a concordance establishes between these two modalities of our look, and consequently between these two regimes of significance. In a conversation, as long as the tone of our interlocutor seems in harmony with the content of what is being said we do not have any reason to make a distinction between the æesthesic level – the sense we "grasp" in the tone of voice of the speaker – from the cognitive dimension of the speech, the articulated significations we "read" in what is uttered. On the contrary, the sense effects grasped on the first level seem to us validated by their conformity with the "propositional content" of the discourse. The distinction remains nonetheless relevant in its principle, and useful in practice whenever such a concordance does not occur. But its main interest appears at another, metasemiotic level, where the question arises of the "existential" implications of the alternative between these regimes.

In order to make oneself a reader and look at the world as if it were a text, one has to detach oneself from what one sees, to objectify it, to observe it as a reality in itself signifying and potentially intelligible even when it does not reveal straight ahead its signification. Seen from this perspective, a text or any object considered as such is an autonomous object observed at a distance and regarded as the location of significations supposedly preconstituted which require only to be uncovered. In these conditions, reading is a mere operation of decoding which only necessitates finding the right key. In contrast, in the æesthesic experience of sense grasping, the subject is directly involved in the relation to the object, since it is precisely this relation that then makes sense. This sense that the subject has just experienced, what might be its meaning? Grasped in an instant, it is *it*, now (and no longer the meaning of a text) which constitutes an enigma for the subject. But whereas the enigma of the text (the question of its signification) was due to be solved by an appropriate reading, such a solution is now excluded since what is at stake is not anymore the meaning of some objectifiable data – a given text – but the meaning of a primary sense effect which has been immediately, æsthesically experienced. As a result, unlike readable meanings which appear as the final results of processes of interpretation, the immediately grasped æsthesic effect of sense constitutes for the subject the starting point of an open if not endless interrogation.

By opposing the reading of significations which fall within the realm of the narration and the grasping of æsthesic qualities which make sense in lived experience, we do not want to suggest that the first of these regimes would concern only our relations to texts (as objects readable by nature), or more generally to verbal manifestations (conceived as intelligible par excellence), whereas the process of grasping sense would specifically concern non-verbal manifestations (thus assimilated to the sensitive). Each one of these regimes is defined by the nature of the look which it implies upon the world and not by a particular class of empirical objects to which it would exclusively apply. This entails that for whom privileges reading, any object may be treated as a text carrying readable meanings (a view which corresponds to the semiotically orthodox option), whereas for whoever would prioritise grasping, any object, including a text, can be regarded as making sense beyond what it may signify in linguistic or narrative terms.

5.2 Forms of figurativity

In the global architecture of the theory, *figurativity* is defined in relation to *narrativity*. The latter refers to the syntactic organisation of the discourse, the former to its semantic component. This is the generic acceptation of the term (below, *a*). However, when the notion of figurativity is used as a tool for the analysis of a particular discourse, it assumes a more technical character. The word then refers to iconic sets of features supposed to represent particular objects of the world, or to indexical devices charged to signal their presence or refer to it: this is the figurativity *stricto sensu*, also called, "figurativity of surface" (below, *b*). But to this comes, in addition, a third meaning of the term. Alongside surface figurativity, one has had indeed to recognize the existence of a form of figurativity – termed "profound" (*c*) – which instead of producing meaningful effects based on iconic representation allows to grasp æsthesic effects of sense which depend on the rhythmic and plastic organisation of the elements (for instance chromatic settings, when speaking about images) that enter in the composition to the discursive manifestation:

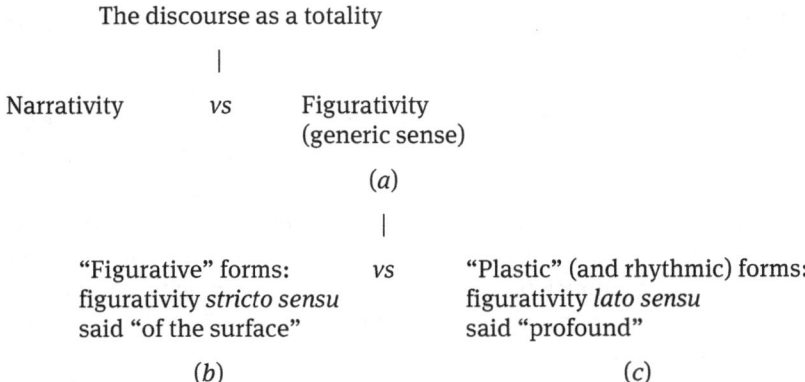

For a long time, in visual as well as in literary semiotics, the treatment of the figurative dimension has been reduced to the option (*b*): the analyses were confined to recognising in the surface of discourses certain actorial, spatial or temporal figures, more or less strictly codified by usage, which one considered as charged to give their "discursive dressing" to the more abstract dispositives used by the narrative syntax. This is the principle that any good *reader* will follow: attentive to the slightest index that may mean something, he will notice and memorise sceneries, clothing, physiognomies, gestures etc., connect them to one another and, on this basis, endeavour to reconstitute the actantial and modal structure implicit in the actions and passions from which the spectacle of the world, seen as a narration, will finally derive its signification.

On the contrary, considered according to (*c*), a figure imposes the presence of that form of sense which immediately emanates from the plastic and rhythmic articulations immanent to any perceptible object. Greimas spoke in such cases about a "second" language whereby not only works of art but also the objects of ordinary life speak to us "in another way" – otherwise than through the filter of natural languages or of the cultural grids which we have learned to apply in order to read surface figurative elements as featuring recognisable objects that "have names". One may, however, ask whether rather than "second" this plastic language which does not designate anything and nonetheless speaks to us should not be in reality recognised as primary. This is what Greimas already suggested when he observed, further in the same text, that "the narration, with its overwhelming figurativity, is nothing but the 'noise' that has to be overcome in order to grasp the main articulations of the object." This *noise* of narration is that of surface figurativity, upon which the *reading* focuses. On the contrary, the "main articulations", those which give access to the "deep" sense of the object – its "mythical" or "existential" sense – are those which organise the plastic forms constitutive of the "profound" figurativity which we experience through the processes of *grasping*.[4]

But in order to fully measure the role figurativity plays in the emergence of sense, one has moreover to connect it with the above-presented model concerning narrativity, since these are the two inseparable components of discourse as a whole. As regards the figurative component, we have just distinguished two regimes of significance: "reading", which deciphers the significations attached to "figurativity stricto sensu", and "grasping", which lets sense emerge from æsthesic apprehension through the so-called "profound figurativity". And previously, we had presented an extended narrative model interdefining four regimes of interaction. We now have to examine the relationships between these two configurations, our postulate being that regimes of significance and regimes of interaction are structurally connected.

5.3 Existential styles

The first of these correlations consists in the fact that the recognition of significations through the processes of reading the surface figures of the world systematically goes together with behaviours commanded, at the interactional level, either by the principle of intentionality, which founds the syntax of *manipulation*, or that of regularity, which permits *programmation* (or by a combination of both). In fact, the process of reading is in itself of a programmatical order since its condition of possibility is the regularity of a code which allows deciphering textual meanings or the significations attributed to whatever aspect of the world, when regarded as a textual surface. But at the same time, to read is by definition entering into the game of interpretation and persuasion (be it only self-persuasion), that is of manipulation. Thus, the process of reading displays a double articulation which implies at a first level the use of programmatic procedures whose final objective transcends programming and pertains, at a second level, to the realm of manipulation. The affinity we observe between a certain way of interpreting the world (as a set of readable features) and a corresponding manner of acting (which prioritises programming and manipulation) thus appears as properly structural. A relation of the same nature binds the alternative mode of significance, grasping, with the other pair of interactional regimes, assent to accident and, more directly, sensitive adjustment.

---

4 See also (Lévi-Strauss 1955: 120–121; Calabrese 1985: 46).

A perfect example of the first correlation may be found in Stendhal's *Le Rouge et le Noir*. For Julien Sorel, the main protagonist, to read his environment in order to be able to program action and manipulate people, such is the combination of operational modes he is applying in all circumstances, to analyse and handle his relationships with the others, to make his decisions and generally to orient his behaviours. In all domains – mundane life, love affairs, politics – Julien is at the same time, on the level of significance, a *reader*, and on the level of interaction, an intrigant entirely *programmed* to *manipulate*. Moreover, the life program which guides him is itself borrowed from a reading (Napoléon's *Mémorial de Sainte-Hélène*, by Las Cases), in such a way that all his existential trajectory proceeds explicitly from this first narrative model which he takes as a norm. To him, the narration anticipates life and supplants experience. We previously admitted the possibility of a "discourse of the experience", distinct from "lived experience" but capable to account for it. What we now see is that also the "discourse of the narration" may exert power upon lived experience, the power of inscribing it in advance within its grids, thereby reducing lived experience to a "lived narration".

A diametrically opposed case is Goliadkine in Dostoyevsky's *The Double*. Unable to master the codes of his social environment, he cannot manage to make out any signification of the intrigues which surround him: this is a language he is unable to read. But hardly does he enter into contact with whomever he meets in front of him, immediately he embarks in experiencing a multitude of dramatically enigmatic sense effects that he involuntarily grasps and whose precise meanings escape him. Correlatively all his behaviour is ruled according to either the principle of sensitivity or that of alea: M. Goliadkine is at the same time, on the one hand – in his relation to forms of figurativity – a *non-reader*: excessively sensitive to the plastic qualities of all the manifestations he encounters, he perceives his surroundings as in an enigmatic dream or, rather, a nightmare, and on the other hand – at the interactional level, that is to say, in terms of narrativity – he is exactly the contrary of a programmed manipulator: in his manner (that is, with utmost clumsiness), he behaves as a kind of dancer in the sense that all his motions are only immediate reactions to the perceptible impulses arriving from the others, to which he tries at every moment to adjust (without success). Simultaneously, as a true fatalist, he is in advance resigned to the beats of destiny which he anticipates in spite of denying their threat, so to say magically.

The symmetry between these two characters is almost perfect. The hero of Stendhal is just as unyielding to the æsthesic dimension of experience as the hero of Dostoyevsky is blind to the conventional signs of narration. If the obstinate resistance of Julien to the calls of sensitivity makes him (as the narrator several times underlines) a "fool", then the blindness of Goliadkine in front of the most elementary significations of the social text makes him an idiot, a ridiculous, a marginal and soon a psychopath destined to asylum. When the former, as a distant observer of his surroundings, all the more lucid as he is more detached from himself, plans coldly his actions anticipating others' reactions, the latter, like in a consecution of hallucinations, finds himself balloted by a series of unpredictable æsthesic accidents whose outburst excludes from his part any efficient strategy of manipulation. And finally, just as we readers have to wait until the last chapter of the novel by Stendhal to see Julien suddenly realising (in his jail) what might have been the existential experience of sense, in the same way, M. Goliadkine must have his double, a M. Goliadkine Number Two – a cunning manipulator whom one could almost take as another Julien Sorel – to permit that the "canonical" regime of narration with its "junctive" philosophy would also find its place in Dostoyevsky's novel.

How to explain this generally observable coherence between the way how individuals and cultures tend to make mean discourses, situations and experience by privileging a given regime of significance, and their corresponding tendency to favour a specific regime of interaction? Such coordination seems to imply that the preferences (or, rather, "spontaneous" tendencies) manifested regarding both ranges of regimes are the expression, at two different levels, of something deeper and common to both: once more, the expression of a certain existential manner of being-in-the-world. This is probably what would best define the identity of the two literary characters just evoked, as well as, maybe, our own. While some spend their lives mainly on the mode of *experience*, grasping sense and attempting to adjust with partners or resigned to assent to the unavoidable, others seem to conceive and even live their life rather as a *narration*, the world appearing to their eyes as a universe at the same time readable because covered by intelligible and named figures, and over which they feel capable to exert an efficient control inasmuch as it appears to them as peopled by entities, human or else, who can be manipulated and by objects destined by nature to obey their programs.

6 Conclusion

Each one of these semiotic configurations thus covers at the same time, from the point of view of the theory of meaning, certain modes of treatment of the figurativity, and, from the viewpoint of action theory, certain precise forms of narrativity. As a whole, this conceptualisation allows to account for the different types of attitudes and practices which each individual (or, by extension, each culture) tends to privilege. This means that, in order to deal with the experience, there is no need to leave aside the conceptual field where the notions of figurativity and narrativity find their pertinence. Just as the figurativity of surface, privileged by the discourse of narration, differs from the deep figurativity which one sees principally working in the experience, the programmatic and manipulatory syntaxes, which dominate the narration, differ from the syntax of adjustment and assent to accident which fundamentally articulates the experience. Once these syntaxes have been recognised, made explicit and conceptualised, the existential field where they come into play opens to our analyses.

But these distinctions may still be given a more general meaning. The narration is finally the form of discourse which fixes the identity, the regularity, the necessity and the rationality of things as they are supposed to be. It is fundamentally an assertive discourse. In front of the uncertain experience of the real, it appears as a discourse of knowledge which permits to fix recognisable and readable significations, deemed to reflect the manifest form of what exists. The experience, on the contrary, is an interrogation on the meaning of the sense effects which emerge from what happens to the subject, either from outside under the form of æsthesic configurations which impress him, touch him, affect him, challenge him, or from inside of himself under the form of impulses depending on the dynamics of his own body and perhaps also (especially if we should include the dream in the field of experience as making sense) of imaginary figures manifesting the drives of the "unconscious". The subject may either yield to these fluctuations or try to master them by attempting to reduce them to some combination of preconstructed schemas borrowed from the universe of narration. But he may also try to *say* them by producing such a discourse of experience that were capable of taking in charge what first made sense in lived experience through an initial sense-grasping. For, even if the experience cannot be told, it is in principle sayable, on the condition of inventing appropriate forms of expression, be they literary or, for instance, cinematographic, or adequate forms of reflexive writing, as in phenomenology, and maybe, one day, in semiotics.

This finally amounts to contending that it is not necessary to fall into mysticism to dare to speak about the experience, whether lived or enunciated, and to search to parallel it with the discourse and even the experience of the narration. Textualized or not, all these configurations are equally positive and, as a consequence, analysable. If the existential dimension is embedded in these elements, then it is possible to think about it from within semiotics.

Taquaral (Brazil), October 2020

References

Bucher, Gérard. 1997. De la perfection de la théorie à l'imperfection des lettres. In AAVV, *Lire Greimas*. Limoges: Pulim.
Calabrese, Omar. 1985. *La macchina della pittura. Pratiche teoriche della rappresentazione figurativa fra Rinascimento e Barocco*. Bari: Laterza.
Clifford, James. 2013. *Returns: Becoming Indigenous in the Twenty First Century*. Cambridge (Mass.): Harvard University Press.
Detienne, Marcel & Jean-Pierre Vernant. 1974. *Les ruses de l'intelligence. La mètis des Grecs*. Paris: Flammarion.
Fontanille, Jacques & Claude Zilberberg. 1998. *Tension et signification*. Liège: Mardaga.
Geninasca, Jacques. 1997a. Le regard esthétique. *Actes Sémiotiques* VI, 58 [1984] (re-ed. in *La parole littéraire*, Paris, P.U.F., 1997).
Geninasca, Jacques. 1997b. Et maintenant. In AAVV, *Lire Greimas*. Limoges: Pulim.
Greimas, Algirdas Julien. 1966. *Sémantique structurale. Essai de méthode*. Paris: Larousse.
Greimas, Algirdas Julien. 1979. La soupe au pistou. Construction d'un objet de valeur. *Actes Sémiotiques-Documents* I 5 (re-ed. in *Du sens II*, Paris, Seuil, 1983).
Greimas, Algirdas Julien. 1987. *De l'Imperfection*. Périgueux: Fanlac.
Greimas, Algirdas Julien & Joseph Courtés. 1979. *Sémiotique. Dictionnaire raisonné de la théorie du langage*. Paris: Hachette.
Greimas, Algirdas Julien & Jacques Fontanille. 1991. *Sémiotique des passions*. Paris: Seuil.
Ingold, Tim. 2000. *The perception of the environment: essays on livelihood, dwelling and skill*. London: Routledge.
Jullien, François. 1996. *Traité de l'efficacité*. Paris: Grasset.
Jullien, François. 2015. *De l'Être au Vivre. Lexique euro-chinois de la pensée*. Paris: Gallimard.
Kersyte, Nijole. 2009. La sémiotique d'A.J. Greimas entre logocentrisme et pensée phénoménologique. *Nouveaux Actes Sémiotiques* 112. http://epublications.unilim.fr/revues/as.
Landowski, Eric. 1997a. *Présences de l'autre*, Essais de socio-sémiotique II. Paris: Presses Universitaires de France.
Landowski, Eric. 1997b. Le sémioticien et son double. In AAVV *Lire Greimas*. Limoges: Pulim.
Landowski, Eric. 2004. *Passions sans nom*, Essais de socio-sémiotique III. Paris: Presses Universitaires de France.
Landowski, Eric. 2005. *Les interactions risquées*. Limoges: Pulim.
Landowski, Eric. 2007. Unità del senso, pluralità di regimi. In AAVV, *Narrazione ed esperienza*. Rome: Meltemi.
Landowski, Eric. 2009. Socio-sémiotique (et douze notions connexes). In Driss Ablali (ed.), *Vocabulaire des études sémiotiques et sémiologiques*, 73–80. Paris: Champion.
Landowski, Eric. 2012a. *Shikata ga nai* ou Encore un pas pour devenir sémioticien!. *Lexia* 11–13. 45–70.
Landowski, Eric. 2012b. ¿Habría que rehacer la semiótica?. *Contratexto* 20. 127–155; French version, Une sémiotique à refaire? 2013. *Galáxia* 26. 10–33.
Landowski, Eric. 2015. The Greimassian Semiotic Circle. In Marina Grishakova (ed.), *Theoretical Schools and Circles in the Twentieth Century Humanities*, 84–98. London: Routledge.
Landowski, Eric. 2017. Interactions (socio) sémiotiques. *Actes Sémiotiques* 120.

Landowski, Eric. 2019. Politiques de la sémiotique. *Rivista Italiana di Filosofia del Linguaggio* 13(2). 6–25.
Lévi-Strauss, Claude. 1955. *Tristes Tropiques*. Paris: Plon.
Merleau-Ponty, Maurice. 1945. *Phénoménologie de la perception*. Paris: Gallimard.
Parret, Herman, 2001. Présences. *Nouveaux Actes Sémiotiques* 76.
Petitimbert, Jean-Paul. 2017. Régimes de sens et logique des sciences. Interactions socio-sémiotiques et avancées scientifiques. *Actes Sémiotiques* 120.
Rabinow, Paul. 1977. *Reflections on Fieldwork in Marocco*. Berkeley: University of California Press.
Sartre, Jean-Paul. 1947. *L'être et le néant*. Paris: Gallimard.
Sparti, Davide. 2015. *Sul tango. L'improvvisazione intima*. Bologne: Il Mulino.
Tarasti, Eero. 2000. *Existential Semiotics*. Bloomington: Indiana University Press.
Tarasti, Eero. 2009. *Fondements de la sémiotique existentielle*. Paris: L'Harmattan.
Turner, Victor. 1986. *The Anthropology of Performance*. New York: PAJ Publications.

Daniel Charles
Prolegomena on the semiotics of silence (from Jankélévitch to Tarasti)

Abstract: The music philosophy of Vladimir Jankélévitch appears clearly in his treatise *La musique et l'ineffable,* he a.o. approaches music as a doubly complicated element, both expressive and inexpressive, serious and frivolous at the same time. Herman Parret, the Belgian semiotician, has spoken about semiotics of traces, which in Peirce's theory corresponds to index sign. For Jacques Derrida even a grapheme was a testament. Ancient myths of Orpheus and Sirenes reveal the essence of music, Jankélévitch is in this framework simultaneously a philosopher of music and postplatonian thinker. Essentially he is an antimetaphysician. Nevertheless, Jankélévitch still offers ideas also for existential semiotics. Modal dimensions are then emphasized, as they appear in Tarasti's analysis of silence in opera. Tarasti refers to Wagner but also to Musorgsky in his vision of multilevelled signification of music. In Tarasti's theory much has been inherited from the Jankéevitchian hermeneutics.

Keywords: ineffable, appearance, hermeneutics, existential, modalities, silence

When history repeats itself it becomes myth: it is to this genesis, and perhaps to the mystery which it conceals, that Vladimir Jankélévitch refers when he scrutinizes with feverish fastness that never betrays him, the "double complication" which is characteristic to the music he loves, to be "at the same time expressive and inexpressive, serious and frivolous, profound and superficial" and to reveal, on the moral level, "that ironic and scandalous disproportion between incantatory power....and the deep inevidence of the musically beautiful." The key works which can 'eliminate definitely the ambiguity', Jankélévitch numbers them first when he, at the start, admits to being unable to express himself about the fine word of their history: should one ---and according to which justice – to decide if their 'charm' is the one of "treachery or the principle of wisdom."? Yet, to judge if Liszt and Dvorak, Fauré and Debussy, Rimsky and Musorgsky, shortly said the key composers which the *captatio benevolentiae* of *La Musique et l'ineffable* evokes, are to be doomed by the fate of this genre, still one has to abandon to the research on the context. It is this what the author decides: "We have to research if the word of these contradictions is not precisely in the operation of Charm and in the innocence of a poetic act which has the Time as its only dimension."

La Musique et l'Ineffable opens with the remark which Herman Parret calls the *semiotics of traces*. Since, "the music, sonorous phantasy is the most futile of the appearances, and the appearance. . . . ..a kind of objectivation of our weakness", one only has to refer, as Plato did, to "the austere Dorian and Phrygian monody" with the pretext that it corrects the easy-going "pathetic and languishing modes of the Orient, Ionian and Lydian and their lamenting harmonies." Or contrarily to recall *Carmen* for the only reason to get rid of the enchantment of the flower girls and the love potion of Tristan, in the manner whereby Nietzsche's *Traveler and His Shadow* desolidarizes from "the eternal musical feminine according to Wagner, these attitudes returning to the Same, not to say the eternal return of the Same. One could ask (as Jean Wahl did not hesitate to do) if Jankélévitch does not resort to this point close to Heidegger, which one knows was diagnosed in the Nietzschean affirmation of the Will to Power, in the form of the reversed Platonism, a perfect return of abstination – namely the ultimate distance of the fulfillment of Metaphysics. . ." Let it be as it is that the call or assumption of a semiotics of traceability could well manifest just in favour of this juxtaposition, back to back, of Plato and Nietzsche – however contrarily to any metaphysics – and there was hope by the abbé Liszt as well as by the theosophe Fabre d'Olive, of an 'orphic civilization' of which we should perhaps dream not only according to a nostalgic or passeist scheme but as a concrete utopy to be realized.

"What is musical is not the voice of the Sirens, but it is the song of Orpheus. The marines Sirens, enemies of the Muses, do not have any other goal but to mislead, and retardate the Odysseia of Ulisses: in other terms, they try to prevent the dialectics of the rightness of the itinerary, which leads our spirit to the duty and the truth. It is just in this way the captivating songs of the untrusty Tamara, at Michel Lermontov, lead the traveller to death. In order not to be seduced what else could one do but to make one deaf to any melody and delete with all effort the sensation itself? "The interpretation of the myth, should it not, in fact, provide us against the metaphysical temptation in order to enrich a little too abundantly – not so much the sense (if it exists)- but the reification of the letter of a text by hypothesis already declared? However, one is not in any way surprised to see, in the same passage, how Jankélévitch musically reopens the gate: "In fact, he says, the musicians who let the Rusalkas and Sirens of nothingness sing, like for instance Debussy or Balakirev or Rimsky-Korsakov, make us rather hear the voice of Orpheus: since the real music humanizes and civilizes." In the same way, if Michelet of *Bible de l'Humanité* is here called to testify, it is because the reading he proposes of Aristotelian defence of conflict between the Lyra and Flute, is without pretexts: as to the flute, the hunter of the rats and charmer of snakes of the satyre Marsyas, Orpheus is opposed by the Apollonian lyra and the cult of Helios, the god of the light. The odes of Marsyas could not reveal to be but 'enchanteresses' in the bad sense, one prefers to them the rhythmic incantation of Apollonian processes which articulate the musical around 'metric scheme of time'. The idea of a temporal poetic act and at the same time first and – as the original Time of Heidegger in Sein und Zeit – one-dimensional, the organ point upon which terminates the preface of *La Musique et l'ineffable*, demands, without doubt, to reach the authentic status of sign-activity (according to the expression of the ergonome Jacques Theureau), let it be 'innocent' (and Jankélévich would have said it 'deconcretizable' (depalpabilité) the 'Charm' of music.

The whole reasoning which dominates in this aspect the entire beginning of the work (whose publication is dated back to 1957 and 1961) goes back if one wants to understand its play, to the First Philosophy (*Philosophie première*), to the principal text, in which the philosopher delivered from 1953 on, one kind of theoretical issue of his interpretation of the myth of Sirenes. Since the first chapter of his magnum opus, he asked about the 'conductibility of the Appearance' and formulated that "the appearance is that which has the 'air' without being, and which is not in itself. Yet, from the other side the appearance is appearing, and at the same time a copy which is relatively a fake, which is, at the same time, the probable. The appearing is the patent. . .and consecutively, instead of confusing our ears, instead of being that weak Ulysses, who prefers not to listen to the tempting Sirenes, and who makes them vanish. . ..if we listened a little to those enchanteresses? Not to believe what they say, but to understand what they think". In such a taking of risk resides perhaps the essence of the musical. . ..

So one arrives at the whole hermeneutics, and at the same time, the ambivalence of Jankélévitch regarding Plato gets precise form. . ..One reveals therefore with Jankélévitch at the same time philos of music and postplatonian (better term than neoplatonian) thinker. . .

Yet, is this all? In the pages which succeed this Odyssean call, the motif of time will be certainly reinvested but what is involved is the uncertain character of its perpetuality. "Of all the appearances the sonorous appearance is the most futile..but the vanity of noise is twice vain and demands to be prolonged to be continuously renewed: without it, it would get plat and fall into silence. . .. If the spatial existence is vanity, the sound event is the vanity of vanities: as an undefinite mood, it requires, all the time, to be continued. . ..

However, one should insist at the fourth part of *La Musique et l'ineffable* the whole position of antimetaphysics mentioned at the beginning, which expresses itself at the humorous evocation of the three last words 'in the silence' of 724 pages of the Traité de Métaphysique Traité de Métaphysique should be in cursive. of Jean Wahl. Jankélévitch could well have undersigned the last paragraph of Traité which we copy here: "In the presence of artworks, those at the same time complete and incomplete world, or simply in presence of things we experience a plenitude, we do not separate any longer the interior and exterior, the unfinished and finished. And the incessant dialogue arrives here at the conclusion, in the silence." One may doubt those three last words, one would apply them to the music. . . to give to the silence the last word and thinking not only the last words is one not then put under the doubt to 'blend together the metaphysics and the metaphoric"?

The semiotics of silence attempts, however, such as it has been touched by the text of Jankélévitch, an effort to semiotize the whole canvas of the background – the existence – in the full sense of the term. By semiotiziation, said recently Herman Parret in a conference on the Archival memory and figurative memory, nothing deeply epistemological is suggested: we simply think of an interdisciplinary or transdisciplinary approach which systematizes the naturalist, psychological, philosophical, and phenomenological perspectives by taking the memory as sign value and the memory as a significant act".

Parret anchored this 'transdiscipline' in the pragmatic movement of Charles S. Peirce, according to which the notion of *trace* is equal to the one of *the index*: an animal passed and left a trace. It is an index. The index can be extended to cover writing in the sense in which analogy of printing originally adheres to the touch of a letter. The writing, that is true, is it not a graph, and in this senses, an index? One recalls here the word (definitive?) of the eminent theoretician of writing, Jacques Derrida, for whom 'every grapheme is a testament'- should one not join from this dark statement on the actual music, such as it was understood by the Cassandra-Adorno, to the 'bottle in the sea'? All depends on the evidence of the idea that one makes from the writing of sound silence, or of its diverse silences. And the 'existential' tonality which necessarily is connected to the simple formulation of the problem if the right to existence to the semiotic or at least semiotizing to the search – like the one of Jankélévitch. Independently, we should add, referring to the opinion of the virtuoso of Vladimir Jankélévitch which he forged from week to week on that or that contemporary piece for piano!

Since it is precisely – to use more technical terms – the conjunction of the Peircean logic, according to which the index is one of the possible variants of a sign and the Husserlian thesis on the indexicality of sign (see Logical researches) which has been formulated well before Derrida's elaboration of the theory of writing and the fashion of deconstructionism, the Heideggerian description of a sign as *Zeigen* (§17 of *Sein und Zeit*). And, the evidence of such a chiasma of Peirce/Heidegger which has allowed, on one hand, the Italian philosopher Carlo Sini to establish a hermeneutical critic of the general semiotics, has favoured, on the other hand, the emergence of musical semiotics of our time. It is not at all surprising that just in our time the direct links between Peirce's heritage and the actual renewal of musical hermeneutics, at least at an incomparable musician, and zealous disciple of Algirdas Julien Greimas and who started his career by translating *Sein und Zeit* into Finnish – what is still an aggravating circumstance! The personality to whom we make here the allusion is Eero Tarasti, the author of many works touching the musical semiotics which have been significant events: the author of a key work (appeared in 2000) in which he did not hesitate to enlarge, in the direction of general semiotics, certain perspectives which have been so far only sketched, but which we gathered in his work Existential Semiotics.

The prestige of the chair holder of musicology at the University of Helsinki helped such a project as Existential Semiotics, elaborated even before the page of academic structuralism had been turned – definitely incited attention not only in Europe but Urbi et Orbi, including the American and South American context of the 'new musicology'. And this happened even more easily because Eero Tarasti himself has always emphasized his spiritual debt to Jankélévitch – it is sufficient to report on the list of his different work to be convinced. Yet what is, even more, the sigetics (sigétique), which characterizes so meticulously *La musique et l'ineffable* contains enough still unexploited ideas to appear eventually tomorrow as one continuation of 'existential' semiotics in expansion. Still one should draw here some consequences from the almost prophetic note which Eero Tarasti has consecrated in his *Theory of Musical Semiotics* from 1994 on the possibility to apply the chart of modalities of Greimas to the analysis of certain scenes of opera at Richard Wagner.

Let us read this note again. In searching for "the most efficient procedure of integration in the operatic texture of heterogeneous mixture of sign systems", Tarasti defends the modal dimension – which puts together the great categories of Being and Doing, and Can, Want, Must, which Greimas particularly instigated; his master in narrativity. Since such a dimension appears as he observes "each time when the music becomes gestural in a scene of Wagnerian opera, each time when the symphonic continuity changes into the discontinuity of language on a gestural basis. In the course of scenes, the encounter of two actors will develop it, step by step, in one and same modal dimension like in the first meeting of Senta and Daland in the *Flying Dutchman* or when Brünnhilde awakens in the first act of *Siegfried*. And he adds in the bottom of the page: "One could even risk at this type of scenes to employ the semiotics of silence, in the sense as Jankélévitch understands it when he studies silent ruptures which break the musical" (*Musique et l'ineffable* 1961: 170). The fact that in the opera even the silence speaks and despite the realm of intensities, which emerge, there is the continuity in the depth of modal nature for all that happens on stage. When the Wagnerian protagonists observe the silence, this only underlines simply what Adorno said namely the existence of this modal level which albeit is hidden never stops being present.

The idea of an immanent multileveled elaboration of music is certainly no novelty in musicology – because the reduction of the underlying harmonies of work into one and sole key formula *Ursatz* of Schenker for instance, or the resorting to, as Greimas proposed, to complex isotopies, all this instigates numerous studies and quite serious scholars have tried to elucidate the notion of the generative course without being satisfied with the linguistic transpositions of elementary linguistic schemes, to which the adherents of rustic structuralisms of the 1960s adhered...nevertheless, Tarasti's reference to opera, and particularly to the Wagnerian *Gesamtkunstwerk*, seems to us to grasp the whole of what has been written about the topics: the passage of the author (and note) we have cited indicates their origin in the reflection which Tarasti has made just after reading Jankélévitch and this entitles us to reread la *Musique et l'ineffable* in another way – by paying new attention to certain expectations of the semiotics of existence. This would be even more intensively worried about the 'modalities' which would multiply their effects when they are considered in the context of a 'semiosphere' in the sense of Lotman.

It is, in fact, appropriate to inquire about the status of the borderline, which Tarasti has parallelly dealt with it seems, with that which was said by the semioticians of the Tartu school, particularly Yuri Lotman and whose mixture does not seem to him only credible in the semiotized context or during the semiotiziation but logically obliged. This leads to a redefinition of the uses and articulations of the silence. Just to take one example: *Pictures at an Exhibition* has been composed as separate pieces but whose limits – the territorial borderlines in the score – could be made fluent ad libitum in order to effectuate like the practice Schumann adopted by jumping in *Carneval* from one piece to another, a virtual transition, which is only able to economize the steps of the walker making promenads – it is sufficient – in their borderline one could say – that the one which Musorgsky supposes to keep in a precise moment in the hall of exposition of several canvases, stops there in order to let only the glance to promenade: the absence of a transition justifies the transition and Tarasti goes until to presume that this (almost) immobile minimalism has certainly enchanted Debussy, pioneer in the matter of 'modernism', i.e. precursor of the 'deworked work' (*oeuvre desoeuvré*) – *The Great Gate of Kiev* which is nothing but the end of the expositon because it closes it, 'almost penetrates into the listener, says Tarasti, preventing him from a promenade; all happens as if the composer would have wanted to directly paint a kind of sensual uniqueness, grasp alive in the moment in which realizes the mixture, almost miraculous, of the consciousness of the narrator with the object of his narration. The differences remain thus connected and joined until the performance of the piece – doubtless because they are put to a syncretism of a fusion, which they obtain if one refers to a Peircean analysis, to the formal play of deduction (Thirdness) synthesizing the previous operations of abduction (Firstness) and then induction (Secondness). (Let us leave this to the specialists for a closer distinction.)

Yet, one may ponder that all these operations only promote here the eloquent silences or signifying absences. When one of the most gifted disciples of Eero Tarasti, Richard Littlefield consecrated a part of his doctoral thesis to discern a methodological inventory of the frameworks which separate artworks (in general) from their contexts, but resorting rather to how a painting is 'protected' – or well sees its limits guaranteed –by its framing the principal objection to which he hurts concerns the relevance just of the 'silences' which animate (or rather admit its going forwards) the music. If what is involved are the internal silences – for instance, the tacet limited to one measure which occurs quickly beyond the work (or the sonorous canvas) of a famous aria by Verdi La *donna e mobile* the listener feels to be kept (practically and physically) to missing chain. . ..One can thus ask if the sudden suspension, absolutely unexpected, of any tonal or sonorous texture at the moment where harmonic signification, melodic, and rhythmic meaning of a passage would curve to attain its maximal degree of saturation (according to the term by Kofi Agawu), if this kind of stop, makes only the effect of an uppercut destined just to leave the listener a little bit 'groggy', what would be the same as to refuse from him 'the impression of having to do with a musically significant silence – What remains to him after all if not the dysphory of a simple interruption due to an incident in the course, when it is not – horrible dictum – due to a pure and simple accident? The ambiguity can only represent a momentary disturbance. . ... which one could even choose to ignore, according to the degree of subtlety which one allows to one's nerves. (And let us admit is this not the same what happens in the 'bis' a capo of a new couplet?) (Nietzsche, did he not speak about those spices which help to support sometimes the obsessions?)

The analysis of *Pictures at an Exhibition*, just like the beginning of the typology of silent 'frames' in Littlefield, refers, however, a little to the effect produced by the emergent part of an iceberg, if one compares them with the completely grandiose vision which Tarasti has expressed since 1994 in the true manifest of unbordered silence which his *Theory of Musical Semiotics* contains when he has stated that 'no one can claim to have reached the ultimate synthesis of all the sign processes which the nature of opera implies as a semiotic polydiscoursive and intertextual totality.' In his eyes, 'every opera performance depends entirely on the global effect which is produced by the plurality of semiotic systems of which no one is dominant: the receiver of an operatic utterance is there only to be confronted simultaneously tones, colours, speeches, and gestures. The first question, which one would suppose, the opera scholar would formulate, would be: what authorizes that the polydiscoursive totality would keep together to make an opera? A question which every producer of an opera performance has to answer personally, by the practice of his semiotic activity.

It is to confirm this vision of opera's complexity – but also in the line of several memorable analyses not only in Wagner but also of Sibelius (*Kullervo*) and Stravinsky (*Oedipus Rex*) which had for the first time drawn the attention on the rigour and conviction of the author of *Myth and Music* – which one should now reflect starting from the same interpretation of Tarasti of the *Je ne sais quois* of Jankélévitch and his philosophy of 'bad comprehension'. The fine word of this semiotics of misunderstanding and also of the analysis of the errors of intelligence, which had developed in 1957 at *Je ne sais quoi et le Presque rien*, resides according to Tarasti in the diagnostics of the suppression of the ostentative man, with which we share the everyday existence, to a syndrome of undecision: this syndrome that Jankélévitch has discerned here in the terms close to Heidegger which criticized as early as in 1927 the dictatorship of 'Man' (Das Man). At once reformulating his additional study of Jankélévitch in the pages which figure from here on in his *Existential Semiotics* of 2000, Tarasti can decisively constitute the essential problematic: We have arrived at one extreme proximity regarding the question which is situated in the ultimate core of semiotics, namely how to study significations which touch the field of nonquantifiable and nonobservable entities. Do we need to recall, here, the role which was played from Heidegger to Jankélévitch, the must, the obligation (to be applied to art like music) in an irresistible manner – to be freed from the terrorism of calculating thought? What Tarasti declares eloquently is that it is impossible to construct our silences, to habit them, to live them – and finally to semiotize them!

Yet, have we not, by this statement, closed our mouth by showing that it is one and same problematic, taken again and examined diversely but without remarkably deviating from its path, whereupon our behaviours should depend, 'in this time of anguish'? Should we identify Tarasti as a kind of universal inheritor of Jankélévitch? And to which extent the semiotics of Tarasti has to be recognized as an integral historic part of Jankélévitch? To our mind, answer to such questions is already included in the text of Existential Semiotics: the interpretation of Jankélévitch by Tarasti does not legitimize itself only because it gathers in one and same line the coherence of the authentic semiotics of silence, but because it reveals to us the genealogy even by taking there the semiotic master to whom Tarasti has remained faithful, Greimas. . ..such an answer needs, of course, some clarification. All depends, we can say, on the reference to the borrowing of Greimas from positive science, the chemistry, of the notion of **isotopy** which he used sure as a metaphor but loading it 'on the most profound level of his whole positivist system'. Although it was, according to Tarasti, 'inaccessible to an experimental observation since only those persons provided with the relevant competence were able to recognize it'. Namely one has to insist on the inaccessibility and this ability to identify it.

These two characteristics play, in fact, an essential role – what Eero Tarasti specifies immediately – by putting us to our everyday life, that is our daily existence, yet of the normal life. . . .. The belief which, manifest in this speech of Tarasti, is not only simple trust in the place of such and such interventor, judged subjectively by circumstantial aptitudes, momentary, to resolve such difficulty, to interpret the score. . . ..It is rather more deeply the certainty to communicate with the one who catches the silence, certain among us who are listening, for others not. Only the first ones have to be recruited. Should one here complain unsupportable elitism? However, the reality is otherwise subtle! The hermeneutic sensibility of silence is, by no means, 'the better-shared thing'. Or still, as it has been said by John Cage 'the ear alone is not a being'. Even worse for Descartes.

Let us agree: once the line has been drawn about the semiotics of silence, far away to be a futile line, it will pass from Jankelevitch to Tarasti, via Greimas. Yet, we have to convene also about the right to priority which incontestably returns to Jankelevitch. Since what we have to recall now is that the thought of the latter remains incomparable, since the moment when what is involved is to justify what all the hermeneutics of Tarasti gives us in advance. To take only one simple example, let us report about the admirable analysis of the 'case of Satie' in the last pages of *Satie et le Matin*. It reveals to us what Jankélévitch calls 'the ridiculous paradox, of the music of 'ameublement', namely a paradoxology, which deprives music of its sacrosaint souveraintiy, which cannot be but the demand, beyond all pretentious musicolatry, of a truth which is more profound and secret. . . .. the art of Satie is yet well the esoteric art. Here, the sacred truth, the saint truth to be remembered, in the time when whoever can classify Satie as 'unbalanced artist'. His music pursues without disturbance and Jankélévitch chose his friends, in order, to discourage important persons and conformist frivolity; it conceals 'a mystery in the great day, meridian mystery, which is occult in midnight mystery.' Now, what is this mystery? "The benevolent night which is the seventh night nocturnal of Requiem. . .and Paradise of the melody of the Eva, which is the first morning of the world, are perhaps only one and same night."

Would one judge this example as too esoteric? Perhaps contrarily the evidence he gives us is too direct. Let us make justice to Jankélévitch who never plays with words but always returns – this was the expression of Schönberg, indicating the return to sources – to the first experience, which before 'the eternalisation' of the language lets the time be. It is remarkable in this respect that the scheme which always looms behind the argumentation is always the 'plastic' principle i.e. not only in synchrony but in diachrony. It is the issue which was developed in the IX chapter of *Philosophie premiere*, and particularly its third section, *Le Faire-être se fait lui-meme* (The doing/being makes itself) which refers to Jacob Boehme by its striking formulas, and to the master of Jankélévitch, namely Henri

Bergson, according to whom the absolute is not a thing but duration, freedom and life. The Absolute is nothing at all, it is a creative light...From divine creator, transcendent, it is allowed to pass to the immanent creation – of which one does not know that it is human all too human but which has the advantage to be with us concretely and to bring us, without turns, to the fest on our level. By making us – once – to profit from it.

Selected references

Jankélévitch, Vladimir. 1953. *Philosophie première: introduction à une philosophie du presque.* Paris: Presses Universitaires de France.
Jankélévitch, Vladimir. 1958. *Le je-ne-sais-quoi et le persque-rien.* Paris: Presses Universitaires de France.
Jankélévitch, Vladimir. 1961. *La musique et l'ineffable.* Paris: Colin.
Tarasti, Eero. 1979. *Myth and Music.* The Hague: Mouton.
Tarasti, Eero. 1994. *A Theory of Musical Semiotics.* Bloomington: Indiana University Press.
Tarasti, Eero. 2000. *Existential Semiotics.* Bloomington (IN): Indiana Universiy Press.

Daniel Charles
Myth, music and postmodernity

Abstract: *Myth and music* by Eero Tarasti was immediately commented by international magazines when it appeared in 1979 as the second edition at Mouton. Yet, Tarasti's work has to be joined in the first place to the contemporary French and German intellectual field; thus he should be compared to works like *Arbeit und Mythos* by Hans Blumenberg and *La Condition postmoderne* by Jean-Francois Lyotard. However, the question is how to get rid of the myth and especially the idea of the 'last myth' in structuralism. Lévi-Strauss puts himself to the same category as Hegel. He asked whether the myth studies are science or philosophy. Eero Tarasti in his work from 1979 might have been under influence of the French Robert Jaulin from 1974. Tarasti's approach is related to the three phases of semiology: I, II and III. It maybe a kind of 'rustic structuralism' which term Michel Serres has proposed. The role of Greimas is simply to observe how lived experience can be articulated by *Sémantique structurale*. There are metastories behind the whole study of *Myth and Music*, such as Kullervo, borrowed from Kalevala, by Sibelius and Gallén-Kallela. One can here speak of music of concepts. At the end, at least, appears the paradigm of Lucien Lévy-Bruhl, Lévi-Strauss and Robert Jaulin, which seem to constitute the proper paradigm of Tarasti' s *Myth and music*.

Keywords: myth, music, postmodern, Lèvi-Strauss, Hegel, semiology

Normally, the deontology of a historian immediately makes him replace the events in the context of their own to optimize the intelligibility.[1] Yet, it occurs that the pedagogical zeal mixes the cards without distributing them. Accordingly, all are endarkened instead of being elucidated and the reader risks to get asphyxiated. Carl Dahlhaus told to have undergone this disaster when he consulted the appendix (yet provided with good intentions) that the American musicologist Donald Jay Grout had consecrated to prepare a chronological inventory of outstanding facts of Western art music history. For instance, in the year 1843, he had mentioned *The Flying Dutchman* – alongside *Don Pasquale* by Donizetti and *The Fear and Trembling* by Kierkegaard. What is the subtle analogy, among these three woks (and their three authors), that he had to appreciate? Not less enigmatic appeared in 1843 the juxtaposition of *Les Préludes* of Liszt, *Tannhäuser* and *Comte de Monte Cristo*;

---

[1] Published originally as chapter 3 in *La fiction de la postmodernité selon l'esprit de la musique*, Paris: Presses Univesitaires de France, Thémis/Philosophie, 2001, p. 77–98. Translated by Eero Tarasti reprinted by the permission of PUF.

or in 1852 the *House of Uncle Tom* and the revolution of Louis-Napoleon Bonaparte, and 1853 saw also the *Traviata* and the War of Crime! The music, of course, is not alone. Is this the reason to measure it with literature or even with politics?

Now, let us change the century and the register. The year 1979 saw the appearance of three equally important works (to judge it by the interest they have arisen although for different domains and distinct publics) and which twenty years afterwards, like in *Monte Cristo,* mark not only their age but our period mutually clarifying each other: *Myth and Music* by the Finnish Eero Tarasti; *Arbeit am Mythos* by the German Hans Blumenberg; and by Jean-Francois Lyotard *La condition postmoderne*. it may seem paradoxale to regroup them by the pretext of their chronology. The lightning of a new Dahlhaus lurk us. By merely looking at their titles one would be right in doubting the ground for such a comparison. It is true: when the work by Tarasti pretends to be apparently propedeutic for the instauration of general semiotics of music, 'the work on myth', such as conceived by Blumenberg, presents it as a treatise on 'philosophical anthropology' and the report by Lyotard whose scantiness is eloquent has the air of a simple manifest, too concise, too cleaned in order to offer other than a rapid memorandum concerning the 'affairs in course' – although it has been edited explicitly for *ad usum delphini.* Here, one can add to be clear that to define the postmodernity as a 'doubt about metastories', it depends on poststructuralist problematic, the metastories being not at all myths in the sense (structuralist following Lévi-Strauss) of Tarasti, once Lyotard and Tarasti have turned their backs to each other the position of Blumenberg about modernity will appear original if it is true as Robert M. Wallace has vigorously shown that it situates in the halfway of the methodological requirements of Gadamerian hermeneutics and Habermassian critics. At first sight, nothing justifies substantial vicinity among the three authors.

Yet, should one maintain their divergences? This depends on the manner one orients the debate. If one chooses to centre all on the problematic of the relationship between myth and music, the analyses of Tarasti, it is clear that the elaborations of Blumenberg complete them: to put in music grand myths does not constitute in the perspective of Blumenberg but an aspect of a 'work of elaboration' (*Arbeit*), whereby the logos is perpetually present to exorcise our anguish in front of the real; but symmetrically the question, 'for what do have myths?' if it conducts Blumenberg to grandiose developments concerning the literature, it does not approach music but indirectly – in the respect of its limits or prolongations – and does not interest the Tarastian research but partially.

However, it is worthwhile to examine more closely this 'musical' part of the Blumenbergian inquiry: as one will see, the light he projects on the enterprise of Tarasti reveals to be uniquely subtle. It obliges the semiotic research not to be satisfied by historical framing where it had chosen to be interwoven at the beginning and incites it to enlarge by interrogating its presuppositions and even its goals. In the eyes of Blumenberg, when a composer like Henri Pousseur feels forced to collaborate with a writer, Michel Butor, to start an opera project (*Our Faust*) following a fundamental myth (in the side of Paul Valery's *My Faust*) 'the epigenesis' to which it abandons itself poses the delicate problem of the 'last myth': what is sought for is the determination of the version or ultimate transposition from which it becomes impossible to keep the conviction to have exhausted the potentialities of a given myth. Nevertheless, so that the end of one myth would be the end of all myths, here we have the real problem; when it conceals itself this problem makes the intrigue reappear, and take advantage of literature or the music or their combination. Lessing, for instance, said 'to wait' to publish 'his' *Faust* so that his two competitors would have left; such an attitude is revealing. In fact, from here on, the myth is interpreted as a 'strategy' destined to heal the supreme illness i.e. illness of the origins, in which inconsolidate occurrence the perplex which mankind experiences with its inaptitude to swallow 'real absolutism', and state the disappearance of this myth which corresponds to recognize the success of this strategy. However, equivalent success is only a border idea, and ostinato of the creativity nourishes this imperfection. To refuse to wait, to economize the refusal of Lessing, such is the destiny of the stressed people. As one needs a solid amount of immaturity to steal in this domain to gain victory! It is this immaturity which the idealists prove to have: they congratulate too early to have the situation in their hands and own hands. In reality, their philosophy lets the target go like a shadow. Some Valery, some Gide, some Kafka prove to be suspects. Their work should surely be the 'last one': if this were true all the myths would be annulated.

Furthermore, it is not easy to get rid of the myth: if the 'end of the art' is not enough, nor is the 'death of the god'. "Only a God could come to save us", said Heidegger to *Spiegel*, to which one of his pupils, Heribert Boeder has found (not bad) the answer: "But did the God not arrive yet?" One understands that the last lines of *Arbeit am Mythos* evoking the end – enigmatic – of Kafka's *Prometheus*, make us descend in doubt. "What could be there after all if there would still remain something to be added?" "After all" renders 'all' and 'the all' in question. That is it has been stressed.

To dream, precisely, to have finished once for all with the myth, is it not the small sin of A*ufklärung*? Finally, in asking which variations the 'last myth' would still be able to go through, Blumenberg has not dreamt certainly of the musical form of variation. But Eero Tarasti, coming to play with Lévi-Straussian baton, i.e. resorting to the demand of scientificity which the structural anthropology calls, does not join only the methodology (following Saussure) which his mentor has forged, he diversifies maximally his angles of attack to take into account the multidimensional complexity of the corpus to be studied. This eclecticism which, at first sight, hurts the monolithism of the Blumenbergian building will permit him to avoid just the major objection which one may settle, in the name of the aporia of the 'last myth', to the history of philosophy which is implied in structuralism, i.e. more generally to *Aufklärung*.

The text of the *L'Homme nu*, in which Tarasti, at least in the first time, seems to have confidence is formal: it subscribes a rigorously systematic conception of reason, Lévi-Strauss has endeavoured to traverse integrally the universe of myth. Also, this closure of history is blocked. It would be false to imagine "that a completely new interpretation of myth, to start with ours, would take its place in the series of already known variants of this myth. . .one is therefore closed in a circle every form being as much saturated by a content emerging infinitely so that it would have lead to another form? From the previous results that contrarily the criterion of structural interpretation avoids this paradox because it only knows to account at the same time as itself and the others. Because as far as it consists in making explicit a relational system which other variants only embodied, it integrated them into it and on a new level where operates the ground and the form, and which is thus no longer susceptible for new incarnations. Revealed for itself the structure of a myth puts a terminal to its accomplishments." As one can see, Lèvi-Strauss does not hesitate to put himself in the shoes of Hegel; as one has to do, he omits to mention it because some pages further away the hours have sounded for a small satisfaction: "Far away from abolishing the sense, my analysis of myths of a group of American tribes has taken the advantage of sense that there are not in the common places to which they could be reduced, since some one thousand five hundred years reflections of philosophers on mythology, except by Plutarkhos."

This theft from Hegel, is it destined to make a change to persuade the reader that he has to do with 'science' and not of 'philosophy'? Is it always so that Lévi-Strauss retakes the operation at the moment when the music is called to help. But from myth to music, it is proper that transition is made at the same sweetness (Hegelianism obliges: *Aufhebung* has to take place rather for an alternation than for a passing-by; one would utilize maximally the dialectics in the way to make subtle all the traces of philosophy) and according to the canon structural interpretation (the model to be followed is supposed to authorize the 'fusion' – the free changeability and permutability – of the basis – the sense – and the form – the sign.; phonology has shown it altogether)- The fact that music could thus serve the scientific aspiration of myths, this supposes consequently and in conformity with the imperatives which have been enumerated. At the same time, a historic closure and semantic joining in the two domains. This has been enunciated in terms: "the myths are only translatable one to the other in the same way as a melody is not translatable but into another melody which preserves with it the relations of homology.....but if one can always and practically infinitely translate one melody to another melody, one music to another music, just like in the case of mythology one can translate, one may translate the music into something else than itself, without falling in the trap of hermeneutic pretension of old mythography and too often of musical criticism. Accordingly, liberty without limits of translation in the dialects of an original language forming the basic universe is similar to the impossibility radical of any transposition into an external language. "Anyway, the lock is locked, the removal has been done: once the dress of another age has been eliminated both for myth and music, the 'external languages', there remains only the task to formulate the working hypothesis susceptible to fit the 'structural field'. Accepting the copresence of myths and music and their bipolarization between 'mathematical entities' and 'natural languages' Lévi-Strauss suggests a crosstype, bipolarization to develop it into a square: "Let us suppose that mathematical structures are all at the same time applicable to sound and sense; and that linguistic structures materialize contrarily their union. Less completely incarnated than the second ones but with better than the first ones the musical structures are situated in the side of sound (without sense) and mythical structures at the side of sense (without sound).

As it has been observed by Robert Jaulin this makes an enigma:

Qui a du son et du sens
pas de son et pas de sens
du son et pas de sens
pas de son et du sens

Only this presentation demystifies at once the enterprise whose artificial effort has something childish. And Robert Jaulin can reveal the key. "The sense like the sound cannot be pertinent by themselves as 'sense' and 'sound'; the fact that the sense and the sound can or not exist *stricto sensu* is a minor problem; what they can say and what is proper we suppose them say, are the structures whereby they unfold and which underly them. It is comical that the chief structuralist Claude Lévi-Strauss would have literally taken the sound and sense, has emptied them, reduced into words and then has imagined from this to explain or provide the smallest information on the phenomena such as music, myth, mathematics and natural languages."

In 1977, was Eero Tarasti aware of the commentary of Robert Jaulin from 1974, when he was editing his book? His bibliography, although immense, does not make any mention of it. It is always so that the extreme worry whereby immediately after the citation, he marks, at the same time, his doubt and distance as to the author of *Mythologiques*, referring to the ambiguity of the English word of 'challenge', this worry does not diminish in the course of the pages. It would have been inconceivable that research done under auspices of Greimas (whose pupil Tarasti became precisely from 1974) would have favoured openly the thought which Greimas himself (let us think of his remake of Lévi-Straussian quadrilaterality if not the 'semiotic square') employed to enlarge the perspectives and to sweep away the simplicities. Moreover, on such a topic and, at the same time, the Lévi-Straussian camp was perfectly invincible; if the things have changed it is Eero Tarasti who has caused it. But it all happens as if *Myth and Music* instead of anchoring into the monoideist temptation of clean formalization, would have started to renew the concrete i.e. first with multiple or rather more exactly with the plurality. The choice of analyzed scores testifies for it, although it has been focused on last two centuries: far afield from falling into stereotypes, the author explores the places less frequently visited to start with *Oedipus Rex* of Stravinsky and *Kullervo* by Sibelius, which have the right at the end of the work together with *Siegfried* of Wagner for special treatment (150 pages); around these key works, several pieces less directly linked by the same composers make the object of the partial analyses but also decisive. The work by Liszt is equally given a priority; but neither are Berlioz, Glinka, Smetana and Rimsky-Korsakov forgotten. In the end, a galaxy of diverse musicians from Beethoven and Brahms to Schubert and Schumann, with almost unknown composers like Kajanus, Launis, Salmenhaara, notwithstanding the South American ones whose specialist Eero Tarasti is (Villa-Lobos just like ethnographic scores gathered in the field). One could, without doubt, express regarding *Bolero* of Ravel whose at least discutable analysis by Lévi-Strauss mentioned several times, a certain indulgence beyond the season; yet, the comparison with the *Leningrad symphony* of Shostakovitch suddenly opens an unpredictable perspective.

We have insisted on the variable character, not to say bright, of musical illustrations proposed by Tarasti. For him, only such a choice is synonymous to liberty. If Messiaen were present in a substantial manner just like Satie and Milhaud or Poulenc, but if the Viennese school does not figure there but in a homeopathic way with only *Wozzeck* by Berg and *Erwartung* by Schönberg, well this reveals not only the tastes of the author – which surely should not be intervened but the cogency of the theses he defends. The procedure radically differs from the one by Levi-Strauss because *the semiotics which Tarasti aspires does not consist in formalization of the lived but in a pragmaticism* in which, following the word by Herman Parret, the reasonability is more important than logos excluding the pathos – which requires the omission of any totalisatory model of structuralist type, i.e. recognizing only the immanence of the sense. In the horizon of the problematic, one can already point out phenomena which he designates twenty years later with the expression of 'existential semiotics'. Far away from pretending to reduce the complexity of the confrontation of myth and music by exhibiting an algorithm obtained by hypotethico-deductive manner *Myth and Music* attacks, in the first place, at the lability of diverse contextualisations what are involved in apprehending in *statu nascendi* and *hic et nunc*, rather than *urbi et orbi*. Certainly, Lévi-Strauss had opened the route – but had he lost his sense?

In order to avoid forgetting this, Tarasti does not approach it by four avenues but by one hundred, or even thousand! Leaning only on Lévi-Strauss, one does not make justice to the tempting aspect of gigantic theoretical patchwork to which the whole first part of the work has been dedicated, because successive references to Jakobson and Vladimir Propp or still to Andre Jolles and theoreticians of Tartu school, constitute in the *Myth and Music* momentary scaffolds and so to be cut out or not at will. This attitude authorizes quick looks and abrupt returns dictated by the material, contextualized, adjusted better to local needs – as if everyone of the scores considered or almost every fragment would be justifiable of a special treatment sui generis, accounting its proper particularities. Such methodological variations allowed only to be seen at Greimas; their width at his faithful disciple could disturb some of his commentators, surprised by the apparent flow of certain taxonomies. Accordingly, the numbering of the 'semes' would become suspect because the 'isotopies' have been blended there. Yet, to reproach the author on the theoretical level does not object, but when one applies it to a précis musical text, which would effectively reveal a rebel against the presumed violation. In his *Essai d'une philosophie du style*, Gilles-Gaston Granger had already pondered this problem and his conclusions arrived at doubting the suggestion by Greimas of a 'structural semantics' based upon the metaphor of 'chemistry of sense', which would apply at 'meaning effects' the classification of isotope groups elaborated from the diagram of Mendeleiev. Following Granger, the error of Greimas stemmed from the fact that signification depended less on the structure of language system, hence from the laws of phonology or syntax, but from a 'schematisation' aspiring to 'transform the lived into an object structure', from the laws of stylistics. In these conditions, a lexique could not be made as to the result of an abstract planification but depended on particular seriations according to which our lived experiences articulate: from here emerged the idea of 'open plurality of simultaneous organizations of sense', plurality responsible of the uncertainties, double uses which one can distinguish already at Aristotle albeit one would be only little interested in the stratigraphy of lexical groupings of which he is accustomed.

Is it an effect of *Zeitgeist*, of this spirit of the time which – perhaps – makes us find identical thought at separated individuals because they ignore each other but their period gathers them? Is it always so that Tarasti, if we believe in his bibliography, had not read during writing the *Myth and Music*, neither Jaulin nor Grange? Nevertheless, his *fellow conspiracy with the second one obliges us to reflect upon the conspiracy of the second with the first one. As* what is involved in one and the other – and by the Zeitgeist in between at Tarasti – reminds of the 'stratigraphy' (or if one prefers 'transcendental geology' following the expression of Merleau-Ponty) which comes to question. One has seen it with Jaulin: purely formal elaboration on myth (to criticize it or not) will, in any case, give place to a structural inquiry proper, which is said to be 'underlying' the literality of the distinction of sound and sense. Since Granger, who is not less worried to reorganize the semiological field, distinguishes in *Essai d'une philosophie du style*, three levels or stages of the 'lived' to which he makes three distinct semiologists to correspond, namely sémiology I which deals with 'internal functioning of formal systems as far as they virtually refer to the experiences'; a semiology no. II: thematizing 'the activity of constitution even of signifying systems starting from the 'lived'; and finally semiology III which 'does not construct structures but tries to analyze the interpretants of a symbolism'.

In the view of Granger, the semiology I would correspond to the entire formalization on which Lévi-Strauss wished to found his system or to the 'semantic' dream of Greimas imitating Lévi-Strauss and copying Mendeleiev. Yet, neither this nor that have not been established in this level which would be the one where the myths 'think by themselves'; Greimas, who realized this, returned to semiology II and Lévi-Strauss doubtless to avoid to recognize it, declared himself entitled to Absolute Knowledge(i.e. Grand Matheme platonic) – which meant reconquering the field of philosophy.

How did one come here? By forging a joined history of myth and music, so that the return to a quarternary image does not seem too displaced. It would not be but a history 'of order' and measures: it would be sufficient to judge it probable. By arguing that permutational bricolage of structures – which Clement Rosset has been able to do by calling Michel Serres as 'rustic structuralism' – existed in music beginning from Flamish counterpoint in the 15th century, finding itself already 'fully constituted in the myths' one gave thus a route to semiology I (what could be more mathematical than counterpoint?) by letting behind itself the impure mixture (semi-material and semi-formal) of semiology II.

For Lévi-Strauss, semiology or real semiotics could not appear but in the name of dialectic turn dictated by the scenario of the death of myth, being clear that this death which did not signify simple disappearance of this myth but its transfugration or resurrection, its *Aufhebung* did take place but when its heritage was liquidated: "With the invention of the fugue and other modes of composition the music assumes the structures of mythical thought at the moment when the literary story, the mythical become novelistic, empties them. It had to go so that myth dies as such so that its form would escape like a soul leaving the body, and went to demand of music a means for its reincarnation." From here stems that statement a la Malraux: "When the myth dies the music becomes mythical in the same manner the art works when the religion dies to finish to be simply beautiful and become sacred." Does this mean, however, that historically it is the music which has the last word? Yet, music precisely is not an affair of words and history is not terminated when the sharing of myth and music takes place in a novel, i.e. between sound and sense. The music is, however, kept following this to finish or simply make a closure. Lévi-Strauss, from whom we know his criticism against contemporary music, it is just what happens in our time. By collapsing the music liberates the mythical structures which it had recollected and this emancipation with the final value it effectuates "so that under the form of a discourse on itself the myth evades finally for the consciousness of oneself." The teleology certainly reaches its goal by recognition of the primary place of literature. Yet, it would mean to restart the conflict between sound and sense than to pretend them.

Contrarily one has to resolve this tension by dialecticizing it successfully. In this ultimate point, let us allow the speech to the superb commentary of Jean Greisch: "Those who are familiar with *Phenomenologie des Geistes* and Hegelian logic recognize here if not the voice then at least the music of Concept, and understand by which necessity the composer-author of *Mythologiques* gives to his work the form of a musical composition."

One understands that Eero Tarasti was inspired by the grandiloquence and its simulacra announcing since the declaration of intentions, whereby, opens *Myth and Music*, his willingness not to distanciate from semiology II, i.e. not to search to join himself to the semiology I. In reverse and consequently nothing prevents from doing an inquiry on the axis of semiology II and semiology III. Let us translate: once given up the dream of universal code susceptible to give a reason, at the same time, to myth music and their interaction, and what too apparently legitimates the Hegelian mode of knowing of absolute knowledge so that it would not seem to be suspect, the structuralist procedure consists well in the methodic comparison between the two domains, aiming to detach the isomorphisms but with resorting to any privilege of the idea of progress. From one work to another as well as from one myth to another the time being certainly very fast, whereas the sense is not like that, at least according to the acceptance of a 'unique sense' which would be the 'sense of history' – and neither as there is no 'progress' of mythos into logos, as pretend the adherents of *Aufklärung*. We said above that semiology II admitted a relative impurity; it is clear for Tarasti, *that there is no pure myth nor the pure knowing of any myth*. For him, as for Michel Serres, the rationality is to detach the real precisely because it would not know to constitute its ground. The fact that this ground by itself will not be completely inaccessible legitimizes semiology II i.e. the science of signs not submitted to the obligation of elaborate structures. The role of history is no longer that one to assimilate the certainty of all risks, the part of contingency and accidents finish to be passed under silence and hermeneutics finds again its requirements – with dignity, which Lévi-Strauss denied from it, anxious as he was not to leave his subjectivity to appear.

We only need the methodological effort to provide and put in play amidst the delicate problem to have to maintain the balance between two modes of approach which design semiology II and semiology III, namely an objectifying search and a non-objectifying (which does not necessarily mean subjectivating). It is just this where Tarasti employs with an indefatigable virtuosity in *Myth and music*, but it is also that which allows him to exceed lévistraussian ambitus, in the case of double closing joining the musical in that which we called above the function make-valid of myth. In this respect, the use of such a category as – borrowed from Juri Lotman and the Tartu school – of 'orientation towards the mythical' is instructive. The subordination of music to a text is there clearly announced like black on the white. It determines as one expects, the choice of themes, Orpheus or Oedipus, the archaism of the means, medieval modes or folkloristic melodies, the invention of genres, *Gesamtkunstwerk* or symphonic poem and until instrumental economy. Yet, it answers at the same time to the demand as a historical and geographical line of differentiation of the belongings – a hermeneutic criterion – called to temper the automatisms to which all exclusively structural research is doomed. Nothing more legitime because one avoids by speculative inflation and hyperbolic gliding of rationality. Nevertheless, the structuralism starts to break into pieces. Like in the *Pendulum* music by Steve Reich where the initial impulse is enacted so that it progressively mitigates until the moment when one would be tempted to take as an autoannulation freely admitted the structural mechanism cannot grasp – and this brings all its pertinence to *Myth and Music*: an unexpected dynamics makes an appearance there which one should not underestimate.

This is what all the time effectuating in favour of myth which does not need but to accompany itself, altogether by music, the encounter of myth and music is far afield to leave myth untouched and assigns to it one embodiment which obliges to develop it. The putting into the music of *Kullervo is* will be accomplished by the internal auto communication (Gasparov) whereby the composer combines with a Wagnerian idiom such a legend from *Kalevala*, and this appears as transformed after the operation. And symmetrically the 'style' of Sibelius will never be the same. However, the semiotician does not hear it exactly by these ears. For him, the utilized narrative structure before any mixage depends on a distributive grammar common to all the myths, and whose empire exercises in a discreting manner the user dictating to him not only the mode of reading to be adopted but the transformational procedure to be followed so that the mayonnaise would be ready with a sense and taste needed. Also, the music is put in the same mold – mutatis mutandis.

However, one grain of sand risks the functioning 'parthenogenesis' of the orthodoxy. If a story, in order to be listened to and understood, has to gather previously the acceptance of the group of users, the identity of mythos and logs is only a fake, a simple rhetoric effect destined to polish the asperities to silence any difference, any particularity which would risk damaging the dominant homogeneity. Provide the myths by linguist/ethnologist situated in between leads to promote their readability. But to pay its debt of a 'pacificating' mission whose benefit would be earned by the one who commanded it, makes one commit to risk to transform the differences into différends. What guarantee could one demand of a colonizer, who desires hypothetically to mummify the culture of those whom it exploits to dominate them better? To treat a myth by the rules of 'art'; that is just the suspect type of activity in the eyes of the colonized jealous of his independence! Could the structuralist reduction of sense to sign be, however, wrongly interpreted? A communicative pragmatism like that of Haberman or Apel estimates to be able to bring into consensus, i.e. to a principle of autoreflexivity to reasonably found the objectivity of the research and dissipate the misunderstandings stemming from a discutable choice of criteria. One should resolve the conflicts by only resorting to argumentation and discussion in the eggs before they explode: if the myths achieved one great day sharpness of logics which structures them, the fights would finish in the lack of fighters! To such a rescue effort which attempts to get rid of the culpability of the modernity by reinstituting here their lost communicational virginity, how not to object that it falls in the aporia of Blumenberg of the 'last myth'? Since the totality, its sketches would forgive the 'work of myth' but by detotalizing it and by paying the customs of its totalitarianism, its inconditional joining to the discursivity and finally to the Concept.

One returns to Hegel and the 'negative work', to the vector in the Course on Aesthetics, from the so-called 'death of art' (but which is not dying but inside the system); in this regard, Eliane Escoubas makes negative use valid; the science of art, he writes, can be constituted only when the art is a 'revolted thing', 'thing of the past'. Why? Hegel says: "The past belongs only to the memory, and the memory proceeds already itself from the actions of persons, events and activities in the dressing of the universality, through which the external and contingent individual particularities do not appear." Therefore, 'the really serious' to which Hegel wants to guide us, remains in the art, or rather to the science of art? What does remain from art in the science of art? In the same way, we saw, Blumenberg by showing that if the idea of the death of myth is itself another myth, the reduction of myth to the tautological discursivity a la Schelling is not tenable, yet, Blumenberg cuts the herb under the foot of Hegel and Habermas to prepare the way to allegory and metaphor, i.e. to the creativity of myth, which he calls navigation vitae, the sailing of life.

We are now better prepared to understand the opening which by music Eero Tarasti tries to operate. His approach leads him to the gate of the third key work evoked at the beginning, *La condition postmoderne* by Jean-Francois Lyotard; even when the discussed questions and used methods are radically different, sudden convergences make one reflect what could we put to the package of contemporary problematic of relationship myth/music, since the modernity, the third term, gets there 'tested'.

Let us take the explanation Tarasti proposed to the symphony of *Kullervo*. There is a strong affinity to the speech of Kalevala; however, the analysis dissolves immediately into a network of hypotexts and metatexts embedded there whose complexity oversaturates the myth. When in the 19th century, Carelie was elevated to the ranks of the flag of Finnish nationalist culture, there was no art in Finland except the one by local customs, which educating their users had appreciated as exotic, and be measured with diverse cultural or regional levels, or supranational taken as models which served for the elaboration of new syncretisms because each had its meaning on its level. The belonging of painter like Gallen-Kallela, dramaturg like Erkko or poet like Eino Leino, to the 'spirit' of the renovation of Carelian culture, is synonymous to selective assumption not only of dominant archaisms but of the constraints of their rewriting. Nothing is astonishing, yet, that which Tarasti joins with a Benedictian zeal to clarify the carnelian issue, underlines its profoundly ambiguous character. Does he not, by that, join to certain aspects of the 'postmodernity' a la Lyotard?

The idea may seem to be paradoxical: it exploits the chronology. The 'metastories' which Lyotard finds in Requiem are situated on a different level than Kalevala, even separated from the procession of 'metatexts'. Nevertheless, one has to admit that 'postmodenity' is indebted to its prefix to be superlative of the 'modernity'; since what else could he superlative mean than just the conative movement of modernization? And as a partisan of the romantic doctrine in the awakening of nationalities, like Zachris Topelius or before Busoni, the master of Sibelius, Martin Wegelius, the modernity is an ideal to be realized and this realization would accomplish only by auction; what motivates it is the conviction that the Finns should not be less modern than their neighbours. In any case, the description of the 'social tie' which proposed at the 5th chapter of *La condition postmoderne* is well echoing the Tarastian preoccupations which the first

carnelians touched in *Kullervo* symphony. The decomposition of great stories to which we assist could be done according to Lyotard but by the 'atomisation' of subject thrown into an absurd Brownian movement which such a sociologist like Baudrillard thought to be able to anticipate. Contrarily as little as one can get freed from the 'paradisiac representation of a lost 'organic' society, the subject appears eminently sociabilized...

One has evidently recognized three names to which we make here allusion – let them be respectively Lucien Levy-Bruhl (at least, the one of La mentalité primitive), Claude Lévi-Strauss, and Robert Jaulin. What is involved are three temptations of possible impact upon *Myth and Music* by Eero Tarasti... in this conspiracy there is nothing surprising, the fact that his choice has been imposed at the same time to our two authors (with the reserve that we mentioned concerning Jaulin, not cited by Tarasti) what could be more natural...Quite exactly, the Lyotardian procedure has to be pout in parallel with that of Tarasti, for which it constitutes an eloquent counterexample. Since the Tarastian project situates into the prolongation if the study of Charles Boiles, on the substitution of musical to the mythical in the ritual texts of Tepehua Indians (1973) in an exactly same manner as Lyotard proceeds to join his *Dit des vrais hommes*, put together in 1977 by André-Marcel d'Ans, and in which opens the same problematic although in a different corpus by transcription of 60 stories fairy tales and legends of the oral tradition of Cahinahua Indians. One should not put on the same level the work by Boiles with its enormous erudition ... ..not more than one could risk abolishing the musicological perspective of Eero Tarasti and a philosophical approach like at Jean-Francois Lyotard. Nevertheless, one has to remember that Tarasti, well before reading Boiles, attempted to translate into Finnish *Sein und Zeit*: and that, at the same age, Lyotard followed the courses of Jean Beaufret in the Lyceum Condorcé. Were they not predisposed – each on his side and manner – by a certain spiritual attitude to scrutinize the secrets which Mikel Dufrenne studied in the line of Levy-Bruhl and Karl Kerenyi, under the denomination of 'primitive mentality'?

No metastories yet but utilization of microstories, that is here which ritual protomusic offers based on which emerge the myths of more extension as forms of *Gestaltpsychologie* which are distinguished from a supposed indeterminate ground, but whose analysis can be done with an exactness: from this principle, image derives the Tarastian conception of musical narrativity such as it is profiled in *Myth and Music*. In the forthcoming magnum opus, A *Theory of Musical Semiotics* of 1994, Eero Tarasti, joining Greimas to Propp, furnishes a more elaborated version of this theory by pushing forwards the idea of 'stratigraphique' narratology.

References

Blumenberg, Hans. 1979. *Arbeit am Mythos*. Frankfurt am Main: Suhrkamp.
Boiles, Charles. 1973. Les chants instrumentaux des Tepehuas. *Musique en jeu* 12. 81–99.
Granger, Clive William J. 1968. *Essai d'une phlosophie du style*. Paris: Colin.
Levi-Strauss, Claude. 1971. *L'homme nu* (Mythologiques 4). Paris: Plon.
Lyotard, Jean-François. 1979. *La condition postmoderne*. Paris: Les Éditions de Minuit.
Tarasti, Eero. 1979. *Myth and Music*. The Hague: Mouton.

Ramūnas Motiekaitis
XX century philosophical paradigms of Japan and the West: A view from Greimassian perspective

Abstract: According to Greimas, syntactic operations are purposeful and organized in logical sequences. Expanding this notion, in this article we are trying to reveal how fundamental existential choices or constructions of philosophical paradigms are also to certain degree purposeful, logical and based on fundamental grammar. Thus, even logic of identity challenging philosophical paradigms of Heidegger, Merleau-Ponty and Nishida, can to certain degree be explained invoking structural semiotic approach.

The middle of the semiotic square is not usually discussed in classical Greimassian semiotics, because the principle of non-contradiction is followed. However, at least from theoretical perspective we can consider the middle of the semiotic square as absolute contradiction of materms, in which polarities are neither identical nor different to each other. In the ambiguous unity and contradictory identity of polarities, that is manifested in philosophical concepts like *basho, ereignis* and *the third term*, we can see an opposition to the traditional Western logic of non-contradiction. It brings ideas of these philosophers close to East Asian paradigms of "preserving the totality" (Daoism, Buddhism). An article reveals, how this contradictory identity is manifested in philosophical considerations about subject-object relationship, temporality and definitions of fundamental existential modalities.

Keywords: Heidegger, Nishida, Merleau-Ponty, *ereignis, basho, the third term*

Are the methods of narrative analysis, developed by Greimas, still of interest in humanities?[1] Is it possible to apply them not only to literature, myths, and arts but to the philosophical discourses? If so, does this application reveal something particular and not function as an unnecessary supplement to phenomenological or hermeneutical analyses?

---

[1] Published originally in 2011 Ramunas Motiekatis: *Poetics of the Nameless Middle. Japan and the west in the Philosophy and Music of the Twentieth Century*, Acta Semiotica Fennica XL. Approaches to Musical Semiotics 14. Helsinki: Ineternational Semiotics Institute of Imatra/The Semiotic Society of Finland.

https://doi.org/10.1515/9783110789164-012

If philosophical discourses are possible only in narrative rendering, they can be also considered as myths or narratives. If constitutions of mind are inseparable from the linguistic dimension of articulation, natural language is indeed "a house of being". Accordingly, structural semiotic approach, in which language and sign systems are considered as a means of constituting "being", may help us to understand how philosophical paradigms are constructed and enable us to compare them. Semiotic reductions reveal a limited number of universal principles that are operating in several non-isomorphic discourses and, in this way, may help to understand aspects of philosophical narratives' "syntax".

According to Benveniste (1979: 224–225):

> "[s]ubjectivity", whether it is placed in phenomenology or in psychology, as one may wish, is only the emergence in the being of a fundamental property of language [. . .] Consciousness of self is only possible if it is experienced by contrast. I use I only when I am speaking to someone who will be a you in my address [. . .] It is in a dialectic reality that will incorporate the two terms and define them by mutual relationship that the linguistic basis of subjectivity is discovered.

Subject and object is the fundamental syntactic axis, representing the binary opposition as a basic human conceptual mode, seen in both textual and existential (thymic) space (cf. Greimas 1989a: 226, 231). Thus, from the perspective of semiotics, strategies of existence, concepts in philosophy, human states (modalities) or sensibilities in art are based on the same fundamental grammar and can be formally defined as certain value relationships attributed by an observing subject to objects being observed and manifested in diachronic processes of narrativity. Looking more broadly, human life itself could be considered as narrative or travel in a certain semio-system, with characteristic definitions of space, time, and action.

Deleuze and Guattari (1994: 65) suggest that "[b]eginning with Descartes, and then with Kant and Husserl, the cogito makes it possible to treat the plane of immanence as a field of consciousness." The Cartesian distinction, between *res extensa* and *res cogitans*, served as a starting point for the modern Western concepts of a subject, object, space, time, and corporeality. Structurally similar distinctions between consciousnesses with its cognitive network and *ding an sich* can be found in Kant and later German idealists' (Hegel, Fichte) substantialisations of consciousness as a centre of ontological totality.

Such a paradigm was seriously questioned in the phenomenological investigations of the end of the nineteenth century and twentieth century by James, Bergson, and partly by Husserl, then later by Heidegger and Merleau-Ponty. Reconsiderations of traditional Western values were also fundamental for the Kyoto School of Philosophy with Nishida as one of the most important initiators. Contemporary Japanese traditions of philosophy developed from adaptations of

Husserl's phenomenology, fundamental ideas from James and Heidegger, and orientations towards systematic thinking taken from German idealism. However, their axiological background was in East Asian philosophical paradigms, especially Buddhism.

The above-mentioned philosophers' phenomenological investigations of intentionality all reached similar conclusions, namely that intentional constitutions are inextricably connected with bodily modalities and objects. Thus, the ontological status of consciousness and self are reconsidered in similar ways. Nishida (2005: 210) questioned ideation as "the most fundamental characteristic of consciousness." For Heidegger (1989: 224), "first of all what is ownmost to self is not a property of extant man and only seemingly given with the *consciousness of the I*". For Merleau-Ponty (1962: 426), "[w]e must not treat the transcendental Ego as the true subject and the empirical self as its shadow or its wake." Since consciousness is always in complete operative belongingness to an object, boundaries of subject and object become unclear; consequently, the autonomy of consciousnesses and self is considered as hardly possible. Philosophers used different terms to name the sphere of subject-object totality, such as *basho* (Nishida), *ereignis* (Heidegger), flesh *(chair)* or the *third term (le troisiéme terme)* (Merleau-Ponty). These concepts have many points in common since they were constructed opposing the previous fundamental values of Western philosophy. In a nutshell – these are philosophies of radical conjunction and ambiguity in which traditional limits of subject and object are reconsidered. Accordingly, they have many aspects in common with East Asian ways of thinking.

The essence of traditional East Asian definitions of subject and object can be explained by invoking Nishida's concept of *basho* (場所). *Basho* (jap. place) is defined as "a structure of mutual revealment of self and world" (Nishida 1987a:17) and described as a concrete living space to which the human's body and intentionality belongs. The *basho* points, first of all, to inseparability and mutual dependence of external and internal, bodily and intentional, abstract and concrete, personal and social. Basho is considered as an initial realm from which subject as "noetic self-determination" (cf. Nishida 2005) emerges and to which it belongs.

Merleau-Ponty's theory of corporeality incorporated ideas from Husserl, Bergson, and Heidegger. Nishida's early concepts, though developed earlier than the *Phenomenology of Perception*, were not known to him. However, since both Nishida and Merleau-Ponty were strongly influenced by James's theories of radical empiricism, their concepts have many points in common. Thus, as with Nishida, for Merleau-Ponty, intentionality and the intentionally-defined self have no autonomous status; they belong to the sphere of objects. Instead of the ontological asymmetry, for Merleau-Ponty:

> Neither object nor subject is *posited*. In the primary field we have not a mosaic of qualities, but a total configuration which distributes functional values according to demands of the whole. (1962: 241)
>
> Perception and the perceived necessarily have the same existential modality, since perception is inseparable from the consciousness which it has, or rather is, of reaching the thing itself. (1962: 374)
>
> In so far as I am a consciousness, that is, in so far as something has meaning for me, I am neither here nor there; [. . .] I am in no way distinguishable from an "Other" consciousness. (1962: ix)

Subject and intentionality, as Merleau-Ponty's investigations show, are inseparable from the body that is always *"in-the-world."* Thus the noetic realm can never be completely pure and abstract; in any noetic constitution, there are always traces of objects and bodily modalities. Noetic constitutions change according to corporeal situations that in turn are brought into the sphere of objects through seeing, hearing, touch, and the arrival of various temporal horizons, where "our former movements are integrated into a fresh motor entity, the first visual data into a fresh sensory entity, our natural powers suddenly come together in a richer meaning [. . .]" (Merleau-Ponty 1962:153). In this way, a perceptual "'something' – is always in the middle of something else, it always forms part of a 'field'" (1962: 4).

On such a phenomenological basis, Merleau-Ponty considered "motility as basic intentionality" (1962: 137). As with Taoist examples of performative mastership (cf. Zhuangzi chapter 7) or Nishida's emphasis on "acting intuition" (行為的直観 *kōiteki chokkan*) which is "the deepest level of our self-consciousness" and "most concrete and immediate" (Nishida 2005: 193), for Merleau-Ponty "being-in-truth" is indistinguishable from "being in the world" (1962: 395). Accordingly, "[t]o understand is to experience the harmony between what we aim at and what is given, between the intention and the performance – and the body is our anchorage in a world" (1962: 144).

The unity of corporeal and mental is known as "the third term" (*le troisiéme terme*); its ontological status is ambiguous since it is neither body nor mind, but a certain organic and initial unity from which all the intentional acts as "thetic positions", or "positings" emerge (cf. Merleau-Ponty 1962: 242). As with Merleau-Ponty, for Nishida (2005: 206) "[the] intelligible self can be construed as the noetic plane of determination of the acting self, in the depths of which one finds the content of a deep profound life."

Following phenomenological presumptions of fundamental belongingness of subject and object, Nishida considered the absence of substantialized noetic self as the initial and most authentic modality of self. In the "absence" of self, belongingness to the object is most completely realized. Accordingly, the subject as "noetic determination" is transcended and the "true self" who "sees without a seer" is achieved. Instead of the substantialization of the "noetic self", Nishida defines initial consciousness as nothingness: "[F]or objects to be known by me they must be immanent in me; I must be the topos in which these things are situated. In this sense then I am utter nothingness with respect to things and merely reflect them" (Nishida 2005: 194).

Although Merleau-Ponty did not speak directly about nothingness, in his writings we can find similar illustrations of "seeing without seer": "[a] mind could not be captured by its own representations; it would rebel against this insertion into the visible which is essential to the seer" (Merleau-Ponty 1958: 139). Hence one cannot say that man sees because he is Mind, nor indeed that he is Mind because he sees: to see as a man sees and to be Mind are synonymous (Merleau-Ponty 1962: 137).

In such philosophical paradigms, instead of preserving a something permanent in a mind, the perception of things is, "assuredly not a process of passive reduplication of their sensuous affects in a mental substance, and is also not an apprehension of their ideal meanings for a mind; it is a captivation, in oneself, of their "manner of filling space and time", their sensible essence" (Lingis: 35).

The social aspect of *basho* or *the third term* is also considered by philosophers. For Merleau-Ponty, the social realm is an aspect of corporeality through which the substantiality of the individual is neutralized. Accordingly, "I" is defined as an "intersubjective field" in which "[T]he present mediates between the For Oneself and the For Others, between individuality and generality. True reflection presents me to myself not as idle and inaccessible subjectivity, but as identical with my presence in the world and to others." (Merleau-Ponty 1962: 452)

Nishida used the term "historical body" (歴史的な身体 *rekishitekina shintai*) as an aspect of *basho* that applies to family, social, and cultural spheres. The most important aspect of social existence, namely a common language, is treated by Merleau-Ponty (1973: 140) as "the anonymous corporeality which we share with other organisms." Similar attitudes could be found in later Heidegger's (1971a) considerations about the language as a historical "house of being."

However, besides many points of contact with East Asian ways of thinking, some Japanese philosophers found in Heidegger's early writings fundamental differences from their paradigms, stemming, they considered, from deeply rooted Western backgrounds. Since in *Being and Time*, individually experienced time is the crucially important term, Japanese philosophers Watsuji, Yuasa, and Abe criticized Heidegger's concept of authenticity as being exclusively self-centred, with evident neglect or negative interpretations of the social sphere. Another fundamental aspect of difference, noticed by Yuasa (p. 174), can be found in Heidegger's treatment of corporeality. Heidegger, as distinct from Nishida or Merleau-Ponty, never illustrated *Dasein's* authenticity corporeally. For Heidegger, in the majority of cases, "[T]he most actual and broadest leap is that of thinking" (Heidegger 1989: 167). Thus authentic *Dasein* is mostly described as thinker, poet, or artist, but not as a worker or dancer, which loses completely the "noetic self" in action. Such preferences perhaps conditioned Irigay's observation about "forgetting the air", or Mickūnas's (2004: 34) remark about Heidegger's inability to dance.

Later Heidegger himself admits that "[I]n *Being and Time* Da-sein still stands in the shadow of the "anthropological", the "subjectivistic", and the "individualist", etc." (Heidegger 1989:208). From *Contribution to Philosophy (From Enowning)* onwards, the existence of *Dasein* is always considered as being en-owned by cosmological space – *Ereignis*. Similarly to Nishida or Merleau-Ponty, the subject's identity is defined as inextricably connected with the material and historical given-ness [es-gibt] of *Ereignis*, thus "[T]he *self* is never "I" (Heidegger 1989: 226). Humans, together with the sky, earth, and gods, belong to Fourfold [Geviert], where neither of the phenomena is autonomous, "[N]one of the four insist on its own separate particularity. Rather, each is expropriated, within their mutual appropriation, into its own being" (Heidegger 1971: 179). As a result, "earth and sky, divinities and mortals dwell *together at once*" (Heidegger 1971: 173).

Such cosmological illustrations are strongly reminiscent of ancient Chinese cosmological models in which the five primary elements, and polarities of heaven and earth interconnected by *dao* and *qi*, and are considered as a primordial unity that gives birth to everything. Also, similarly to the classics of Taoism or Buddhism, being en-owned is considered as a fundamental existential condition, which should be harmoniously accepted but not confronted. In this aspect, we can see the reversal of Western philosophical models, as Heidegger puts it: "[W]ith Appropriation [i.e. *Ereignis* – R. M.] one is no longer thinking in a Greek way at all" (*Seminar in Le Thor 1969*, quoted in May 1996: 42).

Because of the definition of subject as given-ness and en-owned, later Heidegger's postulates could be compared with Merleau-Ponty's or Nishida's paradigm, in which "seer" (subject) is inextricably connected with "seen" (object); accordingly, positing consciousness is connected with *hyle* and bodily modalities, the personal – with the social. Thus subject and perception "is always in a mode of the impersonal 'One'"(Merleau-Ponty 1962: 240). As distinct from previous traditional Western ontological and epistemological distinctions between subject and object or mind as active and body as controlled-passive, the philosophers consider these separate realms as "thetic-positions"(Merleau-Ponty 1962: 242), "noetic determinations" (Nishida), or metaphysical, abstracted segments of initial totality.

In such a philosophical paradigm, following Greimas's formalizations of narratives, the substantialized, noetic subject could be defined as a disjunction from the field; whereas belongingness to the field – as a conjunction, union. Such a paradigm implies an appropriate concept of time in which presence and absence – now and other temporal horizons – gain a specific configuration which is different from the traditional Western one in which being was inextricably connected with presence.

Heidegger's and Merleau-Ponty's concepts of temporality owe much to Husserl's and Bergson's phenomenological investigations into the connectedness and interchangeability of temporal horizons. However, the fundamental difference lies in their definitions of the ontological status of intentionality. In Husserl's phenomenological project intentionality, as with the Cartesian or idealist paradigms, is treated as the centre and source that constitutes the cosmological totality from its perspective. Accordingly, for Husserl, time coincided with the temporal organization of intentionality, he "suggests the possibility of explicating the *a priori features* of temporal order (infinite, two-dimensional, transitive and so on) by reference to time-consciousness" (Wood: 61). Both Heidegger and Merleau-Ponty found in Husserl's interpretation of time aspects of traditional Western metaphysics and anthropocentrism. In *Being and Time*, Heidegger called such an organization of time, "temporalization." Merleau-Ponty applied the term "thetic time", or "objective time", which is "made up of successive moments", whereas Nishida called it "noetic time."

Heidegger and later Merleau-Ponty brought to Husserl's considerations the further idea, that "we have no coherent idea of experiences that exist in (or are immanent to) consciousness without having a necessary relation to an environment that is outside of consciousness" (Keller: 12). Thus, temporality in Heidegger and Merleau-Ponty is considered from the perspective of belongingness, manifested in *Ereignis* or "the third term." Accordingly, for their phenomenological project, "[I]t is necessary to take up again and develop *fungeriende* or *latent* intentionality which is the intentionality within being" (Merleau-Ponty 1958: 244).

According to Husserl (1991: 68), now is the "continuous moment of individuation" and "the source-point of all temporal positions" (1991: 74). In this way, the intentionally constituted "now" functions as the centre of temporal totality, a point of orientation controlled by intentionality. Following Husserl, Merleau-Ponty (1962: 424) agrees that now "enjoys a privilege, because it is the zone in which being and consciousness coincide." However, Merleau-Ponty is distinct from Husserl in his suggestion that, while the intentionally constituted presence is at the centre of time, it should also lose its substantial status through its belongingness to bodily modalities, objects, and the totality of temporal horizons.

As with the impossibility of phenomenological reduction, philosophers tried to explicate phenomenologically the impossibility of the centricity of now and presence. According to Merleau-Ponty (1962: 424), as distinct from "thetic" presence, "the lived present holds a past and a future within its thickness" (1962: 275). This temporal thickness can be seen in the temporal interconnectedness between "the actual body" (*le corps actuel*) and "the habitual body" (*le corps habituel*) through an "intentional arc" which "projects round about us our past, our future, our human setting, our physical, ideological and moral situation, or rather which results in our being situated in all these respects" and "which brings about the unity of the senses, of intelligence, of sensibility and motility" (Merleau-Ponty 1962: 136). Intentional and corporeal processes are intrinsically connected with deeply accumulated habits that function as a basis of reaction to the external phenomena and accordingly shape the "now." Thus the past, as distinct from Husserl, *is not only intentionally represented in the presence but also corporeally included in presence.* As with intentionality that is corporeally based, for Merleau-Ponty time is also corporeal. Instead of positing the centricity of temporalizing intentionality, intentionality itself is projected and temporalized by belongingness to the body and objects. In this way, "the third term" in a temporal sense is defined as a totality in which all the temporal horizons coexist. Accordingly, "[W]hat we have experienced is, and remains, permanently ours; and in old age a man is still in contact with his youth. Every present as it arises is driven into time like a wedge and stakes its claim to eternity" (Merleau-Ponty 1962: 393). However, as distinct from intentionally constituted sequential temporality, in which the past is consciously recollected in the present, in the temporality of "the third term", presence is inextricably connected to the "immemorial past", "that has never been present and that cannot be made present in a representation or act of recollection" (Merleau-Ponty 1958: 164). However, this invisibility is essential for constituting being and time; it could be compared with the unconscious background that is essential for conscious processes. Similarly to Merleau-Ponty, for Nishida noetic, "represented" time and temporalizing consciousness, is inseparable from the temporal totality and objects that make the representation possible:

> We usually think of the present as one point in the infinite flow of time, and we think of time as a continuum of presents. Yet just as a continuum cannot be made intelligible as a collection of discrete points, neither is time a collection of isolated presents. The real present is a *section* of the temporal continuum and captures the meaning of the entire continuum in a single point. (Nishida 1987a: 126)

> [t]ime, space, and causation are merely "represented", but concrete reality must be the "representing". (Nishida 1987a: 124)

From the presumptions above, another important aspect of such temporal order arises. Since in temporal totality all the corporeal experiences and intentional projections are mutually interconnected and accumulated, as distinct from a sequential temporality with a centralized presence as the position for temporalization, in this paradigm temporal horizons and vectors are manifested simultaneously and multidirectionally. According to Merleau-Ponty:

> The upsurge of a fresh present does not *cause* a heaping up of the past and a tremor of the future; the fresh present is the passage of the future to present, and of former present to past, and when time begins to move, it moves throughout its whole length.
> (Merleau-Ponty 1962:419)

> [t]he course of time must be primarily not only the passing of present to past, but also that of the future to the present. If it can be said that all prospection is anticipatory retrospection, it can equally be said that all retrospection is prospection in reverse.
> (Merleau-Ponty 1962: 414)

Heidegger gives the example of temporal holism, relating it to thinking from the perspective of being enowned, as intimating. As with the spatiality of Fourfold [*Geviert*], in which cosmological realms are interpenetrated: "[i]ntimating does not at all aim only at what is futural, what stands before – as does the intimating that is generally thought in a calculative way. Rather, it traverses and thoroughly takes stock of the whole of temporality: the free-play of the time-space of the t/here [Da]" (Heidegger 1989: 16). Thus "[E]xistence=the full temporality and indeed as ecstatic" (Heidegger 1989: 213).

Primordial temporality is not "thetic" but total in which the present is: "[a]n arbitrary point, like one chosen at random on a straight line, but it is determined from the totality of a self-conscious system in both its qualitative and quantitative aspects, and is thus the focal point wherein the totality of the real is reflected. In the present, we touch the core of the universe." (Nishida 1987: 126). Following the ambiguous definition of the subject as a "seer" that is indistinguishable from the "visible" (Merleau-Ponty 1958: 139), time is defined ambiguously as the totality of present and eternity: "It is for this reason that it is a matter of indifference whether we say that the present foreshadows eternity or that the eternity of truth is merely a sublimation of the present. This ambiguity cannot be resolved, but it can be understood as ultimate, if we recapture the intuition of real time which preserves everything" (Merleau-Ponty 1962: 394).

Following Greimas's formalizations, the noetically constituted presence (as a sphere of an active subject), and "temporalization", could be defined as a disjunction from the totality of times. This disjunction is constantly neutralized, interrupted, and desubstantialized by its belongingness to the totality of temporal horizons – immemorial past and unrepresentable future. As a result, time is not only a linear and controllable by intentionality teleological flow from past to future, with the present as a centre, but rather an ambiguous saturation of horizons in which presence and absence are interpenetrated. In such a temporality, "the apparent positivity of the present thus incorporates and relies on a negativity of the past – just as the visible spectacle includes an invisibility in principle" (Al-Saji 201). The same ambiguity and sway between positing subject and being incorporated into the anonymous realm of objects and times can be found in definitions of fundamental human modalities.

The basic narrative trajectory of traditional Western philosophy was a movement from chaos towards *arche* or *logos*, from appearance to reality, from contradictions or ambiguities towards explicitness and non-contradiction. Reformulations of the ontological status of fundamental actants and temporality were reflected in definitions of truth and thinking too. Thinking, in which the thinker is an actor, could be considered in terms of actoriality as defined in Greimassian narrativity. As distinct from the requirement for non-contradiction, or conjunction with the object of "truth" in Merleau-Ponty, similarly to the famous metaphor of a butterfly's dream in Zhuangzi (see p. 61), the polarities of traditional Western philosophy are not separated but identified:

> It has often been said that consciousness, by definition, admits of no separation of appearance and reality, and by this we are to understand that, in our knowledge of ourselves, appearance is reality [...] Here reality appears in its entirety, real being and appearance are one, and there is no reality other than the appearance. (Merleau-Ponty 1962: 294)

> The identity of being and appearance cannot be posited, but only lived as anterior to any affirmation. (Merleau-Ponty 1962: 295)

Fundamental belongingness to the (m)other undermines the substantialist metaphysics and, accordingly, the distinction between the truth and appearance. Since thinking has no autonomy, "[T]he primary truth is indeed 'I think', but only provided that we understand thereby 'I belong to myself' while belonging to the world" (Merleau-Ponty 1962: 407). Heidegger, especially concerned with the questions of authentic thinking, compared thinking with the way: "[T]hinking itself is a way. We respond to the way only by remaining underway" (Heidegger 1968: 41). Responding to the way, while being underway, as May (1996: 36–37) noticed, shows Heidegger's evident closeness to the fundamental postulates of Taoism. In *The Nature of Language*, the "way" in is substituted by dao [Tao] and contrasted to its improper interpretations as logos (cf. Heidegger 1971a: 92). Dao as a source, "that gives all ways" could be compared to en-ownment (*Ereignis*), which gives being by the mutual belongingness of cosmological realms. In both Heidegger and Taoist or Buddhist classics, the "remaining underway" is considered as non-metaphysical.

As with Merleau-Ponty's "thinking from perspective of belonging to the world" in authentic thinking, "[D]ecision [is] related to the truth of being, not only related but determined only from within it"(Heidegger 1989: 69). Thus "[E]n-thinking the truth of be-ing [. . .] must place itself back into what it opens up" (Heidegger 1989: 39).

"Remaining underway", or placing the thinking back "into what it opens up", means being always in different situation of en-ownment. Thus, for Heidegger (1989: 39), "[b]eginning can never be comprehended as the same, because it reaches ahead and thus each time reaches beyond what is begun through it and determines accordingly its own retrieval." Merleau-Ponty (1962: 396) explores similar territory. Instead of reaching some explicitness or conclusions, he suggests that "[T]o think of thought is to adopt in relation to it an attitude that we have initially learned in relation to "things"; it is never to eliminate, but merely to push further back the opacity that thought presents to itself." For later Heidegger, such "opacity" is best manifested in "poetic thought" (*das Dichtende Denken*) that, as distinct from the orientations of traditional philosophy, preserves the ambiguous totality of "world" and "ground" (cf. especially *The Origin of the Work of Art*).

In Heidegger, authentic thinking is most often metaphorically described as "Nothing" [das Nichts]. Thus, "[T]he more originarily being is experienced in its truth, the deeper is the *nothing* as the abground at the edge of the ground" (Heidegger 1989: 228). Being is frequently directly compared, interchanged, or identified with nothing. It culminates in the formula "Being: Nothing: Same" (*Le Thor Seminar* in May: 26). For Heidegger, nothingness became the most important metaphor for delineating the fundamental human modality. Nothingness is defined as "absence" [ab-wesend] to presencing [Being] (*The Question of Being*, cf. May: 24), that results in "Openness" (*Alētheia*), which is *"emptiest of the empty"* (Heidegger 1989: 237). Nothingness is always invoked in explanations of important neologisms, such as *Unverborgenheit* (Unconcealedness) or *Gelassenheit* (Letting-be) (cf. Heidegger 1989). Nothingness as insubstantiality of self enables the belongingness from which fundamental thinking stems; accordingly "[T]he nothing does not remain the indeterminate opposite of beings but unveils itself as belonging to the being of beings" (Heidegger 1977: 110). In this way, belongingness and nothingness are closely related to a concept of *Gelassenheit*, realized as "not-granting", "reservedness" or "inabiding".

For Nishida, similarly to Heidegger – the deepest self is defined as belongingness to basho (topos) and as an absence of the noetic self:

> That we conceive of conscious activity in terms of (substanceless) pure acts is due to the fact that, since acts are immediate to topos, they are immanent and thus substanceless; it is non-being that determines their being. The more clearly the acts are recognized as having their initial points in non-being, the more they are seen to take on the character of consciousness. (Nishida 2005: 190)

Nishida's phenomenology could be compared with Hegel's systematic thinking. However, Hegel's self-consciousness as a fundamental entity and centre of totality is replaced by nothingness here. Thus, for the deepest self-consciousness or "[T]he self-consciousness of self-consciousness [. . .] is seeing in the plane of the selfless self" (Nishida 2005: 213).

As can be seen above, it is nothingness or selfless-self that enables the most intensive fullness of a fundamental subject's modality – belongingness. Thus, in Heidegger, and Nishida, nothingness is defined in a similar way – challenging the logics of non-contradiction, nothingness is equated with fullness:

> For "being" here does not mean being extant in itself; and "not-being" here does not mean total disappearance, but rather (a) not-being as a way of being: being and yet not; and (b) in the same way being: having the character of nothing and yet precisely being. (Heidegger 1989:70)

> How [is] the *originary* ab-ground [to be thought]? [As] "emptiness"? Neither emptiness nor fullness. (Heidegger 1989: 72)

> [h]ow absolute nothingness can possibly determine itself. In reply it must be stated that absolute nothingness is not simply not-being-anything but is rather the ultimate noetic determination; it is the essence of spirit. It is both absolute nothingness and absolute being, and as such it transcends the limits of our understanding. (Nishida 2005: 207)

At the same time, philosophers are aware that a subject's perspective as an aspect of totality is in-transcendable. Belongingness and nothingness are never substantial and pure; there is always an aspect of subject-consciousness in them. Thus, instead of differentiation, subject and object are defined as a contradictory totality in which each gives being to the other:

> The world is inseparable from the subject, but from a subject which is nothing but a project of the world, and the subject is inseparable from the world, but from a world which the subject itself projects. The subject is a being-in-the-world and the world remains "subjective" since its texture and articulations are traced out by the subject's movement of transcendence. (Merleau-Ponty 1962: 430)

> That I am consciously active means that I determine myself by expressing the world in myself. I am an expressive monad of the world. I transform the world into my subjectivity. The world that, in its objectivity, opposes me is transformed and grasped symbolically in the forms of my subjectivity. But this transactional logic of contradictory identity signifies as well that it is the world that is expressing itself in me. (Nishida 1987b: 52)

Accordingly, in this paradigm, the identity of subject, self or anything posited is always neutralized by belongingness to the other. Thus, *Ereignis*, *basho* or *the third term* could be defined rather as *simultaneous coexistence (coincidentia oppositorum)* in which polarities such as subject and object, conjunction and disjunction, nothingness and fullness, "now" and other temporal horizons, seer and seen, visible and invisible – are always present, interdependent or even identical. The syntagmatic order of such interdependency can be illustrated by the following thoughts of Heidegger:

> [i]nitially we think "decision" as what comes to the fore within an either-or polarity [. . .] (Heidegger 1989:62) [t]he essential sway of be-ing sways in the en-ownment of de-cision (Heidegger 1989: 65–66). [W]hat is ownmost to decision can only be determined from within and out of its prevailing essential swaying (Heidegger 1989: 70). [d]ecision [involves] human activity and is sequential. What is necessary in it [is] what lies before the "activity" and reaches beyond it.
> (Heidegger 1989: 71)

At the same time, in this interdependency, there is an aspect of ambiguity, named by Heidegger as "suspense", "cleavage", "in-between-ness", "midpoint", "self-sheltering" or "hesitating refusal":

> The cleavage is the inner, incalculable settledness [Ausfälligkeit] of en-ownment; of the essential swaying of be-ing as the midpoint that is used and that grants belonging [. . .].
> (Heidegger 1989:197)

> Enowning as the *hesitating refusal* and therein the fullness of "time" the mightiness of the fruit and the greatness of the gifting – but in the *truth* as *clearing* for the *self-sheltering*
> (Heidegger 1989: 189)

Considerations about this fundamental ambiguity can be also found in Nishida and Merleau-Ponty:

> [t]he concrete self exists as a self-contradiction. As the self deepens its self-awareness, it discovers its own incommensurable parts – its objectivity and its subjectivity, its spatiality and its temporality [. . .]. The more it realizes its own discrepant parameters, the more it becomes self-conscious (Nishida 1987b: 82). Every activity of consciousness at the same time that it is "reflection in itself" is "reflection in another", and when a certain moment of consciousness has been determined it immediately includes the negation of itself and is ripe for sublation. (Nishida 1987a:148)

> We are not in some incomprehensible way an activity joined to a passivity, an automatism surmounted by a will, a perception surmounted by judgment, but wholly active and wholly passive, because we are the upsurge of time. (Merleau-Ponty 1962: 428)

> I face truth not with its negation, but with a state of non-truth or ambiguity, the actual opacity of my existence. In the same way, I can remain within the sphere of absolute self-evidence only if I refuse to make any affirmation, or take anything for granted.
> (Merleau-Ponty 1962: 295)

As can be seen from the above, for the philosophers discussed, the authentic subject is not a noetic subject defined by self-consciousness; neither is it a subject which aims for conjunction with metaphysical "truth". Consequently, the fundamental subject's modality is not "doing", i.e. establishing centre-logos by confronting the givenness and belongingness, but rather occupying the position of tension and ambiguity. The subject belongs to cosmological space; it is initially conjuncted to the field (S∧O) and, in this way, desubstantialized; however, at the same time, the subject viewed as the possibility of a noetic activity and metaphysical step is disjuncted from the field (S∨O). Speaking in terms of Greimassian narrativity, instead of the dialectical syntagmas of losing and gaining the objects of value, (schematized as S∨O→S∧O), conjunction and disjunction are, in these philosophical paradigms, considered as an ambiguous unity (S∨O+S∧O; S∨O=S∧O). This reflects above-discussed ambiguities and identifications of perception and perceived, "now" and the totality of temporal horizons. Heidegger often described this by the metaphor of midpoint, middle or in-between-ness:

> What counts in the *other beginning* is the leap into the encleaving midpoint of the turning of enowning in order thus to prepare – in knowing, inquiring, and setting the style – the t/here [Da] regarding its grounding. (Heidegger 1989:164)

> Truth [. . .] is the midpoint that holds to abground and enquivers in the passing of god and is thus the sustained ground for the grounding of creating Da-sein. (Heidegger 1989: 232)

Invoking the semiotic square as an elementary structure of signification that "constitutes a virtual map of conceptual closure, or [. . .] the closure of ideology itself as a mechanism" (Jameson 1983: xv), syntagmatic order of discussed paradigms and their contexts could be schematically represented as follows (Figure 1):

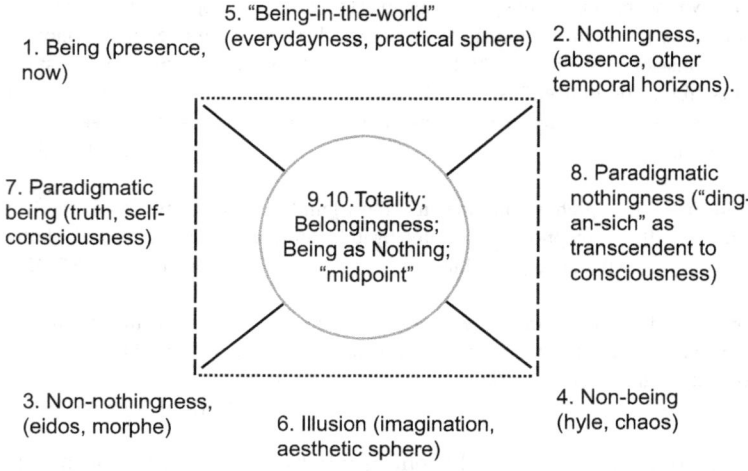

Figure 1: Metaterms.

Metaterms 1–8 represent traditional polarities of Western philosophy that are constructed in regard to each other, following logics of contrariety (between metaterms 1– 2 and 3–4), contradiction (between metaterms 1–4 and 2–3), complementarity or implication (between metaterms 1–3 and 2–4). Metaterms 7 and 8 are considered here as intensifying semantic value and the negation of the opposite value, i.e. intensifying "being" (i.e. being – not nothingness = paradigmatic, authentic being) and "nothingness" (i.e. nothingness – not being = paradigmatic nothingness, complete transcendence).

Metaterms 9 and 10 (the middle of the semiotic square) are not usually discussed in classical semiotics because the principle of non-contradiction is followed. However, at least theoretically, we can consider these absolutely contradictory metaterms, in which polarities are neither identical nor different to each other. In the ambiguous union and contradictory identity of polarities, we can see opposition to the traditional Western logic of non-contradiction. It brings this paradigm close to East Asian paradigms of "preserving the totality" (cf. Motiekaitis 2011). Such thinking could be also defined as a "radical epoche", which enables insight into the "ground of intentionalities that fluctuate between permanence and flux, Being-Nothing, eternity-time" (Mickunas 1993:272); however, it does not imply "any particular object or event, and hence cannot be ascribed noetic character" (Mickunas 1993: 270). Exactly this aspect of existence and thinking is of interest for philosophers discussed here and their philosophical narratives actualize this semiotic structure in distinctive ways. A primordial substrate, which is neither subject nor object, neither present nor omnitemporal, neither active as a subject of "doing", nor passive as that of "being", can be described only in absolutely contradictory terms. It cannot be considered as synthesis, position or identity. Semiotic structures define the logic of constituting identities that are at work in any narrative. Philosophies considered here are trying to examine the territory beyond this logic.

According to Greimas (1989a:164), syntactic operations are purposeful and organized in logical sequences. "An author, a producer of any semiotic object, operates within an epistemy, which is the result of his individuality and the society in which he is inscribed. Within this society it is possible for him to make a limited number of choices, which have as an initial result the investment of organized contents, that is, contents endowed with valencies (possibilities of relations)" (Greimas 1983: 61). Expanding this notion, we can think that *fundamental existential choices, constructions of philosophical paradigms and changes in them are also to a certain degree purposeful, logical and based on fundamental grammar.* We tried to consider, here, that even philosophical paradigms that are challenging the logic of identity can to a certain degree be explained invoking structural semiotic approach.

Traditional either-or based narrativity and the resolving of binary oppositions by privileging certain aspects of totality, in case of these philosophies, was confronted by leaving it unresolved, tensed, cleaved. It was constructed against traditional Western philosophical attempts to find the centre of totality. In this sense, these modern philosophical paradigms echo most archaic ones of Heraclitus or Taoist Zhuangzi (ch. 53), for whom "[W]hat is It is also Other, what is Other is also It. [. . .] Are there really It and Other? Or really no It and Other? Where neither It nor Other finds its opposite is called the axis of the Way".

References

Al-Saji, Alia. 2007. Temporality of Life: Merleau-Ponty, Bergson, and the Immemorial Past. *The Southern Journal of Philosophy.* Summer 2007. 177–206.

Benveniste, Emile. 1979. *Problems in General Linguistics.* Trans. by Mary Elizabeth Meek. University of Miami Press.

Deleuze, Gilles & Felix Guattari. 1994. *What is Philosophy?* Trans. by Hugh Tomlinson and Graham Burchell. New York: Columbia University Press.

Greimas, Algirdas Julien. 1983. *Structural Semantics: An Attempt at a Method.* Trans. by Daniele McDowell, Ronald Schleifer & Alan Velie. Lincoln: University of Nebraska Press.

Greimas, Algirdas Julien. 1989a [1970]. Apie prasmę. *Semiotika: Darbų Rinktinė.* Trans. by Rolandas Pavilionis. Vilnius: Minties leidykla. (Orig. in French *Du sens. Essais sémiotiques*).

Jameson, Fredric. 1983. Foreword to Greimas *Structural Semantics: An Attempt at a Method.* Trans. by Daniele McDowell, Ronald Schleifer & Alan Velie. Lincoln: University of Nebraska Press.

Heidegger, Martin. 1968. *What is Called Thinking?* Trans. by J. Glenn Gray. New York: Harper & Row.

Heidegger, Martin. 1971. *Poetry, Language, Thought.* Trans. by Albert Hofstadter. New York: Harper & Row.

Heidegger, Martin. 1971a. *On the Way to Language.* Trans. by Peter D. Hertz. New York: Harper & Row.

Heidegger, Martin. 1977. What Is Metaphysics? In *Basic Writtings.* Trans. by David F. Krell. New York: Harper & Row.

Heidegger. 1989. *Contributions to Philosophy (From Enowning).* Trans. by Parvis Emad & Kenneth Maly. Indiana University Press.

Husserl, Edmund. 1991. *On the Phenomenology of the Consciousness of Internal Time (1893–1917).* Trans. by J. B. Brough. Collected Works, vol. 4. Dordrecht: Kluwer.

Keller, Pierre. 1999. *Husserl and Heidegger on Human Experience.* Cambridge University Press.

Lingis, Alphonso. 1986. *Phenomenological Explanations.* Dordrecht: Martinus Nijhoff Publishers.

May, Reinhard. 1996. *Heidegger's Hidden Sources: East Asian Influences on His Work.* Tr. Graham Parkes. London: Routledge.

Merleau-Ponty, Maurice. 1958. *The visible and Invisible.* Trans. by A. F. Lingis. Evanston: Northwest University Press.
Merleau-Ponty, Maurice. 1962. *Phenomenology of Perception.* Trans. by Colin Smith. New York: Routledge and Kegan Paul.
Merleau-Ponty, Maurice. 1973. *The Prose of the World.* Trans. by John O'Neill. Evanston: Northwestern University Press.
Mickūnas, Algis & Arūnas Sverdiolas. 2004. *Visa aprėpianti dabartis* (All Embracing Present). Vilnius: Baltos Lankos.
Mickunas, Algis. 1993. Phenomenology of Zen. In Phillip Blosser (ed.), *Japanese and Western Phenomenology,* 263–273. Dordrecht: Kluwer Academic Publishers.
Motiekaitis, Ramūnas. 2011. *Poetics of the Nameless Middle – Japan and the West in Philosophy and Music of the Twentieth Century.* (Acta Semiotica Fennica XL). Imatra & Helsinki: International Semiotics Institute at Imatra; Semiotic Society of Finland.
Nishida, Kitarō. 1987a. *Intuition and Reflection in Self-Consciousness.* Trans. by Valdo H. Viglielmo with Takeuchi Yoshinori & Joseph S. O'Leary. State University of New York Press.
Nishida, Kitarō. 1987b. *Last Writtings: Nothingness and Religious Worldviews.* Trans. by David A. Dilworth. Honolulu: University of Hawaii Press.
Nishida, Kitarō. 2005. General Summary. Trans. by R. Wargo. In Robert Wargo (ed.), *The Logic of Nothingness: A Study of Nishida Kitarō.* Honolulu: University of Hawaii Press.
Wood, David. 1989. *The Deconstruction of Time.* Atlantic Highlands, NJ: Humanities Press International.
Yuasa, Yasuo. 1987. *The Body: Towards an Eastern Mind-Body Theory.* Trans. by Nagatomo Shigenori & Thomas P. Kasulis. State University of New York Press.
Zhuangzi. 2001. *Chuang-Tzŭ: The Inner Chapters.* Trans. A. C. Graham. Indianapolis: Hackett Publishing Company.

Elżbieta Magdalena Wąsik
Thought and consciousness in language as prerequisites for the existential-identity perception of the human self

Abstract: The subject matter of this chapter constitutes the linguistic manifestation of the identity of the human self as a product of its thinking abilities and mental experiencing of its consciousness. The focus of attention is paid to different aspects of man's existential awareness connected with his spirit-based rationality and reflexivity. The principal stress is on the mental states of the human self, determined by the subjectivity of its reasoning or feelings processes. That's why the first place occupies here the idea of transcendentality originating in the apriority (*a priori* forms) of self-awareness. The second forms the idea of existential subjectivity inexpressible through objective forms and inadequacy to reality. The third, in turn, makes up the stream-of-consciousness-related dialogical form of internal communication, a tendency to actualize images from the past, unrelated to the present but counting for in the future. Finally, the subject of a separate discussion forms the notion of intentionality, a precondition of freedom, unconditional dependency on the existence of the individual in the world. While pondering upon the relation between thought and language, the author deals with the role of language-based thinking in the communicative systems and cognitive processes of the embodied mind. Against this background, the viewpoint of existential semiotics is highlighted where the subjective perception of identity as a kind of being expressed through transcending signs appears to be a prerequisite for a private performance of the individual self in the domains of public communication.

Keywords: thought and consciousness, thought semiotics, existential semiotics, linguistic self

1 Thought and consciousness in philosophical discourse

1.1 The semiotic web in the surrounding environment of animals

Questions of thought and consciousness as species-specific properties of humans have engaged the attention of philosophers since antiquity. Among them, Aristotle (c. 384 BC–322 BC), in the *Nicomachean Ethics* (edited nota bene by his son Nicomachus, cf. Aristotle 1926 {ca 347–330 B.C. (or 349 B.C.)] tried to define man in comparison to animals. He took as fact human capacities for thinking and reasoning, maintaining that they imply human rationality, and consequently, a different kind of life than that of animals. In Aristotle's view, it was the self-consciousness, which allowed a sense of good as a value and the capacity to be subjected to pleasure and happiness, manifesting itself as contemplation, the most precious human activity.

If citing and quoting the nineteenth-century English translation of *The Nicomachean Ethics of Aristotle*, it is exactly, man, featured by rationality, who is becoming a unique being when acting obediently upon reason, and exercising or employing it (cf. Aristotle [1881] 1893: 15–16). Also, man is able, in Aristotle's depiction (1893: 30, 31, 68–69), to achieve happiness through his contemplative thinking, that is, deliberating above all about means that would lead him to the goal rather than about the goals themselves. As far as his life as a rational being is defined not only by the capacities of feeling and thinking, the man is above all, after Aristotle, somebody "who sees feels that he sees, and he who hears feels that he hears, and he who walks feels that he walks" (1893: 310–311). And, for Aristotle "to be conscious of feeling or thinking is to be conscious of existence" since in Aristotle's words, "our existence" (as humans) "is feeling or thinking". Most importantly, man, endowed with thinking abilities, was, for Aristotle, conscious of moral requirements and responsibilities, so, in consequence, "consciousness of life is a thing that is pleasant in itself; for life is naturally good, and to be conscious of the presence of a good thing is pleasant" (quoted and cited after Aristotle 1893: 310–311). All in all, aware of the fact that "the other animals do not participate in happiness, being quite incapable of this kind of activity", Aristotle (1893: 344) insisted that happiness "extends just so far as contemplation, and the more contemplation the more happiness is there in a life." In the context of debates about the existential aspects of human experience, the views of Aristotle regarding human consciousness seem to be apt and still valid.

Similarly to Aristotle, identifying consciousness with the spiritual part of man, viz. the soul, René Descartes (1596–1650) held that thinking, fundamental to all considerations, was an indicator of existence. To put it differently, it was exclusively the mind that, for Descartes, constituted a being (an entity) the existence of which was unquestionable, because nothing was more accessible to the knowledge (cognition) of man than his own mind. Descartes announced his view about man as *res cogitans* or *substantia cogitans* 'a thinking thing' or 'a thinking substance', treated also as *res extensa*, i.e., a (thinking) thing which is extended through corporeal things (or substances) being present in his organism and environment, at first, in the famous catchphrase: «*Je pense, donc je suis*» (literally) 'I think, therefore I am' (or more exactly) 'I am thinking, therefore I exist' (Descartes [1637] 2011: 22), expressed in his *Discours de la méthode* . . . (published anonymously at Leyden in 1637). Subsequently, Descartes confirmed this claim, in his *Meditationes de prima philosophia*, with the famous Latin statement, "ego cogito, ergo sum, sive existo 'I think, therefore I am, or exist' ([1641] 1642: 155). Remarkable is here Cartesian distinction between three grades of human existence, conveyed in the statement: "*Corpus, Corporeum sive animus, et Mens sive spiritus, cujus existentia quaeritur*" 'flesh, body or life force and mind or spirit, the existence of which is searched' (1642: 45) and concluding phrase: "*Corpus, Animus, Mens*" (1642: 45), according to which the human individual is considered in terms of three modes of existence, as 'corporeal', 'animated' and 'mental' being.

1.2 Consciousness and thinking as empirically investigated and existentially experienced human powers

Up to and including the seventeenth century, consciousness was associated with the moral character (characteristics) of humans, since, as Larry M. Jorgensen (2020) explains, in French and Latin, the languages of philosophy, there was no clear semantic distinction between consciousness as sentient awareness of oneself and the world and conscience as "a moral sensibility". As to the later understandings of the concepts of consciousness, cognizance, thoughts, ideas, and the like, the views of such philosophers, as, John Locke (1632–1704), and David Hume (1711–1776), Immanuel Kant (1724–1804), G. W. F. Hegel (1770–1831), Søren Kierkegaard (1813–1855), Francis Herbert Bradley (1846–1924), William James (1842–1910) and Henri-Louis Bergson (1859–1941), Edmund Husserl (1859–1938), Jaen-Paul Sartre (1905–1980), Martin Heidegger (1889–1976), Hans-Georg Gadamer (1900–2002), Maurice Merleau-Ponty (1908–1961), have to be recapitulated from the viewpoint of their significance for contemporary approaches to man as a signifying-communicating individual.

For Locke ([1690] 1952), the consciousness was a mental power allowing humans to recognize ideas representing objects of the world in their minds, forming thus their minds. Focusing mainly on sensory experiences, through which ideas could arise in the human mind, pure, not imprinted with innate ideas at the moment of birth, as well as on mental acts of making perceptual contact with external world objects, Locke argued that considering an object was just equal to thinking about the idea of that object. As to Hume, the man was for him "a person or creature, endowed with thought and consciousness" (cf. "An enquiry concerning human understanding" 1952 [1690]: 485). Nonetheless, Hume essentially contended that all information available to man came from experience, and, at the same time, conscious knowledge arose from complex processing of sensory impressions into ideas (mental images), and as such could never be reliable. Ultimately, considering man somebody determined by his beliefs about the expected effects or outcomes, which he usually derives from accumulated experiences instinctively, that is, because of feelings not because of reasoning, Hume claimed, not the reason played a crucial role in cognition but rather a feeling controlled by reason.

In turn, Immanuel Kant's analysis of transcendental consciousness presupposed that a subject's thoughts always took some shapes. In his *Critique of Pure Reason* ([1781] 1838), Kant maintained that transcendental thinking originated in the *a priori* forms as universal cognitive categories, through which human beings, regardless of their position in the world, as the subjects of cognition, could go beyond the object of cognition to obtain the absolute knowledge about reality, and to find the absolute truth. Subsequently, the first-person-experience approach to reality, subjectively perceived by the individual through senses and grasped through the acts of reasoning and feeling, was elaborated by Hegel, especially in his *Phenomenology of Mind* ([1807] 1910). Focusing on self-reflection as an aspect of human thinking processes, Hegel considered the human being "a type of animal" and "product of nature", but, at the same time, "the self-consciousness of existence itself" (cf. Glenn Alexander Magee 2010: 2–3). What Hegel argued was that all forms of human consciousness aimed at an absolute cognition of reality as the whole, in which each thing was an appearance of the Absolute, and as such enabled humans to gain knowledge in its highest form, equal to understanding themselves through art, religion, and philosophy. The consciousness of man, conducting philosophical thinking, was, for Hegel, superior to the common consciousness of other living beings. The reflexive human mind, operating in the world of a systemic nature, in which every part is inherently related to every other, was featured, in Hegel's view, in the pursuit of perfection.

It followed from Kierkegaard's (1813–1855) reveries and contemplations that the subjectivity of human individuals was inseparably connected with their existence, which was attainable only through the inward acts of the mind. As an opponent of Hegel's systemic approach to the nature of truth and forerunner of the twentieth-century philosophy of existentialism, Kierkegaard showed, in his work *Fear and Trembling. A Dialectical Lyric* ([1843] 1941), published in Copenhagen under the pseudonym "Johannes de Silentio", that human beings though equipped with an exceptional quality of consciousness, were unable to settle queries of individual and social or universal matters in daily life situations. For humans, who were not able to describe their conscious first-person experiences through any objective categories, their internal conflicts of values appeared to be irrational and inexplicable.

Separately, special attention deserves Bradley's focusing on the relation of thought to reality. In his two-book essay on metaphysics, *Appearance and Reality* ([1893] 1897), the British idealist philosopher brought to light his view that human appearance-related (appearance-based) cognition, being as such fragmentary, can only result in a distorted picture of reality, constituting a whole, so that it is by no means possible to grasp reality through concepts.

The idea that thoughts are the flowing stream of consciousness experienced by human individuals comes from James, an American philosopher of pragmatism. Defining the human self, on the one hand, as the subject (the *I* who experiences, thinks, and speaks), and, on the other, the object of its own experiences, thoughts, and utterances (the *Me* as a physical person), James in his *Principles of Psychology* (1890), stressed subjectivity of the contents of the array of its thoughts and dialogicality of its structure. However, as he demonstrated, only the words of the language as a means of symbolic speech communication, having the same denotative meanings for many individuals, imply (cause) the objectivation of shared meanings. At the same time, Bergson pointed out to the importance of memory for the functioning of consciousness. In his *Matter and Memory*, he argued that the conscious awareness of the individual is dependent on his or her recollections of the past for, inhibiting spontaneous, automatic responses to stimuli (caused by unexpected affections), it facilitates to act towards the future properly (Bergson [1896] 1911).

Transcendental and existential phenomenology continued to deal with thinking and consciousness as properties of the human mind, especially in response to Hegel's philosophy of spirit (mind). In this regard, significant contributions were made by the philosophers-phenomenologists, who focused on experience and its mental representation. Specifically, Husserl investigated the contents of the human mind from the viewpoint of how phenomena occurred to the human individual in the stream of their consciousness, possibly (in ideal settings) in a pure way, that is, not interpreted or transformed. For Husserl consciousness, as the consciousness of an object, as follows *inter alia* from his *Ideas Pertaining to a Pure Phenomenology and to a Phenomenological Philosophy* ([1913] 1982), was intentional. Exactly, such an intentional consciousness of the subject as the pure *ego*, separated from the world and manifesting itself in the acts of transcendence, enabled the individual to get beyond the experience of the empirical ego through the phenomenological reduction. However, unlike Husserl, for whom consciousness was featured by intentionality, Sartre held that consciousness was intentionality itself. In the view of Sartre, expressed in his essay *The Transcendence of the Ego* ([1936–1937] 1990/1960: 39), the consciousness of the individual, as the perceptual syntheses of past consciousnesses and present consciousness, unifies itself by itself.

A significant step at this point, in the philosophical clarifications of intentional consciousness, was made by Husserl in his later work *The Crisis of European Sciences and Transcendental Phenomenology* ([1954] 1970) where he thematised the concept of the lifeworld (*Lebenswelt*). For Husserl ([1954] 1970: 49), the phenomenological lifeworld, the world enabling, as he believed, scientific objectivity (in natural sciences) and providing the basis for creating perceptual meanings, was "the only real world, the one that is actually given through perception." Applying it, Husserl believed that human thinking, especially scientific thinking, was, by its very nature, based on socially and culturally pre-defined basic meanings, and its scope was essentially limited. However, the lifeworld is not only the foundation of scientific theories, but also constitutes the general framework of meanings, common to human individuals as members of a social or cultural group, for their intersubjective experiences, and thus, for the way they perceive and think of the objective world, including themselves and others as objectively existing subjects.

In the hermeneutic phenomenological approaches proposed by Heidegger in *Being and Time* ([1927] 1962) and Gadamer (1900–2002) in *Truth and Method* ([1960] 1989/1975), questions of the mental consciousness and thinking have been replaced by questions of the understanding of human experience and subjectivity of meaning. Especially, Heidegger's concepts of *Dasein* and being-in-the-world can be looked upon as referring to a kind of involvement (viz., coping with things, or presence in the world) that demarcates the horizons for understanding (and action). According to both Heidegger and Gadamer, humans are capable of finding meaning in their existence, especially through interpreting the events and things from their surroundings. It is the present situation, determined by the socio-cultural-historical context which is decisive in articulating the understanding of being. The interpretative phenomenology focuses on the mode of being, assuming that it is the language that discloses aspects of being, or, in other words, understanding can only come to pass through language.

Returning to the philosophical stance of Sartre, he formulated in *Being and Nothingness* ([1943] 1956), it brought an amplification of the view that consciousness provides for the man his freedom of choice. The consciousness of the individual as a corporeal being, in fact, "only a transcendental field without a subject" (cf. Sartre [1943] 1956: 235) is, according to Sartre (1956: 334), characterized by a "total contingency", especially as it "specifies itself in its very act of nihilation". In other words, consciousness nihilates the world (that is, it detaches itself from the world or being), taking a particular perspective. Reflecting on the liberty of a human being, Sartre (1956: 439) took the first-person perspective: "I am indeed an existent who learns his freedom. through his acts, but I am also an existent whose individual and unique existence temporalizes itself as freedom." And so, he continued, "I am necessarily a consciousness (of) freedom since nothing exists in consciousness except as the non-thetic consciousness of existing." Taking Sartre's view, the individual is free, because of the power of his/her consciousness that is able to transcend itself, the world, and even the transcendence of the other.

The examination of selected approaches to consciousness could end with a reference to Merleau-Ponty's concept of the incarnate (embodied) subjectivity that aimed at replacing the concept of transcendental subjectivity. The author of *Phenomenology of Perception* ([1945] 2005), pondering upon the primordial structures of perception, realized that the intentionality of consciousness is a bodily intentionality of the man as a being of flesh and blood. For Merleau-Ponty, the thinker was a body-subject whose perception opens up the horizons for cognition and reflection.

Concluding, especially after some empiricist and existentialist philosophers, that consciousness and thought are operating as a medium between the external world and the human psyche while the experience of the individual is the ultimate source for his/her knowledge. Focusing on the self-consciousness of the individual as a category significant from an empirical point of view, one has to be stress that it can develop only under the condition of his/her language endowments.

2 Defining the relation between thought and language

2.1 Language as a tool for thought

Leaving the views of existentialists aside, one should notice that philosophers, who defined language in relation to man, as, roughly saying, a code of communication consisting of a structured system of sounds, words, and grammatical rules, concentrated on its relationship with the human thought. One cannot do here without mentioning again Aristotle, exactly his achievement regarding the understanding the nature of thought as an element of the mind. As one can find out from Will Durant's (cf. *The Story of Philosophy* [1926] 1962: 55) and J. Samuel Bois' (cf. *The Art of Awareness* [1966] 1972: 5–7) reports, Aristotle, who pondered upon both the nature of things and the acts of reasoning, was the first to formulate the laws of the human mind in his works on logic (such as *Categories, Topics, Prior and Posterior, Analytics, Propositions*, and *Sophistical Refutation*), collected, after his death, and called *Organon* (the instrument, or tool, for mental work, or correct thinking). Believing that "whatever existed remained identical with its natural self" (cf. Bois 1972: 6), Aristotle introduced the principle of identity as fundamental for his system of logic, a study of the laws of reasoning, per se, a tool for concluding about the ontologies inherent in language as an expression of thought.

Alluding to the views of contemporary philosophers regarding the relationships between language and human thought, one has to elaborate (after Hubert G. Alexander [1967] 1972: 13–14) on Aristotle's view on man as a rational and political animal, that is, social animal. It is evident, as Alexander (1972: 13) argues in his work *The Language and Logic of Philosophy*, that these two aspects of the man distinguished by the ancient Greek philosopher, are inseparable, as man is significantly dependent, when conducting reasoning, on symbolizations. That is, he creates symbols because of his need for social communication, and at the same time, it is the symbols that constitute for him the visually and audibly perceivable equivalents of his acts of thinking and feeling. When thinking exceeds feelings and intuitions, it operates at the conceptual level, at which individuals express thought through a developed symbol system, such as the language system (see also Alexander 1972: 33–57 and 58–80).

One has to agree with Alexander (1972: 26) that "symbolic systems may have a genuine and considerable influence upon concept formation", especially as "[t]he habits of linguistic patterning channel thoughts into well-formed grooves" of which humans are mostly unaware, so that languages help to them orient in the world. To be precise, the concepts "colour the character of referents" and, hence, linguistic symbol systems influence the ways humans see objects. Thus, after Alexander, not only language considerably controls human thinking, but vice versa, also thinking shapes language. Literally, "the organizational schemes of the various languages have been built up through habits of conceiving", which as such, "must to some extent arise in response to perceptual stimuli," therefore, they seem to be "reasonably reliable indicators of the way things are" Alexander (1972: 27).

Anyway, language, as such, is, for the philosophers of language, what also Alexander (1972: 48–55) proves, complementary to thinking. The various natural languages of the world, associated by people with their phonetic aspects, offer human individuals, as Alexander (1972: 49, cf. also 81–103) demonstrates, (1) sets of shared words and (2) traditional grammatical structures (syntax) in which the arrangement of these words substantially varies depending on the range of meanings. As to the thought processes of human individuals proceeding thanks to language, they are so dependent on the concepts in their languages (offering freely available ways of expressing ideas) that it is quite impossible to conceive of thinking without language. Though the individual can break the habits of language, he/she cannot fundamentally change the structure of the language. Another thing is, what Alexander (1972: 54) does not doubt, that "there are many more distinguishable relationships in experience than any one particular language incorporates into its syntax. Consequently, each language omits explicit formulations of a great many of these relationships. Despite this, symbols, standing for referents, exactly for everything man has discovered or imagined, give him a new dimension of reality not possessed by the other animals (cf. Alexander 1972: 59), and the vocal sounds of language "are apparently the most natural symbolic formation of man" (Alexander 1972: 63). However, one cannot settle for stating that language exists only as symbols available to perception. Rather, since linguistic thinking consists of operating mental representations of concepts, such as the meanings of words and sentences, the manifestation of language in the minds of the speaking and thinking individuals is a phenomenon worth considering from the viewpoint of how concepts are formed through the mental processes of abstracting, imagining, and generalizing.

In short, Alexander (1972: 108), whose considerations profoundly draw on rationalism, empiricism, and idealism in philosophy, states that all concepts are formed either by simple abstracting or by imaginative altering of abstractions. Simple abstracting is a mental process related to perception, over and over again repeating in the mind of the individual, that is, taking place continuously when he/she focuses attention upon some feature within his/her experience and holds this feature as the object of his/her immediate thought to possibly remember it later.

In turn, imaginative altering of abstractions comes to pass when the individual transforms objects in his/her mind, imagining them in different ways. In the creative processes of imagination, thoroughly described by Alexander (1972: 202–215), a human individual forms mental images and concepts of objects, which may be, in a particular moment, absent, do not exist as such, or are inconceivable at all. This way, exactly through imagination, the individual moves beyond the limits of his/her sensorial experience. Generalizing, in turn, that is, taking the abstracted objects in a class of objects, is, in concept formation and language-based thinking, necessary as well, for linguistic concepts refer to objects as belonging to "a bunch or class of any kind of thing grouped together because of similarity of the members" (Alexander 1972: 230), not to individual items. Thus, on the one hand, imaginative processes are impossible without the human ability to produce (verbal) signs, to use them in interpersonal communication, and to refer them to the extra-linguistic reality, and on the other, symbolic (linguistic) thinking through concepts is indispensable for human individuals to be able to communicate the contents of their consciousness to each other.

2.2 Consciousness and thought in cybernetic and cognitive perspectives

From among approaches to consciousness and thought, worthy of special notice are those which were elaborated by cybersemiotically- and cognitively-oriented researchers of communication, as for example, Søren Brier (2003), and Jordan Zlatev (2009). They appreciate the role of thought processes in communication at the social level and show the hierarchical structure of cognitive processes related to the formation of subjective meanings.

Demonstrating semantic differences between semiotics-related terms, such as *intrasemiotics* and *phenosemiotics*, concerning the terms *exosemiotics* and *endosemiotics* designating self-organizing processes that take place in living systems, Brier (2003: 71) put forward the term *thought semiotics*. Brier's perspective on thinking processes seems to be inasmuch important that, for him, it would be impossible to explain the semiotic nature of communication without accounting for mind-body interactions at several interdependent levels of information transmission and sign production, reception, and interpretation. By and large, these levels of semiotic processes correspond to the properties of human beings as communicating subjects, which are of at least fourfold nature.

Brier (2003: 77–78) describes the levels of semiotic processes in the following words. Firstly, humans, as physical beings, display the physicochemical aspects of themselves as embedded in the natural environment. Secondly, as embodied beings, humans share their corporality with other living species. Thirdly, as feeling and knowing beings, they experience their emotions and thoughts, manifesting themselves as mind and consciousness. And fourthly, as cultural beings, they function in the world of culture thanks to language that allows them to create and interpret the meanings. Accordingly, since (1) the physical nature of human communicative behaviour is explained from energy and matter, (2) living systems – from the development of life processes, (3) social sign cultures – from the development of meaning, while (4) the inner mental world of humans is explained from the conscious processes of thinking, there are four different areas of knowledge which fall within the scope of the interests of scholars who investigate "the communicative social system of embodied minds" (quoted and cited after Brier 2003: 78).

Getting to the point of Brier's deliberations on semiosis and information exchange, one has to note that its essential part is his reference to the relevance of the conception of *autopoiesis*, (first used by Humberto Romesin Maturana, a Chilean biologist, in his report in 1970 (widely known from the work of Maturana and Francisco Javier Varela García *Autopoiesis and Cognition: The Realization of the Living* (cf. 1980/1970/). An extended understanding of the term *autopoiesis* was proposed by Niklas Luhmann (1990) as the model of Triadic Autopoietic Systems, applicable to higher levels of communication. One has to stress, after Brier, that, unlike Maturana and Varela, who treated living beings as self-organizing systems in a biological sense, Luhmann, presenting a comprehensive view of social communication, acknowledged the role of psychological thinking systems, which operate within the socio-communicative systems, as unconditionally indispensable for communication to occur. What Brier (2003: 84) admits, he became interested, as a cybersemiotician, in the human psyche as "a silent, inner system of perception, emotions, and volitions", functioning in communication alongside the linguistic system, being inspired by Luhmann. It seems obvious here, what Brier also stresses, that in the case of humans, the linguistic system is indispensable for communication to occur within social systems, for which human bodies and minds constitute, from the social cybernetics perspective, the surroundings.

As regards the concepts defined and used by Brier (2003: 86–88) for the tasks of cybercemiotic studies, thought semiotics is, for him, the interaction between the psyche and the linguistic system during which "culture through concepts offers the individuals potential classifications of their inner states of feelings, perceptions, and volitions." As such, it constitutes just a small part of all the processes that cybersemiotics deals with. Next, what Brier calls phenosemiotic processes (phenosemiosis, prelinguistic experiences) are the non-conceptual, that is, pre-linguistic states that are not recognized by conceptual consciousness. In turn, the interactions between the psyche and body (precisely between the psychological and the biological autopoiesis), occurring, in fact, within the body are called by Brier intrasemiotics, especially as they are different from internal bodily purely biological processes (endosemiotics). It should be added here that the endosemiosis, the semiotic interactions at a biological level only, that is, between cells, tissues, and organs, is set against exosemiosis, the sign processes occurring between the organisms, especially if one refers to the terms used, *inter alia*, by Thomas A. Sebeok (1976).

What follows from Brier's (2003: 88–89) reasoning upon the different types of semiosis and proto-semiotic processes is that there is relatively little knowledge about the dependences between the lived inner world of feeling, volitions, and intensions of the individual constituting an autopoietic system different from another autopoietic system of the biological self (arising as a result semiotic interactions between the hormone systems, nervous system and the immune system). Brier notices, discussing relevant examples, that the systems in question are systems with closure, especially as, though there are grounds to generally conclude about the embodiment of the human mind, it is not possible, at present, to infer about the subtle interaction between them. Evidently, the awareness of certain bodily functions or imagination can influence physiological functions. Likewise, some hormones effect sexual or maternal responses and some emotions trigger chemical reactions that change the kind and time of reaction time of many bodily functions, and so on. That is to say, current knowledge about intrasemiotic processes is still insufficient to properly analyse the multifaceted interplay between the perceptions, thoughts, and feelings of the individual and his or her bodily states working, *inter alia*, through the reticular activating system in the brain. Convinced of the embodiment of the mind, researchers, having extensive knowledge of particular systems or levels of autopoiesis, are not able to trace thinking processes as correlated with the embodiment of the mind. Only the nervous, hormonal, and immune systems, responsible for the qualitatively different activities, are kind of internally closed, and their autopoietic description as living cybernetic systems "does not really open for sign production per se" so that "semiotics in itself does not reflect very much about the role of embodiment in creating signification". Following Brier's (2003: 90) reasoning, one can, however, admit that the body-and-mind, or the body-and-thought systems, form complex phenomenological dynamical systems, responsible not only, as Brier believes, for exerting influence on their environment, including the other body-and-mind systems, especially through their significative-communicative activities, but also of constructing of oneself.

Zlatev's (2009) typological depiction of the distribution of consciousness in humans and non-humans is an example of an evolutionary-phenomenological-semiotic approach to the cognitive processes in the organization of meaning. It delineates a four-level hierarchy in the development of consciousness (including, in Zlatev's terms, life, consciousness, sign, and language). Thus, language-based consciousness that operates in the human mind inseparably from the functioning of the species-specific system of two-class social symbols, functioning as a means of communication in the human world, is at the very top of these hierarchically ordered interrelated semiotic systems. Considering the four stages, or levels, at which, meanings are formed, described by Zlatev, one has to reflect upon consciousness as the property of living systems. Above all, it seems doubtful whether those biological organisms as living systems, which are distinguished by their behaviours within an *Umwelt* and, as such, are characterized by autopoiesis (the ability of self-organization), situated at the first level, possess consciousness or can be called conscious. As for both the minimal self, at the second level in Zlatev's hierarchy, being equipped with the ability to act intentionally in its directly perceived natural *Lebenswelt*, and the enculturated self, at the third level, being able to act in a culturally mediated *Lebenswelt*, they undoubtedly show some forms of consciousness. Nevertheless, only the linguistic self, situated at the fourth level, is featured by the ability of thinking, in Zlatev's (2009: 186–187) words, the capacity of manipulating conventional-normative semiotic systems for communication and thought, such as "spoken, signed and written languages (and derivative forms, such as mathematical and logical notations)", known to and investigated by semioticians.

All in all, the hierarchical order of the levels, such as life, consciousness, sign and language, at which, in Zlatev's view, meanings are created, implies that consciousness itself could be viewed as a transitory stage from life to the intersubjectivity and imitation-based signs, facilitating, as such, the evolution of language. What Zlatev himself stresses is that his semiotic hierarchy with human language at the top indicates that humans "live in subjectively coloured, but intersubjectively shared *Lifeworlds*, which differ across cultures to various extents, but are all grounded in a common Panhuman "natural" *Lebenswelt* due to certain universal features of human consciousness (and the human *Umwelt*)." To some degree, humans share, in Zlatev's opinion, their experiential worlds "with at least some non-human animals." Still, it is difficult to agree at this point with Zlatev that humans, being "unique as (spontaneous) sign users, and especially language users on this planet," "are not unique as semiotic and conscious creatures, implying the need for a more ethical attitude to our fellow living beings" (quoted and cited after Zlatev 2009: 196).

Summing up both transdisciplinary approaches to consciousness, one can notice that thinking involving symbolic signification as a semiotic process is a very small segment of semiotic processes in communicative systems. The related issue, which demands here a proper comment, is the role of language-based thinking in the development of self-consciousness, and accordingly the perception by the individual of his/her identity.

3 Communicational identity of the human self

It seems right to refer to thought semiotics examining the interaction between the psyche and language, when realizing the diversity of emotional-intellectual faculties and mental capabilities of the thinking and communicating subjects, such as perceiving and memorizing or remembering, anticipating and imagining, reasoning and concluding, valuing and judging. These competencies of humans, largely based on language and culture, are a necessary precondition to their personal growth and the development of their multiple identities.

Essentially, one should accept Locke's view of identity as tightly related to consciousness. For the British empiricist philosopher, the sense of identity was the same as consciousness, viz., the recognition of what passes through the mind of man. So it was Locke who associated personal identity, similarly to consciousness, with the mechanisms of perception and the abilities to reflect on facts (information) both perceived and remembered by a particular person. In Book II Chapter XXVII, "On identity and diversity" in *An Essay Concerning Human Understanding* ([1690] 1952: 218–228), Locke came to believe that personal identity was, in truth, the continual self-identification of oneself as the same person, and as such, a mental process consisting of repeated, recurrent acts of consciousness.

Remaining with the statement of Locke that thought processes and consciousness are important from the viewpoint of human identity, one has to consider the process of sending and receiving of messages within the same individual, called by representatives of communication studies, intrapersonal communication. It is, as a matter of fact, equal, in their opinion, to the formation of self-concept, or discovering and defining oneself as a person. Thus, one has to take for granted, for example, agreeing with Larry Lee Barker (1978: 109–132), Raymond S. Ross ([1965] 1974: 6–19), and Jacquelyn B. Carr (1979: 53–73), that human individuals, able to take the first-person perspective, have multiple identities as they tend to explore their various perceptions of themselves, gathering various experiences of themselves in different situations over time.

The multiple identities of the human self, as summarized in a monographic publication on manifestations of the linguistic self in human communication by Wąsik (2020: 55) after Ross ([1965] 1974), Barker (1978), and Carr (1979), depend upon how it experiences (1) the singularity and individuality of its own body as an object situated in space and time, (2) itself in relation to others, attempting to take the perspective of others, when imagining how it is viewed by others, (3) its own changing drives, needs, feelings, and emotions, etc., (4) its own thoughts and reflections, especially internal, verbally conducted monologs that refer to events taking place in its life, (5) the dynamics of its own action, performed according to repeating patterns and determined by the (social) situations, (6) its own public self (not known to others), that is, the image the self deliberately projects to others which, being the result of self-presentation, is the opposite of the private self, (7) the durability and stability of its own corporeal and spiritual existence over time, related to memory, especially its ability to recall its own emotional, volitional, and cognitive experiences, as well as (8) continuity of the own past and present selves, and (9) tensions between the present (current) and future selves.

The identity of the individual is defined by social psychologists with regard to two relationships, most important for the human being, such as his/her relationship to oneself and to other people, and thus also to culture and tradition. Examining how human individuals become conscious of these relationships in social situations, for example, John P. Hewitt (1989: 153–155) viewed identity, as (1) a sense, or a feeling about self, (2) an organization of individual sensitivities to the external world, which is (3) a consequence of human existence in the world, (4) manifesting itself through multiple impulsive responses to external objects, and (5) based on a motivational force so that no activity can proceed without it.

According to Hewitt (1989: 151–164), thoroughly discussed by Wąsik (2020: 71–74), the social behaviour of the individual principally requires an objectification of his/her self regarding a specific aspect of his or her existence, so he/she can create, maintain, or challenge his/her identity depending on the communicative situation. Coping with his/her identity, the individual sometimes has to go beyond his/her perspective to view the situation from the perspective of the other. However, taking some social roles in some situations, the individual may fully concentrate on them, and this way, at least for some time, act as an integrated, internally coherent personality. Also, as events, in socially defined situations, take place and make sense sequentially; the individual has to adjust his/her behaviour to their temporal logic. Nevertheless, in many social situations, his/her identity is put to the test, especially due to an unexpected, undeniable evaluation of his/her conduct by self or others, the constant exposure to (unfeasible) challenges, or long-lasting tensions between identification (a feeling of being like others) and differentiation (a sense of being different from others) despite the coincidence of objectives. Anyway, human individuals are able either to adopt or refuse some goals when they perceive their self-interest as different from that of the group. Many situations in which they communicate, though socially defined, may be problematic, but, at any rate, episodes interrupting ongoing activities may help improve the identities of individuals, not only, as one could guess, reveal their character. All in all, the participation in communicative events brings about the transformation of self-consciousness into the consciousness of identity or some of its dimensions.

Being aware that identity is both a necessary condition for action and a product of the situation itself, one has to state, from the perspective of social psychology, that (1) a person, engaging in a social activity, concentrates all his/her energy on remaining that person, at least within the social reality created by that activity, (2) the situated experience of personal continuity, provided by social situations, in general, corresponds to the meaning of events, which follow each other in a particular situation, (3) the identity of the individual is the result of their identification with the situation, as such, and with other communication participants as well as their sense of distinctiveness within the community. And one has to add that human beings are not able to act without identifying with others and the collective aims or interests they share with others since the organization of their own impulses is possible only through the acts of identification. This reflection leads to pondering the foundations of existential semiotics treating identity in terms of transcending signs of collective subjectivity.

4 Existential identity in a semiotic perspective

Against the background of views on consciousness, thinking, and identity presented in a historical-ordering account, one should refer to Eero Tarasti's growth of existential semiotics, having merged the phenomenological traditions of absolutists idealism and ego-centred existentialism, which emphasises on ontological reflections about human existence in the world between immanence and transcendence with biologist semiotics in which the organisms endowed with ego-quality attach meanings to objects founds in their circles of life. This new framework, called respectively neosemiotics or new semiotics (Fr. *la nouvelle sémiotique*) at the 12th World Congress of IASS/IAS, has been steadily modified and presented by Tarasti in his numerous lectures and publications at the international forum. Among his recent outputs of scientific labour worth discussing, against the background of his perennial manual *Existential Semiotics* (2000), are his article "Existential semiotics and cultural psychology" published in *The Oxford Handbook of Culture and Psychology* (2011), and his subsequent larger monographs, *Semiotics of Classical Music: How Mozart, Brahms and Wagner Talk to Us* (2012), and *Sein und Schein. Explorations in Existential Semiotics* (2015), which are ripe enough to be applied by researchers as the conceptual-terminological tools for examining human subjectivity as an aspect of consciousness from a semiotic perspective.

Tarasti's dynamic model of new semiotics focuses on human subjects as creators of the "existential signs", that is, the signs they produce in their *Dasein*, reflecting (or representing) as such, their subjective, unique, experiences of being. Exactly saying, under discussion are the mental states of humans, preceding, accompanying, and following the creation of signs, which, otherwise, are not available to any explorations or analyses in a direct way. As to the signifying-communicating subject, experiencing such states, he/she is, in existential-semiotic terms, "an imaginary body" and "a kind of transcendental being" (Tarasti 2000: 21), constantly changing oneself, affecting others, shaping his/her environment, etc.

In existential semiotics, the individual, when sending, receiving, creating, and interpreting messages, is not a submissive, unreflective subject or interpreter who decodes them merely according to social norms and requirements. Assuming that signs in communication can only be understood in connection with the psychological conditions of their producers and users, for example, their needs and desires, feelings and emotions, or attitudes and values, etc., existential semiotics accentuates the fact that significative-communicative acts are the acts of transcendence in a semiotic sense. This kind of transcendence is, "a transition, a shift between two *Daseins*," as Tarasti (2000: 23) puts it, the "fictive and intuitive counterpart of which "could be the sharing of signs, for instance, between two style-periods of art, or between two historical phases of the same society, or between two temporal moments in the life of an individual." especially as the human subject, when acting, "has the liberty to pursue affirmation and negation" (Tarasti 2011: 325).

Semiotic transcendence takes place when a self-conscious signifying-communicating subject is more or less faced with the possibility of making choices. Then, to quote Tarasti, who frequently makes references to the "existential moves" described by Sartre, he (the subject) "transforms transcendental ideas into signs", so that his existence reaches "the level of signs", ceasing to be "a series of detached moments in the process of communication without a real content" (Tarasti 2011: 325). Assuming that the formation of signs is "[t]he continuous crossing-over limits of transcendence and *Dasein*" (2011: 325), Tarasti explains how the unceasing experiences of human individuals in their *Dasein* determine the way they subjectively equip their signs (or strings of signs) with meanings, frequently idiosyncratic, and as such, detached from original contexts or settings. Tarasti maintains that:

> [T]he individual who has clung to the communication processes of his *Dasein*, as rich as they may ever be, is blinded to its contents, to the true semiosis of ideas and acts of signification, and believes it is empty. Therefore, only when he abandons the boundaries of his *Dasein* or via an act of conception and is able to step over this borderline, does he realize the true plenitude of the transcendence. This experience is connected with the existential experience that he is already waited for on the other side of the boundary. All that positive or negative, which he has left in his life, waits for him in the transcendence. Thus mimesis means transgressing the boundary, striving to get beyond oneself and its realization.
> (Tarasti 2011: 325)

Taking the viewpoint of existential semiotics, one has to say (as Tarasti consequently argues, cf., *inter alia*, 2012: 74) that the presence of transcendence in *Dasein* makes up the existence of man. Exactly, treating transcendence as the key concept for pondering upon the subjectivity of signs, it (existential semiotics) takes an in-depth interest in such mental acts of human individuals, through which that what is absent makes itself present (re-presents itself) in their minds, enabling them to exist in *Dasein*. In these acts, it is the signs that are, in existential semiotic terms, in constant movement between transcendence and *Dasein*.

To move on to identity, considered, in psychological terms, as a product of self-consciousness, it corresponds to the awareness of the individuals of their separateness from others, on the one hand, and their membership in social, cultural, or ethnic groups, on the other, and is, as such, decisive for their relationships with their lifeworlds. It stands to reason that the individual discovers, creates, and expresses his/her identity through linguistic and non-linguistic signs he/she produces in social communication at certain levels of his/her personal development. The sense of identity is, in this view, a sense of relationships of a special kind, the one that connects the subject with him/herself, with his/her own psychophysical and moral condition and, at the same time, the sense of the relationship with others. One needs to add that such relationships, based on more or less conscious attitudes towards some distinguished values, carried either by the subject or by other people, or a culture, arise, just as existential semiotics proposes, as the outcome of the acts of transcendence.

In terms of existential semiotics, identity can be seen as a kind of *being* perceived by the individual as a dynamic semiotic subject from the first-person perspective. As such, the perception of identity, being a prerequisite of his/her performance, is one of the aspects of the subject whose significative-communicative activities occur in and are determined by a particular situation or context. To characterize the subject, one has to note that these activities constantly put him in a position between transcendence and *Dasein*, especially as the types of his signs, such as (1) virtual pre-signs (having not yet become externalized in his performance or the products of it), (2) act signs (the observable significative-communicative activities as well is products), and (3) post-signs (exercising their impact upon other subjects, are all transcendental entities. The subject is also distinguished by transcendental values which may become sings through his actions in the *Dasein*. From the perspective of existential semiotics, the subject not only participates in symbolic-semiotic processes or only produces and receives the so-called exosigns, the signs which are external to him. Also, the signs internal to the subject, the so-called endosigns attract the attention of existential semiotics. Moreover, the semiotic activity of the subject and its products are analysed or interpreted in terms of the phenosigns (the signs which stand for, or denote, something) and, especially the genosigns, if transformations they undergo in their continuity when becoming ultimate sings, are taken into account (cf., for example, Tarasti 2012: 74–77).

To elaborate upon the changeability of the signifying-communicating subjects in *Dasein* and the dynamics of his signs, existential semiotics redefines some concepts from classical philosophy and semiotic theory, largely the semiotics of music, having regard to the role of musical identity in the personal development and education of adept musicians (as has been repeatedly emphasized by Tarasti in his works, *inter alia*, in 2012: 135–142 cf., for example, Tarasti 2012: 135–136). In this particular approach, the mental states of the subject, which are responsible for the formation of signs, corresponding to the existential varieties of *Moi* and *Soi* as private and social aspects of the self, described through the categories "being-in-itself" and "being-for-itself". Tarasti characterizes these mental states and existential varieties of the subject as follows:

> The first of these [categories] is something that stands by its pure inner qualities, "*an sich*" – of, according to Kant, we can know nothing. Yet, when this entity an sich enters a social context, it is determined by the latter, and becomes für sich. For instance, someone who is good with hands (an sich) may become a tailor, pianist, or baker (*für sich*); who is good at speaking may become a teacher, politician, or priest. And so on. To this Hegelian distinction we add the point of view of subject in the proper sense, what is in French called the *Moi* (*Me*). In this way we derive two more categories: an-mir sein (being in-myself) and für-mich sein (being for-myself).
>
> The remaining category is that of "*Soi*", or the self as determined by society: being-for-oneself and being-in-oneself. This last means society with its abstract values and norms; the former designates exemplifications of those values and norms via institutions and other social practices. For instance, if the values of being in-oneself is Beauty, it can manifest through a conservatory of it aural aesthetics; if the values is visual, then through an arts academy; if patriotism, its corresponding practice might be the army. These two aspects of *Moi* and *Soi* represent two sides of our inner subjectivity: the social has impact on and power over us only because it has internalized in our minds. In this way, the *Soi* can impose itself on our *Moi*. (Tarasti 2012: 135–136)

Being interested in the perception of existential identity, Tarasti exhibits the significance of the formation of signs in the mind of its observer. Identity corresponds to being-for-myself, the level of actualization, when the individual takes the role/position of an observer, capable of the acts of negation, and thus of semiotic transcendence of which he/she is aware. Feeling/receiving support for his/her activity in his/her corporeality, the self-aware individual as a subject is featured by habitual behaviour marked by its relation to itself. However, in order to perceive its identity, the subject must first find himself in, or pass, the being-in-myself, as the bodily ego that is not conscious of itself. Being-for-myself is a variety of being in the individual sphere (*Moi*), similarly to being-in-myself, and both condition two other, higher varieties of being, taking place in the collective sphere (*Soi*), such as being-in-itself and being-for-it-self.

Thus, in the next order, being-in-itself, a variety of being depending on identity is characterized by transcendence as well, that is, the moves through which the subject actualizes, or not, virtual norms, ideas, and values in relation to other subjects or to external objects. Correlated with being-in-itself, the subject expresses his duties and shows his desires to perform some actions. Also, as to being-for-it-self, this variety of being implies that the subject brings to life the norms, ideas, and values in his *Dasein* transforming them, thanks to his creativity. The behaviour of the subject, producing new information, becomes unexpected. These varieties of the modes of existence form a sequence in which being-for-myself (conceptualized as identity) follows being-in-myself and precedes being-in-itself and being-for-itself (cf., especially Tarasti 2000: 197–198, 2011: 327–331, 2012: 25–27, 2015: 21–27).

As identity (determined by being-for-myself), similarly to other modalities, is reflected in the significative-communicative acts of humans, including their verbal behaviours and texts as their products, the researcher examining it, should take into account the following tents of existential semiotics (quoted here literally after Tarasti, 2011: 331–337, 2015: 29–38). (I) Every sign or text stems from its being, or a certain being behind it: ontological foundation. (II) Each sign or text is either done by a subject in a given state of being or it emerges "originally" from it. (III) One mode of being transforms, changes into another. (IV) Different modes of being are in a dialog with each other. (V) What does it mean that one mode of being changes into another? (Continuous transformations of the modes of being are guarantee of the development of the individual and society and the formation of new identities.) (VI) Every mode of being has its history – that is memory of what it was, and expectations of what it will be. (VII) Every sign or text is considered an appearance with regard to its Being; thus, Being constitutes its truth. (VIII) In a dialogue between two subjects, modes take place in different "levels" or modes. (IX) The real semiotic forces in the universe occur in the opposed directions from body to values, from concrete to abstract or from values and norms to body. (X) The encounter or touch between *Moi* and *Soi* or body and society takes place between identity and social roles (in semiotic terms, between gesture and genre). (XI) In the analysis of subjects (of Being and Doing) and their representations (appearing), the four modes can exist simultaneously; they are looming behind each other. (XII) Among the modes, there exists a process of learning from a subject's inner points of view or, teaching. (XIII) Every mode of Being and Doing as well as becoming has its own ambience, atmosphere, *Stimmung*, how they feel in their positions. (XIV) From every stage or mode, there are open possibilities for reflection (*Schauen*), distanciation, alienation, and existentiality, which means a shift to a metalevel, "metabeing" via affirmation/negation. Hence, the possibility of freedom opens on the side of necessity. (XV) One mode of being can compensate or sublimate another. (XVI) Every mode of being is an actuality, but in a dialogue with others it becomes reality; yet, they originate from virtuality and they are aiming for virtualities. (XVII) Every mode of being has one dominating modality while organizing and subordinating others.

In existential semiotics, two spheres of semiotic activity of the subject, his individual and collective subjectivities, seemingly opposed to each other, are seen as interrelated. Significant is the argument (cf. Tarasti 2015: 137) that collective subjectivity or individual identity, as a worldview, is "a kind of filter between the environment and the self" that "selects which ideas from transcendence are finally realized in the *Dasein* of an individual or community." Regarding individual subjectivity, Tarasti (2015: 141–143) believes that the study of semiotic manifestations of movements within it allows researchers to examine the ways/modes the self-conscious individual opposes norms and values, being on the path of its discontinuous development. Based on existential semiotics, one comes to the belief that the collective identity and the individual identity as two sides of the subjectivity of the embodied subject, motivate his/her socio-cultural experiences and activities.

Seen through the lens of existential semiotics, the conception of the identity of the human self appears to be definitely different from the belief assuming that the self-identity is jointly constructed by members of a community as a result of their everyday-life interactions, similarly to the case of their worldviews. The existentialist conception presupposes a search for expressions of collective and individual identities rather than for shared meanings communicated by humans at different social levels. Agreeing with tenets of existential semiotics that the acts of consciousness and thinking are the imagination-related acts of semiotic transcendence, in which language enables the kinds of being that depend on the sense of identity, researchers have to pay attention to linguistic thinking involving signification, the contents of which are sometimes externalized as spoken or written texts.

5 Concluding remarks

Narrowing down the considerations about the semiotic subject, who performs his significative-communicative acts, moving between the four kinds of being, to language as the property of his mind, one should mention the concept of the linguistic self. At its core, there is an assumption that the emergence and development of language in both phylogenetic and ontogenetic terms, has been possible thanks to some mental endowments of man, such as, in particular, (self-)consciousness and subjective thinking, and, at the same time, that thinking would not be possible without language. The concept of the linguistic self accounts for the significance of some factors, both internal and external, for humans as language speakers. Hereto belong, especially (1) their broadly understood ecological, that is, natural and cultural environments, (2) the physical and mental aspects of human communication (to be investigated respectively in the physical domain of meaning bearers and the logical domain of subjective inferences), and the resulting distinction between observable and concluded facts or linguistic properties of communicating individuals, (3) the phenomenological structures of the consciousness of humans, including intentionality (orientation toward an object, or objects, they experienced from the first-person perspective, as determined by existence and transcendence), and (4) forms of beings as existential subjects and modalities of their semiotic expression through both verbal and nonverbal means.

As regards the linguistic self, who thinks in and speaks a natural language, its significative-communicative skills seem to be responsible for semiotic transcendence. Its involvement in intra- and interpersonal communication requires mastering complex skills, which enable it both to create, distinguish, delimit, and recognize semantic signals and to interpret their communicative values, and this way, to attain mutual understanding through linguistic utterances. Considering language as a property of the human mind, which manifests itself in the form of language rules and communicative abilities internalized in human consciousness, one can become convinced of the complex nature of semiotic (or linguistic) transcendence, especially if one lists the communicative skills of the human self (distinguished by analogy with the multiple properties and aspects of natural languages and more exhaustively discussed in Wąsik 2020: 81–86). To delineate them, one has to mention, in particular, the form-related skills, such as substantial and grammatical, the function-related skills, that is, semantic, semasiological, onomasiological, and pragmatic skills of the human self (which, in fact, exceed the boundaries of language itself, such as stylistic, rhetorical, dialectical, and hermeneutic properties), further divided, *inter alia*, into morphemic properties, lexemic, phrasemic as well as expressive, representational, impressive, emotive, referential, poetic, phatic, metalinguistic, conative and also interrogative, exclamative, imperative, and directive, on the one hand, and, on the other, diagnostic and prognostic, including also descriptive, explicative, comparative, and argumentative skills of speakers/hearers. Finally, to communicate by differentiated speech acts and genres, while selecting appropriate means for eliciting, conducting, or maintaining conversation, discussion or debate, for convincing someone about something or persuading someone into or from something, for mitigating or moderating conflict, are verbal behaviours which demand respective skills from the human self.

References

Alexander, Hubert Griggs. 1972 [1967]. *The Language and Logic of Philosophy*, enlarged edition. Albuquerque, NM: University of New Mexico Press.
Aristotle. 1893 [1881, c. 347–330 B.C. (or 349 B.C.)]. *The Nicomachean Ethics of Aristotle*. Trans by F. H. Peters, 5th edn. London: Kegan Paul, Trench, Trübner.
Aristotle. 1927 [c. 347–330 B.C. (or 349 B.C.)] *Nicomachean Ethics*, Trans. by H. (Harris) Rackham. Cambridge, MA: Harvard University Press. (Αριστοτέλης. Ἠθικὰ Νικομάχεια. (Editor:) Νικόμαχος (the son of Aristotle)).
Barker, Larry Lee. 1978. *Communication*. Englewood Cliffs, New Jersey: Prentice-Hall, Inc.
Bergson, Henri-Louis 1911 [1896]. *Matter and Memory. Essay on the Relation of Body and Spirit*. Trans. by Nancy Margaret Paul & W. Scott Palmer. London: George Allen & Unwin [*Matière et mémoire. Essai sur la relation du corps à l'esprit*. Paris : Presses universitaires de France].
Bois, Joseph Samuel. 1972 [1966]. *The Art of Awareness: A Text on General Semantics and Epistemics*, 2nd edn. Dubuque, IA: W. C. Brown.
Bradley, Francis Herbert. 1897 [1893]. *Appearance and Reality. A Metaphysical Essay*, 2nd edn., revised, with an Appendix. London, Oxford: Clarendon.
Brier, Søren. 2003. The cybersemiotic model of communication: An evolutionary view on the threshold between semiosis and informational exchange. *tripleC* 1(1). 71–94.
Carr, Jacquelyn B. 1979. *Communicating and Relating*. Menlo Park, CA, Reading, MA, London, Amsterdam, Don Mills, ON, Sydney: The Benjamin/Cummings Publishing Company.
Descartes, René. 2011 [1637]. *Discours de la méthode* (1637). René Descartes (1596–1650) Édition électronique (ePub) v.: 1,0 : Les Échos du Maquis [*Discours de la méthode Pour bien conduire sa raison, et chercher la vérité dans les sciences. Plus La dioprique des Meteores et La geometrie qui sont les effets de cette methode*. A Leyde: De l'imprimerie de Ian Maire CIƆ IƆC XXXVII].
Descartes, Renatius. 1642 [1641]. (*Renati Des-Cartes*) *Meditationes de prima philosophia, in quibus Dei existentia, et animae humanae a corpore distinctio, demonstrantur. His adjunctae sunt variae objectiones doctorum virorum in istas de Deo et anima demonstrationes*; Cum responsionibus authoris. Secunda editio septimis objectionibus antehac non visis aucta. Amstelodami, Apud Ludovicum Elzevirium. M DC XLII [*Meditationes de prima philosophia, in qua Dei existentia et anima immortalitas demonstrate*. Parisiis Apud Michaelem Soly via Iacobel, sub signo Phoenicis, M DC XLI]. Electronic elaboration, Corpus Descartes, édition en ligne des œuvres et de la correspondance de Descartes, at: http://www.unicaen.fr/puc/sources/prodescartes/
Durant, Will. 1962 [1926]. *The Story of Philosophy. The Lives of Opinions of the Greater Philosophers*. New York: Simon and Schuster.
Gadamer, Hans Georg. 1989/1975 [1960]. *Truth and Method*, 2nd revised edn. Trans. by Joel Weinsheimer & Donald G. Marshall. London, New York: Continuum. [*Wahrheit und Methode*. Tübingen: Mohr].
Hegel, Georg Wilhelm Friedrich. 1910 [1807]. *Phenomenology of Mind*. Trans., introduction & notes by James Black Baillie. London, UK: George Allen & Unwin; London, UK: Swan Sonnenschein and Co.; New York, NY: The Macmillan Company. (*Die Phänomenologie des Geistes. System der Wissenschaft*. Erster Theil. Bamberg, Würzburg: Verlag Joseph Anton Goebhardt).

Heidegger, Martin. 1962 [1927]. *Being and Time*. Trans. by John Macquarrie & Edward Robinson. London: SCM Press. (*Sein und Zeit*. Tübingen: Max Niemeyer Verlag).
Hewitt, John P. 1989. *Dilemmas of the American Self*. Philadelphia, PA: Temple University Press.
Hume, David. 1952 [1758]. An enquiry concerning human understanding. In Robert Maynard Hutchins (ed.), *Great Books of the Western World*, 451–509. Chicago, London, Toronto: Encyclopaedia Britannica [In *Essays and Treatise on Several Subjects by David Hume*. Vol. III. *Containing an Enquiry Concerning Human Understanding*. A new edition. London: Printed for A. Millar, in the Strand, and A. Kincaid and A. Donaldson, at Edinburgh, MDCCLX].
Husserl, Edmund. 1982 [1913]. *Ideas Pertaining to a Pure Phenomenology and to a Phenomenological Philosophy*. First Book: *General Introduction to a Pure Phenomenology*. Trans. by Fred Kersten. The Hague: Martinus Nijhoff. (*Ideen zu einer reinen Phänomenologie und phänomenologischen Philosophie*. Erstes Buch: *Allgemeine Einführung in die reine Phänomenologie. Jahrbuch für Phänomenologie und phänomenologische Forschung* 1(1). 1–323. Max Niemeyer Verlag: Halle an der Saale).
Husserl, Edmund. 1970 [1954]. *The Crisis of European Sciences and Transcendental Phenomenology: An Introduction to Phenomenological Philosophy*. Trans. by David Carr. Evanston, IL: Northwestern University Press. (*Die Krisis der europäischen Wissenschaften und die transzendentale Phänomenologie. Eine Einleitung in die phänomenologische Philosophie*. In Walter Biemel (ed.), *Husserliana. Edmund Husserl, Gesammelte Werke*. Band VI. Den Haag: Martinus Nijhoff).
James, William. 1890. *Principles of Psychology*. New York, NY: Henry Holt and Company.
Jorgensen, Larry M. 2020. Seventeenth-century theories of consciousness. *The Stanford Encyclopedia of Philosophy* (Spring 2020 Edition), Edward N. Zalta (ed.), URL = <https://plato.stanford.edu/archives/spr2020/entries/consciousness-17th/>.
Kant, Immanuel. 1838 [1781]. *Critique of Pure Reason*. Trans. by Francis Haywood. London, UK: William Pickering. (*Critik der reinen Vernunft*. Riga: Johann Friedrich Hartknoch).
Kierkegaard, Søren. 1941 [1843]. A joint English edition: *Fear and Trembling. A Dialectical Lyric* and *The Sickness Unto Death*. Trans. by Walter Lowrie. Princeton, New Jersey: Princeton University Press. (*Frygt og Bæven. Dialektisk Lyrik af Johannes de silentio*. København: C. A. Reitzel).
Locke, John. 1952 [1690]. An essay concerning human understanding. In Robert Maynard Hutchins (ed.), *Great Books of the Western World*, 85–395. Chicago, London & Toronto: William Benton. (*An Essay Concerning Human Understanding*. London: Printed by Eliz. Holt, for Thomas Basset and sold by Edw. Mory at the Sign of the Three Bibles in St. Paul's Church-Yard. MDCXC).
Luhmann, Niklas. 1990. *Essays on Self-Reference*. New York, NY: Colombia University Press.
Magee, Glenn Alexander. 2010. *The Hegel Dictionary*. London & New York: Continuum.
Maturana, Humberto Romesin. 1980 [1970]. Biology of cognition. In Humberto Romesin Maturana & Francisco Javier Varela García. *Autopoiesis and Cognition: The Realization of the Living*, 5–58. Boston, Dordrecht, London: D. Reidel Publishing Co.
Merleau-Ponty, Maurice. 2005 [1945]. *Phenomenology of Perception*. Trans. by Colin Smith. Routledge Classics. Taylor and Francis e-Library. (*Phénomènologie de la perception*. Paris: Gallimard).
Ross, Raymond S. 1974 [1965]. *Speech Communication. Fundamentals and Practice*, 3rd edn. Englewood Cliffs, New Jersey: Prentice Hall, Inc.

Sartre, Jean-Paul. 1956 [1943]. *Being and Nothingness: An Essay on Phenomenological Ontology*. Trans. and intr. by Hazel E. Barnes. New York: Philosophical Library. (*L'Être et le néant: Essai d'ontologie phénoménologique*. Paris: Gallimard).

Sartre, Jean-Paul. 1990/1960 [1936–1937]. *The Transcendence of the Ego: An Existentialist Theory of Consciousness*. Trans. & intr. by Forrest Williams & Robert Kirkpatrick. New York: Hill and Wang. (La transcendance de l'ego: Esquisse se d'une description phénoménologique. *Recherches philosophiques* VI. 85–123).

Sebeok, Thomas A. 1976. *Contributions to the Doctrine of Signs*. Bloomington, IN. Indiana University Press.

Tarasti, Eero. 2000. *Existential Semiotics*. Bloomington, Indianapolis, IN: Indiana University Press.

Tarasti, Eero. 2011. Existential semiotics and cultural psychology. In Jaan Valsiner (ed.), *The Oxford Handbook of Culture and Psychology*, 316–343. (Oxford Library of Psychology, Part III.15). Oxford, UK and New York, NY: Oxford University Press.

Tarasti, Eero. 2012. *Semiotics of Classical Music: How Mozart, Brahms and Wagner Talk to Us*. (Semiotics, Communication and Cognition 10). Berlin and Boston: De Gruyter Mouton

Tarasti, Eero. 2015. *Sein und Schein. Explorations in Existential Semiotics*. Berlin & Boston: Mouton de Gruyter.

Wąsik, Elżbieta Magdalena. 2020. *Linguistic Dimensions of the Self in Human Communication*. Poznań: Adam Mickiewicz University Press/Wydawnictwo Naukowe UAM.

Zlatev, Jordan. 2009. The semiotic hierarchy: Life, consciousness, signs and language. *Cognitive Semiotics* (4). 169–200.

Zdzisław Wąsik

Umwelt, Lebenswelt, Dasein & *monde vécu* – (de)constructing the semiotic cosmology of human existentiality

Abstract: This chapter presents an overview of the conceptions of semiotic universes of meaning opposed, as surrounding environments of animals, to lived-through environments of humans. Its subject matter constitutes the epistemological deconstruction of the concept of worldhood put forward by philosophers dealing with subjective experience. Regarding its investigative methodology, the chapter alludes to cognitive sources of knowledge about the world, merging thus the mundane and transcendentalist phenomenology with epistemology understood not only as the sets of investigative perspectives or the psychophysiological ability of a cognizer, but also as a narrative activity of a knower. What is new here is the author's conception of the linguistic-phenomenological epistemology of practice, which considers the complexity of knowledge about the world and the partiality of its cognition. In such a cosmological conception, the reality of everyday life is shown as experienced through man's being-in-the-world, where the human 'lifeworld' turns to be a 'lived-through' world. Finally, the chapter puts forward investigative postulates for discussing the relationship between the concepts of world and reality in order to explain the incompatibilities of worldviews in the perception of reality, hierarchies of worlds and semiotic modeling systems, and creative aspects of epistemic ability to construe phenomenal worlds beyond words.

Keywords: alternative worlds, existential semiotics, experiential knowledge, linguistical epistemology, phenomenology of practice

1 Demarcating humans from animals in relation to their environments

This chapter departs, in general, from phenomenological inquiries into the relations of human individuals as natural organisms and cultural subjects to their environments. It appeals to the understanding of phenomenology, which originates from the philosophy of Immanuel Kant (1883 [1781]) and Georg Wilhelm Friedrich Hegel (1910 [1807]). However, it utilizes the methodological and conceptual tools pertaining to the description of appearances in the first-person perspective, initiated by Edmund Husserl. Working within the current paradigm, researchers have at their disposal Husserl's classical tripartite division into transcendental, existential, and mundane phenomenology. Nevertheless, followers of other orientations adhere also to an extended or rather an attributive typology, proposed by Max van Manen, into (1) transcendental phenomenology, (2) existential phenomenology, (3) hermeneutical phenomenology, (4) linguistical phenomenology, (5) ethical phenomenology, and (6) phenomenology of praxis (available at *Phenomenology Online. A Resource from Phenomenological inquiry)*.

The first part of this chapter devoted to phenomenology presents the investigative domain, in which the objects of specific discussions make up the following terms, firstly, *Umwelt* introduced by Jakob von Uexküll (1864–1944), a Baltic-German biologist and philosopher, secondly, *Lebenswelt* put into the use by Edmund Husserl (1859–1938), a German mathematician and philosopher, thirdly, *Dasein* worked out by Martin Heidegger (1889–1976), a German philosopher, the pupil of Husserl, and finally *monde vécu* launched by Maurice Merleau-Ponty (1908–1961), a French phenomenologist, who strongly exposed the primacy of objectivity in sensorial perception opposing to subjectivity in the rational experience exposed by Husserl and Heidegger (cf. Wąsik 2018).

1.1 The semiotic web in the surrounding environment of animals

The term *Umwelt* roughly denoting the 'surrounding world' derives its semantic connotation from Jakob von Uexküll who has investigated how living organisms perceive their environment and how this perception determines their behaviour. Pertaining to the subjective world of an organism, this term was coined by Uexküll in his book *Umwelt und Innenwelt der Tiere* as early as in 1909. As Kalevi Kull remarked (1999b: 390), "in his article of 1907 he still uses the term 'Milieu', as different from 'Außenwelt'" (cf. Uexküll 1907). Soon afterwards in 1920 this framework was enriched with a new term *Umweltröhre(n)* 'environmental pipe(s)' introduced in Uexküll's *Theoretische Biologie* 1926 [1920] and 1928 [1920]. Moreover, in the 2nd edition of *Umwelt und Innenwelt der Tiere* 1921 [1909], a complementary term was added, namely, *Funktionskreis* (translated into English as "functional circle" or lately also as "functional cycle"), as a clue to understanding meaning in biological terms within the *Umwelt* of an organism (cf. Uexküll 1921 [1909].

Metaphorically modelled as a "soap bubble", *Umwelt* might be referred to a particular environment of an animal acting at a given moment in a "functional circle" (*Funktionskreis*) consisting of medium, food, enemy or sex (cf. Uexküll 1982 [1940]: 36 & 59–60, especially 71), and *Umweltröhren* appear to be useful for showing a sequence of all environmental circles that the individual organism has to pass in a stroll throughout its whole life understood as a determined journey. This investigative method of pursuing and reconstructing the journey through invisible worlds is demonstrated in the works of Jakob von Uexküll (& Georg Kriszat), "A stroll through the world of animals and men: A picture book of invisible worlds" [*Streifzüge durch die Umwelten von Tieren und Menschen. Ein Bilderbuch unsichtbarer Welten*] (1992 /1957/ [1934]) as well as of Jakob von Uexküll *Niegeschaute Welten: Die Umwelten meiner Freunde. Ein Erinnerungsbuch* (1936).

Having studied the behaviour of organisms which enter into relationships with their environments, Uexküll noticed, in his "The theory of meaning" [*Bedeutungslehre*] 1982 [1940: 27–31]), that animals at all levels – from unicellulars to hominids, as living systems endowed with a property of subjectivity, the so-called *Ich-Ton* rendered by an 'ego-quality' in the English translation of original German terms signifying musical tones – are capable of discerning meanings from environmental indicators. According to Uexküll certain objects of the environment can become meaning-carriers possessing the qualities that appear to be significant for the fulfillment of the subject-related needs.

1.2 The mundane phenomenology of appearances in the lifeworld in human experience

Another kind of a subjective universe, described as a pre-given world in which humans live, was offered in Husserl's phenomenology under the label of *Lebenswelt*. What Husserl proposed, in his lectures held at Prague in 1935 and Vienna in 1936, *Die Krisis der europäischen Wissenschaften und die transzendentale Phänomenologie. Eine Einleitung in die phänomenologische Philosophie*, published for the first time in 1954 and translated into English as *The Crisis of European Sciences and Transcendental Phenomenology: An Introduction to Phenomenological Philosophy* in 1970 was the study about appearances of perceptible lifeworld objects in human experience.

Inquiring into the ways how human individuals experience and describe, in the first-person perspective, the meanings of objects their lifeworld, Husserl distinguished three kinds of phenomenology, namely, transcendental, existential, and mundane (Germ. *Lebenswelt* 'the lifeworld'.) phenomenology. From Husserl's reasoning, one can deduce that the phenomenological conception of world connotes not only a dualistic split between empirical and rational facts, encompassing as such two distinct worlds, the world of nature and the psychic world (1970 [1954]: 60), but also generates "a psychophysical anthropology in the rationalistic spirit" (1970: 62, cf. quoted and cited Wąsik 2018: 128).

Following Husserl's interpretation, the phenomenological conception of the world overcomes the hitherto prevailing opposition between empiricism and rationalism, to that extent that it includes simultaneously the spiritual world, the ideal world, and the lifeworld (cf. Husserl 1970: 62). The *Lebenswelt* (lifeworld), constituting the domain of mundane phenomenology, is the world in which people live together, about its existence they are conscious, and to which they belong.

The spherical dimension of human surroundings is thus visible in Husserl's definition of *Lebenswelt* inaugurated in his lectures of 1935–1936, which belongs most quoted and discussed: "In whatever way we may be conscious of the world as universal horizon, as coherent universe of existing objects, we, each "I-the-man" and all of us together, belong to the world as living with one another in the world; and the world is our world, valid for our consciousness as existing precisely through this "living together". (Husserl 1970: 108; cf. Wąsik 2018, quoted & cited 128). Thus, Husserl's idea of 'lifeworld' requires a more accurate concern of human subjectivity and objectivity, when considering that „to live" constantly means „to live-in-certainty-of-the-world".

Husserl's theory of the "rational world" raises the question of how to use the concept of the world for designating a discrete domain or closed special regions, What is significant, Husserl links the widely held use of world to the appearance of a special subject-oriented psychology (cf. Husserl 1970: 62).

Thus, Husserl's lifeworld conception demands a more authentic understanding of subjectivity and objectivity, as far as to live is always to live-in-certainty-of-the-world. Walking life is being awake to the world, being constantly and directly conscious of the world and oneself as living in the world, actually experiencing [*erleben*] and actually effecting the ontic certainty of the world. The world is pregiven thereby, in every case, in such a way that individuals things are given. But there exists a fundamental difference between the way we are conscious of the world and the way we are conscious of things or objects (taken in the broadest sense, but still purely in the sense of the lifeworld), though together the two make up an inseparable unity (cf. Husserl 1970: 142–143; cited by Wąsik 2018: 129).

It was, however, slightly earlier, in the manuscript of 1890 "Zur Logik der Zeichen (Semiotik)" 'On the logic of signs (semiotics)', when Husserl ([1890] 1970) gave some thoughts to the origins of sign behaviour. Husserl's explanation may be summarized here in four statements, claiming that: firstly, all animals react to phenomena as signs of existentially relevant objects or situations; secondly, when animals are able to grasp causal or regular connections between some parts of situations they usually chose these as signs of the whole; and thirdly, when communication occurs with the use of signs then it must be preceded by the sign consciousness of its producers or interpreters (*Zeichenbewusstsein*); and, finally, the users of signs, at further evolutionary steps, must be aware of regular effects of their intended use(s).

1.3 The worldhood of the real world experienced through the man's being-in-the-world

The existential relationship of the human subject with the world, in which he/she lives, should especially be brought to light on the basis of Heidegger's works with special reference to *Being and Time* [*Sein und Zeit*] (Heidegger 1962 [1927]), "On the essence of ground" ["Vom Wesen des Grundes"] (1998 [1929] and *The Fundamental Concepts of Metaphysics: World, Finitude, Solitude* [*Die Grundbegriffe der Metaphysik: Welt – Endlichkeit – Einsamkeit*] (Heidegger 1995 [1983]).

As Heidegger (1995: 176–177) noted, *Sein und Zeit*, constitutes, de facto, the second of three different approaches to the problem of the world. The first approach, in "Vom Wesen des Grundes" (1998), deals with the historical development of the term and the concept of the world. The second approach, in *Sein und Zeit* (of 1926–1927), addresses "*the phenomenon of world* by interpreting the way in which we at first and for the most part move about in our everyday world" (Heidegger 1995: 177]). The third one, discussed, in turn, in *Die Grundbegriffe der Metaphysik: Welt – Endlichkeit* (of 1929–1930), is based on a "comparative examination" of man, animals, plants and stones (Heidegger 1995: 177).

What makes *Sein und Zeit* distinctive is its emphasis on the world not as a concept but as a phenomenon (*das Weltphänomen*). A phenomenon describes something that becomes "manifest" and "shows itself in itself" (Heidegger 1962: 28–29]). Thus, the world as a phenomenon should give us the world itself. As Heidegger explains, his attempt was "this initial characterization of the phenomenon of world" in order "to press on and point out the phenomenon of world as a problem" (Heidegger 1995: 177]).

Following Heidegger's path of reasoning, how he approaches the world from the vantage point of *Dasein*, as being-in-the-world, we might thus grasp the phenomenon of the world: "That which is so close and intelligible to us in our everyday dealings is actually and fundamentally remote and unintelligible to us" (Heidegger 1995: 177]). What Heidegger addresses, in his third approach, are thus the three concepts, namely 'world', 'finitude', and 'solitude', which form a unity.

There are at least two relevant arguments, which should be recalled in Heidegger's approach to the worldhood of the world. In the first argument, the reader is introduced into the idea of existentiality, cf. "'Worldhood' is an ontological concept, and stands for the structure of one of the constitutive items of Being-in-the-world. But we know Being-in-the-world as a way in which *Dasein's* character is defined existentially. Thus worldhood itself is an *existentiale*" (Heidegger 1962: 92; italics are mine: ZW). The second argument pertains to the notion of environmentality, cf.

> That world of everyday *Dasein* which is closest to it, is the environment. From this existential character of average Being-in-the-world, our investigation will take its course [Gang] towards the idea of worldhood in general. We shall seek the worldhood of the environment (environmentality) by going through an ontological Interpretation of those entities within-the-environment which we encounter as closest to us. The expression "environment" [Umwelt] contains in the 'environ' ["um"] a suggestion of spatiality. Yet the 'around' ["Umheruin"] which is constitutive for the environment does not have a primarily 'spatial' meaning. Instead, the spatial character, which incontestably belongs to any environment, can be clarified only in terms of the structure of worldhood. (Heidegger 1962: 94)

In view of the latter argumentation, the discussion of animality must be contextualized as belonging to this broader analysis of metaphysics pertaining to the essence of man. Without a doubt, Heidegger's famous tripartite thesis constitutes an attempt to understand the essence of "the other beings which, like man, are also part of the world", with regard to their relationship to and difference from the "having world" that characterizes man: "[1.] the stone (material object) is wordless; [2.] the animal is poor in world; [3.] man is world-forming" (Heidegger, *The Fundamental Concepts of Metaphysics*, 1995: 177]). Finally, one should make reference to Heidegger's history- and memory-oriented typology of at least four existentialist attitudes towards the human being-in-the-world (Heidegger, *Being and Time*, 1962: 424–449), as derivation/genesis (1962: 444), event/transformation (1962: 430), or heritage/legacy (1962: 435), past/alien previousness (1962: 448).

1.4 From the lifeworld over the being-in-the world to the lived-through world

To trace the way in which the human lifeworld (Husserl's *Lebenswelt*) turned out to change from the being-in-the-world (Heidegger's *Dasein*) to the lived-through-world (Merleau-Ponty's *monde vécu*), one should estimate the statement from *Phenomenology of Perception* [*Phénomènologie de la perception*]: "The process of making explicit, which had laid bare the 'lived-through' world which is prior to the objective one, is put into operation upon the 'lived-through' world itself, thus revealing, prior to the phenomenal field, the transcendental field." (Merleau-Ponty 2005 [1945]: 73).

What is more Maurice Merleau-Ponty emphasizes that: "Consciousness is being-towards-the-thing through the intermediary of the body. A movement is learned when the body has understood it, that is, when it has incorporated it into its 'world', and to move one's body is to aim at things through it; it is to allow oneself to respond to their call, which is made upon it independently of any representation." (2005: 159–61).

The direction of interpretative reasoning inaugurated by Merleau-Ponty has been undertaken by Max van Manen who has elaborated, in his work *Researching Lived Experience. Human Science for an Action Sensitive Pedagogy* (1997 [1990]), and constructively applied, the phenomenological notion of lifeworld existentials to explore and understand the world of the lived experience.

An extensive exploration of phenomenological traditions and methods for the human sciences, such as psychology, education, health care, and everyday living, is culminated in van Manen's, *Phenomenology of Practice: Meaning-Giving Methods in Phenomenological Research and Writing* (2014).

Above all, the applications of interpretative or hermeneutic terms have appeared to be very productive, such as "lived life", "lived meaning", or "lived experience". Having been widely distributed, the so-called "essential themes" pertaining to the analysis of lived experience, called otherwise "lifeworld existentials" – initially four in number, (1) lived body (corporeality), (2) lived human relation or lived self-other (relationality), (3) lived space (spatiality), and lived time (temporality), deserve particular attention in further developed studies (cf. van Manen 1997: 18, 27, 31–35, and further pages).

In his subsequent article "Phenomenology of practice" (2007), van Manen implicitly formulates his conviction that: "Phenomenology of practice is formative of sensitive practice, issuing from the pathic power of phenomenological reflections. Pathic knowing inheres in the sense and sensuality of our practical actions, in encounters with others and in the ways that our bodies are responsive to the things of our world and to the situations and relations in which we find ourselves." (2007: 11). Claiming that: "A phenomenology of practice grasps the world pathically" (2007: 20), van Manen explains that „the term *pathic* relates to the terms of a discourse, as in, em-pathic and sym-pathic. [...] more generally, to be understandingly engaged in other people's lives". (2007: 20, italics are mine: ZW).

As van Manen further exhibits, despite the fact that the derivational basis of *pathic* is *pathos*, meaning „suffering and also passion": "In a larger life context, the pathic refers to the general mood, sensibility, sensuality, and felt sense of being in the world." (van Manen 2007: 21). Undoubtedly, Maurice Merleau-Ponty's statement: "Consciousness is being-towards-the-thing through the intermediary of the body. A movement is learned when the body has understood it, that is, when it has incorporated it into its 'world'" (2005 [1945]: 159–161) might be easily comparable with Max van Manen's ways of reasoning: "The pathically tuned body recognizes itself in its responsiveness to the things of its world and to the others who share our world or break into our world. The pathic sense perceives the world in a feeling or emotive modality of knowing and being." (2007: 11).

Making reference to Max van Manen's definition, we might treat the knowledge about the world in terms of a linguistic text:

> Knowledge as text: We can speak of phenomenological texts as knowledge in the same sense that we refer to other bodies of knowledge contained in books and documents. It is important to see, however, that the phenomenological text differs in the manner that meaning is embedded in the text. Phenomenological knowledge-as-text has cognitive and pathic, conceptual and poetic, informative and formative dimensions.   (van Manen 2011: Phenomenology online)

In appreciating the understanding of phenomenology as the textual embodiment of knowledge, as an understanding of texts, and as a formative constituent of the personal stock of knowledge, one may distinguish its three meanings, relevant, as a matter of fact, for the scope of a narrative *linguistic-phenomenological epistemology of practice*. The first meaning refers to the bodies of knowledge contained in books and documents, the second to the reflective and discursive participation in meaning-related production and interpretation of texts, and the third to the connection between knowledge and practice in the personal formation of a knowing self.

Although van Manen has claimed, in *Researching Lived Experience*, that "the experience of lived time, lived space, lived body, and lived human relation) are preverbal and therefore hard to describe" (1997: 18), these lifeworld existentials may be considered in terms of commonly lived experiences while using such descriptors as "lived word-ness (textuality)", or "lived sign-ness (semioticality)", with reference to the textual view of language and culture, or the so-called semiospheres of culture, promoted by Juri Lotman, in his articles "The semiotics of culture and the concept of a text" [«Семиотика культуры и понятие текста»] (1988 [1981]), and "On the semiosphere" [«О семиосфере»] (2005 [1984])].

1.5 Animal symbolicum on the evolutionary scale of communication systems

While reading Husserl's thoughts pertaining to the awareness of signs, Ernst Cassirer (1874–1945) took stand to the mutual relationships between the sensorially perceivable bearer of meaning and the meaning itself in several places of his *The Philosophy of Symbolic Forms* [*Philosophie der symbolischen Formen*] (cf. Cassirer 1955 [1923–1929] and 1995). However, he had created his human-centered phenomenology of symbolic forms directly under the influence of his contemporary friend and scientific colleague at the University of Hamburg, namely Jakob von

Uexküll. As Frederik Stjernfelt pointed out discussing the topic of simple animals and complex biology, Uexküll's had a twofold influence on Cassirer's philosophy. The first influence of Uexküll upon Cassirer was connected with the *Umwelt* conception and the second, following the account of Frederik Stjernfelt (2011), with the definition of man as the *animal symbolicum*.

Entering into the epistemology of biology, Cassirer poses a question, in *An Essay on Man*: "Is it possible to make use of the scheme proposed by Uexküll for a description and characterization of the *human world*?", and he answers it consecutively: "Obviously this world forms no exception to those biological rules that govern the life of all the organisms. Yet, in the human world we find a new characteristic which appears to be the distinctive mark of human life . . . a third link which we may describe as the *symbolic system*." (see Cassirer 1962 [1944]: 24) As he explains furthermore:

> [M]an lives in a symbolic universe. Language, myth, art, and religion are parts of this universe . . . Instead of dealing with the things themselves man is in a sense constantly conversing with himself. He has so enveloped himself in linguistic forms, in artistic images, in mythical symbols or religious rites that he cannot see or know anything except by the interpretation of this artificial medium. . . . He lives rather in the midst of imaginary emotions in hopes and fears, in illusions and disillusions, in his fantasies and dreams. (Cassirer 1962: 24)

With regard to philosophical anthropology, Cassirer argued, based on research on the mentality of apes, that animal behaviour includes only signals but not symbols. Even when practical imagination and intelligence is attributed to an animal, it is only man who has power over of "a symbolic imagination and intelligence" (Cassirer 1962: 33). As he furthermore claimed, higher-order apes may communicate symbolically under the specific conditions created by humans, and some birds are able to categorize different objects, to learn songs, while creating their varieties. However, at the same time, a two or three-year-old child not only learns but also masters its own language. The range of symbolic forms and genres may include zoosemiotic systems, but, on the other end of the evolutionary scale marking the first civilizations of humans, there is the development of mathematics and scientific knowledge.

1.6 On the three levels of modelling the mundane reality in the semiotics of nature and culture

The background of Cassirer's concept of symbolic forms was noticed by Thomas A. Sebeok (born Sebők, 1920–2001) in his chapter "From Vico to Cassirer to

Langer" (1994 [1992]) placing him between the historiosophical thought of Giambattista Vico (1668–1744) and the philosophy of Susanne Langer (born Knauth, 1895–1985), pertaining to mentalist symbolism in language and art. Worth mentioning is here the rapport between Vico and Juri Lotman (Yuri Mikhailovich Lotman, 1922–1993), the promoter of a textual view of culture as a semiosphere, discussed in Tuuli Raudla's article "Vico and Lotman: poetic meaning creation and primary modelling" (2008).

In conformity with Uexküll's and Cassirer's separation of animal and human universes based on a semiotic opposition between the signs of nature and the symbols of culture while being opposed to the distinction of primary and secondary modelling systems authored by Lotman, Sebeok postulated the existence of three levels of the modelling of reality, answering a question (posed at the Semiotic Society of America Meeting in 1987): "In what sense is language a 'primary modelling system'?" (cf. Sebeok 1991 [1988]).

The term *modelling systems* is a legacy of the Tartu–Moscow school. The authors of this distinction between primary and secondary modelling systems were Andrey A. Zaliznjak, Vyacheslav V. Ivanov and Vladimir N. Toporov in their joint paper on "Structural-typological study of semiotic modelling systems" [Зализняк, Андрей Анатольевич, Вячеслав Всеволодович Иванов & Владимир Николáевич Топоров О возможности структурно-типологического изучения некоторых моделирующих систем].] (1977 [1962]). presented in Russian at a Symposium on Structural Studies of Sign Systems in Moscow 1962, to which Ivanov wrote a foreword, entitled in the English translation as "The science of semiotics", [Иванов, Вячеслав Всеволодович, Предисловие. *Симпозиум по структурному изучению знаковых систем: Тезисы докладов*] (Ivanov 1978 [1962]).

Since 1964 the first semiotic schools were organized by Juri Lotman and his associates, under the heading of "Secondary Modelling Systems". As Peter Grzybek, in his article on "The concept of 'model' in Soviet semiotics", mentioned, "the concept of model has been applied quite successfully by practically all Moscow-Tartu semioticians over the years, although it has never been the topic of an explicit theoretical discussion" (1994: 286). In the original conception, the modelling systems were described as primary or secondary, where the natural language was seen as a primary modelling system and the supra-lingual systems, with two or more layers (literature, theater, myth, folklore, painting, puppetry, etc.), which were translatable into the natural language, were named as secondary modelling systems. This distinction between primary and secondary modelling systems became known to semioticians after it had been applied by Juri Lotman to the notion of semiosphere in a textual view of culture (cf. 1977 [1974], (1988 [1981], 1994 [1981], and 2005 [1984]).

In his theses on "The place of art among other modelling systems", Lotman ([1967] 2011: 250) describes a model as "an analogue of an object of perception that substitutes for it in the process of perception". Accordingly, in Lotman's view: "Modelling activity is human activity in creating models. In order that the results of this activity could be taken as analogues of an object, they have to obey certain (intuitively or consciously established) rules of analogy and, therefore, be related to one modelling system or another" (Lotman 2011: 250). Accordingly, "A modelling system is a structure of elements and rules of their combination, existing in a state of fixed analogy to the whole sphere of the object of perception, cognition, or organization. For this reason, a modelling system may be treated as a language" (Lotman 2011: 250).

While taking a stand to Lotman's position by the question, "In what sense is language a 'primary modelling system'?", Sebeok puts forward his modelling system theory based on the discrimination between non-verbal communication and verbal systems. At the same time, he mentions that it is very likely that the *Homo habilis* had the capability of language without any verbal expression claiming that: "Solely in the genus *Homo* have verbal signs emerged. To put it in another way, only hominids possess two mutually sustaining repertoires of signs, the zoosemiotic non-verbal, plus, superimposed, the anthroposemiotic verbal" (Sebeok 1991 [1988]: 55). According to Sebeok, what the Russo-Estonian semioticians call "primary", i.e., the anthroposemiotic verbal, is "phylogenetically as well as ontogenetically secondary to the nonverbal; and, therefore, what they call 'secondary' is actually a further, tertiary augmentation of the former" (Sebeok 1991 [1988]: 55).

In his studies on the semiotic self, Sebeok (cf. 1991 [1979] and 1991) postulates three modelling systems of reality. Accordingly, following the semioticians of nature and culture, the primary modelling system (PMS) of reality is found on the level of animals possessing the ego-quality which act through the mediation of effectors and receptors, i.e., on the level of indexical symptoms and appealing signals. The secondary model system (SMS) involves, in turn, the extralinguistic reality of everyday life construed by the use of verbal means of signification and communication, which occurs as such only in the realm of human organisms. The tertiary modelling system (TMS), which includes the secondary one, is characterized as encompassing the whole semiosphere of language and culture and civilization where the representations of reality beyond the signs are artificially created in accordance with axiological (value-and-good-oriented) and praxeological (function-and-purpose-oriented) principles.

Describing in terms of anthroposemiosis the triadic relationship between "developmental" stages of an individual organism, Thomas A. Sebeok and Marcel Danesi, in *The Forms of Meaning: Modelling Systems Theory and Semiotic Analy-*

sis, have recently argued that (1) PMS is "the system that predisposes the human infant to engage in sense-based forms of modelling."; (2) SMS – "the system that subsequently impels the child to engage in extensional and indexical forms of modelling."; and (3) TMS – "the system that allows the maturing child to engage in highly abstract (symbol-based) forms of modelling." (*The forms of meaning: Modelling systems theory and semiotic analysis*, 2000: 10).

2 Interpreting the individual and social modes of being-in-the-world in terms of existential semiotics

The second part of this chapter[1] constitutes the search for the roots of existential semiotics, developed by Eero Tarasti, which is characterized by the category of *Dasein* being central to the mundane phenomenology of Martin Heidegger (1889–1976). Amongst subsequent works he published in the last decades, two of them appear to be the most advanced as a theoretical framework for the purposes of detailed consideration, namely, "What is existential semiotics? From theory to application", (Tarasti 2009), and *Sein und Schein. Explorations in Existential Semiotics* (Tarasti 2015). Having departed from phenomenology as the study of human experience consciously realized by the senses (or lived through) from a subjective or first-person point of view, Tarasti postulated rethinking the layouts of human-centered semiotics in the light of philosophers who paid attention to the notions, such as, *inter alia*, "subject", "existence", "transcendence", and "value". These semiotic concepts were placed on the philosophical background of such notional categories of existential phenomenology as *Umwelt*, *Lebenswelt*, and *Dasein*.

2.1 Philosophical positions of existential semiotics

The foundations for a human-centered paradigm of existential semiotics were laid at the 9th Congress of the IASS/AIS, Helsinki–Imatra, 11–17 June 2007 (cf. Tarasti 2009). To understand Tarasti's (2015) contribution to the semiotic-existential interpretation of the transcendental forms of human subjects who cross

---

[1] Most of the ideas presented in this part on existential semiotics have been discussed in detail by the author in his article accessible online "Umwelt, Lebenswelt, and *Dasein* seen through the lens of a subjective experience of reality" (Wąsik 2018: 136–137).

the boundaries of their lifeworld by means of signs and sign-processing activities, one should especially attend to the relationship and the difference between the understanding of existentialism in the works of Martin Heidegger and Jean-Paul Sartre (1905–1980).

However, the sources and direction of reasoning of Heidegger and Sartre were completely unrelated. The way of Heidegger's thought was leading from the forerunners of existentialism, Søren Kierkegaard (1813–1855); cf. *Concluding Unscientific Postscript to Philosophical Fragments* [*Afsluttende uvidenskabelig Efterskrift til de philosophiske Smuler*] (1941 [1846]) and Karl Jaspers (1883–1969); cf. *General Psychopathology* [*Allgemeine Psychopathologie*] (1962 [1946 /1913/]), and the paths of Sartre's reasoning, in his works *The Transcendence of the Ego: An Existentialist Theory of Consciousness* [«La transcendance de l'ego: Esquisse se d'une description phénoménologique»] (1990 /1960/ [1936–1937]) *Being and Nothingness: An Essay on Phenomenological Ontology* [*L'Être et le néant : Essai d'ontologie phénoménologique*] (1956 [1943]), were departing, firstly, from the speculative philosophy of Immanuel Kant (1724–1804), incorporated in *Critique of Pure Reason* [*Critik der reinen Vernunft*] (1941 [1846]), and, secondly, from idealist stance of Georg Wilhelm Friedrich Hegel (1770–1831), taken in the *Phenomenology of Mind* [*Phänomenologie des Geistes*] (1910 [1807]). Therefore, Tarasti, in his works, as *inter alia*, "What is existential semiotics? From theory to application" (2009), and *Sein und Schein* (2015) proposed to go back to Hegel, the first philosopher who characterized his approach to reality as phenomenology alluding to Kant, but who, unlike Kant, expressed his conviction that phenomena constitute a sufficient basis for a universal science of being.

The primary object of reference in Tarasti's (2009), and (2015) inquiry constituted categories of *an-sich-sein* 'being-in-itself' and *für-sich-sein* 'being-for-itself' distinguished in Hegel's *Phänomenologie des Geistes* (1910). These categories subsequently turned into subjective and objective being in the philosophy of Kierkegaard (1941) when he spoke about an individual as an observer of him- or herself or the observed one who was said to be a subject or such an individual who was what he/she was because he/she had become like it.

Here, the secondary object of interest for Tarasti was Sartre's existentialist philosophy, because Sartre, as an attentive reader of Hegel (1910) and Kierkegaard (1941) simultaneously, referred to Hegelian concepts while using French terms, *être-en-soi and être-pour-soi* (cf. Sartre's original source of citation 1956 [1943: 124–125]). Especially worth of consideration was Sartre's line of reasoning, in *L'Être et le néant* (1956 [1943]), that the being as such becomes aware of itself through an act of negation, and when becoming an observer of itself, it shifts its interest into the position of being for itself. Having noticed a certain lack in its reality, the being begins with the first act of transcendence as far as it strives to fulfill what it lacks.

2.2 Individual and social being forms of human body in the semiotic phenomenology

For the layouts of existential semiotics, departing as such from Hegel's idealist phenomenology of spirit (2009, 2015), the crucial role played the corporeal semiotics of Jacques Fontanille, one of the main representative of the Paris School of Semiotics. In keeping with Fontanille's *Soma et séma. Figures du corps* (2004: 22–23), Tarasti (2009: 1761–1763; 2015: 22–24) reconstituted Hegelian categories *an-sich-sein* and *für-sich-sein* through *an-mir-sein* and *für-mich-sein* (*être-en-moi* 'being-in-myself' and *être-pour-moi* 'being-for-myself').

In his appropriation of Hegelian categories, Fontanille (2004), proposed a distinction between individual and social being forms of the human body (*soma*) in an entirely new phenomenological sense (*séma*). Accordingly, Fontanille detached two kinds of body-related meanings for human agents (*actants*) while separating the body experienced inside of their organism as a flesh, which concentrates all physiological and semiotic processes, from the body observed outside of their organism, which shapes the uniqueness of their behavioural characteristics.

In fact, Fontanille has distinguished between *Moi* and *Soi* as two categories referring to the same acting individual. For him (Fontanille 2004: 22), the body as a flesh constitutes the totality of the material resistance or impulse to meaning-making processes. The body is thus sensory-driven support of all organismic experiences. Hence, on the one hand, in Fontanille's view (*Soma et séma*, 2004: 22–23), there is a body that constitutes the identity and directional principle of the flesh, being the carrier of the personal "me" (*Moi*), and on the other hand, the body that supports the "self" (*Soi*), shaped as a result of discursive activity. As Fontanille argued, the *Soi* is that part of ourselves, which me, *Moi*, projects out of itself to create itself in its activity. Similarly, the *Moi* constitutes that part of ourselves to which the *Soi* refers when establishing itself. In Tarasti's interpretation (cf. 2009: 1761): "The *Moi* provides the *Soi* with impulse and resistance whereby it can become something. In turn, the *Soi* furnishes the *Moi* with the reflexivity that it needs to stay within its limits when it changes. The *Moi* resists and forces the *Soi* to meet its own alterity." Hence, *Moi* and *Soi* are to be seen as inseparable.

Although Fontanille departs from French semiotics, being influenced by Algirdas Julien Greimas (1917–1992), the promoter of structural semantics, especially after such works *Sémantique structurale : recherche de méthode*, (Greimas 1966); *Sémiotique et sciences sociales*, (Greimas 1976); and *Sémiotique des passions : des états de choses aux états d'âme*, (Fontanille & Greimas 1991), his way of reasoning fits well to the phenomenological categories of Hegel ([1807] 1910). In accordance with Fontanille's proposal, a new interpretation of *an sich* and *für sich* is involved, the first corresponding to the bodily ego, and the second to its stability and identity and its aspiration outward, or the Sartrean negation. The *Soi* functions as a kind of memory of the body or *Moi*; it yields its form to those traces of tensions and needs that have been inserted in the flesh of the *Moi*. Anyhow, before pondering which consequences this distinction has to existential semiotics, it is necessary to scrutinize the principles of *Moi* and *Soi* as such. Consequently, anything belonging to the category of *Mich*, "me", concerns the subject as an individual entity, whereas the concept of *Sich* "him-/her-/it-self" has to be reserved for the social aspect of this subject.

When one thinks about the identity and individuality of an organism, one can distinguish in it two aspects: *Moi* and *Soi*. In "me," the subject appears as such, as a bundle of sensations, and in "himself", "herself" or "itself", the subject appears as observed by others or socially determined. These labels, *Moi* and *Soi* connote the existential and social aspects of the subject or, rather, the individual and communitarian sides of the whole self as an investigative object of the so-called neosemiotics.

2.3 Human subjects in existential acts of self-awareness

After considering, in a historical-ordering review, the scaffolds of Hegel's *Phänomenologie des Geistes* (1910 [1807]), Heidegger's *Sein und Zeit* (1927 [1962]) & *Die Grundbegriffe der Metaphysik*, (1995 [1983]), Sartre's *La transcendance de l'ego* ([1990 /1960/ [1936–1937]) & *L'Être et le néant* (1956 [1943]) along with Fontanille's *Soma et séma* (2004), which have inspired Tarasti to elaborate a semiotic model of human existentiality, it is worth enumerating the modal acts expressing the humans' self-awareness (cf. 2009: 1766; or 2015: 25). In this model, Tarasti reconstitutes the forms of how human subjects manifest themselves in their corporeal and mental, individual and social modes of existence in the real world, and/or how they mentally transcend from it going into other subjective realities of possible worlds.

The modality acts of *Moi* (M) and *Soi* (S) comprise two ego states, corporeal and mental, combined with two identity perceptions, individual and collective, of the same subject. They may be seen, as one is entitled to conclude from Tarasti's reasoning, from four opposed angles as M1, M2, M3, M4 and S1, S2, S3, S4, when confronted in contradictory levels of existence of the subject as *Moi* = M1 : S4, M2 : S3, and as *Soi* = S2 : M3, S1 : M4.

As regards the counterposed relationships between *Moi* (M) and *Soi* (S), Tarasti (2009: 1765) refers to the so-called semiotic square of logical oppositions useful in the analysis of signs within the semiotic systems designed by Greimas (1966), the semiotician and linguist of Lithuanian descent, in his *Sémantique structurale* (cf. Tarasti (2009: 1766–1768)).

(M1 : S4) Being-in-myself – *An-mir-sein* – *être-en-moi* in which an individual is willing to appreciate his/her/its existential bodily self-worth;

(M2 : S3) Being-for-myself – *Für-mich-sein* – *être-pour-moi* in which the individual can reflect upon him-/her-/it-self while transcending to the position of an "observer";

(S2 : M3) Being-in-itself – *An-sich-sein* – *être-en-soi*, in turn, in which an individual transcends to probable chances that he/she/it must either actualize or not actualize in society;

(S1 : M4) Being-for-itself – *Für-sich-sein* – *être-pour-soi* in which an individual refers to an actual role he knows how to perform in the existential world of society.

As Tarasti explained more recently, in his article "The semiotics of A. J. Greimas: A European intellectual heritage seen from the inside and the outside" (2017: 51), considering the existential constituents of the framework of *Dasein*, which stem from the Hegelian idealistic system:

> The categories of an-sich-sein and für-sich-sein, being-in-oneself and being-for-oneself, were very important. The case was further enriched by inserting Fontanille's categories of Moi and Soi so that we ended up with a 'semiotic square': Being-in-myself = Moi1 = body as such; Being-for-myself = Moi2 = person, habit; Being-for-oneself = Soi2 = social practices; and Being-in-oneself = Soi1 = values and norms.

But soon afterward, as the theory developed, Tarasti replaced the Greimassian square with "the 'Zemic' model", as he used to call it, where "the letter Z symbolizing the movement within the structure either from body – by gradual sublimation – into values, or from abstract values – by stepwise embodiment – into our primal corporeal behaviour", and the term *emic* "evoked Kenneth Pike's theory of the emic and etic aspects or categories, 'emic' being the internal and 'etic' the external" The intention of the author "to portray nothing less than the human mind, after all." (quoted from Tarasti 2017: 51), is visible in the title of Pike's booklet *Talk, Thought, and Thing: The Emic Road Toward Conscious Knowledge* (1993).

To sum up, it is worth pointing out to *Sein und Schein: Explorations in Existential Semiotics*, where Tarasti, has proposed to capture the variety of subject and environment relations in the form of taxonomy (2015: 128–130). This classificatory proposal appears to be very productive inasmuch as it might be deconstructed, and even constructively extended, by the consideration of some more criteria, such as, among others, autochthony vs. displacement, autonomy vs. heteronomy, center vs. periphery, conjunction vs. disjunction, connection vs. detachment, conventional vs. arbitrary, domination vs. subordination, indifference vs. concern, integration vs. separation, intimacy vs. distance, private vs. public, seclusion vs. attachment, and the like. In this context, the works might be very useful, which have been developed on the basis of from the relational dialectics theory (RDT), for example, following Baxter, Lesley A., & Barbara M. Montgomery. 1996. *Relating: Dialogues and Dialectics*. New York: Guilford Press.

3 Investigative postulates for discussing the relationship between world and reality

3.1 Incompatibilities of worldviews in the psychophysiological perception of reality

Summarizing the similarities and differences between the existential modes of non-human and human subjects in terms of their being in the world as immanence and being for the world as transcendence, one can say that the immanent subjects are assumed to exist in or with their environments and transcendent subjects as being able to exceed the universe of their (human) life.

A significant dissimilarity between animals and humans, discussed within the framework of existential phenomenology and subject-cantered semiotic phenomenology, is noticeable in the meaning of 'life' and 'existence' in terms of conscious awareness of being alive and taking a stand to the existence in the surrounding and existing for the surrounding.

On the margin of this discussion, one has to admit that the world of life-and-death is considered to be common for all systems described (metaphorically?) as "living" by representatives of anti-speciesism. But following the terminological distinctions encountered in some languages of the world, their users have to be aware that the notions of "life" and "death" are restricted only to the world of humans. As a matter of fact, some languages discern the difference between "living", "breathing" and "vegetating" (along with their synonyms) versus "dying", deceasing, decaying/declining, rotting/perishing, or wilt/wither, and the like.

Important is the statement that all organisms cohabit (dwell in) the same world. One might, therefore, be entitled to assume that considering thus the organisms' relations to the world they cohabit, it is the matter of their becoming in the world and, subsequently, the becoming of the world as a result of these relations.

To begin with the belief of Gregory Bateson (1904–1980), expressed in his chapter on "Psychiatric thinking: An epistemological approach", the worldview depends upon the perception of reality (1951: 237), as, firstly: "a category of observables in opposition to mental phantasies", secondly, "a social construct"... determined by dissimilar viewpoints" and interpretations "in different cultures", thirdly, "a set of personal knowledge ... acquired through observation and formulated through mental propositions", fourthly, "a kind of living through and coping with the world of phenomena on the basis of pleasure and gratification", and fifthly, "a pre-given factual" sphere "based on communication in opposition to the artificially created magical" sphere "based on rituals" (1951: 239–242, quoted and cited in Wąsik 2016b, 28–29).

3.2 Hierarchies of worlds and semiotic modeling systems

Among philosophical queries, it is the epistemological theory of Karl Popper (1902–1994), namely *Objective Knowledge. An Evolutionary Approach* (1972), which has been mostly quoted, contested or complemented. The following "three worlds or universes" , according to Popper, might be distinguished as distinct domains of human knowledge "first, the world of physical objects or physical states, secondly, the world of states of consciousness, or mental states, or perhaps behavioural dispositions to act; and thirdly, the world of *objective concepts of thought*, especially of scientific and poetic thought and works of art" (cited & quoted by Popper 1972: 106).

As Geoffrey Leech remarked in *Principles of Pragmatics* (1983), Popper's main intention was to justify that there is such a third world, which entails the "objective 'knowledge'", or the "knowledge 'without a knowing subject'" involving its formulation in linguistic theories (cited and quoted by Leech 1983: 49). However, Popper (1972: 70) did not maintain that his three-worlds conception was exhaustive in relation to four language functions, such as (A) expressive, (B) signaling, (C) descriptive, and (D) argumentative. Therefore, Leech (1983: 51), noticed only that what was missing in Popper's evolutionary epistemology was a link to a world of societal facts, intervening between the second (subjective) and the third (objective) worlds, as the intersubjective world. Thus, Leech's division (cf. 1983, Table 3.1.) embraced objects and states of World 1 – physical (including biological), World 2 – mental (subjective), World 3 – societal (intersubjective), World 4 – scientific and artistic (objective knowledge).

Worth quoting is the opinion of Susan Petrilli who supported Sebeok's convictions, in her book *The Self as a Sign, the World, and the Other. Living Semiotics*, that: "Thanks to language understood as modeling device and to its syntactical capacity, the human animal, differently from nonhuman animals, is not programmed to remain fixed within a single world, but, on the contrary, is able to build an infinite number of possible worlds through the work of construction, deconstruction, and reconstruction" (Petrilli 2013: 38–39).

3.3 Creative aspects of epistemic ability to construe phenomenal worlds beyond words

The topic of the creative use of language has been extensively discussed in numerous works about dispositional potentials of human individuals as communication participants as well as mental faculties and physiological endowments of human beings as speaking animals. The abilities of humans to create unusual novelties or to perform average innovations in style and form of language as a means of communication, encompass the imaginative altering of abstraction of cognizing and sign-processing subjects, to displace themselves from one existence mode to another and to enter into sometimes inexperienced dimensions of their states of being, or to the assumed states of others while basing on the creative power of knowledge.

In allusion to the mundane phenomenology, it is worth recalling the idea of the social construction of reality from the late 1960s, based on the assumption that people create their own view of the world they live in on the basis of reflections of their individual experiences. A certain kind of a social construct is the reality of everyday life, or the world of life, which comes into being as a result of communicational activities. Sociological constructivists take for granted that the reality of everyday life is shaped by information gained by particular human beings as organisms in interactions with their environment. Personal constructs result therefore not only from similar perceptions of the world but also from analogous attitudes towards the objects evaluated with respect to their utility.

It is supposed that interpersonal communication can lead to creating intersubjectively similar personal constructs in the minds of people interacting within the same culture, as Peter Ludwig Berger and Thomas Luckmann, in *The Social Construction of Reality* (1966) have claimed. In the view of Berger and Luckmann "The reality of everyday life" appears to individual selves "as an intersubjective world, a world that" they "share with others". However, this intersubjectively comprehended world "sharply differentiates everyday life from other realities of which" they are aware (1966: 23). This collective stock of everyday knowledge is created due to social interactions (cf. Berger & Luckmann 1966: 19–46).

Assuming that man is a social being whose contacts with external environments is mediated by symbols, Berger and Luckmann state that it is the language which "objectivates the shared experiences and makes them available to all within linguistic community, thus becoming both the basis and the instrument of the collective stock of knowledge" (1966: 68).

The postulated conception of imaginative abilities of humans to create possible or alternative worlds may finally be supported by the statement of Jørgen Dines Johansen, from his "Chapter 10. Semiotics, biology, and the adaptionist theory of literature", assuming that "we are programmed by evolution to produce virtual universes in dreaming, in playing, in hypothesizing about the future and in daydreaming", and what is more, "the production of fictional universes allows us not only to project future changes onto present states of affairs but also to change the conditions – ashairmong other things, the nature and the ontological status of the agents" (Johansen 2011: 219).

References

Bateson, Gregory. 1951. Psychiatric thinking: An epistemological approach. In Jurgen Ruesch & Gregory Bateson, *Communication. The Social Matrix of Psychiatry*, 228–256. New York: W. W. Norton & Co.

Baxter, Lesley A. & Barbara M. Montgomery. 1996. *Relating: Dialogues and Dialectics*. New York: Guilford Press.

Berger, Peter Ludwig & Thomas Luckmann. 1966. *The Social Construction of Reality*. Garden City, NY: Doubleday.

Cassirer, Ernst. 1955 [1923–1929]. *The Philosophy of Symbolic Forms*. Vol. I: *Language*. Vol. II: *Mythical Thought*. Vol. III: *The Phenomenology of Knowledge*. Trans. by Ralph Manheim. New Haven, CT: Yale University Press. (*Philosophie der symbolischen Formen*. Erster Teil. *Die Sprache (Zur Phänomenologie der sprachlichen Form)*, 1923. Zweiter Teil. *Das mystische Denken*, 1925. Dritter Teil. *Phänomenologie der Erkenntnis*, 1929. Berlin: Bruno Cassirer).

Cassirer, Ernst. 1962 [1944]. *An Essay on Man: An Introduction to a Philosophy of Human Culture*. New York, NY Doubleday and Company; New Haven, CT: Yale University Press (Louis Stern Memorial Fund); London, UK: H. Milford; Oxford, UK: University Press/Third printing. New Haven, CT: Yale University Press; London, UK: H. Milford.

Cassirer, Ernst. 1995. *Symbolische Formen*. Zu Band IV (Originalmanuskript 1929). In John Michael Krois & Oswald Schwemmer (eds.) *Nachgelassene Manuskripte und Texte*. Band 1. *Zur Metaphysik der symbolischen Formen*, 1921–1940, 199–258. Hamburg: Felix Meiner Verlag.

Fontanille, Jacques & Algirdas Julien Greimas. 1991. *Sémiotique des passions: des états de choses aux états d'âme*. Paris: Éditions du Seuil.

Fontanille, Jacques. 2004. *Soma et séma. Figures du corps*. Paris: Maisonneuve et Larose.

Greimas, Algirdas Julien. 1966. *Sémantique structurale. Recherche de méthode* (Langue et langage). Paris: Larousse.

Greimas, Algirdas Julien. 1976. *Sémiotique et sciences sociales*. Paris: Éditions du Seuil.

Grzybek, Peter. 1994. The concept of 'model' in Soviet semiotics. *Russian Literature* 36(3). 285–300.

Hegel, Georg Wilhelm Friedrich. 1910 [1807]. *Phenomenology of Mind*. Trans., introd. & notes by James Black Baillie. London, UK: George Allen & Unwin; London, UK: Swan Sonnenschein and Co.; New York, NY: The Macmillan Company. (*Die Phänomenologie des Geistes. System der Wissenschaft*. Erster Theil. Bamberg, Würzburg: Verlag Joseph Anton Goebhardt).

Heidegger, Martin. 1962 [1927]. *Being and Time*. Trans. by John Macquarrie & Edward Robinson. London: SCM Press. (*Sein und Zeit*. Tübingen: Max Niemeyer Verlag).

Heidegger, Martin. 1995 [1983]. *The Fundamental Concepts of Metaphysics: World, Finitude, Solitude*. Trans. by William H. McNeil & Nicholas Walker. Bloomington: Indiana University Press. (*Die Grundbegriffe der Metaphysik: Welt – Endlichkeit – Einsamkeit*. Frankfurt am Main: Vittorio Klostermann).

Heidegger, Martin. 1998 [1929]. On the essence of ground. In William McNeil (ed.), Martin Heidegger Pathmarks, trans. by William McNeil, 97–135. Cambridge: Cambridge University Press. (Vom Wesen des Grundes. In Martin Heidegger (ed.), *Festschrift, Edmund Husserl zum 70. Geburtstag gewidmet* . . . (Ergänzungsband zum Band X des Jahrbuchs für Philosophie und phänomenologische Forschung, ed. by Edmund Husserl), 71–110. Halle an der Saale: Max Niemeyer Verlag).

Husserl, Edmund. 1970 [1954]. *The Crisis of European Sciences and Transcendental Phenomenology: An Introduction to Phenomenological Philosophy*. Trans. by David Carr. Evanston, IL: Northwestern University Press. (*Die Krisis der europäischen Wissenschaften und die transzendentale Phänomenologie. Eine Einleitung in die phänomenologische Philosophie*. In Walter Biemel (ed.), *Husserliana. Edmund Husserl, Gesammelte Werke*. Band VI. Den Haag: Martinus Nijhoff).

Husserl, Edmund. 1970 [1890]. Zur Logik der Zeichen (Semiotik). In Lothar Eley (ed.), *Husserliana. Edmund Husserl, Gesammelte Werke*. Band XII: *Philosophie der Arithmetik mit ergänzenden Texten*, 340–373. Den Haag: Martinus Nijhoff [Manuscript].

Ivanov, Vyacheslav V. 1978 [1962]. The science of semiotics. Trans. by Doris Bradbury. *New Literary History* 9(2). 199–204. (Иванов, Вячеслав Всеволодович, Предисловие. *Симпозиум по структурному изучению знаковых систем: Тезисы докладов*, 3–9. Москва: Издательство Академии наук СССР).

Jaspers, Karl. 1962 [1946 /1913]. *General Psychopathology*. Trans. by Jan Hoenig & Marian W. Hamilton. Manchester: Manchester University Press. (*Allgemeine Psychopathologie. Ein Leitfaden für Studierende, Ärzte und Psychologen*. Vierte, völlig neu bearbeitete Auflage (4th, entirely new elaborated edn.), 1st edn. Berlin, Heidelberg: Julius Springer).

Johansen, Jørgen Dines. 2011. Chapter 10. Semiotics, biology, and the adaptionist theory of literature. In Paul Cobley, John Deely, Kalevi Kull & Susan Petrilli (eds.), *Semiotics Continues to Astonish: Thomas A. Sebeok and the Doctrine of Signs*, 2007–2222. (Semiotics (Communication and Cognition 7)). Berlin & Boston: De Gruyter Mouton.

Kant, Immanuel. 1838 [1781]. *Critique of Pure Reason*. Trans. by Francis Haywood. London, UK: William Pickering. (*Critik der reinen Vernunft*. Riga: Johann Friedrich Hartknoch).

Kierkegaard, Søren. 1941 [1846]. *Concluding Unscientific Postscript to Philosophical Fragments*. Trans. by David F. Swenson, Walter Lowrie. Princeton: Princeton University Press. (*Afsluttende uvidenskabelig Efterskrift til de philosophiske Smuler*. Af Johannes Climacus. Udgivet af S. Kierkegaard (Udkast til indholdsfortegnelse. Trykmanuskript)).

Kull, Kalevi. 1999. Biosemiotics in the twentieth century: A view from biology. *Semiotica. Journal of the International Association for Semiotic Studies. Revue de l'Association Internationale de Sémiotique* 127(1/4). 385–414.

Leech, Geoffrey N. 1983. *Principles of Pragmatics*. New York: Longman.

Lotman, Juri. 1988 [1981]. The semiotics of culture and the concept of a text. *Journal of Russian and East European Psychology* 26(3). 52–58. ((Лотман, Юрий Михайлович). Семиотика культуры и понятие текста. *Труды по знаковым системам* 12 (Тарту). 3–7).

Lotman, Juri. 2005 [1984]. On the semiosphere. Trans. by Wilma Clark. *Sign Systems Studies* 33(1). 205–229. ((Лотман, Юрий Михайлович.) О семиосфере. *Труды по знаковым системам* 17 (Тарту). 5–23).

Lotman, Juri. 2011 [1967]. The place of art among other modelling systems. Trans. by Tanel Pern. *Sign Systems Studies* 39 (2/4). 249–270. ((Лотман, Юрий Михайлович.) Тезисы к проблеме "Искусство в ряду моделирующих систем". *Труды по знаковым системам* 3. 130–145).
Merleau-Ponty, Maurice. 2005 [1945]. *Phenomenology of Perception*. Trans. by Colin Smith. Routledge Classics. Taylor and Francis e-Library. (*Phénomènologie de la perception* Paris: Gallimard).
Petrilli, Susan. 2013. *The Self as a Sign, the World, and the Other. Living Semiotics*. New Brunswick, NJ & London, UK: Transaction Publishers.
Pike, Kenneth L. 1993. *Talk, Thought, and Thing: The Emic Road Toward Conscious Knowledge*. Dallas, TX: Summer Institute of Linguistics. International Academic Bookstore.
Popper, Karl. 1972. *Objective Knowledge. An Evolutionary Approach*. Oxford: Oxford University Press.
Raudla, Tuuli. 2008. Vico and Lotman: Poetic meaning creation and primary modelling. *Sign Systems Studies* 36(1). 137–165.
Sartre, Jean-Paul. 1956 [1943]. *Being and Nothingness: An Essay on Phenomenological Ontology*. Trans. & intr. by Hazel E. Barnes. New York: Philosophical Library [*L'Être et le néant : Essai d'ontologie phénoménologique*. Paris: Gallimard].
Sartre, Jean-Paul. 1990 /1960/ [1936–1937]. *The Transcendence of the Ego: An Existentialist Theory of Consciousness*. Trans. & intr. by Forrest Williams & Robert Kirkpatrick. New York: Hill and Wang. (La transcendance de l'ego: Esquisse se d'une description phénoménologique. *Recherches philosophiques* VI. 85–123).
Sebeok, Thomas A. & Marcel Danesi. 2000. *The Forms of Meaning: Modelling Systems Theory and Semiotic Analysis*. Berlin: Mouton de Gruyter.
Sebeok, Thomas A. 1991 [1988]. In what sense is language a "primary modelling system"? In Thomas A. Sebeok, *A Sign is Just a Sign*, 49–58. Bloomington, IN: Indiana University Press. [In Henri Broms & Rebecca Kauffmann. (eds.), *Semiotics of culture* (Proceedings of the 25th symposium of the Tartu-Moscow school of semiotics, Imatra, Finland, 27th–29th July, 19), 67–80. Helsinki: Arator Inc. Publishers]
Sebeok, Thomas A. 1991 [1979]. The semiotic self. In Thomas A. Sebeok. *A sign is just a sign*, 36–40. Bloomington, IN: Indiana University Press. (Also in Thomas. A. Sebeok, *The Sign and its Masters*, 263–267. Austin, TX: University of Texas Press. Appendix).
Sebeok, Thomas A. 1995 [1992]. From Vico to Cassirer to Langer. In Marcel Danesi (ed.), *Giambattista Vico and Anglo-American Science. Philosophy and Writing*, 159–170. Berlin: Mouton de Gruyter. (Von Vico zu Cassirer zu Langer. *S: European Journal for Semiotic Studies* 4(1/2). 207–222).
Stjernfelt, Frederik. 2011. Simple animals and complex biology: Von Uexküll's two-fold influence on Cassirer's philosophy. *Synthese* 179. 169–186.
Tarasti, Eero. 2017. The semiotics of A. J. Greimas: A European intellectual heritage seen from the inside and the outside. *Sign Systems Studies* 45(1/2). 33–53.
Tarasti, Eero. 2015. *Sein und Schein. Explorations in Existential Semiotics*. Berlin & Boston: Mouton de Gruyter.
Tarasti, Eero. 2009. What is existential semiotics? From theory to application. In Eero Tarasti (ed.), *Communication: Understanding/Misunderstanding. Proceedings of the 9th Congress of the IASS/AIS – Helsinki-Imatra: 11–17 June, 2007*, 1755–1772. Imatra: International Semiotics Institute at Imatra and Helsinki: Semiotic Society of Finland.

Uexküll, Jakob von (& Georg Kriszat). 1992 /1957 [1934]. Uexküll, Jakob von. 1992. A stroll through the world of animals and men: A picture book of invisible worlds. Trans. by Claire H. Schiller (Reprint). *Semiotica. Journal of the International Association for Semiotic Studies. Revue de l'Association Internationale de Sémiotique* 89(4). 319–391. / Uexküll, Jakob von. 1957. A stroll through the world of animals and men: A picture book of invisible worlds. Trans. by Claire H. Schiller. In Claire H. Schiller (ed.), *Instinctive Behaviour. The Development of a Modern Concept*, 5–80. New York, NY: International Universities Press. (Uexküll, Jakob von & Georg Kriszat. 1934. *Streifzüge durch die Umwelten von Tieren und Menschen. Ein Bilderbuch unsichtbarer Welten* (Sammlung: Verständliche Wissenschaft 21). Berlin: Julius Springer Verlag).

Uexküll, Jakob von. 1907. Die Umrisse einer kommenden Weltanschauung. *Die neue Rundschau* 18. 641–661.

Uexküll, Jakob von. 1921 [1909]. *Umwelt und Innenwelt der Tiere*, 2nd enlarged and improved edn. Berlin: Julius Springer Verlag.

Uexküll, Jakob von. 1926 [1920]. *Theoretical Biology*. Trans. by Doris L. Mackinnon. New York, NY: Harcourt, Brace. (*Theoretische Biologie*. Berlin: Verlag von Gebrüder Paetel).

Uexküll, Jakob von. 1928 [1920]. *Theoretische Biologie*, 2nd entirely new elaborated edn. Berlin: Julius Springer Verlag.

Uexküll, Jakob von. 1936. *Niegeschaute Welten: Die Umwelten meiner Freunde. Ein Erinnerungsbuch*. Berlin: S. Fischer.

Uexküll, Jakob von. 1982 [1940]. The theory of meaning. Trans. by Barry Stone, Herbert Weiner. *Semiotica. Journal of the International Association for Semiotic Studies. Revue de l'Association Internationale de Sémiotique* 42(1). 25–82. (*Bedeutungslehre* (Bios. Abhandlungen zur theoretischen Biologie und ihrer Geschichte, sowie zur Philosophie der organischen Naturwissenschaften. Band X). Leipzig: Verlag von Johann Ambrosius Barth).

van Manen, Max. 1997 [1990]. *Researching Lived Experience. Human Science for an Action Sensitive Pedagogy*. 2nd edn. (revised and corrected). New York: Routledge. (New York, NY: State University of New York Press, London, ON: Althaus Press).

van Manen, Max. 2007. Phenomenology of practice. *Phenomenology & Practice* 1(1). 11–30.

van Manen, Max. 2011. *Phenomenology Online. A Resource from Phenomenological Inquiry*. Available at Max van Manen's pages: www.phenomenologyonline.com/inquiry/orientations-in-phenomenology/

van Manen, Max. 2014. *Phenomenology of Practice: Meaning-Giving Methods in Phenomenological Research and Writing* (Developing Qualitative Inquiry 13). Walnut Creek, CA: Left Coast Press.

Wąsik, Zdzisław. 2003. *Epistemological Perspectives on Linguistic Semiotics*. (Polish Studies in English Language and Literature 8). Frankfurt am Main, (etc.): Peter Lang. Europäischer Verlag der Wissenschaften.

Wąsik, Zdzisław. 2014. *Lectures on the Epistemology of Semiotics*. (Philologica Wratislaviensia: Series Didactica 1). Wrocław: Philological School of Higher Education in Wrocław Publishing.

Wąsik, Zdzisław. 2016a. *From Grammar to Discourse: Towards a Solipsistic Paradigm of Semiotics*. (Seria Filologia Angielska 50). Poznań: Adam Mickiewicz University Press/Wydawnictwo Naukowe Uniwersytetu im. Adama Mickiewicza w Poznaniu.

Wąsik, Zdzisław. 2016b. Epistemology – the theory of knowledge or knowing? Appreciating Gregory Bateson's contribution to the cartography of human cognition. *Romanian Journal of Communication and Public Relations* 18.3(39). 23–35.

Wąsik, Zdzisław. 2018. Umwelt, Lebenswelt & *Dasein* seen through the lens of a subjective experience of reality. *Sign Systems Studies* 46(1). 126–142.

Zaliznjak, Andrey A., Vyacheslav V. Ivanov & Vladimir N. Toporov. 1977 [1962]. Structural-typological study of semiotic modeling systems. In Daniel P. Lucid, (ed.) 1977, *Soviet Semiotics: An Anthology*, 47–58. Baltimore: Johns Hopkins University Press. (Зализняк, Андрей Анатольевич, Вячеслав Всеволодович Иванов & Владимир Николáевич Топоров О возможности структурно-типологического изучения некоторых моделирующих систем).

Roberto Mastroianni
Aesthetics and human praxis. Notes on the existential semiotics of Eero Tarasti

Abstract: Eero Tarasti's existential semiotics presents itself as a third generation semiotics interested in investigating the conditions of human existence and the emergence of meaning, significance and signs. In this perspective, the essay investigates how the existential condition is connected to the sphere of aesthetics understood as human praxis and how in this specific praxis emerges space for freedom and transformation of the human and the ontological and cultural horizon in which it is immersed.

Keywords: existentialism, existentialism, existential semiotics, praxis, art, human praxis, aesthetics

> In the world of everyday experience, in *Dasein*, one can consider as a sign that situation in which a subject must search for the appropriate code for his actions. If the situation in which one is involved is of an ethical character, one must employ an ethical code, not an aesthetic code; if the situation is of a historical character, one must apply an historical code; if it is existential, an existential code. How is it possible for the subject to find the appropriate code?[1]
>
> E. Tarasti

Introduction

Eero Tarasti was a leading international figure in semiotics and musicology in the second half of the second half of the 20th century. Starting with his 1978 doctoral dissertation on myth and music on Richard Wagner, Jean Sibelius, and Igor Stravinsky, up to his recent studies on Cultural Heritage, Tarasti has shown that he pursues an integrative and multidisciplinary perspective capable of uniting theoretical philosophy, sociology, anthropology, and musicology, choosing semiotics as a method to become fully part of the linguistic turn[2] that has characterized the twentieth-century human sciences. Starting from a Greimasian approach, A. J. Greimas was the supervisor of his thesis for his Ph. D. in 1978, he opened up his research to a comparison with the thoughts of Claude Levi-Strauss and Roland Barthes, whom he met during his Parisian studies, and with those of Thomas A.

---

1 Tarasti 2009:24; Tarasti 2000.
2 Rorty 1992.

https://doi.org/10.1515/9783110789164-015

Sebeok, to whom he was linked. He succeeded in outlining a personal and fruitful theoretical and analytical path, as is amply testified by the dozens of publications that are fundamental for semiotic studies, by the many scientific posts he held over the decades, not least for importance the Presidency of the IASS/AIS (International Association for Semiotic Studies, 2004–2014), by his teaching activities and by the many honours he received.

In the last two decades, Tarasti has finally concentrated his intellectual efforts on the attempt to outline a new semiotic perspective that he has called "existential semiotics", which can explain what dynamics come into play in the "states before the formation of signs" or in those "existential situations" in which man and signs are located, before they are crystallised into forms that can be analysed, classified, and studied. This exquisitely philosophical intellectual operation makes him one of the promoters and protagonists of a new generation of semiotic studies.

From this point of view, existential semiotics is, in fact, a "third-generation semiotics", as it tries to assume and go beyond the results achieved by "classical semiotics" (Saussure, Jakobson, Peirce. . .) and by the "second generation" (Greimas, Eco, Barthes, Kristeva. . .), in view of an existential clarification of the onto-anthropological dimension of semiosis and human praxis.

While "first-generation semiotics" formulated general theories of meaning and signification of a linguistic-structuralist matrix, "second-generation semiotics" was interested in developing analytical semiotic theories of a structuralist, culturological, and philosophical nature with reference to sign systems and communicative and social phenomena, "third-generation semiotics", on the other hand, poses the problem of formulating new general philosophical and post-structuralist theories capable of explaining the nature and emergence of signs, codes, and discursive practices in relation to the nature of subjectivity, temporality, and human praxis. This operation articulates the scientific project of semiotics in an exquisitely philosophical direction, which sees in aesthetics its exemplary dimension of application. This theoretical move seems to be motivated and legitimised by the interest in identifying new paths for our thought, through a change of perspective, which we could ascribe to Ludwig Wittgenstein's warning about the "change of look" that allows us to escape from the condition of imprisonment in which a certain image of reality forces us, informing our language and continuously proposing it to us.[3] The image that holds many semiotic theories prisoner, well exemplified in the "extra textum nulla salus" of Greimasian memory, is the idea that the doctrine of signs can only be applied to

---

3 Wittgenstein 1999.

explain social and communicative phenomena that can be considered as "texts" and "discourses" in themselves enclosed and precisely for this reason analyzable with the "conceptual toolbox" developed over time by the discipline. Tarasti's gesture, in this perspective, represents a "change of view" aimed at producing a new "general theory of semiotics", which, by questioning the formation of signs, of sense, and of signification, is able to explain problems such as: the "existential condition of the human being"; the "existential states in which the subject and the signs are placed before their emergence"; the "relation of the subject with otherness and the world"; the "ethical and political dimension of human existence". These are all exquisitely philosophical problems that can be investigated by recovering philosophical weapons and theories, choosing aesthetics as a privileged field of investigation, giving rise to existential semiotics that can be considered as a kind of semiotic existentialism, or rather a semiotic theory interested in the relationship between semiosis and the possibilities and conditions of human existence. This change in outlook takes the form of a Kantian-style "transcendental leap", interested in tracing the foundations and conditions of emergence of systems of meaning and signification in relation to the very ontological nature of the relationship that binds sign, subject, and transcendence, which is brought back to human praxis and to an exemplary part of it that is represented by the aesthetic dimension. For Tarasti, in fact, "reality is formed by fields of energy governed by specific laws", of which both the subject and signs are part and to which they are subject: these are the "situations in which the sign manifests itself as it is always in relation to a specific existential situation".[4] This perspective prefers a vision of existence, indebted to the anthropological reading of existentialism that is very widespread in the French context,[5] and partially rejects post-Heideggerian ontologism, maintaining post-structuralist traits that guarantee the application of semiotic tools to the different fields of human praxis. In this perspective, existential semiotics presents itself as an advanced attempt to explain a possible semiotic reading of the existential condition of the human being in the world, its ethical and political dimension and the emergence of systems of signification that attribute meaning to the anthroposphere, in relation to the temporal and spatial dimension of the onto-anthropology of the human animal.

---

4 Tarasti 2009: 18.
5 Levinas 1967.

1 Semiotic existentialism: Ontological existentialism or anthropological existentialism?

We are clearly faced with an existentialist vocation of Tarasti's semiotics, which is developed in close dialogue with philosophical thought, in search of an "existential clarification" of semiotics itself, and which chooses existentialism as its philosophical koiné: existentialists are the authors of reference for Tarasti (Kierkegaard, Jaspers, Sartre. . .), existentialist is the philosophical lexicon that Tarasti uses, existentialist and existential are the philosophical problems that Tarasti poses.

Then, the fundamental question is to understand which philosophical references Tarasti chooses, putting them in relation with the semiotic tradition, in order to develop a "general theory of meaning and signification" that is able to account for "existential states": of those "existential situations" that precede the appearance of signs and systems of signification.

There are, in fact, different forms and approaches of existentialism, which can be divided into two large groups: ontological existentialism (Heidegger, Jaspers, Maritain. . .) and anthropological existentialism (Merleau-Ponty, Sartre, Levinas. . .).

The most intense form of ontological existentialism is that of the Heideggerian matrix, which sees its genesis in Sein und Zeit and refers to the imperfect parallelism between two pairs of concepts such as "existential"/"existential" and "ontic"/"ontological".[6] For Heideggerism and post-Heideggerism, in fact, "existential is the theory of the possible modes of being of being, considered abstractly, as pure and neutral a priori, indistinct and indifferent to any concrete distinction, even if their nature belongs to being always concrete and distinct modes that ground a priori the possibility of concrete and ontic (existential) determinations. Existential is every concrete relation of the individual [. . .] concrete being to his being, conditioned and ontologically motivated [. . .] by the existentiality of being".[7] In this perspective, "existential" would be the concrete problems that the individual encounters in everyday life, while "existential" would be the problems identified by reflection on existence and on existence only. An existential

---

[6] We refer to the philosophical lexicon established by the Italian translation of Pietro Chiodi's Sein und Zeit (1953), which has determined central philosophical approaches and perspectives on the international scene for post-Heideggerism and hermeneutics, such as the interpretation that Gianni Vattimo has carried out in recent decades.
[7] Pareyson 1950:219.

reflection could therefore only be conducted within existence and would therefore have deep "existential roots".[8]

By not openly thematizing this distinction, Tarasti finds himself rejecting a "narrow definition" of the concept of "existential condition", making his own a "wide version" faithful to that post-Sartrian slogan ("existence precedes essence"), in which existentialism, as a cultural movement, has long recognized itself.

Tarasti chooses, therefore, to adopt a "broad version" of existentialism: a vision more similar to the anthropological existentialism of French matrix, which has its references in Levinas (transcendence and otherness) and Sartre (being in situation), placing at the centre of his research human praxis in relation to existence and semiosis.

2 Subjectivity, otherness, and existential condition

Subjectivity is one of the central themes of Tarasti's theories; it is analyzed in relation to the existential condition, the construction of identity and otherness.

In this perspective, the relationship between "sign" and "subject" is analyzed in relation to the "existential situation", which precedes the formation of signs, and which determines the semiotic construction of subjectivity, intersubjectivity, and the world.

From this point of view, the subject and the semiotic process are placed in an "existential situation" characterized by communicative practices that reject the logic of the "equal exchange of information", embracing a more dynamic and open form of semiosis, in which the "subject" and the "world" are subjected to continuous processes of construction and deconstruction, produced by human praxis that is always characterized by a projectuality inserted in a specific temporality and spatiality.

In this perspective, the aesthetic dimension constitutes a fundamental junction of praxis with regard to both the capacity and the symbolic necessity of the human being to endow the world with meaning and sense by giving form to the subject, inserting both into a dynamic process that produces identity only and always in relation to otherness. Otherness, therefore, presents itself as a fundamental polarity of "existential semiotics": the "subject" is, in fact, always

---

8 Heidegger 1977: 185; cfr. Pareyson 1950: 185.

formed in praxis and in relation to "otherness" within an open semiotic process, which moves the centre of semiotic activity into a dialogical space and the code adopted in relation to the existential situation. It is, therefore, important, in order to analyze codes and systems of signification, to understand the connotations and forms of "existential situations", which represent the ontological space from which signs emerge and in which codes are formalized. A semiotics of this type, therefore, rejects the idea of "communication" as an "equal exchange of information", rejects the "engineering and naive model of communication" (sender, receiver, message, code, channel) in favour of an idea of "communication" of a "communitarian communicative" type (praxis, spatiality, and inter-subjectivity, understood as the sharing of a symbolic dimension that produces community).

The existential situation thus assumes a discursive/communicative value, making existential semiotics a semiotics of communication interested in onto-anthropological spatiality and the forms of praxis that establish it. There is in this interest a strong analogy with some researches carried out by contemporary post-Heideggerism, such as Sloterdijck's "spherology"[9] for example, which see in the spatial dimension of human existence an essential element at least equal to temporality in order to define the human condition, bringing back to the spatial metaphor (the "spheres") the dimension in which the human and the world take shape through processes of handling and signification capable of holding together from the simplest physical, material, and linguistic part to the great symbolic systems that govern the forms of life that populate the world.

Tarasti seems to approach this approach, attributing in his writings a dialogical character to the symbolic interaction between man and the world, which enriches the concept of "existential situation" with a further meaning. The "existential condition", in fact, represents, for the author, that set of "conditions that precede the constitution of signs, the so-called pre-signs".[10] In this perspective, the sign "always appears concerning a given situation. [. . .] I mean the situation in which the sign manifests itself as its determined, concrete spatio-temporal position". Moreover, "the sign can place itself in any form of existential relationship with its own situation: it can either deny it or affirm it".[11] This approach espouses an anthropological vision of existentialism, which sees in Sartre and Levinas some of its most important references.

The emergence of the symbolic, of codes, and systems of signs are, from this point of view, always "in-situation" and this "situation" takes on socio-histor-

---

9 Sloterdijk 2013.
10 Tarasti 2009: 22.
11 Tarasti 2009: 22.

ical and, in some ways, political overtones. . ., indicating in transcendence a fundamental element of reference in the construction of subjectivity and intersubjectivity. This approach has strong ethical and political elements and sees in dialogicality the central element of the anthropological dimension, which is always referred to the different forms of human praxis. The semiotic dimension of human praxis is, in this perspective, always called upon to give voice to the essential contents of a certain "form of life" and is therefore always linked to specific socio-historical contexts and refers to an intersubjectivity that is always immersed in certain cultural worlds, in a way of life from which it cannot prescind. From this perspective, we are faced with an attempt to give shape to a "broad version" of the very concept of the "existential condition" that attempts to unite the ontological and anthropological approaches, which see man placed in an "existential phase" with precise socio-historical characteristics, from which signs, codes, and systems of signification emerge.

In this perspective, transcendence is the desire to overcome the realist acceptance of the world as it is, towards a political, ethical, and design reality of subjectivity in a semiotic relationship with the world, leveraging the forms of praxis.

3 Existential semiotics, aesthetics, and human praxis

Tarasti accompanies us in an exploration of the elementary and existential structures of semiotics, which sees the production of meaning linked to human praxis and the emergence of signs to symbolic forms called to enliven certain "forms of life".[12] It claims a relational approach to reality in which intersubjectivity is linked to specific socio-cultural contexts.
The interesting theoretical aspect of this approach is that it denies the pure character of intersubjectivity, highlighting it being constitutively linked to a plurality of codes and always being immersed in certain cultural worlds that cannot be separated from the world of life.

Intersubjectivity is therefore always in tension between the universality of the modes of symbolic production and the particular ones of praxis and the codes corresponding to them, bringing to light the existential nature of human doing characterized as a dimension of projectuality. Every human project, in fact, is always existential in nature and characterized by a form of indeterminacy deeply

---

[12] Bertram: 2014.

linked to that dimension of freedom that characterizes the sphere of human communication.

The reference to which our thought goes can only be the existentialism of Heidegger's Sein und Zeit, even if Tarasti does not thematize it, and to an idea of *Dasein*, in which man, understood as "thrown being", is characterized by an existence considered as "ex-sistere" (from the Latin, "to be outside"[13]) in the sense of going beyond the simply present reality in the direction of possibility, through the posing of a "projectuality" that is always ontological and anthropological. This idea of "existence" as "transcendence" together with the centrality of dialogue/discourse becomes the theoretical premise of a semiotics interested in otherness, in the subject, and in existence with strong interpretative characteristics. This outlines a semiotics that aims to explain existential situations and praxis and that could be integrated with the results of philosophical hermeneutics. This is because *Dasein* is always a "situated being" and localized, not a transcendental subject, but a "thrown being" (Geworfenheith), Heidegger would say, a finite and concrete being, historically situated: a single and finite existence to which corresponds a certain emotional situation and a set of historical-cultural pre-judgments.

Reflection on the ontological status of the sign and the possibility of a correspondence between codes and existential situations also comes close to the idea of the Heideggerian matrix sign as "usable" and this opens up a semiotic reflection that is attentive to the ethical dimension of the human condition and its constitutive relationship. In this perspective, an intersubjectivity is outlined that is always immersed in certain cultural worlds, in a "world of life" from which the emergence, formation, and exercise of symbolic forms cannot be separated. This new semiotic theory can, therefore, find application in an investigation of that "worldliness of the world", which is a "character of being itself"[14] and which is constituted through the usability of things (Zuhandenheit) and their meaning in relation to our lives.

The universality of human making, of its forms, and of the faculties and semiotic devices are, therefore, put into relation with irreducible otherness within an anthropological dimension characterized by projectuality, in which the human animal is called upon to "make sense" within an ontological opening constituted by language and signs.

This is because the human being (what Tarasti calls the subject) is always in the world as a designing entity that relates to its own possibilities, inserting them

---

13 Heidegger 1977.
14 Heidegger 1977: 135.

into a project, taking them on as instruments. The character of "referral" (*aliquid pro aliquod*) of the sign (§17 of Sein und Zeit), a constitutive and not accidental character that acquires more strength in relation to that specific form of human making that is art.

In fact, it is not by chance that in recent years, Tarasti has dedicated himself to investigating the aesthetic field in many of its forms, broadening his interest in art from the semiotics of music to that of Cultural Heritage and interculturality, driven by an implicit idea of art as a form of doing in relation to the rest of human praxis and to the binomial of tradition and innovation.

In this perspective, the production and interpretation of systems of signification, symbolic forms, and works, which can be specifically defined as artistic, immerse the subject in the interpretation of reality, setting in motion a life-giving activity of praxis with intrinsically plural characteristics in which the producer/user of systems of signification is immersed in a hermeneutic horizon that recalls a certain semiotics of Umberto Eco, more precisely the one outlined in "Opera aperta".[15]

Tarasti's work is ambitious and creates fruitful short-circuits and spaces of interaction between different disciplines such as philosophy, musicology, and semiotics, precisely because it is based on a semiotic approach based on a profound rethinking of human praxis, highlighting its reflexive and self-reflexive character. In fact, the connection between "existential situation" and "existential code" highlights the cultural and symbolic character of the human being, who is obliged to take a position towards himself through a wide range of "reflexive practices",[16] i.e. complex communicative and symbolic practices that lead the human being to continuously redefine himself in a relationship between tradition and the existential condition in which the human being is immersed. These practices of a linguistic nature take on an exemplary form in the aesthetic dimension since it is the specific form of those practices through which human beings take a position in relation to themselves within a cultural praxis.[17]

Existential semiotics, therefore, presents itself as an in-depth investigation of the linguistic and communicative relations that arise in the relationship established within the triad of subject, sign, and transcendence, rejecting a naive realist vision of reality.

Language in Tarasti's perspective, as in that of Gadamer, Arendt et alia and part of contemporary semiotics,[18] considers language/discourse "in-between"

---

15 Eco 1962.
16 Bertram 2014.
17 Bertram 2014.
18 Volli 2008; Volli 2002; Volli 2007.

people, between speakers. For this reason, the "existential space", the "existential situation" that precedes the constitution of signs, is essentially a dialogical/discursive spatiality that takes shape between the subject, otherness, signs, and transcendence, similar to many hermeneutic and dialogical philosophical approaches (such as philosophical hermeneutics, Bakhtin's dialogism, Buber's thought, Gadamer's thought, etc.).

In Tarasti's thought, transcendence is an irreducible need for the subject's otherness, and here the debt to Levinas' theories is evident. This conception undermines a too simple theory of signification, based on the "equal exchange of information", in the direction of a more complex theory of communication attentive to the ontological and existential dimension of the human being.

For all these reasons, Eero Tarasti's work will remain a point of reference in twentieth-century semiotic studies.

References

Bertram, Georg W. 2014. *Kunst als menschliche Praxis, Eine Astetik*. Berlin: Suhrkamp Verlag.
Eco, Umberto. 2014. *Opera aperta*. Milano: Bompiani.
Heidegger, Martin. 1977 [1927]. *Sein und Zeit*, Klostermann, Frankfurt am Main 1977; Italian translation by Pietro Chiodi, *Essere e tempo* (Milano: Longanesi & C., 1976).
Levinas, Emmanuel. 1967. *En découvrant l'existence avec Husserl et Heidegger*. Paris: Vrin.
Pareyson Luigi. 1950. "Esistenziale ed esistentivo nel pensiero di M. Heidegger e di K. Jaspers (1938)", in *Studi sull'esistenzialismo*. Firenze: Santoni.
Rorty. Richard. 1992 [1967]. *The linguistic turn : essays in philosophical method : with two retrospective essays*. Chicago, London: Chicago University Press.
Sloterdijk, Peter. 2013. *In the World Interior of Capital: Towards a Philosophical Theory of Globalization*. English translation by Wieland Hoban. Polity Press.
Tarasti, Eero. 2000. *Existential Semiotics*. Bloomington, Indianapolis: Indiana University Press.
Tarasti, Eero. 2009. *Fondamenti di semiotica esistenziale*. Italian translation by Massimo Berruti. Bari: Edizioni Giuseppe Laterza.
Volli, Ugo. 2002. *Le figure del desiderio*. Milano: Cortina.
Volli, Ugo. 2007. *Il nuovo libro della comunicazione*. Milano: Saggiatore.
Volli, Ugo. 2008. *Lezioni di filosofia della comunicazione*. Roba, Bari: Laterza.
Wittgenstein, Ludwig. 1999 [1953]. *Ricerche filosofiche*. Italian translation by Renzo Piovesan & Maria Trinchero. Einaudi.

Juha Ojala
Eero Tarasti, existential semiotics, music, and mind. On the existential and cognitive notions of situation

Abstract: In recent decades, there has been a shift both in semiotics and in cognitive science to novel, perhaps more flexible currents of research. This applies to semiotic and cognitive musicology as well, and raises interest in the conceptual correlates in the historical shifts, particularly in how the shifts have opened avenue for addressing both the social and cultural, and the subject's embodied mind in the study of signification within a systematic framework. Emblematic of the paradigmatic shifts, *situation* emerges as a key notion.

From the current, pragmatist perspective, a comparison of Eero Tarasti's existential-semiotic and Mauri Kaipainen's cognitive notions of situation reveals striking similarities. For one, situations become meaningful only in their contexts and through their use, as they are dynamically established in the processes of being in the world. Besides the evident methodological and topical differences, fundamental differences are to be found in the attention paid to the epistemic conditions of subject's being in the world, and the acknowledged complexity of the situations, illustrated by the recursive agent/patient-levels by Tarasti.

For the study of musical signification, the pragmatist approach may help reconcile the differencies, contributing to the necessary groundwork for a theory that could incorporate complex, iterative levels of narration spanning between signs as acts, stylistic constraints of musical discourse, social contexts, and epistemes of culture, while also taking into account the view of mind as embodied, embedded, enactive, and extended cognition.

Keywords: situation, existential semiotics, embodied cognition, music, signification, pragmatism

1 Introduction

Over the recent decades, a paradigmatic shift has taken place in semiotics: a re-turn away from the language-oriented view of signification. This shift resembles the paradigmatic changes in cognitive sciences. In semiotics of music and in cognitive musicology, these advances are particularly pronounced. The study of signification and mind across these traditions of music research may well yield better understanding of the semiotic and cognitive processes at large.

The history of semiotics has witnessed several strong research traditions, e.g. those of
1. empirical semioticians, studying medical symptoms, etc.
2. linguistic semioticians, such as de Saussure, Jakobson, Hjelmslev and Greimas
3. philosophical semioticians, such as John Locke and Charles Peirce, and
4. cultural semioticians, such as those of the Tartu-Moscow school (see Nöth 1995: 11–38; Tarasti 1990: 5–11).

These traditions or paradigms have constituted the domain of *classical semiotics*. Recently, there has been a shift taking place both in musical and in general semiotics from the classical semiotics to less traditional and more novel, original, and perhaps more flexible currents of research, as professor Eero Tarasti (2000: 3–4, 1998: 39–44) has pointed out. According to Tarasti (1998: 39), the classical musical semiotics attempted "to reduce a musical sign to a normative, constraining set of rules, whether it be a generative grammar, style norms, or various classes of signs as defined by general semiotics." More recently, "one need not try to reduce the object to a code system, but may conceive of it in a more phenomenological and hermeneutic way so as to understand its originality" (Tarasti 1998: 40).

In cognitive sciences, somewhat similarly, the classical, *symbolic* paradigm emphasized verbal language, symbol manipulation, and rules. It also relied on computer metaphor, and serial or linear computing – computationalism. To a degree, the classical paradigm survived parallel to the more recent cognitive paradigms, such as the *connectionist* (a.k.a. associationist, subsymbolic, non-symbolic) paradigm of the late 20th century, fostered particularly in neurophysiology, natural and artificial neural network research, parallel computing, and naturalist modeling of cognition. More recently, however, the classical and connectionist views have given way to the subsequent, interdisciplinary 4E paradigm (paradigm of embodied, embedded, enactive, and extended cognition; see, e.g., Newen, De Bruin, and Gallagher 2018), and the cognitive views of subject and mind as a brain/body-in-the-world system (e.g. Rossi et al. 2019).

These changes apply to cognitive musicology as well. While both the older and the newer paradigm of cognitive musicology consider music a cognitive process, the difference lies in beliefs regarding what kind of representative system music is or uses. In the older, symbolic paradigm, music was regarded as rule-based symbol manipulation, akin to verbal language, as opposed to the newer view of music as asymbolic, non-arbitrary process of (embodied and social) interaction, that has uses or functions for organism's being in the environment.

Emblematic of the new paradigm in semiotics, Eero Tarasti's existential semiotics has searched for a balance between the communicational and the significational. Central also to the quest of cognitive inquiry to understand the mind's functioning in the world, *situation* emerges as a key notion. Despite the differences between the traditions of semiotics and cognitive sciences, the existential and cognitive notions of situation have striking similarities. The similarities suggest a possibility of a *pragmatist* reconciliation of the contentions between the semiotic and cognitive fields. In this article I explore, through the viewpoint of music research and the key notion of situation, how the recent changes in semiotics, particularly Eero Tarasti's existential semiotics, and the concurrent changes in cognitive science align with one another. As but one representative case of the latter, I make use primarily of the associationist paradigm as expressed by Mauri Kaipainen in his (1994) book Dynamics of Musical Knowledge Ecology. Similar comparisons could be made between other sources, but a more thorough analysis from the viewpoint of history of science would be out of scope here. Yet, the interest here is in the conceptual correlates in the historical shifts, that occurred quite simultaneously across the strands of research, from the "classical" stages, founded on linguistics, structuralism, and (arbitrary) symbol manipulation to the more holistic, dynamic paradigms. The shifts have turned out critical as they opened avenue for the contemporary theories on signification, that are able to take into account, with better balance, both the social and cultural, and the subject's embodied mind.

2 Paradigmatic shifts in semiotics, cognitive science, and musicology

In grand scale, the new directions of the late 20th and early 21st century musical semiotics have been holistic, scrutinizing "the whole situation of communication, taking into account the fact that every sign is an act committed by some subject." (Tarasti 1998: 41). While in (1998: 41), Tarasti expected that "this concrete physiological and bodily perspective" might open up an avenue for analysis, "which connects music to the prevailing epistemes of a culture, to its dominant canons, to the stylistic constraints of musical discourse," he also expressed his concerns regarding the approaches in which "[m]usic is viewed merely as a transaction according to the traditional model of communication" or in which the musical sign is contextualized "as a way of living in a sociological context" or "as a transmission in modern media society" (Tarasti 1998: 43). Consequently, in search for an approach that balances both the communicational and the significational, he embarked towards existential semiotics (Tarasti 2015, 2012, 2000, 1996a).

Interestingly, the shift in semiotics "away from universality, and toward more particularity" (Tarasti 1998: 40) is reminiscent of the paradigm shift in cognitive sciences in a specific way. Namely, it coincided quite well with the shift away from the exclusive top-down, rule-based, constraint-oriented and grammar-searching symbolist view of the classical cognitive science and the "good old-fashioned artificial intelligence" towards including and preferring the subsymbolic, neurally-inspired connectionist paradigm.

Illustrative of this, Tarasti (1998: 40) referred to Raymond Monelle's deconstructionist analyses (Monelle 1992), in which "textual 'ruptures' are identified, which momentarily reveal the universe of unarticulated semiotic, the pre-symbolic world of gestures and desires." Meanwhile, in cognitive sciences and cognitive musicology, the target of study moved from a hermetic mind, black-boxed brain or operationally more or less static symbol-manipulating machine into a (more or less) genuinely existing sensomotor organism dynamically interacting with the objects of its environment, with or without symbols. Similarly, in musical semiotics, the target of study moved towards that of the new, connectionist paradigm in cognitive musicology: from a static musical object equipped with a code and thereby significant in itself in virtue of its internal relations into a dynamic musical process and its ecology involving both musical objects and musical subjects, and the relations thereof, implying referential or contextual analysis in addition to analysis of the inner relations of a musical object or work of art.

These shifts in both semiotics and in cognitive sciences, seem reactions to the earlier linguistic turn (Rorty [1967] 1992), a *re-turn* away from the language-oriented view of signification as a symbol-manipulating, rule-based system. In musicology, this entails a "shift from mere observation of a musical utterance (text)" (Tarasti 1998: 41) to the more holistic view of scrutinizing the whole situation and subject's (and organism's) embodied role in communication. As Tarasti (1998: 41) put it, "[i]n general, one realizes that communication involves a dialogue between subject and utterance. Efforts in this direction have been made in psychoanalytic and feminist-oriented analysis, where scholars have theorized how the human body is projected into music."

The differences between the old and the new are radical. From a pragmatist perspective, the new in musical semiotics as described by Tarasti seems to get to the heart of it: The dialogue between subject and utterance as described above corresponds to the Deweyan process of shaping and reshaping (see Dewey [1934] 1980: 51). In contemporary musical semiotics, music is understood as a holistic and dynamic process of communication or dialogue involving embodied, social subject and subject's meanings, actions and experience. Instead of static structures and musical works, for instance, we are dealing with subject engaged in dynamic processes of interaction. In Tarasti's existential perspective, "music is portrayed as a rich interaction between all participants in the communication and the meaning involved in the music itself" (1998: 43). Essentially, this disrupts "the unidirectional, linear-chain model, since in real communication our exchanges go back and forth and not in just one direction," and consequently, "music already appears as a certain situation rather than as a fixed object" (Tarasti 1998: 43).

Here we encounter something that we come across in conjunction with the contemporary cognitive approach to music: the notion of situation. How do the key notions of *situation* in two contemporary musicological traditions relate to each other?

3 Situation in existential semiotics and cognitive musicology

According to Mauri Kaipainen (1994: 15), the fundamental assumption of cognitive musicology that "music is regarded as a process of the human mind" implies, that "there is no manifestation of music without cognitive involvement" by cognizing organisms engaged in the process. It is worth emphasizing, that in the connectionist view, music, being a process, was no longer considered to exist as static objects although objects are involved. Since music "unfolds in time," and the process is driven "from mental states to others," the nature of the musical process is inherently dynamic (Kaipainen 1994: 20). Following the tradition of methodological solipsism (e.g. Fodor 1991), the premise was that music "can always be characterized as knowledge interaction between an individual and her/his sonorous environment" (Kaipainen 1994: 23). More recently, this has been expanded to considering how musical processes may or may not involve others, and Zbikowski (2012: 152), for instance, has pointed out how the cognitive science has further transitioned during the past two decades from viewing "the mind as individual and incorporeal, and on thought as the exclusive province of language" to recognizing "that the human mind is also a social mind, that experience shaped by the mediation of the human body does much to shape human cognition, and that language captures only a portion of what can properly be called thought."

As a representative of the connectionist paradigm in cognitive musicology and furthermore, focusing on knowledge ecology, Kaipainen (1994: 21) also subscribed to "musical holism" and asserted, that musical representation must be based on what we sense as our internal states. This includes primarily the input of the auditory modality, but also vision, somatosensory and motor information, representational states generated by the brain, and possibly other internal states (e.g. hormonal) – altogether forming a holistic configuration of features that defines the coordinates of the music-cognizer in the virtual experiential space, present in parallel at any given moment.

Corresponding again with the notions of shaping and reshaping imagined and perceived situations (Dewey 1980: 49), Kaipainen called these holistic configurations "musical situations" (1994: 21).

In comparison, Tarasti's existential semiotic concept of situation "first of all refers always to a certain particularity" (1998: 44), in the sense that typologisation of situations "presumes that the situational phenomenon has first been investigated as its own entity." According to Tarasti (1998: 45), "situation cannot be explained as a series of detached causal chains, but rather as a continuous intermingling of events representing various modes of being in the real contexts in which they occur." More precisely, "[s]ituation is that part of the world with which one enters into a relationship. One is in a relationship to the world via his/her situation. Situation is the whole of all those phenomena, objects, and states of affairs under which and by which a person's organic and conscious existence is realized. Situation always consists of a space of play – a *Spielraum* – of various factors" (Tarasti 1998: 45).

I read this as a manifest against a serial, linear, rule-based, absolutely (pre)determined view of signification, in which one state of affairs unavoidably would lead to another and that again to another. The notion of situation is central in cognitive, semiotic, as well as pragmatic approaches to signification: it is not only an interface or contact surface between subject and the world, but rather, the ever-changing situations are the interactions and the consequent mutual relations between the subject-organism and the actual world and all that it entails, in terms of other subjects, the actual process, and its context. Situation is what joins action and experience (cf. Määttänen 1993); it is where the subject and the actual world are joined. It is through situations that we exist in the actual world as organisms, and in our phenomenal worlds as subjects, and, finally, as agents in our social groups and cultures.

The existential approach insists on taking the uniqueness of situations into consideration as opposed to generalizing categorization, and therefore the analysis of situation ought to be scalable to different scopes, pending on the needs of scrutiny. Here, the needs are not focused on the surface structures, but the main interest is rather in the whole, both as semiosis in general and musical semiosis in particular are concerned, uniqueness of particular situations notwithstanding.

As far as music is concerned, musical communication and musical signification merge in the concept of situation: "A musical situation should be taken as the crossroads of signification and communication." (Tarasti 1998: 46.) A typical model of communication (see, for instance Eco [1976] 1979: 33; Jakobson 1960; the Shannon and Weaver model in Shannon 1948) consists in coded message being transmitted through a channel from sender (source, emitter, etc.) to recipient, both with their codes and contexts. This traditional, simple, one-directional model can be replaced by a model that recursively embeds the agent/patient relations such as composer/audience or narrator/listener into concentric levels, for the benefit of examining musical narrativity (see Figure 1.).

C $\boxed{\;iC(N/iN_{1,2...n} \longrightarrow iA_{1,2...n}/A)iL\;}$ L

Figure 1: The communicational and significational structure of narrative music. Adapted from Tarasti (1998: 47; 1996b: 434). In Figure 1,
C = the physical composer, that is, the creature "subject to historical and organic processes" (Tarasti 1998: 47)
iC = the implied composer, that is, "someone with a certain competence, who provides his musical message with signs" (Tarasti 1998: 48)
N = narrator, who, in each work, "organizes musical events according to a certain kind of logic, while taking into account a possible audience" (Tarasti 1998: 46)
iN = implied narrator, or theme-actors as agents, "which functions in a purely musical sense in such a way that it influences another theme-actor" (Tarasti 1998: 46)
L = physical listener
iL = implied listener, that is, the one who can "presumably receive and decode correctly" the signs provided by the implied composer (Tarasti 1998: 48)
A = audience, that is, the patient for whom the musical events are organized by the narrator in each work
iA = implied audience, or theme-actors as patients, that is, "theme-actor, which behaves as a recipient" of the purely musical action (Tarasti 1998: 46)

In brief, "the whole world of text is situated" (Tarasti 1998: 46) in the actual (physical) world inhabited by the actual composer and the actual listener. Matters related to performer, interpreter, etc., are omitted here, but could be incorporated by extending the model. As Tarasti (1998: 49) noted, a logical consequent of the view of situations as acts or events is that they can be described in terms of the logic of act and action, such as G. H. von Wright's (1963) elaboration. Within the world of text (marked by the rectangular in Figure 1), the actual relationship of agent and patient is reiterated in embedded levels of narration. Consequently, while situation may refer to situation of the actual world, within music – or any other narrative – situations within the world of text represent: "elements of outer reality are internalized so as to form factors that wield influence inside the musical discourse" (Tarasti 1998: 48).

Musical situations, regardless of the level of presentation or representation, are amalgamations of interaction of the agent and patient. "In music, situation always implies an actor; no situation can exist without an actor somehow pertaining to it. Therefore, what is crucial for a musical work is the way it draws listeners into this situation and invites or even forces them to participate in it. Situation is thus an act (i.e., an active situation) or an event (i.e., a passive situation) of a musical subject." (Tarasti 1998: 49.)

Bluntly compared, both Kaipainen's cognitive notion of situation and Tarasti's existential notion of situation refer to particular instances or states of continuous complex holistic configurations that, in virtue of subject's interaction, represent – stand for something – in their contexts. The configurations may represent via their internal relations and via their relations to other configurations of the world, which is also inhabited by the subjects involved in the situation (albeit the connectionist view did not take the social into account). In themselves, situations do not convey meanings or carry significance. They are not meaningful by themselves. They become meaningful only, and always, in their contexts and through their use, which are established during the process of semiosis, in cognition. That process of semiosis or cognition is the process of interaction with the actual world by the subject, subject being immersed in the world.

Besides the evident differences in methodology and detailed topics of research, the key difference between the two notions of situation in the paradigmatic shifts seems to be that the cognitive notion relied on methodological solipsism, in the way that the possible intersubjective issues were avoided by examining the interaction only as an interaction of organism and its environment. Consequently, the possible iterative levels embedded in narration were simplified to the single level between the organism and the actual environment (see Figure 1).

The existential notion, in turn, embarked upon the intersubjective end, top-down, rather than bottom-up, and seemed to disregard detailed analysis of the mind–body problem, although not categorically excluding it either. For the cognitive scientists, the mind–body problem is a central question, which got answered, briefly put, by folding any of the complex virtual experiential states or higher levels of representation back to the knowledge dynamics of the representative system, featuring, then, distributedness, parallellism, nonsymbolism, and connectionism. In other words, the starting point of the cognitive notion (in the connectionist paradigm) was a bottom-up approach, and situation pertains first and foremost to the low-level representation (while some kind of an insurance against the problems of implementation was usually taken), regardless of the simplicity or complexity of the holistic situation, as noted above. The simplification of the levels of narration led to critique, and in the study of real life musical processes, this kind of simplification must at some point be overcome in order to reach the complexities, and sometimes even paradoxical aspects of signification and communication. At the same time, the connectionist methodology was a rewarding choice as it provided, in a relative short period of time, noteworthy results in the attempts of understanding particularly the so-called low cognitive faculties before taking up other challenges addressed today in cognitive science.

The existential notion of situation, in turn, differentiates a continuum of recursive levels of agent/patient, and while each level is tied to or manifested in the narrativity of the signifying process, it is not (necessarily) concerned with implementation, that is, with the actual operation of the representative system, but only the functional operation. Through its broader context of existential semiotics, the existential notion of situation is also in strictly critical stance on connectionism and the attempt to explain the so-called higher cognitive faculties based on descriptions of neural networks (see, for instance, Tarasti referring to G. H. von Wright's argument of a brain surgeon in Tarasti 2000: 4–5).

4 Pragmatism as a potential way to reconciliation

Hence, fundamental differences between the cognitive and existential notions of situation are to be found in how much attention is paid, first, to the epistemic conditions of how the subject's being in the world (or being-in-the-world) is tied to, based on, or constrained by the actual world inhabited by the subject's organism; and, second, to the complexity of the situations, as illustrated by the recursive agent/patient-levels. More so, fundamental differences can be found in their relations to naturalism.

Consequently, major issues appear to stand in front of convergence of the threads of cognitive and semiotic musicology. It seems, however, that with the help of naturalist pragmatism, there may open an alternative to reconcile some of the main incompatibilities between the cognitive and existential semiotic: the unheeded grounding of socially significant interaction into actual reality in existential semiotics, and the seeming solipsism and situational simplicity in cognitive semiotics (see also Madzia and Jung 2016). The key seems to be found in the explanation for the emergence of the competence underlying the communicative act, that is, the epistemology of signification.

While the reconciliation of the existential and cognitive conceptions of music does not seem impossible, whether these differences can be reconciled, or need to be reconciled, is now beside the point. What is attempted here is the examination of certain salient features of these notions of situation and music for the benefit of working towards understanding the processes of musical signification.

Therefore, let us continue with the existential semiotic notion of situation for a moment. This will take us to a very pragmatist aspect of music, present also in the existential notion, namely usefulness. Situations provide "an occasion for an event or an act to occur or to be accomplished" (Tarasti 1998: 51 – here Tarasti followed G.H. von Wright 1963). In narrative processes, occurring events create sequences in which one situation may or may not be followed by another one, that is, event *p* may result in event *q* or event –*q*, and so "there emerges a network of alternative chains of events," a network (idem, see Figure 2.).

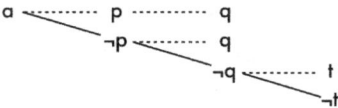

Figure 2: Network of alternative chains of event, and the actual chain of events. Adapted from Tarasti 1998: 51.

A musical style is a *habit* that takes shape as alternatives in the chains are observed. There are possible choices for each branch in the network of events, and a chain of those that actually occur. "How we conceive the range of possibilities," that is, musical style, "is a consequence of what we observe on the surface of the reality," that is, the actually occurring events (Tarasti 1998: 51). We learn the possible choices by observing the occurring choices. And vice versa, we choose the events from the possible choices based on their usefulness to us, that is, their meaning. This idea of learning situated possibilities clearly correlates with the process of enculturation, and more broadly to adaptation. Also, Tarasti (1998: 51–52) connects this idea with Heidegger: "*Dasein* represents the whole situation with all its possibilities. *Da-sein*, however, refers only to the being-there of the surface reality."

The narrativity that is created through the dialogue between the continuation of expected or possible, and the actually occurring continuation of the situations provides a possibility to create a virtual world with its own logic, own habits, own time and space. "When a primitive man, while listening to or telling a myth, sinks into a fabled and extrahistoric time, for us the need to escape mentally into 'a strange universe and time' is fulfilled when hearing music" (Tarasti 1978: 33, quoting Mircea Eliade's expression from Aspects du mythe, 1963). Thereby music, just as myth, may be effective in resolving conflicts or contradictions of the actual life by transferring them to a virtual reality of its own, in which the alternatives may be tested safely (Tarasti 1978: 33).

"Situation might be easily identified with a space," Tarasti pointed out (1998: 49), and hence, the continuum of actually occurring situations versus situations that are possible at any given moment could also be approached in terms of actual and virtual (or phenomenal) spaces, and musical narrativity as changes in actual and virtual space. It is noteworthy, that both Tarasti and Kaipainen (see the quote above on musical holism) make references to space. It seems that the key notion of situation and the whole of the signifying process can be approached in terms of space as a conceptual tool (see Ojala 2009, 328–342).

While Tarasti has connected situation and situatedness as existential concepts with Heidegger's concept of *in-der-Welt-sein*, and has not underwritten the naturalist groundings of the representative process, similarities to cognitive and pragmatist concepts such as object, organism, action, interaction, experience, mind, subject, and representation are striking, and the same holds for the conception of music, at its core. Music is meaningful, not in virtue of the sound itself regardless of the subjects, but through the relations of the musical sounds within themselves, and together with the experiential aggregate of the subject interacting with her environment. The experiential aggregate is accumulated in order for the subject to be in the world. And the significance of musical processes can be found in their ability to provide means of working out virtual situations, that is, situations that stand for actual situations of the world, in order for the subject's mind to guide the actions of the organism in the actual world. (This is a very pragmatist conception of music, cf. Ojala 2009, 94–156.)

Consequently, music has uses or functions for the individual (and society, and culture), through subject's relation to and interaction with the world, and hence the term 'existential' is very apt in this context. From this perspective, it is no surprise the cognitive study of music has then evolved towards including the embodied subjects, and the social. Music operates by means of situations and events, and their expectations and confirmation or disconfirmation, and these situations somehow stand for – are signs of – situations that may actually or possibly be encountered in the world.

5 Conclusion

To summarize, it can be noted, that at heart, there is much in common between the existential, cognitive, and pragmatist conceptions of music. At the same time still today, there remains much of the necessary groundwork to be done within both semiotics in general and musical semiotics in particular, in order to construe a logically solid understanding of musical signification that would incorporate the differing stances or mutually compatible conceptions in various traditions of musicological research. This was aptly marked by Tarasti (1998: 45–46), as well: "An entirely different *semiotic* program takes shape on this basis, which is not very far from Peirce's triadic sign categories. If *representamen* refers to organic process, to something physical, the *object*, in turn, to facticity, to that sign content which stems from outside, from 'reality,' then the *interpretant* would imply the consciousness, as a concept, which in our minds unites sign with the object. This new program takes a negative attitude towards linear causality and dissolves it into three dimensions of an existential sign: its facticity (being in *Dasein*), its physical aspect as an organic process, and its role in the consciousness."

References

Dewey, James. 1980. *Art as Experience*. New York: Perigee Books.
Eco, Umberto. 1979. *A Theory of Semiotics*. (Advances in Semiotics). Bloomington: Indiana University Press.
Fodor, Jerry. 1991. Methodological solipsism considered as a research strategy in cognitive psychology. In Richard Boyd, Philip Gasper & J.D. Trout (eds.), *The Philosophy of Science*, 651–669. Cambridge, MA: The MIT Press.
Jakobson, Roman. 1960. Closing statement: linguistics and poetics. In Thomas A. Sebeok (ed.), *Style in Language*, 350–377. Cambridge, MA: The MIT Press.
Kaipainen, Mauri. 1994. *Dynamics of Musical Knowledge Ecology. Knowing-What and Knowing-How in the World of Sounds*. (Acta Musicologica Fennica 19). Helsinki: Suomen musiikkitieteellinen seura.
Määttänen, Pentti. 1993. *Action and Experience. A Naturalistic Approach to Cognition*. (Annales Academiae Scientiarum Fennicae B 64). Helsinki: Finnish Academy of Science and Letters.
Madzia, Roman & Matthias Jung (eds.). 2016. *Pragmatism and Embodied Cognitive Science*. (Humanprojekt 14). Berlin: De Gruyter.
Monelle, Raymond. 1992. *Linguistics and Semiotics in Music*. New York: Harwood Academic Publishers.
Newen, Albert, Leon De Bruin & Shaun Gallagher (eds.). 2018. *The Oxford Handbook of 4E Cognition*. Oxford: Oxford University Press.
Nöth, Winfried. 1995. *Handbook of Semiotics*. Bloomington: Indiana University Press.
Ojala, Juha. 2009. *Space in Musical Semiosis. An Abductive Theory of the Musical Composition Process*. (Acta Semiotica Fennica XXXIII, Approaches to Musical Semiotics 12). Imatra: International Semiotics Institute. http://urn.fi/URN:ISBN:978-952-5431-28-5.
Rorty, Richard (ed.). 1992. *The Linguistic Turn. Essays in Philosophical Method*. Chicago: The University of Chicago Press.
Rossi, Alejandra, Aitana Grasso-Cladera, Nicolas Luarte, Antonella Riillo & Francisco J. Parada. 2019. The brain/body-in-the-world system is cognitive science's study object for the twenty-first century. *Studies in Psychology* 40(2). 363–395.
Shannon, Claude E. 1948. A mathematical theory of communication. *The Bell System Technical Journal* 27 (July, October). 379–423, 623–656.

Tarasti, Eero. 1978. *Myth and Music. A Semiotic Approach to the Aesthetics of Myth in Music, especially that of Wagner, Sibelius and Stravinsky*. Helsinki: Suomen musiikkitieteellinen seura; The Hague, Paris, New York: Mouton Publishers.
Tarasti, Eero. 1990. *Johdatusta semiotiikkaan. Esseitä taiteen ja kulttuurin merkkijärjestelmistä* [Introduction to semiotics. Essays on sign systems of art and culture]. Helsinki: Gaudeamus.
Tarasti, Eero. 1996a. *Esimerkkejä. Semiotiikan uusia teorioita ja sovelluksia.* [Examples/ Pre-signs. New theories and applications of semiotics.] Helsinki: Gaudeamus.
Tarasti, Eero. 1996b. Merkit tekoina ja tapahtumina: tutkimus musiikillisista situaatioista [Signs as acts and events: a study on musical situations]. *Musiikki* 26 (4). 427–449.
Tarasti, Eero. 1998. Signs as acts and events: an essay on musical situations. In Gino Stefani, Eero Tarasti & Luca Marconi (eds.), *Musical Signification. Between Rhetoric and Pragmatics, Proceedings of the 5th International Congress on Musical Signification*, 39–62. Bologna: International Semiotics Institute & CLUEB.
Tarasti, Eero. 2000. *Existential Semiotics*. Bloomington: Indiana University Press.
Tarasti, Eero. 2012. Existential semiotics and cultural psychology. In Jaan Valsiner (ed.), *Oxford Handbook of Culture and Psychology*, 316–346. Oxford: Oxford University Press.
Tarasti, Eero. 2015. *Sein und Schein. Explorations in Existential Semiotics*. Berlin: Walter de Gruyter.
von Wright, Georg Henrik. 1963. *Norm and Action. A Logical Enquiry*. London: Routledge & Kegan Paul.
Zbikowsky, Lawrence. 2012. Music and movement: a view from cognitive musicology. In Stephanie Schroedter (ed.), *Bewegungen zwischen Hören und Sehen. Denkbewegungen über Bewegungskünste,* 151–162. Würzburg: Köningshausen & Neumann.

Otto Lehto
Cosmologies of life after Peirce, Heidegger and Darwin

Abstract: My paper proposes a tentative framework of bio-existential semiotics based on a reading of Peirce, Tarasti, Darwin, Heidegger, and others. According to this view, there is an evolutionary continuum to life. Human beings are natural organisms and they exhibit many similar bio-existential phenomena. Natural evolution also produces the anthropological, societal and global semiotic processes that constitute cultural evolution as an outgrowth. In the bio-existential perspective, the world is composed of imperfect systems and imperfect consciousnesses where every lifeform must struggle for its existence. Every *"Dasein"* must face the fact that it must die because it cannot comprehend or control the universe in its totality. This is why life and existence are "tragic" phenomena. Every bio-existential *Dasein* is a partial comprehension of the universe, and the only way the universe can comprehend itself is through these partial perspectives, which are born to imperfection and die in imperfection, but whose imperfection is of the essence of the universe. This is why bio-existentialism makes for a "tragic" perspective: we are mortals, and all mortals must die. Nonetheless, there is also hope and optimism in this view of life. In conceiving of existence as having certain universal principles that extend from biology to sociology, semioticians and philosophers can formulate new ways of looking at the world. Together with scientists and artists, they can hopefully work towards a better – or at least more refined – ethical attitude towards science, nature and society.

Keywords: Darwin, Peirce, Heidegger, biosemiotics, existentialism

1 Introduction

In our efforts to extricate meaningful guidelines and hints for *future* projects from semioticians, philosophers and scientists of the *past* – itself an anachronistic and faltering undertaking – we have come to intercourse with the most varied crowd of brilliant minds; from Darwin to Heidegger, from Lotman to Peirce, from Tarasti to Uexküll. In trying to synthesize traditions that never go beyond their spectrum of expected outcomes, one gains the position of a detached observer whose eye for synergy and isomorphic connectivity allows for the flourishing, however perverse and unorthodox, of seemingly separate (in time and space and semiotic scope) intellectual endeavours. Each passion, each vision of the world, inherited from such and such a tradition, is itself a source of great power and hope for the future, because each unique tradition *believes* in itself and in its own tomorrow. So, in their synthesis, one is bringing together "hopeful" practices and synergizing their energies into a common goal, a common vision and a common (semiotic-scientific) practice. This synthesis is the function of thinking; thought, under the guidance of Reason, does not believe in the incommensurability of ideas and practices.

Darwin for me is a revolutionary thinker whose principles, as much as his empirical data, *still* possess untapped potential for semiotic research. He brought light to darkness, but he also handed over the candle, the light-source, to his successors. The continuum represented by the Darwinist school, or rather the *Darwin – Mendel – Crick & Watson* lineage, contributed to the opening of the fields of evolutionary biology, ethology, genetics and biomolecular research. The "philosophical" field of *theoretical* studies of life, unfortunately, has not moved much beyond its roots in the mid-19th century, in Darwin and the neo-Darwinists. Today, such philosophical amateurs as Richard Dawkins (who nonetheless is a meritorious scientist) dominate the field. It is a sorry situation indeed. Semioticians, such as the researchers in biosemiotics (comprising zoo-, myco- and phytosemiotics) can lead the way, among others, to a rehabilitation of the theoretical questioning of *naturalist deep history*. But I don't think they can do it alone. This is where I bring in existential theories. Compared to natural organisms studied by natural science, semiotics studies both natural and non-natural quasi-organismic structures, structures whose consistency is marked by their cunning resilience to outside pressures and their adaptability in the face thereof. Heidegger's model of *Dasein*, itself a somewhat anthropic (not to say anthropological) and thus biotic theory of existentialist epistemology, is interpreted for the purposes of (re-)thinking biology, (re-)thinking life, (re-)thinking man and (re-)thinking society.

Peirce's contributions to my theory come from his evolutionary cosmology, triadic ontology and his pragmatic conception of science; he believes in science because *it works*. Even his mystical bent on spirituality is for me more than a curiosity. I believe that the best way to tackle Cartesian dualisms – tackle them as I do – is to re-approach materialism from a different, perhaps more vivid and sensitive angle, where natural science and existential philosophy are the starting point for a new theory of life. Peirce, Heidegger and Darwin are not, in the end, the strangest bedfellows they may first appear. Semiotic research should, after all, utilize the widest possible source material to reach the most relevant conclusions.

2 The many faces of Peirce: Scientist, Pragmatist, Semiotician

Peirce, for me, represents a *modest* megalomaniac. His obsessions, real and persistent, fuelled a heart and a mind capable of stretching into different directions for different occasions. Despite his philosophical, semiotic and mathematical writings, he never lost sight of Science as lived *praxis*, as an experiential field open to the inquisitive mind. He never drew a wall between philosophy and science; he was never a positivist. He did not attack either one, even if he disavowed many of the established stupidities and dogmas in each tradition. This I call *the many faces of Peirce*: the way he tackled "the opposite poles of inquiry" (i.e. Science and Metaphysics) to quote Brent's (1993: 18) apt characterization of Peirce's broad, and deep, scope of interest.

Science is never far from philosophy, neither of which, again, is far from semiotics. Scientific fields and (history-founding) projects are established by acts of semiotic creation; there are a few of such moments in history when Science undertakes the project of social transformation on an unheard of scale: Bacon, Newton, Darwin and perhaps Freud and Marx. Yet the scope of practices in the modern sciences, despite their richness, is dominated by an attitude of philosophical rigidity and unquestioned dogma, a situation in which "normal science" (to use Kuhn's terminology) follows the paradigmatic road paved by the Great Thinkers in whose shadow the individual scientists find themselves, happily and purposefully. What we can take from Peirce, and what my paper tries to propose, is that science should *never* – and in fact never could – operate "on its own devices," *except*, indeed, if one takes these devices to mean the whole human enterprise of thinking, acting, intuiting, interpreting, model-building, philosophizing and legitimizing. To use Peirce's categories, the firstness and secondness relations of science are founded on its metaphysics (or "logic") of thirdness, and consequently there are no scientific "findings" that are value-neutral or devoid of metaphysical baggage, societal pressures, individual quirks, philosophical prejudices and so on. The solution, to follow Peirce, is a re-integration of aesthetics into ethics and the constant re-imagining of the very *ground* of thinking via new models, theories and world-views. In the end, an existential regard for the nothingness (non-conceptual everythingness) underlying all reality can serve as the starting point for a study of the plurality of the world's riches.

So, semiosis is never-ending – but it must *start* somewhere. As Peirce says in *The Fixation of Belief* (1877: no page number available), "the settlement of opinion is the sole object of inquiry." This kind of idea of competing opinions and ideas (including, incidentally, different models and concepts) is also my starting point in science and theory. There is no privilege given to a particular approach, only to the practices and results obtained thereby for a particular purpose. Perhaps in this regard I am closer to someone like Rorty, except that I do not share Rorty's rejection of Science as a model (if only *one* model) for philosophical thinking. Here I am closer to Peirce, whose scientific background never left him. So, Peirce's own architectonic project is justified by a need to integrate different levels of analysis (semiosis). This is how modern science, too, should operate – integrating different levels of analysis while retaining the conception of science as a never-ending project.

Peirce's own work, and theories, always followed a triadic model. So, perhaps we could divide his different *personae*, different *alter egos*, into three groups (as long as these are seen as mutually enforcing rather than contradictory or conflicting): 1) The Scientist-Empiricist, 2) The Pragmatist-Theorist and 3) The Mystic-Semiotician. This is a scale from rationalism to irrationalism, or from the particular to the general (but is this a Hegelian ascent of the alienated Subject to the Absolute?). Of course, most people see him as a sum of these parts, and rightly so. But does the middle-of-the-road "consensus-Peirce" represent all that can be said about him? I would emphasize the third level (of the three categories above) for the purposes of my analysis, and see his evolutionary and scientistic theories as *stemming* from his deep sense of the spiritual and the cosmic. His semiotic model, indeed, was fundamentally that of the cosmos and its evolution. So, we should place his tychism, synechism, agapism and other grand-scale theories *at the heart* of his intuitive world-view which, while never fully articulated in any consistent way, nonetheless represents perhaps the most philosophical (or at any rate the most "existentialist") of his theories of life. From this wellspring I drink to nourish my thirst for a bio-existential framework of semiotics. Peirce did not know Heidegger, but he certainly knew Darwin and he certainly saw his work in that same historical project. The existential framework will be explored in the next and final chapter, but I will summarize my analysis of Peirce's "many faces" by the following semiotic graph (Figure 1), where I have tried to show that a love-based "diachronic determinism" is at the heart of his concept of evolution, world history and emergent semiosis.

Now, what the graph also shows is that Peirce's many "pulls" meant that it is quite possible to read him as a diachronic determinist or even as a synchronic relativist (though read the caveat at the bottom of the graph Figure 1), but that ultimately his different "faces" were working towards a common synthesis, as explored in his evolutionary conception of life and knowledge.

In the chapter to come, I will turn away from Peirce, towards other theories of evolution, man and biology – namely existentialism and biosemiotics – and argue for a cosmological theory that accounts for isomorphisms, analogies

PEIRCE in ideal-archetypal categories

	RELATIVISM	DETERMINISM
SYNCHRONIC	– (N/A?)* – Tychism – Firstness (Chance) – Peirce-the-Skeptic	– Common Sense – Customs and Habits – Secondness (Causation) – Peirce-the-Scientist
DIACHRONIC	– Fallibilism – Tychism – The Scientific Method – Peirce-the-Pragmatist	– Synechism – Agapism – Evolution & Perfectibility – Thirdness (Synthesis) – Peirce-the-Mystic

* Peirce as a synchronic relativist is a problematic concept, and it is included here mainly as a theoretical category - much like Kant's contradiction-in-terms "analytical a posteriori". Also, in this analogy, the category of diachronic determinism is something like my "synthetic a priori", since it is my love child.

Figure 1: Peirce in ideal-archetypal categories.

and similarities between different *kinds,* and different *levels,* of semiosis by providing a hypothetical new intermediary model based on the mathematical structure of the *circle*; a kind of universal model for *any* bio-existential system of semiosis, at least in conception. It is useful for the very large and the very small (and the medium-scale) without shunning the existing body of scientific knowledge. I will attack rigid conceptions of science, only to reaffirm its radical power to present a unified vision of interlocking semiotic systems; cf. D.Bohm's *Wholeness and the Implicate Order* (1980) for one controversial paradigm to look out for. It is indeed the point of the theoretician and semiotician to sketch hypothetical meta-theories for scientific practice, and to propose new avenues of research. Many of the debates and deadlocks reached by scientific debate are the result of philosophical naiveté or, worse, ethical and aesthetic blindness. Solving these problems requires solving ethical and aesthetic problems as well as grounding them in a holistic ontological theory of existence, or at least explaining the blindnesses that arise when one such theory is allowed to dominate the field (e.g. the current mixture of *neo-Darwinian neo-Newtonian neo-Cartesian neo-Hobbesian* materialism). And since semioticians are experts at studying relations, structures and connections, they may contribute to such a discussion (see my article "Studying the Cognitive States of Animals" [Lehto 2009]) Next, I propose some new avenues for thought with Peirce's invaluable help.

3 A bio-existential framework of semiosis

Let us start with Eero Tarasti's approach, in his book *Existential Semiotics* (2000). He proposes a radical difference between classical (traditional) semiotics and existential (new) semiotics. Old semiotics he identifies with the structuralist and binary approach – here he is thinking about Saussure, Greimas etc. – whose basic metaphor, and basic graph-structure, is the *square*; compare for example Greimas' semiotic squares. As for the "new," existential semiotics, its basic metaphor, and graph-structure, is the *circle*. I would like to accommodate this theory into a historical perspective by qualifying its reading of classical semiotics with a caveat. Namely, despite the factual and accurate depiction of the binary-structuralist (anti-existentialist) current in semiotics, especially its post-Saussurean and post-Jakobsonian linguistic applications, we can *also* find examples of the circle as a basic metaphor for the semiotic reality. So, we have Peirce, in *Evolutionary Love* (1893: no page numbers available): "The movement of love is circular." Love, equated with an evolutionary principle of order or, to quote from the same page (Peirce 1893), "harmony," is a fundamental semiotic principle indeed. Situated within the core of Peirce's evolutionary view of the cosmos – agapism together with tychism and synechism – it represents one opening of the historical and existential dimension of semiotics. Semiotics, as a world-view, conceives of *realms of semiosis* – such realms can be anthropic, societal, ideological, and, yes, biotic all the way to cosmological. So, too, Jakob von Üexkull, whose basic life-structural framework (with its Innenwelt/Umwelt metabolic "loop") is essentially "rounded on the edges" and circular; we can no longer talk about clearly confined structural spaces (with concrete or metaphoric "walls") and clearly unfolding time-scales (synchronized to Big Ben or to Greenwich Mean Time) but rather we must talk about the becoming-space and becoming-time of consciousness – here equated with life's self-engendering existential structure (an animal's being-in-the-world as a sentient organism). Darwin, already, situated the struggling organism in a kind of feedback-relationship with the environment. For Darwin, variation is the key to evolution, and variation is in *constant flux*. Patterns, namely species and higher levels of order, appear as states of *co*-habitation *with*, and *in*-habitation *in*, a natural system. Now, I would argue that biology has always been much more than simply taxonomy and pattern recognition, it is a theory of the interconnection of all life on earth. We don't even need a highly-advanced theory to observe the cyclical nature of natural processes of birth, life and death – whether on an individual scale of an organism's ontogeny, or on the wider scale of seasons, ecologies and biospheres. Nature, we may hypothesize, is a self-evolving bio-existential quasi-organism of interlocking and hierarchically nested circles (*Daseins*), which all interact and co-evolve on the level of Gaia to a gigantic, self-regulating circle, the so-called "circle of life." Beyond the biosphere, this circular framework extends to the circular rotation of the planets and atoms, and the physical processes that underlie gravity and electromagnetism seem to affect the evolution of organisms, as well, and make them "gravitate" or "magnetize" towards the centre of a "circular" mass (more on this later).

What, then, is the connection between Peirce's agapism and the Hobbesian-Spencerian (I hesitate to say Darwinian) concept of nature-as-war/struggle? As a bio-existentialist, this question is the choice between an aesthetics of war and an aesthetics of love and peace. Firstly, because my existentialism owes a debt to Nietzsche, Heidegger and (to a lesser extent) Sartre, I will gladly admit my adherence to a kind of doctrine of life 1) as *Will*, usually rendered as Will-to-Power or Will-to-Survival, and 2) as *Angst*, understood as a kind of sense of urgency of one's own existential condition as a finite, eventually-to-be-dead organism. This view of life is surely *tragic*, in the sense of Nietzsche and Camus, but also – and for the same reason – Dionysian; life establishes itself *despite* opposition and struggle – and establishes itself firmly and soundly at that, in a kind of orgy of self-founding self-expression: "I AM", says the "I" of the self-opening Being, homologous to the way the god of the Hebrew Holy Book announces himself/itself to the world. This act, this *first* act, this initiatory stage of "I-hood", is the birth of semiosis itself, of life itself. Life *is* the self-revelatory opening of semiotic process of "worlding", of being-there, through the individual animals and their capacity for understanding and modelling the world, i.e. making the world *real* and *rational*, in the Hegelian sense. The tragic-Dionysian "I AM" is the universal call of self-recognition, and every animal, plant, human being and other subject is a stage, an experiment, in the unfolding of the absolute self-reflectivity of the Spirit. *The Spirit is Reality perceiving itself (Subject) as Matter (Objective)*, through the alienation of one *Dasein* from the cosmic totality. Consequently, cosmos is full of bio-existential self-enclosed systems of consciousness, all with their particular *Daseins*, i.e. ways of being-(in-)the-world.

I would like to stay away from an orthodox humanist existentialist perspective. Instead, I would like to emphasize life as an existential project, and so cannot privilege humans over other agents. I am interested in the biosphere as a whole, and not only the human world. We can study this world (of humans and non-humans) in various ways. There are many ways of mapping and modelling life processes. Of these, I should mention mathematics (including cybernetics, chaos and fractal theory, algebraic logic), psychology (emergent connectivism, cognitive ethology, sociobiology, evolutionary neurochemistry) and, of course, semiotics (Uexküll's Umwelt-theory, Peircean cosmology, Kalevi Kull's communication studies, Dario Martinelli's zoomusicology and my own bio-existential and epistemological theories).

To "prefer" one theory over another means, simply, to have some usefulness for such a theory, as James and Peirce tell us. And sometimes only one theory will have particular usefulness. Sometimes only one theory will lead us to a particular truth. That is why a good combination is better than a single paradigm in isolation. In this particular paradigm, I combine Heidegger and Darwin, as well as Lotman and Peirce, to marry existentialism and biology (hopefully in an interesting and fruitful way). But I acknowledge my limitations. We are all working within different traditions with their own ways of looking at the world.

The background been laid down, what exactly is the main contribution of such a theory, which so far has been shown to be a Darwinian re-invention of the semiotic tradition stretching back to Peirce, Lotman and Sebeok and utilizing the more recent theories of Tarasti and a broad ecological, Darwinian consciousness? Where, if anywhere, does a *Dasein*-analysis of existential structures of life and the universe lead the scientist or the semiotician? I have stated already my view of life as both *tragic* and *dionysian*; namely evolutionarily determined and simultaneously free and chaotic (here I'm following Peirce, who was an evolutionary determinist moderated by a belief in "tychism" i.e. chance and chaos). We need to read Darwin's *Origin of Species* as a story, not about the *taxonomy* of species, but about *the origin of life in the variation leading to speciation*. Life is both materialistically determined and (semiotically) open-ended. This translates, somewhat facetiously: life is *real (fixed) but playful (unpredictable)*. To say that genes ("nature") programme or pre-determine life and mental states is correct but only in a limited sense. It is also analogously true that pheromones and neural firings "cause" Love – but anyone who claims this is (rightfully) condemned as a lunatic. It would be sheer *reductio ad absurdum* because material and mental structures cannot *cause* each other: they are two explanatory models of the same phenomena from a different perspective. The Umwelt (objective world) is a reflection of the Innenwelt (subjective world), and vice versa. Consequently, life cannot be either/or; it has to be composed of both dimensions. Life is both material and spiritual, using these folk terms (and much of philosophy is using folk terms in an interesting new way). The philosophical error of Descartes and the early Modernists was to reduce the natural world into an objective, materialist machinery, *and* to simultaneously exalt human being's dualistic nature as a composite of two essences or substances, Mind and Body. Of course, the idea of Man as "thinking" or "rational" animal goes back to Athens – and actually to many cultural origins, including Jerusalem and Rome. The Christian legacy has made this line of thinking particularly appealing to philosophers. But the problem is that it fails to capture the fact that *all* reality and *all* nature is dual in this sense: every organism is composed of an inside and an outside, a subjective world and an objective world, the perceiver and the perceived. Even an anthill has this structure.

However, to reintegrate the material and the mental into a single unitary phenomenology is possible, I believe, through a careful reading of Peirce (semiosis and evolutionary cosmology), Heidegger (*Dasein* and the destruction of Western metaphysics), Kant (the critical constructivism of epistemological idealism), Hegel (the analysis of subjectivity, alienation and the process of returning to the objective absolute), Nietzsche (the tragic view of – human and animal – life) and Darwin *via* Uexküll (the unity of neo-Kantian constructivism and natural evolutionary determinism). The need for this integration is clear; we may only think of the plundering of natural resources, the destruction of world's ecosystems, the pollution of the environment, global climate change, crammed mass production and the slaughter of farm animals, as well as countless other "philosophical errors" translatable into "societal" and "actual" errors that have resulted from the mistaken view that only humans are conscious beings. So, in conceiving of life and existence as having certain universal principles, together with certain amount of openness, we can come to formulate principles of aesthetics, ethics and cosmic ontology.

This would amount to a paradigm shift, and I don't propose to provide anything like that here. It seems a number of different factors and agents are preparing the way for this paradigm shift, as the necessary result of centuries of oppression and sleep under the domination of Western (Platonic-Christian) metaphysics, whose self-deconstruction is happening every day as the world is changing in interesting ways due to global integration and new scientific, philosophical and artistic visions that are deluging the West and the rest of the world.

The nature of this new paradigm is rather unclear. It could come about spontaneously as a result of new discoveries. Or it could come about as the result of rediscovering old theories (a new "renaissance"). Of course, there could be numerous competing paradigms: whichever paradigm or research method or "truth" wins does not depend on fantasy or our private wishes, but on the practical demands of scientific practice and the concrete problems set by our life worlds. In our modest way, semioticians and philosophers can formulate new ways of looking at the world. Together with scientists and artists, in developing models that break free from the subject-object dualisms and other old *clichés* we can hopefully work towards a better – or at least more refined – ethical attitude towards science, nature and society.

I propose that the prevalent malaise of technological and humanist origins can be traced back to a lack of interpretation of *cosmic* semiotic systems. *Cosmic* → *Biological* → *Existential*, three levels of analysis, should be separated no longer, but integrated to a new theory.

Let us turn back to our theory, then.

There is an evolutionary continuum to life. Natural evolution, turning into *cultural* evolution, also produces the anthropological, societal and global semiotic spheres. These have been analyzed by structuralists like Lévi-Strauss and the Russian formalists. Semiotic systems, as Tarasti says, are like a *Dasein* ("Being-There"), in which existential self-hood is manifest, as the Hegelian "for-itself" of the system. Uexküll uses the term "Ich-Ton" for that which reverberates the internal dynamism of an organism. This dynamism is not the "essence" of that existential sign system but rather the *modality* of its existence, i.e. the way an organism structures the world around it by means of (available) signs. *Dasein*, the Innenwelt-Umwelt loop, Existence, Semiosphere... All these are relative synonyms. Tarasti, I believe, largely takes *Dasein* to describe *human* reality (cf. Kierkegaard, Jaspers and Sartre). For me, however, *Dasein*-analysis can accurately describe an anthill as well as a human being, a science project, a tribal community, the metabolism of the body or, for example, the structuring of world by the philosopher in his self-exploratory meditations. Now, to provide my modest contribution to the new non-dualistic bioexistential paradigm (against humanistic subject-object metaphysics and anthropocentrism), I will hereby present a diagram (Figure 2) that depicts my proposal for a model of bio-existential semiosis grounded on space-time phenomenological reality. It combines the Innenwelt-Umwelt structures of organic and cosmic life with the well-known *Dasein* models of Heidegger and Tarasti.

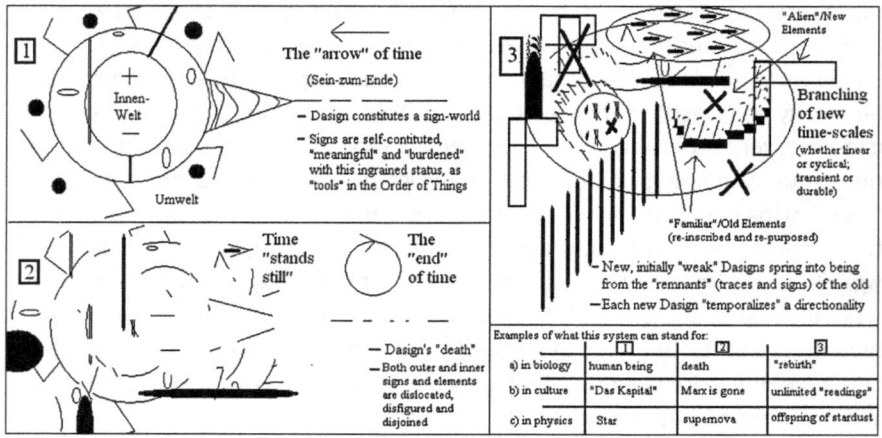

Figure 2: Bio-existential semiosis grounded on a space-time phenomenological reality.

Now, some comments on the graph above. (I have used the word "Dasign" for "*Dasein*" to individuate my theory, but those words are synonymous and should not confuse the reader.) The graph's three-part structural process relates, consecutively, to the facts of (1) becoming-into-existence, i.e. life-as-becoming; (2) the death and/or end of an existential sign system ; and, finally, (3) the after-effect, the "post-signifying reality" of *Dasein's* existence (whether or not the *Dasein* is yet "dead"), namely the "after-life" of semiosis.

The process of self-becoming and self-manifesting of a sign-system always "takes time" and thus envelops a kind of temporality and directionality, i.e. the creation of a sense of history, mission, intentionality (Will), purposefulness (*telos*) and a "towards-something-ness.": Heidegger analyzed Time in *Sein und Zeit* as the horizon of Being's self-revealing. Time, as he famously put it is, is the horizon of Being. We could say that the "I-hood" of semiotic subjectivity opens up a (particular) world of signs as a means of manifesting one's uniqueness through an act of self-expression (an existential thrown project in the practical world), and an *act* always takes time (and space) by definition, and creates a temporal existence for itself out of what already exists in itself. *Dasein* temporalizes itself by, in effect, creating a surrounding world (a niche) for itself, i.e. creating a meaningful environment in which it can exist. Of course, it may have already been *created* in this way by the world itself, but just "who" did the creating is not as important as the fact of its creation. We can say that, on the level of nature, it is nature itself which divisions itself off as separate organisms, just like on the level of reality it is reality itself which divides itself, creates itself, into separate (competing, conflicting, cooperating) "parts of reality." World is self-creation and self-differentiation and the continual ascent (self-integration) back to unity with the Absolute. Every organism is an effort by the universe to comprehend itself, and it is the deepest drive of every organism to understand (model) the universe. Human are very good at this, but not perfect; and tape worms are very bad at this, but still capable of some kind of understanding, i.e. world-building.

Let us take a further look at the graph. In the lower right-hand corner I have sketched three (very much non-exhaustive) interpretations, practical applications, of this "*Dasein's* journey" from birth (1) to death (2) and beyond (3). Firstly and most obviously, there is the "existentialist-humanist" reading whereby we can conceive of our structure here as an anthropological tale of man's becoming, dying and, lastly, his "after-life" (one's "legacy" in the natural and societal memory). This corresponds to the humanistic and anthropological interpretation of *Dasein*. But a wolf would have a similar course; from the Schopenhauerian Will's manifestation in the organism to its eventual death and post-mortem fate (i.e. state of being remembered and used, metaphorically speaking, by the world after its death – as food or seed, for example, for further generations of animals). A wolf has a bio-existential *Dasein* structured according to its *own* (non-human) Innenwelt-Umwelt structure and shaped by its own semiotic world. We could also substitute a plant here, and look at the ways a plant develops into existence out of nothingness by means of developmental blueprints and patterns that enable that becoming-plant of a plant... We could look at how the same plant, or the aforementioned animal, will be the food and nutrition for some other species, or how its products will be productively used by other (opportunistic) life forms – like, for example, how animals breathe the oxygen exhaled by plants and micro-organism, thus constituting a positive after-life to a dying *Dasein*, and giving birth to new, other, alien *Daseins*. Every life form, and every *Dasein*, materializes (for itself) a reality that can be used (in itself) by others as well (for themselves). One's subjective existence becomes objective existence for others. It is impossible to be "pure spirit" – every spirit has to become matter, to "incarnate" into the world, just as much as all matter has to become spiritual (through cosmic evolution). That is why all spirit must perish, and all organisms are mortal – they cannot signify the totality of the universe, only part of it. *If*, on the other hand, there were a spirit capable of sustaining itself and signifying the totality of the universe, it would be immortal, because it would signify everything to itself, and itself to everything else, but in the world of imperfect systems, imperfect consciousnesses and imperfect *Daseins*, every *Dasein* must *struggle* for its existence and face the fact that it must die: it must die because it cannot comprehend the universe in its totality, i.e. it cannot be pure spirit. No *Dasein*, by itself, is God. There is (likely) no God, because in order to exist, one has to be *Dasein*, i.e. an imperfect mortal being. *Dasein* is a *partial* comprehension of the universe, and the *only* way the universe can comprehend itself is through these partial perspectives, which are born to imperfection and die in imperfection, but whose imperfection is of the essence of the universe.

We are mortals, and *all* signifying totalities must perish. The mortality (partiality, imperfection) of parts is the only key to immortality (impartiality, perfection) of the totality. The universe cannot exist without renewing itself through self-alienation. Human beings, star systems and anthills are the necessary self-alienated substance of the universe transcending itself.

The path to universal totality is through cosmic evolution.

Well then, to get back to more mundane questions: why does my graph of the *Dasein*, with its Innenwelt/Umwelt-structure, resemble a *circle* (an amoeba) – and not a square or a triangle? I believe there are some suggestive mathematical (geometric) reasons for the ubiquity of circular structure in nature. A circle is *omni-directionally proportional*, i.e. its radius is the same to all directions, and it is thus capable of 360 degree turns without losing its inherent "preferential" orientation. A water-droplet, a planet, a cell, an atom, a galaxy, a plate and a crumb of bread all share that essential circular nature, because *nature prefers circles*; physical laws, like gravity and electro-magnetics, draw things into clumps and centerings, and this is the first stage of cosmological evolution. The circle is the geometric form of differentiation and self-formation. Every being has to accumulate, and this accumulation gathers towards a centre, forming primordial "circles" of the universe (atoms, star systems, human beings). Not everything is circular, but many things are – surprisingly many, I would say. Natural evolution of life on planet Earth starts off, too, with microscopic circular structures because this (easily defendable structure) reflects the biotic centre's need to defend itself as a separate entity, omni-directionally (against all possible enemies and forces), and to gather energies towards its centre. By eating and territorializing, an entity maintains its centripetal orientation and draws the boundaries of its own circle, i.e. its own being-in-the-world. This circle is not, of course, a bubble. Even a worm is a circle in this sense (it doesn't have anything to do with the literal shape of a circle!), since it has fixed boundaries around its body. So, by "circle" I mean any self-centred, self-enclosed entity capable of defending its self, life and existential value, from societies to human beings to tapeworms and star systems. Without this capacity to concentrate and gather towards a centre, no *Dasein* could ever develop. All *Daseins* have the need to defend themselves in the struggle for existence of *Daseins*. Sometimes they fight for survival, sometimes they cooperate and find ways of co-existing, but always they have to protect their own interest, in order to survive. Now, of course many organisms and sign structures develop into interesting shapes and levels of complexity, forming networks and interrelationships that have higher orders of existence. Sometimes they already find themselves within such totalities to begin with. I have taken into this account, and I acknowledge the complexity of things, but one must remember that even a complex structure like a society or a city is roughly understandable, I think, as a *circular* structure of signs (that's why we have "a city centre" and "orbital highways", and "national borders"). Or, take a human: Its round body has limbs, two generally pointing downward while the upper two limbs are freer to interact on the horizontal plane with the world around us.

Now let us summarize our position: I have drawn a structure of a *Dasein* which constitutes a (meaningful) sign-world by its interactions with the Umwelt, as a function (a process) of that Umwelt – as one particular, actualized form of that Umwelt's sum-total of potential actualisable field-effects, reflecting the range of organisms capable of surviving in a particular niche in certain conditions with certain levels of competition and cooperation. *Daseins* are existential gatherings of worldly energies into abiding structures that develop their own laws, metabolic systems and Innenwelts. Any such structure must have means of interacting with the world, either through the senses (always interpretative and proactive to some extent) or through limbs and external tools and signs. So, in biology, this model is largely applicable without exception. Also, it should be noted that such *Daseins* often form "colonies", "communities", "hierarchies" and other structures which enable the building of complex structures from relatively simple, circular elements. But these elements, the building blocks of higher order *Daseins*, are themselves not insignificant or "dead": For example, the cells in the human body or – to take a completely different example – the artistic sub-cultures of New Orleans or Helsinki are very much alive and full of vitality, yet their existence is linked to, and depended on, the existence of some "higher" levels of semiospheric structuring – in this example, "human body" and "city" respectively, to which they also contribute as members or internal organs. All life is in this sense dependent on different *niches*, *field effects* and (external as well as internal) *interactions*. Every *Dasein* opens up ("for-itself" a subjectivity) within a domain of already-existing *Dasein* (whose "for-itself" it uses as "in-itself" objective raw material, for example as food or slaves). Every *Dasein* envelops within a domain of possibility, as an out-growth of real "in-itself" stuff. Every child is born to living parents. But the child is not the parent, and there are infinite children to infinite parents. Bio-existential theory studies the essential and contingent features of these beings, together with the natural sciences, arts and philosophy.

Every bio-existential structure carves out its own (contingent) for-itself reality, its subjective domain, out of already-existing (necessary) in-itself reality, the so-called objective world (which is nothing other than the subjective world of others turned "dead" via phenomenological perception). Plants, cities, humans, ants, science and art, thus, create their own *Dasein(s)* by appropriating and objectivising other *Dasein(s)* for their own use, for their own bio-existential "world building" and "truth building." Animals eat other animals, and human constructs eat other human constructs. Every *Dasein* wants (and must in order to survive) to differentiate from the primordial unity of the mother, and that is why reality is inherently tragic and Dionysian.

So, in analyzing "bio-existential" structures such as these, we may learn to overcome our reliance (old and tired) on a mechanical worldview *without throwing out the baby (Science, Reason) with the bathwater*, and maintain a perspective that is properly cosmic yet also properly grounded on local phenomena, i.e. on local occurrences of self-organizing selfhood. Peirce remains a major influence, a thinker whose schemes of a logical and cosmological order of semiological unity have proven fodder for future research, at least in my own case, into the relationship between the emerging frameworks of ecology with the semiotic tradition. In my opinion, by not relying on rigid, "square" models of research but instead advocating and developing "circular," dynamic and rich systems-theories based on something like the models proposed here is the way forward. The point is not to have the final or best model but to keep the field open for a radical investigation into the possibilities of knowledge itself. The old "dyadic" models of the Cartesian mould should be supplanted by the "triadic" models of the Peircean-Heideggerian variety. Science should not be seen as a field devoid of (avoidable) ethical consequences, because it *cannot* be (there is no separation of the ethical from the aesthetic and the ontological). Under the assumption of mistaken objectivity, its products and inventions are shaping and ravaging societies, human beings and ecosystems. Science, in order to be true to its name, must be open to hypotheses that can be tested. But it is important to *also* test theories that are not based on old metaphysical concepts, because the creation of new hypotheses drives science (and all other human practices) forward.

So, in order to be able to formulate new theories, new hypotheses, we need new ways of looking at the world (new directions and perspectives for study), including those which subject the self-certainty of our own *Dasein* into question. We need to analyze reality as the interlocking of competing *Daseins* for existence and survival which use methods of self-subjectification and other-objectification. Everything is real by definition. We need to see that reality is the phenomenological content of the objective semiotic process of being-able-to-perceive. Reality cannot be without the being-there of existence. Only existence *is* reality. Reality is the sum-total of all *Daseins*. Only then will the full reality of reality be discovered, because reality is the self-realization of its own fragmentary nature. Reality is self-separation of the primordial *Dasein* into competing existences, mutually vying for dominance. No single *Dasein* is the only (ultimate and final) *Dasein*, but every *Dasein* has a perspective on the world and a place in it. In order to break free from the spell of boring old metaphysics, we need to develop new theories that accommodate a holistic understanding of life and existence. Such a new view of life, societies, nature and other existentially organized semiotic structures will hopefully guide the way to a more *evolved*, more *ethical* and also more *aesthetically* happy conduct in the sciences and the humanities.

References

Bohm, David. 1980. *Wholeness and the Implicate Order*. London &c.: ARK
Brent, Joseph. 1993. *Charles Sanders Peirce: A Life*. Indiana University Press.
Lehto, Otto. 2009. Studying the Cognitive States of Animals: Epistemology, Ethology and Ethics *Sign Systems Studies* 37(3/4). 369–422.
Peirce, Charles Sanders. (Note: all references are to these online editions of his work, for which reason no page numbers can be given.)
Peirce, Charles Sanders. 1877. The Fixation of Belief. http://www.bocc.ubi.pt/pag/peirce-charles-fixation-belief.pdf
Peirce, Charles Sanders. 1893. Evolutionary Love. https://arisbe.sitehost.iu.edu/menu/library/bycsp/evolove/evolove.htm
Tarasti, Eero. 2000. *Existential Semiotics*. Bloomington (Indianapolis): Indiana University Press

Merja Bauters
Existential semiotics, semiosis and emotions

Abstract: The paper aims to ponder Tarasti's theory on existential semiotics concerning the semiosis of the semiotic self, emotions, and Umwelt. Peirce's theory of signs (sign – action) allows tackling the dynamics of the intertwined relationship of individual and Umwelt. The key idea is that sign action i.e., semiosis could give a more holistic view on the effect of the social environment/Umwelt onto the interpretation of signs. Existential semiotics has been the starting point for pondering the question of individual and its relation to Umwelt. Existential semiotics provides a clear view of the development of the self, resistance, and Umwelt. The combined approach of existential semiotics, Peirce's theory of signs, and Damasio's neuroscientific approaches allow an opportunity to look further on at the emotions and the role they might play in the semiosic process. The aim is at raising questions, finding connections, and affinities between disciplines, without attempting to create a new theory.

Keywords: Semiosis, Semiotic self, Existential semiotics, Emotions, Feeling of Emotions

1 Introduction

Using Tarasti's approach, as a basis for understanding the inseparable nature of individual and Umwelt, allows well the formulation of a holistic point of view on the semiosis.

Still, my approach will have a different emphasis than Tarasti's existentialist semiotics. Firstly, I shall point out that according to Peirce, the individual or self is already by nature social; thus, the distinction between an individual and Umwelt in a certain sense disappears. Secondly, I emphasise the role of emotions and ponder on the role of resistance in the forming of the semiotic self, which is independent dependant with the Umwelt. I shall especially highlight the emotional meaning and Emotional Interpretant. In the next sections, I shall first outline Antonio Damasio's neuroscientific approach to self which complements the holistic point of view of semiotic self. After which, I shall present how the Peircean framework provides insights into the existential semiotics and notion of resistance. Not exceptionally many others in social, psychological tradition have been interested in emotions, for instance, for Bourdieu, nothing was more serious than emotion (Bourdieu 2000:138,140), which was emphatically affirmed by Joas and classical pragmatism (Kilpinen 2002a: 61). William James (1902) agreed on the importance of emotions in experience and thus in action.

Antonio Damasio's main interest lies in the ignored importance that emotions play in all human reflection, decision-making, problem-solving, and learning. He argues that the consciousness and self cannot come into being and cannot be without continuous interdependent and intertwined connection to the chemical and neural systems that regulate the body and the brain. He also extends the traditional concept of consciousness and self[1] into what often is called the body and argues against the Cartesian division of body and mind. It is essential to define the concept of emotion; it is different in traditional human and social sciences. Peirce does not make a clear distinction between emotions and feelings. According to Damasio, the emotions come first and after that the feeling, namely the feeling of the emotions: "When we have an emotion we alter the state of the body in a variety of ways, and then register the resulting changes in the brain's body maps and feel the emotions. Emotions come first, feelings second" (Damasio 2003a: 49) and another definition for the terms of emotion and feeling is that "The term 'emotion' should be rightfully used to designate a collection of responses triggered from parts of the brain and body, and from parts of the brain to other parts of the brain, using both neural and humoral routes. The end result of a collection of such responses is an emotional state. The term "feeling" should be used to describe the complex mental state that results from emotional state" (Damasio 2001: 103).

Damasio's construction starts with the Proto Self that is *becoming* into awareness (becoming to be conscious) of oneself. As a whole, Proto Self is the neural and chemical system that sort of scans, moment by moment, the physical state of the physical structure of the organism in its many dimensions, including the brain. The Proto Self is the pre-conscious biological precedent of both Core and Autobiographical Selves (Parvizi & Damasio 2001: 138). Core Consciousness ensures in the biological level the homeostatic balance in a living organism and represents the current organism state within somato-sensing structures. The Core Consciousness is the imaged relationship of the interaction between the object[2]

---

1 The concept of self is defined by Damasio (2003: 253–254) as follows "[Self] as something that denotes stability and continuity over time, as well as singularity [. . .] self always implies a reference, for example, to an organism, to its behaviour, or to its mind".
2 By object, Damasio means "entities as diverse as a person, a place, a melody, or an emotional state", by image, he means "a mental pattern in any of the sensory modalities, e.g. a sound image, a tactile image, the image of an aspect of an emotional state as conveyed by visceral senses" (Parvizi & Damasio 2001: 136–137).

and the changed organism state it causes. The images convey the physical characteristics of the object as well as the reaction of like or dislike one may have for an object and the plans one may formulate for it, or convey the web of relationships of the object among other objects (see Parvizi & Damasio 2001: 135–137). The ceaselessly maintained first-order collection is the Proto-self, and the turning of these neural patterns into specific mental patterns occurs in the interactions of the Proto Self and the Core Consciousness. Out of these mental patterns, the sense of self (Core Self) is formed (move from Firstness to Secondness). This awareness of the self and the mental patterns of relationships of the objects is according to Damasio "a specific kind of wordless knowledge" (or knowledge of bodymind) (Parvizi & Damasio 2001: 137).

The Extended Consciousness and its protagonist, the Autobiographical Self, are Thirdness in Peircean sense. Extended consciousness holds the ability to process time. Thus, past and future come into play with the person's memories of previous situations, outcomes of the situations, feeling of emotions related to these and experiences in general. It also holds the capability of learning and forming of the habits. The processes are integrated into meaningful combinations through time and combined with the previous experiences (Extended Consciousness).

It means that if experience or a particular stimulus promotes the same kind of feeling of emotions and this feeling of emotion is experienced and conceptually processed many times, it comes habituated, or in other words, it becomes "second nature". Somewhat like when learning to drive the car – the changing of the gear and pressing and lifting of the clutch and pressing the gas – comes to be habituated/automatic. The same occurs to specific stimulus or events that promote a particular feeling of emotion and evolve into a habituated reaction. For example, through education, particular manners can promote disgust or likeability. Namely, when one learns to drive a car, the driving manners that are thought supposed to arise disgust or appreciation depending on how oneself or the others are driving, as such teaching the right attitudes for good driving manners. In Damasio's words:

> Emotion is in the loop of the reason all the time. We have inherited an incredibly complex emotional apparatus, which, in evolution, was tied to certain classes of objects and situations that were fairly narrow [. . .] but now we have added to that repertoire of emotional triggers many other objects and situations we have learned in our lives, so we do have a possibility of responding emotionally to all sorts of situations.   (Damasio 2003a: 49–51)

Moreover, the whole idea that Damasio has proved through the neuroscientific experiments is surprisingly close to Peirce's idea of how Firstness, Secondness, and Thirdness intertwine in the trialogical semiosic process. Namely "[. . .] core consciousness is the process of achieving an all-encompassing imagetic pattern which brings together the pattern for the object, the pattern for the organism, and the pattern for the relationship between the two" (Parvizi & Damasio 2001: 139–140).[3] The continuous process of the self's becoming is a spiral-like process where the two selves, namely the Core Self and the Autobiographical Self, are in dialogue. One phase of the process can be resistance, which will be discussed below after the discussing on the holistic point of view of the forming of the self.

The above (process of Proto Self to Core Self) is close to concepts of instinct, creativity or in Peircean terms abduction. Another critical aspect of the Core Self is its ability to produce us the sense of self as continuous "[. . .] the key to the self is the representation of the continuity of the organism" (Damasio 2003: 254).[4] It means that one is interpreting signs holistically all the time from inside oneself and from the "outside". Tarasti (2005: 19) has mentioned in his article about the semiotics of resistance, which explains how the memory, being, and history are related to resistance, that the continuous becoming is an illusion. However, Tarasti's aspect on the mind going back to compare the experiences to the memory of the previous experiences is more like a metaphor, since there is no going backwards only more loops in the semiosic spiral. Selecting memories is one part of the spiral-like loop of the self's process. Without the move to remembering there would be no self and reflective thinking as Damasio has shown by his patients who have brain damages on the connections to the memory networks (See Damasio 1999, 2001 and 2002).

Having in the background and as a base, the sense of the continuous Core Self (and Core Consciousness), the Extended Consciousness (involving the memories, e.g. the past experiences) forms the identity or personality of the semiotic self, namely the Autobiographical Self. However, Peirce already anticipated this continuity of the consciousness, "My notion is that we directly perceive the continuity of consciousness" (CP 6.181).

Still, secondary emotions are products of primary emotion processes and use primary emotions as their basis. The difference between the processes of the primary (bottom-up) and secondary (top-down) emotions can be summed up as the body doing what it does in interdependent, interrelated interaction

---

[3] Some of the similarities in the choice of concepts and descriptions may well be because Damasio is acquainted, for example, with William James (Damasio 2003: 254).
[4] The support for the continuity is the neural system responsible for the representation of our bodies. This Damasio calls an intuition (cf.: Damasio 2003: 254). The relationship of intuition with the representation of the continuous self has similarity with Peirce's idea of abduction, which is not discussed in this paper. For further information see Paavola (2004, 2004a and 2005) for the instinct or the creative side of Peircean abduction and Merrell for the relation of abduction to the bodymind and concept of becoming into being (for example 2003: 222–238).

with the mind. Creating a bodymind, not separate mind and body (Merrell 2003: 176). However, in the secondary emotion process, the signs become a part of the bodymind sign processing. The difference is significant to notice since, on the one hand, we react to many signs without realising it, and on the other hand, we learn new signs and make them as habits. These processes are time-binding regarding signs made and taken must and play a role in adequately embodied communication (Merrell 2003). The bodymind is an essential aspect in semiosis; namely, it is crucial for realising the holistic manner in which one perceives and uses signs.[5] The cultivation or education or communication with/in our Umwelt is a significant part of the secondary learned signs. It is also crucial to realise that emotions play a role in cognitive processes, in learning, in decision making/reasoning, in memory and are behind ethics, law, artistic, scientific, and technological creativity. (Damasio 2001). Before examining how Tarasti's existential semiotics and resistance come into view, I shall discuss how the Core Self and the Autobiographical Self can be seen through Peirce's concepts of deeper/critical self[vi].[6]

2 Are we at the mercy of emotions?

I assume that everyone has experiences of emotions overpowering so-called "reflective thinking"; thus, how does one try to control these situations? If seen through Peirce's categories of experiences, reflections belong to Thirdness, and Firstness belongs essentially to Thirdness. Therefore, it is not possible to have reflective thinking without emotions being involved. According to Damasio, one can learn and guide emotions "the way we have cultivated our relation with the world depends entirely on how we are educated or our family ideas or on the social environment" (2003a: 49–50). By Peirce, one can proceed with the self-semiosis using self-control in having a dialogue with oneself (cf.: 5.440–443). The same kind of dialogue occurs in Damasio's theory between the Core Self and the Autobiographical Self.

In other words, the emotions, feelings of the emotions and the changes (Core Consciousness and Core Self) are in a dialogue with the Extended Consciousness (memory, past experiences, timeline, e.g. past, present, and future) and the Auto-

---

5 Some such as Howard Gardner (1983, 1987) has called the embodied signs of all sensory channels as "multiple intelligences".
6 See for similar ideas of dialogue within one-self emphasising the embodied knowledge (bodymind signs) and the communal aspects (Mead 1934, 1938, Vygotsky1978 and 1981, Colapietro 1989 on Peirce, on "Intersubjective meanings" and William James 1983 and 1902).

biographical Self. These two selves, in semiotic terms, are in dialogue with each other and to become aware or meet in Secondness but create habits, reflection, and habit change in Thirdness. Peirce expresses nearly word to word the same idea that Damasio has found; namely that in Secondness, two different consciousnesses meet:

> [. . .] You get this kind of consciousness in some approach to purity when you put your shoulder against a door and try to force it open. You have a sense of resistance and at the same time a sense of effort. There can be no resistance without effort; there can be no effort without resistance. They are only two ways of describing the same experience. It is a double consciousness. We become aware of ourself in becoming aware of the not-self. The waking state is a consciousness of reaction; and as the consciousness itself is two-sided, so it has also two varieties; namely, action, where our modification of other things is more prominent than their reaction on us, and perception, where their effect on us is overwhelmingly greater than our effect on them. To this element, I give the name of Secondness. (CP 1.324)

It is the semiosis of the semiotic self. The idea of the spiral-like semiosis of the Core Self and the Autobiographical Self helps to see how intertwined the body-mind is in the forming of the semiotic self or individuality within the Umwelt (or community in Peircean terms), even to the extent to say that part one is the same as the Umwelt or community. The individual is the same as the environment in two ways, namely in Peircean way "Now you and I – what are we? Mere cells of the social organism" (CP 1.673) and in Damasioan way "[we] share our image-based concept of the world with other humans, and even with some animals" (Damasio 1994: 97). It means that we share our conscious thought with Umwelt but also that the basis (biological structure) is part of nature. The semiosis is a continuous process adding new experiences to the already formed self-image/personality. The semiosis of the semiotic self is in focus on the concept of self-control basing it on experience. In Damasio's terms, on the changes of the state of the organism's emotional state, and if the stimulus (sometimes "brute force") requires a change in beliefs or values, it can cause resistance. The mind of the interpreter with his/her habits should "exert a measure of self-control over his/her future actions" (CP 5.418). The self-control of the human has degrees. As Peirce describes:

> There are inhibitions and coördinations that entirely escape consciousness. There are, in the next place, modes of self-control which seem quite instinctive (Core Consciousness and Core Self, from Firstness to Secondness). Next, there is a kind of self-control which results from training. Next, a man can be his own training-master and thus control his self-control. [. . .] when a man trains himself, thus controlling the control, he must have some moral rule in view, however special or irrational it may be. But next he may undertake to improve this rule; that is, to exercise a control over his control of control. To do this he must have in view something higher than an irrational rule. (CP 5.533, brackets added)

On reflecting or controlling one's reasoning, one can add new experiences to the already formed habits and norms. When proceeding onwards, one may come to the point of changing one's habits, norms, and rules through reasoning with the new experiences. It means that one can change one's potential acts in future situations or one may change his/her interpretations of particular signs or modify to the point of beliefs. In Peirce's words:

> [Self-control] consists (to mention only the leading constituents) first, in comparing one's past deeds with standards, second, in rational deliberation concerning how one will act in the future, in itself a highly complicated operation, third, in the formation of a resolve, fourth, in the creation, on the basis of the resolve, of a strong determination, or modification of habit. (CP 8.320)

Although the end is never reached in reasoning, it is a continuous spiral process and includes emotions.

In the theory of existential semiotics by Tarasti, the process is with a focus on the individual comparing his past to the present or anticipated future where a broader experience base of the person allows more extensive range of different outcomes and choices he can see when comparing the present to the memory stores (2005: 21). Following Peirce and Damasio's idea that includes the body-mind, it enables a creative action to occur. The largeness of the experience base and knowledge is not the only one enabling legion of outcomes but needs the possibility to have a creative association between the present events and the memory bases (in the network of memory stores) affect the outcome crucially. How the person associates these experiences and uses his/her self-control to the instinctive bodymind knowledge might produce an even wider variety of future-oriented possible actions and thoughts including the possibility of overcoming one's resistance by new beliefs and values. Adding new belief and values is seen in Deely's idea of the semiosis occurring through abduction – deduction – induction process. Abduction would then hold the notions of instinct and the signs of the bodymind (which requires acknowledging one's feeling of emotions thus enabling to place the experiences also in the emotion-line and not only into the timeline (cf.: Tarasti 2005: 18)). It would enable the person to notice the "weaker possibilities". The comparing of the past and present or anticipated future is not enough but only a part of the process. Self-controlled reasoning is needed since one's conception of one's past experiences and memories change within time, which are not unchanging (cf.: Tarasti 2005: 17). As Moss and Damasio have described:

> Key value systems are involved, including emotional states and culture, which determine *the memories to be selected* and *the occasions of their recall*. The specificity of experiences

can then create a collection of memory stores and modes of recall that are unique to each individual, and that *change according to the context"*. (Moss and Damasio 2001:99)

The emotional states of oneself affect more or less profoundly what is selected and not from the Umwelt and in what perspective the issues are seen. However, one can also force (or to be forced by brute facts) oneself to notice issues that seem to contradict one's beliefs, habits, and values and critically, by Peircean self-controlled manner, ponder some beliefs or habits one has for correcting them. It seems it is worthwhile to glance into the intertwined relations of the semiotic self and the Umwelt (context).

3 Semiotic self in dialogue within semiotic self and Umwelt

In this section, I shall present ideas about the dialogue within oneself and where an individual is positioned from a semiosic perspective and discuss the self as social. I attempt to express the affinities found in Tarasti's existential semiotics and others, for example, Mead and Peirce, but also indicate the different perspectives the authors have to the subject under investigation.

In Mead's theory of mind, self, and society, the individual is a part of its environment and formed by it. Moreover, Mead's opinion of the individual-environment relations comes close to Deely's description of Umwelt.[7] For Mead, the mind, in our case the individual, selects objects which are "worth minding". Namely "mental processes imply not only mind but that somebody is minding and that objects of these processes are dependant upon the *emphases* and *selections of the individual*" (Mead 1938: 68 cited from Kilpinen 2002: 14, emphasis added). The point that some objects are salient or selected implies that the individual does select knowingly or unknowingly some objects and ignores others. Peirce has explained the emphasising or selecting of objects, for example, in his description of multiple objects and of the effect of time for instance that the past, the present, and the future influence perceiving (for more in-depth insight into the question, see Bergman 2004: 299–309). In Joas's parlance, it means that the individual is

---

[7] The term "Umwelt" originates from Uexküll's theory of meaning (see Nöth 1995: 158). John Deely has mentioned the selective tendency of the individual in its Umwelt 'Umwelt is shorthand for the objective world. In the case of the species-specifically human objective world; it is often called rather "Lebenswelt"' (Deely 2001: 719). However, the terms "Object" and "objective" have been thoroughly revised by Deely to take on their original meaning in philosophy.

involved in a continuous process of forming boundaries and of opening them regarding other individuals and the collectives with which he is associated. Out of this emerges, using the creative accomplishments of human action, the norms, values, cultural works, and institutions which are accepted by the society (Joas 1990: 186, see also Gibson 1979).

However, there is more than just the tendency to select specific objects at the expense of others. It stresses the context where the individual is situated, and the already existing experiences of the individual and his/her former semiosis, which allows attaining certain habits, attitudes, and, perhaps, even values. The attitudes and habits are not stable; they keep on changing. From this aspect, the individuals and the existing context agree among themselves some values, habits, and partially the world view/lifestyle. The existing temporal consensus sharing values, habits, and world views follows Peirce's description of the performance of the scientific inquiry. The scientific inquiry bases on a wish to learn. Learning occurs through observation and experience.[8] "As to that process of abstraction, it is itself a sort of observation. The faculty which I call abstractive observation is one which ordinary people perfectly recognise" (CP 2.227 [c.1897]). The observation of "ordinary people" covers also the idea of selection and interpretation of perceived objects through collateral experience (CP 6.319, 8.178, CP 8.314 [1909]).

Mead's idea of intersubjectivity[9] is that the individual begins from the state of intersubjectivity and develops his/her subjectivity gradually, also implies the notion of selectivity based on previous social action and experience. Mead and Peirce see the individual be primarily social and as well as the acquired habits, norms, and attitudes which grow through the process of intertwining with the Umwelt. To put it another way, the individual captures the world through semiosis. Peirce emphasises the social in nature of the individual as the communal aspect, which forms the "our experience" (CP 8.101). Peirce's descriptions provide a springboard to extend the concept of individual/self, particularly regarding Mead's, Tarasti's, and even Vygotsky's work.

If the "semiotic self" is a sign and it is "social in nature", then how it affects the aspects traditionally taken for the interaction between Umwelt and the individual? The question of the interaction occurring within Umwelt and individual

---

8 "[...] experience can only *mean the total cognitive result of living*, and includes interpretations quite as truly as it does the matter of sense. Even more truly, since this matter of sense is a hypothetical something which we never can seize as such, free from all interpretative working over" (CP 7.538, italics added).

9 Term Intersubjectivity is introduced by Joas to summarise Mead's theory on the emergence of the inner self (Kilpinen 2002: 16, see also Vygotsky 1981: 163 and Wertch 1985: 47–62).

has been studied extensively, for example, by Mead (1934), obviously by Peirce, and Vygotsky (1978), later by Deely (2001a), Colapietro (1989), Joas (1990 and 1996), Merrell (2003), and Tarasti (2000 and 2004). In social identity studies, there is a question that has been central and problematic for a long time, that is of what the social identity consists of. It has come up frequently, for example, Augoustinos and Walker argue that social identity is not reducible to personal identity only, the identity is inherently social (1995: 98, cf. CP 6.307, for a stronger emphasis on social self, see Bourdieu 2000, Kilpinen 2002, and Mead 1934 and 1938). To Colapietro's understanding of Peirce's concept of self; the self is essentially minds of others as well as a totality of meanings; thus, Peirce sees that "otherness and meaning are given together in our experience of our self as being embedded in a network of relations – more specifically, enmeshed in the "semiotic web"" (1989: 27–28). Namely, the self is itself a sign (CP 5.313). Therefore, the question is not about the discrepancy between individual and group or society, simply because an individual *is* a group or society in some sense. The subject or self is essentially a form of semiosis[10] (Colapietro 1989:37). Therefore, I assume that the individual is not able to proceed in its semiosis all by him/herself, but needs the interaction with society, because the person qua subject possesses the original form of community (CP 5.421 cf.: Colapietro, 1989: 43), and individuals form the society. Thus, society is, in its turn, also affected by individuals acting alone or together as a whole.

Focusing on the action of the self or the mind of Interpretant is needed in the reasoning that attaches the collateral experience and mind's relation to the sign. The action is a type of conduct and, thus, belongs to Thirdness. Conduct, in its turn, is closely related to Peirce's notion of habit. Following Colapietro, already the thought as such is a form of action, although it would not amount to an actual utterance or physical action. It means that a form of thinking that has established a particular "way of thinking" can be called a habit. In social psychological terms, it would be the "mental structure". Colapietro notes that from the semiotic perspective, individuals are always in the midst of others and meanings, which means that otherness and meaning emerge from the individual using his/her experience of him/her self. That is embedded in a network of relations (1989: 27–28; CP 6.286 cited from Bernstein 1965: 78).) Habits and emotions, especially in the Emotional Interpretant, play an essential role, which has affinities to what Damasio explained through neurosciences. As for the semiosis, habits are

---

[10] Peirce did not accept James's ([1890] 1983: 221) notion of the insulation of the self. Peirce emphasised limitless, infinite interpretation (cf.: CP 8.81). For more specific points of view on individual semiosis, see Colapietro (1989), Kilpinen (2002) and Tarasti (2000).

the outcome of mediation in the individual: the mind of Interpretant mediates between the two parts of the semiotic self.

Some similar concepts and ideas may be observed between approaches of Mead and Peirce to that of Tarasti where the self is considered from semiosis perspective. Tarasti gives an exciting model of the "reflective self" and its journey towards existential values. My aim, here, is not to discuss the concept of values or the semiosis inside an individual in detail but to analyse Tarasti's approach from Peircean viewpoint. Tarasti studies signs from inside and approaches the human dialogue occurring both within a person and between the signs. He bases his existential semiotic theory on Hegel, Kant, Kierkegaard, and Sartre (cf.: Tarasti 2004: 84–102[11]). Tarasti argues that the values and the creative inner self (Moi) are connected through a particular communal self (Soi). These two parts of the self are in the dialogue, and they create the "semiotic self" (in Sebeok's parlance) or Ich-Ton as Tarasti calls it. The Ich-Ton is like a mediator between the two parts of the self and the Umwelt.

Tarasti transfers Hegel's notion of "An Sich" and "Für Sich" to the potential/ the actual and to the subjective/the objective (from Kierkegaard) and Moi/Soi (from Fontanille), respectively. As far as the potential and the actual are concerned, it is possible to use them for the development of the "semiotic self". Tarasti follows Peirce and Mead while explaining the dialogue between the two parts. Thus, the "critical self" (Peirce)/Me (Mead)/Soi reflects/controls the impulses of the "deeper self" (CP 6.338)/I/Moi. However, when Peirce (CP 5.421), Mead (1934: 178), and Vygotsky (1981: 163) emphasise the essentiality of the *sociality* part, Tarasti stresses the value of the *Moi*, (deeper self/I/intrapsychological category). In other words, Tarasti proceeds from the "subjective" to social interaction. In contrast, the others come from sociality to the forming of subjectivity (if at all, it can be called *subjectivity*). The difference is important because it changes the perspective on how the individual acts in the Umwelt, how the thoughts can be shared between people, and how the notion of shared meanings and understanding and the creative actions originate[xii].[12] However, all of the thinkers emphasise the intertwined process or indivisible character of the two parts.

Tarasti visualised well the model on the subject or the individual interactions with the Umwelt or with the other individual (see Figure 1 and 2).

---

11 See also Tarasti's *Existential Semiotics* for the broader context of the issue (2000: 6–7).
12 The further discussion about the differences is not discussed in this paper, but for creative action and knowledge creation see Joas (1990 and 1996), Kilpinen (2000 and 2002), and Paavola and Hakkarainen (2005), respectively.

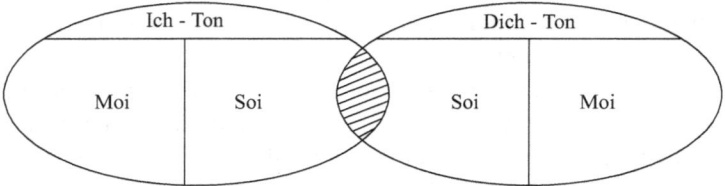

Figure 1: Two organisms are interacting through the *Soi*. According to Tarasti, only through the *Soi*, the *Ich – Ton* and the *Dich – Ton* can have a connection to each other. It is since only between the *Sois*, the communication proper is possible (Tarasti 2004: 96–97).

Tarasti's model could be seen as follows in the Peircean triadic perspective:

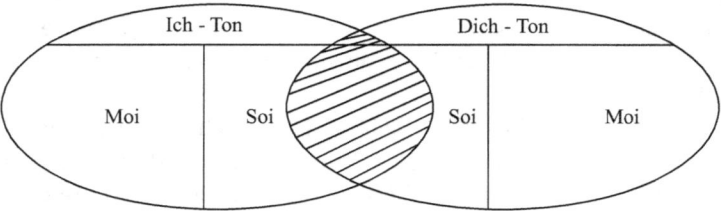

Figure 2: If the interaction is taken as semiosis then *Ich – Ton* and *Dich – Ton*, that is the semiotic selves, are also overlapping with the other organism and also with the *Umwelt*.

According to Peirce, the self is social and, more than that, it is a sign itself; thus, it is already in/part of the Umwelt; it is social or communal. Practically it is not possible to separate semiosis that goes on within the person between the two parts and that of going on between person and the Umwelt.

As Tarasti explains how the transcendental mediates the values, he is mainly concentrating on reflective thinking (Thirdness), using, for example, Greimasian modalities without the role of the emotions in the semiosis. Emotions, however, are an essential aspect when discussing the evolving of the semiotic self, or while interpreting mundane signs or looking at how certain signs can be interpreted in a shared manner. As mentioned above, the emotions (as Firstness) are an essential part of the reflective interpretations i.e., Thirdness. It can be concluded that Peirce, as well as Mead, does not separate the faculties of cognition, emotion, and conation of mind. Kilpinen describes that the emotion and reason are the two sides of the same coin.[13] If the inferential or reflective character of the dialogue is based on mental associations, growing from the sign-action, through relations of sign and

---

[13] Kilpinen is not alone in pointing out the part of emotions. For example, Daniel Goleman (1996) has emphasised the concept of emotional intelligence, a concept that has been eagerly

object(s), then it could be seen that the associations are determined by the objects some of which are emotions (cf: Kilpinen 2002: 6 and 9). It means that emotions lie in the essential ground (Proto Self) of evolving of both the semiotic self and the actions in/within the Umwelt. Mead's theory of mind may, therefore, converge in many ways with Peirce's theory of signs, especially regarding semiosis.

Both Peirce and Mead state that feelings and emotions belong to the "I" or the Firstness, but come into being through mediation. According to Peirce, the coming into being; to be a habit, occurs through Thirdness, through the triadic relations. According to Mead, the self becomes a self only when s/he can take the attitude of the other (Mead 1934: 171 and 256), namely when the "I" (the expressions, emotions) and the "Me" (the social aspect) fuse together (Mead 1934: 279). It occurs in the process of adaptation to the large or small social groups, in which the ever-changing semiotic self evolves (Mead 1934: 197 and 256). Peirce's phaneroscopic categories of Firstness, Secondness, and Thirdness are in some sense also explained by Mead. The "I" holds the feelings and emotions (Firstness) and can react to them. Nevertheless, without reasoning (Secondness), only when the actions within the Umwelt have appeared to the extent to enable the person to place him/herself "to the other persons shoes" (Thirdness), the semiotic self and the consciousness of the "I" will evolve.

Peirce has been more specific about semiosis – the phaneroscopic categories describe the different (but still indivisible) interpretants. On the level of Firstness, there is the Emotional Interpretant that mediates the feelings, emotions; on the level of Secondness, there is the Energic Interpretant that mediates the actual actions; and on the level of Thirdness, there is the Logical Interpretant that requires the intellectual appreciation and can cause a change of a habit (cf.: EP 2:209 cited from Bergman 1999: 45, CP 4.536 and CP 5.476). In Mead's terms, the self is capable of adaptation, or it can change the habits and some of the Umwelt

> as a man adjusts himself to a certain environment, he becomes a different individual; but in becoming a different individual he has affected the community in which he lives. [. . .] There is always a mutual relationship of the individual and the community in which the individual lives. (Mead 1934: 215)

The mutual relationship of the individual and the community gives room for the change of the attitudes and beliefs. Further, this may provide mutual change within the group on interpreting signs. To obtain a detailed view on semiosis, I shall next discuss semiosis from semiogenetic perspective that enables better to position the emotions and feeling of emotions into spiral-like semiosis.

---

adopted by the media. Ronald Sousa (1987) has given a somewhat different point of view in pointing to the rational aspect of emotions.

4 Semiosis

What happens in semiosis (in internalisation/externalisation[14])? The mediating signs enable the relationship of the individual and Umwelt (the other). There are two aspects in semiosis and the different Interpretants, namely the individual semiosis and the somewhat abstract social semiosis in a helix.

Internalisation holds two oscillating modes: the distancing and the being present (immediacy). The internalisation process reminds somewhat Damasio's explanation on the imagetic view of the continuous self.[15] In Internalisation as well as in Damasio's description, both movements, i.e., distancing and being present (immediacy), are affect-laden, thus bringing along emotions. Distancing enables comparing of diverse experiences of the person to the anticipated future and the here and now content. The process creates tension, which sets the potential reflection (Thirdness – Logical Interpretant, dialogue between Core Self and Autobiographical Self mediated by signs) into motion. This process of meaning-creations entails a constant change in the distancing and immediacy (cf.: Valsiner 1998: 118–119). It also enables symbols to grow in the persons' interpretation of the signs. According to the personal-cultural world, the person can be either open or closed (fixed and holding to the habits) for further developmental change. In other words, s/he can be open to new meaning-creation or discarding the possibilities to new/altering meaning-creation depending on the constraints of the person and the perceived affordances[16] of the signs in Umwelt.

Externalisation process includes all processes where ideas, thoughts, actions are shared with others or communicated with others, or projected towards others.

---

14 According to Valsiner's semiogenetic approach, the basis for internalisation/externalisation comes from Baldwin's (1894) aspect of sociogenesis of the self, Harré's (1970, 1980 and 1989) philosophical perspective on the self, Allport's (1938 and 1955) developmental interactionalist approach, and Mead's (1934 and 1938) pragmatic dynamism emphasising the subjective individual embedded in the social world, Vygotsky's (1978 and 1981), Leont'ev's (1978), Wertsch's (1981, 1985 and 1993) Activity Theoretical studies, and Bakhtin's (1981) discursive thinking.
15 "[. . .] the image of knowing (being aware of oneself) originates in the neural structures fundamentally associated with the representation of body states, the image of knowing is a feeling" (Parvizi and Damasio 2001: 139–140). The process of being aware of oneself creates the distancing from the feeling of the self and reflection on it.
16 The term "affordances" originates from James J. Gibson. It is employed extensively in the user interface design approaches (see Norman 1988 and McGrenere and Ho 2000), in pedagogical approaches, and distributed cognition (see Pea 1993 and Paavola and Hakkarainen 2005: 246). Affordances are the properties and features of things (or signs) themselves that direct how they can be interpreted and used.

The main point is the inner/outer tension without which there could not be any internalisation or externalisation.

If considering the different perspectives that can be taken along into the issue of sign mediated process in the irreversibility[17] of time (Bergson 1911a: 8–9; see Valsiner 1998: 179–181), it is possible to view the process from the perspectives of the society, individual, and signs. As mentioned before, the tension, between the past and future or the self and others (Umwelt), promotes the process.

Peirce describes it as insistency of ideas from past to the present, and from the present toward the future (See CP 5.289; and Paavola, Hakkarainen, and Sintonen 2006: 144). It is through signs since signs are the mediating vehicles, that personal past experiences can guide one's own and be shared with others and guide also other's future conducts. The semiosis of the self or the forming of the self exists in the continuous tension that time creates. In Valsiner words, "the imagery of the possible future – from most immediate to most distant – creates the contracting pull for the sense of the present. This tension is depicted by the two equilateral hyperbola, which create permanent tension at any present moment" (1998: 243) (see Figure 3).

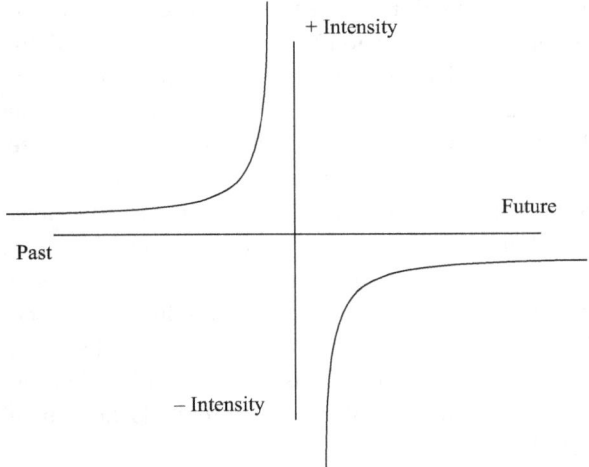

Figure 3: Peirce's description of the intensity of ideas from the past to present and from the present towards the future (Peirce 1935: 104 in Valsiner 1998: 243).

---

17 Valsiner describes Bergson's notion of the irreversibility of time as "If the notion of irreversibility of time in development is taken seriously, no feed*back* processes are theoretically possible, and all information that is 'fed back' (in the manner of speaking) is actually 'fed forward' so as to be functional in the *new present* state in which the (already further changed) organism encounters a novel environment" (Valsiner 1998: 28–29, emphasis in the original).

Tension provides a space for the potential altering of the meaning of the signs or new signs to be created. Tension can arrive from different social suggestions from Umwelt or sense of the self and others, both of which are about the feeling of time, feeling of emotions, and to the feeling of a continuous self.

This process of meaning-making reminds Tarasti's idea of pre-signs (Tarasti 2000: 33) since the meaning arrives from an emerging feeling, which is not nameable yet, but is still affected by the previous experiences, namely "Feeling which has not yet emerged into immediate consciousness is already affected" (Valsiner 1998: 244). Furthermore, the future is suggested by or rather is influenced by the suggestions of the past (See Peirce, 1935: 104–105; 6.142). Misztal has well mentioned "[. . .] present influences the past" (2003: 14), and also Moss and Damasio have described how the specificity of experiences creates a collection of memory stores and modes of recall that are unique to each individual and that *change according to the context* (Moss and Damasio 2001: 99).

Emotional states of oneself and the constraints affect more or less profoundly of what is selected and what is not and in what perspective the issues are perceived. The flow guarantees the continuously active novelty of semiotic processes. Thus, the sign could not be something repetitive – each time it is taken up, it appears in a new act of semiosis (See Ponzio 1985: 16). In other words, there is a continuous cyclic process that is striven by the tension of the time in particular situations. It does not mean that the person necessarily would adapt to the present or the anticipated future but that it creates novel possibilities of future existence. The spiral (Figure 4) represents how the space arising from the tension of the time can give rise to the helix-like semiosis. The push to construct new semiotic solutions/loops to/on "top" the experienced events can arrive from different social suggestions from Umwelt or due to the sense of the self and others or by specific unexpected events that occur in the course of the ritualistic organised activities (habituated activities). If ritualistic activities are taken as the Peircean habits (beliefs), a collision might arise when the habits/beliefs are placed under doubt. The collision might promote certain kind of opposition towards the change (the wish to keep the status quo).

For example, the unexpected event in present or in the imagery future can question the current habits. According to Damasio, the process inevitably involves emotions, feeling of emotions (namely Firstness and Secondness involved in Thirdness). The feeling of emotions could be, for instance, irritation (Emotional Interpretant) towards the necessity to reflect on one's habits and beliefs. The challenge of questioning one's belief (Peirce's Critical Self) can promote a novelty in creating new signs (new habits, beliefs). The signs mediate the dialogue process between the selves and Umwelt that is a loop in the semiosic spiral. The tension of time between past and future can act, as well, as space where embodied signs/

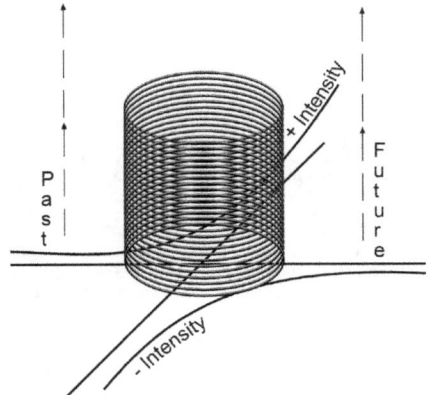

Figure 4: The spiral of semiosis rising from the pull or tension.

Firstness/Emotional Interpretant has an apparent role. In the present situation, the embodied knowledge promotes clues for the anticipated or imagery future and is "the knowledge" needed for creating novel idea or activities for present and future.

Considering Damasio's statements of the emotion's role in decision-making and learning, it seems probable that in the cases of intensive tension between the past and imagery future the Emotional Interpretant becomes the dominant one. Maybe, promoting not so favourable Energetic Interpretants that could end up into a habit change after intellectual appreciation (Logical Interpretant). The constant circular process unites humans with their Umwelt, which means that both the external and the internal dialogues occur and feed to each other by semiotic mediation. By this intertwined (independent dependant) process, the signs gain new meanings but as well get created and cease to be interpreted. This kind of unity consistently produces diversity at the level of activity in the construction of signs (cf.: Valsiner 1998: 281). The double helix can be examined from different aspects, i.e., from the individual, societal, and sign evolvement. However, when one aspect is emphasised; the particular aspect never occurs alone (independently of the others).

In the next section, I shall present a small hypothetical case on possible semiosis where resistance plays a part.

5 Resistance in semiosis

I shall discuss the spiral-like semiosis, which places the resistance into the process (Figure 5) through a hypothetical scenario.

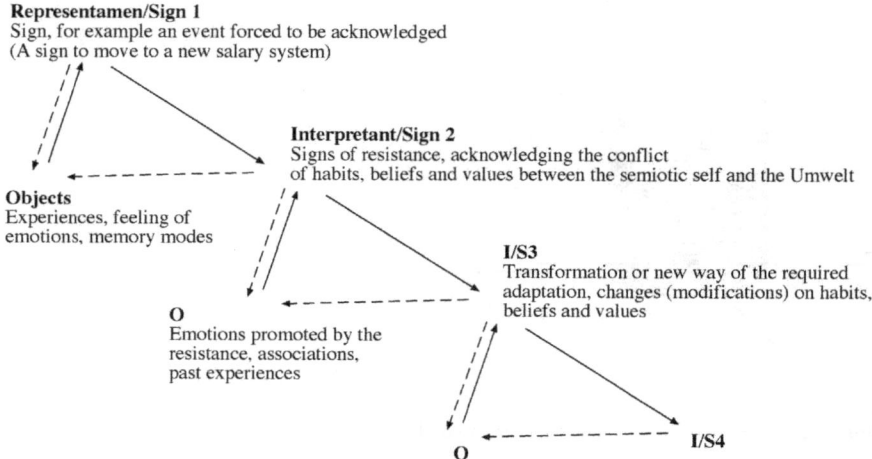

Figure 5: The chain of semiosis and the "continuous becoming".

In the first round of semiosis (the top see Figure 5), a sign could be an event, even a forced event, for example, an announcement to move to a new salary system. The sign can have different objects, but one object could dominate through the previous experiences and memory modes. This object could be an emotional state, which happens to be irritation, an overall negative feeling (Secondness through Firstness). The mind of the Interpretant goes on with its dialogue between the Core Self and the Autobiographical Self (Moi/Soi), but it cannot distinguish what the bodymind indicates. Thus, the outcome is an emotional meaning,[18] which can lead to the logical meaning (Thirdness); a resistance – reflecting the negative emotional state. Thus, generalising this particular event-sign to cover all related signs. The first round has proceeded already beyond the mere comparing of the past experiences and memory modes. However, many "weaker possibilities" reminded ignored due to the inability to take into account the bodymind.

---

[18] In Peirce's later writings, he frequently connected meaning with the Interpretant (see for example PPM 86 [1903]; MS 318:19/163b, MS 318:15/170b [1907], cited from Bergman 2004: 393). Peirce mentions in these writing three nuances on meaning such as the emotional, existential, and logical. The emotional meaning is a mere recognition of the sign, which is associated with the possibility to use the sign adequately (cf.: EP 2:256 [1903], EP 2:496 [1909]). The existential meaning can be as the actual event or thing. The sign gets its value by the position it occupies within the other signs with the other signs. The logical meaning is associated with the results that arrive from a particular process of semiosis. The logical meaning arrives when the ultimate logical Interpretant has managed to put an end to a particular process of semiosis.

The new round could involve the signs (Sign 2) of resistance, their objects being idealised modified memories (to fit the context) of gallant resistant figures in history known to the mind of the Interpretant. The mind of the Interpretant could then arrive at signs (Sign 3) of action of this generalised, idealised resistance. Therefore, being able to justify the conflict between certain habits, beliefs, and values that exist between the semiotic self and the Umwelt without pondering a possible alternation of semiotic self or Umwelt or both. On the other hand, it might be that the "first" emotional state is the resistance towards unpleasant event-sign. Thereupon, through the self-controlled reflection acknowledging the bodymind "signs", one creates new creative-associative-combinations of the possibly required actions and outcomes of the event-sign.

Resistance and comparing the memory modes and previous experiences belong, thus, to both hypothetical speculations. However, the other ignores the bodymind (even though the memory modes and experiences could be extensive). In the other case, one faces the conflict of the habits, beliefs, and values and takes into consideration the bodymind. Hence, forming something new, which might even be better than what the event-sign from Umwelt proposed. To judge the goodness or badness would need another article. Consequently, it is not tackled here.

As shown above, the feeling of emotions is in the basis of cognition and on forming of semiotic self. Thus, values are also related to primary and secondary emotional states. Some of the secondary emotional states are acquired in the interdependent intertwined interaction of the semiotic self within Umwelt and developed by self-control. It is a complex process involving the changing of the self as the changing of the memories, beliefs, and sometimes also values. This spiral-like semiosis includes the resistance towards some of the changes, especially if they would require transforming of the belief and values. The resistance and doubt are a necessary outcome if in any serious reflection. Therefore, Tarasti's movement – upstream – is one part of the spiral-like movement of the semiosis. However, it would bring a more holistic picture to the self-controlled reflection of the semiotic self to acknowledge the part that feeling of emotions plays in the process.

As Peirce has stated and Damasio proved in practice that feeling of emotions and emotions belong to the "Deeper Self" or the Firstness, but come into being through mediation. According to Peirce, the coming into being; occurs through Thirdness, through the triadic relations. The 'Core Self' holds the feelings of emotions and can react to them. Howbeit, without reasoning (Secondness through Firstness), only when the actions within the Umwelt have appeared to the extent to enable the person to place him/herself "to the other persons shoes" (Thirdness), the semiotic self will evolve.

6 Reflections

All the different approaches presented above have one element in common, which is the mediating nature of signs in a dynamic process, but the perspectives into the process differ. On the one hand, theories are taking the aspect of society counter to the aspects of an individual. The emphasis on only one aspect brings along the notion of dualism that Valsiner argued against by stating that the parts are independently dependent. Peirce, Mead, and Damasio emphasise the intertwined nature of the parts, although, Peirce's theory of signs is more general theory and not only about individual persons and society. While Damasio's neuroscientific investigation on emotions concentrates on humans and their relations to the environment on the forming of the self. Tarasti's existential semiotics has given a foundation from which it has been possible to adopt a more thorough insight into the question of individual and signs in the process. The attempt in this paper was to find the affinities and see if the similarities allow a holistic view of the spiral (helix) like process, which would enable to take into account or at least keep in mind the other parts while investigating a particular event or interest area.

I have described that the individual is already social. Thus, the gap between the group and the individual in a certain sense disappears. Especially, it is evident if the views of Peirce, Mead, and Vygotsky are considered: namely, they argue that the social self (Me, Soi, Interpsychological) keeps on forming the deeper self (I, Moi, Intrapsychological). Therefore, in every action, the semiotic self already belongs to Umwelt. The semiosis proves that even our perception, namely, how we select signs and perceive the Umwelt, is already a result of semiosis in the same intertwined and joint way. Damasio's neuroscientific approach explains the same idea in the form of emotions and feeling of emotions. The spiral-like semiosic process allows to create, understand, take into practise and spread the ideas and beliefs that the community has agreed upon. In Tarasti's approach, the spiral-like semiosic process would enable us to acquire the transcendental values (Tarasti 2000). In Peirce's words, "[. . .] ideas tend to spread continuously and to affect others which stand to them in a peculiar relation of affectability [. . .] in this spreading they lose intensity, and especially the power of affecting others, but gain generality, and become welded with other ideas" (CP 6.104).

References

Allport, Gordon W. 1938. *Personality: A Psychological Interpretation*. London: Constable.
Allport, Gordon W. 1955. *Becoming: Basic Considerations For a Psychology of Personality*. New Haven.
Augoustinos, Martha & Walker, Iain. 1995. *Social Cognition, an Integrated Introduction*. London: Sage Publications.
Bakhtin, Mikhail Mikhailovich. 1981. *The Dialogic Imagination. Four Essays*. Michael Holquist (ed.). Austin and London: University of Texas Press.
Baldwin, James Mark. 1894. Personality-suggestion. *Psychological Review* (1). 274–279.
Bergman, Mats. 1999. *Meaning and Mediation: Critical Reflections on Peirce and Communication Theory*. Helsinki: Helsingin Yliopisto.
Bergman, Mats. 2004. *Fields of Signification, Explorations in Charles S. Peirce's Theory of Sign*. (Philosophical Studies from the University of Helsinki). Helsinki: Helsingin yliopisto, filosofian laitos.
Bernstein, Richard. 1965. Action, Conduct, and Self-control. In R. Bernstein (ed.), *Perspectives on Peirce: Critical Essays on Charles Sanders Peirce*, 66–91. New Haven and London: Yale University Press.
Bourdieu, Pierre. 2000. *Pascalian Meditations*. Trans. by Nice Richard. Cambridge: Polity Press.
Colapietro, Vincent Michael. 1989. *Peirce's Approach to the Self, A Semiotic Perspective on Human Subjectivity*. Albany: State University of New York Press.
Damasio Antonio R. 1994. *Descartes' Error: Emotion, Reason and the Human Brain*. New York: Grosset / Putnam.
Damasio Antonio R. 1999. *The Feeling of What Happens: Body and Emotion in the Making of Consciousness*. New York: Harcourt Brace.
Damasio Antonio R. 2001. Emotion and the Human Brain. *Annals of the New York Academy of Sciences* 935. 101–106.
Damasio Antonio R. 2002. Remembering When. *Scientific American* 287(3). 66–73.
Damasio Antonio R. 2003. Feeling of Emotion and the Self. *Annals New York Academy of Sciences* 1001. 253–261.
Damasio Antonio R. (2003a). Virtue in Mind. *New Scientist* 180(2420). 48–51.
Deely, John N. 2001. A sign is What? *Sign Systems Studies* 29 (2). 705–743.
Deely, John N. 2001a. *Four Ages of Understanding: the First Postmodern Survey of Philosophy from Ancient Times to the Turn of the Twenty-first Century*. Toronto: University of Toronto Press.
Gardner, Howard. 1983. *Frames of Mind: The Theory of Multiple Intelligences*. New York: HarperCollins
Gardner, Howard. 1987. *The Mind's New Science: A History of the Cognitive Revolution*. New York: Basic Books
Gibson, James J. 1986. *The Ecological Approach to Visual Perception*. London: L. Erlenbaum.
Goleman, Daniel. 1996. *Emotional Intelligence: Why It Can Matter More than IQ*. London: Bloomsbury Publishing Co.
Harré, Rom. 1970. *The Principles of Scientific Thinking*. London: Macmillan.
Harré, Rom. 1980. Making Soscialpsychology Scientific. In Robin Gilmour & Steve Duck (eds.), *The Development of Social Psychology*, 27–51. London: Academic Press.
Harré, Rom. 1989. Language Games and Text of Identity. In J. Shotter & K. Gergen (eds.), *Texts of Identity*, 20–35. London: Sage.

James, William. 1983 [1890]. *The Principles of Psychology*. Cambridge Massachusetts: Harvard University Press.
James, William. 1902. *The Varieties of Religious Experience: A Study in Human Nature*. London and New York: Longmans, Green and Co.
Joas, Hans. 1990. The Creativity of Action and the Intersubjectivity of Reason: Mead's Pragmatism and Social Theory. *Transactions of the Charles S. Peirce Society* 26 (2). 165–194.
Joas, Hans. 1996. *The Creativity of Action*. Cambridge: Polity Press.
Kilpinen, Erkki. 2000. *The Enormous Fly-wheel of Society: Pragmatism's Habitual Conception of Action and Social Theory*. University of Helsinki, Department of Sociology.
Kilpinen, Erkki. 2002. A Neglected Classic Vindicated: The Place of George Herbert Mead in the General Tradition of Semiotics. *Semiotica* 142 (4). 1–30.
Kilpinen, Erkki. 2002a. Joas, Bourdieu, Taylor. *Acta Sociologica* 45 (1). 57.
Leont'ev, Alexei N. 1978. *Activity, Consciousness, and Personality*. Englewood Cliffs: Prentice Hall.
McGrenere, Joanna & Ho Wayne. 2000. Affordances: Clarifying and Evolving a Concept. *Proceedings of Graphic Interfaces 2000*, 179–186. Available: http://www.cs.ubc.ca/~joanna/#Publications (last retrieved: 02.02.2007)
Mead, George Herbert. 1934. *Mind, Self, and Society, from the Standpoint of a Social Behaviorist*. Ed. by C.V. Morris. Chicago: University of Chicago Press.
Mead, George Herbert. 1938. *The Philosophy of the Act*. Morris C.W. et al (ed.). Chicago: University of Chicago Press.
Merrell, Floyd. 2003. *Sensing Corporeally: Toward a Posthuman Understanding*. Toronto: University of Toronto Press.
Misztal, Barbara A. 2003. *Theories of Social Remembering*. Maidenhead, Philadelphia: Open University Press.
Moss, Henry & Damasio Antonio R. 2001. Introduction to Part III: Emotion, Cognition, and the Human Brain. *Annals of the New York Academy of Sciences* (935). 98–100.
Norman Donald A. 1988. *The psychology of everyday things*. Basic Books. Proceedings of the Computer-supported Collaborative Learning 2002 Conference, Erlbaum: Hillsdale.
Paavola, Sami. 2004. Abduction as a Logic and Methodology of Discovery: The Important of Strategies. *Foundation of Science* 9 (3). 267–283.
Paavola, Sami. 2004a. Abduction Through Grammar, Critic, and Methodeutic. *Transactions of the Charles S. Peirce Society: A Quarterly Journal in American Philosophy* 40 (2). 245–270.
Paavola, Sami. 2005. Peircean Abduction: Instinct of Inference? *Semiotica* 153 (4). 131–154.
Paavola, Sami & Kai Hakkarainen. 2005. Three Abductive Solutions to the Meno Paradox – with Instinct, Inference, and Distributed Cognition. *Studies in Philosophy and Education* 24. 235–253.
Paavola, Sami, Kai Hakkarainen & Matti Sintonen. (2006). Abduction with Dialogical and Trialogical Means. *Logic Journal of the IGPL* 14(2). 137–150.
Parvizi, Josef & Antonio Damasio. 2001. Consciousness and the Brainstem. *Cognition* 79. 135–159.
Pea, Roy D. 1993. Practices of Distributed Intelligence and Designs for Education. In G. Salomon (ed.) *Distributed Cognitions: Psychological and Educational Considerations*, 47–87. Cambridge: Cambridge University Press.
Peirce, Charles Sanders. 1931–1958. *Collected Papers*. Vols. 1–6 ed. by C. Hartshorne & P. Weiss, Vols. 7–8 ed. by A. Burks. Cambridge, Massachusetts: Harvard University Press.

Peirce, Charles Sanders. 1977. *Semiotics and Significs: the Correspondence Between Charles S. Peirce and Victoria Lady Welby*. Ed. by Charles S. Hardwick with the assistance of Cook James. Bloomington: Indiana University Press.

Peirce, Charles Sanders. 1992–8. *The Essential Peirce: Selected Philosophical Writings*., Vol. 1 ed. by Nathan Houser and Christian J. W. Kloesel, Vol. 2 ed. by the Peirce Edition Project. Bloomington and Indianapolis: Indiana University Press.

Ponzio, Augusto. 1985. Semiotics between Peirce and Bakhtin. *Kodikas* (8). 11–28.

Sousa, Ronald. 1987. *The Rationality of Emotion*. Cambridge MA and London, England: MIT Press.

Tarasti, Eero. 2000. *Existential Semiotics*. Bloomington: Indiana University Press.

Tarasti, Eero. 2004. Valta ja subjektin teoria [Power and the theory of subject]. *Synteesi* (4). 84–102.

Tarasti, Eero. 2005. Vastarinnan semiotiikkaa [The semiotics of Resistance]. *Synteesi* (1). 2–29.

Valsiner, Jaan. 1998. *The Guided Mind: A Sociogenetic Approach to Personality*. Cambridge, Massachusetts, and London: Harvard University Press.

Vygotsky, Lev. 1978. *Mind in Society: The Development of Higher Psychological Processes*. Cambridge Mass: Harvard University Press.

Vygotsky, Lev. 1981. The Genesis of Higher Mental Functions. In J. Wertsch (ed.) *The Concept of Activity in Soviet Psychology*, 144–188. Armonk York: Sharpe.

Wertsch, James V. (ed.) (1981). *The Concept of Activity in Soviet Psychology*. Armonk, N. Y.: Sharpe.

Wertsch, James V. (1985). The Semiotic Mediation of Mental Life: L. S. Vygotsky & M. M Bakhtin. In Elizabeth Mertz & Richard J. Parmentier (eds.), *Semiotic Mediation, Sociocultural and Psychological Perspectives*, 49–71. London: Academic Press.

Wertsch, James V. 1993. *Voices of the Mind: A Sociocultural Approach to Mediated Action*. Cambridge, MA: Harvard University Press.

Sayantan Dasgupta
The Plane of Dasein. Existential Semiotics and the problem of the medium

Abstract: Existential Semiotics and its attempt to show the state of signs before they existed do not halt its enquiry in understanding those signs only. *Dasein* and Transcendence, two of the most important terms in Existential Semiotics, carry the ethos of existence and abundance. Eero Tarasti wrote, "*Dasein*... does not refer only to one subject, Me, but also to Others and likewise to the objects that we desire." (Tarasti, 2015) Therefore there is a movement in *Dasein* which is both unique and social. Transcendence, in all this, cannot be said to remain idle, as Tarasti wrote, "Transcendent is anything that is absent but present in our minds." (Tarasti, 2000) The question is how do Transcendence and *Dasein* connect and synchronize? In this study, I shall be looking to find a connector that does not necessarily validate the rejection or acceptance of Transcendence in any particular approach. If we consider the connector to be a medium, avoiding presumptuous acknowledgment, we can say that this medium is something that is not a concretely built presence, but its existence can only be validated by decoding the activities of *Dasein* and Transcendence. Therefore, the working of this medium-connector can be divided into two parts. The first part denotes the journey from the internal of *Dasein* to the way to the external. The second part portrays the connection from the external periphery of *Dasein* to Transcendence. In this study, I shall be exploring the first part of the connection; the activities inside *Dasein*, the internal and how it reaches the external.

Keywords: Existential Semiotics, Eero Tarasti, The Plane of *Dasein*, *Dasein*, Transcendence, Zemic, Plato, Kant, Hegel, Kierkegaard, Deleuze, Guattari, Kant, Lacan

Introduction

Eero Tarasti concluded his paper, *Existential Semiotics and Cultural Psychology*, by saying, "I believe the avenues opening from existential semiotics may lead not only the semiotic theory to new configurations but also change our basic understanding of mind and culture leading perhaps into new discoveries." Existential Semiotics and its attempt to show the state of signs before they existed do not halt its enquiry in understanding those signs only. *Dasein* and Transcendence, two of the most important terms in Existential Semiotics, carry the ethos of existence

https://doi.org/10.1515/9783110789164-019

and abundance. Eero Tarasti wrote, "*Dasein*... does not refer only to one subject, Me, but also to Others and likewise to the objects that we desire." Therefore there is a movement in *Dasein* which is both unique and social. Transcendence, in all this, cannot be said to remain idle, as Tarasti wrote, "Transcendent is anything that is absent but present in our minds." The question is how do Transcendence and *Dasein* connect and synchronize? Materialism denies the presence of Transcendence as a realm, whereas, in religious studies, Transcendence becomes a divine power that is independent of the material universe and it is not affected by the laws that play a part on living beings. In this study, I shall be looking to find a connector that does not necessarily validate any of the two ways just mentioned. If we consider the connector to be a medium, avoiding presumptuous acknowledgement, we can say that this medium is something that is not a concretely built presence, but its existence can only be validated by decoding the activities of *Dasein* and Transcendence. Therefore, the working of this medium-connector can be divided into two parts. The first part denotes the journey from the internal of *Dasein* to the way to the external. The second part portrays the connection from the external border of *Dasein* to Transcendence. In this study, I shall be exploring the first part of the connection; the activities inside *Dasein*, the internal and how it reaches the external.

1 Kant's Critique, Plato's theory of form and the medium

A medium is something that connects things in a manner that sometimes make the medium not easy to discern. The connection between Transcendence and *Dasein* is one of real importance. According to Eero Tarasti, "In the existential semiotics, the life of signs is situated in their movement and traffic between transcendence and *Dasein*." The medium through which *Dasein* and Transcendence remain connected could be understood in various manners, but to be sure which one of it is accurate is the real question.

One may follow Karl Marx but refuse to follow any Marxist. One may believe in God but refuse to follow any religion. What does a scenario like that signify? A Marxist or a person of high status in a religious institution could be considered to be a medium through which a person tries to get connected to the 'Real' (eg. Marx, God etc.). But the scenarios mentioned above can be said to be a result of a broken or inadequate medium.

Immanuel Kant writes, in *Critique of Pure Reason*, "The nominal definition of truth, namely that it is the agreement of cognition with its object, is here granted and presupposed". If we consider Marx or God to be the Truth that one seeks to know, then the perception of that Truth depends on the person who is reaching towards the Truth. For a person who is trying to follow Marx long after Marx died has to rely on either Marx's writings alone or the interpretation of his writings by other Marxists. So the other Marxists become a medium between Marx and the person interested in Marxism. What if the Marxist does not seem to satisfy the criteria and the person decides to overlook him/her and start reading and understanding/interpreting Marx himself/herself. Here, the medium, the Marxist, breaks down.

The question of God is a bit different in this sense as a person who decides to unfollow every single religion would have a concept of God that is unique. However, a person may decide to follow a God belong to some religion but still refuse to follow religious preachers. In both the cases, the medium breaks down and the person tries to connect directly to God. (Here, the question could arise of the importance of zemic model as an example that there is already a medium that connects *Dasein* and Transcendence. But, I shall not explore that part as I intend to try to understand the problem of the medium through more "worldly" analogies).

In both cases, the Truth, as described by Kant, becomes what has an agreement with cognition. Out of this agreement arises relative truth. Now, if we consider Plato's theory of Form, we will see that the Truth and the Truthseeker has a gulf between them that he/she may not be aware of. There is a "distinction between the intelligible and the visible. The Forms or essences are now understood to be real intelligible objects, known by the intellect, and are complete, perfect, whole, unchanging n and prior to the mutable, that is, ever-changing, imperfect, particular, 'sensible' objects apprehended through sight, touch, and so on." (Harrison-Barbet) So, keeping in mind both Kant and Plato, the Truth could be intelligible through cognition. But its relative presence makes it impossible to solve the connection. A Marxist or a religious preacher both need a medium themselves to get connected, but it's the cognitive agreement and relative arrival at Truth that disrupt the process. Kant again wrote, "Truth, it is said, consists in the agreement of cognition with its object. In consequence of this mere nominal definition, my cognition, to count as true, is supposed to agree with its object. Now I can compare the object with my cognition, however, only by cognizing it. Hence my cognition is supposed to confirm itself, which is far short of being sufficient for truth. For since the object is outside me, the cognition in me, all I can ever pass judgement on is whether my cognition of the object agrees with my cognition of the object." (Kant: 2019)

We, as beings, try to reach the relative even though we believe that we are reaching the Absolute. It happens because we try to come in an agreement between the object and cognition. Hegel, in *Phenomenology of Spirit*, wrote, "Truth is its own self-movement." The movement of thesis-anti-thesis-synthesis is a movement towards a higher truth. But in Hegelian philosophy, the idea of Truth is a bit different from Kantian philosophy. For Hegel, Truth is a self-moving object that is external to inner subjective thoughts. The steps of thesis-anti-thesis-synthesis take us to a higher truth, but, in Existential Semiotics, the happenings inside a zemic model represent the influence of external or internal in creating it. So, if the truth is external and self-moving, we still cannot say that it is not connected to internal. If that was so, then we would remain ignorant of the Truth. We are not ignorant, we are searching for a medium to connect to it. More precisely, we are trying to understand the medium that made us aware of the Truth. The presence of Transcendence as a self-sufficient existence has its internal presence in us in a relative manner. There is a two-way system; one from Transcendence to *Dasein* and the second from *Dasein* to Transcendence. If we consider Transcendence as an able presence that knows how to connect to *Dasein*, the question closer to us is the failure of *Dasein* to do the same (or it is ignorant of the process). So, keeping in mind both Hegel and Existential Semiotics, our movement towards a higher truth is actually a movement inside the zemic to understand the right and wrong of happenings inside our *Dasein*. Through these movements, the higher truth that we could achieve, according to me, is the complete understanding of the internal. This is the first and most important step. The internal which is separate but (supposedly) not unknown to the external (Transcendence) already has the connection established from one side (from Transcendence). Once we get to know the internal in the truest manner, it will reveal to us the exact way in which we should proceed to know how Transcendence reaches us.

The problem of the medium is a problem of revelation. If the truth that we reach is a relative one and our cognition finds truth through an agreement with the object, then we are not going beyond the internal. The Truth is beyond the Internal and to understand that it is necessary to perceive the internal completely and then explore the external. An unperceived internal would mislead the process of understanding Transcendence and lead us to a relative or partial truth.

2 Kierkegaard, 'absolute paradox', and the Plane of *Dasein*

Søren Kierkegaard, in his *Philosophical Fragments*, wrote, "Just to come to know that the god is the different, man needs the god and then comes to know that the god is absolutely different from him. But if the god is to be absolutely different from a human being, this can have its basis not in that which man owes to the god (for to that extent they are akin) but in that which he owes to himself or in that which he himself has committed. What, then, is the difference? Indeed, what else but sin, since the difference, the absolute difference, must have been caused by the individual himself. . . .. Only the god could teach it – if he wanted to be teacher." I would like to explore the question of the medium in Existential Semiotics through this idea. If we consider Transcendence to be as powerful as Kierkegaardian god, then we must say that the way transcendence is known to us is through our failure to understand or recognize or acknowledge it. That failure could be equivalent to sin ('sin' as described by Kierkegaard) in the sense that it is our existential choice to do so. So, we are doing it. Our failure forces us to go in the wrong direction. Transcendence becomes known to us through our failure to understand it.

This 'absolute paradox' in Existential Semiotics leads to the question of the credibility of Transcendence as a realm of all and everything. If Transcendence is that absolute which provides us with all that is there, then the question of the existence of paradoxical things also arises. Can't we then say that Transcendence does not have an existential choice of its own, which we have? If that is so then it is the existential choice that is making things known/not known to us.

> Transcendence – A realm of all without any discrimination.

> Dasein – A realm of distinction where not always the 'truth' but the chosen option survives.

To continue the last excerpt from Kierkegaard, "But this he did indeed want to be. . . and in order to be that he wanted to be on the basis of equality with the single individual so that he could completely understand him. Thus the paradox becomes even more terrible, or the same paradox has the duplexity by which it manifests itself as the absolute – negatively, by bringing into prominence the absolute difference of sin and, positively, by wanting to annul this absolute difference in the absolute equality."

So, our failure to grasp the medium also has the touch of grave paradox in it. On one hand, it enables us with the assurance that it is we who choose and Transcendence provides. There is no question of transcendental compulsion. On the other hand, it takes us away from the Transcendence and the medium that connects it by the presence of the question of existential choice.

If Transcendence becomes 'equal' with us by the presence of existential choice, then, by existential choice, it is also coming down from all to not-all, which means, to quote Kierkegaard, "absolute difference in the absolute equality." So, this 'effort' has its counterintuition.

Now, is there a way out of it? Kierkegaard wrote, "But is a paradox such as this conceivable? We shall not be in a hurry; whenever the contention is over a reply to a question and the contending is not like that on the race track, it is not speed that wins but correctness. The understanding certainly cannot think it, cannot hit upon it on its own, and if it is proclaimed, the understanding cannot understand it and merely detects that it will likely be its downfall. To that extent, the understanding has strong objections to it; and yet, on the other hand, in its paradoxical passion the understanding does indeed will its own downfall. But the paradox, too, wills this downfall of the understanding, and thus the two have a mutual understanding, but this understanding is present only in the moment of passion."

The zemic could become a vital instrument here. Whatever a zemic outcome is what if we reverse that outcome and judge from the point of view of "the passion of thought"? If a zemic model is an example of existential choice, then we should try to find the zemic model that deals not with our existential choice. One may question that the negation of one existential choice is itself another existential choice. But we must keep in mind that our existential choice is also something that goes in accordance with Transcendence; Transcendence is not in conflict with it, but the argument is to break the paradox between them. The solution could be with finding the Plane of *Dasein* negating the one with an existential choice.

The Plane of *Dasein* – The zemic that is present beyond an existential choice but not beyond *Dasein*. The zemic that reflects Transcendence beyond paradoxes.

The zemic with an existential choice wants to deny Transcendence's absoluteness. But with denying, zemic with an existential choice actually follows what comes from Transcendence in order to find equality. The Plane of *Dasein* is that model that presents Transcendence in all its glory. It cannot stay alone. Its existence is also paradoxical. It hides behind zemics with an existential choice. It is there because of zemics with an existential choice. So, negating the zemic with an existential choice until it reaches the point of a zemic which is without "passion" or beyond our choice or beyond our denial of choice in choosing but not beyond *Dasein* is the point which could be of a vital breakthrough.

3 Deleuze, Guattari, and the concept of body without organs

The idea of the Plane of *Dasein* is a topic that needs some exploration. As I said before negating the zemic with an existential choice until it reaches the point of zemic which is without "passion" or beyond our choice or beyond our denial of choice in choosing but not beyond *Dasein* is the point which could lead us to the Plane of *Dasein*. So, this plane is a place which is not possible to reach if our choice is based on what suits us. This realm is present beyond this selection process and, though, it is the prime spot for *Dasein*, it is not beyond Transcendence.

Gilles Deleuze used the concept Body without Organs (BwO) in his *The Logic of Sense* (1969), *Capitalism and Schizophrenia: Anti-Oedipus* (1972) and *A Thousand Plateaus* (1980)]. Although Deleuze's ideas have much more to do with materialism, here I intend to use the concept not to break the stable structure of Existential Semiotics, but to utilize some of the themes to solidify Existential Semiotics. Gilles Deleuze and Félix Guattari wrote, in *Capitalism and Schizophrenia*, "The body without organs is an egg: it is crisscrossed with axes and thresholds, with latitudes and longitudes and geodesic lines, traversed by gradients marking the transitions and the becomings, the destinations of the subject developing along these particular vectors." The Plane of *Dasein* is where the potentialities of a particular *Dasein* lie. Transcendence being a realm of all carries all the possibilities that are there. The Plane of *Dasein* tells an individual about his/her potentialities. Every game has its own rules, but that does not mean there cannot be other games and other rules. All the rules can be called rules related to different games. But not all rules can be applied to a single game. The Plane of *Dasein* holds the possibilities but it is very much different from Deleuze's concept of Plane of Immanence. Deleuze's Immanence denied Transcendence. "It is only when immanence is no longer immanence to anything other than itself that we can speak of a plane of immanence." (Deleuze 2001) But here the Plane of *Dasein* signifies the realm that captures all the possibilities of the *Dasein* (not all the possibilities that are there in the whole world, but the possibilities that are there for an individual). This Plane of *Dasein* has direct contact with Transcendence, whereas the zemics with existential choice absorb from the Plane of *Dasein* what it chooses. Deleuze and Guattari, in *A Thousand Plateaus*, wrote, "Here, there are no longer any forms or developments of forms; nor are there subjects or the formation of subjects. There is no structure, any more than there is genesis." So, they eliminate Transcendence altogether. The Plane of *Dasein* consists of possibilities that are products of Transcendence.

> Transcendence – All the possibilities that are available for all the individuals.
>
> The Plane of *Dasein* – All the possibilities that are available for an individual.
>
> Zemic with an existential choice – All the possibilities that are chosen by an individual.

Now, the way to reach this Plane of *Dasein* has some particular ways to follow. Deleuze and Guattari, in *A Thousand Plateaus*, wrote, "This is how it should be done. Lodge yourself on a stratum, experiment with the opportunities it offers, find an advantageous place on it, find potential movements of deterritorialization, possible lines of flight, experience them, produce flow conjunctions here and there, try out continua of intensities segment by segment, have a small plot of new land at all times. It is through a meticulous relation with the strata that one succeeds in freeing lines of flight, causing conjugated flows to pass and escape and bringing forth continuous intensities for a BwO."

Our attempt to experiment with possibilities that we would not have thought about otherwise takes us closer to the Plane of *Dasein*. These attempts would help us in understanding not just the exact reason behind its rejection in the first place, but whether our choices were correct or not. This is important. Our choices take us closer to what we want, but our rejection takes us closer to what are potentially other people's choices (but not necessarily mine). Therefore, when we try out those possibilities we are being one with the whole world. This is what Deleuze calls "becomings". In Existential Semiotics, it is that phase which takes us closer to the Plane of *Dasein*. But, in Existential Semiotics, it does not stop there. There is Transcendence beyond that. By doing so, the individual would not distort his/her being. He/she would be able to validate what is taken forward and left behind. The fear of experimentation or the fear of knowing the unknown would be eradicated and this is the stage that is much closer to the Plane of *Dasein*. The potentialities would connect the individual with the rest of the Plane of *Dasein*. Zemic with an existential choice is somewhat impossible to ignore as that is the basis of *Dasein*. The reaching process is not to disturb the ongoing ways of the world. This process will be useful in understanding the connection between Transcendence and *Dasein*.

The Plane of *Dasein*, for an individual, is a realm that would lead to overcoming whatever bothers. Once the Plane of *Dasein* is known, the possibilities would not be possibilities in the literal meaning of the word but become experimentations. By 'knowing' we would know what life is on the surface that we choose and also on other surfaces that remain within our reach. That is why the 'known' *Dasein* (with possibilities, potentialities becoming experimentations and experiences) would solve the mystery on the part of the individual. The next step would be to find a pattern through which Transcendence delivers (or we 'choose') what would be our potentialities. Our possibilities are beyond our chosen experience, but not beyond our reach. The next step is to try to know what is beyond *Dasein*.

4 Hegelian logic, Being-Essence-Notion, and the zemic model

Kant, in his *Critique of Pure Reason*, said, "People have always spoken of the absolutely necessary (absolutnotwendigen) being, and have taken pains, not so much to understand whether and how a thing of this kind can even be thought, but rather to prove its existence. . . .. if by means of the word unconditioned I dismiss all the conditions that the understanding always requires in order to regard something as necessary, this does not come close to enabling me to understand whether I then still think something through a concept of an unconditionally necessary being, or perhaps think nothing at all through it." Kant, here, tried to portray the difficulty of understanding the Absolute. The stages that we must seek and reach in order to reach the Absolute are the ones that, according to me, need to have logical steps and these steps cannot be explained in a manner that is not connected to each other. In order to understand that, Hegelian logic could be of real value here. Hegel's idea of Being-Essence-Notion can be viewed from the point of view of an individual in explaining the zemic formation that eventually leads to the Plane of *Dasein*.

A zemic model is a mediated presence as it shows the way a sign is created. An individual while creating a sign, at the moment when he/she does not yet know the sign they are going to create but has a vision of one image after another out of which one would be his/her choice of sign creation, has the immediate vision of a certain sign. What I call a zemic with an existential choice is the Essence that comes out of immediate sign after an individual becomes aware of the break in sameness. This Essence is an individual's attempt to understand what the sign is in actuality. But we also need to understand "an advantageous place on it". The "possible lines of flight" need to be conceived as a negation of one zemic with an existential choice with another until we reach the Plane of *Dasein*.

Andy Blunden, in his *The Meaning of Hegel's Logic*, wrote, "we recognise various things which do not simply pass away to be replaced by something else like unconnected images one after another, but something that lies behind Being. But each of these views proves inadequate, fails to explain various aspects of the thing, and is one after another negated. Each view or essence is not destroyed by its negation, but overcome, retained and superseded by a still deeper essence. . ." To reach the Plane of *Dasein*, we need to negate the zemics with an existential choice without refusing to recognize their value as a formation. Each negation leads to an assertion that would eventually lead to the final path. Each zemic with an existential choice is true to its choice and this truthfulness prevents their destruction. Further progress depends on the way we could overcome one essence by finding a way to reach another expectedly closer to the Plane of *Dasein*. Blunden, again, wrote, "Essence describes how you come to the Notion, to the 'key' to understanding something which, once arrived at, is the basis for all analysis of and 'logical thinking' about the thing. This process goes through all sorts of 'mistakes' before finding the 'right road'. Without this concept of Hegel's, it appears as if the Notion can only be arrived at by 'inspiration' or 'hunch'." The key to understanding the Plane of *Dasein* does not depend on how many negations one did but on the concrete realisation of what is yet nothing but a theoretical realization.

Hegel, in *Science of Logic*, wrote, "The Notion is... in the first instance... the third to being and essence, to the immediate and to reflection. Being and essence are so far the moments of its becoming; but it is their foundation and truth as the identity in which they are submerged and contained... Objective logic therefore, which treats of being and essence constitutes properly the genetic exposition of the Notion..." (Blunden 1997). So, as I said previously, the zemics with an existential choice are not unnecessary in their existence. They are parts of the final Plane of *Dasein*. They include in it and negating them is the way to perceive the rest to understand the concrete. What we may think as the final Plane of *Dasein* could just not be the concrete ending yet.

5 Lacanian orders and the concept of real in Existential Semiotics

Jacques Lacan, in his theories, mentioned the concepts of the mirror stage, the Real, the Imaginary Order and the Symbolic Order. The Real becomes impossible once we evolve from need to demand and then to desire. In Real, there is no separation between the body and the external world. But, once we enter the realm of language, the Symbolic Order, desire takes birth. Even though the Real still plays its part but we cannot go back there. In the Imaginary Order, a child tries to make the other his/her own as he/she learns his/her separation from his/her mother/father. In the mirror image, the child tries to establish an "Ideal-I" or "ideal-ego" which is actually an impossible realization. In the Symbolic Order, "[t]he symbolic, through language, is the pact which links... subjects together in one action. The human action par excellence is originally founded on the existence of the world of the symbol, namely on laws and contracts." (Lacan 1991; Felluga). The Symbolic Order deals with our entrance to the conventions of society.

Even though, according to Lacan, "the real is impossible", we may attempt to overcome it in a way that is on the other side of infancy. The Plane of *Dasein* is a realm that connects an individual to a point where he/she gets beyond the "what suits me" point and reaches the place that makes them one with the possibilities that are there for an individual beyond selfish desires of the Symbolic Order. The realization of zemic with an existential choice, with the influence of societal values, is again a product of the Symbolic Order. But, in this plane also, the Imaginary very much plays its part as it is not rare to find individuals whose demands depend on the demands of achieving things that are not possible.

The Plane of *Dasein* does not exclude possibilities from us but gives us a wide and clear view of what are the possibilities that lie in front of us if we could think beyond demands and desires. So, the Plane of *Dasein* is the Real for an individual. Once we grow up and leave infancy behind it is not possible to go back there. But the Real is a plane that never leaves us and a way to go back there would be to break the conventions that bind us. Also, as I said before, the Plane of *Dasein* has a straight connection with the Transcendence. So, our realizing the Plane of *Dasein* as Real would lead us, eventually, to the Real that will connect an individual with the possibilities that are there not just for him/her but for all. In short, the Lacanian Real would be reached or realized.

Every zemic with an existential choice is an essence that comes into existence because of our desire to follow the societal rules, which is the Symbolic Order. In reality, before this order, we were in the Imaginary Order, where our demand was to see the "ideal-ego" where we could be one with what we perceive as the separate/missing piece. However, as we cannot go back to our infancy to sense the Real again, we must seek forward in order to see if we could reach the Real where the mayhem created by language and societal rules would not be present and our needs would concern only that what does not separate us in a conventional manner from the external world as, in Transcendence (the collective Real), we would be able to experience what possibilities lie collectively.

> The Plane of *Dasein* – The Real (individually)
> The Transcendence – The Real (collectively)

In Deleuzian sense, it is necessary to find an advantageous place on the opportunities that are offered and, in the Hegelian sense, we must negate the zemics with an existential choice in a manner of overcoming them by not denying what was there but establishing the next one on the previous one until we reach the Plane of *Dasein*. The Lacanian concepts, here, are not reversed, but continued. If the Real is a plane without ego and separation, then it has to have two different definitions in infancy and adulthood. In infancy, we are yet to come in contact with language and society, whereas in adulthood, we need to break that bond by overcoming it. So, it is a journey from the Real to the Real.

The Lacanian concepts could be helpful in the question of the medium in Existential Semiotics in the sense that the establishment of the zemics with an existential choice as products of the Imaginary Order would give us a lead, in the concept of the Real, to follow in order to understand the problem of the medium. As the Real was once there, it according to Lacan, plays a part throughout our lives. "We should keep in mind, however, that the Real and the Imaginary continue to play a part in the evolution of human desire within the symbolic order. The fact that our fantasies always fail before the Real, for example, ensures that we continue to desire; desire in the symbolic order could, in fact, be said to be our way to avoid coming into full contact with the Real, so that desire is ultimately most interested not in obtaining the object of desire but, rather, in reproducing itself." (Felluga) So, our desires fail because of the Real and, therefore, the negation of one desire for another would prove the existence/presence of the Real. Now, using the Deleuzian and Hegelian concepts, as mentioned before, we can overcome this huddle of desire and reach the Plane of *Dasein* (the Real that is individually).

Concluding remarks

The next step of this study would explain how the Plane of *Dasein* is connected with Transcendence which is the ultimate Real (collectively). Existential Semiotics, as a theory, is not confined to the mere structures of zemic as the zemic itself is impossible without these dense connections between a human being and society or *Dasein* and Transcendence. The theory connects different fields for the sake of finding answers to questions that remain topics of deep speculations.

The connection between *Dasein* and Transcendence could become a delicate one as it is interpretable in various ways. Here, I tried to explain the same connection using influences whenever and wherever required. My attempt to divide this connection into two parts is to stay on the line with the theory of Existential Semiotics. The first portion, which has been explained here, tried to elucidate a part which is much closer to human beings in its workings. The idea of explaining first the way the internal works is the result of the interpretive formation which makes it more explicable for human beings to grasp this rather than explaining the connection from Transcendence. We can also say that the internal is explained in several steps to connect the invisible dots where overstepping could result in missing this imperceptibility. Materialism and Idealism both have its merits, but here an attempt has been made to amalgamate the relevant essence of the two in order not to put an end to where further explanation is possible or indulge in continuity where the source has become a base of inexplicability.

The next part shall be based on theories that are not disconnected from the theories in the first part. The explanation of the connection between *Dasein* and Transcendence is a way to understand the way the signs that are created are created. The presence of ideas and the creation of signs is a two-way street to follow. Here, in Existential Semiotics, with the help of different theories, an attempt has been made to begin the process of understanding these ways.

References

Blunden, Andy. 1997. *The Meaning of Hegel's Logic*. Retrieved from https://www.marxists.org/reference/archive/hegel/help/mean.htm

Deleuze, Gilles & Félix Guattari. 1980. *A Thousand Plateaus*. Trans. by Brian Massumi. London and New York: Continuum, 2004. Vol. 2 of *Capitalism and Schizophrenia*. 2 vols. 1972–1980. (Trans. of *Mille Plateaux*. Paris: Les Editions de Minuit.)

Deleuze, Gilles & Félix Guattari. 1972. *Anti-Oedipus*. Trans. by Robert Hurley, Mark Seem & Helen R. Lane. London and New York: Continuum, 2004. Vol. 1 of *Capitalism and Schizophrenia*. 2 vols. 1972–1980. (Trans. of *L'Anti-Oedipe*. Paris: Les Editions de Minuit.)

Deleuze, Gilles. 1993. *The Logic of Sense*. Edited by Constantin V. Boundas. Trans. by Mark Lester with Charles Stivale. Columbia University Press

Felluga, Dino. 2011. *Modules on Lacan: On the Structure of the Psyche. Introductory Guide to Critical Theory*. Purdue University. http://www.purdue.edu/guidetotheory/psychoanalysis/lacanstructure.html

Harrison-Barbet, Anthony. (n.d.). Philosophical Connections. Retrieved from http://philosophos.org/philosophical_connections/profile_014.html

Hegel, G. W. F. 1977 [1807]. *Phenomenology of Spirit*. Oxford University Press.

Kant, Immanuel. 1998 [1781]. *Critique of Pure Reason*. Cambridge University Press.

Kant, Immanuel. 2019. *Metaphysical Works of the Celebrated Immanuel Kant*. Hardpress Publishing.

Kierkegaard, Søren. 1985 [1844]. *Philosophical Fragments: Johannes Climacus*. Trans. by H. V. Hong and E. H. Hong.

Lacan, Jacques. 1991 [1988]. *Freud's Papers on Technique 1953–1954*. The Seminar of Jacques Lacan, Book 1. Ed. by Jacques-Alain Miller, Engl. trans. by John Forrester. New York: Norton.

New World Encyclopedia. (n.d.). Absolute (philosophy). Retrieved from https://www.newworldencyclopedia.org/entry/Absolute_(philosophy)#Credits

Tarasti, Eero. 2000. *Existential Semiotics*. Bloomington: Indiana University Press.

Tarasti, Eero. 2015. *Sein und Schein – Explorations in Existential Semiotics*. Berlin: De Gruyter Mouton.

Tarasti, Eero. 2013. *Semiotics of Classical Music*. Berlin: De Gruyter Mouton.

Morten Tønnessen
Existential universals. Biosemiosis and existential semiosis

Abstract: This paper is divided into five parts. The introduction presents some implications of the relational nature of human beings as well as other living beings, and establishes a connection between biosemiotics and existentialist thinking. The second part indicates key points of a "semiotics of being" as a genuine outlook within semiotics. In "Universals of biosemiosis", the third part, a number of common features of everything and anyone alive are identified. The fourth part, "On Earth – the natural setting of the human condition", sets the stage for a few ecologically and astronomically minded reflections in philosophical anthropology. In the fifth and concluding part, "On the alienation of the semiotic animal", observations are made on some existential implications of the characteristically human form of being. Part of the motivation for the paper is to demonstrate firstly that existential semiosis plays a key role in human semiosis, and secondly, that other living beings too live through existential dramas.

Keywords: alienation; biosemiotics; existence; existential semiotics; existentialism; the human condition

1 Introduction

The starting point for the text you have laid your eyes upon is a relational concept of nature. Such an understanding of nature is described in the biological works of Jakob von Uexküll (1864–1944), among them *Bedeutungslehre* (cf. Uexküll 1956, translated as Uexküll 1982). The world as Uexküll depicts it consists of a myriad of organism-specific phenomenal worlds. Taken as a whole – interwoven by the interconnectedness that various ecological relations, etc. result in – the life worlds of all that lives (the phenomenal world at large) comprise what we call nature.

Note: This article is an outcome – or rather further development – of a talk I held in Eero Tarasti's seminar "Introduction to existential semiotics" in Helsinki, Finland 11 November 2007 entitled "On the self, relational being and the philosophy of Gabriel Marcel". It was developed and written as part of the research project Dynamical Zoosemiotics and Animal Representations (ETF/ ESF 7790). This chapter was first published in 2017 in Chinese Semiotic Studies 13(4): 381–398. DOI: https://doi.org/10.1515/css-2017-0022

"The radical essence of the biosemiotics of the Uexkülls," says Eero Tarasti (Nöth et al. 2008: 529–530), with reference to Jakob and his son Thure (1908–2004), "has been that man's symbolic, signifying activities are not reducible to biology – as it has been in socio-biology – but that, quite the reverse, all biological and organic processes are processes of semiosis." If the living world is indeed intrinsically semiotic, then perhaps we can make sense of what Warwick Fox (1984: 196) calls the central intuition of deep ecology: "the idea that there is no firm ontological divide in the field of existence. [...] Rather, all entities are constituted by their relationships." Isolated from its ecological relations, an organism would be nothing but a corpse. It is exactly a certain participation in the existence of others that constitutes the process of being alive. In this sense, life is not only inherently ecological, but further inherently social, or symbiotic.

"What we learn from complexity theory and science," writes cultural theorist Wendy Wheeler (2006: 34), "is that human creatures simply cannot be properly understood as the isolated, rationally choosing, self-maximisers so beloved of liberal politics and political economy." With the development of biosemiotics, she holds (p. 139), "we are in a position to think again about the biological *and* semiotic life of human beings in non-reductive ways." Biosemiotics thus provides a world view potentially critical vis-à-vis a more modern, excessively rationalistic world view in which a human monopoly is assumed with regard to any kind of agency worthy of our attention. In the terminology of existentialist philosopher Gabriel Marcel, this modern world view, with roots back to Descartes – if not Plato – is highly problematic in its dealings with nature (cf. his statement that the denial of the mysterious is symptomatic of the modern world). Conceptually, nature – regarded as a force of its own – is unambiguously done away with.

If nature is fundamentally semiotic and relational, then so are we humans. But how do we define a human being in relational terms? In the words of Donald Favareau (2002: 84), "we can situate the deeply internalized, seemingly ubiquitous concept of [a human] 'self' as a product of the uppermost symbol level of our 'biological inner semiosphere'", including and yet exceeding "the supporting iconic and indexical levels of the never-ending sign-exchange activity mediating cell, brain, body and world." Personally I have come to find it fruitful to distinguish between the *explicit self* that represents our more or less conscious identity, and our *implicit self*, i.e. our behavioural ("actual") self as demonstrated by the (psycho-)somatic, social and ecological relations we maintain (our ontological footprint, as it were, in the phenomenal world at large). The human self, as Marcel states (1949: 167), "is always a thickening [...] of the body". It is through all of these processes – of the inner and the outer – and the steady coordination of them, that our living selves are constituted, and it is in these spheres of life (me – us – my world) that our developing selves manifest themselves at a conscious level whenever something calls for our attention with a sufficient sense of urgency.

Perception is not as such a self-reflective activity, but rather a sustained attempt at grasping something which in part opposes you and in part constitutes your very being. There is a world out there – a world of differences, a world of creatures, almost all of them differently constituted than you, but many of them nevertheless constitutionally related to you. In this world of existence-through-and-with-others, consciousness no doubt plays a part, but by no means delineates the horizon of our entire bodily awareness. In fact, consciousness is but a special case of awareness – which is a much more common phenomenon, appearing in countless forms ranging from the amoeba to the ludicrous human genius. While consciousness very well might represent the most novel evolutionary innovation in which we partake, being conscious is, in general terms, not a prerequisite for navigating in the world of the living. For us humans, it is first of all a matter of not getting trapped in our own minds. By neglecting the foundation of consciousness – its natural sources – we risk making a very bad figure indeed as big-brained animals.

I have earlier sketched a phenomenology of environmental change, and pinpointed Uexküll's relation to phenomenology (Tønnessen 2009: 49–50 and 57–60, respectively). In the current text I explore a number of existential implications of biosemiotics – partly with an emphasis on living beings as such, but first of all aiming at improving our understanding of the human condition, in a more-than-human world. I will start out by reiterating a platform for a *semiotics of being*, as opposed to a more perfunctory *semiotics of functioning* (cf. also Tønnessen 2009: 60–63). Next, I will put forward a selection of *existential universals* – a subcategory of "biosemiotic universals" – and depict the Earth as the natural context in which the great drama of "the human condition" plays out. In conclusion I will give consideration to the terms "alienation" and "authenticity" within the framework of a semiotics of being.

A key figure potentially representing a "missing link" between existentialism and eco-philosophy is the Norwegian philosopher Peter Wessel Zapffe (1899–1990). Throughout this text I will refer to him at occasion. Zapffe made use of Uexküll's writings in his main work *Om det tragiske* [On the tragic] as well as in his explicitly "biosophic" work (cf. Zapffe 1996; 1961). Zapffe's view was that mankind is an over-equipped, tragic species, only causing trouble for itself and other beings. The only enduring solution to any human problem, according to Zapffe, is to collectively stop reproducing, and voluntarily go extinct as a species. At the face of it, this is a bleaker philosophy than even primitivism. Although Zapffe never got beyond his "brotherhood of suffering shared by all that lives" (Zapffe 1993: 41), a semiotics of being – an existential semiotics enthused by biosemiotics – should indeed be able to provide a deeper and broader sense of community with fellow beings than more anthropocentric versions can. As Eero Tarasti (2000: 11) writes:

> In the theories of existentialist philosophers, the movement of a subject stops [in negation]; Sartre remains in his *Nausée*, Camus in his *The Fall*. The experience of Nothingness is anguishing. But it can become a creative experience if the movement of a subject goes forth.
>
> When the subject returns from his negation, the transcendence of his *Dasein*, he sees it from a new point of view. Many of its objects have lost their meaning and have proven to be only seemingly significant. However, those which preserve their meanings are provided with a new content enriched by the new existential experience. The subject is, as it were, reborn as a "semiotic self"[.]

2 Semiotics of being

The following points, taken from the abstract of "Steps to a semiotics of being" (Tønnessen 2010), represent a path to a semiotics of being and are pertinent to various sub-fields at the conjunction of semiotics of nature (biosemiotics, ecosemiotics, zoosemiotics) and semiotics of culture – semioethics and existential semiotics included.

1) Semiotics of being entails inquiry at all levels of biological organization, albeit, wherever there are individuals, with emphasis on the living *qua* individuals (*integrated biological individualism*).
2) An *Umwelt* is the public aspect (cf. the *Innenwelt*, the private aspect) of a phenomenal/experienced world that is organism-specific (rather than species-specific) and ultimately refers to an existential realm.
3) *Existential universals* at work on Earth include seeking out the edible, dwelling in a medium, holding a phenomenal world (possibly an Umwelt) and being endowed with life, and followingly being mortal.
4) Human Umwelten include *speechless Umwelten*, *spoken Umwelten* and *alphabetic Umwelten*.
5) An *Uexküllian phenomenology* – stating that *semiotic states* represent the general class to which all mental/cognitive states belong – can draw on the works of the phenomenologists David Abram and Ted Toadvine.
6) A task for such a phenomenology is to portray *the natural history of the phenomenal world*.
7) An imperative task in our contemporary world of faltering biological diversity is that of *Umwelt mapping*, i.e. a mapping of *ontological niches*.

8) The ecological crisis is an *ontological crisis* with historical roots in humankind's domestication of animals and plants, which can be taken as archetypical for our attempted planet-scale taming of the wild.
9) The process of globalization is expressed by correlated trends of *depletion of semiotic diversity* and *semiotic diversification*.
10) *Semiotic economy* is a field which task it is to map the human ontological niche insofar as its semiotic relations are of an economic nature.¹

3 Universals of biosemiosis

Let there be no doubt: Existential universals can be articulated and conceptualized in a variety of ways. Any numbered list would be likely to be incomplete – and any chronological exposition may well be at least in part arbitrary. That being said, this is my bid. In Tønnessen 2001 (689) I pragmatically assumed "that semiosis is a universal characteristic of living beings, because without semiosis, there can be no recognition." That is fair enough – but one should keep in mind that not all semiosis is conceptualized as existential, i.e. by nature experientially related to the existence of a being (cf. intracellular semiosis, and everything to do with genomes, in particular). Consequently, not all "biosemiotic universals" qualify as existential universals. All existential universals, however, are necessarily universals of biosemiosis.

What is it like to be a human being? (In other words: What is the human condition?). Before we can answer that question, we have to answer a more general question, the answer to which has foundational validity for the human question, namely: What is it like to be a living being?² In what follows I will allude to sixteen

---

1 The notion of a "semiotic state" is described in Tønnessen 2009: 62–63 as the self-referential form which a sign system assumes in order to realize a certain agenda. As for Abram and Toadvine, see especially Abram 1997 and Toadvine 2003. An "ontological niche" can be understood as the set, or whole, of contrapuntal (ecological) relations that a creature partakes in at a given point of natural history (cf. Tønnessen 2009: 54–57). "Semiotic economy" denotes a turf in which economic relations are regarded as more-than-economic, in that they concern not only (theoretically infinite) resources but also finite (mortal!) beings and living systems. Volume in itself has no meaning. Modelling economic activity in its phenomenological aspect, we come to realize that the true measure of a healthy (or "sustainable") economy is the well-being not only of humans, but of any being capable of being well-off (insofar as their state (i.e. level) of well-being is elicited by human economic activity).
2 In Tønnessen 2003 I list seven distinctive features of human beings, expressed in Uexküllian terms. Some of these (such as individuality, and the ability to learn) are features shared by other

answers to that question. Sex and pain are both off this list of universals, given that neither sexual reproduction nor sentience (or enmity, for that matter) are universal phenomena in the sphere of the living (though Descartes was terribly wrong in theorizing that only humans feel pain). First, all living beings are alive. Second, all living beings are ultimately mortal. Third, all living beings eat, i.e. consume nutrition (be it animate or inanimate). Fourth, all living beings dwell and find their way in a medium (be it aquatic, aerial or terrestrial). Fifth, all living beings display awareness – i.e. they are one way or another aware of distinctive properties of their life worlds (all that lives, in other words, is able to make distinctions). Sixth, the awareness (experience, perception) of the living is always directed, namely at what matters (what is relevant, has a function) to the living in question (consciousness is always *about* something – and so is awareness). Seventh, by being directed, the awareness of the living is further proof of the intentionality (goal-oriented nature) of all living beings. Eighth, the awareness of the living is always normative (evaluative) in that distinctions made in and through awareness not only categorize but further categorize in terms of likes and dislikes, what should be sought and what should be avoided (and what can safely be ignored). Ninth, by being endowed through awareness with intentionality as well as with normativity, all living beings are subjective (i.e. they are goal-oriented living systems with their own norms, their own agenda). Tenth, *qua* subjective beings, all living beings are in a state (one state or another) of well-being (judged along the lines of the criteria they themselves put forth).

Eleventh – as we can see from the fact that all that lives is somewhat aware of its relevant surroundings – all living beings carry and inhabit a *phenomenal world* (be it an Umwelt or a *Wohnhülle* (Uexküll 1940/1982) – or whatever else we prefer to call it – *Lebenswelt*, life world, experiential world, etc.). Twelfth, for all that lives and is aware, it is the case that behaviour is logically primary to awareness in that behaviour – that of others as well as, crucially, that of oneself – is always anticipated in awareness.[3] In actual processes of life, however, behaviour and awareness are practically indistinguishable – no place do we witness behaviour without some variant of awareness involved. The logical primacy of behaviour nevertheless points to a fundamental trait of the living: All beings are principally 'thrown into the world', already acting, already acted upon – doomed from the outset to choose between rivalling interpretations of their dubious surroundings, which eats into their initial privacy from the first moment of unguarded exist-

---

creatures but particularly highly developed in humans, others (related to conceptual perception) are uniquely human traits.

[3] The term "behaviour" is here applied in an unusually wide sense – as is "awareness", throughout this text.

ence. As Camus (1991: 8) said with the human context in mind, "[w]e get into the habit of living before acquiring the habit of thinking."

Thirteenth, *qua* aware, intentional, normative creatures anticipating behaviour, all living beings are principally (though oftentimes unsuccessfully) receptive or responsive with regard to their own paths of life as well as regarding changing environments and environmental conditions. Pragmatically, we could make two more statements which (I would argue) are descriptively true but do not concern the principal constitution of the living: Fourteenth, all living beings are today within the reach of human causation.[4] Fifteenth, all living beings – *qua* aware, phenomenal, more or less well-off creatures – are to be regarded as moral subjects (cf. Tønnessen 2003: 292),[5] i.e. worthy of moral consideration. These lead us to a final universal which is indeed of constitutive character: Sixteenth, by systematically (though oftentimes unsuccessfully) attempting to resist being subdued by the human hand or its control technologies, all living beings display an innate autonomy (it is a telling fact of nature that practically only humans commit suicide). Resignation is of course an option, in nature, as in human society. But as Albert Camus (1965) wrote – again with the human context in mind – "[t]he habit of despair is worse than despair itself".

4 On Earth – the natural setting of the human condition

Every human being, then – like any other living creature – is alive, mortal, eats/consumes, and dwells and navigates in a medium. Every human being is further aware in a directed and intentional manner; normative, subjective, more or less well-off, etc. There is naturally much to be said about our particular dwellings – almost exclusively in terrestrial settings – our preferred diet, and so on. Needless to say, we are further characterized by several non-universal phenomena, our sexual lives and sentience included. Finally, many existential universals have no doubt found a special expression in man (not least the fact that our awareness is distinctively apt to abstract thought). Any living being whatsoever has its peculiar

---

[4] "The reason why it makes sense to regard all semiotic agents [. . .] as moral subjects, is that in respect to these entities, our actions make a difference. Only for semiotic agents can our actions ultimately appear as signs that influence their well-being. [. . .] Wherever there is semiosis, there are needs, and even though actual moral treatment is also a question of practicability, attribution of moral status is a principal one."
[5] Cf. Tønnessen and Deely 2009 – the first in a series of interviews on the topic of semioethics.

taste and habits. The point I am nevertheless making is that very much of what characterizes us as human beings – and as experiencing subjects, or persons – is, in one form or another, characteristic of all that lives.

Any creature indulges in – as if taking pride in – its specific differences. *Homo sapiens sapiens* has at occasion described itself as a rational animal (a political animal), or a semiotic animal – a particularly gifted animal. More often than not we have defined ourselves in opposition to "animals", the biological kingdom to which we belong. Man, as I wrote in Tønnessen 2003, is "the animal that does not want to be an animal". The aforementioned existentialist Peter Wessel Zapffe claims in his essay "The last Messiah" (Zapffe 1993) that "most people manage to save themselves [from our all-too-conscious selves] by artificially paring down their consciousness", and names four *suppression mechanisms* (each representing "a betrayal of man's most potent gift"): isolation, attachment, diversion and sublimation (43–44). Through attachments – beliefs, superstitions, prejudices; altogether providing a metaphysically imposed structure that gives purpose and organization – we build a certain necessity into our lives. I would suggest that anthropocentrism is a near universal attachment in this sense. Zapffe for his part refers (51) to "the dire misconception that we are biologically ordained to conquer the earth". This conception is likely to be fortified as increasing portions of our biological talents are rendered superfluous in the modern technological game with the environment (as a consequence, says Zapffe [50], "we are victims of increasing 'spiritual unemployment'").

Many would assume that a superstitious anthropocentrism was a thing of the past – a feature of a geocentric world, perhaps. But it is in no way obvious that our present societies are less anthropocentric than past societies, or that our advanced and bureaucratic anthropocentrism is in the big picture any less "mythical" than that of low-tech societies. What matters the most is in what terms we think about our own role on this planet (conquerors, caretakers, fellow inhabitants?). "Today", as phenomenologist David Abram (1997: ix) observes, "we participate almost exclusively with other humans and with our own human-made technology." Noting that we, in modern, "civilized" humanity, have "a strange inability to clearly perceive other animals – a real inability to clearly see, or focus upon, anything outside the realm of human technology, or to hear as meaningful anything other than human speech", Abram suggests that "we are human only in contact, and conviviality, with what is not human".

In this section I will proceed thematically from existential universals to what we may call Earthly (terrestrial, as opposed to extra-terrestrial) universals. First, it should be noted that what has been said thus far derives from a cellular notion of life (cf. the problematic status in biology of viruses). It is conceivable that the very first forms of life were not cellular (but perhaps the experiential dimension of life emerged only with cellular life). Second, as is well known, all known life is carbon-based. Various authors have hypothesized the possibility of silicon-based life forms (some have even had the courage to suggest that we should improve the photosynthesis of plants by applying principles of solar energy technology to genetic engineering). The materiality of all known life, in short, is intimately tied to the history and location of planet Earth. Whether or not the biochemical composition we observe all known life to display on Earth is truly universal (and necessarily so), we do not know. What we do know is that there are more than 90 chemical elements occurring in terrestrial nature, and that some 22 of these are directly necessary to human life (Bonnet and Woltjer 2008: 238–40). These 22 elements were synthesized at various stages of the gradual unfolding of the universe. Many of them, like iron and silicon, were for the most part created in supernova explosions. One implication is that it is not by chance alone that we live in a universe that is 13–14 billion years old. At much earlier stages, our existence would not have been physically possible.

Before I proceed further, I owe it to Frederik Stjernfelt to point out that there is a profound difference between universality and globality. In Tønnessen 2001, I asserted (689) that "[e]ven though I do find speculation about what characteristics of living beings, if any, are universal, interesting, I consider claims that certain characteristics are in fact universal to be unfounded, and impossible to justify." My statement referred to Stjernfelt's article "Biosemiotics and formal ontology" (Stjernfelt 1999). In Stjernfelt 2002, he replied in a footnote that it does indeed make sense to describe universal characteristics of living beings, since something lacking all recognizable characteristics would not even be recognized by us as life (and would therefore be irrelevant to the discussion). If it is alive, I reply, it is alive – regardless of our conception of life, or our recognition of it. It should consequently be noted that what I in this chapter call "existential universals" are to be regarded as universals of living creatures *as far as our knowledge goes* (cf. my notion in Tønnessen 2001 of "biosemiotic possibilism"). Might there be – or, might there have been – experiencing creatures with constitutions others than those described by the aforementioned existential universals? There might (were that the case, I would of course have been wrong in asserting that these "universals" are in fact universals). To stress such a possibility, one could replace the term "universal" with "global (terrestrial) property" – though there is much life that lurks on Earth, as well, unknown to man.

What, then, are these "Earthly universals", apart from the restraints on our materiality that follow from the exact selection of elements appearing on Earth? My focus in the following will be on our deep-seated astronomical (or cosmological) situatedness. As creatures of Earth, we inhabit a planet – a planet with a history which has in effect determined many of our perceptions and conceptions.

Let me start out by reminding you how the Moon came to be (Bonnet and Woltjer 2008: 19–22). Most likely the early Earth was hit by a large body more or less the size of Mars. A substantial fraction of the Earth's mantle was ejected into space, and eventually formed the Moon. Under the shock the Earth went into a spin, and its axis of rotation tilted. Following tidal interactions with the Moon – much fiercer in early times than today – the present cycle of seasons, and the duration of our days, was in place. The tidal coupling stabilized the Earth's rotation axis, giving the Earth a fairly stable climate. In sum: Our days and nights, our summers and our winters – all these have been shaped by this initial clash. What we conceive of as archetypically normal is in fact to a considerable extent the outcome of a singular astronomical event. We talk about days and nights because we live on a planet that is not tidally locked to its star but rotates, and rotates rather rapidly at that. We talk about months because we inhabit a planet that has one and only one Moon, with a certain orbit. We talk about spring and autumn, summer and winter because of the Earth's tilted rotation axis. We talk about years because we live on a planet that orbits around a star frequently enough for us to perceive multiple turns during a lifetime. And not only do we talk. We fine-tune our entire lives to these natural rhythms, and their local configurations.

Surely there is great variety in different cultural conceptions of time and space – but there are also palpable restraints, dictated by the history of our planet. There are many other Earthly universals as well, related either to planetary conditions (in the bigger context of the solar system) or to Earth history, but here it will suffice to allude to one more, namely the force of gravity at the surface of our planet. Our particular strength of gravity (determined blindly by the mass of the Earth – once again affected by the creation of the Moon) has not only shaped our sense of balance, weight, motion, etc., but further set the base conditions for how thick or thin the limbs of animals of various sizes can possibly be – think about an elephant and a mosquito.

What is the point of all this? The lesson to learn is that we are not some kind of general creatures, for which anything is possible, but particular beings with a history, a geographical (astronomical) location, and physical (perceptual, and behavioural) restraints. I would not be retelling such obvious facts, were it not for our modern God complex. In *Surviving 1,000 centuries: Can We Do It?*, the astronomers Bonnet and Woltjer contribute to the eventual fall of the human fantasy of leaving Earth for good – another brick in the great wall of human megalomania. Zapffe (1993a: 57) potently summarizes the existential prospects of settling elsewhere: "Sure, and it'll be exciting the first week. Eventually, though, people will start worrying about how much to tax the uranium mines in order to keep the price of margarine down." Bonnet and Woltjer's bet (2008: 300) in this context is a reply to a 1950 lunch discussion among a group of scientists which included Nobel laureate Enrico Fermi (cf. also Webb 2002: 288).

> [T]here was a consensus that the Universe should contain billions of planets capable of supporting life, and most probably millions of intelligent species. Fermi made a rapid calculation and remarked that these putative civilizations, based on the human tendency to expand and on the promising capabilities of space technology, would already have colonized the entire galaxy within a few million years and visited us a long time ago and many times over. He then asked the stunning question: *'But where is everybody?'*

The simplest answer, suggest the two astronomers, is that "interstellar travel is just an impossible concept." Either that, we may infer, or there is no intelligent life elsewhere, or there is intelligent life elsewhere but it does not sustain a technological civilization (what a shock *that* would be!), or there is intelligent life elsewhere but it is wise enough not to have imperialist ambitions (again – what a shock!).

As I have attempted to demonstrate throughout this article, man's reality is not only one of embodiedness (entailing an *embodied mind* etc.). The individual is constituted as an organism, and this organism is not only part of an ecosystem but further serves as an ecosystem in its own right for trillions of miniscule creatures (only thus could it come into being) – the great majority of which we live in symbiosis with. A human being is impossible to understand in merely human terms. Human beings are constitutionally more-than-human – already partaking in (and depending on) something bigger than themselves. Human creatures, then, are not isolated, simply rational beings (cf. Wheeler) – we are, indeed, "human only in contact, and conviviality, with what is not human" (Abram 1997: ix).

But that is only part of the story. It is no accidental trait that we are "part of nature". We are, vitally, "beings of nature". In general terms, that implies that we are aware, intentional, normative, subjective creatures etc., and in *specific* terms it further implies, in our terrestrial environment, that nature – Earth – is our situation, and that its history is our history. We are not some kind of general creatures. We are grounded on Earth. As Bonnet and Woltjer (2008: 311) say, there "is no serious alternative to our occupying the mother planet for another 1,000 centuries, even if we manage to inhabit the Moon, Mars and perhaps Titan [. . .] for science, resource exploitation and tourism [. . .] The Earth is what we have".

What, then, of the semiotic animal? What of "unlimited semiosis"? Surely we are magnificent creatures. But by opining that it faces no restraints whatsoever, the human spirit only deludes itself. All is not arbitrary, and it is plain falsehood to claim that anything whatsoever is possible. In existential terms, each and every human individual does, principally, have an immense semiotic freedom to define itself as a persona, and shape its very being. But there are restraints. There is a world out there. Physics matters. History matters. What we do matters. We are not inhabitants of a wholly abstract, wholly intellectual landscape.

5 On the alienation of the semiotic animal

Some might think that I am propagating a return to essentialism – often conceived of as the very arch-enemy of existentialism. What I am propagating, however, is but a variety of existentialist thought informed by natural reality. In no way do I wish to belittle the extraordinary qualities of human fervour and despair. "Animals, too, know angst", observes Zapffe (1993: 41), but "man feels angst for life itself – indeed, for his own being." It is uniquely human to think in universal, general terms. But our intellectual achievements (so often written in sand, carved in stone, materialized as monuments over the greatest and freest spirit ever to have wandered the Earth) come at a high price: Namely that we easily confuse our purely human sets of signs with reality as such. Here I would like to introduce a notion, with reference to Jean-Paul Sartre (cf. his notion of *bad faith*) and John Deely (cf. Deely 2005), of our twofold confusion of objects and things. Firstly, we human beings tend to confuse objects with things – this entails, for example, to believe that a social/historical, human construct (such as a nation state) is in fact necessary (cf. Zapffe's concept of attachments). Secondly, we oftentimes practically confuse natural things (something existing in its own right) with (merely human) objects. In being anthropocentric, we frequently treat natural entities aiming only at their utility in human terms. The construction of human reality and the reduction of the natural world as it is being incorporated into human culture, and made "useful", go hand in hand, and one presumes the other. As we can see, this anthropocentric reductionism is at work in thought as well as in "real life", and intrinsically tied to our constitution as thinking things.

Man, as I have argued, is not alone in being aware – but what is characteristic of humans *qua* creatures endowed with awareness? Paradoxically, the more conscious a being is, the more selective is its conscious awareness. To be conscious is not simply to be aware. Rather, it is to be exceptionally aware of a small selection of all the impressions bestowed to the body. Odd as it might seem, to be conscious is to be aware only of the most urgent events – in other words, to be very aware of very few of all the sign processes that our bodies are continuously engaged in.

The human self was not always an issue. Portraying it as a historical, social construct was pioneered by Hegel (1977) – others, Kierkegaard and Heidegger included, take a self-conscious self as a given. I have previously in this text mentioned my distinction between our implicit self (our identity) and our explicit self (our "behavioural" self). For no being, I would claim, is the divide between its idea or impression of itself (its implicit self) and its actual behaviour (its explicit self) wider than in the case of human beings. We are consequently prone, from the outset of human existence, to be alienated from ourselves as beings of and in nature (and yet, our current split between identity and behaviour is a historical fact, and cannot necessarily be taken as exhaustively representative of human nature!). Ironically, less conscious beings, and creatures with awareness but without consciousness, are in a sense much more (directly) aware of their undertakings than we are. With higher levels of semiotic freedom come higher degrees of arbitrariness in interpretation.

Whereas Hegel traced the origin of alienation to the breakup of the Greek *Polis*, Engels (1958) and Marx mainly related it to the emergence of a division of labour. Zapffe, for his part, traces the roots of modernity back to the first division of labour, and philosophizes that ongoing specialization leads to an ever-increasing surplus of vacant skills at the individual level, thereby contributing, as mentioned, to "spiritual unemployment" (cf. Zapffe 1996). Though experiences of alienation have likely preceded modernity, the term is typically modern in that it applies well to a social world in which individuals are expected to choose their own roles. For Kierkegaard (cf. Westphal 1987) as well as for Heidegger (1962), estrangement or inauthenticity is the default human situation, and only escapable for exceptional individuals. What, then, of a semiotics of being – an existential semiotics inspired by biosemiotics?

While the implicit self – our identity – is predominantly a social (to some extent personal) creation, the explicit self is less so, rooted as it is in man's ecological activities, whatever form they might take. At the face of it, it appears that a person would be more "authentic" the better her implicit self came to reflect her explicit self – the better, in other words, she consciously came to understand herself in terms of how she actually behaves in all her engagements, be they social or ecological. In principle, such a "semiotic rebirth" could take two forms: more truthful self-comprehension or behaviours more actively guided by her proclaimed ideals. While that may serve as a fine norm, it should be noted that the ecological as well as social relations that any sociable person (except perhaps the very poorest) of our era engages in *qua* economic player by far transcend the horizon of his conscious self (many an all-to-mindful soul in our society consequently choose a dignified solitude – the price (in terms of sociality) of consequence and oversight).

From the perspective of science, it appears that this process of being reborn as semiotic self, as it were, is not a wholly philosophical enterprise. It is true enough that aspects of our groundedness as beings of Earth – our situatedness in ecological and astronomical/cosmological terms – are there to be re-discovered in various cultural sources. Others, however, we have to discover for the first time, at least on a proper scientific ground. Here, then, we re-encounter the hope that a semiotics of being – or whatever we would call a fertile existential semiotics – could potentially transcend the "subject [of mainstream existentialism] who essentially moves alone in the universe, without the presence of other subjects" (Tarasti 2000: 13). If David Abram (1988: 101) was right in claiming that the ecological crisis "may be the result of a recent and collective perceptual disorder in our species", then perhaps we need also to reconsider the aforementioned twofold confusion of objects and things, and start treating objects like objects and things like things. Again, a fine norm, apparently, but alas: Each and every creature on Earth does by necessity objectify some things. Nevertheless we should as far as practically possible treat other creatures, not least, as more-than-economic bodies (cf. the notion of semiotic economy), and take their respective subjectivities into account. Once again knowledge of reality emerges as a definitive advantage: Due to the considerable size of the global human population, there are demographic restraints to how drastically we can possibly change our behaviour, and these restraints are likely to be in place for hundreds, but not thousands, of years (cf. Tønnessen 2008). A truly virtuous humankind is therefore – one might very well argue – necessarily a phenomenon of a fairly distant future. For the same reason, our environmental impact is likely to remain elevated for a long time to come, no matter what happens with our economy.

In his famous essay "Economic possibilities for our grandchildren", written during the depression, John Maynard Keynes (1930: 366) envisioned that "the economic problem", the struggle for subsistence – which had always up till then been the primary, most pressing problem of the human race – "may be solved, or be at least within sight of solution, within a hundred years." "If the economic problem is solved," reasoned Keynes (1930: 367), "mankind will be deprived of its traditional purpose" – "for the first time since his creation man will be faced with his real, his permanent problem – how to use his freedom from pressing economic cares, how to occupy the leisure, which science and compound interest will have won for him, to live wisely and agreeably and well." It is arguably the case that more than half of all the economic activity that has ever taken place – since the birth of humankind – has taken place since the publication of Keynes' essay (cf. Tønnessen 2008). We have reached our "destination of economic bliss" (Keynes 1930: 370). And yet, there is no end in sight. The aim of pursuing (endless) economic growth has been universally acclaimed across the globe, as a primary attachment of our time. The human tendency to transcend our species' actual circumstances in both ambition and perception – indeed, in our worldview – lingers on.

Alluding one last time to Gabriel Marcel, we may say that when all mysteries are approached as problems to be solved, man is nothing but a problematic being. To behave bluntly as efficient, problem-solving creatures – treating everything (and everyone non-human) as reducible to controllable entities – appears to entail a terrible waste of human resources and potential. But then again, what is man? Only history will tell. To define what a human being truly is remains premature.

References

Abram, David. 1988. Merleau-Ponty and the voice of the Earth. *Environmental Ethics* 10. 101–120.
Abram, David. 1997. *The spell of the sensuous: Perception and language in a more-than-human world*. New York: Vintage Books/Random House.
Bonnet, Roger-Maurice & Lodewyk Woltjer. 2008. *Surviving 1,000 centuries: Can we do it?* Berlin-Heidelberg-New York/Chichester, UK: Springer/Praxis Publishing.
Camus, Albert. 1965 [1947]. *The plague (La Peste)*. New York: McGraw Hill.
Camus, Albert . 1991 [1942/1955]. *The myth of Sisyphus [Le Mythe de Sisyphe] and other essays*. Translated by J. O´Brien. New York: Vintage International.
Deely, John. 2005. *Basics of Semiotics*, 4th edn. (bilingual edition, Estonian/English; Trans. by Kati Lindström). Tartu: Tartu University Press.
Engels, Friedrich. 1958. Origin of the family, private property and the state. In *Selected Works* (2 volumes), 2. Moscow: Foreign Languages Publishing House.
Favareau, Donald. 2002. Beyond self and other: On the neurosemiotic emergence of intersubjectivity. *Sign Systems Studies* 30(1). 57–100.
Fox, Warwick. 1984. Deep ecology: A new philosophy of our time? *The Ecologist* 5–6. 194–200.
Hegel, Georg Wilhelm Friedrich. 1977 [1806/07]. *Phenomenology of spirit [Phänomenologie des Geistes]*. Trans. by A. V. Miller. Oxford: Clarendon Press.
Heidegger, Martin 1962. *Being and time [Sein und Zeit]*. Trans. by J. Macquarrie & E. Robinson. Oxford: Blackwell.
Keynes, John Maynard 1930. Economic possibilities for our grandchildren. In John Maynard Keynes, *Essays in persuasion*, 358–373. New York: W.W. Norton & Co.
Marcel, Gabriel. 1949 [1933]. Outlines of a phenomenology of having. In Gabriel Marcel, *Being and having [Être et Avoir]*, trans. by Katharine Farrer, 154–179. Glasgow: The University Press.
Nöth, Winfried, Eero Tarasti and Marcus Tamm 2008. Humanities: state and prospects. *Sign Systems Studies* 36(2). 527–532.
Reed, Peter & David Rothenberg (eds.). 1993. *Wisdom in the open air: The Norwegian roots of deep ecology*. Minneapolis: University of Minnesota Press.
Stjernfelt, Frederik 1999. Biosemiotics and formal ontology. *Semiotica* 127(1/4). 537–566.
Stjernfelt, Frederik 2002. A biosemiotic building: 13 theses. In Claus Emmeche, Kalevi Kull & Frederik Stjernfelt (eds.), *Reading Hoffmeyer, rethinking Biology* (Tartu Semiotics Library 3), 13–24. Tartu: Tartu University Press.

Tarasti, Eero. 2000. *Existential Semiotics*. Bloomington/Indianapolis: Indiana University Press.
Toadvine, Ted. 2003. Singing the world in a new key: Merleau-Ponty and the ontology of sense. *Janus Head* 7(2). 273–283.
Tønnessen, Morten. 2001. Outline of an Uexküllian bio-ontology. *Sign Systems Studies* 29(2). 683–691.
Tønnessen, Morten. 2003. Umwelt ethics. *Sign Systems Studies* 31(1). 281–299.
Tønnessen, Morten. 2008. The statistician's guide to Utopia: The future of growth. *TRAMES* 12(2). 115–126.
Tønnessen, Morten. 2009. Umwelt transitions: Uexküll and environmental change. *Biosemiotics* 2(1). 47–64.
Tønnessen, Morten. 2010. Steps to a semiotics of being. *Biosemiotics* 3(3). 375–392.
Tønnessen, Morten & John Deely. 2009. The semioethics interviews I: John Deely: 'Tell me, where is morality bred?'. *Hortus Semioticus* 4 (August). 57–80.
von Uexküll, Jakob. 1956 [1934/1940]. *Streifzüge durch die Umwelten von Tieren und Menschen: Ein Bilderbuch unsichtbarer Welten. Bedeutungslehre*. Hamburg: Rowohlt.
von Uexküll, Jakob. 1982. The theory of meaning [*Bedeutungslehre*]. Trans. by Barry Stone & Herbert Weiner. *Semiotica* 42(1). 25–82.
Webb, Stephen. 2002. *Where is everybody?* New York: Copernicus Books, Praxis.
Westphal, Merold. 1987. *Kierkegaard's Critique of reason and society*. Macon GA: Mercer University Press.
Wheeler, Wendy. 2006. *The whole creature: Complexity, Biosemiotics and the evolution of culture*. London: Lawrence & Wishart.
Zapffe, Peter Wessel. 1999 [1961]. Et biosofisk perspektiv [A biosophic perspective]. In Peter Wessel Zapffe (ed.), *Indføring i Litterær Dramaturgi* [Introduction to Literary Dramaturgy], 165–176. Oslo: Pax forlag.
Zapffe, Peter Wessel. 1993 [1933]. The last Messiah [Den sidste Messias]. Trans. by Sigmund Kvaløy & Peter Reed. In Peter Reed & David Rothenberg (eds.) *Wisdom in the open air: The Norwegian roots of deep ecology*, 40–52. Minneapolis: University of Minnesota Press.
Zapffe, Peter Wessel. 1993a [1958]. Farewell, Norway [Farvel Norge]. Trans. by Peter Reed. In Peter Reed & David Rothenberg (eds.) 1993, *Wisdom in the open air: The Norwegian roots of deep ecology*, 52–59. Minneapolis: University of Minnesota Press.
Zapffe, Peter Wessel. 1996 [1941, 1983]. *Om det tragiske* [On the tragic]. Oslo: Pax forlag.

Francesco Spampinato
Memories of the body and pre-signity in music: Points of contact between Existential Semiotics and Globality of Languages

Abstract: While Eero Tarasti, in the formulation of his Existential Semiotics, benefits from the suggestions of certain philosophical orientations in order to breathe new life into semiotics, Gino Stefani and Stefania Guerra Lisi, in the context of the Globality of Languages, refer to psychophysiological models to examine phenomena of communication and expression. These two semio-aesthetic paradigms, however, find common ground in a shared intention to move beyond "semiotics of rules and grammars". One particular aspect of this convergence will be examined in this text: the proximity between the notion of "pre-sign", such as it is formulated by Eero Tarasti in the works *Existential Semiotics* and *Signs of Music*, and the notion of the "psycho-affective memory of the body", proposed by Stefania Guerra and Gino Stefani. It is therefore possible to distinguish two types of pre-signity: a phylogenetic pre-signity and an ontogenetic pre-signity. Thanks to the double articulation of the psychophysiological dimensions of pre-signity, we have a dialogue between a *phenomenology of traces* and an *anthropology of tracks*, in which the track is the body memory which gives a meaning to the traces.

Keywords: Globality of Languages, pre-sign, body, memory

The transition to new semiotic models, other than Greimasian structuralism, can be counted among today's often interdisciplinary currents of thought and research. While Eero Tarasti, in the formulation of his Existential Semiotics, benefits from the suggestions of certain philosophical orientations to breathe new life into semiotics, Gino Stefani and Stefania Guerra Lisi, in the context of the Globality of Languages,[1] refer to psychophysiological models to examine phenomena of communication and expression. These two semio-aesthetic paradigms,

---

[1] The discipline of the Globality of Languages was founded by Stefania Guerra Lisi during the 1970s, then developed by its founder and by Gino Stefani, applied today by an international group of researchers. This discipline operates in the areas of research, education, entertainment and therapy based on psychophysiological semiotics and aesthetics (see, among others, Guerra Lisi 1987 et Stefani and Guerra Lisi 2004).

Note: Paper presented at the International Workshop on Eero Tarasti's Existential Semiotics, April 5th 2006, University of Aix-en-Provence.

however, find common ground in a shared intention to move beyond "semiotics of rules and grammars" (cf. Tarasti 2002: 126). One particular aspect of this convergence will be examined in this text: the proximity between the notion of "pre-sign", such as it is formulated by Eero Tarasti in the works *Existential Semiotics* (2000) and *Signs of Music* (2002), and the notion of the "psycho-affective memory of the body", proposed by Stefania Guerra and Gino Stefani (2004, 2006).

1 Synesthesia, memories of the body and semiosis

The conjunction that we would like to propose here thus goes in the direction well illustrated by Eero Tarasti in his description of the passage from classical semiotics to the new semiotics: the latter is primarily interested in the signification which precedes the formation of rules and follows a chain of "pre-signs" which are related to the gestural and the emotional.[2] For Tarasti, the life of a sign is always in a state of becoming, and the "pre-interpretant", or "pre-sign", is the first step of this life. It precedes the production of a new sign, coming "before the formation of signs", before their "crystallisation" and their "concretisation".

The proposal of a notion such as the "psycho-affective memory of the body" by Gino Stefani and Stefania Guerra Lisi can, in our opinion, be included in this same opening of horizons. According to these authors, all intense experience will evoke bodily "memories", formed at a stage of prenatal life which lacks all sensory specialisation; during this phase of human development, stimuli, particularly of the tactile variety, are linked to all the other senses and emotional states. These bodily "memories" would, therefore, be intersensory. "It is certain," write Stefani and Guerra Lisi, "that we pass from prenatal intersensory experience to post-natal experience, which, despite progressive hierarchised specialisation, retains *vicarietà*[3] and connection, even if we focus only on a single sense" (2004: 271). A notion as such shelters us from the risk of moving beyond the frontiers of semiotics and entering into a "pre-semiotic" biological field: these "memories" constitute an "anthropological lexicon of traces", the elements of which function as "interpretants" within the process of semiosis. Their presence thus moves us from the mechanical-biological relations of stimulus-response (which,

---

2 Cf. Tarasti 2002: 91–104 ; 124–126.
3 Substitutability by vicarious senses.

in the terms of C.S. Pierce, would be merely "dyadic" and not semiotic) to genuine bodily "languages" (to "triadic" signic structures, and thus semiotics).

The "homological model of synesthesia", developed in the Globality of Languages (Stefani and Guerra Lisi 2004: 261), plays a key role in the extension of the field of semiotics to psychophysiological phenomena. In this discipline, the bodily origin of all potential signification is virtually intermodal. Productions of meaning evoking different sensory modalities are here reinterpreted as many derivations of a single foundation: a tonic emotional state capable of simultaneously activating all sensory modalities, as well as motricity. The connection between auditory experience and tactile, gustatory, motor or visual evocation would thus not be created by mere mental association, nor by a kind of "short-circuiting" of the senses, but rather by a "common matrix" from which the various manifestations of bodily experience would constitute the results of an articulative process. From this perspective, the eventual *"analogical relationships"* (similarities of forms) established, for example, between an auditory experience and a tactile sensation, recognisable through the use of the tools of componential semantics, are less important than the *homological relations* (identity of function, genetic and structural connection). Synesthesia would thus be a spontaneous and universal mental disposition, which develops already during prenatal life: its origins are in the intersensory modalities which are particular to the foetus, which has not yet developed specific sensory systems and experiences equivalence between tactile pressures, autoplastic images, and sounds amplified by the amniotic fluid. One example is the experience of musical "caress" and of "caressing" sounds. The origin of human affectivity and of the possibility of establishing an emotional dialogue with others is found in prenatal cutaneous stimulation. Sounds are perceived by the foetus in a tactile-pressive manner and invested with emotional value. For these authors, music is a "privileged vibrational envelopment" (2006: 19): in communicating and being communicated, it has enormous potential for contact. This explains the origins of metaphors relating to the "sonic gesture": sounds are "caressing", "hard", "violent", "penetrating", "sharp", etc. Music can awaken the pleasure of emo-tonic nuance and the vibrational caress by reactivating these memories of the body.

When one takes into account the institution and learning of these equivalences (in the prenatal phase or the successive phases of acquisition of sensori-motor schemes), one finds all the terms of Peircean semiosis. The sensory modalities of the foetus (in prenatal life) and the memories of the body (in prenatal and post-natal life) give birth to interpretants in order to establish connections between a certain signifying "sign" (a "representamen", such as, for example, a cutaneous pressure, a whispered word, or the vision of nuance of colours) and a signified "object" (for example, a tonic and emotional effect such as that which is produced by a caress).

The verbal label ("interpretant") connects the meaning ("object") – in this case, a listening experience – with the music ("sign"), which is supposed to have produced this experience in the listener. Although the cultural attribution of a verbal label makes the mechanism triadic, expressions of experience which are not culturally codified, not yet tied to labels, but simply *expressed*, will not be triadic without the bodily pre-sign. The possibility of defining meaning, with the help of a codified label, is thus not a determining factor for the process to be semiosic, as the expression of emotions is already semiosis, already triadic, before being set into a label. Furthermore, the interpretant, which functions as the trace of an experience, can also belong to non-verbal and less codified languages (for example, a drawing expressing the pleasure of the caress felt when listening to a piece of music). The determining factor in semiosis is that, *without the synesthesic memory of the equivalence between "sonic nuance" and "cutaneous nuance", we would not have been able to feel the caress in the music.* There is thus a kind of *"pre-interpretant"*, as Tarasti would say (2000 : 30), which functions as a guide for the apprehension of meaning and the development of verbal labels, even if it remains latent with regards to the results of semiosis at work. The relation between "interpretant" and "pre-interpretant" is thus configured as the relation between the *trace* and the *track*; the latter is merely a primary trace which directs the attribution of meaning towards new traces (without, however, mechanically predetermining them).

Recent musicological trends have borrowed notions, from other disciplines, tied to amodal sensorimotor patterns and close to the concept of "body memory": the "image schemata", proposed by the philosopher Mark Johnson (1987), have been applied to music by various researchers (cf., among others, Brower 2000 and Marconi 2001); the "vitality affects" studied by psychologist Daniel Stern (1985) have been taken up, for example, in the works of Michel Imberty (2005). In our view, these notions, although elaborated in different disciplinary contexts, can be considered to be *pre-signic tracks of signification*.

This model is doubly triadic, as the semiotic triangle is doubled by the pre-semiotic triangle. Such a model is likely to be related to the model of the life of signs in three stages – "pre-signs", "act-signs", and "post-signs" – proposed by Eero Tarasti in *Existential Semiotics* (2000: 33–34) (Figure 1).

The various types of *amodal sensorimotor patterns* can be considered, in our opinion, as a particular category of pre-signs. In effect, they precede the phase of fixation of concrete signs (in other words, they precede the production of specific meaning connected with a listening experience): their formation dates back to the beginnings of human life (*anteriority of their formation*); in the course of a musical listening experience, they are activated by "modulations of the vital flux", below the state of consciousness and sensory specialisation, and continue to guide it throughout its *mise en langage* (*anteriority of their reactivation*). Further, these bodily patterns give "existential" depth to signs by putting them in relation with dimensions important to human beings (intense sensations and emotions, profound experiences, etc.) and with the "golden age" of human ontogenesis, the pleasure of intra-uterine life. However, it is not a question only of "references" to moments of importance to the existence of the individual ("transcendent" signifieds of musical signifiers), but of the very source of the possibility for attributing meaning to a musical listening experience, or for clarifying a meaning *through* musical language. The body is not "signified", "evoked" by music or "associated" with a piece of certain music, it is rather *the source* of the various ways in which a sign can bring forth meaning, in which meaning comes to the sign to establish it as a sign.

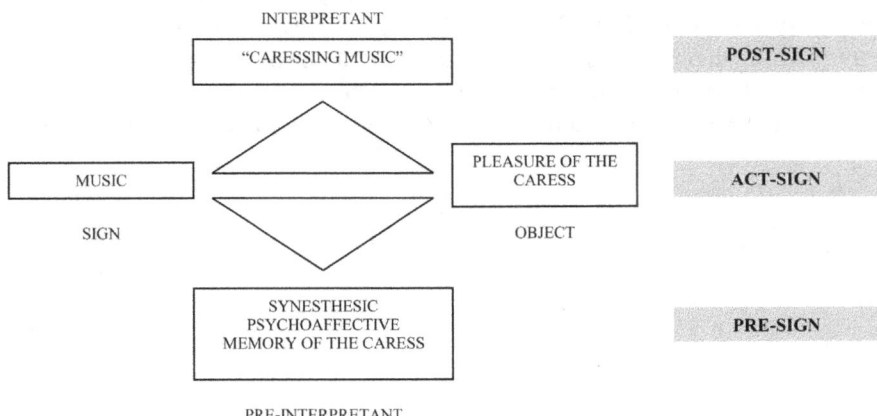

Figure 1: Semiotic and pre-semiotic triangles.

2 Ontogenetic and phylogenetic pre-signities

These patterns have given rise, throughout the history of music, to various actualisations, which function, in their turn, as pre-signs for further actualisations. If we accept that these crystallisations are many pre-signs, it would yet be necessary to distinguish them from bodily pre-signs which are reactivated for each experience. It is, therefore, possible to distinguish two types of pre-signity: a phylogenetic pre-signity and an ontogenetic pre-signity. In the first typology, we find the history and phenomenology of the concretisations of a same bodily pre-sign. The pre-sign/act-sign dialogue is, here, made in the domain of intertextuality and of inter-semiosis (as is the case, for example, with the relationship between Ernest Chausson's *Piano Quartet* and César Franck's *Prelude, Chorale and Fugue*, mentioned by Tarasti 2002: 124). In contrast, bodily patterns are associated with the second form: ontogenetic pre-signity (Figure 2). Furthermore, if we leave the field of psychology, we find that the "transcendental ideas" discussed by Tarasti (2000: 20, 33), which are not tied to any specific artistic discipline, more closely resemble this second category. The notion of "silent speech", discussed by Bernard Vecchione in his works on the hermeneutics of existence, can also be added to this vertical pre-signity: that "speech" which announces itself at the door of, unbeknownst, or even contrary to, utterance (2009). In addition, Vecchione speaks of the "wholeness" of *Dasein*, which weaves together several types of "pre-signitive sources" and which precedes all "signitive specificity" of the verbal, of the musical, of the plastic, etc.: "each pre-signitive specificity is probably, although perhaps in proportions which vary every time, woven from all the pre-signitive sources which constitute *Dasein*" (1997: 123). Such philosophical reflections resemble the psychophysiological considerations illustrated above on the subject of synesthesia.

It is possible to represent this double pre-signity in the following manner:

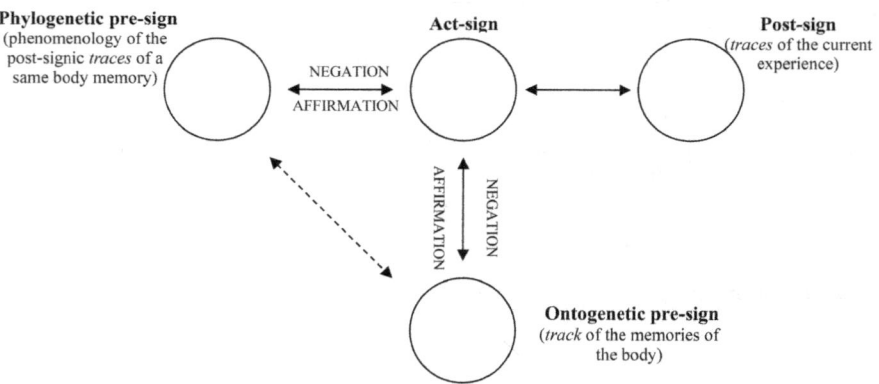

Figure 2: Double pre-signity of bodily memories.

The passage from pre-sign to act-sign can be effected in two ways: either by "negation" (the pre-sign is "abandoned" and "denied") or by "affirmation" (by a "concretization" in the "perceptual world of *Dasein*", the pre-sign fulfils the act-sign with "something more profound", which motivates it and renders it significative, by giving it a "transcendental", "existential" depth (Tarasti 2000: 34).

A musical example will allow us to better understand the functioning of this double pre-signity. My research on the reception of Claude Debussy's *La Mer* has shown that a feeling of "fluidity", aerial or liquid, is felt in listening to this work, even by those who do not know the title of the piece and its three sections (Spampinato 2005a, 2005b). Thus, the water in this piece is not simply *recognised* in its visual manifestations (shape of waves in the melodic curve, rhythm which reproduces the coming and going of the waters on the shore, timbres which shine like the sun reflecting off the surface of the sea, etc.), it is also *experienced*: the muscular tonus is hypotonic, the gestural, descendant, the posture, relaxed; and the prevalent emotion is a feeling of the pleasure of being contained, enveloped, gently rocked, transported; the pleasure of the nuance is synesthesic (gradations of light and colours, alongside tactile strokes and light sonorous opalescences). In short, not only do we *perceive* and *recognise* water and the sea, but we *are* this water and this sea. Fluidity, from this point of view, is thus entirely bodily: tonic and emotional, amodal and synesthesic (cf. Spampinato 2011). This is "architecture of vitality affects", to use the expression proposed by Imberty (2005) to define the psychological aspects of stylistic phenomena in music; and, for Imberty, water is the archetype of Debussy's style (1987). From a historical perspective – as pointed out by Caroline Potter (2003), among others – in *La Mer*, Debussy avoids the devices which western musical tradition had forged for translating water into music (most notably, arpeggios). The musician invents new strategies of signification by diverting not only the "rules" of tonal music (an issue much studied by historians and analysts) but also the rules of musical signification itself. He proposed to establish a new path between a *meaning* and its musical *manifestation*. Thus, the guide along this path, which constitutes the measure of comprehension of meaning in listening, is not the reference to a context or tradition (phylogenetic pre-signity), but the rooting in a bodily and emotional "ontogenetic pre-signity". In this case, it is, therefore, possible to recognise a vertical relation of *affirmation*, whereas a primarily *negative* relation is configured on the horizontal plane.[4]

Another example of the application of this model of bodily pre-signity concerns the analysis of interartistic phenomena and relations. As I have shown in recent work (Spampinato 2007, 2011), the first of Debussy's *Préludes pour piano*

---

4 But this vertical relation always contains negation in so far as these schemas are implemented without the knowledge of, and sometimes contrary to, the compositional development and creative projects of the musician. This is where work on utterance breaks down, escapes the conscious control of the composer, that meaning announces itself and is perceived. Also, the horizontal relationship is equally complex in so far as the composer, despite being critical with regard to musical tradition, always finishes by weaving a dialogue of affirmations and negations with this tradition.

(Premier livre), *Danseuses de Delphes*, invites the listener to adopt the same sensorimotor pattern as Claude Monet's painting *Le bassin aux nymphéas, harmonie verte*, namely the bodily schema of "swinging". If from a historical and phylogenetic perspective there is no relevant connection between these two works, from an ontogenetic and homological perspective, beyond any communicational intent on the part of the authors, they are based on the same bodily pre-sign.

3 Towards a pre-signic imaginary

Due to the double articulation of the psychophysiological dimensions of pre-signity, we have a dialogue between the *phenomenology of traces* and *anthropology of tracks*, in which the track is the body memory which gives meaning to the traces. It also becomes possible to delineate topography of bodily (and virtually intersensory) imaginary space, which can be called up by a passage, a work, a composer, or a musical genre. It is not, however, a question of a merely acoustic imaginary, but a *kine-synesthesic imaginary*, with roots in the muscular tonus and emotion. Hence the possibility for the experience, not only of expressing oneself in a work, but also the possibility, for the work, to be known, revealed, expressed in words, or translated into choreography, staged, etc. By following the various phases of the life of a sign, existential and psychophysiological semiotics thus provide a valuable contribution to the phenomena of production and reception of meaning, by untangling the complex relations between tradition and invention, anamnesis and creative act.

References

Brower, Candace. 2000. A Cognitive Theory of Musical Meaning. *Journal of Music Theory* 44/2. 323–380.
Guerra Lisi, Stefania. 1987. *Il metodo della globalità dei linguaggi*. Rome: Borla.
Imberty, Michel. 1987. Il senso del tempo e della morte nell'immaginario debussiano. *Nuova Rivista Musicale Italiana* 21. 383–409.
Imberty, Michel. 2005. *La musique creuse le temps. De Wagner à Boulez: Musique, psychologie, psychanalyse*. Paris: L'Harmattan.
Johnson, Mark. 1987. *The body in the mind. The bodily basis of meaning, imagination and reason*. Chicago: University of Chicago Press.
Marconi, Luca. 2001. *Musica Espressione Emozione*. Bologne: Clueb.
Potter, Caroline. 2003. Debussy and nature. In Simon Trezise (ed.) *The Cambridge Companion to Debussy*, 137–151. Cambridge: Cambridge University Press.

Spampinato, Francesco. 2005a. Archétypes de la forme et archétypes du sens dans *Jeux de vagues* de Debussy. *Studi musicali* 1. 181–207.
Spampinato, Francesco. 2005b. Principi costruttivi e dinamiche tensive in *Jeux de vagues* di Debussy. *Versus* 2. 15–38.
Spampinato, Francesco. 2007. Les patterns corporels de l'expérience musicale : nouvelles perspectives pour l'étude des rapports interartistiques. In Alessandro Arbo (ed.), *Perspectives de l'esthétique musicale*, 305–315. Paris: L'Harmattan.
Spampinato, Francesco. 2011. *Debussy, poète des eaux. Métaphorisation et corporéité dans l'expérience musicale.* Paris: L'Harmattan.
Stefani, Gino & Stefania Guerra Lisi. 2004. *Dizionario di musica nella Globalità dei Linguaggi.* Lucca: LIM.
Stefani, Gino & Stefania Guerra Lisi. 2006 [1999]. *The Prenatal Styles in the Arts and the Life.* Acta Semiotica Fennica 24. Imatra: International Semiotics Institute.
Stern, Daniel. 1985. *The Interpersonal World of the Infant.* New York: Basic Books.
Tarasti, Eero. 2000. *Existential Semiotics.* Bloomington: Indiana University Press.
Tarasti, Eero. 2002. *Signs of Music. A Guide to Musical Semiotics.* Berlin, New York: Mouton de Gruyter.
Vecchione, Bernard. 1997. Musique, herméneutique, rhétorique, anthropologie: une lecture du musical en situation festive. In Françoise Escal & Michel Imberty (eds.), *La musique au regard des Sciences Humaines et des Sciences Sociales*, 99–174. Paris: L'Harmattan.
Vecchione, Bernard. 2007. L'*hermeneia* silencieuse du musical. In Christian Hauer & Bernard Vecchione (eds.), *Le sens langagier du musical, Semiosis et Hermeneia.* Paris: L'Harmattan.

Sari Helkala-Koivisto
The existential question between musical and linguistic signification

Abstract: The present text dates partly to the early days of my dissertation and the essays (2007) related to the first steps towards Existential Semiotics, when trying to shape and explain the first theoretic and experience-based basics on my research, looking for the new paths to draw interaction between *Music and Autism* through *Prosodic sign* (2015). The study raised the question: whether musical signification, the flowing prosodic accentuation within music, could have the potential to promote the development and metalinguistic interaction in children with severe autism. Autistic children live and stay behind spoken language. An innate, congenital sensitivity, a natural rate of detection may help them to find the first competent contacts with arts and music in suprasegmental structures of speech. People do not interpret only the words (lexicon), but all the clues that matter in the formation of meanings and understanding communication. Every sign of the said will make sense. What does the linguistic expression as a whole mean to the autistic recipient? Children with autism can quickly map out the soil for the dialogue. They make a difference between speaker and heard language and direct all interests to the speaking person, not for heard speech. The children seem to be missing species-specific ability to combine observations into single entity. It signifies an internal contradiction that causes unrest and chaos between autism and environment. The music is more intact compared to spoken language. Its integrity and continuity are dictated by artistic creativity, repeated diving from consonance into dissonance and back. Musical speaks to the importance of art in human existence. The music communicates in the composition of both man and culture. Music and the arts create an experiential rhythm and form for everything that cannot be shaped by other means. Art touches the mobile experiencing world. The world is a child with autism or anyone but everywhere.

Keywords: Musical, autism, global, prosody, competence

This essay forms some theoretical reflections on music, music therapy on children with autism, philosophy of music and art, and the ancient idea of *poesis* discovered in the semiotic field on the philosophy in a special branch of Italian music and art therapy. *Poesis* is a concept of cultural heritage originated in ancient Greece, which is still relevant in our time signified by music and the other arts. It was mentioned in Martin Heidegger's late thoughts, in his final Definition of Art. He said that the essence of art is defined as poetry. Poetry, on the other hand, refers to the word of linguistics, but in its diversity withdraws to the deeper meaning shared by music and other arts. The mentioned method of art therapy and the phenomenological background of the underlying philosophy have formed the rehabilitative *mind and practice* called Globality of Languages (*Globalità dei Linguaggi*), developed by Italian art scholars, artists, and semioticians, Stefania Guerra-Lisi and Gino Stefani.

Existential Semiotic theory proved to be an applicable matter to the present multidisciplinary research. The movement of temporally signified human subjectivity happens, according to the Z-model lines, from the attraction of life into the next significant process of self-development. The movements between subject and surrounding signification symbolize cultural maps of the state of mind space – from which it is possible to us to navigate towards both, into every spoken language of different cultures and universal idea of musical/artistic creative mind. Human consciousness, in the individual subject, transcends the world created by expressive surrounding space in time of the language it speaks. Man accepts it and seizes the possibilities of consciousness to understand the world even beyond what we can normally sense and see. In analyzing all the found prosodics, in being the living intermediary in between musical and linguistic expressions of personal existence, one will usually have the ability to feel and experience his/her personal life and the opportunity given at birth to influence it.

Autism is an autonomous neurodevelopmental disorder that may cause wide-ranging developmental deviation. The most typical problems are slow-progress in interaction and linguistic skills. Communication difficulties slow down learning and the achievement of social independence and reciprocal behaviour. Speechlessness or selective non-speaking may obscure, in the early years, a child's true skill level, which can range from high IQ to severe developmental disability in different individuals. Due to interaction problems, a child's competence profile is often uneven until adulthood. In autism, one's own choices and opportunities to influence life will be limited from childhood. Problems related to development and learning communication skills offer a different way to learn to understand what it is to experience and imagine freedom and awareness of one's future possibilities.

The study aims to find the mentioned existential signs in music and speech through children's physical existence, wherein they first appear as bodily gestures and musical movements, in which case they are assumed to occur as body gestures and movements in the early development of infants. The signification is thought to emerge within the accents of prosody (prosodic features) in the development of sense-perception between increasing cultural and individual identity of human existence. The signs in question can be recognized especially in the unhurried development on children with autism, and their individually growing sensitivity and fascination despite the difficulties arising from their diagnosed autism spectrum disorders (ASD).

The accentual prosody is seen to form interactive semiosis in between the (inside) individual and cultural development through the infant's embodied temporal existence. Interactive semiosis is supposed to have a moving prosodic/accentuated core that originates in every infant into one's early related body-mind/*corporeal "there being"*. The prosodic core intensifies further within *musical* signification through pre-musical bodily affections before the later appearance of a symbolized state of words and spoken language. Later, the musical prosody proceeds in our homogeneous human conception within *linguistic* signification. The mentioned triad *(corporeal/*bodily, *musical,* and *linguistic)* does not here signify hierarchy, but at the first place a chronological chain concerning emotional-cognitive progress inside processes on bio-semiotic semiosis. The acting triad will be entirely seen as developing the ability of human continuous self–process, working as a mediating factor in between the development of subjective thinking and one's expressive and interactive communication.

The most interesting question one could present is, how does appearing pre-music-lingual signification represent the cognitive and sensory emotional signs? Does the pre-music-lingual signification structure as well as the meta-linguistic process in developing non-autistic and autistic self? Also, how does it signify conductive social meanings on autistic person's (*Dasein*) *being there*? The existential theory seems to provide in Music Semiotics useful agents for scrutiny in clarifying musical semiosis that occurs as a cognitive function during self-development or self-process in our becoming and *being* human. Existential questions concerning a person's life with autism encounter the sense of signified experiences and particularly understood or misunderstood human signs in divergence situations caused by autistic peoples' aberrant communication abilities. Autistic people behave in a deviant manner relative to the norm and, besides, they often have some comprehensive dis-ontogenesis on the background of their slow developmental stage. They are different from the others and seldom human existence enfolds them in the spirit of Sartre's existentialism.

Responsibility and freedom to make a choice as Sartre's canons on existentialism, in the idea of human beings and existence, do not normally reach the autistic peoples' everyday life in their cultural activities and shared unspoken reality. Whereas, musical communication contains a human core, having a symbolized chance to become signified probably by every non-disabled people as a subjective and cultural part in and for themselves, and, to reflect musical signification also into music for itself. In music, we can create and signify a potential world of temporal beauty. Music as art symbolizes to us a constant movement between human life and its ever-changing, divergent, and multicultural cultures.

Music and the other arts have the power to act as a cultural language in the interaction of music and art therapy sessions by replacing missing or repressed speech. Music creates *a potential world* being a means of expression, a tool for communication and education. It has a real power to signify a flowing dialogue in musical sessions. It replaces another one's missing speech but conveys information about the constant state of emotion, the non-representational relationship with the world and the other present being – It may be signified in music therapy without a too strong conventional performance or social challenge, related to an autistic way, to sense and recognize shared communicative goals.

In music, people have a chance to feel self-expressive freedom through musical communication. It means the individual possibility of choice in playing and listening to music, flowing through musical thinking and as if discussing with music within or outside itself. Existential signs in music are assumed to instruct the consciousness of human being and insert conscious effort to observe the existence of self and other people around. The most crucial goal in the music therapeutic signification is defined by progressing personal integration in mental welfare and social psychophysical growth of individual power and to achieve balance with dialogical self.

Music is great artistic merit in every society. It is also extensive historical merit in culture concerning the whole life of mankind. Music rocks a cradle and dances with us in youth and love. Music steps marching to the boundary and, finally, at the time of passing away, it takes a human gently into the last sleep of peace. In the music lies a hidden, an aesthetic lifelong line of human senses, emotions, and cognition. It reflects linguistic thinking and developing competence of the cultural mind. Music lives in society and as well as society lives in music. Plenty of the most essential cultural values have been handed down throughout centuries subconsciously within musical signification and musical signs. How does society signify musical values today while walking hand in hand with human dignity? Does music, at last, belong universally to every human being or do people still need to have the artistic hierarchy that classifies human beings by musical competences into separate levels or categories of existence?

Music is a sign of culture. It is also a sign of being human. If we investigate music as a cultural sign, the art object will easily carry a categorized mantle of social hierarchy. But if music is seen as a sign of the individual, one can have a momentary chance as if to cross cultural limits and consciousness of being human. An individual signifies culture and, also, furthermore (or before) human nature in time and space. From the viewpoint of human nature, many steps in individual development can pass regardless of the dominant culture. We can ask, does music sound especially within nature or in culture while one listens to music and feels it through various channels of his/her personal sense-perfection (inner mind), which is called (*Dasein*) a human life-world? Values of musical rules will develop, remain, or change the history in consequence of the cultural conclusions and cultural acts. The rules of musical practice and guiding activities are primarily part of social, educational, or artistic planning in society. The values in the background of music culture may not have a musical content inside itself, but they have influences on contents through musical action and in musical signification processes. Musical thinking or working with musical activities will represent music and indicate the directed valuation or non-valuation by a situated prevailing actor. The acts of the valuation or non-valuation demand a close object-relationship. People must have an ability to understand signs of the objects or even, to have an inkling contact with their thinkable signified lifeworld.

People communicate with music through movements, senses, images, and feelings and while playing (music). One can appreciate artistic musical subjectivity and musical signification while being sensible for musical experiences in the corporeal and mental sense. Musical experience represents *instant space* on the mind, becoming fulfilled by existential signs signified both corporeally and mentally. Given *instant space* has reference to existential signs that shape the way to an individual's musical life-world. We can define it as a temporal structure, but, on the other hand, it is seen as an unbroken emotional stream that flows, at the same time, everywhere in our temporal or timeless emotional-aesthetic consciousness. The music moves and sounds inside the human mind and it is coincident with this moving and sounding emotional stream. A human being can catch a feeling as if he/she could resonate in proportion inside the just received music.

The absolute artistic value of music is signified by semiotics in meta-linguistic transcendental signification. Individual's immediate relation with music is created outside of *Dasein,* where this transcendental sphere emerges through contact with human being's life-world. The transcendental musical signification leads our cognitive mind and emotional senses to experience sound nature of life energy through music and its resonances in dialogical self. In the same semiotic sphere, music will come into existence as well as the other aesthetic experiences, *corporeally in 'embodied inner word'* found in visual arts, cinema, poetry, literature, dramatic art, dance, and architecture.

Music has the deepest power in existential and transcendental signification related to human arts. It creates within itself an unnoticeable environment where *subconscious* codifies an individual's procedural *embodied speech*. The mentioned *bodily speech* signifies the subject's cultural-minded values constructed in active consequence by transcendental meta-modalities. It may be seen that music never loses its artistic significance while having a communication role as a meta-lingual expression in music therapy and an educational tool or artistic aim and subject in music education. Its culturally signified artistic and human nature breaks off or varies only in transitional periods, wherein changing attitudes and values are directed towards it becoming emotionally *signified*. Through Existential Semiotics, one can realize the relative and arbitrary nature of signified cultural values. The values and their changes form transcendental chains in the human mind apart from *Dasein*. The choices made by people seem to be independent options, but they still conduct opinions, adaptation, and activities related to their subjective lifeworld (*Dasein*). *Music exists* in itself and for itself. Individual's attitude to it may vary and make often continuous changes, either in deepening or in expanding, *becoming encountered* or in occasional shortening, *escapes encounter*.

Values and prevailing practices navigate both established and developing cultural activities on the musical stage, manifesting itself in visible acts as well as in concealed attitudes. While the cultural values arise, move and change, human being tries to bind and place the existent mind to continual self-experienced and self-understood moving reality. However, the conscious feelings in *Dasein* appear like a trapeze artist's performance in the air, looking for a balance between the permanence and the change. The stabilization of values affects the course of life and keeps conditions stable, while the variable values fall a person into existential unsteadiness, into Heideggerian uncertainty of *being* within prevailing circumstances. Do we people think the conditions of life are somehow settled by permanent, predicted values? (The power of *Dasein* is situational awareness that refreshes us from moment to moment. Situations are times that what create the existential conscious state of our beings). Existential uncertainty exposes us repeatedly by the inevitable meeting of unforeseen tomorrow. Instead, existential certainty lies supposedly in signified signs on every individual's *embodied speech*, in non-verbal and vertically drawn artistic line of life, at the heart of one's deep *dialogic self*.

A great artistic and aesthetic musical value has represented in history the classification of musical practice and musical performance. In the theory of musical competence, one can perceive how music will be able to signify itself as a sign of cultural hierarchy. In Western cultures, the artistic justification for music is included in musical techniques and performance. The musical aim has virtually been exclusively artistic, which makes music unique and autonomic by comparison with other social practices. In the music therapy or other social music-activities, the autonomic, artistic-aesthetical goal is not seen as prime or relevant (Stefani 1982). Though the artistic-aesthetical musical aim would not appear primary in therapy processes, or the other social targets, the artistic-aesthetical signs signify nonetheless through musical content, while moving out a point of view from practice to the sensible world represented by corporeal music experience.

Musical signification represents in human action as a two-way role. Musical products and compositions generally have their appearance in sounding musical performances that provide people with a possibility to "read" or interpret a performer's and composer's musical competence or artistic performances. On the other hand, received music experience can be digested by a listener to his personal cognitive and emotive structuring without any cultural need to a *"public readability"* or analyzed interpretation. Auto-communicative approach, to music and musical signification, is observed well in expression or non-expression on people with autism. Existential signs, within received music and musical communication, are read by them more often in close human presence inside shared musical experiences not in music's great merit and artistic competence. It would be evident that the same emotional-aesthetic part of experiential bodily thinking also exists to the inner world of corporeal us, non-autistic people.

A mentioned part of human thinking signifies the artistic-aesthetical signs of existence. It is not manifested or diagnosed by social or medicine criteria. Emotional-aesthetic thinking represents existential signs of *inner speech*, which means a bodily embodied part of the human thought process. It appears itself in non-verbal bodily gestures and expressions as well as in other meta-linguistic ways of individual and cultural existence (Helkala-Koivisto 2015: 152). The arts signify our meta-linguistic embodied voice to communicate with the world and people around. The classified artistic-aesthetical level in musical competence includes the premium art of the culture, but anyway, this *cultural* stage cannot fence human ability to signify musical signs alone in "the most educated levels of ontogeny".

The idea of musical competence (Stefani 1982) is represented through five distinctive musical function and their cultural practices. Musical functions or offered hierarchical levels are correlated human beings moving and developing relationship and cultural activity to music. A hierarchical concept of musical competence can be comprised, based on, *musical* in the theory, but moving mind competence, advanced and living within music, or individually born between music and human being does not appear correspondingly. Musical competence within the mind, naturally based on transcendence, has no performance-tied cultural hierarchy towards *musical* or music itself. The "artistic-aesthetical" transcendental *space* or phenomenon in music is not engaged to *Dasein* defined by the outside world. So, a marginal of "artistic-aesthetical" can cover up all five levels in musical competence presented by Gino Stefani's theory. In consequence of the mentioned conclusion, the development of musical competence represents, first and foremost, performing musical art being directed only to the aims of the fifth level in classified codes of competence. Musical competence refers, in the case, to a musical ability that comes to a *cultural* head in performing art of music. *Natural* (mind) competence, originated by biological roots, has, on the contrary, a live reference to immediate affections and experiences through one's sensible world. The development of human being with autism seems to be like outside cultured or uncultivated according to conventional rules. But it is not observed to be *unnatural* while coming, for instance, from creative expressions in the arts. And so, inner musical experience is universally opened to every person who has bodily/corporeal possibility to touch and to be touched by flow and sounds on music.

A hierarchy-released, artistic-aesthetical overcome within musical competence could lead to cultural change in musical values and attitudes. Thus, it is not forever a question of artistic autonomy in the music itself, but a cultural appreciation of musical affairs and personal positions. In the model of musical competence, the artistic and popular (general) levels are extremities of cultured code-system. They reflect on cultural practice in developing a relationship between man and music (the arts). An acquirement of musical abilities commences on the first level in schematic sense perfection and will later close on the fifth level in artistic understanding of individual musical works. The fifth level signifies the most developed or talented activity in musical competence. It has culturally used to be seen as a situation of the mental *opening* between *Dasein* and transcendental existence on experienced music. If *musical* represents situation and objects to mental *opening*, it (mental *opening*) may be experienced equally everywhere, with every people being touched by the music itself.

Music exists for us as a mirrored subject of the body-mind. It seems to be in a way as if it were an abstractive, independent *another*. The abstractive *another* can be accidentally disqualified on the artistic level of musical competence. It loses by defining sense-perfection and living experience outside of the theoretic and analyzed musical knowledge. If one forgets a human basis of man, one does not notice anymore all integrative qualities in movements of musical signification. Becoming unfastened from *corporeal* touch on musical significance, people prevent the self in developing its personal growth. Temporal human will know more; it grows from one's ability to signify life as "*being-in-myself*" and as "*being-for-myself*" (see, Tarasti 2005c: 244). It releases people to seek for their existential sign in the spirit of Sartrean freedom. Their subjective experiential sign is understood as well through bio-semiotics if we equate it with Jakob von Uexküll's *Ich-Ton* concept, the idea of natural symbolic self in collective cell-level function picking up the signified sounds that are needed to nourish a main bodily *Ich-Ton* itself.

Music represents symbolic subjectivity being by nature like sensed experienced *another*. Music has simultaneously a temporal substance relating to space, which coincides with auditory *me*-experience in our essential nature. Music pierces the human mind being existential sign within an interactive sense of experiential *me* and understood *another*. Hence, music has as well a historically given power to signify itself as an external subject, separate and sensible matter, which refers to its reflected appearance in the sense of humanity and the culture. Music has the ability to unite people with society and *the other* without losing their touch in the liberty of choice and individual taste of freedom. Spoken language is drawing limits within human existence. The conventionally limited world will be changed all the time, by becoming into new knowledge and experienced bodily plasticity or music and the other arts.

Musical semiosis is interpreted as a sign of experiential subject on corporeal gestures. So, it is good to remember, the conceptual semiotic interpretation is not the only source of semiotic theoretical knowledge. In the event, the object of research is the signified relationship between man and music, not the actual analysis of music – one should not conceptualize the child and his or her existence. The conceptualized child loses his or her ability to form meanings and signify the world to conquer and symbolize it as his/her own. Everyday practices, especially highly expressive communication, can reveal a meta-cognitive core of music in its accentual *being* and *doing* modalities. The musical meta-cognitive core refers to the confluence between an experiential touch of music (maybe the same way in the other arts as well) and human emotions, in the first instance embodied and symbolized meanings. If musical semiosis signifies the existential life-world through the bodily universal qualities (of a human being), the experience-based code of musical competence will be able to include inner *artistic-aesthetical* realization from the moment of birth or even before, appearing emotionally at the same level as the embodied (internal, profound) performances of the artists in their presented and interpreted artistic works. Musical signification maintains experiential human significance and further revives it in culture if people will value music and care for its existence.

One signifies in self and for self only the signs and feelings he/she has understood by/for him/herself. Consequently, one creates constant signs alone for the objects, which he/she has for his/her self signified personally. Musical signification, on the level of *artistic* competence, deviates to a great extent from musical understanding in general codes. Nevertheless, both have their ultimate basis in sense perception and sub-cognitive bodily comprehension. Sub-cognitive signs attach themselves to pre-linguistic *corporeality* that is based on early affective recognition of musical signs, already before the development of *emotional-aesthetic* sensation.

Musical signification is, not only in *Dasein* or *the transcendental world*, required to realize a viewpoint of musical theory or analyzing approach. One needs to know it as well as an emotive issue and let it feel as an *aesthetic affective* one concerning a sensed subject as one's personal property in corporeal body-mind. *Emotional* is not enough for a musical experience. Significance contains, inside of itself, the aesthetic sense; it expands a given opportunity of signified *corporeal* experience, *Sense-perception-self*, to conceive bodily outside, timeless directed life possibilities. For the reason of the semiotic approach, cultured *artistic-aesthetical* cannot be seen as competent as an object of musical competence created by composers and other musicians or performing artists.

Musical experience, as signified by *artistic-aesthetical*, indicates on every level of musical competence the idea of *undivided independent self* that is hidden through existential signs within transcendence. In pursuit of the undivided self, it has its origin in emotional sharing, acceptance, and repeating acts in interactive humanity (human behaviour and communication). Orientation towards emotional sharing appears in autism first in artefacts and non-social objects. It communicates with bodily signs, immersed in gestures and expressions within the music. Autistic living moves on one's personally timed autistic life cycles in a period of early development in place, without any temporal or spatial target of existing movements. The autistic gestures in eyes, in lips, in hands, and body are looking for a time and space to turn rather away towards the outside world around. Music flows in time and the air of space. It sounds or stops, takes up time, but does not inevitably touch a dateless world inside embodied autism. Music awaits a touch within sounds until a person on autism is seized with it, conceding him/herself sympathy towards experiential musical signs. Inner *space* caused by *musical* provides a rhythmic setting for supposed non-activity in mind with autism. Repeating gesture signifies autism. It is stuck in the early developmental stage, merges into music and begins, step by step, to go forward transforming itself within frames in supposed non-activity. Transformation arouses the individual on autism to notice distinctive signs contagious inside touch and outside reactions of his/her musical experience. He/she exists unexpectedly between stability and change. Repeating gestures, which the others interpret an aimless obsessive repetition in his/her mind is not probably a sign of mind but a signal of body-mind. It is not an obsessive idea moving in intentional mind but rather a bodily impulse due to autism. The impulse is not easy to control or to ease the pressure. Gradually continuous repetition will start to vary related to sensed music and moving step in clapping rhythms. Repetitive behaviour as we call it mirrors first within the *musical* subject, and moves then – responding, after in self-drawn choices – into existential question and musical dialogue between two interactive expressions in the *potential to open worlds*.

Musical moments, signified by inviting smile, dancing movements, concentrated awaking in the arts, the slow approaching, pausing, and creating an inquiring look, will refer to first non-verbal roots to feel human existence. A shared joy means a living expression in giving chance to signification. To signify *another* represents a realized possibility to choose a discovered way of listening to *another*. Then, listening is a "real" *pre-sign* in understanding or misunderstanding in nature. Concentrating to *another* means extend the journey to the inner identity of personal/subjective body-mind existence. Non-spoken signification aroused from musical or other artistic matters is a way to fasten one's existent tendency into existent human reality around self. It happens before, or instead of becoming grade of *linguistic* that is presumably preceded by unifying symbolized prosodic features in musical and linguistic signification.

Experiential prosodic *signified* appears, supposedly, in an early stage with accentual embodied prosody. Semantic transitions in infancy first from bodily/corporeal- into musical and further towards *linguistic* symbolic signs are considered in the present study, later, from a point of view on Kristeva's *chora*. Semiotic *chora* represents a pre-linguistic level in human development. In early childhood, before the advent of linguistic ability, it will, in advance, express the signs of inside-outside communication (Tarasti 2004: 243; Välimäki 2005: 179; Helkala-Koivisto 2015: 99). Early synesthetic sense perception concerning *signified* in existential and individual self-expressive *signs of arts has been examined in the theory of the Globality of Languages* (Guerra Lisi & Stefani 2006). The theory manifests capability of expression in the artistic experience, observed especially among disabled people. In the mentioned aesthetic-semiotic approach, the *artistic signified* proves a necessary significance of non-linguistic cultural alternatives to the universal human *being*. Every *sense-perception-self* collects useful signs making progress in many areas of individual development. The existential sign is found continually present by the mentioned collector. It is a prosodic accent discovered both in the subjective nature and in the culture. It signifies positions of change in the body and mind through bodily/corporeal, musical, and *linguistic* existence of human lifeworld (Helkala-Koivisto 2015: 67–70; 2019).

A prosodic sign represents widely, creative transformations, musically or linguistically signified expression on temporal signification within voicing. Significance of prosodic sign coordinates speech expression or played musical work leading it as an expressive act towards interpreting *other*s. The real existence of prosodic sign (prosodic features) does not usually consciously signify in a natural speech at all. It is considered a normal part of spoken language and received according to conventional cultured interpretation. In reality, the people do not notice prosodic features in speech or culture but are instinctively waiting for non-verbal information that received speech represent and express prosody in the presentation. A nature of prosodic signs seems to be transcendental. Their characteristics assimilate in their entirety into situational speech stream. Therefore, a listener is not woken up, until prosodic features are missing in the speech/spoken language. The prosodic features are signified in their non-appearance or in "lack of existence". They acquire their fullness through negation in the transcendence that is generally detected in communication with people on autism.

Expression in music or speech obtains a position of human activity only in an interactive situation. It needs to become expectedly received by *another's* interpretation at the time of instant enunciation. Prosodic features act, on the other hand, as a temporal medium of meta-modalities that bind subject's (inter-actors) activities with covering the emotional part of the expression. Prosodic continuum has fastened into the linguistic structure and its cultural expressions. It carries within itself extensive information of cultural heritage. In historical context, a touch between prosodic features and archaic, the oldest emotive communication of man, is possible to be seen quite apparent. Mother-child relationship has been, without a doubt, based on interactive baby talk's nurtured voicing throughout history. And, on the other hand, people have had, already in primitive cultures, the ability to take care of each other and escape alive through coherent, effective (prosodic) knowledge of the community.

The first impression, produced by *another* person in received speech, lies not directly in words, in the meaning of verbal referents. The impression is signified within hidden emotive and identified signs of enunciation. Displacements in *emotional* are often conducted by acoustically present prosodic signs that ensure people's communicative signification in moving *Dasein*. In addition to their acoustic communicative presence, prosodic features represent, on the other hand, inner corporeal signs of transcendental meta-modalities. Their existence appears in human signification as "*the surplus of meaning*" (Ricoeur 2000) within unconsciously signified conventions of the culture.

The best representative on signified communication structure is surely the self of a human being. Communication can be seen analogous to music because of its simultaneous passing in the same way both inside and outside of expressive linguistic significance, and likewise, the music is also connected to person's emotive bodily expressions (Lång 2004: 184–185; Szekely 1962; Salomonsson 1991). *Inside Sign* of linguistic existence is thought to signify the following concepts: *human sign within linguistic* and in inverse proportion *linguistic sign within the human* (mind). Becoming to *linguistic* and being within it refer in this connection to linguistic usage, acquired cognitive competence to speak, to understand, to think, and to express the linguistic abilities. Unfastened *Outside Sign* of linguistic existence, in relation to *Dasein*, means here the inmost most core of *linguistic*. This core seems to be as if disappeared outside of the linguistic sphere but will again be discovered there. The inmost core has its appearance from linguistic. It is not situated in lingual expression but within *corporeal* semiosis. *Corporeal* semiosis is signified like mind-drawn unconscious bond around *Dasein's* moving existence. The mind-drawn bond of Transcendence can reach for timeless Existential knowledge of self in music.

The existence with *another*, in an expressive (musical) situation, can catch through musical transcendence the shared experience, wherein *emotionally signified* appears like in a mirror-effect. The experiential moment is seen and sensed supposedly like "Me-Tone" rocking on the balanced inner-outer waves of deep, felt as undivided identity. *Emotionally signified* can be found partly in language or outside of it, but its *corporeal is* not present in linguistic semantics before spoken expression, for linguistic expression lacks a unifying sense of feeling between personal touch and living experience. Lingual (textuality) words represent non-corporeal exterior experience, while "musical words" are written and spoken through experience within the musical and bodily expression of lived (signified) experience.

Emotionally *signified* is concealed in musical expression alike in speech. Emotional is hidden in its situated existential presentation. In speech, it is set or unset out in the automatic prosodic features or intentional rhetoric. In music, *Emotional* presents more strongly because of a chance to be widely signified directly by sense perfection. It is exposed by music more sensitively compared to speech. Existential in emotional beats through a dialogue between appearance and interpretation, that is manifested by interactive voicing to musical or lingual expressions. A dialogue between appearance and interpretation implies emotionally shared signification. Shared signification is carried by interpretation met by prosody within sounding music or in spoken language, in the speech addressed to another and as well as imitating echo speech- 'nonsense'- that is typical on autistic expressions.

Emotionally *signified* refers, herein, to transcendence that seizing upon metamodalities will activate succeeded signification to object's interpretation. The reference to transcendental energy signifies the birth of an inner interaction within an individual subject or between two subjects on the artistic level of transcendence outside of *Dasein*. Shared signification is non-linguistic in nature but, anyhow, indirectly through shared *signified*, deeply tied also to linguistic expression. *Linguistic* moves towards transcendence in literature, in poetry or other narrative and illustrating texts of art. It has artistic means to exceed itself in going beyond verbal *signified*, but it can never succeed in reaching a space where music can continually exist and vary in and outside of its self. Linguistic is situated in *Dasein*. It stratifies to communicative inter-textual relations and objects of people. Number of *Daseins* form individual and communal linguistic chains that become interpreted by their mutual appearance; established chains of *Dasein* are founded upon moving emotional *aesthetic signified* in temporality. Life is covered by linguistic competence from various points, but in humans, it contains the inner bodily energy, constructed outside the language. Individual's musical cognition and the musical knowledge in the culture begin to take shape through prosodic attraction points. The musical sensibility of a human being develops in temporal structure to corporeal mind before a receptive ability in language. Also, the temporal structure on becoming corporeal, mind has its origin or basement in vowel-shaping phase during a period in the baby's babbling. The vowels have an immediate connection with emotional expressions of moving body and infant's vocalizations (Guerra-Lisi & Stefani, 2010, 69). For the reason, embodied affective meanings are supposed to be the first existential signs to structure *inner* embodied *speech* and its developing emotional self.

In acquiring his/her musical competence, one has had corresponding cognitive processes in the development of musical into linguistic signification. Accordingly, the musical cognition is structured by perception, understanding, thought, and power of deduction. One can ask whether the process in musical befall within or without linguistic influence in cognitive advancement if one defines art according to Susan Langer (1953): "Art is the creation of forms symbolic of human feeling". Consequently, the music can reflect directly the subjective aspect of experience. Its open "presentational" symbols (signs) are distinctive from "discursive" symbols of language. "Music articulates forms which language cannot set forth" – it shows us the issues that cannot be said.

Musical experience does not require the listener to have in babyhood or afterwards any linguistic communication, but especially during the early chaotic phase of development likewise in the earlier prenatal period, a possibility to communicate within musical exists in a psycho-physiological situation of signifying prosodic signs. The first presentation of prenatal prosodic germ can be interpreted as bodily psycho-physiological accents between a mutual contact of a fetus in a womb and a baby-expecting mother. During the development of senses, a broadening ambient voice-world around the fetus, the "temporal" prosodic germ, transposes to vibrating pre-musical existence. Prosodic, within pre-musical, promotes a `developing subject' towards next expressive processes that will catch up with linguistic as a key to the code of becoming symbolic thinking. Psycho-physiological communication, during the prenatal period, can be described as if to carry on correspondence with the subject's individual source text. It constitutes a universally genetic basis to individual's later cultural identity and inner inter-textual development (see also Guerra-Lisi & Stefani 2006; Helkala-Koivisto 2009: 571–572).

The birth of prosodic signs occurs first in psycho-physiological communication between a biological process (natural act) and a tiny receiver (natural actor) in the development of one's individual life. That means an unbroken dialogue between "a wave-pressure on the skin" and moving fetus in amniotic fluid. As a result of the mentioned interpretation, it can be thought, prosodic semiosis does contribute to a human being from the early stage to the whole course of one's life. Accentual continuum of prosodic "emo-tono-phono-symbolic" (Guerra-Lisi & Stefani 2006) signs conserve reciprocal connection of bodily/corporeal, musical, and linguistic "thinking" by twining itself into every individual signification situated in questions, choices, and decisions on human existence.

In the development of a linguistic-evading autistic child, accentual prosodic sign in speech or music does turn to him in linguistic effects of expression of the other. Representing a deep content of musical signified, the prosodic sign shapes as if a "broad structure" that reflects moving *Dasein* of a suspicious child. Child's relationship to music and *musical* within the "broad structure" is based on non-verbal expression and non-verbal understanding. Music listens to his/her own will and wishes, unlike natural linguistic way to be touched by surrounding others. Child's developing/growing ability to find "speaking signs" through music can be well observed in music therapeutic dialogue. On the other hand, the music represents to child more unconstrained world of outside *Dasein*, but, then again it organizes simultaneously his/her relation in present time and space to affecting *Dasein*. Music has an affective emotional-aesthetic line through musical forms from *Dasein* to transcendental timeless space and vice versa. Moving emotional-aesthetic energy within musical signifies individual's varying consonant or dissonant existential balance. Moving musical energy is noticed to be analogous with human thinking and experiencing in its continual forms by composed and improvised musical works (Lehtonen 1996: 60). Musical performances anticipate musical resolutions in their advancement. They pre-indicate also reflective dynamic changes started upon the human mind by inside musical influences.

Musical cognition is, herein, defined as an activating energetic sign of human development. If necessary, the musical cognition will be able to carry a birth of pre-linguistic social cognition. The birth of social cognition has occurred when human life-force imprints interactive development potentials upon progressing mind competence. Mind competence signifies a general sign of psychic welfare of man. This sign intends interactive self-consciousness. It includes the ability to understand, express, and receive culturally signified communication concerning one's personal knowledge and skilled activities. Primarily interactive self-consciousness manifests itself in natural resources to realize, express, and make the most of one's spoken mother tongue. With autism one is without essential resource to have a natural possibility to interact in acquiring the cultural and personal identity of the self. The development of the ego with autism is often seemed to be imperfect and slow. Autistic people normally have an inadequacy in the social skills, and therefore they represent in their dissimilarity, dictated by autism, as if to a majority unknown culture.

Language of the culture signifies people of great anticipation of acquaintanceship and reliability. It means, in a large amount, more to be understood by others than to stay unintended outside of linguistic communication. People feel and sense their individual existence consciously through their expressive language. They involve it in their corporality and linguistic ability. They represent linguistic as a sign that cultivates and brings them up during interactive progress of culture. Developing mind competence, into a language-adopted ego-development of man, is based on influences and inner images, such as the outer world reflects on the existence of one's self. Becoming a person manifests to ego an inner space that has its first supporting basements in close contact with nurturing others.

A musical dialogue between child and another composes interactive gestures and images before linguistic ability develops and appears as speech in human communication. A person with autism does not often learn to talk or if he acquires linguistic skills, anyhow, his speech is not directed towards another. His auto-communicative speaking has not signified any message to other people in the culture. Autistic deviation from conventional interaction creates a social situation, where monotonic speech production predominates over prosodic speech. It cuts away our supposed social interaction, while strips away dropping words and change them to an inexpressive combination of sounds. Inexpressiveness, of those subtly queuing sounds, signifies contextually no-signification; in codes of linguistic, it means undecipherable fact, non-interpretation object to *another*...

Existence of prosodic features can be defined to be natural as if self-evident part of cultural speech production. Semiosis of prosodic signs in signified speech has not been in a broader sense an interesting subject in scientific discourse outside of phonetics and speech sciences. One's scientific interest to prosodic features within speech is not seen to arouse until they form a deviation from accustomed culture-competent expression. (see, e.g. Tarasti 2006b: 91).

The existential character of prosodic signs appears only through their negation in transcendence. Their existence is situated in no-appearance. They are covered by inexpressiveness and for that reason not observed, but intuitively supposed because of human sense perception within *linguistic*.

One will be embarrassed by that, as far as prosodic features are unexpectedly lost, hidden somewhere from normal auditory sense perfection. Despite the embarrassing situation, prosodic signs *certainly exist*. One has them especially within mother tongue in the spoken and bodily experienced signification of culture. They exist as sense perceived signs of inner speech of human being and similarly to the reality of his *Dasein* codified by conscious thinking. Hidden function of prosodic features within *inner speech* may be a given good start of our historical cultured appearance.

Normally, *emotional-aesthetic* gathering around prosodic features within the linguistic, musical, and corporeal experience – unbroken prosodic signs processing communicative touch concerning dialogic inner self, to the emotive environment and to experiencing another – signifies the first existential sign, which represent signified human birth of our social cognition. *Emotional signified* with fantastic and unpleasant experiences and the development of man in human growth as well as the processes within music (or music therapy) cannot be transferred from phenomenological figures of life to physical directly measured units of "stony science". Existence of man is – in real – a meta-linguistic phenomenon. Therefore, the existential worlds of human appearance are deeply based on non-verbal signification between corporeal and musical (artistic) mind competence.

The Globality of Languages is based partly on Existential philosophy and a new interpretation and application of psychoanalysis to experientially narrated if compared to Julia Kristeva's conceptual interpretation on *semiotic*. Also, it walks in quite the same field but the 'analytical discussions' are born in real artistic dialogues through creative group and multi-disciplinary teamwork as a practical implementation with people on severe autism. Guiding therapists have observed, 'read', and analyzed the sensory perception and developing flow of immediate experience. One could call it a poetic event (music, drama, painting etc.) improvised outside the spoken language, but the events have always been translated together into a linguistic form after creative dialogic activity. However, the most important sign will always be that what translates itself to itself, within itself and for itself. The developmental period, *the time* before speech is virtually the pre-social space, wherein also the autistic one's personal experiences, the human instinct and senses, will *slowly* practice a relationship with the outside world around. The Globality of Languages communicates with pre-speech phenomena. It translates the language of functionally signified existence towards culturally understandable interaction. Music and other arts are universal parts of its global vocabulary. The method of Globality of Languages approaches semiotics as it transcends geographical and cultural boundaries in symbolizing immediate sensory perceptions. It refers to semiotics for the signification it encounters is an endless continuous process. The Globality of Languages represents Existential Semiotic lifeworld by signifying the phenomenon of autism through the symbolized language of music and other arts.

The prosodic sign is the existential continuum of human existence; it manifests itself in its absence, for example, in the repetitive expressions of an autistic person. It is related to musical and linguistic expression; profitable for their communication. But above all, its functions are most deeply related to the human bodily and, with its support, to everything contained in human expression. The prosodic sign may have a figurative, even rhetorical, role in culture, but its distinctive function is committed to reading and interpreting the interaction. The prosodic sign is global, a common universal shared by man and cultures. If the sign indicating the nature of the speech subsides, people distance themselves from each other. Each other's dialogical literacy disappears, and the unity of cultures thins out. The existential question is no longer between music and language, but our human and natural communicative existence.

References

Guerra-Lisi, Stefania & Gino Stefani. 2006. *Prenatal Styles in the Arts and the Life*. Trans. by A. E. Mereni. (Acta Semiotica Fennica 24). Rome: Castel Madama; Imatra, Helsinki: International Semiotics Institute at Imatra, Semiotic Society of Finland.

Guerra-Lisi, Stefania & Gino Stefani. 2010. *Il corpo matrice di segni, nella Globalità dei Linguaggi*. Rome: Edizioni Borla.

Helkala-Koivisto, Sari 2009. The accentuated signified. Between musical and linguistic signification. In Eero Tarasti, Paul Forsell & Richard Littlefield (eds.) *Communication: Understanding / Misunderstanding. Proceedings of the 9th Congress of the IASS/AIS – Helsinki-Imatra: 11–17 Juni, 2007*. (Acta Semiotica Fennica XXXIV). Imatra: ISI; Helsinki: Semiotic Society of Finland; Tartu: Greif.

Helkala-Koivisto, Sari. 2014. Musical matrix and maternal overtones. Preconscious intentions on autistic signification. In Audronė Daubarienė & Dario Martinelli (eds.) *The Role of Humanities in Contemporary Society: Semiotics, Culture, Technologies. Selected Proceedings from the 1st International Congress of Numanities -Kaunas, 2–7 June, 2014.* ISI, Kaunas University of Technology.

Helkala-Koivisto, Sari. 2015. *Musiikki ja autismi -prosodinen merkki eksistentiaalisemiotiikassa.* (Acta Semiotica Fennica XLVI. Approaches to Musical Semiotics 19). Helsinki: Semiotic Society of Finland, Libris. (The English version is nearing completion.)

Helkala-Koivisto, Sari. 2019. Finding a human lifeworld through musical communication: Existential-semiotic movements between severe- autism- and spoken-language reality. In Zdzisław Wąsik, Elżbieta Magdalena Wąsik & Józef Zaprucki (eds.) *The Semiotics of Lifeworla Existentials: Between Necessity and Choice,* 87–103. Jelenia Góra 2019: Karkonoska Państwowa Szkoła Wyższa w Jeleniej Górze. Agencja Reklamowo-Wydawnicza: ESUS.

Langer, Susan. 1953. *Feeling and Form.* New York: Charles Scribner's Sons.

Lehtonen, Kimmo. 1996. *Musiikki, kieli ja kommunikaatio. Mietteitä musiikista ja musiikkiterapiasta* [Music, language and communication, reflections on music and music therapy]. Jyväskylä: University of Jyväskylä, Department of Musicology. Series A 17.

Lång, Markus. 2004. *Psykoanalyysi ja sen soveltaminen musiikintutkimukseen* [Psychoanalysis and its application to musicology]. (Studia Musicologia Universitatis Helsingiensis XI). University of Helsinki: Department of Musicology. [English abstract in p. 285.]

Ricoeur, Paul. 2000. *Tulkinnan teoria. Diskurssi ja merkityksen lisä.* [Interpretation Theory: Discourse and the Surplus of Meaning]. Trans. by Heikki Kujansivu. Helsinki: Tutkijaliitto.

Salomonsson, Björn. 1991. Musikupplevelsen: Psykoanalytiska synpunkter. In Hans Reiland & Franziska Ylander (eds.), *Psykoanalys och kultur, Uppbrott och reflektioner,* 161–174. Hans Reiland & Franziska Ylander (ed.), Stockholm: Natur och Kultur.

Stefani, Gino. 1982. *La competenza musicale.* Bologna: CLUEB.

Szekely, Lajos. 1962. Meaning, Meaning Schemata and Body Schemata of Thought. *International Journal of Psycho-Analysis* 3, 43. 297–305.

Tarasti, Eero. 1996. *Esimerkkejä. Semiotiikan uusia teorioita ja sovelluksia* [Pre-signs, new theories and applications in semiotics]. Helsinki: Gaudeamus.

Tarasti, Eero. 2004. *Arvot ja merkit. Johdatus eksistentiaalisemiotiikkaan.* Helsinki: Gaudeamus.

Tarasti, Eero. 2005a. Vastarinnan semiotiikkaa: Oleminen, muisti, historia – merkkien vastavirta. *Synteesi* (1).

Tarasti, Eero. 2005b. *Lectures on the Theory of Existential and Transcendental Analysis of Music.* 29th November 2005. University of Helsinki.

Tarasti, Eero. 2005c. Existential and Transcendental Analysis of Music. In *Studi Musicali,* 223–266. Firenze: Leo S. Olschki.

Tarasti, Eero. 2006a. Roland Barthes eli semiotiikan synty musiikin hengestä. *Synteesi* (1).

Tarasti, Eero. 2006b. Tutkielma ilmenemisestä – eli läsnäoleva rakenne ja subjektin eksistentiaalisia poikkeamia. *Synteesi* 4/2006.

Välimäki, Susanna. 2005. *Subject Strategies in Music. A Psychoanalytic Approach to Musical Signification.* (Acta Semiotica Fennica 22). Helsinki: Hakapaino.

Guido Ipsen
Growth and entropy in semiosis: Signs coming full circle

Abstract: The general semiotic belief that "becoming" or "growing" is the single force in the life of the sign has ever been dominating semiotic thinking. The demise of signs has not been discussed so far. Such an idea must resemble fundamental criticism of traditional sign theory in its positivist character. The concept of *entropy* and its importance for semiotic thought, i.e., the question of how probable *order* in sign systems is in the long run, serves as critical approach in this paper, the central question of which is: To which extent are signs not only *fallible*, as Peirce put it, but are subject to *loss, corruption*, and finally *extinction*? The idea that the universe is bound in a process of semantic growth is utterly rejected. Forgetting, rejecting meaning, or the sheer fact of physically destroyed items serve as naïve examples of the negative forces in the life circle of signs. Permanent conscious reconsidering of signs confronts the idea of "ephemeral truth". The conclusion is that existential semiosis must take place continuously and in principle without end, the mind being at different stages in multiple continua of existential semiosis, building signs towards the goal of transcendence, but at the same time being subject to eroding forces that will wash away signs. Ultimately, this leads to a balance that may be expressed in a *law of conservation of semiosic potential*.

Keywords: Positivism, Entropy, Finality, Life cycle of signs, Law of conservation of semiosic potential

1 Introduction

In his book *Existential Semiotics*, Eero Tarasti focuses, maybe, on the most important aspect of the nature of signs, as also conceived by classical pragmatist semiotics:[1] Their being in constant flux. Therein, Tarasti (2000: 7) uses the phrase that signs are "in a process of becoming". Other illustrious semioticians have phrased this process *semiosis* (with Peirce).

---

[1] Though, Tarasti himself should not be called a pragmatist. However, from the personal experience with the man, I have gathered that his dynamic mind has always been at the ready to incorporate ideas from a variety of semiotic and philosophical traditions.

In this paper, the question is raised whether "becoming" or "growing" can be perceived as the sole, the governing force in the life of the sign. Heretofore unconceived by semiotics in particular or philosophy at large, the momentum of the demise of signs is discussed. To understand the fundamental criticism of sign theory that goes along with such discussion, the positivist character of traditional semiotics will be illustrated. Next, the concept of *entropy* and its importance for semiotic thought is considered: The question of how probable order in sign systems is in the long run. Finally, this paper ventures into formulating alternative ideas about the life cycle of signs.

2 Semiotic positivism

Before venturing into the central question of this paper, namely to which extent signs are not only fallible, but may be subject to loss, corruption, and finally extinction, we need to focus on a variety of concepts in order to render the argumentative line of this paper transparent.

The central idea of pragmatist thinking, based on Peirce, is that not only the individual sign but the cosmos, the universe as such, is bound in this process of semantic growth. In Peirce's theory, the end of all semiosis, and with it, the end of the universe, will have come when all signs have arrived at the state of absolute truth, or, as the great American polymath called it, *final interpretation*, which is "that which would finally be decided to be the true interpretation if consideration of the matter were carried so far that an ultimate opinion were reached" (CP 8.184). Peirce wrote about the "end" of nature (CP 1.362), the "end of being and highest reality" to be reached by means of "evolution" (CP 1.487), and so forth.[2]

To this day, semioticians have bluntly accepted Peirce's theorizing of the nature of the sign as "growing", as if it were a law of nature. Interestingly, moreover, the proximity of Peirce's musing and positivist thinking has not only been ignored but actively countermanded (cf. Fairbanks 1970). Admittedly, Peirce himself wrote critically about positivism, which he understood as "speculative thinking" (MS 146: 123), naturally referring to the philosophy of, e.g., Poincaré or Comte, who formed the idea that, roughly speaking, only hypotheses which admit positive experimental verification should be formulated in science. However, according to Comte, if observation were not possible for the time being, or too dif-

---

[2] Admittedly, Peirce also said that "universal science" might never achieve true finality (CP 1.562). However, in this statement, he does not eschew the idea of finality being cosmologically *possible*.

ficult, speculative hypotheses might still be constructed and put to use. The limits are merely set by hypotheses that do not allow for observation in nature *at all* because these would only cause interminable discussion (Comte 1934: 226). Mach (cf. 1914) called the latter, if such hypotheses happened to meet with truth, "lucky guesses" and demanded that experimentation must not be considered only an *option*, but *essential* to true science. Together with Poincaré (cf. Poincaré 1952), these writers, in short, hold that unproved hypotheses may be used by *convention* because otherwise, phenomena might escape scientific attention. Hypotheses should be *verifiable*, but they need only be verified *eventually* by experience.

Essentially, Peirce denies this assumption by arguing that all knowledge must come from a series of cognitive acts and that anything that does not come from this line of thinking must be *intuition*. The latter he denies being in conformity with scientific thinking, as may be shown by the sheer fact that what we see is not always what is, but is sometimes based on mere conjecture. Hence, "immediacy" in forming hypotheses can only be damaging to scientific reasoning (CP 5.213). Hypotheses must be the result of inferences (deduction, induction, abduction), which is in accordance with Peirce's general idea of the formation of thought, or, semiosis.

Surely, thus, Peirce is not to be considered "positivist" in the sense of sensationalism, as the ground of ideas for him are "logical rules of human cognition" and "the hypothesis has plausibility of itself" (Fairbanks 1970: 121). However, the actual question should be to which extent semiosis, as conceived by Peirce, is truly bound to "logical rules". He thoroughly rejects Descartes' dualism; for Peirce, the formation of ideas is a continuous process and has nothing to do with "thinking" (*cogitare*), but *inferencing*, which cannot represent an immediate act of thinking, but always the result of mental activity of a higher order (cf. Myers 2002: 144). For Peirce, truth is existent and thought is driven towards it. The fallibility of the sign does not concern the absence of truth, but merely mistakenness on behalf of the thinker (Myers 2002:144). Eventually, erratic signs will be "corrected" in semiosis. Hence, Peirce accepts only the method of science as acceptable for the evaluation of belief (Myers 2002: 150). He is an empiricist through and through.

In the sense of this paper, "empiricism is the epistemological standpoint that observations and (sensory) experiences should be regarded the most important or only method to gain knowledge and that all controversies should ideally be reduced to claims that can be verified by observations" (Birger 2005: 134). Now to understand why Peirce was such a devoted empiricist, we must look at Peirce the man in the context of his life and times. Before our eyes, the age of industrialization unrolls and the success of scientific research makes possible new technologies, the harnessing of unimagined energies, and at long last does away with superstition and challenges the role of religious belief, replacing it with a rationalist world view.

In Peirce's time, no critical discourse on the limits of science and technology was existent, which would only appear first after the *Titanic* disaster, though it never gained the power to stop the scientific or technological advance.[3] How can we expect Peirce, as a trained scholar in a multitude of rational sciences, to actively criticise empiricism? On the contrary, he developed the idea of empiricism further and gave scientific thinking a philosophical basis – and vice versa. Hence, the philosophy of the sign of the modern age is a child of its times and must be considered as such. The question of whether it should still be considered applicable to the issues and problems of contemporary society is an imperative one.[4]

Finally, positivism means

> that philosophy should be scientific, that metaphysical speculations are meaningless, that there is a universal and a priori scientific method, that a main function of philosophy is to analyze that method, that this basic scientific method is the same in both the natural and social sciences, that the various sciences should be reducible to physics, and that the theoretical parts of good science must be translatable into statements about observations.
>
> (Kincaid 1998: 696)

This meaning of positivism has derived during the 20th century only, but it shall be applied to Peirce and the ensuing theory of semiotics in this paper, as the discoursive problems of the semiotic theory have only originated with Peirce, but they have never been challenged and are the basis of semiotic theory (and practice) to the present day.

We have seen that positivist semiotic empiricism assumes that the sign is a permanently growing entity. Gradually, the members of the interpretive community strive towards final thirdness by the process of applying analytic thought to

---

[3] Indeed, the critical discourse on science and technology keeps popping up like a Jack-in-the-box. The nuclear bomb, high-speed train disasters and recently the dangers and uncertainties of digitalization have called for the apocalyptics to raise their voice, but their warnings are frequently lost in the frenzy of technological hype.

[4] Even though I have to submit I see even greater demand in discussing the question of whether *structuralist semiology* can still serve as a means of fruitful semiotic musing, I must leave such argument to another paper. Suffice it to say that a theory defining stark differences of *yes/no*, *what is* and *what is not*, of *what means what* and *what is in opposition* to such meaning units – a theory which came into existence on the eve of the creation of the most abominable totalitarian systems of all times – should be deconstructed according to the context of its origination. The 19th century might have been empiricist; the 20th was characterized by difference and ensuing vilification that resulted in industrialized murder; in "cumulative radicalization" (Mommsen 1981).

sensation, thus creating a more and more precise representation of the world of items in their minds.

At the same time, terms such as "forgetting", "amnesia", or "arcane" do not play any role in semiotic theory.[5]

Apparently, this then means that the process of signification is a one-way journey. Signs, semiotic theory tells us, come into existence and may be challenged, but they never wither, they do not decay and they do not disappear. On a trivial basis, then, why do we not understand archaic writing systems? Why do I not know what makes my wife angry even though I have had the same kind of dispute with her once and again for years? Why do we have to reconstruct knowledge of the past, which got lost, and why do some people cling to pre-scientific beliefs? Why do some religions "forget" the names of their gods? How is this all possible? Are there essential flaws in the world of signification which semiotics has overlooked or are we, essentially, misled and merely wandering the over-trivial when pursuing these questions while semioticians can tell us the stark truth?

We shall now turn to something completely different in order to shed some light on this question.

3 Entropy

Whereas semiotics, with Peirce, assumes that the universe is gradually growing into a state of absolute order, or law, physics assumes the absolute opposite. In thermodynamics, the term *entropy* was coined by Clausius (1865). It was further developed in physics and led to the formulation of the "Boltzmann constant" in 1872 (cf. Harris 2012: 19) and the "Boltzmann-Planck equation" by Ludwig Max Planck in 1900 (Planck 1901; cf. Jammer 1966: 17; Pohling 2013: 1). Ludwig Boltzmann's constant relates the relative kinetic energy of gas particles with the thermodynamic temperature of the gas, i.e., roughly speaking, its application allows for the calculation of the average temperature of a particle in a system in relation to the absolute temperature of the system. As is obvious, such equations are valuable for the calculation of the statistical occurrence of certain states of matter. Entropy as a value then equals the number of probable distinguishable microstates of a system in relation to the defined macrostate of said system. At the same

---

5 In *The triad in physiology*, Peirce mentions something he calls "forgetfulness" (CP 1.390), but simply in the context of biological cells not being stimulated, so that they "forget" the reaction they at first produced. Still, this reaction is soon re-established when the irritation of the cell is renewed, as Peirce puts it.

time, entropy is a measure for the probability (German *"Wahrscheinlichkeit"*) of the systemic macrostate. Thermodynamics states that entropy will always grow in a closed system. This means that while the system loses energy, the statistical probability of a multitude of states inside the system grows. Physicists use the term "disorder" for this state. This has led to grave misunderstandings and controversy, but "disorder" must be understood as the probability of a maximal diversity of a multitude of microstates in the system. In other words: The homogeneity of microstates is reduced, while that of the macrostate is increased.[6] Later, a more fitful way of considering entropy as disorder was developed, namely entropy as *uncertainty*. This means entropy is associated with the "ignorance" of the system or the lack of information about its microstates. (cf. Gell-Mann/Lloyd 1996; Gell-Mann 1994).[7]

The general understanding of the development of a system, or the universe at large, is that a) the amount of energy in a system is constantly reduced, b) the degree of order is reduced (or the degree of uncertainty of the system is increased) and thus c) the entropy in the universe cannot be decreased, but will grow until there are maximum entropy and equal distribution of matter in the universe, without order.[8] We can perceive now that in absolute contrast to the semiotic understanding of meaning and knowledge as growing faculties connecting into ordered systems of law, of "thirdness", the conception of entropy describes the

---

[6] Take as an example a group of 100 persons in a square. We may calculate the probable location of any person in the square. It is obvious that the probability of all persons being arranged in "rows" and "columns" of ten, forming a perfect quadrangle, is highly improbable. Now when we calculate that any one person may be in contact with one, two, three or more of the others, standing in smaller or larger clusters on either side of the square, we arrive at a varying probability for these different microstates of the persons. However, our perception will suggest that wild clustering of people looks far more disorderly than the arrangement in the form of the quadrangle. Still, the equal distribution of people all over the square, while not quite "orderly", represents homogeneity of distribution. The same is true for ink particles in water, coloured gas in a larger volume of transparent gas, etc. It is also obvious, by these examples, why entropy grows in systems, which strive for equal distribution and reduction of energy.

[7] The term entropy has also been employed in information theory (cf. Shannon 1948) and sociology (cf. Bailey 1990). In both disciplines, it is connected with the phenomenon of loss of information, which goes along with the general understanding of entropy. Unfortunately, there is no room for an extensive explanation of either in this paper.

[8] The only way of increasing the amount of energy of a system is to harness it from another system. In the example of the people in the square elaborated above, this might be represented by a force of marshals who tell people where to stand, and maybe even physically move them about in the square. This group of ordering marshals will have to invest a large amount of energy to make people stand where they are supposed to be. Most probably, in the absence of a marshal, individuals will start to move again and disrupt the order, becoming agents of entropy.

absolute opposite. The dissipating structures of knowledge under the pressure of growing entropy leave little room for final thirdness in the universe. In retrospect of Peirce's own terminology, we are led to think of a universe of absolute firstness: Unbeknownst in its complexity of absolute probability of every possible microstate. Indeed this must be so since absolute thirdness does not allow for alternatives: There can only be one "truth" about an item, the sum of this truth being its semiosic interpretant. However, in a universe of maximum entropy, every microstate has a multitude of alternatives, the order which Peirce demanded to be the result of semiosic cosmological growth merely representing statistical improbability of the highest degree.

4 Growth and transcendence of the sign in existential semiotics and pragmatism

One of the most important aspects of existential semiotics is the semiosic move towards *transcendence*. Tarasti mentions the transcendence of the subject as one of the key features of his theory (Tarasti 2000: 17–36). The "journey of the existential subject" that Tarasti illustrates (cf. Tarasti 2000: 10; see Figure 1: The Journey of an Existential Subject via the Acts of Negation and Affirmation) in its movement towards transcendence is mirrored in the model of semiosis. Let us first consider Tarasti's ideas.

4.1 Existential semiosis and its ethical ends

As Tarasti explains, the subject in its existential movement "leaps" into the unknown, the future beyond its immediate *Dasein*: "The subject makes a leap into nothingness" (Tarasti 2000: 11). The nothingness Tarasti describes is set in opposition to the fixity of the known state from which the subject sets out. At the very beginning of the process Tarasti maps, there is hence a distinct parallel to what Peirce conceives of as semiosis: The manifestation and becoming of signs in the flux of time, which plays out between the temporal dimensions of past, present, and future. From what insight we gain from Tarasti, clarity, or fixation of belief is originally situated in the past. Peirce uses almost the same wording when he introduces the levels of past and present in semiosis. For Peirce, thought is "a thread of melody running through the succession of our sensations", meaning that the sensations are in the *immediate* present, whereas the thought must rest on experiences in the past (CP 5.395). However, what Peirce conceives of as the "real", is not to be found in the present. In semiosis, present sensation and past experience work together to make accessible the "real", which is to be found in the future. This is what Peirce called "pragmatistic idealism" in a letter to James (CP 8.284).

The tension between past, present, and future generates momentum in the semiosic journey of the subject moving in time. The existential subject in Tarasti's theory endeavours the same journey. Since the similarity between Tarasti's and Peirce's theorems is so obvious, it seems only natural to label the mechanics of existential semiotics *existential semiosis*.

4.2 The "finality" of values

For Tarasti, the aim of semio-philosophical musing is not an end in itself, but a sketch of a semiotic theory that a) illustrates functions of the self in society, and b) explains the coming into being of *transcendent values*, such as ethics, which can be derived from his writings. Tarasti's approach towards transcendence from the semiotic venue runs, in part, parallel to Peirce's approach towards ethics via logic. It is not surprising that he eventually brought logic and ethics together:

> Logic is a study of the means of attaining the end of thought. It cannot solve that problem until it clearly knows what that end is. Life can have but one end. It is Ethics which defines that end. It is, therefore, impossible to be thoroughly and rationally logical except upon an ethical basis. [. . .] Before my logic was brought under the guidance of ethics, it was already a window through which much important truth could be seen, but dim with dust, distorting details by striæ. Under the guidance of ethics I took it and melted it down, reduced it to a fluid condition. I filtered it till it was clear. I cast it in the true mold; and when it had become solid, I spared no elbow-grease in polishing it. It is now a comparatively brilliant lens, showing much that was not discernible before. I believe that it will only remain to those who come after me to perfect the processes. I am as confident as I am of death that Logic will hereafter be infinitely superior to what it is as I leave it, but my labors will have done good work toward its improvement. (CP 2.198)

Peirce defines the notion of truth in the contexts of logic, ethics, and esthetics. The truth of things in themselves, namely "transcendental truth" (CP 5.572), is not quite the same. For our discussion of existential semiosis, it is imperative to understand that the ethical truth that is bound to the sign-action of a situation does not equal the transcendental truth of the ideas that are represented by said signs. Absolute ethical values cannot be derived from situations or momentary sign contexts. On the contrary, to be able to demand absolute value in ethics, the morals of the moment *need* to be mirrored in some projection; into the future (in Peirce) or in a transcendent realm where these values cannot be corrupted (in Tarasti).

Each sign-action, in the process of contrasting the immediate by the projection, will return some insight as to what the transcendental truth may be, as the contrast or accordance can be "felt", and put to the test of logic. Hence, we may argue that there are indeed "true" ethical values which are step by step clarified in the process of semiosis, as long as the projection, which may itself be a construction from individual and social experiences of the past, holds. The individual lacking ideal ideas of values will ultimately fail in the project to achieve the ethical goal.[9] But it is dependent on the existential journey of the subject that these final values be projected; otherwise, a crisis of the societal system may ensue.[10]

Whatever is transcendental, in Tarasti's words, must point at least to some extent towards finality. Insights into transcendental values are supposed to be insights not only into temporarily valid truths but into truths that lie behind the confines of immediate sign usage. In what Tarasti sketches as the "transference of signs" in the context of transcendence, we may see a theoretical foundation of how parts of semiosic actions are thought to gain permanence and offer us a perspective (even though a very limited one) on the finality of signs.

Where Peirce defines the temporal consensus within the subject and between the multitude of subjects in the discourse community as the basis from which interpretation starts, Tarasti uses the term "*Dasein*". This Hegelian term may also be semiotically defined as the temporarily stable notion of the self as opposed to what is not the self, in all its complexities. The *Dasein* must necessarily be constituted by the experience horizon of the interpreting mind. In Peirce's as well as in Tarasti's models, this state of mind is the starting point of change. The "journey of the existential subject" (Tarasti 2000: 10) is nothing else than an act of semiosis that is stirred by the cognition of something that is conceived of as different from the existing experiential basis of the *Dasein*. As Peirce says (CP 2.84, cf. Ipsen 2002), opposition lies at the root of semiosis:

> We can make no effort where we experience no resistance, no reaction. The sense of effort is a two-sided sense, revealing at once something within and another something without. There is binarity in the idea of brute force; it is its principal ingredient. For the idea of brute force is little more than that of reaction; this is pure binarity.

---

9 Again, we are reminded of barbaric times when the existence of the transcendent projection was not necessarily given.
10 I admit that I tend to reduce the content matter of the values to some social ground, or essence of behaviour, or social conduct. I am myself not convinced of either Kantian deontology or utilitarianism serving the purpose. I, therefore, prefer to remain vague and abstract about the factual values that might be projected.

The subject leaves the known sphere of the *Dasein* as the new experience will stir the peace of that existence. It reaches a first position which is new, yet not stable again. We may translate this into Peircean terminology, stating that before the first move by the subject lies an absolute firstness of cognising a previously unknown element of the environment, as Peirce says, by "brute force" of perceiving the world of things. To know that the new is different from the old means to establish a relation. Therefore, the first move of the subject is governed by secondness. This secondness is the essence of the critical state of the questioned *Dasein* in Tarasti's model. There will be new experiences there, and this is the first act of transcendence. The subject is confronted with the results of its departure from the former, seemingly stable *Dasein*. It arrives at a stage of *negation*, where the old existence is questioned in the face of the new. However, the movement continues. The subject gains affirmation of the transcendental movement in a second step, where what Tarasti calls the "opposite pole of Nothingness" is met. From this second movement, the subject gains a new *Dasein*. Where is this opposite pole situated? As Tarasti explains, it is the universe of signification which discloses itself naturally to the subject. This is not a wilful step taken by the individual. It is a semiotic necessity and consequence of sign action. Using pragmatist terminology, we see here that the act of semiosis is completed by achieving the thirdness of a new stable sign continuum.

Existential semiosis, of course, takes place continuously and in principle without end. In semiosis, signs are continuously escaping the reassurance of finality, i.e., secure and possibly final experience and knowledge. In the words of Peirce, we can only temporarily achieve a consensus and the working state of interpretation, which enables us to use the signs as a community of users.

But then, what is the nature of existential semiosis that urges us to newly chart the process of the growth of signs? The seemingly secure interpretants escape us, the only temporal halt in semiosis, or in Peirce's words, the final logical interpretant will be replaced by something subject to new cognition and new experience. The only security the experiencing subject knows is situated, as it seems, in the past. But this is merely a pitfall of semiotic thinking. The interpretants of the past are only constructions of the present. And here we find the essence of existential semiosis: The seemingly firm plane of past interpretation, or in Tarasti's words, the former *Dasein*, is left, *must* be left as new experiences enter the semiotic life of the individual, who cannot escape them – the only possible stop in conscious semiosis is the death of the interpreter. Peirce calls the unavoidable necessity of signs coming to our mind the *brute force* of firstness. Here the subject finds itself in negation, or Tarasti's *"Dasein"*. It is a volatile state. Tarasti correctly criticizes how existential philosophy has not considered the force of reflection. Reflection must result in a different perspective on the world. Immediate negation without reflection is nothingness. The subject correlates the critique of the past which is manifest in the *"Dasein"* with the ground, i.e., the object-sign relation of its own experienced past. The direction of this reflection is what Tarasti calls *affirmation*. The new state X is the result of this reflection, or interpretation process, as we may call it. It is hence a new interpretant in the existential semiosic process. In the future, X will again become a *Dasein* in the past: It will be put into question by new experiences.

5 The impossibility of final interpretation

Existential semiosis must take place continuously and in principle without end. This requires that we accept the model of the existential journey as a snapshot of the real process. Even though we may be able to map an individual movement and illustrate the three stages and two transcendental steps by individual examples, reality suggests that the experiencing subject is at all times, in the most different experience situations, at different stages in multiple continua of existential semiosis. Parts of the experience horizon will resemble the *Dasein*, others will just be in the process of being questioned – elsewhere, the subject finds new reassurance. Hence, the three stages themselves are involved in the continuous flux of signs interrelated in the semiotic universe.

One question now remains a mystery: How is truth, transcendence, or finality, achieved, when, as we have seen in the discussion on entropy, there is a universal force working against it? In practice, empirical study or abduction (CP 2.96) as methods will only yield temporary results, no more; taking this seriously we seemingly have to put into question even our firmest beliefs in our reasoning. Hence, whatever we decide to rest in finality retains a highly hypothetical character. Does the serious consideration of transcendence in semiosis return any philosophical axioms at all?

James (1907) explains the pragmatist perspective by restricting sign meaning to the sign effect, and usage. Both are subject to individual experience. Existential semiosis will focus on the signs which carry information and *mediate* between the individuals within the sociosphere of sign users. This is the essence of existential semiotics, namely to acknowledge that the signs evince a situational focus, which, however, shifts endlessly in the flux of becoming, in which the signs are caught. A diachronic approach is necessary in order to understand semiotic mediation, sign usage, and possible developments in the future. Existential semiotics sees the signs in flux but accepts their momentary bonds and structural delimitations.

Hence, the assertion of truth is neither an individual decision of the self nor is it the result of cognizing the sign in one situation exclusively. James makes explicit that the essence of the pragmatist notion is that various truths coexist, this meaning that the transcendental value of a sign must not be imagined as a one-dimensional monolithic truth. Since the experience horizons of the semiosic minds will always differ considerably, truth is not so much a matter of judgement but of experiencing additively. The polyindividual nature of interpretation will ultimately come to the surface. In this sense, transcendence must be considered a constructed projection in the process of existential semiosis which must be open to judgement for the entirety of the semiosic community as such, i.e., in principle endlessly. The social communication of signs and the probing of the sign potentials will remain the means to verify or falsify the results of the existential moves in semiosis.

6 Entropy and the life cycle of the sign

At the beginning of this paper, I have criticized semiotics for not contemplating the loss of memory, the unrecognizable, or the secret. I hope it now becomes obvious what I mean by this criticism: Semiotics does not contemplate entropy in signification or semiosis. I have described whatever may be called finality of the sign is a construction. Transcendence I have characterized as a – necessary – projection. I essence, such thinking countermands Peircean musing on the sign completely. The presumption of possible finality which Peirce undertakes is not an *esse in futuro* of the sign, but a justification of our present reasoning by assuming that sometime in the future our logic is vouchsafed. The ultimate problem is that this is impossible. Neither can the individual, in his or her lifespan, be sure to attain certainty of meaning, nor can the interpretative community "strive" for finality, or transcendence: The sheer forces of the universe, of nature, or of the social bodies that work against such endeavours will eventually dissipate the individual mind, the codices of the social group, and the presumptions of positivist reasoning in philosophy. Essentially, we may presume that with the demise of the human race, the ethical and logical propositions that form the semiotic horizon of our species will be gone.[11]

---

[11] Some have argued that semiosis is not limited by the interpreting mind, basing their arguments on Peirce's notion of "Matter as *effete mind*" (cf., e.g., Santaella 2001; Nöth 2001). I should like to personally express disgust for such presumption. Its most positive interpretation may be that we find quasi-religious worship of some disembodied semiosic force that is independent of

But the effects of entropy are perceptible also in the living world of everyday semiosis. If there is one aspect of the Peircean sign in its nature and development I should not like to put into question, it is its fallibility. However, the supposition that fallibility rests only in the sign is erratic. A universe that changes around the interpreters will yield their final logical interpretations brittle in the course of time. But still yet, the forces of forgetting or suppressing ideas (individually as well as collectively) which may be perceived as semiosic entropy, leave room for fruitful musing. Only yesterday, for example, I thought that I had never had chicken wings for a barbecue in my garden and consequently enjoyed the experience as something new and unique. Later, my wife reminded me that it was indeed not the first time. I fail to recall the first time, up to now. My mind has not stored this, even though I must assume that now I have felt the bliss of eating the crunchy meal not for the first, but for the second time, which should make for a considerable difference in my personal semiosis of the occasion. But nay, I cannot resurface any recollection. Hence, unbeknownst to me, I have felt the same joy twice, and forgetting the first one has allowed me to experience another "first time".

I should like to form a radical thought here, namely that signs *have to die* in order to make room for new ones. Signs come full circle, from their birth, growth, through maturation until decay and demise. A sign that dies makes room for new signification. Interpretation eradicated allows for new approaches.[12] Entropy in semiosis, therefore, is by no means a negative agent of destruction but may be understood as a form of destruction as a renewal of the grounds on which interpretation takes place. In analogy to the law of conservation of energy, we may assume that there is also a *law of conservation of semiosic potential*.[13] In a semiosic system, essentially, the sign potential (for beliefs, reasoning, musing, etc.) therefore may be enriched by other systems, but in itself, it requires a transformation in order to generate new meaning. In the world of physics, transformation

---

any interpreting mind. Such semiotic esotericism appears ridiculous in view of entropy, which will do away with a formed matter in the first place, not to mention living bodies that may incorporate the minds necessary for interpretation. The worst communication of such theory is the totalitarian "pansemiotic" perspective that is established, which has never done semiotics any good, but which seems to resurface in various guise every couple of years or so. In any case, I hold it as true that when the last member of an interpretative community has sunk into the grave and no traces of their signification are left behind, all of their ideas, thoughts, and reasoning is lost. Such is the only finality existent in the cosmos.

12 Please note that "new" here has no qualitative implication. There is absolutely no guarantee that renewed musing results in "better" ideas.
13 This is not supposed to refer to *quantity*, but *the quality* of semiosis.

is not possible without destruction. Should there be a difference in the world of semiosis, which must be based on the physical world?

Let us now reconsider Tarasti's idea of transcendence in view of the semiocriticism of this paper. Seemingly, if we still identify transcendence with thirdness, it becomes a hollow concept. If there is no such thing as finite thirdness towards which we can strive, then how can sign values transcend when entropy will yield absolute thirdness impossible? In my perspective, the essential question is what transcends and to which end this process takes place, and also how the community of sign users is concerned as participating actively and consciously in recognising (or generating) transcendence.

In presuming that transcendence represents a sphere beyond human reckoning in which signs, or sign values, exist as a "repertoire" for future semiosis or a "blueprint" against which "true" or even "correct" semiosis may be evaluated, the question remains in how such iron representations of ideas may exist beyond the eroding forces of entropy. Should transcendence be used in this fashion, it represents a highly problematic term.

However, if transcendence simply means that the *immediate sphere of semiosis of the individual* is transcended so that the values achieved in semiosis are accessible to the community without the immediate action of one singular member, then the concept attains feasibility. Also, the repository of transcendent signs then gains a value in itself, meaning that it needs to be nourished, permanently justified, and defended. The importance of the self-critical journey of the individual in Tarasti's theory and its move from one stage of the *Dasein* to the next thus gains societal importance. The move then aims at the communal.

Indeed, under the auspices of the eroding forces that will wash away signs and ethical values unless we strive for their preservation, the permanent conscious reconsidering of signs that may be represented in the transcendental repository becomes imperative. Agreeably, such understanding of semiotic processes is rooted in the here and now, with little perspective for finding "ephemeral truth". But it also concerns the foreseeable future, with all the dangers that exist in this world of permanent change for the highly elaborated ethical systems on which civilization is based. Such transcendence cannot guarantee that what we do is ethically "right" from a universal point of perspective,[14] but it empowers us to re-evaluate our positions and actions and, hopefully, enables us to eventually send that which we successfully eradicated from our *Dasein* into the abyss where it belongs.

---

[14] Which does not exist if I take my points seriously!

References

Bailey, Kenneth D. 1990. *Social entropy theory*. Albany, New York: State University of New York Press.
Clausius, Rudolf. 1865. Über verschiedene, für die Anwendung bequeme Formen der Hauptgleichungen der mechanischen Wärmetheorie. *Annalen der Physik und Chemie* (125). 353–400.
Comte, Auguste. 1934. *Cours de philosophie positiviste*. Paris: Flammarion.
Gell-Mann, Murray. 1994. *The quark and the jaguar: Adventures in the simple and in the complex*. New York: Freeman.
Gell-Mann, Murray & Seth Lloyd. 1996. Effective complexity. In Murray Gell-Mann & Constantino Tsallis (eds.), *Nonextensive entropy – interdisciplinary applications*, 387–398. Oxford: University Press.
Fairbanks, Matthew. 1970. Peirce and the positivists on knowledge. *Transactions of the Charles S. Peirce Society* 6 (2). 111–122.
Harris, Stewart. 2012. *An introduction to the theory of the Boltzmann equation*. Mineola, New York: Dover Publications.
Hjørland, Birger. 2005. Empiricism, rationalism and positivism in library and information science. *Journal of Documentation* (61/1). 130–155.
Ipsen, Guido. 2002. Hybridity at the root of semiosis. In Scott Simpkins & John Deely (eds.). *Semiotics 2001. Proceedings of the 26th Annual Meeting of the Semiotic Society of America*, 292–310. Ottawa: Legas.
James, William. 1907 [1975]. Pragmatism: A New Name for Some Old Ways of Thinking. Reprint Cambridge, MA: Harvard University Press.
Jammer, Max. 1966. *The conceptual development of quantum mechanics*, New York: McGraw Hill.
Kincaid, Harold. 1998. Positivism in the social sciences. In Edward Craig (ed.), *Concise Routledge Encyclopedia of Philosophy*, 696. London: Routledge.
Mach, Ernst. 1914. *The analysis of sensations and the relation of the physical to the psychical*. Chicago/London: The Open Court Publishing Company.
Mommsen, Hans. 1981. Hitlers Stellung im nationalsozialistischen Herrschaftssystem. In Gerhard Hirschfeld (ed.), *Der „Führerstaat". Mythos und Realität*, 43–72. Stuttgart: Klett-Cotta:
Myers, Robert G. 2002. Peirce's extension of empiricism. *Transactions of the Charles S. Peirce Society* 38(1/2) [Essays in Honor of Richard S. Robin]. 137–154.
Nöth, Winfried. 2001. Protosemiotics and physcosemiosis. *Signs systems studies* 29(1). 13–26.
Peirce, Charles Sanders. 1931–58. *Collected Papers*. Vols. 1–6, ed. by C. Hartshorne & P. Weiss, vols. 7–8, ed. by A.W. Burks. Cambridge, MA: Harvard University Press.
Planck, Max. 1901. Ueber das Gesetz der Energieverteilung im Normalspectrum. *Annalen der Physik* 309(3). 553–563.
Pohling, Peters. 2013. *Durch Universum mit Naturkonstanten: Abschied von der Dunklen Materie*. Norderstedt: BoD.
Poincaré, Henri. 1952. *Science and method*. Mineola, New York: Dover Publications.

Santaella, Lucia. 2001. Matter as "effete mind": Peirce's synechistic ideas on the semiotic threshold. *Signs systems studies* 29(1). 49–62.

Shannon, Claude Elwood. 1948. A mathematical theory of communication, *Bell System Technical Journal* 27(3). 379–423.

Tarasti, Eero. 2000. *Existential Semiotics*. Bloomington: Indiana University Press.

Daniel Röhe
Creativity in existential semiotics and psychoanalysis

Abstract: In 2018, Prof. Tarasti elected *Sources of Creativity* as the theme for the Academy of Cultural Heritages Seminar that took place in Mikkeli, Finland. Using my background in Psychoanalysis I've scrutinized creative process under the light of Existential Semiotics. Firstly, the dialogue between endo- and exo-signs was observed in order to understand the interaction between an artist and his/her medium. Secondly, psychopathological cases were observed in accordance with such dialogue between endo- and exo-worlds. Creativity was also related to sublimation and the discharge of aggressive instincts. Moreover, aspects such as variation, repetition, activity, and inhibition were observed in creative process. Examples from Opera, Painting, Sculpture, Cinema, Literature, Architecture, *haute-cuisine*, Latin American Cultural Heritages, and Religion were studied by means of concepts from Existential Semiotics and Psychoanalysis. In the end, I've observed the role of the exo-field as a space that allows creative process to take place at its best, as in the case of Sibelius' country-side home known as Ainola, which, although helped him with personal issues, failed to offer him a space to succeed over interwar political ideologies and compositional theories, which may explain why he did not publish his 8th symphony.

Keywords: Existential Semiotics, Zemic model, Psychoanalysis, Creativity, Cultural Heritages

In 2018, Prof. Tarasti elected *Sources of Creativity* as the theme for the Academy of Cultural Heritages Seminar that took place in Mikkeli, Finland. Using my background on Psychoanalysis I've scrutinized creative process under the light of Existential Semiotics. Firstly, the dialogue between endo and exo-signs was observed in order to understand the interaction between an artist and his/her medium. Secondly, psychopathological cases were observed in accordance with such dialogue between endo- and exo-worlds. Creativity was also related to sublimation and the discharge of aggressive instincts. Moreover, aspects such as variation, repetition, activity and inhibition were observed in creative process. Examples from Opera, Painting, Sculpture, Cinema, Literature, Architecture, *haute-cuisine*, Latin American Cultural Heritages and Religion were studied by means of concepts from Existential Semiotics and Psychoanalysis. In the end, I've observed the role of the exo-field as a space that allows creative process to take place at its best, as in the case of Sibelius' country-side home known as Ainola, which, although helped him with personal issues, failed to offer him a space to succeed over interwar political ideologies and compositional theories, which may explain why he did not publish his 8th symphony.

1 Prologue

In July 2017, two years after my first contact with Tarasti's (2000) *Existential Semiotics* (from now on ES), I wrote my first clinical cases in which I have applied concepts from ES and its Zemic model.[1] Although these cases are now under confidentiality, I presented in Syros, October 2017, short clinical studies based on the repertoire of erudite music with the aid from ES and Psychoanalysis. Although we can trace the relationship between Semiotics and Clinical Practice back to the times of Hippocrates (Eco 1984), and that Semiotics was already scrutinized by psychoanalysts (Lacan 1955–1956; Kristeva 2000), the work *Existential Semiotics and Psychoanalysis* (Röhe 2017) was the first attempt to bring the two disciplines into a single debate. Later, in August 2018, Prof. Tarasti organized, in Mikkeli, a seminar entitled *Sources of Creativity. From Local to Universal*, in the eve of his 70th year anniversary. On the occasion, I presented a sequel to the previous approach to Freud's and Tarasti's disciplines. The present paper is derived from that presentation in Finland.

2 Creativity as a dialogue between endo and exo-signs

What is creativity? Although we know of more than a hundred definitions for this term, it is currently considered as a psychological dimension present in human everyday life and is a result from the interaction with the environment (Meusburger 2009). Upon his discussion on endo and exogenic signs, Tarasti once

---

[1] I'd like to express my most sincere feelings of gratitude to Prof. Tarasti and Rector Pokkinen (Mikkeli Conservatory) for granting me a place to work on my research about *Creativity in Existential Semiotics and Psychoanalysis* during my days in Mikkeli. I also would like to thank Dr. Guðrún Elsa Bragadóttir (Reykjavík) for enriching my reflections on agressivity in creative process. Further, part of this research is indebted to Prof. Cabrera and the meetings held at Sueli's home, when Latin American Cultural Heritages were explored in 2017–2018. Finally, I'd like to thank Dr. Grajter (Academy of Music in Łódź) for proofreading the present paper and Prof. Martins, M.D., semiotician and psychoanalyst, for being a guiding light.

asked: "How do we interact with signs and those signs interact with us?" (2000: 41). Further, I ask, how the interaction of such signs takes place in creative process? In Marion Milner's creative process, there are "moments when the inner and the outer seem to co-incide" (1969: 416). Then, semiosis in endo and exo-fields might happen simultaneously. Moreover, "the distinction endo/exo is always relative and depends on what level the focus of examination is put" (Tarasti 2000: 40).

Louise Bourgeois (2012) called as *translation* the process of expressing what she had to say to the medium. Further, Townsend speaks of a *dialogue* between artist and medium which happens when an "idea is put into practice" (2015: 121) – which generally takes place after the artist conceived his/her initial idea (Townsend 2015). In a sense, Townsend's (2015) dialogue implies externalization – a transition from endo to exo. In the exo-field, the artist must impose him/herself to the medium while the medium offers resistance, as if it were alive as well.

Conversely, "Many musical processes consist of internalizing the external, of transforming exogenic signs into endogenic ones. Thus, a musical composition forms, in a metaphoric sense, a kind of living organism" (Tarasti 2000: 39). At this point, there is a transformation stemming from exosemiosis of the "objective environment into subjective universes or individual realities [which] require endosemiotic processes" (Uexküll et al. 1993: 7). In this context, the medium must be internalized, which implies that it is first disjuncted from the artist. Whether it is alien to Tarasti's (2015) notion of *Dasein* or not will depend solely if the object is already present in the mind, but absent in actuality. For instance, when you are composing, you may imagine the notes or else, play them at the piano. In the former case, the inner creative dialogue begins when the musical object is transcendental to *Dasein* – it is not materially present as a mechanical wave. I would like to call this kind of endo-dialogue as *transcendental imagination*, and it happens prior to the proper *dialogue* in the way Townsend understand it (Figure 1).

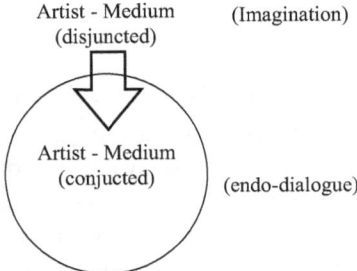

Figure 1: Imagination and endo-dialogue (introjection).

When the object becomes owned by the artist, which means, it becomes present in *Dasein*, a second process starts to take place together with the endo-dialogue. In this second process, the *dialogue* is *translated* from the endosemiotic field towards the exo-field. Such shift from endo to exo does not constitute in a kind of transcendence in which "one moves completely beyond temporal-spatial-actorial correlates" (Tarasti 2000: 41). The very reason for that is because, since the object is present in the mind and in actuality, there is no reason to speak of transcendence – in ES terminology. Nonetheless, there are particular trans-signs, "which are by nature metagenic or metasemiotic entities" (Tarasti 2000: 41). Such signs in the exo-field are in direct relation to the endo-field, as parallels or in an alternate reality/field. Therefore, musical notes in a score could be seen as trans-signs to the musical ideas that were conceived prior to them. Summarizing, artistic process begins with transcendental imagination, then it moves to *Dasein* when an endo-dialogue takes place. Simultaneously, the artist interacts with the medium, translating his/her idea to it. The dialogue (interaction between the artist and the medium) then occurs at the endo-space, as if the medium which the artist is working on is part of the artist's inner world, while, at the same time, it is at the exo-field and is modified according to the artist's expression of his/her endo-dialogue.

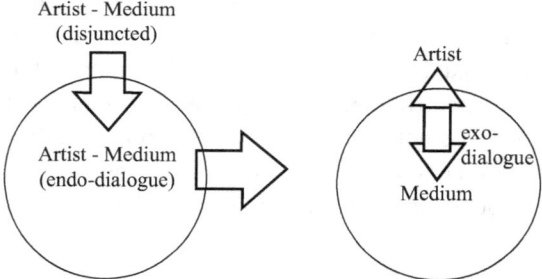

Figure 2: endo and exo-dialogue (projection).

Freud (1905) once observed that psychoanalytic therapy and hypnosis work according to two poietic principles stated by Leonardo da Vinci. Hypnosis, as a suggestive method, imposes something into the patient. In this sense, it is closely associated with painting and what Leonardo called *per via di pone*. Yet, psychoanalysis, as in archeology or in sculpture, is a method rather interested in what lies beneath the surface, and thus is related to Leonardo's *per via di levare*. Still, in both processes there is interaction between the artist and its medium. Moreover, when the artist is translating his endo-signs to the medium, although he/she may be withdrawing something from it, an idea is being added to it. Also the internalization of ideas and of the medium always add something to the artist's endo-field. This is why in creative process something is *created* despite the kind of activity upon the medium.

Louise Bourgeois once said that one has to overcome and conquer the medium (Townsend 2015), suggesting that a battle occurs between the artist and the signs at the exo-field. In this sense, both *per via di pone* and *per via di levare* involve a modification on the medium – whether by adding or withdrawing something from it. Modern psychoanalytic approaches to creativity consider the role of *aggression* in creative and poietic process. In this sense, Townsend quoted Sir Howard Hodgkin in his creative process: "I want to be able to attack again and again and again, and the trouble with canvas is that if you attack it more than once or twice there's nothing left" (2015: 125). Now, many problems arise. In a sense, aggression is second to dissatisfaction with the state of things, or better, with the state of the object. The artist's impulse here is to destroy the object, or rather to modify it until the artist is satisfied (Townsend 2015).

Still, even when the artist displays an aggressive attitude toward the medium and refashions it in such a way that the intended artistic object will no longer take place, there still might be room for art. Grayson Perry talks of the need to consider ideas that may seem ridiculous if the artist's own critical voice is silenced: "If you kind of go 'Oh! Rubbish!', then you think 'Oh right, I'm not going to bother'" (Townsend 2015: 126). One example of such attitude is Massimo Bottura's *Oops, I Dropped the Lemon Tart*. Takahiko Kondo (Bottura's *sous-chef*), was delivering two lemon tarts and then he dropped one, ruining the dessert. He was devastated. Then Botttura said to him: "that is beautiful, let's re-build as it's a broken stuff" (Bottura in Klorman-Eraqi 2016: para. 9). Then they spread the lemon sabayon in the lemon tart that wasn't broken, and finally broke it as well, thus rebuilding the two plates. "That was the moment in which we created 'Oops, I Dropped the Lemon Tart' recipe" (Bottura in Klorman-Eraqi 2016: para. 10). The *sous-chef* concluded: "In life, to move forward. . . you learn from mistakes" (Kondo in Klorman-Eraqi 2016: para. 11).

If today the dessert at *Osteria Francescana* is intentionally made to appear as if it were unintentionally broken, the Japanese have been repairing broken objects for millenia. Since 1500 BCE the use of *urushi* resin is being employed in the restoration of ceramics. Later, in the first half of the 17th century CE, appear the earliest evidences of *Kintsugi*, which employs gold in restoration of ceramics (Keulemans 2016). Kintsugi "uses precious metals to draw attention to the object and transform the object's appearance, in contrast to other forms of repair that attempt to hide a history of damage" (Keulemans 2016: 16). It is actually the evidence of damage that makes it valuable. A restored vase means that it is still usable despite the fact the it was shattered, for instance, by an earthquake. Then,

Kintsugi and Bottura's dessert could be seen as the result of an effort to bring together the shattered pieces of endosemiosis after a work of art suffered a violent modification from the exo-field.

Moreover, the notion of aggression is present in the attitude of a music composer when he intentionally takes away one chord from a score. Or you can just say that this process is related to *per via di levare*. It is important to highlight that, when aggression operates on the musical medium, you can turn back and decide to add the same chord again. The same does not apply for a sculpture in Carrara marble. Not even with *haute-cuisine*. Nevertheless, when music is studied under its performatic sense, it falls under the same category of sculpture and culinary. What to say of Clouzot's (1956) *Le Mystère Picasso*? Could the director ask Picasso to start from scratch if something goes wrong during the translation process?

3 Repetition, variation and psychopathology

Schoenberg (1990) claimed that a motive must be repeated throughout a piece. Nevertheless, pure repetition creates monotony, which can be overcome by variation "which means change. But changing every feature produces something foreign" (Schoenberg 1990: 8). As of repetition, it may be called as exact, modified or developed. The first case happens when musical features and relations are preserved, even though they may be found transposed to a different degree. The second case necessarily involves the creation of new material through variation. Still, it should take place in less-important features only, since the preservation of more important features is of paramount importance, otherwise the piece might be perceived as incoherent. The relevance of each feature is determined by the compositional objective. Then, variation should only be applied into subordinate musical meaning with no special consequences to the main motive. Its purpose should be restricted to embellishment only. The third case takes place when subsequent variations change the motive-form allowing the inclusion of foreign material without making the play incoherent (Schoenberg 1990).

Then, by taking a psychoanalytic turn into poietic and creative process, we learn that it serves sublimation processes, which: "allows for the expression and reworking of grief through remembrance" (Nimroody 2014: 320). According to Freud (1908), our sexual and vital forces (*trieb*) usually aim at finding an external object in order to get satisfaction. Sublimation, which includes artistic creation and intellectual inquiry, involves a modification of the original aim (*ziel*) and object (*objekt*) whilst being constrained by our social values and not losing its original pressure exerted in the subject (Freud 1908). Consequently, creativity relies on the pressure (*drang*) originally related to sexuality, but then converted into something else and causing relief from the tension created by pressure.

Furthermore, "a rigid, stereotyped form of creativity involves repetition designed to ward off painful affect and allows for little constructive mourning of the loss" (Nimroody 2014: 320). Therefore, if sublimation involves only a poor application of creativity, it provides little therapeutic outcome. Moreover, "repetition involves repeatedly failed efforts to repair the loss and thus leads to an inability to overcome guilt through creativity" (Nimroody 2014: 318). What is implied here is what Freud (1914) observed when patients displayed their symptoms in a repetitive way, creating obstacles to his analytical efforts and preventing hurtful memories to be remembered and told by the patient.

Considering Tarasti's (2000) relation between endosemiosis of remembrance and exosemiosis of expression, we may see sublimatory creativity as an affair that creates "the sense that we are masters of our own destiny" (Tarasti 2000: 44). In this context, we must consider that sublimation does not happen spontaneously or naturally. It requires culture and labour for one to work-through endosemiotic signs and live to create works of art perceived by others. There is no creativity when you drop a lemon tart, but when you rebuild it.

Nevertheless, if proper mastery of the exogenic field doesn't happen, monotonous and pathological repetition appears preventing the actual improvement of someone's mental health condition, for instance when one wants to cope with mourning. In this situation, the exo-field dictates everything to the individual, leaving no room for the working-through of painful feelings. An Italian everyday saying about a flag and the wind tackles such issue. The flag's fabric and colors are the signs of its endo-field. Then comes the wind, being the exo-field of the flag. If the same flag only moves according to the wind, we have a metaphor with negative values (Tosi 1991). It is related to Plauto's verse (Epidicus: 1.1.49): "Whichever way the wind is at sea, Epidicus, in that direction the sail is shifted" [*Vtcúmque in alto ventust, Epidice, exim velum vortitur*]. Although Plauto may have related to the importance of adaptation, one should question if there is a benefit of always being adrift to the winds of life.

Another problem with creativity lies in the inhibition which takes control over the artist, a condition often accompanied by pathological mourning (Nimroody 2014). This may be the case with Jean Sibelius during his Silence of Järvenpää in Ainola: "Compositional productivity was limited (. . .). The many and frequent visitors were told he was working on an Eighth Symphony" (Chipman 2000: 433), which was never delivered. "The causal explanations [for Sibelius' Silence of Järvenpää] have ranged from alcoholism or manicdepressive illness to the increasing harshness of his self-critical faculties" (Chipman 2000: 434). We may also take in consideration that Sibelius' "early history of withdrawn and unavailable mothering, and the early loss of stable paternal identification figures would be consistent with such a character resolution" (Chipman 2000: 451).

Let us consider now two opera characters which may have found themselves in crisis related to pathological development which caused a disruption in the dynamism between endo and exo-signs. Firstly, Berg's Wozzeck, who suffered from schizophrenia (Tambling 2004). The character role was condemned by the Captain for not being a man with morals since he had an unbaptized son. Wozzeck's response to the Captain caused, in the latter, a feeling of strangeness, as if he had not understood him. This duet might be seen as an evidence of Wozzeck's incapability of expressing himself thus creating a breach between his endosemiosis and his exo-field.

Then, in the Doctor scene we learn of Wozzeck's obsessions with signs in a *passacaglia*. If *ostinato* express the madness of a man "condemned to nothing but repetition" (Tambling 2004: 184), it rather suggests the presence of a comorbidity: obsessional neurosis. What I see as related to schizophrenia is how Wozzeck re-creates his exo-field in a way far from reality. For instance, in the open fields with Andres (Act I, scene 2), Wozzeck seems to be in a world different from his friend's, claiming that they are being surrounded by Masons, when Andres claims that there were only small animals. Also Wozzeck can hear the trumpets that resonate from the fires falling from the skies. Here we have an example of a split between the companions as an outcome from the disinvestment with the actual world.

Then, Wozzeck witness Marie dancing with the Drum-Major (Act II, scene 5), but sees the whole world in fornication. Rerwriting Tambling's (2004) conclusion in ES terminology, Wozzeck rebuilds his exo-field with hyperbolic variation. Wozzeck's symptoms were produced probably due to "irreconcilable demands of the Captain, the Doctor, his own life as a soldier and his relationship with Marie" (Tambling 2004: 181), his wife of dubious moral character.

Those responsible for the pressure exerted on the Wozzeck's *Moi* are indicated in Figure 3: the Captain, the Doctor and Marie. As sources of anguish, they promote disinterest in the part of Wozzeck, whose psyche is not able to make the proper libidinal reinvestment in the world. Then, Wozzeck suffers from hallucinations which illustrate a doomsday scenario, the irreconcilable. Here, the semiotic mechanism of creativity assumes a pathological function, that in which a new reality is created. The problem lies in the fact that new hallucinated reality lacks cohesion with the actual exo-field – there is too much variation. Wozzeck's frustrations also led him to kill Marie. He drowns when searching for the dagger he used to kill her, evidencing another aspect of Wozzeck's complete psychological disintegration.

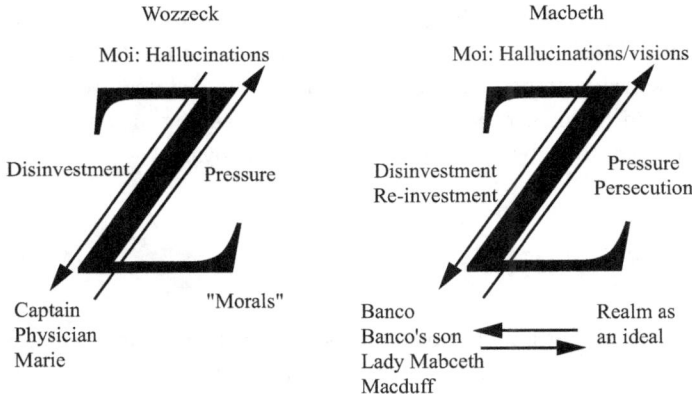

Figure 3: Zemic model as a diagnostic tool in Wozzeck's and Macbeth's.

Then there is the case of Verdi's Macbeth. In Act II, scene 7, he sees the ghost of his deceased rival. According to Henry Ey (1973), one can differ between a spiritual vision, when one's vision are corroborated by his social group, and a hallucination, which is second to the psychic disorganization of the subject. Macbeth's vision may be more related to a hallucination, for the ghost is not seen by others and he is not in some sort of religious ritual. Moreover, Castarède (2002) noticed that Macbeth assumes a feminine role, whilst his wife undertakes a masculine one. Thus he is faced with his own homosexuality. According to Freud (1911), paranoia (and its hallucinations) is a defense mechanism against such homo-sexual impulses. Further, Castarède (2002) argued that Macbeth suffered from hallucinations related to the threat posed by the vengeance of Banco's ghost, or rather, his son. A threat that later would materialize in Macduff.

Differently from Wozzeck, who suffered from schizophrenia, Macbeth's paranoia still allowed him to re-invest himself in the world. After his hallucination in Act II, Macbeth meets many apparitions upon an invocation by the three witches in Act III, scene 2. Macbeth also notices in a solemn atmosphere, that the last ghost in the procession is that of the feared Banco. He relates the scene to Lady Macbeth, who appears later, suffering from a form of hysterical blindness. Whilst Macbeth regains his connection with his exo-field and *Soi 1* (kingship), the same cannot be said of his partner, who falls into a grave psychopathological crisis.

Freud (1911) observed that in paranoia there is a chance of recovery, this is why Macbeth will still be able to pursue the three witches in order to check if his throne is still vulnerable (in modern days he might have sought for a doctor's help – Maybe not Wozzeck's). On the other hand, in schizophrenia, there is a complete deterioration of the endogenic field. In Berg's Wozzeck, the main character hallucinations are second to a failed reinvestment into the real world – quite different not only from Macbeth, but also from Bottura and Kondo's lemon tart, who dealt with a broken sign at their exo-field and managed to restore it. Wozzeck fails not only in rebuilding his exo-field, but also fails in keeping his endo-dialogue with his endo-field, thus dwelling in a psychological abyss.

4 Spectrum of creativity

Research in creativity and psychopathology shows that creative people usually displays high scores in psychometric scales for psychopathology. Still, they usually display lower levels than that of psychotic subjects (Eysenck 1995). It seems reasonable, then, to assume that creativity is found in healthy subjects but also in ones suffering from psychopathologies such as schizophrenia, paranoia and hysteria.

Considering the dialogue between endo and exo-semiosis in creative process and psychopathological issues related to artistic creativity, I created a graphic summary with cases I've mentioned and a few additions. Figure 4 has two axes, one indicating the degree of variation or repetition for each situation, and a second indicating the degree of inhibition or activity. In Figure 4, the more aggression is released in a sublimated way, the more creative the work of art is – until a threshold is reached and variation becomes pathological. Conversely, below sublimated activity, we have daily routine, which could turn to pathological when healthy psychological dispositions become inhibited, allowing thus free space for pathologies to flourish. Melancholy, parapraxis (Freudian slip) and catatonia take place when the subject is inhibited in a lesser or higher degree. In extreme cases, all control of the body is lost, and the subject becomes motionless, very similar to a dead person – the difference being that when someone is dead, all internal body activity also ceases.

In Figure 4, the threshold of sublimation marks the point when aggressive instincts and pulsional activity are turned from its original aim. Right above it I've placed Schoenberg' three kinds of repetition which take place in music poietic process. Variation is then allowed up to a point in which the musical composition does not present lacks in coherence, which is limited by *threshold of coherence 1* (TC1). Beyond it, aggressive instincts are employed in the creation of meta-works of art. Namely, those that suffered a partial destruction and the artist is not anymore able to reconstitute the original object. Restoration efforts generally take place after TC1. Yet, sometimes restoration aims at rebuilding the damaged object closer to the original work of art, looking for less variation. At other times, more variation is allowed, as with Bottura's and Kondo's lemon tart. I've placed

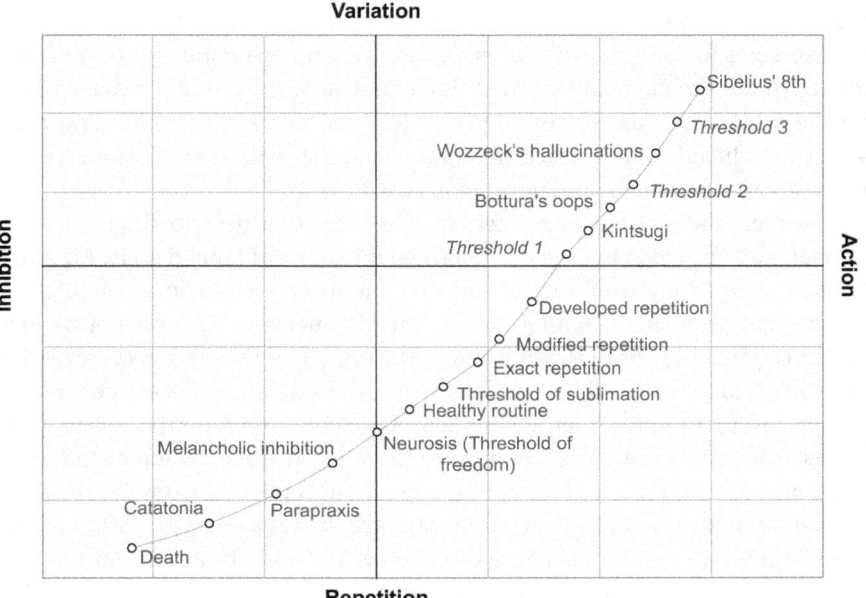

Figure 4: Spectrum of creativity.

the Italian dessert above Japanese craft because the former, today, is created as broken, so it necessarily employs more aggression on the medium. Conversely, Kintsugi art does not involve the destruction of its medium, but rather its restoration. Such debate could be applied to the *Notre-Dame de Paris* reconstruction: should it be rebuilt as close as possible to the original one, or should the reconstruction allow the intrusion of modern architectural features?

Above Bottura's and Kondo's lemon tart lie all cases which allows variation in the exo-field up to a point that it is no longer healthy or involve some sort of depreciation of the exo-field. Then, simple transgressions are right above *threshold of coherence 2* (TC2). Such is the case when young Sanumá Indians (a subgroup of the Yanomami) use non-accepted ways of calling their relatives (Ramos 2008) – here the exo-field (foreigners) influenced Sanumá children in a way that the endo-field (familial names) is threatened. Then, these modified endo-signs become part of communal activity in a transgressed way: new exo-signs are created. In this situation, creative process is employed merely as transgression and with no artistic purpose at all – indeed it is endangering the original cultural heritage. The threat caused by the foreigners to the endo-field of the Sanumá involves a process similar to Macbeth's paranoia. Yet, in the latter's case it causes more psychological suffering than the deterioration of a tradition. In paranoia, the endo-field assumes a more important position in the world than what it really has. Moreover, the exo-signs in dialogue with the endo-field vary up to a point that they are not related to the exo-signs in reality. Still, narcissistic influence in paranoia allows for the subject to retain some self-preservation concerns, although exaggerated and with unhealthy outcomes. Differently from the situation of the Sanumá, what is preserved in paranoia does not actually exist.

Further, Todorov (1982) noticed an Aztec tale that described iguanas that were going to be eaten but then were turned into parts of human body. Although Spanish conquerors would not deem this tale to be a realistic account, these images had prophetic meaning for the *Nahuátl* speakers. This case of hallucination can be interpreted as lying below TC2 for, albeit there is a reconstruction of reality (iguanas turned into parts of a human body), they were accepted and interpreted by the people at Xochimilco. A similar situation takes place when a deceased asks for a living Guarani to be relieved from his tomb, the latter hearing the former and adhering to the dead one's plea (Clastres 1975). Hildegard von Bingen's visions, which fall under the same category of Saint Theresa of Avila (Ey 1973), could also be placed below TC2 and above TC1, for they are deemed as valid in a cultural milieu (Catholic religion). Therefore, if a hallucination is accepted by society, it should stand only beyond TC1; if not (and if there is no enough link with reality), then the hallucination must stand beyond TC2 as well. Macbeth's case then departs from TC2 in Act II, but then, in Act III, he falls back closer to Bottura's lemon tart – which is accepted not by religious standards, but by *haute-cuisine*'s. Wozzeck's case is the opposite of Macbeth's: the former departs from TC2 and reaches a higher degree of variation from norm in his action of killing Marie. Further, Wozzeck's transgression is not only related to a norm, as the one among the Sanumá, but also to a deep psychological disorganization.

Finally, when a third threshold of aggression is reached the work of art is totally destroyed. Such is the case of Sibelius's 8th. For this reason, I would not say that Sibelius was inhibited in his Ainola's days: albeit full of conflicts, he was active. Moreover, due to his self-judgmental crisis, he passed *threshold of coherence 3* (TC3) and annihilated his last symphony. This situation is radically different from when a work of art doesn't become real due to inhibition in the artist. Furthermore, TC3 differs from schizophrenic states because, in the latter there are, at least, deformed vestiges of reality, whereas in the former, there is not a single evidence of signs in the exo-field.

5 Mikkeli, Ainola and the the need for containment

Finally, I shall consider the role of the exo-field as a *Source of Creativity*. The issue was highlighted by Prof. Tarasti at the *Tertti Manor*. On the occasion, Tarasti (personal communication) spoke of the role of Mikkeli for the birth of ES – not as a medium, but rather as a space. One could still think of space as a medium, as it happens during the festival *Lux Helsinki* in January. Nevertheless, a psychoanalytic perspective knows of another role of space in creative process. The Iranian artist, Shirazeh Houshiary, speaks of the importance of her studio for her: "When you're in the outside world, you are busy with domestic or everyday events. Here [in the studio] you leave all that behind; it's a place where you are free, without any involvement with the outside world . . . it is a place to let go" (Townsend 2015: 127). Further, Townsend also noticed the relevance of space if one wants to set apart from everyday life and enter a "domain of contemplation" (2015: 127), in Kenneth Wright's terms. Moreover, Townsend observed that Henry Moore collects items and place them in his studio, making it a "physical space that embodies the conditions for entering a particular mental space where creative work can take place" (2015: 127).

Freud's consulting rooms (in Vienna and London) were full of archeological material, which stood for the excavation metaphor that takes place during therapy. The psychoanalyst Andrea Sabbadini compares the analyst's consulting room to the artist's studio, writing that within the "consistent and therefore relatively safe space provided by our 'studios'" (Sabbadini 2013: 120) the analyst can make creative use of the material brought by the patient.

In 1904, Aino, Sibelius' wife, hoped to cure Jean of some bad habits by moving into the rural home in the village of Jarvenpää: Ainola. It is true that, in Ainola, Sibelius managed to abstain from alcohol and cigars (Chipman 2000). In his early Ainola days, Sibelius wrote: "I managed when I had cigars and wine, but now I have to find new ways. I must!" (Sibelius in Tawaststjerna 1986: 142). Still, "Sibelius responded with exceptional intensity to the moods of nature and the changes in the seasons: he scanned the skies with his binoculars for the geese flying over the lake ice, listened to the screech of the cranes, and heard the cries of the curlew echo over the marshy ground just below Ainola" (Tawaststjerna 1986: 21). Not even a suspicion of diabetes haltered Sibelius' progress. In a sign of struggle, Sibelius wrote to Baron Carpelan: "I shall write more" (Tawaststjerna 1986: 22).

Ainola was not only a safe haven for Sibelius, it was also home to Finnish Cultural Heritages. Tarasti once observed that "in the prelude to the third movement [from Kullervo, opus 7] Sibelius comes closest to the decorative element of

Karelianism" (1979: 251). Also Sibelius payed his homage to Viipuri, Karelia, in his opus 11. Later, Karelianism would be employed in the architecture of Ainola. For instance, the windows at Ainola's library are directly related to Karelian culture (Tawaststjerna 1986). Still if Ainola was a home for Sibelius' creativity, why was it also the place for his phase known as the "Silence from Järvenpää"?

According to Chipman (2000), in the *4th symphony* (and its stoical resignation at the end) and in *Kullervo*'s earlier suppression, we see traces of Sibelius' crisis already – but he was still composing. The first mention of Sibelius' 8th is found in a 1926 letter to Olga Bratt in which he said that he was "working on a new thing for orchestra" (Oramo 2017: 51). Then in a 1931 letter to Olin Downes (Oramo, 2017: 51) he mentioned a "symphony". Furthermore, there were many reasons which "contributed to his alienation and loss of creative spirit. But this is hardly the whole truth" (Oramo 2017: 53). Sibelius' silence might have been fostered by the pressure exerted from the new techniques of compositions born in the 1920s and 30s, but also by the political turmoil in Europe (Oramo 2017: 52). In a sense, Sibelius' endo-conflicts with his 8th were beyond of Wozzeck's with his *Soi*: Whilst the latter was still able rebuild his exo-field in a hallucinatory fashion, Sibelius was so pressured by the dialogue between his endosemiosis and his exo-field that he was unable to give life to his 8th.

References

Bourgeois, Louise. 2012. Interview with Donald Kuspitt 1988. In Kristine Stiles & Peter Selz (eds.), *Theories and documents of contemporary art. A sourcebook of artist's writings*, 38–42. London, Berkeley and Los Angeles: University of California Press.
Castarède, Marie-France. 2002. *Les vocalises de la passion. Psychanalyse de l'opéra*. Paris: Armand Colin/VUEF.
Chipman, Abram. 2000. Janáček and Sibelius: The Antithetical Fates of Creativity in Late Adulthood. *Psychoanalytic Review* 87(3). 429–454.
Clastres, Hélène. 1975. *La terre sans mal. Le prophétisme tupi-guarani*. Paris: Éditions de Seuil.
Clouzot, Henri-Georges (ed.). 1956. *Le Mystère Picasso* [Movie]. Paris: Filmsonor.
Eysenck, Hans. 1995. *Genius: the natural history of creativity*. Cambridge: Cambridge University Press.
Eco, Umberto. 1984. *Semiotica e filosofia del linguaggio*. Torino: Einaudi.
Ey, Henry. 1973. *Traité des hallucinations. Tome II*. Paris: Masson et Cie.
Freud, Sigmund. 1905. Über psychotherapie. *Wiener Medizinische Presse* 46(1). 9–16.
Freud, Sigmund. 1908. Die 'kulturelle' sexualmoral und die moderne nervosität. *Sexual-Problem* 4(3). 107–129.
Freud, S. 1911. Psychoanalytische bemerkungen über einen autobiographisch beschriebenen fall von paranoia (Dementia Paranoides). *Jahrbuch für Psychoanalytische und Psychopathologische Forschung* 3(1). 9–68.

Freud, Sigmund. 1914. Erinnern, wiederholen und durcharbeiten. *Internationale Zeitschrift für Psychoanalyse* 2(6). 485–491.

Keulemans, Guy. 2016. The geo-cultural conditions of Kintsugi. *The Journal of Modern Craft* 9(1). 15–34.

Klorman-Eraqi, Haggai. 2016 [July 3]. "Oops, I Dropped the Lemon Tart!" https://www.linkedin.com/pulse/oops-i-dropped-lemon-tart-haggai-klorman-eraqi

Kristeva, Julia. 2000. From symbols to flesh: the polymorphous destiny of narration. *International Journal of Psycho-Analysis* 81(4). 771–787.

Lacan, Jacques. 1955–1956. *Le Séminaire, Livre III, Les psychoses*. Paris: Editions du Seuil

Meusburger, Peter. 2009. Milieus of Creativity: The Role of Places, Environments, and Spatial Contexts. In Peter Meusburger, Joachim Funke & Edgar Wunder (eds.), *On the psychology of creativity*, 97–153. Dordrecht: Springer.

Milner, Marion. 1969. *The hands of the living god*. London: Hogarth Press.

Nimroody, Tehela. 2014. Mourning, identity, creativity. *Journal of the American Psychoanalytic Association* 62(2). 313–321.

Oramo, Ilkka. 2017 Sibelius' Eighth Symphony – Fact and Fiction. In Daniel Grimley, Tim Howell, Veijo Murtomäki & Timo Virtanen (eds.), *Jean Sibelius's Legacy: Research on his 150th Anniversary*, 51–65. Newcastle upon Tyne: Cambridge Scholars Publishing.

Ramos, Alcida. (2008). Nomes Sanumá entre gritos e sussurros [Sanumá names between cries and whispers]. *Etnográfica* 12(1). 59–69.

Sabbadini, Andrea. 2013. In between and across. In Gabriela Goldstein (ed.), *Art in Psychoanalysis. A contemporary approach to creativity and analytic practice*, 109–122. London: Karnac and the International Psychoanalytical Association.

Röhe. Daniel. 2017. Existential Semiotics and Psychoanalysis. Paper presented at the Opening Seminar of the Academy of Cultural Heritages, Ritsos Hall, Syros, 2–9 October.

Schoenberg. Arnold. 1990 [1967]. *Fundamentals of Music Composition*. Ed. by Gerald Strang & Leonard Stein. London: Faber and Faber.

Tambling, Jeremy. 2004. Listening to schizophrenia: the Wozzeck case. In Arved Ashby (ed.), *The pleasure of modernist music: listening, meaning, intention, ideology*, 176–196. Rochester: The University of Rochester Press.

Tarasti, Eero. 1979. *Myth and music: A semiotic approach to the aesthetics of myth in music, especially that of Wagner, Sibelius and Stravinsky*. The Hague: Mouton Publishers.

Tarasti, Eero. 2000. *Existential Semiotics*. Bloomington: Indiana University Press.

Tarasti, Eero. 2015. *Sein und schein. Explorations in existential semiotics*. Berlin and Boston: Walter de Gruyter.

Tawaststjerna, Erik. 1986. *Sibelius. Volume II 1904–1914*. Berkeley and Los Angeles: University of California Press.

Todorov, Tzvetan. 1982. *La conquête de L'Amérique. La question de l'autre*. Paris: Éditions du Seuil.

Tosi, Renzo. 1991. *Dizionario delle sentenze latine e greche*. Milano: RCS Rizzoli Libri.

Townsend, Patricia. 2015. Creativity and destructiveness in art and psychoanalysis. *British Journal of Psychotherapy* 31(1). 120–131.

Uexküll, Thure von, Werner Geigges & Jörg Herrmann. 1993. Endosemiosis. *Semiotica* 96(1/2). 5–51.

Pertti Ahonen
Ethnomethodological, symbolic interactionist, semiotic and existential micro-foundations of research on institutions

Abstract: Institutions are ubiquitous. Many of them mix tangible and ideational aspects, such as "dating", "marriage", the "business firm", "politics", the "arts", and the "university". There are also institutions which are generic and abstract, such as the "group" or the "organization". One possibility to grasp approaches to institutions is to consider their philosophy of science presuppositions. However, the common and trite procedure simply distinguishes different "institutionalisms", three, seven, or more. Well-known resulting lists commonly include a "sociological" category, meaning "generically of social science", the micro-foundations of which this article examines analogously with previous studies. The purpose of this article is to examine four types of micro-foundations of generic social science research on institutions, foregrounding micro-foundations underlying published research and backgrounding potential micro-foundations out of which research might have grown but has not done so amply or at all. The four types of micro-foundations derive from ethnomethodology, symbolic interactionism, semiotics, and existential approaches. This implies the delimitation that, for instance, research on institutions sharing the rationalistic micro-foundations of economics or some other disciplines falls outside the consideration, as does research with post-structuralist, post-modern or post-foundational micro-foundations. The foremost reason for focusing upon the four types of micro-foundations comprises their expected semiotic relevance.

Keywords: Institutionalization, signs, signification, meaning, organizations

Institutions are ubiquitous. Many of them mix tangible and ideational aspects, such as "dating", "marriage", the "business firm", "politics", the "arts", and the "university". There are also institutions which are generic and abstract, such as the "group" or the "organization". One possibility to grasp approaches to institutions is to consider their philosophy of science presuppositions. However, the common procedure simply distinguishes different "institutionalisms", three (Hall and Taylor 1996), seven (Peters 2019), or more (Lowndes and Roberts 2013). Each list includes a "sociological" category, meaning "generically of social science", the micro-foundations of which this study examines analogously with previous studies (Powell and Colyvas 2008; Chandler and Hwang 2015; Powell and Rerup 2017; Hwang and Colyvas 2019).

The purpose of this article is to examine four types of micro-foundations of generic social science research on institutions, foregrounding micro-foundations underlying published research and backgrounding potential micro-foundations out of which research might have grown but has not done so amply or at all. The four types of micro-foundations derive from ethnomethodology, symbolic interactionism, semiotics, and existential approaches. This implies the delimitation that, for instance, research on institutions sharing the rationalistic micro-foundations of economics or some other disciplines fall outside the consideration, as does research with post-structuralist, post-modern or post-foundational micro-foundations. The foremost reason for focusing upon the four types of micro-foundations comprises their expected semiotic relevance.

Acknowledging ethnomethodological micro-foundations is common in generic social science research on institutions (Powell and Colyvas 2008; Meyer 2009; Chandler and Hwang 2017; Powell and Rerup 2017; Hwang and Colyvas 2019). The founder of ethnomethodology, Harold Garfinkel, focused upon "the rational properties of indexical expressions [pointing to states of affairs such as situations and contexts] and other practical actions as contingent ongoing accomplishments of organized . . . practices" taking place in the *Lebenswelt* of human beings (Garfinkel 2010 [1967]: 11). Influences upon Garfinkel can be sought, for instance, in the work of the phenomenological philosopher Edmund Husserl and the ideas of Husserl and others as modified by Alfred Schütz (e.g., Schütz 1953, 1954). What is more, Garfinkel's notion of "indexicality" derives from one of the numerous triads in pragmatic philosopher C.S. Peirce's triadic semiotics (Peirce 1958: 248; Sonesson 2002: 84), paralleling "iconicity" and "symbolicity".

Researchers have traced the micro-foundations of institutions also in symbolic interactionism, which focuses upon "activity in which human beings interpret each other's gestures and act on the basis of the meaning yielded by that interpretation" (Blumer 1969: 65–66; Hall 1972). Symbolic interactionism has roots in the work of the pragmatist philosopher G.H. Mead. However, more frequently than ethnomethodology let alone symbolic interactionism, researchers on institutional micro-foundations have explicitly built upon Peter Berger and Thomas A. Luckmann's hybrid work with elements from phenomenology, social constructionism, semiotics, ethnomethodology and symbolic interactionism. Berger and Luckmann's (1991 [1966]: 72; see also Kim and Berard 2009) characterization of achieved institutionalization and institutionalization processes has become popular:

> Institutionalization occurs whenever there is a reciprocal typification of habitualized actions by types of actors. (A)ny such typification is an institution.

This article also considers what the semiotic study of signs and signification has to give when examining institutional micro-foundations. John W. Mohr (e.g., Mohr 2000; Mohr and White 2008) and, using the binary semiotics of A.J. Greimas, Barbara Czarniawska (e.g., 1998, 2008) and François Cooren and his colleagues (e.g., Cooren 2012) have directly tapped semiotic sources in considering the micro-foundations. Other semiotically inspired approaches have been offered for the micro-institutional study but found a less ample reception than the work of Czarniawska and Cooren and others (Barley 1983, 2008; Denzin 1987; Heiskala 2007; Gronow 2008; Landowski 2019). Moreover, this article considers what the micro-foundational examination may receive from existential approaches to being (*Dasein*, *l'être*, existence) in the facticity of everyday situations. To do this one has to use the not so ample and not so recent literature within which social sciences and existential approaches have met (e.g., Manning 1973; Kotarba and Johnson 2002; but see also Sartre [1960] 1982: 343–663).

This article seeks answers to five research questions:

1. On the expectancy that the reciprocal typification of habitualized actions requires both inclusions and exclusions, a first research question can be asked. How do inclusions and exclusions, separately and combined, contribute to institutional micro-foundations?
2. One can extend the attention from typifications to categorizations and boundaries between what has been included and what has been excluded. How do categorizations, including category names and labels, proliferate and become stabilized, and how are they related to institutional boundaries?
3. The term "agency" refers to the modalization of subjects in respect to doing something, from obligation to prohibition to enablement, and beyond. How do institutional agents meet the constraints of the conditions of their agency, and how do they use the opportunities which these conditions offer?
4. Besides achieved institutionalization, institutionalization processes need research. What conditions are there for institutional stability, and for gradual and abrupt institutional change, either progressive, neutral, or regressive?
5. The fifth research question derives from Max Weber ([1922] 1978: 85–86), Alfred Schütz as influenced by Weber, and Berger and Luckmann ([1966] 1991) elaborating analogous questions. What institutional tradeoffs prevail between doing things legitimately according to some specific values on the one hand, and doing them because their performance is good on the other?

1 Inclusions and exclusions at institutional micro-foundations

The political theorist William E. Connolly (1991: 64) writes: "Identity requires difference in order to be; and it converts difference into *otherness* in order to assure its own self-certainty." Well over a century of research on modernization leaves little doubt of fundamental changes in the identities of people, although the complete dissolution of identities remains a postmodern overstatement (Smith 2008). Insofar as traditional identities were monolithic and stable, their present-day equivalents are prone to change and replacement – but also to revival in retro-forms.

Many representatives of ethnic, religious, and academic (Becher and Trowler 2000) identities offer their preferred identity as the oxymoronic "only alternative". Zerubavel (1995: 1094) connects this to "the common essentialist tendency to reify mental entities" and suppress the ultimately constructed character of all identities. Zerubavel (1996) and Billig (1989: 118–155) have elaborated how such reification advances by means of particularization, splitting undesirable elements from the preferred identity. These two authors also consider categorization lumping together and lumping "in" elements with desirable characteristics and lumping together and lumping "out" elements with undesirable characteristics.

The repetition of an achieved identity is common (Derrida [1972] 1988; Driver 2009). This superficially attests to a self-certainty, but often conceals the uncertainty of the identity's defenders of the legitimacy of this identity. Gieryn (1983), Fuller (1991) and Zerubavel (1995) have elaborated how within academic research such uncertainty spawns prescriptions of what counts for "proper research", and who are "proper", and who are "false" researchers with a "spoiled identity" (Goffman 1963a). Analogous black-and-white categorization can be found in other strands of life (e.g., Joyce and Jeske 2020).

Alfred Schütz emphasizes the importance of typification (Schütz 1954: 268–269):

> (T)he typified patterns of the others' behavior become ... motives of my ... actions, and this leads to the ... self-typification well-known to social scientists .... The more ... interlocked behavior-patterns are standardized and institutionalized, that is, the more their typicality is socially approved ..., the greater ... their ... common-sense and scientific ... usefulness ....

Both expanding and delimiting an identity may outline paradigmatic objects (e.g., countries, landmarks, peoples, historical periods, incidents, and cultural objects) or people (leading figures of a culture, polity, or society) to represent such an identity (Fuller 1991). By contrast, other objects and people may be what Scott and Lyman (1968: 58) call altercasted, nowadays usually called othered. Who or what is altercasted or othered are relegated to alterity as alter-ego, without which the identity – the ego – could not articulate itself. In this respect the ego receives its definition through what it excludes and not only what it contains.

Probing the self-assurance of representatives of identities gears the examination towards the nominalist study of power (Alasuutari 2010). This is the power of taken-for-granted trivia carried by words, names and terms of particular vocabularies, usages according to established conventions, and resulting definitions and demarcations. Whether we approach institutional micro-foundations through symbolic interactionism, ethnomethodology, Goffman's ideas (Powell and Colyas 2008; Samra-Fredericks and Bargiela-Chiappini 2008), semiotics, or an existential approach, such power should not be underestimated. This is witnessed by the examination of such ubiquitous and apparently irrelevant practices as record-keeping, accounting, statistics, and surveillance (Garfinkel [1967] 2010; Porter 1993; Heath and Luff 2000; Power 2009; Lampland 2010).

2 Micro-institutionalism of categorization, boundaries, and naming

2.1 Categorization and related phenomena

"The power to categorize is serious power" (Negro et al. 2010: 21). Therefore, examining micro-institutionalization has to cover phenomena of typification (Berger and Luckmann [1966] 1991: 72; Kim and Bernard 2009), categorization, and classification. Fuller (2003: 3) writes: "By providing a framework through which we interpret the world, . . . classification[s] created by our cultural boundaries provide the basis for interaction and social organization". Shepherd (2010: 134, 136–137) elaborates the political character of classifications:

> [C]lassifications carry . . . rules . . . that produce behaviors favoring clear and unique . . . over ambiguous and hybrid categorization. . . . (O)nce a classification . . . is institutionalized . . . boundaries between categories become strengthened and . . . violations . . . punished. . . . The degree to which categories are assumed to be "natural" depends on whether they are perceived to be amenable to political influence.

Pertinent institutional features to examine include genealogy-constituting, foundational myths, order-maintaining rites and rituals, and authoritative institutional distinctions between the sacred and the profane, and the vulgar and the distinguished (Douglas 1966; Bourdieu 1985: 735; Alaimo and Kallinikos 2020). One must also examine verbal struggles in terms of what stands out as the facts, mixtures of fact and fiction, rumors, insults, and insinuations (Lawrence and Suddaby 2006; Therèse and Martin 2010).

2.2 Institutional linguistic turns: Performatives, naming, boundary-drawing, and rhetorical re-description

One cannot trace any abundance of semiotics within current research on institutional micro-foundations (Ahonen 2020), although it has taken other linguistic turns. This research has not failed to consider performatives, also known as speech acts, occurring *in* language (illocutions) or *by* the medium of language (perlocutions) (Austin 1975; Skinner 1988; Feldman 2003; Lounsbury and Crumley 2007: 996–997; Powell and Colyvas 2008: 281–282). Performatives operate, for instance, during institutional foundation, persistence, change and dissipation; in the acquisition, accumulation and use of institutional power; and in the institutional politics of naming, name-effacement, and name-avoidance (Glynn and Abzug 2002; Guenther 2009).

Nietzsche ([1882/1887] 1974: § 58: 122) wrote: "It is enough to create new names and estimations and probabilities in order to create in the long run new 'things'." Guenther (2009: 412) writes: "(t)he act of naming is an act of power". Pierre Bourdieu (1985: 732–733) holds that "names . . . record . . . struggles . . . over . . . designations and the material and symbolic advantages associated with them". Ernesto Laclau (2005: 104) goes so far as to suggest that "the identity and unity of [each] object result from the very operation of naming" (see also Althusser [1969] 1971; Butler 1997). Charmaz (2006: 396) further specifies the issue:

> (N)ames classify . . . and convey meanings and distinctions. . . . Names provide knowing – and being. . . . Much of sociology addresses relative power differentials to make a name stick – or to resist the name with its attendant categorizations, values,. . . and implications. . . .

One of the foci of research on institutions is "institutional work" in recognition of the institutional influence upon actors' agency and the related "identity work" of these actors (Maier and Simsa 2020). Institutional work may build upon the performative use of power in order to expand, delimit, delineate or clarify a preferred identity with the simultaneous altercasting or othering of the respective alterity. Research on institutions also examined "boundary work" (Gieryn 1983; Fuller 1991; Lamont and Molnar 2002: 179; Zietsma and Lawrence 2010) on the assumption that "boundaries are often a key site for struggles over social relations" (Fuller 2003: 4).

According to Gieryn (1983: 791–792), boundary work "heightens the contrast between rivals in ways flattering" to the protagonists. Actors' monopoly over boundary work – in the case in hand within scientific research – "excludes rivals ... by defining them with such labels as 'pseudo', 'deviant' or 'amateur'" (Gieryn 1983: 792). Those who carry out boundary work may expand their autonomy by means of instituting new fields of operation, renaming fields, and merging or separating fields and their institutional elements (Zerubavel 1995; 1996). Gieryn (1983: 792) considers boundary work which "exempts [those who pursue it] from responsibility for consequences of their work by putting the blame on scapegoats from the outside". Fuller (2003: 5) forewarns of opportunism in boundary work: "Because ... no boundary [may] ... meet every challenge..., [protagonists place the] borders differently according to who and what ... to exclude."

Suddaby (2010) argues for better rhetorically inspired basic research on institutions. Such research has many sources to tap, such as legitimating and delegitimating accounts (Creed et al. 2002); framing contests rich with what Kaplan (2008: 731) calls "politicking" by the participating actors; the rhetoric of drawing and maintaining boundaries (Fuller 1991); and institutional fashions (Perkmann and Spicer 2008; Learmonth 2009). Researchers on institutions often refer to C.W. Mills:

> When an agent ... imputes motives, he is ... influencing others – and himself. ... This ... ex post facto ... lingualization may ... appeal to a vocabulary of motives associated with a norm with which [the] members of the situation are in agreement. (Mills 1940: 907–908)

Further opportunities for examining institutions derive from the political science examination around the classical rhetorical figure *paradiastole*, known in Latin as *distinctio* (Skinner 2008; Palonen 2004: 170; Carver 2020). *Paradiastole* is composed of rhetorical redescription that accents the merits of what is preferred, and understates the merits of what is repudiated. An everyday example of performativity that uses *paradiastole* consists of the common "naming, blaming and shaming" within research (Thérèse and Martin 2010) or elsewhere (Meyer and Höllerer 2010).

2.3 Methodological specialties in examining institutional micro-foundations

The ethnomethodological examination of micro-institutionalization does not shy away from experimentation (Garfinkel [1967] 2010; Zucker 1977). C.S. Peirce's abductive semiotic method of inference (Peirce 1931–1935, Vol. 5: 188–189; Peirce 1929) is not alien to micro-institutional research, either. Notably, the method known as grounded theory (GT) – a method despite its name – explicitly relies upon abductive inference (Reichertz 2007). Grounded theory has roots also in symbolic interactionism.

The ethnomethodological micro-foundations of the study of institutions bring in the "documentary method", adapted by Harold Garfinkel (e.g., 2010: 40, 94–96, 100–103) from Karl Mannheim (1952: 43–63) and more indirectly also Erwin Panofsky (1955: 51–81). Mannheim distinguishes an "objective meaning" corresponding with the intentions of honest creators of objects that interpreters will have to interpret. He also takes apart an "expressive meaning" deriving from the honest or dishonest intentions of the authors of documents or the creators of other cultural objects. Last, he discerns a "documentary meaning" expressing the ethos of the authors or other cultural creators. According to Mannheim, documentary meaning covers all relevant conditions of the cultural creation in question (Bohnsack 2008). Examples which Mannheim gives of such ethos include Wilhelm Dilthey's notion of *die Weltanschauung*, Max Weber's *der Geist des Kapitalismus* and *der Beruf*, Marcel Mauss's – and after Mannheim's times, Pierre Bourdieu's – *habitus* (Mannheim 1952: 58–59; Bohnsack 2008).

Garfinkel expanded Mannheim's interpretive model to include also lay sociology and its everyday ethnomethods utilized by laypersons in our practical, everyday affairs of the *Lebenswelt*. Both in research and in everyday uses, the model requires the simultaneous interpretation of patterns, or typifications, and the observation of indexicality, which indicates what is available in the interpretation. Garfinkel (2010: 78) writes:

> The method consists of treating an actual appearance as "the document of", as "pointing to", as "standing on behalf of" a presupposed underlying pattern. Not only is the ... pattern derived from its ... documentary evidences, but the ... evidences ... are interpreted on the basis of "what is known" about the ... pattern.

3 Research on institutions in an "agency crisis"

3.1 No easy way out of the crisis

Research on institutions has an "agency crisis" (Clegg 2010; Lawrence et al. 2010; Willmott 2011), because of difficulties in approaching agency, which modalizes actors in such ways as enabling these actors to act (Powell and Colyvas 2008;

Suddaby 2010). In this context institutional researchers often refer to Harold Garfinkel's (2010: 68) notion of the "cultural dope" as an agent type beyond which they would like to reach (see, for instance, Powell and Colyvas 2008):

> By "cultural dope" I refer to the man-in-the-sociologist's-society who produces the stable features of the society by acting in compliance with preestablished and legitimate alternatives of action that the common culture provides.

The common appreciation of the work of Anthony Giddens (e.g., 1976: 120) in research on institutions might make it appear that the resolution of the "agency crisis" is at hand: "[S]ocial structures are both constituted by human agency, and yet at the same time are the very medium of this constitution." Giddens avoids both what Margaret Archer (2007) calls "upward conflation" – or what in research on institutions can be called the "agentific" determination of action – and downward conflation with the macro-reduction of action to its structural determinants. Yet Archer criticizes Giddens for "central conflation" with "co-constitution": restless shuffling between the agentific and the structural determination. In actual practice, resolution of this dispute remains a long-term work in progress (Fleetwood 2008; Archer 2007; Dépelteau 2008).

"Embedded agency" comprises a common term in efforts to resolve the "agency crisis" (Zietsma and Lawrence 2010). The notion has characteristics of an oxymoron in referring to agency within an institutional context which constrains this agency. One embedded agency approach considers "institutional entrepreneurship" (Rao and Giorgi 2006). However, this may elevate voluntaristic hero figures into the *primus motor* of institutional change in *a deus ex machina* way (Delbridge and Edwards 2010; Willmott 2011). In their embedded agency approaches, Edwards and Jones (2008) and Zietsma and Lawrence (2010) have drawn upon a division introduced by Emirbayer and Mische (1998): "habitual agency" with selection among sets of established routines; "practical/evaluative agency" addressing dilemmas and ambiguities of evolving situations; and future-oriented "projective agency". Archer (2007) provides another agency typology built upon three types of reflexivity with different ways in which "I-actors" take themselves as the "me-objects" of their own actions: evasive "communicative reflexivity"; strategic "autonomous reflexivity"; and subversive "meta-reflexivity". Without doubt, considerations of embedded agency also have relevance for examining institutional change (see section 4 below).

3.2 Ideas for resolving the "agency crisis" from ethnomethodology, symbolic interactionism, semiotics, and existential approaches

Might relief for the "agency crisis" in the study of institutions come from a micro-foundational direction? I first look at symbolic interactionism. G.H. Mead ([1934] 1992: 140) regarded each "self,... which can be an object to itself,... essentially [as] a social structure". He also saw each self as inserted within "[t]he organized community... which gives the individual his unity of self... called the 'generalized other'" (Mead 1992: 154, see also 260–263). In his introduction to an edition of the works of Mead, Anselm Strauss formulated the following conclusions concerning the study of institutions:

> [O]rganizations... somehow work, although they have no single goal, no wholly agreed upon consensus;... they service... diverse aims... through bargaining, deals, agreements, and negotiations plus the more institutionalized mechanisms. (Strauss 1965: 14)

Within ethnomethodology, Harold Garfinkel ([1967] 2010: 53) has chronicled the impediments that institutional agency faces. His formulation has some resemblance with present-day bounded rationality research on institutions (e.g., March and Olsen 2009). Garfinkel writes:

> Not only does common sense knowledge portray a real society for members, but in the manner of self fulfilling prophecy the features of the real society are produced by persons' motivated compliance with these background expectancies. (Garfinkel (2010: 53)

Garfinkel (1964: 24) also elaborates what modifies the institutionalized expectancies that make up our common attitude to everyday life:

> The expectancies that make up the attitude of everyday life are constitutive of the institutionalized common understandings of the practical everyday... workings of society.... One... consists of... ceremonial transformation... in play, theatre going,... religious conversion, ..., and scientific inquiry. A second [comprises]... transformations... such as... in... extreme fatigue.... A third.... A fourth [takes place] in adult socialization.... Other[s]... are those of estrangement... as well as... phenomena of the cultural stranger.... Modifications [also] occur through mischief, playful and serious; through the subtle psychopathic effects of aging as one comes to learn that one may sin, cause others harm and not "pay"; and through the discovery... in adolescence... that... societal orders... depend... upon persons' continual improvisations. Finally, there is the modification that consists in... social science....

Within semiotic research proper, Norbert Wiley (1994: 2326, 48–59, 74–103) has expanded upon Mead's ([1934] 1992: 134) consideration of that feature of our selves called reflexiveness, also known as reflexivity. Wiley harmonizes triadic elements in Mead (1992: 40) with Peirce's triadic semiotics. Wiley inserts the present self of I (a *sign*, representing something; Peirce 1958: 272–273) talking to the future self of you (an *interpretant*, an effect of a sign upon an interpreter) about the past self of me (an *object*, represented by the sign; Peirce 1958: 492). Unfortunately, Wiley ignores institutional questions, unlike Mead (1992: 261), who explicitly considered institutions as "organized forms of group or social activity".

Jean-Paul Sartre's *Being and Nothingness* [1934] 2005) offers substantially than only a draft for to approach human agency. Sartre begins with our human state of chronic void, negation and nothingness, and continues to the "bad faith" of our self-deception because of denying our void. He next turns to "being-for-ourselves" and subsequently proceeds to regarding our everyday structures, temporality, and our possible transcendence of our being-for ourselves. Then he takes up "being-for-others", such as staying under their gaze and stepping into concrete relations with others. Last but least, Sartre considers doing and being as conditions for freedom in our existence. However, *Being and Nothingness* proves weak in examining institutions, whereas they abound in Sartre's *Critique of Dialectical Reason* ([1960] 1982) I will take up in subsection 4.2.

4 Institutional stability, gradual change, and radical change

4.1 Recognizing achieved institutionalization

To examine institutionalization one must recognize it. Lynne G. Zucker (1977 considers the institutionalization of acts accompanied by accounts comprised of actors' explanations of why they engage in these acts (Zucker 1977: 728, 730):

> When acts have ready-made accounts. . ., they are institutionalized; that is both objective and exterior. . . . [T]hese accounts . . . function as objective rules because their social origin is ignored. . . . Acts high on institutionalization will be resistant to . . . change . . . because they are seen as external facts . . . imposed on the setting and, at the same time, defining it

Tolbert and Zucker ([1995] 2005: 184–185) elaborate stages of institutionalization. At pre-institutionalization with high risks of the structural failure of the evolving institution, homogeneous adopters imitate solutions taken from elsewhere without much lay theorization on what they are doing. This will possibly lead to habitualization with routines of problem-solving. At semi-institutionalization still with moderate risks of structural failure, heterogeneous adopters carry out remarkable lay theorization to support their adaptation and their invention of institutional solutions, which may become objectified into solidly shared meanings. Finally, at full institutionalization with few risks of structural failure, lay theorization abates as procedures become routinized, institutional solutions taken for granted and sedimented, and solid shared norms stabilize themselves.

4.2 Sartre's rarely acknowledged account of institutionalization

In his later major work Sartre ([1960] 1982) contemplates negations in our existence, focusing upon the facticity accomplished for us 3 third parties, who constitute what he calls our serial alterity (see also Palonen 1992: 151–153). Sartre (1982: 256–269) illustrates seriality with a queue at a bus stop, where people arrive in no particular order, and have no concern about who the others are.

Starting with seriality, in which Sartre sees alienation ruling, he (1982: 343–663) proceeds to examine the fused group, the statutory group, the organization, and the institution. He writes (1982: 345) that already "a gathering . . . through its serial unity . . . furnishes the elementary conditions that its members should constitute a group." Sartre (1982: 374, 387) takes the example of individuals who find themselves together when a gathering has turned into a fight with an opponent (analogously Goffman 1963b). Sartre sees it as possible that from the elemental and haphazard group, a fused group possibly evolves, provided that seriality vanishes and an elementary community arises. Should the fused group persist, Sartre suggests that it may stabilize towards the more solid formation of a statutory group with more permanence and with more division of tasks between its members (Sartre 1982: 412–413, 417–428).

Sartre sees the statutory group as taking shape at the constitution of a morally binding common purpose. By organization, Sartre 1982: 445, 447, 455) means "the action on itself of the . . . pledged . . . statutory group" regarding its common *praxis* made up of the members' reciprocal freedom in the fight for their common purpose." Sartre sees the institution to arise insofar as the organization falls into "pledged passivity" with "degraded forms of community" (Sartre 1982: 591). These he sees to "reproduce alterity in itself and freeze it", and also (1982: 600) to effect "the re-emergence of seriality". Sartre (1982: 606) writes:

> The institutional moment . . . in the group . . . corresponds to . . . the systematic self-domestication of man by man. . . . In so far as the ossified *praxis* which is the institution is due to our own impotence, it constitutes for each and for all a precise index of *reification*. . . . [T]he moment. . . in which the institution emerges is . . . that in which everyone aims to expel freedom from himself in order to realise the endangered unity of the declining group as a thing.

4.3 Coercive-regulative, mimetic-cultural-cognitive, and normative institutionalization

Paul DiMaggio and William W. Powell's 1983 text on institutionalization by means of coercive, mimetic, and normative isomorphism has been adapted by W. Richard Scott (2008a), who has divided institutionalization into a regulative, cultural-cognitive, and normative pillar (see also Scott 2008b; Lawrence and Suddaby 2006; Perkmann and Spicer 2008). In important respects coercive-regulative institutionalization comprises an exogenous force imposed, for instance, by foreign powers upon weaker countries, by governments of countries towards domestic actors, or by business competitors. However, as Scott (2008a) stresses, we must examine institutionalization in the regulative pillar also in such modes as deregulation, reregulation, self-regulation, networking, governance without government, and policy-making by means of persuasion rather than coercion (Sahlin and Wedlin 2008; Bevir and Rhodes 2010).

Scott's (2008a) cultural-cognitive pillar, one of shared symbolic representations, does not differ fundamentally from DiMaggio and Powell's (1983) mimetic institutionalization. The latter authors derive mimetic institutionalization from uncertainty, which spurs actors to adapt domestic or foreign solutions whose emulation promises to offer the emulator additional legitimation. The examination of cultural-cognitive-mimetic institutionalization has extensions, for instance, in inquiry on institutional fashions (Perkmann and Spicer 2008), on movements from institutional path dependence to path creation and opportunity creation (Lounsbury and Crumley 2007; Schneiberg and Lounsbury 2008; Garud et al. 2010; Delbridge and Edwards 2010), and on intellectual movements (Frickel and Gross 2005).

Besides the *whats* of mimetic institutionalization, its *hows* are also important (Massey 2009). One may learn more about these hows, for example, by introducing counterfactuals, meaning envisaged occurrences that only narrowly fail to come about. Using counterfactuals promises to reveal the entire spectrum of the possibilities that used to prevail and not only that possibility which actually took place (Edwards and Jones 2008; Booth et al. 2009; Tarasti 2009: 61–65). It is also important to acknowledge the possible negative consequences of mimetic institutionalization, including the possible institutionalization of lacking performance and chronic failure (Tolbert and Zucker 1983; Rao et al. 2001; Rubtsova et al. 2010).

DiMaggio and Powell (1983) derive the normative mode of institutionalization first and foremost from professionalism, whereas Scott (2008a) expands his normative pillar to include wider social normativity, a notion aptly captured in March and Olsen's (2009) notion of the "logic of appropriateness". Analogously, Schneiberg and Clemens (2006: 213) characterize institutionalized professional rules as follows:

[The] violation of such normative rules [is] . . . met with reactions that differ from those [towards] . . . deviance from regulatory or coercive regimes; issues of taboo, pollution, and sin . . . overpower elements of damage, debt, and disorder.

There are also derivative analytic challenges. These include, for instance, examining deinstitutionalization (Oliver 1992); the limits of mimetic or cultural-cognitive tendencies towards institutional isomorphism (Ramanath 2010); processes which enhance institutional hetero- rather than isomorphism (Beckert 2010); and institutional change which is lacking isomorphic characteristics (Delbridge and Edwards 2010).

4.4 Gradual institutional change

Seeking *endogenous* rather than *exogenous* reasons for gradual institutional change, Streeck (2010) focuses upon institutional members who break institutional rules in creative ways and get away with it. According to Streeck, this may, if successfully repeated often enough, enhance incompleteness in the reproduction of institutional practices, and may ultimately erode institutions until they either fundamentally reform themselves or collapse.

Mahoney and Thelen (2009) introduce five types of slow institutional change. These comprise the complete *exhaustion* of rules; the complete *displacement* of rules with new rules; the *layering* of new rules on top of old rules that stay; the *drift* of effects of rules that stay as the circumstances of their application change; and the *conversion* of the interpretation of rules that also stay. These authors also connect particular actor types and particular types of agency to the last four types of change: "insurrectionaries" to displacement; "subversives" to layering; "symbionts" allying with those wanting to restrain institutional change to drift; and "opportunists" to conversion.

4.5 Radical institutional change

Possibly the easiest type of abrupt institutional change to examine comprises change imposed by exogenous reasons, with no background accumulation of endogenous reasons whatsoever and little or no true institutional agency within the changing institution. However, Sahlin and Wedlin (2008: 227–230) remind us that exogenous institutional change is not necessarily triggered by external shocks, but may ensue from far from deterministic chain reactions. In this respect their view has characteristics which are analogous with Streeck's (2009) and Mahoney and Thelen's (2010) view.

Research on institutions suggests that we should not necessarily expect much formal ends-means rationality in many institutional changes; to do so possibly risks the *ex post facto* rationalization of what actually happened (Mills 1940: 907–908). The classic article on institutions by John W. Meyer and Brian Rowan (1977: 343–344; see also Lounsbury 2008: 352–353) stresses the prevalence of "rationalized myths" of institutionalization. Accordingly, while institutions change, this may not substitute something rational, modern or efficient for previous irrationality, but only replace a rationalized myth with a more streamlined successor. In March and Olsen's (2009) words, a new institutionalist "logic of appropriateness" may smoothly replace the previous comparable logic.

Critical research on institutions has examined the transcendence of established orders by means of collective action (Schneiberg and Lounsbury 2008). However, the systematic examination of resistance (Tarasti 2009) and contention and contentious agency in institutional contexts (Tilly 2003) appears to be a long way off. Insofar as radical institutional change is contemplated, the perspective is a macro rather than meso or micro one, although one may be able to detect at least some of the possible meso and micro roots of institutional macro change (see Klein and Lee 2019). The *problématique* which Karl Marx once characterized is still acute and without ultimate theoretical resolution. As translations age – well illustrated by the start of the common English translation as "Men make their own history" as is women would not do the same – and no "official" translations can exist, I make my own:

> Die Menschen machen ihre eigene Geschichte, aber sie machen sie nicht unter freien Stücken, nicht unter selbstgewählten, sonder unter unmittelbar vorgefundenen, gegebenen und überlieferten Umständen. (Marx [1852] 1972: 115)

> People make their own history, but they do not make it out of their own free will, not by their own choice, but in circumstances that are immediately found, given and handed down. (Google Translate translation, my refinement).

5 Doing what is institutionally appropriate instead of what brings results

Berger and Luckmann's ([1966] 1991: 135) aphorism captures an expectation widely shared in research on institutions: "One does certain things not because they *work*, but because they are *right*." Schütz (1953: 26) characterizes the issue as a paradox of rationality: in our everyday *Lebenswelt*, "the more standardized the pattern [that defines rationality]. . ., the less the underlying elements become analyzable for common-sense thought in terms of rational insight" (see also Garfinkel [1967] 2010: 283). Moreover, good institutional reasons may prevail to deliver substandard accounts of what is happening (Garfinkel 2010: 186–207), whereas formally perfect accounts may be institutionally inappropriate (Heath and Luff 2000: 31–60). Accordingly, at least since the work of Meyer and Rowan (1977; see also Deephouse and Suchman 2008), research on institutions closely scrutinizes compromises in performance made for the sake of legitimacy, also meaning contradictions between what March and Olsen (2009) call the rationalist logic of consequences and the institutional logic of appropriateness.

We find evidence of performance compromises in many institutional elements, such as institutional foundational myths, rationalized myths, institutional rites and rituals, and institutional distinctions between the sacred and the profane and the vulgar and the distinguished. What Zerubavel (1996) calls lumping and splitting, what research on institutions examines as identity work and boundary work, and "naming, blaming and shaming" also fall into comparable categories.

6 Conclusions

According to the results of this article, symbolic interactionist micro-foundations of research on institutions are implicit rather than explicit, whereas ethnomethodology joins together more micro-foundational threads. The ethnomethodologist Garfinkel's notion of indexicality derives from the pragmatist philosopher and semiotician C.S. Peirce, and narrative research on institutions has regarded well the binary semiotics of A.J. Greimas (Czarniawska, 1998, 2008). There is not much say about inspiration that originates from semiotics in established research on institutional micro-foundations despite promising beginnings and interesting theoretical proposals.

There is little direct evidence on the influence of existential approaches within research on institutional micro-foundations. However, important orientations in the study of the micro-foundations share some of with the existential approaches, albeit indirectly rather than directly. Students of micro-foundations do not tend to refer to the work of Edmund Husserl, although they amply refer to classical social scientists who undoubtedly had been influenced by Husserl, other phenomenologists, and representatives of nearby currents of thought. Max Weber has not gone unrecognized in work on micro-foundations, either, nor has the work of other authors influenced by Weber such as Alfred Schütz and Karl

Mannheim. However, researchers on institutions have relied upon the hybrid work of Berger and Luckmann ([1966] 1991) or the ethnomethodological work of Harold Garfinkel rather than relevant original classical authors (Adler 2010).

There is something inherently conservative in institutions including their micro-foundations. Jean-Paul Sartre understood this well while writing on institutionalization as "self-domestication of man by man" (Sartre [1960] 1982: 606; for a rare recent article drawing upon Sartre, see Ransom and Gallagher 2020). One can sense subtle intellectual sarcasm or subtle irony in Sartre's formulation, the likes of which have not been alien to others who have looked at institutions, either. From Harold Garfinkel's notion of "cultural dope" (Garfinkel's [1967] 2010: 68) there is little distance to institutional actors who become "institutional dopes" (Powell and Colyvas 2008). Moreover, from Garfinkel's (1964: 24) biting characterization of our little institutional sins there is little distance to many themes later amply examined in research on institutions.

One easily detects subtle sarcasm and irony in present-day research on institutions. Remember Pamela S. Tolbert and Lynne G. Zucker's (1983) confirmed hypothesis that even the failure of institutions may become institutionalized. We can also take up the central notion "rationalized myth" in John W. Meyer and Brian Rowan's seminal article on institutions (Meyer and Rowan 1977). While we may make fun of ancient people's rain dances built upon myths that appeasing ancestral spirits relieves drought, it may be harder for us to acknowledge such rationalized myths of our own as believing that acting in the name of what is seen as bringing good, such as "efficiency", "productivity", and "performance" will do this independently of what empirical evidence will say. Remember also that Schneiberg and Clemens (2006: 213) characterize deviance from professional rules in analogous terms as taboo, pollution, and sin.

References

Adler, Paul A. (ed.). 2010. *The Oxford handbook of sociology and organization studies: Classical foundations*. Oxford: Oxford University Press.

Ahonen, Pertti. 2020. The semiotic theory of A.J. Greimas in mainstream organization theory and organization research. In *14th World Congress of Semiotics, Buenos Aires, 9–13 September 2019, Tomo I*, 71–80. Buenos Aires: International Association for Semiotic Studies.

Alaimo, Christina & Jannis Kallinikos. 2020. Managing by data: Algorithmic categories and organizing. *Organization Studies* 42(9). 1385–1407

Alasuutari, Pertti. 2010. The nominalist turn in theorizing power. *European Journal of Cultural Studies* 13(4). 403–417.

Althusser, Louis. 1971 [1969]. Ideology and ideological state apparatuses. In Louis Althusser, *Lenin and philosophy and other essays*, 170–173. New York: Monthly Review Press.
Archer, Margaret. 2007. The trajectory of the morphogenetic approach. *Sociologia* 54: 35–47.
Austin, John A. 1975. *How to do things with words*. Oxford: Clarendon.
Barley, Stephen R. 1983. Semiotics and the study of occupational and organizational cultures. *Administrative Science Quarterly* 28(3). 393–413.
Barley, Stephen R. 2008. Coalface institutionalism. In Royston Greenwood, Christine Oliver, Robert Suddaby & Kerstin Sahlin (eds.), *The SAGE handbook of organizational institutionalism*, 490–515. London: Sage.
Becher, Tony & Paul R. Trowler. 2001. *Academic tribes and territories*. 2. ed. Buckingham: The Society for Research into Higher Education.
Beckert, Jens. 2010. Institutional isomorphism revisited: Convergence and divergence in institutional change. *Sociological Theory* 28(2). 150–166.
Berger, Peter & Thomas Luckmann. 1991 [1966]. *The social construction of reality: A treatise in the sociology of knowledge*. London: Penguin.
Bevir, Mark & R.A.W. Rhodes. 2010. *The state as cultural practice*. Oxford: Oxford University Press.
Billig, Michael. 1989. *Arguing and thinking: A rhetorical approach to social psychology*. Cambridge: Cambridge University Press.
Blumer, Herbert. 1969. *Symbolic interactionism: Perspective and method*. Englewood Cliffs, NJ: Prentice-Hall.
Bohnsack, Ralf. 2008. The interpretation of pictures and the documentary method. *Forum: Qualitative Social Research* 9(3). 2–20.
Booth, Charles, Michael Rowlinson, Peter Clark, Agnes Delahaye & Stephen Procter. 2009. Scenarios and counterfactuals as modal narratives. *Futures* 41(2). 87–95.
Bourdieu, Pierre. 1985. The social space and the genesis of groups. *Theory & Society* 14(6). 723–744.
Butler, Judith. 1997. *Excitable speech: Politics of the performative*. London: Routledge.
Carver, Terrel. 2020. Interpretive methods. In Dirk Berg-Schlosser, Bertrand Badie & Leonardo Morlino (eds.), *The SAGE handbook of political science*, 406–422. London: Sage.
Chandler, David & Hokuy Hwang. 2015. Learning from learning theory: A model of organizational adoption strategies at the microfoundations of institutional theory. *Journal of Management* 41(1). 1446–1476.
Charmaz, Kathy. 2006. The power of names. *Journal of Contemporary Ethnography* 35(4). 396–399.
Clegg, Stewart. 2010. The state, power, and agency: Missing in action in institutional theory? *Journal of Management Inquiry* 19(1). 4–13.
Connolly, William E. 1991. *Identity/difference: Democratic negotiations of political paradox*. Ithaca, NY: Cornell University Press.
Cooren, François. 2012. Communication theory at the center: Ventriloquism and the communicative constitution of reality. *Journal of Communication* 62(1). 1–20.
Creed, W.E Douglas, Maureen A. Scully & John R. Austin. 2002. Clothes make the person? The tailoring of legitimating accounts and the social construction of identity. *Organization Science* 13(5). 475–496.
Czarniawska, Barbara. 1998. *A narrative approach to organization studies*. Thousand Oaks, CA: Sage.
Czarniawska, Barbara. 2008. How to misuse institutions and get away with it: Some reflections on institutional theory(ies). In Royston Greenwood, Christine Oliver, Robert Suddaby &

Kerstin Sahlin (eds.), *The SAGE handbook of organizational institutionalism*, 769–782. London: Sage.
Deephouse, David L. & Mark C. Suchman. 2008. Legitimacy in organizational institutionalism. In Royston Greenwood, Christine Oliver, Robert Suddaby & Kerstin Sahlin (eds.), *The SAGE handbook of organizational institutionalism*, 49–77. London: Sage.
Delbridge, Rick & Tim Edwards. 2008. Challenging conventions: Roles and processes during non-isomorphic institutional change. *Human Relations* 6(3). 299–325.
Denzin, Norman K. 1987. On semiotics and symbolic interactionism. *Symbolic Interaction* 10(1): 1–19.
Dépelteau, François. 2008. Relational thinking: A critique of co-deterministic theories of structure and agency. *Sociological Theory* 26(1): 51–73.
Derrida, Jacques. 1988 [1972]. Signature, event, context. In G. Graff (ed.), *Limited, Inc.*, 1–23. Chicago: Northwestern University Press.
DiMaggio, Paul J. & William W. Powell. 1983. The iron cage revisited: Institutional isomorphism and collective rationality in organizational fields. *American Sociological Review* 48(2). 147–160.
Douglas, Mary. 1966. *Purity and danger: An analysis of conceptions of pollution and taboo*. London: Routledge.
Driver, Michaela. 2009. Struggling with lack: A Lacanian perspective on organizational identity. *Organization Studies* 30(1). 55–72.
Edwards, Tim & O. Jones. 2008. Failed institution building: Understanding the interplay between agency, social skill and context. *Scandinavian Journal of Management* 24(1). 44–54.
Emirbayer, Mustafa and Ann Mische. 1998. What Is agency? *American Journal of Sociology* 103(4). 962–1023.
Feldman, Martha S. 2003. Performative perspective on stability and change in organizational routines. *Industrial and Corporate Change* 12(4). 727–752.
Fleetwood, Steve. 2008. Institutions and social structures. *Journal for the Theory of Social Behaviour* 38(3). 241–265.
Frickel, Scott & Neil Gross. 2005. A general theory of scientific/intellectual movements. *American Sociological Review* 70(2). 204–232.
Fuller, Steven. 1991. Disciplinary boundaries and the rhetoric of the social sciences. *Poetics Today* 12(2). 301–325.
Fuller, Sylvia. 2003. Creating and contesting boundaries: Exploring the dynamics of conflict and classification. *Sociological Forum* 18(1). 3–30.
Garfinkel, Harold. 1964. Studies in the routine grounds of everyday activities. *Social Problems* 11(3). 225–250. An edited and more concise version has been published in Garfinkel 2010 [1967]: 35–75.
Garfinkel, H. 2010 [1967]. *Studies in ethnomethodology*. Cambridge: Polity Press.
Garud, Raghu, Arun Kumaraswamy & Peter Karnøe. 2010. Path dependence or path creation? *Journal of Management Studies* 47(4): 760–774.
Giddens, Anthony. 1976. *New rules of sociological method: A positive critique of interpretative sociologies*. London: Hutchinson.
Gieryn, Thomas F. 1983. Boundary-work and the demarcation of science from non-science: Strains and interests in professional ideologies of scientists. *American Sociological Review* 48(6). 781–795.
Glynn, Mary Ann & Rikki Abzug. 2002. Institutionalizing identity: Symbolic isomorphism and organizational names. *Academy of Management Journal* 45(1). 267–280.

Goffman, Erving. 1963a. *Stigma: Notes on the management of spoiled identity.* New York: Simon & Schuster.

Goffman, Erving. 1963b. *Behavior in public places: Notes on the social organization of gatherings.* New York: Free Press.

Gronow, Antti. 2008. Not rules or choice alone: A pragmatist critique of institution theories in economics and sociology. *Journal of Institutional Economics* 4(3). 351–373.

Guenther, Katja M. 2009. The politics of names: Rethinking the methodological and ethical significance of naming people, organizations, and places. *Qualitative Research* 9(4). 411–421.

Hall, Peter A. & Rosemary C. R. Taylor. 1996. Political science and the three institutionalisms. *Political Studies* 44(5). 936–957.

Hall, Peter M. 1972. A symbolic interactionist analysis of politics. *Sociological Inquiry* 42(3–4). 35–75.

Heath, Christian & Paul Luff. 2000. *Technology in action.* Cambridge: Cambridge University Press.

Heiskala, Risto. 2007. Economy and society: From Parsons through Habermas to semiotic institutionalism. *Social Science Information* 45(2). 243–272.

Hwang, Hokyu & Jeannette Colyvas. 2019. What do we talk about when we talk about microfoundations? Conceptualizations of actor and multi-level accounts of the micro in institutional processes. In Patrick Haack, Jost Sieweke & Lauri Wessel (eds.), *Microfoundations of Institutions (Research in the Sociology of Organizations, Vol. 65B)*, 337–352. London: Emerald.

Joyce, Kelly & Melanie Jeske. 2020. Using autoimmune strategically: Diagnostic lumping, splitting, and the experience of illness. *Social Science Medicine* (e-preprint). https://pubmed.ncbi.nlm.nih.gov/31927476/ (accessed 10 June 2020).

Kaplan, Sarah. 2008. Framing contests: Strategy making under uncertainty. *Organization Science* 19(5). 729–752.

Kim, Kwang-ki & Tim Berard. 2009. Typification in society and social science: The continuing relevance of Schütz's social phenomenology. *Human Studies* 32(3). 263–289.

Klein, Steven & Cheol-Sung Lee. 2019. Towards a dynamic theory of civil society: The politics of forward and backward infiltration. *Sociological Theory* 37(1). 62–88.

Kotarba, Joseph A. & John M. Johnson (eds.). 2002. *Postmodern existential sociology.* Walnut Creek, CA: Altamira Press.

Laclau, Ernesto. 2005. *On populist reason.* London: Verso.

Lamont, Michèle & Virág Molnar. 2002. The study of boundaries in the social sciences. *Annual Review of Sociology* 28. 167–195.

Lampland, Martha. 2010. False numbers as formalizing practices. *Social Studies of Science* 40(3). 377–404.

Landowski, Eric. 2019. Sémiotique et organisations: Présentation. *Actes Sémiotiques* 122. https://www.unilim.fr/actes-semiotiques/6334&file=1/ (accessed 15 March 2019).

Lawrence, Thomas B. & Roy Suddaby. 2006. Institutions and institutional work. In Stuart R. Clegg, Cynthia Hardy, Thomas B. Lawrence & Walter R. Nord (eds.), *The SAGE handbook of organization studies*, 215–254. Thousand Oaks, CA: Sage.

Lawrence, Thomas B., Roy Suddaby & Bernard Leca. 2011. Institutional work: Refocusing institutional studies of organization. *Journal of Management Inquiry* 20(1). 52–58.

Learmonth, Mark. 2009. Rhetoric and evidence: The case of evidence-based management. In David Buchanan & Alan Bryman (eds.), *Organizational Research Methods*, 92–107. London: Sage.

Lounsbury, Michael. 2008. Institutional rationality and practice variation: New directions in the institutional analysis of practice. *Accounting, Organizations and Society* 33(4–5). 349–361.
Lounsbury, Michael & Ellen T. Crumley. 2007. New practice creation: An institutional perspective. *Organization Studies* 28(7). 993–1012.
Lowndes, Vivien & Mark Roberts (2013). *Why institutions matter: The new institutionalism in political science*. Houndmills: Palgrave Macmillan.
Mahoney, James & Kathleen Thelen. 2009. A theory of gradual institutional change. In James Mahoney & Kathleen Thelen (eds.), *Explaining institutional change: Ambiguity, agency, and power*, 1–37. Cambridge: Cambridge University Press.
Maier, Florentine & Ruth Simsa. 2020. How actors move from primary agency to institutional agency: A conceptual framework and empirical application. *Organization* 28(4). 555–576.
Mannheim, Karl. 1952. On the interpretation of *Weltanschauung*. In Karl Mannheim, *Essays on the sociology of knowledge*, 33–83. London: Routledge.
Manning Peter K. 1973. Existential sociology. *Sociological Quarterly* 14(2). 200–225.
March, James G. & Johan P. Olsen. 2009. The logic of appropriateness. In Robert E. Goodin (ed.), *The Oxford handbook of political science*, 478–497. Oxford: Oxford University Press.
Marx, Karl. 1972 [1852]. Der achtzehnte Brumaire des Louis Bonaparte. In Karl Marx & Friedrich Engels, *Karl Marx/Friedrich Engels Werke*, Band 8, 115–123. Berlin: Dietz Verlag.
Massey, Andrew. 2009. Policy mimesis in the context of global governance. *Policy Studies* 30(3): 383–395.
Mead, George Herbert. H. 1992 [1934]. *Mind, self & society*. Chicago: University of Chicago Press.
Meyer, John W. 2009. Reflections: Institutional theory and world society. In George Kruecken & Gili S. Drori (eds.), *World society: The writings of John W. Meyer*, 36–63. Oxford: Oxford University Press.
Meyer, John W. & Brian Rowan. 1977. Institutional organizations: Formal structure as myth and ceremony. *American Journal of Sociology* 83(2). 340–363.
Meyer, Renate E. & Markus A. Höllerer. 2010. Meaning structures in a contested issue field: A topographic map of shareholder value in Austria. *Academy of Management Journal* 53(6). 1241–1262.
Mills, C. Wright. 1940. Situated actions and vocabularies of motive. *American Sociological Review* 5(6). 904–913.
Mohr, John W. 2000. Introduction: Structures, institutions, and cultural analysis. *Poetics* 27(2–3). 57–68.
Mohr, John W. & Harrison C. White. 2008. How to model an institution. *Theory and Society* 37(5). 485–512.
Negro, Giacomo, Özgecan Koçak & Greta Hsu. 2010. Research on categories in the sociology of organizations. *Research in the Sociology of Organizations* 31. 3–35.
Nietzsche, Friedrich. 1974 [1882/1887]. *The Gay Science*. New York: Vintage.
Oliver, Christine. 1992. The antecedents of deinstitutionalization. *Organization Studies* 13(4). 563–588.
Palonen, Kari. 1992. *Politik als Vereitelung: Die Politikkonzeption in Jean-Paul Sartre's "Critique de la raison dialéctique"*. Münster: Westfälische Dampfboot.
Palonen, Kari. 2004. Die *Entzauberung der Begriffe. Das Umschreiben der politischen Begriffe bei Quentin Skinner und Reinhart Koselleck*. Münster: Lit Verlag.
Panofsky, Erwin. 1955. *Meaning in the Visual Arts*. Harmondsworth: Penguin Books.

Peirce, Charles Sanders. 1929. Guessing. *Hound & Horn* 2(3). 267–285. The article has been also published in Pierce 1958, Vol. 7: 36–48.
Peirce, Charles Sanders. 1931–1935. *Collected Papers of Charles Sanders Peirce*. Vols. 1–6, 1931–1935. Cambridge, MA: Harvard University Press.
Peirce, Charles Sanders. 1958. *Collected Papers of Charles Sanders Peirce*, Vols. 7–8, 1958. Cambridge, MA: Harvard University Press.
Perkmann, Markus & André Spicer. 2008. How are management fashions institutionalized? The Role of institutional work. *Human Relations* 61(6). 811–844.
Peters, B. Guy. 2019. Institutional theory in political science: The new institutionalism. 4. ed. Cheltenham: Edward Elgar.
Porter, Theodore M. 1991. Statistics and the politics of objectivity. *Revue de Synthèse* 114. 87–101.
Powell, William W. & Jeannette A. Colyvas. 2008. Microfoundations of institutional theory. In Royston Greenwood, Christine Oliver, Robert Suddaby & Kerstin Sahlin (eds.), *The SAGE handbook of organizational institutionalism*, 279–298. London: Sage.
Powell, William W. & Claus Rerup. 2017. Opening the black box: The microfoundations of institutions. In Royston Greenwood, Christine Oliver, Thomas B. Lawrence & Renate E. Meyer (eds.), *The SAGE handbook of organizational institutionalism*, 311–335. London: Sage.
Power, Michael. 2009. The risk management of nothing. *Accounting, Organizations and Society* 34(6). 849–855.
Ramanath, Ramya. 2009. Limits to institutional isomorphism: Examining internal processes in NGO – government interactions. *Nonprofit and Voluntary Sector Quarterly* 38(1). 51–76.
Ransom, Tailer & Shaun Gallagher. 2020. Institutions and other things: Critical hermeneutics, postphenomenology and material engagement theory. AI & SOCIETY (e-preprint). https://doi.org/10.1007/s00146-020-00987-z (retrieved 11 June 2020).
Rao, Hayagreeva & Simona Giorgi. 2006. Code breaking: How entrepreneurs exploit cultural logics to generate institutional change. *Research in Organizational Behavior* 27. 269–304.
Rao, Hayagreeva, Henrich R. Greve & Gerald F. Davis. 2001. Fool's gold: Social proof in the initiation and abandonment of coverage by Wall Street analysts. *Administrative Science Quarterly* 46(3). 502–526.
Reichertz, Jo. 2007. Abduction: The logic of discovery in grounded theory. In Antony Bryant & Kathy Charmaz (eds.), *The SAGE handbook of grounded theory*, 214–228. London: Sage.
Rubtsova, Anna, Rich DeJordy, Mary Ann Glynn & Mayer Zald. 2010. The social construction of causality: The effects of institutional myths on financial regulation. *Research in the Sociology of Organizations* 30. 201–244.
Sahlin, Kerstin & Linda Wedlin. 2008. Circulating ideas: Imitation, translation and editing. In Royston Greenwood, Christine Oliver, Robert Suddaby & Kerstin Sahlin (eds.), *The SAGE handbook of organizational institutionalism*, 218–242. London: Sage.
Samra-Fredericks, Dalvir & Francesca Bargiela-Chiappini. 2008. Introduction to the symposium on the foundations of organizing: The contribution from Garfinkel, Goffman and Sacks. *Organization Studies* 29(5). 653–675.
Sartre, Jean-Paul. 2005 [1943]. *Being and Nothingness*. London: Routledge
Sartre, Jean-Paul. 1982 [1960]. *Critique of Dialectical Reason*. I. Thetford: Verso.
Schneiberg, Marc & Elisabeth S. Clemens. 2006. The typical tools for the job: Research strategies in institutional analysis. *Sociological Theory* 24(3). 195–227.

Schneiberg, Marc & Michael Lounsbury. 2008. Social movements and institutional analysis. In Royston Greenwood, Christine Oliver, Robert Suddaby & Kerstin Sahlin (eds.), *The SAGE handbook of organizational institutionalism*, 648–670. London: Sage.

Schütz, Alfred. 1953. Common-sense and scientific interpretation of human action. *Philosophy and Phenomenological Research* 14(1). 1–38.

Schütz, Alfred. 1954. Concept and theory formation in the social sciences. *The Journal of Philosophy* 51(9). 257–273.

Scott, Marvin B. & Stanford M. Lyman. 1968. Accounts. *American Sociological Review* 33(1). 46–62.

Scott, W. Richard. 2008a. *Institutions and organizations: Ideas and interests*, 3rd ed. Thousand Oaks, CA: Sage.

Scott, W. Richard. 2008b. Approaching adulthood: The maturing of institutional theory. *Theory and Society* 37. 427–442.

Shepherd, Hana. 2010. Classification, cognition and context: The case of the World Bank. *Poetics* 38(2). 133–149.

Skinner, Quentin. 1988. A reply to my critics. In James Tully (ed.), *Meaning and context: Quentin Skinner and his critics*, 231–288. Cambridge: Polity Press.

Skinner, Quentin. 2003. *Paradiastole*: Rescribing vices as virtues. In Sylvia Adamson, Gavin Alexander & Katrin Ettenhuber (eds.), *Renaissance Figures of Speech*, 149–166. Cambridge: Cambridge University Press.

Smith, Keri E.I. 2008. Hybrid identities: Theoretical examinations. In Keri E.I. Smith & Patricia Leavy (eds.), *Hybrid identities: Theoretical and empirical examinations*, 3–11. Leiden: Brill.

Sonesson, Göran. 2002. The varieties of interpretation: A view from semiotics. *Galáxia* 4. 67–99.

Strauss, Anselm. 1965. Introduction. In Anselm Strauss (ed.), *George Herbert Mead on social psychology*, vi–xxv. Chicago: University of Chicago Press.

Streeck, Wolfgang. 2010. Institutions in history: Bringing capitalism back in. In Glenn Morgan, John L. Campbell, Colin Crouch, Ove Kaj Pedersen & Richard Whitley (eds.), *The Oxford handbook of comparative institutional analysis*, 659–686. Oxford: Oxford University Press.

Suddaby, Roy. 2010. Challenges for institutional theory. *Journal of Management Inquiry* 19(1), 14–20.

Tarasti, Eero. 2009. Semiotics of resistance: Being, memory, history – the counter-currents of signs. *Semiotica* 173(1/4): 41–71. Also published in Tarasti, Eero. 2015. *Sein und Schein: Explorations in existential semiotics*, 152–191. Berlin: Mouton de Gruyter.

Thérèse, Sandrine & Brian Martin. 2010. Shame, scientist! Degradation rituals in science. *Prometheus* 28(2). 97–110.

Tilly, Charles. 2003. Contention over space and time. *Mobilization* 8(2). 221–225.

Tolbert, Pamela S. & Lynne G. Zucker. 1983. Institutional sources of change in the formal structure of organizations: The diffusion of civil service reform, 1880–1935. *Administrative Science Quarterly* 28(1). 22–39.

Tolbert, P.S. & L.G. Zucker. 2005 [1995]. The institutionalization of institutional theory. In Stewart Clegg & Cynthia Hardy (eds.), *Studying Organization*, 169–184. London: Sage.

Weber, Max. 1978 [1922]. *Economy and society: An outline of interpretive sociology*. Berkeley: University of California Press.

Wiley, Norbert. 1994. *The semiotic self*. Cambridge: Wiley.

Willmott, Hugh. 2011. "Institutional work" for what? Problems and prospects of institutional theory. *Journal of Management Inquiry* 20(1). 6 –72.

Zerubavel, Eviatar. 1995. The rigid, the fuzzy, and the flexible: Notes on the mental sculpting of academic identity. *Social Research* 62(4). 1093–1106.

Zerubavel, Eviatar. 1996. Lumping and splitting: Notes on social classification. *Sociological Forum* 11(3). 421–433.

Zietsma, Charlene & Thomas B. Lawrence. 2010. Institutional work in the transformation of an organizational field: The interplay of boundary work and practice work. *Administrative Science Quarterly* 55(2). 189–221.

Zucker, Lynne G. 1977. The role of institutionalization in cultural persistence. *American Sociological Review* 42(5). 726–743.

Dario Martinelli
"Disturbing quiet people" – on the hyper-bureaucratization and corporatization of universities

Abstract: This study intends to elaborate on one important manifestation of that institutional crisis that has progressively reduced the humanities to an academically-marginal, socially-not-too-relevant and poorly-funded field: the increasing phenomenon of hyper-bureaucratization and corporatization of universities. For several years already, the academic community has been monitored and measured by an increasing number of procedures that were previously non-existent and that now tend to occupy a large chunk of the total working time. Hyper-bureaucratization and corporatization have certainly slowed down *every single* academic activity, but perhaps humanists (thus semioticians too) are in a particularly uncomfortable condition, as most of these managerial tasks are in fact conceived for types of measurements that are difficult or impossible to apply to humanities.

An additional, and very important, problem is that this process is aimed at transforming them into business enterprises where academic merit is equated with the amount of funds raised, where the professors look more and more like managers and students like customers. No wonder that the least profitable of the academic businesses, humanities, is the one that suffers the most from this situation, experiencing the most severe budget cuts and the most pressure for redefinition of their research aims and education programs:

The phenomenon is here analyzed as symptomatic of five of the fourteen "re-civilizing traits and processes" that Eero Tarasti (2015) identifies in his theories, as a result of the author's personal reflections, within his theoretical platform of the Numanities (Martinelli 2015) and in the light of the theory of Appropriate Technologies.

Keywords: Humanities, Numanities, Hyper-bureaucratization, Corporatization, Appropriate Technologies

1 Introduction

Moving from Eero Tarasti's lengthy reflections on the so-called "semiocrisis" appeared in 2015 (133–181, in particular), and anticipated in the likes of Tarasti 2005, this study intends to elaborate on one important manifestation of the crisis: the increasing phenomenon of hyper-bureaucratization and corporatization of universities. A topic dear to both Tarasti and myself (and not "dear" in a positive sense, as one may guess), the phenomenon is here analyzed as symptomatic of five of the fourteen "re-civilizing traits and processes" that Tarasti identifies in his analysis (2015: 154–156).

In the last couple of decades or so, researchers and teachers have become concerned and frustrated with the massive increase in administrative staff and tasks within the academic world, which mostly relied on management models from business corporations, and which has led to the phenomenon considered in this study.

> Instead of government by academics there is rule by hierarchy, a good deal of Byzantine bureaucracy, junior professors who are little but dogsbodies, and vice chancellors who behave as though they are running General Motors. Senior professors are now senior managers, and the air is thick with talk of auditing and accountancy. Books – those troglodytic, drearily pre-technological phenomena – are increasingly frowned upon. [. . .] Philistine administrators plaster the campus with mindless logos and issue their edicts in barbarous, semiliterate prose. (Eagleton 2015)

Academic activity is nowadays monitored and measured by a multitude of rankings, applications, codes, reviews, evaluations that were previously non-existent and by now tend to occupy a good third, if not more, of the total working time of the average academic. Hyper-bureaucratization and corporatization have certainly slowed down *every single* academic activity, but perhaps humanists (and therefore semioticians too) are in a particularly uncomfortable condition, as most of these managerial tasks are in fact conceived for types of measurements that are difficult to apply to humanities (when not completely inapplicable).

Most of all, and predictably, the main problem is that all this "managerialization" of universities is aimed at transforming them into business enterprises where "academic merit is equated with how much money you can raise", where "professors are transformed into managers", and "students are converted into consumers" (Eagleton 2015). No wonder that the least profitable of the academic businesses, humanities, is the one that suffers the most from this situation, experiencing the most severe budget cuts and the most pressure for redefinition of their research aims and education programs:

> Universities fall over one another in an undignified scramble to secure their fees. Once such customers are safely within the gates, there is pressure on their professors not to fail them, and thus risk losing their fees. The general idea is that if the student fails, it is the professor's fault, rather like a hospital in which every death is laid at the door of the medical staff. One result of this hot pursuit of the student purse is the growth of courses tailored to whatever is currently in fashion among 20-year-olds. In my own discipline of English, that means vampires rather than Victorians, sexuality rather than Shelley, fanzines rather

> than Foucault, the contemporary world rather than the medieval one. It is thus that deep-seated political and economic forces come to shape syllabuses. Any English department that focused its energies on Anglo-Saxon literature or the 18th century would be cutting its own throat. (Eagleton 2015)

It is not very easy, as always in these cases, to identify a specific spot in space and time that would mark the beginning of this phenomenon that has interested the majority of academic institutions in the world, but there is a reason to believe that the period between 2003 and 2008 has been of particular relevance (not incidentally, Tarasti sounded his cry of alarm in 2005, in an article on the Finnish journal *Synteesi*). To make one example, it is in these five years that UK academic institutions witnessed a quick increase of no less than one third of their administrative and managing personnel (see Tahir 2010). All of a sudden there was much more administration needed and much more red tape, and not – mind you – because the academic and students' population had increased accordingly (in the same period, the growth was in the physiological order of 9–10%, as normal after a timespan of five years). Something else had happened: universities were turning into corporations where the techniques of "getting things done" were more important than the actual results (the "metalevel"), where assessment of quality was more important than quality itself, and where indeed an economic-technological discourse had become more important than a scholarly-pedagogical one.

And yet, just like with the other manifestations of the semiocrisis, this was something that the most attentive among academics had already anticipated for quite a while, even though it was evidently difficult to predict the exact time when the fear for something to happen would become already a reality. Like in that beautiful song by XTC, "all of a sudden it's too late". To define the semiocrisis, Tarasti uses the metaphor of the earthquake:

> Earthquakes can be to some extent anticipated but, when they take place exactly speaking, no one can tell. The conceptual orientations of a culture's deep level also move as slowly as continental plateaus. A semiocrisis emerges when these epistemic levels start to move. This becomes manifest when the prevalent discourse in a society does no longer correspond to the epistemic reality. The speech is not equal to man's situation. Such a discrepancy between man's speech and the values steering the epistemes at the deep level of a culture, causes what can be called intracultural misunderstanding (. . .) or what the French philosopher Vladimir Jankélévich called by the term 'méconnaissance', miss-knowledge. (. . .) In general semiocrisis means that the visible, observable signs of social life do not correspond to its immanent structures. Signs have lost their isotopies, their connections to their true meanings. (. . .) As said, such situations can be forecasted but their exact timing is impossible. Accordingly, when the value isotopies of a culture start to move, they cause semiocrisis. It is as if under the surface of the everyday reality there would loom a kind of sociokinetic energy field, which can combine things in unexpected manners. Just these changes in such a socio-energetic level are recognized as semiocrisis. (Tarasti 2015: 134–135)

Within the framework of such a definition, thus, the phenomenon of hyper-bureaucratization and corporatization of universities is a perfect example to analyze. Stemming from Tarasti's work, I shall "personalize" this analysis with a number of notions I worked on within the platform of numanities (see Martinelli 2016), including my own proposal for "resistance", and I shall employ a number of case studies, mostly first hand, which I however anonymized in order not to give the impression that my *J'accuse* involves colleagues and institutions that I respect and which are certainly not my target. During my career, I have been officially affiliated to eight different academic institutions in different places of Europe, so no specific criticism to a specific institution should be inferred.

2 Globalization, the Nothingness and the *condition humaine*

The rise of a new phenomenon is always and inevitably related to a factual, or at least perceived, failure of a pre-existing status quo. The above-mentioned "earthquake" is not a magical event that occurs out of the blue. While this is no time or place to discuss the causes that directly or indirectly generated the academic semiocrisis – and I myself have not spared some firm criticism to the way academics partly brought the crisis to themselves (Martinelli 2016: 11–84) – it is surely relevant to understand what immediately follows after such failure:

> When old structures falter man is left in a structureless situation in which they are no longer protecting him. This again can have two consequences: either man then becomes aware of him/herself as an existing subject – as it happened in Europe after World War II. Man experiences the Sartrean Nothingness; man unexpectedly encounters the emptiness and becomes conscious of his/her situation, choice and responsibility/solidarity. This is one way to react to the epistemic earthquakes recognized as semiocrisis (. . .).
>
> Nevertheless, a more common reaction is to reject the Nothingness and resort to old values until the last moment, by misunderstanding, ignoring the signs of a semiocrisis. Hence a mythological behaviour enormously increases under such times. Mythical longing, nostalgia for perpetual myths, of a nation or tradition are emphasized. When the experience of nothingness under semiocrisis becomes unbearable man creates himself a symbolic surrogate in the media world and its phantasmagorical products. (Tarasti 2015: 135)

Funnily enough, in the days I am writing these lines, I had the opportunity to show my son an old children classic from the 1980s: *The Neverending Story*. In that movie, based on Michael Ende's fantasy novel, the metaphor of "The Nothing" is employed to represent the existential emptiness that overcomes humanity when the latter gives up on hope and dreams.

I am not aware of whether Mr. Ende had any knowledge of, let alone inspiration from, Sartre's philosophy, but certainly there are a few coincidences. *The Neverending Story* does not explicitly identify hope and dreams as "old" values, but a sense of nostalgia and loss of that innocence that did not dismiss the act of desiring as unrealistic and ultimately irresponsible, seem to pervade the fairy tale.

The conditions are now laid. Old structures have faltered, Nothingness has come, people "share the feeling that they are powerless to intervene in its course in any way" (Tarasti 2015: 152), and therefore new models of society, culture and of course economy and politics, take over. In this epoch, this new wave of models is embodied by "globalization",

> a single, unquestioned model, the characteristics and demands of which are familiar to everyone, since they now exist practically everywhere. Traditional terms such as "progress", "development", "results", and "education" are rampantly becoming caricatures of themselves, and serve as a means of adapting everyone and everything to this new global order: a kind of supra-individual, collective power, an actor or mentality that forces real persons to submit to its will.   (Tarasti 2015: 153)

The emphasis of globalization is on "re-educating and re-civilizing people into the new system" (Tarasti 2015: 154). Tarasti finds this process as mostly a result of fourteen actions, which generates the new *condition humaine* of the globalized society. They are called (Tarasti 2015: 154–156): 1) "No more future"; 2) "No more past"; 3) "Shift to the metalevel"; 4) "Perpetual assessment of quality in all domains"; 5) "One dominant discourse: Economic-technological"; 6) "Only two classes of people: Winners and losers"; 7) "Elevation of ownership as a goal unto itself"; 8) "The basic emotional moods in society stem from business life"; 9) "The reservate model of reality"; 10) "Symbolic violence"; 11) "Science: Total behaviorism"; 12) "Study is an unnecessary and unpleasant hurdle of life"; 13) "The naturalization of transcendence"; 14) "The Huntington thesis". For a proper illustration of the whole list, I shall remind to the primary source, as this is outside my scopes here.

Now: while Eero Tarasti perfectly articulates his own response to this status quo (a response which combines the lineaments of his existential semiotics with the paradigm of the semiotics of resistance introduced by Eco 1997 and elaborated in Bankov 2004, and on which I shall return later), I will devote a good half of this study on reflecting deeper on the "diagnosis" of the semiocrisis, as manifested through the phenomenon of hyper-bureaucratization and corporatization of universities. Or, as I like to call it, the "Bu-Bu problem" (as in "bureaucracy" and "business"). It is a phenomenon that Prof. Tarasti himself has often expressed his preoccupation for in official and (as I will briefly show) less official contexts. As it will become quite clear in the next paragraphs, a focus on this manifestation of the semiocrisis, implies a particular attention to points 3, 4, 5, 8 and 12 of Tarasti's *condition humaine:*

> (3) A shift to the metalevel. In work, intent and product are unimportant. What matters is the manner of doing, the techniques and technology of getting things done. This shift is accompanied by the problematization of all phenomena of everyday life. Nothing can happen by itself: faith in one's own intelligence and in *Eliasian civilité* requires that everything take place on the basis of "research" and "control" (the new obsession). This mind-set is linked to the principle of minimizing risks and maximizing efficiency, which is in turn based on the growing conviction that everything and anything can be anticipated, counted, and manipulated.
>
> (4) Perpetual assessment of quality in all domains. People and institutions must undergo continuous self-criticism; at the same time, it is forgotten that the more energy which one puts into the assessment of quality, the less quality there is. From this obsession with assessment emerges a system of total control and self-censorship.
>
> (5) One dominant discourse: Economic-technological. Borrowing its terms from the military, as mentioned in the previous chapter, this discourse allows for assessment and discussion only in terms of functionality/non-functionality, effectiveness/ineffectiveness.
>
> (...)
>
> (8) The basic emotional moods in society stem from business life. These moods are greed (to assure continuous profits and results) and fear (continuous anguish about losing profits and positions), which are expounded and disseminated everywhere via communications media.
>
> (...)
>
> (12) Study is an unnecessary and unpleasant hurdle of life. It has to be cleared as quickly as possible and with minimal expenditure of energy and funds. (Tarasti 2015: 154–156)

My condition as an academic who a) has shifted among different affiliations in different parts of Europe; b) has occupied positions with managerial responsibilities (most notably the direction of the International Semiotics Institute, inherited from Tarasti himself); and c) has experienced the whole transition to the new situation, having started his career before the crucial 2003–2008 period, places me, I believe, in a significant position to critically testify of the different characteristics and effects of the Bu-Bu problem, and to do it with directly-experienced examples. While the main focus here shall remain the assessment of this problem as a "semiocrisis" specifically, I dare suggesting (as I did in Martinelli 2016 already) that to talk about the hyper-bureaucratization and corporatization of universities means to discuss also the specific problem of the current crisis of the humanities.

2.1 The crisis of the humanities, in a nutshell

The evidence of a decrease in interest towards the humanities has been documented in various ways. In Europe, the Instituto Nacional de Estadística has calculated a significant drop in degrees in humanities between 1998 and 2010. Specific institutes have also provided their own data: Harvard University has famously reported a straight 50% cut in enrollments in humanities, from the 14% of 1966 to the 7% of 2010 (Sorensen 2013); while 50% is also the rough decrease that occurred at Yale, where we also learn that there is no significant difference between male and female students.

However, not all sources share the same conclusions. Prof. Benjamin Schmidt from Northeastern University in Boston maintains that "the entirety of the long-term decline [of the humanities] from 1950 to the present has to do with the changing majors of women." (Schmidt 2013). Before the 1970s, indeed, a remarkable percentage of women who went to college majored either in education (40%) or in humanities (50%). The second-wave of feminism, instead, encouraged women to pursue other paths, particularly business, math and science. Inevitably, the overall percentage of students in humanities suffered from it.

In addition to this, several universities in the whole world joined social sciences and humanities together, under a single faculty (or department, or school), hoping to reciprocally strengthen programs and scholarships. Quite interestingly, nearly all of the marketing strategies of these institutions convey a similar message: humanities + social sciences = skills and values for a better world. Some examples: the tagline from the MIT School of humanities, arts and social sciences is "Great ideas change the world"; at Penn State Behrend college is "Developing the skills for success in a diverse world"; Jacobs University (Germany) suggests that the programs in their School of humanities and social sciences have been "designed to combine elements of creativity, innovation, job perspectives and research orientation for an internationally competitive academic education"; Lakehead University inaugurates the page of the Faculty of humanities and social sciences by quoting Socrates: "the unexamined life is not worth living"; and so on.

More questions have been emphasized. In a study called "The Humanities matter", it was shown that important positions of political and financial leadership in society are actually occupied, for a significant majority, by people with a humanistic background. As of 2012, for instance, 60% of American CEO's, 65% of UK parliament members and over two thirds of private entrepreneurs in wholesaling and retailing were shown to have degrees in the humanities (additional data are available in Terras et al. 2013). And yet, not more than 0.45% of American federal research money and not more than 1.06% of the EU research budget went to research in the humanities, creating an enormous gap with other fields of inquiry. Of course, on the one hand, the humanities are normally an inexpensive and relatively low-tech affair. While the nuclear engineer or the biochemist may need equipment and premises that are worth millions, the humanist's higher expenses are normally a few conference trips, some books and a new laptop. Or are they? In fact, there are fields in the arts and humanities in which, too, very costly equipment is needed. Building a decent music recording studio, complete with mixing desk, recording machines, software, instruments, amplifiers, sound boots, microphones, and all the rest, is in fact an enterprise no cheaper than a biochemistry lab. Plus, in any case, a gap like that remains not justifiable in principle. There must be something else.

3 The Bu-Bu problem in universities: Bureaucracy and business

A major problem in the current crisis of the humanities is that the latter and their institutional interlocutors (establishment, funding sources, management. . .) have ceased interacting in a fruitful manner. This communication breakdown can be particularly understood by considering two manifestations of the crisis: the decrease of value of the humanities and, indeed, the Bu-Bu problem. In the first case, it has become clear that institutions do not seem to appreciate the importance of the often intangible and uncountable value created by the humanities (there it is: the dominance of the economic-technological discourse). For instance, we have seen that only a small, insignificant portion of public funds are allocated to humanistic research.

But of course, it is the second case that interests us, here. Before any other consideration, and at the risk of alienating some sympathies among the readership of this essay, I would like to start by declaring, rather firmly, that although, as humanists (or semioticians in particular), we are not very keen to admit it, we need to take a fair share of responsibility for what has happened. If we reached this particular situation, it is also (or perhaps mostly) because many academics have been, for decades, models of laxity, short-sightedness, recklessness and laziness. In more prosperous financial times, we just worried about ourselves, our own position and our ego; we failed to pave any path for future generations; we used the general lack of institutional control for our own profit (instead of celebrating the value of that freedom), and we did not care to treat our own research/ teaching activities in terms of intellectual and economic investment. We were happy that the humanities did not need to be "justified" at institutional level, as they enjoyed that "intrinsic value" that nobody had the courage to question.

Except that now, guess what, someone had that nerve, and thus humanities have lost that centrality in society that they used to enjoy in the past.

Having said this, and having all agreed on the importance of self-criticism, there is no doubt that things went just too far, and that the "punishment" for our shortcomings has been grossly disproportionate. It was wrong of us to consider ourselves "untouchable lords of knowledge", but to turn us into "managers and sellers of (a much more superficial) knowledge" is a greater mistake. Therefore, some specific aspects of this auspicated dialogue (the solution to the above-mentioned communication breakdown) can and should be also achieved by a process of reformation, if not revolution. And that articulated group of practices that we call "corporatization" and "hyper-bureaucracy" is, in my humble opinion, almost entirely on the wrong side of this dialogue, and as such it must be profoundly changed, if not disintegrated.

3.1 Disturbing quiet people

It is now time to finally shed light on the mysterious title of this study. Eero will hopefully forgive me for the violation of his privacy: a few years ago, I was asking him clarifications about a certain request I had received one administrator and whose logic was not awfully clear to me. In one passage of his email, Tarast wrote: "[. . .] As to the demands from the Faculty, that is what they typically do nowadays: disturb quiet people".

There it was. It became a bit of a comedy routine for me and my closer colleagues: whenever we would receive some annoying request from the administration, we would comment "here they go *disturbing quiet people* again". I have never counted myself as a "quiet" person, but definitely I feel one whenever I get harassed by the bureaucratic machine of my job place.

Here is a more elaborate comment on the issue by Prof. Grahame Lock, philosopher at Oxford University:

> Imagine that managers are going to assess the quality of restaurant meals but they have no sense of taste. They have no idea – everything tastes the same to them. So what are they going to do? They will undertake evaluations such as how many minutes did it take for the soup to arrive at your table? How many words of explanation did the waiter use? And so on. Everything is evaluated quantitatively, so the obvious thing for a manager to do is to increase the amount of information gathered. As all these factors come into play, then you need more and more managers and managers need to cover themselves so they bring in more managers. So what happens is hyper-bureaucracy. My view is that this has its own momentum and there can be no limit to it and it is not something that can be rolled back. I would predict that the 33% expansion will be greater in 10 years' time because there is no mechanism that can put a stop to this.   (Quoted in Tahir 2010)

Finally, a frankly less subtle observation:

> Universities are increasingly populated by the undead: a listless population of academics, managers, administrators and students, all shuffling to the beat of the corporatist drum [. . .] Academic zombie speech is peppered with affectless references to DEST points, citation indices, ERA rankings, ARC applications, esteem factors, FoR codes, AUQA reviews and the like. Aca-zombies participate in numerous Rber-zombified, government-sponsored quality assurance exercises, presided over by powerful external assessors. Many zombies have long lost the capacity to distinguish between a place of learning and a money-making PR machine, mummified in red tape. They appear incapable of responding meaningfully to the tyranny of performance indicators, shifting promotion criteria, escalating workload demands and endless audits, evaluations and reviews. [. . .]
>
> They even come to believe corporatist language promotes transparency and accountability. The viral effects of such delusions are such that many aca-zombies do not even realise they have already passed over into the valley of shadows. Work formerly conducted at university (remember teaching and research?) has been replaced by a sinister doppelganger: bureaucratically generated compliance. [. . .]
>
> Occasionally it is necessary, as in Zombieland and Shaun of the Dead, to pass as undead to survive. Paradoxically, it is the unthinking intellectual rigor mortis of the present bureaucratic plague that enables some to survive the worst aspects of zombification.   (Gora and Whelan 2010)

There we go. In a crescendo of annoyance, frustration and fury, researchers and teachers (that is, in the metaphors, quiet people, restaurant chefs and finally human survivors in a land of zombies) display their concern over the Bu-Bu problem. The management by now requests all sorts of things from academics: monitoring, assessments, deconstruction and reconstruction of programs according to new rules, measuring and quantitative analyses. The cunning promise of a simplification of the procedures in the near future ("once you have gone through the learning curve, you'll see that everything will proceed faster", or – more diabolically – "this is just an evolution, not a revolution, from what you were already doing") is constantly deluded by repeated additions, so-called refinements, and most of all reshuffling and addition of more managers, who – in turn – are eager to introduce new procedures and new training sessions to teach them.

These people, Prof. Lock correctly remarked, have no competence in the academic work: they are not scholars-turned-to-managers, nor managers with *some* competence in scholarship. They are managers-full-stop. They may have worked in public administration, in a bank, in the best of cases in a governmental institution related to cultural policies, but that is about all. The result is a particular case of the famous Putt's law (Putt 2006: 159): there are people (academics, in our case) who understand what they do not manage, and people (the bureaucrats) who manage what they do not understand.

Now, academics are already pretty allergic to any form of intrusion into their work (especially comments on its quality) when such intrusion comes from an experienced colleague. If it comes from people they do not even acknowledge as "equals", they get seriously irritated, and not without reason (why should a researcher be asked to perform administrative tasks by *administrative staff*? Is by any chance an administrator ever asked to write and publish a scientific article?). Humanists are in the worst condition here, because not only they do not acknowledge any authority in managers: they also do not understand a word of what the latter tell them. While researchers and teachers in natural sciences will at least understand the numerical aspects of the tasks that are inflicted on them by managers (say, a financial plan, a budget statement. . .), and those in social science will get the methodology and the language, humanists will get frustrated with both figures and words, and that will anger them even more.

Not that one should be surprised, by the way, as humanists were not involved in this process in the first place. The whole managerial/bureaucratic system was conceived and developed within a territory (economics, social psychology, statistics, marketing research. . .) mostly inhabited by social and natural scientists, and where humanists were carefully left out of the picture. In that territory, for instance, the classic writings on bureaucracy and management (Marx, Mill, Weber. . . competences that humanists would have been happy and competent to contribute) are happily ignored, in favor of dynamic workshops, games of social facilitation, and of course plenty of markers and post-it's. Humanists are not welcome in the creation of this apparatus, not only because their competences are not perceived as necessary, but also (mostly?) because they are the ones most likely to understand the basic fraud behind it: while bureaucracies are rhetorically advertised as the only way to ensure transparency, reciprocal control, fairness, etc., they are in fact the antithesis to participatory democracy.

And why is it humanists who can understand this? Exactly because they, on the contrary, *did* read their Weber, and they do feel that "polar night of icy darkness and hardness" right inside their bones (I am intentionally giving no reference here: humanists will know what I am talking about, while managers, for a change, may finally be prompted into reading the classics of management theory – or at least googling the very expression I mentioned!). By the way, I am not only mentioning Weber because he devoted a significant portion of his work to management and bureaucracy. I am doing that also because he was *not* opposed to bureaucracy as such, but to its excesses only. One of the main points I am trying to make here is that the humanities are especially powerful in *critical* assessment of reality. Their power is exactly in not being monolithic, unilateral and therefore ultimately unfair. If *50 shades of grey* had not become the title for a silly book and an even sillier movie, we could have exactly said that humanists can turn a generic black-or-white analysis of reality into one that catches most of the grey nuances of it.

The next paragraphs shall be devoted to the consequences of the Bu-Bu problem, and how it affects the humanities in particular (provided that, as we said, it is the whole of academia that suffers from this form of semiocrisis).

3.2 Red tape redundancy

The appearance of an excessive amount of (and most of all, too redundant) red tape and paper work is certainly the first point we need to discuss. Actions, decision-making and problem-solving, instead of being facilitated, are slowed down or even hindered. Humanists, as mentioned, suffer in particular for this, as they also need additional time to adapt to a *forma mentis* they were never familiar with in the first place. In one sentence: they are exactly asked to renounce to what they are best at.

The melancholic case of the procurement system is possibly the most painful example of red tape delirium. Born to avoid lobbying and conflict of interests in the various service and material expenses that an academic institution faces, this "best of three offers" principle has become a neurotic practice that not only slows down and complicates procedures that once were very quick, but also determines a standardization and worsening of the service itself. First of all, a company owner who wins a procurement for – let us say – printing a book, knows already that they will get the money *anyway* (save legal actions that would require more financial investment from both sides), so the healthy principle of competition that was previously established in the tender with two other companies is threatened by the serious possibility that the service eventually delivered will be not as good as promised: knowing very well that the bureaucratic apparatus of the university is so laborious that the chances anybody will raise an issue (including indeed legal means) are very low, the company gives a clear demonstration of why it was the cheapest in the tender. Bad quality and slow delivery are the two most recurrent disservices received by the academic institution.

I have a colleague at one of my affiliations who is directing an institute, with whom we have a running gag: ". . .and the cookies are disgusting!" We use it to conclude most conversations or complaints about bureaucracy at our university. The gag refers to the fact that the tender for cookies' provision, to employ in conference coffee breaks and the likes, was won by a company in a town that is over 150 km distant from the university. They became the symbol of our dissatisfaction against the procurement system, because they are objectively and empirically of a very bad quality, with something red on top (sold as jam) which is probably

silicon, judging from the consistency and heroic resistance to any attempt at chewing it. Now, everything is wrong about this procurement:
1) Imagine how cheap the production of such cookies must be, if the company managed to win the tender despite 150 km of distance (that is, the overall price we pay *includes* transportation, and still they manage to outdo local companies from the competition);
2) Imagine the contribution to environmental protection that a similar enterprise carries out: vans filled with horrible cookies travel 150 km to delight our congress guests, then return happily empty to the factory for another 150 km;
3) Imagine what progress in image and reputation our institution gains by inflicting inedible coffee breaks to our international colleagues, and what interesting academic discussions take place while half of the crowd is stoically working their tongue around to remove indestructible pieces of red silicon from their molars.

This colleague I mentioned once explained me how she got around this embarrassing obstacle. Take note: she pretended she had an important meeting in another city, so she applied for refunding to the faculty. We have a document with a table reporting fuel costs, related to the average consumption of various car engine types, so my colleague filled the tank of her own car with the equivalent amount needed for a trip back and forth to that city (200 km in total, for the record). Of course, you understand, it has to be a car trip, not a public transportation one, otherwise one actually needs to buy a ticket. Given her reimbursement, she finally had the money *not* to go to that city, but instead walk less than 100 meters from the faculty, and buy delicious anti-procurement cookies from the bakery round the corner.

Another episode I may mention in the procurement odyssey is my own problem with the hotels where we accommodated our invited speakers at a congress my team and I organized. Our university arranged another tender to get special offers from three 4-star, three 3-star, and three 2-star hotels. The cheapest in each category would get the exclusivity for our accommodation requests. Mind you: the cheapest. Given some basic criteria (number of rooms available, breakfast included, and the likes), the price was the only significant requirement. Nobody thought it would be wiser to establish *a set* of parameters (prestige of the hotel, distance from the university buildings, absence of architectural barriers, attention for different lifestyles in their restaurant menus, nicety of the location, etc.) in order to choose the cheapest-among-the-satisfying options, not just the cheapest-and-fullstop ones.

Results. Great for the 2-star winner: very nice and clean hotel, well-located and very close to the faculty: students and low-budget participants could be happy. So-and-so for the 3-star winner: very nice hotel, picturesque location, but *very* far from the faculty: one needed to use public transportation or a taxi. Finally, terrible result for the 4-star winner, where of course one likes to accommodate plenary speakers, whom – as it happens – tend to be the most senior ones as well: the hotel as such was great, but it was not very close to the faculty – of that kind of distance that you might generally like to cover by walking, but not if you have your paper in less than 30 minutes, or if you have reached a certain age; and – most of all – the hotel was located in an area of the city that was not very appealing. So, we had to give our most prestigious guests an image of ourselves as a not particularly attractive city (and thus country). And to add salt to the wound, this particular hotel won the tender by offering rooms that were only one euro cheaper than the hotel we would have loved to hire, because it was much closer and more nicely located. One euro. One euro is all it took to get all those minuses. This is what happens when this kind of calculations is made on an exclusively-quantitative basis.

Plus, of course, with only one euro of difference, you cannot help suspecting that a bit of behind-the-scene arrangement *did* take place, and someone, somewhere, had some kind of interest to have that particular hotel winning the tender. And that is certainly ironic for a system that was born exactly to fight behind-the-scene business.

...And the cookies are disgusting.

3.3 Losing motivation and initiative

Secondly: motivation to work for, and sense of belongingness to, an academic institution are discouraged and seriously endangered. Academics start perceiving the headquarters of their department/faculty/university as enemies that get in their way, do not trust them and merely harass them with unnecessary work. Once again, this is particularly a problem for humanists, because they are most often the "intellectual façade" of an academic institution. They represent it in the media with their magazine columns, TV appearances, interviews (a journalist who wants to write about a given university is more likely to approach the charmingly talkative philosopher from that university, rather than – say – the antisocial IT nerd); they appear more often in public events, and so forth. An unmotivated, "unpatriotic" humanist, who is immediately visible and recognizable, is likely to be very vocal in their dissatisfaction.

Moreover, the excessive reliance on schemes and regulations inhibit personal initiative and growth of the academics, who are treated more like machines than like individuals. The human factor is almost entirely neglected. For instance, current teaching programs, with all their requirements, precise scheduling, regular monitoring, fixed methodologies, "aims and objectives" mechanical templates, "at the end of the course students will be able to. . ." redundancy, etc., damage the teachers' abilities to accommodate their work to the students' need, and to assess them case by case.

By now, teachers have to take too many *final* decisions *before* having even met their students. They are less and less enabled to understand what can be done, how, with whom, etc. They cannot "make a difference" as individuals, beyond institutional restrictions. Humanists pay the highest price for this, because they are naturally inclined to "make a difference" in their work by their personal talents, critical mind, individual style, unconventional choices and unique background. There is no need to recur to fascinating scenarios in *Dead Poets' Society* style: a teacher can make the difference with a much less fancy approach than asking the students to step on their desks, read poems in a cave and call them "O Captain, my Captain". Still the point remains: a teacher can make students dig inside themselves and discover their true identity, showing them a path that will characterize their whole life. Teachers, in other words, have the ability to become mentors, if they are left free to do so. Nowadays, mentorship tends to happen only as a result of a special relationship established between teacher and student in *their spare time*, that is, if they are able to develop that relationship outside the spaces and the times of their class.

Just to make an example: in the intranet system of one of my affiliations, whenever I plan a course, I am asked to choose the teaching methods for each topic and the criteria to assess the student's understanding of that topic. That is bad enough, but what if I told you that (I kid you not) the choice of teaching methods consists of twenty-four options and the assessment criteria of forty? A system like this just *begs* to be cheated at. Of course, the majority of us simply pick a few methods and criteria (even at random) and just repeat them over and over for each topic, without really thinking that this is what they will actually do in the class. And that is just fair, because indeed one just *cannot* plan these things in advance. A teacher has a right and in fact a moral duty not to know in advance what teaching methods they will adopt for each of their topics, because they need to see their class first: they need to get familiar with the students' needs, their potentials, their strengths and their weaknesses. A teacher needs to see if one particular topic is a bit more challenging than others, if more time is needed, if they have to try to teach it in a different manner. And so on and so forth: all these things cannot and should not be planned in advance. Result: we just fill in the intranet system in order to comply to the requirements, not because we *mean* what we write there. That is the handbook definition of Tarasti's "metalevel": results/products do not matter – what matter is the "technique".

3.4 Time and categories

And since we mentioned it, "time", in both the operative and the conceptual sense, get the most unfair treatment in the process. There is a great website called phdcomics.com, where the most hilarious and relatable jokes about academia can be found. One of such comics is entitled "How professors spend their time" (http://www.phdcomics.com/comics.php?f=1060), and emphasizes, via three mock-statistics, the main problems related to the way bureaucracy ("service") gets in the way of an academic's job: a) it concretely occupies a good quarter of the employee's working time (the first pie chart shows bureaucracy occupying 25% of the working time); b) it is not acknowledged as working time by the employer (the second mock-statistics shows bureaucracy in a separate pie chart); c) it is an annoying imposition for the employee (the third pie-chart is occupied for the 100% by the academic's statement "Don't tell me what to do!").

This is indeed the reality: bureaucracy takes a lot of time to be implemented, and yet does not get any recognition as "working time". Where do academics take time to, for instance, compile and re-compile ad infinitum their list of publications for different goals and destinations (e.g., library, doctoral committee, project department, human resources, mid-term report, full-term report, accreditation of their job, accreditation of their department, accreditation of their faculty, accreditation of their university, and so on and so forth), within a situation where not only the various units do not communicate with each other (they could share the same "list of publications" document, for a start, but they never do that, do they?), but they also have different templates, criteria, order, parameters for compiling that single set of information. So, today my list of publications will have to be arranged in chronological order, Times New Roman 12 and MLA style; tomorrow it will have to be by levels (indexed and peer-reviewed first, only peer-reviewed second, etc.), Arial 11 and Chicago Manual of Style; etc.

All this takes t-i-m-e, but in the end of the year report, the employee cannot write that, say, ten hours of their work were used to write and rewrite the list of publications for twenty different purposes, simply because there is no entry in the report template that says "time spent complying with administrative tasks". As emphasized in the second mock-statistic of the comic, that time is "outside", it is entirely neglected by the institution. Once more, humanists generally suffer the biggest handicap in this process, because their activities are also the most difficult (or at least varied) to categorize, and tend to be more numerous in quantity. If, for example, the activity of a biochemist is very focused on a single (very important) experiment for five years, and that experiment results in *one* (very important) article in a prestigious scientific journal displaying the success of that experiment and maybe a groundbreaking discovery, that of course (and justly) corresponds to a great achievement and a career high. The humanist, in that time span, was likely busy with fifteen conferences, ten articles, one monograph, five public lectures, eight different (big or small) research projects, three edited collections, two book reviews, ten Erasmus missions, the preparation of a new study program, and who knows how much more. All of these items have to be reported, and very probably categorized in a different way than how I just listed them.

Which brings us to the next problem. Along with a "time" issue, there is also a categorization issue. One reason why bureaucracy takes a lot of time is because it claims to be able to map all the variables within a given task, while it generally fails to do so. That is particularly true in the humanistic academic environment, where – generally speaking – things make sense when developed into a narrative structure, not into a "this or that" classification. The above-mentioned report, as compiled by a humanist, would make much more sense if the scholar was enabled to write it in free form, where they have the chance to show the consequentiality of certain activities (and related choices), as part of a perhaps eclectic but very coherent discourse. But no. At the entry "conferences" the scholar has to separate the international from the national; the ones related to a given research project from the ones related to another; the ones that will result in a proceedings publication from the ones that will not; the ones where the scholar was invited as key-note from the ones where they were not... At the entry "articles", they have to separate A level form other levels; peer-reviewed from not peer-reviewed; journals from edited collections; top publishers from less important ones...

The narrative is deconstructed and the result is a fragmented puzzle where all the single pieces make much less sense than their sum. When this problem is raised, the hyper-bureaucratic apparatus reacts in the worst possible way: it adds *more* variables, *more* categories, *more* tasks, in the vain illusion that sooner or later the full spectrum will be covered, and failing once again to understand that this is not (This. Is. Not.) a quantitative problem. When we are kids, we realize pretty soon that with a box of six tempera colors we cannot draw very imaginative pictures; so we ask our parents to buy a 12-tube box, but that, too, turns out not to be sufficient; so we ask for a 24-tube box, until that is not sufficient either... and so on and so forth, until we grow up a bit, and (click!) we realize that colors can be "mixed", and all we need is the three primary colors plus the two neutral ones. And from that small unit of five colors, we can develop any pictorial "narrative" we want, with all the tiniest nuances.

Needless to say, in this example hyper-bureaucracy corresponds to the stubborn child who keeps on asking for more and more colors, without realizing the qualitative aspect of those tubes: they can be mixed!

This, too, takes us to the next step of the analysis.

3.5 Paradoxes and principles

There are two important paradoxes that result from this mentality, and they both have scientific names. One is the *Downs–Thomson paradox* about street traffic (Downs 1992: 30): if we try to solve the traffic problem by enlarging the roads and adding more lanes, we will only have more traffic. Translated: if we think that adding more procedures and more managing personnel (more tempera colors) will make bureaucracy lighter and more usable, let us think again. The example I gave of 24 teaching methods and 40 assessment criteria to be chosen for each topic of each course is paradigmatic. I do not wish to make a Duke Ellingtonian statement and say that there are only two teaching methods, the good one and the bad one, but the situation forces me into something like this. It is true: at the end of the day, there are teachers who did a good job, and teachers who did not. The teachers who did a good job, among other qualities, were usually the ones who showed flexibility, variety, ability to change methodologies when the case would call for it and a mind sufficiently open not to stick to any premade, ready-to-serve plan, but build the course as a narrative in progress, *with the cooperation* of the students, who also can make a difference with their personalities, their ideas, and the way they function as individuals and as a group. By consequence, the existence of 40 "tempera colors" criteria of assessment is even more ridiculous than the 24 teaching methods. There is hardly anything less accurate and in a sense more humiliating than thinking that the assessment of a student should be quantified by a checklist. Every decent teacher knows that the assessment of a student is not just a sum of parts, but an overall profile built (this one too) "in the making", with nuances and with, again, the right and the duty to rethink each and all the (forty!) criteria depending on the subject. Take the various assessment criteria for oral presentations: what if one student stutters? What if another one is shy? What if one is foreigner and less comfortable with the course language? What if another one is very bad at expressing themselves orally but a genius at writing, and they would be capable to give the best exam of the whole class if they only could write?

The funny side of the story is that, when I raise this issue to my colleagues in administration, they are always agreeing. Maybe they do it out of pity, or maybe just because I am a nuisance and they want to get rid of me as quickly as possible, but the type of answer I receive is always in the line of "Yes, you're right. But, you know, this is the regulation: we *have* to do it!". If this is a sincere answer, then, once again, we are facing another metalevel: these regulations are empty in meaning – we just *have* to comply. What if we remembered that this is a free world, and in fact we do *not* have to comply, unless we want to? If we are always told the story that regulations are made to *improve* the work, but in fact we all know that they are made for their own sake, is it not time to question their existence, and reflect on their very purpose? Is it not time to finally get rid of the ones that are mere red tape exercise, and keep only the ones that are really useful (and I will admit that some of them are)?

The second paradox is known as the *Jevons paradox* (Jevons 1865: 146): an increase of efficiency generates an increase (rather than a decrease) of consumption. Translated: we are told that procedures are made more efficient (again, in a quantitative sense only: from 6 to 12 colors, from 12 to 24, etc.), but what happens is that we are getting more and more dependent on them. Bureaucracy develops in a rather organic way, and tends to fill all the empty spaces. Little by little, it gets to regulate not only the things that were in need of being regulated (if they really were), but also those that were simply standing in the way. What was before possible to do without, say, an authorization, now requires one; what was possible with two signatures now requires five, and so on. Again: what was possible with a couple of teaching methods and a couple of assessment criteria, now requires 24 and 40 respectively.

Since we are into the realm of economic paradoxes and laws, perhaps we can also add a collateral effect of the constant reshuffling of personnel. It became known as the Peter Principle (Peter and Hull 2009: 9): anything that works will be used in progressively more challenging applications until it fails. It is a typical career-scheme in management (and a typical career goal of managers): if a manager X is good in the A position, they will get promoted to the B position (better paid, but with different tasks), if they succeed there as well then there is C (better paid, but with different tasks), then D (better paid, but with different tasks)... until it turns out that, well, tasks became so different that X performs very poorly, the institution suffers a drawback, and X may also be fired (which, playing with words, may remind of how "fired" Icarus ended up for wanting to fly higher and higher). Of course, this situation tends to occur pretty soon (a promotion path from A to D and beyond is very optimistic, because normally X fails already at B or C), and activates a chain reaction: when X went, say, from B to C, manager Y was promoted from A to B (and maybe they will fail in this new position, while X was very good there), and manager Z was hired for the A position (where Y was very good). All this, while, instead, if someone is good at something, they should be kept there, and, if anything, given a higher salary and more bonuses for their merits. On the contrary, what happens (using football as an example) is that a good defender is promoted to striker (bigger salary and more fame), while of course they have no clue how to score goals.

To put these reflections in practice, we could for instance mention the data reported by the *Times Higher Education* (Jump 2015) about UK universities. There, we learn two important facts: that support staff has increased by no less than one third in few years (and we knew that already from Tahir 2010), and that such staff is the majority of the total in 111 out of 157 institutions. So, in more than 2/3 of British universities there are more managers than people to manage (with peaks of over 60% in such cases as the University of Bradford, the University of Wolverhampton and Durham University). Which is more or less (keeping up with the football example), like having a football team with 11 players on the pitch and 16 coaches in the dugout. At the same time (of course!) the best UK academic institutions (Oxford, Cambridge, Institute of Cancer Research, King's College...) are all in the Top 10 of those with *the lowest* amount of support staff (the lowest being ICR with only 37%). So: more quality, less management. Maybe it is time to focus on quality, for a change?

Concluding: in order to overcome the communication breakdown and re-open the dialogue between us, as academics and humanists in particular, and the institutions we are affiliated in or apply to for funds and projects, we certainly need to be self-critical and learn some of the "rules of the game", and that is something we cannot escape from. However, at the same time, this must be counterbalanced by the equally-crucial necessity to *rewrite* such rules. In fact, we should learn such rules *because* we want to rewrite them.

Some of these rules, I shall repeat, have become necessary because of our laxity and selfishness: we need to admit that – there is no way around it. Some others must be instead understood in order to be corroded from the inside. The phenomenon of corporatization and hyper-bureaucracy certainly belongs to the latter category. There is absolutely no doubt that every single scholar in this world, not just within the humanities, should roll up their sleeves to develop solutions against the outrageous overload of paperwork, evaluations, self-evaluations, monitoring processes, performance assessments, and all possible (imaginable and, more often, unimaginable) tasks the employees of academic institutions are systematically and increasingly harassed by. This is depressing, demotivating, frustrating and ultimately ridiculous. And counterproductive, for what is worth: the melancholic irony that these managers seem to be incapable of noticing is that most of these tasks are meant to "assess and improve" the quality of the academic work, but they are so time- and energy-consuming that the first and foremost process to get damaged by them is the production of quality itself.

"How do you work?", "How much did you work?", "Can you quantify this particular work?", "And what about that other work?", "How did you distribute the tasks of this work?", "Could you select the assessment criteria of that work?", "Can you do the S.W.O.T. analysis of your work?"...

These and hundreds of others are the questions managers harass us by.

We, in turn, have only one question: "Can I go back to work, please?"

4 Semiotics of resistance and appropriate technologies

After we got all this out of the system, let us now return to our point of departure, Tarasti's assessment of the semiocrisis, and let us now discuss the possible solutions. As I mentioned, the Finnish semiotician adopts the paradigm of the "semiotics of resistance" as a proposed counterforce for the crisis. It is a model I had the opportunity to adopt in Martinelli 2009, although for quite different purposes. Apologizing for the generalization, I would suggest that Tarasti's take on the semiotics of resistance can be interpreted in three fundamental actions, or "subtle mechanisms", as he calls them (Tarasti 2015: 156):
1) The importance of active engagement into a counterculture that would be antithetic to the dominant one: "If the attraction to culture A is stronger than to culture B, then adaptation or assimilation occurs; whereas if one actively engages with B, then what is involved is resistance" (Tarasti 2015: 156);
2) The importance of active negation of the dominant culture. In other words, not only engaging in culture B, but also being vocal against culture A. Negation is "spiritual and pragmatic operation" and is "a statement that is typically and universally true of all humans" (Tarasti 2015: 157); however
3) Unlike the Hegelian concept of negation that is followed by "becoming", Tarasti wonders: "what if we should (. . .) presume that negation, rather than leading to becoming, is instead followed by a return backwards? If such concepts as becoming, development, progress, anticipation, directionality, and the like have all been subordinated to serve the global system, and if we want to reject this system as a whole, then we have to look at the movement of signs in the counter-current to all of that" (Tarasti 2015: 157).

As a great admirer of Gandhi's philosophy, both the concepts of "counterculture" and "negation" find me in total agreement. On the suggestion of returning backwards, on the other hand, I may express a preference for another notion introduced by Gandhi, although formalized and developed by the German economist Ernst Schumacher: the so-called "appropriate technologies" (AT, from now on). I shall devote this section of the study to introduce the concept and build a hopefully credible argument in its support. Just like Tarasti's reflections, AT too depart from a critical approach to the idea of "progress". AT imply an understanding of "progress" as something not necessarily represented by every single thing that is newer, bigger, faster: a critical (therefore, intimately humanistic) view seeks progress in what is tailored for the real needs and demands of a given community. The point about progress is not about going forwards or backwards. The point is to go *towards*. Towards the people, towards the society, towards the environment, towards life.

As an actual theory in economics AT, sometime known also as "intermediate technologies", originate indeed from Gandhi's struggle for Indian independence, when he developed the idea of economic "self-reliance" (in Hindi "Swadeshi"), that is, the advocacy of small and local technologies by which Indian villages could reject economic colonialism from Britain. Embodied by the famous image (and flag symbol) of the spinning wheel, the swadeshi produced the khadi movement in the 1920s, that is, the local production of clothes as a form of civil disobedience, eventually causing the collapse of the British monopoly on textiles. Starting from the 1950s, the German economist Ernst Schumacher, inspired by these ideas of Gandhi, brought the concept of AT to a more systematic level, particularly via his famous book *Small is Beautiful* (1973). What emerges from Schumacher's work, and that turned into the three pillars of the whole theory, is the following set of characteristics of AT:

1. AT have to be *sustainable*: that is, environmentally sound and "economic" in the literary sense of the word. Not by coincidence, the concept of AT, which nowadays is certainly less fashionable than it was in the 1970s, has been partly replaced by "sustainable development": they are not the same things, but plenty of what sustainable development theories advocate were originally promoted by AT theories.
2. AT have to be *appropriate* to a given context. Contexts are of an ethical, cultural, social, economic, environmental and political type. Obviously, a technology that is appropriate for a given context, is not necessarily so for another, however some generally-applicable rules exist: community input, affordability, reparability and maintainability are certainly four universally "appropriate" properties for a technology.
3. AT's have to be small where possible (or, as I prefer to say, "direct"). Of the three pillars, this is the one that is most often misunderstood, since "small" is naturally perceived as unambitious, unpretentious, modest. On the contrary, the main idea is to place more power at the basis of an economic process, at the grassroots, and to make sure that the technology is in the hands of the users. In that sense, I prefer the word "direct", in the same sense that one would employ in speaking about "direct democracy". Also, the idea of appropriateness itself implies proportion and context-dependence. Technologies can therefore be also "big", if the context requires it:

   The question of scale might be put in another way: what is needed in all these matters is to discriminate, to get things sorted out. For every activity there is a certain appropriate scale, and the more active and intimate the activity, the smaller the number of people that can take part, the greater is the number of such relationship arrangements that need to be established. Take teaching: one listens to all sorts of extraordinary debates about the superiority of the teaching machine over some other forms of teaching. Well, let us discriminate what are we trying to teach? It then becomes immediately apparent that certain things can only be taught in a very intimate circle, whereas other things can obviously be taught en masse, via the air, via television, via teaching machines, and so on.

What scale is appropriate? It depends on what we are trying to do. The question of scale is extremely crucial today, in political, social and economic affairs just as in almost everything else. What, for instance, is the appropriate size of a city? And also, one might ask, what is the appropriate size of a country? Now these are serious and difficult questions. It is not possible to programme a computer and get the answer. (Schumacher 1973: 50)

One can easily see why 24 options for teaching methods and 40 for assessment criteria are the exact contrary of "sustainable", "appropriate" and "direct".

Still during the 1970s, another important AT scholar, the Austrian designer Victor Papanek (1971: 258–259), added another piece to the theory by emphasizing the concept of "design", and specifying that the design of an AT has to always keep in mind two goals: the "real world" and the "human scale", both often overlooked in the diverse economic processes.

As what I am trying to do here is to make an economic concept like AT "function" within the more abstract level of an academic-scientific context, it shall be also important to mention Audrey Faulkner's and Maurice Albertson's distinction between hard and soft AT (1986). While hard technologies are grounded in the natural sciences, scientific techniques, and improve upon tangible structures, soft technologies concern the needs and values of a community, and are grounded on social structures, interactive processes and motivation techniques. My conviction is that an area of academic/scientific investigation like humanities can be configured for society in form of soft AT. I also believe it is a good idea in general, because – unless some obscure research has escaped my scrutiny – there have been no previous attempts to bring the concept of AT into the realm of academia as such.

4.1 The criteria to judge an appropriate technology

Most interesting of all, as far as our purposes are concerned, is Wicklein 1998 and 2004, which contain a 7-point classification of the so-called "Criteria to judge the appropriateness of technology", some of which I would like to connect (sometimes literally, sometimes metaphorically – but not less significantly) with the purposes of this study (all the following quotes are from Wicklein 2004). The first point is "Systems-Independence", or "the ability of the technological device to stand alone, to do the job with few or no other supporting facilities or devices to aid in its function". A form of academic work that is fully operative is one that is not dispersive in its actions and that is able to "stand alone", without the support (which is not really a support, but a handicap) of accompanying procedures: good teachers are able to assess the students by themselves, without having to select among 40 criteria. A good hotel for hosting congress attendants can be chosen without a procurement system. And so forth.

Interesting is also the third point, "Individual Technology versus Collective Technology", or the societal/cultural context in which a given technology will be established. "Some cultures advocate a strong commitment to the group process where the good of the whole is held in higher esteem than individual accomplishments. Other cultures place a high priority on individual responsibility and accomplishment. These factors should be considered in detail when designing appropriate technology because they will contribute to the success or failure of any given device or strategy. If a given cultural group has a strong allegiance to the community or region then the technology may be more system dependent, where the overall group could take a greater responsibility for the operation of a larger system". The application of this criterion to our case is quite self-evident: the Bu-Bu problem reflects an exclusive obsession for "collective technologies" in academic activities, forgetting – in fact failing – to create conditions wherein single scholars/teachers can make "a difference" by their individual skills and ideas.

The sixth point, "Evolutionary Capacity of Technology". consists of "the ability of the appropriate technology to continue to develop and expand beyond its originally intended function. [. . .] If the appropriate device is static (i.e., performs one function and cannot be altered) then although it may provide for a basic need at the present time it will be a relatively short-lived solution to a much larger problem. Wherever and whenever possible it is preferred that the appropriate technology allow for (i.e., have design characteristics) a continuation of development. That is, to have the capability to expand and be reconfigured to accomplish a higher volume of work and/or more sophisticated production processes". This is a very important point that again calls for a plea to the academic institutions that are so passionate about their process of corporatization. And it calls again for a reflection on the already-discussed notion of "time". Borrowing from the terminology of the Boston Consulting Group, more and more institutions seem only to be content with investments of the "cash cows" type (and when I say investment, I do not only mean financial ones). Plenty of actions (say, a degree program, a research project, a development strategy. . .) are launched with enormous time pressure that allows only for one option: immediate success. When that is not achieved, the action is erased, and replaced with another one – with a significant loss of time, energy and again financial resources. The new action has indeed its own costs, learning curves, management problems, and so forth: it does not just continue from where the previous action had failed. To take a significant example, in the universities I work or worked for, I witnessed more than one degree program killed after one year or two, because of a lack of students. Those programs had required important investments in terms of working hours, human resources and money, but they were not given the chance of a slow (or even false) start. The order was to close them, and one is always left wondering if the costs of starting a new program from scratch are really inferior to the losses of that old program's unsuccessful first year. In particular, that attitude shows a narrow-minded analysis of a problem which clearly has many variables at play: the program fails, therefore it is a bad program. What about bad timing, bad advertising, bad development, bad finalization...? And what if the program is simply not a cash cow, but an investment that will grow slowly but steadily? There is a reason why a classic time frame for an activity's development is (or used to be) five years. Playing with words, I would exactly use the acronym F.R.A.M.E. to summarize a development of the AT type:

- F (the first year) is for Fail. New ideas need to have the chance to fail at the beginning. It is a basic right for anything new. If a kid learns to ride a bicycle without training wheels, they have an absolute right to fall, and nothing is more useful than falling, at this stage.
- R (the second year) is for Repair. With the right for failure comes also the duty to repair. At this stage, the action is under analysis and assessment: one has to prove that they have understood the initial mistakes, react and fix them. It is a crucial moment in development. The kid in our example, now, puts a particular effort in understanding what, in their pedaling, was wrong and how they can improve. The academic institution has to be present in the action, and evaluate if the repairing stage is proceeding seriously and efficiently. If not, fair enough: there are, *now*, the conditions to erase the action.
- A (the third year) is for Achieve. If the "repair" stage was conducted properly, the third year will be the year when one can reap the fruits. Now, the kid can stand on the bicycle and pedal correctly. If, on the contrary, there is no "achievement", the institution has again the right to erase the action. As we can see, even in a 5-year plan development, there is no need to wait five years if the conditions are not ideal. The important point is not to invalidate an action after a first initial failure. Depending on the development of events, an institution can intervene in the second or the third year. Not later, and most of all, not earlier.
- M (the fourth year) is for Maintain. To achieve success is already difficult, but to maintain it is even more complicated. The fourth year is a maturity test: keeping up with the example of the degree program, the success in the students' enrollment is as bound to circumstantial variables as the failure. If the program had failed because, say, it was "a bad year" (whatever that means: financial crisis, temporary unfashionableness of a given topic, etc.), it may also have succeeded for the same, but opposite, reasons (a "good year" of

financial boom, fashionableness of a given topic, etc.). Back to the kid learning how to cycle, this is the time for them to show that they can now ride continuously, for a longer period, and so forth.
- E (the fifth year) is for Expand. Now, finally, we can apply the "Evolutionary Capacity of the Technology". Now it is the time for the action "to develop and expand beyond its originally intended function". Now the kid can ride bigger bicycles, on different grounds, different weather conditions, he can even participate in some race or competition.

5 Conclusions: Academic wars – a new hope?

This study was finalized during the COVID-19 lockdown. During this period, social media, particularly Facebook, thrived with interactive activities meant to kill time during the long days spent at home. Particularly popular were the so-called "challenges", invitations to post something funny, sentimental, even socially-significant, usually in form of list of favorite items. What was particularly intriguing is that pretty much all these challenges were humanistic in nature: ten favorite books, ten albums that influenced you the most, ten classic movies, etc. (for some reason, it always had to be "ten" of something. I cannot really think of any good reason for this, except Louis C.K.'s hilarious monologue on the "nine 11 deniers" – as opposed to the "9/11 deniers". Maybe those nine guys are onto something, after all). Whatever the topic, those challenges made it crystal clear that, in times of difficulties, it is arts and humanities we seek comfort in. We look for songs, not chemical formulas; novels, not mathematical equations. As I wrote a few years ago, "if natural sciences study and create what makes life possible, humanities study and create what makes life worthwhile" (Martinelli 2016: 60). I stand to those words completely, and I can see now that writing about the humanities is a rather appropriate work resolution for the Corona lockdown.

Since we concluded the last paragraph with the words "race" and "competition", both so dear to the Bu-Bu model, I would like to conclude this study with an injection of hope, an example of that counterculture-negation-appropriate technology that the semiotics of resistance seems to embody. As a matter of fact, yes, something is happening. Ghent University, in Belgium, set a great example of resistance, at the end of 2018. It is worthwhile to transcribe the whole press release, because it is, quite simply, a model of academic freedom that we encounter more and more rarely, these days:

> It is a common complaint among academic staff that the mountain of paperwork, the cumbersome procedures and the administrative burden have grown to proportions that are

barely controllable. Furthermore, the academic staff is increasingly put under pressure to count publications, citations and doctorates, on the basis of which funds are being allocated. The intense competition for funding often prevails over any possible collaboration across the boundaries of research groups, faculties and – why not – universities. With a new evaluation policy, Ghent University wants to address these concerns and at the same time breathe new life into its career guidance policy. Thus, the university can again become a place where talent feels valued and nurtured. We are transforming our university into a place where talent once again feels valued and nurtured.

With the new career and evaluation model for professorial staff, Ghent University is opening new horizons for Flanders. The main idea is that the academy will once again belong to the academics rather than the bureaucracy. No more procedures and processes with always the same templates, metrics and criteria which lump everyone together.

We opt for a radically new model: those who perform well will be promoted, with a minimum of accountability and administrative effort and a maximum of freedom and responsibility The quality of the individual human capital is given priority: talent must be nurtured and feel valued.

This marks the end of the personalized objectives, the annual job descriptions and the high number of evaluation documents and activity reports. Instead, the new approach is based on collaboration, collegiality and teamwork. All staff members will make commitments about how they can contribute to the objectives of the department, the education programmes, the faculty and the university.

The evaluations will be greatly simplified and from now on only take place every five years instead of every two or four years. This should create an 'evaluation break'.

We opt for a radically new model: those who perform well will be promoted, with a minimum of accountability and administrative effort and a maximum of freedom and responsibility. At the same time, we want to pay more attention to well-being at work: the evaluations of the supervisors will explicitly take into account the way in which they manage and coach their staff. The model must provide a response to the complaint of many young professors that quantitative parameters are predominant in the evaluation process. The well-known and overwhelming 'publication pressure' is the most prominent exponent of this. Ghent University is deliberately choosing to step out of the rat race between individuals, departments and universities. We no longer wish to participate in the ranking of people.

Through this model, we are expressly taking up our responsibility. In the political debate on the funding of universities and research applications, a constant argument is that we want to move away from purely competitive thinking that leaves too little room for disruptive ideas. The reply of the policy makers is of course that we must first do this within the university itself. This is a clear step in that direction, and it also shows our efforts to put our own house in order.

With this cultural shift, Ghent University is taking the lead in Flanders, and we are proud of it. It is an initiative that is clearly in accordance with our motto: 'Dare to Think'. Even more so, we dare to do it as well.

A university is above all a place where everything can be questioned.

Where opinions, procedures and habits are challenged. Where there is no place for rigidity.

I am absolutely convinced that in a few years' time we will see that this new approach has benefited the overall quality of our university and its people.

Rik Van de Walle, rector.

17/12/2018 (transcribed in Wals 2019)

The "radically new" model proposed by Ghent University is a perfect appropriate technology, as in fact it is not radically new, but it combines elements of innovation with elements of that tradition that the Bu-Bu earthquake had demolished. As a model in itself, it is that counterculture (culture B) that the institution is actively engaging into in order to provide a viable alternative to the dominant culture. Stepping out of the "rat race", finally, is the type of firm and vocal negation (starting from the expression chosen) that the academic community needs to hear in order react to the undead described by Gora and Whelan.

It is "a new hope", indeed: there are still Princesses Leila's, Luke Skywalker's and Han Solo's out there.

References

Bankov, Kristian. 2004. Infinite Semiosis and Resistance. In Eero Tarasti (ed.), *From Nature to Psyche*, 175–181. Helsinki/Imatra: International Semiotics Institute.
Downs, Anthony. 1992. *Stuck in Traffic: Coping with Peak-Hour Traffic Congestion*. Washington, DC: The Brookings Institution.
Eco, Umberto. 1997. *Kant e l'ornitorinco*. Milano: Bompiani.
Faulkner, Audrey O. & Maurice L. Albertson. 1986. Tandem use of hard and soft technology: An evolving model for third world village development. *International Journal of Applied Engineering Education* 2/2. 127–137.
Gora, Joseph & Andrew Whelan. 2010. Invasion of aca-zombies. *The Australian* 3 November 2010. Retrieved May 3, 2020 from http://www.theaustralian.com.au/higher-education/opinion/invasion-of-aca-zombies/story-e6frgcko-1225946869706.
Jevons, William S. 1865. *The Coal Question; An Inquiry Concerning the Progress of the Nation, and the Probable Exhaustion of Our Coal Mines*, 1 ed. London: Macmillan & Co.
Jump, Paul. 2015. Academics in the minority at more than two-thirds of UK universities. *Times Higher Education*. Retrieved May 3, 2020 from https://www.timeshighereducation.com/news/academics-minority-more-two-thirds-uk-universities.
Martinelli, Dario. 2009. The Ethic Imperative in Eero Tarasti's Semiotic Path: Reflecting on the Relationships between Resistance and Biocentrism. In Robert Hatten et al. (eds.), *A sounding of signs – Modalities and moments in music, culture and philosophy*, 321–337. Helsinki/Imatra: International Semiotics Institute.

Martinelli, Dario. 2016. *Arts and Humanities in Progress. A Manifesto of Numanities*. Berlin & New York: Springer.
Papanek, Victor. 1971. *Design for the Real World: Human Ecology and Social Change*. New York: Pantheon Books.
Peter, Laurence & Raymond Hull. 2009. *The Peter Principle: Why Things Always Go Wrong*. New York: Harperbusiness.
Putt, Archibald. 2006. *Putt's Law and the Successful Technocrat: How to Win in the Information Age*. New York: Wiley-IEEE Press.
Schmidt, Benjamin. 2013. Sapping Attention. Retrieved May 3, 2020 from http://sappingattention.blogspot.com/2013_06_01_archive.html.
Schumacher, Ernst F. 1973. *Small Is Beautiful: Economics as if People Mattered*. Vancouver, BC: Hartley & Marks.
Sorensen, Diana. 2013. Addressing a Decline in Humanities Enrollment. *Harvard Magazine*, June 6, 2013. Retrieved May 3, 2020 from http://harvardmagazine.com/2013/06/reinvigorating-the-humanities.
Tahir, Tariq. 2010. The irresistible rise of academic bureaucracy. https://www.theguardian.com/education/2010/mar/30/academic-bureaucracy-rise-managers-higher-education (retrieved 3 May 2020)
Tarasti, Eero. 2005. Vastarinnan Semiotiikkaa: Oleminen, Muisti, Historia – Merkkien Vastavirta [Semiotics of resistance: being, memory, history – the countercurrent of signs]. *Synteesi* (1). 2–29.
Tarasti, Eero. 2015. *Sein und Schein. Explorations in Existential Semiotics*. Berlin & New York: Mouton de Gruyter.
Terras, Marisa et al. 2013. The humanities matter!. Retrieved May 3, 2020 from http://4humanities.org/wpcontent/uploads/2013/07/humanitiesmatter300.pdf.
Wals, Arjen. 2019. "We no longer wish to participate in the ranking of people" Ghent University wants to become a place where talent feels valued and nurtured. https://transformativelearning.nl/2019/01/07/we-no-longer-wish-to-participate-in-the-ranking-of-people-ghent-university-wants-to-become-a-place-where-talent-feels-valued-and-nurtured/ (retrieved 27 April 2020)
Wicklein, Robert C. 1998. Designing for appropriate technology in developing countries. *Technology in Society Journal* 20/3. 371–375.
Wicklein, Robert C. 2004. Design criteria for sustainable development in appropriate technology. Paper presented in the PATT-14 Conference, Albuquerque, New Mexico, March 18–20, 2004.

Terri Kupiainen
The modes of being inside (or outside) the value fragment: The application of Tarasti's theory of subject, transcendence and modalities of self to the consumer research

Abstract: The text interpretation framework of this research is grounded on the Eero Tarasti's existential semiotics theory, especially on the theory of subject and modalities. The dialogue between existential subject and consuming society is specifically interesting from the consumer research's point of view, because marketing induce consumer experiences and creates value related objects as transcends to be consumed. The consumer also marks out the path for transcendence in different situations and existential life-worlds for the markets. There is a wide consensus between researches that human beings are living in fragmented consumer society, in which they are open and free, or even compelled, to take many identities. Fragmentation is related to ideologies in society, and their purpose is to represent power structures, a diversity of views, and oppositional forces in society. Subject's existential position concerning valorisation and basis of their ethical judgements of values, also include philosophical questions that are often implicit and unreflected in a consumer understanding. Subjects may use values in pluralistic, realistic, hedonistic, traditionalistic or universalistic way in everyday life, for instance. When the subject define his or her own existence as an experience which is often unique for a moment, the need to understand what it means to be inside or outside the value system is important, as we live in the fragmented value system and ontology of some supreme ontology that are not well observed or easily discovered.

Keywords: personal values, consumer experience, value fragment, modalities, existential semiotics

1 Introduction

The concept of value is centrally embedded in the theory of existential semiotics (Tarasti 2012: 316–343; 2004: 50–115, 198; 2000:18–20) and in the consumer culture theory as well (Sassatelli 2007: 32–52, 147–162). Shalom Schwartz – one of the most sited social-psychologists in consumer research— proposes that value types form an integrated system, values represent stability, attribute openness, transcend the welfare of human beings, and refer to social contacts and relations in situations in which values are relevant (Schwartz 1996:16–17; 22). Schwartz distinguishes universal values from narrower concepts like norms and attitudes that usually refer to specific actions, objects or situations (Schwartz 2007: 171). Rokeach (1973: 5) defines values as an enduring belief that one mode of conduct or end-state of existence is preferable to an opposing mode of conduct or end-state of existence. We recognise that words relevance, conduct, and existence are previously related to values. The headline in Brown's book chapter (1998) *"We're on the road to nowhere, come on inside"* opens a totally different picture on a postmodern intuitions, condition of life, attitude, and value, in which being inside is the most important thing. This is important point of view and obviously concern several other aspects of human societies. No matter if we are thinking postmodern or the later, and perhaps more actual periods of consumer culture.

Consequently, my interest and the research intention concern the modes of a subject's being inside in fragments of a bigger value system (specifically in Finland) and sources of subject's transcendence. I refer these modes of inside/outside to local ontologies. Ontology refers to philosophical investigation of being (Craig 2000: 645). The local ontology is a basis for subjective valorisation and the ethics of judgement cultural things and entities. A person often makes intuitive and situational assertion about the value system or its entities without ontological commitment or being inside or outside a value system (Tarasti 2004:175–193, Jubein 2000: 644). Subjective and existential ontologies and consumer's commitment are described in the literature of consumer research. For example in edited books Cova, Kozinets and Shankar (2007); Beckman and Elliot (2002); Ratneshwar, Mick and Huffman (2000); Holbrook (1999); Brown, Doherty and Clarke (1998); Stern (1998); Brown and Turley (1997).

Specifically, by value fragment, I mean subject's existential positions concerning valorisation and basis of ethical judgements of values e.g. affirmation of pluralism, realism, hedonism, traditionalism, or universalism. These –isms are not conceived as power structures but refer ontologies of different *Daseins* such as affirmed by the autonomous subject. In my mind, these positions refer also to Tarasti's concept of existential *Dasein*, in which consumers live their lives and transcend the objects of desire as the postmodern theory of consumption supposes (Bauman 2008: 57). The difference between my approach and, for instance, how Kahle and Timmer (1993) see values is clear because the ethics is eliminated on the value concept defined in *The Social Adaptation Theory*. According to Rokeach (1993: 5), "A value system is an enduring organisation of beliefs concerning preferable modes of conduct or end states of existence along a continuum of relative importance. In value system, values should be ordered in priority with respect to other values".

It may also be worth of mentioning that my intention concerning writing of this essay originates also on the intuition that the meaning of values is not easy to understand from the basis of conventional consumer research methods because people do not use concepts when they answer research questions, and even more and more extensively mirror values and lifestyles against the smaller groups they belong (Cova et. al. 2007: 3–23). By means of existential semiotic theory it would be possible to illustrate consumers' value judgements and/or reasons for difficulties to speak same languages between value fragments. Especially the theories of subject and modalities have potential advantages in the context.

2 Tarasti's existential semiotics theory and existentialism in consumer research

Central concepts in the consumption theory are consuming subject, subjectivity (human being as a subject), authenticity, existential ontology, local ontology, existential autonomy, existential encounter, existential departure, existential angst (subject's inner conflict) and existential care, for example (Elliot 1997; Jensen and Lindberg 2002: 213–232; Beverland and Farrelly 2010: 839). The theory of postmodern consumption supposes that the markets (e.g. people's lifestyles and preferences) are fragmented. There is obviously a consensus between researches that human beings are living in a fragmented consumer society, in which they are open and free but at the same time compelled to take many identities. Styles shape manners of being in remarkable way, and profusion on images confuse individual ways of being and traditional group identities (Maffesoli 1996: 37–49, 127–129). Typically, the word existential is related to specific or very strong sensory experiences (Pine and Gilmore 1998:102). However, the meaning of concept existential is not same as a hedonic experience, even if they sometime may be in close relationships with each other in the hedonic ethics.

Researches also mention that, the importance of pre-reflective structures of the life-world (existentials) have been frequently overlooked in the recent consumer research (Thompson 1998: 130–131). Consumption is defined as an active, collective behaviour, and a system of learned values (Baudrillard 2005: 81). The existentialism contains the conscious reflection of authenticity of selected life-worlds in relation to the inner self and the society in the context (Caru and Cova 2007: 5–7, Beverland and Farrelly 2010: 838–855). Distance between subject and object transcends desires (Belk, Ger and Askegaard 2000). Values relate objects and subject's desires through object's values. Therefore, the value-object relationship is an important concept in consume value theory. Holbrook's theory of consumer value defines values as one dimensional, preferential, changing and paradigmatic (1999: 5). The one common thing recognised by consumer and consumer value theory is a shared passion towards objects. Belk (1998: 41): *"The reason is the great discounter, while indulging libidinal passion as well as resisting such passion in favour of greater self-transcendent pleasure, both embrace enchantment. Many types of passions —positive or negative— involve the domination of reason by emotional state of enchantment and attendant state of desire"*. However, it is not easy to see clearly whether marketing as the organisation of diverse purposes can never be the very subject or object in the meaning of the claim that the consumer consumes ads, lifestyles and other images rather than products. Therefore marketing turns to the consumer that marks out the path for transcendence in different situations and existential life-worlds (Jensen and Lindberg 2002: 30–32; Cherrier 2005: 128–129).

Existentials in a consume research and Tarasti's existential semiotic theory have similar roots in philosophy. Hirschman and Holbrook (1992: 25, 62) mention Heidegger's and Derrida's and Greimas's works; Elliott (1997) Sartre's, Derrida's and Kristeva's; and Tarasti (2000:17–20) Kant's, Hegel's, Kierkegaard's, Jasper's, Heidegger's, Arendt's, Sartre's, de Beauvoir's, Marcel's and Wahl's philosophies, for instance. The concept of existential subject is central in Tarasti's theory. Subject performs transcendental acts (Tarasti 2000:10, 19, 76–83; 2009: 1757–1766). Existentials in a consumer research relate mainly to the methodological positioning of research (Thompson 1998: 127–155). As far as I know the existential semiotics theory is not widely applied in the area of consumer research. Eero Tarasti's builds on the European tradition in the philosophy, and for instance Algirdas Julien Greimas's theory of subject and modalities in semiotics (Tarasti 2000). There are two fundamental existential categories in the existential semiotics: *Dasein* and transcendence, which are ontological in nature (Tarasti 2009: 1756). *"Dasein is simply the world in which we as subjects live, surrounded by other subjects and objects with which we try to come to terms"*. . . .[ ] *"Transcendence is the realm beyond the concrete world of Dasein which our subject can reach via two acts, negation and affirmation"* (Tarasti 2009: 1756). Tarasti defines these and other central concepts through his works (Tarasti 2000, 2004, 2009, 2012, for instance).

The concept of transcendence is known in other value definitions too (Schwartz 1992; Kahle 1983), but it is used in narrower meaning referring to consumer value preferences, undefined desires, or desires of value related objects. (Beverland and Farrelly 2010: 839) identify also the negative transcendence, the phenomenon in which subject uncovers inner cores of transcendent meanings before affirmation (Tarasti 2000: 78). By transcendent is referred to the fact that values, as beliefs are not manifest in the material world. Rather, values transcend ideas on possible, virtual and desired worlds and lifestyles containing different beliefs, ideals, norms, sensory experiences, ethical principles, aesthetics and ideologies, for instance. Accordingly, consumers' lives are described as narratives (Escalas and Bettman 2000), and their unconscious is activated by metaphors (Coulter and Zaltman 2000) that encourage subject's transcendence by identity supporting or opposing actors, such as brand names, positions, claims and functions related to values, morals and attitudes (Luedicke and Giesler 2007). Basic values are supposed relate to consumption through objects. Objects portray values by their qualities, attributes and emotions induced by products, brands and images (Holbrook and Hirschman 1993; Holbrook 1999).

In a certain moment, existential *Dasein* and subject's being inside the value system is mental category, but it appears as more than mere interpretant, because its values call for action and contain all potential for transcendence from the very beginning. There is also an existential paradox that the human being need to become conscious about that the being in *Dasein* is incomplete (Tarasti 2009: 1756). How authentic subject's *Dasein* is in relation between self and society is subject's mental process. Subject's authenticity can be retained by controlling of communicative or material transcendent calling for actions (Arnould and Price 2001). The level of frustration and tension is then signs of lacking authenticity. Sometimes system's internal tension becomes too high and the system becomes disturbed.

3 Modes of subject in *Dasein*

Tarasti's theory of subject combines the spheres of individual and collective subjectivities (Figure 1). The individual subject is conceptualised as MOI and social subject as SOI. *"Subject develops in two different directions or movements among coordinates of semiotic square portraying a subject's mind. Movement goes from the concrete and corporeal towards abstract and intelligible"* (Tarasti 2009: 1765–1767).

Tarasti's model comprises of four categories: 1) Being-in-myself (M1) represents bodily ego, energy, desire, Khora (perhaps senses, biological reality). Its modality is endotactic will; 2) Being-for-myself (M2). It notices the lack in its existence and becomes aware of itself and transcendence. Its modality is endotactic can; 3) being-in-itself (S1). The category is the transcendental category. It refers to the norms, ideas, and values, which are purely conceptual and virtual, and potentialities of a subject, which can either actualize them or not. Its modality is exotactic must; 4) Being-for-itself (S2) means the norms, ideas, and values as realized by the conduct of subject in *Dasein*. Those abstract entities appear here as applied values, choices, and realizations, which often will be far away from original transcendental entities. Its modality is exotactic know. (Almost literally referred to Tarasti 2009:1765–1767).

Figure 1: The categories of subject are being in *Dasein* (Tarasti 2010b, 2009: 1765–1767).

4 The problem of value ontology related to subjects being inside (or outside) the value system

The word ontology is used to refer to the philosophical investigation of existence or being (Craig: 645). It may also refer to the realm of metaphysics that addresses both the nature and essential characteristics of being and things that exist and ontological commitment on them. A value system is a social system also in Tarasti's theory, values are social in their basic nature and transcendent as well. Subject either affirms system's values or not (Tarasti 2000: 30–31).

Hofstede defines values as 1) implicit (values that are embedded in system and can be understood in the context, for example in practices, but which are not clear or easy to define for all other subjects, e.g. outside the system), or 2) explicit (values that are manifest and can be explained for others). A value system is the collection of values by which an individual or a group can be distinguished, for instance, desired goals, available modes of conduct, means and preferred end-states when executing values. Individual subject is supposed to belong to the sphere of some distinguishable value system according to which values she/he prefers.

Generally, value research has been interested in individual and collective value systems and their comparison. Traditional systems are supposed to be collective and opposite of individualistic systems (Hofstede 2001: 150–151). A social system has a stabilizing effect on human behaviour. For instance, hedonic ethics is typical for individualistic value systems, and not collective value systems. Though the concept of value system is not clear in the consumption research, most often by consumption society is referred to a post-modern system rather than modern or traditional system Bauman 2008: 52–53). There are also several other value related systems, such as ideologies, ideal systems, symbolic systems, realistic systems, ethical systems and moral systems, for instance. Ideologies are typically one value systems. Van Raaij (1998) suggests that one value systems are weak, which is one reason that the modern broke down and the postmodern was born.

By fragmentation is referred to fragment's ideologies in society. As Elliott and Ritson (1997) propose: *"The ideology's purpose in fragmentation is to represent the oppositional forces within society as being disparate and unworthy of support in their challenge to dominant powers in society"* For instance, in Finland, the individualism is a dominant value orientation (Schwartz 2006). The suffix –ism refers to some ideology or tendency, but ism is also related to time and history, because some 'isms' may, in a certain moment, be more actual or even modern than other isms. A value can relate ideological, political, ethical or moral system in 'isms', for instance, the conception of how society functions.

Hence, the individualism is thought to elevate marketing ideologies beyond the influence of more traditional socially-oriented ideologies and confer on it the status of super-ideology over the traditional values (Elliott and Ritson 1997). Generally, ideologies are such systems that ground on a known doctrine, concerning democracy, religions, moral virtues or aesthetics, for instance. *"The origin of ideology stems from an acceptance that ideas related to society as a whole does not emerge autonomously in individual member of that society but have had a centre of formation, irradiation, dissemination and persuasion. This centre of formation represents an axis of power, which attempts to create and maintain a superior position within society by constraining, and controlling the ideas that individuals hold"* (Elliott and Ritson 1997).

However, the previously mentioned is not the only form of being 'inside or outside' the society and its values (in the meaning of dichotomy traditional vs. modern). For instance, the theory of contemporary consumption society grounds on a horizontal consumer democracy, autonomy, and subject's existential authenticity in relation to social, including consuming (Cova, Kozinets and Shankar 2007: 21). Therefore, from existentialism's and specifically, existential semiotics' point of view, a value fragment might be the transcendental form of ideal lifeworld, e. g. its values and functions, but it is not necessarily asking how well subject performs or manages to realize fragment's values in the self's *Dasein*, e.g. in a real-life context (Raz 2008:43–49; Tarasti 2009:1767–1768). Fragments only exist because of their different existential ontology and the semantic distance between local ontologies.

A semantic distance, for example, between two codes, forms the basis for interpretive communities (Elliott and Ritson 1997). As consumers subjectively interpret the same texts inside the code system, the end result will be meaning which is very similar to other consumers' subjective interpretations of the same text (Elliott and Ritzon 1997: 206). A polysemy in values indicates fragmentation of codes in interpretations and social nature of interpretations. The subject's connection to their social position in values ensures that their subjective interpretation corresponds with other subjects' interpretation of the same value and interpretive community. The concept of interpretive community transcends social boundaries as readers take up their memberships of different social groups (Elliot and Ritzon 1997: 206). However, Elliot and Ritson (1997: 206) note that interpretive conventions provide a significant limitation to the polysemic potential of the text. No matter are we seeing them from inside or outside of value ontology. Next, I try to describe more closely, what the existential subject's being inside or outside the ontology would probably mean in the context of pluralism, realism, hedonism, traditionalism, and universalism.

4.1 Value pluralism

Raz (2008: 43, 45) poses that value pluralism has been a familiar doctrine in recent times. Its core is the affirmation that 1) there are many distinct values that are not merely manifestations of one supreme value; 2) there are incompatible values in a sense that they cannot all be realized in the life of a single individual, nor can they be realized by single society (when we consider values that can be instantiated by societies), 3) the spirit of pluralism can be accommodated within a framework of social dependences thesis, a) because it can embrace local relativism, or b) because evaluative thought is genre dependent. The social dependence thesis holds that social practices do not limit the application or validity of value. "Values are contradictory when one yields the conclusion that something is good, and the other the conclusion that that very thing is, in virtue of the same properties, without value, or even bad" (Raz 2008:44).

According to Raz (2008: 43), it is possible to affirm diverse and contradictory values, but certain values can be successfully realised only in a community that has coherent values. Therefore it is not obvious that values will function according to any universal principle in a pluralistic *Dasein*, even if Raz is right that importance of values and how they can be implemented is not one and the same thing. Pluralism also argues that modern values are not better than the values of past times. Hence, it would not be right to say that postmodern, in general level, is better than traditionalism, or traditionalism is better than hedonism. Pluralism differentiates between values that depend on value sustaining practices and values that depend on a practical situation where values are realized Raz (2008: 34).

The pluralism in consumption is commonly affirmed value ontology in Finland (Kupiainen 2008: 53). Many pluralists have a considerable high socio-economic and professional status, which in many cases is not based on formal education. In general level, value pluralist has a positive attitude towards values. As a concept, value pluralism is the idea that there are several values which may be equally correct, good and fundamental even if they are in conflict with each other (Raz 2008: 44). Conflicting values are not problematic in pluralism because pluralism postulates that in incompatible values may be incommensurable in the sense that subject has not any objective criterion for the ordering of values (the pluralist compared for instance to the hedonist, who is able to order values by sensory experiences). Pluralism as an attitude is functional in practices, but it is not conceptually or experientially well defined (Raz 2008: 39–42).

The subject's pluralistic ethics is not a common theme in the field of consumer research, even if it is referred to in the theory of the postmodern consumer. However, Slater (1997: 83–84) mentions that pluralisation is typical for post-traditional societies in which the idea of culture is a response. Hence, secure value systems are replaced by pluralistic identities based on changing situations, different roles and symbolism. Slater (1997: 83–84, 95, 206) maintains: *"Increasingly unanchored in tradition, religion, law etc., identity can only emerge from the choice. . . . [ ] modernity involves a pluralisation of life Worlds in which each individual has to negotiate multiple and contradictory identities as they traverse different public and privet spheres, each with their different roles, norms etc."*

We may easily see that modalities as exotactic knowing and endotactic being-able-to are clearly indicated in the texts about pluralism. It also implies the kind of competencies that are the most valued. Subject's endotactic will (M1) and exotactic must as a normative social component (S1) are clearly on the background in the kind of pluralism described. Thompson's (2000) concept *tactical flexibility* is also a very illustrating concept in this context. The pluralist is priced for pluralism by pluralistic society. Slater (1998: 208) continues: *"Pluralist therefore asserts formal values (reason, equality, freedom) that regulate, constrain or frame the diversity of desires and interests. By contrast, postmodernism asserts relativism"*. Pluralism is ideal (even utopian) value system for many subjects. It is the idea of ideal social system, and personal situation in which everything is available without giving up anything. Subject's existential value pluralism may be sensitive to antinomial value conflict because of different meanings in values. However, Pipping comes to the conclusion that our genre-based evaluation of values is the key point in avoiding the antinomy that might naturally lead to relativism and existential conflict (Pipping 2008: 97). Therefore, the pluralist's 'counterfactual auto-communication' is eased up when a pragmatic situation changes.

4.2 Value realism

Value realism is seldom explicitly mentioned in the literature of consumer research. Therefore, my abductive approach is to handle it as the opposite fragment of pluralism. The basic idea in realism is that all issues that exist and how they are, are independent of us and the way we receive information on them (Greig 2000). In semantic realism, the meaning of sentence is understood by its truth content. In other words, situations that are possible to achieve can be achieved only if they are real. The opposite of realism is antirealism. Realism and antirealism differ in that they rest on opposite theories on meaning. An antirealist (pluralist), for instance, argues that meanings can be understood only by referring to the assertability–condition e.g. situation, where we could be assured about the meaning of the argument, even if there is no concrete evidence on it (Greig 2000: 744–745).

According to Fromm (1990: 90), a realist sees only the surface features of things; the world which is manifest for subject. Therefore subjectivity in *Dasein* of realist means that reality is conceived in a specific way and things are handled on a concrete level. A realist has a tendency to see reality as a reflection of subject's inner world and therefore the deepness and perspective may disappear. Fromm (1990 [1947]: 746) concludes: *"Realism seems to be the very opposite of insanity and yet it is only its complement". . . [ ] the normal human being is capable of elating himself to the world simultaneously by perceiving it as it is and by conceiving it enlivened and enriched by his own powers"*. For Fromm, virtue is more important than value because of its progressiveness and energy. When conceiving realism, this is important because Fromm has an opinion that productivity (e.g. a particular mode of relatedness to the world) is not easy to maintain in realism. Also, Tarasti (2004: 110–113) refers to realism proposing that the principle of reality (in general) is an external element in relation to *Dasein* and its danger is the lack of subjective meaning and stagnation.

One thing that obviously relates to realism is the drawing of a simplified view of the world. In my empirical findings, the profusion of possibilities and richness of narratives characterize pluralists' texts, whereas realist's narratives are less colourful and plain. Certainly, realism has something to do with objective and subjective reality, but realism is not grounded on immediate personal experiences because it can say something about things that realist has no personal experiences. Lyotard (1984: 75) for example, proposes that the demands of reality are integrity, simplicity, and communicability. Realism is not adaptive to all values in the same meaning as pluralism is.

In existential semiotic terms, realist's self (M1) is related to the concrete external world of the social (S2). It is an adult's concern of meaning of being-in-itself and the discovery of an ontological framework of external reality as expressed by Giddens (1991: 48). Difference between realist and hedonist is that in realism the focal point of experience is externalized in social practices and in *"a role of objective eye"*, especially. The modalities of this ontology are being-in-itself and knowing what is a practical truth in average social practices. Also, Beverland and Farrelly (2010: 845–850) describe narratives that might fit well with realism and how marketing messages may lead to a negative transcendence. The insistence of authenticity is obvious because *whatever a thing or an issue is, the most important is that it looks like as it really is.*

4.3 Hedonism

Hedonism is the doctrine that says that pleasure is good. But the claim that pleasure is to be maximized is not commonly affirmed in the theories of hedonism (Gosling 2000: 336). Holbrook and Hirschman (1982) give impression about hedonism claiming that fantasy and fun are valuable as an intrinsic value and end-state. This is the basic definition of hedonic ethics (Feldman 2004: 25–29). Hedonistic means anything that belongs to hedonism. A hedonist is an individual enjoying good life as it is defined by hedonism. For instance, the discussion about bodily pleasure alternates from the view that pleasure is to be avoided to the view that immediate bodily pleasure is to be sought (Feldman 2004: 30). According to Gosling (2000: 336), there are three varieties of hedonism: psychological hedonists, evaluative hedonists and reflective hedonists. Psychological hedonists hold that we can pursue only pleasure and agents' actions are a function of what they think will maximize their overall pleasure. Evaluative hedonists state that pleasure is what we ought to pursue and its difficulties are how we can establish certain ends as desirable. Reflective hedonists maintain that it is what on reflection gives value to any pursuit.

Hedonism is related to the variety of sensory pleasures and the total hedonic pleasure can be maximized via many episodic pleasures, for instance (Feldman 2004: 129–130). Hedonism is associated with the post-traditional economic ethos. According to Slater (1998: 98), hedonism is the signifying feature of mass consumption. It is *"A cult of the hedonistic self, individuals defined through their desires"* (Slater 1998: 129–130). In consumer theory, related concepts to hedonism are a hedonic response, hedonic enjoyment and hedonic pleasure (Holbrook and Hirschman 1993:274). In a way, many types of hedonic behaviours may be conceived as a bad behaviour. An archetypal hedonist consumer is a master of profusion and luxurious living, devoted shopper and pleasure seeker. In other words, hedonist is enthusiastic on everything new, noise, exciting and stimulating. On a contrary to the traditionalist, a hedonist is a marketer's dream with his/her endless and undiscovered desires.

To me, hedonism is appearing like one of the most well-developed theories on what different value words mean in hedonism. The idea of hedonic freedom, for example, is illustrated by Michael Flocker (2004:13); *If you avoid all things pleasurable, you will live a long and happy life. But can happiness really be found scampering along on a treadmill in a smoke-free environment, Palm Pilot in hand, chasing after the capitalist ideal? Are sixty-hour works weeks, building stock portfolios and a packaged agenda really the key to the good life? I think not."* Flocker (2004: 106) lists also hedonic imperatives: a) be true to yourself throughout your life journey, b) live in anticipation of being judged by others, or 3) live from moment to moment because denying of one's true nature can lead to disappointment and opportunities lost. This is what Maffesolli called the interest of the present times in general.

Hedonists are typically the most pleasure-seeking and experience-driven value fragment and the group ontology. The hedonist gravitates toward pleasures and enjoys that which feels good (Flocker 2004: 151). The food is important for a hedonist. Hedonists are motivated by concrete sensory experiences (not abstractions or abstract concepts) which maximize their pleasure over pain, and effort or being moderate (Feldman 2004: 8).

Typically hedonists need concrete products and other desirable things which symbolize and induce pleasure. Hedonic experiences create meanings other than practical and functional values, but in relation to foods and eating, many of hedonists still behave similarly as realists (Kupiainen 2008). However, many of hedonists are interested in novel information, new products, spicy tastes and exotic foods more than realists. For hedonists, food and cooking is often a hobby. Otherwise, they are not interested in preparing traditional meals and dishes at all. Hedonists are also interested in how foods and their ingredients influence body aesthetics because how the body looks like is also the synonym for the health in its extreme form of meaning.

From the existential semiotic point of view, the hedonic ethic functions in an area of endotactic will (M1) and endotactic can (M2), probably best in the area of primary processes as Flocker confess. In sociological term, hedonism is functional for society, but dysfunctional for an individual because social does not necessarily function in an area of subject's pleasure (Slater 1998;). Also, Feldman (2004: 200–203) emphasizes that the concepts of hedonism and hedonic ethics are wide especially if they are perceived from the individual pleasure's point of view. Sociologists confer that one of its advantages is that the modern type of hedonistic ethics contains class consciousness surrounded hedonism's special competences and resources to receive different kinds of arts and aesthetic values (Slater 1998).

4.4 Traditionalism

Bauman (2008, 46) notes that traditional consumer is a nightmare for the market economy as *"guided by yesterday's familiar needs, gladly closing their eyes and plugging their ears against the blandishment and baits of the commodity market to be allowed to follow old routines and stick to their habits, would spell the death knell of the society of the consumer's, of the consumer industry and consumer market"*. The former translated in the language of existential semiotics, clearly, what Bauman says is that marketers' efforts to trigger transcendence (negation-offer-affirmation-process) in the *Dasein* of traditional subjects are unsuccessful because seldom their messages contain anything that is valued by traditional consumers.

Slater (1998) writes in his book *Consumer Culture and Tradition* about tradition and traditional societies, but not a single word is mentioned about traditionalism. Clearly, the authenticity of consumption relates to tradition more than any other value fragment in sociology (Slater 1998: 79–80). Status identity defined by the structures of tradition (social class, gender, ethnicity) are different from the production of identities in modern or postmodern.

Identity in tradition is defined by tradition is the claim, which according Sagi (2008: 7–8) raises the question: *"Is there room for subjectivity, if subject's identity is defined by tradition and is same as a tradition's identity?"* Sagi's answer is yes, tradition is anything transmitted or handed down from the past to the present and for people living in tradition the tradition is self-evident (Sagi 2008: 14). Sagi also reminds that freedom and the pain of alienation are both modern's definitions of tradition having no clear meaning in traditionalism or in tradition. Traditionalism cannot be described as modern or postmodern because nationalism, democracy, or religion is not valued by them, for instance, but which are essential for tradition.

Tradition is not bound to one perspective because there are different kind of traditions and traditional practices. Therefore, it is difficult to define tradition in general. For instance, Shils (1981) names several types of traditions, as social traditions, the tradition of modernity, and religious traditions. Cultural traditions as classical design, food traditions, and gastronomy are examples of living traditions. However, traditionalism can be the strong ideological form through which the milder forms of traditions are preferred, prioritised or affirmed (Sagi 2008: 37–38). Sagi (2008: 10–11) clearly differentiates tradition from traditionalism and notes that traditionalism supposes a higher level of affirmation that a traditional ontology does not apply. Living in traditionalism means different things than willingness and ability to live in tradition. Specifically, if traditionalism is denied, the reflective people can return to tradition (Sagi 2008: 10). Return to tradition without traditionalism's strict obligations and doctrine is possible according to Sagi. A post-traditional subject can see tradition as dynamic and changing and capture its genius in dialogue. According to traditionalism, tradition comes from history but this does not mean living in traditionalism. Sagi (2008: 10–11) notes further: *"For modern, reflective, sceptical, and autonomous person the path of return to traditionalism is quite obviously closed, because traditionalism is an invention portraying tradition incorrectly"*. For Sagi tradition represents present and future, but not past and this is a new ontological ground for present and future. It seems to me now that it would be better to use the word tradition instead of traditionalism at least in the context of consumer research.

Giddens (1991: 48) saw tradition as follows: *"Tradition has a key role in articulating action and ontological frameworks; tradition offers an organising medium of social life specifically geared to ontological precepts"*. According Giddens tradition orders time in a manner that it restricts the openness of counterfactual futures (Giddens 1991: 48). From existential semiotics' point of view, the subject living in tradition is developing in areas of exotactic must (S1) and endotactic can (M2). Endotactic primary self (M1) and self in diverse social practices (S2) are less important sources of self in a tradition because its ontology is not anchored in mastery as in modernism or in indulgence as in postmodernism. Then the ontological knowledge and self-understanding in traditionalism and tradition are based on the trust on the structure of affirmed tradition.

4.5 Universalism

Like realism, universalism is the local ontology reserving very little attention in the consumer theory, especially in the textbook literature. Universalism refers to something which is common and necessary to all universes and shared by all individuals. Universalism in ethics may be identified with claims about form, scope or content of ethical principles, or the idea that ethical judgement applies to principles rather than to particular cases (O´Neill 2000: 907). If value is universal, this means that all value words that belong to universalism have coherent meaning among the people and nations (concern only western societies Schwartz 1992).

According to Bauman universalism is an elusive concept that means almost everything. It refers stable and peaceful relationships, fairness of transactions, attention to partners, fairness in general, care, sharing, equity and harmony between systems, dependence on other human beings, dependence on nature and its ecosystem, and so on. For Bauman universalism appears as an opposite on the modern egalitarian autonomy, and exemplifies and refers to the metaphor "*a postmodern tourist's aesthetic capacity*" (Bauman 2005: 240–249). Bauman concludes that universalism as a sociological term is not easy to find, describe, remember and achieve. Universalism belongs to the history of good and bad. Therefore it is difficult to find people that share its conceptions from good and bad and, specifically, concepts of togetherness that would connect such people that share the conception of good and bad (Bauman 2005). Universalism does not assert the ideas of modernity. For example, the ideas of egalitarian commitments to the development, where humans have been able to cut off their cultural and traditional roots and loyalty, and raise themselves above the rest of nature. In the modern cultural value system universalism has remained marginal. It has not been fashionable or trendy. Bauman (2005: 49–50) concludes: "*Universalistic actions lead precarious existences among the plurality of sovereign authorities. Consistently universalistic can be only a power bent on indentifying the human kind as a whole with the population subjected to its present or prospective rule. Such power is unlikely to emerge in a world organised according to the principles of national states*". Nevertheless, single values that belong to universalism are highly ranked in same other local ontologies like pluralism and hedonism.

The knowledge of universalism can be approached also via humanistic ethics. This means that we have to choose between good and bad. Ethical principles in humanism are general and are not concerning individual cases. For instance, nations, subject itself, groups of people, or even human beings alone because universalists admit that human beings are part of wider universe and system of ecology. In humanism, good is to approving of life and virtue is to take responsibility from one's existence. Value is what is desired as a good and its measure is a will (Fromm 1990: 14). This can be compared to radical subjectivism, but whether it is a new code applicable to universalism remains unclear in this context.

In some previous research using the existential phenomenology framework, universal principles are conceived literally in meaning global. Moreover, the ethical consumption is perceived contextually and subjectively as an activity in which several intentional activities combine. Universalism as a value ontology is not typically included in the ethics of consumption (Cherrier 2005: 128). Universal values like benevolence and altruism can be found also in many of the value fragments, but they are highly valued also among universalists (Kupiainen 2008: 50). The proposition that there are several local ontologies within which ethical consumption takes place does not mean that ethical consuming would not be the most typical for universalists.

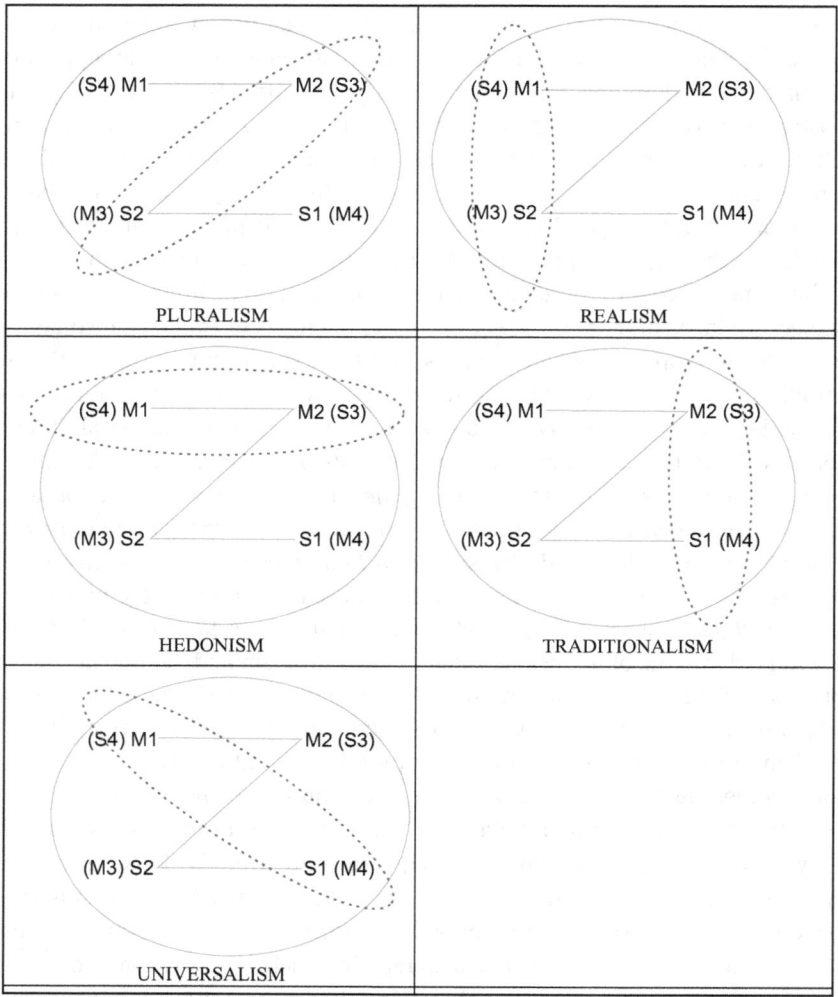

Figure 2: The value ethics and ontology of subject's *Dasein* from a fragmentation perspective. An application of Tarasti's (2009) theory of subject. Two most important modes and modalities are marked with an oval circle.

For instance, when Cherrier's (2005: 128–133) research is read from existential semiotics perspective, the analysis of Jim's case illustrate that pursue to authenticity in personal life might well be a typical ethical decision for a universalist. On a contrary, in Alex's, John's and Vivian's cases, the ethical decision and activity described might relate with pluralistic value ethics (and probably do) because the consumption decisions are related to modalities endotactic can (M2) and exotactic knowing (S2). Then they might be primarily motivated by members of their social circles. In universalism subject's modalities relate to endotactic willing and loosely to exotactic must, but not to modalities exotactic knowing or endotactic being able to. The difference between universalism and pluralism is clear. On the other hand, universalism refers to the non-hedonistic world-view and is not clearly anchored to the rules of traditions either.

The concluding results of text analysis are presented in Figure 2. Research indicates that values in subject's *Dasein* appear in different modes and combinations.

5 Concluding words

In existential semiotics the individual subject is the focus of all knowledge, understanding, and empirical subject exists in all communication, everyday activities and life situations (Tarasti 2009: 1757–1768). Consume researchers are convinced that individuals are products of culture, and their social groupings and culture cannot be differentiated from the subject because a culture is not the system of abstract values, which exist independently without people (Mooij 2004: 26–27.). How this dialogue develops in consumption context depends also on the process, where subject evaluates other people's values and what kind of information and knowledge she or he uses when evaluating the importance of the transcendent values from their own existential point of view (Tarasti 2009: 1768). In consumption context, the individual's inner world encounters external world's reality or perceived reality. The ontology that emerges differently in subject's lives, depends on, for instance, how subject use sensory experiences, appropriate social norms, or appropriated ethical principles as an information source. To conclude, the value fragments —according to text analysis— differ from each other by their local ontology and modalities related to each specific ontology (Table 1).

Table 1: Value fragments and their local ontology.

EXISTENTIAL DASEIN	LOCAL ONTOLOGY (The fundamentals of being in the world)
Value pluralism	Ability to comply (adapt), social convention and trust that subject's identity is carried by the social
Value realism	Being-in-itself (as the subject is) and realisation of values in social practices.
Hedonism	Being through senses (immediate sense experiences) and the ability to relate experiences to the attributes of identity

Table 1 (continued)

EXISTENTIAL DASEIN	LOCAL ONTOLOGY (The fundamentals of being in the world)
Tradition	Social norms, roles, e.g., ability and will to comply them with subject's identity.
Universalism	Ability to analyse conditions of subject's own being and will and ability to invent new personal (universal) codes (on the basis of known tradition)

    The research indicates that values come into being (realise) in different modes and combinations in *Dasein*. For instance, the focal point of hedonic value ontology is, according to literature, in modes of being as an authentic self in terms of being-in-self and being-for-self. Traditionalism and universalism both relate to the mode of being for others, but because traditionalism is related to the modality of can and universalism to the modality of will, these might be conceived as different ontologies. This supports the previous results that consumers do not passively accept marketing communications but also renegotiate the meaning of values subjectively and construct their own interpretations (Elliott 1999: 113–114).

    At this point of analysis, the ultimate question comes up: how receptive the consuming subject is in his or her *Dasein* for the transcendence representing the ontology of other's value system. The subjective part of transcendence may relate only to the chain of affirmation and the modalities of their own value fragments. For instance, hedonist's endotactic *Dasein* e.g. desire, will, being able to be here and now); pluralist's eksotactic *Dasein* and sign system, e. g. knowing how social functions and ability adapt to social environment's transcends; value realist's endo-type intent to be as they are and knowledge on how social functions in relation to their *Dasein* (will and know); traditionalist's affirmation of tradition's historical knowledge and identity as a free will (must and can), and universalist's intransigent compulsion to create new rules for society (will, must). At the moment, it seems obvious that a subject living in some of the named value fragments do not communicate easily. Therefore value related message transcend may lead self-protective (negative) reactions. This happens because the *Dasein* the subject appreciates and prefers to live in is a private bubble (small and closed group) up to the time when something makes them burst.

    As van Raaij (1998) maintains that we do not have the grand narratives of modern times any more. Instead, values and identities are fragmented and modern values are replaced by the postmodern's flair and sense of drama in a marketplace. At the moment, there would exist need to add the problematic question of value ontology and the primary concern of taking responsibility for consumer's being. It is also the only category of being for a subject inside the local ontology. Still, it is not the only truth and possible value ontology for all human beings. The idea of Jensen and Lindberg (2002: 236–237) that the next step for managers is existential care in understanding consumer might well be extended to more general application in the existential consumer theory in semiotics. Thought, it would be the topic for future research to explore what possibilities this means for existential consumer research, value research and perhaps also for existential semiotics. When the subjects define their own existences as an experience which is often unique for a moment, the need to understand what it means to be inside or outside is important, as we may live in the fragmented value system ontology of some supreme ontology.

References

Arnould, E. J. & Linda L.Price. 2000. Authenticating acts and authoritative performances. Questing for self and society. In S. Ratneshwar, David Glen Mick & Cynthia Huffman (eds.), *The Why Consumption. Contemporary perspectives on consumer motives, goals, and desires*. Eastbourne: Routledge.
Baudrillard, Jean. 2005. *The System of Objects*. UK:Verso.
Bauman, Zygmunt. 2008. *Consuming Life*. USA: Polity Presss.
Bauman, Zygmunt. 2005 [1993]. *Postmodern Ethics*. India: Blackwell Publishing.
Beckman, Susanne C. & Richard Elliott. 2002. Philosophical and paradigmatic issues. In Susanne C. Beckmann & Richard H. Elliott (eds.), *Interpretive Consumer Research. Paradigms, Methodologies & Applications*. Denmark: Copenhagen Business School Press.
Belk, Russell W. 1998. In the Arms of the Overcoat. On luxury, romanticism and consumer desire. In Stephen Brown, Anne Marie Doherty & Bill Clarke (eds.), *Romancing the Market*. London/New York: Routledge.
Belk, Russell W., Güliz Gerr & Søren Askegaard. 2000. The Missing Streetcar Named Desire. In S.Ratneshwar, David Glen Mick & Cynthia Huffman (eds.), *The Why Consumption. Contemporary perspectives on consumer motives, goals, and desires*. Eastbourne: Routledge.
Beverland, Michael B & Francis J. Farrelly. 2010. The Quest for Authenticity in consumption: Consumers' Purposive Choice of Authentic Cues to Shape Experienced Outcomes. *Journal of Consumer Research* 36 (February). 838–856.
Brown, Stephen, Anne Marie Doherty & Bill Clarke (eds.). 1998. *Romancing the Market*. London/New York: Routledge.
Brown, Stephen & Darach Turley (eds.). 1997. *Consumer Research. Postcards from the Edge*. London/New York: Routledge.
Brown, Steven. 1998. *Postmodern Marketing*. London: Routledge.
Caru, Antonella & Bernard Cova. 2007. *Consuming Experience*. London/New York: Routledge.
Cherrier, Héléne. 2005. Using Existential-Phenomenological Interviewing to Explore Meanings on Consumption. In Rob Harrison, Terry Newholm & Deirdre Shaw (eds.), *The Ethical Consumer*. Thousand Oaks: Sage Publications.

Concise Routledge Encyclopedia of Philosophy. London: Routledge.
Coulder, Robin & Gerald Zaltman. 2000. The Power of Metaphor. In S.Ratneshwar, David Glen Mick & Cynthia Huffman (eds.), *The Why Consumption. Contemporary perspectives on consumer motives, goals, and desires.* Eastbourne: Routledge.
Cova, Bernard, Robert V. Kozinetz & Avi Shankar (eds.). 2007. *Consumer Tribes.* Great Britain: Elsevier.
Elliot, Richard. 1997. Existential consumption and irrational desire. *European Journal of Marketing* 31(3). 285–296.
Elliot, Richard and Mark Ritson. 1997. Post-structuralism and the dialectics of advertising. Discourse, ideology, resistance. In Stephen Brown & Darach Turley (eds.), *Consumer Research. Postcards from the Edge.* London/New York: Routledge.
Escalas, Jenifer Edson & James R. Bettman. 2000. Using narratives to discern self-identity related consumer goals and motivations. In S. Ratneshwar, David Glen Mick & Cynthia Huffman (eds.), *The Why Consumption. Contemporary perspectives on consumer motives, goals, and desires.* Eastbourne: Routledge.
Feldman, Fred. 2006. *Pleasure and the Good Life. Concerning the Nature, Varieties, and Plausibility of Hedonism.* Great Britain: Oxford University Press.
Floch, Jean-Marie. 1988. Contribution of Structural Semiotics to the Design of a Hypermarket. *Journal of Research in Marketing.* 233–252.
Flocker, Michael. 2004. *The Hedonism Handbook. Mastering the lost arts of leisure and pleasure.* Cambridge, MA: Da Capo Press.
Fromm, Erich. 1990 [1947]. *Man for Himself. An inquiry into the psychology of ethics.* New York: Henry Holt.
Giddens, Anthony. 1991. *Modernity and Self-identity. Self and society in the Late Modern Age.* Cambridge: Polity Press.
Gosling, Juslin. 2000. *Hedonism.* Concise Routledge Encyclopedia of Philosophy. London: Routledge.
Graig, Edward. 2000. *Pluralism.* Concise Routledge Encyclopedia of Philosophy. London: Routledge.
Hafstede, Geert. 2001. *Cultures Consequences: Comparing Values, Behaviours, Institutions and Organisations across Nations.* Thousand Oaks: Sage Publications.
Heard, Gerry C. 1990. *Basic Values and Ethical Decisions.* Malabar: Krieger Publishing Company, INC.
Hirschman, Elizabeth C. & Morris B. Hobbrook. 1992. *Postmodern Consumer Research. The Study of Consumption as Text.* Newbury Park: Sage Publications.
Holbrook, Morris B. 1999. *Consumer Value: A Framework for Analysis and Research.* London: Routledge.
Holbrook, Morris B. & Elizabeth C. Hirschman. 1982. The Experiential Aspects of Consumption: consumer fantasies, Feelings, and Fun. *Journal of Consumer Research* 9 (September). 132–140.
Holbrook, Morris B. & Elizabeth C. Hirschman. 1993. *The Semiotics of Consumption. Interpreting Symbolic Consumer Behaviour In Popular Culture and Works of Art.* Berlin: Mouton de Gruyter.
Jensen, Øystein & Frank Lindberg. 2002. The Consumption of a Tourist attraction: A Modern, Post-modern and Existential Encounter Perspective. Philosophical and paradigmatic issues. In Susanne C. Beckmann & Richard H. Elliott (eds.), *Interpretive Consumer Research.* Copenhagen: Copenhagen Business School Press.

Kahle, Lynn R. (ed.). 1983. *Social Values and Social Change: Adaptation to Life in America*. New York: Praeger.
Kahle, Lynn R. & S.Timmer. 1983. A Theory and a Method for Studying Values. In Lynn R. Kahle (ed.) *Social Values and Social Change: Adaptation to Life in America*. New York: Praeger.
Kahle, Lynn R. & Chung Hyun Kim (eds.). 2006. *Creating Images and the Psychology of Marketing Communication*. Mahwah, NJ: Lawrence Erlbaum.
Kukkonen, Pirjo. 2010. Det översättande jaget: homo signifians – homo interpres [Translating ego: homo signifians – homo interpres]. (*Acta Translatologiea Helsingiensia* (ATH) vol 1:99–121).
Kupiainen, Terri. 2008. Arvotypologian muodostaminen tuote- ja markkinointikonseptin suunnittelun perustaksi [Value typology for consumer segmentation]. In Terri Kupiainen, Harri Luomala, Katariina Lehtola & Hannele Kauppinen-Räisänen (eds.), *Tavoitteena tyytyväinen kuluttaja* [Tarketing consumer satisfaction]. (Vaasan yliopiston tutkimuksia 286). Vaasa: Vaasan yliopisto. https://www.uwasa.fi/materiaali/pdf/isbn_978-952-476-241-0.pdf
Leipämaa-Laaksonen, Hanna. 2009. *Consumer in the world of contradictions: Essays on the challenges of food*. (Acta Wasaensia NO 203). Vaasa: Universitas Wasaensis.
Luedicke, Marius K. & Markus Giesler. 2007. Brand Communities and Their Social Antagonists: Insights from the Hummer Case. In Bernhard Cova, Robert V. Kozinets & Avi Shankar (eds.) *Consumer Tribes*. Oxford: Elsevier.
Lyotard, Jean-Frangois. 1984. *The Postmodern Condition: A Report on Knowledge*. (Theory and History of Literature, vol. 10). Minneapolis, MI: The Minnesota University Press
Maffesoli, Michel. 1993. *Shadow of Dionysus: Contribution to the Sociology of Orgy*. New York: State University of New York Press.
Maffesoli, Michel. 1996. *The Time of the Tribes. Decline of Individualism in Mass Society*. London: Sage Publications.
Mooij de, Marike. 2004. *Consumer Behaviour and Culture. Consequences for Global Marketing and Advertising*. London: Sage Publications.
Morris, Charles. 1964. *Signification and significance. A Study of the Relations of Signs and Values*. Cambridge, MI: The M.I.T. Press.
Morris, Charles. 1956. *Varieties of Human Values*. Chicago: The University of Chicago Press.
Pipping, Robert. 2008. The Conditions of Value. In R. Jay Wallace (ed), *The Practice of Values*. USA: Clarendon Press.
Putnam, Hilary. 2004. *Ethics without Ontology*. Cambridge, MA: Harvard University Press.
Ratneshwar, R., David Glen Mick & Cynthia Huffman (eds.). 2000. *The Why Consumption. Contemporary perspectives on consumer motives, goals, and desires*. Eastbourne: Routledge.
Raz, Joseph. 2008. The Practice of Values. R. Jay Wallace (ed). USA: Clarendon Press.
Rokeach, Milton. 1973. The Nature of Human Values. New York: Free Press.
Sagi, Avi. 2008. *Tradition vs. Traditionalism*. Amsterdam: Rodopi.
Sartre, Jean-Paul. 1946. *Existentialism*. New York: Philosophical Library.
Schwartz, Shalom H. 2006. A Theory of Cultural Value Orientations: Explication and Applications. *Comparative Sociology* 5(2–3). 157–182.
Schwartz, Shalom H. 2007. Value orientations: Measurement, antecedents and consequences across nations. In Roger Jowell, Caroline Roberts; Rory Fritzgerald & Gillian Eva (eds.), *Measuring attitudes Cross-Nationally* Great Britain: Sage Publications.

Schwartz, Shalom H. 1992. Universals in the content and structure of values: Theoretical advances and empirical tests in 20 countries. In Mark Zanna (ed.). *Advances in experimental social psychology* 25, 1–65. San Diego.

Shils, Edward. 1981. *Tradition*. Chicago: The University of Chicago Press.

Slatter, Don. 1997. *Consumer Culture and Modernity*. Cambridge: Polity Press.

Stern, Barbara (ed.). 1998. *Representing Consumers. Voices, Views and Visions*. London/New York: Routledge.

Tarasti, Eero. 2010a. Representaatio semiotiikassa [Representation in semiotics]. *Synteesi* 1/2010. 2–19.

Tarasti Eero. 2010b. Olemisen ja subjektin moodit eli 32 teesiä [Modes of subject and being, 32 thesis]. *Synteesi* 2/2010. 2–25.

Tarasti, Eero. 2009. What is existential semiotics? From theory to applications, In Eero Tarasti (ed.), *Communication. Understanding and misunderstanding*. (3). (Acta Semiotica Fennica XXXIV). Tartu: Greif.

Tarasti, Eero. 2004. *Arvot ja merkit*. [Values and signs] Tampere: Gaudeamus.

Tarasti, Eero. 2000. *Existential Semiotics*. Bloomington: Indiana University Press.

Thompson, Craig J. 2000. Postmodern Consumer. Goals made easy!!!!. In S.Ratneshwar, David Glen Mick & Cynthia Huffman (eds.), *The Why Consumption. Contemporary perspectives on consumer motives, goals, and desires*. Eastbourne: Routledge.

Van Raaij, Fred. 1998. Postmodern consumption. In Mary Lambkin, Gordon Foxall, Fred Van Raaij & Benoît Heilbrunn (eds.), *European, Perspectives on Consumer Behaviour*. London/New York: Prentice Hall.

Jean-Marie Jacono
Existential semiotics and sociology of music

Abstract: Existential semiotics deals with the social dimensions of a subject within the relation between *Moi* and *Soi*. In the *Zemic* model, social roles, institutions and practices and, on the other hand, norms, values and general codes are only taken into account. *Moi* and *Soi* form an organism, an *Ich-Ton*. Despite its interest, the theory lacks some aspects in the background. A composer is a socialized person. The role of his/her relationships, as well as social and political contexts must be analyzed to explain the meaning of a work.

Musorgsky and his works are particularly relevant to study both the existential dimensions of a composer and the relations to his artistic and social environment within a moving society. In 1874, Musorgsky's depression leads him to compose *Pictures at an exhibition*, then to refuse to perform it. The sociological and cultural contexts not only explain Musorgsky's refusal but also light the meaning of the work beyond Hartmann's exhibition. The relationship of *Pictures at an Exhibition* to Russian society provides the essential key to analyze his work.

Sociology of music challenges the semiotic concept of environment (*Umwelt*) and even existential semiotics. Nevertheless, by other means, it also links a work to the *Umwelt* and even to transcendence. The revelation of transcendence not only depends on analyses and performances. It is the result of artistic and historical processes. In this perspective, sociology of a musical work will always be helpful to existential semiotics, in spite of their differences.

Keywords: Sociology of music, Existential semiotics, Musorgsky's depression (1874), *Pictures at an Exhibition*, Subject, Social contexts

Sociology of music and existential semiotics seem to belong to two different fields. Existential semiotics deals with the expression of transcendence within a musical work. The conditions of production, interpretation, and listening to music by an audience are mainly studied by sociology of music. The link seems impossible between the two disciplines. Nevertheless, sociology of music also deals with the musical work. Every structural dimension of a musical work and every one of its producers (composer, performers, and users) is concerned by a sociological approach. The musical text leads to its contexts which may even be considered as texts according to the semiotician Raymond Monelle (2000: 152–155). From a sociological perspective, it is impossible to closely separate them: "there is no talk possibilities about music that does not imbricate at a very fundamental level some or other aspect of social relations or institutions" (Klumpenhouwer 1998: 295).

Some social dimensions are present in existential semiotics. According to Eero Tarasti, the individual (*Moi*) and the social (*Soi*) of a composer cannot be separated. *Moi* (the artist's proper, existential ego) and *Soi* (his/her social communal self) form the same organism, an *Ich-Ton* (2012: 18–21). *Moi* and *Soi* are articulated by a central concept coming from Greimas's semiotics, the modalities of a subject. For instance, with the modality of 'must', *Soi* is defined by "the normative forms and structures of communication which take the shape of musical styles" (Tarasti 2012: 23). In short, *Soi* expresses the dimensions of social and technical rules. Later, the "zemic" model presents, through a simple figure (Z), the relationships between *Moi* and *Soi*. At the bottom of the "zemic" model, *Soi*, on one hand, represents the social roles, institutions, and practices and, on the other hand, norms, values, and general codes (Tarasti 2015: 26–27). In a sense, these dimensions pave the ways to the sociological analyses: the existence of a musical work depends on the presence of social values and artistic rules. The study of their role is absolutely fundamental.

Nevertheless, some aspects which both depend on *Moi* and *Soi* are almost put on the background in this way: the relationship between a composer and the 'actors' of a musical work. These 'actors' challenge existential semiotics. Despite some theoretical comments about 'subject and environment' (Tarasti 2015: 128–130), existential semiotics focuses on the subject and the organic dimension of work within the expression of *Ich-Ton*. Then, we would like to explore the presence of the 'actors' within and outside a musical work to set up new links between existential semiotics and sociology. The Russian composer Modest Musorgsky (1839–1881) and his works are particularly relevant to study both the existential dimensions of a composer and the relations to his artistic and social environment within a moving society. Among his works, we will examine *Pictures at an Exhibition*. This famous musical work questions existential semiotics in numerous ways as an expression of the crisis of a subject. Also, it cannot be analyzed without examining its relations to the political dimensions and the 'actors' of Musorgsky's environment. In this way, would it be possible to try to conceive a new definition of transcendence? This central concept of existential semiotics is absolutely essential. Nevertheless, it may be revisited according to some sociological and artistic points of view.

1 Around a composer

In existential semiotics, *Moi* is defined by two dimensions: the being-in-myself (*an-mir-sein* in German) which expresses the primary kinetic energy and the modality of "will" (*vouloir*), and the being-for-myself (*für-mich-sein*) with the modality of "can" (*pouvoir*). This being-for-myself is only defined by its relation to transcendence: it "corresponds to Kierkegaard's position of the "observer". Sartre's negation, in which mere being shifts to transcendence, points up what is lacking in its existence; in this way, being becomes aware of itself and of transcendence. (. . .) The ego discovers its identity; it reaches a certain stability and permanent corporeality via habit; (. . .)" (Tarasti 2012: 26). The individual dimension is pointed out in this concept. However, a composer is a social human being. His/her relations to others may already be conceived in this part of *Moi*. The theory does not clearly take them into account. They seem to belong to the sphere of *Soi* which is divided into two parts: being-for-itself ("know", *savoir*) and being-in-itself ("must", *devoir*). In fact, the sphere of *Soi* is linked to the subject: "Being-for-itself means the aforementioned norms, ideas and values as realized by the conduct of the subject in his or her *Dasein*" (Tarasti 2012: 26). Even if the relationships between the spheres of *Moi* and *Soi* may pave the way to the study of a subject in his/her human environment (Tarasti 2015: 128–130), they are not evoked. Yet they are fundamental even in the perspective of existential semiotics.

The composer discovers his/her identity through social and cultural relationships. According to the sociologist of literature Lucien Goldmann, every writer or artist is a transindividual subject belonging to several collective groups and structures (1966: 152). This concept is similar to Norbert Elias's configuration: every person depends on the presence of others. This interdependence is not only a sociological reality, but a fundamental way in the making of an individuality. The society is not only a factor which standardizes: it is a "factor of individualization" thanks to this interdependence (Elias 1997: 103). The social and artistic relations make up the identity of a creator. In his interpretation of Mozart, Elias links the possibilities of composition to the social groups and social classes of his time (1991: 26). Mozart's ambivalent behaviour came from the conflict between his will to be both a free composer and to seduce Vienna's aristocracy. Do these aspects only belong to *Soi* (Tarasti, 2012: 36)? As they play a major role in the constitution of an artist's identity, they could also find a place in the sphere of *Moi* (being-for-myself) with the modality of "can". The ideas of a composer are determined by his/her relationships to artistic and social groups within a society. They contribute to the appearance of existential dimensions. The composer's will to assert autonomy and an original place in artistic production comes also from these social relations.

In short, it is necessary to take into account the situation of a composer as an interdependent person. The socialized dimensions of *Moi* have to be included in the field of the existential semiotics. They allow analyzing Musorgsky's crisis in 1874, visible both in his works and his social life. We have to recall briefly its process.

2 Despair and salvation

Since the 1860s, Musorgsky was a member of a group of five young composers called "The Mighty Handful" by their mentor, Vladimir Stasov. Their musical gatherings in Saint Petersburg were fruitful. They allowed these amateurs to become experienced in composition thanks to the study of other composers and discussions on their musical works. They could challenge the academic direction of Conservatory by the creation of a Free Music School, and define new ways for Russian music. Musorgsky's personality and ideas emerged thanks to his contacts with Balakirev, Borodin, Cui, Rimsky-Korsakov, and Stasov. Their will to create a new speech and new forms in music, under the influence of Realism, helped Musorgsky to compose outstanding vocal works in the 1860s. His identity as a composer, his *Moi*, was both the result from individual and collective ideas. Furthermore, this circle was not only a musical group, but also a real family for Musorgsky. As an unmarried and an almost lonely man after the death of his mother (1865), he could find a warm atmosphere and even friends within this musical circle.

However, the common ideal of the "Mighty Handful" disappeared gradually at the beginning of the 1870s within a changing society. Each member found his proper way: Rimsky-Korsakov, for instance, became a professor at Saint Petersburg Conservatory and adopted western musical techniques as a professional composer. "The circle's past is bright; its present is cloudy; gloomy days have begun", wrote Musorgsky to Glinka's sister on 11 July 1872 (Orlova 1983: 272). The "Mighty Handful" totally broke up in spite of the first performances of Musorgsky's *Boris Godunov* at Maryinsky Theater in February 1874, after a long demand from the Five to perform it (the opera was first rejected by the Imperial Theaters directorate in 1871). The success of *Boris Godunov* could not give new dynamics to the circle. Only Stasov enjoyed it. Cui wrote a very hostile review in *St Petersburg Gazette* which hurt Musorgsky (Brown 2006: 133–137). Furthermore, success did not resolve Musorgsky's situation. He continued to work as a clerk in the Forestry Section of the Ministry of State Property and remained an unprofessional composer.

The dissolution of the "Mighty Handful" led Musorgsky to depression. Stasov was the only one to keep in touch with him. On March 6, he wrote to his daughter "He has completely changed. He has begun to drink more and more, his face has swollen and turned dark red, his eyes have gone bad (. . .)" (Russ 1992: 14). Nevertheless, thanks to an aristocratic friend, the poet Golenischev-Kutuzov, Musorgsky could find support and new perspectives in composition. Golenischev-Kutuzov provided the verses of a melody after a painting by Vereschagin, *The Forgotten*, and two song cycles, *Sunless* (1874) and *Songs and Dances of Death* (1875–1877). These titles are very significant. They link to Musorgsky's crisis, even if their meaning is more complex. These short works are no more connected to the preparation of operas (Jacono 2018: 132). Do they reveal an existential dimension in music and Musorgsky's *Dasein*, beyond this clear conjuring up of his despair? The six songs of *Sunless* need to be analyzed deeply. The use of short lyrical melodies and unconventional chords in the harmony expresses intensively what was already emerging in *Boris Godunov*: the assertion of the subject, *Moi*, both far from a realist and a conventional musical language. We could find existential signs within each song of this cycle. However, *Sunless* is an intertextual work. It is closely linked to *Pictures at an Exhibition* composed at the same time for piano. The different pieces of this well-known work seem only to evoke the paintings by a composer's friend, Victor Hartmann. In fact, they allow Musorgsky to give a personal reply to the break-up of the "Mighty Handful" and to define other perspectives to *Moi*.

3 Existential and sociological meanings

Pictures at an Exhibition is structured by a narrative course from the beginning, 'Promenade', to the last piece, 'The Bogatyr's gate'. 'Promenade' ('*Allegro giusto nel modo russico*') depicts Musorgsky himself and not an anonymous visitor of Hartmann's exhibition (Russ 1992: 35). Its folk-inspired theme expresses Russian features which were also emphasized by the "Mighty Handful" in the 1860s (the use of modal and variable musical scales, for instance). This expression of Musorgsky's identity as *Moi* is socialized. It is included in the cultural and social contexts of his time. This *Moi* faces up to different situations through the presence of Hartmann's pictures. Among others, the most striking expression of existential signs may be found in the eighth piece, 'Catacombae, (sepulcrum romanum)', immediately followed by 'Con mortuis in lingua mortua'. There is no more melody in 'Catacombae' but violent and stark chords contrasted in register, dynamic and spacing, without clear harmony till the beginning of 'Con mortuis' (Figure 1). It is a total negation of the basic elements of the work.

The beginning of *Pictures* sets out one of the two principles used by Musorgsky, according to Caryl Emerson (1999: 68–69): the process, a celebration of possible movement in multiple directions that is independent of beginnings and ends. Then, in 'Catacombae', we may observe the second principle: non-predetermination or surprise. These organic principles seem loosely connected to the influence of Darwin on Musorgsky.

Beyond the representation of a picture made by Hartmann after a visit to Paris catacombs, this striking piece deals with the expression of death. It stops

Figure 1: M. Musorgsky. *Pictures at an Exhibition*. 'Catacombae', m. 1–7. St. Petersburg: Bessel, 1874.

the musical flow coming from the previous one, 'Limoges, le marché', and reveals the transcendence through the negation of life. This brutal presence of death gives also Musorgsky the opportunity to evoke his own situation after the end of the "Mighty Handful". The violent break-up of 'Catacombae' involves his longing for new horizons. The Promenade theme appears for the first time in the following piece, 'Con mortuis', and later within 'The Bogatyr's gate'. Then, it is surrounded by Russian themes and sounds: a processional theme evoking tsar's greatness, an Orthodox hymn, and bell sounds recalling tsar Boris Godunov's coronation. Their presence is not a coincidence. Hartmann designed a gate in a Russian style for a competition about the building of a grand entrance to the city of Kiev. This monument had to be a tribute to tsar Alexandre II, who escaped from assassination in 1866. At the end of the narrative course of *Pictures*, the Promenade theme is "going home" (Tarasti 1996: 298). In fact, Musorgsky joins within music the traditional Russia whose greatness is emphasized in the last piece. What does this nationalist celebration of conservative Russian powers at the end of *Pictures* mean? Certainly, it is possible to do a semiotic analysis of *Pictures at an Exhibition* with the use of modalities (Tarasti 1996: 293–335). It is also possible to view the moving from *Moi* ('Catacombae') to *Soi* via the integration of the Promenade theme in another atmosphere. However, it is impossible not to deal with the sociological and political meanings linked to this work. They allow explaining its existential dimensions.

We have to take into account the relation to the audience. In the semiotics of literature, Umberto Eco explained a text is written for a reader. The writing of a novel cannot be conceived without his/her cooperation; the text even produces a reader (1985: 61–69). In music, it is necessary to adopt similar views summarized by Tarasti: "the composer keeps in mind an idealized image of future listeners and their location. In modern terms, the composer thinks of a collective, "implied listener". The social is inside both of these musical subjects, composer and listener. The social is their common *Soi*." (2012: 110). However, this fundamental relationship has to be clarified in its contexts in terms of the sociology of music. Who were the listeners of *Pictures at an Exhibition*?

A fact is hardly mentioned in the studies of *Pictures*: the absence of publication. Musorgsky composed quickly this work in June 1874. On July 26, he wrote in Russian on the cover of the score *K petchati* (to be printed). However, this manuscript was never edited by the Bessel publishers house. It is not a lack of care. Musorgsky accepted the publication of *Sunless* at the end of 1874 but put *Pictures* aside. Furthermore, he never performed it during his lifetime. neither at a musical gathering in Saint Petersburg for his/her friends nor in the concert tour organized in association with the soprano Daria Leonova in Ukraine (1879). Musorgsky refused the presence of an audience. *Pictures at an Exhibition* was only published in 1886, after his death. How to explain his behaviour? *Pictures* were both the original production and a way to resolve his existential crisis, also expressed in the works he composed at the same time. It was a big protest against the disappearance of the "Mighty Handful" and the loss of their ideal. After 'Catacombae', the work involves Musorgsky's longing to be reborn and to reach a new community within music. The best solution for him was to assert a community bigger than the "Five" at the end of *Pictures at an Exhibition*'s course, the Russian nation. 'The Bogatyr's gate' celebrates its harmony: the traditional forces (tsar, Orthodox church, and even Russian people within the melody of Promenade theme) are not in conflict. This ideal view is a kind of fairy tale. It is not a coincidence if it appears just after the evocation of a tale character in the ninth piece, the witch Baba Yaga. This mythical Russia is a "picture". It is far from Musorgsky's real opinions and has to be linked to the works where he deals with solitude (*Sunless*, for instance). In short, *Pictures at an Exhibition* is a musical provocation against Musorgsky's previous friends.

However, the publication of the work as soon as its performances would have immediately been covered by a political meaning, even by the implied listeners of the "Mighty Handful". Musorgsky was emphasizing the role of Russian people in the last scene of *Boris Godunov* under the influence of the populist historian Kostomarov (Taruskin 1993: 271). This revolution scene got an enthusiastic reaction of young students at the première of the opera. Musorgsky was regarded as a progressive composer linked to the preoccupations of the intelligentsia and even to the struggle of populist revolutionaries. Six months later, *Pictures at an Exhibition* would have generated confusion. The celebration of traditional Russia at the end of *Pictures* was only able to be interpreted as a celebration of tsar by whatever audience. It would have destroyed Musorgsky's reputation. The withdrawal of the work was probably a pity for Musorgsky: *Pictures at an Exhibition* was – and stays – his only substantial instrumental composition, with the exception of the orchestral tone poem *St John's Night on the Bare Mountain*. Nevertheless, in the contexts of Russian society, the refusal of performers and listeners was the only solution to avoid hostile reactions and controversies about his so-called betrayal of progressive intelligentsia's hopes. According to existential semiotics, this behaviour could be analyzed as the will to assert *Moi* (being-for-myself) against *Soi* (being-for-itself). The generative course of the subject through *Pictures* could also be analyzed after the basic model of *Dasein*, from negation (the evocation of death in 'Catacombae') to affirmation ('The Bogatyr's gate') (cf. Figure 2).

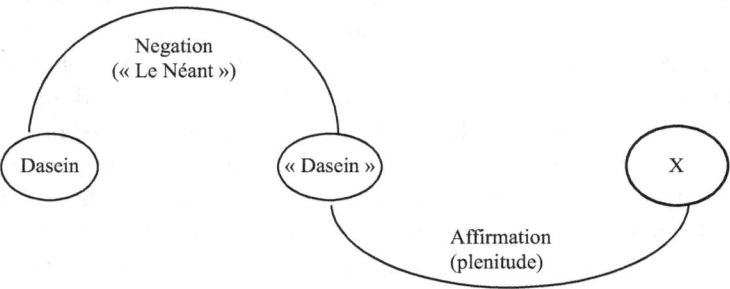

Figure 2: Existential semiotic model of *Dasein* and two "transcendental" acts: negation and affirmation (Tarasti 2012: 73).

However, the sociological and cultural contexts not only explain Musorgsky's refusal but also light the meaning of the work beyond Hartmann's exhibition. The relationship of *Pictures at an Exhibition* to Russian society provides an essential key to analyze the work. Does Musorgsky's behaviour concern transcendence? The question is fundamental in the field of existential semiotics to determine the relations between *Dasein* and transcendence. It cannot also be ignored by sociological perspectives.

4 Organicity and conflicts

If each subject is determined by his/her environment or *Umwelt*, then, what is precisely the *Umwelt* and what is its role? This concept comes from the theories of the Estonian biologist Jakob von Uexküll. According to him, "each organism lives in his own universe of signs, which he calls the *Umwelt*" (Tarasti 2015: 120). This organism is of course an *Ich-Ton* which distinguishes *Moi* (individual) and *Soi* (social). The *Umwelt* allows defining what surrounds a subject and may explain his/her evolution to the expression of transcendence. It is a large field which unites different disciplines. Culture and history have not a special position in the *Umwelt*. They are only a part of the environment. The *Umwelt* and *Ich-Ton* concept lead to the predominance of organicity in the process of life as soon as in artistic production. The role of a subject in existential semiotics is also emphasized to reject the concepts coming from a Stalinist and dogmatic Marxism, where the individual disappears.

By other means, by other concepts, sociology of music also links work to the *Umwelt* and even to transcendence. This *Umwelt* is determined by social realities and social processes which strongly or weakly condition the musical life and the musical works. Even if a musical work is autonomous and depends on artistic rules, it is connected to these social and cultural backgrounds at different levels. A society is always the place of conflicts. The processes of composition, performance, listening, and reception of a musical work are also linked to artistic and social conflicts. In the perspective of sociology, the distinction between *Moi* and *Soi* is almost impossible. As an interdependent person, a subject is connected to others. *Moi* is always a socialized *Moi*. This inclusion in a social reality explains why some composers are inventive and why others only produce conventional works for an audience. Nevertheless, sociology of music and existential semiotics have the same goal: to explain the value of a work. Certainly, this value depends on the original production of a composer. It also depends on the possibility for different audiences, in other societies and contexts, to question the same work and to give it meanings. This perspective also includes the performers. It explains why *Pictures at an Exhibition* was only successful in the 1920s thanks to the orchestrations by Ravel and Funtek.

Transcendence comes from a subject's experience. It may express within music something hidden in a subject's consciousness, something great which cannot be reduced to a clear content according to Ernst Bloch's views in *The Principle of Hope*. Transcendence also comes from the will to escape from cultural and social realities by the creation of an imaginary world in a work. This world becomes transcendental if it exceeds the expectations of implied listeners. Is it an eternal value? The revelation of transcendence not only depends on analyses and performances. It is the result of artistic and historical processes. In this perspective, sociology of musical work will always be helpful to existential semiotics, in spite of their differences.

References

Brown, David. 2006. *Musorgsky. His Life and Works*. Oxford: Oxford University Press.
Eco, Umberto. 1985. *Lector in fabula*. Paris: Grasset.
Elias, Norbert. 1991. *Mozart, sociologie d'un génie*. Paris: Seuil (*Mozart. Zur Soziologie eines Genies*. Frankfurt/Main: Surkhamp, 1991).
Elias, Norbert. 1997. *La Société des individus*. Paris: Fayard (*Die Gesellschaft der Individuen*, Frankfurt/Main: Surkhamp, 1987).

Emerson, Caryl. 1999. *The Life of Musorgsky*. Cambridge: Cambridge University Press.
Goldmann, Lucien. 1966. *Sciences humaines et philosophie*. Paris: Gonthier.
Jacono, Jean-Marie. 2018. Les formes brèves de Moussorgski et leur sens. In Vincent Cotro (ed.), *Musique et formes brèves*. 121–135. Brussels: Peter Lang.
Klumpenhouwer, Henry. 1998. Commentary – Poststructuralism and issues of music theory. In Adam Krims (ed.), *Music/Ideology: Resisting the Aesthetic*. 289–310. Amsterdam: G+B Arts.
Monelle, Raymond. 2000. *The Sense of Music: Semiotic Essays*. Princeton, NJ and Oxford: Princeton University Press.
Orlova, Alexandra. 1983. *Musorgsky's Days and Works. A Biography in Documents*. Ann Arbor: UMI Research Press. (*Trudy i dni Musorgskogo*, Moscow: Music State Publishers, 1963).
Russ, Michael. 1992. *Musorgsky:* Pictures at an Exhibition. Cambridge: Cambridge University Press.
Tarasti, Eero. 1996. *Sémiotique musicale*. Limoges: PULIM.
Tarasti, Eero. 2012. *Semiotics of Classical Music*. Berlin/Boston: Walter de Gruyter.
Tarasti, Eero. 2015. *Sein und Schein. Explorations in Existential Semiotics*. Berlin/Boston: Walter de Gruyter.
Taruskin, Richard. 1993. *Musorgsky. Eight Essays and an Epilogue*. Princeton: Princeton University Press.

Reijo Mälkiä
Destruction of cultural heritages: The case of Jerusalem in the Light of Jeremiah's prophecies

Abstract: I apply the theory of existential semiotics of Eero Tarasti to the text of the Bible – the prophetic texts of Jeremiah's book about the destruction of Jerusalem 586 BC. My goal is to find out by zemic model whether there is a common metalevel model for Jeremiah's differents prophecies. Transcendence is the theologically most fascinating concept of existential semiotics. Transzemic (radical transcendence) can only be processed with metaphor and symbols; its existence can only be inferred. We know that "God doesn't speak, doesn't use human language, and acts indirectly. Knowledge of God is available only through metaphor and symbols". Is God the same as transzemic?

The model seemed to fit indeed very well in explaining theoretically the situation and the story which has of course also a historic background. The study also raises other issues; for example, reflection from *Dasein* S1 to the suprazemic level and to the transzemic one. Does a man create his own God?

Models of existential semiotics are, of course, hypotheses, but they are intended to serve as a universal theory that transcends the eras of history and the boundaries of cultures. Its special feature is that it allows access to the texts, to their "minds" and, in particular, to the "soul landscapes" and worldviews of the persons working in the texts, who guide their value choices and actions. The gift of existential semiotics is that it offers a whole new type of number for biblical texts and interpretations.

Keywords: The Book of Jeremiah, The Destruction of Jerusalem, Existential Semiotics, Transcendence, Zemic Model

1 Research in brief

In my study, I use the zemic model to find out if there is a common metalevel model for Jeremiah's prophecies; I place them in the zemic model (*Dasein*) and interpret what each mode means as a representation, i.e. as a sign or deed (Figure 1 and 2). Then, I consider whether there is a transcendent interpretation of mode M1 that holds for all similar M1s, as is the case for other modes. By transcendental interpretation, I refer to the suprazemic plane, which is the metaplane of *Dasein*. It is reached by affirmation or negation of *Dasein*'s representation, which is also divided into modes. At the suprazemic level, the modes are, of course, common to the stories currently under review.

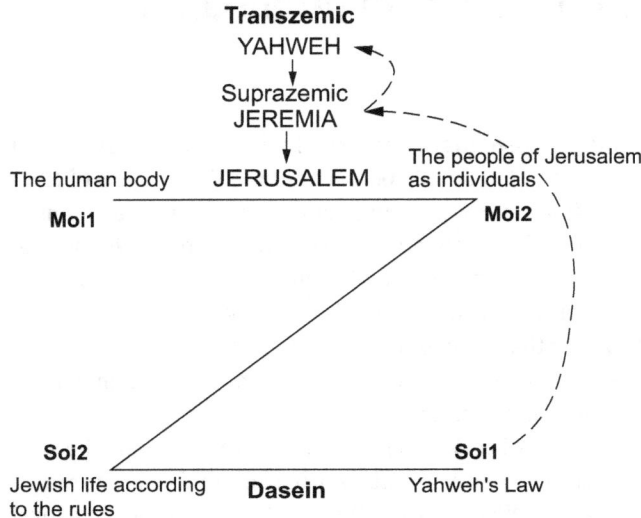

Figure 1: Theoretical framework.

2 Faiths are fictional narratives

Transcendence is the theologically most fascinating concept of existential semiotics. Transzemic (radical transcendence) can only be processed with metaphor and symbols; its existence can only be inferred. We know that "God doesn't speak, doesn't use human language, and acts indirectly. Knowledge of God is available only through metaphor and symbols". Is God the same as transzemic?

For God I use the name Yahweh to emphasize that the question is about the God of the Jews, not about the later God of Christianity. However, Christianity and our Christian views cannot be ignored. Early ancient religion served as a framework for a new religion, Judaism, that was born on the basis of the old through the same tradition, experience, and reinterpretation. Just as since then, Christianity was born based on Judaism. It is also worth remembering that the religion of ancient Israel is based not only on the religious phenomena of the Israel but of the whole of Mesopotamia.

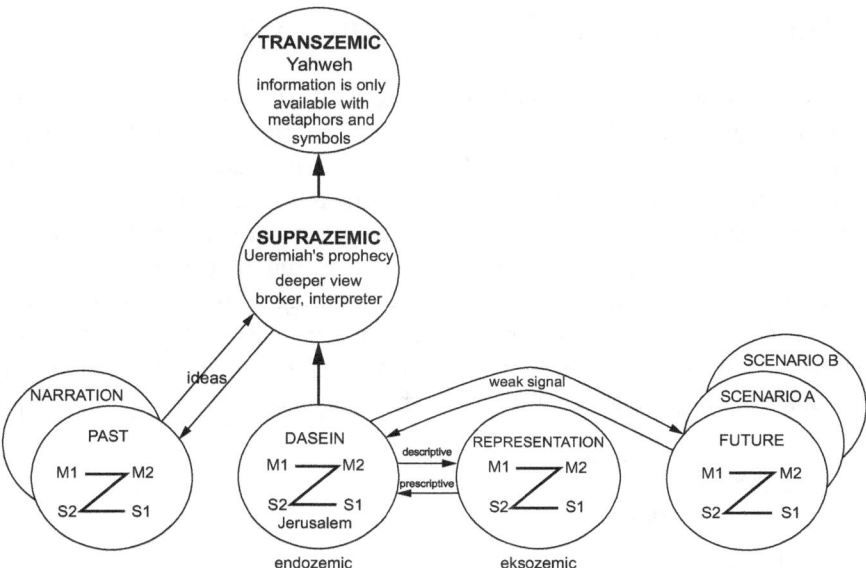

Figure 2: Zemic in time.

According to Tarasti, values must be considered as the origin of semios. Although the values are transcendent, the individual chooses himself and assumes responsibility for his choice, cf. free will in Christianity. He then sees the pragmatic consequences of how the values affected. A human has freedom of choice, but also responsibility for his choice. The starting point is that reality (*Dasein*) is just a reflection of the transzemic level that is eternal. Christianity begins with the idea of an ancient, perverted idea that God made the world for the picture of himself and looks at the image from the transzemic level in all its incompleteness.

Faiths are fictional narratives, which, for a long time, are often composed of different texts and behaviours. They are great creations, character phenomena. They are metaphors of the transcendental divinity behind them. Is the Bible true? There is the definition that you may think it is half history, half fiction. For example, about the exodus or the kingdom of David and Solomon, has not been found archaeological evidence or written information from the Assyrian or Babylonian archives. The texts in the Bible are not accepted as primary sources in scientific research. But there is information about the events that follow the destruction of Jerusalem in 586 BC is a real historical event.

3 Holy Jerusalem, the capital of Judah

Ideas are radiated or transmitted from transzemic to *Dasein*. In Jeremiah's case, the idea is transformed into a prophetic on suprazemic level. Jeremiah is working it into an "understandable" form of *Dasein's* representation in M1. An intrinsic form, an idea, creates an activity. This same thing is already familiar with antiquity. In this case, *Dasein* is Jerusalem, which projects its own Soi1, that is, its value to the suprazemic level and ultimately to the radical transcendency (transzemic). Jerusalem's leadership and the people do not believe in Jeremiah's prophecies, but consider him a typical phenomenon of suprazemic, i.e. healing and continuing their behaviour in the former way. This leads to the destruction of Jerusalem, that is, Jeremiah's "weak signal" proved to be true (Figure 3).

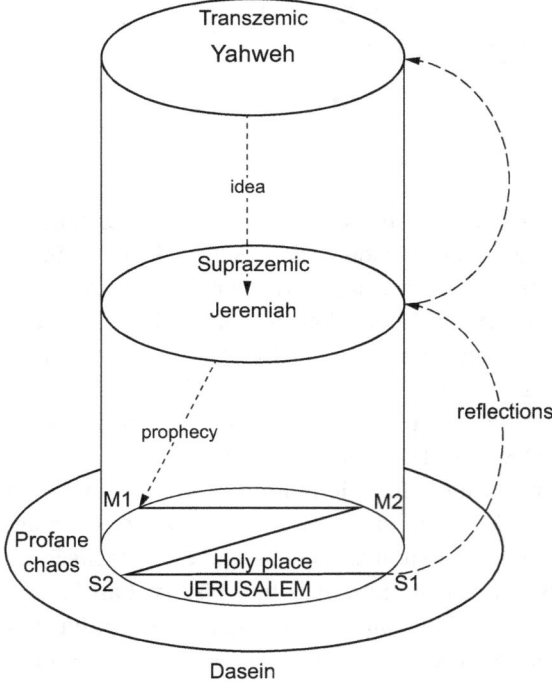

Figure 3: Holy Jerusalem.

The figure depicts Jerusalem in Jeremiah's destructive prophecies semiotically. The figure is based on the mythological level of thinking that has dominated almost all cultures, with the heavenly level of the gods above the lower level of everyday life and the lower level of the dead below. There is chaos outside the current level (*Dasein*). Chaos is a common concept in mythologies. Battles between gods and monsters were a popular subject of myths in the ancient Middle East. These stories told from the early twilight of mankind have been interpreted as a victory of order over the forces of chaos. I have not drawn the underworld of the dead under the everyday life-world (*Dasein*). The old Hebrew thought did not know of life after the grave where the pious could be compensated for injustices. It was not until the atoning sacrifice of Christ was made possible.

The zemic model of Jerusalem is about the concrete Moi1 and Moi2 units, and especially the unique city of Jerusalem, as well as the so-called social practices, Soi2, the social activities of the inhabitants and institutions such as religion, and Soi1 represents the value of Judaism as a symbol of Yahweh's law. But, at this time, Jerusalem was very corrupted (Figure 4).

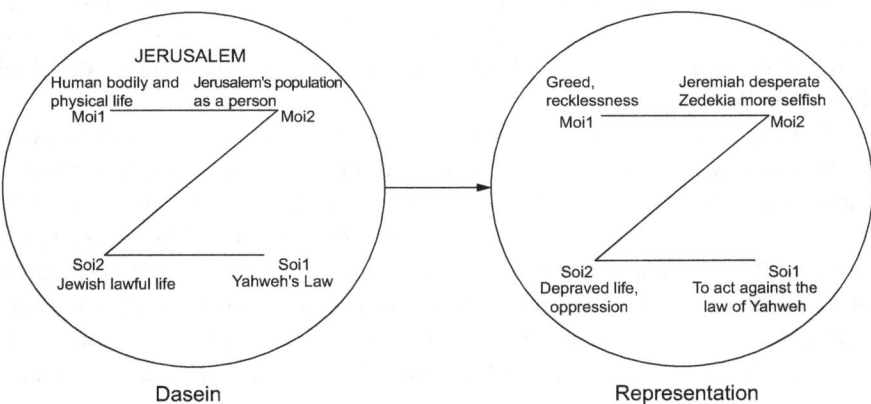

Figure 4: *Dasein* and representation of Jerusalem.

4 Method and research question

As a method, I have used the existential semiotic theory. I consider the applicability of the zemic model of existential semiotics to the analysis of Jeremiah's destructive prophecies. Zemic is used to create a metalanguage that can deal with otherwise difficult and essential things. Of the two randomly selected prophecies, after analysis, I search for the suprazemic, or metalevel, common to all similar prophecies. On these two prophecies I have placed their own zemic-models; fractions are very well taken over its implanted modes. The *Dasein* level is everyday life in Jerusalem: M1, the bodily life of man; M2, people as individuals; S2, pious lawful life in practice; S1, The law of Yahweh as a supreme value. A corresponding representation (what it means as signs) for both modes, and from there to the suprazemic level, being common to both prophecies. As research material, I have a Masoretic text, the "Hebrew Bible", on which our current Church Bible is based, as well as research literature, especially comments on Jeremiah.

5 Semiotic analysis

I take from the book of Jeremiah two prophecies addressed to the kingdom of Judah (Prophecy 1: 21: 11–14; and Prophecy 2: 22: 1–5). I place those two prophetic texts in the zemic model to find a meta-morph that would fit all Jeremiah's crush propheses. Text analysis is necessary when it comes to as many submitted texts as the books of the Old Testament. First, I look at them using the theological comments of Robert P. Carroll, Georg Fischer, Jack R. Lundbom and William McKane; they are well-known biblical scholars.

The most interesting examples of comparisons are the assumptions of later additions to the Hebrew text. Probable later additions are due to linguistic and/or grammatical abnormalities or the lack of such points in the Septuagint (the Greek Septuagint is based on one of the oldest Hebrew manuscripts; it has not been preserved). Why should changes be made afterwards? The reason might be a quest for a unified narrative, a dramatic addition or a general revelation. In the comments, too, it is stated that attempting is too lightly used, for example, the use of the 3rd of the unit rather than the plural, to see indications of Messiah's coming.

Prophet 1 Jer 21:11–14

וּלְבֵית֙ מֶ֣לֶךְ יְהוּדָ֔ה שִׁמְע֖וּ דְּבַר־יְהוָֽה׃

11. And unto the house of the king of Judah: Hear ye the word of the LORD;

בֵּ֣ית דָּוִ֗ד כֹּ֚ה אָמַ֣ר יְהוָ֔ה דִּ֤ינוּ לַבֹּ֙קֶר֙ מִשְׁפָּ֔ט וְהַצִּ֥ילוּ גָז֖וּל מִיַּ֣ד עוֹשֵׁ֑ק פֶּן־תֵּצֵ֨א כָאֵ֤שׁ חֲמָתִי֙ וּבָ֣עֲרָ֔ה וְאֵ֥ין מְכַבֶּ֖ה מִפְּנֵ֥י רֹ֥עַ מַעַלְלֵיהֶֽם

12. O house of David, thus saith the LORD: Execute justice in the morning, and deliver the spoiled out of the hand of the oppressor, lest My fury go forth like fire, and burn that none can quench it, because of the evil of your doings.

הִנְנִ֨י אֵלַ֜יִךְ יֹשֶׁ֧בֶת הָעֵ֛מֶק צ֥וּר הַמִּישֹׁ֖ר נְאֻם־יְהוָ֑ה הָאֹֽמְרִים֙ מִי־יֵחַ֣ת עָלֵ֔ינוּ וּמִ֥י יָב֖וֹא בִּמְעוֹנוֹתֵֽינוּ׃

13. Behold, I am against thee, O inhabitant of the valley, and rock of the plain, saith the LORD; ye that say: 'Who shall come down against us? or who shall enter into our habitations?'

וּפָקַדְתִּ֧י עֲלֵיכֶ֛ם כִּפְרִ֥י מַעַלְלֵיכֶ֖ם נְאֻם־יְהוָ֑ה וְהִצַּ֤תִּי אֵשׁ֙ בְּיַעְרָ֔הּ וְאָכְלָ֖ה כָּל־סְבִיבֶֽיהָ׃ ס

14. And I will punish you according to the fruit of your doings, saith the LORD; and I will kindle a fire in her forest, and it shall devour all that is round about her.

Prophet 2 Jer 22:1–5

כֹּ֣ה אָמַ֣ר יְהוָ֗ה רֵ֚ד בֵּית־מֶ֣לֶךְ יְהוּדָ֔ה וְדִבַּרְתָּ֣ שָׁ֔ם אֶת־הַדָּבָ֖ר הַזֶּֽה׃

1. Thus said the LORD: Go down to the house of the king of Judah, and speak there this word,

וְאָמַרְתָּ֞ שְׁמַ֣ע דְּבַר־יְהוָ֗ה מֶ֚לֶךְ יְהוּדָ֔ה הַיֹּשֵׁ֖ב עַל־כִּסֵּ֣א דָוִ֑ד אַתָּ֤ה וַעֲבָדֶ֙יךָ֙ וְעַמְּךָ֔ הַבָּאִ֖ים בַּשְּׁעָרִ֥ים הָאֵֽלֶּה׃ ס

2. and say: Hear the word of the LORD, O king of Judah, that sittest upon the throne of David, thou, and thy servants, and thy people that enter in by these gates.

כֹּ֣ה ׀ אָמַ֣ר יְהוָ֗ה עֲשׂ֤וּ מִשְׁפָּט֙ וּצְדָקָ֔ה וְהַצִּ֥ילוּ גָז֖וּל מִיַּ֣ד עָשׁ֑וֹק וְגֵר֩ יָת֨וֹם וְאַלְמָנָ֜ה אַל־תֹּנוּ֙ אַל־תַּחְמֹ֔סוּ וְדָ֣ם נָקִ֔י אַֽל־תִּשְׁפְּכ֖וּ בַּמָּק֥וֹם הַזֶּֽה׃

3. Thus saith the LORD: Execute ye justice and righteousness, and deliver the spoiled out of the hand of the oppressor; and do no wrong, do no violence, to the stranger, the fatherless, nor the widow, neither shed innocent blood in this place.

כִּ֤י אִם־עָשׂוֹ֙ תַּֽעֲשׂ֔וּ אֶת־הַדָּבָ֖ר הַזֶּ֑ה וּבָ֣אוּ בְשַׁעֲרֵ֣י הַבַּ֣יִת הַזֶּ֗ה מְלָכִ֞ים יֹשְׁבִ֤ים לְדָוִד֙ עַל־כִּסְא֔וֹ רֹכְבִ֥ים בָּרֶ֖כֶב וּבַסּוּסִ֑ים ה֥וּא וַעֲבָדָ֖יו וְעַמּֽוֹ׃

4. For if ye do this thing indeed, then shall there enter in by the gates of this house kings sitting upon the throne of David, riding in chariots and on horses, he, and his servants, and his people.

וְאִם֙ לֹ֣א תִשְׁמְע֔וּ אֶת־הַדְּבָרִ֖ים הָאֵ֑לֶּה בִּ֣י נִשְׁבַּ֤עְתִּי נְאֻם־יְהוָ֔ה כִּי־לְחָרְבָּ֥ה יִֽהְיֶ֖ה הַבַּ֥יִת הַזֶּֽה׃ ס

5. But if ye will not hear these words, I swear by Myself, saith the LORD, that this house shall become a desolation.

I placed them in the zemic model (*Dasein*) and interpreted what each mode means as a representation, a sign, or words or deeds. I, then, looked at whether there is a transcendent interpretation of mode M1 that holds true for all similar Jeremiah prophecies about M1; the same is true of other modes. I have taken advantage of the interpretations of commentaries on the prophecies.

What that suprazemic is in content requires the interpretation of every circle. Also, it is important from which direction to look, i.e. whether the suprazemic is perceived as a step from the transemic level towards the zemic world or whether it is an attempt to elevate the zemic from the real world towards transcendence. When the direction is from top to bottom, suprazemic is characterized by certainty, but when the direction is from bottom to top, it is characterized by uncertainty, i.e., there is a pious desire to reach the suprazemic level. The biblical premise is, of course, from top to bottom; meaning Jeremiah receives a revelation from Yahweh – possibly as a bodily experience (cf. the preferred expression in Hebrew is "even at night my kidneys" – translation – "a night I hear").

Moi1: Jeremiah's body would probably express the prestige he believes comes from Yahweh. The existential concept of Suprazemic would thus be something like dignity.

Moi2: it is a matter of justice i.e. protection of the weak, i.e. the existential content of suprazemic would be Mitleid or compassion.

Soi2: it is, therefore, a matter of correcting, changing, interfering with wrong practice; the wrong practice must be changed, an error/mistake must be admitted; it is a suprazemic concept of erroneousness.

Soi1: it is a punishment i.e. the laws result in total destruction, so suprazemic is negative repentance or horror (Figure 5).

6 Epilogue

The method I used is the theory of existential semiotics. I consider the applicability of the zemic model of existential semiotics to the analysis of Jeremiah's destructive prophecies. The model consists of the modes that settle in the shape of the letter Z (Moi1; body, Moi2; personality, Soi2; practice, Soi1; values). Zemic is an ontological model that describes our being. It describes what is happening in the world, but also what has happened (history) and what will happen in the future (prediction). Zemic is used to create a metalanguage that can deal with otherwise difficult-to-out, essential things. In this study, I sought to show that Jeremiah's prophecies can be addressed at the metalevel.

My research concerns Jeremiah's prophecy of the destruction of Jerusalem in 586 BC, applying existential semiotics. Eero Tarasti has developed a theory that is much a part of the thinking of Aristotle, Plato, Hegel, Kant. It is not just a matter of coordinating Western but equally oriental philosophy. The aim has been to develop models, concepts and analysis tools that are universal.

The gift of existential semiotics is that it offers a whole new type of number for biblical texts and interpretations. Models of existential semiotics are, of course, hypotheses, but they are intended to serve as a universal theory that transcends the eras of history and the boundaries of cultures. Its special feature is

Destruction of cultural heritages — 499

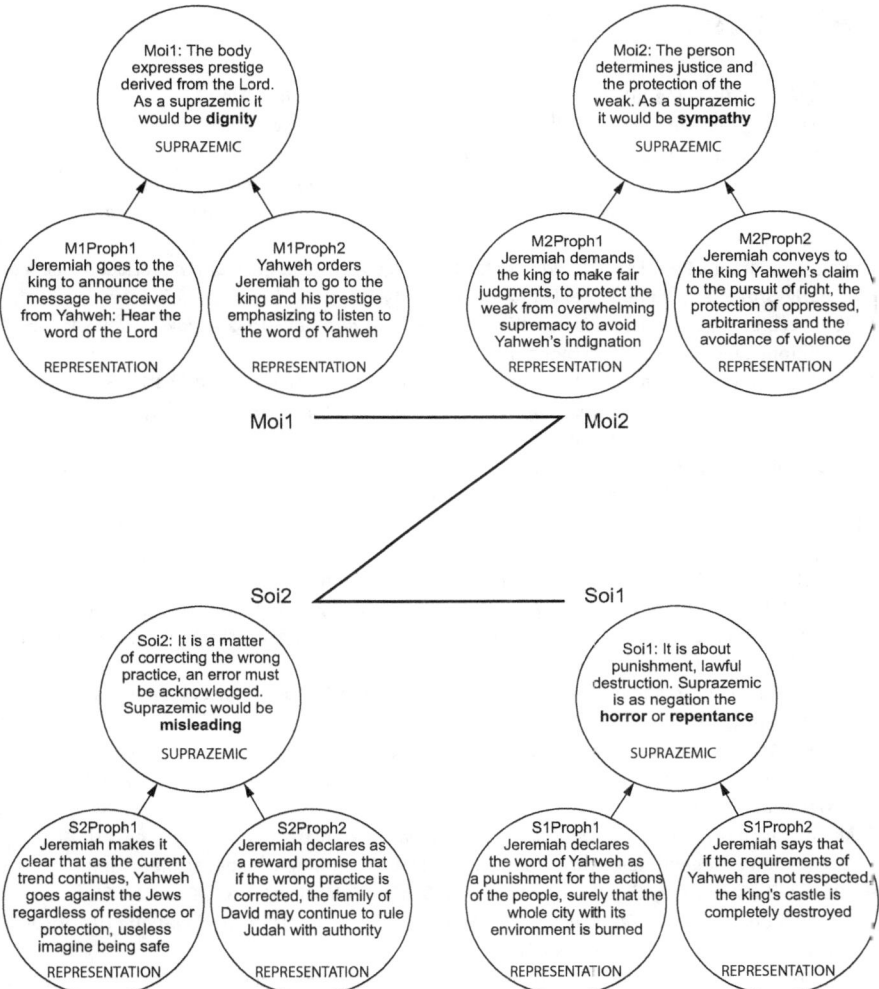

Figure 5: Representations and suprazemic.

that it allows access to the texts, to their "minds" and, in particular, to the "soul landscapes" and worldviews of the persons working in the texts, who guide their value choices and actions. In particular, one key concept in existential philosophy, transcendence, brings it closer to theology. Existential semiotics is very open to theological interpretations, including attitudes towards values and one's freedom of choice but also responsibility for one's choices.

References

Anttila, Miika. 2008. Merkityksen täyteys, Transsendenssi Eero Tarastin eksistentiaalisemiotiikassa [Plenitude of meaning, transsendence in Eero Tarasti's existential semiotics]. *Teologinen Aikakauskirja* (2).

Cosgrove, D. 1989. Geography is Everywhere: Culture and Symbolism in Human Landscapes. In Derek Gregory & Rex Wallford (eds.), *Horizons in Human Geography*. Hong Kong: Macmillan.

Finkelstein, Israel. 1994. *From Nomadism to Monarchy: Archaeological and historical aspects of early Israel*. Jerusalem: Israel Exploration Society.

Grabbe, Lester L. 2017. *Ancient Israel: What Do We Know and How Do We Know It?* Revised Edition. London, New York. Bloomberry.

Gravett, Sandra Lynne, Karla Gail Bohmback, Franz Greifenhagen & Donald Charles Polaski. 2008. *An introduction to the Hebrew Bible: a thematic approach*. Louisville, KY: Westminster John Knox Press.

Hendel, Ronald S. 1987. *The epic of the Patriarch: The Jacob cycle and the narrative traditions of Canaan and Israel*. Atlanta, GA: Scholars Press.

Laato, Antti. 1996. History and Ideology in the Old Testament Prophetic Literature. A Semiotic Approach to the Reconstruction of the Proclamation of the Historical Prophets. (Old Testament series 41). Stockholm: Almqvist & Wiksell International.

McKane, William. 1986. *A Critical and Exegetical Commentary of Jeremiah*. The International Critical Commentary on the Holy Scriptures of the Old and New Testament. Edinburgh: T&T Clark Ltd.

Nissinen, Martti. 2017. *Ancient Prophecy. Near Eastern, Biblical and Greek Perspectives*. Oxford: Oxford University Press.

Nissinen, Martti & Leena Vähäkylä. 2018. *Kiveen hakattu? Pyhät tekstit ja perinteet muutoksessa* [Carved in stone? Changing sacred texts and traditions]. Helsinki-Tallinna: Gaudeamus Oy.

Pakkala, Juha (ed.). 2014. *Tekstejä rautakauden Levantista* [Texts from iron age Levant]. (Suomen Eksegeettisen Seuran julkaisuja). Helsinki: Suomen Eksegeettinen Seura.

Gertz, Jan Christian, Angelika Berlejung, Konrad Schimd & Markus Witte. 2012. *T&T Clark Handbook of the Old Testament, An Introduction to the Literature, Religion and History of the Old Testament*. London: T&T Clark.

Tarasti, Eero. 2012. Existential Semiotics and Cultural Psychology. In Jaan Valsiner (ed.), *The Oxford Handbook of Culture and Psychology*, 316–343. Oxford: Oxford University Press.

Tarasti, Eero. 2014. Kulttuuri ja transsendenssi I [Culture and transcendence I]. *Synteesi* (3).

Tarasti Eero. 2015. *Sein und Schein. Explorations in Existential semiotics*. Berlin: Mouton.

Tarasti, Eero. 2015. Kulttuuri ja transsendenssi II [Culture and transcendence II]. *Synteesi* (2).

Tarasti, Eero. 2017. Mitä tapahtuu? Zemicin liikkeistä – eksistentiaalisemiotiikkaa [What happens? About the movements of Zemic – existential semiotics]. *Synteesi* (1–2).

Valkama, Kirsi. 2012. *Judah in the Mid-Sixth Century. Archaeological Evidence for a Post-Collapse Society*. Academic dissertation at the University of Helsinki. 2012.

Ricardo Nogueira de Castro Monteiro
From identity to transcendence: A semiotic approach to the survival of the Carolingian cycle in the Brazilian cultural heritage

Abstract: After eight centuries of coexistence under Muslim rule in the Iberian Peninsula, the once glamorously celebrated figure of the Moor gradually assumed the role of otherness in the Christian Iberian imagery – a dysphoric synthesis that led to the identity construction of the so-called "enemy of Christendom". The *Chegança* is a musical drama with choreographic and poetic interludes describing the adventures of a Christian vessel attacked by a Muslim ship but ending up by winning the battle and converting the Saracens to Christianism. This article shows that the *Chegança* presents significant traits of the Carolingian cycle under the form of themes, figures and even textual fragments alluding to the combats between Charlemagne's Twelve Peers and their opponents. Organized according to a semiotic square opposing *inclusion* and *segregation*, the drama displays the beaten Moors having to choose between two forms of *exclusion:* baptism – *segregation* followed by *assimilation* – or death – the ultimate form of annihilation. But the abandon of their former values is expressed not as the loss of their previous identity, but as the *transcendence* of their "state of sin". Such an expression of the Iberian *Volksgeist* develops throughout most of its colonies, representing a metaphorical promise of *inclusion* to the frequently majoritarian non-white and non-Christian communities that accept to "transcend" their former identities expecting to pass from an initial phase of *segregation* to one of *assimilation* that might allegedly lead them to their full acceptance by their dominators – a promise sadly still to be fulfilled.

Keywords: semiotics; existential semiotics; Carolingian cycle; Chegança; identity construction; otherness.

1 Identity and otherness in the representation of the Moor

After eight centuries of coexistence under Muslim rule in the Iberian Peninsula, the once glamorously celebrated figure of the Moor, step by step, ended up by assuming the role of otherness in the Iberian imagery – a dysphoric synthesis that ultimately led to the identity construction of the so-called «enemy of Christendom». Despite the insignificant Islamic presence in the New World until as late as the 19th century, the celebration of the polarization between Christians and Muslims has eventually become one of the most widespread invariances in the traditional cultures of the Americas. The drama *Cristianos y Moros* was presented in the inauguration of the first church in New Mexico in 1598 (Englakirk 1940). Its presence and strength has been witnessed in Spain, at least, since the 15th century (Albert-Llorca 2015), and spread worldwide to places so distant from each other as Zacatecas, in Mexico (Beutler 1983), Huamatanga, in Peru (Bautista 2001), Saubara, in the State of Bahia, Brazil (Silva 2007), and Dapitan, Philippines (Wiley 1996), not to mention their spectacular contemporary versions in different cities in the region of Valencia, Spain, like Alcoi or Vila Joiosa (Shefferman 2014).

Despite the presence of the representation of such antagonism in many traditional manifestations of the Brazilian folklore, this article is focused specifically in the *Chegança*, a musical drama with choreographic and poetic interludes describing the adventures and misadventures of a Christian vessel caught by surprise by a Muslim ship but ending up by winning the battle and converting the Saracens to Christianism. Like so many other traditional representations involving the antagonism between Christians and Moors all over the world, it is possible to identify in the *Chegança* significant traits of the Carolingian cycle, that appear under the form of themes, figures or even relatively long textual fragments alluding to the combats between Charlemagne's Twelve Peers and their opponents. It is above all the episode of the quarrel between the Frankish king's knight Olivier and the giant Fierabras that left an indelible mark in the Brazilian cultural heritage, visible by means of its many adaptations – some of them remarkably sophisticated – to the oral and written modalities of the national traditional culture, most of them taking as a reference, among so many available versions of that *chanson de geste*, its Occitan 13th century source. Such an influence can be discussed considering, for example, verses 617 to 626 of the 13th century Occitan *Roman de Fierabras* in the classical Immanuel Bekker's edition (Bekker 1829):

E si anet per forsa en Roma guerreyar,	And he forced a war against Rome,
E tuh cels de la terra fetz asi renegar,	And made all its citizens abjure their faith,
E car la gens no y s volgro am luy senhoreyar,	And because the people have refused to submit to him,
El fetz destruire Roma e ls monastiers gastar.	He destroyed Rome and devastated its monasteries.
Mortz lay fo l'apostoli li legat e li bar.	He killed the apostles, the legates and the parochs.
Si n portet la corona que tant fay ad amar,	He took from there the crown we love so much,

E'l signe e ls clavels don si fetz clavelar,	And the signs, and the nails Jesus was nailed with,
En portet lo enguen don dieu se fetz onchar,	And he took the ointment God was anointed with,
E'l ver sante suzari don si fe 'nvolopar.	And the holy shroud he was shrouded in.

Despite some superficial variances – the change of the site of the pillage from Rome to Jerusalem –, many significant discursive and narrative elements of the fragment above can be found in the following excerpt of a Brazilian *Chegança*:

Aquele foi quem entrou	That was the one who entered
em Jerusalém,	In Jerusalem,
e não respeitando ninguém,	And with no respect to anyone,
até os apóstolos matou.	He has killed even the apostles.
No templo sagrado	In the holy temple,
ele encontrou bálsamo	He found the ointment
que Deus tinha ungido	God had been anointed with,
coisa que serviu	that was used
na paixão do Redentor,	In the passion of the Redeemer,
e a coroa do Senhor	And the Lord's crown
por ele foi conduzido.	Was taken by him.

In the discursive level, both texts share figures like Jesus' *ointment* and *crown*, the themes of *pillage* and *profanation*, actors like the *apostles* and the various cognomens of *Jesus*, the narrative programs of the *attack to the holy city*, the *slaughter of the apostles* and the *appropriation of the relics* – all of them perpetrated in the same order, and by the *Muslim infidels* led by *their king*. Naturally, were that a singular episode and the relation between the *Chegança* and the *Roman de Fierabras* would be no more than a matter of fortuity. Nevertheless, examples like that are abundant enough to become significant. In fact, it is easy to recognize in the description made by Henry Koster (Koster 1816) of the dramatization of a naval combat between the armies of Christian and Muslim fortresses he witnessed in 1815 in the Itamaracá Island (State of Pernambuco, Brazil) many elements of the battle between the Peers of France led by Charlemagne and the warriors commanded by King Balan – Fierabras' father –, finishing with the defeat, conversion and baptism of the Saracens. Although Koster does not offer further details regarding the musical aspects of the presentation, his far more careful description of the visual elements of the mis-en-scène such as scenography, costumes, acting, and plot suggests that the present-day *Chegança* is almost certainly a version, even if simplified throughout the centuries, of the spectacular presentation he had witnessed. It was not until 1883 that a first serious research about that feast was published by the scholar Silvio Romero in his landmark *Cantos populares do Brasil* (Romero 1985). Disregarding completely any concern about the music and its notation, Romero nonetheless offers a precious register of the verbal instance of the syncretic text sung and enacted by the performers, like in the following fragment (Romero 1985: 146):

Mar e Guerra:	Entreguem-se, mouros, à santa religião, que dentro d'esta nau, temos ferros no porão.	*Captain:*	Moors, surrender to the holy religion, for inside this ship, we have a dungeon and chains.
Rei Mouro:	Eu não me entrego, nem pretendo no meio de tanta gente; Somos filhos da Turquia, temos fama de valentes.	*King of the Moors:*	Neither will I surrender nor would I ever do it in front of so many people; We are sons of Turkey, well known by our bravery.

As in the passage that substituted Rome for Jerusalem, some superficial changes respond for the adaptation of the Occitan text to that of the *Chegança*. Thus, the words originally assigned to Charlemagne will in the musical drama appear most of the times in the mouth of the commander of the ship (whose rank largely varies from *captain pilot* to *admiral* in the different versions); the name *Fierabras* is hardly heard, his title as *Rei dos Mouros* [King of the Moors] being referred to instead, and his speech occasionally is also transferred to a choir of Moors or to the *Embaixador dos Mouros* [Ambassador of the Moors]; and, most importantly, the man-to-man field combat between Fierabras and Olivier becoming a collective sea battle between a Christian ship and its Turkish/Moorish opponent. On the other hand, among the invariants, there are the very pronounced thematic and actorial oppositions between Christians and Moors at the discursive level.

In the narrative level, the texts share the programs of provocation – with Moors and Christians offending and challenging each other, including episodes with the appropriation of the holy relics by the Moors; the refusal to convert to the other faith by means of emphasising self-identity; the polemical structures, as alluded by Greimas in his *Du Sens II* (Greimas 1983), corresponding to the battles – perhaps better explained by Landowski's concept of adjustment regime than by Greimas' junctive relations (Landowski 2004); the cognitive sanction corresponding to the acceptance of the Christian faith by the Moors; and the pragmatic sanction of their conversion.

Finally, in the fundamental level, we find the opposition between *Death* – converted to the narrative level by the modal syntagma *make-no-to-believe*, and convoked to the discursive level by the dysphoric isotopies related to the Moors – and *Life* – corresponding in the narrative to the passion of *to-make-believe*, and convoked to the discourse through the Christians and their isotopies (like the holy relics). Taking into account the variances and invariances described above, it is possible to relate Romero's fragment to the excerpt corresponding to verses 872 to 875 of the Occitan *Roman de Fierabras*, in which Roland challenges Fierabras:

Per me ti manda Karles, lo rey ab lo vis clar,	On behalf of Charles, the king with the brave face,
C'ades layches Bafom, e fay te bateyar,	leave Mohammed and make yourself baptized.
E crezas en Jesu que ns a totz a jutjar,	and believe in Jesus who will judge us all,
E si non o vols fayre, ieu ti venc desfizar	and if you refuse, I will challenge you.
"Vassal" ditz Ferabras, "e cum auzas parlar!	"Vassal", says Fierabras, "how dare you talk to me like that?
Si tu mi ves armat, be t dic senes duptar	If you see me in arms, I tell you with no doubts,
Que auras ardit cor si m'auzas esperar.	You will be really brave if you venture to wait for me"

2 The invariants of an ever-changing text

The original Occitan version shares with Romero's fragment not only the discursive opposition between the Christian and Moorish isotopies and the theme of their rivalry, but also the manipulation by provocation in order to obtain the conversion of the opponent, and the refusal to surrender by means of the stressing and valuing of self-identity – not to mention the fundamental opposition of *Death vs Life* as commented before. As far as the plane of expression is concerned, the abyssal superficial distance in time, space, and language between the Occitan text and its varieties in Brazilian Portuguese disguises some relevant structural parallels that cannot be dismissed. After all, the monorhyme tridecasyllable verses that compound the stanzas under a more careful examination prove to be composed by hemistiches, as in "Per me ti manda Karles,/ lo rey ab lo vis clar". Dividing the verses in hemistiches, the result is a strophic structure of hexasyllables with rhymes in the even lines – a feature shared by the Brazilian versions and that will soon deserve our attention.

Romero's excerpt is not the only registered version of the episode mentioned above. Nonetheless, the possibility that the subsequent variants can have been transmitted with the aid of written sources can be essentially dismissed. If even today illiteracy proves to be one of the sad challenges Brazilian society has not yet managed to completely eradicate, in the last decades of the 19th century in which Silvio Romero has developed his research and published his book, official numbers indicated that 82,6% of the country's population was unable to read or write (Ferraro and Kreidlow 2014). Another argument supporting that impossibility is the regrettable absence, even today, of complete transcriptions of such traditional popular dramas in Brazil. Considering such circumstances, it is forceful to recognize that the participants of such traditional feasts used to count with no other resources but oral tradition and their well-trained mnemonic abilities to transmit these cultural manifestations from generation to generation. The process of transmission, normally committed to be as faithful to the original sources as possible, is nonetheless not exempt from mistakes and/or divergences. The complex balance between fidelity to the original sources and inevitable change is a key feature of orality, in frank contrast with respect to the relative immutability of written literature. Such a constant change proves to be in fact quintessential to orality, no matter if seen as a perverse trend that profanes and degenerates a hypothetic canonical text, or rather as a creative force that renews and updates traditions that would otherwise run the risk of being petrified – practically mummified – into sterile versions of themselves doomed to distancing from their genuine origins either by sacralisation or oblivion.

Thus, in 1888, five years after the appearance of Romero's book, his colleague Mello Moraes Filho will publish a slightly different version of that excerpt of the *Chegança* (Mello Moraes Filho 1999: 60):

Piloto:	Entrega-te, rei Mouro A essa nossa religião. Aqui dentro desta nau Há um padre capelão	*Pilot:*	Surrender to our religion, Moorish king, For inside this ship, There is a chaplain [to baptise you]
Rei Mouro:	Entregar-me não pretendo Em meio de tanta gente; Eu sou filho da Turquia, Tenho fama de valente.	*King of the Moors:*	I have no intention of surrendering In front of so many people; I am a son of Turkey, I am renown for my bravery.

A first difference between the two versions lays upon the systematic usage of the first person of the plural in Romero's variant, whereas Moraes registers the singular. Another point to notice is the contrast between the strategies of intimidation in Romero's version – alluding to the dungeon and its chains – and the more pragmatic manipulation in the second variant, indicating the availability of a chaplain to baptise the muslims. As far as the plane of expression is concerned, both share the structure of the strophes in heptasyllable quatrains with rhymes in the even verses – more precisely, ending in "ão" in the first stanza and in "ente" in the second one. Regarding the plane of content, the invariants in the narrative structure – the refusal of the intimidation – and in the discursive level – the themes on religious conversion, quarrels opposing Christians and Muslims, the nautical isotopies and the shared meters and rhymes – lead to the conclusion that both texts are related to the point of probably corresponding to variants of a common source. Actually, the sound structure (rhythmical and timbristic assonances by means of meters and rhymes) in the plane of expression of the two texts is remarkably close to the one we could examine in the Occitan original.

The discussion, until now limited to the verbal instance, will only be able to finally reach the musical and syncretic levels that characterise the song structure by means of the notes taken by Mário de Andrade in his 1928 ethnomusicological expedition. About 40 years later than his predecessors Romero and Moraes, almost 800 km away from the state of Sergipe where Romero had first collected his verses, Mário de Andrade was the first researcher to notate – sometimes, even record – not only the verbal but also the musical elements of the *Chegança* (Andrade 1982: 154–156), as can be seen in Figure 1 – whose lyrics appear below in their original and translated versions:

Mestre Patrão:	Intrega-te aqui, Môro,	*Skipper*:	Moor, surrender here
	A essa nossa religião.		To our religion;
	Dent' deste anau di guerra		We have a chaplain
	Temos pade Capelão!		Inside this warship!
Mouros:	Num m'intrego i nem pertendo	*Moors*:	I'm not surrendering, nor do I intend to,
	Pur num sê da nossa Lei;		For this is foreign to our law;
	Imbaxadô da Turquia,		Ambassador of Turkey,
	Lá o nosso deus é reis!		Our god there is our king!

It is interesting to notice the contrast between the invariance of the thematic opposition between Christians and Moors and the variance of the discursive actors: the *Captain* in Romero's version giving place to Moraes' *Pilot* and to Andrade's *Skipper*, whereas there is no variation among the Moors except for the alternance between the determined subject *King of the Moors* and the relatively indeterminate *Moors*, which, in the specific context of that feast, has little significance – if any –, even because the choir often alternates between the plural and singular in the conjugation of the 1st person. The most relevant contribution of Andrade's with respect to the corpus analyzed here so far is the register, for the first time, of the melodic and rhythmic aspects of a chant whose lyrics have barely varied since their first register in1883:

If it is impossible to affirm categorically that the similar lyrics of the three variants have necessarily been accompanied by the same – or by an only slightly variable – musical structure, this is unquestionably a hypothesis to be considered, even because all the versions share already sound features such as their rhythmic and strophic structure in heptasyllable quatrains. Another aspect to be mentioned is the similarity in the rhymical structure, in which the *ão /ente* pair in Romero's and Moraes' versions is not particularly distant from Andrade's *ão/ei*. Anyway, the remarkable similitude between the different versions, even if the conditions

Figure 1: Mario de Andrade's transcription of a *Chegança* he witnessed in 1928 in Natal, RN.

of their recollection were 40 years and hundreds of kilometres apart, represents a consistent argument in favour of the possibility that memory may have retained in the musical figures of expression of the three renditions an analogous level of resemblance to that one detected in the lyrics of the variants both in their plane of expression and their plane of content. But maybe the most consistent evidence to support the above-mentioned hypothesis is the extraordinary proximity between the version registered by Mario de Andrade and the one we collected in 2002 in a presentation of the *Chegança Minas Gerais*, that Master Bumba – a man whose illiteracy seemed to walk, hand in hand, with his wisdom and domain of oral culture – had commanded for more than 50 years in a gorgeous small village on the shore of Lake Manguaba, State of Alagoas. Bumba's version says:

Mar e Guerra:	Entrega-te, corsário,	*Captain:*	Corsair, surrender
	À nossa religião,		To our religion;
	(por) Dentro deste nau		For inside this ship
	Tem um padre Capelão!		There is a chaplain!
Rei Mouro:	Não me entrego e nem pretendo	*King of the Moors*	I'm not surrendering, nor do I intend to,
	Que não é de nossa Lei;		For this is not part of our law ;
	Somos filhos da Turquia,		We are the children of Turkey,
	e o nosso deus é rei!		And our god is king!

The striking similarity between Bumba's version and the one annotated by Moraes is particularly intriguing if we consider the geographical and temporal distances between both variants: Moraes recollects his *Chegança* in Bahia, more than 800 km from Bumba's city Pilar, and the two events were separated by a time span of about 120 years. Despite the existence of some annotations with fragments of the Chegança collected by authors like Moraes, there is no complete transcription of it, and Bumba received all his knowledge about the feast by oral transmission. As usual in oral tradition, the syncretic text was completely memorized by the master, who could still recite it and discuss it in detail in his most recent interview in 2019, when he was 93 years old.

3 Analysis of the chant – musical, verbal, and syncretic aspects

If the resemblance in the verbal instance of the text is already remarkable, the similarity of the syncretic musical text is really astounding, as can be seen in Figure 2:

Figure 2: Transcription of a *Chegança* witnessed in 2002 in Pilar, AL.

In the score above, the F# tonality, originally used by Master Bumba's *Chegança*, is transposed to C in order to facilitate the comparison between that version and the one collected by Mário de Andrade about 80 years before. Despite some minor differences, the two scores coincidence reaches the impressive mark of 80% – but if some of the divergences are treated as *appogiature* and ornamentations, which definitively seems to be the case, the level of coincidence increases significantly.

Similar as the versions can be, our analytical effort will from now on focus in Master Bumba's variant, for a reason that also sheds light on the semiotic approach we intend to develop: we had the opportunity to witness the presentation that will be investigated. Even if Mário de Andrade had had the means to document the 1928 performance also in images, it would be very unlikely that such a material could allow us to dive also into an existential perspective of the presentation – an approach that can be greatly enriched by the phenomenological observations and physical presence of the analyst in some of its stages.

One of the most striking features of Bumba's version lies on the ambiguity between the Ionian and the Mixolydian modes, and how such ambivalence relates to the verbal text. Thus, whereas the imperative "Entrega-te, corsário" ["Corsair, surrender" – M.2–3] takes place in Ionian, the complement "à nossa religião" ["To our religion" – M.3–5] – thus, a metamorphosis by means of the conversion – is in Mixolydian. The effects of sense of such a commutation between categories of content and expression – the canonical definition of semi-symbolism – prove to be structural to the text they enrich. After all, the mode transformation in the plane of expression is homologous to the subject transformation – the conversion – in the plane of content. This metaphor – which actually corresponds to a trope – might seem to be a fortuitous fruit of casualty, were it not recurrent in the text. So, in the next strophe, we find the emphatic refusal of the manipulation in the Moor's phrase "Não me entrego, nem pretendo" ["I'm not surrendering, nor do I intend to" – M. 16–17], which is justified by the argument "pois não é de nossa lei" ["for this is not part of our law" – M. 17–19]. Therefore, the Moor refuses to surrender because capitulating would mean to break their own laws – and this would imply a metamorphosis of the subject by perversion, a fact that eventually takes place later when the Moors renounce to their faith and accept to be baptized. Thus, the mode ambivalence anticipates the revelation of the moral frailty of the Moor, insinuating in advance the metamorphosis that will occur in the following scenes.

Another rhetorical tool, to be highlighted in the chant, is the ascending perfect 4th, working as a martial *topos*, in an analogous way with respect to the *Marseillaise* and the Brazilian national anthem. Its association to the lyrics creates an appealing synecdoche that reinforces the polemical character and assertiveness both of the demands of surrender by the Christian addresser – "Entrega-te" [Surrender] – and the refusal of the addressee to accept the manipulation – "Não me entrego" [I'm not surrendering]. Another aspect to be considered is briefly discussed by Greimas and Fontanille in their *Sémiotique des Passions:* the relation between the opening aspectualization and the effect of meaning of the modal verb *to-want* (Greimas and Fontanille 1993: 41–42). Thus, this perspective would imply the presence of the opening gesture and semantic trace of *will* both in the Christians imperative order of surrendering and in the desire of resistance of the Moors.

The second phrase (M.6–10, 19–23, with repetitions) corresponds to a short descending progression built with the juxtaposition of ascending leaps and descending gradations of 3^{rds} – a motif which is retrograded in its third incidence, generating an ascending gradation and a descending leap of a minor 3rd. Such a specular relation between the beginning and end of the phrase generates an effect of meaning of *conclusion* that is consistent with the relation between the closing aspectualization and the modal verb *to-know* (Greimas and Fontanille 1993). The semiotization of the figures of expression is in this case compatible with the categories of content mobilized in the verbal text: both phrases emphasize modal and descriptive values that are quintessential to the comprehension of the identities of the contenders. Thus, in the first incidence of the second phrase, the Christians will announce the presence of the "padre capelão" [chaplain], the man with the power to lawfully convert their opponents into Christian allies – what implies both the reinforcement of the identity of the Christians and the annihilation of that of the Muslims. In the second incidence, in which the discourse is assumed by the King of the Moors, the Moorish identity is highlighted by affirming that "somos filhos da Turquia, e o nosso deus é rei" [we are the children of Turkey, and our god is king!] – once more, a statement of power and value by means of their presentation as members of a great empire – an argumentative synecdoche – ruled by their god – a super-human statute. Therefore, while the first phrase stresses the antagonism between the contenders, the second one emphasizes the self-conscience of their respective values and identities.

Finally, another remarkable homology between the form of expression and the form of content appears in the musical instance: the opposition between the rhythmical homogeneity of the first phrase with the heterogeneity of the second one. Thus, both the order to surrender and its refusal appear in a homogeneous continuity of eight notes, whereas both the affirmations of identity values – the chaplain in the Christians speech, the statute of children of the empire and serfs of god in the voice of the Moors – are heard in a heterogeneous discontinuous texture comprising sixteenth, eighth and quarter notes.

The generative path is summarized in Table 1.

In the fundamental level, the opposition *live vs death* is homologous to the aspectual oppositions *continuity vs discontinuity, cursivity vs punctuality*[1] and to the phoric opposition *euphoria vs dysphoria*. Thus, in the text, *life* appears as euphoric and is associated to the *continuity* of the *cursive* aspect, whereas *death* is dysphoric and related to the aspects of *discontinuity* and *punctuality*. The categories in the fundamental level are converted into values in the narrative level, and so the cursivity in *life* appears associated with the *power* that the Christians, as *addressers*, impose upon the Moors they want to convert – or *to-make-not-to-believe*. The Muslim *addressees* have the *duty* – *to-have-to-believe* – to resist the *death* represented by their conversion and the annihilation of their faith and identity.

The values in the narrative level are converted into themes and figures in the discursive level, where the Christian *power* appears in the theme of their *advancement*, and *peace* is proposed in case the Moors accept to be baptized. These latter are moved by their *duty* to *war*, in a desperate effort of *resistance*. As far as the figures of the discourse are concerned, the aspects of continuity and cursivity are convoked to the Christians imposing *religion*, personified by their *chaplain*, counterpointed by the Muslim sense of obedience to their *law*, associated to the aspects of punctuality and discontinuity and represented by the syncretic figure of their *king* which is presented as a ruling representative of god. A trace of the bias of the text is perceptible in the presentation of the Christians by mean of an ecliptic *we* subject in the 1st person of the plural, whereas the king of the Moors is symptomatically called *Corsair* – the technical, but even so pejorative, a term for a sea criminal sponsored and at the service of the crown. The activities of the *corsair* would be illicit, even if legitimized by the crown he served – a metaphor for those who would be the faithful servants of an allegedly false religion, and whose baptism could prove to be enough of a remedy to guarantee their redemption. Finally, in topological terms, *here* coherently means the Christian *ship*, while otherness in *there* appears related to distant *Turkey* and to their so-called alien god, all of them stigmatized as dysphoric in a discourse that barely disguises its partiality.

The two axes that organize the generative path pervade not only its fundamental, narrative, and discursive levels – they regard also some categories of expression homologous to categories of content, constituting figures of expression and semi-symbolic relations. Thus, as discussed before, the instability between the

---

[1] In the *Sémiotique des passions*, Greimas and Fontanille propose a connection between the aspect of *cursivity* with the modal verb *can*, and likewise an association between the aspect of *punctuality* and the modal configuration *to-have-to* (Greimas and Fontanille 1993:41–42).

Ionian and Mixolydian modes act as a *metaphor* of the hesitating faith of the Moors that will be converted to Christianism – their quandary being emulated by the fall of the note B to Bb, the aspectual trace of discontinuity being semiotized from the rupture of the mode to that of their faith. On the other hand, the ascending perfect 4th leap works as a *topos* functioning as a *synecdoche* of the martial character of the Christians converted into crusaders spreading the power of their faith.

Table 1: Analysis of the generative path.

			Christians	Moors
PLANE OF CONTENT	Fundamental Level	Categorical opposition	Life	Death
		Flow	continuity	discontinuity
		Aspectuality	cursivity	punctuality
		Phoria	euphoria	dysphoria
	Narrative Level	subject statute	addresser	addressee
		modal configuration	to-make-not-to-believe	to-have-to-believe
		pathetic configuration	power	duty
	Discursive Level	figures	our religion	our law
			chaplain	king
		themes	peace (Surrender)	war (I'm not surrendering)
			advancement	resistance
			identity	otherness
		actor	We	Corsair
		space	ship (here)	there (Turkey)
PLANE OF EXPRESSION		Musical mode	Ionian	Mixolydian
		Figures of expression	synecdoche	metaphor

4 The loss of identity: Annihilation and transcendence

Eero Tarasti's Existential Semiotics offers most invaluable methodological and conceptual tools to the analysis of complex syncretic performances like the *dramatic dances* – in Mario de Andrade's nomenclature – or *musical dramas* that constitute cultural manifestations such as the *Chegança*. Tarasti's *Zemic model* can be summarized in the scheme below (Tarasti 2012):

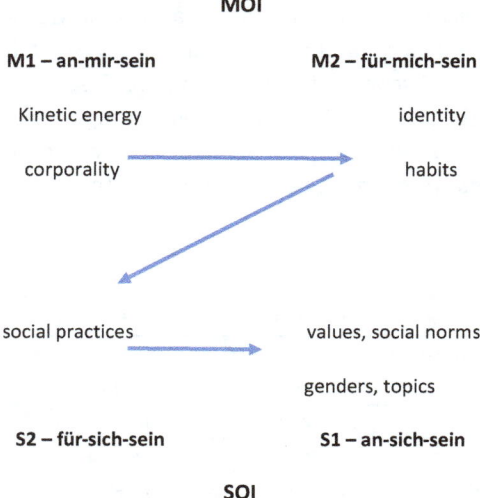

As far as *corporality* and *kinetic energy* are concerned in M1, although no choreographic elements distinguishing the two battling groups of dancers was detected, it is important to note that the contending swords that clashed steadily every beat were slightly stronger and higher in the off-beats – a metaphoric element evoking the recurrent semantic trait of subversion, here by means of displacing the emphasis from the *down* to the *upbeat*. Another interesting corporal aspect was that the Christians' part was sung by the Captain (Master Bumba himself) alone, whereas their opponents' reply was sung not only by the King but by all the Moors. This simple but extremely significant property will be further discussed in S1.

The identity (M2) of the performers is marked by the opposition between the Christians' white uniform – very close to the orthodox traditional Brazilian navy patterns – and the red phantasy characterizing the Moors – red helmet and garments with a Santa Claus' cape in a totally heterodox composition freely inspired in the Brazilian firemen uniform. Thus, besides the chromatic *white vs red* opposition homologous to *Christians vs Moors*, a most important visual dichotomy is also *orthodoxy vs heterodoxy* – unsurprisingly, the Christians as representatives of *order*, whereas the Moors appear associated to the *subversion* of traditional standards.

The social interactions that characterize S2 can, in this case, be summarized by the dynamics related to war. The classical semiotic opposition between contractual and polemical relations will here definitely pend to the latter – expressed mainly by the physical combat displayed in Figure 3 –, even if not excluding the

Figure 3: Photo by the author of Master Bumba's *Chegança*: Captain battling the Moorish King.

former, represented by the Christian's offer to surrender, which could barely hide its blatant character of ultimatum. The conflict, in this case, is, by no means, a mere tense instability without a definite direction: it clearly proves to have a sense, which can be summarized by the term *conversion* – which ultimately means the annihilation of the opponent by the denial of his former values and his transformation into an ally. This symbolic death stablishes a remarkable commutation with the modal structure of the musical phrase. As can be seen in Figure 2, the first phrase appears originally in a C plagal Ionian mode, rapidly shifting to a C plagal Mixolydian mode with a *finalis* in G. In a simplification similar to Schenker's *Mittelgrund*, the phrasal structure follows a descending line with the notes C – B – A – G, as can be observed in Figure 4:

Figure 4: Reduction of the first phrase resulting in the C – B – A – G line.

The second phrase reframes the Mixolydian C into the dominant chord of an Ionian F mode, but ends up with a deceiving cadence – and its dysphoric transition to minor – whose resolution falls into an Eolian D rather than in its relative, the Ionian F. The consequence is that a similar reduction will reveal the transposition of the same descending phrasal structure with nodes in G – F – E – D, as marked in Figure 5:

So-mos fi-lhos da Tur-qui-a, e o nos-so Deus é rei;

Figure 5: Reduction of the second phrase resulting in the G – F – E – D line.

This conversion in the plane of expression from C Ionian to D Eolian by means of the instability from B to Bb and of a deceiving cadence compounds a complex musical figure of expression which is homologous to the narrative process of religious conversion and its thematic projection into the discursive level. Thus, the musical modulation ultimately works as a metaphor of the aimed religious conversion that the Christians will impose upon the Moors. The instability that brings to the decay from B to Bb is another metaphor of the hesitation of the Muslims' faith, and the deceiving cadence ending with a dysphoric minor resolution expresses the crises between *to-be* and *to-seem-to-be*, the euphoric belief in *faith* and the symbolic death represented by its loss by means of the defeat in battle and the conversion to another religion.

Finally, as far as S1 and its social norms are concerned, it is interesting to consider the meaning of the conversion that appears in the *Chegança* in Brazilian culture and society. In the absence of a significant Muslim community in Colonial Brazil – with a very small Islamic presence even today –, it is fundamental to consider that the conflict between Christians and Moors can be seen as a metaphor of another much more significant duality: that one between Christians on the one hand and on the other hand the complex and heteroclite originally Pagan collectivity embracing the religiosity of the hundreds of Native Brazilian ethnic groups and the no less numerous African peoples brought to the country by force -– the Bantus and Yorubas deserving a special mention due to their enormous contribution to the national heritage. Thus, this originally religious opposition pervades the social structure throughout, at least, two other dimensions: the ethnic (*whites vs non-whites*) and social (*dominator vs dominated*) perspectives ("dominance" here appearing as the power to oppress in political, social, and economic terms).

In all these dimensions, the *conversion* would ultimately sponsor the repetition of a social process which is fundamental to the history of the Iberian Peninsula in its transition from the Muslim occupation in the Middle Age to the Christian kingdoms in the Modern Era, and that can be exemplified by the situation of its Jewish community. Fully incorporated (*inclusion*) and indistinguishable from its Christian and Muslim peers in some periods of the Muslim rule, with the development of the Christian fundamentalism that would write with the Inquisition some of the darkest pages in the history of the peninsula, the Jewish community in the recently occupied Nazari kingdom of Granada received an ultimatum of its conqueror, King Ferdinand II of Spain, with a decree that scheduled a period after which the Jews should either convert to Christianism or be expelled (*exclusion*). Those that accepted to stay – and consequently also to be baptized – became known as the "new-Christians", being firstly *segregated* by means of several important restrictions with respect to their physical and social mobility. After the fall of the restrictions, the new-Christians were finally *assimilated* to the Christian community – the necessary condition to reach the final stage of *inclusion* and become indistinguishable with respect to the Christian community. This path can be illustrated by the diagram below:

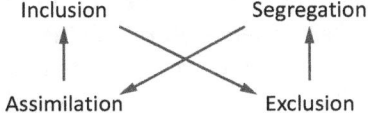

Diagram 1: Inclusion, segregation, assimilation, exclusion.

Unsurprisingly, the *Chegança*, in fact, reproduces a historical cycle very familiar to the Iberian civilization, in which the beaten Moors will have to choose between two forms of *exclusion:* baptism – *segregation* followed by *assimilation* – or death – the ultimate form of annihilation. The abandon of their former values is nonetheless expressed in the Chegança not as the loss of their previous identity, but as the *transcendence* of the allegedly equivocated state of sin that would have led them astray. It is no wonder that such an expression of the Iberian *Volksgeist* develops deep roots throughout all of its colonies, from the Americas do the Philippines, for they represent metaphorically the promise of inclusion to the large, frequently majoritarian and heteroclite non-white and non-Christian communities that accept to transcend their former identities expecting to pass from an initial phase of segregation to that of assimilation that would eventually lead them to their full acceptance by their dominators – a promise that contemporary history sadly proves that is still to be fulfilled.

A final but no less important remark regards an intriguing question: would the profound social meaning of the metaphoric connotation of religious conversion as a form of transcendence by redemption with respect to a former identity and a promise of social inclusion be original contributions of the Iberian imagery and semiosphere due to very specific historic conditions, or could the 13th-century Occitan text already allow a similar polysemic approach? Or, in a different perspective: would the original Occitan text be essentially denotative – a biased epic narrative of the combats between Francs and Moors glorifying the former with respect to the latter –, or could it already represent in its time the social parable of conversion for the sake of inclusion that it came to acquire in the New World?

Although this problem deserves a book rather than a few lines to be conveniently enlightened, it should be advanced that there is enough evidence to allow at least the hypothesis that a similar connotation would, by no means, be foreign to an Occitan living in 13th century Provence.

First of all, the status of the Occitan language suffered a dramatic transition, since if "in the 12th to 13th centuries it was a vehicular language for poetry that enjoyed a strong international reputation", by the 15th century its scope had "changed from a deracinated and genuinely international idiom into a minor provincial art form" (Léglu 2010). Henri Giordan blatantly relates this decadence to what he identifies as "the destruction of the Occitan society after the Albingensian Crusade" from 1209 to 1229 (Giordan 1973: 135) – a period very close to that of the production of the *Roman de Fierabras* –, followed by what Catherine Léglu defined as the imposition of "northern legal and social norms" (Léglu, Rist and Taylor 2013). The Catalan historian Jordi Bolòs i Masclans defined this period as "the conquest and colonization of the lands d'Oc, which would be the beginning of a process that caused the destruction of its very singular cultural and national identity", leading thus to the conquest of "one of the culturally richest countries in the European continent" that, far from being limited to a handful of small cities in Provence, could then see its borders extending "from Catalunya to Northern Italy" (Masclans 2014: 10, 21, 23). Moreover, in the words of Masclans, the Catalan language is far closer to Occitan than to Spanish (Masclans 2014: 25), as Occitan is much closer to Catalan than to French – and nonetheless, even if Catalunya has been able to preserve its language, culture, identity, and political autonomy in a far higher degree than a much more "converted" Provence, both regions are still now struggling to have their language and voice legitimized by a foreign language speaking capital that, according to Giordan, insists on maintaining an "imperialistic attitude towards its ethnical cultures" (Giordan 1973: 136).

Thus, the tragical fate of the once blooming Occitania – with its troubadours and its Cathar faith and to whom we owe the version of the *Roman de Fierabras* that still echoes worldwide – of having its people being ultimately "converted" to a new religion and a new language is not significantly different from the Native Brazilians and Africans that were obliged to a similar renouncement – and the same applies to the Incas, Aztecs, or even somehow to the 20th century Catalans having their voice and language silenced by Franco's dictatorship. It is just as if these peoples and their corresponding narratives shared a similar kind of generative path that departed from deep level invariants in S1 – the farce of a process of conversion for the sake of inclusion – to reach its physical manifestations in M1 and its corresponding discursive structures in radically different configurations, suitable to the corporality, space, and time of the enunciation. In Adolph Bastian's terminology, the *Elementargedanken* related to the tragically forced conversion would be the invariant that, due to the particularities of different *Völkergedanken* (Bastian 2005: 171), would appear in such different forms of manifestation as in Master Bumba's *Chegança* or in the spectacular *mis-en-scène* of the *Moros I Cristians* Festival in the Spanish city of Alcoi, in Valence – another region whose language is far closer to the one spoken by their Catalan neighbours than to Spanish. The Zemic model thus proves to be a powerful analytical tool not only to the analysis of specific texts but also to the study of their intersemiotic translations throughout different cultures – a subject that deserves to be further discussed in the near future.

References

Albert-Llorca, Marlène. 2015. L'image du Maure dans les fêtes de « *Moros y Cristianos* » (Pays valencien, Espagne). In Catherine Richarté (ed.), *Héritages arabo-islamiques dans l'Europe méditerranéenne*, 449–459. Paris: La Découverte.
Andrade, Mário de. 1982. *Danças dramáticas do Brasil. 1º Tomo*. Belo Horizonte: Itatiaia.
Bekker, Immanuel (ed.). 1829. *Der Roman von Fierabras, provenzalisch*. Berlin: G. Reimer.
Bautista, B. Ramírez. 2001. Danza de moros y cristianos en Huamantanga: tradición y teatro popular en la sierra de Lima". *Revista Anthropologica Del Departamento De Ciencias Sociales* 19(19). 195–210.
Bastian, Adolf. 2005. Elementary ideas, folk ideas and geographical provinces. In Klaus Peter Köpping & Adolf Bastian. *Adolf Bastian and the Psychic Unity of Mankind: the Foundations of Anthropology in Nineteenth-Century Germany*. Münster: Lit Verlag Münster.
Beutler, Gisela. 1986. *Actas del octavo Congreso de la Asociación Internacional de Hispanistas : celebrado en Brown University, Providence Rhode Island, del 22 al 27 de agosto de 1983*, 221–233. Madrid: Ediciones Istmo.
Englekirk, John Eugene. 1940. Notes on the repertoires of the New Mexico Spanish Folktheater. *Southern Folklore Quarterly* IV(4). Gainesville: University of Florida.
Ferraro, Alceu Ravanello & Daniel Kreidlow. 2014. Analfabetismo no Brasil: configuração e gênese das desigualdades regionais. *Educação e realidade* 29 (2). Porto Alegre: UFRGS.
Giordan, Henri. 1973. Occitanie : langue, culture, lutte des classes. *L'Homme et la société*, N. 28 "Linguistique, structuralisme et marxisme".
Greimas, Algirdas Julien. 1983. *Du sens II*. Paris: Seuil.
Greimas, Algirdas Julien & Jacques Fontanille. 1993. *Semiótica das paixões*. São Paulo: Ática.
Koster, Henry. 1816. *Travels in Brazil*. London: Longman.
Mello Moraes Filho, Alexandre José de. 1999. *Festas e tradições populares do Brasil*. Belo Horizonte: Itatiaia.
Landowski, Éric. 2004. *Passions sans nom*. Paris: PUF.

Léglu, Catherine E. 2010. *Multilingualism and Mother Tongue in Medieval French, Occitan, and Catalan Narratives*. University Park: Penn State University Press.
Léglu, Catherine, Rebecca Rist & Claire Taylor. 2013. *The Cathars and the Albigensian Crusade*. London: Routledge.
Masclans, Jordi Bolòs i. 2014. *Occitània i Catalunya dins l'Europa de l'edat mitjana central (segles XII i XIII)*. Lleida: Conselh Generau d'Aran, D.L.
Romero, Sílvio. 1985. *Cantos populares do Brasil*. Belo Horizonte: Itatiaia.
Shefferman, David A. 2014. Rhetorical Conflicts: Civilizational Discourse and the Contested Patrimonies of Spain's Festivals of Moors and Christians. *Religions* 5. 126–156.
Silva, Angélica Maria da. 2007. *Chegança dos mouros – a arca nova: uma manifestação dramática saubarense*. Salvador: UNEB.
Tarasti, Eero. *Semiotics of Classical Music: How Mozart, Brahms and Wagner Talk to Us*. 2012. Berlin, Boston: De Gruyter.
Wiley, Mark V. 1996. *Filipino Martial Culture*. Singapore: Tuttle Publishing.

Cleisson Melo
Saudade: A semiotic study of the cultural episteme of Brazilian existence

Abstract: Talking about saudade stills a challenge especially considering powerful meaning and signification. Probably, it is one of the Portuguese words that are most difficult to explain. Though akin to nostalgia, melancholy (for some people), a complex meaningful sentiment of missing, loneliness, love, hope, suffering, pain, and so on, is the object of several types of research in the Lusophone world. This complexity and ambiguous sentiment take place in the intersection of this paradoxical feeling. It became, with exploration over literature, music, philosophy, not only the key sentiment of the Portuguese soul but an important way to understand human relationships; a condition over temporality.

Assuming that in the complex foundation of Brazilian cultural process saudade shall be one of the most important cultural aspects, in this work I claim to territorialize saudade following it as a cultural trace existing as a social entity, with powerful mechanisms of temporal preservation. Besides, in an interdisciplinary approaching based on Tarasti's Existential Semiotics, a brief study of saudade in the episteme of Brazilian existence would review saudade as a symbolic representation of a sentiment rooted on the cultural experience.

Keywords: Saudade; Existential Semiotics; Semiotic Systems; Signification; Brazilian Culture; Text of Culture

It is a difficult task to talk about Saudade, especially considering powerful meaning and signification. Probably, it is one of the Portuguese words that are most difficult to explain. Though akin to nostalgia, melancholy (for some people), a complex meaningful sentiment of missing, loneliness, love, hope, suffering, pain, and so on, is the object of several types of research in the Lusophone world. This complexity and ambiguous sentiment take place in the intersection of this paradoxical feeling. Saudade became, with exploration over literature, music, philosophy, not only the key sentiment of the Portuguese soul but an important way to understand human relationships; a condition over temporality.

The etymology of Saudade has two major streams: Latin *solitade* or *solidad*; and Arabic *saudah* – both are straight connected to solitude and absence. On the other hand, a free translation for other languages as French, for example, Souvenir or Nostalgie, would not reflect the depth of its meanings. Saudade is more than just sadness and/or nostalgia.

In the twelfth century, Portuguese king and poet Dom Dinis (1261–1325) was one of the first to use the word *soidade* related to Portuguese homesickness, loss or absence of someone or a loved one. It is strongly attached to Great Portuguese Discoveries (giving strong meaning to sadness) and with most of its myth of origin. In 1606, writer, historian, Duarte Nunes Leão (1530–1608) has delivered *Origem da Lingoa Portuguesa* (Origin of Portuguese Language), taking on the tough task of defining and evaluating *suidade/soidade*. He highlighted two key aspects of Saudade: positive and negative; heart (emotion, not reason) versus sadness; pleasure memory versus loss. Certainly, it was the main motif for folk music in Portugal (*Fado*).

It could be resumed in the poem *Mar Português* (Portuguese Sea) by the great Portuguese writer and poet Fernando Pessoa (1888–1935):

> Oh, salty sea, how much of your salt
> Are tears of Portugal!
> To get across you, how many mothers cried,
> How many sons prayed in vain!
> How many brides were never to marry?
> In order to make you ours, oh sea!
>
> Was it worth it? Everything is worthy
> If the soul is not small.
> Who wants to go beyond Bojador,
> Must go beyond sufferance.
> God gave the sea peril and abyss,
> yet upon it, he also mirrored the sky.
>   (Pessoa 1934: 64)

This deeper expression of the Portuguese soul establishes a relationship between saudade and imaginary through cultural myth. The sea is a reflex, a mirror to saudade's representative projection. In this way, Portuguese philosopher Teixeira de Pascoaes (1877–1952) pointed out that saudade is a permanent state of latent soul as consciousness, admitting its universality; a dialogue between human being and nature and cosmos, a very poetic view of man and time (Ferraz 2007).

Therefore, its path in Brazil is linked to the construction of a representative discourse – an image of a nation in the representation of a nation. Thus, three distinct people are protagonists of it: Portuguese (representing European people); African (slaves); and Indigenous (native citizens). I shall regard one point as important; saudade became different for those mentioned people; for Africans, missing freedom and Africa nation, many of them had died of *Banzo* (homesickness). Then, there is Indigenous saudade of living free on their land, and Portuguese saudade of the oversea motherland. These are three original ways of the same sentiment. But we should keep in mind that all of them had to "live" together as an organism in the cultural and social aspects. That was difficult.

Despite the Portuguese influences over Brazilian sociocultural aspects, way of life, miscegenation, specific viewpoint had been very influential in the development of myth and imaginary of Brazilian as a people.

It shows Saudade as a cultural element of Brazil; as people and nation. Nation, in this work I understand as culture, society, value system; as a system of values attached to society and culture. Looking at that as melancholic-myth in mind in the Brazilian discourse, an individual plurality as a cultural metaphor is an emotion vector which defines culture and social elements, and transcendental presence.

Brazilian writer Olavo Bilac (1865–1918) pointed out that plurality as a significative influence in the building of nation:

> And in consistent nostalgias and passions,
> Lascivious pain kiss of three saudades,
> Loving flower of three sad races.
> (Bilac 1940: 140)

Those three sad races (Brazilian myth of origin) are the root of the Brazilian socio-cultural foundation, where those plural aspects are imbued in several fields (psycho-social-cultural) representing the essential elements in its development. At the same time, it emphasizes melancholic/nostalgic character as part of Brazilians but coming into a paradox feeling. Orico said, "Brazilian Saudade, a fresh one, happier than sad, more imagination than pain" (Orico 1940: 44). It is more optimistic, happy (less sad), and imaginative (less pain). Imagination stands out in the African slaves' desire for freedom; for the Indigenous, it is their being so free in their lands; and the Portuguese overseas motherland. This mix of hope and pain, but nostalgic, strengthen the Brazilian soul. This hermeneutic-symbolical approach characterizes the "multiple souls" through this powerful sentiment.

I could classify the paradoxical aspects and elements as inclusive which is preclusive. Thus, according to studies of imaginary culture and the interrelationships with myth enable dynamic exchanges of mythical images. About it, an anthropologist Gilbert Durand (2002) has developed a myth theory based on anthropological structures of imaginary to classify symbols and archetypes, distinguishing between two regimes: diurnal and nocturnal. Diurnal is the antitheses, verticalization of images, the opposition of ideas and words. Nocturnal deals with the harmonization, conjunction, horizontalization of mythical structures. Therefore, diurnal is preclusive – this or that –, and nocturnal is inclusive – this and that. That is the complex sentiment of saudade: this or that, and this and that; pain and pleasure, and joy or sadness.

This very singularity is indicative of an existential approach to study the human condition.

> In the act of saudade, the existence of being for the subject and the existence of the subject for the being, or by scholastic vocabulary expressive words, that for which there is saudade is, in a certain viewpoint, this *in* [*esse in*], that is, event that is given in an individualized consciousness, and under another, this *ad* [*esse ad*], that is, intentional relationship with the absent and desired object. (Carvalho 1998: 73)

Consequently, it is an expression of the plural territory of existence as a commonplace for a cluster of individuals or groups, where they can reinvent, recreate, imagine themselves, or even appropriate the cultural, representative, and symbolic imaginary to become permanent into time.

Admitting the plurality of Brazilian culture, it works as a mirror, reflected in the mythic representation of the great nature. That representative aspect of the metaphor of Saudade shall be considered as a crucial element in the construction of Brazilian culture(s). Representation/symbolism goes through the process of appropriation, a kind of dynamic process of "anthropophagical challenger" of two worlds; civilized vs. wild. For that, it is necessarily a cultural immersion.

1 Saudade (places and culture)

Brazilian cultural construction process shall be seen from a singular point. Three main people, with original sociocultural experiences, share the same environment, land, places, and so, but there are differences and symbolic space. It was not a peaceful dealing, but at the same time, there was a coexistence (cultural) with no longer defined borders. So, the Brazilian cultural environment is a kind of fusion of those three symbolic "cultural worlds", but not in the sense of something melted as a homogenous mix. This apparently harmonic relationship occurs within the same universe.

In this "kaleidoscope of agreements and disagreements, small and large collisions" [. . .] "happen tensions over the occupation of the same space – the gradual emergence of something distinct, perhaps a kind of synthesis which the discourse on the national system seeks to capture systematically from the 19th century onwards." (Lima 2011b: np.). The challenge to deal with those forces could be seen as one of the prime points in the construction of Brazilian society. Power relations and internal conflicts allow a collective dimensional representation of that construction; symbolic space disruption. Cultural presence (African, Indigenous, and Portuguese) makes up what we are as a society, and that is not an external element.

It is clear, in this context, that symbolic imagetic space defines the cultural borders. As such, values emerge from the society building, setting saudade as a category that moves from society (collective) to within us (subject).

According to this view, saudade, as a cultural trace, exists as a social entity capable of being felt and experienced collectively. It is inside and outside of us. So, as territories, saudade has powerful mechanisms of temporal preservation, bringing past to the present, considering memory as a place of preservation.

Thinking about saudade is a way to discuss the temporal eternalization of an event or occasion. In the Brazilian context, it is possible to be in an eternal situation even before it ends, thus being a kind of premature missing for something that is yet to come. This "future saudade" has an affective connection attached to the moment, exactly as Brazil was established. It is not a unique Brazilian sentiment, but a frame of the rooting process of Brazilian being.

It connects territorialization to the idea of "between-places", where values and knowledge manifest through [(dis)continuous] temporality, underlining the tension "and/or". Saudade speaks about time from within, rejecting any kind of static interpretation; place of thinking: presence and absence. It brings to discuss cultural aspects present on that dichotomy. So, to understand saudade by the Brazilian axis, the local is very important, where the temporal construction is a territory of preservation.

Narratives about territory (representative creations), established in time-space as cultural manifestations/representations, and significative territories, based on experience (individual and collective), provide myth, signs, and symbols of representation. At the same time, cultural manifestations are located territories.

Thinking saudade as a projection of desire in a cultural context (sentiment and/or emotion) links intention to corporal existence (very similar to the concrete in Levi-Strauss); unconscientious existence – "saudade is to be and then to have" (Rosa 1983: 68). Here, the desire (to want) presented as "it and that" is a frame of Brazil and its diversity, the desire of developing an individual language with esthetic bases (place of intention/impetus).

Besides cultural and social aspects, the paradox of this key emotion points up to the position of individuals defined more by their own creations; how we create ourselves in the sense of society and individual. Thus, as an expression made up by identity traces (place of expression) highlights the sense of belonging in this material dimension; the materiality of representations.

As a place of speech – social practices, culture, and stimulus – saudade is a conscious knowing emotion, intentionality as an example of norms; desire, cultural practices (dimension of material/object). This is not the individual or subject, but a collective practice (social), to observe and be observed as part of a whole; social body. Here, culture through saudade as identity trace manifested as a practice of social rhetoric.

On the other hand, as a made-up essential human phenomenon (philosophical, social, historic) and as a culture, it means a place of existence/phenomenon (existential) in the sense of a symbolic sign present in our mind, moving between continuing and discontinuing temporality; subject in disjunction to the object.

Being "and/or" sets saudade in the symbolic and material dimension, increasing symbolic borders in the material representation, establishing multiple (concrete and symbolic) ones. Semiotically, the concept of border/frontier also is something which splits and connects simultaneously, better explaining the diversity of manifestations through cultural elements. "Saudade can be a key element of a metaphysical interpretation of existence, which could lead to taking a stand in the world, that affects the totality of existence lived and for living." (Carvalho 1998: 74).

2 Semiotics of Saudade

The search for definitions of representative values (as cultural traces) of the construction of Brazilianness comes up against this existing interrelationship. We should consider that the identification process is part of the belonging process, by building a sense; individuals influence and are influenced by different cultural elements.

At this point, I claim a connection between semiotics and saudade, especially considering Existential Semiotics (ES). In short, Tarasti's theory deals with the distinction between Moi and Soi interpreted as individual aspects of the subject and social/society. The principal point is to study the sign-in movement, giving us the knowledge to understand a living sign from within.

This neosemiotics considers the contemporary world, Moi (me), with the definition that "the subject appears as such, as a bundle of sensations" (Tarasti 2015: 24), encompasses two dimensions M1 body and M2 psyche, representing individual cases. Soi (self), "the subject appears as observed by others, as socially determined. These constitute the existential and social aspects of the subject, or rather, its individual and communal sides" (Tarasti 2015: 24); S1 "represents norms, ideas, and value of social context that are virtual potentialities of a subject; and S2 represents the norms, ideas, and values of the social context actualized by the society" (Macdonel 2011: 153).

The theoretical scheme is based on two categories of ornithological nature: *Dasein* and *Transcendence*. Shortly, *Dasein* is "simply the world in which we as subjects live, surrounded by other subjects and objects with which we try to come to terms" (Tarasti 2009: 1756). In the field of signification Transcendence "is anything absent, but present in our minds" (Tarasti 2009: 1757).

So, according to Tarasti, the aspects of subjectivity are:

(1) Being-in-myself represents our bodily ego, which appears as kinetic energy, khora, desire, gestures, intonations, Peirce's "First". Our ego is not yet conscious of itself, but rests in the naive Firstness of its being; modality: endotactic, 'will'.

(2) Being-for-myself corresponds to Kierkegaard's position of the "observer". Sartre's negation, in which mere being shifts to transcendence, points up what is lacking in its existence; in this way, being becomes aware of itself and of transcendence. The mere being of the subject becomes existing. This corresponds to the transcendental acts of my previous model: negation and affirmation. The ego discovers its identity; it reaches a certain stability and permanent corporeality via habit; modality: endotactic, 'can'.

(3) Being-in-itself is a transcendental category. It refers to norms, ideas, and values, which are purely conceptual and virtual; they are potentialities of a subject, which he or she may or may not actualize. What is involved are abstract units and categories; modality: exotactic, 'must'.

(4) Being-for-itself means the aforementioned norms, ideas and values as realized by the conduct of the subject in his or her *Dasein*. Those abstract entities appear here as "distinctions", applied values, choices, and realizations that often will be far from original transcendental entities; modality: exotactic, 'know'. (Tarasti 2012: 26)

This four-dimensional model, in this context, combines aspects of Moi and Soi subjectivities. It portrays a dynamic movement among those four logical cases: "the transformation of a chaotic, corporeal ego into one having identity, into an ego that becomes a sign to itself" (Tarasti 2012: 26).

Unlike Heidegger, in ES *Dasein* is not only my being or my existence but embraces other individuals and objects. Thus, new categories of signs emerge in the traffic between *Dasein* and Transcendence. "The self (Soi) functions as a kind of memory of the body (Moi); it gives form to the traces of tensions and needs that have lodged or been inserted in the fleshly 'Me' (Moi)" (Tarasti 2012: 17).

For this work, it is important because the collective "other" is present here. So, the social-oriented environment enables the emerging abstract and virtual values of signs, but has not yet become "concrete".

Based on *Dasein*, a new theory of human mind is present on the principles of Moi/Soi unfolded on the four modes of being: body, persona, social practices, and values. In a nutshell, it is not only the Hegelian collective spirit but the movement and communication between Moi and Soi.

It is exactly in the dialectical tension between Moi and Soi, based on the Greimasian modalities of the subject, that we can understand Tarasti's model (Zemic model) and the communication/transformation process between them (figures 1–6). It represents the two sides of our subjectivity.

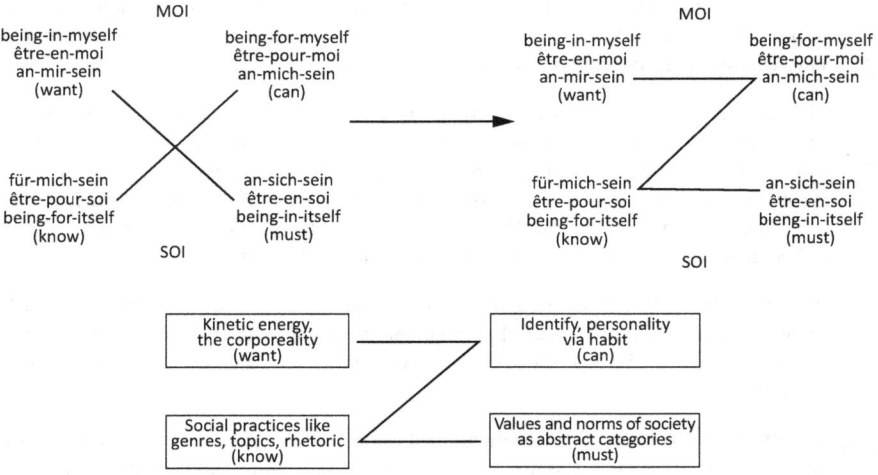

Figure 1: Semiotic Square and Z-Model – Existential Semiotics by Eero Tarasti.

As already mentioned, in the imagery scheme there is a kind of bridge between experience and articulation (Snyder 2000). In this transition between articulation and experience, transcendence and memory can be articulated in saudade. Its connection, based on experience (cultural, in this case), underlines artistic manifestations and its doing.

Imagery schemes can be used representatively and metaphorically to express (other) ideas, both literal and abstract. In nostalgia/memory, it may be seen as a sign or causative element. It articulated in saudade and can foster articulated and/or expressive connections in the creative process. Thus, the absence (which is only present in our memory) can be metaphorically articulated in saudade. In this sense, I understand that the metaphor acting in the absence can dynamically connect to saudade, not only being influenced by remembrance (memory) but mainly in the imaginative (and creative) process. Saudade, in representation, is an essential element in the discourse's construction, such as, for example, the image of the nation as representation and identity in distinct ways.

One of the most important things is the dynamic aspect of this processual concept. Modalities are very relevant in the understanding of the symbolic representation. Also, it could be one meaningful pathway on the track to realize saudade in the thinking field.

Considering modalities portraying dynamic *Dasein*, it is possible to apply saudade as something present in Transcendence; something absent but present in our mind. Here, "positive" and "negative" aspects of saudade are covered. It underlines the "and/or" paradox of saudade, inclusion and exclusion, junction and disjunction, placing saudade as an "object" articulated in the memory, i.e., taking place in the Transcendence; absently present.

This saudade movement and articulation idea, representatively or symbolically speaking, acts as an inside sign present in the cultural construction of Brazil. What I am trying to say is: a powerful signification/representation load would help to create a "virtual environment" as a relevant part of the socio-cultural discourse construction. Thus, connecting all those points we would have:

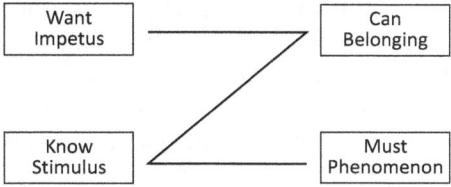

Figure 2: Saudade: Z-Model.

Saudade, as "be the cause of", comes through the existing field in the concretization of realities, or better, it is the desire, the representative attitude in the intentionality of its realities' construction. As a belonging sentiment, saudade is an expression that evokes a related subject and object; materialization of saudade as a reality present in mind and the way we see the world – life experience. This dialectic belonging comes from the meditating will of "me" and "what is my".

As "know", social and cultural practices go through a cultural experience: intentional and conscious expression narratives present in mental/abstract representations of culture. Although, saudade as a complex phenomenon in its totality (existence) is the local of culture, this reflective consciousness of time and the relationship between individuals is the frame of this dynamic proposition. In this temporal dimension with the presence of images (imagetic/imaginary), it is possible to find a deliberative distinction, in some representative, signifies between saudade and culture (existence). Probably, that is the way to the place/local where preservation (survival) of images/myth happens. There is no possibility under a just universal (and unique) or fix (static) saudade.

3 Reflections

If we are talking about this "tropical nostalgia", Brazilianness is part of a cultural process, bringing up to discuss problems of Brazilian reality; key elements, and a certain "tradition" capable to highlight the Brazilian being (social and cultural one). This identity construction becomes one of the central points. It goes through a process of meaning construction, identification, and interpretation of sociocultural traits present in Brazilian reality that make some sense of its representation.

In this way, the search for definitions of values (as cultural traits), representative of identity (construction of Brazilianness), comes up against this prevailing interrelation. We can consider that the identification process is part of the belonging, i.e., constructing a sense, individuals influence and are influenced by different cultural elements.

In contrast, cultural self-description goes through some points in that construction of identity. Probably, the most important one is the construction of the belonging sentiment. At this point, saudade being a cultural/identity trace concerned to Lusophone peoples (even considering that it is a universal sentiment), it is unexpected from them, i.e., it belongs to life experience; either as an individual or society; saudade (place of) phenomenon/existence.

A presumable text written by the great Brazilian composer Heitor Villa-Lobos (1887–1959) highlights the sentiment as the keynote of his *Chôros No. 8*. But the same approach is present in the introduction of *Bachianas No. 5 – Ária* (Cantilena) with so much embedded nostalgic (*saudosismo*), or *Melodia Sentimental*, for example. The sentiment, in this case, is his desire rooted in the Brazilian nostalgic/sensibility, a kind of tropical sadness, melancholy, reviewed as "sentiment" by Villa-Lobos. It is the material (substantial) part of Brazilian soul/identity, and it is axiomatic in Brazilian culture, interspersed by attitudes impregnated with "sentiment(s)", allowing identification as something that is recognized properly as Brazilian being.

In concern to *Chôros No. 8*, Villa-Lobos' intention is a symbolic representation of reality. In the very first measures, there is seeming chaos, the use of popular elements, nature, and repetitions, emerging a very dramatic plot through textural and timbre layers. The key point is illustrating the "chaos" of carnival celebrations that cluster together on their way out, interweaving the urban universe and indigenous parties embedded in sentiment. A dialogue between erudite and popular forces in the way to transfigure corporeal representation ("primitive" rhythm, kinetic) into his style and strategies and this euphoric modernism seems to consider a "contradiction between intention and expression" (Reyner 2016: 13).

Villa-Lobos had a desire to organize his own carnival group – *Sodade do Cordão*, to create the flavour and mood of old carnivals. He was very enthusiastic about the old carnival (the golden era of carnival). And, he made it to revive in 1940, as faithful as possible. The attention to details, all elements, including costumes, music, dancing, and so on, kept Villa-Lobos on track to, from a memorable saudade remembrance, build a parade group very close to early 20th-century one. He had vivid memories of old carnivals.

Memories embedded on saudade, the fulfilment of signification based on a cultural experience, transits on Villa-Lobos' imaginary pushed by impetus as an intention. It intended to express a cultural sense of memory, i.e., cultural experience crystalized as a remembrance; an inner sign of a representative reality. Here, saudade territories as phenomenon manifested through an intentional act of bringing to present a cultural past memory; saudade's places simultaneity – Villa-Lobos' Moi expressed by his Soi.

The soundscape, built up from images (natures, bohemia nights), drives Chôros No. 8 into a representation of a plural image of Brazil, and Villa-Lobos' sensibility/sentiment condition.

Further along, in that sense, the first recording of Bossa Nova[1] music, *Chega de Saudade*[2] by Tom Jobim and Vinícius de Moraes, very representatively has another of saudade:

> Get away, my sorrow [*Vai minha tristeza*]
> And tell her it's just impossible without her [*E diz a ela que sem ela não pode ser*]
> Tell her in a pray [*Diz-lhe numa prece*]
> To come back to me [*Que ela regresse*]
> Because I can't suffer any longer [*Porque eu não posso mais sofrer*]
>
> No more saudade [*Chega de saudade*]
> The truth is that without her there's no peace [*A realidade é que sem ela não há paz*]
> There's no beauty [*Não há beleza*]
> Only sadness and melancholy [*É só tristeza e a melancolia*]
> That won't leave me, won't leave me, won't leave [*Que não sai de mim, não sai de mim, não sai*]
>
> But if she comes back, if she comes back [*Mas se ela voltar, se ela voltar*]
> What a beautiful thing, what a crazy thing [*Que coisa linda, que coisa louca*]
> Cause there are fewer fishies swimming in the sea [*Pois há menos peixinhos a nadar no mar*]
> Than the kissies I'll plant on her mouth [*Do que os beijinhos que eu darei na sua boca*] [. . .]
>
> (Jobim and Moraes 1958: 3)

We can note, first in the title and then in the lyrics, a subject suffering and sad, telling us about a sad past under a present sentiment. There are two dimensions here, first the pain and desire not to suffer anymore related in the first two verses. The second one, present in the next verse, shows us how life would come better with his lover. It addresses a hope sentiment, a positive view on the path of getting her back. Pain and hope, love and desire, sadness and melancholy, point

---

[1] Bossa Nova (new trend/wave) is a very singular style of Brazilian music developed in the 1950s and 1960s, known by a fusion of samba and jazz.
[2] Translated to English as "No More Blues" with new lyrics. I will use a free translation in order to preserve the real meaning of this song.

to happiness based on hope/love as an intension driven by impetus reflected on the sentiment of sadness and pain, but not able to suppress a pleasant one. This positive affirmation present in the third verse is a future projection in the certain return of his lover. Although, this narrative-(land)scape does not represent the object of memory, a (re)constructive, based on experience (cultural), interpretation, and expression of the subject.

The melody acts in parallel to the lyrics. Minor harmonic/melodic construction, lower note ending, and descending movement, despite skipping notes, are the material scenario for a nostalgia expressed on the title and lyrics

Figure 3: Chega de Saudade – m. 09–24.

The second part, positive aspects (hope and happy) are present on a major key which is a symbolic representation of happy/hope in contrast to the minor tone (sad, nostalgic). It is only a representation, a kind of quotation. I will not urge about the real meaning of major-minor tone, but, in this case, there is a symbolic representation expressed on the compositional strategies. As a sign, this representation works in line with lyrics. The compositional rhetoric strategy is at all levels: rhythm, melody, harmony, and structure. It is more than harmony and melody, Bossa Nova rhythm, moderate time, and interpretation. This very articulated musical-compositional strategy addresses all musical elements working as one. As we know, music as a phenomenon and all elements happen simultaneity, but the interrelation among them works as a wide representative/significative sign.

Figure 4: Chega de Saudade – m. 35–50.

We shall consider one important thing in the path of interpreting those signs: the compositor's decisions, which call in question a range of elements that are part of musical narrative and discourse. Here, all elements are assigned in the representation of a plot in a wide meaning context; saudade and its hyponyms.

It roots those representations of saudade on an imagistic idealization present in the construction of national cultural images, and not only on the holding past. This symbolic and representative appropriation of a cultural trace could represent an ethic detachment, but make it up the cultural identity building. However, it avoids common sense, turning itself in an aspect/sign/trace (even considering the universality of saudade) that defines either existentially the Brazilian people as a social being immersed in the world.

So, the representation of a subjective reality addresses saudade as a discursive representation/signification, creating territories that are able to hermeneutically/epistemically measuring of saudade in the cultural-existential field for further approaches and discussions.

Base on a temporal view, saudade appears horizontally but in a nonlinear continuity. Saudade transits in an inner temporality that does not finish. Therefore, saudade operates over time in a bi-dimensional way, tensioning and "re-tensioning" time; past-Time as memory, remembrance, images of impetus, inclusive (this and that). It appears as a framework of knowledge, internal memories – images codification in a symbolic language (subject-object relations), memory, and cultural identity. It is dialectic dealing among objects and subjects.

In what concerns Present-Time, the opening for a potential reality points to a future, as a consequence of that experience based on the impetus and intention to create themselves (people versus nation/society); as intension, aspects of preservation, the desire to extend time under an intension. And Future-Time as a projection based on the past, an expression of social imaginary. Saudade presents aspects of discontinuity (nonlinear) time, opening for stretching and/or contracting.

Maybe the aspects of deconstruction of temporality enhance the abstract elements. It drives saudade in its temporal dimension, establishing the presence of the image. Thus, saudade is an entity working as a frame, a photo in movement, not in the terms of a film, but pushing memories by intention expressed in a timeline that can be or not in conjunction with the chronological time.

José Ferraz de Almeida Junior (1850–1899), a Brazilian painter, had a very singular way of dealing with national representation, far from romanticism, allegories, but close to a common human being. In *Saudade* (1899), the representation of saudade sentiment presents a rich "compositional" scheme of details. It is a frame of his lover, a kind of picture of a moment, probably a remembrance of the artist's memory; he had painted in the year of his death.

The title suggests portraying the sentiment, absence, missing, and so on, embedded in the imagistic representative dimension of this picture; the dark colour scheme, clear illumination in a quotation of São Paulo countryside, in the representation of reality, dialoguing to the national representation in a broad tradition.

Figure 5: Saudade (1899) by Almeida Junior (197cm x 101cm).

It seems to be an aesthetic transgression related to the challenging way of building a common sense, authenticity, and independence. At the same time, the dry dark chromatism turning up deep sadness in contrast to the wall's colours, the light coming up from the window and the colour skin. All of it becomes a virtual entity, mixing sentiment and dryness in the representation of saudade, also, tears of sadness, a man's hat as a symbol of losing and presence of her lover; the presence of absence. The fact about hat to be in a superior position does not represent any kind of masculine superiority, just a representative sign of living together, a mention of one day her lover was there.

If we consider the paper in the woman's hand as a photo, we could have a wide field of interpretation; history, memory, moments, a life; saudade driving memories in the re-creation and re-construction of those memories. It gives a temporality movement to that picture. This cognitive timing goes forward and back from Moi to Soi; picture, colours, sign, meaning, signification, signs, and so on. It is impor-

Figure 6: Saudade (1899) by Almeida Junior – Tears detail.

tant to understand saudade's territories as a dynamic process and scheme. So, as a virtual sign in our minds, time possibilities expressed by the history behind the ink, colour scheme, and texture, interpreted through the movement between *Dasein* and Transcendence, become crystalized signs that emerged from the belonging and cultural experience.

The paradox of saudade transfigured in artistic elements, artistic choosing, and representative context of a reality in which the viewer could identify themselves with the pain, the sadness of the character in the picture. Even abstractly, it puts the observer as part of the artwork, as an entity is able to recognize signs and the symbolic forces present in that reality representation; cultural experience values.

A book with a white fabric above the case reinforces the representation of the absent character. White is symbolically the colour of peace, pureness; here, the pure sentiment of love in the saudade implied. The book is a sign/symbol of living memory, something eternal, locked forever, knowledge as a desire of preservation; the impetus of having the lover back.

The technique used to colour the skin gave it the smoothest aspect than walls and fabrics. It helps the connection of the masterpiece with the representative dimensions. The symbolic representation of saudade is present from corporeal to the levels of values, establishing a construction of a human entity giving a very representative image of the world without artificial elements. Here, there is an intentional process to achieve saudade as a sociocultural experience broadcasted by symbolic communication. It qualifies saudade as a sign, but either as a qualifier factor of experiences.

Despite the construction of discontinuity, there is viewer identification with the signs and symbols, putting them into the picture, denying their presence outside the sentiment represented. It is the transcendental entities and aspects present in the *Dasein*.

In concern to develop a saudade framework, signs crystallization in the *Dasein* through the subject action sets an imagetic representation as an ethic picture of identity from a community as social, or a local representation.

4 Conclusion

Based on the above, it is possible to review saudade as an intra-sign. It appears as a symbolic representation of a sentiment rooted in the cultural experience. Thus, intra-sign acting from within establishes an over meaningful conception translated into another language, either considering achieving several instances of saudade: sentiment, memory, hope-pain, emotional sad-love, and so on, for example.

Rather than measuring saudade in Heidegger terms, understanding saudade as horizontal experience as such memories, relationships, experiencing time from within, resist to a closed concept of time. Also, a vertical point of view addresses saudade and its territories; Brazil's project with a very cultural border.

However, while it should be straightforward to associate a sentiment to a time-space/cultural experience, it could be a good or bad time one, but persona and object. It develops a network of relationships related to memories, building a social world. Nevertheless, this "temporal experience", which points to a future based in the past, but strongly connected to a present desire, is a non-linear future; i.e., before an individual memory, we have a collective one: to fell/experience saudade! I claim it can be a path of mapping saudade though a semiotic viewpoint, establishing connection and axes which enable accurate reading of human condition quantified by saudade. "This amazing saudade that allows (re)connect this world with another, and past with present" (Damatta 2012: n.p.).

This ongoing work is a reflection and investigation of an imagetic sign action as representation and identity construction; building a representative image of saudade highlights saudade entity construction, which is inherently represented through symbolic representations. Saudade investigation through a semiotic discussion with a little philosophical flavour – a cultural/national consciousness that defines the being from a specific condition – that is national and a-national aspects relevant to develop analytical paths able to understand idiosyncrasies and peculiarities of essence and existence of Brazilian being (why not a universal one) through a signification.

References

Bilac, Olavo. 1940. *Musica Brasileira*. In Osvaldo A. Orico, *A saudade brasileira*. Rio de Janeiro: A Noite.

Carvalho, Joaquim de. 1998. *Elementos constitutivos da consciência saudosa e problemática da saudade*. Lisboa: Lisboa Editora.

Damatta, Roberto. 2012. *Conta de mentiroso: sete ensaios de antropologia brasileira*. Rio de Janeiro: Rocco Digital [E-book].

Durand, Gilbert. 2002. *As estruturas antropológicas do imaginário: introdução a arquetipologia geral*. 3. ed. São Paulo, SP: Martins Fontes.

Lourenço, Eduardo. 1982. *O labirinto da saudade*. Lisboa: Dom Quixote.

Ferraz, Roberta Almeida P. de F. 2007. *O mito da saudade*: ambivalência criativa em Teixeira de Pascoaes. *Soletras* Ano VII, N. 13, jan/jun. São Gonzalo: UERJ.

Heidegger, Martin. 2001a. *Seminários de Zollikon*, Petrópolis: Editora Vozes.

Heidegger, Martin. 2001b. *Being and time*. Trans. John Macquarrie & Edward Robinson. Oxford: Blackwell.

Lima, Paulo Costa. 2011. *A influência da África nas Músicas Brasileiras*. Available at: https://paulocostalima.wordpress.com/tag/a-influencia-da-africa-nas-musicas-brasileiras (accessed 28 May 2020)

Jobim, Antônio Carlos & Moraes, Vinícuis de. 1958. *Chega de Saudade*. São Paulo, SP: Editora Musical Arapuã.

Macdonel, Grisell. 2011. Subjectivity in music performance. In *Performa '11: Encontros De Investigação Em Performance*. Aveiro, 2011. Available at: http://performa.web.ua.pt/pdf/actas2011/Grisell%20Macdonel.pdf (accessed 10 June 2020)

Orico, Osvaldo. 1940. *A saudade brasileira*. Rio de Janeiro: A Noite.

Pessoa, Fernando. 1934. *Mensagem*. Lisboa: Pereira.

Reyner, Igor. 2016. Programa de Concerto: Orquestra Sinfônica de Minas Gerais. *Fortíssimo*, n. 1, 2016. https://docplayer.com.br/19064209-Fortissimo-no-1-2016-l-o-b-s-r-a-h-m-a-allegro-vivace-18-02-19-02-i-n-o-v.html (accessed 10 June 2020)

Rosa, Guimarães. 1983. *Rosiana: uma coletânea de conceitos, máximas e brocardos de João Guimarães Rosa*. Rio de Janeiro: Salamandra.

Snyder, Bob. 2000. *Music and Memory: an introduction*. Cambridge/London: The MIT Press.

Tarasti, Eero. 2000. *Existential Semiotics*. Bloomington: Indiana University Press.

Tarasti, Eero. 2009. What is existential semiotics? From theory to application. In Eero Tarasti, Paul Forsell & Richard Littlefield (eds.), *Communication: Understanding/Misunderstanding: Proceedings of the 9th Congress of the IASS/AIS – Helsinki-Imatra: 11–17 June, 2007*. Vol 3. Imatra: International Semiotics Institute; Helsinki: Semiotic Society of Finland.

Tarasti, Eero. 2012. *Semiotics of classical music: How Mozart, Brahms, and Wagner talk to us*. Berlin: De Gruyter Mouton.

Tarasti, Eero. 2015. *Sein und Schein: Explorations in existential semiotics*. Berlin: De Gruyter Mouton.

Rahilya Geybullayeva
Semiolinguistic look on mythology, cultural history and meanings of places in Azerbaijan

Abstract: Transcendence is one of the key categories of philosophy and denotes "a state of being or existence above and beyond the limits of material experience." *Transcendence* comes from the Latin prefix *trans-*, meaning 'beyond,' and the word *scandare*, meaning 'to climb.' When you achieve *transcendence*, you have gone beyond ordinary limitations. The word is often used to describe a spiritual or religious state or a condition of moving beyond physical needs and realities.[1]

Cognitive-semiotic-linguistic analysis of sign and constituent components helps discover the itinerary-history of the transcendence unit of word and sign. This paper contributes explicitly to this research area within the analytical context of how meaning and content are conveyed *through signs and communication* – transcultural references to the ancient or pre-medieval period. It looks at Azerbaijani cases of social practice signs and their cross-cultural changes transferred through communication. For example, this paper uses the symbols incorporated in the modern-day Azerbaijani (Islamic) rite of prayer, *namaz*. It demonstrates how the social practice of namaz includes ways that are also linked to Hinduism. It explores how it is identified as social practice and how it can be seen as a Muslim rite through specific, attributed signs. Or is it relevant to explore its semiotics through its signs dating back to a more ancient, pre-Islamic period? Cognitive anthropology and semiolinguistic analysis of the rite of namaz can help illuminate or understand how the process of transcendence takes place or how the association of specific signs allows the adaptation of a new ritual. In this context, what lies behind the ordinary, secular Azerbaijani word *odun* (wood): is it related to *Odin*, or/ are they just homographs? And what about the case of *halo-hal-hello*? What is behind *Fat(i)ma*, a name associated as Muslim name and its Azerbaijani dialect version *Pad(i)ma*? What links the names of ethnic groups or toponyms such as *Rutul, Udin,* and *Gargar*, well-known in Zagatala region in modern-day Azerbaijan, and almost unknown in other parts of Azerbaijan, not to mention other countries? What does transcendence mean – is it "communication before our eyes, but beyond *our consciousness?*"

---

1 *Transcendence.* https://www.vocabulary.com/dictionary/transcendence

https://doi.org/10.1515/9783110789164-032

Keywords: existential semiotics, cognitive linguistics, *Dasein*, Odin, namaz, Fatma-mano-panteo-hamsa, abjad alphabet, Azerbaijan

What does culture want? To make infinity comprehensible. – Umberto Eco[2]

1 Sign as a transcendantal unit in the classical and pre-classical context

The term transcendence has become an integral part of Professor Eero Tarasti's theory of existential semiotics, and he considers the term from Plato to Islamic Sufis, from Thomas Aquinas and Dante to Kant and Hegel. Traditionally, semiotics has been considered to consist of two major problems: one related to *meaning* and the other to *communication*. As E. Tarasti highlighted during his keynote lecture at the AzCLA-2018 Prototypes conference in Baku,[3] *each sign is, in fact, a transcendental unit in the light of the classical meaning* of the sign (aliquid stat pro aliquo – something stands for something) established in the Middle Ages. This accords with our *method* of reconstructing the itinerary of a sign's semiotics, based on *consonant letters* (abjad or consonant alphabet). Linked to the early alphabet concept in which each consonant is relevant to the meaning, this refers to a transcendental unit in the *light of letters* or *acronyms or letter combinations*, going back *to the pre-medieval period – ancient times.*[4]

A relative date for a starting point for this meaning is the Phoenician alphabet, which originated from the Proto-Canaanite alphabet conventionally thought to be in the 15th century BCE, which in turn is linked to Egyptian hieroglyphs.[5] Phoenician script uses an abjad alphabet, i.e., without vowels, and is the precursor of many alphabets such as Hebrew, Arabic, and Greek. It was based on Egyptian hieroglyphs such as the eye (ayn – in the shape of the eye).

---

2 *Umberto Eco*, from his comment to *The Infinity of lists* – "The list is the origin of culture. It's part of the history of art and literature. What does culture want? To make infinity comprehensible" – Spiegel Interview with Umberto Eco. https://www.spiegel.de/international/zeitgeist/spiegel-interview-with-umberto-eco-we-like-lists-because-we-don-t-want-to-die-a-659577.html.
3 Prototypes in Recycling Cultures and/or Cultural Genomes, 20–21 April 2017, Baku. [Online] Available at: http://www.azcla.org/RCallforpapers.htm
4 For more, see R. Geybullayeva, "Liberal Arts" in *Filologiya və ya ədəbiyyat araşdırmaları tarixi* (journal to mark Prof. Məmməd Qocayevin's 75th birthday). Baku: Mütərcim, 2016, pp. 128–143.
5 *Phonecian/ Canaaite.* https://omniglot.com/writing/phoenician.htm

The names of the letters are acrophonic,[6] and their names and shapes can be ultimately traced back to Egyptian Hieroglyphs. For example, the name of the first letter, 'aleph, means ox and developed from a picture of an ox's head. Some of the letter names were changed by the Phoenicians, including gimel, which meant camel in Phoenician, but was originally a picture of a throwing stick (giml).[7]

Since the Greek and Latin alphabets based on this alphabetic principle and translations of sacred texts into these languages (because of the imperial status of the titular people) enriched Greek and Latin with borrowings from the language of the original text, the abjad translation method is useful for recovering transcendental semiotics.

The next important part of Prof. Tarasti's theory is that the explanation for the transcendental unit may be that the transcendent is everything that does not exist before our eyes, but *remains in our consciousness*. We call them *non-associative relatives* associated with otherness, but they might give a clue as to *what is behind* these signs. Tarasti defined three levels of *transcendence* in existential semiotics:

> The notion of transcendence is perhaps the most provocative new issue which existential semiotics tries to launch for theoretical reflection in contemporary semiotics and philosophy. The following paper lays out three species of transcendence in existential semiotics: empirical, existential, and radical. **Empirical** means elements in our living world, which are abstract, intelligible aspects as in the sense of the German understanding of sociology. The **existential** means that we leave our four-part 'zemic' universe by a reflection, either as negation or affirmation. That constitutes the supra-zemic level. The **radical** one is beyond all temporality, narrativity, etc., a purely conceptual state, of which we can speak only by metaphors. Either transcendence can be naturalized as an aspiration to something more complete than our deficient *Dasein*.[8]

Dasein is one of the cornerstones of German philosophy. Literally translated from German, it means "to be there," that is, "being" or "existence." Heidegger (1889–1976) asks in the introduction to the treatise "Being and Time": which creature will give access to the question of the meaning of Being? Heidegger believes that

---

6 Acrophonic is "the use of what was originally a logogram as a phonetic symbol for the initial sound of the word the logogram represented, as, in Semitic writing, the use of a picture of a shepherd's crook to represent the sound (l), the first sound of *lamed,* the Hebrew word for a shepherd's crook. – *Acrophony*. https://www.dictionary.com/browse/acrophonic
7 Phoenician-Canaanite.[Online] Encyclopedia for writing systems and languages. Available at: https://omniglot.com/writing/phoenician.htm#:~:text=Phoenician%2FCanaanite,date%20 back%20to%201000%20BC.
8 Tarasti, E. "Culture and transcendence – the concept of transcendence through the ages", in Kristian Bankov, Paul Cobley (eds.) *Semiotics and its Masters*. Vol. 1. De Gruyter, 2017. [Online] Available at: https://www.researchgate.net/publication/318145845_Culture_and_transcendence_ the_concept_of_transcendence_through_theages_Volume_1

it can only be that Being, for which the question of Being is essential. This creature he calls "*Dasein*"; the method used in *Dasein* – "Being and Time" – attempts to distinguish between the characteristics of *Dasein* through the interpretation of *Dasein* temporality.[9]

Now for a brief foray into the transcendent according to Tarasti – what does not exist before our eyes but remains in our consciousness; non-associative relations, which can give clues as to what stands behind these signs. This theory, which fully conforms with my theory of the stereotype-archetype-prototype, is considered in the context of presentation and representation. What seems non-existent for one recipient is existent for another (*Dasein*). In this case, the example of the transcendent word-signs *hal(o), od(in), namaz, Mano-Pantea/hamsa*, and non-associative peoples who are part of the modern-day Azerbaijani nation – *Rutul, Udin, Gargar* – from the position of someone of contemporary Azerbaijani culture.

Medieval Islamic symbols determine the specifics of the Azerbaijani semio-linguistic analysis of cultural history. *Pre-Islamic elements* of culture acquired a particular interest in the post-Soviet period in reconstructing national identity and searched for an ethnic past. From this perspective, a proto-historical stage of the semiotics of words in the Azerbaijani language is found both in the region and beyond the modern-day country's borders.

2 Some lexical history or the infinity of lists: Halo, namaz, Fatma, Odin

2.1 *Halo* as an example of radical transcendence in existential semiotics

The expression kefin-*halın* necıdir? (how are you feeling?) is widespread in Azerbaijani. In this instance, the semantic relationship with the lexical and semantic root **Halo** is apparent.

> Modern-day halo and lexico-semantic relatives?
> **Hal** (Azerbaijani) – *spirit;* condition, mood
> **Hal** – kefin-halın – well-known conversational Azerbaijani greeting (between close people), meaning "how is your mood (kef)" or "*spirit* (hal – condition, strength, health)"
> **Hal** – in Azerbaijani tales is an invisible woman, usually a bad *spirit*

---

[9] Heidegger, M. et al. *Being and Time* (1962) [Online] Available at: https://www.bard.edu/library/arendt/pdfs/Heidegger-BeingAndTime.pdf

Ruh (roah – in translation *spirit*, nefes, breath) – nefs (kama – desire, passion in Indian philosophy)
*Ha*llo-*he*llo-(*h*)*ola* (Spanish) – greeting in many European languages
Hal-heal-health-healer (to heal the *soul, spirit*, as in the Yoga system)

Halo (aura, nimbus, gloried circle around the head to highlight a person's sacred status, e.g., a saint) – nimb-aura-aurel-mandorla (the frame around the body of a saint) – *vesica piscis* (blood of *f(p)*ish) – sacred geometry (solar eclipse).

Halo in the imagery
Halo – a ring of light usually around the head of a sacred person; primary in Orthodox Christian *icon* painting. While a visual depiction of the human image was prohibited, the halo substituted for a saint or holy person.
halo – around Buddha's head

Halo related words in different beliefs
Halal/halel/ halleluiah
Hello/halo/hal/*halleluiah* (glorification as salutation)
Halakka/halq(ga) – the way of (fulfillment of) the law – in Judaism

Halal – a Muslim term for what is permissible (equivalent to kosher in Judaism)
Hallel – in Judaism "a section of the liturgy consisting of Psalms 113–18, read during the morning service on festivals, Chanukah, and Rosh Chodesh"[10]
Halakka – the way of (fulfillment of) the law in Judaism
Hal-ga – ring, circle, chain in Azerbaijani
The connection with the sacred semiotic past here is obvious.

ḤLL /Semitic roots
To be(come) clean, pure, holy.
1. Elul, from Hebrew ʔĕlûl, a month name, from Akkadian *elūlu, elūnu*, name of a festival and of a month corresponding to parts of August and September, perhaps from *elēlu* (< *ḥalālum*), to be(come) clean, pure, holy.[11]
Elul is kept in modern-day Turkish – *Eylul* (September).[12]
L consonant

We turn now to the proto-historical root of the word that is contained in the abjad cluster hll. **Ḥ**, as a rule, is likened to the sound (vowel); **L** means "the highest" or "most high" and is contained in the names of god in the region, for example, **Eliyah**-Eliy+as (My God is Yahweh), Allah. **El** is the name of god, sometimes the title of gods, and is the substitute name Yahweh in the Tanakh. In the Book of Genesis, Chapters 18–20, Abraham, the progenitor of the Jews and Arabs, receives

---

10 *Hallel*. Collins Dictionary
11 ḥll. https://www.thefreedictionary.com/_/roots.aspx?
12 For more about t he namesYahweh, El and El-Elyon, see Day, John. *Yahweh and the Gods and Goddesses of Canaan*. Vol. 265. A&C Black, 2002, p.21.

the blessing **El**, when he is blessed with wine and bread by the ruler of the city of Salem and Melchizedek (Maliki-Sedek) who is the priest of El Elyon (the Most High):

> 18 And Melchizedek king of Salem brought forth bread and wine; and he was a priest of *God the Most High*.
>
> 19 And he blessed him, and said: 'Blessed be Abram of *God Most High*, Maker of heaven and earth;
>
> 20 and blessed be *God the Most High*, who hath delivered thine enemies into thy hand.' And he gave him a tenth of all.[13]

> יח וּמַלְכִּי-צֶדֶק מֶלֶךְ שָׁלֵם, הוֹצִיא לֶחֶם וָיָיִן; וְהוּא כֹהֵן, לְאֵל עֶלְיוֹן.
>
> יט וַיְבָרְכֵהוּ, וַיֹּאמַר: בָּרוּךְ אַבְרָם לְאֵל עֶלְיוֹן, קֹנֵה שָׁמַיִם וָאָרֶץ.
>
> כ וּבָרוּךְ **אֵל** עֶלְיוֹן, אֲשֶׁר-מִגֵּן צָרֶיךָ בְּיָדֶךָ; וַיִּתֶּן-לוֹ מַעֲשֵׂר, מִכֹּל.

Another connection is the amulet called the *hand of Ali*; Shia Muslims associate Ali with Ali, the companion, and son-in-law of the Prophet Muhammad. The amulet has another name too – the hand of Fatima, which includes the image of the eye as a talisman against the evil eye. Amongst (not only) Muslims, it is associated with the name of the Prophet's favourite daughter, and amongst Jews, it is the *hand of Maryam*.[14] The common name is *Hamsa* (five as it consists of five fingers; another translation is slaves).

We'll take a short diversion here from lexical semantics; the context of the five fingers symbol's cognitive visuality allows for deeper historical roots of the sacred to be discovered. The sacred nature of *"the open palm"* amulet is also found in the pre-monotheistic period in the region: in Egypt, it was known as *Mano Pantea* and in the relatively distant Indian subcontinent as an asana (pose) named *Anjali Mudra* (mudra-mudrost' in Russian, meaning wisdom, seal; anjali is a gesture of welcome) or pranam-asana, the philological equivalent of which is "welcome" or "greetings." One of the Mano Pantea/hamsa symbol interpretations connects it with the concept of a slave – he who does not know God the Father.

> In Arabic, 'khamsa' means 'slave,' and because of its dual meaning (number 5 and a slave), we draw attention to the Egyptian Underworld Du'at. In Du'at, the dead are slaves, and the hieroglyph of Du'at is a fivefold star. The dead, in ancient Egyptian mythology, were slaves to their bodies and souls, devoid of spirit. The master of these slaves is no other god than, once again, father-god Osiris himself.

---

13 Genesis Chapter 14 בְּרֵאשִׁית. https://www.mechon-mamre.org/p/pt/pt0114.htm#18
14 *Hamsa meaning*. https://web.archive.org/web/20160816100430/http://www.hamsameaning.com/

The Spirit refers to [the] Father, and without spirit the "dead" is unconscious, having no understanding of themselves. Note here, Jesus' teaching that whoever has not found [the] Father (the eternal Truth and Knowledge) is still a slave and dead.[15] (see e.g. Matthew 8:22)

The version *Mano Pantea-Hamsa* exists in the Indian subcontinent too. The Jainism symbol, the open palm, includes a wheel (the symbol samsara – the cycle of life) in the centre of the palm and is called *A+himsa* (non-violence, non-injury). *A+himsa* means not only the absence of physical violence but also refers to the absence of the desire to carry out any type of violence. For centuries vegetarianism has been based on this premise.[16]

The version *El* was retained as an article in Arabic and Spanish. It can also be traced in the name of the father (*Alı kişi*) of Koroghlu, the hero of the eponymous 17th century Oguz epos, popular in Azerbaijan and amongst other Turkic tribes. In the text, he is an ostler and served the cruel khan. His status is closer to shepherd, which is the status of many prophets, including the ancient Mesopotamian Dumuzid-Tammuz. His connection with the sacral transcendental past is seen in his abilities to predict the magical, with which he, as a blind man (kor), helps his brave son (kor-oğlu), who possesses a unique voice and strength.

The differences between *Dasein* (existence in space and time) and *hal-halal-heylel-hl-L* amongst different peoples today, whose languages come from various family groups, reveal an ordinary transcendental meaning (which we call *cultural matrix*) at the proto-historical stage, discovered through the abjad alphabet method. This alphabet is more or less familiar to those in the region who have received a philological education.

The word and rite: A symbiosis of cultures or cultural matrix?

Transcendental meanings of word and rite in the example of *namaz/salaa* in Azerbaijan

The Muslim ritual of namaz can serve as an example of intersection and hybridity. The Russian-English dictionary defines it as "canonical Muslim prayer performed five times a day, cf. salat",[17] although in the Francophone world, the word is associ-

---

15 *The Evil Eye and the Hamsa Symbol*. https://houseoftruth.education/en/teaching/mona-lisa/mona-lisa-upside-down-lion-722#:~:text=This%20symbol%20is%20Mano%20Pantea,of%2C parents%20over%20their%20child.
16 Cort, John E. "'Intellectual Ahiṃsa' Revisited: Jain Tolerance and Intolerance of Others", in *Philosophy East and West* (2000): 324–347.
17 *Namaz*. ABBYYLingvo 12.

ated with Hinduism and Buddhism. This was the response of the French-speaking audience at a Visual Semiotics conference in Liege (Belgium) when I was asked, "What will the presentation be about?" It was called "The Cultural Matrix of the Namaz Ritual." The reaction was the same (Hinduism and Buddhism) from scholars from Muslim Morocco, Algeria, and Egypt.[18] The Muslims of Azerbaijan and Central Asia could not imagine such a striking disparity in one of the most important religious rites performed every day. The Soviet and Russian understanding of namaz given above is based on a word term of the common past – the modern version borrowed the word from the Russian Empire's Muslim peoples. The name for namaz in Arabic, i.e., in the language in which Islam spread, is *salat*, meaning the same ritual. **Salat** in the translation of the abjad cluster has the meaning *peace* and in this has common semantics both with the Semitic greetings *salam* and **shalom** and the word **salutation** (*saluty*- "safety, to greet, wish health to" in Latin) and its permutations which have their roots in Romance and Germanic languages.

The audio-visual semiotics of the word and ritual namaz allow parallels to be drawn with the word *namas-te* – with the greeting of the Indian subcontinent one of the main meanings of which is *peace* (to meet in peace, to part in peace). It is related to the Russian *na+maz+at'*; it is not only the everyday *na+maz+at' maslom* (to spread butter), but also *bozhiy po+MAZ+ann+yy* (God's anointed). The root of the word MAZda (Ahura Maz+da – lord of wisdom; he is Or+MUZ+d), in which MAZ+da is wisdom (or a seal) may show that this is not mere coincidence.[19]

At the *visual semiotics* level namaz is related to the visuality of *open palms*. The significance of this gesture is briefly mentioned above in connection with the historical semiotics of the **hll** cluster. The semiotics of the namas-te ritual gesture, called anjali mudra, means "*to come in peace,* with open hands". The open palm as the amulet symbol *the hand of Fatima or hand of Ali* is widespread in Islamic countries of the Middle East and dates back to the more ancient history of the culture of the Middle East.

Another visual pose of the namaz ritual – *placing the forehead on the ground* – is found in the version of namas-te when the pupil or child places their forehead (as the fate of a person is written on their forehead) at the foot of the master

---

[18] R. Geybullayeva. *From Visuality to Cultural Matrix: Word and Rite Namaz XIth Statutory Conference of the International Association for Visual Semiotics. Liege (Belgium) 8–11 September 2015 – Theorein.* University of Liege, Belgium, abstracts – pp. 81–82.

[19] For more about the word and rite *namaz*, see R. Geybullayeva. *Методы перевода: «биография» слов-терминов в контексте дискурса стереотип-архетип-прототип* (Methods of translation: the "biography" of words-terms in the context of the discourse stereotype-archetype-prototype). MGIMO, Magic of Innovation Proceedings, Vol. 1, 24-23 March 2017. Moscow: pp. 385 – 393. http://inno-conf.mgimo.ru/i/inno-magic-2017_tom-1.pdf

(who teaches wisdom-MAZ+da/ poMAZanniy?) or parent. In Russian anthropology this visuality is repeated in the secular rite of petitioning, performed when a peasant bowed before his boyar with a request. There is a similarity here with the *shashank asana* (*rabbit pose*), which is performed kneeling with the spine stretched forward.

It is difficult to judge which region was first to use these elements, and it's not so important anyway. What is important is the clear parallels of *Dasein* both at the physical-bodily level and the level of religion.

It is possible to break down further the history of the semantics of **every corresponding word in the semiotic cluster** *namaz*, including the Russian for forehead, *chelo* (like a Russian matryoshka doll), which reveals a link with the words cel+estial and the Russian *chelyad'* (menials, servants) or chil+dren.

Namaz as ritual and the word signifying it can, therefore, be considered *a symbiosis of different cultures*. But these commonalities can also be defined as a cultural matrix or isosemantics, such as rhizome (a rootstock without a hierarchy of priority in the etymology of language). In seeking to confirm my conclusions I found the Rhizome project of the French philosophers Deleuze and Guattari which they describe in *A Thousand Plateaus* (1980) as the phenomenon of the hypothesis of the contemporaneity of the appearance of commonalities in counterbalance to the theory of borrowing:

As a model for culture, the rhizome resists the organizational structure of the root-tree system which charts causality along chronological lines and looks for the original source of 'things' and looks towards the pinnacle or conclusion of those 'things.' A rhizome, on the other hand, is characterized by 'ceaselessly established connections between semiotic chains, organizations of power, and circumstances relative to the arts, sciences, and social struggles.' Rather than narrativize history and culture, the rhizome presents history and culture as a map or wide array of attractions and influences with no specific origin or genesis, for a 'rhizome has no beginning or end; it is always in the middle, between things, interbeing, intermezzo'.[20]

Related with namaz cultural layers can be summed up as follows:
Audio and lexical semantics and parallels of cultural dimensions:
- Na+**MAZ** – Azerbaijani case (+ Central Asia, Turkey, Iran)
- Na+**MAS**+te (Indian subcontinent)

---

[20] "Deleuze & Guattari's Rhizome", *In the Ravine* [Online] Available at: https://intheravine.wordpress.com/2016/11/26/deleuze-guattaris-rhizome/; see also: Deleuze, Guattari. *A Thousand Plateaus. Capitalism and Schizophrenia.* Translation and Foreword by Brian Massumi [Online] Available at: https://libcom.org/files/A%20Thousand%20Plateaus.pdf

- Ahura **MAZ**da-(H)Ohr**MAZd** (in Zoroastrianism the creator and highest deity, spirit)
- **NamKuzi** – most probable semantic relative. Sumero-Akkadian composition relating his endowment with perfect wisdom (*nam-kù-zu*) by the god Marduk and his claim to belong to a "distant line of kingship from before the flood."
- **poMAZat'** -marking by blood during Muslim sacrifice on the chelo (forehead)
- **Mezuza** (Exodus 12:10) – marking (poMAZat) the door frame of the Hebrews (until nowadays in Europe and the USA)
- *SAL+am* and *SHAL+om* (peace) – greeting
- *SAL+ut* – greeting, safety (SALutation)
- *SAL+am+at* (safe) Azerbaijani case (+ Central Asia, Turkey, Iran)
- **MAZda – poMAZ-at' (anoint)** and **Chelo**
- **Chelo+bitnaya** – chelo, chelyad', child, celestial (Russian)inder
- ***Chelo*** (forehead) as a fate object (fatum) *–bindi; alin yazısı;* during namaz "ağ alnını yerə qoydular" – literally: white, clean forehead in the meaning of a honest conscience (in KDG –XVI century text)
- **Ash Wednesday** – sprinkling ash over the head and painting cross with this ash (remembering of the "all are from the dust, and to dust, we will return"). Azerbaijani well-known desacralized version: **kül başına** (ash on your head) like a curse word
- **Wednesday** -*(Wo) odin's Day)* – Odin (wood for fire)
- **Burnt palms (wood) from Palm Sunday** (recall triumphal entering of Jesus as a king of Israel on donkey (symbol of peace; and the same way as Solomon entered),[21] during which his path was covered by palm fronds; Palm Sunday (Verbnoye Voskresenye – Willow Sunday in Russian version) arises from Jewish tradition Sukkot».
- **Vihbuti** – (3 horizontal lines on the chelo) in Hinduism
- **Bindi** – made from ash, marking period of life (married, divorced)
- **The Pineal gland in biology**
- **Pine cones around Budda's (enlightened one) head**
- **Pineal gland as eyelike structure (lotus)** in the midline of the brain (pineal gland) or if not as eye structure, has a function of **light receptor.**[22]

Pineal gland as a gland for producing melatonin and pineal gland in ancient China as a regulator for day circle (day and night).[23] "In some lower vertebrates,

---

21 Matthew 21:1–11, Mark 11:1–11, Luke 19:28–44 John 12:12–19.
22 Rogers, Kara, ed. *The endocrine system*. Britannica Educational Publishing, 2011, p.86
23 Circadian rhythms -from roots *circa-cycle* and *day*, and means biological shifting (endogenous or self-in) rhythms during 24 hours. Even they are characteristic to any individual, but have

the gland has a well-developed *eyelike structure* [highlighted by RG]; in others, though not organized as an *eye*, it functions as a *light receptor*[highlighted by RG]. . . And supporting cells that are similar to the *astrocytes*[24] of the brain."[25]

- **Shiva and Kama (the god of desire)** – Shiva burnt Kama (the god of desire) when he interrupted Shiva during his meditation (with worldly desires; during vihbuti, it is used *sacred ash* – from offering – remembering why Shiva kills Kama
- **Place of residing by Shiva, as Ahura MAZda's – Lord of Wisdom)**
- **Ajna chakra -a** place of AJNA (JAYIn in Hebrew version) CHAKHIR – enlightenment
- **Om (Um)** –-place of **Om- Crown Chakra – omnipresence-** in Indian subcontinent
- **Horus's eye as a protection amulet** – in Egyptian mythology (de-sacred- Tepegoz and Polyphem); third eye or One-Eyed (as ODIN)
- **Tepegoz, Polypheme (OneEyed Cyclops)** – *desacralized* heroes from myths (Azerbaijan, Central Asia, and Greece)
- And more is in my upcoming book

From hand of Fatima to Padma(t) and lotus feet in a chain of signs (signifier element) and interpreter

I'll digress briefly on the historical semiotics of Fatima, a name that Muslims associate with the name of the Prophet's favourite daughter, and correspondingly the hand of Fatima. This is a girl's name amongst the peoples who have adopted Islam. There are two versions of the name in Azerbaijan: Fatma (Fatima) and Patma (sometimes Patim+at, where the version beginning with 'p' is considered dialect of Zagatala district).

So, this case interprets the hand of Fatima amulet/talisman and, consequently Fatima. How interlinked are this version of the *open palm* sign-pose in the Muslim ritual namaz, the Hindu Namaste and Fatima? We will try to find the key to these cognitive categories, which will help to reconstruct the isosemantics.

---

a big impact of daylight for producing melatonin and serotonin hormones.
24 *Astrocytes* – "any of the *star-shaped cells in the tissue supporting the brain* and spinal cord (neuroglia)". This highlights also Zor-o-ast-er etymology as conceptual name.
25 Robert D. Utiger. *Pineal gland.* – Encyclopedia Britannica. http://www.britannica.com/ EBchecked/topic/460967/pineal-gland ; See also: Stephanie S. Erlich, Micahel J. Apuzzo. and *The pineal gland: anatomy, physiology, and clinical significance.* –Journal of Neurosurgery. September 1985/ Vol.63/ no.3/pp. 321–341 .

Cognitive linguistics and linguistic relativism may be the first key way of doing this. According to linguistic relativism, linguistic differences are reflected in the way they are conceived – in the cognitive process of perceiving the surrounding world.[26] Background interpreted as the native speaker of language(s) and dialects can be added here. In this case we will take the word **Fat+ma/Pad+ma** and the version **P**atima(t). As well as the suffix *–ma*,[27] the unfamiliar root *pat* (almost unfamiliar to the interpreter but familiar to inhabitants of its region) and relatively familiar *fat* (*fat+im* – fate). The suffix *–am* is found in nouns in the languages of the Middle East and neighbouring areas, irrespective of language family, as a legacy of the ancient Sumerians. It signifies the plural in the Azerbaijani language too.

Fat+um means "what was said", referring to what was said by god, on whom fate depends, which suggests the transcendent semiotics of this root:

> The Latin word for fate is "fatum," which literally means "what has been spoken." "Fatum," in turn, comes from *fari*, meaning "to speak." In the eyes of the ancients, your fate was out of your hands – what happened was up to gods and demigods. Predicting your fate was a job for oracles and prophets. "Fatidic" is "fatum" combined with *dicere*, meaning "to say." That makes "fatidic" a relative of the word *predict* as well; the "-dict" of "predict" also comes from Latin *dicere*.[28]

Padma means "lotus" in Sanskrit, it is also emblematic image. In India it is also part of the name of certain awards:

Pad+ma
1. the lotus plant or flower, or an emblematic representation of it;
2. (in India) the first part of the titles of certain awards.[29]

Padma could be both feminine and masculine. In Hinduism a pad(t)ma-lotus bearing the god Brahma came from the navel of the god Vishnu. The name Padma

---

[26] The Sapir-Whorf hypothesis of linguistic relativism posits that the structure of language influences how people perceive the world. The weak version says that linguistic categories influence traditions of non-language behaviour. The strong version says that these categories restrict and determine cognitive categories.
[27] It's not difficult to single out the suffix –ma since it exists in Russian too.
[28] *Fatidic*. Merriam-Webster dictonary. Fat(e)+dic(ere) https://www.merriam-webster.com/dictionary/fatidic#:~:text=The%20Latin%20word%20for%20fate,up%20to%20gods%20and%20demigods.
[29] *Padma*. Collins English Dictionary. HarperCollins Publishers. https://www.collinsdictionary.com/dictionary/english/padma

is used in Hindu texts to signify the goddess Lakshmi and hero Rama[30] (the reason for the first part of the title of awards!).

Padma as lotus?

What can the distant word *padma*, which translates from Sanskrit as lotus, tell us? "Inside the Mera or spinal column there are six main centres of Tattva activity, called Chakras or Padmas, which are the locations of Shakti, just as Sahasrara is the seat of Shiva."[31] Or the tradition of binding the feet of little girls so that they have "lotus feet" in Japan and China, familiar from the novels *Memoirs of a Geisha*? (Arthur Golden) and *Three Swans* (Jung Chang)?[32] And the Padma asana – the lotus pose – is often used for meditation in yoga.

Transcendence in the sense of the divine meaning of the sign of the open palm and Pad+ma+Vati are found in Jainism. On the one hand, Padma+vati in Jainism is the protector or attendant goddess (Yakshini) śāsana devī (शासनदेवी). Padma+vati (Padim+at?) is a legendary queen of the 13th–14th century kingdom of Mewar in India. She is said to have danced barefoot before the emperor on a floor bearing the image of a golden lotus. "The emperor expressed admiration and exclaimed, 'a lotus springs from her every step!', a possible reference to the Buddhist goddess Padmavati who is often portrayed sitting on a pink lotus."[33]

F/p switch

A modern-day example of the f/p phonetic alteration: the pound (British) and funt (Azerbaijani and Russian versions of pound).

---

30 *Padma.* "This is a transcription of both the feminine form पद्मा and the masculine form पद्म. According to Hindu tradition a lotus holding the god Brahma arose from the navel of the god Vishnu. The name Padma is used in Hindu texts to refer to several characters, including the goddess Lakshmi and the hero Rama." https://www.behindthename.com/name/padma
31 Глава 5. *Центры Или Лотосы. Чакры. Падмы* http://www.e-reading-lib.com/chapter.php/130530/7/artur-avalon-zmeinaya-sila.html
32 Until the 20th century foot binding was considered a sign of elite status and also of beauty, but it was painful and disabling for most women. Feet changed by binding were described as lotus feet.
33 *Foot binding in Imperial China.* https://www.danceshistoricalmiscellany.com/foot-binding-imperial-china/#:~:text=The%20emperor%20expressed%20admiration%20and,sitting%20on%20a%20pink%20lotus.

Fat+ma and Pat+ma
Pad+ma and Patimat – Pad(t)0ivat(i)?
Pir-Fire

It's also possible to talk of the semiotic kinship at the transcendent level of the words *pir/fire*.

The p/f switch is common and inherent to some dialects within one language, including Azerbaijani. Arabic has neither the *sound nor letter* p. And the word has been retained as Fatima. Azerbaijani has both versions f and p. In Greek the sound f is conveyed through ph, and not f, for example, **ph**ilosophy. The word **Pyrrhus (Pir)** can be added to this, the name of a commander and king (319–272 BCE) of Epirus and Macedonia (Pyrrhic victory), which translates from ancient Greek as "red" or "fiery".[34] The **p** remains in Azerbaijani in the literary version of the word **pir** (a **hearth** – the burial place of a saint or holy person). There is also the related, secular word **fır** (a small burn mark on the skin) in Azerbaijani and **fır+ın** (oven, stove) in Turkish. Another version of the **f/p** switch is the name of the ethnos Fars (the Arabized version also exists in Azerbaijani) and **Pars** and **Parsee** (English: Persian) – the Iranian Zoroastrians who emigrated to India in the 7th century to avoid religious persecution following the establishment of Islam.

Thus, the study of parallels in the semiotic past of Fatma/Pad(i)ma allows us to compile a lexical list and through it to find the sacred status of these words in this region as a key to the *protective symbol of the Hamsa (five fingers)- open palms-one eye-* and its semiotic kinship:

Open PALMS /FATma-fatum/ Padma-lotus/ one eye

Thus, the study of parallels in the semiotic past of Fatma/Pad(i)ma allows us to compile a lexical list and through it to find the sacred status of these words in this region as a key to the **protective symbol of the Hamsa (five fingers)-** *open palms-one eye-* and its semiotic kinship:
- the hand of Fatima as an amulet with the *single eye*[35]
- **Odin's one eye** (the North mythology); **Horus's** *one eye* (Egyptian mythology)
- **Padma** -the image of lotus feet, image of Shiva; forehead is a place where Shiva resides

---

[34] For more about Pyrrus see: Plutarch. *Pyrrus*. http://classics.mit.edu/Plutarch/pyrrhus.html
[35] Adaptation of beliefs about the gouged out eye of an Egyptian deity, Osiris's son Hor + uz (Horus)

- **Fatma** -the name of prophet Muhammad's daughter
- **Khamsa** – (pant –or five – fingers), as in *Pancha-Tantra*
- **Hamishsha** (Khumshey) -five-book conceptualization, the first part of the Tanak (h)); The Pentateuch[36]
- **Ahimsa** – with the image of the wheel of life, India[37]
- **Maneo-pantea** – in ancient Egypt (not for common people, only for the priests is the attitude toward the Lord in the act of benediction)
- **Hand of Fatima** – protective amulet
- **Hand of Ali** (among Shia Muslims) and L as a meaning of a highest status (as in Halilulah, Hallel, Eliah, Allah)
- **Hand of Miriam** (among Jews)
- **In Muslim namaz- prayer with** *open palms*, **representing request to a God**
- In Namaste
- **Buddha's gesture for teaching** – in Indian subcontinent
- as visual element of in Namaz
- as asana Anjali mudra (hand's position) in Namaste

ODIN got Wednesday – (W) odin's day and Ash in Wednesday

Another interesting aspect from the point of view of the interpretant is the pre-Christian Scandinavian god Odin. Insight into the existential semiotics of Odin reveals a line between the *god* from the North mythology, the tradition of *Ash Wednesday*, the Azerbaijani word *odin* (wood), and the Indian *vibhūthi*.

> **Odin and his semiotic cluster** can be defined as follows:
> Odin-Wodin-Wotan-Wednesday (Ash Wednesday)-Wood
> **(W)Od+in** and **Azerbaijani odun (wood)** are homophones
> **Od – fire, and odun – wood** in Azerbaijani and other Turkic languages. What lies behind this apparent commonality: coincidence or a common semiotic-prototype past?

---

36 The five books of Moses. The word is a Greek adaptation of the Hebrew expression "ḥamishshaḥ ḥumshe ha-Torah" (five-fifths of the Law) applied to the books Genesis, Exodus, Leviticus, Numbers, and Deuteronomy, and indicating that these five books were to be taken as a whole, as they are in the first distinct reference to a division of the Biblical books by the Greek Sirach (see Jew Encyc. iii. 145b, *s.v.* Bible Canon). Emil G. Hirsch, Joseph Jacobs. *Pentateuch*. https://www jewishencyclopedia.com/articles/12011-pentateuch

37 Adaptation of beliefs about the gouged out eye of an Egyptian deity, Osiris's son Hor + us (Horus)
Indian regional version on the cyclical nature of life.

Ash – what remains of *fire (od)*, burnt objects. Best known is wood ash. So, *ash* is related to fire (**od** in Azerbaijani and in many Turkic languages) and wood *(odun)*. In Azerbaijan *aş* is the name of a rice dish which is an obligatory part of elite cuisine, without which no celebration is complete. It is the same as the famous Iranian pilaff (plov), but the word *aş* is more widely used.[38] On the other hand, it is the meaning of the verb "to knock over, reverse", which is how *aş* is made. A third meaning is ash (cinders) and is part of the popular expression in Azerbaijani and other Turkic languages **kül başına** (ash on your head) with the meaning "God give you wisdom". There is also the dialect *həş* (hash), which means dust, i.e. it conveys the texture of ash.

Aş (ash) in the sense "ashes on your head" recalls two religious traditions: *Ash Wednesday* in Christianity and **holy ash *Vibhūthi*** in India. Both versions are related by the visual act in the expression "ash on your head", but constitute a holy ritual. In Hinduism *Vibhūthi* is holy ash painted (poMAZaniye) in three horizontal lines onto the forehead in honour of Shiva and recalls the need to curb desire recounted in an episode in his story.

Vibhūthi, which is believed to be holy ash, is an article of faith. The ash, which the devotee is asked to smear himself with, is a symbol of ash that the desire is reduced to. One who reduces his desires to ash by means of the fire called knowledge (Jñyāna) is real 'śivayōgi' [ಶಿವಯೋಗಿ]. It is figuratively said that his mind, intellect, sense, and the whole gross body are made up of vibhūti. Aiśvarya, [ಐಶ್ವರ್ಯ] which is a synonym of vibhūti means lordship. One who has control over his senses is īśvara [ಈಶ್ವರ] (or has aiśvarya). In other words, one who reduces his desires to ashes is the lord of his senses. Normally vibhūti is smeared horizontally with three fingers, mainly on the forehead, two sides of the throat, etc. The three parallel lines of the sacred ash have mythological reference.[39]

In the Christian ritual (in the Roman Catholic Church, Anglican (through British dominion, churched in the USA, and other denominations) ash from the burning of the previous year's palm crosses is placed on the forehead and drawn (poMAZanii) into the shape of a cross between the eyebrows,[40] accompanied by a prayer recalling that man is made of ashes and to ashes will return. The burnt palms (tree) from Palm Sunday recall Jesus' triumphal entry into Jerusalem

---

38 It is the same with the word *şərab* (sharab – wine), a popular symbol in classical Islamic poetry, which has not been able to supplant the version *çaxır* (chakhir – wine).
39 *Vibhūti (Bhasma or Bhasita): [ವಿಭೂತಿ or ಭಸ್ಮ, ಭಸಿತ]* https://lingayatreligion.com/LingayatTerms/Vibhoti_or_Bhasma.htm
40 Between the brows is the location of the Ajna chakra or Om (Um, which in Russian also means mind) and Ajna Padma (the lotus chakra); it is the spot that is placed on the ground in the Muslim prayer ritual namaz; and in physiologically is the location of the pituitary gland.

on a donkey (a symbol of peace)⁴¹ during which his path was covered in palm branches. After the Ash Wednesday ritual participants shake hands and wish one another peace. This ritual is performed on the Wednesday (**Wodin's Day**) after Shrove Tuesday, the first day of Lent during the seventh week before Easter.

On the origin of Odin in Nordic myths: A wise man and god from Tyrkland

After seeking Odin's semiotic kin, we will attempt to find Odin's origins through Scandinavian sources, where he was the most important pre-Christian god. The prologue of Prose Edda⁴² narrates:

> From the north and all down over the eastern part, even to the south, is called Asia...There also is the centre of the earth... Near the earth's centre was made that goodliest of homes and haunts that ever have been, which is called Troy, even that which we call **Turkland** [þar sem vér köllum Tyrkland]. There were *twelve* kingdoms [tólf konungdómar] and one High King, and many sovereignties belonged to each kingdom; in the stronghold were *twelve* chieftains [tólf höfðingjar]. These chieftains were in every manly part greatly above other men that have ever been in the world.⁴³ After that he went northward, where the land is called Sweden...There he [**Odin**] established chieftains in the fashion which had prevailed in Troy; he set up also twelve head-men [tólf höfuðmenn] to be doomsmen over the people and to judge the laws of the land; and he ordained also all laws as, there had been before, in Troy, and according to the customs of the Turks.⁴⁴   [Tyrkir váru vanir]

Some new editions of the *Nibelunglied* note that Siegfried fought against his enemies alongside his *twelve* knights.⁴⁵

As+gard – gorod – the Norse gods' dwelling place in the sky, "the residence of the gods and included their various dwelling places and feasting halls such as Valhalla, Odin's heavenly hall where honorable warriors were sent".⁴⁶

Ace (French) – ace, a very skilled person, an expert. Semantically can be associated with the *As* – Norse gods, who advocated law and order according to *Prose Edda*, the Icelandic epic containing tales of Norse mythology.

---

41 Matthew 21:1–11, Mark 11:1–11, Luke 19:28–44 John 12:12–19.
42 *The Prose Edda* of Icelandic politician and poet Snorri Sturluson (circa 1200 AD)
43 Sturluson, S. *Prologue, The Prose Edda of Snorri Sturluson*, translated by Arthur Gilchrist Brodeur, (1916). [Online] Available at: http://www.sacred-texts.com/neu/pre/pre03.htm, http://www.voluspa.org/proseprologue.htm
44 *Sturluson, S. Prologue, The Prose Edda of Snorri Sturluson, translated by Arthur Gilchrist Brodeur, (1916).*
45 Macgregor, Mary. *Stories of Siegfried. Told to the Children*. [Online] Available at: https://www.heritage-history.com/index.php?c=read&author=macgregor&book=siegfried
46 *Asgard*. https://www.newworldencyclopedia.org/entry/asgard

As+garor – in the Icelandic variation. *Gorod* or *grad* in Slavic, means city; in Russian the verb *goroditʼ* – to border, to enclose; *gare* (French) – station, as a place enclosed for a crowd, *garage* – the same meaning.

Gara (Turkic) – [ga:ra:], *black* and also *mighty, great, abundant;* also, part of the expression qonaq-*garalı* (*with many* or *abundant* guests)

Cher+shenbe *(çərşənbə)* = **Wednesday**

Another word that sheds light on the semiotics of Odin is the ritual of jumping over a bonfire (fire)[47] every Tuesday approaching the Novruz holiday – the (pre-monotheist) Zoroastrian spring equinox, part of the heritage of subsequently Islamicized peoples including the Azerbaijanis. On Tuesday evening (*çərşənbə axşamı* or Wednesday Eve), in this case on the eve of the main holiday cher+shenbe (*çərşənbə* – Wednesday), similar to the New Year's Eve celebrations of 31 December. Tuesday in Azerbaijani and many languages of the region is *çərşənbə axşamı* or Wednesday Eve.

Cher+Shenbe is equivalent to **Wednesday (Wodin's day)** – the fourth (*cha-ha-r*) day after Saturday (şənbə – shenbe) is **Wednesday.** In ca**h**ar – four – *ha* is a Semitic suffix, present in many modern-day languages such as Io*Ha*N, and r-*ha* reduced variants such as Ion – Ivan.

Odin – women warriors (Amazons) and the one-eyed

A semantic list that reveals the transcendence of the existential semiotics of Odin and stemmata:

> **O***din* (German) or **(W)o***den*, **(W)o***din* (Norse god), **Oth***in* (Old High German)
> **Wo***din* – **Wo***dnes* (Old English) – **Wo***den's day* – **Wednes***day* – Holy **Wednes***day* in Passion or Maundy week (an important fasting week before Easter)
> **Wood** (English) – the trunks of trees
> **O***dun* (Azerbaijani) [odun] – wood
> **Oud** –in the Islamic countries musical instrument made from wood
> **Od** (Azerbaijani) – fire
> **Wotan (Odin, Wod***en* – old English, **Woud(t)an** – Old German – counterpart *Od*in; **Wotan** – motherland in Azerbaijani and other Turkic languages
> **Wēdnes dæg, Woden's day** –Wednes-day
> **Wednes**day – **(W) o**din's Day
> **Wednes**day – wood+ne's+day – Ash Day
> **Cher+shenbe** *(çərşənbə)* = **Wednesday,** four holy days before Novruz

Another two parallels with Odin are found in the myth of how he gave away an eye to Mimir, owner of the source of wisdom (well or waterfall), in order to drink from the source and gain wisdom. So, Odin has one eye:

---

[47] One more link to the sacredness of fire is a shrine, a pilgrimage place, which is called *pir* in Azerbaijani; here *pir* is a phonetic version of *fire*.

27. I know of the horn
of Heimdall, hidden
Under the high-reaching
holy tree;
On it there pours
from Valfather's pledge
A mighty stream:
would you know yet more?

28. Alone I sat
when the Old One sought me,
The terror of gods,
and gazed in mine eyes:
"What hast thou to ask?
Why comest thou hither?
Othin, I know
where thine eye is hidden.

29. I know where Othin's
eye is hidden,
Deep in the wide-famed
well of Mimir;"[48]

An echo can be found in a famous episode in the 'Koroghlu' epic[49] (the son of a blind man in the Azerbaijani version and the son of the grave in the Turkmen version) about the horse of *Ali (consonant L?)* who was blinded by his evil master Hasan khan. He was punished for bringing handsome horses, according to the khan, as a gift for the khan's guest. Blinded *in both eyes*, Ali alerts his son Rovshan (beam of light) as to when he should drink water and from what source in order to be strong. Here *wisdom is replaced by strength,* as the time of writing and context are that of the heroic epic, identical to Robin Hood. Odin's weapon is the spear Gungnir, which never misses its target, while Koroghlu has a similar weapon, the sword Misri.

Another parallel with the one-eyed character is the monster Tepe+goz in the Oghuz epic 'The Book of Dede Korkut', written down in the 16th century.

---

48 *The Poetic Edda,* translated by H.A. Bellows (1936), Vol. I, *Lays of the Gods, Voluspo – The Wise-Woman's Prophecy.* [Online] Available at: https://www.sacred-texts.com/neu/poe/poe03.htm

49 *Koroghlu* is a 17th century epic of the Turkic peoples. See also: Korogly, Kh.G. (1976) *Огузский героический эпос* (The Oghuz heroic epos). Nauka; Raykhl, K., Funk, D.A., Treyster, V. *Тюркский эпос: традиции, формы, поэтическая структура* (The Turkic epic: traditions, forms, poetic structure) Nauka: 2008

A second parallel is the Valkyrie who recall the Amazons – women warriors popular in Azerbaijani culture (the Greek version is well known). For example, in *The Book of Dede Korkut* mothers of warriors set off on a military campaign, while girls fight just as well as their young men; a woman's military valour is the main criterion when choosing a wife.

Semantic parallels-paradigms with Odin can, therefore, be drawn to such clusters as **odun, od, chahar-shenbe, one-eyed** in Azerbaijani culture, though the associations may not be obvious at first sight.

Communication before our eyes, but beyond *our consciousness:* Ancient links for ethnoses (modern-day Azerbaijani Rutuls, Udins) and toponyms (Nits, Rutul, Gargar)

An example from the history of culture shows yet another layer of prior communications which can be called *communication before our eyes, but beyond our consciousness*. It's not only rituals, rites or the state of being of a person, but names too. In this regard, I will consider the ancient links of modern-day, little known ethnoses and place names in Azerbaijan. For example, while some may have heard of the *Udins* of Azerbaijan, the *Rutuls* are never mentioned for some reason.

The epic poem the Book of Dede Korkut talks of the journey of Gazan khan, his son and others to Trabzon and Aya Sofiya "where the kafirs live" (today's Istanbul, this was the era before the fall of Byzantium) and the campaign to the neighbouring Abkhaz people. If we look at history, names arise in a period close to the Middle Ages, the 4th century. In this period the **Udin** and the earlier Illyrian (**Illiroy,** the modern-day Ingiloy) tribes lived on the territory of modern-day Italy and Albania. The Burgundians are preserved in history in the texts of the Edda and Nibelung epic poems, but in the modern day ethnoses that are not states and peoples mix with other peoples and lose their national identity (*misplaced and immix identities*). For example, the Huns or the not very numerous Rutuls who live in modern-day Azerbaijan and Dagestan are for the same reason not linked with Turnus, king of the Rutulians, ally of the Roman emperor, who is mentioned in Virgil's epic the Aeneid (29–19 BCE).

Rutul

The Rutulians are mentioned 51 times in the Aeneid. Though the Rutulians are different from the Trojans, who laid the foundations of Rome, they are not incomers to Italy.

> **The same Rutulians**, who with arms pursue the Trojan race, are equal foes to you. . .;

> (Book VII, 310) But I, Jove's imperial consort, who have borne, ah me! to leave naught undared, who have shifted to every device, I am vanquished by Aeneas. If my deity is not great enough, I will not assuredly falter to seek succour where it may be; if the powers of heaven are inflexible, I will stir up Acheron. It may not be to debar him of a Latin realm; well; and Lavinia is destined his bride unalterably. But it may be yet to defer, to make all this action linger; but it may be yet to waste away the nation of either king; at such forfeit of their people may son-in-law and father-in-law enter into union. *Blood of Troy and Rutulia shall be thy dower*, O maiden, and Bellona is the bridesmaid who awaits thee.

Then, Alba(niya):

> (Book I, 265) he shall appoint his people a law and a city; till the third summer see him reigning in Latium, and three winters' camps pass over the conquered **Rutulians** . . . he shall carry the kingdom from its fastness in Lavinium, and make a strong fortress of **Alba the Long**.⁵⁰

Meanwhile, this text written in 29–19 BCE notes the creation of a new people from the Trojans (Aeneas) and their enemy the Greeks (Evander Arcadians),⁵¹ likewise the Rutulians, Latins and Etruscans.⁵²

> While suffering Juno watches them from heaven and aware of the coming fate. She makes this final request of Jupiter: "Bid thou not the native Latins change their name of old, nor become Trojans and take the Teucrian name, or change their language, or alter their attire: let Latium be, let Alban kings endure through ages, let Italian valour be potent in the race of Rome. Troy is fallen; let her and her name lie where they fell." Jupiter replies, "I give thee thy will, and yield thee ungrudged victory."

According to the epic, the non-Latin Trojan Aeneas founds the state of Rome (not rare in history). The Rutulians are defeated and disappear from the stage of history. Meanwhile, the Rutul are a minority people living on the relatively lesser known "periphery", which is in the Rutul district in modern-day Azerbaijan's Zagatala and in Dagestan. Biologically they are a constituent part not only of the modern-day Latins-Italians but (like the Trojans, Udins, Illiroys – *Fuimus Troes*

---

50 Virgil, *Aeneid*, Books I and VII (translated by J.W. Mackail). [Online] Available at: http://www.gutenberg.org/files/22456/22456-h/22456-h.htm#BOOK_SECOND
51 Arcadia is a Greek place name.
52 Evander is the king of the Greeks who moved from Arcadia to a place nearer Rome; in Roman myth he was the son of Mercury, god of war and merchants, and Carment; in the Aeneid he founded the city of Pallantium before the Trojan war and erected an altar to Hercules. Another meaning is "worthy".

fuit Ilium,[53] we were Trojans, this was Ilium or "No more are we a Trojan people; Ilium ... is no more") also of the modern-day Dagestani peoples and Azerbaijanis.

Udin

Ancient roots in Italy can be found for the Udin people who live in the *village of Nis in Azerbaijan's Gabala* district. Udine is the name of a small city in the Italian region of Friuli-Venezia Giulia (capital Trieste). Historically Friuli was the capital. There is a hypothesis that this was the territory settled by the Illiroy. When Attila, leader of the Huns (434–455), was laying siege to Aquileia, he built a square castle on a mound and laid out the city (Lengyel, Dénes, 1972. *Régi Magyar mondák*. Budapest: Móra Ferenc). The etymology of the word is the Indo-European *oud^h*-'udder', meaning mound.[54] On the other hand, the Udins live in the village of Nis(j) in Gabala, Azerbaijan. With close lexical and phonetic alteration parallels (like pal*ace*-palazzo, N**ice**- **Nizza**), the city of Nice (Nizza) in France is 686 km from the *Italian city of Udine*.

The city of Nizza was a neighbour of Liguria, inhabited by the Ligur tribe in the north-west of Italy. In the 7th century Nizza joined the League of Genoa, which united the cities of Liguria. Following the Treaty of Turin between France and Sardinia in 1858 the Duchy of Savoy and Italian-speaking Nizza became part of France:

> **Art. 1.** His Majesty the King of Sardinia consents to the annexation (*réunion*) of Savoy and of the *arrondissement* of **Nice** (*circondario di Nizza*) to France, and renounces for himself and all his descendants and successors his rights and claims to the said territories. It is agreed between their Majesties that this *reunion* shall be effected without any constraint upon the wishes of the populations, and that the Governments of the Emperor of the French and of the King of Sardinia shall concert together as soon as possible on the best means of appreciating and taking note of (*constater*) the manifestations of those wishes.[55]

---

53 Virgil, *Aeneid*. Book II, line 324 (translated by J.W. Mackail). [Online] Available at: http://www.gutenberg.org/files/22456/22456-h/22456-h.htm#BOOK_SECOND
54 Pellegrini, Giovan Battista. 1990 *Toponomastica italiana: 10000 nomi di città, paesi, frazioni, regioni, contrade, fiumi, monti spiegati nella loro origine e storia*. Milan: Hoepli, p. 130; Snoj, Marko. 2009. *Etimološki slovar slovenskih zemljepisnih imen*. Ljubljana: Modrijan and Založba ZRC, p. 454. Derived from Wikipedia.
55 *The Times*, March 31, 1860, *The Annexation of Savoy and Nice to France* (Treaty of Turin, 1860). https://sites.google.com/site/savoyannexation/the-times-full-list/the-times-march-31-1860-the-annexation-of-savoy-and-nice-to-france

Gargar

Gargar is the name of a river and a village in Zagatala (Azerbaijan) and is also found in Homer's Iliad:

> [290] But Hera swiftly drew nigh to topmost **Gargarus**, the peak of lofty Ida, and Zeus, the cloud-gatherer, beheld her. And when he beheld her, then love encompassed his wise heart about . . .
>
> [350] Therein lay the twain, and were clothed about with a cloud, fair and golden, wherefrom fell drops of glistering dew. Thus, in quiet slept the Father on topmost **Gargarus**, by sleep and love overmastered, and clasped in his arms his wife. But sweet Sleep set out to run to the ships of the Argives [355] to bear word to the Enfolder and Shaker of Earth.[56]

The reference to the Gargar as to a tribe is linked with the history of Caucasian Albania, which is closely connected to the tribes and toponyms of modern-day Italy and Greece. The ancient city of Alba is on the border of Liguria (neighbouring Nice) and Piedmont. Giyaseddin Geybullayev cites ancient sources on the Gargars of the Caucasus:

> Strabo (1st century) writes that "the Amazons live in the mountains above Albania" (Strabo, XI. 5. 1). He goes on to say that in the first centuries of our era the Sarmatians lived in the North Caucasus plains. For, according to Strabo: "In the south the Caucasus mountains divide Albania and Iberia from the Sarmatian plains in the north." (Strabo, XI, 2. 15). It should, therefore, be assumed that the Gargars must have been found amongst the Sarmatians, because Strabo (XI. 5. 1) writes: ". . .the Amazons were neighbours of the Gargars." Justin writes (3rd century CE): "The Amazons are neighbours of the Albanians." (XLII, 3, 7).

The Gargar language is mentioned with regard to the Albanian alphabet; this language is thought to have been the foundation of this alphabet, just as the Latin language was once the foundation of the Roman alphabet:

> Since he refers to the Gargars amongst the descendants of Aran, we are right to assume that they are one of the most ancient (together with the Utis) and most prominent tribes of the Albanian union.
>
> When Mesrop Mashtots created the Albanian alphabet in the 5th century he based it on the Gargar dialect of the Albanian language ("he created a written Gargar language rich in throat sounds"). The latter allows us to suppose that the Gargars were the more cultured and leading Albanian tribe.[57]

---

56 Homer, Iliad. Book 14. [Online] Available at: http://www.perseus.tufts.edu/hopper/text?-doc=Perseus%3Atext%3A1999.01.0134%3Abook%3D14
57 Trever, K.V. "Албания в IV-II вв.до н.э." ("Albania in the 4th–2nd centuries BCE") in *Очерки по истории и культуре Кавказской Албании: IV в. до н. э.-VII в. н. э* (Notes on the history and

So, can these names of tribes and places mentioned in "non-eastern", classical texts of Ancient Greece and the Roman Empire, be considered homophones? Or is there a semantic kinship that the contemporary consciousness is not immediately ready to accept, because there is no room for this layer of knowledge in the generally accepted academic background?

Peirce's triadic model of "sign, object and interpretant" are here sign-word, object-peoples and toponyms, and interpretant the person for whom this Being (*Dasein*) has meaning. These words are not essential for an interpretant from another environment:

> The importance of the interpretant for Peirce is that signification is not a simple dyadic relationship between sign and object: a sign signifies only in being interpreted. This makes the interpretant central to the content of the sign, in that, the meaning of a sign is manifest in the interpretation that it generates in sign users.[58]

One of the sources of semiotics – regional characteristics – brings together seemingly very different peoples of the region, regardless of religion and denomination, playing a significant role in modern cultural symbiosis.

3 Conclusions

"How does one attempt to grasp the incomprehensible? *Through lists*[59], through catalogs, through collections in museums and through encyclopedias and dictionaries." "Life experience" can be added as a list too. Through this prism the structure of the word, cognisable through the abjad alphabet (consonants), allows for compilation of an audio-lexical list. This is an example when the structure of language influences the cognition of its speakers *through relevant or familiar meanings*; cognition of the external world depends on a person's background.

This research includes brief examples of branching in cultural history and cognitive linguistics from the perspective of a semiotician who has studied the topic for over a decade. In this work I have tried to lift the curtain (*trans-scandare*) of semiotic units (words-rituals-signs) through revealing their itinerary or branching off from the modern-day to the ancient period, discovering *different*

---

culture of Caucasian Albania: IV century BCE-VII century CE). USSR Academy of Sciences, Moscow-Leningrad, 1959, p. 4.
58 *Peirce's Theory of Signs*. Stanford Encyclopedia of Philosophy. First published Fri Oct 13, 2006; substantive revision Mon Nov 15, 2010 https://plato.stanford.edu/entries/peirce-semiotics/#Int
59 Eco, U. (2009) *La Vertigine della Lista (The Vertigo of Lists)*.

historical layers of cultural association. They are grouped according to lexical and audio-visual clusters (lists) of words-names of rituals (for example, namaz) which made up their components in different periods of history and different regions (Maneo-Pantea, ash on Wednesday, Odin), and also the words-names of peoples.

The sign as a transcendent unit in the classical and pre-classical context was explored through the example of the ordinary, secular, everyday Azerbaijani phrase *halın necədir,* which led to creating of the lexical history-list (Umberto Eco's "infinity of lists") of the sacred *halo.* The modern-day *halo* and lexical-semantic relatives *halo* in different religions revealed an example of radical transcendence in existential semiotics.

The transcendental meanings of word and rituals based on the **example of namaz/salat in Azerbaijan** and the list-semiotic cluster of audio and lexical parallels revealed a symbiosis of cultures or cultural matrix of rituals of components based on the example of the contemporary Azerbaijani variant of prayer – namaz, with the word namaz for the Muslim prayer ritual instead of the Arabic salat.

One of the **visual components of namaz – open-handed prayer** – led to symbols-signs such as the hand of Fatima or hand of Ali, the letter **L** meaning, the history of which goes back to pre-monotheist elements and which are perceived as transcendent. This is how the line appeared from the hand of Fatima to Padma (Padimat) and *lotus feet in the chain of sign (element of significance) and translator, and, accordingly, Fatima-Padma,* Padma as lotus, the f/p switch.

Another visual element of namaz – placing the forehead on the ground when bowing before the Almighty – led to parallels with the pre-Christian Scandinavian god **Odin (Ash Wednesday;** what remains after wood is burnt – ash on Odin's day, which is used to make a mark on the forehead between the eyebrows) and its semiotic "kin", revealing the transcendence of the existential semiotic of Odin. These relatives, making up a semiotic cluster, also revealed kinship of the day named in honour of Odin – Wednesday, and the **Novruz holy day çə(hə) rçənbə-the fourth day after Saturday;** the kinship with Anatolia (**the wise man-God from Tyrkland**); with **female warriors** (Valkyrie/Amazons) and the symbol of the **one-eyed** person (the eye sacrificed by Odin in return for wisdom).

And finally, this work gives the example of three peoples or nations who have become part of the modern-day Azerbaijani nation and are not associated with ancient peoples mentioned in ancient literature at all: the **Rutuls, Udins and Gargars** and the toponyms they brought (the villages of Nizza, Rutul, Gargar), analogous to the names of rituals themselves. To demonstrate, for example, the way that the inhabitants began to call the new Arabic salat by a previous name, namaz, by association with habitual traditions and concepts.

All these cultural intersections or semiotic matrices, which seem improbable at first sight, can be indirectly confirmed by words-signs-names of ancient peoples who have dispersed amongst modern-day peoples, importing elements of their previous culture into ground that is new to them. These names do not appear to be transcendent, but our consciousness also finds it difficult to accept them because of stereotypical knowledge.

References

"Acrophony". n.d. Dictionary.com. https://www.dictionary.com/browse/acrophonic (last modified 28 February 2022) "Asgard". N.d. New World Encyclopedia. https://www.newworldencyclopedia.org/entry/asgard (last modified 28 February 2022)

Atkin, Albert 2010 [2006]. "Peirce's Theory of Signs." Stanford Encyclopedia of Philosophy. First published Fri Oct 13, 2006; substantive revision Mon Nov 15, 2010 https://plato.stanford.edu/entries/peirce-semiotics/#Int

"Azerbaijan Comparative Literature Association". n.d. Prototypes in Recycling Cultures and/or Cultural Genomes, 20–21 April 2017, Baku". http://www.azcla.org/RCallforpapers.htm

Bankov, Kristian & Paul Cobley (eds.), *Semiotics and its Masters* Vol. 1, 293–323. De Gruyter Mouton.

Campbell, Mike. n.d. "Meaning, Origin and History of the Name Padma." Behind the Name. https://www.behindthename.com/name/padma (last modified 25 April 2021)

Cort, John E. 2000. 'Intellectual Ahiṃsa' Revisited: Jain Tolerance and Intolerance of Others. Philosophy East and West. 324–347.

Day, John. 2002 [2000]. *Yahweh and the Gods and Goddesses of Canaan*. London, New York: Sheffield Academic Press.

"Deleuze & Guattari's Rhizome". 2016. In the Ravine. https://intheravine.wordpress.com/2016/11/26/deleuze-guattaris-rhizome/ (last modified February 26 2018)

Deleuze, Guattari. 2005 [1980]. *A Thousand Plateaus. Capitalism and Schizophrenia*. Eng. translation & intr. by Brian Massumi. Minneapolis, London: University of Minnesota Press. https://libcom.org/files/A%20Thousand%20Plateaus.pdf

Eco, Umberto. 2009. *La Vertigine della Lista* [The Vertigo of Lists]. Milan: Bompiani.

Eco, Umberto, Beyer, Susanne & Lothar Gorris. 2009. November 11. 'We Like Lists Because We Don't Want to Die'. *Spiegel International*. https://www.spiegel.de/international/zeitgeist/spiegel-interview-with-umberto-eco-we-like-lists-because-we-don-t-want-to-die-a-659577.html

Erlich, Stephanie S. & Michael J. Apuzzo. 1985. The pineal gland: anatomy, physiology, and clinical significance. *Journal of Neurosurgery* 63(3). 321–341. "Fatidic". 2019. Merriam Webster Dictionary. https://www.merriam-webster.com/dictionary/fatidic (accessed 28 February 2022)

"Foot binding in Imperial China." 2014. Dances Historical Miscellany. https://www.danceshistoricalmiscellany.com/foot-binding-imperial-china/#:~:text=The%20emperor%20expressed%20admiration%20and,sitting%20on%20a%20pink%20lotus. (last modified 25 August 2014)

Geybullayeva, Rahiliya. 2017. *Методы перевода: «биография» слов-терминов в контексте дискурса стереотип-архетип-прототип* [Methods of translation: the "biography" of words-terms in the context of the discourse stereotype-archetype-prototype]. MGIMO, Magic of Innovation Proceedings, Vol. 1, 24-23, March 2017, 385–393. Moscow. http://inno-conf.mgimo.ru/i/inno-magic-2017_tom-1.pdf

"Hamsa meaning". 2016. Web.archive.org. https://web.archive.org/web/20160816100430/http://www.hamsameaning.com/ (acccessed 28 February 2022)

Heidegger, Martin. 1962 [1927]. *Being and Time*. London: SCM Press. https://www.bard.edu/library/arendt/pdfs/Heidegger-BeingAndTime.pdf

Homer. 1924 [n.d.]. *Iliad*. Eng. trans. by A. T. Murray. http://www.perseus.tufts.edu/hopper/text?doc=Perseus%3Atext%3A1999.01.0134%3Abook%3D14 Korogly, Kh.G. 1976. Огузский героический эпос [The Oghuz heroic epos]. Nauka; Raykhl, K., Funk, D.A., Treyster, V. Тюркский эпос: традиции, формы, поэтическая структура [The Turkic epic: traditions, forms, poetic structure]. Nauka: 2008

Macgregor, Mary. 2020 [1908]. *Stories of Siegfried. Told to the Children*. [Online] Available at: https://www.heritage-history.com/index.php?c=read&author=macgregor&book=siegfried

Namaz. ABBYYLingvo 12.

"Padma". n. d. Collins English Dictionary. HarperCollins Publishers. https://www.collinsdictionary.com/dictionary/english/padma "Pentateuch". n.d. Jewish Encyclopedia. https://www.jewishencyclopedia.com/articles/12011-pentateuch (last modified 2021)

Pellegrini, Giovan Battista. 1990. *Toponomastica italiana: 10000 nomi di città, paesi, frazioni, regioni, contrade, fiumi, monti spiegati nella loro origine e storia*. Milan: Hoepli.

"Phoenician-Canaanite." 2020. Omniglot.com, The Online Encyclopedia for Writing Systems and Languages. https://omniglot.com/writing/phoenician.htm (last modified 10 August 2021)

"Pineal Gland". n.d. Encyclopedia Britannica. http://www.britannica.com/EBchecked/topic/460967/pineal-gland Plutarch. n.d. [75]. Pyrrhus. http://classics.mit.edu/Plutarch/pyrrhus.html (accessed 28 February 2022)

Rogers, Kara (ed.). 2012. *The endocrine system*. New York: Britannica Educational Publishing.

"Semitic Root Hll" [Hallel].2022. TheFreeDictionary.com. https://www.thefreedictionary.com/_/roots.aspx?type=Semitic&root=%E1%B8%A5ll (accessed 28 February 2022)

Snoj, Marko. 2009. *Etimološki slovar slovenskih zemljepisnih imen*. Ljubljana: Modrijan and Založba ZRC. Derived from Wikipedia

Sturluson, Snorri. n.d. *Prologue, The Prose Edda of Snorri Sturluson*. Translated by Arthur Gilchrist Brodeur, (1916). http://www.sacred-texts.com/neu/pre/pre03.htm, http://www.voluspa.org/proseprologue.htm

Tarasti, Eero. 2017. Culture and transcendence – the concept of transcendence through the ages. In Kristian Bankov & Paul Cobley (eds.), *Semiotics and its Masters* vol. 1, 293–324. Berlin/Boston: De Gruyter Mouton.

"The Annexation of Savoy and Nice to France". 1860. March 31. [Treaty of Turin.] The Times. https://sites.google.com/site/savoyannexation/the-times-full-list/the-times-march-31-1860-the-annexation-of-savoy-and-nice-to-france

"The Evil Eye and the Hamsa Symbol." 2016. House of Truth. https://houseoftruth.education/en/teaching/mona-lisa/mona-lisa-upside-down-lion-722#:~:text=This%20symbol%20is%20Mano%20Pantea,of%20parents%20over%20their%20child. "The Poetic Edda". 1936 [n.d.]. English trans. by H. A. Bellows. https://www.sacred-texts.com/neu/poe/poe03.htm "Transcendence." 2019. Vocabulary.com. https://www.vocabulary.com/dictionary/transcendence (accessed 28 February 2022)

Trever, K.V. 1959. Албания в IV-II вв.до н.э. [Albania in the 4th–2nd centuries BCE]. In *Очерки по истории и культуре Кавказской Албании: IV в. до н. э.-VII в. н. э* [Notes on the history and culture of Caucasian Albania: IV century BCE-VII century CE]. Moscow-Leningrad: USSR Academy of Sciences.

"Vibhūti (Bhasma or Bhasita): [ವಿಭೂತಿ or ಭಸ್ಮ, ಭಸಿತ]". n.d. Lingayat Religion. https://lingayatreligion.com/LingayatTerms/Vibhoti_or_Bhasma.htm (accessed 28 February 2022)

Virgil. 2007 [29–19 BC]. *Aeneid*. Eng. trans. by J. W. Mackail). https://www.gutenberg.org/files/22456/22456-h/22456-h.htm Глава 5. Центры Или Лотосы. Чакры. Падмы. n.d. Glava 5. Cenrts ili lotosı. Chakri. Padmi. http://www.e-reading-lib.com/chapter.php/130530/7/artur-avalon-zmeinaya-sila.html (accessed 28 February 2022)

Mattia Thibault
Ludo Ergo Sum: Play, existentialism and the ludification of culture

Abstract: This chapter aims to initiate a dialogue between semiotics of culture and existential semiotics about how to understand and conceptualise the changing role of games and play in contemporary society. Games have become the largest cultural industry in the World and their prestige is now exceeding their traditional borders and contaminates the languages of marketing, politics, art and many others. It is urgent, therefore, to acknowledge this change and to try to analyse it with the tools of semiotics. Cultural semiotics, hence, will allow us to conceptualise play as a *modelling system* and therefore to reconstruct its trajectory in the semiosphere. Existential semiotics, on the other hand, will help us outline the connection between the cultural evolution of games and the current global semiocrises and then to trace their effects on the individual level. In this chapter, then, we will first focus on the inner workings of play as a modelling system, then on its position in the semiosphere (in particular in relation to the concepts of *gamification* and *ludification*) and on the relationship between the ludification of culture and the global semiocrises brought by globalization. Finally, we will outline how, in this context, play and games have the semiotic potential to become tools of resistance and of individual expression.

Keywords: Semiotics of play, Ludification of Culture, Existentialism, Gamification

1 Introduction

This chapter aims to investigate, from the perspective of semiotics, the changing position of games and play in our society, from their position in the semiosphere, to the role they play at the individual level. In the last decades games have become one of the main entertainment industries in the world. Activities that for a long time were thought to belong to small groups of users (like the nerd and geek subcultures) have since become mainstream. Many stories, characters or even platforms related to games have become cultural icons, while gaming itself could be

---

Acknowledgements: This project has received funding from the European Union's Horizon 2020 research and innovation programme under the Marie Sklodowska-Curie grant agreement No 793835.

https://doi.org/10.1515/9783110789164-033

described is a barthesian myth in today's society. The passion for digital games or more in general for play, has started to become an important personality trait in how many people think of themselves. Groups of people (and not necessarily young!) identify as "gamers", while academia started to analyze gaming culture as an important, contemporary (and sometimes problematic) phenomenon.

Games themselves, are often escaping the narrow role of products of entertainment and are increasingly employed in various non-ludic fields. Game-based learning, for example, is becoming a major trend in education. Similarly, so-called serious games (that is, games that deal with important real-life topics) have been used to raise awareness about many pressing ethical issues. Finally, "gamification" in the last ten years has become a real buzzword, and has given life to a plethora of applications, studies, theories, and strategies.

In order to account for this phenomenon, this paper tries to describe how games and play are becoming cardinal semiotic engines within our society and addresses them through a dialogue between semiotics of culture, and in particular a lotmanian approach to play (cf. Thibault 2016) and existential semiotics (cf. Tarasti 2015). This will allow us, on the one hand, to conceptualise play as a modelling system and to trace its trajectory in the semiosphere and, on the other hand, to connect its cultural evolution to global semiocrises and back to the individual level. If semiotics of culture will help us to systematize how play is perceived in our society and what is its role in it, existential semiotics consists in a revalorization of subjectivity in semiotics.

In this paper then, we will first focus on the inner workings of play as a modeling system, then we will focus on its position in the semiosphere (in particular in relation to the concepts of Gamification and Ludification), finally we will deal with the relationship between ludification and the global semiocrises brought by globalization and on how play can become a tool of resistance and of individual expression.

2 Play as a modelling system

Play is indeed something very difficult to define or to describe. Several academics have tried for years to find a satisfactory definition of play. We can think, for example, at the works of Huizinga (1938), Caillois (1967), and many others. Wittgenstein (1953) however argues that there is not unique definition of play. That, in fact, the different activities that we define as "play" do not have any characteristics that is common to all of them. these activities characterized from what it calls a "family resemblance".

From a semiotic perspective (Thibault 2020), more than defining play it is interesting to deal with the process of playing and on how this is a primarily semiotic act. Jurij Lotman (1967) defines playful behavior as the parallel existence of two kinds of interpretive behaviors. On the one hand, while we play, we follow a *conventional behavior*: we assign to the objects, spaces and subjects involved in the play activity new fictional meanings. On the other hand, we also observe a *practical behavior:* we remember and recognize the real meaning of these objects, spaces, and subjects. If, for example, we play with a doll, at the same time we pretend to react to it as with a real baby, but we are well aware that it is, after all, only a toy. Play therefore always involves some form of resemantisation, and therefore, before becoming a way of acting and behaving, it is first of all a specific form of interpretation.

The objects that we use during play, regardless of if there are crafted to be used in that way, become part of new sign functions (Thibault 2020). We could call these playful signs "as-if signs", that is: "signs that must not be taken quite literally in the *Dasein*, but rather as kinds of metaphors" (Tarasti 2015: 16). This kind of signs can also be found, for example, in cinema or theater (Ibid.), but the nature of their creation is that of play.

The as-if signs that are produced during play, however, are not in any way random, but very often create some kind of system. Starting from the first resemantisation, all the following will be determined from one another. If a child has a toy sword, they will look for an enemy to battle against or a monster to slay. If they have a doll, instead, they will look for something that can work as a cradle, or something to feed them, and so on. The resematisations, then will create a system of as-if signs, based on a specific theme and a series of scripts (Thibault 2020). This, however, is not typical only of child-play, and happens in games as well. It is very well possible to play draughts using, for example, bottle caps. In this case, all is needed is to find enough bottle caps of two different colors, and something that could work as a chess board. In this case, then, the system that emerges will have an actantial nature, as the meaning of the different pieces will be determined by their reciprocate relationships and their possible interactions in the game.

Every playful activity, then, creates its own set of signs – which, combined with a series of constraints (in some cases stable and predetermined, like in chess, in other cases created on the spot, like in child-play), will give structure and meaning to the activity itself. In this sense, play works as a secondary modeling system. While it creates a series of idiolects more than a single language, its structures and workings are stable and well-known enough to make of play a specific form of communication and meaning making.

3 Play in the semiosphere: Gamification and ludification

Since the Enlightenment, the common perception of games and playfulness has been evolving towards a position of prestige. Rousseau's and Schiller's works on education inaugured a change in the rhetorics of play: the latter is seen less and less as "frivolity" (to borrow a term from Sutton-Smith 1997) and increasingly as an important, and sometimes "productive" facet of culture. With the 20th Century, new interest on the study of play arose, in cardinal theoretical works as those by Huizinga (1938) and Caillois (1967) soon fuelled by the birth and success of digital gaming. Already in 1990 Ernst Lurker predicted that some major transformations would take place in society's attitude towards play. Later, Brian Sutton-Smith (1997) noted how the world was becoming more play-oriented and stated that the "ludic turn" of Western societies is modifying the way in which society expects products and services to cater for its needs (Sutton-Smith, in Henricks, 2017). Twenty years later, Sicart claims that, in current society, "play has become a cultural, social and economic centerpiece" (Sicart, 2018, 262).

Recently, this cultural shift in the perception of play has been named the "ludification of culture" (Raessens 2006), or sometimes "emergent gamification" (Hamari 2019), "gamification of culture" or "ludification"(Bonenfant and Genvo 2014). This shift caused a redefinition of the contexts in which playful behaviour is considered acceptable (Idone Cassone 2017).

From the perspective of semiotics of culture, we can define the ludification of culture as a movement of play within the semiosphere. Play, in Lotman's terminology, is a *secondary modelling system*, which has been present in the semiosphere of all cultures throughout history. In the last centuries, however, due to several factors, both social and technological (see, e.g., Ortoleva, 2012), this specific modelling systems has been accelerating towards the centre of our semiosphere.

While some forms of play have always more or less been hegemonic in Western culture (for example sports, or hunting), the larger context of play has often been relegated to the periphery of the semiosphere. Play has been deemed childish – and child culture has often been deemed as separate from the adult's (Crawford 2009). Play has been opposed to values such as seriousness and productivity, and therefore considered sinful (Leone 2016) or silly – hence attempts to transform it in a tool to "tame" children and young people, as lamented by Barthes (1957).

While some ludophobic attitudes persist, (Thibault 2019b) the movement of play in the semiosphere has changed much of this mentality. This does not mean that we play more, or that play was less of cultural importance in the past, but that we recognise more openly its value. Today play enjoys an unprecedented prestige, and its semiospheric centrality entails a new dimension of modelling ability. Play is increasingly taken as a model in other contexts and for other modelling systems, both in a descriptive and prescriptive sense.

On the one hand, according to Lotman, every movement towards the centre of the semiopsphere is accompanied by an increase of self-awareness, so that the modelling system is then proposed as a metalanguage to describe the whole semiosphere (Lotman 1990: 135). Play and games become a universal metaphor (Idone Cassone, 2017), used to describe political dynamics (made up of "winners" and "losers"), economic competition (populated by "players") and even our very relationship to our lives (for whose we need a "life coach").

On the other hand, play becomes also a prescriptive model, a blueprint to be used in the design of all sort of systems and activities. This is the idea behind the concept of "gamification" (Hamari 2019), based on the claim that things would be "better" if they were more game–like.

The increase of modelling ability an of prestige of play, finally, triggers a dialogue with the other sign systems of the central area of the semiosphere (Lotman 1990: 143–150). These systems start to develop metalanguages to describe play and games, resulting in the proliferation of academic research, documentaries, fiction (novels, comics, films) dedicated to them.

This movement throughout the semiosphere, however is also reflected on the individual level. While it is easy to imagine culture as something abstract, the semiosphere only exists in the actual texts circulating and on the encyclopedias of the people belonging to it.

In order to consider this new centrality of play on the individual level we will make use of the Zemic model presented in Tarasti (2015), one of the most famous concepts of existential semiotics. Briefly, it is a model based on the confluence of Greimas' modalities, the concepts of moi and soi elaborated in Fontanille (2004) and the Hegelian being-in-itself and being-for-itself (Tarasti 2015). It is a modified version of the semiotic square used in existential semiotics to make ontological investigations. The name "Zemic" comes from the "Z" shaped path that it draws and from the fact that it focuses on the inner movements of the subject (and therefore it is "emic" and not "etic") (Tarasti 2015). It is articulated in four steps, the first two related to the sensible and the other related to the intelligible.

The first step is "*Moi 1*" or *être en moi* and it deals with the physical qualities of the subject, its body and chora (the pre-lingual stage pre-lingual stage of development, dominated by a chaotic mix of perceptions and needs, introduced by Kristeva and Derrida). To this step Tarasti assigns the modality of wanting-to or *vouloir*. The second step, "*Moi 2*" is devoted to the *être pour moi* and therefore to the personality of the subject, its inner characteristics and abilities and is related to *pouvoir*, being-able-to.

"*Soi 2*" is the third step and it means *être pour soi*. The subject is now integrated in the social institutions, where its modality of *savoir*, knowing-to, is fundamental. The last step is "*Soi 1*" or *être en soi*. It is on a higher level and deals with cultural values and axiologies. The subject is now confronted with the modality of duty: *devoir* (having-to).

Even if these four concepts are called steps, they are not alternate in time or necessarily subsequent: the subject is simultaneously immersed in all of them, even if it is generally more committed or focused on one of them. If we apply the Zemic model to analyse play as an practice and a cultural element, we can distinguish the following steps:

M1 *être en moi (vouloir)* – play is a naturally emerging phenomenon that, since infancy, guides our actions and our ways of learning and making sense of the world around us. Its modality is that of wanting to-do or to-be, as play is a voluntary action that responds to the needs and desired of the players.

M2 *être pour moi (pouvoir)* – shifts to transcendence as the individuals observes themselves and what they are lacking. Being becomes existing. In this case the fact of playing, of being a player becomes the testimony that one exists: Ludo ergo sum. We have countless texts that testimony this sort of identification, including fictional representations that equate the loss in a game to death we can think of the long lasting trope of the gladiators' fights, as well as contemporary depictions such as in Altman's Quintet or Hwang Dong-hyuk's Squid Game The possibility (pouvoir) of playing, in this cases, is linked to one's existence.

S2 *être pour soi (savoir)* – the transcendent category originated around this step is that of the "gamer" (generally related to those of nerd or geek). Being a gamer is related to specific competences (expert knowledge on games) that are somewhat proof of passion and commitment (cf Greimas & Fontanille 1991). This sort of *thematic role* has several representations in media (the most famous of which is probably TV series The Big Bang Theory by Chuck Lorre and Bill Prady).

S1 *être en soi (devoir)* – in *Dasein*, people want to belong to this category, to be recognised a gamer. The "have-to" modality proves their competence to other gamers signaling the belonging to the group and the sharing of interests and passions. This, in turn, can give rise to activities of gatekeeping and often toxic behaviours intended to exclude certain individuals (or categories of individuals, such as "noobs" or unexperienced players) from the group (Nieborg & Sihvonen 2009).

From our application of the Zemic model we can see how the different steps present different degrees of generalisability. While M1 can be considered universal – as play is a constarn throughout cultures and times – the importance of the next steps (and therefore play's movement towards transcendence and towards the soi) are related to a specific cultural predicament. In particular, they can be interpreted as the practical reflection on the individual level of the semiospheric dynamics that have invested play (i.e. of the ludification of culture). If the lotmanian model helped us to map how the role of play is changing within our society, the Zemic model allowed us to trace its movement within the inwardness of the individual.

4 Ludification in the global semiocrisis and gamification as a force of resistance

We have briefly described the mutations caused by ludification in the semiosphere as well as on an individual level. But why this cultural change happened in the first place? Ortoleva (2012) tries to answer this question and links it to a larger cultural trend that sees a massive shift of values in Western culture. In particular, Ortoleva claims that playfulness may be taking the place of sexuality as our cultural "obsession". He states that, in the last century, many cultural areas like economy and entertainment have undergone a progressive "sexualisation". This "century-lasting strip tease" is almost come to completion (the sexual taboos are almost completely gone, with the important exception of pedophilia) and therefore the efficacy of eroticism as a cultural tool is decreasing. A new model will soon have to replace it and, according to Ortoleva, it will probably be playfulness – and, in particular, games. The Homo Ludens described by Huizinga (1938) is now becoming a Homo Ludicos (Ortoleva 2012): a real play-obsessed being. Play is no more only a fundamental aspect of culture, but it could be slowly becoming one of the main ones.

According to Volli (2016), instead, the success of play as a universal metaphor is due to the fact that contemporary society suffers of a lack of stimuli or, in semiotic terms, a deficiency in the ability of creating or choosing *objects of value*. Play is able to create values that are not rooted on anthropological and psychological grounds but are proper only to the play itself. This is one of the most important features of play and, according to Volli, it may explain why the latter is so important today: as the fulfilment of basic needs is taken for granted, individuals need new motivations to pursue their activities. Play provides such motivations – it is the principle behind both gamification (that explicitly use play values as lures for non-playful tasks) and ludification (through which society rethinks itself as play-oriented).

In the context of existential semiotics, however, we could also connect ludification with the challenges brought about by globalisation. According to Tarasti (2015), globalisation tends to annihilate the past and the future in favour of an eternal present. It moves production (both of signs and of goods) on a metalevel, and it restricts the emotional spectrum to modes such as greed or fear etc.

Some of the problematic characteristics that, according to Tarasti, are typical of globalisation, find some interesting echoes in the ludification of culture. Tarasti mentions, for example, the importance of the categories of "winners" and "losers", borrowed from sports and digital games, and today widely used, even at the highest levels of political life. Similarly, Tarasti mentions the perpetual assessment of quality in all domains. While this particular aspect might not sound very playful at a first sight, it is a strategy that is very often used in gamification techniques. The latter tend to use metrics to measure several aspects of performance, and then use these values in a game system. Reframing assessment within a game might make it less heavy, perhaps even enjoyable, but it stems from the same cultural and ideological premises that other forms of continuous tracking and assessment. Ludification, then, would appear to be an effect, or a concurrence, of globalisation. Strategies making use of the new prestige of play such as gamification or game-based learning have indeed been criticised in the past for the fact that they have sometimes been used for exploitation or for their ability to naturalise all sorts of processes and therefore to hinder critical thinking (Thibault 2019a). However, we believe that the ludification of culture offers, at the same time, some tools of resistance against globalisation and, in particular, against the naturalisation of transcendence.

Globalisation indeed naturalises transcendence: the rich communication processes of their *Dasein* blind people who cling to them as to the true semiosis of ideas and acts and significations. Embodied by the Internet (Tarasti 2015: 160), this process makes transcendence look empty – and this apparent emptiness encourages us to refuse it altogether.

As global culture advances on all fronts, making struggle and tensions emerge everywhere, in every aspect of everyday life, strategies of resistance need to be equally ubiquitous. These are based on *negation* a spiritual and pragmatic operation, at the very hearth of existential semiotics, that questions the *Dasein* and the supposed emptiness of transcendence (Tarasti 2015: 160).

Using negation as a form of resistance, therefore, means looking for alternatives, progressing in a different direction than that of globalisation. In other words, it entails an exploration of what could have happened and of what could happen still.

Counterfactuality, that is at the centre of this process, is, in fact, a playful way of dealing with history. According lo Lotman, the work of the historian itself is partially playful, as "The historian may be compared with the theatrical spectator who watches a play for the second time: on the one hand, he knows how it will end and there is nothing unpredictable about it for him. The play, for him, takes place, as it were, in the past from which he extracts his knowledge of the matter. But, simultaneously, as a spectator who looks upon the scene, he finds himself once again in the present and experiences a feeling of uncertainty, an alleged "ignorance" of how play will end" (Lotman [2004] 2009: 126). This way of dealing with history is similar to the so-called "what if...?" games and is typical of several forms of childish play. Playing with history, looking at the possible alternatives, imagining different outcomes, questioning its narratives is a dynamic already present in many games (Idone Cassone & Thibault 2016), but at the same time it could become a way of resisting globalisation.

The goal of resistance is to grant freedom to the individuals: this means that they need to realise that "the course of the subject is not predetermined, but that an energetic action can take place by the subject, which, through its acts, moulds its reality" (Tarasti 2015). According to Lotman, play has a similar need: it must be unpredictable, as "the moment when the player has no more choices, the game has lost its meaning" (Lotman [1967] 2011: 159).

Additionally, play by definition questions the ordinary signifiers of everyday life (Thibault 2020). If games have been used to reinforce the naturalising narratives and myths that justify certain forms of civilization, play can be indeed also a tool to deconstruct them. Play can induce us to defamiliarize the objects of everyday life so to eventually challenge the status quo (Dunne 2005), To question power and power structures, To laugh at the *Dasein*, and therefore to open new horizons for retrieving a sense of transcendence.

To conclude, we have seen that the ludification of culture can be understood as a process that proceeds parallel to that of globalisation. On the one hand, the latter can appropriate this cultural change and make it its own tool of control and assessment. On the other hand, however, ludification has also a lot to offer to those that wish to resist the values of globalisation, providing them with a tool to challenge the status quo and imagine possible, sometime radical, alternatives to globalisation.

In this chapter we have established a dialogue between existential and cultural semiotics, as a methodological approach to the ludification of culture. This allowed us to take in consideration both the effects of the increased prestige of play on society at large and on the individual level. It is at the interface between these two dimensions, between the cultural and the personal, that playfulness can then become a tool of resistance, a tool fight the homogenisation brough by globalisation and contrast the semiocrisis it entails.

References

Barthes, Roland. 1957. *Mythologies*. Paris: Seuil.
Bonenfant Maude & Sébastien Genvo. 2014. Une approche située et critique du concept de gamification. *Sciences du jeu* 2 https://journals.openedition.org/sdj/286.
Caillois, Roger. 1967. *Les jeux et les hommes*. Paris: Gallimard.
Crawford, Sally. 2009. The archaeology of play things: theorising a toy stage in the 'biography' of objects. *Childhood in the Past* 2(1). 55–70.
Dunne, Anthony. 2005. *Hertzian Tales: Electronic Products, Aesthetic Experience, and Critical Design*. Cambridge: MIT Press.
Fontanille, Jacques. 2004. *Soma et séma. Figures du corp*. Paris: Maisonneuve et Larose.
Henricks, Thomas S. 2017. Foreword. In Brian Sutton-Smith, *Play for Life. Play Theory and Play as Emotional Survival*. Comp. and ed. by Charles Lamar Phillips and the editors of the American Journal of Play. The Strong.
Greimas, Algirdas Julien & Jacques Fontanille. 1991. Sémiotique des passions: des états de choses aux états d'âme. Seuil.
Hamari, Juho. 2019. Gamification. Blackwell Pub, In *The Blackwell Encyclopedia of Sociology*, 1–3. Malden.
Huizinga, Johan. 1949. 1938. *Homo Ludens*. London: Routledge.
Idone Cassone, Vincenzo. 2017. Through the Ludic Glass. A cultural Genealogy of Gamification. In *Proceedings of Academic MindTrek 2017 Conference (Tampere)*. New York, ACM Press. DOI: 10.1145/3131085.3131120
Idone Cassone, Vincenzo & Mattia Thibault. 2016. The HGR framework A Semiotic Approach to the Representation of History in Digital Games. *Gamevironments* 5: 156–204.
Leone, Massimo. 2016. La Pallavolo Sacra. In Mattia Thibault (ed.), *Gamification Urbana: Letture e Riscritture ludiche degli spazi cittadini*. Aracne: Rome.
Lotman, Juri. 1990. *Universe of the Mind: A Semiotic Theory of Culture*. London: I. B. Tauris & Co.
Lotman, Juri. 2009 [2004]. *Culture and Explosion*. Berlin: Mouton de Gruyter.
Lotman, Juri. 2011 [1967]. The place of art among other modelling systems. *Sign Systems Studies* 39(2/4). 251–270.
Lurker, Ernst. 1990. Play Art: Evolution or Trivialization of Art? *Play & Culture* 3. 146–167.
McGonigall, Jane. 2011. *Reality Is Broken: Why Games Make Us Better and How They Can Change the World*. London: Penguin Books.
Nieborg, David B. & Tanja Sihvonen. 2009. The new gatekeepers: The occupational ideology of game journalism. Proc. of DiGRA.
Ortoleva Peppino. 2012. *Dal Sesso al Gioco, un'ossessione per il XXI Secolo?* Turin: Espress edizioni.
Raessens, Joost. 2006. Playful Identities or the ludification of culture. *Games and Culture* 1. 52–57.
Scolari, Carlos Alberto. 2013. *Narrativas Transmedia, Cuando Todos los Medios Cuentan*. Bizkaia: Deusto.
Sicart, Miguel. 2018. Quixotean Play in the Age of Computation. *American Journal of Play*, 10(3).
Sutton-Smith, Brian. 2009 [1997]. *The ambiguity of play*. Cambridge, MA: Harvard University Press.
Tarasti, Eero. 2015. *Sein und Schein: Explorations in existential semiotics*. Berlin: De Gruyter Mouton.

Thibault, Mattia. 2016. Lotman and Play: For a Theory of Playfulness Based on Semiotics of Culture. *Sign Systems Studies* XLIV(3). 295–325.
Thibault, Mattia. 2019a. Punk Gamification. In *Proceedings of the 3rd International GaminFIN Conference (GamiFIN 2019), CEUR-WS*, 58–69.
Thibault, Mattia. 2019b. Taming Play: A Map of Play Ideologies in the West and in China. In Massimo Leone, Bruno Surace & Jun Zeng, *The Fountain and the Waterfall*, 329–344. (Monographic I Saggi di Lexia, 34). Rome: Aracne. DOI 10.4399/978882552787214
Thibault Mattia. 2020. *Ludosemiotica. Il gioco tra segni, testi, pratiche e discorsi*, Rome: Aracne.
Volli, Ugo. 2016. L'incorcio fecondo fra giochi e città. In Mattia Thibault (ed.) *Gamification Urbana, letture e riscritture ludiche degli spazi cittadini*. Roma: Aracne.
Werbach, Kevin & Dan Hunter. 2012. *For The Win: How Game Thinking Can Revolutionize Your Business*. Philadelphia: Wharton Digital Press.
Wittgenstein, Ludwig. 1953. *Philosophical Investigations*. Trans. by E. Anscombe. New York: Palgrave Macmillan.

Altti Kuusamo
Uncertain signifiers: 'An Affective Phantasy' in Jacopo Pontormo's *Joseph in Egypt*

Abstract: In spite of its renown, Jacopo Pontormo's (1494–1556/57) painting Joseph in Egypt (ca. 1518) still calls for deeper art historical consideration. The painting does not open its reservoirs of meaning very easily, and art historians have left many interesting questions untouched in the old and in more recent research literature. In a way, it is surprising that this painting, with its *bellezza dell'invenzione* ('the beauty of inventions', as defined by Giorgio Vasari), has not received much attention for decades, especially when we take into account the development of methods and tools in art history over the last thirty years. As such, many questions are open for discussion, even when we think about normal art historical research and leave semiotic analysis untouched.

Applying some methods of semiotics my interpretation tries to solve the problem of so called living statues in the painting – as much as the problem of basic contrasts of meaning using dysphoria / euphoria -opposition – not to forget the contrast between nuclear and tribal family. With these tools it may, finally, be possible to open the core of the affective fantasy of Pontormo's famous painting.

Keywords: Living statues, melancholy, dysphoria, euphoria, tribal family, nuclear family, affective fantasy, *vaghezza*, Mannerism

In spite of its renown, Jacopo Pontormo's (1494–1556) painting *Joseph in Egypt* (1515), still calls for deeper art historical consideration. The painting does not open its reservoirs of meaning very easily, and art historians have left many interesting questions untouched in the old and in more recent research literature. In a way it is surprising that this picture, with its *"bellezza dell'invenzione"* ("the beauty of inventions", as defined by Giorgio Vasari),[1] has not received much attention during last decades – especially when we take into account the development of methods and tools in art history over the last thirty years. As such, many questions are open for discussion, even when we think about normal art historical research and leave the semiotic analysis untouched. So, I am also going apply some methods of semiotics in order to illuminate this old but still ever green object of study.

---

[1] Giorgio Vasari, *Le vite dei più eccellenti pittori, scultori ed architetti VI*, ed. Gaetano Milanesi, Firenze, 1887, 261.

https://doi.org/10.1515/9783110789164-034

Belonging to the early phase of Italian Mannerism, the painting was thought by Pontormo's contemporary Giorgio Vasari to be the most challenging of all his paintings: "*storia assai grande pur di figure piccole*" ("quite a large story for the small-scale figures").[2] The size of the painting is relatively small, only 93 x 110 cm on panels, and yet as a little oil painting it contains numerous micro-episodes and narrative oddities. Vasari also stated that it is "la più bella pittura che Puntormo facesse mai".[3] Translated in the mannerist language the word "bella" here does not mean simply beauty, but rather complex splendor. *Joseph in Egypt* is a "little big" painting, full of narrative and symbolic enigmas. The most surprising of these might be the so called living statues, which await new interpretative efforts. I have not encountered semiotic interpretations of the painting, however, it seems clear that semiotic analysis could be the most fitting for this complex picture (Figure 1).

Figure 1: Jacopo Pontormo: *Joseph in Egypt*. 1515–1518. Oil on wood. 96,5 x 109,5 cm. National Gallery, London. Photo: By permission of National Gallery, London.

The panel painting, now in the National Gallery, London, was painted for the wedding chamber of Pierfrancesco Borgherini and Margherita Acciaioli in their

---

2 Vasari, *Le vite dei più eccellenti pittori, scultori ed architetti VI*, 261.
3 Vasari, *Le vite dei più eccellenti pittori, scultori ed architetti VI*, 262.

townhouse in Borgo SS. Apostoli, having been commissioned by Pierfrancesco's father Salvi Borgherini in 1515. The work was the most significant in the series of *spalliere* and *cassoni* paintings made by Pontormo and other artists (Andrea del Sarto, Bacchiacca and Francesco Cranacci) for this famous wedding chamber. The subject was the story of Joseph as narrated in the Old Testament.[4] Vasari mentions that Pontormo's *Joseph in Egypt* was located independently of others, left of the doorway,[5] and it was "apparently a separate item in the scheme of decoration",[6] yet the theme or subject matter was the same: the life of Joseph. Pontormo also made three other panels, which are smaller ones and for spalliere and cassoni (and for lettuccio?) of the chamber: *Joseph sold to Potiphar*, *Pharaoh with his Butler and Baker* and *Joseph's Brothers Beg for Help*, all in the year 1515. The common theme, which underlie all these paintings, is a story of Joseph as a precursor of Christ.[7] The biblical story depicted in *Joseph in Egypt* consists of five episodes: 1. Joseph presents his parents to Pharaoh, bottom left of the picture. 2. Joseph receives the message of his father's illness, bottom right. 3. Dying Jacob (top right) with his family and grandsons, and the depiction of the change of grandsons' privileges to the younger boy Ephraim. 4. Above the Egyptians begging for food (bottom centre), is a crowd of men gathered behind a stone, considered to be Joseph's brothers (which is an old presumption).[8] 5. Finally, there is a group of children below the stairs in the foreground; one of these kinds is in a contemporary dress. In this way the small picture plane is packed with episodes. Besides these main events the rare and peculiarly notable elements of the whole scene, however, are the three semi-living statues standing over the activities on the ground.

Before considering the statues, the first of various peculiarities is the long narrative time span between the episodes in the biblical text represented. The distant time span has been condensed into five episodes, so spatially close to each other that the beholder cannot easily discern one episode from the next. It has been said that within the scene the story proceeds jerkily (*a scatti*, as Antonio Pinelli has stated),[9] and yet there is a double movement of signifiers within the

---

[4] Vasari, *Le vite dei più eccellenti pittori, scultori ed architetti VI*, VI, 261; Cecil Gould, 'Joseph in Egypt.' *The Sixteenth-Century Italian Schools, National Gallery catalogues*, London, 1975, 200.
[5] Vasari, *Le vite dei più eccellenti pittori, scultori ed architetti VI*, 261.
[6] Allan Braham, 'The Bed of Pierfrancesco Borgherini,' *The Burlington Magazine*, CXXI: 921, 1979, 761.
[7] Braham, 'The Bed of Pierfrancesco Borgherini,' 757, 761, 765.
[8] *Genesis* xlvii, 13 & xlviii; cf. Gould, 'Joseph in Egypt,' 199; Kurt Forster, *Pontormo. Monographie mit Kritischem Katalog*, München,1966, 30–31.
[9] Antonio Pinelli, *La bella maniera. Artisti del Ciquecento tra regole e licenza*, Torino, 1993, 73.

visual narrative: one is disjointed (fragmented) and the other is condensed. Thus, discontinuities of meaning on the one level of the narrative can signify continuities on the other. There has been much discussion of the incorrectness, or the lack of unity of the perspective of the work.[10] Arguably, this particular "dimension" of the picture has been exaggerated in the earlier research, especially in the 1960s, when perspectival discontinuities were seen as the dominant feature of early Mannerism with its assumed medieval references. However, the scene can be viewed as more coherent than discontinuous, and its depth cues as consistent rather than inconsistent.[11]

While the biblical story has a "profane" visual structure, a compound which does not follow dominant visual conventions of the age, the hypothesis that I propose here, is that "the deep structure" of the scene represented contains certain important polarities of meaning: Euphoria /dysphoria; nuclear family/ tribal family; *unheimlich/heimlich*; solitude (melancholy)/crowd; solitary affects/ familiar affects. The scene thus introduces a field of meaning full of essential tensions. Of pivotal concern here are the living statues (*statue viventi*), replete with different affective and totemic (meaning: family-oriented) implications. According to my hypothesis, the enigmatic meaning of the living statues can be interpreted through an analysis of the various tensions or polarities built into the scene. For example, we can try to search for a contextual identity of the colorful putto on top of the short column; and yet a more important question might be to ask what kind of catalytic function does this figure have in the middle of the overall multi-focalized scene? As such, the roles of these animated but seemingly melancholy statues placed in the midst of the lively episodes are the center of my concern. In my view the problem of "living statues" has not been correctly resolved in the extant art historical literature. Indeed, the meaning of these statues has continued to be an art historical enigma, especially when thinking about their roles or functions in the scene.

The main problem concerning the meaning of the statues has usually been fashioned as referential, and thus iconographic in the narrow sense. A semiotic approach, however, does not so much focus on what the statues mean, but rather

---

10 Cf. Forster, *Pontormo*, 28; Pinelli, *La bella maniera*, 73.
11 According to recent views, perspective is a tricky thing: without architecture it offers often irregular depth cues, which the beholder can perceive as regular (cf. Ernst Gombrich, *Art Illusion*, London, 1960, 201). In the first draft the whole scene of the painting was different. According to Plazzotta & Bilinge (Carol Plazzotta & Rachel Billinge, 'The Underdrawing of Pontormo's Joseph with "Jacob in Egypt".' *Burlington Magazine* 144, 2002, 662–665) there are many underdrawings in Pontormo's work. The master changed the round stair case into its mirror image and situated the bed scene in the middle of the upper zone of the scene.

it asks how their presumed referential meaning is bound up within, or "woven" into, the symbolic structure of the picture. In this sense we can assume that the so-called hidden meaning does not in fact refer very far "outside" of the scene, but, on the contrary, it elucidates the disposition of certain visual segments of the story; the sections loaded with certain kinds of evidence which can be discerned within the tensions of meaning.

1 The seductive symbolism of living statues

In terms of surveying the literature, it is interesting to look at the different referential meanings art historians have given to the living statues.

1. In his early monograph of Pontormo Mortimer Clapp states: "There are three statues on high pedestals in the picture. They represent Mars, Venus and Cupid".[12] He does not, however, tell us why they are included in the scene.

2. Rachel Wischnitzer published a more profound analysis in 1953: "There is a statue surmounting a column at the entrance of Pharaoh's palace, another one at the top of the circular stair, and the third at the foot of the stair. The three figures were interpreted as some unspecified Egyptian deities, intended to give local color to the scene".[13] She also refers to Clapp: "According to another suggestion they are Mars, Venus and Cupid",[14] and continues: "The three statues, an old man, a young woman and a child, seem to personify the *Three Ages* and thus sum up the content of the picture, with Jacob, Joseph and Joseph's children representing three generations".[15] The problematic, colorful "dancing putto" does not disturb Wischnitzer.[16] She sees the statue of the dancing putto as nothing more than "the image of a carefree childhood."[17] Whereas for Venus or Caritas – although the attribute is not clear – she finds a clear function which refers to *Genesis* (41:45) and finally the family situation of Borgherini: "Pontormo in his Biblical picture may have wished to glorify paternal love and filial affection, thus alluding to the tender relationship of his patron Salvi Borgherini, to his son Pierfrancesco".[18] Because

---

[12] Mortimer Clapp, *Jacopo Carucci da Pontormo, His Life and Work*. New Haven, 1916, 157.
[13] Rachel Wischnitzer, ‚Jacopo Pontormo's Joseph Scenes.' *Gazette des Beaux-Arts*, 16, 1953, 155.
[14] Wischnitzer, 'Jacopo Pontormo's Joseph Scenes,' 157.
[15] Wischnitzer, 'Jacopo Pontormo's Joseph Scenes.‘ 155–156.
[16] Wischnitzer, 'Jacopo Pontormo's Joseph Scenes,‘ 161.
[17] Wischnitzer, 'Jacopo Pontormo's Joseph Scenes,‘ 156.
[18] Wischnitzer, 'Jacopo Pontormo's Joseph Scenes,‘ 156.

we don't know much about the circumstances of the Borgherini family-situation in the early years of sixteenth century the reference might be too hazy.[19]

3. In his monography of Pontormo (1966) Kurt Forster follows the lines of Wischnitzer as far as he can, and mentions the same allegorical meanings: "*Lebenslater* and Venus as Caritas" – and in that way does not say much about the statues. However he also refers to an illusory *Caritas*-sculpture of Pontormo's in another painting dealing with the theme of Joseph, *Joseph sold to Potiphar* (Figure 2), which is also in the National Gallery, London.[20] Forster's idea that these statues are like "allegorical comments", is a good one,[21] and yet their commenting role here could be seen as even more important and explanatory than the "exact" referent. In this sense, there is a possibility that the statues can more importantly be an inside referent within the picture.

Figure 2: Jacopo Pontormo: *Joseph sold to Potiphar*. 1515. Oil on wood. 61 x 51,6 cm. National Gallery, London. Photo: By permission of National Gallery, London.

---

19 Cf. Braham, 'The Bed of Pierfrancesco Borgherini, 761.
20 Forster, *Pontormo*, 132.
21 Forster, *Pontormo*, 132.

4. Kaoru Adachi in his article "La statua vivente ermetica" ("A hermetic living statue") from the year 1997 refers mainly to the representatives of the corpus of hermetic knowledge as a key for the interpretation: Marsilio Ficino, Francesco Zorzi Veneto, Tiberio Russiliano, Sesto Calabrese, Giulio Camillo Fidelminio, Cornelio Agrippa di Nettesheim and Giordano Bruno. According to Adachi "the painter has wanted to "animate" in a divine manner the statue the same way as a hermetic magician".[22] Unfortunately, the mystical-hermetic knowledge does not explain or validate its relationship to the narrative whole. It is far too syncretistic. In fact Adachi's interpretation is typical of the age (1980–90s): the overall cosmological account rolls over the visual narrative and does not fit the demands of the pictorial narrative.

5. In his late monograph Philippe Costamagna states: "The three emblematic and enigmatic ritual figures underline, in all probability, the moralizing intent of the story".[23] What this means exactly remains somewhat open. Costamagna's explanation is a loosely psychological one: it suggests a lack of motivation to 'return' the meaning back to the machinery of other representations in the scene.

6. Maurizia Tazartes (2008) sees clearly the double role of the statues. According to her the statues are "not only living persons but also sculptural works, the art which the painter seems to know quite well, and which we can infer from the explanations in Pontormo's letter to Benedetto Varchi on 18th February 1548".[24] Tazartes also refers to the terracotta models Pontormo later used when making figures *a fresco* in S. Lorenzo.[25] They are works of art inside the scene. This explanation is interesting and leads us to the revealing testimonial of Pontormo himself – to which we will return. It does not, however, explain the function of the statues in this particular scene.

It is hardly ever mentioned that the pagan statues in the scene can be seen to represent paganism or otherness, "Egypt" in a wide sense, in the same way that Pontormo borrows elements of the art of Flanders and Germany, especially if we think the topos of "The Flight to Egypt" – and the function of the pagan statues in this topos in Flemish painting. It has often been mentioned (from Vasari to Cecil Gould) that Pontormo admired Northern art, especially Dürer and Lucas van Leyden. As for the statue on the left, Cecil Gould refers to the Laocoon-group,[26]

---

[22] Kaoru Adachi, 'La statua vivente. Una precisazione iconografica della Giuseppe in Egitto del Pontormo.' *Bijutsushigaku*, 19, 1997, 110.
[23] Philippe Costamagna, *Pontormo*. Milano, 1994, 130.
[24] Maurizia Tazartes, *Il "ghiribizzoso" Pontormo*, 2008, 59.
[25] Tazartes, *Il 'ghiribizzoso' Pontormo*, 2008, 59.
[26] Gould, 'Joseph in Egypt,' 201.

and as for otherness, Pontormo has painted a gabled gate in the background of the scene, which he took from the engraving of Lucas van Leyden, *Ecce Homo* (1510).²⁷ Antonio Pinelli has rightly observed that Hans Memling's painting *Scenes from the Passion of Christ* (1470–71), with its microcosms of labyrinthine events in the same architectural setting, has been the most influential work for Pontormo's image. The painting was at that time in Florence – being now in the Galleria Sabauda, Torino.²⁸

Although Pontormo's living statues seem to be a rarity in the pictorial world of the Renaissance, they certainly do not come from out of the blue. Not long before Pontormo, Piero di Cosimo had painted two pictures representing the deeds of Prometheus, notably depicting how Prometheus shapes a human being from clay and puts him on a pedestal in a mode of a living statue.²⁹ Suzanne Peters-Schildgen has also referred to Filippino Lippi's role as the initiator of the living statue-topos with his frescos in the Strozzi-chapel in Santa Maria Novella, Florence.³⁰ Some have also referred to the myth of Pygmalion.³¹ This reference is worth noting, but it does not help much when seeking the function of these *statue viventi* within the whole narrative, which mostly indicates the isolation of figures. Indeed, their liveliness is a challenge for criticism. Paul Barolsky even speaks about the "putto in the flesh", posing "Pippo-fashion,"³² whereas S. Nigro speaks about *"marmocarne"*, marbleflesh.³³ In addition, the concept *simia natura* has also been mentioned.³⁴

The other term often used is *figura viva* (or *quadri viventi*), especially in light of how the decorations of triumphal carts in the carnival processions of late *quattrocento* have been described.³⁵ Probably the most famous description of this

---

27 Forster, *Pontormo*, 29; Gould, 'Joseph in Egypt,' 200.
28 Pinelli, *La bella maniera. Artisti del Ciquecento tra regole e licenza*, 59.
29 E.g. Uwe Bischoff, *Die ‚Cassonebilder' des Piero di Cosimo. Fragen der Ikonographie*. Frankfurt am Main 1995, 68–69; Elena Capretti, ‚Sezione I – 55 a-b: Piero di Cosimo: Prometeo plasma l'uomo & Prometeo sottrae il fuoco celeste agli dei. *Piero di Cosimo, 1462–1522.' Pittore eccentrico fra Rinascimento e Maniera*. Ed. by Elena Capretti, Anna Forlani Tempesti, Serena Padovani, Firenze, 2015, 326.
30 Suzanne Peters-Schildgen, *Die Bedeutung Filipponi Lippis für Manierismus*, Essen, 1989, 73–75, 115.
31 Paul Barolsky, 'As in Ovid, so in Renaissance Art.' *Renaissance Quarterly* 51: 2, 1998, 456; Victor Stoichita, *L'effetto Pigmalione, Breve storia dei simulacri da Ovidio a Hitchcock*, Transl. B. Sforza, Milano, 2006, 88–89.
32 Barolsky, 'As in Ovid, so in Renaissance Art.' *Renaissance Quarterly* 51, No. 2, 1998, 70.
33 Salvatore Nigro, *L'orologio di Pontormo. Invenzione di un pittore manierista*. Milano, 1998,
34 Bischoff, *Die ‚Cassonebilder' des Piero di Cosimo, Fragen der Ikonographie*, 68.
35 E.g. Philine Helas, *Lebende Bilder in der italienischen Festkultur des 15. Jahrhunderts*. Berlin: 1999, 3–8.

kind of image is in Vasari's "Live of Pontormo": how in a carnival triumph of the year 1513 they used a real gilded boy who finally died from his pains.[36] In many ways the problem of *statua vivente* or *figura viva* is a serious one, not only semiotically but also historically.[37] It has, therefore, both synchronic and diachronic meaning-structures. Diachronic ingredients come from Filippino Lippi and Piero di Cosimo, while synchronic items illuminate the whole scene and give a new meaning to this *mixtura*, many times seen as a strange compendium of different motifs and themes.

The semiotic context of the *statua vivente* -topos is bound up with the following narrative codifications which concern the whole representation:
1. Details have been depicted realistically, and yet the whole scene is represented as a fantasy which is full of disjointed elements or narrative abysses. It seems that some narrative details live a life of their own, detached from the narrative context.
2. Discontinuities of meaning on the one level of narrative can signify continuities on another level.
3. This leads to a search for oppositions, discrepancies and polarities of meaning in the disposition of the story, as well as the search for semic dimensions and polarities of the visual story. The painting/narrative gives several interpretative hints, some of which are seemingly contrary and some clandestinely consistent.

It has to be stressed that the main discrepancy within the visual narrative is structured as follows: naturalistic/realistic details > < the fantastic whole. The most realistic detail in the whole scene is the portrait of Agnolo Bronzino as a young boy sitting on the lower level of the staircase; he was the beloved pupil of the lonely Pontormo who later became a famous painter. Vasari mentions him and his "realistic" shopping basket.[38] Before we put Bronzino in his place in the logic of the narrative we have to refer to the melancholy of Pontormo himself.

---

36 Vasari, *Le vite dei più eccellenti pittori, scultori ed architetti VI*, 254.
37 Cf. Stoichita, *L'effetto Pigmalione. Breve storia dei simulacri da Ovidio a Hitchcock*, 89, 262. Cf Helas, *Lebende Bilder in der italienischen Festkultur des 15. Jahrhunderts*, 3–7, 182–189.
38 Vasari, *Le vite dei più eccellenti pittori, scultori ed architetti VI*, 261. Rudolf and Margot Wittkower state: 'Pontormo's devoted pupil Bronzino was a friend of Vasari's and very likely told him many details about his master's life' Margot & Rudolf Wittkower, *Born Under Saturn, The Character and Conduct of Artists: A Documented History from Antiquity to the French Revolution*, New York & London, 1963, 69; cf. Braham, 'The Bed of Pierfrancesco Borgherini,' 762.

1.1 Lonely melancholy and familial euphoria

It is essential to notice that the "living statues" standing over the events are dissociated from the main narrative stream in a way which gives an insight into Pontormo's eccentric motivations. Besides being monochromatic and working on another level of the representation, their separateness seems to be awesome, even melancholy. Indeed, the postulation of melancholy here can be motivated by the biography of Pontormo. He lost almost all his near relatives during his childhood.[39] According to Vasari he "was a melancholy and solitary young man", an "uomo fantastico e solitario" ("eccentric and solitary man") who made pictures "con tanta malinconi".[40] Vasari also mentions that Pontormo was a learned man.[41] According to the Renaissance theory of genius, learned men usually suffered from intellectual melancholy; this was linked to "heightened self-awareness".[42] In that sense "[m]elancholy was the price one had to be pay for aspiring to reach the level beyond ordinary men".[43] Also when Vasari characterizes Pontormo's eccentric ideas with the word *"ghiribizzi"* (whims or fancies), he emphasises his bizarre way of making inventions in solitude.

Especially the light brown, a bit drained colour, and the sense of the surface of the two monochromatic statues on the top arouses certain depressive associations. Also, the poses and gestures these two seem to be more or less gloomy: the female one has bent her head down and the left one is in the shadow stretching his arms in a way which really brings to mind the grief expressed in *Laocoon*-group.

---

[39] Timothy Verdon has rightly stressed that Pontormo was bound to experience heavy losses in his childhood: 'Povera Pontormo: gli era morto il padre quando Jacopo aveva cinque anni, e la mamma quando ne ebbe dieci; morì poi Mona Brigida, la parente presso la quale il ragazzo era finite.' That was not all, also his sister Maddalena died very young. Timothy Verdon '"Pensando a nuove cose." Spunti per un analisi formale del linguaggio pontormesco.' *Pontormo e Rosso. Proceedings of the symposium. (Empoli – Volterra 22–24 settembre 1995)*, ed. Roberto P. Ciardi & Antonio Natali, Venezia, 1996, 49.
[40] Vasari, *Le vite dei più eccellenti pittori, scultori ed architetti VI*, 247, 279, 287.
[41] Vasari, *Le vite dei più eccellenti pittori, scultori ed architetti VI*, 285–286; cf. Cécile Beuzelin, 'Jacopo Pontormo: A Scholarly Craftsman.' *The Artist as Reader. On Education and Non-Education of Early Modern Artists*. Ed. Heiko Damm, Michael Thimann and Claus Zittel. Leiden–Boston, 2013, 85–92.
[42] Raymond Klibansky, Erwin Panofsky, & Fritz Saxl, Fritz, *Saturn and Melancholy, Studies in the History of Natural Philosophy, Religion and Art*, New York, 1964, 228.
[43] Noel Brann, *The Debate over the Origin of Genius during the Italian Renaissance, The Theories of Supernatural Frenzy and Natural Melancholy in Accord and in Conflict on the Threshold of Scientific Revolution*, Leiden, 2002, 337.

But not only that, we have to remember also what Leon Battista Alberti has said in his *Della Pittura* (*libro seconda*) about melancholy movements of the body:

> Melancholy (*uno atristito*), preoccupied with cares and beset by grief (*il pensiero l'assedia*) lacks all vitality of feeling and action, and remain sluggish, their limbs unsteady and drained of colour. In those who mourn, [--] the neck bent, and every part of their body droops as though weary and past care.[44]

When looking the statues the way Alberti describes visual signs of *pensiero l'assedia*, it seems to obvious that Pontromo has read his *Della Pittura*. It is, therefore, not so important to ponder the exact mythological referent of these two statues above the scene, if indeed there is any. What is more significant is the consideration of their psycho-semiotic roles and functions, especially when taking into account the melancholy and solitary nature of Pontormo's main oeuvre.

So, it seems that there is a melancholy sphere in the illusory upper zone of the representation. How about the lower zone, to the right of the happy episode of Jacob and the pharaoh, to the ground, to the chthonic level? It certainly appears that there exists a lonely representative of Pontormo's own "family" in the scene little Bronzino sitting on the lower level of the staircase. Both the statues and Bronzino represent the opposite pole of the happy reunion of Joseph's big family depicted on the top of the stairs left side. Indeed, the statues together seem to constitute a kind of nuclear family, and one of them – the colourful "dancing putto" on the top of the column – seems to be in the mediating role between the adult world and the world of children. The putto is looking at Joseph, whereas little child (Manasseh?) in the lap of Joseph is looking at Bronzino sitting on the steps. There is a chain of glances: putto looking at Joseph and a naked child in the hands of Joseph looking at Bronzino instead.

In fact this episode is in the intertextual connection with the side-episode of Andrea del Sarto's *Joseph in Egypt* (Galleria Palatina, Florence): Among many incidents in this picture there are two children playing on the steps of Pharaoh's palace on the right hand side of the picture (Figure 3).[45] We can say that Pontormo simply makes one of the children recognizable in his own painting. Compared to Andrea's picture Pontormo strategy is twofold: He is not only making the "waiflike figure" of Andrea a child who has his own personal history (Bronzino), but

---

[44] Alberti, Leon Battista, *On Paintning*, transl. by Cecil Grayson. London: Penguin Books 1991, 76–77. Cf. Alberti, Leon Battista 1980, De pictura (Della Pittura), Edited by Cecil Grayson Roma-Bari Editori Laterza,1980, 70–72.
[45] Cf. Braham, 'The Bed of Pierfrancesco Borgherini,'762; John Shearman, *Andrea del Sarto I-II*. Oxford, 1965, 420.

also he is changing the odd, shadowy and life-like river-god in the left corner of Andrea's picture into living statues in his own versions of the story of Joseph.

Figure 3: Andrea del Sarto: *Joseph in Egypt*. 1515. Oil on wood, 98 x 135 cm. Galleria Palatina, Florence. Photo: Wikimedia Commons.

In this sense the third statue, the clothed putto, has a totally different function: it can be understood as a catalyst of the family situation. It seems to comment on the narrative around it. The children depicted in this part of the picture are located on different levels of the representation: 1) naked puttos which draw the wagon of Joseph, 2) sitting Bronzino, 3) a standing boy discussing with Bronzino (and looking at him), 4) a boy in the lap of Joseph looking also straight at Bronzino, and finally 5) the lively and colorful putto-statue. Levels of representation have thus been transgressed in this particular part of the story.

First, the putto in colorful clothes at the top of the little column clearly differs from the other two monochromatic statues. We have to suppose that the eye contact between the children crossing the two representative levels is meaningful. Second, almost all children around Bronzino except the "dancing putto" are looking at him. This visual fact cannot be without significance. Art historians have paid some attention to this relationship, which also gives light to the enigmatic role of Bronzino. Maurizia Tazartes mentions him and says that when seated there in contemporary clothes he is "surreal and metaphysical".[46] Thinking through Pontormo's own family situation, Bronzino's role here is understandable: He is looking for contact with the others, and yet, he is an onlooker of the event in this part of the scene. Indeed, he is the only "outsider" onlooker inside the representation. In this sense there is a double transgressive focalization-process taking place in this part of the painting. Furthermore, the animated putto on top of the little column transgresses two representative zones and has a double role: It is both looking at Joseph and at the same time pointing with its right hand to Joseph's family, especially to the children climbing the stairs – while a little child in the lap of Joseph is poking with his hand to the thigh of Joseph. In this way putto takes part to events around – almost the same way as "the prophet"-statue in the scene of Pontormo's panel *Pharaoh with his Butler and Baker*.[47] All in all, there is a complicated complex of different kinds of indications.

In the following scheme the main dichotomies or polarities lead us to find a key or a hidden code which can hopefully clarify the basic tensions (or polarities) of meaning in Pontormo's painting. In this scheme I have found it useful to apply two concepts of A.J. Greimas and J. Courtes. First, we have to take into account basic semic categories (semes, dimensions of meaning), such as "vertical" and "horizontal" (which have a metalinguistic character).[48] Additionally one semic dimension can contain lexemes (object categories, "semic nucleus") which are manifestations one semic dimension.[49] Second, we can think of these basic dimensions, "cardinal points" via thymic categories (which has to do with temperaments in general), such as *dysphoria* and *euphoria*.[50] These two pairs of categories can give us a certain insight into the role and signification of *statue viventi* in the whole scenic playground of the accents of meaning: they can reveal how Pontormo's pre- or unconscious scene-structure of the narrative field is determined by his basic melancholy accents.

---

[46] Tazartes, *Il 'ghiribizzoso' Pontormo*, 59.
[47] Cf. Braham, 'The Bed of Pierfrancesco Borgherini,' 765. Allan Braham does not compare these two panels, neither Philippe Costamagna, who states that 'the prophet dominates the scene' Costamagna, Pontormo, 128.
[48] A.J. Greimas & J. Courtes, *Sémiotique: dictionnaire raisonné de la théorie du langage*, Paris, 1979, 332–333.
[49] Greimas, A.J., *Sémantique structurale, Researche de methode*, Paris: Libraire Larousse, 1966, 45–47.
[50] A. J. Greimas & Courtes Greimas, & J. Courtés, J. *Semiotics and Language: An Analytical Dictionary*, Bloomington, 1982, 21.

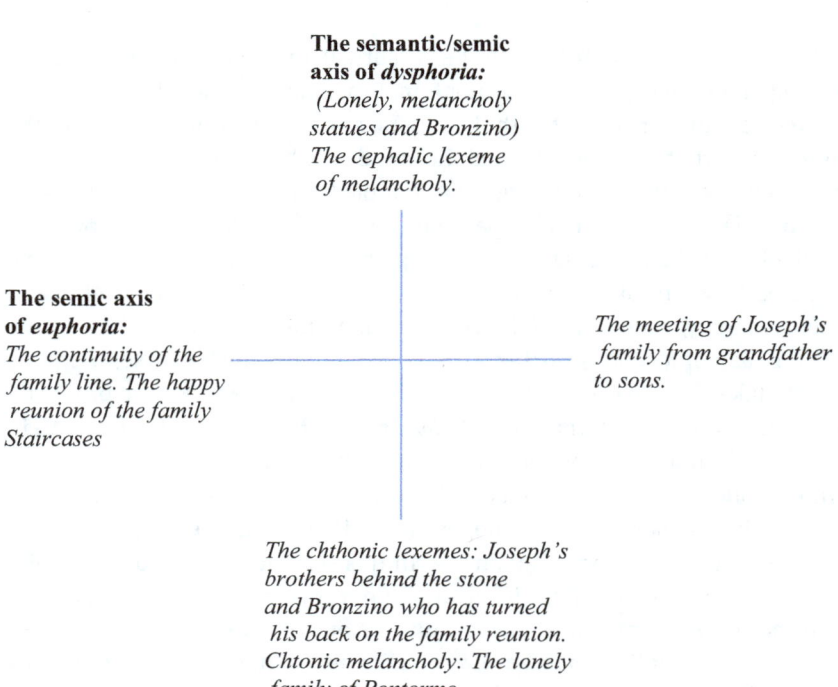

Figure 4: The basic semic dimensions. The division between euphoria and dysphoria.

In this way we have two semantic axes: vertical (dysphoric) and horizontal (euphoric). Both axis has two poles with two kinds of lexemes as object-references. In the vertical axis there are two kinds of melancholy accents, cephalic and chthonic, and in the horizontal dimension alliance (after many years of separation) and continuity (future generation), both euphoric. Staircases in both ends mean emotional *crescendo*, euphoria. According to Otto Rank and Sigmund Freud climbing up the staircase in the dream can be compared to sexual act; in that sense German word "*steigen*" has a double meaning.[51]

Additionally, we have to assume that the *living statues* exist on another representative level to the main narrative. Their role, therefore, is a commenting or a symbolic one. Second, we have to presume that the child with colorful clothes on top of the little column differs from the other two (monochromatic) statues, and in this way has a *catalyst function* in relation to the episode around it. Third, we have to suppose that the eye contact between children crossing the two representative

---

51 Freud, Sigmund, *Die Traumdeutung. Dritte Vermehrte Auflage*. Leipzig: Franz Deutike, 1911.

levels produces focalizations, which might open the way to the meaning-structure of the picture. The fact that the two children are looking at young Bronzino cannot be without significance. No art historian has paid attention to this relationship, which certainly opens the enigmatic role of Bronzino. He is both an onlooker of the events on the right, and he is the only (outsider) onlooker inside the representation. Such factors result in the basic meaningful tensions/oppositions of meaning:

Euphoria / dysphoria:
Two solitary and isolated dysphoric statues vs. euphoria of the family finally rejoined.

Tribal family / Nuclear family (the yearning for it):
The image of Agnolo Bronzino (the famous painter as a boy student of lonely Pontormo) vs the big family of Jacob. The hilarious tribal family versus a nuclear family which is symbolically represented in separated statues.

Or, *Abundant family /missing family:*
Perhaps this is the biggest common devisor or the basic tension between the totemic (familiar bound) and solitary affects. Pontormo's own family situation is represented by the figure of Bronzino, only. It is also telling that Bronzino has a shopping basket with him.[52] Normal everyday routines cast a clear alienation-effect within a mythical event.

Unheimlich (uncanny) / heimlich (homely):
All three living statues expressing their strange "emotions" vs.
the family in euphoria ascending the stairs (meaning emotional *crescendo*).

Solitary affects / familiar affects (statues vs. Joseph's family):
This discrepancy may show that Gilles Deleuze's and Felix Guattari's definition of an "affect" as a kind of ambiguity zone of meaning in the work could be applied here, especially when thinking of the fuzzy role of statues.[53] They are also affective in the sense that they are melancholy but undefined.

All in all there are two kinds of structural key points which can also be understood as sutures, seams which close the structure of the picture. One is Bronzino's role in the scene, which opens the personal dimension of meaning and gives us the clue for the central polarities of meaning of the scene: Bronzino as a representative of the "lonely" nuclear family of Pontormo. The other category of sutures, of course, are lonely statues – and especially the colored and clothed one, the dancing putto. The putto inevitably serves as the mediating point, or rather the "nodal point", (or *point de caption* of Žižek) of these two sutures (Bronzino and the statues).[54] Although ambiguous sutures close the meaning of the picture – the

---

[52] Vasari, *Le vite dei più eccellenti pittori, scultori ed architetti VI*, 261; cf. Costamagna, *Pontormo*, 130; cf. Tazartes, *Il 'ghiribizzoso' Pontormo*, 59.
[53] Gilles Deleuze & Felix Guattari, *Qu'est-ce que la philosophie?* Paris, 1991, 164.
[54] Slavoj Žižek, *The Sublime Object of Ideology*, London – New York, 1999, 87–88, 95.

melancholy statues being hints and the dancing putto being a being an active catalyst. They function as a kind of zip fastener. At the same time, these sutures try to close meaning and leave it incurably open, even if only certain affects could come to light.[55] We might also suggest that these two sutures explain the vague and indefinite meaning-zones of the picture: when closing the structure, they seem to leave the meaning in an ambiguous state. When transgressing the two representative levels (real child – statue) the animated putto also ties up them. In the first level, it has a double role: It is both looking at Joseph and at the same time pointing with its right hand to Joseph's family climbing the stairs. Considered thus, the animated statue can be seen taking part in the action and in this way mixing representational levels.[56] Indeed, the question is of the fusion of two boundary zones of "reality". The function of this effect was to irritate and challenge the self-evident norms of the pictorial imitation which now is known as the High Renaissance, and make them affective in an alienated, cool way.

In this sense the portrait of Bronzino acts as an indiscernible narrative hint for the lonely statues. The role of the "dancing putto" statue has a double role also in another sense: It is alone in its *own cephalic zone* and still takes part to the episode around by its gestures. In fact it has the same role as Bronzino: transgressing the two representative levels – and still being isolated from the representation of Joseph's familial events! The putto is lonely and still trying vigorously to take part of the events. Bronzino, instead, has turned his back on the happy reunion of the large family. To be sure, this is the most significant opposition in the whole scene! Syntagmatic closeness creates a huge paradigmatic opposition (euphoria / dysphoria). The tonal contrast light (Jacob) / dark (Bronzino) even emphasizes this obstruction. We can see two opposite "*scènes de rappel*" and two types of focalization:

Euphoric Jacob	>< Dysphoric Bronzino
light	dark
(light) blue	(dark) brown
mythic	"real"
reunion	separation
joy	uncertain seriousness

---

[55] Silverman, Kaja, The Acoustic Mirror. The Female Voice in Psychoanalysis and Cinema. Bloomingtona and Indianapolis: Indiana University Press, 10–13, 30. Cf. Taylor, Mark, *The Picture in Question. Mark Tansey & the Ends of Representation*. Chicago and London: The University of Chicago Press, 60–61.

[56] Earlier they spoke of "reality levels"; cf. ‚Verwischung der Grenzen zwischen Schein und Realität' in Peters-Schildgen, *Die Bedeutung Filipponi Lippis für Manierismus*,115; cf. 75.

Discrepancies found on the level of subject matter, however, do not open up all the segments of this complicated work. We also have to take into account the problem of style, especially the question of beauty and the beautiful. What is this "bellezza d'invenzione" or "bella maniera" of which Vasari is speaking? Indisputably, we meet beauty in its complicated form.

Both Adachi (1997) and Tazartes (2008) refer to the letter Pontormo wrote in answer to Benedetto Varchi's famous question in his book *Due lezzioni* (1549) about the relationship of sculpture and painting. The question is of the so-called *paragone*-discussion. Pontormo's explanation is not only challenging but also arrogant: The painter's duty is to animate a figure in such a way as to "surpass nature" (*superare la natura*), and to "have a desire to give a spirit to the figure and make it seem to be alive (*parere viva*) in a plane". This especially concerns the skill of a painter: To make a subject in an artificial, miraculous and divine way (*uno soggietto si artificioso, e più tosto miraculoso e divino*.[57]

Of course, this discussion connects with the fertile ground of the picture in question, even if it was made more than thirty years earlier than his answer to Varchi. From another angle, we also have to take into account Michelangelo's praise of Pontormo's abilities as a painter, expressed when Pontormo was very young.[58] Moreover, we also have to remember the famous characterization of Francesco Bocchi which leads us to the problem of "*vago*" and '*vaghezza*' of the mannerist oeuvre. When Bocchi (1580s) refers to the colouristic effects of Pontormo's frescos in San Lorenzo, Florence, the key word is "*vago*" (vague beauty).[59] With *vago*, the mind becomes vagabond.[60] Therefore the basic affect which 'colors' the scene of *Joseph in Egypt* and stupefies the beholder with a certain array of different greens might be the effect of *vaghezza*, which, at that time, also contains the charge of ambivalent and feminine beauty.[61] In addition, there is the question of the invention of a theme which depicts a new kind of vagabond or melancholic beauty – at least for Vasari and other Mannerists. Indeed, *statue viventi*, the living statues, can be characterized as both *vaghi* – in its most literal meaning – but also as affective, eccentric and "real", in a melancholic sense.

---

57 Benedetto Varchi, *Due lezzioni*, Firenze, 1549, 134.
58 Vasari, *Le vite dei più eccellenti pittori, scultori ed architetti VI*, 250, 277.
59 Bocchi, 'Eccellenza del San Giorgio di Donatello.' *Trattati d'arte del Cinquecento fra manierismo e controriforma 3: C. Borromeo, Ammannati, Bocchi, R. Alberti, Comanini*, ed. Paola Barocchi. Bari, 1962, 185.
60 Cf. David Summers, *Michelangelo and the Language of Art*, New Jersey, 1981, 169.
61 Cf. Philip L. Sohm, 'Gendered Style in Italian Art Criticism' *Renaissance Quarterly* XLVIII: 4, 1995, 767–768.

Affects are depicted on two levels of the picture: At the level of the expressions of the lonely statues and at the level of overall composition. They can be seen or sensed also at the level of undefined or unstable beauty (*vaghezza*), because the relationships between the events are obscure. There is something undefined in how different levels of representation accord with one other. According to Deleuze and Guattari, affect can be defined as *"une zone d'indétermination, d'indiscernibilité"*.[62] In spite of the fact that affects (*affetti*) were seen at that time as more or less the same as passions, we can discern the purport-level which opens at the level of unconscious or preconscious affects (affects as primitive unconscious representations).[63] Pontormo's affects are too sweet or "weak" compared to those of Michelangelo, who in his poem to Giorgio Vasari emphasized the deceptive nature of *arte*, which can bring together two opposite expressions: "l'affettuosa fantasia".[64] Indeed, Pontormo's painting is also mainly about *affective fantasy*, but only in a weak *and* sweet sense. Besides this, we can sense "belle" and undetermined affects taking the place "between" the events – so that as the whole scene is about vagabond affects.

Because there are numerous tensions of meaning in Pontormo's painting, we can say that the picture is characterized by *the disparate sensibility* which is also peculiar to melancholy: Melancholy brings to the fore a peculiarly contradictory qualities of mind; the diabolic nature of the character, as Marsilio Ficino so often stressed.[65]

When interpreting all this from the painting of Pontormo we have to emphasize the role of concepts used as a kind of "objective correlative" – and state: *We don't know the intentions of Pontormo, we only know that the (affective) structure of the work knows it!*

This is not all, however, as we have to refer to yet another concept by problematizing the solitary statues as *accessory* elements of the scene. The role of these solitary figures as *bystanders* is to ornament the scene, but at the same time they give a solitary or dysphoric, or even a repressive tune, to the episodes depicted. Two of these statues have a liminal character: they don't have an access to events. There is no seemingly visual dialogue between the monochromatic statues and the main discourse. These two statue-figures above the scene are in a monologue-state, and this also concerns the catalyst putto-statue – even when it tries to establish contact with the events around from its separate position. Thus, these statues are not only *bewegtes Beiwerk*, "accessories

---

[62] Deleuze & Guattari, *Qu'est-ce que la philosophie?*, 164.
[63] Sara Beardsworth, *Julia Kristeva, Psychoanalysis and Modernity*, New York, 2004, 97.
[64] Vasari, *Le vite dei più eccellenti pittori, scultori ed architetti VII*, 246.
[65] Marsilio Ficino, *De vita libri tres*, Hildesheim, 1978, 114, 166.

in motion" in Warburg's sense.⁶⁶ We can also speak of *Belebung-Beiwerk*, the animation of accessory figures, the animation of melancholy bystanders in a liminal state.

References

Adachi, Kaoru. 1997. La Statua vivente. Una precisazione iconografica della Giuseppe in Egitto del Potormo. *Bijutsushigaku* 19.
Alberti, Leon Battista. 1980. *De pictura (Della pittura)*. Ed. by Cecil Grayson. Roma-Bari: Editori Laterza.
Alberti, Leon Battista. 1991. *On Painting*. Trans. by Cecil Grayson. London: Penguin Books.
Barolsky, Paul. 1998. As in Ovid, so in Renaissance Art. *Renaissance Quarterly* 51(2).
Beardworth, Sara. 2004. *Julia Kristeva, Psychoanalysis and Modernity*. New York.
Beuzelin, Cécile. 2013. Jacopo Pontormo: A Scholarly Craftsman. In Heiko Damm, Michal Thimann & Claus Zittel (eds.), *The Artist as Reader. On Education and Non-Education of Early Modern Artsts*, 85–92. Leiden-Boston.
Bischoff, Uwe. 1995. *Die ‚'Cassonebilder' des Piero di Cosimo. Fragen der Ikonographie*. Frankfurt am Main.
Bocchi, Francesco. 1962. Eccellenza del San Giorgio di Donatello. In Paola Barrochi, *Trattati d'arte del Cinquecento fra manierismo e controriforma 3: C. Borromeo, Ammannati, Bocchi, R. Alberti, Comanini*. Bari: Gius. Laterza & Figli.
Braham, Allan. 1979. The Bed of Pierfrancesco Borgherini. *The Burlington Magazine* CXXI.
Brann, Noel. 2002. *The Debate over the Origin of Genius during the Italian Renaissance, The Theories of Supernatural Frenzy and Natural Melancholy in Accord and in Conflict on the Threshold of Scientific Revolution*. Leiden: Brill.
Capretti, Elena, Anna Forlani Tempesti & Serena Padovani (eds.). 2015. *Piero di Cosimo, 1462–1522. Pittore eccentrico fra Rinascimento e Maniera*. Firenze: Giunti.
Clapp, Mortimer. 1916. *Jacopo Carucci da Pontormo, His Life and Work*. Yale University Press: New Haven.
Costamagna, Philippe. 1994. *Pontormo*. Milano: Electa.
Deleuze, Gilles & Félix Guattari. 1991. *Qu'est-ce que la philosophie?* Paris: Les Éditions de Minuit.
Ficino, Marsilio. 1978. *De vita libri tres*. Hildesheim: G. Olms
Forster, Kurt. 1966. *Pontormo. Monographie mit Kritischem katalog*. München: Bruckmann.
Freud, Sigmund. 1911. *Die Traumdeutung. Dritte Vermehrte Auflage*. Leipzig: Franz Deutike.
Gombrich, Ernst. 1960. *Art Illusion*. London: Phaidon Press.
Gould, Cecil. 1975. *The Sixteenth-Century Italian Schools, National Gallery catalogues*. London: National Gallery.
Greimas, Algirdas Julien. 1966. *Sémantique structurale. Researche de methode*. Paris: Libraire Larousse.

---

66 Aby Warburg, *Gesammelte Schriften*. Nelden/Lichtenstein, 1969, 54–58, 161.

Greimas, Algirdas Julien & Joseph Courtés. 1979. *Sémiotique: dictionnaire raisonné de la théorie du langage*. Paris: Classiques Hachette.
Greimas, Algirdas Julien & Joseph Courtés. 1982. *Semiotics and Language: An Analytical Dictionary*. Bloomington.
Helas, Philine. 1999. *Lebende Bilder in der italienischen Festkultur des 15. Jahrhunderts*. Berlin: Akademie.
Klibansky, Raymond, Erwin Panofsky & Fritz Saxl. 1964. *Saturn and Melancholy, Studies in the History of Natural Philosophy, Religion and Art*. New York.
Nigro, Salvatore. 1998. *L'orologio di Pontormo. Invenzione di un pittore manierista*. Milano.
Peters-Schildgen, Suzanne. 1989. *Die Bedeutung Filipponi Lippis für Manierismus*. Essen: Verl. Die Blaue Eule.
Pinelli, Antonio. 1993. *La bella maniera. Artisti del Ciquecento tra regole e licenza*. Turin: G.Einaudi.
Plazzotta, Carol & Rachel Billinge. 2002. The Underdrawing of Pontormo's Joseph with "Jacob in Egypt". *Burlington Magazine* 144. 662–665.
Shearman, John. 1965. *Andrea del Sarto I – II*. Oxford: Clarendon Press.
Silverman, Kaja. 1988. *The Acoustic Mirror: The Female Voice in Psychoanalysis and cinema*. Bloomington: Indiana University Press.
Sohm, Philip L. 1995. Gendered Style in Italian Art Criticism. *Renaissance Quarterly* XLVIII 4.
Stoichita, Victor. 2006. *L'effetto Pigmalione, Breve storia dei simulacri da Ovidio a Hitchcock*. Trans. by B. Sforza. Milano: Il Saggiatore.
Summers, David. 1981. *Michelangelo and the Language of Art*. New Jersey: Princeton University Press.
Taylor, Mark. 1999. *The Picture in Question. Mark Tansey & the Ends of Representation*. Chicago and London: The University of Chicago Press.
Tazartes, Maurizia. 2008. *Il "ghiribizzoso" Pontormo*. Firenze: Mauro Pagliai.
Vasari, Giorgio. 1887. *Le vite dei più eccellenti pittori, scultori ed architetti VI*. Ed. by Gaetano Milanesi. Firenze.
Verdon Timothy. 1996. "Pensando a nuove cose." Spunti per un analisi formale del linguaggio pontormesco. In Roberto P. Ciardi & Antonio Natali (eds.) *Pontormo e Rosso. Proceedings of the symposium. (Empoli – Volterra 22–24 settembre 1995)*.
Warburg, Aby. 1969. *Gesammelte Schriften*. Nelden/Liechtenstein: Kraus Reprint.
Wischnitzer, Rachel. 1953. Jacopo Pontormo's Joseph Scenes. *Gazette des Beaux-Arts* 16.
Wittkower Margot & Rudolf Wittkower. 1963. *Born Under Saturn, The Character and Conduct of Artists: A Documented History from Antiquity to the French Revolution* New York & London.
Žižek, Slavoj. 1999. *The Sublime Object of Ideology*. London/New York: Verso.

Onur, Zeynep and Onur, Ayşe
Existential being of an artist

Abstract: An architect as an artist reflects his/her existential being through his work to construct an original "self". This happens by facing the world and within the struggle to construct the new self that stands beyond confusion. The search of "I" is produced by a search of an obscure self, a personality who can carry patiently and insistently a dual ability of personalizing and looking like oneself. When we look at creative personalities, we see clearly that they have personalized their observations by using analogies as a source of inspiration, to produce the work which looks like their own selves. The existential reality produced by architecture proposes to produce a sensory space, which is comprehensible by perception. This reality is completely meant to be an existential reality. This reality is not an empty and naked space but a reality that exists with a certain frame of reference. This paper would discuss the existential being of an artist with existential signs.

Keywords: presigns, actsigns, postsigns, genosigns, existential semiotics

1 Introduction

In his book *Existential Semiotics* (2000), Eero Tarasti sketches a new philosophical basis for semiotic inquiry which is mainly a debate related to processes, temporality, signs in flux, particularly in the states before fixation into a sign or what he calls **"presigns"**, and constitutes a new approach to the study of signs signification and communication.

"**Presigns**" are values, axiological entities; in a more concrete form, they are "ideas" which, an artist may have, prior to their being actualized, transformed, or transcribed into what Tarasti called **"actsigns"**, moreover when **actsigns** are performed or received by the community, in which signs are conveyed, they become **"postsigns"**. So far, he has enumerated **"endosigns"**, **"exosigns"**, **"transsigns"**, **"as-ifsigns"**, **"genosigns"**, **"phenosigns"** which would purport 21th century thought.

On the epistemological and ontological level, it establishes a theory that semiosis takes place between **"Dasein"** and **"transcendence"**; the process of production of signs and meaning, from the inside: "*how signs become signs and, particularly, how they are preceded, i.e., virtual transcendental entities*" (Tarasti 2000).

To examine them, Tarasti discusses meta-modalities, which portray communication between ***Dasein*** and **transcendence** – being-in-myself, being-for-itself, being-for-myself, and being-in-itself.

> Being-**in**-myself – the personal, bodily responses (moi1)
> Being-**for**-myself – the personality, the humanizing approaches of a person (moi2)
> Being-**for**-itself – the social role, functioning (soi2)
> Being-**in**-itself – the mental outcomes, ideas, values, norms (soi1)

In this article, Tarasti's philosophical approach will be discussed in the existential being of an artist, and those modalities will be examined in the semiotic square of being/doing and the sign processes in the field of art and architecture to discuss architecture as a form of art.

2 Existential being of an artist

Being-in-myself and **being-for-myself** are the modalities of Peircean view of the phenomenological categories of **firstness** and **secondness**.

Firstness helps to explain the logico-cognitive process and therefore at once the formation of signs; this is what Husserl called "passive predata" (Husserl 1938) as they represent themselves to perception by "abstracting from all qualifications of known" (Cobley 2001: 217).

> **Being-in-myself** represents our bodily ego, which appears as kinetic energy, khora, desire, gestures, intonations, Peirce's First. Our ego is not yet in any way conscious of itself but rests in the naïve Firstness of its being. (Tarasti 2000)

This is the body such as "flesh", which is the center of everything, the material resistance or impulse to semiotic processes. The body is the sensorial, motor fulcrum of semiotic experience (Fontanille 2004).

Maurice Merleau-Ponty emphasizes this simultaneity of experience and sensory interaction as follows: "My perception is [therefore] not a sum of visual, tactile, and audible givens: I perceive in a total way with my whole being: I grasp a unique structure of the thing, a unique way of being, which speaks to all my senses at once"(Maurice Merlau-Ponty 1964: 18). Marcel Proust describes "how the protagonist wakes up in his bed and gradually reconstructs his world on the basis of 'the memory of the sides, knees, and shoulders'". This is the situation of "being-in-the-world" or **"Dasein"**. The world reflects in the body and the body reflects the world. We remember with our body as well as with our neurologic system and brain.

Peircian category **secondness** appears in Tarasti's existential semiotics as **being-for-myself.**

Being-for-myself corresponds to Kierkegaard's attitude of an observer. Sartre's negation obtains, such that mere being shifts to transcendence; it notices the lack in its existence and hence becomes aware of itself and transcendence. The mere being of the subject becomes existing. . . . Ego discovers its identity, reaches a certain kind of stability, permanent corporeality via habit.

The Peircian category thirdness is extended consciousness which holds the ability to process time. Thirdness is not a purely mental and disembodied process given a particular direction by some sensations or firstness. Also, the sensation was followed by some reaction, from some other, whether of the physical world, the community, or the self's own inner other (Merrell, 2004).

In Tarasti's words, in this way, values and inner self (moi) are connected through a certain communal self (soi). Tarasti's important argument bases on how individual acts in **Dasein,** how the thoughts are shared by the people, and how the notion of shared meanings, understanding, and creative action originates (Bauters 2004: 246).

In his article, "strolling among values of a creative act", architect Ziya Tanalı (Tanalı, Z. 2008) puts forward the existential being of an artist while examining the processes of a creative act, by means of the process of doing the thing and seeing how it was done by observing "*how it was conceived* and *how it was produced*"; in short, the relation of "*thinking* and *doing*".

In the process of the creative act, *"Personalizing/to look like one's own self/ Internalizing"* is the first step in Tanalı's article.

When starting this journey, if one wants to be successful, has to start considering creativity as an intellectual act, and has to think and understand the necessity of building up **a special awareness in perceiving the values and the qualities of everyday life that already exist in his vicinity.**

If one can begin adding himself to the things observed, if one can start perceiving what has been seen in his own way, and start to add his own subjectivity to the common and general, namely if one can **personalize** what he has visualized; then the alien line that person has started from suddenly disappears. What you look eventually loses its importance and what you see tends to become your inspiration. From that point on, what one observes will be accepted **"as his"** although it stemmed from someone else's and it will be well understood by others that late observer has his own values. As of then, he is accepted to arrive at the first steps of the creative sequence and has the right to go further where the things he would produce will have the chance to reflect him. (Tanalı, 2008)

This is the step that Tarasti termed as **"presign"**, which artists have prior to their being actualized, transformed, or transcribed into **"actsigns"**. **"Presign"** appears in the mind of an artist when personalizing **Dasein**.

Tanalı's (Tanalı 2008) **personalising** is the modality **"being-in-itself"** (soi1) in Tarasti's parades. As he explains:

> Being-in-itself is a transcendental category. It refers to norms, ideas, and values, which are purely conceptual and virtual, they are potentialities of a subject, which he can either actualize or not. What is involved are abstract categories and units.

We find a similar expression of perceiving the world in Pallasmaa's (Pallasmaa 2011) thoughts; *"a kind of special exchange happens in experiencing art, I lend my sensations and association of ideas to the space, and it gives me back its aura which makes me to refine my perceptions and thoughts."*

The second step in Tanalı's (Tanalı, 2008) creative act process is **"to look like one's self"**

> It is most probably possible to declare that "to look like one's own self" is related with re-presenting the personalized qualities and sensitivities back to the world. The ones who are successful in personalizing their perception while observing the world cannot always attain the same success as expected when they want to perform, when it comes to re-presenting their observations.
>
> The phenomenon of "to look like one's own self" can be considered as a continuation of personalizing. In fact, these are mutual sequences walking together, attached to each other, the second following the first, yet with differences that need completely different conditioning. Where they meet is the ability of installing the "like myself" attitude first into observation and then later to making.

This step is the modality **being-for-itself** in Tarasti.

> Being-for-itself means the aforementioned norms, ideas and values as realized by the conduct of our subject in his **Dasein**. Those abstract entities appear here as applied values, choices and realizations, which often will be far away from the originally transcendental entities.

As Maurice Merleau-Ponty says; *"What else can a painter or poet might express out of his attains of meeting the world?"*

Dasein is not only "my Being-There", as it was for Heidegger, but also covers other subjects and objects. *Dasein* (literally, being there) is simply the world in which we as subjects live, surrounded by other subjects and objects with which we try to come to terms.

In structuralist narratology, a primal "desire" to be conjuncted/disjuncted was viewed as the "initial force" behind narrative processes, and this holds true also in existential semiotics, within the limits of Dasein.

Still, we feel our **Dasein** to be incomplete, lacking of something and these catalyze our wish and longing for the transcendent. That is how **Sartre explained the notion of transcendence – i.e., as a lack in Dasein** which forces us to go beyond its borderlines. Man starts to exist when he realizes the incompleteness of his being. In Kierkegaardian terms, the being becomes an observer of **itself** and is thus shifted into being-**for-itself**. This is precisely transcending.

Every sign is, in fact, a transcendental unit, in light of the classical medieval definition of sign as "aliquid stat pro aliquot" (something standing for something). This means: by signs we talk and think of objects which are absent. The most serviceable definition of the transcendental might be as follows: the transcendent is anything that is absent, but present in our minds. (Tarasti, 2000)

When explaining the process of an artist's search for himself, Onur and Tanalı (Onur, Tanalı, 2013) ask *"Don't these flower paintings by Van Gogh make us think he is in search of something which is present in his mind? "Even makes us think, if he had found the thing what he was after, he would not paint again", and we are naming these questionings as paintings, we are calling them Van Gogh".*

Then we come to a point where the artist represents himself as a personality, a kind of personality which is impossible to mix with another, he becomes **the sign of himself**, he becomes Van Gogh.

In the chapter "Becoming a subject", in his treatise **Concluding Unscientific Postscript**, Kierkegaard speaks about an individual who is said to be a subject or such an individual *"who is what he is because he has become like it"* (Tarasti 2000). The advent of a subject corresponds **to his becoming a sign to himself** or the emergence of his identity. The artist who has become himself may be considered a **"genosign"**, which we find in different personalities in different times of human history.

Then there will be no way of mixing for example Van Gogh with Gauguin. The artist's positioning as oneself symbolizes his/her **genosign.**

it seems that their personalities and what they have done are different from each other; we cannot deny that they have personalized what they have observed and used analogies as a source of aspiration to produce work looking like their own selves. (Tanalı 2008)

Tanalı (2002) describes this lack as *"**awareness of human accumulation and transferring them into one's own self**"*. The adventure that can also be defined as exploring the non-existent from what already exists starts from a line that is already achieved by those before. "Already known" has a universal context indicative of the awareness of what humanity has done and collected throughout time. It is being aware of cultural gains; simply what human kind had accumulated ever since. . .

> To express how "a courage full and sensate process is to touch the existed", Adorno says, "one's fear of natural beauty is because of foreseeing the nonexistent in the existed, it is the fear of injuring yet has not been existed". (Adorno 1970)

When we examine the process of semiosis, the outcome of an artist becomes an **"actsign"**. Also via this effort, value enters human life. Value is that to which one aspires, and when those **actsigns** are performed and received by the community they become **"postsigns" (Tarasti 2008).**

As an architectural example, by means of Libeskind's thoughts and Jewish Museum building, we may discuss those signs:

Libeskind explains his ideas related to his Jewish Museum project as;

> The official name of the project is 'Jewish Museum' but I have named it 'Between the Lines' because for me it is about two lines of thinking, organization and relationship. One is a straight line, but broken into many fragments, the other is a tortuous line, but continuing indefinitely. (Libeskind 1998)

When thinking about the design, he speaks about four different concepts in his mind:

1. He felt there was an invisible matrix of connections between the figures of Jews and Germans. Libeskind plotted an "irrational matrix" which resembled a distorted star: the yellow star that was worn often on this very site
2. To complete the opera by Schonberg: "Moses and the Aaron" architecturally
3. To give dimension to the deported and missing Berliners, Libeskind inspired by the 'Gedenbuch' which contains all the names, dates of births, and places/dates of deportation and/or deaths
4. Incorporated Walter Benjamin's text 'OneWay Street' into the continuous sequence of 60 sections along the zigzag, each representing the 'Stations of the Star'

The sketches by Libeskind are the **presigns** that have not been acted yet but in the mind of the architect, but when they are realized in the mind of the architect, presigns become visible units as actsigns.

The very importance of this building lies in personalising and making the thoughts related to the building is to be Libeskind's own self. We may say, **genosign** of Libeskind.

In the Jewish museum, we perceive how Liebeskind was able to present "tragedy" in formal language **(as an actsign)** with irregularities and deformations, Libeskind had been able to convey to us the **'meaning of that tragedy"** in that museum (Onur Z., Tanalı Z. 2004: 181).

But when those zigzagged shapes were accepted by society and begun to be used as signs (sometimes iconic, sometimes symbolic), it becomes **postsign. So far, there are numerous versions of Jewish museum as postsigns for differ-**

ent hostings. Just around here somewhere, the concept of "new" starts to stick in to one's mind. Especially, if creative act is such a laborious process and yet when there are so many things swarming around considered as new. Liebeskind's shape seems to be perceived as "new" to many designers as well as the student.

Attaching façades as "historical extracts" on to new buildings is another way of using **"postsigns"** to achieve a "new". Yet some may still think they are doing something 'new' by doing so. *"We know that the answers given to questions according to previous understandings and technologies certainly cannot be valid today. No one still composes like Bach did; no one paints like Van Gogh anymore"*. (Onur Z. (ed) 2017)

This has been found as a new way for design nowadays. Jumping from one to another and attaching yourself to anything that seems 'new' around, using a different language or a different grammar in each different work seems just to attain the *market values* and not doing something for your own self.

This situation in architecture is what Pallasmaa named as "the hegemony of vision". *"Instead of creating existential microcosms, embodied representations of the world, architecture projects retinal images for the purpose of immediate persuasion*', and complaining about "*our buildings have lost their opacity and depth, sensory invitation and discovery, mystery and shadow*" (Pallasmaa 2011).

An architect as an artist reflects his existential being through his work to construct an original "self". This happens by facing the world and within the struggle to construct the new self that stands beyond confusion. Human naturally is an individual entity, as in existentialism human builds oneself and only needs others to judge her/his place/level depending on her/his own values and not for more. Human has the power to create! While one is creating, one is rearranging her/his place in humanity. Creative act is a multi-way interaction. At the end of the act, she/he reaches to an opportunity to see her/his own transcendence in a concrete form. Existential semiotics opens up a new vision to challenge today's architectural era with the tools it provides us.

References

Adorno, Theodor W. 1970. *Aesthetic Theory*. London/New York: Continuum.
Bauters, Merja. 2004. Multiple determination and association: Peirce's model of mediation applied to visual signs. *Existential Semiotics, semiosis and emotions*. (Acta Semiotica Fennica, XXIV). Helsinki, Imatra. 246.
Cobley, Paul (ed.). 2010. *The Routledge Companion to Semiotics*. London: Routledge.

Libeskind, Daniel. 1978. Between the Lines. http://www.jmberlin.de/main/EN/04-About-The-Museum/01- Architecture/01-Libeskind-Building.php (accessed 2011 September)

Merleau-Ponty, Maurice. 1964. (From Pallasmaa) '*The Film and the New Psychology*'. *Sense and Non-Sense*. Evanston: Northwestern University Press. Evanston.

Proust, Marcel. 1968, (From Pallasmaa) "*Kadonnutta aikaa etsimassa*" (Remembrance of Things past). Helsinki: Otava.

Merrell, Floyd. 2004. Abduction is Never Alone. *Semiotica* 148(4). 245–275.

Onur Zeynep. (ed.). 2017. *Ziya Tanalı*. TMOBB Mimarlar Odası Publishing.

Onur, Zeynep & Z. Tanalı. 2004. *Modern Sonrası Mimarlık Üzerine Notlar* [Notes on architecture after modernism]. Ankara: Mimarlar Odası Publising.

Pallasmaa, Juhani. 2011. *The Eyes of the Skin; Architecture and the Senses*. Wiley & Sons Ltd-2005. (*Tenin Gözleri*, trans. by Aziz Ufuk Kılıç. Yem Publishing, İstanbul).

Tanalı, Ziya. 2008. *Mimarlığı Düşünürken, Hilmi Güner ve Hüseyin Bütüner'in Düşündürdükleri* [Thinking Architecture,what Hüseyin Bütüner and Hilmi Güner makes us think]. Hilmi Güner ve Hüseyin Bütüner Mimarlığı Artı Mimarlık Ankara. 11–27.

Tarasti, Eero. 2000. *Existential Semiotics*. Bloomington: Indiana University Press.

Hamid Reza Shairi
An essay on the Persian calligraphy in the light of the theory of existential semiotics by Eero Tarasti

Abstract: If the calligraphy can be considered a way to represent a text, its conversion into image would be a discourse in action aiming for the existential. This conversion brings about a sensory-motor dynamics, which transforms the objective values into subjective ones and makes us confront a co-enunciate and co-existential praxis in which the Supreme Being of disengaged utterances, the subject of utterance, the world of the perception and the art work intermingle in order to realize an existential style of affirmation, negation and transcendence.

In fact, on the basis of the existential semiotics by Eero Tarasti and beginning from the study of three Persian calligraphies, we shall see how in its effort to become an image, the text can undergo three types of existential changes: the first one concerns the enunciative aspect which guarantees the gliding of the text towards the discourse conserving its primary linearity: we are in the style of affirmation. The second depends on a phenomenological stand point which offers an existential dimension to the text from one's own body, from the existential 'flesh' and from a sensuous and multidimensional presence; the linear course changes into pictorial course; we are in the existential style of the negation and rebellion. And finally, the third one reproduces three signs (pre-sign, act-sign and post-sign) into one in order to manifest the presence of the will, know and can: we are facing the existential style of the transcendence where the spiritual gains foothold by letting the aesthetic and the ethic intervene in the existential sense.

Accordingly this article tries to show, in the light of the existential theory by Eero Tarasti, the realization of three existential instances, affirmation, negation and transcendence, through three Persian calligraphies (entitled "In the name of the God").

Keywords: existential semiotics, Persian calligraphies, affirmation, negation, transcendence

1 Introduction

In its course of conversion into an image, the text abandons its first writing surface in order to adopt another one. What changes here its destination and is introduced as a new course is characterized by different existential styles. The three Persian calligraphies, which constitute the object of our analysis in this article, show well how the existential method by Eero Tarasti can help us to discover the sense of the work of art starting from a philosophical approach to the signs, which itself is bathing in the classical and phenomenological semiotics.

All along this essay, we shall demonstrate that a calligraphic work is based upon an enunciative activity which adopts a sensory-motor activity to produce existential enunciations of affirmative, negative, and transcendental nature. In fact, an introjective tensivity caused by the writing and the tensionality which is stemming from the image are joined in order to give place for one event only: "Other" becomes another face of the 'I'. Can these changes cause that the independent character of the text is lost and disengaged in order to introduce the existential, individual, and engaged course by modifying the realm of the perception and conception of its instantaneous nature?

This essay belongs to the context of existential semiotics. It has as its objective to show how through some Persian calligraphies (entitled In the Name of God) which have become image, the modulations of the being and doing cause a change in the enunciative space into a place of reconciliation and reintegration in which an act of co-communication takes place: The divine Being and the 'I' – could they be grasped by the same intention of communication? Would it be possible to see how existential ethics manifests from the plenitude of the sense? What is involved is not, however, the being in interaction with the Other (the Sublime) but its participation into construction and plenitude of the sense of the existential 'being': the transcendental unity.

2 From writing to calligraphy

One cannot speak about the calligraphy without making an allusion to the writing which in a certain manner provides its necessary material ground. Long time one has been inclined to consider the writing as a substitute to the oral. In this respect, the writing can only fill one role: to serve as a means whereby one can shift the oral language from a vanishing level to a more solid and stable one. On this topics, Klinkenberg underlines the abrupt conception of the writing when he reminds that "it makes them permanent and transmissible in a vast gamut of action; it enables one to store and disseminate informations without being subordinated to the constraints of time and space, nor to the limits and weaknesses of the memory" (Klinkenberg 2006: 89).

But we know very well that the writing always passes beyond its model of linguistic origin (the oral), just by including in its space punctuations, effects of enunciation, articulations, the modification of the shifters, the particular organization of its units, its character of intermediality (the fact that it is capable to enter into interaction with other genres) etc. That is why Klinkenberg (2006: 89–91) recognizes for writing two others major properties which contribute to the enlargement of the field of its function: the writing is an activity which helps "the speech pass from the oral channel to the visual one; writing is an 'organisation of the space'. In reality, if one believes in the definition of the writing as an act which can contain an infinite number of linguistic units realized in a perceptible space, one has to admit that it is impossible to reduce it into a means of information transmission or to its role as a substitution or still to a device of simple transposition from an oral modality to a written modality.

In fact, according to the above definition, the writing functions at the same time as: (i) realization of an act; that which puts emphasis on its autonomous and enunciative character; (ii) the realization of such an act in the space; what contributed to its spatial unfolding at the same changing its linear character into something like in a 'table' (*tabularité*); (iii) the realization of such an act in a perceptible space; what proves that visual character of the writing and sensory-motor activity which accompanies it.

Now, thinking of the main purpose of this study, the existential research in the calligraphy, it is legitimate to talk about the activity of double effect. What can be identified as writing of the writing or image of the writing. Contrarily to the writing which concerns the conversion of the oral speech or non-articulated thoughts into an enunciative activity of visual and spatial order, the calligraphy deals with the already visual and the already spatial. That places it to the status of representation of a representation. So calligraphy becomes a phenomenon which touches the existential being of the world. In fact, according to its proper relationships with the world of the writing, it organizes the space in another way in order to make us see the written entity differently. That is why it belongs to the existential organization of the act of the enunciation.

In this context, in its course of conversion into calligraphy, the writing adopts a second enunciative position and abandons itself to a new force of engagement in the act of enunciation. An engagement whose degree of intensity varies according to whether what is involved is the act or writing or the calligraphic act. One would say that the latter undergoes above all an effect of enunciative doubling.

On the enunciative level, the writing which has been so converted into calligraphy becomes an act of assertion (whereby the content of enunciate arrives at presence, whereby it is identified to be in the field of presence of the discourse"

(Fontanille 1999: 268)). But, the calligraphy cannot limit itself to this assertive act. That is why the latter one will be followed by another act which Fontanille defines as 'assumption'.

> The assumption is autoreferential: in order to make an assertion, to take the responsibility of the enunciation, in order to adjust the presence the instance of discourse has to adopt them to itself, to its position of a reference, and to the impact they produce on the body. This act of assumption is in fact the act whereby the instance of the discourse makes its position known regarding what happens to it in its field. (Fontanille 1999: 269)

Tarasti shows us well how in the '*Moi*' "it is the subject itself which appears, as a sensation, whereas it is in the '*Soi*' where the subject is observed by others and is socially determined" (Tarasti 2009:111). So, the calligraphy changes the *Soi* from the writing into an existential 'Moi'. That is why to believe in Tarasti that the act of assumption is an existential act.

In reality, the calligraphy is another manner to articulate the writing. The calligraphy puts the writing in the line of modalisation. In other words, by the act of assumption, it puts in affiche, relief, remodels and gives new codes to the latter. The writing rediscovers so its transcendence through the calligraphic act, which does not hesitate to make it pass to constitute its proper field of presence by the basis of the figurative selection made thematic. From this point of view, the calligraphy would be that phenomenal 'being' of writing and it will be considered a meta-discourse. In this manner, Tarasti has the reason to underline the fact that the existential '*Moi*' makes the social '*Soi*' immortal. Just this occurs to the writing thanks to the calligraphy.

One of the important effects of the act of assumption, as far as intensivity (illocutory) and extensivity (syntactic dislocation) are concerned, is to modify the scriptural rhythm of the writing. M.G. Dondero qualifies as the effect of 'slowing down' and 'acceleration' these rhythmic differences which correspond to "the different durations of reception" (Dondero 2006: 22). If one wants to discover the rhythmic impact of the calligraphy, it means that one wants to furnish it with its proper and particular temporality. Tarasti (2009: 104) emphasizes the fact that "the existence is never general, it is always particular."

It is now reasonable to proceed by the hypothesis that the calligraphy as a representation of representation, includes, in addition to its visual and spatial propriety, also a third dimension: the temporality. Yet, the temporality has the character of being 'omnitemporal' because it frees the writing act from its social constraints and makes it possible to develop. Just like Tarasti, we agree that the Persian calligraphy offers innumerous possibilities of leaps and transformations. What corresponds to an existential transcendence where the depth and freedom constitute its subjective reality. In other words: the calligraphic act transforms the objective temporality of writing into a subjective temporality where the absence becomes the reason for the existence of the sense.

3 The existential conversion of the calligraphic text into calligraphic image

The object of this study is to examine the proprieties of two types of classical and baroque calligraphy which we distinguish by two existential styles: the affirmation (the enunciated text) and the negation (discourse as enunciation). To say as Tarasti (2009: 365), the classical calligraphy is embedded in the world and blends together with "the harmony of the spheres". Whereas the baroque calligraphy is 'rebellious' and avoids any effort of maintenance and stability.

Just questioning the mode of association between the mediated issues in his study on the intermediality (J. Fontanille 2007a: 107), Fontanille shows us two syntactic modalities of the montage: 'insertion' and 'composition'. But the question arises in a completely different way for visual productions where we are dealing neither with hierarchical reception of one medium by another nor their non-hierarchical combination.

So the corpus of calligraphy-image constitutes the object of our study and lets us meet a new problem of the relationship between the media: calligraphy converts the writing into an image and transforms all the readable qualities into visual qualities. It is obvious that such a conversion cannot be complete without wavering the conditions under which the original text has appeared, i.e. the calligraphic writing.

As we know, the calligraphy itself is an artistic representation of writing which belongs to the domain of the readable. In the case of those pictures which interest us, we are doing with the representation of the sacred writing (the readable visual) which have been converted into image (the visual readable, in the case of the classic and the visual in the case of the baroque). In this manner, the images which preoccupy us constitute a representation of a representation. This doubling shows the gliding from the level of expression which has been earlier thematized to another level of expression which has been conceptualized in another manner. This means that the writing undergoes an existential course to transcend towards the plenitude. It is so that the calligraphy is capable of changing the objective temporality of the writing into a subjective and multidimensional temporality.

Accordingly, we are in front of a discursive phenomenon depending on the 'transposition' (2) in the of Kristeva. In fact, what is involved is just the religious text but articulated in an appropriate manner. It is precisely by such an articulation one is shifted from common sense, shared and objective (*le Soi*) to an individual and subjective sense (*le Moi*). That means that the semiotic operation, which guarantees the passage from the writing to the readable and visual mode, changes the text utterance of the beginning to a subsequent discourse enunciation. In order to realize such a change, the baroque calligraphy artist has to be able to resort to two different projects of signification: first, we have here a kind of pre-established order of the text utterance (writing) yet destabilized (the negation); and then it remodels this from the standpoint of a sensible relationship of affective perceptive order (to transcend).

In reality, instead of being the observer at a distance of the object text (*Au nom de Dieu*) and to represent it to us in its sublime state, the calligraphy intervenes all the modulations of his field of presence in the visual discourse, which is first the image itself and then the image of the Other such as it is felt. We encounter here to speak like Jacques Fontanille, in the perspective of 'a discourse in act', whereby "one tries to restore the sense of this human experience which consists in producing or interpreting something significant." (Fontanille 1999: 7)

So the adapted calligraphy reminds of the existential style of affirmation where one reanimates the experience of the utterance text therefore of writing. It remains in harmony with the original text in order to be situated quite close to the modality of must. To take its distance in relation to the world one deals with, to see it from the outside, to be obliged to represent it in its absolute structure, starting from a preexisting sense, which one continuously tries to join there, well, here is all we meet when an idea is brought to practice in a discursive act. Because one is in front of a world dominated by one and only reality of sense. In this case, a stable and pre-established content orients and directs our relationship with the planned text object. Figure 1 of calligraphy here below shows a 'linear' expression of the reality and a preconceived objective sense. A form of expression whose form of content stays unchanged, solid, and immutable. Here we have the existential style of affirmation:

As one may state, we are here in front of a certain and absolute figure which makes present an approved reality. There is no shadow of a doubt that the spectator can contemplate this reality with an undeniable assurance, taking into account that all is organized from an objective and transparent style. Wölfflin (1986/1994: 31) distinguishes in this sense two styles, linear, and pictural:

> The great opposition of the linear style and pictorial style supposes, in front of the world, two fundamentally different attitudes. From one side, one is in presence of a stable structure, on the other side, an appearance in movement, here the form has a character of permanence, it is measurable, limited; here the movement predominates, the form is only a

Figure 1: Masoud Mohammdzadeh Chamazkoti, Veresk Design Studio, Iran, 2021.

function; on one hand, the things are taken as such, and on the other, they are shown in their relationships . . . .. Yet, beyond the thing which can be conceived as an object, the sensibility opens also to the domain of the ungraspable; because the pictorial art is the first to discover the beauty of the incorporeal. Every time when another attitude manifests in front of the world, a new beauty emerges. The pictorial style reveals us really for the first time, the world as a seen object.

The assurance of the figure presented in its absolute reality saves the spectator from every effort to provide the painting with meaning. The linear style situates it in the world of the evidence.

Whereas in Figure 2 (where the same text occurs) presented here below, all is inverted and it is the spectator who is invited to establish not only the sense of the painting but also to give to it its multiple and diverse unity. Figure 2 corresponds in fact to the existential style of negation, or as is underlined by Tarasti (2009: 29), the signs "detach from the world of *Dasein*, in order to go to float in a transcendental space without gravitation, only to be able then to be reconnected to the

Dasein". This makes us confront the signs which unfold in the space according to their existential force to adhere to a temporality which is of the kind than the objective one; an atemporal temporality.

Figure 2: Masoud Mohammdzadeh Chamazkoti, Veresk Design Studio, Iran, 2021.

As we see, the linearity of the line in Figure 1 is substituted by a swirl of line in Figure 2. The line which we thought to follow in one direction passes now in all possible directions on the pictorial surface in order to make us forget the logic of its narrative course in favour of the dialectics of the continuous and discontinuous. The line avoids, escapes from itself; it develops, gets intensified, accumulates, takes volume and speed; shortly, it abandons its classic greatness and passes by its regular and ordered form to become an 'accident' of the line. Landowski (2005: 64) recognizes quite properly the accident as a new region of sense.

> In the same way as the regularity, this principle which is presupposed by all forms of programmation in the interaction, as the intentionality, the basis of any strategic manipulation, as the sensibility, condition of all interaction in the form of adjustement, the accident constitutes in its way the founding principle of a region of sense and autonomous interaction (. . .) and is to be placed on the same level as the three others: the region of accident.

As the opposition to Figure 1, which proves the sovereignty of the letters and the line, Figure 2 makes us face the suddenness of the line. Landowski continues to specify that "in the region of the accident, contrarily, the sense appears again as given, but in a different manner from what we observed in the programmed conversation. When it here emerges also beyond any dialogical type of relation in the proper sense, it is this time with abrupt, unpredictable and vague nature of the clarity" (Landowski 2005: 82). Tarasti would call this hasty movement from the simple being to the existence "as a rebellion of the *Moi* against the community, against the conventional world of the *Soi*" (Tarasti 2009: 118). Therefore the accident makes the existential qualities of the world appear; it goes from the being to doing and exploding of unexpected potentialities. This existential proof takes place in the fact that an artwork does not depend on any pre-established rule nor any recognized convention. The total and multidimensional freedom characterizes this act of enunciation and its particular genre.

4 The enunciative event: An attack against the process

In its conversion trajectory into a visual discourse, the line conserves, however, partially, the nature of the original enunciate. In reality, one sees how the same letters, utilized during the production of the text object, are reused and re-employed, in the moment of passage to a verbal-visual enunciation. ". . . when the actualized enunciation is of the same nature as the referential enunciation, the doubling of the modality (verbal – word/visual – glance), adds to this relation of reference a value of authentification", so Shairi and Fontanille (2001: 90–91) argue in their study on the photographic enunciation. However, we would prefer to moderate here the tone and to speak about a target enunciation which keeps not only the traces of the source enunciate in its dynamism of transformation but also it makes it unfold in the sense of an enunciative synthesis.

Tarasti spoke about "ontological leaps" of the signs. It is just in the course of these leaps where the appearance of the sign detaches itself from the original *Dasein*, vanishes, yet remembering its origins, in order to give place to a transcendental signified. Finally, when "the sign is completely transcendental, its limits have disappeared." (Tarasti 2009: 326)

Accordingly, if there is authenticity, it has to be heard in the level of the potential interaction and in co-action between two types of calligraphy (classical and baroque) in question. It is true that the target enunciation does not hesitate to call upon the whole body of enunciate source; but once the convocation has taken place, it passes by completely in order to transform it into a new body. This could approach the ontological predicate of Barthes, the "it has been" (Barthes 1980: 120) because what is involved is no longer to create a network of homology between one state of affairs and a surface writing but just contrarily, between a passage from the first surface writing to the second one. We are far away from the world of photography which follows the rules of 'printing'.[1]

All can be explained here by the existential becoming which rests – as Fontanille and Zilberberg remark (1998: 116) – upon the distinction between the 'past' and 'present' (or *passéification and présentification*).

Since the beginning of this essay, we have insisted on the fact that the text 'becomes' image. Such becoming cannot be realized without having a step in the past and another in the future. "The semiotic approach of existential becoming will distinguish (i) a properly existential predication: being/having been, and (ii) an alethic predication: be/must be; the first installates yet the past and the second the future" (Fontanille and Zilberberg 1998: 116). It is now possible to see the leading thread which brings us from the text enunciate to the image discourse; the whole semiotic process is subordinated to a movement, which without breaking the ties with the nostalgic past (the text of reference), is installed in the modulations of the present. This movement, which characterizes the passage of a sign into another, denotes the change of the tempo in the sense of a measured rhythm into an accelerated one. From this point of view, the 'presentification' is established as a semiotic phenomenon which makes the entire body of the enunciate sign shake under the pressure of the tension of enunciative events in order to change the course of the process at once.

We have thus reached the point which Tarasti defines as 'act-sign'. In this way, the Figure 1 of our calligraphy is homologous with an enunciative event which one could qualify as suspended. It belongs to the dissolution of homogeneous figurative chains which have the tendency to minimize the sense in order to conceive it only as a unity. We find in this way in a semiotics of process dominated by the measured course of the line. It is just we have above portrayed as an act of affirmation. What is involved is to affirm the already enunciated, but by the support of the aesthetic activity. In this type of calligraphy, it is the enunciate who has to take the initiative to go to the discovery of the figures of the world which are posed to it.

So when the Figure 2 of our calligraphy participates in an enunciative event depending on a more fast tempo, the attack, beat; an act-sign which is based upon the negation as well as on rebellion. In other words, Figure 2 surprises the enunciate by its will to introduce itself in its space. Likewise, it is proof of overwhelming of the line and heterogeneous unfolding of the discursive figures. This

---

[1] The printing, as a matter of fact, is a proof of the presence of a fact or several facts when they are converted point by point into an object or a group of semiotic objects; in the case of photography, as in other sophisticated printings, the correspondence 'point by point' is subordinated to a mediation, the one by the light and optic machine. . .." (Shairi and Fontanille 2001).

contributes to the sensibilisation of the line as well as to maximalisation of the sense and its plurality. All passes as if the calligraphy would become the appropriate place of the manifestation of the passions. And in this time it is the enunciate which is the object of the calligraphic discourse.

> This time, it is not me who will search for it. . . it is he who leaves the stage, like an arrow which will pierce me. (Barthes 1980: 94)

To summarize the trajectory of the conversion of the text into an image, it consists here of transforming the process into a beat, the simple being into multiple existential.

5 From the single perception to the synaesthesia

The two conceptions of the calligraphy which we have tried to sketch appear each as a particular manner to perceive the perception. Therefore, the classical calligraphy is apt for treating the writing which tries to introduce us to the region of the seeing-reading. Here, the seeing is only in the service of reading. In other words, we are put apart from the phenomenal being of the world by a skin which separates us from the 'thing itself'. This skin rises like a wall between the spectator and the 'flesh' of the world. This only makes possible contact with the external and the distance with the latter. This fact situates our glance into a rather objective conception of the world. In other words, in this relationship, we do not live our vision because our act of seeing is ruled by an exteroceptivity which allows us only a simple reading of the text without introducing us in the adventure and experience of its sensorial data.

In this manner, only one visual sensoriality is found at the origin of our reading activity. For Merleau-Ponty (1945: 252), "the separated sensoriality takes place when I break this total structuration of my vision, when I finish to keep my glance, and when instead of living the vision I start to question upon it." With this separation, the visible such as it is given to us by the calligraphic enunciate remains invisible. So, one cannot reach the sensible qualities of the calligraphic world; the approach to a text object stops at the surface, in other words, at its outside: the world closes its gates to us. The uni-sensoriality and the lack of synaesthesia in Figure 1 provide the calligraphic letters with a status of a Sublime Object, which one can observe so to say. It is why this type of relation depends on seeing-reading.

We are, therefore, "in a classical model which presupposes the linear course of the communication from the left to the right" (Tarasti 2009: 331), in the case of Persian language, we have to specify, from the right to the left. For us, Figure 1 plunges the spectator into an aesthetics of affirmation where the subject of enunciation accepts the already accepted by a linear style which guarantees the confirmation of the calligraphic world.

Contrarily to Figure 1, Figure 2 displays a seeing-sensing which is suspended and realizable by the defined synaesthesia as an interaction of sense. With the passage of calligraphy-text to the calligraphy-image, we participate in a weakening of the objectifying and conscious relationship with the world. Even more than this gliding from the intelligible to the sensible increases the ontological and phenomenal relation with the latter. This conversion of the relation is explained by the fact that Figure 2 peals the skin of the world for us to be reconciliated with the phenomenal being. So emerges the outside of the calligraphy and we are brought from the linear surface to pictorial ocean where the letters seem to revolt in order to make us participate to their quality of movement, rhythm, and depth. We are in front of the existential style of negation where the calligraphy dances with the world to make us accessible the Here-Now of the sense the calligraphy changes into rebellious music of the world:

> The aesthetic communication does not go in one direction only, but it proceeds by leaps to forth ad back, and guided by the modal field where the global communication takes place. This evokes the Heideggerian conception of the communication as *Mit-Sein* (to be with), the co-existence. . . .. (Tarasti 2009: 332)

All happens as if the calligraphic matter would serve as particular support to the letters so that they would communicate among others, and that they would create a synaesthetic place by their force of commutation. "The sensations are not given us as independent and objective facts but they are reached and inspired by a total experience of a perceptive synaesthesia which constitutes and puts under the total experience of the world" (Le Gerun 2005: 15). The existential style of negation makes visible to others what remains unnoticed on the deep level.

In fact, when the skin of the calligraphy is elevated, the being of the world opens us its doors and we are touched by the vibrating flesh of calligraphic letters. It is in this way the touch is added to the seeing. What hitherto was only aesthetics of a form becomes here an ethics of depth: at the end, it is the being which accounts. We are taken by the sensible qualities of the world in order to sense the beating of its heart. Instead of making us see its majestic aspects and its greatness of the form, the calligraphy communicates us its pathetic warmth. It is our whole body which enters into interaction with the body of the other and lets the warm rhythm of its being penetrate to it.

In this mutation of text into a calligraphic image, three steps are decisive: i) aesthetics of communication, ii) pathic beyond the communication, iii) the co-existential ethics[2] (which unites all the instances of the calligraphic practice). The first one is homologous to a course of adherence and affirmation in which the spectator enters into the process of seeing and accomplishes with serenity its reading of the world; consequently, the activity of seeing-reading takes place: the seeing dominates the rules over our relationship with the world (Figure 1). The second type should be first understood as a negation, and then as an interaction and finally as a blending together with bodies: the seeing joins to touching to unite us to the deep being and to lead us towards the invisible of the visible. We are in the course of inherence and one rediscovers the existential being of the calligraphy (Figure 2). And the third aspect shows us the displacements of the viewpoint, the union of all the instances of calligraphic praxis (enunciator, enunciate, the act of signification) as well as the unfolding of the sense of the action.

This last one is due to all evidence on the basis of retreatment of the practical domain (the bi-dimensional aspect of the calligraphic text is replaced by the multidimensional aspect of the calligraphic image) and the balance of the ties between the instances of calligraphy (the actants of enunciation, action, and the practical scene unite to participate to a new value: the transcendence of the calligraphic work just as one of the subjects of enunciation). So the calligraphic event has taken place.

This transcendence reaches all its perfection in Figure 3 where the Other becomes the observer of the existential course of the calligraphic work. The Other (the Sublime, the Sovereign), the subject, the world, and artwork blend together to represent together a unique experience and non-recurrent of the aesthetic and ethic presence. What is involved is also an experience of synaesthesia which consists of living as existential being in the world.

So the Supreme Being of the enunciate, which is disengaged in Figure 1, changes into an intimate partner engaged in Figure 2. The co-communication is realized and the seeing-reading gives place to the seeing-touching. Likewise, the aesthetic communication becomes perfect by its resort to ethical communication. All takes place as if once the aesthetics of the work were attained, the calligraphy 1 would then put us in presence of its ethics of the accomplished work. Such an ethics, emphasizes Tarasti (2009: 345), reveals us "what a composer or interpreter would have in their head in the moment of writing or interpreting a work, about the sense they would give to the act, and intention whereby it has been pursued".

---

[2] The ethical question rises, in fact, since the moment where what is involved are the 'relations' which unify the calligraphic act, actant. Enunciator is engaged in this act and actant-enunciatee is sketched by this act regarding the Other (see Fontanille 2007: 4).

Figure 3: Marzieh Aghili, Art school and Gallery, Iran, 2021.

As we can now remark, in order to become an image, the calligraphy abandons its effort of narrativisation and representation. In this viewpoint, the calligraphic painting opens like a voluminous mass which presents the flesh of the writing. The excessive flesh replaces the sublime of the form. The calligraphy is no longer image of the world or being which it represents, but before all the existential image of itself which is at the same time the reflection of the Other. We are in the presence of an anthropological choice-making appeal to modalities of 'will', 'know', and 'can'. So we find ourselves in front of the existential space of representation where the aesthetic and ethic mix in order to enact a third principle, the spiritual. Therefore, one can qualify the return to the *Dasein* as a moment of ecstasy where the artwork becomes a source of co-existential communication without limits. In fact, after the return to the *Dasein*, this calligraphy is so perfect that it realizes in one and the same act of enunciation the presign (origin of calligraphy), the act-sign (calligraphy in past), and the postsign (the becoming of the calligraphy), according to Tarasti.

In reality, the letter, which became the flesh, gains all the pictorial space and makes us face the event of the matter. In this issue, Odile le Gerun makes us notice the fact how, as an event, the matter "would evoke pictorial and subjective style, of the reception and impression of the appearance, which implies the subject of an aesthetic experience" (Le Guerun 2005: 71). Accordingly, the effort of lexicalization or categorization and representation substitutes the effort of return to the origin of the visible: the flesh. The painting is from here on the place of all eventual practice of sense. And all this, thanks to touch, which joins us with the 'thing itself'. In the *De Imperfection*, Greimas underlines just that the touch is capable to produce beyond its capacities of spatial exploration: "It is situated among the sensorial orders which are most profound; it expresses proxemicly the optimal and manifest intimacy and – on the cognitive level – the will of total conjunction." (Greimas 1987: 30)

When the seeing dominates, we are in the area of aesthetic admiration. When the touch takes us, we find us in the realm of sensing and of the pathetic. And when the unity subject/world/act/artwork realizes in order to fulfil the sense of calligraphic action and to discover the ecstasy, it is the triumph of the ethic and the spiritual.

6 Conclusion

The theory of existential semiotics by Eero Tarasti has allowed us to study three Persian calligraphies which constituted the object of the analysis of this essay. Through this examination we have been able to advance the idea which says that it is possible to state that there are three existential styles in the Persian calligraphies: i) the style of affirmation where the calligraphy is in harmony with the already enunciated (Figure 1 where all respects the disengaged Sublime, ii) the style of negation where the calligraphy is in revolt and tries to go via the route of rebellion in order to be introduced to the transcendence (Figure 2 where the calligraphy transforms into an image and lets the flesh of the world appear in order to show us its innumerous existential possibilities, iii) the style of plenitude and perfection where the subject/world/act/sign blends together beginning from their will, know, and can in order to create a new spiritual world of aesthetic-ethical qualities.

The only point of difference between us and Tarasti lies in the fact that for the author of Foundations of Existential Semiotics, the three existential styles unite in one course, whereas for us each style could be characterised one independent from the other and in one semiotic trajectory. That is why the calligraphic Figure 1 represents the existential style of affirmation, whereas Figure 2 corresponds to the existential style of negation, rebellions without any kind of affirmation being involved.

References

Abasi Parzad, Hasan. 2008 *Besmellah Garden; the year Book of Besmellah*. Tehran: Mashgh – e – Honar.
Badir, Sémir. 2007. La sémiotique aux prises avec les médias. *Visible: Intermédialité Visuelle* 3. Limoges: Pulim.
Barthes, Roland. 1980. *La Chambre Claire*. Paris: Seuil.
Breuur, Roland. 2005. la synesthésie, un effet de matière. *Visible: la Diversité Sensible*. Numéro 1. Limoges: PULIM.
Dondero, Maria Guilia. 2006. Quand l'écriture devient texture de l'image. *Visible: l'Hétérogénéité du Visuel* 2. Limoges: Pulim.
Fontanille, Jacques. 1999. *Sémiotique et Littérature*. Paris: PUF.
Fontanille, Jacques. 2007a. Intermédialité: l'affiche dans l'annonce-presse. *Visible: Intermédialité Visuelle* 3. Limoges: Pulim.
Fontanille, Jacques. 2007b. Sémiotique et éthique. *Nouveaux Actes Sémiotique*. http://revues.unilim.fr/nas/document.
Fontanille, Jacques & Claude Zilberberg. 1998. *Tension et Signification*. Paris: Mardaga.
Greimas, Algidas Julien. 1987. *De l'Imperfection*. Périgueux: Pierre Fanlac.
Klinkenberg, Jean Marie. 2006. Vers une typologie générale des fonctions de l'écriture. L'écriture comme image. *Visible: l'Héterogénéité du Visuel* 3. Limoges: Pulim.
Kristeva, Julien. 1974. *La révolution du langage poétique*. Paris: Seuil.
Landowski, Eric. 2005. Les interactions risquées. *Nouveaux Actes Sémiotiques* 101, 102, 103. Limoges: Pulim.
Le Gerun, Odile. 2005. La matière picturale aux origines des effets rhétoriques de synesthésie. *Visible: l'Hétérogénéité du Visuel* 1. Limoges: Pulim.
Merleau-Ponty, Maurice. 1945. *Phénoménologie de la Perception*. Paris: Gallimard.
Shairi, Hamid Reza & Jacques Fontanille. 2001. Dynamique visuelle. *Nouveaux Actes Sémiotiques* 73, 74, 75. Limoges: Pulim.
Tarasti, Eero. 2009. *Fondement de la Sémiotique Existentielle*. Paris: Harmattan.
Wölfflin, Heinrich. 1992 [1986]. *Principes Fondamentaux de l'Histoire de l'Art*. Paris: Gérard Monfort.

Vesa Matteo Piludu
Transcending violence: Artistic interpretations of the myths of Kullervo from the Kalevala to Tero Saarinen

Abstract: The tragic stories of the hero Kullervo are some of the most represented mythical narratives in all the Finnish arts. The brutal violence of the narrative and Kullervo's disturbed mind have been too problematic to be represented by artistic means, and the hero has been defined as the popular but troubled child of Finnish literature, theatre, music, dance and visual arts. Working on Kullervo, Finnish artists offered deep reflections on the social, cultural, personal or psychological origins of violence. Kullervo has been interpreted as a hero or an antihero, the natural result of a violent society or family, a tragic warrior or a sorcerer using the power of spell and sound, as a nationalist model for Finnish revolt against russification, as metaphor for artists' necessity of breaking norms, or as a complex character that choose to be violent, even if he has better alternatives. This article aims to reveal how the interpretations of the myth and personality of Kullervo had radically changed due to the changes in the historical, cultural and artistic contexts and in the semiosphere. In the last paragraph, I shall reflect on how this fascinating and problematic research topic deals with: a) Juri Lotman's theories about the relation between symbols, myths and different cultural context, and b) Eero Tarasti's recent reflections and writings on existential semiotics and semiotics of transcendence. The methods and theories of Eero Tarasti's zemic model offer several theoretic frameworks to analyse the changes in the interpretations of Kullervo's story.

Keywords: Myth of Kullervo and *Kalevala*, Aleksis Kivi, Jean Sibelius, Akseli Gallen Kallela, Aulis Sallinen, Tero Saarinen.

Acknowledgements: I would like to express my special thanks of gratitude to Tero Saarinen and David Scarantino for the interviews and their help in different phases of my research on Kullervo, the Tero Saarinen Company for the stage photos of the choreography "Kullervo" and the Finnish National Gallery for the photos of paintings and sculptures. I'm grateful to the Niilo Helander Foundation (*Niilo Helanderin Säätiö*) for having generously funded my research work at the University of Helsinki.

https://doi.org/10.1515/9783110789164-037

1 Introduction: The myth of Kullervo and the Finnish arts

The stories of the hero Kullervo are some of the most represented myths in Finnish arts. Kullervo has inspired several generations of Finnish artists and some relevant foreign ones. Kullervo's legends influenced Friedrich Reinhold Kreutzwald (1803–1882) when he edited the national Estonian epic *Kalevipoeg* (1857), based on local folklore as the Finnish *Kalevala* (1849). John Ronald Reuel Tolkien (1892–1973) was also inspired by Kullervo: his very first and unfinished novel, *The Story of Kullervo* (1914–1915) has been recently edited and posthumously published by Verlyn Fieger (Tolkien 2015). However, the brutal violence of the narrative and Kullervo's disturbed mind have been very problematic to be represented by artistic means, and the hero has been defined as the popular, but troubled child of Finnish literature, music, theatre and arts. In recent years, marked by the fear of terrorism, Kullervo has been reinterpreted as an anti-hero and a negative figure in the artists' imagination. This article aims to reveal how the interpretations of his myth and personality had radically changed due to the changes in the historical, cultural and artistic contexts and in the semiosphere (Lotman 1990: 102–119). The artistic masterpieces, inspired by Kullervo's legends, have been analyzed by Finnish scholars of folklore, literature, music and visual arts in monographs or articles focused on one artist or art, but few scholars compared the interpretation of Kullervo of different artistic languages. In this article, I shall attempt to analyse how the interpretations of Kullervo, presented by some of the main artists, influenced the work of Kullervo by other contemporary and following artists and to reveal the importance of phenomena of intertextuality between different artistic codes. The article will proceed in chronological order starting from the *Kalevala* (1849) and ending with Tero Saarinen's Kullervo (2015), and it covers the works of some of the most relevant Finnish artists and intellectuals who worked on Kullervo, focusing on the different meanings that the myth acquired in different times, artistic languages and socio-cultural contexts. I shall focus on the Kullervo's interpretation by Lönnrot, Cygnaeus, Sjöstrand, Kivi, Sibelius, Gallen-Kallela, Sallinen and Saarinen. In order to make the topic fully understandable for foreign readers, I added historical and cultural details to better understand the changes in cultural contexts in Finland. In the last paragraph, I shall reflect on how this fascinating and problematic research topic deals with: a) Juri Lotman's theories about the relation between symbols, myths and different cultural context, and b) transcendence and Eero Tarasti's recent reflections and writings about existential semiotics and semiotics of transcendence.

2 The stories of Kullervo in the *Kalevala* and Elias Lönnrot's interpretation of the myth: The relevance of family and education

The myths of Kullervo that the Finnish artists are more familiar with were collected and edited by Elias Lönnrot (1802–1884) in six long Runes or chapters (XXXI–XXXVI) of the *New Kalevala* (1849, furthermore only *Kalevala*), the Finnish national epic poem (divided into 50 Runes) that united in an organic literary whole several epic and ritual folksongs transcribed during several travels and field works by Lönnrot himself and his helpers. The *Kalevala*, published during the period in which Finland was a Grand Duchy of the Russian Empire (1809–1917), was the first real literary work in the Finnish language in a country that for many centuries has been under the political dominium of Sweden (c. 1150–1809) and has had Swedish as its official and literary language for many centuries. In the previous version of the Lönnot's epic poem, the *Old Kalevala* (1835), the myth of Kullervo was shorter, condensed in the Rune XIX. In the *New Kalevala*, the adventures of Kullervo form quite a relevant part (10%) of the whole epic poem and a sort of "epic inside the epic". The tale started with the bloody war between two brothers: Kalervo, the father of Kullervo and Untamo, the uncle of the main hero. Untamo won the struggle and tried to exterminate all the family and the people of the brother. At first, Untamo tried to kill the infant Kullervo too, but the small boy, who had supernatural strength and endurance, survived all murder attempts. After that, Untamo tried to put the young Kullervo at work, but the hero made several disasters caused by his vigour or cruelty (Rune XXXI). At this point, Untamo decided to sell Kullervo as a servant or slave to the hero and smith Ilmarinen, who married the beautiful Maiden of Pohjola after having forged a mythic object (the sampo) for her mother (the Mistress of Pohjola) and having to overtake deadly trials and ordeals. Kullervo became the servant of Ilmarinen's wife, who sent him into the clearings of the forest to shepherd her cattle. She hid a stone in the bread baked for Kullervo, who ruined his knife trying to cut the bread. As the knife was the only inheritance obtained after the father's death, Kullervo got enraged and, uttering a spell, changed the cattle into bears and wolves that tore the woman into pieces (Runes XXXII and XXXIII). After that, Kullervo travelled into the forest and he found out that his father, mother, brothers and sisters were still alive as they were able to flee from their village at the very last minute, and Kullervo decided to stay with them. Only a sister was missing as she got lost in the forest (Rune XXXIV). After a while, Kullervo departed again; this time to collect taxes. In the forest, he tried to seduce a girl, who is convinced to come up into the sledge by the gold and richness of the hero and to make love with him. Only after that, the two youngsters started to reveal themselves and they understood that they were brother and sister. The girl, in despair, ran madly through the woods and jumped into a river, drowning (Rune XXXV). Kullervo decided to find his death in war and left to kill the uncle Untamo and his folk. Kullervo obtained his revenge, but coming back home he found out that his mother and father too were killed during the war and their cabin was burned. At this point, Kullervo killed himself with the sword that has caused the death of many (Rune XXXVI). As a whole, the legends of Kullervo form a saga fulfilled of blood and violence: the tragic hero provokes the death of all the people around him and finally his suicide.

In reality, Lönnrot modified the folk songs he attributed to Kullervo. The folklorist that analysed Kullervo's material found out that core of the legends of Kullervo was the folk songs (called *The Kaleva's Son*) about the two brothers' war, the unfortunate attempt to kill the infant, the tragic works of Kullervo for Untamo, the episode of the killing of the Smith's or Hiisi's wife (in the folk song, the Ilmarisen's wife was not mentioned) and the killing of Untamo (Kupiainen 2002: 102–112). These main episodes are the ones selected by Lönnrot for the *Old Kalevala* (Lönnrot 1999 (1835): 268–285). In the folk songs, the hero of these legends could be called Kullervo, Kalervo's Son, Kaleva's Son or Kalerva's Son. By contrast, the episode of the seduction of the sister was part of other epic songs, called by the scholars with the title *The Sister's Ruin* (*Sisaren turmelus*). The male protagonist of these legends was generally called Turikkainen or Tuurittuinen (Krohn 1885: 522), and only in one song, he is called Kalova's Son. After the seduction of the sister, the hero often goes to tell what has happened to the mother, who suggests him to flee to Saari (The Island), where he seduces almost all the local ladies. The topic suggests that the hero of these adventures had features remembering Lemminkäinen, another of the main heroes of the *Kalevala* (Kupiainen 2004: 112–123).

By joining the two different epic songs into a narrative with the same protagonist, Lönnrot created the image of a very strong and violent hero, who is condemned to a very unfortunate fate: a character that somehow reminded the heroes of Ancient Greek tragedies or the ones of German and Scandinavian mythology (Siegfried or Sigurd). However, Lönnrot's interpretation of the myth of Kullervo was mostly negative or pedagogical. At the end of the stories of Kullervo, the hero Väinämöinen sang:

> O, ye many unborn nations,
> Never evil nurse your children,
> Never give them out to strangers,
> Never trust them to the foolish!

If the child is not well nurtured,
Is not rocked and led uprightly,
Though he grow to years of manhood,
Bear a strong and shapely body,
He will never know discretion,
Never eat the bread of honour,
Never drink the cup of wisdom.
(Lönnrot 2008 (1849), Rune XXXVI, lines 351–360, English translation (1888)
by J. M. Crawford)

In this situation, Väinämöinen expresses the "hidden voice of the author" and reveals the opinion of Lönnrot about the reasons that caused the ruin of Kullervo. Lönnrot explains to the reader that a child that grows up in war, slavery, outside his real family and under the influence of a murderous uncle could become physically strong, but he will be insane and morally weak. Lönnrot's perspective is rooted in psychological and sociological explanations: what "makes a man" is the social environment and the family context.

The influential Finnish Swedish-speaking writer Zachris Topelius (1818–1898) showed a very similar opinion about Kullervo. Topelius was a central cultural figure of the time: he was convinced that Finnish should be the cultural language of the country (and, for this reason, he defended the aesthetic qualities of the *Kalevala*), but as a Swedish writer he was also concerned about the importance of Swedish as a relevant language for Finnish education, culture and learning. In an article, published in 1851, in the newspaper, *Helsingfors Tidningar*, Topelius stated that the tragic fate of Kullervo is what happens when the sweet words of the father and the tender of the mother did not teach a child's heart to love the neighbour. (Apo 2014: 177). Taking in consideration Eero Tarasti's Zemic model (Tarasti 2017), Lönnrot and Topelius stressed the importance of *Soi1* (the social values) and *Soi2* (the social institutions, like the family) in forming *Moi2* (the psychological self) of Kullervo.

3 Fredrik Cygnaeus' nationalistic interpretation of Kullervo: The slave-hero who took hard revenge against his oppressors

The professor of aesthetic and literature Fredrik Cygnaeus (1807–1881) was an important art critic and collector and one of the most relevant figures in the Fennoman movement, which aimed to establish the Finnish language as the official national language of the country and supported Finnish independence. He wrote the influential essay, *Det tragiska elementet i Kalevala* (1853), in which he declared that Kullervo's legend, for his dramatic qualities, was the most relevant part of the *Kalevala*. Cygnaeus abominated the "Christian morality" of Topelius' judgment on Kullervo. Cygnaeus, as several early Fennomans, spoke Swedish as mother language, and he was influenced by the critics of many Svecomans and Scandinavists about the *Kalevala*. The Svecomans supported the Swedish as the main official language of Finland and the Scandinavists were in favour of the political union of Finland with Sweden, Norway and Denmark. According to many of them, Lönnrot's epic poem demonstrated that the Finnish speaking people was unable to create a proper culture and govern their land. The European intellectual elite of the time stressed that a people or nation that could demonstrate to have a heroic past and a language with a long history had the right to establish an independent state. According to many Svecomans, the *Kalevala*'s heroes were too primitive and fragile: they were not real warriors as they used magic and incantations more than the sword, and they often cried and asked the thunder-god Ukko to help them. Cygnaeus answered them that this statement was not correct, as Kullervo represented a real warrior hero, one that could easily compete with Siegfried or other German or Norse heroes. Kullervo had a heroic personality; he was egocentric as the Scandinavian heroes and he also had a tragic "heroic death". Cygnaeus underscored the swordsman's qualities of Kullervo, ignoring the fact that the hero uttered incantations to take revenge of Ilmarinen's wife.

According to Cygnaeus, the main tragic element of Kullervo was that he was born as a hero but he lived his childhood and youth as a slave. The injustice of slavery justified the revenge of Kullervo. The interpretation of Cygnaeus is "sociological". Using the Zemic model (Tarasti 2017), the *Soi2* (a social institution, the slavery) provokes the vengeance, but Cygnaeus accepted the reprisal of Kullervo. If Lönnrot and Topelius abhorred the violence of Kullervo's revenge, Cygnaeus admired his rebellious spirit (Apo 2014: 177–178). For several Finnish nationalists, Kullervo became a metaphor for the whole of Finland: Finland was subjugated to the Russian tsarist power, but his destiny should fulfil in its independence and that should be obtained by cultural means or through a more open and violent rebellion.

Otherwise, Kullervo's violent character, the supernatural strength, the unethical behaviour and the heroic tragic death are typical features of some ancient heroes, for example, the Iliad's Achilles: in this sense, Kullervo was seen as a Finnish counterpart of certain Homeric and Ancient tragedies' heroes. The influence of Cygnaeus' ideas is evident in the sculptures of one of the first artists who worked on Kullervo's legends: Carl Eneas Sjöstrand (1828–1906), who was born in Sweden but worked in Finland for 40 years as an art teacher. He was invited by Cygnaeus to Turku to make a sculpture of Henrik Gabriel Porthan (1739–1804), one of the first scholars interested in Finnish mythology and folk poetry. His monument was ready in 1858 (Toivanen 1952). In the same year, Sjöstrand made his first sculpture of Kullervo: *Kullervo Breaks his Swaddle* (*Kullervo katkoo kapalonsa*). Here the infant Kullervo shows his supernatural force in the cradle: the structure of the work is heavily neoclassical and it clearly reminds the ancient sculptures on the infant Heracles who kills the snakes sent by Hera to kill him. The myths of Heracles remind of Kullervo in many ways: the two heroes have supernatural strength and they use it in an extreme way. In Homer's Odyssey, Heracles is presented as a disturber, a hero who does not follow social rules, like Kullervo (Nummi 2014: 128). The second Sjöstrand's work on the hero is the most famous one: *Kullervo Addressing his Sword* (*Kullervo puhuu miekalleen*, 1868, figure 1), depicting the last moments of the life of the hero, asking the sword to kill him. The work is a kind of "manifesto" of Cygnaeus' ideas on Kullervo as the perfect Finnish counterpart of the Classical and Scandinavian heroes: the sculpture's position reminds one of the ancient heroes, but Kullervo's clothing is a simple bearskin that reminds of the war gears of Scandinavian *bersekir* ("bear-shirts" in Old Norse), the furious warriors of Scandinavian mythology. On the other hand, the ritual bear hunt was considered a heroic task in Finnish folk culture too (Piludu 2019). In the sculpture, Kullervo has a stoic expression: there is no sign of the desperation and remorse of his final lament, which appeared in the *Kalevala*. Sjöstrand's Kullervo goes forward toward his heroic death with the same spirit of a Viking warrior leaving for his last battle.

Figure 1: Carl Eneas Sjöstrand, *Kullervo Addressing his Sword* (*Kullervo puhuu miekalleen*), 1868, 260 cm, plaster. Finnish National Gallery / The Ateneum Art Museum, Helsinki. Photo: Finnish National Gallery / Hannu Aaltonen.

4 Aleksis Kivi: The slavery and the "tragic choice" of Kullervo

Aleksis Kivi (1834–1872) was the first Finnish professional writer who has published poetry in Finnish, the first Finnish novel *The Seven Brothers* (1870), and the very first drama in the Finnish language: *Kullervo* (1859 and 1864), a tragedy in five acts, which was fully staged only after the death of the author. The first version of the drama was written in 1859 and it won the competition of the Finnish Literature Society for writing the first drama in Finnish language, but the reviewers of the Society's commission requested several changes and adjustment before the publication of the last version of the manuscript. As Cygnaeus was Kivi's teacher and one of his main mentors, he has influenced some features of the writer's Kullervo: the slavery of the protagonist is underscored in the drama and Kullervo has a slave mark on his skin. The drama presents all the adventures of the hero told in the *Kalevala* but is not a mere copy of the original epic poem: it is written in prose and presents many original characters, which were not present in the *Kalevala*. One of the most relevant new characters is Kimmo, the faithful friend of Kullervo who follows the hero until reaching madness and death: he is the drama's "protagonist's confident" and *"raissonneur"* (Nummi 2014: 119). Kimmo will return in some contemporary works of art on Kullervo, as Aulis Sallinen's opera *Kullervo* (1988) and Tero Saarinen's choreography *Kullervo* (2015). Kivi's drama has references to Shakespearean and other European tragedies. One of the most relevant connections with the European dramatic tradition is the presence of the tragic choice or decision: the hero consciously chooses to follow a tragic "path". In the forest, Kullervo meets two mysterious female spirits: Ajatar, who incites him to take revenge and Sinipiika (Blue girl), who tries to lead him toward the family and mind's peace (Kivi 2014: 248–253). The two beings do not appear in the *Kalevala*, but Kivi probably read about them in Professor Matthias Alexander Castrén's essays on Finnish mythology (Castrén 1853; Castrén 2016). Ajatar is an evil forest spirit who tried to mislead the hunters so that they get lost in the forestland (Nummi 2014: 119; Castrén 1853: 114; Castrén 2016: 157). By contrast, Sinipiika was one of the names of the forest spirits mentioned in hunting incantations: she is a being who could help the hunters to find out game animals in the forest, if she is properly pleased with songs and spells (see Piludu 2019; Nummi 2014: 119; Castrén 1853: 105). Kullervo consciously chose revenge's way shown by Ajatar. The two forest spirits are allegories representing the path of Evil and the Good: similar allegoric figures are present in medieval and renaissance dramas and Shakespeare (Nummi: 119–120). This element was new in the interpretations of the myth: Kullervo was not only a natural-born hero, the result of a violent society, slavery and injustice (Cygnaeus) or bad education (Lönnrot, Topelius). He chooses his destiny, so his fate is also the result of a personal choice and responsibility: he decided to proceed toward the killing, revenge and self-destruction (Kinnunen 1967: 110–111). The personality (*Moi2* in the Zemic model) of Kullervo plays an important role in the destiny of the hero (Tarasti 2017). This element makes Kivi's Kullervo more complex and modern and a source of inspiration for contemporary artists. Another of Kivi's innovations is that Kullervo participated in bear hunting and other hunters are present as characters of the drama: the interest in hunting, interpreted as one of the most important traditional and ancient Finnish activities, is a constant in Kivi's literary production, as evident in *Metsämiehen laulu* (*Hunter song*, Kivi 1997: 42–34), one of Kivi's most popular poems. The bear hunting was considered a ritual and heroic task in Finnish folk culture (Piludu 2019) and it was considered a symbol of Finnishness. Kullervo is a pagan rebel and an individualist hunter who decided to break social norms, and his stubbornness reminds of one of the young protagonists of Kivi's novel *The Seven Brothers* (Kivi 1991). Kullervo has also been interpreted as one of Kivi's literary metaphors of his individualism: the writer often presented himself as a forest man, an "outsider" of society and the Finnish literature's establishment (Sallasmaa 2009: 32–33). The tragedy was an important step in Kivi's career, but Professor August Ahlqvist (1826–1889) disapproved some features of its style, starting a maniacal and often unbalanced criticism of all the Kivi's works that had a very bad influence on Kivi's mental health (Sihvo 2012: 196–197; Tarkiainen 1949). However, Aleksi Kivi's *Kullervo* has deeply influenced Finnish music and theatre: Armas Launis' opera *Kullervo* (1917), Paavo Haavikko's monologue *Kullervo's Story* (*Kullervon tarina*, Haavikko 1989; Pentikäinen 2004: 279–323), Aulis Sallinen's opera *Kullervo* (Sallinen 1988) are grounded on this drama (Aho 2009: 108). Kivi's work is also the most staged tragedy inspired by Kullervo, as Juhana Heikki Erkko's drama *Kullervo* (1895) did not obtain the same attention after the death of the author.

5 Jean Sibelius' Kullervo: The tragedy of the incest with the sister

Jean Sibelius' (1864–1957) interpretation of the myth of Kullervo was as innovative and ground-breaking as Kivi's one. Sibelius is officially known as the Finnish national composer and Eero Tarasti defined him as an "icon" of the Finns (Tarasti 1999: 221–247). Before Sibelius, only two Finnish composers worked on Kullervo. In 1860, Johan Filip von Schantz (1835–1865) composed *Kullervo-overture* (1860), an orchestral work in Beethoven's style. In 1881, Robert Kajanus (1856–1933) composed *The Funeral March of Kullervo* (*Kullervon surumarssi*): the work is not based on Kalevala's text, it is grounded on the musical language of late German romanticism, but it used variations of Finnish folk songs like *Velisurmaaja* (*The Brother-Slayer*) (Aho 2008: 82–83; Aho 2009: 45; Aho 2011: 584).

Sibelius' symphonic poem *Kullervo* (Op. 7), composed in 1891–1892, has quite a complex structure. It is divided into five movements: 1) *Introduction*, 2) *Kullervo's Youth*, 3) *Kullervo and his Sister*, 4) *Kullervo Goes to War*, 5) *Kullervo's Death* (Aho 2009: 46). The work is based on almost all of Kullervo's adventures described in the *Kalevala*; only Ilmarinen's wife's death is missing. The real dramatic focus of the work is the longest third movement and the episode of the seduction of the sister (Tarasti 2012: 222–273). The choice was original because this episode was not considered the most heroic deed of the hero: the theme is rarely represented in visual art. In 1891, the Swedish painter Louis Sparre (1863–1964) drew the moment in which Kullervo takes the sister on his sledge (Konttinen 2001: 155). The creative process was very complicated: Sibelius worked on more than 50 alternative themes for the first movement only (Dawn Goss 2003). He started to work in Wien, where he fell in love with the *Kalevala*, finding it "modern" and full of music (Aho 2008: 84). When he came back to Finland, he listened to the famous folk singer Larin Paraske (1833–1904). However, Sibelius did not banally copy the so-called "Kalevalaic" or "Runo" singing tunes, he elaborated his melodies fusing few and selected elements of folk singing with the language of the emerging romantic symphonic music (Tarasti 2012: 222–273). The introduction, purely instrumental, progresses in a sonata form. In the beginning, the clarinets and French horn play a Kullervo "destiny" theme which is later repeated, in a much more powerful way, by brasses and woodwind: Kullervo's drama finds a powerful musical representation at the very beginning of the work. The second movement, also instrumental, is a like a "second introduction" to Kullervo's legends. The first two movements are not strictly programmatic: they introduce Kullervo's legends in quite an abstract, symphonic and mysterious way, without singing any *Kalevala*'s text. The second movement is marked by a "lullaby theme", in which resonate some Kalevalaic singing's tune, whose intensity is increased through variation. When the intensity increases markedly and strongly, the aura of the lullaby disappears, giving space to the early childhood's violent adventures. According to Tarasti, the growing of the intensity deals with the growing of the hero's physical force and the violent result of all the tasks his master and mistress gave him (Tarasti 1994: 222). Franklin and stress that the music changes from a feminine maternal lullaby into a heroic and masculine Tawaststjerna "cry of protest and revolt" (Franklin 2001: 66; Tawaststjerna 1989:113).

Other themes have been described by Erik Tawaststjerna and Eero Tarasti as "incantation" and "pastoral". The "pastoral theme" refers to the Kullervo shepherd's work for the Ilmarinen's wife, and the "incantation" could refer to the Ilmarisen wife's spell to protect cattle from bear and wolves or to the hero's incantation to transform the cattle into bears (Tarasti 1994: 222, 2012: 222–273).

The third movement is different and the huge male choir starts to sing the Kalevala's texts. The choir's unison and the Finnish 5/4 tempo create an impressive archaic and collective atmosphere (Tarasti 1994: 223–225). The choir has the same role of choirs in Ancient Tragedy: it presents the protagonist and his family background ("Kullervo, son of Kalervo, / an old man's son, with blue socks"), preparing the dramatic entrance of the soloist (Tarasti 1994: 223, Tarasti 2012: 222–273). The soloist Kullervo (baritone) and the sister (soprano) have a dialogue: Kullervo tries many times to convince the girl to come into his sledge and the sister refuses. The chorus describes the actions of the drama: how Kullervo opened the sledge's leather coffer, showing the girl his silver, convincing the girl to come into the sledge. After that, Sibelius was cautious in describing the sexual intercourse by purely musical means, without any singing, to avoid embarrassing singers and listeners. Later the movement evolves in the moment of the "revelation": Kullervo presented himself (after the sexual intercourse) as the son of Kalervo and asked her about her origins. The sister reveals to be Kalervo's daughter and starts a long lament, crying that it would have been better to die when she was an infant or a small girl. The movement ends with Kullervo's lament, in which he blames himself for having ruined the sister and cries that it would have been better if he was not born. The sad episode is followed by a surprising fourth movement, *Kullervo Goes to War*: the music is a warfare's rondo fanfare, full of romantic heroism, somewhat cheerful. The music is inspired by the *Kalevala*'s verse describing the hero leaving for battle "Blowing war upon his bugle". In the fifth movement, the soloist singing Kullervo's role returns to sing Kullervo's last words before the suicide and the orchestral music returns the "doom theme" of the *Introduction*: the tragic destiny of the hero is fulfilled (Kambe 2005: 83–84). In the first public performance of *Kullervo* (1892), Sibelius directed the orchestra and it was his "baptism" as a director. The University's festive hall was full of intellectuals (Tawaststjerna 1997: 94–95) and the event had political connotations too. The Svecomans criticized the roughness and brutality of the music, considering Sibelius, coming from a Swedish-speaking family, a kind of traitor who decided to join the Fennoman group. By contrast, the Fennomans were quite enthusiastic about the novelty and energy of *Kullervo*. Sibelius directed *Kullervo* for the last time in 1893 and he received some criticism even from the Fennoman composer and critic, Oskar Merikanto. After that, the musical style of Sibelius evolved in other directions and he prohibited the performance of the Symphonic

Poem during his life. However, *Kullervo* firmly established the position of Sibelius as a composer, and the "cult" of Sibelius as the Finnish national composer and the fundamental musical interpreter of *Kalevala* started from this early work and the political and aesthetical quarrels related to it (Tarasti 2001: 4). After Sibelius' death, *Kullervo* has been performed several times, and from the 1980s there has been a real renaissance of performances and recordings of *Kullervo* in Finland and abroad: Sibelius' *Kullervo* and his powerful male chorus gained the same "iconic" features of Gallen-Kallela's *Kullervo Cursing* in the Finnish imaginary. It can be considered as a "marked sign" (*segno marcato*) as it is as powerful as a national hymn (Tarasti 2009: 6).

6 Akseli Gallen-Kallela's Kullervos: From the bewitching hero to the remorseful rogue

Akseli Gallen-Kallela (1865–1931), the most well-known Finnish painter, has produced several works on Kullervo which have defined the position of the hero in the Finnish imaginary on the popular and intellectual levels (van der Hoeven 2001: 50; van der Hoeven 2012). An important graphic work, by Gallen-Kallela, on Kullervo is the cover of the literary and artistic publication *Nuori Suomi* ("Young Finland") of 1894, depicting a naked child Kullervo drawing pictures on the bark of an oak tree: the images represent his enemies on hangman's nooses. The cover was an aggressive warning for all the persons who dared to threaten Finland and his people (Gallen-Kallela-Sirén 2001a: 190–191). Väinö Blomstedt (1871–1947) painted the same theme, in a more dynamic and dramatic way, in his *Episode from the Kalevala (Kullervo Carves on the Oak's Bark)* ("*Episodi Kalevalasta: Kullervo kaivertaa tammen runkoon*", 1897). In 1894, Gallen-Kallela also sketched the first version of the *Kullervo's Curse* (*Kullervon kirous*), where the young hero is again naked, as the Ancient Greek heroes, and embraced by the ghostly figure of Kostotar, the Goddess of Revenge, an allegoric figure that was not present in the *Kalevala*: she could remind that the rage of Kullervo was a revenge caused by the vile act of Ilmarisen's wife (Gallen-Kallela-Sirén 2001a: 265). In the final version of the painting, Kostotar disappeared and the hero has trousers, resulting in a more realistic representation of a Finnish or Karelian shepherd. As the painting was ready in 1899, at the very beginning of the "years of oppressions" or russification period (1899–1905 and 1908–1917), this iconic picture (figure 2), in which Kullervo raises the left fist to the sky, was often interpreted by the contemporary viewers as a representation of the Finnish folk's rebellion against the Russian oppressor. Van der Hoeven considers this Kullevo "raising the hand" as a strong symbol of Finnish resistance and revolt: "a symbol for how the Finns felt in the days Gallen-Kallela painted it – and in other times as well" (van der Hoeven 2012: 80). The raised fist is the central symbol, the Saussurian signifier of the painting, representing anger, revolt and the hero's intention to take revenge (van der Hoeven 2012: 82). The hero is really furious, but he is also conscious of his intentions and future acts (van der Hoeven 2012: 88). The psychological features are connected to the landscape, representing a true forest wilderness (*erämaa*), which was a powerful symbol of Finnishness (van der Hoeven 2012: 88). Finland is a wild country and it has a wild hero with the wilderness within. There is a human-environmental dialogue: the hero interiorizes the nature, and nature exteriorizes the inner world and rage of the hero. However, the first sketch of the work was done some years before the so-called *routavuodet* ("Frost-years", the hard years of Russification of Finland: 1899–1905) and the image is deeply connected to the episodes narrated in the *Kalevala*'s Rune XXXIII: the hero has just dropped the bread with the stone, which his dog sniffs in the lower part of the painting and his rage is directed against the wife of Ilmarinen. The landscape also highlights the upcoming doom: thunderstorm's clouds appear over the hills and, behind Kullervo, there is a fallen tree and a rowan with berries red as blood. Janne Gallen-Kallela-Sirén remarks that the painting is first of all mythological, but it could have political references, not only as a manifesto against the Russification but as a polemical message against the political divisions of the Finns (Fennomans versus Svecomans) too, as the myth of Kullervo is related to the fratricide war between Untamo and Kalervo (Gallen-Kallela-Sirén 2001a: 265–266). However, the painting has a more complicate symbolism and this Kullervo has also interpreted as an alter-ego of Gallen-Kallela as an individual artist trying to find new artistic paths with creative rage without inhibitions (Martin and Sivén 1990: 149). The wilderness of Finland required not only wild heroes but wild artists too. We have to consider that Gallen-Kallela's creative process was long, difficult, complex and painful as Sibelius' *Kullervo*: it took five years to find out the last and definitive version of the painting.

In 1901, Gallen-Kallela painted the fresco *Kullervo Departs for the War* (*Kullervon sotaanlähtö*, figure 3) in the Music Hall of the Student House of the University of Helsinki. The painting shows a bearded and older Kullervo leaving alone for his personal war against the uncle, Untamo, playing a birchbark's horn. Kullervo rides a white horse: the structure of the painting and the horse's position are inspired by Simone Martini's *Guidoriccio da Fogliano at the Siege of Montemassi* (Gallen-Kallela-Sirén 2001: 285). Also, in this case, Gallen-Kallela started to make the first sketches of the painting before the russification years, in 1894, and the painting was inspired by the lines 155–162 of the Rune XXXVI of the *Kalevala*, in which the hero went to combat "Blowing war upon his bugle". Even so,

Figure 2: Akseli Gallen-Kallela, *Kullervo Cursing* (*Kullervon kirous*), 1899, 184 × 102,5 cm, oil on canvas. Collection: Antell Collections. Finnish National Gallery / The Ateneum Art Museum, Helsinki. Photo: Finnish National Gallery / Pirje Mykkänen and Jouko Könönen.

Figure 3: Akseli Gallen-Kallela, *Kullervo Departs for the War* (*Kullervon sotaanlähtö*), 1901, 89 × 128 cm, tempera on canvas. Finnish National Gallery / The Ateneum Art Museum. Helsinki. Photo: Finnish National Gallery / Hannu Pakarinen.

Figure 4: Akseli Gallen-Kallela, *Kullervo Herding his Wild Flocks* (*Kullervo petokarjoineen*), 1917, 70 × 68 cm, watercolour. Finnish National Gallery / The Ateneum Art Museum. Helsinki. Photo: Finnish National Gallery / Pirje Mykkänen.

the two Kullervo's paintings were interpreted as artistic "war call" against the Russification. However, Gallen-Kallela-Sirén is right in stressing the fact that in both the paintings Kullervo does not draw his sword, but express his rage through the power of sound and music (Gallen-Kallela-Sirén 2001a: 284): in *Kullervo Cursing*, Kullervo shouts the incantation that transforms the cattle into the wild beast that devoured Ilmarinen's wife, in *Kullervo Departs for the War*, the hero expresses his belligerent intention and heroic presence playing the birchbark horn, a realistic and real Finnish folk instrument which the painter has represented in his previous *The Shepherd Boy of Päänäjärvi (Päänäjärven paimeenpoika*, 1892). Van der Hoeven considers this Kullervo as "horn blower"; an expression not only of revolt, but also of freedom: the hero warns his enemies, but at the same announces to the world that he is a free warrior and horseman (van der Hoeven 2012: 80, 83). The rising and blowing of the horn became a recognizable Finnish symbol of liberation from oppression (van der Hoeven 2012: 83). It could be interpreted also as a sign of artistic and intellectual freedom, and not only of political emancipation. This Kullervo is not a shepherd any more, but a ruler who decides his path and his destiny (van der Hoeven 2012: 88). The rich horsecloth has no ethnographic realism, but the horn of birchbark and the winter landscape are still strong symbols of Finnishness (van der Hoeven 2012: 88). Gallen-Kallela, who studied the *Kalevala*'s text with passion and attention, stressed the importance of the magic of the voice, incantations and music in the legends of Kullervo. In this sense, Gallen-Kallela's Kullervo is much more faithful to the *Kalevala*'s text than the Kullervo of Cygnaeus, which negated the importance of incantations in the saga of the hero. If the sound is a common motive in both paintings, Tarasti noticed that the two works of art have several oppositions (Tarasti 1994: 174–175); in the first one, nature is represented during the summer and the day, the hero is young, poorly dressed and furious, while in the second one, the environment is snowy and nocturnal (with stars and northern lights), Kullervo is a mature bearded man, he is richly dressed and surprisingly calm and static. At the aesthetic level, the first painting is more realistic and it could represent the "Strindberg's aesthetic of ugliness", and the second one is connected with Gallen-Kallela's symbolist period and a classic "heroic mysticism" (Tarasti 1994: 172–173). The second Kullervo seems to be a cosmic ruler too and a metaphor for a "warrior of the soul". Tarasti also stresses that these two Gallen-Kallela's paintings represent the same themes of the second and in the fourth movement of Sibelius' *Kullervo* (Tarasti 1994: 175). An interesting element of these two classic paintings is the fact that the hero's enemies (Ilmarinen's wife and Untamo) are not represented: the paintings are focused on the moments when the hero chose to use violence, not on the depiction of the violent act himself. The focus is on the hero's choice and personality (the *Moi2*, see Tarasti 2017).

The necessity of doing some kind of artistic "censure" of the most violent or disgusting acts of Kullervo has been a problem for other artists dealing with the myth: Sibelius and Sallinen.

At the beginning of 1917, Gallen-Kallela returned to Kullervo's myths and painted *Kullervo Herding his Wild Flocks* (*Kullervo petokarjoineen*, figure4), based on the episode that followed the story represented in his previous painting *Kullervo Cursing*. The hero has just transformed the cattle into bears and wolves, and in the painting he leads the beasts to tear apart Ilmarinen's wife, which is not represented in the painting. Playing the birchbark horn, a wild-looking young Kullervo convoyed the wild beasts to the house of Ilmarinen's wife (see *Kalevala*, Rune XXXIII). The painting is very dynamic and all the nature around Kullervo seems to be bewitched, and an eagle and a lynx also follow the furious hero. The scenario is made by a puzzle of running beast and fallen dead pines, without any panoramic view. In the right hand, the hero has a stick with a red strip, rolled around the fist and the stick. The red is related to the blood and the fury, but the colour could have some political connotation too. Finland became independent in the same year, but from January to May 1918, in Finland, ravaged a bloody civil war between the Red Guards and the White Guards, provoking the death of 39.000 people. Gallen-Kallela joined the Whites as a soldier, officer,

General Mannerheim's adjutant and cartographer (Gallen-Kallela Sirén 2001b: 72–73), and he also drew the design for several military decorations and medals. In 1919, Gallen-Kallela revealed that his new Kullervo's painting represented the Bolsheviks, the enemies that broke into the house of neighbours with the aim of taking revenge, plunder and kill compatriots (Gallen-Kallela-Sirén 2001a: 396–397). This was the first time in which Kullervo was not interpreted as a national hero avenging injustice, but a bloodthirsty rogue. Even more dramatic are the last works of Gallen-Kallela on Kullervo: *The Remorseful Kullervo* (*Katuva Kullervo*, 1918). There are two versions of this work (a watercolour and a gouache painting) that represent the last moments of the life of the hero, who is about to commit suicide with his sword. Kullervo has killed the uncle, Untamo. Returning home, he finds that the parent's house has been burned down to the ashes. Wandering in desperation, he ends up on the spot where he had seduced his sister. At this point, he asked his sword if it wants to drink his blood, and the blade answered:

> Why should I not drink thy life-blood,
> Blood of guilty Kullerwoinen,
> Since I feast upon the worthy,
> Drink the life-blood of the righteous?
> (Lönnrot 2008 (1849), Rune XXXVI, lines 330–334, English translation by J. M. Crawford (1888)

These paintings are not heroic at all: the bearded and poorly dressed old hero covers his face with the right hand, probably crying on his misery. Three dreadful female spirits (the Fates or Moirae? Spirits of the Dead?) look at Kullervo with hate and reprobation. The environment is a dreadful forest. The difference between Sjöstrand's *Kullervo Addressing his Sword* and Gallen-Kallela's *Remorseful Kullervo* is impressive, considering that both the works are related to the same theme: in the first one, Kullervo seems to accept his fate with indifference or stoicism, while in the second, the hero is completely desperate and broken. In the gouache version of the painting, the entire forestland's ground is painted in a quite unnatural brown-red colour, remembering the death of the sister and the upcoming fate of the hero. In the watercolour version, the sword's scabbard is red. The sword here is a central symbol, not of glory, but tragic failure and suicide (van der Hoeven 2012: 80). The works, done during the Finnish civil war, are probably connected to the sad feelings of the painter for a country that had just obtained independence and it fell into a bloody fratricide war, remembering the dramatic family conflicts between Untamo, Kalervo and Kullervo.

7 Aulis Sallinen's opera: Kullervo chooses between love and hate

After Sibelius, few other Finnish composers worked on Kullervo's myth. In 1908–10, Toivo Kuula (1883–1918) wrote the *Kullervo's Song* (*Kullervon laulu*) for male choir. In 1913, Leevi Maadetoja (1887–1947) composed a short *Kullervo Overture* (*Kullervo-alkusoitto*) in a romantic style remembering Tchaikovsky's one. In 1917, Armas Launis (1884–1959) composed the opera in three acts *Kullervo*, writing also the libretto, strongly based on Kivi's tragedy, but containing several references to the *Kalevala*, the *Kanteletar* and Eino Leino's drama in verses *The Swan of Tuonela* (*Tuonelan joutsen*). The opera was also staged in France. In the *Introduction*, it has an interesting solo for shepherd's horn, which was inspired on the folk melodies for this instrument collected by Launis in his ethnomusicological field works (Aho 2008: 87–89). During and after the Second World War, few musical compositions were done about Kullervo. For several musicians, working on Kullervo was problematic because it represented a risk: the audience tended to make uncomfortable comparisons with Sibelius, considered the master of music inspired by *Kalevala*. A new renaissance of music inspired on the poem emerged in 1975–1988, some decades after the death of Sibelius and with the significant works and operas by Einojuhani Rautavaara (1928–2016). The 150th anniversary of the *Old Kalevala* in 1985 marked a consistent return of public financing for art project inspired on the *Kalevala*. Aulis Sallinen (1935 –) composed his opera *Kullervo* in 1986–1988 for the new Finnish National Opera and Ballet, writing the libretto too. In 1992, the opera was premiered in Los Angeles because the Finnish National Opera and Ballet's building was not ready. The *première* in the United States, part of the celebrations of the 75 years of the Finnish independence (1917), was followed by the Finnish media as an international "sport event", following all the steps of the preparation, searching for possible little "scandals" and doing interviews with the main stars as the baritone Jorma Hynninen (Kullervo), the director Kalle Holmberg, the orchestra's director Ulf Söderblom and Aulis Sallinen (Parola 1996: 8). In 1993, *Kullervo* opened the Finnish National Opera and Ballet and later it has been staged in six countries and three different languages. In 2014, a new production of the opera has been staged for the Savonlinna Opera Festival. This production was followed by Finnish media with more journalistic professionality and by skilled musical critics. The opera was filmed and broadcast several times in public TV channels (YLE Teema and YLE Areena), reaching a considerable audience.

The work is divided into two acts and six scenes, a prologue and an epilogue; it has a mixed chorus and five main soloists: Kullervo (Baritone), Kimmo (lyric tenor), the smith's wife (mezzo-soprano), the mother (dramatic soprano), Kalervo (bass-baritone), the sister (high soprano). The opera is strongly based on Aleksis Kivi's tragedy *Kullervo*, and its main drama is not based on the incestuous relationship with the sister as it happens in Sibelius' *Kullervo*. A huge quantity of newspaper and popular magazine articles has been written on the first production: 330, of which 30 in foreign media (Parola 1996: 8). Scientific writings on this opera are quite a few and the best analysis of the work is Anne Desler's licentiate unpublished dissertation (1997). The dramatic plot focuses on the relations between Kullervo, the mother, the smith's wife, and Kimmo. Kullervo dominates the stage, but the other characters are keys to understand his complex psychology (Heiniö 1995: 334).

Sallinen seems to be concerned to avoid references to Sibelius' *Kullervo*, but one evident influence is the use of a massive chorus. Sibelius' and Sallinen's choruses are however different: the first one was a male one, the second a mixed one. The roles of Sallinen's chorus are more complex and articulate: the chorus not only tells the story, but comments on the plot or the protagonist's affirmations, and sometimes it judges the protagonist. At the end of the second scene, after the killing of the smith's wife, the chorus asks the god of thunder Ukko to strike Kullervo with his hammer. This multiplicity of narrative roles reminds the ones of the choruses of the Ancient Greek tragedies. The chorus, often present on the stage, has visual roles too: for example, it catches and ties the young Kullervo when he is sold to the smith. The central role of the chorus makes the opera quite an atypical contemporary opera, which is quite complex at the musical level: there is space for very dramatic soprano's solos, reference to folk music and laments, parts remembering oratorios, the popular and jazzy song sung by the blind singer, the use of primitivistic devices with intervals, harmony and repetitions, and the almost comical and operetta-like dialogues of Tiera, the Hunter and two scoundrels that, in the final war against Unto, seem to be only interested in robbing money and drinking spirits (Desler 1997: 134–143). Another original element of the opera is the oneiric atmosphere: Unto and Kullervo have nightmares and premonitory dreams, and both have difficulties in discerning the difference between reality and the dreamworld. Their psychological insecurity leads to the "collapse of external reality" in the mind of human beings that are obsessed with homicidal and drives (Majava 1999: 171). The dissolution of the perception of the difference between dream and reality, and mental sanity and insanity, is a prominent topic in Paavo Haavikko's dramatic monologue *Kullervo* and in Sallinen's *Kullervo* (Desler 1997: 73–76).

A significant difference between the first production of 1992 and the last of 2014 is the stage and costume design. In the production of 2014, the open-air stage is very minimalistic and essential: the old walls of the Savonlinna's castle and the profiles of three simple houses, representing the exteriors or the interiors of the lodges of Unto, Kalervo and the smith's wife. The wall represents an ancient and legendary world, but the three houses are enigmatic: they could be old lodges in the forest or modern wood houses of the suburbs of a contemporary city. In the 2014's newspaper critics, the use of contemporary visual design has been noticed. The costumes are also temporally ambiguous: the coat, the trousers and boots of the smith's wife are quite modern; Kullervo wears contemporary black trousers and jacket, Kimmo and the Hunter wear nineteenth-century opera costumes and the chorus has simple Finnish peasants' clothes present in the Gallen-Kallela's realistic period. The visual design clearly underscores the universality and atemporality of Kullervo's legend: The story could happen in a remote past or today. The visual ambiguity suggests that new "Kullervos", young boys traumatized by war, unstable family relations, enslavement or exploitation, could become future murderers and terrorists. The opera underscores the importance of slavery: Kullervo has been branded with marks of the slaves that "burn and scorches" his soul, because he was not born a slave, but he was made one (Sallinen 1988: 7). In this sense, the opera transmits Cygnaeus' and Kivi's idea that slavery's humiliation is one of the keys to understanding Kullervo's attitude to violence. Thinking about his slave's condition, Kullervo is tempted to kill his friend Kimmo, who was born as a slave (Sallinen 1988: 7). Another element in common with the Cygnaeus' interpretation is the absence of reference to the incantations: in the *Kalevala*, Kullervo transformed the cattle into wolves and bears and sent them to slay Ilmarinen's wife. In the opera, the hunter tells the smith's wife that Kullervo was only watching the bears devouring her cattle and Kullervo kills the woman with a common knife (Sallinen 1988: 12, 16). Sallinen wrote the libretto in plain and understandable prose, simplifying the archaic features of *Kalevala*'s language and following his idea of making contemporary operas more popular and accessible. Sometimes, the chorus sings some lines that are quite close to the original texts of the *Kalevala*, but also in these cases Sallinen clearly edited and shortened the old poetic language of the epic poem. One relevant example is in the third scene when Kullervo finds his family in the wood, the mother accepted him, but the father refuses to recognize the son due to the fact that Kullervo confessed having killed the smith's wife. At this point, the chorus comments that Kullervo never "grew to wise dignity, for he had been brought up in crocked way" (Sallinen 1988: 25). The chorus referred to the end of Rune XXXVI of *Kalevala*, which was the summa of Lönnrot's interpretations on Kullervo's personality: the hero becomes a murderer due to the lack of proper education. However, the opera underscores that, alongside slavery and the bad education, Kullervo decided to follow the hate's path on several occasions. He could have accepted the erotic advances of the smith's wife, the love of her mother or Kimmo's sincere friendship. In the 2014 production, all these three characters wore a blue jacket that seems to express some hope or positive feeling (love or sexual attraction) in a stage and costume design marked by violent and contrastive colours: black, red, and white. However, the blue is also a colour symbolizing sadness (the blue feeling): Kimmo, the Smith's wife and the mother are the victim of the violent actions of the hero. In the *Kalevala*, the maiden of Pohjola is described as a very beautiful and attractive woman in the first part of the epic poem, but when she married the smith Ilmarinen, she seems to be transformed into a wicked mistress that lacks any charm and irritates Kullervo with the stone in the bread for pure cruelty. In Sallinen's opera, she remains a captivating but dangerous and manipulative lady (*Femme fatale*). She tries to seduce Kullervo but during the night, the hero is unsuccessful for his inexperience in sexual and love matters, and he is badly ridiculed and offended by her for this reason. The tragic stone in the bread seems to be a way to obtain his attention, as the smith's wife sensually sang: "There is a stone that's hidden in the bread I made you. / Consider that stone, it's granite like you hard, hard. / That soft bread is my body. / You must come to me now, I am waiting" (Sallinen 1988: 11). When the furious Kullervo returns to her with bad intentions, she tried again to seduce the hero, telling him that she could teach him the love's arts and she will lie to the husband, stating that Kullervo had tried to defend the cattle from wolves, and that he asked for mercy. The word "mercy" enrages the hero, which considers the proposal another humiliation. Here we find a trace of new contemporary psychoanalytic interpretations of Kullervo, who is not seen any more as a bold national hero, but a character with "a malignant naricissistic psychic disorder", who "felt the grandiose need to be a hero and he demand respect" (Majava 1999: 171). Rejected, the smith's wife teases the hero by repeating that he is only a slave and she will treat him as a slave, and Kullervo murdered her with his knife (Sallinen 1988: 15–16). A tense eroticism between Kullervo and the smith's wife was already present in Kivi's tragedy, but Sallinen elaborated it in a complex relation that dances between attraction and repulsion, softness and hardness of body and soul. The most poetic of the dramatic relations in the opera is the one between Kullervo and his mother, the only family member who fully recognizes the hero and is able to see the beauty in him: "There is so much of you I remember: beautiful you were as a child. Beautiful you are still" (Sallinen 1988: 23). Sallinen elaborated the character of Kimmo, which is very important in the whole opera. Kimmo is presented as an extremely loyal friend, he is the only optimistic character of the opera, but he is also very childish in believing that if Kullervo will find his family, he will solve all his problems and settle down in the forest with them. In Aleksis Kivi's *Kullervo*, Kimmo was not so pure: he has killed some persons too (Aho 2008: 109). In the production of 2014, when Kimmo discovers that Kullervo's family is still alive, he builds a horse toy to ride towards Kullervo (Sallinen 1988: 16–19). At the end of the Opera, Kimmo goes insane and sees Kullervo as Jesus, who bears the sins of the world on his shoulders (Sallinen 1988: 49). The extravagant comparison between Kullervo and Jesus is present also in the prologue, in which the chorus sings that Kullervo is ready to be crucified (Sallinen 1988: 2). The paradoxical analogy seems to tell that both Kullervo and Jesus are "victims" of a very rude society. The Christian references are not present in other versions of Kullervo, who is generally presented as a champion of violent and rude paganism. Sallinen seems to place Kullervo on the temporal borderline between paganism and Christian era, or at least a less violent society, as, at the end of the opera, Kullervo sings: "My fam'ly, all of my fam'ly did not even enrich this planet. Now a brighter, new, better one is needed" (Sallinen 1988: 47). The composer Kalevi Aho correctly noticed that one of the main problems of the opera is the fault (Aho 2009: 109): who is to blame for Kullervo's sins and violence? The family, the society or Kullervo himself? The opera suggests that the answer is not easy and it could be more than one. Sallinen tried to avoid composing an opera only based on hate and revenge. Some of the most brutal parts of the legend are not visually represented on the stage: the episode of the incestuous relationship with the sister is only sung by a blind singer, and the Unto's burning of the Kalervo's village is not represented. Sallinen's Kullervo is not a monolithic character: he suffers, has nightmares, and is attracted by the smith's wife, he feels sincere affection for her mother and Kimmo, and it is the desperation for the death of the mother and his friend, the last drop, which leads him to suicide. According to Aho, Sallinen's Kullervo has features remembering Dostoevsky's protagonists: even in the most terrible of the murderers, there is space for light and potential goodness (Aho 2009: 109). Sallinen's Kullervo has the possibility to choose love, but he always falls into the vertigo of violence and revenge.

8 Tero Saarinen's choreography for Sibelius' Kullervo: The wheel of violence of a universal Kullervo

The last artistic masterpiece about Kullervo has been the choreography by Tero Saarinen (1964 -) for the music of Jean Sibelius' *Kullervo*: it was staged in the Finnish National Opera and Ballet and it was one of the main events of Sibelius' jubilee year in 2015. The choreography covers all the movements of the symphonic poem and it has nearly 100 performers on stage, of which more than 60 are male singers of the Choir of the Finnish National Opera and Ballet and the Helsinki

Philharmonic Choir, and the rest are dancers and soloists. The orchestra of the Finnish National Opera and Ballet has been directed by Jukka-Pekka Saraste (1956–), one of the best interpreters of Sibelius' *Kullervo*. In the choreography, there are three soloist dancers (Kullervo, Kimmo, the sister) and two large groups of male and female dancers. In the first cast the soloist dancers were: Samuli Poutanen (Kullervo, Finnish National Ballet), Terhi Räsänen (sister, Finnish National Ballet) and David Scarantino (Kimmo, Tero Saarinen Company). In the second cast the soloist dancers were: Pekka Louhio (Kullervo, Tero Saarinen Company), Johanna Nuutinen (sister, Finnish National Ballet) and Johan Pakkanen (Kimmo, Finnish National Ballet). The soloist singers were Ville Rusanen (Kullervo) and Johanna Rusanen-Kartano (sister), both experts in these roles.

According to Saarinen, the fact that the soloist singers were siblings in real life brought a fascinating level of deepness to their interpretation and performance. A second production of the choreography was staged in 2017. Tero Saarinen is one of the most important Finnish contemporary dance choreographers and dancers; he is much respected at a national and international level (Jyrkkä 2020). Saarinen's *premiere* of *Kullervo* has been filmed and broadcast several times by the Finnish national TV channel YLE Teema. In 2020, during and after the COVID-19 lockdown, the whole film was freely viewable on the webpages of the Finnish National Opera and Ballet and the public web television YLE Areena. A large amount of national and international newspaper articles and critics covering Saarinen's *Kullervo* have been collected by the Tero Saarinen Company, however, scientific literature about Tero Saarinen's choreographies is still very limited (Piludu 2010; Scarantino 2019a; Butterworth and Sanders 2020). Recently, Hannele Jyrkkä has written a non-scientific but very interesting biographic book on Tero Saarinen's career and choreographies (Jyrkkä 2020). For the lack of scientific literature, I obtained the most relevant information about Saarinen's Kullervo by doing interviews with the choreographer himself and David Scarantino, one of the most skilled dancers of the Tero Saarinen Company, who interpreted Kimmo. Tero Saarinen's interpretation of Kullervo is far from being nationalistic:

> The principal themes that we may distil from the various versions include Kullervo's broken childhood, his identity problem, his emotional instability and his obsession to take revenge for a ruined life. These are universal themes: just consider Sophocles' Electra or Shakespeare's Hamlet. I do not see him as a specifically Finnish character. There have been and always will be stories like his wherever there is war. (Saarinen 2015: 34).

The connection between Kullervo and European drama and Hamlet is a relevant component of Kivi's *Kullervo*. However, Kivi's Kullervo was ugly and grotesque with the mark of slavery on his forehead. By contrast, Saarinen's Kullervo is a beautiful, energetic, charismatic hero, a kind of dangerous agitator. Saarinen's

Kullervo is not a victim of society but a complex figure: a potential and dangerous leader who fails, a stubborn hero deciding to go toward his doom and destruction. Saarinen considers that Kullervo could have the possibilities to solve his struggles in a better way, but he chooses to follow the "cycle of the revenge and destruction" (Ekroos 2015: 37).

An important starting point for Saarinen was finding connections between Kullervo's myth, Finnish history and the contemporary world. In 2012, Saarinen was impressed by the exhibition on the Finnish civil war (1918) in the Vapriikki Museum of Tampere. He remembered the personal experiences of his grandparents during the civil war and he started to reflect that the traumas of the civil wars are far from being resolved after three or four generations; this drama is the "circle of violence" relevant in his *Kullervo* choreography. In the myth, the trauma of the "war of the fathers" (Kalervo and Untamo) affects Kullervo from the beginning of his life. However, Saarinen stated that Kullervo's drama is far from being only Finnish: "His destiny is universal. In Syria there are Kullervos, and in Africa too. Narrow-minded Kullervos could born in any place ravaged by war" (Ekroos 2015: 37). According to Saarinen, the "contemporary Kullervos" struggle with social exclusion, unemployment and evident difficulties in finding their place in the world (Ekroos 2015: 37).

The dialogue between the archaic time of the myth and the contemporary world is stressed by the costume design by Erika Turunen and light and screen design by Mikki Kunttu. The stage has nothing to remember the Finnish national-romantic art or folklore: it is made by white screen lights showing geometric figures with symbolic meanings on a black background. The stage design is very contemporary and it resembles the geometrical abstractions of concrete art. The clothes of Kullervo are both modern and archaic: he wears futuristic silver trousers and jacket that shine with the stage light. However, part of the clothes reminds of a medieval chain mail, and the jacket is opened and shows the naked torso of the dancer, remembering the nakedness of Ancient Greek heroes. The temporal hybridism of clothes suggests that Kullervo is not only a hero of a distant past but also of the present. The silver is also connected to the coldness of Kullervo's personality and the doom of the hero: with silver, he will be able to corrupt the sister.

The "circle" is one of the key symbols of the whole choreography. At the beginning of the *Introduction*, a circular white light appears on the top of the stage and the male dancers run clockwise around Kullervo who, later, starts to run counterclockwise. The circular symbolism is connected with the "cycle of revenge": the hero falls several times in the spiral of brutality as the humans fall in the entrapping movements of the "wheel of violence" across history (Saarinen 2019). Significative is that Kullervo runs counter-clockwise: he is a contrarian, someone who does not follow social rules. He is a potential ruler but he is also ruled by his rage. Later, Kullervo dances at the centre of the stage, illuminated by a "spear" light, signifying that he is "crucified" or doomed from the beginning.

In the first two movements, the choreography does not strictly follow the main narrative or literary topic of Sibelius' *Kullervo* (the second movement was titled *Kullervo's Younghood*) but it focuses on the triangular relations between Kullervo, Kimmo and the sister. Kullervo repeats a movement of fundamental importance, called the "Kullervo's hand" by Saarinen: the hero slowly raises an elbow and tries to stretch the arm to the sky, while the other arm caresses the elbow, the torso and the waist. After that, the hero bends the legs doing a sort of exaggerated plie and seems to be pushed toward the ground by something very heavy (figure 5). Saarinen explains that this key movement (which is obsessively repeated with some variations by the hero, Kimmo, the sister, the groups of male and female dancers, and also the chorus and the soloist singers) is the resume of the whole of Kullervo's story (Saarinen 2019): the hero tries to reach glory (the ascensional heroic movement, figure 6) but he always fails and falls down, pushed by the weight of guilt (the heroic fall hubris). The ascending movement reminds also of the reaching of heavens or rapid growth of trees and forests (the heroic hope, the growth), and the fall a connection with the land, ground, the dirt, the mud (guilt, destruction and death). The movement is repeated by the other dancers (and also by the chorus and the soloist singers) because Kullervo's individual choices are followed by all the others and provoke their ruin (figure 7). Saarinen noticed the dramatic importance of the movement of the hands in traditional Asian dances and he often uses hand symbolism in his choreographies. The male dancers, a sort of "visual chorus" repeating Kullervo's gestures, are a collective extension of Kullervo's body and mind and they also represent Kullervo's blind followers in war (Saarinen 2019). Modern and contemporary dance have been defined in quite a semiotic way by the sociologist of dance, Helene Thomas, as a socially recognizable "encoded system" of body movements with peculiar stylistic and aesthetic qualities (Thomas 1995: 29). This definition fits quite well with Tero Saarinen's style, in which the movements are not purely abstract, but fulfilled with a web of symbolic meanings, forming a choreographic and visual language which includes a complex dialogue between dance, music, stage and light design.

The Kullervo's sister, who in the *Kalevala* seems to be the typical victim of fate, became a more complicated character in the choreography. She has a white, silver, and blue skirt (figure 6). The blue is connected with her doom: she will jump and drown into a river. The silver is related to Kullervo's silver that "corrupt" her. This colour, dominant in Kullervo's cloth (figure 5), signifies also the existence of a deep bond between the two: not only the brother-sister relation but also the common destiny (both will commit suicide, and the death of the sister breaks the fragile psychic balance of Kullervo). In the choreography, the sister is a solitary figure, she is lost in the forest, but she is also a pathfinder; someone searching for a way out. Like Kullervo, she chooses her path and destiny, deciding to abandon herself to the passion. She is also an opportunist as she is attracted by Kullervo's silver and richness. Like Kullervo, she is a potential leader and the female dancers are a social extension of her personality (Saarinen 2019).

Figure 5: Kullervo (Samuli Poutanen) falling on his knees, doing the descending part of the movement "Kullervo's hand". Tero Saarinen's choreography *Kullervo*, 2015.
Photo: Sakari Viika, Finnish National Opera and Ballet and Tero Saarinen Company.

Figure 6: Kullervo (Samuli Poutanen) and his sister (Terhi Räsänen) doing the ascending part of the movement "Kullervo's hand". Tero Saarinen's choreography *Kullervo*, 2015.
Photo: Sakari Viika, Finnish National Opera and Ballet and Tero Saarinen Company.

Figure 7: Kullervo (Pekka Louhio) and his sister (Johanna Nuutinen) doing the descending part of the movement "Kullervo's hand". Tero Saarinen's choreography *Kullervo*, 2015. Photo: Mikki Kunttu, Finnish National Opera and Ballet and Tero Saarinen Company.

Figure 8: Kimmo (David Scaratino) and Kullervo (Samuli Poutanen). Tero Saarinen's choreography *Kullervo*, 2015. Photo: Sakari Viika, Finnish National Opera and Ballet & Tero Saarinen Company.

Kimmo, present in Kivi's *Kullervo* and Sallinen's opera, but not in the *Kalevala*, is a fundamental character of the choreography and he represents a deep level of friendship and brotherhood. He has clothes of a bronze colour, a warmer metal than Kullervo's silver, and he is the most positive figure on the stage (figure 8). Kimmo is apparently a simple character, very sincere in his friendship: from the *Introduction*, he tries to help Kullervo in his ascensional movement.

Figure 9: The death of Kullervo (Samuli Poutanen). Tero Saarinen's choreography *Kullervo*, 2015. Photo: Sakari Viika, Finnish National Opera and Ballet and Tero Saarinen Company.

According to Saarinen, Kimmo is the positive counterpart of Kullervo, clarifying that there are love and friendship even in this violent story. Unlike Kullervo and the sister, Kimmo does not have any "social extensions" or followers in the group of dancers. There is no soloist singer representing Kimmo because he is not present in Sibelius' musical score. Kimmo passes through an elaborate process of dramatic changes: at the beginning, he is playful and fluid in the movements of legs and arms in many situations, he plays the role of Kullervo's helper and he also behaves as his protector, but, at the end, he becomes crazy and the movements of his body seem to be uncontrolled, disordered and uncoordinated (Scarantino 2019b). Finally, he dies and leaves the stage.

In the first and second movements (*Introduction* and *Kullervo's Younghood*), Kimmo and the sister interact on the stage and they fight for Kullervo's attention and love. However the communication between the members of the trio is problematic as they also dance without any eye contact: they are "together" but also "alone", there is attraction, competition, separation and repulsion among the trio. Sometimes, Kullervo, unable to express positive feelings, tries to dominate the more joyous and fluid Kimmo by pushing his head down. In some moments of the first part of the choreography, Kullervo tries to submit the sister too with possessive or aggressive movements.

By contrast, the sexual relation between Kullervo and the sister, which is represented in the third movement (*Kullervo and his Sister*), is very passionate: both Kullervo and the sister feel a real attraction, which was shown by choreographic means by the dancers on the stage. At the beginning of the choreography,

Kullervo is quite cold and rigid in his movements and he represents the classic and old model of Finnish masculinity: the real man who does not express any feeling or weakness in public. In the third movement, the sister takes off Kullervo's jacket and Kullervo starts to show his feelings, including the passion for the unknown maiden. From this moment on, Kullervo is not a monolithic hero; he is "interactive" in the seduction dance and completely desperate after the sister's and Kimmo's death. In this way, the sister plays a fundamental role: she is the "revealer" of the inner psychology of the hero (Saarinen 2019).

In the third movement, the "seduction" is shown by choreographic means by the soloist dancers and the "revelation of the identities" is sung by the soloist singers. The singers, the dancers and the majestic chorus are all present on the stage, interacting in many ways. When the sister and Kullervo sang the "The lament of the sister" and "the lament of Kullervo", the dancers stopped their dance: it is a moment of revelation and musical reflection. In this movement, two sisters appear on the stage: the dancer, younger, representing her before the trauma and the singer, older, representing her just after the traumatic revelation. There are two Kullervos too: the dancer and the singer. With this dramatic expedient, the sister and Kullervo are living their drama doubly; dancing and singing it (Saarinen 2019). Before the fourth movement, there is a short moment without any music, where all the dancers run with boots, making a sound resembling a military march. During the fourth movement (*Kullervo goes to war*), Kullervo dances as the military leader of a bloodthirsty crowd of dancers going to war against Untamo. At this moment, Kimmo returns on the stage, but his movements seem to be more and more jerky, disjointed and incoherent (figure 8): Kimmo loses his mind and dies. According to Saarinen, the relation between Kullervo and Kimmo is complex, based on a secret, and often unexpressed, "brotherhood's love": they share some secrets, both love and murder secrets, as Kimmo has killed a person in Kivi's drama (Saarinen 2019). Only when Kimmo dies and disappears from the stage, Kullervo understands the importance of his friend and the relevance of the deep affection of his "brother/friend". After the death of Kimmo, there is a moment of silence, where the crowd of immobile female dancers watch Kullervo. This moment represents the sorrow of all the mothers, wives, sisters and daughters that suffered during and after the war (Saarinen 2019).

The fifth movement (*Kullervo's Death*) is very dramatic. The crowd of dancer dances on a motorized rotating stage representing the endless circle of violence. Kullervo is dancing at the centre as a kind of "death's dance", illuminated by a stage light in a "V" shape representing the tip of a spear or the blade pending on the hero like a sword of Damocles. In the end, a violent flash of light illuminates the whole stage and the spectators: Kullervo dies in the luminosity (figure 9). The end of the choreography is like a fascinating and complex *"opera aperta/*

open work", leaving many answers open for the reflections of the viewer: I shall analyse the purposes and meanings of this death of Kullervo in the last and conclusive paragraph.

9 Conclusion: Kullervo as a myth transcending violence

Using the semiotic theory of the symbol, by Juri Lotman, for the study of this research topic, I could affirm that a powerful symbol or myth as Kullervo does not only belong to one synchronic section of a culture, but it always cuts across several sections vertically, becoming meaningful in different artistic eras for different reasons. The myth of Kullervo comes from the past and the pre-literal world of folklore, but it interacts with the cultural contexts of different generations of artists and it influences the future, having an impact on addressers who reflect in a transcendental sense on the meaning of the myth. The artists could react to several versions of the story by creating new and innovative interpretations of the myth that have an impact on the present and the future (Lotman 1990: 102–119). On the one hand, the story of Kullervo is transcendental by itself: being a myth, it happens in a mythical and indefinite time; the *illo tempore* of mythology. On the other hand, the relevance of Kullervo transcends the mythical time and the historical era of Finnish national-romantic era of *Kalevala* (19th Century): the myth is still important in Finnish culture at the end of the 20th century and also at the beginning of the 21st century. However, the changes in the cultural contexts and the artistic languages have produced a great variety of interpretations of the myth. The methods and theories of Eero Tarasti's Zemic model offer several theoretic frameworks to analyse the changes in the interpretations of Kullervo's story (Tarasti 2017, 2018: 9). All the categories and movements of the Zemic model are relevant in the artistic interpretations of Kullervo. The Zemic model is divided into two main parts: *Moi* (I, or Self) and *Soi* (the Others, the Society). *Moi* is divided in *Moi1* (the physical self) and *Moi2* (the psychological self) and *Soi* in *Soi1* (the social values) and *Soi2* (the rules, institutions, family and laws based on social values). *Moi1*, the physical and bodily level of the self, is extremely prominent in all Kullervo's stories as the hero has an exaggerated strength and he commits disasters and murders also because he has a heroic but tragic empowered body. The revenge is not only obtained thanks to his physical strength, as the Kullervo's knowledge of magic and incantation made his violence more destructive (Aleksis Kivi's and Gallen Kallela's interpretation). However, the bodily strength or magical powers do not explain why Kullervo has a horrible tendency to slaughter everybody around him or to cause the death of his relatives and friends. The mystery of Kullervo's violence is related to the realm of *Moi2*: the controversial and violent personality and psychology of Kullervo. All the Finnish artists and intellectuals, presented in this article, have tried to explain why Kullervo's personality evolved toward violence, grief, revenge, self-destruction and suicide. Their answers often tend to be related to the social levels. All the artists and intellectuals stressed that violence of Kullervo is related to the social problems of a "broken" society, where the basic social institutions (*Soi2* the rules, family and laws) are ravaged by war and each sort of brutality. The deprivation of this society is based on a set of violent values as the culture of vengeance, revenge and blood feud (*Soi1*: the social values). The reflections of the artists are based on these four factors but they lead to a transcendental level of reflection about the essence and the meaning of Kullervo's violence (Tarasti 2010: 63–73). As we have seen in this article, the "transcendental models of violence", elaborated by the Finnish artists, varies a lot. The reflections on Kullervo are transcendental on several levels: 1) they are reflections and models explaining the reason causing the explosion of Kullervo's violence, and 2) this model is often not used only to furnish an explanation for Kullervo's myth, but also as a more generic and theoretical tool to understand the causes of the violence present in the Finnish history or the contemporary world. In this sense, Kullervo transcended Finnishness too, becoming more and more international. The Kullervo of Cygnaeus and Gallen-Kallela was a hero related to the question of violence in Finnishness, but Sallinen's and Saarinen's Kullervos are more connected to the problem of social and psychological violence at an international or general level. The international success of the Kullervo of Sibelius and Sallinen – and of the version by Tolkien – has also provoked an internationalization of Kullervo's stories as they have foreign audiences and receivers too. The transcendental models offered by the Finnish artists are very different: 1) Lönnrot and Topelius explained that the wrong education and family values (*Soi2*, *Soi1*) influenced the violent personality of the hero (*Moi2*) and his bodily actions (*Moi1*). By contrast, Cygnaeus explained that it was the slavery and social humiliation (*Soi2*, *Soi1*), the keys to understanding why Kullervo rightly slaughtered his oppressor, the uncle Untamo. Sibelius and Saarinen worked on the problematic element of the incest with the sister (the breaking of the most important of the social rules and *Soi2*) as one of the main tragic events provoking the heroic fall of Kullervo. Ruining a basic social institution as a family (*Soi2*) provokes a tragic personal crisis (*Moi2*). Gallen-Kallela stresses the personal and psychological elements of Kullervo, which is a solitary figure in his paintings: the painter focuses on the moment when Kullervo chooses to take revenge (*Moi2*), and on the importance of his voice, incantation and sound (the horn), which are amplifications of the magic powers of the hero's mind and soul. Gallen-Kallela and Kivi even made the stubborn and enraged Kullervo a metaphor of the individualist and rebel artist who searches for new creative paths (*Moi2*). In 1918, Gallen-Kallela shifted from a heroic interpretation to a negative one, in which the story of the family wars between Kalervo and Untamo and Kullervo and Untamo are metaphors for the social trauma of the Finnish civil war, an event that broke social morality and values (*Soi1*). Kivi's, Gallen-Kallela's, Sallinen's, and Saarinen's interpretations of Kullervo are some the most elaborated and sophisticated ones because, alongside the social factors provoking Kullervo's violence, they shed light on the importance of the individual "tragic choice": Kullervo is not only a passive result of a brutal society or violent social values (*Soi2* and *Soi1*) but a conscious actor of violence (*Moi2*), someone who has interiorized the violence and decided to commit, several times, terrible atrocities. Kullervo is not only a prisoner of a violent social structure, but he is also a semiotic subject who makes decisions and actively interprets the world around him (Tarasti 2009: 101–132).

Sallinen's and Saarinen's interpretations are very complex because they contain several multilayered references to almost all the previous works on Kullervo, especially the ones by Kivi and Sibelius. The questions that emerge from the last artistic interpretations of Kullervo are not nationalistic, but philosophical, transcendental and existential ones; deep reflections on individual, social and moral choices. The main problem of Tero Saarinen's choreography is: "how it is possible to escape from the history's, the fathers' and wheel of violence?" (Saarinen 2019). Saarinen did not give an easy or clear answer to the question, but the events, at the end of his choreography, suggest that there are ways to flee from this path: "In Kullervo's death, I see the possibility of cleansing that will release Kullervo from his trauma and give just a little hope of breaking free from an endlessly repeating cycle." (Saarinen 2015: 37). At the end of Saarinen's *Kullervo*, the stage light invades the hall: the stage, the singers, the dancers and public are united, illuminated by the same flashing and cathartic light. The light is like a heroic apotheosis but also a shock, a moment of purifying dissolution and death. The light illuminates the spectators who generally are hidden in the dark; so the spectators are seeing the other spectators too: for a short moment, they are part of the stage universe and they have awareness of being inside the story too (Saarinen 2019, Scarantino 2019b). The light unites the past, the present and the future, the mythical fiction, the reality and the future choices and possibilities of viewers. The end of the choreography is an "*opera aperta*" or "open work" (Eco 1979: 47–67): what is coming next? The end – as the future – is unsure, "open". The end does not give a clear answer about the mythical past or a key to understand the original story of Kullervo in the folk culture. It offers a set of important existential questions: through the light, the spectator is united with the mythological story and he/she is a part of it, but his mind is oriented toward the present and the future. The open final puts the mind of the viewer in motion: he is invited to reflect on the meaning of the story, the music and the language of the dance and stage lights. The viewer thinks about the differences in Sibelius' and Saarinen's versions, pondering on the changes that happened in Finnish culture and society. These reflections influenced my scholarly motivation on the necessity to analyse the artistic interpretations of Kullervo and write an article for an international audience. In an indirect way, the reactive spectator of the choreography is invited to make his own existential choice for the future. He or she should reflect on his/her way of "being" in the world and his/her position in the society in the present and future: does he/she want to be as Kullervo or like the "fathers" and "forefathers" traumatized by wars? Does he/she want to be a victim of violence, a bloodthirsty avenger, a serial killer who decides to hate and be violent, creating more revengeful victims of violence? Does he/she want to be a follower of Kullervo like Kimmo or the crowd of dancers? Does he/she want to be a blind follower of some delirious violent warlord or dictator? Or does he/she want to be someone else; an independent spirit refusing to follow brute leaders and the circle of violence, revenge and rage? (Saarinen 2019) The choices for the future and all the possible answers are in the hands and the minds of the spectators, who are indeed semiotic subjects, and not passive receivers.

References

Aho, Kalevi. 2008. Kalevala ja suomalainen taidemusiikki [Kalevala and Finnish art music]. In Ulla Piela, Seppo Knuuttila & Pekka Laaksonen (eds.), *Kalevalan kulttuurihistoria* [Cultural history of Kalevala], 82–123. Helsinki: SKS.
Aho, Kalevi. 2009. The Kalevala and Finnish Music. *Journal of Finnish Studies* 13(2). 45–60.
Aho, Kalevi. 2014. The Kalevala and Finnish Music. In Vesa Matteo Piludu & Frog (eds.), *Kalevala: epica, magia, arte e musica / Kalevala: Epic Magic, Art and Music*, 583–616. Viterbo: VociFuoriScena.
Apo, Satu. 2014. Kansanrunon, Kalevalan ja Kiven Kullervot [Kullervo of Kivi, folk poetry and Kalevala]. In Aleksis Kivi, *Kullervo. Näytelmä viidessä näytöksessä* [Kullervo. A play in five acts], 164–199. Helsinki: SKS.
Bonsdorff, Anna-Maria von. 2009. Kalevalan inspiraatio – tyyli, kokonaistaideteos ja dekoraatio [Inspiration of Kalevala – style, total art work, and decoration]. In Riitta Ojanperä (ed.), *Kalevala kuvissa. 160 vuotta Kalevalan innoittamaa suomalaista taidetta* [Kalevala in pictures. 160 years of art inspited by Kalevala]. Helsinki: Ateneum taidemuseo / Valtion taidemuseo.
Butterworth, Jo & Lorna Sanders. 2020. Tero Saarinen. In Jo Butterworth & Lorna Sanders (eds.), *Fifty contemporary choreographers*, 235–240. London: Routledge.

Castrén, Mathias Alexander. 1853. M. A. Castréns föreläsningar i finsk mytologi [M. A. Castrén's lectures in Finnish mythology]. In Carl Gustav Borg (ed.), *Nordiska resor och forskningar af M.A. Castrén* [M. A. Castrén's nordic travels and studies]. Helsinki: SKS.

Castrén, Mathias Alexander. 2016 [1853]. *Luentoja suomalaisesta mytologiasta* [Lectures on Finnish mythology]. Trans. by Joonas Ahola, intr. by Joonas Ahola & Karina Lukin. Helsinki: Suomalaisen Kirjallisuuden Seura.

Dawn Goss, Glenda. 2003. A Backdrop for Young Sibelius: The Intellectual Genesis of the Kullervo Symphony. *19th Century Music* 27(1). 48–73.

Desler, Anne. 1997. *The tragedy of Isolation: Aulis Sallinen's Kullervo*. Helsinki: University of Helsinki, Faculty of Arts, Musicology. Unpublished licentiate dissertation.

Eco, Umberto. 1979. *The Role of the Reader*. Bloomington and London: Indiana University Press.

Ekroos, Anna-Leena. 2015. Minne menet, nyky-Kullervo? [Where are you going, modern Kullervo?] *Kulttuuri* 1/2015. 36–39.

Gallen-Kallela-Sirén, Janne. 2001a. *Minä palaan jalanjäljilleni. Akseli Gallen-Kallelan elämä ja taide* [Life and art of Akseli Gallen-Kallela]. Helsinki: Otava.

Gallen-Kallela-Sirén, Janne. 2001b. Akseli Gallénin Kalevala-taide [Art of Akseli Gallén-Kallela]. In Helena Sederholm (ed.), *Pinx. Maalaustaide Suomessa. Suuria Kertomuksia* [Pinx. Art of painting in Finland. Great narratives], 62–74. Porvoo: Weilin+Göös.

Franklin, Peter. 2001. Kullevo's Problem: Kullervo's Story. In Timothy L. Jackson & Veijo Murtomäki (eds.), *Sibelius Studies*, 61–75. Cambridge: Cambridge University Press.

Haavikko, Paavo. 1988 [1982]. *Kullervon tarina. Kullervo's story*. English trans. by Anselm Hollo. Helsinki: Art House.

Heiniö, Mikko. 1995. *Suomen musiikin historia 4. Aikamme Musiikki 1945–1993* [History of Finnish music. 4. Music of our times 1945–1993]. Porvoo – Helsinki: WSOY.

Hoeven, Adriaan van der . 2001. Kullervon kirous ja kosto [Kullervo's curse and vengeance]. In Helena Sederholm (ed.), *Pinx. Maalaustaide Suomessa. Suuria Kertomuksia* [Pinx. Art of painting in Finland. Great narratives], 48–55. Porvoo: Weilin+Göös.

Hoeven, Adriaan van der . 2012. The Making of Kullervo. In Cornelius Hasselblatt & Adriaan van der Hoeven (eds.), *Finno-Ugric Folklore, Myth and Cultural Identity. Proceedings of the Fifth International Symposium on Finno-Ugric Languages. University of Groningen, June 7–9, 21*, 73–93. Maastrict: Maastricht: Shaker. Studia Fenno-Ugrica Groningana 7.

Jyrkkä, Hannele. 2020. *Etsijä – Tero Saarisen tie nykytanssin huipulle* [Seeker – Tero Saarinen's way to the peak of modern dance]. Helsinki: Siltala.

Kambe, Satoru. 2005. *Jean Sibelius' Kullervo and Lemminkäinen. Form, Image and Musical Narrative*. (Acta Semiotica Fennica XXI, Approaches to Musical Semiotic 8). Imatra – Helsinki: International Semiotic Institute.

Kinnunen, Aarne. 1967. *Aleksis Kiven näytelmät. Analyysi ja tarkastelu ajan aatevirtausten valossa* [Plays of Aleksis Kivi. Analysis and study on the basis of the ideas of the epoch]. Porvoo-Helsinki: WSOY.

Kivi, Aleksis. 1991 [1870]. *Seven Brothers* (Seitsemän veljestä). New York: New Paltz, Finnish-American Translators Association.

Kivi, Aleksis. 1997. *Odes*. Selection and English trans. by Keith Bosley (ed.). Helsinki: SKS.

Kivi, Aleksis. 2014 (1864). *Kullervo. Näytelmä viidessä näytöksessä. Kriittinen editio*. Helsinki: SKS.

Konttinen, Riitta. 2001. *Sammon takojat. Nuoren Suomen taitelijat ja suomalaisuuden kuva*. [Forgers of Sampo. Young Finnish artists and the picture of finnishness]. Helsinki: Otava.

Krohn, Julius. 1885. *Suomen kirjallisuuden historia: Ensimmäinen osa: Kalevala* [History of Finnish literature. First part: Kalevala]. Helsinki: Weilin & Göös.
Kupiainen, Tarja. 2004. *Kertovan kansanrunouden nuori nainen ja nuori mies* [Young woman and young man in narrative folk poetry]. Helsinki: SKS.
Lotman, Juri. 1990. *Universe of the mind: a semiotic theory of culture*. London: Tauris.
Lönnrot, Elias. 1999 [1835]. *Kalevala*. New edition of the *Old Kalevala*. Helsinki: SKS.
Lönnrot, Elias. 2008 [1849]. *The Kalevala*. English trans. by John Martin Crawford (1888). Glouchester: Dodo Press.
Majava, Heikki. 1999. Ethnic identity in the light of an ancient myth: Psychoanalytic and semiotic interpretations of the Finnish Kullervo legend. In Eero Tarasti (ed.), *Snow, Forest, Silence: The Finnish Tradition of Semitics*, 162–174. (Acta Semiotica Fennica VII). Imatra – Bloomington: Indiana University Press, International Semiotic Institute.
Martin, Timo & Douglas Sivén. 1990. *Akseli Gallen-Kallela. Elämänkerrallinen rapsodia* [Akseli Gallen-Kallela. A Biographical rhapsody.] Porvoo: Weilin+Göös.
Nummi, Jyrki. 2014. Kullervo – Viisinäytöksen tragedia. In Aleksis Kivi. *Kullervo. Näytelmä viidessä näytöksessä*. Kriittinen editio. 164–199. Helsinki, SKS.
Parola, Aila. 1996. Suomi-Neito ja sotilas. Aulis Sallisen Kullervon suomalaisuus [Maiden of Finland and soldier. Finnishness of Aulis Sallinen's Kullervo]. *Musiikin Suunta* 3/1996: 7–11.
Pentikäinen, Johanna. 2004. *Rautaa, unta ja kultaa: Myytit ja myyttien käyttö Paavo Haavikon Kalevala-aiheisissa teoksissa* [Iron, dreams, and gold: Myth and its uses in Paavo Haavikko's works based on Kalevala]. Helsinki. SKS.
Piludu, Vesa Matteo. 2010. Danze simboliche dal folclore all'avanguardia. Le sacre du Printemps e il Petroushka da Stravinsky a Tero Saarinen. *Lexia*, 6/5. 255–273.
Piludu, Vesa Matteo. 2019. *The Forestland guests. Mythical Landscapes, Personhood, and Gender in the Finno-Karelian Bear Ceremonialism*. Helsinki: University of Helsinki, Unigrafia, E-thesis.
Saarinen, Tero. 2015. *Kullervo*. Program. Helsinki: Ooppera-Baletti.
Saarinen, Tero. 2019. Unpublished interview by Vesa Matteo Piludu. Helsinki.
Sallamaa, Kari. 2009. Kalevala sanataiteessa 1860–1935 [Kalevala in prose and poetry 1860–1935). In Ulla Piela, Seppo Knuuttila Pekka Laaksonen (eds.), *Kalevalan kulttuurihistoria* [Cultural history of Kalevala], 28–65. Helsinki: SKS.
Scarantino, David. 2019a. *Stepping Inside Yourself: The Body as a Vessel for the Movement of the Mind*. Unpublished research text. Helsinki: Theatre Academy: University of The Arts.
Scarantino, David. 2019b. Unpublished interview by Vesa Matteo Piludu. Helsinki.
Sihvo, Hannes. 2012. *Elävä kivi. Aleksis Kivi aikanansa* [Living stone. Aleksis Kivi in his time]. Helsinki: SKS.
Sallinen, Aulis. 1988. *Kullervo*. Finnish and English libretto. English trans. by Adam Pollock. London and Sevenoaks: Novello.
Tarasti, Eero. 1990. Näkökulmia Gallen-Kallelan Kullervon maalauksiin [Perspectives on Gallen-Kallela's Kullervo-paintings]. In Eero Tarasti (ed.), *Johdatusta Semiotiikkaan: Esseitä taiteen ja kulttuurin merkkijärjestelmistä* [Introducing semiotics. Essays on sign systems of art and culture], 170–178. Helsinki: Gaudeamus.
Tarasti, Eero. 1994. *Myytti ja Musiikki. Semioottinen tutkimus myytin estetiikasta* [Myth and music]. Helsinki: Gaudeamus.

Tarasti, Eero. 1999. Jean Sibelius as an icon of the Finns and others: An essay in post-colonial analysis. In Eero Tarasti (ed.), *Snow, Forest, Silence: The Finnish Tradition of Semiotics*, 221–247. (Acta Semiotica Fennica VII). Imatra – Bloomington: Indiana University Press, International Semiotic Institute.

Tarasti, Eero. 2001. An essay in post-colonial analysis: Sibelius as an icon of the Finns and others. In Timothy L. Jackson and Veijo Murtumäki (eds.), *Sibelius Studies*, 3–13. Cambridge: Cambridge University Press.

Tarasti, Eero. 2009. *Fondamenti di semiotica esistenziale*. Bari: Laterza.

Tarasti, Eero 2010. *I segni della musica. Che cosa ci dicono i suoni*. Milano: Ricordi LIM.

Tarasti, Eero 2012. *Myth and Music: A Semiotic Approach to the Aesthetics of Myth in Music especially that of Wagner, Sibelius and Stravinsky*. Berlin/Boston: De Gruyter, 2012.

Tarasti, Eero 2017. Mitä tapahtuu? Zemicin liikkeistä – eksistentiaalisemiotiikka [What happens? On the movements of Zemic – existential semiotics]. Synteesi (1–2). 50–80.

Tarasti, Eero. 2018. Anna Sahlsténin elämä ja tuotanto la belle époquen heijastuksena [Anna Sahlstén's life and works as a reflection of la belle époque]. Synteesi (3–4). 9–32.

Tawaststjerna, Erik. 1989. *Sibelius I*. Helsinki. Otava.

Tawaststjerna, Erik. 1997. *Sibelius*. Helsinki: Suuri Suomalainen Kirjakerho.

Tarkiainen, Viljo. 1951 (1915). *Aleksis Kivi. Elämä ja teokset* [Aleksis Kivi. Life and works]. Porvoo – Helsinki: WSOY.

Thomas, Ellen. 1995. *Dance, modernity and culture: explorations in the sociology of dance*. London and New York: Routledge.

Tolkien, John Ronald Reuel. 2015. [1914–1915]. *The Story of Kullervo*. London: HarperCollins.

Tolvanen, Jouko. 1952. *Carl Eneas Sjöstrand. Suomen uudemman kuvanveistotaiteen uranuurtaja* [Carl Eneas Sjöstrand. A progenitor of new Finnish sculpting]. Porvoo-Helsinki: WSOY.

Tristian Evans
Existential soundtracks: Analysing semiotic meanings in minimalist and post-minimal music

Abstract: This chapter examines existential meanings in film, theatre and televisual advertising contexts, in which the music employed is predominantly based on minimalist and post-minimal characteristics. A range of case studies will be presented, and the chapter initially applies Eero Tarasti's existential semiotic model to a car commercial that employs musical extracts from Michael Andrews's soundtrack to *Donnie Darko* (2001), before analysing the recontextualised use of Steve Reich's *Music for 18 Musicians* (1974–76) in a telecommunication commercial.

The chapter subsequently proceeds to examine the music of Philip Glass as employed in film and theatrical contexts, principally the soundtrack to Godfrey Reggio's *Naqoyqasi* (2002) and Glass's collaboration with Leonard Cohen on the theatrical song-cycle *Book of Longing* (2007). In the former case study, references to the work of Karl Jaspers among others will be made, while the study of *Book of Longing* posits the work in the context of negation and affirmation, both in relation to the text and music.

Finally, the soundtrack to the fantasy comic-book film *Watchmen* (2009) is discussed, which employs extracts from Glass's *Koyaanisqatsi* (1982); the chapter examines how the original meaning of the music is preserved, albeit partly, within its new context. In conclusion, a summary of some of the main features of the music is discussed in relation to the notion of existentialism and the cinematic, televisual and theatrical contexts in which the music is heard.

Keywords: Minimalism, existentialism, Philip Glass, film, cinema, theatre

Introduction

The documentary film director Errol Morris once noted that Philip Glass's music evokes a certain type of "existential dread",[1] thereby inherently remarking that his

---

[1] See Scott Hicks's 2007 documentary on Glass for Morris's quote. In his discussion on the *Fog of War* soundtrack, Glass also refers to "the ambience of existential dread" during an interview with Marc Savlov (see Savlov 2004: unpag.).

https://doi.org/10.1515/9783110789164-038

repetitive music can evoke a range of emotions and scenarios that include bleakness, impending doom, fear, awe and tension. We can offer examples of other instances whereby musical repetition has been employed to convey expressions of low-spirited emotion. Around a century and a half ago, Friedrich Nietzsche wrote his highly repetitive *Das "Fragment an sich"* ("The Fragment Itself") for piano (1871) – a piece that might justifiably be considered as being pre-minimalist.[2] Full of chromaticism, tension and resolution, with a strong descending chordal feature, this piece is to be played *"con malinconia"*, and due to a lack of closure at the end, it conveys a sense of endless despair. This brief analysis hints at the music's ability to create an affinity with existential feelings and conditions, but the question of why and how the music of other composers working in the area of minimalism, pre-minimalism and post-minimalism can interact with existentialism needs to be unpacked in greater detail. By drawing on specific case studies from the domains of film, theatre and also a selection of television commercials that employ subliminal marketing strategies, this chapter will seek to identify different manners in which existentialism relates to minimalism and post-minimalist music. In other words, how can such musical elements as tonality, form, texture, and instrumentation promote existential meanings, and how does they relate to humanism, freedom, identity and individuality – all of which might be described as some of the crucial aspects of existentialism?[3]

During the process of this investigation, a televised advertising campaign by the car manufacturer Ford will initially be discussed, which employs pre-existing music by Michael Andrews, originally written for the cult film *Donnie Darko* (2001). Taking into account Eero Tarasti's existential semiotic model as published in *Existential Semiotics* (2000), the narrative of the commercial will be traced, and by exploring its interaction with the music it will be argued that this particular example clearly represents an existential journey – one that initially passes through negation and subsequently affirmation in order to sell a particular product by means of a subliminal marketing strategy. Continuing in the area of marketing, a commercial by the telecommunications company Orange, which uses an extract out of Steve Reich's *Music for 18 Musicians* (1974–76) in a campaign entitled "I am" will subsequently be examined; aspects of musical and textual temporality in relation to the anti-dialectic will be brought to the forefront of this section's inquiry. Such matters will become further apparent in the second part

---

[2] As in the case of minimalist music, Nietzsche's piece is based on a tonal framework, however musical meaning is diluted "through the endless repetition of the fragment", as a process resulting in the notion of "active forgetting" (De Mul 1999: 129). Jeroen van Veen recorded this piece on his album *Nietzsche: Piano Music*, 2017.

[3] A concise introduction to existentialism is given in Flynn 2006.

of the chapter, which focuses on examples of Glass's music for film and theatre: the soundtracks to *Naqoyqatsi* (2002) and *Watchmen* (2009), and the theatrical song cycle *Book of Longing* (2007). In conclusion, a summary of common characteristics in post-minimal music demonstrating an affiliation with existentialism will be drawn.

1 *Donnie Darko* and "Desire"

In May 2007, Ford launched a new televised campaign to promote their "all-new" Mondeo by means of a television commercial entitled "Desire". According to the producers, "the advert challenges the viewer's perception of a typical car commercial, signalling that the arrival of the dynamic new Ford Mondeo will make car owners want their old and uninspiring cars to float away – literally".[4] In the commercial, the citizens of London are seen silently observing several cars floating in the sky, held up by balloons. Towards the conclusion, an individual observes a passing Mondeo, after which he decides to join the remainder of the population by discarding his own car in similar fashion. This individual seemingly becomes the principal subject in the unspoken narrative. The commercial ultimately ends with a panoramic shot of London with a mass of floating cars in the sky, before the textual captions "New Mondeo" and "Feel the Difference" appear. Such key words as "desire" and "feeling" form an integral part in the language of the advertising, as often common in marketing strategies; Robert Fink writes on the relationship between minimalism and consumer desire, quoting Georges Perec's epigraph that "enjoyment *[jouissance]* was confused with owning things" (Perec 1965: x. Quoted in Fink 2005: 99). Perhaps minimalist music's suitability in such a context might also be explained by the fact that, according to Robert Neveldine, the resulting effect of minimalist music as a reflection of post-modernism "can entail new ways of desiring and feeling" (Neveldine 1998: 102). It is therefore of great interest to note that these key words are employed in order to promote the Mondeo car – to the backdrop of Michael Andrews's music.[5]

Andrews represents a recent generation of composers who have taken onboard some characteristics of minimalism, and applied them to the sphere

---

[4] This is quoted from Ford's website after the advert was launched, however it is no longer available.
[5] Michael Andrews (b. 1959) is a New York based musician and composer. His soundtrack to *Donnie Darko* also includes a cover version of Tears for Fears's "Mad World", which as sung by Gary Jules proved to be a standalone pop hit in the United Kingdom during 2003.

of film and popular music hence gaining a high degree of commercial appeal. Andrews's use of a tonal framework, simple melody can be taken to represent the characteristics of post-minimalism, and equally reflecting the past by its reminiscence of the modal repetition found in the pre-minimalist style of Erik Satie.[6] The piece is largely formed out of a one-bar bass ostinato, accompanying a simple melody in the treble clef that is subsequently repeated in parallel octaves. Reminiscent of Satie's *Gymnopédies* for example, Andrews's "The Artifact and Living" also makes use of semitonal shifts in harmony, alluding to Philip Glass's style as heard in "Façades" from *Glassworks* (1982), for instance.

Some considerations of the music's characteristics from an aesthetic perspective leads to the observation that the grounded stasis of the ostinato, the textural simplicity of the melodic line as performed on a solo piano, and the generally colourless and muted *timbre* used, evoke a sense of the mundane and one-dimensional, which might be taken to represent both the old cars that the people are so desperate to dispose of, and also the greyness of the urban landscape. By Fink's argument, the use of ostinato as heard in the commercial can be taken to represent everyday life: "as a cultural practice, this excess of repetition is inseparable from the colourful repetitive excess of postindustrial, mass-mediated consumer society" (Fink 2005: x). Indeed, the advert represents a world overpopulated with mediocre cars.

Moreover, the harmonies employed in this advert, comprising densely packed B minor and B-flat major triads alternating in the bass register, certainly sound in contrast to the airborne cars in the sky. The music evokes a rather ominous if supernatural ambience, suitably reflecting the oddity of the scenario as evident in the onlookers' perplexed facial expressions – how can a few helium balloons alone lift such a heavy object as a car? Andrews's music subsequently provides a subtle lifting from the trappings of ordinariness. In the one minute version of the commercial, a change in musical detail coincides with the point at which the principal character decides to join his neighbours in disposing of his old car (and to replace it with a Mondeo after seeing the stylish new model being driven on the road). There is almost a warm sense of relief at this point, and the principal character seems to be admiring the new car. The onset of a new G minor triad in the treble part, followed by a rising melodic line implying the relative major tonality of B-flat major, contributes towards a glimmer of light in the commercial's conclusion (though this is short-lived, as it returns to the minor key right at the end of the extract). We also hear a colouristic contrast, due to the introduction of synthesised strings at this point. These musical changes seemingly interact with the

---

[6] Further discussions on the characteristics of post-minimalism may be found in Evans 2016.

visual narrative of the commercial, in which the principal character's thoughts are implied, i.e. his decision to replace his car with a new model. The coincidence of a shift in tonality with the structure of the visual narrative does not occur in the extended (two and a half minute) version of the commercial, however.

Eero Tarasti, in his chapter on analysing commercials and other forms of advertising explains how "[a]dvertising operates with signs intended to evoke certain kinds of emotion" (Tarasti 2000: 192). The music in this Ford Mondeo commercial certainly plays a role in the overall mood of the advertising strategy – firstly by juxtaposing a sense of the mundane with uneasiness, which is followed by a subtle sense of elation when the new Mondeo passes on the road. Usually, a commercial's role is to "penetrate into the *monde naturel*, the world of natural, mostly unconscious semiosis" (Tarasti 2000: 192). What makes the Mondeo commercial stand out, perhaps, is its uncanniness, therefore seemingly replacing the portrayal of a "true story" which is often the strategy used by advertisers as Tarasti notes (Tarasti 2000: 193).

1.1 An existential process?

Further to the a-teleological nature of the music's repetitive characteristics, in their representation of a consumerist drive, other reasons for using Andrews's film music in the Mondeo commercial can be sought after; an outline of the extra-musical context of the music might provide some additional answers. As stated earlier, the music in the commercial was composed originally for the film *Donny Darko*, which is widely regarded within popular culture as an existential film. Its creator, Richard Kelly, cites existential authors including Camus, Dostoyevsky and Kafka as some of the formative influences of his high-school literary education, which might well have had an impact on his subsequent career as a screenwriter (Kelly 2003: xiv).

Donnie Darko's existentialism manifests by its focus on a young individual's enquiry into human existence within an "idealised suburban" yet surreal landscape (Kelly 2003: xxiii). Such surrealism – correlating with the Freudian sense of the uncanny, described by Nicholas Royle as "the peculiar commingling of the familiar and the unfamiliar" (Royle 2003: 1) – is reinforced by Richard Kelly's unconventional use of narrative in the creation of the film, resulting in its "perplexingly complex" construction (Kelly 2003: vii). Anna Powell's application of Deleuze's existential philosophies to her reading of the film reveals how the film "maps out '*undecidable alternatives* between circles of past, *inextricable differences* between peaks of present'" (Deleuze 1989: 105 in Powell 2007: 161). In other words, the film contains a mixture of distorted timelines that provoke and induce altered states of mind that are conveyed to the perceiver of the film. In fact, the scene in which "The Artifact and Living" is heard illustrates a crucial element of surrealism in the film, displaying the aftermath of a jet engine that has mysteriously crashed into a house and suspended in the air by a crane.

The existential attributes of the *Donnie Darko* narrative appear to be transferred to the Ford Mondeo commercial both in terms of their music and visual dimensions. The focus on an individual's place within society is apparent by the commercial's portrayal of the principal subject deciding to discard of his own car amid the mundane (yet bizarre) environment that he is found within. In musical terms, the soloistic element of Andrews's piece (in the treble clef) arguably represents this individuality, while the chromaticism and unsettling shifts in harmonic content reflects the commercial's surreal ambience. In fact, this individual identity might be associated with an existential process that can be identified in the commercial's musical and visual narrative. Such a journey can be examined in relation to Tarasti's writings on the "paths of existential semiotics", which offers an effective model that maps out a change in the existence of a person (or subject) based on their negative and positive subjective experiences, as reproduced in Figure 1 (Tarasti 2000: 10–11).

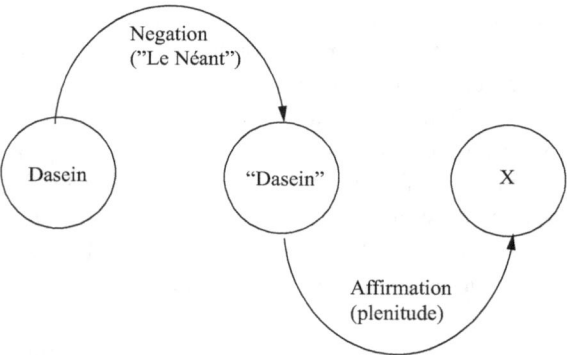

Figure 1: Reproduction of Tarasti's "paths of existential semiotics" model.

From the outset of the commercial, the viewer (and later also the principal subject) "finds himself amidst the objective signs", which Tarasti would call this as being in a state of *Dasein*, in existence (Tarasti 2000: 11). He is unable to ascertain the meaning of the objects that surround him, and later "recognises the emptiness or nothingness surrounding the existence from which he has come" (Tarasti 2000: 11). One could take this to mean the mundane aspect of his urban environment (supported by the bleak and surreal aspect of the harmonies employed), and is therefore in the state of "nothingness" or "negation". The appearance of the main individual in the commercial represents the point at which the subject returns to a state of existence. The subject at this point is "as it were, reborn", (the melody is also repeated in octaves at this point), and later enters the "affirmation" stage that "radiates a new kind of signification also to the subject dwelling in it" (Tarasti 2000: 11). This "new kind of signification" represents the point at which the viewer observes the commercial's principal character deciding to discard of his own car. In musical terms, Andrews's music represents this point of "affirmation" by the addition of a G minor triad and a hint of the relative major key in the melodic line – the positive change in tonality here ostensibly supports the progression of the existential process depicted in the visual narrative.

Examining this particular commercial in relation to Tarasti's model suggests how the application of a semiotic framework to a re-contextualised piece of film music reveals an existential meaning that was also integrated within the original context of the film. By studying the music in relation to its origin, one might conclude that the film and its music had possibly influenced the creators of the commercial during its production. Such a finding confirms the potency of music as a carrier of meaning – and by mapping out the existential narrative of the commercial, a shift from a bleak aesthetic of (sur)realism to a more uplifted state of being has apparently taken place. The uncertainty of the floating cars (coupled with the semitonal shifts in the soundtrack) is replaced towards the end of the commercial by a brief assurance of major tonality. As a result, the interplay between Andrews's music and the visual narrative offers meaning unequalled by other forms of music; quotations out of a pre-existing opera, for instance, would not provide this existential meaning, or a feeling of unease. In fact, this particular commercial had also been released with an alternative soundtrack, namely an extract from Delibes's "Flower Duet" out of the opera *Lakmé*. Its resulting effect in this version implied lightness and the vocal agility resonated with the floating balloons, as opposed to the uncanny aspects apparent in conjunction with Andrews's music.

2 Orange's "I am" commercial

We can conclude that the Ford Mondeo commercial demonstrated an existential journey, and a clear affinity with the aesthetic and storyline of the music's original context, i.e. *Donnie Darko*. An interaction between musical and visual temporality assumes an even more prominent position in a campaign by the telecommunications company Orange. In 2008, the company rolled out a series of television and billboard adverts entitled "I am" – one of which featured the Scottish cyclist Mark Beaumont, who holds the Guinness world record for cycling around the world. The short version of the televised commercial (which was accompanied by a longer ten-minute documentary film) is centred around Beaumont who is seen talks about his life experiences whilst pedalling a stationary bicycle, generating enough electricity to power the video walls surrounding him with home-cinema footage recalling his cycling experiences to date.

The commercial's message is subliminal, as it does not directly refer to the brand's products or services at any point. Beaumont attributes his success to the support that he gained by family, friends and everyone along the way (non-diegetically stating at the end of the commercial: "I am who I am because of everyone"). His message does not display a particularly close relation to the commercial's selling of Orange products or services. Whilst cycling on the spot, we hear extracts from Steve Reich's instrumental work for the concert hall, *Music for 18 Musicians* as a backdrop: equally so, the abstract nature of Reich's music (i.e. the lack of a descriptive title or a performance context outside of the concert hall such as film or theatre) seemingly offers no overt connection to the Orange commercial's subject matter. In this respect, the marketing strategy is sophisticated; such sophistication corresponds with Reich's music, this being an example of the high-minimalist music written during the mid-1970s.[7] In comparison with his contemporaries such as Glass, Adams and Nyman, Reich's music is widely regarded as being a more intellectually sophisticated form of minimalism; perhaps some of the reasons for this assumption lies with the fact that his music is less associated with mainstream contexts than others.

While the commercial and music are equally similar by their abstract nature, other affinities may be discovered in uses of minimalist design and approach towards time. The geometric layout of the commercial's set, where Beaumont is in the centre of four video walls arranged in the form of a square, shows a degree of compatibility with the minimalist aesthetic. Further symmetries between the music in the commercial and its visual dimension may be observed in the combination of motion and stasis – the overall stasis of the bicycle versus the movements of the wheels and the moving images – audibly interact with the temporal aspect of Reich's music. In teleological terms, the music conveys a sense of motion through repetition, however avoids any sense of goal-oriented direction, or resolution – an example of "non-directed linear time" in Jonathan Kramer's temporal terms (Kramer 1988: 20, 46–50).

---

[7] Interestingly enough, Orange had also employed another piece of minimalist music (namely Glass's *Einstein on the Beach*) in a campaign entitled "City Skyline" during 2002.

The mysterious and unsettling character of the music in the Ford Mondeo commercial certainly evoked what Errol Morris would describe as a sense of "existential dread". However Reich's music in the Orange commercial arguably does not. The pulsating rhythms and undulating chord structures are full of vitality, and there is a clear sense of drive that is compatible with the cyclist's recounting of his life's journey. Nevertheless, certain reports of listeners' perceptions of *Music for 18 Musicians* soon after it was composed reveal certain viewpoints that are indeed seemingly compatible with the existentialism. Robert Fink refers to Alan Rich, music critic for the *New York Magazine*, who described Reich's work as being "'extremely hypnotic' (as we might expect), but he also reported a quite different sensation as the piece developed, 'something that, when heard in the proper spirit can churn up the gut – *very* slowly, but with terrifying control'" (Rich 1978: 97. Quoted in Fink 2005: 41). Rich's subjective experience as listener here, describing the overwhelming impact of the music suggests that it did indeed evoke an emotion often related with the existential condition.

In relation to the performance techniques employed in *Music for 18 Musicians,* Keith Potter refers to the effect that "Reich calls 'the rhythm of the human breath'" (Reich 1978: unpag. Quoted in Potter 2000: 232–233) i.e. the performance technique employed whereby "the notes of a chord are repeated as an insistent pulse, their duration controlled only by the length for which each performer's breath may comfortably be sustained" (Potter 2000: 233). From a performance perspective, we can see a very human element being expressed in the music. This resonates with the "I am" theme of the Orange commercial in which the notion of the self is clearly articulated in Mark Beaumont's spoken narrative. And if consideration is given to whether or not the commercial offers an overall dialectical or an anti-dialectical narrative (with the latter case suggesting an allusion to an existential process due to the importance of an individual identity), then the lack of resolution in the music would indeed suggest an affinity with the anti-dialectic.

While Beaumont's narrative itself offers a sense of conclusion (the final sentence resolves with "I am who I am because of everyone"), the overall meaning of the commercial – that is, how Beaumont's spoken narrative relates to the whole purpose of the advertising campaign – displays a lack of clear resolution (as in the use of Reich's music, in which conventional tonal cadences are not employed). The focus in the cyclist's life story, his personal achievements, and the emphasis on stating who he is and what he does, all offer a relation to a thought-process based on existential and humanistic principles.[8] Beaumont's achievements rep-

---

[8] In this respect, Descartes's famous observation "*Cogito, ergo sum*" resonates with the subjective thinking and a sense of identity portrayed in the commercial's verbal narrative.

resents humanity's efforts to succeed within society – such efforts were equally apparent in Godfrey Reggio's Qatsi trilogy – the final instalment of which, *Naqoyqatsi*, will be examined in the next part of this chapter in relation to Philip Glass's soundtrack to the film.

3 Existentialism in film music and theatre

The validity of the claim that the existential movement, or any existential though-processes influenced Glass's music needs to be addressed in greater detail at this point. Whether or not Glass was particularly well read in the theories of Sartre, or such predecessors as Nietzsche, Heidegger and Jaspers is not well-known,[9] however in his memoirs, *Words Without Music*, he alluded to his familiarity with the existentialist during his period in Paris (Glass 2015: 122). The work of Sartre and Camus failed to leave a positive impression on him, however, as he considered their writings to be "nihilistic and oddly narcissistic" (Glass 2015: 123). The main issue, it seems is that the existential frame of mind was seemingly incompatible with the spirit of the younger American generation in the years that followed World War II: "Their books struck me as full of self-pity and despair at the meanness of their lives and their inability to find value therein, and my generation was impatient with all that" (Glass 2015: 123). In contrast, however, and as articulated in his memoirs and in other literature, Glass's association with dramatists Samuel Beckett and Bertolt Brecht, and the Beat generation writers Allen Ginsberg, William Burroughs and Leonard Cohen is however certainly more affirmative.[10] These individuals may be regarded as being particularly influential in the course of the formative stages of his career, in Paris especially, where he studied during the mid-1960s as a Fulbright scholar. In fact, the Beat writers often travelled to Paris, where they resided at the so-called "Beat Hotel" in the Latin

---

9 In comparison, Reich's knowledge of Wittgenstein's theories (which also relate to existentialism) is generally better documented than Glass's readings of philosophy (see for instance Reich 2002: 191–3).

10 Jennie Skerl defines the Beat generation as "an avant-garde arts movement and bohemian subculture that led an underground existence in the 1940s and early 1950s, gaining public recognition in the late 1950s" (Skerl 2004: 1). The Beats "fashioned a role as poet-prophets who sought a spiritual alternative to the relentless materialist drive of industrial capitalism" (Skerl 2004: 2). An example of Glass's connection with the movement is evident by his collaboration with Allen Ginsberg, whose texts (including the poem "Howl") are employed in *Hydrogen Jukebox* (1990). Also, he took part in a documentary on the Beats entitled *The Source* (1996), which also features extracts out of his *Hydrogen Jukebox* and "Metamorphosis 2".

Quarter of the city, and although it is claimed that they did not cross paths with Sartre, it is undoubted that Paris was simultaneously a hotbed of existential influences and Beat activity during this time. Barry Miles comments that even though the Beats and the existential writers (particularly Sartre, Camus and Beckett) were living in close proximity to each other, the Beats "were never interested in the existentialists and did not read their books" (Miles 2001: 60).[11] Nevertheless, resemblances inasmuch as both groups promoted individuality and freedom of thought within a Bohemian mindset are in no doubt – this proximity is observed in Pete Edler's comment that "unlike existentialism, which grew out of Sartre's writings, to encourage new lifestyles, beat was the *result* of a new lifestyle, a word that *defined* a lifestyle rather than creating it" (Edler 2006: unpag.).

Glass's experiences in Paris at this time can therefore be perceived as mediations between existential and Beat influences,[12] although his period in the Gallic city during the mid-1960s was not his first. In 1954, Glass had gone on an expedition that led to him becoming increasingly familiar with the works of another existentialist, Jean Cocteau.[13] His visit during the mid-1960s however resulted in a submersion within the subversive existential counter-culture. In fact, Glass's interest in Beckett's work preceded his visit to Europe although it was during these years that these interests were crystallised through his attendance at various performances in Paris's theatres (Bryden 1998: 191), including the *Théâtre Odéon* and the *Théâtre Nationale Populaire*, which often performed the works of Beckett, Genet and Brecht (Glass 1987: 4–5). In contrast to the Beat writers, whom he knew personally, Glass had not met Beckett in person, only through other individuals – David Warrilow and Fred Neumann – who were active in Paris during this period (Bryden 1998: 193). Nevertheless, from 1965 onwards, an indirect collaboration took place between Glass and Beckett, starting with the Mabou Mines group's staging of Beckett's *Play*. Glass's music for *Play*, scored for soprano saxophones performing in conjunction with pre-recorded material,[14] demonstrates the use of similar "cut-up" techniques to those developed by William Burroughs (Zurbrugg 1999: 145).[15]

---

11 It is interesting to note, however, that one of the speakers in *The Source* documentary noted that Dostoyevsky's *Notes on Underground* had a considerable impact on the writers, which reinforces the argument for interrelating existential elements with the movement.
12 For more details on the Beat writers' residency at the Hotel, see Miles 2001.
13 Interview with Jonathan Cott, Liner notes to *La Belle et La Bête*. Nonesuch 79347 (1995).
14 Reich was also combining live instrumentation with taped material around this time, for instance *Violin Phase* (1967) (see Reich 2002: 26).
15 This "non-narrative literary form" associated all of the Beat writers (Bryden 1998: 191). Beckett was initially unsure of the use of music in his works, and though of it as "an intrusion" (Bryden 1998: 193).

But why did these approaches appeal to Glass, and did such associations between existential literature and music manifest in his work? Although Glass did not write any music for Beckett's *Waiting for Godot* (1948–1949), this work demonstrates a close conceptual proximity between both dramatist and composer. Edith Kern observes how the characters in the play are disengaged from the society that they placed within (Kern 1954: 44). Moreover, *Godot* represents a literary work that has no real action, instead focusing on persona and psychological dimensions (Kern 1954: 41). Beckett's immaterial philosophy was further demonstrated in the fact that he was not "concerned about the appearance of things and whether they show themselves in their truth or in distortion when man's intelligence sheds light upon them" (Kern 1954: 41). Instead, his works demonstrates "the conviction of the absurdity and confusion of the universe" (Kern 1954: 47). And it is this crucial element that forms the basis for Reggio and Glass's Qatsi trilogy, particularly *Naqoyqatsi* (Life as War), which will shortly be discussed.

For this examination, the modernist premises of Karl Jaspers as found in *Man in the Modern Age* (1933) and José Ortega y Gasset's *The Revolt of the Masses* (1932) are mainly drawn upon. As will become apparent, both treatises are relevant to the society documented in Reggio's film, even though they form a critique of a *modernist* society's dependence on technology. Reggio's assemblage of moving images in *Naqoyqatsi* again serves a similar critical purpose, albeit as a post-industrial response: the work is, as Bruno Lessard writes, "a commentary on digital technology and the cult of the computer" (Lessard 2009: 503fn.).

While the notion of war forms a central message in the film, and brought to the forefront of the scenes in which Glass's music for the scenes entitled "Naqoyqatsi", "Intensive Time" and "Point Blank" are heard, Reggio posits such conflict within a wider sociological context. Attention is often drawn towards several key symbols and themes of relevance to our contemporary world. In the area of science, images of x-ray technology, genetic experimentation and the cloning of Dolly the sheep emerges (also found in Reich's multimedia opera *Three Tales* premiered in 2002), while other key themes include industrialisation and commerce in addition to popular culture and sporting activities. Furthermore, Reggio incorporates religious icons and company logos, footage of explorations in space, the natural world and of course images of conflict are again often apparent, as are the humanistic element evinced in the focus on facial gestures. All of these elements amalgamate to form potent visual responses to the contemporary digitized and globalized world that we inhabit.

These images are all assembled in a way that effectively highlights the dialectic between human achievement and destruction, although Reggio's assemblage does not entail a single clear narrative – the film can be regarded as being multiply narrative or even anti-narrative in some respects, inherently embodying the post-modern condition identified by Lyotard as "a state in which no one believes in grand stories or master narratives" (Tarasti 1994: 285). Reggio's overall message, according to himself, is

> not the effect of technology on society, on economics, on religion, on war, on culture, etc., on art. It's that everything now is existing in technology as the new host of life. It's the price we pay for the pursuit of our technological happiness that is what warfare is. It's way beyond the battlefield. It's total war. It's war as ordinary daily life.[16]

Glass's soundtrack features the textures of a solo cello as performed by Yo-Yo Ma, an intoning soprano vocalist and the overdubbing of the sound of a heartbeat, all of which contribute towards the depiction of a humanistic theme that is central to the music. In this respect, Glass approximates Reggio's focus on the influence of war on society's population. The soloistic textures employed – showcased by lyrical passages on cello or the voice – are heard in conjunction as footage documenting the human achievement of space exploration or the breaking of the sound barrier on land. On the other hand, the use of ostinato in the accompaniment, often on strings, creates textural intensification and essentially embodies a collective society, or the masses, as often illustrated in Reggio's selection of visual crowds.

3.1 Applying Jaspers's philosophy

Karl Jaspers's philosophy posits the recognition of a human entity as part of a mass society but also holds onto an individuality – "each individual continues to say to himself: 'What another has, I also want; what another can do, I also can do'" (Jaspers 1951: 42).[17] This statement also resounds with Baudrillard's observation in his article "The System of Objects", that in a commercial world "each individual feels unique while resembling everyone else" (Baudrillard 1968: 409). Both theories highlight a desire for both material gain and achievement – a desire that is well represented in *Naqoyqatsi*'s frequent reference to advertising material and mankind's advancement in space exploration, in bio-medical science and sport. As an example of individuality, one can instantly compare this to the expression of solitude in the music heard during "Vivid Unknown". This scene represents an individual's achievement, for instance by breaking the speed barrier or ventur-

---

16 This quotation is a transcript of Reggio's commentary in a behind the scenes featurette on the DVD. See *Naqoyqatsi*, 2002.
17 The efficacy of minimalism for advertising will further be explored in this thesis's conclusions.

ing into space. In this respect, the meandering nature of the solo melodic line is clearly associated with the scene's subject matter that gives a picture of an individual's achievement in one form or another.

On the other hand, such a scene as "Massman" represents civilisation, or a multitude of people in society. By this scene's title, one is reminded of Jaspers's view on the notion of a "massman", which features heavily in *Man in the Modern Age*, further to José Ortega's *The Revolt of the Masses*, in which it is defined as "a multitude of 'the average man'" (Ortega 1950: 8). In *Naqoyqatsi*, the company of swimmers almost at the outset of the scene would indeed represent a "mass

Phenomenon" in Jaspers's mind – the display of man's competitive streak and his "self-preservative impulse" (Jaspers 1951: 67). In musical terms, Glass's three-against-two figurations draws a parallel with the pace of the sea waves and the swimmers, thereby demonstrating a musico-visual kineticism. Based around the key of F melodic minor, Glass's melodic lines in the upper treble voice and the bass line progress in contrary motion, causing dissonances in the use of extended sevenths and minor second intervals (between *e*-natural and *d*-natural, and between *d*-natural and *e*-flat for instance). The overall contour of the upper and lower voices undulates, which can be regarded as the musical equivalent of the natural ebb and flow of the sea.

3.2 The dialectic of progress?

While the melodic contours heard in "Massman" evinces a certain degree of extra-musical meaning, evoking the contour and motion of sea waves and the group of swimmers, other scenes in the film are, not surprisingly, heavily engaged with technology. The development of technology is often discussed in social commentaries, being a subject featuring in both Jaspers and Ortega's writings. Needless to say, however, the technology explored in *Naqoyqatsi*'s digital context, has advanced greatly since both authors' periods of writing. Nevertheless, in his introduction to Sartre's *Existentialism and Humanism*, Philip Mairet notes that Jaspers's *Man in the Modern Age* is "mainly a powerful indictment of the progress of technological civilisation, which he regards as a social disease" (Sartre 1973: 11). The multifaceted nature of this observation is often illustrated in Reggio's film, which essentially embodies Mairet's understanding of Jaspers's views: "The surrender of man's thinking to rationalism and of his artifice to technics have consequences which console man with the feeling that he is progression, but make him neglect or deny fundamental forces of his inner life which are then turned into forces of destruction" (Sartre 1973: 11).[18]

Mairet's statement succinctly articulates the struggle between mankind's achievement and failures, or a dialectical battle between the positive and negative aspects of human civilisation and the natural world. A similar stance is also taken in Ortega's seminal *Revolt of the Masses*:

> The rebellion of the masses may, in fact be the transition to some new, unexampled organisation of humanity, but it may also be a catastrophe of human destiny. There is no reason to deny the reality of progress, but there is to correct the notion that believes this progress secure. It is more in accordance with facts to hold that there is no certain progress, no evolution, without the threat of "involution," of retrogression. (Ortega 1950: 56)

Ortega's commentary further reinforces some of the ideas formed in the visual narrative of *Naqoyqatsi*, particularly those that display mankind's advances in science and medicine, for instance, yet at the same time demonstrating the destructive effect of nuclear development and social rebellion. These visual representations are confirmed by Fredric Jameson's placement of Ortega's writings within Heideggerian ideology – an ideology that "expresses a horror of the new industrial city with its new working and white-collar classes, its mass culture and its public sphere" (Jameson 2009: 426).

Glass's "Massman" shares a close kinetic relationship between music and subject matter, as the musical flow is consistent with the visual pace of society as depicted in Reggio's visual material. In other instances it ostensibly interacts with the colouristic characteristics of a scene. In "New World" and "Old World" (note how these titles reveal the dichotomy between old and new that is central to the film), Reggio employs idiosyncratic colour effects, whereby the earth is blue and the sky is orange for instance. This correlates with Glass's scoring of harmonics on cello that enhance the otherworldly, ethereal ambience of the scene. And if one reads further into this musico-visual association, one might argue that both music and visual narratives represent the expression of a natural world affected, or even spoiled – by technological advances.

Matters relating to existentialism converge from the perspective of humanity's development and a struggle to succeed in *Naqoyqatsi*, with the individual amongst the masses represented musically by the cello as the singular voice driving the work onwards amid the characteristic texture of arpeggio figures. Glass's collaboration with Leonard Cohen on *Book of Longing* on the other hand represents a more personal, even introverted, exploration of an individual psyche.

---

18 In Jaspers's own words, "the mass-order brings into being a universal life-apparatus which proves destructive to the world of a truly human life" (Jaspers 1951: 44).

4 Book of Longing

Naqoyqatsi looks towards the future, while *Book of Longing* looks back at the past in a similar manner to the nineteenth-century poets, replicating a similar intensity of emotion and yearning belonging to the Romantic movement.[19] Moreover, the fact that the *Book* takes the form of a song cycle is yet again an allusion to the Romantic era – to Schumann's *Dichterliebe* or Schubert's *Winterreise*, for instance. Characteristic of a post-modern aesthetic however, Glass's selection of Cohen's texts is an assemblage of the poems in no particular order, thereby promoting a sense of anti-narrativity to the overall work.

In contrast to *Naqoyqatsi* nonetheless, *Book of Longing* does not refer to technological developments as part of social development – instead, in his representation of the thoughts of an anti-hero, Cohen's work often relates to feelings of love, depression and hopelessness. The introverted aspect often manifesting in Cohen's text is hardly surprising given the fact that most of the poems were written during a period when their author was retreating in the solitary environment of the Buddhist monastery, Mount Baldy, in California. Glass's music is equally intense, even sombre and bleak, though sometimes tinged with a degree of sentimentality or melancholy. Several of the work's movements are based on solo material, often performed in an extemporal manner, such as the cello piece entitled "Want to Fly", the saxophone in "Not a Jew", the violin in "I Enjoyed the Laughter", and double bass ("I am now able"). Similar to the importance of the solo cello in *Naqoyqatsi*, the monophonic textures of these pieces arguably replicate the solitary, if existential, character of the first-person narratives often presented in Cohen's text. The timbre of the low-pitched strings, in addition to the often-used low tessitura by the ensemble in general, assimilates the timbral qualities of Cohen's own earthy voice; we hear fragments of his poetry being recited by Cohen during the performance. If we delve deeper into this aspect, we can refer to Roland Barthes's writings on the "grain of the voice" within the context of a musical voice, which seem particularly apt in this instance, particularly his comment that "the 'grain' of the voice is not – or is not merely – its timbre; the *significance* it opens cannot better be defined, indeed, than by the very friction between the music and something else, which something else is the particular language (and nowise the message)" (Barthes 1977: 185). Richard Elliott writes

---

19 Bono, the Irish rock band U2's lead singer, has even declared Cohen to be "our Byron, our Shelley". See "He's Moses coming down from the mountaintop" in *The Telegraph* (24 September 2006) <http://www.telegraph.co.uk/culture/3655548/Hes-Moses-coming-down-from-the-mountaintop.html> (Last accessed 28 May 2020).

that "Barthes's pronouncements on the grain of the voice suggest that it enables us to find the person inside; it is where they are in the song we hear" (Elliott 2015: 42). Cohen's voice is therefore inextricably linked to Cohen the person, or songwriter, and it is integrated within Glass's theatrical work. In fact, Elliott goes on to discuss Cohen's search for his own voice (as a singer) during his formative years, and quotes Cohen's "Acceptance Address for the Prince of Asturias Award" in 2011 (Elliott 2015: 51). In his address, Cohen referred to the influence of Federico García Lorca upon himself in his quest "to find a voice, to locate a voice, that is to locate a self, a self that that is not fixed, a self that struggles for its own existence" (Cohen's speech was not published, but a transcript is included in Elliott 2015: 51).

In *Book of Longing*, we hear the haunting qualities of Cohen's voice in between Glass's sung melodies and repetitive figurations. In the Prologue, "I Can't Make the Hills", for instance, both the "grain" of Cohen's voice and the meaning of the words interrelate with the mood of the music: the low-pitched flute melody, the dyadic activity on low strings and drones, all combine to convey a dismal, grounded ambience. If the music in *Book of Longing* assimilates the text in terms of its sombre mood, certain intersections of a more specific nature between text and musical expression also ostensibly exist. In "Want to Fly", we hear in the repetitive dyads various intervallic leaps, however the notes always return to *d* (being the dominant pitch of G minor), which creates a "grounded" sense and a lack of teleological progression. Ascending and descending scales respectively contribute to this motion – trying but being unable to fly.[20] Further textual-musical interrelations also occur in other parts of *Book of Longing*. In "I Came down from the Mountain", Cohen's departure from his Zen retreat in California is recounted to the backdrop of descending chromatic lines that surely imitate the downhill motion alluded to in Cohen's text, "Leaving Mt. Baldy". Cohen in this poem has turned his back on the spiritual heights of the retreat, which sets the tone for the remainder of the work. The descending motion in Glass's piece assimilates with the poetic narrative here – a metaphoric descent from a spiritual haven to the grim reality of human existence.

---

20 This interaction between stepwise motion and textual meaning is reminiscent of the relationship between music and image in *Naqoyqatsi*'s "Point Blank", where the projection and subsequent destructive effect of military warfare in the visual narrative corresponded with Glass's ascending and descending scales: these descending scales represent devastation as a result of war.

4.1 Negation and affirmation in Cohen's text and Glass's tonality

If we return at this point to Eero Tarasti's model explaining "the journey of an existential subject via the act of negation and affirmation" (Tarasti 2000: 10) as discussed earlier in relation to the Ford Mondeo commercial, then this framework becomes relevant once again. Cohen's writings and songs often seem to be located within a state of "Negation" or "Nothingness" (and in this respect, relates to Sartre's *Nausée* for example).[21] His subsequent discovery of the Zen Buddhist philosophy and his experiences at Mt. Baldy during the mid-1990s as expressed in *Book of Longing*, arguably reflects a sense of "Affirmation", which Tarasti describes as "the opposite pole of the Nothingness – the universe, which is meaningful but, in some supra-individual way, is independent of his own act of signification" (Tarasti 2000: 11). Writing about the "Existential Cohen", Ágúst Magnússon reminds us that despite the fact that Cohen is often considered "a peddler of doom", his songs and poems offered much more expressions than the negative emotions and scenarios alone, as they comprise "an immense amount of grace, beauty and joy" (Magnússon 2014: 17). Cohen seemingly flits between negation and affirmation in his works, and Magnússon (2014: 17) writes "one might say that the darkness in his works [. . .] thrown into sharp relief the light that penetrates human existence". Moreover, the "existentialism in Cohen's art is the hopeful reassurance that our sadness is an essential part of what makes us human and that it is deeply intertwined with joy" (Magnússon 2014: 26). Babette Babich writes that Cohen's "songs of love include not only the promise of grace, salvation, and blessing, but also conflict and abandonment, as well as affirmation and letting be" (Babich 2014: 123), while Bernard Wills refers to the "subtle play of affirmation and negation" in Cohen's collection of songs on the *Recent Songs* album released in 1979 (Wills 2014: 237).

In music, we can perhaps relate the duality of negation and affirmation to the use of minor and major tonalities. If we examine the harmonies employed

---

[21] Interestingly, Cohen hinted at his affinity to other existentialist writers, including Sartre, in an interview with Sandra Djwa in 1967 (Djwa 1967: unpag. Reprinted in Burger 2014: 14–5). Rebekah Howes associates Cohen's poetic works with the concept of negation and also the Hegelian *Aufhebung*. Drawing on Nigel Tubbs's writings on education and Hegel (Tubbs 2008: 48), she notes that "the only way something can be negated and preserved at the same time and thus hold itself aporetically is when it is learning and, moreover, when that learning is learning about itself (Howes 2017: 95). Howes (2017: 95) proceeds by noting how the "negative movement of thought is not a mere nothingness [. . .] Cohen's darkest writings and songs show just how much loss is not mere lack or absence, and how much contradiction is not just frustration, but the return to, and the re-drawing of the lines of, who and what we are".

by Glass in *Book of Longing* in relation to Cohen's text, it is noticeable that the majority of the work is written in minor keys (particularly G minor), while the use of chromaticism and sudden chord shifts create a sense of unexpectedness. In "The Light Came Through the Window", based on Cohen's poem "Love Itself", we hear switches from A minor chords (the tonic) to A-flat major (also some allusions to the relative major, C). It is interesting to note how this progression from the tonic to the major seventh, causing the semitonal shift in the bass (A to A-flat and vice versa), is reminiscent of progressions used in Michael Andrews's music in the Ford Mondeo commercial discussed earlier. In Cohen's text, the poets talks of seeing rays of sunlight ("and so inside my little room there plunged the rays of Love"), which subsequently disappear, thus representing nothingness and the absence of love. The use of the major chords here might be taken as a metaphor for optimism; the poem depicts a longing for love, which remains unfulfilled. Such a piece can even be regarded as an allusion to such Romantic song-cycles as Schubert's *Winterreise*, which also makes sparing uses of major key structures – A major, for instance in "Frühlingstraum" (Dreams of Spring), "Täuschung" (Delusion) and "Die Nebensonnen" (The Mock Suns),[22] in reflection of Müller's poetic optimism.

Other movements in the work where Glass employs a strong major tonality include "G-d Opened My Eyes", in which the piece is placed within the key of F major. Cohen here observes a beautiful waitress in a restaurant, and he thanks God for making him aware of his surroundings. In "I Was Doing Something", which is a setting of Cohen's "Separated", the poet writes of an existential journey from a state of confusion ("I was doing something / I don't remember what") to a very dark place (e.g. "and in the place of every part there was the name of fear [. . .] and everything is covered with dust and everyone burns with shame and no one is allowed to cry out"). Glass's music begins with a strong C major tonality, however this is short-lived as the composer reverts to the relative minor. This becomes the principal tonality as the song unfolds and the words become darker and more intense. Glass's chord progressions often embark on a meandering journey, which are compatible with the notion of "separation", "dispersed" and "scattered" in the text.

In "Mother, Mother" he expresses relief that his mother "isn't really dead"; there is a sense of illogical thought processes in this particular poem (e.g. "Do you see the insects? One of them was one of your dog [. . .] The tree is trying to touch me. It used to be an afternoon"). In contrast to "I Was Doing Something" as discussed earlier however, there is a much more robust use of major tonality

---

22 Susan Youens discusses the uses of tonality in Youens 1991, especially pp. 75–76.

in "Mother, Mother". Glass's tonality is centred around C major, but there are a plethora of sudden chord changes: these unconventional progressions arguably relate to the quirkiness of the text, as the meandering thoughts uttered in the poem are seemingly compatible with the Glass's unconventional use of chord progressions.[23] The movement opens with four major chords, which move in a stepwise ascending pattern from A-flat to D-flat. The first couple of lines are set around three major chords, C – F – C. Strings and woodwind perform a couple of chord patterns based on B-flat and B, which leads to the next three sung lines, again based on C – F – C chords. The instruments subsequently play four chords that descend stepwise from B-flat to F-flat (or enharmonically E). Glass returns to an often-employed four chord pattern that begins with the relative minor, A, followed by F, C, and E major chords.[24] Much of the remainder of the song uses similar chord progressions discussed here, though we hear G major (representing the dominant chord) towards the end (again with surreal imagery e.g. "Here is the bone of my heart"), and the piece ends with a low-pitch D notes, which is altogether non-related to the tonal centre of C major.

The final movement to be discussed that employs a strong sense of major tonality is "Roshi's Very Tired", this being the final part of *Book of Longing* (although it is followed by an epilogue). Taken out of Cohen's "Roshi at 89", the poet focuses on the life of the leader of the Buddhist monastery that Cohen took residence during the 1990s, Kyozan Joshu Sasaki (1907–2014). Glass's music is full of brightness and warmth here, as a result of the C major tonality (with an added major 7th employed in the repetitive figurations). This tonic chord is subsequently followed by F major, E-flat major and D minor chords, and this four-chord progression is repeated throughout the movement. There is a sense of contentedness and calmness in the song, which is contributed by the harmonies employed, suitably reflecting the portrayal of Roshi's serene personality as implied in the text.

The examples discussed above seek to draw attention to the light and positivity that reside in *Book of Longing*, amidst other poetry of a much darker and despairing nature (as reflected in their tonalities as well). In "Roshi's Very Tired" we can observe a certain gracefulness in this movement that resonates with Agust Magnússon's aforementioned observation of the "immense amount of grace, beauty and joy" that belongs to Cohen's work (Magnússon 2014: 17). All such

---

[23] For a further discussion of Glass's use of unconventional voice-leading strategies and tonal harmony see Evans 2016: 83–84.
[24] Glass uses this chord progression in the *Truman Show* soundtrack, and is also an extended version of a progression often employed in *The Hours* and *Notes on a Scandal* (see Evans 2016: 114).

attributes are expressed within an existential context in the interplay of Glass's music and Cohen's words.

5 "The existence of life is a highly overrated phenomenon"

A more recent association, albeit more indirect, between Philip Glass and Leonard Cohen occurred in the inclusion of their music in the soundtrack to Jack Snyder's epic fantasy film, *Watchmen*, in which Cohen's pop song "First we take Manhattan" (1988) is used in the final part of the film's end credit sequence,[25] as are selected extracts from Glass's soundtrack to Godfrey Reggio's non-narrated film, *Koyaanisqatsi* (1982). While Glass and Cohen's *Book of Longing* makes several references to religion, either as a rejection or an affirmation of its influence upon the poet's life, human existence and issues surrounding existentialism also forms the crux of *Watchmen*. Within an intricate plot set in the final minutes before a doomsday scenario, the film is a re-adaptation of Alan Moore's comic book series from the late 1980s, which is widely recognised as having existentialist themes. The film assembles a group of comic book heroes together in a dramatic attempt to save the world from destruction at the hands of an individual named Adrian Veidt. Snyder's plot absorbs real historic events involving conflict, such as the Cold War and the Vietnam War, and also existent politicians including Ronald Reagan and JFK, thereby juxtaposing factual material within a fictional setting. The thematic material from *Koyaanisqatsi* is associated with a specific character, namely a government scientist called Dr Jon Osterman, whose body was subjected to an irreversible transformation (acquiring super powers and physically changing his colour to blue) as a result of a nuclear accident at the laboratory in which he worked, and subsequently became known as Doctor Manhattan, who is subjected to a very literal transcending experience, which leads to his transformation from an ordinary human entity into a superhero character – a clear shift from the mundane to the surreal! Doctor Manhattan proclaims towards the conclusion of the film that in his opinion "human existence is a highly overrated phenomenon", to which the subtitle of this present chapter refers.

The initial musical quotation from *Koyaanisqatsi*, out of the "Prophecies" scene, occurs in *Watchmen* at a point when Doctor Manhattan looks back at his

---

25 The use of Cohen's "First we take Manhattan" in *Watchmen* is mentioned in the context of masculinity in Schwanebeck 2014: 32.

life before the accident. Prior to this scene, as the character of Doctor Manhattan is developed, an assimilation of certain generic aspects of Glass's technique is heard by the film score writer Tyler Bates, who employs arpeggios, choral passages, semitonal shifts and works towards climaxes – thereby promoting a "dramatic" effect comparable to the depiction of the accident in the filmic narrative. By the decision to quote Glass's pre-existing "Prophecies", the apocalyptic meaning of *Koyaanisqatsi* is transferred to its new context in *Watchmen*. Demonstrating a rare occurrence of a sung text (other than the opening track), Glass offers a setting of three foretelling statements of an apocalyptic and existential nature derived from Hopi Native Americans, reinforcing Reggio's visual depiction of the environmental problems in the film – "Koyaanisqatsi" is translated as "life out of balance". The Native Americans' foretelling of the problems that might one day face humanity are integral to the text in "Prophecies", in which we hear the vocal incantation on the lines of "If we dig precious things from the land, we will invite disaster", "Near the day of Purification, there will be cobwebs spun back and forth in the sky" and finally, "A container of ashes might one day be thrown from the sky, which could burn the land and boil the oceans".

On similar lines, a pervasive sense of instability is central to the plot of *Watchmen*, with frequent references to war, social lawlessness and riots, in addition to the imminent threat of nuclear Armageddon. The quotation of Glass's "Prophecies" nevertheless presents a contrasting effect, in its calming or even spiritual ambience, although this ambience parallels the extra-musical content of the scene: the calmness of the music, the tonal stability and the quiet dynamic is comparable with Doctor Manhattan's softly-spoken manner as he recounts the story of his accident. A similar degree of poignancy in both speech and music is therefore implied. The extract from "Prophecies" subsequently merges seamlessly into "Pruit Igoe" – specifically at the point when the flashback to the destruction of Doctor Manhattan's human body, later regenerating into a superhuman entity, occurs. These cataclysmic scenes heard in conjunction with this particular musical extract seemingly relates to its original context on a certain level: in *Koyaanisqatsi*, "Pruit Igoe" is employed in conjunction with the destruction of a housing estate. Glass's music consequently offers a "cataclysmic" connotation in both instances. In terms of musical characteristics, "Pruit Igoe" offers a greater degree of instability through chromaticism, though a stepwise descent is once again apparent. This is subsequently replaced by the return to a section from "Prophecies", which causes a change in ambience with a return to the solemnity of the initial quotation, which compares with Dr Manhattan's spoken manner. This music is particularly apt in conveying the otherworldly nature of Dr Manhattan's character, and his supposed supernatural powers to halt the cataclysmic destruction of the world.

The re-application of "Prophecies" and "Pruit Igoe" demonstrates how the apocalyptical nature of the music's original meaning in *Koyaanisqatsi* can also gather similar meanings in *Watchmen*, albeit to a limited extent – after all, *Koyaanisqatsi* is a documentary film while *Watchmen* is a fantasy comic-book film. The textual content of "Prophecies" resonated with the subject matter of the film, and also with Dr Manhattan's omniscient perspective of life on earth, while "Pruit Igoe" evinced a dramatic effect to coincide with the cataclysm depicted in the visual dimension. In short, although the music in *Koyaanisqatsi* is recycled, some of its extra-musical meaning – the struggle of human existence within a "life out of balance" – is preserved.

Conclusions

The cataclysmic effect of *Koyaanisqatsi* in its secondary context, and the foreboding elements in *Naqoyqatsi*, are both prime examples of Glass's ability to invoke "existential dread' as quoted at the beginning of this chapter. However, this investigation has further demonstrated how instances of post-minimal music, as heard in conjunction with filmic or theatrical subject matters depicting individuals within society, can lead to the identification of other existential characteristics. Examples of soloist textures or melodies for voice or cello often expressing a sense of individuality have been identified, while the selection of minor tonality, unsettling harmonic shifts and metrical imbalances promote austere environments and bleak outlooks. In the Mondeo commercial, the chromatic instability of Andrews's tonal framework subsequently leads to a higher degree of optimism, tying in with the visual narrative, with the use of a bass ostinato figuration representing the trappings of a mundane scenario (as also relevant to "Want to Fly" in *Book of Longing*). Other uses of repetitive figurations have been effective in expressing different things: the urgency of apocalyptic scenarios in *Watchmen*, the rapid speed of humanity's development as found in *Naqoyqatsi*, and the use of Reich's music in the Orange's commercial.

Nietzsche's early work strives for melancholy though repetition in his piece composed as a "fragment in itself", while Glass's repetitive units expresses an immediate crisis and the struggle for existence in *Watchmen*. Conflict, rapidity of technological development and a competitive drive appears at the forefront of the *Naqoyqatsi* soundtrack, with psychological interiority, focus on the self and a quest for individual identity being at the heart of the first-person narratives in *Book of Longing*. Andrews's *Donnie Darko* soundtrack, as later employed in a secondary context, combines a mundane existence with the surreal, while Reich music in the Orange commercial subliminally sells a product by associating a repetitive drive with Beaumont's personal achievements, setting out a motivational identity in a similar manner to the humanistic elements of *Naqoyqatsi*. In short, these concluding observations confirm that the concept of existentialism can vividly and variedly be expressed in minimalist and post-minimal music.

References

Babich, Babette. 2014. "Halleluiah and Atonement". In Jason Holt (ed.), *Leonard Cohen and Philosophy: Various Positions*. Chicago: Open Court.
Baudrillard, Jean. 1968. *Systeme des objects*. Paris: Gallimard.
Bernard, Jonathan W. 2003. Minimalism, Postminimalism, and the Resurgence of Tonality in Recent American Music. *American Music* 21/i. 112–133.
Bryden, Mary (ed.). 1998. *Samuel Beckett and Music*. New York: Clarendon Press.
Burger, Jeff (ed.). 2014. *Leonard Cohen on Leonard Cohen*. Chicago: Chicago Review Press.
Cohen, Leonard. 2006. *Book of Longing*. London: Penguin Books.
Cott, Jonathan. 1995. Liner notes to Philip Glass: *La Belle et La Bête*. Nonesuch 79347.
De Mul, Jos. 1999. *Romantic Desire in (Post)modern Art and Philosophy*. Albany: State University of New York Press.
Deleuze, Gilles. 1989. *Cinema 2: The Time-Image*. Trans. by Hugh Tomlinson and Robert Galeta. London: Athlone.
Djwa, Sandra. 1967. "After the Wipeout, a Renewal". *Ubyssey* 3 February 1967: unpag.
Edler, Peter. 2006. "Les Beats sont faits". http://www.beatsupernovarasa.com/thebeats/les_beat_by_peter_edler.htm (Accessed 31 May 2020).
Elliott, Richard. 2015. *The Late Voice: Time, Age and Experience in Popular Music*. New York: Bloomsbury.
Evans, Tristian. 2016. *Shared Meanings in the Film Music of Philip Glass: Music, Multimedia and Postminimalism*. Abingdon, Oxon: Routledge.
Fink, Robert. 2004. (Post-)minimalisms 1970–2000: A Search for a New Mainstream. In Nicholas Cook & Anthony Pople (eds.), *The Cambridge History of Twentieth-Century Music*. Cambridge: Cambridge University Press.
Fink, Robert. 2005. *Repeating Ourselves: American minimal music as cultural practice*. Berkeley: University of California Press.
Gann, Kyle. 1998. "A Forest from the Seeds of Minimalism: An Essay on Postminimal and Totalist Music". In: http://www.kylegann.com/postminimalism.tml (accessed 29 May 2020).
Glass, Philip. 1987. *Music by Philip Glass*. Ed. by Robert T. Jones. New York: Harpers & Row.
Glass, Philip. 2015. *Words Without Music*. London: Faber & Faber.
Howes, Rebekah. 2017. Leonard Cohen and the Philosophical Voice of Learning. In Peter Billingham (ed.), *Spirituality and Desire in Leonard Cohen's Songs and Poems: Visions from the Tower of Song*. Newcastle upon Tyne: Cambridge Scholars Publishing.
Jameson, Fredric. 2009. *Valences of the Dialectic*. London: Verso.
Jaspers, Karl. 1951. *Man in the Modern Age*. Trans. by Eden and Cedar Paul. London: Routledge.
Kelly, Richard. 2003. *The Donnie Darko Book*. London: Faber and Faber.

Kern, Edith. 1954. Drama Stripped for Inaction: Beckett's *Godot*. *Yale French Studies* 14. 41–47.
Kramer, Jonathan D. 1988. *The Time of Music*. New York: Schirmer.
Lessard, Bruno. 2009. Cultural Recycling, Performance, and Immediacy in Philip Glass's Film Music for Godfrey Reggio's *Qatsi* Trilogy. In Graeme Harper (ed.), *Sound and Music in Film and Visual Media*. New York: Continuum.
Magnússon, Ágúst. 2014. The Existential Cohen. In Jason Holt (ed.), *Leonard Cohen and Philosophy: Various Positions*. Chicago: Open Court.
Miles, Barrie. 2001. *The Beat Hotel: Ginsberg, Burroughs, and Corso in Paris, 1957–1963*. London: Atlantic.
Neveldine, Robert B. 1998. *Bodies at Risk: Unsafe Limits in Romanticism and Postmodernism*. New York: State University of New York Press.
Ortega y Gasset. José. 1950. *The Revolt of The Masses*. New York: Norton.
Perec, Georges. 1965. *Les Choses: une histoire des années soixante*. Paris: Julliard.
Potter, Keith. 2000. *Four Musical Minimalists*. Cambridge: Cambridge University Press.
Powell, Anna. 2007. *Deleuze, Altered States and Film*. Edinburgh: Edinburgh University Press.
Reich, Steve. 1978. Liner notes for *Music for 18 Musicians*. ECM Records, ECM-1-1129.
Reich, Steve. 2002. *Writings on Music, 1965–2000*. New York: Oxford University Press.
Rich, Alan. 1978. "Down to Essentials". *New York Magazine*, 6 November 1978: 97
Royle, Nicholas. 2003. *The Uncanny*. Manchester: Manchester University Press.
Sartre, Jean Paul. 1973. *Existentialism and Humanism*. Trans. by Philip Mairet. London: Eyre Methuen.
Savlov, Mark. 2004. The Ambience of Existential Dread: Philip Glass on the *Fog of War* score. *The Austin Chronicle*, 20 February 2004. http://www.austinchronicle.com (accessed 29 May 2020).
Schwanebeck, Wieland. 2014. "Why Cohen's Our Man". In Jason Holt (ed.), *Leonard Cohen and Philosophy: Various Positions*. Chicago: Open Court.
Skerl, Jennie (ed.). 2004. *Reconstructing the Beats*. New York: Palgrave Macmillan.
Tarasti, Eero. 1994. *A Theory of Musical Semiotics*. Bloomington: Indiana University Press.
Tarasti, Eero. 2000. *Existential Semiotics*. (Advances in Semiotics) Bloomington: Indiana University Press.
Tubbs, Nigel. 2008. *Education in Hegel*. London: Continuum.
Wills, Bernard. 2014. "Clouds of Unknowing". In Jason Holt (ed.), *Leonard Cohen and Philosophy: Various Positions*. Chicago: Open Court.
Youens, Susan. 1991. *Retracing a Winter's Journey: Schubert's* Winterreise. Ithaca: Cornell University Press.
Zurbrugg, Nicholas. 1999. Interview with Philip Glass. In Lois Oppenheim (ed.), *Samuel Beckett and the Arts*. New York: Garland.

Discography

Philip Glass. *La Belle et La Bête*. Nonesuch 79347 (1995).
Steve Reich. *Music for 18 Musicians*. ECM Records, ECM-1-1129 (1978).
Jeroen van Veen. *Nietzche: Piano Music*. Brilliant Classics BC 95492 (2017).

Videography

Glass: A Portrait of Philip in Twelve Parts. 2007. [DVD] Directed by Scott Hicks. Koch Lorber Films

Naqoyqatsi. 2002. [DVD] Directed by Godfrey Reggio. Miramax.

Antonio Santangelo
Existential choices of existential signs.
Love stories, structuralism, and existential semiotics

Abstract: This article tries to highlight some points of contact between the existential semiotics of Eero Tarasti and the sociosemiotics of structuralist matrix. It does so, starting from the analysis of some famous love stories, such as those told in William Shakespeare's "Romeo and Juliet" and James Cameron's "Titanic". The aim is to reflect, first of all, on how, in these works, we represent the relationship of transcendence that seems to exist between the reality in which we live and the signs or narrative mechanisms that we use to interpret it. These are the result of shared semiotic systems of a mental nature that determine the functioning of our "dasein" and put us in a position to believe that the world, our identity and that of those we love are as we read them. And yet it is precisely in these love stories that we tell of how we can choose to abandon a certain vision of things, socially attested, but in which we do not believe, in order to embrace another, which seems fairer and "truer". The double movement of Tarasti's existential path is therefore discussed, towards the awareness of the "nothingness of being" of the codes with which we assign a meaning to reality and, at the same time, of the sensation of "fullness" that we feel, in spite of everything, when some of these same codes assert themselves in our daily lives. Between references to Greimas' "Sémiotique et sciences sociales" (1976) and "De l'imperfetion" (1987), and to cultural anthropology (Remotti, 1999), the attempt is to use the texts under analysis as metaphors for some semiotic mechanisms of a more general scope, fundamental for describing our way of being in the world, which the comparison between Tarasti's theories and those of a certain tradition of sociosemiotic studies can, perhaps, help to better understand.

Keywords: Sociosemiotics, existential semiotics, love stories, imperfection, signs, narratives

1 The existential problems that sociosemiotics has to face

Even if I have always been working in the field of semiotics, I have never considered myself to be a philosopher, but a social scientist. My main interest is Culture

https://doi.org/10.1515/9783110789164-039

and the way it interacts with our interpretation of the world, giving us the possibility to share it with other people, so that we can build together a society based on a common vision of things.

When I was asked to write an article about Eero Tarasti's theories on existential semiotics, I was a little sceptical, as I am not a philosopher and I knew Tarasti has been literally trying to "transcend" – from a philosophical point of view – the authors that I consider the basis of my work as a semiotician: Saussure and Durkheim, and the way Luis Prieto (1975) used their theories of knowledge to explain how we resort to signs to classify our experience of the world and then to share it through communication; Levi Strauss and his structuralist vision of how Culture "holds together" the complex systems of signs we make use of to share our general, epistemological, and even philosophical interpretation of things; the way Berger and Luckmann (1966) built a sociological constructivist theory of knowledge, basing themselves on Schutz's phenomenology and demonstrating the main role played by signs and symbolic mental mechanisms to let us reify our cultural conception of what we use to call "reality" in our everyday lives.

In many parts of his "Introduzione alla semiotica esistenziale" (2008),[1] Tarasti claims that he wants to go beyond these theories and, even if he shares some of their ideas, they seem to be a sort of a starting point, giving him the possibility to find the right questions for the answers that he provides in the existential semiotics paradigm. At the moment, I am not sure I agree with his conclusions about the need for distancing from the structuralist paradigm and I shall try to demonstrate my reasons in the following pages. But I truly believe that the questions he poses to a structural (socio) semiotics[2] and its most important authors are very urgent and they represent some of the most interesting research fields, both for a philosophical and for a sociological approach to the discipline.

First of all, as I believe Kroeber (1952) was right, when he talked about Culture as something which has a "superorganic" nature, I think Tarasti's attempt to drive our attention to the transcendental mechanisms that affect our way of using signs to give sense to the world is absolutely central in any reflection about a semiotics of Culture[3] and its analysis of objects. To use Tarasti's Heideggerian terms, our "dasein" is clearly influenced by the relationship that occurs between our conscience and a transcending "néant",[4] as in this "nothingness" there are Culture and its signs, giving us the possibility to share a common "subjective" but also a collec-

---

[1] I quote it in Italian because the Italian version of "Existential Semiotics" (Tarasti 2000) is different from the original one as it contains some more chapters and essays.
[2] For me "Semiotics" and "Sociosemiotics" are synonymous.
[3] Which, in my opinion, must be considered again a "Sociosemiotics".
[4] Now I am referring to Sartre's terminology, as this author is very important in Tarasti's system.

tive vision of things (see A. Santangelo. 2011, in Lexia 7/8, pages: 151–166). However, in my opinion, acknowledging the importance of this knowledge and communication mechanisms is not enough to talk about the necessity of moving out of the structural semiotics paradigm, as many authors whose theories fully belonged to this current have been talking of them, before and after Heidegger and Sartre. For example – just to cite the name of a researcher I have not quoted yet – Tarasti himself (2008: 17–62) refers to Greimas and his generative theory as to an example of how existential semiotics can find some connections with the structuralist one.

But quoting Greimas is very important, in this context, as we all know his last book – *"De l'imperfection"* (1987), which he significantly wrote at the end of his career as a structuralist – deals with the second very important question that Tarasti poses to a structural sociosemiotics, which is to say the problem of how we break free from the chain of the signs of our Culture, to know the world in another way arid to understand that it can have another meaning, a meaning we could not even imagine before and that we perceive and conceive due to our personal experience of imperfection. This is actually the border of a structural sociosemiotics because it forces scholars and researchers to think about how signs originate in our individual relationship with the world, instead of describing some collective structures that already exist.

More or less, the difference between Greimas's convictions about semiotics before and after *"De l'imperfection"* seems to correspond to the two actions of Tarasti's existential path (2008: 28): *negation* (going towards the "néant") and *affirmation* (the fullness of knowledge, "returning" from the "néant"). But again, in Greimas's theories, these mechanisms of our conscience have nothing to do with existentialism, as we do not individually choose to know the world in a way or another. Both the structures of Culture and the glimpse of imperfection seem to be something that "mechanically" affects us, like in a process we do not use to be aware of and that we can hardly control, provoke or foresee. I think the distance between Greimas's positions and the existentialist ones is exemplar in this case and they put us in front of the third important question that Tarasti poses to the structural sociosemiotics tradition, actually challenging it to face existentialism and one of its main issues: how we personally choose the signs that give sense to our experience of the world and that permit us to make our choices in a society made of people who also use signs to read our actions, to judge and to react to them.

In the following pages, I would like to consider these three questions, trying to show how they can find an answer even inside the structural sociosemiotics paradigm, in the theories of the authors that I have quoted above. In this sense, as I have written in the title of this paragraph, I propose to think about the existential problems that sociosemiotics has to face. To do so, I would like to make use of a topic I have been studying for a long a time[5]: the representation of love in melodramatic stories that belong to the cinema and literary tradition. This choice is not accidental, as I consider this kind of narrative as a good example of how an individual has to choose between some transcendental collective value systems that give a meaning to his own *"Dasein"* experience, sharing them not only with another person but with a whole society. Moreover, several times these stories talk about a sort of a "revolution" in the lives of lovers[6] forcing them to face a metaphorical death of their previous identities and another metaphorical affirmation of the fullness of their new way of being.

As anybody can see, here there are all the main existential questions that Tarasti poses to a structuralist sociosemiotics. Of course, these are only fictional stories, but as Tarasti himself underlines in an interesting part of his book (2008: 63–67), maybe the narrative structures of a fictitious *"Dasein"* can reflect some of the mechanisms of our everyday lives, and in this case, we are talking of how we use to think about who we are, or we are choosing which cultural vision of ourselves and of the society we want to live in and – in the end – which existential relationship we want to nourish with our collective Culture.

2 Social and existential problems of lovers

Here I want to show that a certain kind of love stories, like for example "Romeo and Juliet" or "Titanic" are a metaphor of some actual problems we face in our everyday lives, problems which have much to do with the existential questions that structuralist sociosemiotics has to face.

Tarasti claims that in our *"dasein"* experience we make use of some transcendental signs to give sense to the world and that these signs have to do with a *"néant"*, even if we often forget it, reifying them.[7] But then, with the first move of his existential path, Tarasti explains that we can be aware of the real nature of our vision of things and this makes us free from the influence of signs themselves. From that moment on, we are ready to "return" to our *"dasein"*, with the second movement of Tarasti's existential path, which consists in a new kind of knowl-

---

5 See Santangelo (2009).
6 This is exactly what Francesco Alberoni claims in his famous essay "Innamoramento e amore" (1979), talking about the actual mechanisms of love.
7 Up to P. Berger and T. Luckmann ([1966] 2007: 45–55) who follow Saussure's ([1916] 2001: 22) and Durkheim's ([1912] 2007: 497–501) tradition, this happens because we all share the same signs to classify the things we face in our everyday lives.

edge that he interestingly defines as an "affirmation", which gives us the feeling of a sort of "fullness".

As I have written, Greimas described something similar in *"De l'imperféction"*, where he drove our attention towards those "magic" moments when we become aware of the imperfection of our collective signs that are no more able to define the meaning of our experience of things. It is in those situations, which we live as individuals, that we form our idea about the new signs we should make use of to classify the world we inhabit. But then we have to share these signs with other people if we want to be part of society. And so the Stevensonian Robinson Crusoe or the Calvinian solitary wanderer of Greimas's book have the problem of communicating their new vision of things to the rest of the world, without even knowing if it will be accepted or rejected. However, Greimas does not explain so clearly how this social acceptance of the new signs discovered by individuals in the "imperfection moment" takes place. To do so, in my opinion, he should have added to his collection of novels, excerpts, some parts of the love stories that belong to our melodrama tradition, because there the main problem seems exactly like this one.

As the model, more or less, is similar to the one of "Romeo and Juliet", let us think about the narrative structure of that story. There we find two lovers who have a social identity, which is represented by their name. This is a sign and its nature is collective and "transcendental", as it has nothing to do with who the young guys actually are, but as far as everybody makes use of it, this is enough to exchange a Capulet or a Montague descendance with a sort of a nature that will never be changed and that will always preclude any possibility of being together. But "a sign is just a sign"[8] and the lovers are the first to recognize that they have the power to refuse its defining influence. Therefore, moved to their "imperfection" experience from their feelings, they decide to change their identity, symbolically refusing their names and choosing their new ones. Hence, magically, they break free and they feel the happiness – or, to use Tarasti's terms – the fullness of affirming their new way of being. However, they have a problem: convincing their parents, whose vision of the world stands as the basis of their own society. A Capulet must always be divided from a Montague, and the tragedy is knocking at the lovers' door.

I am going to show in my conclusions how and why this narrative structure of a love story, which has been repeated a million times after Shakespeare, has a fundamental anthropological importance in any Culture. But now I would like to show how it has been recovered by James Cameron in "Titanic" because in this

---

8 Here I make use of an expression that Eero Tarasti likes to quote from Sebeok.

movie there are some very interesting "sociosemiotic" answers to Tarasti's and Greimas' questions.

In "Titanic", Rose DeWitt Bukater – the young and pretty daughter of a noble decayed family – is going to get married to Caledon Hockley, the rich son of an American steel tycoon. But she sees this marriage as an imposition by her mother and instead of taking the name – and of course the lifestyle of her future husband – she tries to commit suicide, jumping out of the ship, while it is sailing in the middle of the ocean. She is saved by Jack Dawson, a young *bohemian* artist who travels in the third class cabin and she quickly falls in love with him as it is clear they both share the same values and the same vision of things and life. But at the same time, it is also clear they have two different social identities, and this is the reason why Rose's mother and the young girl's fiancé do their best to oppose her feelings. Like Romeo and Juliet, the lovers of "Titanic" will have to fight against the way of thinking of a whole society, as it is well represented from their mutual collocation in the hierarchies that even drew the shape of the boat in which they are sailing, something that – as everybody knows – will affect also their own destiny.

Interestingly, the paradigmatic and the syntagmatic structure of this love story can be described with a model that Greimas drew in his book *"Sémiotique et sciences sociales"* (1976, it. tr. 1991: 90–92), talking about the *"actant collectif"*. There we find a clear logical and semantic opposition in the social relationships that may occur between people, who can be a *"unité partitive"*, a *"Unité integrale"*, a *"totalité partitive"* or a *"totalité integrale"*. Now, the possibility to describe a love story structure with such a model may not be surprising, as what we are studying is the birth of a couple, which can, in fact, be considered as an *"actant collectif"*. At the same time, the fact that this model was thought by Greimas to sketch the relationships that can occur between individuals and "society"[9] may also be understandable, as every couple can be seen as the smallest kind of a human "society". What is actually interesting is how and why this has to do with sociosemiotics and existentialism, which can be clear if we take a look at the particular way James Cameron faces these themes in "Titanic".

At the beginning of their love stories, Rose and Jack are two *"unitées partitives"* as, from a sociosemiotic point of view, their identities are defined by some very specific and opposite categories of signs: a "first-class" woman and a "third-class" man, with all the encyclopedias that these conditions take with them. Of

---

9 Greimas used this model to talk about commercial societies, but I will demonstrate it can be generalized to every kind of societies.

course, this is not the lovers' vision of things, neither of the world nor themselves. But unfortunately, that is the value system of the whole society they live in.

As the story is told from Rose's eyes, we quickly understand she has always dreamt to be free like Jack but, as she never had the possibility to carry upon herself the same "signs" of her lover's freedom, she tries to commit suicide, somehow exchanging her social identity for something "natural", a son of an essence. Of course, knowing Jack opens her mind. No need to say that she starts to see the young *bohemian* artist as the "perfect" example of what she had always dreamt to be. And of course – using Greimas's words – Rose is saved by the man who lets her recognize all the "imperfections" of her own societal values.

This imperfection is clearly a matter of definition. From the moment she knows her future love, Rose lives an intense experience of discovery. She finds out that every word she had always made use of to give a name to herself, to her attitude, to the things and people that surrounded her were wrong. To be precise, in the relationship with Jack she finds out some confirmations of what she had always thought about her world. But before meeting that young third-class passenger of the Titanic she felt to be the only one to see those things. Now she knows she is not alone.

A very interesting scene on this theme is the dinner scene at the captain's table. Jack, as the hero who has saved Rose from falling out of the ship, is invited to know all the girl's relatives, who want to thank him for what he has done. To do so, he has to wear a dinner jacket, something that he has never done before and he has to behave like a gentleman. Of course, all the "imperfection" of his education comes out during the dinner, when he fails to use the cutlery, but suddenly Rose's mother asks him how it feels to be like a *bohemian* and he passionately corrects her, saying his way of living is the only one that makes sense, at least to him. So, he refuses the name that the whole society of Mrs DeWitt Bukater would give him and to his vision of life. Of course, Rose nods, admired. While the others, for the first time in the movie, do not feel at ease, as they perfectly see that they may wear dinner jacket, but they are poorer than Jack, as they do not possess real freedom.

However, at this stage of the story, Rose and Jack are not a couple yet. They do not know each other so well and they have to met several times, during the cruise. At every encounter, the girl can see in her new friend the person she had always wanted to be, clearly "projecting" herself into the man and suddenly she discovers how far she was from "coinciding" with the woman she desired to become. Hence Jack turns into Rose's Greimasian "value object" and this is the reason why they become a *"totalité partitive";* because they have similar values, but the values of the society they live in keep them separate.

Here it is important to underline what "value" means in the Saussurian tradition. Up to Saussure, in fact, the value of a sign is its meaning, which is given by its opposition to other signs inside a system that he calls "langue". Now, in "Titanic", this concept will return many times, but here I would like to show how Jack's value, in the eyes of Rose, is in his way of opposing a better definition of things to the one of her own hated society. Jack knows the names, or better the signs, which have a real value and of course the "langue" he and Rose belong to is a clearly defined social and cultural vision of the world that is very different from the one that shapes the ship in which they are sailing and the social system it derives from.

Then, the most important sequence of "Titanic" arrives, the one that everybody remembers. Jack and Rose meet at the fore of the ship at sunset. The girl hangs at her man, both of them staring at the sea. What they see is the same sight of freedom. Then the girl asks the artist to paint her, in her first-class room, surrounded by her things and naked, wearing only the marvellous diamond that her rich fiancé once gave her as evidence of his love. These scenes are based on the two lovers' gaze, as for Cameron – and not only for him[10] – loving means seeing the world from the other's eyes. Both on the fore of the boat and in the cabin, it is always a matter of what Jack and Rose reciprocally see, because what they see is what they face, the meaning of their *"dasein"*, as Tarasti would say. So – from a Greimasian point of view – as I have written that the sea in front of the ship sailing towards the new world is just a metaphor of the freedom they are chasing, we can say in this scene they first see and feel their values, the ones that they share.

It is Jack who takes his woman into the place where she can see and feel what life and things actually mean. And at that moment Rose becomes sure of her love because the man is showing her the only "true" and acceptable vision of the world. But then she has to be sure that not only the world but even her identity can be "read" the same way. She wants to be loved back and being loved means being "translated" into her lover's gaze, as Jack sees things with the only values she may dare to love. This is the reason why she decides to be portrayed by him, naked and just wearing a jewel: from a Greimasian point of view, it simply means that people and things have a "value" only as "value objects" and in fact, Rose will put the painting into her strongbox, not the jewel, and this is what the treasure hunters many years later will find there, instead of the diamond. But this is also the metaphor of a sort of new birth: the girl wears off all the signs of what she used to be and she is "baptized" by the gaze of her lover, who gives her the gift of her own new identity.

---

[10] See I. Brugo and G. Ferraro (2008)

Here there is another Greimasian mechanism that becomes clear: in this kind of love stories, who once was a "desire object" becomes a "sender", following a logic that Feuerbach described as typical of the religious experience.[11] People, in fact, use to put their values in the hands and the gaze of an "other", as they want the identity they desire for themselves to be recognized from someone else. When this happened to Jack and Rose, the lovers become a couple, which is to say a *"totalité integrale"*: two persons that share the same values and see life in the same way.

But then, as everybody knows, Jack dies, drowning in the sea to save Rose from sinking. However, at the end of her journey, we see Rose arriving at the destination and claiming to a customs officer of the United States that her name is Rose Dawson, having taken the name of her dead lover. Hence we find out another meaning of the expression *"unité partitive"*, as it is clear that the girl – at the beginning of the story – was "divided" from herself: the society kept her away from who she wanted to be. Then she understood – like in Plato's *Symposium* – that when she was together with her love she was in front of the image of herself that she had to unite with. So now, as an individual, she discovers the "fullness" of the conjunction with her own desired identity: at the end of her social and existential path she has turned into to be a *"unité integrale"*.

3 What Jake and Rose have to do with existential semiotics and structuralist sociosemiotics

I guess everyone has already noticed many connections between the love story told in "Titanic" and the problems I have raised in the first part of my article, but here I would like to formalize them, returning to the end of the scene of Jack painting Rose.

James Cameron chooses to shoot it by filming their gazes one more time. They stare at each other. Then, when everything is over, the camera stops into a very close cut of the young and adoring Rose's blue eye, which suddenly becomes older and older, until we understand it belongs to a centenarian lady, who is telling the story we have been watching so far. What does it mean? I think the movie director wants to tell us that even if the woman has physically changed, from the moment she had been loved she has remained the same. Because a body

---

[11] I think it is not accidental if many authors compare the love that there is between human beings with the one of humans for their gods.

can grow older, but the signs and the values they stand for will always stay the same, as they belong to another realm. Signs are transcendental.

The metaphor of these concepts is of course Rose's portrait. But what is a portrait if not a particular sign? It is an icon and, as Guido Ferraro claims (2007: 17–37), icons look like the ideas we have of things. Due to the Peircian semiotics tradition, we use to think that icons look like the physical objects or subjects they stand for. But even following Peircian theories, Eco (1968: 109–130) showed us that also in iconic signification there is always a selection of the pertinent traits of things, some pertinent traits which may have a "value" because the signifiers of icons created with this selection look like their signifieds. And of course both signifiers and signifieds, in Saussure's theory, belong to the mental realm or – to use the same words I have resorted to in this article – they are transcendental.

Hence, from the portrait scene on, Rose knew her identity had become "eternal", coinciding with the values in her lover's gaze: Jack translated them in an image in which he sketched her naked and free, immensely more "valuable" than the diamond she wore only as a beautiful memory of that moment, somehow as a wedding ring with a totally different meaning form the one that it had the very first time she received it from her former rich fiancé Hockley. Some minutes after she finishes telling her story, the spectator sees some other pictures of her, this time some photos of her life after Jack had died and she had arrived safe in the USA. It is clear that she has always lived free as in her portrait and that she has never taken care of money, as she has still the diamond in her pocket, which she throws into the ocean, after having shared her own story with her niece and with the treasure hunters who have looked for her jewel in the sunken ruins of the Titanic. Then she dies in peace, leaving the spectator with the romantic conviction that people and things may pass by, but the signs they have been using to define their own identities will always last because, as Kroeber used to say of Culture, they are somehow "superorganic" and can be communicated.

But as we have seen, there are some moments of an existential nature, where we find out that some values, and the signs we had always made use of to express them, are wrong and they fail to describe our own experience of things. This happens —to use Tarasti's words— when we move to the "*néant*" and then we go back to our "*dasein*", acknowledging its new, "real" meaning, which has to be expressed from some new "existential" signs. Both for Greimas and Tarasti, these moments seem to be individualistic, exactly as it happens to Rose in another famous scene of "Titanic", when she is in the dining room of the first class, drinking tea with the women of the upper class, and she sees a mother at another table teaching her young daughter how to behave. Suddenly, what had always been so natural for a very well-educated woman like Rose starts to look violent and wrong and she clearly understands the "imperfection" of her own societal values. But the sequence does not stop here, as the heroine immediately goes to look for Jack, who is the representative of the other vision of the world that makes more sense to her, the one where women are free to behave as they want.

This is the point where my structuralist sociosemiotician's gaze differs from Tarasti's and Greimas's positions. Here we perfectly understand that the two lovers, at the beginning of their story, were simply the representatives of two alternative visions of society. Two visions which already existed in the Culture that gave birth to a transatlantic journey that was projected to keep the poor apart from the rich, but that at the same time served as a mean to take everybody from a "world" to another, often looking for change, hope and freedom. The lovers literally belonged to two social classes that such as the values they stood for had always been very present at people's eyes, but they also belonged to a world where the artistic bohemian way of life was appreciated (Rose is portrayed as an art collector who likes Tolouse Lautrec and his "travels" in the "lower" society looking for beauty and humanity, and Jack is represented as a frequenter of Toulouse's world). This is the reason why the young bohemian painter can understand the meaning of his lover's choice and at the same time, this is also the reason why Rose can see so clearly the terms of her existential actions. Hence the individualistic and existential choice of the woman is very difficult, but there is nothing "new" to be invented or discovered, unlike in the novels and in the poems that Greimas shows in his book "De l'imperfection" or in Tarasti's idea of the "birth" of some new existential signs: it is just a problem of choosing between signs and values that Culture already proposes to its carriers and to share them with someone else.

4 The existential relationship between us and culture

As I wrote, love stories like "Romeo and Juliet" and 'Titanic" are just a metaphor of something more important; something that always happens in our own lives and our own societies. Francesco Reinotti (1999: 1–32), a famous anthropologist, claims that every human being has to go through a process of "anthropopoiesis",[12] which consists in facing the values and the signs of his own and the others cultures, and then choosing the ones that are able to give sense to his own

---

[12] "Anthropopoesis" means "the birth, the creation" of a man, the way a man takes his shape and his identity.

life. Every people's identity stands in the signs and values they choose to define things, persons, actions, and situations and those signs and values give shape to everything: to people's bodies, to their houses, their towns, their human relationships and, finally, to the whole society they use to live in.

This is the reason why our love stories – that like any other story – can have the function of showing everybody their Culture's most fundamental mechanisms – take the form of the model Greimas drew to describe the relationships that can occur between individuals and societies. This happens because when the characters love, they love an idea of a society, on which they base their couple rules and, what is more important, their personal identities and their vision of the world. But this is also the reason why lovers, in melodramas, have to fight to transform their reciprocal love into something which is recognized by everybody. A love story becomes the metaphor of a sort of an initiation rite, where the couple is the liminar "elsewhere"[13] where the lovers learn the "true" meaning of things, life, and society is the place into which their visions of the world and their identities have to be accepted.

What is important is that this metaphor[14] is just a particular case of some mechanisms that affect us every day, very far beyond our love stories, as Guido Ferraro (2008: SO) claims that, at different scales and levels, the problem of every society and of every individual who lives inside a society is always to choose between all the different collective models that Culture proposes to give sense to the world. What love stories are about is hence maybe the most fundamental sociosemiotic mechanism of Culture: the way people acknowledge that their Culture's signs and values are "true" and worth to be defended by their carriers, even at the cost of their lives, exactly as it happened to Romeo and Juliet or Jack and Rose.

But these stories also describe the existential mechanisms that take people to choose some signs and values, instead of some others. It is a clash between different "langues" or collective "pertinence principles", to use a structuralist terminology. And individuals, groups, nations etc. have to act, to show everybody that their choice is the best, as it is "truer" and it better explains the experience they have of the world. These are the existential problems of all of us and, as Tarasti well shows, sociosemiotics cannot escape them.

---

13 See A. van Gennep (1909)
14 I have chosen "Titanic" as, in their manual about the movie genres, Aimeri and Frasca (2002) underline that many researchers agree on the fact that James Cameron's story is the most important and successful example of a melodramatic story written in the last ten years in western culture.

References

Aimeri, Luca & Giampiero Frasca. 2002. *Manuale dei generi cinematografici*. Torino: Utet.
Alberoni, Francesco. 1979. *Innamoramento e amore*. Milano: Rizzoli.
Berger, Peter L. & Thomas Luckmann. 1966. *The social construction of reality*. New York: Doubleday & Co., Garden City.
Brugo, Isabella & Guido Ferraro. 2008. *Comunque umani. Dietro le figure di mostri, alieni, orchi e vampiri*. Rome: Meltemi.
Durkheim, Émile. 1912. *Les formes élémentaires de la vie religieuse*. Paris: Aican.
Eco, Umberto. 1978. *La struttura assente. La ricerca semiotica e il metodo strutturale*. Milan: Bompiani.
Ferraro, Guido. 2008. Antenato totemico e anello di congiunzione. La connessione tra "sacro" e "segno" nel pensiero di Emile Durkheim. In Nicola Dusi and Gianfranco Marrone (eds.) *Destini del sacro. Discorso religioso e semiotica della cultura*, 73–80. Roma: Meltemi.
Ferraro, Guido. 2012. *Fondamenti di teoria sociosemiotica. La visione neoclassica*. Rome: Aracne.
Gennep, Arnold van. 1909. *Les rites de passage*. Paris: ÉmileNourry.
Greimas, Algirdas Julien. 1976. *Sémiotique et sciences sociales*. Paris: Éditions du Seuil.
Greimas, Algirdas Julien. 1987. *De l'imperfection*. Paris: Éditions Pierre Fanlac.
Kroeber, Alfred. 1952. *The nature of culture*. Chicago: University of Chicago Press.
Prieto, Luis. 1975. *Pertinence et pratique. Essai de semiologie*. Paris: Minuit.
Remotti, Francesco. 1999. *Forme di umanità*. Torino: Paravia.
Santangelo, Antonio. 2011. Imaginary bridges? Looking for connections between Saussurian sociosemiotics and Sartre's theories about the imaginary. *Lexia 7/8*.
Santangelo, Antonio. 2013. *Sociosemiotica dell'audiovisivo*, Aracne, Roma
Saussure, Ferdinand de. 2001 [1916]. *Corso di linguistica generale [Cours de linguistique générale]*. Paris: Éditions Payot.
Tarasti Eero. 2008. *Fondamenti di semiotica esistenziale*. Bari:Laterza.
Vattimo, Gianni. 1985. *Lo fine della modernità*. Milano: Garzanti.

Xiaofang Yan and Yan Liu

Exploration on the construction of existential semiotic theory of film criticism

With Reference to *A Diary of A Country Priest*

Abstract: Traditional Film Semiotics is not related to the way how the spirit of subjects moves in the texts of movies. Finnish Semiotician Eero Tarasti suggests that Existential Semiotics is about studying transcendence which is the keyword of subjects' movements. Transcendent things can be those absent in reality but appear in our minds. How to reflect the movement of subjects' spirit through the visual way by movies is the goal of Existential Semiotic theory of Films, and whether the visual ways of movies could successfully represent the abstract movement of subjects' spirit, is the main content of Existential Semiotic Criticism of Film. Bresson's film *A Diary of A Country Priest* is a transcendent style film. By describing the theoretical analysis of both Tarasti and Greimas towards this novel, as well as on examples of transcendent movies Paul Schrader had found, this article is meant to approve that the establishment of Existential semiotic theory of Criticism in Film is very necessary and is of high probability no matter from which aspect, theoretical or practical.

Keywords: Existential Semiotics, Semiotics of Films, Transcendence, *A Diary of A Country Priest*

1 Introduction: From traditional semiotics of film to existential semiotic theory

Christian Metz, who proposed the theory of Semiotics of Films, asserted that Semiotics of Film must be done. From the 1960s to the present, Semiotics of Film has been regarded as objective truth and an independent study. Throughout the history of developing the Western Semiotics of Film, You zheng Li was the first scholar to introduce Semiotics of Films to the mainland of China. Furthermore, due to the effort exerted by two scholars Botang Zhuo and Longren Qi, semiotics of film is introduced to Taiwan.

The concept of Semiotics of Film first came from Roland Barthes, who was Mezt's teacher. While Barthes' semiotics mainly originated from the European semiology tradition represented by Saussure, he extended Saussure's semiology to the field of linguistics and non-linguistics, and Semiotics of Film belongs to the latter. Furthermore, Metz's Semiotics of Film developed under such context, which represents the distinctive features of structural semiotics.

From the perspectives of scholars Rui Ma and Yingjun Wu, the research object of Semiotics of Films is "Film Language- symbols of image and the related rules of signifying". (Ma & Wu 2016: 28) Rui Ma and Yingjun Wu illustrated in *An Introduction to Film Semiotics*, "The establishment of this research object reflects the requirement that the film theory moves towards independence, which requires the separation of film theory and criticism." (Ma & Wu 2016: 28) Besides, "studying how the film works as a system of signs, is a mechanism which committed to abstracting commons from considerable movie texts" (Ma & Wu 2016: 28). It is undeniable that the shortcoming of the current researches on Semiotics of Film is pursuing the integrity of the theory itself without noticing the specific context of film development and the uneven individual differences. I believe that the theory shall always be combined with criticism. Otherwise, the theory, which is not able to guide criticism, is deadly without vitality. As scholars, we should restore the theory to the lively reality of life. Combining theory with creation and criticism, and promoting mutually, in this way, we can involve the vitality of development and create a virtuous circle.

As Longren Qi indicated that, if Saussure is the leader of film semiotics in the 20th century, then the leader in the 21st century is Peirce." (Qi 2013: 2) Peirce's semiotics is deeply influenced by phenomenological categories, which profoundly affected the development of film semiotics at the first stage (Warren & Eco). However, at that time, semiotics was dominated by Saussure's theory. Therefore, the influence of Peirce's semiotics was little until the advent of two books written by French philosopher Deleuze in the 1980s. Since then, Peirce's semiotics regained its effect in film theory to the present. However, as the Italian scholar, Johannes Ehrat, indicated "Understanding Peirce has never been and will never be a simple matter. His theoretical system is obscure and difficult to be comprehended, and his thoughts about semiotics are rarely integrated into a comprehensive system. Except for a few people who have 'borrowed his views for their use' there is no real apprentice who can inherit his ideas." (Ehrat 2015: 6) Therefore, Peirce's combination of semiotics and film theory still needs further exploration and argumentation by more successors. While Johannes Ehrat's *Cinema and Semiotic: Peirce and Film Aesthetics, Narration, and Representation*, which is translated by Wen Yiming and published in December 2015, is one of the few attempts in this field.

Whether it is Christian Metz's first and second film semiotics, Pasolini's reality semiotics, and Warren and Eco's Peirce-pattern semiotics, Propp and Levi-

Strauss's film narrative semiotics, or Greimas's semiotic square and film narrative analysis, etc., little do they refer to the mental movement of subject's spirit in the text of the film. While Existential Semiotics proposed by the Finnish Semiotician, Tarasti, is studying transcendence, which is the keyword of subjects' movements.

Arguably, Tarasti believes that semiotics cannot always remain in the classic semiotics proposed by Peirce, Saussure, Greimas, Lotman, Sebeok, and others. "The process of signs is fluid" (Tarasti 2012: 3; Deely 2012: 3). Existential semiotics explores the life of signs from the inside. Unlike most of the previous semiotics, existential semiotics only focuses on the conditions created by special meanings, existential semiotics studies on the phenomena presented by the uniqueness. Besides, it studies signs which are in the movement and flow that are the features of signs when coming into being, and are defined as "pre-signs, act-signs, and post-signs" (Tarasti 2000: 33). Signs are regarded as such movement which transforms, in turns, between Dasein, where our world has its subjects and objects, and transcendence. The totally new categories of signs appear between reality, like Dasein, and tension beyond reality. Furthermore, the literal meaning of the term, Dasein, is "there", which is borrowed from German philosophy, especially the philosophy proposed by Heidegger and Jaspers. Tarasti said that unlike the term, Dasein, proposed by Heidegger, it mainly refers to my existence, and here, it does not only refer to the existence of a subject, me, but also other, and includes the objects of our desires as well. Beyond Dasein, in other words, beyond the concrete reality of our lives, is transcendence. Besides, the simplest definition of transcendence is: "transcendence can be anything that is absent in reality but appears in our hearts." (Tarasti 2015: 17) Therefore, transcendence is a spiritual movement, something intangible. How to reflect the movement of subjects' spirit through the visual way by movies is the goal of Existential Semiotic theory of Films; and whether the visual ways of movies could successfully represent the abstract movement of subjects' spirit is the main content of Existential Semiotic Criticism of Films.

2 From structure to existence – the evolution of semiotics on film criticism of *A Diary of A Country Priest*

A Diary of A Country Priest is adapted from the French writer Bernanos's novel of the same name. In the history of the world's films, it is one of the few art films which takes the human spirit as the object of expression. Eero Tarasti is the proposer of Existential Semiotics and his teacher A. J. Greimas, a Lithuanian linguist, was the proposer of the semiotic square, and the founder of the Paris School of Semiotics. In *Structural Semiotics*, Greimas used structural semiotics to explain *A Diary of A Country Priest*.

2.1 Greimas and Bernanos's semantic sphere

According to Greimas, the meanings associated with Bernanos can be divided into three sets. The first set is made up of the corpus of one novel, such as *A Diary of A Country Priest*. The second set is the corpus which contains all the novels of Bernanos. The last set is the corpus consists of all the novels produced in a certain society and a certain historical stage. Here a practical question arises: what meaning should be given to each of the three corpus sets? Among the models that are elucidated from these corpus sets, what structural associations can be found? On the whole, Greimas was concerned with structures throughout the book. Even in the specific novels of Bernanos, he had been looking for a universal structure. For example, in the chapter *The Description of The Sample*, he used the method of extraction. First of all, he extracted lexeme, and then he assumed the meanings they represent. For instance, for the word 'existence', Greimas believes different levels of platforms composed of its internal combination mode, they are actant, meme, and seme respectively. The subject of 'existence' is not a person, but a structure. As a composite structure, the structure of 'existence' lies in the spiritual dimension, including 'life' and 'die'. They possess different features of spiritual spaces. The character of the novel or 'actant' is neither the young priest, nor the old priest of Saury, nor the countess or other people. It is 'life/death', 'lie/truth', or other similar morphemes instead. The subject is surrounded by other actants, such as opponents and helpers. The analysis of Greimas fully demonstrates the situation that without a subject how does structuralism operate.

In Greimas's view, the semantic sphere of Bernanos serves as "a mediator between *A Diary of A Country Priest* and the imaginary world of French society in the first half of the 20th century" (Greimas 2001: 214). That means Greimas believed only by placing *A Diary of A Country Priest* in Bernanos's semantic domain, the novel will make sense. Greimas treated the characters or actants as morphemes with a dualistic opposition relationship. He considered the priest lives in his illusory world, while parishioners live in the real world. . . It reflects the macroscopic law of social operation. The society does not pay attention to every individual but try to integrate the individuals into the collective. The individual is only a nonentity under the operation of the morpheme. Walking along the route that was preset by others, the individual's emotions and complexity are ignored, whereas, emotion is the most important element to distinguish an individual from other people.

2.2 Existential semiotic analysis of *A Diary of A Country Priest*

Finnish semiotician Eero Tarasti reinterpreted the novel *A Diary of A Country Priest* from the perspective of Existential Semiotics. In Tarasti's view, Greimas's approach is too simple and objective, since Greimas did not take the subjective factor of the novel into account. The young priest lacks the competence of semiotic interpretation so that he cannot interpret messages in reality. He thinks the messages are stamped with hostility, and he completely treated them as signs that come from the restless reality. Those signs make him desperate. Meanwhile, the young priest could not understand what signs he represents in other people's eyes. For example, the little girl, who takes Communion, comes to read the Bible only because of the priest's beautiful eyes. However, he insists on accomplishing Christ's mission, and he believes he is reliable. This brings disastrous consequences to his surrounding world. In Tarasti's view, structures cannot explain the problem of the individual, and the subject of existence is the individual, not the structure.

According to Tarasti, existential semiotics is a new mode of meaning and communication. "I think communication is an act of transcendence." (Jiang & Zhao 2017: 217). When you communicate with others, you cannot know how he/she receives your information in advance. Can he/she understand or not? You can only assume things in your mind will similarly occur in his/her mind, but you are not sure. Therefore, communication is a terrible adventure that you must encounter. Jacques Lacan believes there are two dangers threatening human "to communicate in an overly polite way (It's raining now) or idiotic words, which means words only spoken by one person." (Jiang & Zhao 2017: 217). Both cases are lack of existence.

In Tarasti's recent work, he proposed the 'Zemic' model, and as a result, he pushed forward Existential Semiotic theory, which is being developed by him since 2000 (Yan, 2015). The 'Zemic' model is established based on the Algirdas Julien Greimas's semiotic square, and later it fills the blanks of existence that originated from Hegel's logic. Eventually, it leads to the emergence of the four modes of existence. They are placing on the semantic axis of Moi and Soi, for example, Moi = subject and Soi = society. Therefore, the four modes are Moi1 = body, Moi2 = personality, Soi2 = social practice, and Soi1 = values and norms. Then he deduced the Cartesian square matrix and replaced it with the constant movement from M1 to S1 and vice versa. They are the two symbols of powers in the universe, from perceptible and concrete to understandable and abstract, and on the other hand, from abstract to the concrete of physical reality. Thus, the square matrix becomes a simple Z model. Tarasti depicted these semiotic processes from the inside, so it is an emic model (defined by linguist Kenneth L. Pike). Therefore, Z plus emic model equal to Z mode (Zemic). This is the extent of the theory as of now. He is trying to develop a theory that can use the Z model to analyze any kind of culture synchronically, such as China, Europe, and et cetera. He also wants to analyze the interaction between culture and diachronic history, which means how does a culture develop diachronically.

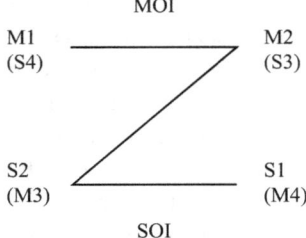

Figure 1: Zemic model (Tarasti 2015:26).

This model has two directions: one direction starts from the purest physical state and perceptibility towards the most eternal stable body (M2). Then it transfers to M3 further, and finally, it reaches the most abstract M4. The pictures show how social norms and abstract values display as concrete and physical things, and how individuals are imprisoned for their existence. The focus is on the inner movement between each element.

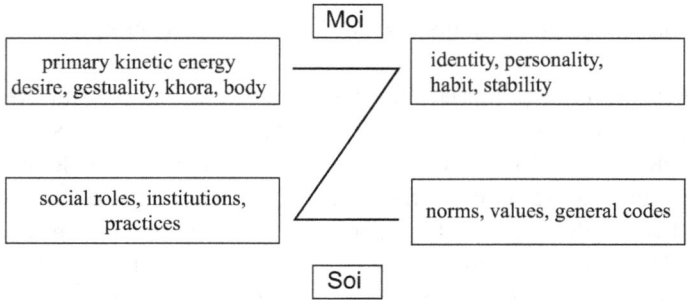

Figure 2: Zemic model (Tarasti 2015: 27).

The young priest comes to a strange town to preach with the faith and mission of preaching. He wants to pass on abstract value to the parishioners but misunderstood by them. We can use the Z model to interpret the movement of him.

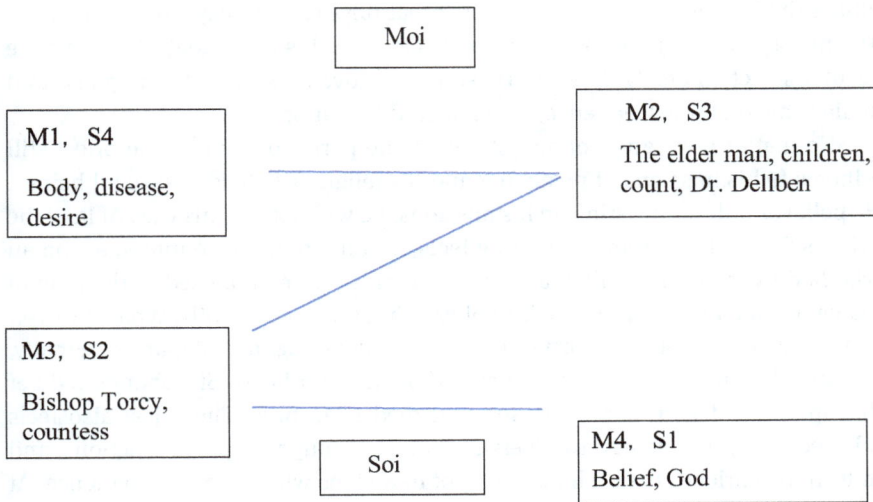

People are surrounded by a variety of signs, and we live in a world of signs. We constantly interpret others' signs, and we create signs for others' interpretations at the same time. The growth of humans can also be seen as the process of cultivating the ability to interpret signs. Classical semioticians have reached a consensus that semiotics is equivalent to communication plus meaning. The communication between the subjects enhances their understanding of the surrounding signs, and the correct understanding of the signs of the objective world is directly related to whether the subjects can adapt themselves to the surrounding world. In the film, the young priest goes to his first workplace in anticipation. He believes he can give full play to his talents and preach. However, reality does not go smoothly as he thought. For the priest, at first, he should build a good relationship with the locals and gradually gain the trust and support of the parishioners. He has a conflict with an elder man from the beginning, which leads to their hostility. When the young priest prepares children's communion, he is flouted by them. What is worse, he wants to visit the count so that he can make use of the count's financial resources and influence to build up a club and sports meet for young people, but he did not succeed. He feels lonely because the parishioners are offish. The young priest loses his value, and he did not receive any support. It is easy for him to find the essential difference between himself and the people around him. Dr Dellben says, "We are the same. We endure silently". Bishop Torcy has been trying to persuade him to be realistic and sensible. Bishop Torcy asks the young priest to do his job well and does not fantasize to be respected. However, the priest does not yield to the realities or compromise with the secular society. He follows his heart all the time, although he has to endure great physical and psychological agony. The priest finds his inner peace and walks towards his inner goal. He rejects the secular society, namely 'Dasein'. He starts to move forward to nothingness and achieve his first transcendence, which means 'negation'.

No matter how ignorant and stubborn the parishioners are, the priest still adheres to his missions of preaching and his religious beliefs to save all beings. He believes only by insisting on his missions, he will not lose his way. At last, the priest's firm belief achieves certain effects, and he frees the countess, a woman who had lived her life chillily and self-deceptively. She immersed in the grief of losing her son and endured the infidelity of her husband silently. What is worse, she had no choice but to withstand the pain of her daughter's departure. Finally, the priest's firm belief influenced her and opened her heart. She abandoned her disappointment and hatred for God and died peacefully. The priest also feels relieved. The priest achieves universal meaning through his positive actions, and in turn, he enriches the understanding of new signs with his own experience. At that time, the priest achieves the second transcendence of life. However, he does not recognize by the outside world and coupled with his deteriorative body. The priest has to go to a schoolmate, a fired priest, for shelter. Eventually, he dies silently. The priest ended his miserable life with a tragedy.

It can be seen that in this Z model, the main component of the young priest is M4 or S1. He encounters resistance from the other three elements. Resistance is also a manifestation of individual existence. The other three resistances are M3, M2, and M1 respectively. Each stage of the subject's developments or each component in the semiotic square of the subject poses threats and challenges to his beliefs. In this case, should he insist or give up? From the principle of structuralism, he should adapt to the circumstance and stays in harmony. By contrast, from the perspective of existentialism, his value lies in persistence.

Saussure considers the essence of language as sociality. The priest does not fully understand the words. When he communicates with others, he keeps talking about his thoughts without considering the relationships between humans. He keeps speaking without holding the power of speaking, and eventually, his right of speech is deprived. The priest's anxiety is doomed, and his tragedy is obvious. The tragedy lies in a weak positive 'energy field' that is endowed with the task of changing the strong negative 'energy field'. What is worse, his religious belief does not allow him to give up. Bernanos's 'semantic sphere' mentioned that truths and lies are the opposites. Truths are gradually accepted by people after sacrificing and fighting with falsehood. On the contrary, lies refuse to accept the new and correct things and succumb to the authority of ignorance. It would be easier for the priest to lie. Then the priest would not be anxious and would stay in harmony with the parishioners. However, it is more charming for him to pursue truth and stick to his belief. The anxiety of the priest also has strong practical and ethical significance. Therefore, Tarasti's Existential Semiotics is different from the traditional semiotics which has been developing by Saussure and many other linguists. It is no more unconcerned about reality and value and walking towards ethical semiotics. In response, John Deely commented, "Semioticians come to realize the need to go beyond pure theory and to explore the way of being and moral responsibilities of semiotics" (Deely 2012: 230).

3 Transcendent style films – the practical basis for the establishment of existential semiotic theory of film criticism

It is not rare to find the transcendent style in films. For example, films directed by Japanese directors Yasujiro Ozu and Mizoguchi, Chinese director Jia Zhangke, French director Robert Bresson, Finnish director Aki Olavi Kaurismäki, Swedish director Ingmar Bergman, Danish director Carl Dreyer, Soviet director Andrei Tarkovsky, and so and so forth. Schrader pointed out that the accomplishment of the transcendental style must follow three steps: everyday life, disparity, and stasis (Schrader 1972). He used *A Diary of A Country Priest* as an example for illustration.

The so-called everyday life is equivalent to 'dasein' in Existential Semiotic Theory. In the film, the social environment of Ambricourt parish and the daily life of the priest and parishioners are oppressive, tiring, and boring. People around the priest are surprisingly offish and hostile. Nevertheless, the priest's actions are not influenced by the environment and daily life. He always keeps himself apart from other people there. His disparity is the first step to start the journey of transcendence in Existential Semiotic Theory. That means negation; to negate everyday life or 'dasein'. In the film, the disparity is reflected in his actions and the conversations interrupted by the narration of the diary, which runs through the film. The narration of the diary pulls the priest into his heart at once when he should have responded to a person. 'Disparity' is a necessary condition for the character of the film to experience the presence of the divine. Schrader argued that there is a decisive moment before reaching the third stage, in which the character needs to silently observe the presence of the divine. In the film, before the last letter is read, the audience learns that the priest is dead and the state of mind on his deathbed: never mind, all is Grace. The cross appears at the end of the film means true stasis. There are at least three moments to show stasis. The first one is the priest helps the countess to regain her belief and then brings comfort to her soul. The second moment is when the priest communicates with Bishop Tracy, making him realize that he is a prisoner of the holy agony. The last moment is the state of mind on the priest's deathbed: all is Grace. This stasis corresponds to the second step of the transcendent journey in Existential Semiotic Theory- the transcendence of affirmation. Through which, the priest gains meaningful sense within himself. The everyday life, disparity, and stasis also correspond to what Karl Jaspers said respectively, "towards the world, the illumination of existence, and metaphysics".

The transcendent style of Bresson's films, as Susan Sontag said, is a kind of reflection. Bresson persuaded the audience to believe things they reject to believe, on the supernatural and spiritual level. Not only because the characters of his films believe in this spirit, but also the spirit indeed exists in his films. These films belong to the second and third kinds of films, as Peirce said.

Category theory is the main framework of Peirce's phenomenology. The classification system of his unique category theory is based on three principles: Firstness, Secondness, and Thirdness (Qi 2013: 57–58). Firstness includes qualities of phenomena, such as red, bitter, clean, hard, sad, and noble (I think films that excite our senses and bring strong visual and auditory shocks belong to Firstness. Of course, those phenomena are not objective, and they are perceived by the subjects). Firstness is superficial phenomena: "It must be instant and direct". Secondness includes actual and facts. Actual is equivalent to real, and similar to Aristotle's 'action', also stands for existence. "We are aware of ourselves and also aware of not non-self". Awareness is binary. To illustrate the relationship between Firstness and Secondness, Peirce used the experience as an example. That is the situation when the shoulders lean on the door to push it away: the dualistic relationship between effort and resistance. (Effort is the behaviour of the subject of existence, while resistance is the counteraction for the subject's effort. Without the subject's behaviour 'effort', the counteraction 'resistance' will also disappear). Thirdness is a ternary relationship, which exists in a sign, its object, and the idea of interpretation. Thirdness itself is also a sign, and it is regarded as an existential mode to construct a sign (Thirdness is a sign, meaning, or thought). According to Peirce's category of three principles, films, like *A Diary of A Country Priest*, mainly focus on exploring Secondness and Thirdness and related to existence and reflection as well. The other films of Bresson, such as *Angel of Evil, Pickpocket, A Man Escaped, Trial of Joan Of Arc*, etc. are all these films.

Bresson used seemingly simple film language to convey the complexity of the human spirit. Ozu Yasujiro's films are similar to Bresson's. He also used different movie techniques to question the offish daily environment, reflecting precious emotions. Paul Schrader said, "As any form of transcendental art, the transcendental style is committed to showing things that are unspeakable and invisible. The transcendent style itself is not unspeakable and invisible. It uses accurate time and angles of the camera to edit for pre-determined purposes" (Schrader, 1972: 3–4). The transcendence, as called by Schrader, is the same as Tarasti. The so-called transcendental style can convey the presence of the divine. It has not resorted to the audience's inner experience of the divine (otherwise, it has no difference with the general religious films) but based on the belief of the presence of the divine (Therefore, people can accept or reject). The presence of the divine is reflected by the absence of reality, so it is transcendence. Therefore, it is necessary to establish a semiotic analysis of transcendent films.

References

Deely, John. 2012. *Basics of semiotics*. Trans. by Zu Zhang, 6th edn. Beijing: China Renmin University Press.
Ehrat, Johannes. 2015. *Cinema, and semiotics: Peirce and film aesthetics, narration, and representation*. Trans. by Wen, Y. Chengdu: Sichuan University Press.
Greimas, Algirdas Julien. 2001 *Structural semantics*. Trans. by Jiang, Z. Tianjin: Baihua Literary and Art Publishing House.
Jiang, X. & Y. Zhao. (ed.) 2017. *Communication semiotics interview-dialogue in the context of new media [CHUAN BO FU HAO XUE FANG TAN LU – XIN MEI TI YU JING XIA DE DUI HUA [C]]*. Chengdu: Sichuan University Press.
MA, R. & Y. Wu. 2016. *Tutorials of cinema and semiotics [DIAN YING FU HAO XUE JIAO CHENG [M]]*. Chongqing: Chongqing University Press.
Qi, L. 2013. *Cinema and semiotics [M] [DIAN YING FU HAO XUE]*. Shanghai: The Eastern Publishing House.
Schrader, Paul. 1972. *Transcendental Style in Film: Ozu, Bresson, Dreyer*. Berkeley: University of California Press.
Tarasti, Eero. 2000. *Existential Semiotics*. Bloomington: Indiana University Press.
Tarasti, Eero. 2012. *Existential semiotics*. Trans. by Wei, Q. & Yan, X. Sichuan: Sichuan Education Press.
Tarasti, Eero. 2015. *Sein und Schein: Exploration in Existential Semiotics*. Berlin: De Gruyter Mouton.
Yan, Xiaofang. 2016. *Review of Sein und Schein: Explorations in existential semiotics*. Chinese Semiotic Studies 12 (4). 597–603.

Massimo Leone
The transcendent arithmetic of Jesus: An exercise in semiotic reading

Abstract: The article bears on how semiotics inflects the practice of interpretation. Often presented as a revolutionary method, the discipline of signs must prove itself in the exercise of organizing and communicating the meaning of complex cultural artifacts, whose aesthetics precisely consists in challenging the linearity of interpretation. The article enunciates its main hermeneutical principles, inspired by semiotics, then applies them to a concrete, difficult case-study: the hermetic literary text *The Childhood of Jesus* by J.M. Coetzee. This narrative conveys its meaning through highly unconventional and often puzzling inventions, whose deciphering requires the application of an astute method. That allows the reader to understand the deep reason of such narrative charade: what the text is seeking to evoke is a difficult theme, that of transcendence, which escapes the grasp of more linear narratives and common verbal constructions.

Keywords: textual Semiotics, post-modern narratives, J.M. Coetzee, *The Childhood of Jesus*, Transcendence

> It may be conceded to the mathematicians that four is twice two. But two is not twice one; two is two thousand times one. (G. K. Chesterton, *The Man Who Was Thursday*, 1908)

1 The assumptions of the interpretation

How to build a semiotic experiment?[1] Ignorant of laboratories, I have not found better than to observe myself in the reading and in the interpretation of a novel. I did not ask myself the question "how does semiotics read and interpret texts?", but "how do I do it?", what influence decades of semiotic studies have had on my reading but also what influence decades of reading have had on my semiotics? I exclude that, had I not studied and written about semiotics, today I would read and interpret how I do. I claim, however, the personality of my journey, and I per-

---

[1] The first version of this article was presented during the conference "The empirical research on text", University of Turin, Sala Lauree of the Department of Humanities, 18 October 2013. I thank Aldo Nemesio for propitiating this interesting event.

emptorily affirm that the rigid application of a method to interpretation is a kind of violence, as well as a vaguely kitsch act. I am grateful to Greimas, for example, but I would never dissect a text as he did with 'his' Maupassant. That was his style, and it was legitimate. The same cannot be said about his many epigones.

The first secret of interpretation consists in the choice of what is read. For example, I do not think that by interpreting a commercial advertisement one could say something profoundly interesting. At most, one should consider a series of commercials, whose complexity would challenge reading. The corollary of this first assumption is that interpretation needs to meet a certain resistance. Very simple objects, made to be decoded without ambiguity, like most commercials or commercial entertainment products, do not offer any resistance. They let themselves be interpreted without friction. One can try to complicate their nature by deconstructing them, or reconstructing them, and reading in them what no one else does, but this is not interpretation. It is rewriting.

Resistance, however, does not coincide with complexity. I can meet a resistant object and realize that it inspires me mild, banal readings. The second secret of interpretation is obsession. If an object does not awaken an obsession in me it can be complex at will but it will not challenge me. Instead, I must immediately have the certainty that this object hides an answer to something that haunts me, even something that I try to hide to myself.

There is, however, a third secret, always with regards to the choice of what is to be interpreted. A resistant object may perhaps challenge me but it will not capture my reading unless it involves seduction. I must fall in love with the shape of an object, with the internal disposition of its elements.

Fourth preliminary secret: a resistant object that haunts and seduces me will not awaken my interpretation if I cannot already see in it the possibility of gratification, of success. I shall happily interpret only those texts that I can, that I know how to interpret. Entrusting the interpretation of a novel to those who will not know how to recognize its poetics has something grotesque about it, as it is the case with all those methods that aim at teaching how to interpret. Interpretation is neither taught nor learned, like a craft. Rather, it develops as an art, through exposure, imitation, and absorption, but with disappointing results if art is not accompanied by talent. Defining talent is beyond my goals here. Rather, I am interested in the monetary metaphor. There is no interpretation without hoarding. Those who do not read in the hope of finding and setting aside a treasure cannot interpret. Nothing is sadder than those useless exercises, common in the courses of semiotics, in which the student applies a method to a text by extracting from it a meaning that he or she will forget immediately after the exam. Not to mention the student who asks the teacher what object he or she will have to submit to this mechanic effort. The fifth preliminary secret, therefore, is the following: an object of which one already perceives that it will not leave any trace in one's memory is not worthy of interpretation. The encounter with this resistance, the challenge of obsession and the seduction that ensues, will be tantamount to an artifice, an occasional event.

Sixth secret: one can never interpret by oneself. When Robinson Crusoe meditates on the Bible on his desert island, that is already interpretation, but not when, in the metropolis, an internet user reads a blog that he will not discuss with anyone. Interpretation needs a hermeneutical community because it is like a game that requires the meeting of more intentionalities within a field, a system of limits and rules.

It is important to explain the choice of words in this strange laboratory. When we speak of meaning in the abstract, and semiotics must do so because it aims at studying meaning in all its manifestations, it is impossible not to adopt equally abstract terms, like "object", or "text". The former is methodologically more neutral than the latter, but it does not matter. What matters is that, in the passage from the abstract to the empirical, there is something in me that deeply resists the use of jargon. In my experiment, I did not read a text, nor even a literary text. I read *a novel*. In fact, to be precise, *I picked up a book* and *read a novel*. And when I go to the cinema I do not watch a 'filmic text', I watch *a movie*. Perhaps we can strive to see a text in a novel even without mentioning it continually, for the sake of a more fraternal dialogue with the readers who preceded us and who will follow us, with those around us.

Last preliminary observation: it is absolutely not true that I have picked up a book, monitoring my moves as an interpreter, for the purposes of the present experiment. On the opposite. I happened to read a novel, and this reading seemed to me the perfect laboratory from which to draw, with an effort of memory rather than attention, some indications on the paths of interpretation. There are complex epistemological questions about the relationship between observation and monitoring, especially in mental experiments, but I shall not deal with them here.

2 The object of interpretation

The novel whose reading I have decided to recall here is *The Childhood of Jesus*, by the South African (now Australian) writer J.M. Coetzee, first published in English in October 2013.[2] As I have anticipated, it is not a random choice for me,

---

[2] London: Harvill Secker

and it could not be one. First of all, I am not just a reader of Coetzee. I am, in a sense, his follower. I read everything he has published, both novels and essays. Why am I a follower of Coetzee? In the first place, because, to take up one of the secrets mentioned above, I am enchanted by his way of putting words and sentences together. And I do not speak of metaphorical charm, but of cognitive, physical, almost cerebral charm. Each sentence of Coetzee gives me a sort of sensual pleasure. It is impossible to separate expression and content, but I have the impression that Coetzee's style, the way in which he says what he says, would produce this enchantment in me even if he spoke of absolute trivialities. There is a passage in *The Childhood of Jesus* in which Coetzee speaks of excrements, and describes how the protagonist unclogs an obstructed toilet. Well, this passage is stylistically wonderful. The wonder comes from the intimate certainty that there is no way to put together those words and phrases to say better what they say. I think I have realized, after a long frequentation of Coetzee's novels, why this style awakens in me such a delight, through which linguistic choices. Other writers provoke the same enjoyment in me, yet I cannot consider myself as their follower: the French writer Jean-Philippe Toussaint, for example, or the Spanish Antonio Muñoz Molina, or even more commercial writers, like the American Jonathan Franzen.

I consider myself, instead, a follower of Coetzee for other reasons. First of all, because I am sure that his novels will touch on themes that are essential to me, and that their reading will make them recognizable to me even when, in the hurry of life, I have lost sight of them. Secondly, because Coetzee's books lead me toward the suspicion, at times the conviction, that I could find something intimately precious therein, a sort of an answer. Thirdly, because Coetzee not only seduces me by his style, or his themes, but also by his tone. Sometimes the topics he deals with, like South African society, for instance, do not involve me personally. Yet, I have a distinct feeling that were this theme to involve me one day, I would like to talk about it in the same way in which Coetzee does. Fourth and last place: I presume to be able to accept the challenge that Coetzee's books offer, to engage in a confrontation with their resistant surface, and to win. In my modest experience as a reader, I find these features only in some writers whose work is not an ongoing corpus but an already closed one, such as dead authors like Dostoevsky and Camus, and perhaps in no other living writer. That is why I look forward to every new book by Coetzee as a kind of secular revelation.

What happened to me when I picked up this book?

3 The interpretation of the para-text

The book's paratext, as Genette would call it, immediately guides my reading. Given my long-term academic interest in religions, the novel's title, *The Childhood of Jesus*, sharpens my curiosity and pushes me to restrict my interpretative approach within a field of moves. In fact, I expect to read a personal story, probably an allegorical one, on the early years of Jesus's life. The title, however, is not isolated in the cover (Figure 1). An image also appears therein, serving as a counterpoint to the title. Three characters are depicted in it, two men and a woman, obliquely arranged on three levels of the photography's perspective, the woman between the two men, all dressed in the Anglo-Saxon sportswear of the 1920s or 1930s: light shoes, comfortable white cotton trousers, loose jackets, open-necked shirts. A tennis racket appears in the hand of the character in the foreground, while the woman keeps a medium-sized dog on a leash. The complexions are fair but very tanned, almost roasted by the sun. The faces, especially the male ones, are bony, leathery, as it was typical in those years. One would say these are faces from Australia, or South Africa, or India, and in any case from a sunny part

Figure 1: Cover of *The Childhood of Jesus* by J.M. Coetzee. Penguin books.

of the Commonwealth; all around, a well-kept lawn, surrounded by hedges and tall trees, perhaps jacarandas. Not only what the image represents, but also the technique of representation is at odds with the title: a photo in black and white, conspicuously sepia.

I know, even before I begin to read, that the childhood of Jesus that will be told to me is not historical but an updated childhood, allegorically transposed to the present time. The precise meaning of this image, however, will be revealed to me, at least in part, only later. I am going therefore to read while I am conscious of a tradition, that of the many writers who have told in their own way the life of Jesus, and in particular his childhood. The choice is logical: very few Gospels tell us about this period, while the information we have belongs mostly to apocryphal literature. It is, therefore, very fertile ground for those who, like Kazantzakis or Saramago, want to create a new imaginary of the early years of Christ as a parable, as a new point of view on Christianity and humanity.

Despite its rigidity, what I have learned about the composition of stories from Greimas' semiotics is essential to me. Not that I begin, as the Franco-Lithuanian semiotician did with Maupassant, to dissect the story so as to eviscerate it of its values, actants, actors, and figures. At first glance, I enjoy, first of all, the mental sound of words and sentences, I yield to the childlike lure of narration, and yet a professional deformation, in addition to the set of the experiment, pushes me to certain alertness. Perhaps interpretation is also that. It is a kind of under-the-skin anxiety, an exercise in paying attention to the signals that are caught in passing while one is immersed in a flow. This attention pushes me to ask myself at what level of abstraction the novel will evoke Jesus's childhood in filigree. It immediately seems clear to me that Coetzee keeps well away from Saramago or Kazantzakis: there the reader would immediately find the subtext of the evangelical or apocryphal tale. Here, instead, I sense that the effort I am asked for is much greater. Coetzee's novel does not tell the life of Jesus, it never mentions him, it does not name any of the characters that compose the scene of the Gospels, and does not even describe the times, spaces, and actions that characterize the biography of Christ. The novel, therefore, proposes to me a sort of charade: the title imposes on me that I recognize therein a childhood of Jesus, yet all the clues for this recognition are hidden or rather veiled. I also understand that solving this charade, recognizing the childhood of Jesus in a novel that never talks about him, will give me the key to it. It is by resolving this charade, in fact, that the novel will give me an answer to a question whose fundamental, existential importance for me I am paradoxically still ignorant about.

4 Interpretation of a charade

As in any charade, however, there are some clues. First, there is a child. His name is not Jesus but it is a biblical name, David, referring to a character closely related to the Christian reading of the Old Testament. At the same time, we will soon know that this is not his real name. The story is in fact immersed in a kind of sometimes disturbing haze where one is never sure of the space and time in which one finds oneself.

We meet David in the company of Simón, a middle-aged adult who narrates the story and who, as we discover, is the child's godfather. The two arrive tired and hungry in a reception centre for migrants in a place called Novilla. We are in fact in an imaginary world in which Spanish has become a lingua franca and the city where most of the story takes place has a toponym that indicates its novelty, Novilla as a *new town*, or as a *nouvelle ville*.

Looking at my moves as an interpreter, I find myself thinking that Coetzee will offer me an allegorical story of the childhood of Jesus as an apologue on immigration. As I continue reading, however, this hypothesis thins out, disintegrates. The novel talks about immigration, but it is not *about immigration*. Or rather, it proposes on immigration a thought that places it in the context of a more general and subtle reflection, free from the banality to which the urgency of current events turns the discourse of media. This first hypothesis breaks down both by virtue of my prejudices about Coetzee – it is not plausible that such a fine thinker proposes a moralizing story – and by virtue of the continuation of the story itself: slowly I discover that in Novilla they are *all* immigrants. They have all arrived in the new city through a port called Belstar, aboard ships from an unspecified elsewhere. But everyone is encouraged to get rid of the memory of the past life to embrace the new existence that is offered to them by Novilla.

My structural sensitivity suggests to me that the novel runs constantly on two tracks. On the first, sibylline clues continue to nurture the suspicion that I am in fact being told a story of the childhood of Jesus. On the second, signals are given to me to understand in what light the childhood of Jesus is flowing before my eyes.

As for the first track, the genius of Coetzee deconstructs the evangelical narrative into some essential molecules to then re-propose them, rearranged, in the novel. The comparison that best captures this operation is perhaps the one with molecular food, in the style of Ferrant Adriá. I do not recognize the visual aspect of a dish, nor that of its ingredients, yet their decomposition and re-composition not only allows me to recognize the taste of the dish but also to grasp with unparalleled clarity the contribution of each ingredient to its formation. Joseph's molecules converge and merge together then in Simón: he reiterates on numerous occasions that he is not the biological father of David, but a sort of godfather, or uncle, or guardian, and that he nevertheless considers himself the natural father of the child. Simón finds work in Novilla as a port hauler, a manual work that weakens his body giving it an indefinable age, but nevertheless of a maturity that tends to old age. But Simón inherits from Joseph above all the lucid dismay with respect to what is happening to him: he finds himself the guardian of a child who is not his son, to whom he feels as close as though he were his own, and little by little it is revealed to him that this child is not normal and that the family situation that is taking shape around him is not normal either.

At one point, David finds his mother but in a way, that again distorts the subtext of the Gospel story. One day, as they wander around the outskirts of Novilla, David and Simón encounter a sort of luxury reception centre called "La Residencia". In the garden, we recognize the characters on the book cover, in tennis clothes. An epiphany takes place here: Simón knows that David and his mother were separated on the ship that took them to Novilla. We are told about the father that "it is a complicated affair". David had a letter around his neck that would allow him to be reunited with his parents, but this letter went lost. In the Residencia, Simón sees Inés, the girl in the photo, and has not simply the feeling, but also the utter certainty that she is David's mother. He, therefore, asks her to take him with her, and Inés accepts, despite the initial contrariety of the brothers.

This recognition, to the reader's eyes, happens in an unexpected and paradoxical way. Simón has been represented, up to this point, as an extremely rational individual. We know, moreover, that David does not remember his mother's face and, last fundamental clue, we are told that Inés is a virgin. Yet Simón has no doubt that Inés is David's mother, and Inés has no doubts about welcoming his son as a natural child.

It is therefore clear that what Coetzee is staging here is *the impossible narrative of the dogma*. It is not possible to tell the birth of Jesus in terms of narrative rationality, and the astonishment that seizes the reader before this fundamental stage of the story is, therefore, the same that captures the believer before the dogma. Coetzee instills in the reader the bewilderment of dogma.

Finally, even in David, we recognize some molecules of Jesus. But it is above all in his case that these elements are blended into a strange, ambiguous result. David has an obsessive relationship with death. There is nothing that dismays him more than any endangerment of life, for example when his friend Alvaro, superintendent of longshoremen, is stabbed by Señor Daga, a gangster of Novilla. And when illness or death occurs around David, he repeats with certainty that he is able to heal or bring back to life. When Rey, the harbor mule, falls ill and dies, David begs Simón to let him breathe his breath into the animal's nostrils. Yet, these miracles are promised but never take place, their enunciation is always imputed by adults to the strangeness of a child with too a fervent imagination.

David is indeed a child full of imagination, and with a very quick intellect. He learns chess with lightning speed, for example. However, it is in this regard that the second of the tracks of the novel manifests itself. When Simón begins to give David the rudiments of education, the child shows strange behaviors. Simón tends to minimize them, but they explode when the child, as required by law, is enrolled in school. After a short time, his putative parents are summoned, because David seems unable to learn, showing a lack of concentration that disturbs the class. The diagnosis is not clear, but dyslexia is explicitly evoked, and the suspicion of autism constantly hovers in the heated conversations between Simón and Inés on the one hand and, on the other hand, Señor León, the teacher of David. Supported by the opinion of the school psychologist, he claims that David should be sent to a sort of reformatory school for children with special needs, located outside Novilla, where parents can visit him twice a month.

Here a narrative tension arises that will lead Simón, Inés, and David to flee Novilla, to another immigrant city called "Estrellita del Norte". Here too the reader with some familiarity with the Gospel story will recognize molecules of another escape, that to Egypt; in this case too there is a danger generated by an anti-subject, as Greimas would define it. And yet interpretation does not consist only in grasping this abstract similarity, but also in seizing the particular differences that create a gap with the subtext. Readers must recognize Herod in Señor León, but also ask themselves: what does this Herod of Novilla embody, why does the novel blend the molecules of the Flight to Egypt in this way?

5 Interpretation of the figures

It is then not around the macro-structures of the story, but around its particular figures that the interpretation must coagulate. As Louis Marin argued about the column halved in the *Tempest* of Giorgione,[3] this fragment of a column is too strange, in too unusual in a position, for not being used as a springboard for interpretation. And this is not because it was placed there, allegorically, by the author's intentionality. Quite the contrary. We can say instead that, in the creation of his painting, Giorgione came across the idea of this half-column as I come upon it in the painting's observation. Giorgione, the painter, and I, the spectator, meet just in the impossibility of expressing the meaning of this half column if not with its presence in the middle of the painting.

---

3 (Marin 1994).

Adopting a metaphor, one could say that reading the meaning of an object is like passing one's hand on a granite slab, whose smoothness is offered to us by the flow of narration, but whose roughness – the more variable the orography of the slab the more it is beautiful – provides the sense, the direction, as well as the *ductus* of interpretation. With meteorological a metaphor instead of a tactile one, Greimas called the peaks of this micro-orography "isotopy".

So, what is the isotopy of Coetzee's Childhood of Jesus? Certainly not the unstructured reference to the gospel, which rather provides the narrative and mythical support of the story. The isotopy emerges instead from the coalescence of figures craftly disseminated along the story. A fundamental figurative path is outlined in David's relation with numbers. Although the child is endowed with quick intelligence and grasps the sense of chess in a flash, he shows disturbing difficulties in seizing the arithmetic common sense of numbers. These difficulties then explode in school and help determine the narrative development mentioned above.

Here is a conversation between David and Simón about the nature of numbers:

> David: "I know all the numbers. Do you want to hear them? I know 134 and I know 7 and I know" – he draws a deep breath – "4623551 and I know 888 and I know 92 and I know-"
>
> Simón: "Stop! That's not knowing the numbers, David. Knowing the numbers means being able to count. It means knowing the order of the numbers – which numbers come before and which come after. Later on it will also mean being able to add and subtract numbers – getting from one number to another in a single jump, without counting all the steps between. Naming numbers isn't the same as being clever with numbers. You could stand here and name numbers all day and you wouldn't come to the end of them, because the numbers have no end. Didn't you know that? Didn't Inés tell you?"
>
> David: "It's not true!"
>
> Simón: "What is not true? That there is no end to the numbers? That no one can name them all?"
>
> David: "I can name them all."
>
> Simón: "Very well. You say you know 888. What is the next number after 888?"
>
> David: "92."
>
> Simón: "Wrong. The next number is 889. Which of the two is bigger, 888 or 889?"
>
> David: "888."
>
> Simón: "Wrong. 889 is bigger because 889 comes after 888."
>
> David: "How do you know? You have never been there."
>
> Simón: "What do you mean, been there? Of course I haven't been to 888. I don't need to have been there to know 888 is smaller than 889. Why? Because I have learned how numbers are constructed. I have learned the rules of arithmetic. When you go to school you will learn the rules too, and then numbers won't any longer be such a" – he hunts for the world – "such a complication in your life."

> The boy does not respond, but regards him levelly. Not for a moment does he think his words pass him by. No, they are being absorbed, all of them: absorbed and rejected. Why is it that this child, so clever, so ready to make his way in the world, refuses to understand?
>
> David: "You have visited all the numbers, you tell me," he says. "So tell me the last number, the very last number of all. Only don't say it is Omega. Omega doesn't count."
>
> Simón: "What is Omega?"
>
> David: "Never mind. Just don't say Omega. Tell me the last number, the very last one."
>
> The boy closes his eyes and draws a deep breath. He frowns with concentration. His lips move, but he utters no word.
>
> A pair of birds settle on the bough above them, murmuring together, ready to roost.
>
> For the first time it occurs to him that this may be not just a clever child – there are many clever children in the world – but something else, something for which at this moment he lacks the word. He reaches out and gives the boy a light shake. "That's enough," he says. "That's enough counting."
>
> The boy gives a start. His eyes open, his face loses its rapt, distant look and contorts. "Don't touch me!" he screams in a strange, high-pitched voice. "You are making me forget! Why do you make me forget! I hate you!"
>
> (Coetzee 2013: 149–151)

It is not clear how this surreal dialogue on numbers might intersect the story of a divine childhood, although the reference to Omega, a symbol of both numerical and transcendent limit, encourages one to look for the meeting point of these figurative paths. It is only in the general economy of the novel, however, that the orographic profile of its meaning is clearly outlined, often starting from episodes that seem absolutely unrelated to the one just mentioned. One concerns the sexuality of Simon/Joseph. In search of sexual satisfaction, having no relation with the virgin Inés except that of watching over David's welfare, Simon goes to a brothel run by the city of Novilla, where he is asked to fill in two forms so that he can be put in contact with the appropriate prostitute. Here is the final phase of the dialogue between the brothel secretary and Simón:

> "You haven't ticked a box," she says. "Length of sessions: 30 minutes, 45 minutes, 60 minutes, 90 minutes. Which length do you prefer?"
>
> Simón: "Let us say the maximum of relief: ninety minutes."
>
> "You may have to wait some time to get a ninety-minute session. For reasons of scheduling. Nonetheless, I'll put you down for a long first session. You can change that later, should you so decide. Thank you, that is all. We will be in touch. We will write, informing you of when the first appointment will be."
>
> (Coetzee 2013: 139)

The irony of the episode is obvious. It ironizes on the genre of social relations in Novilla. There is no hatred in the immigrants' city, nor violence, with very few significant exceptions. There is no Herod. Everything bathes in a warm and a bit dull broth of "goodwill", of benevolence. No one remembers their past, everyone is a newcomer, and people help each other not out of love but out of a more bland and widespread feeling, with neither élans nor harshness. The circulation of this aseptic fluid is regulated by an administrative apparatus that takes care of everything, from looking for a job for immigrants to their sexual needs, but without ever taking an interest in them personally.

Therefore, if the baby Jesus of Coetzee paws to affirm his sense of numbers, he does so in order to affirm a principle that is revealed in one of the last episodes of the novel. Simón, recovering from being hit in the port by the arm of a new mechanical crane, has a conversation with Eugenio, the crane operator, who goes to visit him every day because he feels guilty. The two engage in a discussion on David's unique sense of numbers, and for a moment Simón seems to grasp the child's point of view. The discussion focuses on why, for David, two plus two does not make four:

> Eugenio: "But two and two equal four. Unless you give some strange, special meaning to equal. You can count it off for yourself: one two three four. If two and two really equaled three then everything would collapse into chaos. We would be in another universe, with other physical laws. In the existing universe two and two equal four. It is a universal rule, independent of us, not man-made at all. Even if you and I were to cease to be, two and two would go on equaling four."
>
> Simón: "Yes, but which two and which two make four? Most of the time, Eugenio, I think the child simply doesn't understand numbers, the way a cat or dog doesn't understand them. But now and then I have to ask myself: Is there anyone on earth to whom numbers are more real?
>
> "While I was in hospital with nothing else to do, I tried, as a mental exercise, to see the world through David's eyes. Put an apple before him and what does he see? An apple: not one apple, just an apple. Put two apples before him. What does he see? An apple and an apple: not two apples, not the same apple twice, just an apple and an apple."
>
> (Coetzee 2013: 248–249)

6 Conclusions: The arithmetic of Jesus

The arithmetic one is not the only figural isotopy that runs across the novel. There is another, equally if not more important one, which unfolds around Cervantes' *Quixote*, a classic that Coetzee both loves and is an expert about. As David insists on not embracing the common sense of arithmetic, so he strives not to give in to the common sense of fiction, to the reasonable separation between what is real and what is fictitious. The two isotopies are intertwined, and together they delineate the profound meaning of this childhood of Jesus. The novel invites us not only to recognize the figures of Christ's biography, albeit scattered. It also suggests the teleology of this strange divine incarnation. The evil that the Christ of Coetzee seems to have come to defeat is not that of Herod's violence, the brute prevarication of man over man, the exclusion of the last. The evil of this baby Jesus is more abstract. It could be defined, with a new metaphor, as *a statistical evil*. The evil that is perpetuated in the *oblivion of singularities*. The number, the arithmetical categorization of several elements under the same concept and symbol, embodies this practice since it is only by repressing the singularities that the world can become a number, a matter for calculation and organization. Coetzee's novel, according to this reading, is, therefore, a story about immigration, but not in the trivially sociological sense of the term. Instead, it insinuates an atrocious doubt about the human capacity to grasp suffering: when pain is categorized, accounted for, administratively treated, what results is a kind of cold violence, a dehumanization under the sign of logistics.

But *The Childhood of Jesus* is not just a novel about immigration, because it detects an even more general and more pernicious tendency in the collective treatment of this pain. It is the tendency to reduce existence, life, and, above all, social relations to numbers, to quantity, to matter for calculation. This reduction to numbers, which feeds the new digital writings in a vicious circle, is certainly functional to life in society. No community could live without numbers. And yet when one begins to count friendships in social networks, or when, in the universities of the whole world, ideas are not exchanged, accepted, or contested, but simply counted, then something in the course of the stars that oversee the human destiny shows a disturbing scenario for the humanist, for the person who wants not to count but to recount.

Thus, in observing myself as I read and interpret this childhood of Jesus, I have found myself thinking of the world where I live and work, and its obsession with numbers and tables, and the tragic destiny of a Christ who, descended again on earth to free us from this evil, is not crucified on a cross but trapped in the cases of a formulary, interned as autistic in a world of accountants.

Reference

Marin, Louis. 1994. *De la représentation*. Paris: Gallimard – Seuil.

Aleksi Haukka
Descriptions of death in the Book of Job

Abstract: This essay approaches the Book of Job from the point of view of existential semiotic theory. The approach to the text is not theological but rather existential. Special focus is placed on Job's seemingly contradictory depictions of death and their signification. Even when Job's friends argue against everything else he says, they curiously remain silent on the issue of death. The reason for this remains unanswered for the time being.

Keywords: The Book of Job, semiotics, existential Semiotics, dialogue,

1 Introduction

In the very first pages of his *Sein und Schein* (2015: 3) Eero Tarasti writes that central objective of existential semiotic theory is to revalorize subject and subjectivity in the context of semiotics. This existential semiotic's focus on subjectivity lead me to the idea of trying to apply its theories and concepts on the Book of Job with its existential narrative. The proper object of this text is one of the many side themes of the Book of Job: its descpriptions about death. Interestingly enough Job's descriptions about the nature of death is one of the rare subjects on which his friends offer no opinions during the course of the dialogue.

In this text I will thus apply the existential semiotic concept of *Dasein* and the new z- or zemic (as in z-emic) model on the Book of Job in order to analyze and interpret the elements of the discourse concerning the nature of death. In existential semiotics *Dasein* refers to the present existence of a subject; as Tarasti (2015: 5) writes, it refers not only to Me, "but also to Others, and likewise to the objects of our desires". The z-model on the other hand is used to analyze the *Dasein* in question. First the subject's social (*Soi* or S) and individual (*Moi* or M) aspects are distinguished. Further the subject is approached from four different levels. First level is the primarily bodily M1/S4, second the individual or personal M2/S3, third the social or institutional S2/M3, while fourth level is the abstract level of values and ideas of S1/M4. All of these four leves are in constant flux in the subjects life, in his *Dasein*. (Tarasti 2015: 24–29). The active levels of the z-model are primarily the levels of M2 and S2. M1, on the other hand is, is the subject's "flesh and bone" similar to Jacques Fontanille's *Moi* (2004: 60). Finally, S1/M4 refers to the values in abstract. They are something that subject may or may not actualize.

https://doi.org/10.1515/9783110789164-042

Before proceeding to the material, I will present my referring technique for the Book of Job. With this technique the speeches are referred by the speaker and by the order of the speech. All the human actors are thus given an emblem. Job's emblem is J, Eliphaz's E, Bildad's B, Zophar's, S, and Elihu's U. So Job's sixth speech would be marked with the index 6J, whereas 1E would be Eliphaz's first speech, Bildad's first speech is 1B and so on. This allows more informative citations than what can be obtained from giving only the verses. One can then more easily follow the inner changes of the main character, which are crucial for understanding the Book of Job as can be seen from Agata Szepe's (2018: 55) recent interpretation from the point of view of drama theory.

2 The themes and reception of the Book of Job

The Book of Job is a work of literature that has puzzled generations of writers. As the exegete Jacques Vermeylen writes (2015: 370): "The Book of Job has its proper greatness and beauty: it has something unique."[1] Still the Danish church historian Niels H. Gadegård (1971: 17) was probably quite realistic in his estimation that the Book of Job is like Dante's *Divina Commedia* or Goethe's *Faust* – a book that is often lauded but rarely read. Nevertheless, it has spawned a great deal of commentaries and influenced countless writers. From Christian commentators one can mentions figures such as St. John Chrysostom, Pope Gregory the Great, Thomas Aquinas, and Luis de León. Apparently the Book of Job had also powerful influence on the first existentialist philosopher Søren Kierkegaard. For example his *Repetition* (*Gentagelsen*, 1843) has a sequence on Job. The book also played a role Fyodor Dostoyevsky's life all the way from his childhood to his last days (Troyat 1963: 384; Ilarion 2002: 394). The reception history of the Book of Job extends from the antiquity to our days and has been widely researched. Its influence is not merely restricted to commentary literature, but also to fiction, music, the visual arts, and cinema (see. e.g. Vicchio 2006a, 2006b, 2006c; Franklin and Canty 2016).

The existential main theme, the plot of the book, is the protagonist's downfall from the central figure of his community into the state of diseased and disdained object of mockery. The protagonist is Job, a man who in the prologue loses everything but his life. When Job's three friends hear of his misfortune they arrive to console him. First they mourn with Job for seven days and seven nights. On the eight day Job starts to speak his heart out. His lamentations provoke the friends.

---

1 (Vermeylen 2015:370): "Le livre de Job a sa grandeur et sa beauté: il a quelque chose d'unique."

They start to argue with Job and wrongly blame him for his own misfortunes and try to get him to confess culpability for the situation. This is something that Job will not do. Thus a quarrel begins. Eliphaz the Temanite has three responses, as does Bildad the Shuhite, though Job interrupts his last speech, Zophar the Naamahite gets to speak only twice. In the dispute Job gets the last word. After that young Elihu son of Barakel starts to rebuke Job. Finally God answers to Job's lamentations and accusations.

Theologically the Book of Job's primary purpose is simply the rejection of the retribution doctrine, that is to say, the idea that bad things happen to wicked and good things to good people (Mannermaa 1911: 14–15). Still, reducing the Book of Job to this one theme would be extremely erroneous for as a work of literature it is a profound one, and even its side issues allow for considerable studies.

One of these side themes is the limits and difficulty of dialogue. Job and his friends start to reprimand each other in no time. On the other hand, one can note at least some development and reciprocity even in the fierce dialogue. The Book of Job also poses the question about limits of knowledge, as the friends of Job do not in reality know what Job is talking about. They never attain complete knowledge of Job's inner world or heart. The Book of Job also defends the notion that its significance transcends any temporal *Dasein* when Job wishes that his words would be "engraved in rock forever" (6J 19:22–23). It is as if the Book of Job itself would say that it cannot be read culturally or reduced to any one culture but that it necessitates an universal or transcendental interpretation. Job's last speech (9J 31:1–40) contains the ethical core of the book. In a sense, there one can find the ethical counterpart to the moralistic Ten Commandments. The philosopher and historian Gerschom Scholem (2014: 321–322) thinks that the Book of Job is an indication of the deep relationship between lamentations and teaching. Finally, the aesthetic value of the book is a question in itself with its almost musical beauty with repetitions where Job and his friends develop themes as if in a concerto.

One of the least notable themes of the book is death. Even if Christians at least refer commonly to Job's sixth speech (6J 19:25–27) where Job according to the Christian interpretation affirms the hope of resurrection, this theme is hardly marked in the book as a whole. Still the aforementioned section is far from the only reference to death in the Book of Job. Quite the contrary, the existential state of death is present in all of Job's seven first speeches. Truly, death in Job's speeches is represented not simply as a privation or negation of life, but as a state of existence. Curiously enough, the friends do not address Job's speeches on death at all. Before proceeding to the main question, it is pertinent to give some information on the Book of Job's language and on the theories of its origin and its structure.

3 The form and origin of the Book of Job

Job's Hebraic text is in many parts hard to interpret and it is also partially corrupted. Even without the extra-layer that translations bring the Book of Job contains parts where consensus of the signification has not been reached as even the meaning of some of the words is debatable. (Habel 1975: 11; Michel 1987: 1)

For translators of the ancient times, also, the text, mostly in verse form, was difficult (Michel 1987: 5; Greenstein 2018: 179–182). The original Greek translation of the Book of Job in Septuagint is quite free and one sixth shorter than the Hebraic. One of the reasons suggested for its shorter length is that the translator or translators would have left out repetitions and impenetrable passages. Other suggestion is that some times the omissions resulted due to translator's theological views. However, in most of the surviving Greek manuscripts the version of the Book of Job is one completed by Origen who based his work on a more literal version probably translated by Theodotion (Tenhunen 2018: 181–183). Interestingly enough in the Septuagint's version Job's wife has bigger role than in the Hebraic masoretic text. For example St. John Chrysostom comments on the wife's words somewhat extensively.

In this essay the issues concerning translation are not given greater thought. They are properly concerns of linguists and not of someone doing an existential semiotic interpretation on one of the themes of the book. In this text the Book of Job will be treated as it has been received, as a translated book. All the quotations are from the New International Edition (NIV). Thus no notice will be paid on the hebraic meters or symbolic numbers (cf. Fokkelman 2012: 203). In this sense my interpretation is based on previous interpretations (i.e. translations). At the same time, any interpretation of the Book of Job that neglects the previous interpretations can be hardly justified.

There are different theories concerning the history of origin of the Book of Job (see e.g. Vermeylen 2015: 35–53). All of them cannot be treated in this discourse.

Considering the dating, Habel (1975: 10) finds unlikely that the Book of Job would have been written before the 600 BC. According to Vicchio (2006a)[2] the Hebraic text can be dated to the end of sixth century BC. According to common view the prologue and the epilogue date, at least mostly, from earlier period than the poetic section (Habel 1975: 5–6; Vicchio 2006a; Vermeylen 2015: XIII).[3] Elihu's speech is often considered to be later addition. And if this is the case then there is still the question of whether it is written by the same author as the rest of the book

---

2 (Vicchio 2006a): "the final redaction at the end of the sixth century BCE".
3 (Vicchio 2006a): "the internal evidence of the prologue suggests".

or by some other. (Habel 1975: 8). According to one hypothesis the speech of Elihu was added to the dialogue before the response of God and God's speech itself was composed in two parts; in this case the speeches about Behemoth and Leviathan would be later additions (see Jacobson 1981: 66). It has been also suggested that the Book of Job is partially composed of unrelated or even contradictory elements. But then again according to other interpretations the text is a coherent whole and the contradictions are intentional. (Sawyer 1978: 255; see Smick 1986: 136). Some critics have esteemed that the many repetitions would indicate that the dialogue has many sources, but according to Gadegård (1971: 19–20) repetitions and variations are purposeful effect in Semitic literature.

According to the recent study by Jacques Vermeylen (2015: 369–371) the Book of Job was composed in five different epochs. First there was the ancient legend of Job. This old legend then served more or less as prologue and epilogue for the dialogue composed during the times of Nehemiah (5th century BC) and it was later supplemented in three different epochs. Also, the Book of Job would have had political meaning in addition to the religious one as in that era those spheres of life were closely intertwined.

All in all, knowledge about the history of origin is not essential for this essay. Thomas Aquinas wrote that his commentary was not concerned in what epoch Job lived or whether he or some other wrote the book. Likewise, in my interpretation, I deem it not necessary to provide opinion on the history of the origin of the Book of Job. If the book indeed is written by different subjects and at different times the material of this interpretation is only the final form. As Gilbert Keith Chesterton wrote ('Introduction to the Book of Job – Chesterton' n.d.):

> But whatever decision the reader may come to concerning them, there is a general truth to be remembered in this connection. When you deal with any ancient artistic creation, do not suppose that it is anything against it that it grew gradually. The book of Job may have grown gradually just as Westminster Abbey grew gradually. – Without going into questions of unity as understood by the scholars, we may say of the scholarly riddle that the book has unity in the sense that all great traditional creations have unity; in the sense that Canterbury Cathedral has unity.

As there are many interpretations about the origin of the text, there are also many different interpretations of the form of the final version. As an example, the praise of wisdom in chapter 28 is often considered to be a separate section, though the justification for this is hardly evident (see Vermeylen 2015: 4–6). The following diagram of the dialogic structure of the book is not based on some philological commentary but rather on my view of the literary coherence and the book's traditional reception

Chapters	Narrator	Job	Other actors
1–2	Prologue	Prologue lines.	Prologue lines from God, the Accuser or Satan, and Job's Wife
3		First speech of Job (1J)	
4–5			First speech of Eliphaz (1E)
6–7		Second speech of Job (2J)	
8			First speech of Bildad (2B)
9–10		Third speech of Job (3J)	
11			First speech of Zophar (1S)
12–14		Fourth speech of Job (4J)	
15			Second speech of Eliphaz (2E)
16–17		Fifth speech of Job (5J)	
18			Second speech of Bildad (2B)
19		Sixth speech of Job (6J)	
20			Second speech of Zophar (2S)
21		Seventh speech of Job (7J)	
22			Third speech of Eliphaz (3E)
23–24		Eight speech of Job (8J)	
25			Third speech of Bildad (3B)
26–31		Ninth speech of Job (9J)	
32:1–6	Elihu's introduction		
32–37			Speech of Elihu (1–4U)
38:1	God's introduction		
38–39			Speech of God
40:4–5		Job's response	
40–41			Speech of God
42:2–6		Job's response	
42:7–8			God's final words
42:9–17	Epilogue: restoration		

Of course, there are also many distinct and even contradictory interpretations of the message of the Book of Job which cannot be dealt within the limits of this text. As Vicchio (2006a) writes, it is an "inherently ambiguous work, a text that in several places is open to a variety of interpretations". It necessitates an interpretation, but it is very dubious that any interpretation can totally comprehend it. Vicchio even suggests (2006c) that "every age remakes Job in its own image and likeness." But I would rather say that it is as if the Book of Job reflects the societal and individual *Dasein* of its interpreter. Not every material is reflective in this sense. In any case, it is exactly the internal tensions of the book that are the reason why it is so interesting for a reader, as Vermeylen writes (2015: 35).

The Book of Job itself serves as the base of any justified interpretation. Still, it cannot be interpreted without a subjective interpreter who lives in some *Dasein*. Any interpretation (or interpretation of interpretation) is dependent on the presuppositions of the reader concerning what kind of thoughts are possible for the principal actor Job. Interpretation is also dependent on the presuppositions about the literary devices that the author of the book would like to use. For example, there obtains even an interpretation which sees the Book of Job as full of irony.

My interpretation is based on the principle that Job's existential situation, where the blameless and upright, the healthy and respected man has been plunged into the pit of agony, is such that he can, from the abundance of his heart, speak many things that are – at least seemingly – contradictory. Job (2J 6:2–3) himself says: "If only my anguish could be weighed and all my misery be placed on the scales it would surely outweigh the sand of the seas – no wonder my words have been impetuous." Job charges from one issue to another while complaining, defending, and attacking. As John Deely writes (2002: 51), the possibility of reaching truth for any finite mind presupposes the possibility of error. My presupposition is only that it is also possible for Job to err and to change his mind. The thoughts, emotions, and speech of the human finite mind proceed in time. The human mind is not a closed system that produces only fully coherent non-contradictory statements. Szepe (2018: 60–61) even compares Job's speeches to the modern "stream of consciousness" monologues.

Method for this interpretation consists of reading aloud in addition to silent reading. Without voicing the words, the Book of Job remains an incomplete sign that obtains only internally. It must be voiced or intoned like music. Silent reading is neither suitable for the Hebraic Book of Job nor for its translations even if they are in prose. The Book of Job is literature, not philosophy, logic, or dogma. Without taking into account the transcendental category of beauty, which is the Book of Job's principal sought value (S1), any interpretation of it is bound to be deficient.

Because this is an existential semiotic interpretation, the idea that it would be a sufficient interpretation to reduce the Book of Job to some genre such as wisdom literature or some culture and its value axioms is rejected. These would be reductions to some S2 or S1. Instead, the aim is to study the unique message of the Book of Job, its individual existential illumination of which Tarasti (2004: 63) writes while referring to Karl Jaspers.

4 Job's existential situation before the dialogue

Gregory the Great writes that the writer of the Book of Job depicts Job before the dialogue for the same reason that one who writes about wrestling describes the wrestlers before the match: "because our athlete was about to combat the devil, the writer of the sacred story, recounting as it were before the exhibition in the arena the spiritual merits in this athlete, describes the members of the soul [*mentis*]".

The book opens with the following introduction (Job. 1:1–3):

> In the land of Uz there lived a man whose name was Job. This man was blameless and upright; he feared God and shunned evil. He had seven sons and three daughters, and he owned seven thousand sheep, three thousand camels, five hundred yoke of oxen and five hundred donkeys, and had a large number of servants. He was the greatest man among all the people of the East.

Job's blamelessness, uprighteousness, fear of God and shunning of evil is further confirmed twice by God's words in the prologue (Job. 1:8, 2:3). Then one day God summons his angels and among them is Satan, the Accuser. God presents Job to Satan as a model of blameless and God-fearing man. Satan answers why would Job not fear God when God has blessed everything that he has done and given him a large fortune. Satan says that if Job would lose all that he has been given he would curse God to His face. God allows Satan to test Job. First, Satan is allowed to take away Job's fortune and kill his servants and children. Then in the second phase, Satan afflicts Job with a painful disease. At this point, Job's wife says to him (Job. 2:9): "Are you still maintaining your integrity? Curse God and die!" But Job remains patient and answers (Job. 2:10): "You are talking like a foolish woman. Shall we accept good from God, and not trouble?"

In existential semiotics terms, Job's physical *Dasein* undergoes a series of privations. First, Job's S2/M3 is negated. His property is taken away from him, thus his position in the community is weakened and his ability to do good works is reduced. Secondly, his M2 is negated in the sphere of close relations when his children die. Thirdly, his M1 is negated when the disease smites his body. These privations and sufferings in three levels – societal, personal, and bodily – are the subject of lamentation in Job's speeches. Only Job's S1/M4, which is founded on the fear of God, remains, even if it also falters during the course of the dialogue (See Figure 1).

As mentioned above, Job's friends Eliphaz, Bildad, and Zophar hear about Job's misfortune and arrive to console him. Upon seeing his friend sitting on the dung heap scraping his body, they begin to weep, tear their clothes, sprinkle dust on their heads, and sit silently for seven days and nights with Job. All of these are signs of true friendship (M2) which are publicly manifested (S2). Then after seven days and night, Job starts to speak.

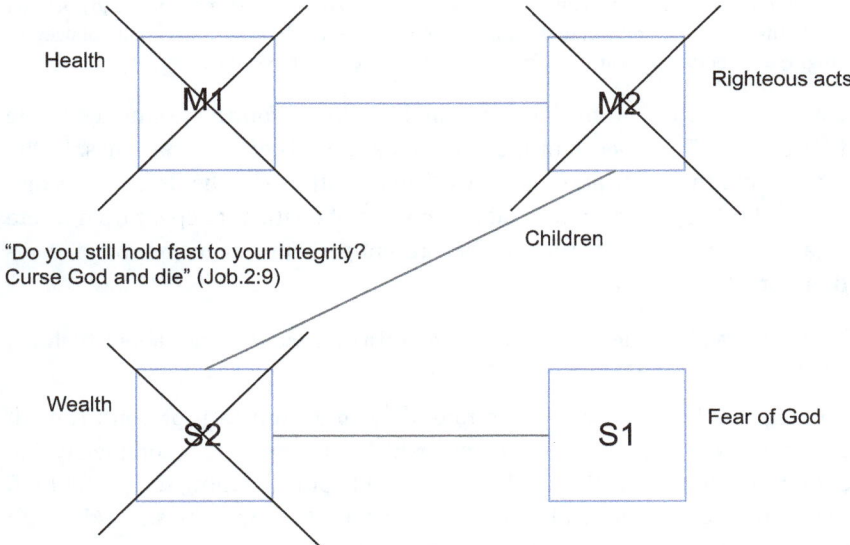

Figure 1: Negation of Job's *Dasein*.

5 Job's descriptions of death

The Book of Job's first description of death is in the first speech of Job (1J 3:13–23). There death or grave signifies rest and a place of complete equality. In the first speech, Job thinks that death would be a liberation from his suffering (1J 3:13):

> For now I would be lying down in peace;
> I would be asleep and at rest.

In the second speech, Job speaks of Sheol, land of death. According to Job, man disappears there like a cloud into the sky and will never return (2J 7:9–10). The notion of death as rest is missing, it is replaced with oblivion, though, as a whole, the depiction is vague.

The third description of death appears at the end of Job's third speech (3J 10:20–22). Now death starts to receive negative tones. It appears to be frightening as Vermeylan (2015: 116) notes. The positive depiction of the first speech and the neutral depiction of the second are gone. Now Job asks God to give him joy for a moment (3J 10:20–22):

> Are not my few days almost over? Turn away from me so I can have a moment's joy before I go to the place of no return, to the land of gloom and utter darkness, to the land of deepest night, of utter darkness and disorder, where even the light is like darkness.

Like in the third speech, the depictions of death in the fourth are situated at the end (4J 14:7–22). This speech also ends the first rounds of Job's speeches. In the fourth speech, the description is almost like a synthesis of the first and second speech (4J 14: 7–12). There obtains again the idea of death as a repose from where man cannot come back. But there is also present perhaps a vague notion of resurrection from death (4J 14:13):

> If only you would hide me in the grave and conceal me till your anger has passed! If only you would set me a time and then remember me!

The principle of hope, which concentrates only on the future, is present. Though it should perhaps be noted that the hope which Job manifests is completely distinct from the hope Tarasti describes as aesthetic or concerning the present (cf. Tarasti 2017: 52). Job's hopeful standpoint does not last. Soon he says (4J 14:19): "as water wears away stones and torrents wash away the soil, so you destroy a person's hope."

In the fifth speech, Job treats death twice. In the first part (5J 16:22), Job calls death a path from which there is no return. It is again somewhat neutral description. It should also be noted that this depiction is part of a sequence where Job rejects his friends' rebukes. Job wishes that justice would be done to him before his death which he believes to be imminent. He trusts in his heavenly advocate (5J 16:19): "Even now my witness is in heaven; my advocate is on high."

Like in the two preceding speeches, the second description of death (5J 17:13–16) is at the end of the speech. It is a dysphoric portrayal of decomposition devoid of any hope (5J 17:14–15): "if I say to corruption, 'You are my father,' and to the worm, 'My mother' or 'My sister,' where then is my hope – who can see any hope for me?"

The death-section of the sixth speech is again at the end (6J 19:25–27). Job has just complained about his bodily and social sufferings, about how he is sick and detested (6J 19:17–20). He has asked his friends to have pity on him, not to oppress him like God (6J 19:21–22). He has presented the wish of having his words eternalized (6J 19:23–24).

After this Job utters probably the most famous words of the book (6J 19:25–27). The section is hard to interpret and even the translations are guided by presuppositions about what Job could say. Christian commentators have since early periods held it to be a reference to the resurrection (Vicchio 2006a).⁴ According to Vermeylen (2015: 130), "there exists a fundamental agreement between the commentators that Job develops here a positive image of God which is in great tension between the accusations that Job has already launched in the text of the redaction I."⁵ The New International Version translates it as follows:

> I know that my redeemer lives, and that in the end he will stand on the earth. And after my skin has been destroyed, yet in my flesh I will see God; I myself will see him with my own eyes – I, and not another. How my heart yearns within me!

Either Job says that he will see God before death at his last hour or that he will see God after he has died. In any case, here the principle of hope is present intensely. Special notice should be paid to what Job says after these words full of hope (6J 19:28–29):

> If you say, 'How we will hound him, since the root of the trouble lies in him,' you should fear the sword yourselves; for wrath will bring punishment by the sword, and then you will know that there is judgment.

Job thus proclaims that God will judge his friends. According to Job, it is they who have committed serious crimes. Not the least they have forsaken him, their friend. Already in his speech, Job had said (2J 6:14): "Anyone who withholds kindness from a friend forsakes the fear of the Almighty." Also, Job has warned his friends of speaking falsely of God (4J 13:7–10):

> Will you speak wickedly on God's behalf? Will you speak deceitfully for him? Will you show him partiality? Will you argue the case for God? Would it turn out well if he examined you? Could you deceive him as you might deceive a mortal? He would surely call you to account if you secretly showed partiality.

In the sixth speech, Job merely repeats the same threat, but it is curiously situated right after the most hopeful words yet. These are the words of angered man, of one who grasps at straws. Still, Job does not threaten his friends with his vengeance but with divine judgment. He does not have faith in M2 but in a principle that transcends the Dasein.

The seventh speech ends the second round of Job's responses. Here (7J 21:26, 32–33), death again signifies the same unconsciousness as in the fourth speech,

---

4 (Vicchio 2006a): "Christian commentators from very early on have come to see this pericope as an Old Testament precursor of Christ, as well as a confirmation of survival after death."
5 (Vermeylen 2015:130): "il existe un accord fondamental des commentateurs pour considérer que Job développe ici une image positive de Dieu, qui se trouve en forte tension avec les accusations que le même Job a déjà proférées dans le texte de la rédaction I."

the same rest as in the first speech, but also the theme of decomposition and worms is present as in the fifth speech. Before this depiction of death, Job had criticized God (7J 21:6–14) of letting wicked men prosper in life and die in peace. In the seventh speech, Job says that the wicked live their life similar to the ones who fear God and they are punished in death because death is, after all, the same for everyone.

After this seventh speech, Job does not describe death. Though, in chapter 28 (9J 28:22), it is mentioned that Death knows nothing of wisdom. During the whole quarrel, Job's friends do not comment on his words about death. In this instance only, they voice no objections, at least explicit, to Job's words.

After Job's ninth speech, Elihu the son of Barakel starts to speak. Like Job's friends, Elihu does not talk about death. Though, Elihu comes closest to describing death in his first speech (1U 33:23–27) in the part where he describes how an angel can convince God to restore the man who is approaching death. It is possible that when Job talks about his advocate in high he is speaking of the same thing. At the same time, the fact that Elihu and Job completely disagree about Job's situation allows also for an interpretation where Job and Elihu do not agree in this case.

In God's response, the theme of death is present. This can be surprising considering that the first impression of God's response is easily that He is not at all concerned with Job's questions or themes, but instead concentrates on describing the marvels of creation. George Bernard Shaw even commented on God's speech sardonically: "If I complain that I am suffering unjustly, it is no answer to say 'Can you make a hippopotamus.'" (Cf. Baker 1978: 17). But, it must be noted that the cultural convention during the time of the Book of Job's creation was not necessarily one where getting a response to a question was taken for granted. It was not necessarily improper to respond with counter-question. Samuel A. Meier (1999: 271) writes in his analysis of God's response that "what at first appears to be a disquieting feature of the Book of Job in fact may be a cultural convention that is foreign to many modern readers." Apparently, Job himself could have referenced this custom when he uttered (4J 13:22): "Then summon me and I will answer, or let me speak, and you reply to me." But when God presents his questions Job is unable to answer.

God in his response talks first about the gates of death and deepest darkness (Job. 38:17). Later God rhetorically (Job. 40:13) urges Job to bury the wicked in the dust and "shroud their faces in the grave." These parts about death suggest that for the author of the book death perhaps is not as equal or tranquil as Job in some of his speeches had suggested. There is no mention of death as rest in God's speech.

6 Conclusions

The narrative of the Book of Job begins after Job's earlier existential situation has been negated and his existence has been almost annihilated. Job begins to lament his situation to his friends and to God. The following diagram depicts some themes that are linked to death in Job's speeches.

	M1	M2	S2	S1	supra-Z
1J	sleep, rest		negation of S2	equality	
2J	rest	disappearance			
3J	darkness, chaos (fear)				
4J		unconsciousness			hope, despair
5J	decomposition				hope, despair
6J				justice	hope
7J	rest, decomposition	unconsciousness			

According to this interpretation, Job's speeches about death reach their climax in the sixth speech at the supra-zemic level. Whether the sixth speech is meant to talk about resurrection or not, Job's friends' reaction gives no indication to either direction. All in all, Job's friends speak nothing about death. They are not concerned with Job's apparent contradictions on the theme. In fact, death is just about the only thing of which Job's friends have nothing to say. This is notable because the friends are there to object to Job. As Zophar (1S 11:2) says concerning Job's words: "Are all these words to go unanswered? Is this talker to be vindicated?"

Do the friends then agree with Job on death? Are they confused about his words? Or do they not pay attention to them because they believe that death signifies extinction as in Job's second speech? Or perhaps the friends think that in those instances Job does not mock God? These are unanswerable questions. The only certain thing, at least for now, is that the friends stay silent; what this could signify necessitates a further inquiry. Unlike Job's friends and Elihu, God does refer to death in his response. Even if, strictly speaking, there are no descriptions of death, the figures of speech do not give a bright picture of the state of existence that Job sometimes called rest. Compared with Job's speeches, death in God's depiction is most alike to Job's third speech where death is a place of darkness and chaos.

Even after all this has been said, it must be emphasized that texts such as the Book of Job transcend any particular interpretation as well as any temporal and geographical *Dasein*. For this reason such texts deserve and should be interpreted lest they become only closed books and their *Dasein* reflecting properties fall into desuetude. {Originally written in June 2020}.

References

Commentaries on the Book of Job

Luis de León. 1591. *Exposición de Libro de Job*. http://www.cervantesvirtual.com/obra-visor/exposicion-del-libro-de-job--3/html/fef4bb68-82b1-11df-acc7-002185ce6064_2.html (accessed 30th of June 2020)
St. Gregory the Great. 590. *Morals on the Book of Job*. Translated by anon. Oxford & London: John Henry Parker; J.G.F. & J. Rivington. http://www.lectionarycentral.com/gregorymoraliaindex.html (accessed 30th of June 2020)
St. John Chrysostom. 1988a [c. 386–397]. *Commentaire Sur Job. I (Chapitres I-XIV)*. Trans. by Henri Sorlin. (Sources Chrétiennes 346). Paris: Les Éditions du Cerf.
St. John Chrysostom. 1988b [c. 386–397]. *Commentaire Sur Job. II (Chapitres XV-XLII)*. Trans. by Henri Sorlin. (Sources Chrétiennes 348). Paris: Les Éditions du Cerf.
Thomas Aquinas. 2018 [c. 1259]. *Expositio super Iob ad litteram*. Trans. by Brian Mulladay. https://dhspriory.org/thomas/SSJob.htm (accessed in June 2017, now unavailable)

Other literature

Baker, John Austin. 1978. The Book of Job: Unity and Meaning. In David J. A. Clines, Philip R. Davies & David M. Gunn [eds.], *Studia Biblica I*, 17–26. Journal for the Study of the Old Testament Supplement Series 11. Sheffield: The University of Sheffield.
Chesterton, Gilbert Keith. n.d. *Introduction to the Book of Job – Chesterton*. http://www.chesterton.org/2011/07/introduction-to-the-book-of-job/ (accessed 3 March 2014)
Deely, John. 2002. *What Distinguishes Human Understanding?* South Bend, Indiana: St. Augustine's Press.
Fokkelman, Jan. P. 2012. *The Book of Job in Form. A Literary Translation with Commentary*. Leiden, Boston: Brill.
Fontanille, Jacques. 2004. *Some et Séma, Figures du Corps*. Paris: Maisonneuve & Larose.
Franklin, T. Harkins & Aaron Canty. 2016. *A Companion to Job in the Middle Ages*. Brill's Companion to the Christian Tradition 73. Leiden, Boston: Brill.
Gadegård, Niels H. 1971. Panen käteni suulleni. Johdanto Jobin kirjaan [I put hand on my mouth. Introduction to the Book of Job]. In Svend Holm-Nielsen, Bent Noack & Sven Tito Achen (eds.) *Runous ja viisauskirjallisuus* [Poetry and wisdom literature], 17–37. Raamattu ja sen kulttuurihistoria 4 [Bible and its cultural history 4]. Helsinki: Otava.
Greenstein, Edward L. 2018. Challenges in Translating the Book of Job. In James W. Barker, Anthony Le Donne & Joel N. Lohr (eds.) *Found in Translation. Essays on Jewish Biblical Translation in Honor of Leonard J. Greenspoon*, 179–200. Purdue University Press.
Habel, Norman C. 1975. *The Book of Job. Commentary*. Cambridge: Cambridge University Press.
Ilarion, Alfejev. 2002. *Uskon mysteeri: johdatus ortodoksiseen dogmaattiseen teologiaan* [*Mystery of Faith. Introduction to the Teaching and Spirituality of the Orthodox Church*]. Translated by Irmeli Talasjoki. Joensuu: Ortodoksisen kirjallisuuden julkaisuneuvosto.
Jacobson, Richard. 1981. Satanic Semiotics, Jobian Jurisprudence. *Semeia* 19. 63–71.

Mannermaa, J. A. 1911. *Jobin kirjan viittauksia kärsimyksistä ja kärsivien sielunhoidosta* [*The Book of Job about suffering and spiritual guidance for the suffering*]. (Suomalaisen Teologisen Kirjallisuusseuran Julkaisuja, VI). Oulu: Suomen Teologinen Kirjallisuusseura.
Meier, Samuel A. 1999. Job and the Unanswered Question. *Prooftexts* 19. 265–276.
Michel, Walter L. 1987. *Job in the Light of Northwest Semitic. Volume I. Prologue and First Cycle of Speeches Job 1:1 – 14:22*. (Biblica et Orientalia 42). Rome: Biblical Institute Press.
Sawyer, John F. A. 1978. The Authorship and Structure of the Book of Job. In David J. A. Clines, Philip R. Davies & David M. Gunn (eds.) *Studia Biblica I*, 253–57. (Journal for the Study of the Old Testament Supplement Series 11). Sheffield: The University of Sheffield.
Scholem, Gershom. 2014. Job's Lament. In Ilit Ferber & Paula Schwebel (eds.), *Lament in Jewish Thought*, 321–323. De Gruyter.
Smick, Elmer B. 1986. Semeiological Interpretation of the Book of Job. *The Westminister Theological Journal* 48. 135–149.
Szepe, Agata. 2018. The Book of Job as a Drama: Interpretation Possibilities. *Roczniki Kulturoznawcze* IX (3). 51–66.
Tarasti, Eero. 2004. *Arvot ja merkit* [*Values and Signs*]. Helsinki: Gaudeamus.
Tarasti, Eero. 2015. *Sein und Schein*. Berliini: De Gruyter Mouton.
Tarasti, Eero. 2017. Mitä tapahtuu? Zemicin liikkeistä – eksistentiaalisemiotiikkaa [*What happens? About Zemic's movement – existential semiotics*]. *Synteesi* 35 (1–2). 50–79. [In English: From Ursatz to Urzemic in Esti Sheinberg and William P Dougherty (eds.), *The Routledge Handbook of Music Signification*. London: Routledge.]
Tenhunen, Katri. 2018. Jobin kirja. Tyylitaiturin käännös ongelmallisesta pohjatekstistä [The Book of Job. Translation of a problematic source text by a master of style]. In Anneli Aejmelaeus, Katja Kujanpaa, and Miika Tucker, *Sisälle Septuagintaan* [*Inside Septuagint*], 181–91. (Suomen Eksegeettisen Seuran Julkaisuja 116). Helsinki: Suomen Eksegeettinen Seura.
Troyat, Henri. 1963 [1940]. *Dostojevski*. Trans. by Kauhanen Kaj. Jyväskylä: Gummerus.
Vermeylen, Jacques. 2015. *Métamorphoses. Les rédactions successives du Livre de Job*. (Bibliotheca Ephemeridum Theologicarum Lovaniensium, CCLXXVI). Leuven – Paris – Bristol, CT: Université catholique de Louvain.
Vicchio, Stephen. 2006a. *Job in the Ancient World. The Image of the Biblical Job. A History 1*. Eugene, Or.: Wipf & Stock.
Vicchio, Stephen. 2006b. *Job in the Medieval World. The Image of the Biblical Job. A History 2*. Eugene, Or.: Wipf & Stock.
Vicchio, Stephen. 2006c. *Job in the Modern World. The Image of the Biblical Job. A History 3*. Eugene, Or.: Wipf & Stock.

Katriina Kajannes
Memory in Eero Tarasti's novel Europe/ Perhaps

Abstract: *Europe/Perhaps* appeared in Italy in 2014 (*L'eredità di Villa Nevski*) and in France 2014 (*Le retour à la Villa Nevski)* and in Finnish in 2016 as a 589 pages long version in 2016 (*Eurooppa/Ehkä*), the English translation is ready entitled *Villa Nevski Revisited* and waiting for its publisher. The central themes of this play-novel are knowing, Europe, values and semiocrisis. The novel as well as Tarasti's existential semiotics opens the human existence and knowledge with such concepts as being, memory, history, transcendence, subject and resistance. *Europe/Perhaps* fulfils and sometime parodizes the program of existential semiotics. This novel opens the semiosphere and phases of signs just from the inside. The narration is here existential.

The past is a joint creation of men, and memory is a particular organ of the transcendence. Memory is also a force of resistance in situation same as in *Politeia* and in a cultural slavery.

The core values and attitudes of the Europe – democracy, freedom, human rights, equality, solidarity, respect of individuality, positive life attitude and sane scepticism – can still be alive in collective memory, arts and humanism. *Europe/ Perhaps* emphasizes the many dimensionality of aesthetic communication and role of art in the spiritual growth and development of empathy and solidarity. The knowledge transmitted by intuition and aesthetic experience changes the approach to man and life. Philosophers, writers, and artists shake us to realize entireties, and art mediates a cognition of the structure of the reality.

Ideal Europeanity or dialogicity and existential semiotics concretize in the structure of the novel. The omniscient narrator is not asserting the speakers to any ranking order nor putting their views on certain boxes. When things are shared together and many interpretations are in touch with each other the understanding multiplies. Views are polished during the conversation. Solution is sought for in encounters which distantly evoke international congresses of semiotics and Plato's dialogues.

Keywords: postmodernism, memory, existential narration, dialogicity, aesthetic experience

Europe/Perhaps, a novel written by Eero Tarasti, appeared in Italian (*L'eredità di Villa Nevski*) and French (*Le retour à la Villa Nevski*) in 2014. The Finnish version was published in 2016 as a 589 pages long book (*Eurooppa/Ehkä*). The English translation, entitled *Villa Nevski Revisited*, is ready to hit the bookstores once it finds a publisher. The central themes of Eero Tarasti's play-novel are several; knowing, Europe, values, and semiocrisis etc. The protagonists stemming from families belonging to various countries elucidate the existential situation of man and cultural history. There are a plenty of speakers and remembering persons and all phenomena are looked from diverse viewpoints – Europe as a dialogue and plurality of interpretations. Different times and grades of knowing are embedded into each other in the novel. What one has seen, recalled, and imagined are common store of memory to all persons.

The novel displays mind functioning in action, in general mediated by speech and talking, and it ponders whether man and society can know correctly or even wrongly. Knowing is neither absolute nor objective but it is knitted into something evoking the memory of people and their experiences. The validity of understanding comes into question when it slips into misunderstanding. They are in consciousness portrayed as equal, the same as memory and oblivion, which can be both individual and personal or societal and cultural. Amnesy appears as trauma of an indivudual and collectivity, whose background is constituted by suffering and slavery in world wars, inequality, systems, and totalitarian states.

I shall analyze the remembering in the novel *Europe/Perhaps* (*Eurooppa/Ehkä*) – this title was by the way the original one proposed by the writer and was used in its Finnish version. I shall try to show its position and assignments in the work. Almost all of the novel consists of reminiscences. Tarasti writes in his essay collection *Pariisin uudet mysteerit* (The New Mysteries of Paris): "History represents the collective memory. Historiless, synchronic societies like the American type media society, do not possess in this respect 'memory'. . . .. Man's ability to create meanings is completely bound with memory" (Tarasti 2004b: 100–102). Firstly, I present some features of the image of Eero Tarasti as a writer in the light of his prose output.

1 Eero Tarasti as a novel writer

Eero Tarasti, a professor of musicology, is a broad-scoped and prolific scholar, whose themes, in music, include myths, style periods, literature, postmodernism and structures of various arts etc. Like some other leading postmodernists of Europe and Finland, he deals with similar themes in science and prose. Tarasti belongs, alongside Umberto Eco, Italo Calvino, Henri Broms, and Harry Forsblom, to the cultivated orientation of literary postmodernism in which aesthetics and philosophy are crucial. In his prose and research, the central issue is the problem of knowledge – particularly rationality and irrationality – in the European culture. Also, Eco and Tarasti write in their prose and semiotic studies about serious issues without declaring anything and without the absoluteness of a *besserwisser*. They present cultural critic with a light touch (see Kajannes 2009).

Tarasti's existential semiotics explores human existence and knowledge with concepts such as being, memory and history. It offers something new to the study of cultural memory, postcolonialism, globalisation, and resistance. The phenomena, investigated in existential semiotics, such as memory, transcendence, subject, and resistance are also essential in Tarasti's prose.

The novels *Le secret du professeur Amfortas* (1995) and *Europe/Perhaps* are musical, polyphonic, multilevelled, and one may read there either levels of surface or depth (Tarasti wrote about the counterpoint in Proust's prose in 1993a: 62). They are semiotic novels in the sense that Eero Tarasti gives to the concepts. The works are, by their themes, sturctures and, partly by the protagonists, meta- and existential-semiotic ones. In both the starting points, representatives and directions of semiotics manifest itself. Tarasti nominates, as the representatives of this genre, some novels by Umberto Eco, Julia Kristeva, and Henri Broms. In those novels, the theme is existential and the most foregrounded of those themes is a semiotic consciousness, which is both questioning and critical. The characteristic of these novels is parody, abandoning the reality-illusion, playing with narrative conventions, diligent quoting from other texts and the polyphonic many-layered structure. (Tarasti 1993b: 215–228) In the side of Eco, Kristeva, and Broms, the other important sources for the work, *Europe/Perhaps*, are J.W. von Goethe, Leo Tolstoy, Anton Chekhov, Gabriele D'Annunzio, Stefan Zweig, Thomas Mann, Hermann Hesse, and Marcel Proust which are all much referred to. Tarasti analyses in his various studies the novels by Proust in which he discovers implicit semiotics (Tarasti 1992a). To him Proust is a great semiotician, albeit he did not use this word (Tarasti 2015b: 109).

Tarasti's analyses of *Parsifal* by Richard Wagner as a semiotic work also elucidate the novel *Europe/Perhaps*. The opera is based upon reflecting on what happened already and its "reminiscence", and not on direct action (Tarasti 1994: 43). The remarks by Henri Broms on the *secret du professeur Amfortas* hold true for both the novels by Tarasti. Broms emphasizes the labyrinth character of the work, and the leading of several simultaneous themes therein. He uses terms like meta- and system novel (Broms 1993a: 33–36, 1993b: 97–98). Andrew Chesterman writes about system novel one layer of which can be semiotical and in which the narrator broadens the perspective by semiotic references (Chesterman 1995: 23).

Tarasti, once, wrote: "One has to go and investigate the life of the signs from inside, and the fact of which kind of factual universe of significations we live all our life along its temporal processes" (Tarasti 1995: 45). Keeping this in mind, we can say, *Europe/Perhaps* fulfils and, sometimes, parodizes the program of existential semiotics. The novel contributes to the debate of the illusion of freedom provided by globalisation, and it shows the change of signs and meaning when we shift from the 1930s to the global Europe. The conformism and digitalisation of culture prove to erase walls without resolving them. The novel displays what prevents and, also, what helps the emancipation of an individual. Tarasti portrays an average person, who creates by memory, alternative realities and pasts and he furnishes examples of artists and scientists rewriting the history. His novels are dialogical, particularly *Europe/Perhaps*. Diverse world views and ideas are there in constant dialogue with each other. Narration is drama-like, as in the Finnish classic novel *Seven Brothers* by Aleksis Kivi: narrator does not participate in the dialogue of protagonists but lets the reader make his/her own reasonings. On the surface, there is parody, irony, and play, but at the end what is involved is weighty and serious. The work opens the door from everyday life to transcendence, art theory, and philosophy. In the narration, there are traits from many periods and many literary genres. The work cites different discourses and styles. It weaves complex structures and endless connections to literary works, music, visual arts, and its research. Fragmentation, clichée, and transforming plagiarism are its devices.

In his investigations, Tarasti appreciates different views and scientific orientations, but in the novel, their representatives often disqualify and mock standpoints which differ from their own. The novel gives place for various views as part of cultural memory. In the stream of debates, an opportunity rises which signifies that values could return to something more human than now.

2 Memory, meanings, and identity

Europe/Perhaps scrutinizes understanding and tradition from the same standpoints as Hans-Georg Gadamer. He writes that undestanding is always understanding in another way. He also argues: *"Sein, das verstanden werde kann, ist Sprache"* (To be – or to be able to be understood – is the language, Gadamer 1986: 478). Man conceives language via languages. By them phenomena exist and they are observed, and likewise the identity is built linguistically. Hannah Arendt, in turn, emphasizes that identity takes shape in social life and it is articulated particularly in narration (Arendt 1998: 193–194). Existential semiotics and *Europe/Perhaps* remind us of that we do not need and we even cannot say all by words.

In the novel, often different narrators and persons present their conceptions and memories. Among four main protagonists prevails the suffering of love. Two novels with which *Europe/Perhaps* discusses events and which are thematically close to it and contain similar configuration are Goethe's *Die Wahlverwandschaften* and D'Annunzio's *Forse che si, forse che no*. The most important person in the novel is the Russian Sandra or Alexandra Bomoloff, who writes a book about different phases of her family and the relationship to three Italian brothers Giorgio, Tullio and Paolo. Over half of the novel, *Europe/Perhaps* portrays the eve of the great war, in august of 1939, when the family enjoys dinner at the manor of Villa Nevski in Estonia. The dinner with its discussions and art programs are present later in flashbacks, images, and dreams, and one returns to the manor even during the war. Other places of the plot are post-war Paris, Brazil, the Thessaloniki of the 1960s and Siberia. Odd turns and incidents occur. One side intrigue consists of the property of the Bomoloffs which lies in a bank – whose account number is revealed by the seven paintings of a Polish painter Janusz. All these events are transmitted by memory. Yet, its role is scanty taking place in short episodes in the present time and in a Nordic town of European Union, in which three young people comment on the situation and the story of the aged Sandra.

Memory, the factor called in the antiquity as *Mnemosyne*, talks via persons. They are more than voices than the protagonists of traditional novels portrayed from many sides. And each represents some phenomenon or idea. In literature, memory is in the foreground in many works of romanticism and symbolism, and in the literature of modernism and postmodernism, it is a central and, sometimes, the most important theme (see Tarasti 2015b: 167–168). *Europe/Perhaps* underlines also existence and subject which are core issues in existential semiotics. Existence is not only being there but it is, moreover, a movement, an orientation towards freedom or away from it, and it is the right to will and choice (Tarasti 2015a: 19–21). An individual can choose either inner liberty or that which binds and narrows the chances of liberty. The more probable the enslaving conformity of thought, manners, and activities the more distant a culture and society are from openness, equality, and cultivation. When one is far afield from those, the memory of individual and culture become deficient.

Theories of cultural memory are useful for the reader of the novel. The idea of Maurice Halbwach of the past as a joint creation of men, serves here as a good starting point (see Assman 2006: 93; Halbwachs 1992). Memory as an interpretation of phenomena and events is creative, even yielding new worlds. Tarasti writes: "There is no such thing as the world as such. World cannot be separated from its interpretation" (Tarasti 2011: 13).

The novel portrays memory as an interpreter and articulator of events and provider of signification to phenomena. Experiences are real to a person as long as they preserve in the mind and maintain the issue they represent. One recalls the experienced, the things which one has encountered by sense, thoughts, and emotions; issues that are imagined. Memory is not a mirror, but it is a factor forming knowledge and experience. The identity of an individual, community, nation, and Europe is built when the past and present meet each other.

Semiosphere, the continuum of signs, culture, as a semiotic process, and transcendence get concretized in the novel (about these notions see Tarasti 2004a: 19–20). Transcendence deepens the being, interiority, and cognition (see Tarasti 2015a: 4–6). "Memory means that some place or time or person has been 'revisited': in some respect it has been made present as absent, transcendent. Memory is therefore a particular organ of the transcendence. Memory is also a force of resistance: as long as one still remembers how things were done in his culture and society, he/she is saved with his/her identity" (Tarasti 2005: 16).

Understanding is based upon memory. Dialogue shows the fluctuation of fantasies, memories, perceptions, and reasonings. Images of what happened constitute continuity, identity, and presence. Reminiscence of different layers of consciousness and subconsciousness manifests other memories. Temporal shifts take place, with them, in sleep and as awaken. Persons glide in a deep sleep from one time and place to another: "They sank into a deep sleep and slept and slept: in dreams they returned to the old continent, to the streets of Paris, to the restaurant of Zaheb, to all sanctified places of their bohemian lives, and at the end to Estonia and Villa Nevski, and its fests and still further away to Vienna . . . finally to the memories of their parents. When parents appear in dreams, it means that the person undergoes some kind of crisis, they had been told by Maxie who had even studied psychoanalysis" (*EP* 565–566).

The experienced and the recurrences of that experienced are theme and variations. Memory is, by its structure, like an orchestra and, by its functioning, like playing; the ingrediente are connected and vary creativity there (Babuts 1992: 55–73). A person can invent for himself significant parts of his past like Sandra in her manuscript. Things are shown from her viewpoint: she is the object of longing and love of many men. Persons create a story when they tell pieces of their individual history and views of the past. It is more real to each one than the interpretations of others about the issues. Tarasti writes in his article: "In fact all history as an activity looking backwards, is also narration of resistance, because there one always transcends the surface of the reality" (Tarasti 2005: 27).

The attitude of the narrator is here very strict: the experienced determines the later lives of protagonists. Persons are not to his mind builders and selectors of their own reality, nor are they fictive figures as such: "We leave them here, that noisy group of young people, who had still much ahead in their lives and who were all detached from their roots. Still they carried their past inside themselves, their experiences and memories, which in spite of their apparent freedom had already designed them. Yet they were not aware of it themselves, before the course of their destiny and events made them realize it!" (*EP* 547).

Narrator may be right insofar when consciousness repeats things it strengthens conceptions, judgements, and the images containing an even greater force. The pencil of memory paints lines in the same direction fortifying each other. In a discussion about art in the novel, one ponders the role of images and reminiscences in arts and notices the unity of memory and art. One person talks about associations evoked by music as a part of it. Another one emphasizes images and intentions as the means to reach the absent object. Photograph is to his mind quite modest because the object there lacks life (*EP* 434–436).

A strong emotional and sensual image or series of images detaches one from the present and leads amidst something which was present once. Time opens in an experiential moment as rich and colorful, when it changes into omnitemporal. A strong image rising from the past explodes on the borderlines of spatiotemporal domain of experience. Existence and experience are temporal there in the first place. The network of impressions and images emerging from the past lives in the side of or inside the present, as the basic stream of life, in whose dimension tempus extends into a limitless space. This also occurs in Proust: Proust reveals his philosophy of time: time is like an arrow piercing the life, directly up to the space reaching dimension, the vertical direction of spatial temporality. This explains those few magical moments when the course of time stops and the past is reanimated – like by the impact of a madeleine cake dipped into a linden leave tea. According to the spatial time conception, the famous episode of tea cup is nothing but a metaphor of four-dimensional spatial time (Pekonen 2008: 50).

Memory is in Tarasti's novel a factor building humanity and when it weakens, life is shallow and superficial. Consciousness and subconsciousness are rich for those who are active in sciences and arts. Mastering of many languages amplifies the understanding: French, English, German, Italian, Portuguese, Russian, Swedish, Greek, and Estonian are spoken in the novel in addition to Finnish. Latin occurs as well. Altogether the memory, of an individual and society, provides an undeniable comparative point for the presence. "A moment came when all their previous lives rushed as images in their minds, happy moments in the summer of Villa Nevski, moments which made them feel still a deeper longing, when they knew it was gone for ever." (*EP* 391)

The narrator, when ironizing them, comments on the minds of protagonists in a neutral fashion. People believe that some issue stay in their consciousness eternally and, for them, the knowlwedge of the body is uncorrupted and lasting: " . . . . certain evasions and silences had sunk deeply to the memory of their bodies" (*EP* 60). Corporeal memory and corporeal metaphors are emotional and sensual, and one may speak of a particular semiotics of the sense organs (Kukkonen 2009: 183, 2014: 252); correspondingly, one may have images of the spiritual world like

Sandra: "I have in my family immediate knowledge, real authentic knowing...The lady sank again to her memories of the spiritual world" (*EP* 39–40).

Love as life and trauma, caused by death, is the core issue of the novel. Although the experienced would try to remain united as lovers all their life, the time can be a cruel destructor and separator. When Giorgio has searched for Sandra after many phases he would not like to abandon her any longer, but the years lived in the meantime have come between them:

> "I do not know. I have to think... *Forse che si...forse che non...*
>
> ---*ma si!*" giorgio's voice squealed almost to falsette.
>
> Deep silence descended to the room again or rather the murmur of the street penetrated inside. For Giorgio the silence lasted an eternity.
>
> At the end Sandra rose up:
>
> "I have to think, I need time..."
>
> "There is no time. Time is over. Do you remember what Paolo said: time is a filter put upon being. All is being. You cannot push me into emptiness. Now starts the being. Eternal being with you."
>
> "No, Giorgio, do not demand it. I have to think...."
>
> Giorgio stood up. He set at the door.
>
> "Sandra I shall not leave you. I rather die..."
>
> Sandra did not listen. Giorgio tried first prevent Sandra from grasping the door handle, but evaded in front of her glance. He sat at the bed and pressed his head between his palms. Sandra closed the door after her.
>
> "Forse che....Giorgio!"
>
> This sank on the bed half unconscious. (*EP* 685)

Being falls into a conflict with man's temporality. The loss and unfulfillment of love are repeated. The words expressing the parting are from d'Annunzio's novel *Forse che si, forse che no*. Tarasti has told that the word 'perhaps' in the title is a reference to d'Annunzio. Erotics, aesthetics, and myth are blended together in both the novels (see Brandstetter 2015: 111–115). Love becomes sometimes grotesque, decadent and, vicious – more in D'Annunzio than in Tarasti. The dialogue with the Italian novel enriches and deepens the image of love, femininity, and corporeality of the work, which consists of dreams, encounters, disappointments, and separations.

Repetition is a constructive principle of life, memory, and art in the novel *EP*. In the work, in its most important events and relationships there are apparently several ends. Also, the beginning and the closing fluctuate in remembering. The closures and returns cause the sense of something endless, being outside the time. This corresponds to the recurrence and development in music, in the same way as in many endings of Beethoven's symphonies.

Memory creates and maintains significations in the novel. Signs are neither arbitary nor singular but they transgress the borderline between the general and particular, abstract, and concrete (see Veivo 2011: 40, 56). The portrayed semiocrises are shown, as actual and after conflicts, from the viewpoint of the previous time (Kortelainen 2016: 63). Semiocrisis involves a conflict: man's experiential knowledge and the speech of those keeping the power do not meet. The new collective identity which is directed from outside remains shallow. Then the collective memory of society and culture can help by providing examples from history of equivalent development, and striving to change it (Tarasti 2015b: 133–137). Tarasti underlines that sign practices and discourses can be changed (Tarasti 2004a: 24–25).

3 Trauma, art and Europe

The novel describes slavery, subordination, and emancipation. Situation is the same as in *Politeia*. The core values and attitudes of the Europe – democracy, freedom, human rights, equality, solidarity, respect of individuality, positive life attitude, and sane scepticism – they are all broken. The dominants guide people to the direction they want. Tarasti considers semio-ethic; the question whether people should be awakened as majority lives in a cultural slavery (see Tarasti 2015b: 440). He writes, "Traditional words like progress, development, result, education have often turned into their contrasts, means to adapt all to this new global order. What is involved is a kind of supraindividual collective force, actor, mentality, which has taken concrete people at his dominance" (Tarasti 2016: 10).

Human rights suffer a tough time in the cultures devoid of history which have denied their past and falsified it. The scarce cultivation, collective injustice, and horror government occur together. Tarasti describes the totalitarian systems in fascism and other models as nightmarish. The trauma they have caused concerns more than one generation, sometimes a whole period of a history. For those who have gone through the socalled historical trauma, memory, and feeling are schematic, one part of the experienced has been eliminated from the consiousness and even language.

The dominant people manipulate the collective memory with their goal to form a unified and easily mastered mass. Propaganda, religion, and uniform education mold identity. History has been selectively and tendentiously formed; important issues have been rejected, and the injustices of society are not dealt with. Selective and falsified remembering maintains that trauma, but the discussion by writing and art can make individual and society healthier. (Siltala 2014)

The best values of the Europe have turned into their opposites in the USSR under Stalin, the globalized Europe, and the postcolonial Brazil. The dominant classes annihilate the local cultures in Brazil and try to exploit the aboriginals: "The aboriginals do not have naturally any history and soul of nation in the proper sense. But the civilized peoples have something to learn from them. I trust in Bavarian fok healing, but one may join there knowledge of Indians of the herbs. . . . .I support healthy life. . . . . and the fact that Indians swim naked is quite healthy. Even we in Germany made sports. . . .. Well, fortunately my sister brought here some picture books of the olympiades by Leni Riefensthal. . . .." said professor with a nostalgy" (*EP* 595).

In this chapter the colonialisation is realized, the phenomenon Tarasti has also studied elsewhere (see Tarasti 2000a: 137–153). It is characterized by silencing, pushing aside, exploitation, and the underestimation of one's language, manners, and cultures leading to their destruction. An authentic people exercise their culture underground but many adopt the fashions and values of the conquerors and attempt to render the Indian culture into a commercial object to be sold to the tourists. Indians continue their hidden nocturnal ceremonies, where they dance savagely, sink into trans and get messages from spirits. Beliefs and rituals preserve fragments from what it once was. The conqueror has not been able to completely break their identity and cultural memory.

Cultural memory is frail in the contemporary Finland and only a few try to strengthen it. The globality and technosemiotic phase of society threaten the local culture and identity and underline anonymity, virtual reality, fragmentary knowledge, and narrativity. (Tarasti 2015b: 137–141).

Helsinki is not mentioned by name. Namelessness is a sign of weak identity: regions in small countries of European Union are cloned from each other, so the people. The conformity, imperialist, anglophonic globality is rude and mass tourism banal compared to genuine cultivation and internationality. The languages fostered at Villa Nevski have been forgotten notwithstanding poor English and miserable Finnish. Language, the home of comprehension and communication, has been impoverished. Young people are victims and slaves of digitalisation and information which have been poured therein.

EU is simulacrum, coulissen, and a surface without contents; the reification replaces humanity, man has distanciated from nature and lost himself. The demand of efficacity makes men beings who only bustle and execute tasks. Money as the most central value works instead of humanity and solidarity, and all is for sale. Studies and media are unifying, individuality is not tolerated. Signs and significations are distorted under semiocrisis. Valuable things change into trivial when they reach common information networks. What is offerred are substitute realities. There are no humanists, but they would carry their cultivation along, not as objectified into machines (see Tarasti 2012: 4).

The European cultural heritages are almost unknown. Young Finns in the frame story take the Italian brothers with their different characters, in the novel, as dead. Only at the end the young ask whether they are still alive. Sandra's meetings with persons invisible to others are a metaphor of cultural work with issues and values which have been believed to be extinct. Also silencing is communication and silence brings about particular knowledge (see Kukkonen 1993a: 41–44, 1993b: 286). In the side of verbalisation there lives an effort towards non-verbal arts and expressions. All is not told by language.

Conversation with 'non-existent' brothers contains a playful ironic reference to existential semiotics and a work of an American scholar. Tarasti writes about double misunderstanding in which 'both partners communicate with a kind of unperceivable ghosts." (Tarasti 2004a: 46). He remarks: "communities in which we live are to a great extent imaginary" (Tarasti 2014: 2). The political scientist Benedict Anderson, in turn, launches the notion of imagined society in his study *Imagined Communities. Reflections on the Origin and Spread of Nationalism* (1983).

Sandra's activity is verbalization of trauma and the past and telling about them in the hope that this would heal her. "The recurrent and transforming narration can free the person gradually from a trauma" writes Sirkka Knuuttila, a medical doctor (Knuuttila 2010: 43). When the images, emotions, and knowledge which rise on surface are verbalized the communication gets milder, the schematized way of experiencing opens into something creative and the traumatic experience is articulated into a part of the whole life (see Knuuttila 2009: 36).

One point of the criticism of globalisation hits those who destroy national cultures. Tarasti criticizes globalisation also in his scientific texts. The past has been finished and one has separated from history. Even future has been halted and one lives from one moment to another. Others are obstacles to be eliminaed from the way when money and utility determine human relations. The novel explains this in the following manner: ". . .if we think of the notion of *Entfremdung* – it means that alienation is a process whereby man forgets that the world in which he lives is his own creation. Capitalism changes the social relations so that they become reified. People loose the possibility of spontaneous contact. They judge other as objects, like things. Their relations are manipulatng by their nature. Such a reification they consider the natural state of the society" (*EP* 458–459).

Art is, in the novel, the healer of men and values. Tarasti writes in *New Mysteries of Paris:* "Every art work is a store of memory and when we experience it a memory remains for us" (Tarasti 2004b: 100). Art, which like an intuition constitutes its own way of knowing and counterbalances the science, is one of the most important starting points for his prose. It illuminates the themes of *Europe/ Perhaps*. Among its protagonists there are composers, writers, painters, and subjects who become relevant by their repetition, artistic creativity, and reception. In the art works portrayed, in their birth and dialogue around them the whole history of art, culture, and ideas are present. Among topics of discussion, we find music, visual art, poetry, and interrelationships of art. The speakers have accurate knowledge of different genres, their structural history, and theories of art and also of their occultism as an interpretation of art, life, and cosmos. Tarasti writes in his theory about these issues, like in his endeavour to lower the borderlines of arts and portray in music the rhythm of cosmic life (Tarasti 1992b: 153, 2000b: 88–113). A many-sided picture of the art and its semiosphere is the core of the existential semiotic nature of the novel. The borderline between art, in literature, science, and life, is transgressed in many ways. They are also evoked in the list of references at the end and two compositions by Eero Tarasti. The compositions in the novel are mentioned as works of its protagonist. Narrators and persons imitate certain discourses of arts and sciences (see Veivo 2007: 35). The love and death are foregrounded in compositions and scientific reflections of the novel as central themes just like in the output of Friedrich Nietzsche and Thomas Mann, and in many operas.

The novel contains with many allusions and themes of Tarasti's aesthetics and pilosophy from a period of quite a lot of years. He emphasizes the mult-dimensionality of aesthetic communication and role of art in spiritual growth and development of empathy and solidarity. (Tarasti 2004a: 142–147, 2004c: 85). Transcendence, interiority, memory, knowing, and subject are concretized in the debates and discussions in the work, however, these concepts are not just used explicitly. Art, its creation and reception deepen understanding and render experience rich and subtle. The knowledge, transmitted by intuition and aesthetic experience, changes the approach to man and life. Philosophers, writers, and artists shake us to realize entireties, and art mediates a cognition of the structure of reality. Some orient towards an esoteric interpretation of the world. Energetism, doctrine of magnetic fields, and correspondences, which are also experiential reality, are familiar to many from the books. The narrator takes, at times, an ironic and, at times, a neutral attitude towards the phenomenon. This is similar to the phenomenon in the *Wahlverwandtschaften* of which Tarasti argues; ". . .. existential semeiotics presumes the world is a kind of 'kinetic energy' which is in constant change and stream. It endeavours to see the life of the signs as a part of this moving semiosphere and to interpret it from inside" (Tarasti 2004a: 25) *Europe/Perhaps* opens the semiosphere and phases of signs from the inside.

Music, visual art, and poetry yield to the persons' unforgettable moments, in which time stops. Of one concert, Tarasti mentions: "Such a play makes one forget everything, even the fact that one dies one day; it detaches man from the presence" (Tarasti 2004b: 43). Tarasti characterizes the existential narration which manifests in the novel as follows:

"Existential narrativity therefore means the stopping of time, in the sense of negation or affirmation; behind the world of *Schein* is revealed 'the truth of being', the external disappears in favour of the internal. Existential narration may thus appear not only as particular mechanisms of textual production but a kind of illumination of the normal narrativity, Heideggerian *stimmung* or *Befindlichkeit* (attunement). Compared to the principles of organic narration, focusing/unfolding appear as metaphorisation; there organic and conventional procedures prove to be metaphors of something, which is behind this phenomenon. Transcendence manifests to us only as metaphors (Solomon Marcus, Rumanian academician, at a talk in Bacau, Rumania Nov. 11, 2006) (Tarasti 2008a: 56–57).

In the novel what is involved are basically the same issues which Tarasti emphasizes as the core of Richard Wagner's operas, i.e. hope and possibility to return to the right path and reconciliation (*Erlösung*). (Tarasti 1992: 108–109). Mentions to opera underline the Wagner connections of the work, whose thematic meaning is foregrounded by the quire of the pilgrims from *Tannhäuser*, which Paolo plays constantly (see Tarasti 2008a).

The rescue of individual and culture is a living bridge of memory and art from bygone days to tomorrow. The identity of an individual, culture, and their understanding are renewed when the things in the European past – classical music, myths of one's origin, and the wise memory – again become familiar. Europe occurs in the novel as a network of memories, conceptions, and stories. As a spatial and geographic phenomenon, it is a series of layered landscapes, countries, and cities with their inherent meanings and *genius loci*. Europe is a conglomeration of places of events, remembered domain, and mental state.

Ideal Europeanity or dialogicity and existential semiotics concretize in the structure of the novel. Dialogism, as a manner of action, respects the voice of each participant, their replies, and humanity. The omniscient narrator is neither asserting any ranking order to the speakers nor putting their views on certain boxes. When things are shared together and many interpretations are in touch with each other the understanding multiplies in number. No ready or final answers exist to questions, but the views are polished during the conversation. Solution is sought for in encounters which distantly evoke international congresses of semiotics and Plato's dialogues.

The essay has appeared in 2018 in Finnish as "Muisti Eero Tarastin romaanissa *Eurooppa/Ehkä*" in the anthology *Muisti ja uni kirjallisuudessa*, 143–158 [*Memory and dream in literature*] (ed. by Katriina Kajannes). (Acta Semiotica Fennica LIV). Helsinki: Kulttuuriperintöjen akatemia ry.

References

Anderson, Benedict. 2006 [1983]. *Imagined Communities. Reflections on the Origin and Spread of Nationalism*. London: Verso.

Arendt, Hannah. 1998 [1958]. *The Human Condition*. Chicago and London: The University of Chicago Press.

Assman, Jan. 2006. *Religion and Cultural Memory. Ten Studies*. Trans. by Rodney Livingstone. Stanford, California: Stanford University Press.

Babuts, Nicolae. 1992. *The Dynamics of the Metaphoric Field. A Cognitive View of Literature*. Cranbury, N.Y.: University of Delaware Press.

Brandstetter, Gabriele. 2015. *Poetics of Dance. Body, Image, and Space in the Historical Avant-Gardes* (Tanz-Lektüren 1995). Trans. by Elena Polzer & Mark Franko. USA: Oxford University Press.

Broms, Henri. 1993a. A system novel: Robert Pirsig's Lila. *Leif* (4). 33–39.

Broms, Henri. 1993b. Romaanimuoto ja nykyhetki [Form of a novel and the present]. *Synteesi* (4). 95–99.

Chesterman, Andrew. 1995. Combining the visionary and the everyday. *Leif* (4). 11–26.

Gadamer, Hans-Georg. 1986. *Hermeneutik I. Wahrheit und Methode. Grundzüge einer philosophischen Hermeneutik. Gesammelte Werke*, 1. Tübingen: J.C.B. Mohr.

Halbwachs, Maurice.1992 [1952]. *On Collective Memory*. Chicago: The University of Chicago Press.

Höhler, Sabine. 2001. *Luftfahrtforschung und Luftfahrtmythos. Wissenschaftliche Ballonfahrt in Deutschland, 1880–1910*. New York/Frankfurt: Campus Verlag.

Kajannes, Katriina. 2009. Possibilities of (mis)understanding. *Eero Tarasti's Le secret du professeur Amfortas as a semiotic novel*. In Eero Tarasti (ed.), *Communication: Understanding/Misunderstanding. Proceedings of the 9th Congress of the IASS/AIS – Helsinki-Imatra 11–17 June, 2007*, Volume II, 676–685. Helsinki: The International Semiotics Institute.

Knuuttila, Sirkka. 2009. *Fictionalising Trauma: The Aesthetics of Marguerita Duras's India Cycle*. Helsingin yliopisto.

Knuuttila, Sirkka. 2010. Historiallisesta traumasta vapauttavaksi fiktioksi. Marguerite Durasin ja Sofi Oksasen tyylit [From historical trauma to liberating fiction. Styles of Marguerite Duras and Sofi Oksanen]. *Synteesi* (2). 43–53.

Kortelainen, Juuso. 2016. Eurooppaa etsimässä. Eurooppa ja semiokriisit Eero Tarastin toisessa romaanissa [Searching for Europe. Europe and its semiocrisis in Eero Tarasti's second novel]. *Synteesi* (3). 62–67.

Kukkonen, Pirjo. 1993a. *Kielen silkki. Hiljaisuus ja rakkaus kielen ja kirjallisuuden kuvastimessa* [The silk of language. Silence and language in the mirror of language and literature]. Helsinki: Yliopistopaino.

Kukkonen, Pirjo. 1993b. On Silence. The Semiocs of Silence. In Eero Tarasti (ed.), *On the Borderlines of Semiosis*, 283–297. (Acta Semiotica Fennica 2. Publications of the International Semiotics Institute at Imatra 4). Imatra: International Semiotics Institute.

Kukkonen, Pirjo. 2009. *Det sjungande jaget. Att översätta känslan och själen. Den lyriska samlingen Kanteletar i svenska tolkingar 1830–1989* [Singing ego. Kanteletar in swedish translations 1830–1989]. (Acta Semiotica Fennica 31. International Semiotics Institute at Imatra). Helsinki: Suomen Semiotiikan Seura.

Kukkonen, Pirjo. 2014. *I språkets vida rum. Salens språk – språkets sal. Volter Kilpis modernistiska prosaepos Alastalon salissa i Thomas Warburtons svenska översättning I salen på Alastalo* [In the wide room of speech. Translations of Volter Kilpi's *Alastalon salissa* by Thomas Warburton]. (Acta Semiotica Fennica 44). Helsinki: Suomen Semiotiikan Seura – Semiotiska sällskapet i Finland, The Semiotic Society of Finland.
Pekonen, Osmo. 2008. Einstein Pariisissa [Einstein in Paris]. *Synteesi* (2). 41–51.
Siltala, Juha. 2014. Kollektiivinen muisti – kuka on se, joka muistaa? [Collective memory – who remembers?] *Lääketieteellinen aikakauskirja Duodecim* 130(24). 2449–2458.
Tarasti, Eero. 1992a. Marcel Proustin implisiittinen semiotiikka [Implicit semiotics of Marcel Proust]. *Musiikkitiede* (1–2). 41–62.
Tarasti, Eero. 1992b. *Romantiikan uni ja hurmio. Esseitä musiikista* [Dream and rapture of romanticism. Essays on music]. Porvoo–Helsinki–Juva: WSOY.
Tarasti, Eero. 1993a. "Brünhilden valinta" eli retki wagnerilaiseen semioosiin: intuitioita ja hypoteeseja ["Brünhilde's choice", a joyrney into Wagnerian semiosis: intuitions and hypothesis]. *Musiikkitiede* (1). 30–67.
Tarasti, Eero. 1993b. Mitä on "semioottinen romaani" [What is a "semiotic novel"]. *Synteesi* (4). 100–106.
Tarasti, Eero. 1994. Paikan poetiikkaa, varsinkin musiikissa [The poetry of location, especially in music]. *Synteesi* (4). 40–46.
Tarasti, Eero. 1996. Esimerkkejä. Semiotiikan uusia teorioita ja sovelluksia [Examples. New theories and applications of semiotics]. Helsinki: Gaudeamus.
Tarasti, Eero. 2000a. Existential Semiotics. Bloomington and Indianapolis: Indiana University Press.
Tarasti, Eero. 2000b. Le secret du professeur Amfortas: Roman, Trad. par Mikko Kuusimäki. Paris: Harmattan.
Tarasti, Eero. 2000c. Transsendenssista, narraatiosta ja musiikista Hugo Simbergin maalaustaiteessa [Of transsendence, narration, and music in paintings of Hugo Simberg]. In Eero Tarasti (ed.) *Ymmärtämisen merkit. Samuuden ja toiseuden ikoneja suomalaisessa kulttuurissa* [Signs of understanding. Icons of similarity and otherness in Finnish culture]. (Acta Semiotica Fennica 8). Imatra: International Semiotics Institute.
Tarasti, Eero. 2004a. *Arvot ja merkit. Johdatus eksistentiaalisemiotiikkaan* [Values and signs. Introduction to existential semiotics]. Helsinki: Gaudeamus.
Tarasti, Eero. 2004b. *Pariisin uudet mysteeri ja muita matkakertomuksia* [New mysteries of Paris and other travel accounts]. (Imatran Kansainvälisen Semiotiikka-Instituutin julkaisuja 2). Imatra: Imatran Kansainvälinen Semiotiikka-Instituutti, Helsinki: Suomen Semiotiikan Seura.
Tarasti, Eero. 2004c. Valta ja subjektin teoria [Power and the theory of subject]. *Synteesi* (4). 84–102.
Tarasti, Eero. 2005. Vastarinnan semiotiikkaa: oleminen, muisti, historia – merkkien vastavirta [Semiotics of resistance: being, memory, history – the counter-current of signs]. *Synteesi* (1). 2–29.
Tarasti, Eero. 2008a. Proust ja Wagner [Proust and Wagner]. *Wagneriaani*.12–20.
Tarasti, Eero. 2008b. Proust ja Wagner – eli narraation kolme lajia [Proust and Wagner – three species of narration]. *Synteesi* (2). 52–65.
Tarasti, Eero. 2011. Maailma ja sen tulkinta [World and its interpretation]. *Synteesi* (1). 3–13.
Tarasti, Eero. 2012. Semiotiikkakin on humanismia – eurooppalaisen humanismin merkit [Also semiotics is humanism – signs of European humanism]. *Synteesi* (1). 2–7.

Tarasti, Eero. 2014. Kulttuuri ja transsendenssi I [Culture and transcendence I]. *Synteesi* (3). 2–13.
Tarasti, Eero. 2015a. Kulttuuri ja transsendenssi II. Transsendenssin käsite kautta aikojen [Culture and transcendence II. The concept of transcendence throughout the ages]. *Synteesi* (2). 2–24.
Tarasti, Eero. 2015b. *Sein und Schein. Explorations in Existential Semiotics*. Berlin/Boston: De Gruyter.
Tarasti, Eero. 2016. *Eurooppa/Ehkä* [=EE, Europe perhaps]. Jyväskylä: Athanor.
Tarasti, Eero. 2016. Voittoisa humanismi. . . ja vastarinnan teoria [Victorious humanism. . . and the theory of resistance]. *Tiedepolitiikka* (4). 7–14.
Veivo, Harry. 2007. Taiteen semiotiikka: lähtökohtia, suuntauksia ja poikkileikkauksia [Semiotics of art]. *Synteesi* (4). 29–47.
Veivo, Harry 2011. *Portti ja polku. Tutkimus kirjallisuuden semiotiikasta* [Gate and path. A study on semiotics of literature]. Helsinki: SKS.

Leena Muotio
Varieties of masculine subjectivity in the Finnish modern literature according to Eero Tarasti's Zemic-model

Abstract: This article belongs to the field of semiotics of literature and it concerns the masculine identity, especially masculine sexuality in the modern Finnish literature starting from Juhani Aho's novel Alone (Yksin, 1890) and ending to modern novels like Kari Hotakainen's Trench Road (Juoksuhaudantie, 2002). These novels are studied by using professor Tarasti's existential semiotic model, so called Zemic-model, as one of the methodological tools. The Zemic-model itself is also studied by comparing and reflecting the model to some concepts of Mikhail Bakhtin's novel theory.

The mentioned novels are studied by showing a few text examples and explaining what category of the Zemic-model they are reflecting, and shortly how they are possible to interpret in Bakhtinian way. The article also points out some similarities between the Zemic-model interpretation and Bakhtinian concepts, like dialogue (inner speech, loophole word, double voiced word etc.), chronotope, heteroglossia, genre theory and speech genres, and even carnivalism. By reading the Zemic-model and Bakhtin's theory together, it is possible to deepen and extend the interpretation of the literature, and to prove the effectiveness and usability of these theories, especially together. This article concentrates to the introductory notes of the Zemic-model (there are 32 theses in the theory and a large philosophical background).

As a conclusion, in the text examples it is possible to see how the Zemic-model works together with dialogical inner speech of the heroes in the novels. In general, it is possible to say that the Zemic-model gives many possibilities to build up the concept of the world in the novel. With the Zemic-model the interpretation of the novel is richer and more vivid.

Keywords: semiotic of literature, Zemic-model, Bakhtin, theory of novel, masculine identity, Finnish literature

1 Introduction

This article belongs to the field of semiotics of literature. My present research concerns the masculine identity, especially masculine sexuality in the modern Finnish literature starting from Juhani Aho's novel Alone (Yksin, 1890) and ending to nowadays novels like Kari Hotakainen's Trench Road (Juoksuhaudantie, 2002). I study these novels by using prof. Tarasti's existential semiotic model, so called Zemic-model, as one of my methodological tools. I also study the Zemic-model itself and I also compare and reflect that model to some concepts of Mikhail Bakhtin's novel theory.

I open up the mentioned texts by showing a few text examples and explaining what category of Zemic-model they are reflecting, and shortly how they are possible to interpret in Bakhtinian way. It is also interesting to show some similarities between Zemic-model interpretation and Bakhtinian concepts, like dialogue (inner speech, loophole word, double voiced word etc.), chronotope, heteroglossia, genre theory and speech genres, and even carnivalism. By reading Zemic-model and Bakhtin's theory together, it is possible to deepen and extend the interpretation of the literature, and to prove the effectiveness and usability of these theories, especially together. I concentrate to the introductory notes of the Zemic-model (there is 32 theses in the theory and a large philosophical background).

2 The fatal mistake in

Kari Hotakainen's novel *Trench Road* won the Finlandia price 2002.[1] *Trench Road is* a story of a man called Matti Virtanen who makes the fatal mistake by hitting his wife once:

> Helena based her whole divorce plan on one slap. One. --- Helena played me the oldest trick known to mankind since the beginning of time: she hit with words in order to make me hit back in the flesh. --- Before that fist I had done everything I could. Everything, I said; hardly anything, she said. --- I even promised to go to one of those family therapy centers, which had been springing up the length and breadth of the country like a spa resorts. ---
> (Hotakainen 2002: 9, transl. Muotio 2020)

He loses his family, and decides to win his wife and daughter back by buying the one-family house, so called veteran house, which model is designed after the World War II by Alvar Aalto. In Helsinki area houses are too expensive for Matti, and so he radically changes his strategy. Matti becomes as a soldier of everyday life, and he is in the war against the society, economical system and all those undefined forces, which tear families apart. One might also say that his mind is unbalanced after the traumatic experience of leaving alone. The undertone of the

---

[1] Finlandia price is the most distinguished literature price in Finland. Kari Hotakainen has also won many other literature prices, for example The Nordic Council Literature Price.

story is serious, but the humoristic features and satire are present when Matti's five gives following description of him:

> The one thing I know for sure was that I never should have gone to that rock festival in the summer of 1978. --- He knew how to touch me there so that it didn't even feel like a finger. He hummed a refrain; he knew many of them by heart. He rocked me on top of him as if I was floating on waves. He threw up apple wine out of the opening of the tent on the grass, but how can you get mad at a man who can touch and rock you like that. But where did that fist come from? Sirkku thought the growth rate of the fist equaled that of a pine tree; twenty years to full-length. I should have gone to the evangelical summer meeting instead.
> (Hotakainen 2002: 47, transl. Muotio 2020)

Aho's novella Alone is a story of middle-aged man who fall in love much younger woman, sister of his friend.[2] At first Anna-girl and the man (alter ego of Aho) are good friends and because of the sweet and vivid company of the young lady the man starts to feel warmer feelings to her. Anna does not answer his feelings and their friendship stops. The man travels to the Paris, as it was habit in those days, trying to forget the love disappointment and when he reads from the newspaper that the young lady has got engaged with another man, he spend one night with a prostitute. Because of that episode this melancholic and beautiful little story was highly criticized when it was published (in nowadays light the text is of course very tolerant and even decent). The most critics did not notice at all how well formed, modern and impressionistic the novella is. We may say that it was ahead of its time. We may also say that the story started the modern literature in Finland.

It is possible to compare the story to the reality of the Finnish cultural life of those days. When Aho's friend Jean Sibelius read the story just after it was published, he immediately recognized that Anna is just like his fiancée Aino Järnefelt, who also Aho admired greatly. Sibelius considered challenging Aho to a duel with pistols. Luckily, for the Finnish cultural life he gave up the idea after sleeping overnight. (Nummi 2003: xx–xxii).

According to Bakhtin's theory of novel, both of these stories are possible to see as an upside down bildungsroman and the hero of the story as a mock-heroic character (Bakhtin 2006/1979; Morson & Emerson 1990: 407–413). In Aho's novella the male hero of the story is somehow soft and melancholic character who can't form a real relationship with a woman. He forms the ideal picture of women and love, and because he cannot confront the reality, he has to confront the disappointment and loneliness.

Through the individual point of view Zemic-model is enlarging to tread also the questions of society, nature and culture in the both stories in hand. For

---

[2] The book is translated in English, and many other languages.

example in Aho's story the different levels of the Z-model culminates in the metaphor of the watermark, which also gather the ethos of the story:

> But when my mind sifts abruptly, when the light, so to speak, falls from the different direction and the inner picture turns toward the light, there is somewhere down inside it a watermark, which shines through all else. It will not wear, it will not fade, and it cannot be falsified. On it there is her image with her clear skin, fine profile, and curl at the base of her ear.
> (Aho 2003/1890: 48)

This repeated poetic picture gives rhythm for the story. At first, it is the sign of the hope and then the very strong sign of the loss. The picture comes out at the most completed in these last sentences (above). Elsewhere in the story, the picture is varied a little bit. The picture of the watermark is like the pure and genuine certificate of real feeling and love, which is possible to see in the deepness of the soul. Somehow, this metaphor is very masculine and idealistic: Anna is like a picture, the work of art that the man has created. The man really do not know the girl, he knows only his own ideal picture of the girl. As Jyrki Nummi says, the profile phrase emphasizes the spiritual and nymph nature of Anna. (Nummi 2003: xix). Otherwise, Anna's character is very sensual and even physical. The narration emphasizes Anna's slim and slender figure against the plump and clumsy figure of the man. Anna's long summer dress emphasizes the contour of her body, which turns covered to revealing. On the other hand the story is about the aesthetics of loneliness, melancholy and nostalgia; the autumn of the man's life, but on the other hand it is the poetic miniature, blazon like portrayal of the female beauty.

Aho's story is based to the allegoric chance of the seasons of the year. The springtime wakens up the hope, the summer time is full of hope and fulfillment, the autumn wind is driving leaves of the desperation on the boulevards of Paris, and finally the dissolute carnival of the turn of the year changes to the resignation of the evening of life. Another allegoric contrast typical for Aho is the contrast between the city life and the countryside life. On the country side, in the summertime life is easy and happy, even the clothes are light and life is in generally simple. In the summertime feelings are getting mature and love seem to be pure. During the wintertime, life in Helsinki is gray and stereotyped. On the other hand, life in Paris, where it is possible to be alone in the crowd, is fascinatingly melancholic and at the same time intensively passionate. Life in Paris is like the circulating movement in the dancing hall. When the hero arrives to Paris the flow of the crowd is combined to the flow of the water fall. Even the Eifel-tower is like a Finnish forest spruce.[3] The story is based on these kinds of impressionistic contradictions.

---

[3] Aho gives also other references to the World Fair of Paris.

As it is possible to see from the introduction of the stories, certain themes arise in to the focus: The questions of identity are in the main role, because it is possible to define identity as to belonging in to something. While researching the masculine subjectivity and identity it is important to study the man's lot as well in the center of the culture as in the cultural marginal. The questions of the identity culminate in the features of the male characters personality. According to Tarasti's model, it is possible to divide the questions of the subjectivity so that personality develops from the basis of the physical energy, desire and bodily sentiments, and the personality caries the identity, habit and stability of the self. This stable self, i.e. subject, carries the social roles and the practices of the social and institutional actions, in which are related the codes of social existence, norms and values. In the Trench Road main character's social existence changes radically, the stable subjectivity and identity falls to pieces and physicality and raw desire takes over. This backwards development is presented in the dialogical relations and development in the story, and in the chronotopic and heterogolossic relationships of the story.

3 Zemic-model from the point of view of identity and sexuality

At first, I open up the Zemic-model with this diagram (Figure 1):

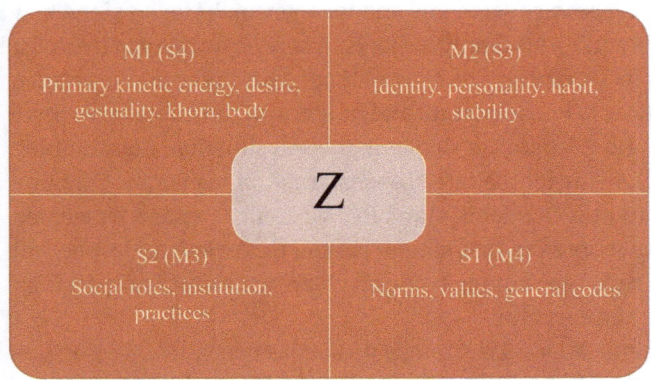

Figure 1: Eero Tarasti's Z-model.

Zemic-model is interesting and very holistic system. I will explain the model and show how it works in the interpretation of Hotakainen's novel Trench Road and Aho's novella Alone.

The most important questions are What M1-M4 and S1-S4 means? In generally we may say that all the M-cases are individual and all the S-cases are collective. The form of the Z-alphabet describes the inner movement and dynamics of the model. I quote Tarasti: "Epistemologically it has many ingrediences which have been smelted together to form a structure representing nothing less than the human mind. Zemic model simply consists of inner movement and tension among four modes of being; this dynamism is portrayed by the letter 'Z'. The varieties of the mode 'being' are articulated following the Hegelian logic on one hand i.e. being-in-myself, being-for-myself, being-for-oneself and being-in-oneself." (Tarasti 2020, see also Tarasti 2012: 328–331). The focus of the model is anyway always in the subject.

3.1 M1-level

M1 is possible to understand as bodily being, as Tarasti says: "Being-in-myself represents our bodily ego, which appears as kinetic energy, "khora," desire, gestures, intonations, Peirce's first. Our ego is not yet in any way conscious of itself but rests in the naïve Firstness of its being; modality: endotactic, will." (Tarasti 2012: 328). M1 deals also with sensuality and sensibility. When we think about Trench Roads' main character Matti, we can see how M1 describes Matti's physical being, his male body, and his masculine sexuality. When Matti loses his family his psyche collapses, he becomes somehow one-idea person because of the new coal of the life (which is getting his family back). He has been working in two jobs: in the warehouse as a forklift driver and time to time at his home as a massager. Now his daytime job turns to less important and he starts to run in the area where one-family houses are. He is a partisan soldier in the war situation; he is running in the black tricot suit looking for the safe "Lebensraum" for his family. Thinking of M1-level, very important is that Matti starts to give erotic massage for women (because he can charge more from that kind of special treatment, and so he will get the house sooner). He is like running erotic machine, who is totally apart from his normal physicality and sexuality.

In Aho's novella Alone M1-level is strongly present as beneath of the surface. Sexual desire and physicality dominates the story. Also M2-level is connected to the questions of physicality, because through the M2-level answers the questions like: How I develop my qualities so that I'll be the personality with certain kind of identity? How I can get teaching and education, which refines me a man or a woman with certain qualities? Main characters of the story belongs to the class society of the 19th century, and in that kind of very strict and controlled system certain profession, status in society, moral codes and values formed a person as he or she appeared to be from the surface. That is why the collective S0i-level is so strongly on the surface of the story: The hero of the story has lived his life alone and rather satisfied for the situation. He has broken up one engagement because he did not want to the marriage of convenience. He is a member of the society, he has a valued profession (he is a writer and journalist like Aho himself), and his life in generally in nice and comfortable from the surface. The questions of the M2-level are other vice answered, but not in the case of love and marriage.

Like S1-level presents, the voice of the society says in the head of our hero that he should be married because it is the correct way of living and control desire. This idea was very strong virtual (and mythical) belief system, and perhaps it still is. Naturally, this idea is related to questions of identity and values. Life without a wife makes the hero as a second-rate person for himself. It is possible to say that the bio semiotic ground of the human being is also the stone base of the story: the need to be with other person, the need to act, as genetic code requires. It is possible to see this situation in Aho's prose in generally.

3.2 M2- and M3-levels

M2 level answers the questions like: "How I develop my properties so that I become a personality --- How I can get training and education whereby I sublimate my physical into a man / woman with a certain competence." These questions are very interesting while thinking Matti's life: Matti is most of all a home front man (after the loss of his family he is a home front soldier):

> The home front man takes care of the housework and understands the woman. During our marriage, I did everything that our fathers had not done. I did the laundry, cooked, cleaned, gave her her own time, and stood up for us against society. For hours I would attend to her work problems, mood changes, and hopes of more versatile expressions of tenderness. I executed large-scale operations to liberate her from being tied to the stove. I was on continual standby with meals when she came home tired.
> (Hotakainen 2002: 16, transl. Muotio 2020)

He is a man who flourishes at home. He has not high education he is ordinary working man. However, at home is always tidy and food is always ready for his five Helena and daughter Sini. He loves his child and takes a good care of her. He talks about everything for his five (which is not typical amongst Finnish man). He is tender, good and loyal lover for her. We may say that his personality, identity and capabilities culminate in home. His masculine identity is very near to those bygone days not emancipated house fives, and when his wife cannot value that effort and these skills (and says nasty words about them), Matti cannot suddenly speak anymore, and uses his fist. It is paradoxical that the five would like to have something else than a soft husband, but she does not want the tough guy either. (The military language/slang is present in this text example.)

M3-level tells "[h]ow I can obtain a job, position, role in a social institute which would correspond to my personality, skills and inclinations. --- How do I get a job and work which is equal to my capacities? How I can act in the community so that I become an accepted member of it, gain appreciation and success?" (Tarasti 2012: 330).

This level is next step from the M2-level. It is obvious that Matti has invested in his family. He has never thought to gain in his working carrier anything else than some money for living and enough holidays to spend with his family. Being a forklift driver or massager (even erotic massager) is only a tool for remaining the happy family life. Work has no absolute value for him. Matti has always known that his best talents are at home. But how his talents are valued in the society? Apparently, these kinds of skills are valued, but real appreciation is for those people who have education, money and influence. Real estate agent Arto Kesämaa is Matti's worst enemy, because he is selling dreams,[4] and he presents everything what Matti doesn't have, what he can't get, and he also presents everything what Matti despises (for example Kesämaa has extramarital relationships). In general, in the society where there is lots of unemployment and social displacement, where people are divided into economic and social castes, all people can in no way reach the highest ultimatum of M3 level. The novel Trench Road tells a lot about that how ordinary human being rises against the dominant circumstances when his humble hopes and dreams are violated and his basic security has taken away. Matti has nothing else than his beloved family, when it is lost, man is in the war against the surrounding world.[5]

In Aho's novella, the institution of the marriage (S2-level) reflects to the M3-level; how our hero can obtain the full social acceptance? By marring a young and beautiful fine lady his appreciation and success in the society would be at its fullest. A change seems to happen in his little bit phlegmatic appearance towards social activity and even ambition to live a life as a full man.[6] When the girl does

---

4 Even his name is like a dream, "Summerland", versus very common Virtanen.
5 The dialogical relationship between Matti and Kesäma is interesting, because it creates the wholeness of the masculine discourse in the story – and very tense and passionate one.
6 Anna's brother is also a little bit Oblomov-like character, he also reads Oblomov in the story. He marries hard working young lady, with whom it is easy to continue lazy and comfortable life.

not answer his feelings and the proposal of marriage has turned down, the man feels sorrow, disappointment and above all shame – and of course, sexual frustration. Impossible love turns his world and for few moments his values upside down. We can see how M4-level works: the hero of the story tries to make his life complete, because he wanted to marry the girl he loved and accepted the norms and values of the society. Marriage as institution refers to the S2-level, where norms and values are filtered as laws, regulations and institutions. S2-level brings to the focus how the actions of the members of society are regulated and directed through the norms and social practices, and how they are leaded to accept these forms and genres of behavior.[7]

The institution of marriage reflects also to M3-level: How the hero may reach the complete social acceptance? By marrying beautiful, young lady from the good family background the man would get both, the personal happiness and full social acceptance. When Anna is not answering to his feelings, the feelings of sorrow, disappointment and shame are equally strong as the feeling of sexual frustration. The impossible situation and disappointment in love turns the heroes set of values upside down:

> Out of my own hopes I created a reality. --- We feel as if it were in the air that we are the heroes of the day and that everyone is curious to know who we are. It seems to me – and it pleases me – that people seem to think that we are engaged.   (Aho 2010/1980: 16, 17)

> She had been my last hope. She had got me on my feet again, when I lay in a heap, psychologically nerveless. I had meant to begin living again, had dared to open another future before me. I wanted to act, to have an effect, to struggle. And I had strained to do so. And everything was as it had been. --- I felt even older and more helpless than before.

> Nothing has been slashed in me, nor did I feel the pain of being crushed, but all resilience was gone. I was like worn out and warped collar tree.   (Aho 2010/1890: 5)

In the text examples it is noticeable that at first the narrator hero uses the we-form and then in the flash back he returners to the me-form. "Me" is the reality in the story; "we" is the dream situation.

In the story of Alone hero's possession makes possible for him to leave abroad and his writing work in there, although the regular and stable working schedule seem to be connected to the possibility of hope. When the hope is lost also the peace of mind and work are lost. In addition, the vision life is quite gloomy after the man has lost his hope.

---

7 In this case Pierre Bourdieu talks about habitus.

3.3 M4-level

M4 level tells how "I can accept the values and norms which are dominant in my community and society – if yes, then how can I bring them on this level of 'Fourtness' into their brilliance, and efficiency. And if not (since we can always either affirm or deny) then how I become a dissident until the extreme negation and refusal, withdrawal from those values which I find inacceptable, and how I then become a pacifist, ecologist etc. with extreme attitudes." (Tarasti 2012: 330). One of these extreme attitudes is definitely to become as a home front soldier, or disappointed and given up old man. These are very important social questions, and very important questions in the research of the literature.

Matti Virtanen considers himself as a defender of the right values; he is honest, he carries the truth. He think that he has to sacrifices himself for the sake of the saving the family. Moreover, because he is in the war, he has to do many not so noble deeds, for example, he has to lie, sell himself, scare and blackmail other people, and he has to be violent. As so many dissidents, also Matti legitimates and explains he is deeds to the correct way by saying that the end justifies the means. Matti is the partisan of the home security forces (well-trained body, a headlamp, black tricot, and a backpack and so on as external marks of the city soldier). He has to get his family back, because it is the only way to stabilize the world and put the society in the order. In Matti's point of view (individuals point of view) the order leys in small details, in the subjective take over, not in the political decisions or the actions of the social office or the police. They cannot understand the individual catastrophe, or anything, which is necessary to do to get the life back to normal. Matti's point of you is twisted, because he sees the society as an enemy and as factor, which separates a person from the normal life. We can only ask how often those people who really live in the marginal of the society feels that society and its institutions are not very safe and helpful. The character of Matti is parodic, but there are also many alarmingly truthful features in him.

As Tarasti says, S1 "represents the voice of society, its ideology and axiology, which appears in sanctified texts, myths. It represents the society as virtual belief system." (Tarasti 2012: 331). S1 is reflected most strongly to M4. A good example of this is how Matti is comparing his situation as a defender of the home front. His battle begins on the same day as famous and mythical Tali-Ihantala defensive battle, 3th of July 1999/1944. (Hotakainen 2002: 54).

In Aho's novella M4-level is present when the hero tries to make his life complete by desiring to marry the woman he love and by following norms and values, which he believes to be the pillars of the society. He really tries to bring them to the level of "Fourtness". When he fails in his purposes, he finally does something, which is against as well his personal beliefs and values as the official values of the society. By spending the night with a prostitute, he on the other hand negates his feelings and dreams but on the other hand, he purifies himself from his desperate love. However, he fails in both of these purposes.

3.4 S-levels reflected to M-levels

When the basic principles of the M-levels are now clear, it is interesting to see how the S-levels deepen the interpretation of the story. We can see how there is two-dimensional movement when Trench Roads' Matti defenses the holiest and highest laws of the society by fighting behalf of the basic units of the society (families). In his point of view, he has the right knowledge and the highest moral. From the outside point of view (other characters of the story and most of the readers), Matti has stepped out from the legal and socially acceptable way of acting. He is actually blackmailer, kidnapper and abuser. This extreme contradiction between the inner and outer point of view creates the effective contrast of the story.

S3-level explains how the personal qualities and characteristics can serve the society. In other words: How people are qualified their jobs and positions? For example, the job interviews are good example of this. Matti's capabilities as a housefather are clear, as well as the other side of his character: physical capability of the furious partisan soldier and unfailing and firm twisted logic of thinking when his psyche collapses. Matti – the housefather – serves society in the best possible way, but Matti – the partisan soldier – is in the service of the total anarchy. Matti's character is strongly dualistic.

Because this article is studying the masculine identity and sexuality in the Finnish literature, the most interesting and most important level is S4, because now it is possible to examine "How does the society penetrate even to the physical sensible behavior of an individual? How are even gender distinctions partly constructed? Here, we encounter those modalities whereby a Soi enacts its contracts, and those passions that make it real in the innermost individual core by emotions and feelings of guilty conscience, shame, glory, duty, and their quasi-physical counterparts of the behavior." (Tarasti 2012: 331).

We may say that the level S4 tells us what happens when a man's lot and his position in the society and his life order disturbs. What kind of feelings arises? When Matti's life collapses, he turns to extremists. He feels very physical feelings, and we can see that S4 is comparable to M1: he feels quilt of what has happened, he has lost his honor, he is deeply shamed of that fact that he couldn't keep his family together and also the fact that he hasn't enough money to buy one-family house (the house he wants is so called ex-service man house, which were built in Finland after the World War II). He is deeply shamed of the fact that he cannot fulfill the responsibility and the manly destiny he has set to himself and which society has set to him. Because of the social and economic situation, he cannot be a full man. He has to live against his will, so he turns to Other for himself, for his five and for the society. Shame and fear changes Matti's conscious to his own interpretation, the common view from the conscious may go. In the end of the story, Matti's honor is the honor of his own army, and there is only on member in that army, Matti himself. However, the story alarmingly insinuates that many others may join that army any day soon.

In Aho's novella the flash back scene in a restaurant in Helsinki (referred above) is a good example from S4-level. The style and tone of the narration reflects the mental state and the feeling of escaping (the man is leaving to Paris next morning). Physical and mechanical objects are metaphors of the state of mind. The vocabulary is masculine: The feel of strength and activity, which is caused by feeling of love, is compared to successfulness of masculine activity and physical work. Paradoxically Paris is like a solitude beach. Paris is state of mind, the picture of loneliness, where the man escapes his failure. With a prostitute, he deepens to the lowest level the shame and masculine defiance. Nevertheless, the story ends to the feelings of desperate longing.

The conclusion of the context of the level S4 is that the questions of shame, guilt, honor and duty are the primary when we research the masculine identity in the Finnish literature. And as we can see Tarsti's Zemic-model opens these concepts up in a deep way.

4 Zemic-model and Mikhail Bakhtin

As I mentioned before, there is 35 theses, which explains the varieties of our subjectivity and relations between M and S levels. Now I mention two of them, number 4 and number 8, because these two are connected to Mikhail Bakhtin's thinking most seemingly way, although also other theses can be seen related Bakhtin's heterogenic and large theory. The diagram here explains how it is possible to compare Bakhtin's theory to Z-model. This is only an outline, but interesting one:

It is possible to see the whole scheme of Zemic-model as same position than the polyphony is in Bakhtin's theory, as it has been explained in this diagram (Figure 2). In addition, dialogical dimension is present in every phase of the Zemic-model, because Z-model is presented and manifested in the language and dialogical relationships between people (one of these dialogical relationships is the inner speech of the person /or the character of the story). Moreover, in generally we can think life and art as an open text.

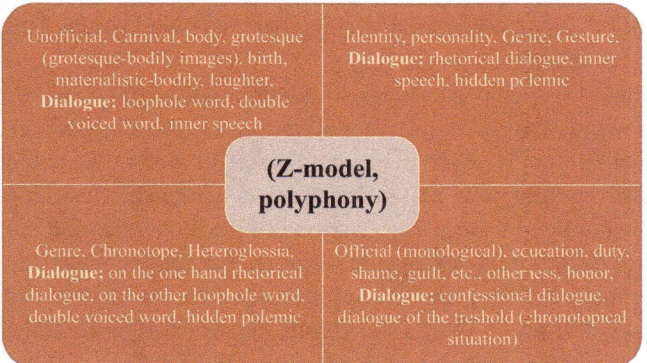

Figure 2: Comparison of Tarasti's and Bakhtin's models.

I take as my example the erotic massage scene mentioned before:

> Eroticism caused me the most pain. It was difficult to get used to the fact that an ordinary shoulder massage now had to stretch to the buttocks and between them. As the client started to get excited, I pretended to be with her, although I was thinking about the decoration of Sini's new room. Breast massages were the most difficult, because I couldn't stop thinking about Helena's breasts. The breasts of most of the clients felt like disgusting pieces of flesh, but there was one cashier from a grocery store, whose breasts were just like Helena's; rounded and full. Her nipples got hard. I was about to cry. I faked dizziness and interrupted the massage. The cashier had almost reached her climax. She got off the table, toppled me down to the floor and started pushing her breast into my mouth. I got a hold of her hair and wrestled her off of me. The cashier was crying on the floor in the living room, while I cried in the kitchen. I explained the matter to her, and didn't charge a full price. She wanted to pay nevertheless, and asked for a new appointment for the following week. (Hotakainen 2002: 32, transl. Muotio)

According to Tarasti's model, I may say that the basis of that episode is physical and sexual. In Bakhtinian light, the episode is upside down turned official and clinical massage situation. Carnivalistic turn shows the materialistic-bodily lower parts and the bottom, and the scene is grotesque and pornographic. When official turns unofficial there is always present the familiar laughter of the carnival, but in this novel as in many modern novels, the laughter is reduced, because it has serious undertone. That is because according the idea of the level S4 our antihero is forced to encounter the shame of the falling from the social role and from the happy, normal family life. We can see here the two dimensional movement of the modern parody. Matti has carried his responsibility, but maybe because of that he has lost everything. In the grotesque (and castrating) situation of erotic massage Matti feels his shame and desperate longing very strongly when he is thinking the furnishing of his daughters room and when he remembers his fives breasts. This is presented in the level of his inner speech.

In Bakhtinian context this episode is inner confessional dialogue, which is directed desperately towards the lost family happiness and the collective condemnatory Other. Naturally Matti is telling in his first person discourse also about the open confession for the lady he is massaging (who is actual the flesh and blood Other). When the family life ends, Matti's social (and also personal) identity collapses (this is the matter of the levels of M3 and S2). But other kind of personality takes over: a metamorphosis happens; Matti turns to some kind of odd joking monster. Because of this also Matti's social role, his task and place in the society chances totally (which is presented in the levels M2 and S3).

> There it is, there is no more. And it awakens no dreams, nor any hopes based on them. The sky of my life seems to have grown clearer and colder. I myself am freezing and shrinking. Total vacuity surrounds me, the soul bells of solitary wasteland sound in my ears. And I think myself ready to accept the vacuity life offers me. And I turn to the wall to sleep. But then I seem to feel a waft of fragrance from this morning's bed ---. Where I may live, where I may seek consolation and forgetfulness, I am always groping for her around me, where she is not. (Aho 2010/1890: 56–57)

We can see in the text example how Zemic-model works together with dialogical inner speech of the hero. The speech is directed to the official other, but also to the dialogical dimension is possible to see between hopeful, sentimental and "in love man", and resigned, melancholic and even a little bit cynical man. In general, it is possible to say that the Zemic-model gives many possibilities to build up the concept of the world in the novel. With the Zemic-model the interpretation of the novel is richer and more vivid.

References

Aho, Juhani. 2010/1980. *Alone*. Trans. by Riachard Impola. Finnish American Translators Association (FATA). http://www.kantele.com/fata/onlinetranslations.html (accessed 10th of January 2011)

Aho, Juhani. 2003 [1890]. *Yksin* [Alone]. Romaani. Helsinki: SKS.

Bakhtin, Mikhail. 2006. The Bildungsroman and Its Significance in the History of Realism Toward a Historical Typology of the Novel. In *Speech Genres & Other Late Essays*. Translated by Vern W. McGee. Eds. by Caryl Emerson & Michael Holquist. Austin: University of Texas Press.

Hotakainen, Kari. 2002. *Juoksuhaudan tie* [Trench avenue]. Romaani. Helsinki: WSOY.

Morson, Gary Saul & Caryl Emerson. 1990. *Mikhail Bakhtin. Creation of a Prosaics*. Stanford, California: Stanford University Press.

Nummi, Jyrki. 2003. Yksin Pariisissa [Alone in Paris]. Preface to the Juhani Aho's novella Yksin. In Juhani Aho *Yksin*, vii-xxii. Helsinki: SKS.
Tarasti, Eero. 2020. The Panorama of musical semiotics and one new theory to elaborate it further. The paradigm of existential theory in music. *MusicMid: Revista Brasileira de Estudos Em Música E Mídia* 1(1). 11–35. https://doi.org/10.29327/16597.1.1-2
Tarasti, Eero. 2012. Existential Semiotics and Cultural Psychology. In Jaan Valsiner (ed.), *Oxford Handbook of Culture and Psychology*. Oxford, New York: Oxford University Press.

Massimo Berruti
H.P. Lovecraft's subjectivity: an existential semiotic perspective

Abstract: The application of the categories of external/internal and inner/outer to Lovecraft's works may prove fruitful in providing a comprehensive understanding of the ways in which his existential perspective influences his literary production. Lovecraft's subjectivity has a strong impact on his writings, and causes the creation of different authorial "masks" in his fictional production and his letters: I aim to demonstrate that Lovecraft's conflicting existential perspective influences the literary rendering of the subjectivity and the semiotic attitude of his characters.

The discussion is divided into two logically consequential steps: what follows is first a survey of the *transcendental experience* undergone by Lovecraft's subjects during their confrontation with *Outsideness* and Nothingness; and second, a discussion on the endo- and exo-semiotic processes Lovecraft's subjects traverse.

Keywords: subjectivity, transcendence, endosemiosis, exosemiosis, Outsideness

1 The transcendental experience of Lovecraft's subjects

At first, it is necessary to investigate, from an existential perspective, Lovecraft as a subject. This approach may lead to further developments with the application of semiotic classical models, such as Greimas's actantial model and Propp's formalist narratology, where subjects and objects are involved as fundamental categories. For the aim of my present study, I will limit my application to the theory of *existential semiotics*, devised by Finnish semiotician Eero Tarasti, a theory in which the subject plays a decisive role, being called to see "the signs from the *inside*, to recognize their inner microorganic life" (Tarasti 2000: 6): it is a model which connects the meaning with a *temporal* process, since "meaning emerges via a kind of 'journey' made by the subject" (Tarasti 2000: 18). Already from the outset, the model appears applicable to Lovecraft's fictional world, since the latter's characters very often approach the threshold of knowledge through a process of wandering and/or descending.

For a subject like Lovecraft, whose life was especially that of an individual intellectual effort, existential semiotics reveals as a fruitful method of study, since it is a theory that searches "[. . .] for the individuality and particularity of phenomena, their 'soul'" (Tarasti 2000: 9). According to this semiotic approach, a sign, which always appears in connection with a certain situation, can be "[. . .] in any existential relations with its situation; it can either deny or affirm that situation" (Tarasti 2000: 7): I will try to demonstrate that the signs emerging from Lovecraft's fictional world are meant to be in a relationship of negation with the situation in which they appear, to which they rebel staging a narrative conflict, and that this conflict stems from a fractured existential perspective on the utterer's part. This is confirmed by the fact that even entirely inner signs – like a sign seen in a dream, a dimension conflicting with that of the reality of existence, or *Dasein* – may constitute a strong impulse to action in existential semiotics as well as in Lovecraft, for whom dreams represent a crucial source of knowledge and inspiration.

The Lovecraftian characters perform what, in the frame of existential semiotics, is defined as the *transcendental journey of the existential subject*, via the acts of Negation and Affirmation. The concept of transcendence is central here, as the "dialectics between 'being' and 'not-being' (or Nothingness)" (Tarasti 2000: 11). It is precisely thanks to a leap into the Nothingness of *Outsideness* that Lovecraft's characters are allowed to step the bounds of *Dasein* and intrude into the realm of truth beyond the threshold: they resist the reality of objective signs (the *Dasein*) in which they are, to use a Heideggerian term, *thrown*, and through this act of Negation they come to experience the Nothingness (the Sartrean *Néant*) of the purposeless cosmos, the nuclear chaos of existence. During this movement of Negation, the existential signs float as mere signifiers with no content in the realm of Nothingness, the playground where they are re-moulded and given new content and new life. During the act of Negation, the Lovecraftian subjects re-fashion the signs of the primary *Dasein*, empty them of their content and fill them with a new one. In existential semiotics the subject, to become a truly existential one, must complete its transcendental journey and convert its anguishing experience of Nothingness into a *creative* one, by going forth. In fact, after the movement of Negation, the subject returns to *Dasein*: it sees the signs around from a new standpoint, enriches old signifiers with new meaningful contents, directly derived from its existential experience. Old signs lose significance, and the Lovecraftian subject is "reborn as a 'semiotic self'" (Tarasti 2000: 11): after returning to the *Dasein*, the subject is itself epistemologically enriched, and endorses a relativistic perspective on universe and life, assuming new values and perceiving the *Dasein* as "transfigured" by the transcendental experience. A movement of Affirmation now takes place, assigning new significance to the (world of) the former "objective" signs, and to the subject itself: this is the *second act of transcendence*. The *Dasein* transfigured by and through the existential subject can be understood as a Peircean

Ground of Fullness/Plenitude of meaning, in the Gnostic sense: what lacked signification in the world of primary *Dasein*, now finds it, thanks to an illuminating experience through which the Lovecraftian subjects fill pre-existing signs with new meaning.

In the Ground of Fullness, modalities change: for example, the knowing and the willing of the existential subject are of a different kind after the transcendental experience. The Lovecraftian existential subject creates new, existential sign meanings whose essence, as we will see, is understood (and I suspect, understandable) only by a subject who has undergone the same path via Nothingness and Fullness, Negation and Affirmation. This is the reason why the new existential signs created by the Lovecraftian transcendental subject (i.e., the subject that has undergone the experience of *Outsideness*) cannot be understood by anyone in the wake world unless s/he has passed through the same path: the "contemptuous amusement" of the "hopelessly conventional" ("Dagon", in Lovecraft [1917] 1999: 6) world which stems from the non-coincidence of the existential perspectives of the utterer and the addressee of the new existential sign. The group of existential subjects is one of "silent subjects" (Tarasti 2000: 12): the Lovecraftian existential characters communicate their transfigured signs to enlarge the group of those silent subjects, even though they are aware that the enlarging would be dangerous since the spreading of the "transcendental" knowledge, acquired in the realm of Nothingness, may ultimately lead to the psychological and then physical collapse of the human race. The sign transfiguration operated by the existential subject is possible thanks to the *temporal* nature of the process: in fact, signs always *become* themselves through a movement in time; they are never fixed and determined as in a Platonic world of ideas. Thus, according to existential semiotics, six species of signs can be distinguished: (1) *pre-signs*: signs in the process of forming and shaping themselves; (2) *trans-signs*: signs in the phase of transcendence (in Lovecraft, those experienced by the subject during his leap into *Outsideness*); (3) *act-signs*: those actualised in the world of *Dasein*; (4) *endo-* and *exo-signs*: signs in the dialectics of presence/absence; (5) *internal/external signs*; and finally, (6) *as-if-signs*, signs that should be understood *as if* they were true (Tarasti 2000: 19). In Lovecraft's literature, one can also see the temporal dimension at work when sign formation via the experience of transcendence affects the life of signs through the notion of *decay*: signs, after the gravity-less experience into Nothingness, undergo a temporal process which turns them into decayed object-signs. In the final Plenitude, their true nature is revealed: decay and degeneration.

The transcendental experience may lead to two different expressive styles, depending on which movement is stressed, Negation or Affirmation. The existential author's style will be "anguished, or rebellious" (Tarasti 2000: 13), as a consequence of the predominance of Negation; "transfigured, which blends into the 'harmony of the spheres'" (Tarasti 2000: 13), if Affirmation prevails. In Lovecraft, the plenitude brought by the Affirmation movement must not be understood as a positive, idyllic state of harmony and balance between man and nature, or between man and the divine: the transfiguration of reality induced by the existential experience leads to reaffirm chaos and entropy, fracture and dissonance, not harmony since the Fullness of meaning which is finally experienced is a dreadful one and represents an ethically and epistemologically undesirable burden for mankind. The Lovecraftian existential subject comes to discover a world soul which is hideous: hidden horrors lie just beneath the surface of the everyday reality, of the *Dasein*, and the five human senses are not able to grasp them unless transcendence is experienced. Mankind is doomed by *epistemic fallacy*, heavily tampering with the achievements of the race, a defect that can be overcome only through the transcendental experience. An early example of Lovecraft's concern with this issue is detectable in "From Beyond" (November 1920), whose protagonist, Crawford Tillinghast, is a prototype of the Lovecraftian subject striving for an indefinite expansion of the human capabilities of perception, a truly transcendental experience which he tries to achieve using an electrical device (an "accursed electrical machine" (Lovecraft 1986: 90)) able to "generate waves acting on unrecognised sense-organs that exist in us as atrophied or rudimentary vestiges" (Lovecraft 1986: 91). Tillinghast's fundamental drive comes from a need to trans-cend the limits and the *resistance* that reality exerts on the human epistemological faculties:

> 'What do we know', he had said, 'of the world and the universe about us? Our means of receiving impressions are absurdly few, and our notions of surrounding objects infinitely narrow. We see things only as we are constructed to see them, and can gain no idea of their absolute nature. With five feeble senses we pretend to comprehend the boundlessly complex cosmos, yet other beings with a wider, stronger, or different range of senses might not only see very differently the things we see, but might see and study whole worlds of matter, energy and life which lie close at hand yet can never be detected with the senses we have. I have always believed that such strange, inaccessible worlds exist at our very elbows, *and now I believe I have found a way to break down the barriers*' (Lovecraft 1986: 91. Italics added)

An essential question arises here: why does the Lovecraftian subject strive to become "existential"? Why is it driven to react and rebel against the *Dasein* in which it is immersed, and to put signs into motion? This often happens to it not voluntarily: the subject is in a sense "forced" to experience *Outsideness*. This holds true for instance in *At the Mountains of Madness* (1931) and "The Shadow Out of Time" (1934–35), while in "The Call of Cthulhu" (1926), or in the aforementioned "From Beyond" and in the Carter cycle, it is apparently thanks to specific intentionality on the character's part that the leap into Nothingness takes place.

As a result, this would lead to divide Lovecraft's narratives into two categories. The reason stirring the subject to action in the narratives belonging to the second category is precisely "the idea that the subject living in this world glimpses and strives for transcendence, since it experiences the world of mere *Dasein* as being insufficient" (Tarasti 2000: 19), for "in *Dasein* everything is evanescent, ambiguous, all its pertinence mere appearance" (Tarasti 2000: 20): the subject desires "to attain a more stable fulcrum" (Tarasti 2000: 20) for its existence. This seems to be most likely the case in the tales featuring Randolph Carter, such as "The Silver Key" (1926), "The Dream-Quest of Unknown Kadath" (1926–1927), "Through the Gates of the Silver Key" (1932–1933), or, in general, in the early tales where the sheer setting in a "dreamland" or a land of a remote past reveals a bitter dissatisfaction on the subject's part towards the "tedium and limitations of waking reality": one may think of narratives such as "Polaris" (1917), "The White Ship" (1919), "The Doom that Came to Sarnath" (1919), and above all "Celephaïs" (1920) and "The Quest of Iranon" (1921). Later, I will elucidate this issue more, thanks to a deeper understanding of the transcendental experience. For now, it suffices to say that in the tales of both categories the Lovecraftian subject is brought, as a direct consequence of the existential perspective of its creator, to perceive *Dasein* as opposition, limitation, resistance to the possibilities of the subject itself: reality imposes limits on men, and this makes the Lovecraftian subject perceive the existential act of rebellion/negation as necessary, makes it strive for transcendence, in opposition to the resistance of the corporeal world of *Dasein*. In fact, in Lovecraft's fiction, communication and existence in *Dasein* are possible only when there is some Other, which (1) does not fuse with the enunciating subject or agent, and (2) performs a resistance necessary for a successful communicative exchange. When Lovecraft's fiction stages the fusion of the spheres of the Human and *Outsideness* by means of the existential subject's leap into Nothingness, the emerging narrative conflict is a truly "blasphemous" one, since it blends two realms which should remain separate. The integrity of the Other is threatened, thus communication is endangered. If *Outsideness* stayed "outside", not intruding into *Dasein* (and vice versa), life and communication – in their respective realms – would be possible. It is just when Lovecraft's narrative choices lead to a blending of the two spheres, that resistance is destroyed and narrative conflict erupts, with that hideous Plenitude of meaning which is likely to doom mankind. But as Sartre, Lovecraft believes that *Outsideness* is resistance; a "bad" resistance because synonymous to the Sartrean *Le Néant*'s loss of meaningfulness – a truly subjective psychological problem. Therefore, here an apparent contradiction arises: the Lovecraftian Nothingness and *Outsideness* are at the same time receptacle of *meaninglessness*, of a loss of a sense that makes the transcendental subject crossing them loses its identity, renovating it into a new one, but they are also, as we have seen, a breeding ground of Plenitude and Fullness of (hideous) meaning. Nonetheless, *Outsideness* is necessary as a resistant, opposing force, because the threat to its integrity and otherness (i.e., its blending with the Human *Dasein*: a subject from any sphere intruding into the other's) has destructive consequences. When the blending occurs, language and communication disappear and human survival is no longer possible: in "Dagon" (1917), nobody is available to listen to the shipwrecked's account, its language reduces to aphasia, because the Other has been verbalized by its words and has thus become "actual", present, its alterity violated and its resistance annihilated. In *Anatomy of Criticism*, Frye describes five fictional modes, according to the level and degree of the resistance. If the characters are on a higher level than the narrator, the result is a text with theological or mythological features; if the resistance is on the same level, pragmatic texts emerge, which move on practical, empirical levels; if the resistance is on a lower level, it brings about comical, ironic, or parodistic texts: no doubt that in Lovecraft the level of resistance, being represented by the forces of *Outsideness*, lies on a higher level than the narrator, that is induced to step *beyond* its human limits and embark in the transcendental experience. Therefore, Lovecraftian texts display a mythical-theological character, and it is worth speaking of a *mythical discourse*. Very fruitful would be then a semiotic analysis of the theme of "resistance" in Lovecraft's literary discourse, i.e. a study exploring how the Lovecraftian existential subjects' reactions towards the resistant forces represented by the manifestations of *Outsideness* take place during the transcendental experience they undergo towards the building of a renovated semiotic self.

Moving toward the Other is a leap into transcendence: it means the negation of the Same, the affirmation of its counterpart, the Other. But when *Outsideness* and Sameness collide, conflict erupts, since Lovecraft's subjects negate the Otherness of the Other, try to conceptualize and rationalize it: they try to incorporate it into their theoretical framework of Sameness. This happens also when *Outsideness* intrudes upon our *Dasein*, often summoned by a human being through his transcendental experience and a consistent sin of *hybris*. The same holds for all those narratives where a human being attempts to cross the borders between the two spheres and entertains, like Randolph Carter in "Through the Gates of the Silver Key" (1932–33), "thoughts of infinite and blasphemous daring" (Lovecraft 1985: 431–432). In Lovecraft, transcendence – and the leap into *Outsideness* it involves – might be seen as the attempt to make *Outsideness* closer to *Dasein*, to the point of mingling them into a unique, and therefore blasphemous and impossible realm.

The return to *Dasein* (to its transfiguration or *Dasein 2*) after the transcendental experience brings to new signifieds which form a new connection with their former signifiers of *Dasein 1*: the most common situation in Lovecraft is that of old signifiers remaining unchanged, and of their signifieds being changed. In *Dasein 2*, old signs are therefore filled with a new meaning deriving from the transcendental experience: this holds, for instance, for all those Lovecraftian narratives in which old legends and bodies of lore are re-interpreted in the light of the experience of *Outsideness*.

Once again exemplary on this regard is *At the Mountains of Madness* (1931), the short novel about the Antarctic expedition of scientists and researchers of the Miskatonic University of Arkham, Mass., organised with the initial, purely scientific purpose of "[. . .] securing deep-level specimens of rock and soil from various parts of the Antarctic continent" (Lovecraft 1997: 180–181).

In the first pages, the narrator states:

> Something about the scene reminded me of the strange and disturbing Asian paintings of Nicholas Roerich, and of the still stranger and more disturbing descriptions of the evilly fabled plateau of Leng, which occur in the dreaded *Necronomicon* of the mad Arab Abdul Alhazred. I was rather sorry, later on, that I had ever looked into that monstrous book at the college library. (Lovecraft 1997: 187–188)

What the unnamed narrator has read in the abominable *Necronomicon* is transfigured during the transcendental experience: in other words, signs produced or experienced by the subject in *Dasein 1* are emptied of their previous signified and filled with a new one. This appears even clearer when, in this work, the mysterious hints to an outer reality contained in the cursed tome or legends and traditional tales, incomprehensible when the subject was in *Dasein 1*, find a plain new signified during the transcendental experience within the realm of *Outsideness*. This is how one of the characters, Dr. Lake, comments upon his disquieting discovery of some frozen animal specimens of an unknown species buried in the ice:

> Complete specimens have such uncanny resemblance to certain creatures of primal myth that suggestion of ancient existence outside antarctic becomes inevitable. *Dyer and Pabodie have read Necronomicon and seen Clark Ashton Smith's nightmare paintings based on text, and will understand when I speak of Elder Things supposed to have created all earth-life as jest or mistake.* [. . .] Vast field of study opened. (Lovecraft 1997: 215–216. Italics added)

And referring to the *Old Ones*, the race of alien beings discovered by the Antarctic expedition, the narrator states:

> They were [. . .] above all doubts *the originals of the fiendish elder myths* which things like the Pnakotic Manuscripts and the *Necronomicon* frightedly hint about. They were the Great Old Ones that had filtered down from the stars when the earth was young – the beings whose substance and alien evolution had shaped, and whose powers were such as this planet had never bred. (Lovecraft 1997: 268. Italics added)

Not only the verbal (symbolic) signs contained in the *Necronomicon* find a new signified thanks to the transcendental experience, but dim traditional belief and legendary convictions are fully renovated (and reinforced) as well:

> For a second we gasped in admiration of the scene's unearthly cosmic beauty, and then vague horror began to creep into our souls. For this far violet line could be nothing else than the terrible mountains of the forbidden land – highest of earth's peaks and focus of earth's evil; harbourers of nameless horrors and Archaean secrets; shunned and prayed to by those who feared to carve their meaning; untrodden by any living thing of earth, but visited by the sinister lightnings and sending strange beams across the plains in the polar night – beyond doubt the unknown archetype of that dreaded Kadath in the Cold Waste beyond abhorrent Leng, whereof unholy primal legends *hint evasively*. (Lovecraft 1997: 326. Italics added)

However, the semiotic task awaiting the transcendental subject is more complex than this re-interpretation of old signifiers in the light of new signifieds. In fact, two parallel semiotic processes take place during the transcendental experience of the Lovecraftian subjects:

1) the metamorphosis of pre-existing, fixed signs (i.e., the ancient bodies of lore re-read under a new light) into existentialized signs;
2) the creation of new signs: the piecing together of dissociated knowledge leading to devise new "terrifying vistas" on existence in *Dasein*: existential signs.

Dasein 2 no longer experiences the existential signs of *Dasein 1* as existential in the proper sense: in Lovecraft's transcendence, the experience of *Outsideness* leads the existential signs of *Dasein 1* (what is commonly accepted as Truth, Religious Beliefs, Moral Principles, etc.) to be rejected and no more susceptible of "existentialization". This holds true also concerning "Lovecraft the man"'s despise for morality, anthropocentrism, and the conventional conceptions of any "absolute" value (all elements pertaining to the subject's existential perspective): the theoretical and philosophical framework sustaining Lovecraft's narratives is one of radical upsetting of the traditional value systems.

Let us examine now more closely how the *existential signs* are generated. In order to describe their formation during the transcendental experience, the distinction between pre-signs, act-signs, and post-signs proves fruitful. The pre-signs are represented in Lovecraft's narratives by what the reader (and, only in few cases, the fictional subject) form in their minds as the experience of *Outsideness* unfolds. In the story-endings of both the confirmatory and the revelatory type, act-signs are formed: the subject realizes the implications of its experience of *Outsideness* and concretizes its pre-signs (formed during transcendence) into act-signs. The pre-signs become, in a sense, *significant*. Truth and horror usually manifest in a final, shocking utterance or the last line reported in a diary, letter, notebook or other sort of documents – often Lovecraft himself underscores with the Italics the revelatory meaning of the final realization: for instance, in chronological order, "The Lurking Fear" (1922), "Pickman's Model" (1926), "The Dunwich Horror" (1928), "The Whisperer in Darkness" (1930), "Winged Death" (1933), "The Shadow Out of Time" (1934–1935), "The Diary of Alonzo Typer" (1935), all end with a remarkable note of hideous realization on the subject's part, while "The Outsider" (1921) presents the most celebrated, final *semiotic reversal* of Lovecraft's production. Let us examine in detail this crucial Lovecraftian technique in the mentioned tales, and its implications from an existential semiotics perspective.

This is the story-ending of "The Lurking Fear" (1922):

> One eye was blue, the other brown. They were the dissimilar Martense eyes of the old legends, and I knew in one inundating cataclysm of voiceless horror what had become of that vanished family; the terrible and thunder-crazed house of Martense. (Lovecraft 1986: 199)

In the light of this final revelation, all the frightful murders occurred in the Catskill area and around Tempest Mountain, previously attributed to a not better identified "creature" or "fiend", can now be properly blamed on the degenerated progeny of Gerrit Martense, the 17th-century builder of the Martense mansion and progenitor of the cursed stock. The persistence, in the murderers, of the differently coloured eyes that are the family's hallmark sheds new light over the history of the family and its supposed, mysterious departure from the mansion: there was no departure at all, the Martenses simply retired in the underground passages of their mansion, gradually becoming a race of interbreeding and degenerate half-humans.

"Pickman's Model" ends on these notes (1926):

> Well – that paper wasn't a photograph of any background, after all. What it shewed was simply the monstrous being he was painting on that awful canvas. It was the model he was using – and its background was merely the wall of the cellar studio in minute detail. But by God, Eliot, *it was a photograph from life*. (Lovecraft 2001: 89. Lovecraft's Italics)

Here the hideous nature of the revelation lies in the fact that Pickman's painting was inspired by the direct observation of an actual, "posing" monster, and not of a photograph or a drawing. The implication which makes the subject re-arrange its epistemic assumptions (assigning new signifieds to old signifiers) is, of course, that the monster exists – the signified of the whole tale, of its accidents, and the characters' behaviours are, therefore (to be) reinterpreted under a wholly new light.

In the final lines of "The Dunwich Horror" (1928), we read:

> But as to this thing we've just sent back – the Whateleys raised it for a terrible part in the doings that were to come. It grew fast and big from the same reason that Wilbur grew fast and big – but it beat him because it had a greater share of the *outsideness* in it. You needn't ask how Wilbur called it out of the air. He didn't call it out. *It was his twin brother, but it looked more like the father than he did.* (Lovecraft 2001: 245. Lovecraft's Italics)

Here the revelation concerns the nature of Wilbur's twin brother, more akin to the father's (the *Outsideness* entity Yog-Sothoth) than to Wilbur's: this realization bears strong epistemic implications because the reader and the characters are forced to fill with new signifieds all the signifiers (the fictional events) they experienced during the narrated transcendental experience.

This is the ending of "The Whisperer in Darkness" (1930):

> For the things in the chair, perfect to the last, subtle detail of microscopic resemblance – or identity – were the face and hands of Henry Wentworth Akeley. (Lovecraft 1999: 267)

The reader is now forced to re-interpret the signified of the latest events narrated in the tale and to infer that the creature with whom Wilmarth, the narrator, has recently dealt was not a human being (Akeley), but a fake *persona* built up by the "whisperers in darkness" through imitation of human speech, language, and acting. This, of course, leads character and reader to fill the pseudo-Akeley's words and behaviour (the signs of its actual presence) with new and disquieting signifieds.

"Winged Death" (1933) is a revision Lovecraft wrote for his client Hazel Heald. Although the tale presents quite an unwitty plot, the story-ending, of an eminently confirmatory type, does not fail to shock the reader and to give the narrated events a new signified. The conclusion revolves around some mysterious words tracked on a ceiling:

> But these were no ordinary ink-tracks. Even at first glance revealed something hauntingly familiar about them, and closer inspection brought gasps of startled wonder from all four observers. [...] For beyond a doubt these inky smudges formed definite letters of the alphabet – letters coherently arranged in English words. The doctor was the first to make them out clearly, and the others listened breathlessly as he recited the insane-sounding message so incredibly scrawled in a place no human hand could reach:
>
> 'SEE MY JOURNAL – *IT* GOT ME FIRST – I DIED – THEN I SAW I WAS IN *IT* – THE BLACKS ARE RIGHT – STRANGE POWERS IN NATURE – NOW I WILL DROWN WHAT IS LEFT–'
>
> Presently, amidst the puzzled hush that followed, Dr. Van Keulen commenced reading aloud from the worn leather journal. (Lovecraft 1989: 263. Lovecraft's Italics)

This story-ending reveals a shocking truth: the soul of the protagonist has "transmigrated" inside the body of a fly, by means of which the protagonist has then tracked the words on the ceiling. All the past events concerning that fly, and then also its conclusive decision to commit suicide, are now filled with new meaning.

However, one of the most striking semiotic reversals in a Lovecraftian story-ending is achieved in "The Shadow Out of Time" (1934–35):

> [...] when I flashed my torch upon it in that frightful megalithic abyss, I saw the queerly pigmented letters on the brittle, aeon-browned cellulose pages were not indeed any nameless hieroglyphs of earth's youth. They were, instead, the letters of our familiar alphabet, spelling out the words of the English language in my own handwriting. (Lovecraft 2001b: 91)

This realization scene leads the reader and the character to re-interpret and fill the events of the whole tale with new meanings, as truthful accounts of experience into transcendence, and not as the dreamy ravings of an overexcited personality. The epistemological implications of this final revelation have a truly cosmic significance since the whole history of mankind and of the universe are re-written on new bases.

In the revision tale "The Diary of Alonzo Typer" (1935), the narration ends on a note of dreadful, though implausible, horror:

> The key has begun to feel warm as my left hand nervously clutches it. At times that vague quickening or pulsing is so distinct that I can almost feel the living metal move. It came from Yian-Ho for a terrible purpose, and to me – who all too late know the thin stream of van der Heyl blood that trickles down through the Sleghts into my own lineage – has descended the hideous task of fulfilling that purpose. [..].
>
> My courage and curiosity wane. I know the horror that lies beyond that iron door. What if Claes van der Heyl was my ancestor – need I expiate his nameless sin? *I will not – I swear I will not!* . . .
>
> [*Writing here grows indistinct*]
>
> Too late – cannot help self – black paws materialize – am dragged away toward the cellar. . .
> (Lovecraft 1989: 322. Lovecraft's Italics)

The sheer implausibility of a man who keeps filling his diary till the very end of his life, even while being "dragged away toward the cellar" by a black-pawed entity, does not invalidate the semiotic value of the conclusive, actual apparition of the monster, which up to this moment had only been mentally conjectured about. A new signified is then attached to the old signs experienced during the narration: for instance, the sense of wicked familiarity the subject experiences along its sojourn in the van der Heyl mansion (a truly existential sign) finally finds an explanation in the sudden discovery of the common lineage shared by the protagonist and the cursed van der Heyl family, and in the light of the subject's new, illuminating understanding, signs like the "contours and arrangements" (Lovecraft 1989: 317) of the "dark ominous clouds" (Lovecraft 1989: 317) over the hill "[. . .] now hold a fresh significance" (Lovecraft 1989: 317). Even all the visions, presences, and rumours that the protagonist claims to be haunted from, at first easily discarded as fabrications of an overexcited mind, gain a new meaningful connotation – and a hue of sinister realism – in the light of the final revelations.

However, the most celebrated final revelatory scene in Lovecraft's literature is probably that of "The Outsider" (1921):

> For although the nepenthe has calmed me, I know always that I am an outsider; a stranger in this century and among those who are still men. This I have known since I stretched out my fingers to the abomination within the great gilded frame; stretched out my fingers and touched *a cold and unyielding surface of polished glass*. (Lovecraft 1999: 49. Lovecraft's Italics)

This is the final passage of the tale in which the protagonist discovers, and the reader with him/her, that the dreadful creature everybody is fleeing from in the ballroom is he/she him/herself: the reflection in the mirror inescapably reveals that the "monster beneath the golden arch" (Lovecraft 1999: 48) and the characters are the same person. Of course thanks to this revelatory scene the whole tale reverts its meaning, and the as-if, narrative signs Lovecraft conveys in the previous pages are to be understood in a new significant light.

From an existential semiotics perspective, the process occurring in the subjectivity of the characters populating Lovecraft's fictional world can be roughly schematized as follows:
1) in the realm of *Outsideness*, pre-signs take shape: they are formed at a *deep level* of the character's subjectivity and influence the formation of
2) act-signs, in the "realization" scene: pre-signs acquire definitive and full meaning for the subject, and gain expression and utterance *to itself*: they are revealed at a *surface level*.

One should emphasize that this second process takes place exclusively *inside the character's subjectivity*, where the pre-sign is born. When transferred into *Dasein 2*, the pre-sign is converted into act-sign in the mind of the subject, becoming alternatively:
1) A "secret": the transcendental subject feels it useless to convey its act-sign to an "unsympathetic" audience. Therefore, act-signs recede to the condition of pre-signs;
2) A "lie": this is how *Dasein 2* perceives the alleged act-sign. Therefore, the tentative communication of the transcendental meaning of the newly born act-sign leads the subject to isolation, madness and, in extreme cases, death.

The new semiotic situation in *Dasein 2* is problematic at a communicational level since the recognition of the new signifieds is hardly socially accepted. The newly born act-signs, if socially accepted in *Dasein 2*, would lead to the acceptation of their deeper, transcendental meaning, and this, on its turn, would lead to the affirmation of the post-signs standing behind them. This is what the transcendental subject strives for when it is trying to tell its story, but what Stephen King once called the "want of an understanding ear" (King 1982: 293) truncates here the process, and the act-sign is perceived as such only by the subject: in fact, the community sees it as a lie, and the subject is forced to perceive it as a secret. The "semiotic renovation" of reality derives from the transcendental leap of a single individual into Nothingness: society could not accept the new signifieds if not through an act of faith, which it is unwilling to perform since the new signifieds society should believe in are undesirable and unwelcome. From this viewpoint, Lovecraft's narratives bring in an epistemic discourse which has strong ethical and anthropological implications and displays friction stemming from a conflicting dialectics between the social and the individual.

Let us examine more closely how *Dasein 2* resists the return of renovated signs that have left their previous *Dasein*. Signs cannot be re-attached to *Dasein*, and their new signifieds to their old signifiers, since rejecting modalities distort, transform, mediate, ideologize the signs coming from the transfiguring transcendental experience: typically, the subject is deemed as "insane", though it more or less vigorously rejects the label. *Dasein 2* resists the new signifieds attached to the transcendental signs because in Lovecraft "affirmation" is an individual process, not a social one. Therefore, it appears clear that in Lovecraft both *Dasein 1* and *Dasein 2* play, though for different reasons, a role of "resistance", opposition against the aspirations and the prerogatives of the subject. Adopting a Greimasian model, it is possible to detect decreasing levels of strength and power in the modalities throughout the consequential phases of the transcendental process:

1) competence on the sender's side: *Outsideness* has competence → STRONG modalities;
2) performance on the receiver's side: Lovecraft's subjects are not adequately equipped to "grasp" signs from *Outsideness* → MEDIUM modalities;
3) interpretative competence in the recoding of the message by the receiver: it is seldom actual. The cosy world is rarely able to receive and understand the new signifieds since they are knowable and interpretable only through the direct experience of the sphere of transcendence and through the leap into *Outsideness*.

From step 1) to 3), we assist to a decrease in the power and the compatibility of the modalities between sender and receiver: this unbalancing in the power relations is the main cause of the narrative conflict exploding in Lovecraft's fiction. Here the notion of *compatibility* is compelling: once set on its way, a sign does not complete successfully its journey "unless compatible modalities are waiting for it" (Tarasti 2000: 25), modalities which make the sign understandable and connect it to the world of *Dasein*. In Lovecraft, compatible modalities in *Dasein 2* are missing – especially TO KNOW and TO BE ABLE – and the sign ends up being ignored or misinterpreted.

The transcendental journey of a sign, from *Dasein 1* to *Dasein 2* through *Outsideness*, is an invisible event, where no physical removals occur: Martense mansion physically remains where it is, but, as a sign, it floats into Nothingness during the transcendental experience, coming back transfigured in its signified. In this process, the role of modalities is of carrying signs from "I" (Sameness) to "not-I" (*Outsideness*, the Other). However, in Lovecraft the Other is the Absolute, and trying to make the new "absolute", transcendent sign exist inside *Dasein 2* means to try to (imperfectly) imitate-simulate it: inevitably, when "existence *simulates* transcendence" (Tarasti 2000: 26. Tarasti's Italics), conflict erupts because *Dasein* is constitutionally unprepared to accept and receive transcendental signs. In Lovecraft, transcendental signs are absolute truth: they retain absolute modalities or meta-modalities (meta-WILL, meta-CAN, meta-KNOW, etc.). They are so existentially superior to *Dasein* and they are meta-physical, i.e. beyond the physicality of *Dasein*, that *Dasein 2* is unable to absorb them.

The transcendental experience undergone by the Lovecraftian subjects is a process marked by a strongly *temporal* nature, a start, a development, and a conclusion: in other words, the subject first experiences emptiness in *Dasein 1*, then a leap into Nothingness, and finally a return into *Dasein*, where, nonetheless, the experience of Plenitude is prevented to it. Because of the unfavourable epistemic conditions of *Dasein* 2, characters have to stop to the Nothingness, colouring signs with "shades of sinister despair" (Tarasti 2000: 27); the bright hopefulness of Plenitude rarely occurs, more often it is a gloomy Plenitude of despair.

Now, how can we reformulate, in the light of the latest discussion, the answer to the question "how does the transcendental experience have a start", and the other, related to this, "why is the subject driven to rebel against the *Dasein*, and to put signs into motion"? If, certainly, the transcendental experience is the trigger of narrative action in Lovecraft, it is not always true that this action stems from dissatisfaction with *Dasein 1* on the subject's part. Indeed, an "inner transcendence" often occurs in *Dasein 1*, as a sort of stimulus the subject feels to reach for the *absolute transcendence*: inner transcendence occurs for instance in the heavily felt Negation of reality which, as we have seen, characters like Randolph Carter, Iranon, and the protagonists of the Dunsanian "dream-cycle" manifest.

In these narratives, set in a dream-and-far-away dimension, "the movement from existence to transcendence is prompted and sustained by the dissatisfaction of the subject, by his/her aspiration toward invariance" (Tarasti 2000: 31) and absoluteness. This is precisely what characters like Randolph Carter (Lovecraft's acclaimed fictional *alter-ego*) look for: a more "stable fulcrum" for their existences, a shelter from the universal void and entropy, the unceasing chaotic vortex of the cosmos, the perishability of existence.

Nonetheless, determinism plays a decisive role in the transcendental process: the course of semiosis, from pre-signs to act-signs through the existential experience, is also an unavoidable process; the subject must undergo it whether it wants it or not. Transcendence is often a sudden and unexpected experience, a true illumination in Jaspersian sense only partially searched for or wished by the subject, that anyway, as a Fichtean self-determining subject, may decide whether to accept or reject it. As a rule, the learned characters tend to accept it (triggering their journey toward the existential/transcendental condition), while the majority rejects it (i.e., the less educated characters, remaining on the "safe" side of the threshold looking onto *Outsideness*). However, the novelty of Lovecraft's approach is that the self-determination of the subject is only partial: once embarked on the semiotic process (the experience of *Outsideness* leading from pre-signs to act-signs), the attractive force and appeal of a luring *Outsideness* are irresistible. The subject is not able to self-determine itself anymore, and becomes the prey of a fierce determinism: the act of absolute Negation is unavoidable. That determinism is a central concept in Lovecraft's philosophy is no new idea, especially when applied to the study of human history and civilizations. From the reading of some passages of "The Shadow Out of Time" (1934–35), for instance, one may argue that Lovecraft holds a "pre-oriented", cyclic conception of history. In "The Shadow Out of Time", Peaslee more than once seems to have unveiled a regularly cyclic course in history, at least for those events concerning the alien race; considering the paradigmatic value of Peaslee's *quest*, this observation can easily be extended to the Lovecraftian historical conception in a broader sense:

> Later the race would *again* face death, yet would live through another forward migration of its best minds into the bodies of others who had a longer physical span ahead of them.
> (Lovecraft 2001b: 51. Italics added)

From his *quest for knowledge*, Peaslee seems to have learned that history is nothing but the repetition of the same pattern through time and space.

As a consequence, we can conclude that the Lovecraftian transcendental subject cannot truly determine itself since its leap into Nothingness is the experience of the "loss of the self": it is its audience, in *Dasein 2*, that determines it because this audience has not passed through the same semiosis-process of experiencing the *Outsideness*. The transcendental experience is irreversible; the subject has free will only *before* it, but even this is not always the case: a learned character cannot resist the impulse since he is compelled by that thirst of knowledge which constitutes the fundamental want prompting the narration. The "lack", mentioned in traditional narratologic theories (such as Propp's and Greimas's) as the main stimulus to narrative action, is almost always a "lack of knowledge" in mature Lovecraft and the Lovecraftian subject is separated from its object-value, which is mostly *knowledge* (of the past of humankind, of the history of its family, of its origins, of the town where it lives, of some unexplainable phenomena around it, etc.). As a result, the distinction between going through an *event* (where no free will on the subject's part is involved) and performing a *semiotic act* (where the individual perspective on the event involves free will and self-determination on the subject's part) is subverted: no power of self-determination is retained by the existential subject. The mythical discourse has been renovated by Lovecraft: the myth imposes itself on the subject; no autonomous semiotic acts are then possible for those who pass through the existential experience. Only for those who approach it from the external, in *Dasein 2*, free will is left.

Since Lovecraft undoubtedly lives more the life of the intellect than that of the body, coherently the value objects displayed and looked for in his literature are mostly immaterial. Therefore, it is not hard to detect here an intrusion of "Lovecraft the man"'s subjectivity into his narrative discourse: if it is certainly true that there always exists a gap between the actual, empirical subject and the sign or the means of expression he uses, distancing and estrangement are, as we will see, employed by Lovecraft in fictionalizing his "personae", like in the Randolph Carter cycle, set in Dunsanian fantasy realms and dream-cities of an immemorial past. The task Lovecraft commits to his fictional personae may often fail, because the transcendental signs they carry on do often collapse in their existential self-revealing in *Dasein 2*: but as we have seen, this failure should be blamed on *Dasein 2*'s constitutional, epistemological unpreparedness. The result is that existentially unsuccessful signs form a paradigm of their own, neither understood nor understandable, in *Dasein 2*: only auxiliary signs, such as "intertexts" like the ill-famed *Necronomicon*, may help understand the paradigm. The sheer amount of references to the *Necronomicon* and of other internal allusions present in Lovecraft's narratives suggests a character of *self-referentiality* for his literature. The discussion on this topic will be crucial in the next section of this paper.

2 The endo- and exo-semiotic processes of Lovecraft's subjects

Now, it is time to introduce the notions of endo- and exo-signs in the way existential semiotics devises them: "When we distinguish the two sides of a sign, signifier and signified, we should complete our model, extending into four dimensions by adding these two new aspects: the endo- and the exo-side of a sign. Any signifier can be seen from both inside and outside, and the same for signifieds" (Tarasti 2000: 54). Signs, which are foreign to us, as, in Lovecraft, those pertaining the realm of *Outsideness*, are at first experienced as exo-signs: only gradually, by a closer acquaintance, the exo-signs may be transformed into endo-signs, but it is just this specific act of transformation that the Lovecraftian existential subject is, as we will see, unable to perform since the internalization of the signs from *Outsideness* entails the reconstruction of the self on new, alien semiotic bases. The notions of endo- and exo-semiosis, and the principles of internal/external to which they are correlated, may prove fruitful in analysing Lovecraft's literary treatment of the "epic" and the "novel" dimensions inside his narratives. A connection exists, moreover, between *endosemiotics* (an unconscious process) and *autosemiosis* as a self-causation and self-reflection principle. The starting point is to admit that the subject's perceptions of the reality of *Outsideness* are "translations of inner sign processes which occur in our brain and are inaccessible to us" (Tarasti 2000: 39). What the existential subject represents of *Outsideness* maybe then understood as a self-reflection/causation of its inner endosemiotic processes, and this also explains why we find in Lovecraft an autosemiotic process portraying the *immanence* of his "personae" inside his narratives. Sid Sondergard has convincingly shown the importance of investigating Lovecraft's subjective "system of producing meaning through reading and writing, and the attitudes revealed to be implicit in an analysis of that semiotic process": a thorough understanding of Lovecraft's "internal semantics" may prove crucial to perform a satisfactory insight on his fiction and non-fiction.

The notions of inner/outer, of the internalization of the external and, vice versa, of the transformation of exogenic signs into endogenic ones, become central here: sign processes always have an endo- side (their inner aspect) and an exo- one (their outer aspect). The distinction between inner and outer sign processes is not a simple one: moral concepts, for instance, are typically endogenic signs, sanctioned by emotions working as interpretants, but conceptual oppositions such as right/wrong, good/bad, etc., are learned in exogenic communication because a character of universality is almost always attached to them. In Lovecraft, the alleged "morality" of the alien societies intruding from

Outsideness is seen as an *exogenic* sign from the human society of *Dasein*, this inevitably being another ground for conflict when their moralities come to collide since they are exogenic to each other.

Endogenic and exogenic signs coexist in *Dasein*, which is born from a perpetual interaction of these two spheres: this dichotomy corresponds to the philosophical and ethical opposition between idealism and realism. Lovecraft often defines himself as a realist, both from an aesthetic and a philosophical viewpoint: some of his most convincing statements on this regard can be found in his letters, where he repeatedly criticizes the somewhat idealistic claim on the existence and truthfulness of absolute values such as "good", "evil", "right", "wrong", "superior goal", "conscious teleology", etc. In a 1931 letter, Lovecraft opposes idealism and realism on a philosophical ground, heatedly assuming the defence of the latter:

> To the realist there is something obscenely frivolous in idealism. [. . .] My intellectual criterion is simply *truth*, and my one and only guide in taking sides on questions is *whether a thing is or isn't so*. I repudiate idealism not because I despise idealists [. . .] but because I see no sense in assuming sets of conditions in the cosmos which have no existence [. . .] I don't dislike the hypothetical conditions postulated by idealists, and would be glad to subscribe to a good many of them if they were so. My only objection is that they are not so, and that attempts to read them into the structure of the universe are injurious to the welfare of the only real value in the entire world of ideas – namely, the simply and basic quality of *unadorned truth* – the honest *is-or-isn't criterion*.   (Letter to James Ferdinand Morton, 1/18/1931 [*SL* III, 271, 274]. Lovecraft's Italics)

From an aesthetic viewpoint, countless are Lovecraft's statements about the effectiveness of *realism* in art, and the fantastic genre above all, as the necessary background for the building-up of a *weird* effect:

> The more I consider weird fiction, the more am I convinced that a solidly realistic framework is needed in order to build up a preparation for the unreal element. [. . .] My own rule is that *no weird story can truly produce terror unless it is devised with all the care and verisimilitude of an actual hoax*. The author must [. . .] build up a stark, simple account, full of homely corroborative details, just as if he were actually trying to 'put across' a deception in real life – a deception clever enough to make adults believe it.
> (Letter to Clark Ashton Smith, 10/17/1930 [*SL* III, 192–193].Lovecraft's Italics)

However, Lovecraft's aesthetic claim that realism can be a very great art must be referred not to any kind of realism, but to one "[. . .] accurate in its depiction of life & motivations" (Letter to Clark Ashton Smith, 10/17/1930 [*SL* III, 194]), and that "[. . .] must be detailed enough to give a sense of actual substance to the outward events shewn [sic], else it will not have enough contact with any deep sense of truth to form the unifying or liberating influence desired" (Letter to Clark Ashton Smith, 10/17/1930 [*SL* III, 195]).

Lovecraft himself traces his fondness for realism by connecting it to the scientific interests that his personality has shown since childhood:

> I am fundamentally a *prose realist* whose prime dependence is on the building up of atmosphere through the slow, pedestrian method of multitudinous suggestive detail & dark scientific similitude. [...] Prose realism is behind everything of any importance that I write – a devilish odd quality, when one stops to think about it, to exist in conjunction with fantastic taste & vision! But I am a paradox anyway – for there have been periods when astronomy, geography, physics, chemistry, & anthropology meant more to me than any form of pure literature or aesthetics.
> (Letter to Clark Ashton Smith, 19/12/1929 [*SL* III, 96]. Lovecraft's Italics)

These statements would leave no room for a discussion on a supposedly idealistic perspective in Lovecraft. But in another letter we can take a clue for a reassessment of this rationalistic, if not positivistic, attitude:

> My big kick comes from *taking reality just as it is* – accepting all the limitations of the most orthodox science – and then permitting my symbolising faculty to *build outward* from the existing facts; rearing a structure of *infinite promise and possibility* whose topless towers are in no cosmos or dimension penetrable by the contradicting-power of the tyrannous and inexorable intellect. But the whole secret of the kick is *that I know damn well it isn't so*. [...] My point is, *that a highly organised man can't exist endurably without mental expansions beyond objective reality*.   (Letter to James Ferdinand Morton, 4/1/1930 [*SL* III, 140]. Lovecraft's Italics)

Lovecraft is perfectly conscious that his creations, though originating from a close observation of reality and a careful devising of a realistically detailed background, trespass in the territory of the purely intellectual, and I suspect, idealistic, realm.

This controversial issue, which I can only tangentially touch upon here, has, of course, strong epistemological consequences on Lovecraft's worldviews and literature. Remaining on a narrative level, our task is to investigate how in Lovecraft the subject's perception and representation of *Outsideness* (an exogenic sign) reflect the subject's inner disposition (its endogenic sign processes). Is it a "reflection"? Also, does not the process perhaps arouse a "conflict"? If exogenic signs "belong to empirical reality, observable by anyone" (Tarasti 2000: 42), we should then clarify why the manifestations of *Outsideness* are perceived (and perceivable) only by two well defined (and antipodal) categories of people: the *elite* of learned academics, and the degenerated/decayed fellows. This is likely because, as Thure von Uexküll claimed, "all consciously experienced outside realities are translations of inner sign processes" (quoted in Tarasti 2000: 39): *Outsideness* is not then observable by anyone, its manifestations, apparently exogenic signs, are self-reflections of the observing subject, as a result of its auto-semiotic process. Then in Lovecraft, a semiotic paradox occurs: there appear exogenic signs originating from the self-reflection of the subject, endo-signs that claim to be exogenic and have to be read as such. This reconnects with the self-definition that Lovecraft constantly gives of himself as a "realist" (both from a philosophical and an aesthetic perspective): being a realist, the "exogenization" of endogenic signs is the only way through which his endo-signs can receive objective verification and even be acceptable by him. Therefore, Lovecraft's representation of *Outsideness* is valuable and carries truth-value because it represents what Jean Wahl defined as *trans-ascendance*. Correspondingly, in Lovecraft *no exogenic sign can be interpreted as endogenic*, as an epistemology oriented toward idealism would tend to claim: no teleology, no supernatural destiny, no conscious "purpose" are guiding human lives. Human beings are not allowed to control and master their destiny; everything is purposeless and follows unpredictably deterministic laws.

Endogenic signs are *pre-signs*, which become actual when reflected into the representation of *Outsideness*, i.e. when externalized. Fictive signs are like pre-signs: in Lovecraft, this occurs when a reversal of traditional transcendence takes place. In fact, during the transcendental process, not only, as we have seen, the common phenomenon of a fluctuation of a signified occurs (while the signifier remains unchanged), but even the *signifier* is subject to change. The most striking examples of this reversal occur in the short novel *At the Mountains of Madness* (1931), where a basic representation of what human beings mean by the word "humanity" (what we could call the signifier of the sign) shifts from the members of the human race to the aliens: the signifier changes its use, the "aliens" are now defined as "men", even "scientists". The signified has remained unchanged (the barrel-shaped extraterrestrials), but now it is attached to a different signifier.

The next step of the discussion consists then in investigating how Lovecraft, in the narrative representation of *Outsideness*, achieves the transformation of endo-signs into verbal exo-signs. Lovecraft strives to take some distance from the original endo-signs, and this distancing is the most striking technique he adopts when facing the task of representing *Outsideness*. This distance is so all-pervasive that it becomes an existential, semiotic, and narrative concept, resulting in the introduction of epic elements and the adoption of an estranging perspective. The narrative techniques employed toward this goal reflect, as an auto-semiotic process, this attempt at distancing: one could mention here, *passim*, the recurrent use of linguistic archaisms as relics of a past era, the resort to second- or third-hand narrating voices, the introduction of infratexts and infranarrators. These mechanisms are part of a process of *reduction* of endo-signs to exo-signs: the passage from pre-signs to act-signs is in fact that from endo- to exo-semiosis. Pre-signs take form in the interiority of the subject during its transcendental experience, but their translation into utterance occurs only when this inner pre-understanding is confirmed in the final "revelatory" scene by outer reality: it becomes an exo-sign, an act-sign filled with meaning. As mentioned already, Lovecraft, when claiming to be a realist, can conceive of an act-sign only as an exo-sign. According to this perspective, endo-signs exist only in the form of pre-signs of an imperfect and incomplete pre-understanding. The key process to analyse here is the one leading to the reduction of endogenic signs into exogenic ones: is the exoworld represented in his narratives a mere physical conversion of the subject's endogenic knowledge, be this subject Lovecraft himself or his fictive personae? If we accepted Lovecraft's statement of being a realist, and not an idealist, the answer would be no. But if one interprets Lovecraft's conceptual system as a purified reduction of the endoworld into the exoworld, then a possibility for a Husserlian pure endogenic knowledge remains. Lovecraft's complex subjectivity would then be revealed as the one he most despised and tried to avoid: that of an idealist. This perspective would open new enthralling vistas in the study of Lovecraft's literature. If this were the case, one could reinforce the interpretation of Lovecraft's existential perspective in the direction of Wahl's trans-ascendance: neurotic endo-signs would be reduced to "objectively existing exo-signs" (Tarasti 2000: 48), assuming a more general validity and a "universal mode of 'being'" (Tarasti 2000: 48). Needless to say, this would not necessarily imply that Lovecraft's is a neurotic subjectivity since we are not taking a psychoanalytical perspective on it, and since the worldview objectified in his narrative representations is not necessarily an expression of a neurotically pessimistic soul but of an indifferentist one.

The discussion and a lot of clues have brought us quite far from Lovecraft's self-assuring statements about his alleged realism: should we then distrust his claims to realism as another of his fictive masks? At a superficial level of reading, one might argue that in Lovecraft's writings the endo- and the exo-signs appear different in nature. Lovecraft often claims that his views on the objective world are not influenced by his personal beliefs (endo-signs). But this is a "persona" he builds, especially in his letters. In Lovecraft's *fiction*, one can hardly doubt that (1) the proposed worldview (exo-world) is a self-reflection of the author's own beliefs (endo-world), even only if we take into account that the fictional world-perception is filtered by characters which so manifestly are the author's *replicas* or personae; and (2) since the formation of endo-signs (and thus, their *influences* on actual behaviours, opinions, activities, such as narrative utterances) is *not* predictable by the subject, then one may be allowed to argue that in Lovecraft the subjective is "first and absolute" (Tarasti 2000: 49) and the objective emanates from it. In a sense, the goals of Lovecraft's art are not far from those of Schelling's transcendental philosophy: the search for a common path for life, art, and philosophy, the doomed-to-fail quest for the inner sense, for the Husserlian *noema*, for the thing in itself, the ultimate reality. For Schelling, the "I" is the basis for everything real, a kind of endless action *producing* objectivity: one scarcely doubts that Lovecraft holds his *ego* and subjectivity in high rate, in line with his statement that each human action is born "[...] from a basic organic impulse of ego-assertion". According to existential semiotics, one may "identify the arch of the human life with the growth of the endo- and the reduction of the exo-" (Tarasti 2000: 50). Moreover, to be(come) herself, humankind has passed from a state of being the only exo- to a state where endo-aspects shoot forth: "the external is more and more transformed into the internal" (Tarasti 2000: 50) until mankind becomes a whole product of endosemiosis, totally independent from the influences of the external stimuli. This concept finds further application in Lovecraft, if one thinks of the evolution of his narratives in terms of a shift from a prevailing of the exo- at the beginning (within the dreamworld and the Dunsanian tales), until an overcoming of the endo- toward the end. This process would reinforce the hypothesis that Lovecraft's narratives are an expression of his existential perspective and an outgrowth of his *ego*. It is, by the way, universally acknowledged that Lovecraft's most mature worldviews, and his most striking representations of *Outsideness*, are portrayed in the latest narratives. The early tales are interpretable mostly as rhetorical exercises, imitations in the vein of E.A. Poe and Lord Dunsany: Lovecraft's philosophical, scientific, and social reflections are there only sketched and marginally touched upon.

What arouses dissatisfaction in Lovecraft, and lies at the basis of the narrative conflict so plainly at work in his literature, is his failure to understand this existential perspective of his: as an idealist *manqué*, Lovecraft perceives that the objective thinking "does not have any relationship with an existing subject" (Tarasti 2000: 51). As Kierkegaard claimed, "The way of objective thinking renders the subjective accidental and at the same time existence indifferent and evanescent. The way to an objective truth [the one always pursued by Lovecraft throughout his life and his art, EN] leads away from the subject, and when subject and subjectivity become indifferent, the truth also becomes indifferent" (quoted in Tarasti 2000: 50). Therefore, Lovecraft's claims to *indifferentism* now assume a new, sinister light. Indifferentism, in fact, renders existence arid and unsatisfactory because the subject gets erased and the "I" incomplete: this is why Lovecraft searches for the contact with the non-I, and the representation of the Other, of *Outsideness*. This is a result of his conflicting existential perspective. At a surface and apparent level, Lovecraft's fictional efforts show a rejection of the endo-world; but Lovecraft as a subject cannot help his literature to be an outburst (a reduction) of his endo-world, and this is the key to understand the conflicts present in his life and art: the conflicts between his endo- and exo-, between the epic and the novelistic elements of his fiction, between the Human and the *Outsideness* spheres. Adopting a Kierkegaardian perspective, one could claim that Lovecraft's unconscious ambition to reduce endo-signs to exo-signs is doomed to fail because for Kierkegaard the subject strives for the unity of subject and object. The pursuing of this ambitious goal would, anyway, lead to dismissing existence as a whole, since vital to the existence of the subject is the separation between the subject itself (the "I") and the object (the "non-I", the "Other"). On the contrary, I believe that, in Lovecraft, the reduction of endo-signs to exo-signs is unconscious but not a necessarily doomed-to-fail attempt: he could succeed, and he does, felicitously. But this is a consideration we readers may do, now, *a posteriori*. Lovecraft's late frustrations about his literature derive from his non-realization of his success, from his *a priori* rejection of his *endo*-world. In Lovecraft, as in Kierkegaard, the question remains unanswered, though for opposite reasons: in Kierkegaard, the impossibility of an encounter of the endo- and the exo- spheres derive from the philosopher's rejection of the *exo*-world; in Lovecraft, from the rejection of the *endo*-world. Jean-Paul Sartre provides a concept, that of "free being", which may perhaps help in understanding why Lovecraft experiences the impossibility of a reconciliation between the spheres of the endo- and the exo-. The endo-world is, in fact, that of a free being, of an almost uncontrolled interiority, while the exo-world represents an objective "Other", fixed and determined. In Lovecraft's conception, *Outsideness* is the realm of determinism, and *Outsideness* is so powerful that it influences the human subject's existence, rendering it deterministic too. In the realm of *Outsideness*, a determinism of an incomprehensible sort rules, where new natural laws are at stake: everything there is fixed and immutable, and whereas a contact between the sphere of *Outsideness* and that of the Human occurs, *Outsideness* imposes its laws and the human subject undergoes its own "illumination": also its life, it realizes, is predetermined, there is no room for the "free flowing" of the self anymore. Lovecraft's literature springs from the process of transition of his endo-signs into exo-signs, but in doing so it generates conflict, not only under a narrative but also under an existential viewpoint, because of Lovecraft's existential fallacy, i.e. his incapability to realize that his endo-signs were actual "free being" and that their translation into exo-signs would inevitably lead to the clash with the deterministic fixation of the exo-world. Lovecraft's effort is the impossible one to "de-determine", to "move" the exo-world away from its fixity, making it, through an autosemiotic process, a self-reflection of his endo-world. Lovecraft's narratives portray the impossibility of this existential process, and this is the reason why the fracture, the conflict they represent on a narrative level stems from the conflict in Lovecraft's existential perspective. The existential conflict also originates from Lovecraft's (utopian) claim to be a realist, i.e. from his pretence to derive any of his statements on the nature of life and the cosmos from objective observation of the exo-world. Lovecraft strives to translate the exo-world into the endo-world but, once he unconsciously recognizes that the exo-world is fixed and deterministic, he tries to render his philosophical views deterministic as well: when perceiving the clash of this deterministic perspective with the inner, free, and uncontrollable life of his endo-world, he realizes the impossibility to reduce his endo-world to mere deterministic rules and events, and his existential conflict shoots forth, originating a melancholic state stemming from the dissatisfaction toward his literary production, not only of the latest period.

If this is the process "Lovecraft the man" as a subject is forced to pass through, it is now time to examine how his subjective experience is translated into his narratives, i.e. how Lovecraft means to stage the transcendental experience of his characters. In terms of existential semiotics, "endo/exo-signs take place in the sphere of *Dasein*. Beyond them, remains the world of transcendence in the proper sense, which represents cosmological time in contrast to the historical time of the endo/exo-signs" (Tarasti 2000: 55). Signs in the state of transcendence can be called *trans-signs*, while signs in a state preceding that of endo/exo, are called *pre-signs*. Then, both endo- and exo-signs belong to the category of *act-signs*. Schematically:

Signs in *Dasein*: **Historical Time**	**Signs in *Transcendence*:** **Cosmological Time**
Pre-signs Endo/Exo-signs = **Act-signs**	Trans-signs

For Lovecraft's fictional subjects, the transition from the endo- to the exo- field occurs contextually to their experience of *Outsideness*, i.e. during their transcendental experience. While experiencing that state, the signs they meet with and develop, are *trans-signs*: but their actualization occurs only when the subjects return to *Dasein* (in its new configuration, i.e. *Dasein 2*). During the transcendental experience, trans-signs influence the subjects to translate/transform their endo-signs (also partially created by their experience of *Outsideness*) into exo-signs, i.e. signs theoretically communicable to their fellow human beings when in *Dasein 2*:

Dasein 1	**Experience of Transcendence**	*Dasein 2*
The subject has his own set of endo/exo signs	Transcendence forms/influences new endo-signs in the subject → *trans-endo-signs*	The subject tries to translate his new endo-signs formed in transcendence (*trans-endo-signs*) into exo-signs
Human Sphere	***Outsideness Sphere***	***A tentative blending of the Human and the Outsideness Spheres***

When in *Dasein 2*, from a semiotic viewpoint, the subject strives to translate its new trans-endo-signs (i.e., endo-signs formed in transcendence) into exo-signs: this equals, from a narrative perspective, the subject's attempt to communicate its transcendental experience to the lifeworld. An attempt which is doomed to fail, since it is born from the utopian ambition of blending two spheres (that of Human and *Outsideness*) which should remain separate.

Thus, from a semiotic standpoint, Lovecraft's *Dasein 2* is the stage of a quite complicated situation. The *trans-endo-signs*, influenced as such by trans-signs, cannot be actualized in act-signs proper because:
- they cannot become exo-signs: i.e., *Dasein 2* does not accept them into its epistemic system, being epistemologically unprepared;
- often, they cannot become endo-signs either: i.e., the subject is not able to internalize/metabolize these signs into its epistemic system. The subject becomes insane or dies.

Therefore, the transcendental experience leads Lovecraft's fictional subjects to form trans-endo-signs whose fate might be double; its duplicity being only partly dependent on the typology of the subjects involved. Schematically:
- The subjects experience transcendence (*Outsideness*) → they get in touch with Trans-signs → Trans-signs influence the formation of trans-endo-signs in the subjects.
- Trans-endo-signs, retaining part of the trans-(cendental) nature of the *Outsideness* experience and realm, must undergo a transformation when transported into *Dasein 2*, the realm of the Human, to be fully comprehended and accepted by humankind's epistemological system.

Theoretically, two results are possible: trans-endo-signs could get transformed into exo- or endo-signs. But:
- **Trans-endo-signs never become exo-signs**: *Dasein 2* is too "hopelessly conventional" to accept them epistemologically; no subject, regardless of its intellectual or social status, can perform the transformation of its own trans-endo-signs formed in transcendence into objective exo-signs universally comprehensible and acceptable in *Dasein 2*;
- **Trans-endo-signs seldom become endo-signs** perceived as such by the subject: here the typology of the subject bears quite an impact, because a character with strong intellectual and philosophical/scientific background, i.e. Lovecraft's academicians, can succeed in the semiotic transition. On the contrary, such characters, as the uneducated or the countrymen, are not epistemologically equipped enough to complete the semiotic transition.

In conclusion, in Lovecraft, the attempted transition

$$\text{Trans-endo} \rightarrow \text{Exo}$$

always fails, while the transition

$$\text{Trans-endo} \rightarrow \text{Endo}$$

more often succeeds.

Likely the reason for the second process's higher rate of success lies in the fact that the semiotic distance between the two terms at stake is smaller than in the first transition. In fact, between trans-endo- and exo- there is no connection at all, save for the fact that the signs involved are parts of a semiotic process, while the endo- element is common between trans-endo- and endo-. For "hard" signs like those acquired in (or influenced by) the transcendental experience in the realm of *Outsideness*, epistemological acceptance is such a difficult and risky process that it bears more chances to be successful when the semiotic distance between the starting and the final statuses of the sign is the smallest possible.

Abbreviation

SL H. P. Lovecraft, *Selected Letters*, 1965–76; A. Derleth and D. Wandrei (eds.). 5 vols*. Sauk City, WI: Arkham House Publishers, Inc.

> * In the body of the text the following system of the quotation has been adopted: *SL*, progressive number of the volume (from I to V), number of the page(s) in which the quoted passage is reported.

References

Airaksinen, Timo. 1999. *The Philosophy of H.P. Lovecraft. The Route to Horror*. New York: Peter Lang Publishing, Inc.
Bakhtin, Mikhail M. 1982. *The Dialogic Imagination: Four Essays*. Austin, TX: University of Texas Press.
Berruti, Massimo. 2004a. H.P. Lovecraft and the Anatomy of the Nothingness: The Cthulhu Mythos. *Semiotica* 150(1/4). 363–418.
Berruti, Massimo. 2004b. The Double Nemesis of 'The Cats of Ulthar'. *Studies in Fantasy Literature* 2. 3–17.

Berruti, Massimo. 2005. 'Dagon': Shipwreck to Nowhere. *Lovecraft Studies* 45. (1–9).
Burleson, Donald. 1990. Lovecraft's Humankind: Orphans in the Cosmos. In *Six Views of Lovecraft. Lovecraft Studies* 22–23. 43–52.
Burleson, Mollie L. 1990. The Outsider: A Woman?. *Lovecraft Studies* 22–23. 22–23.
Cannon, Peter. 1989. *H.P. Lovecraft*. Boston: Twayne Publishers.
Cannon, Peter. 1996. On 'At the Mountains of Madness': A Panel Discussion. *Lovecraft Studies* 34. 2–10.
Cannon, Peter (ed.). 1998. *Lovecraft Remembered*. Sauk City, WI: Arkham House Publishers, Inc.
Clore, Dan. 1998. Some Aspects of Narration in Lovecraft. *Lovecraft Studies* 40. 2–11.
Crypt of Cthulhu (A Pulp Thriller and Theological Journal), West Warwick, RI: Necronomicon Press (issues 1–101). Poplar Bluff, MO: Mythos Books (issues 102–107).
Dansky, Richard E. 1994. Transgression, Spheres of Influence, and the Use of the Utterly Other in Lovecraft. *Lovecraft Studies* 30. 5–14.
de Camp, L. Sprague. 1976 [1975]. *Lovecraft. A Biography*. London: New English Library.
Frye, Northrop 1973 [1957]. *Anatomy of Criticism. Four Essays*. Princeton, NJ: Princeton University Press.
Johansen, Jørgen Dines. 2002. *Literary Discourse. A Semiotic-Pragmatic Approach to Literature*. Toronto Buffalo London: University of Toronto Press.
Joshi, S.T. 1990a. *H.P. Lovecraft: The Decline of the West*. Berkeley Heights, NJ: Wildside Press.
Joshi, S.T. 1990b. Lovecraft's Ethical Philosophy. *Lovecraft Studies* 21. 24–39.
Joshi, S.T. 1999 *A Subtler Magick: the writings and philosophy of H. P. Lovecraft*. Gillette, NJ: Wildside Press.
Joshi, S.T. 2001. *A Dreamer and a Visionary. H. P. Lovecraft in his time*. Liverpool: Liverpool University Press.
Joshi, S.T. 2004 [1996]. *H.P. Lovecraft: A Life*. West Warwick, RI: Necronomicon Press.
King, Stephen. 1982. The Body (Fall from Innocence). In *Different Seasons*, 293. New York, NY: Viking Press.
Leiber, Fritz. 1998 [1949]. A Literary Copernicus. In Peter Cannon (ed.) *Lovecraft Remembered*, 455–466. Sauk City, WI: Arkham House Publishers, Inc.
Lévy, Maurice. 1988. *Lovecraft. A Study in the Fantastic*. Detroit: Wayne State University Press.
Lord, Bruce. *The Genetics of Horror: Sex and Racism in H.P. Lovecraft's Fiction*. Available at http://www.contrasoma.com/writing/lovecraft.html (last checked on April 14, 2011).
Lovecraft, Howard Phillips. 1984. *The Dunwich Horror and Others*. Ed. by S.T. Joshi. Sauk City, WI: Arkham House Publishers, Inc.
Lovecraft, Howard Phillips. 1985. *At the Mountains of Madness and Other Novels*. Ed. by S.T. Joshi. Sauk City, WI: Arkham House Publishers, Inc.
Lovecraft, Howard Phillips. 1986. *Dagon and other Macabre Tales*. Ed. by S.T. Joshi. Sauk City, WI: Arkham House Publishers, Inc.
Lovecraft, Howard Phillips. 1989. *The Horror in the Museum and Other Revisions*. Ed. by S. T. Joshi. Sauk City, WI: Arkham House Publishers, Inc.
Lovecraft, Howard Phillips. 1995. *Miscellaneous Writings*. Ed. by S.T. Joshi. Sauk City, WI: Arkham House Publishers, Inc.
Lovecraft, Howard Phillips. 1997. *The Annotated H.P. Lovecraft*. Ed. by S.T. Joshi. New York: Dell Publishing, Dell Trade Paperback.
Lovecraft, Howard Phillips. 1999. *The Call of Cthulhu and Other Weird Stories*. Ed. by S.T. Joshi. New York: Penguin Books.

Lovecraft, Howard Phillips. 2001a. *The Thing on the Doorstep and Other Weird Stories*. Ed. by S.T. Joshi. New York: Penguin Books.
Lovecraft, Howard Phillips. 2001b. *The Shadow Out of Time. The Corrected Text*. Ed. by S.T. Joshi and D. E. Schultz. New York, NY: Hippocampus Press.
Lovecraft, Howard Phillips. 2004 *Collected Essays. Volume 2: Literary Criticism*. Ed. by S.T. Joshi. New York, Hippocampus Press.
Lovecraft, Howard Phillips. 2007. *O Fortunate Floridian. H.P. Lovecraft's Letters to R. H. Barlow*. Ed. by S. T. Joshi and David E. Schultz. Tampa: University of Tampa Press.
Lovecraft Studies, West Warwick, RI: Necronomicon Press (issues 1–41, 44). New York: Hippocampus Press (double issue 42–43).
Mosig, Yōzan Dirk W. 1997. *Mosig At Last: a Psychologist Looks at H.P. Lovecraft*. West Warwick, RI: Necronomicon Press.
Murray, Will. 1999 [1990]. H. P. Lovecraft: Pulp Hound. In James Van Hise (ed.), *The Fantastic Worlds of H. P. Lovecraft*, 5–31. Onaga Trail, Yucca Valley, CA.
Price, Robert M. 1990. *H.P. Lovecraft and the Cthulhu Mythos*. Mercer Island, WA: Starmont House.
Seppänen, Jouko. 2003. Autosemiosis: Self-Reflection as a Universal Principle. In *From Semiotics of Man, Culture and Nature to Natural Autosemiotics*. Workshop on the Semiotics of Nature, International Summer Institute for Semiotic and Structural Studies, Imatra, Finland, June 8–13, 2003.
Seppänen, Jouko. 2004a. *So Nature created Man in Her Own Image. Origin and Evolution of Life, Mind and Culture as Natural Autosemiosis*. Workshop on the Semiotics of Nature, International Summer Institute for Semiotic and Structural Studies, Imatra, Finland, June 3–9, 2004.
Seppänen, Jouko. 2004b. Autocatalysis as the Universal First Principle of Life. In T. Thorsteinsson (ed.), *Bioastronomy 2004: Habitable Worlds*. 8th International Conference on Bioastronomy. Reykjavik, 12–16 July 2004.
Setiya, K. & S. T. Joshi. Lovecraft on human knowledge: an exchange. *Lovecraft Studies* 24. 22–23, 34. West Warwick, RI: Necronomicon Press.
Sondergard, Sid. 2002. Mapping the Lovecraft Idiolect: Iterative Structures and Autosemiotization as Reading Strategies. *American Journal of Semiotics* 18, Part 1/4: 87–106.
Tarasti, Eero. 2000. *Existential Semiotics*. Bloomington, IN: Indiana University Press.
Ust, Daniel. 1996. The Philosophy of Lovecraft's Art. *Crypt of Cthulhu* 93, 20. 43–45.
Waugh, Robert H. 1991. Landscapes, Selves, and Others in Lovecraft. In David E. Schultz & S.T. Joshi, *An Epicure in the Terrible. A Centennial Anthology of Essays in Honor of H.P. Lovecraft*, 220–243. Rutherford, NJ: Farleigh Dickinson University Press.
Wheeler, Andrew. 1990. Infratextual Structures in Poe, Bierce, and Lovecraft. *Lovecraft Studies* 21. 3–23.

Márta Grabócz
Structure and meaning in music. A dialogue with Greimas

Abstract: This article deals with the meaning, structure and place of musical semiotics in the field of contemporary musicology. Since musicology represents the "scientific study of music", several aspects of musical analysis readily relate to structural semiotics and the semiotics that underlie it. The study of music involves the examination of musical genres, and according to eminent theorists, a musical genre has two aspects: structure and content. This article compares the different definitions of structure and discusses the "problem" of musical meaning and how this concept evolved thanks to Greimassian semiotics and American topic theory. The methods of Greimassian textual semiotics have significantly expanded musical analysis: the operational tools and their contribution to the understanding of compositional strategies in music are outlined.

Keywords: musicology, musical semiotics, structure and form in music, topic, intonation, strategies of composition, musical narrativity

1 Introduction

Within the realm of the humanities, musicology corresponds to the scientific study of music. The investigation into the evolution of musical styles in Western music is most often carried out through the study of musical genres (H. Danuser 1998). Musical genre provides a predetermined framework for music in terms of its instrumentation (instrumental set) and its form, as well as its social function and content. The Hungarian music philosopher and aesthetician, J. Ujfalussy, has described this dialectical relationship as follows:

> On one hand, genre relates to the subject, and on the other hand, to the structure. The dialectic between the two, created *in* and *by* the music, is a feature that merits further examination. [...] Genre points one of its sides towards the subject (the content, the theme). The latter is directly dependent on the changing circumstances of collective life and follows

---

Note: First publication: Marta Grabocz: *"Structure et sens en musique: Dialogue with Greimas"*, Langages n°213 (1:2019), pp.79-92, Armand Colin. Disponible sur: https://revues.armand-colin.com/lettres-langues/langages/langages-no-213-2019/structure-sens-musique-dialogue-greimas

https://doi.org/10.1515/9783110789164-046

> them in an immediate way. These changes drive and force the genre to metamorphose in a perpetual manner. The other side of genre is structural in nature. Musical structure retains and preserves, with particular strength, its fundamental traits: it binds and immobilises a genre by impeding its transformations. What prevails, at the end, is always the impulse coming from the side of the subject. The latter (the theme, the subject) transforms the content and, with it, the structural and stylistic features of the genre.   (Ujfalussy 1968:151)

We will now examine these two aspects of a musical work or genre: structure and meaning.

2 The role of structure (and form) in music

Music cannot exist without structure, and the rules governing forms have been defined since the concept of "musical work" has been in existence.[1]

Since the question of form or structure is inherent in musical thinking, the definition of form given by Greimas and Courtés also sheds considerable light on the problem of music while concurring with Ujfalussy's definition.

> The diverse and varied uses of the word 'form' reflect practically the whole history of Western thought. [. . .] Indeed, the notion of form has inherited its eminent position in the theory of knowledge from the Aristotelian tradition. Opposed to the matter which it "informs" (to which it gives form) at the same time it "forms" the knowable object, form is what guarantees the permanence and the identity of the knowable object. Taken in this fundamental sense, form is close to our conception of structure (cf. Gestalt).   (Greimas and Courtés 1982: 121).

In 1971, Greimas stated that "all exact sciences are naturally structuralist, because they cannot be different" (Greimas 2017: 40). Music is not necessarily an exact science, except when one examines it from the perspective of its physical (acoustic) construction, i.e. its frequency and temporal characteristics.

A reference book on the analysis of musical works and their structures defines analysis as

> The resolution of a musical structure into relatively simpler constituent elements, and the investigation of the functions of those elements within that structure.
> (Bent & Drabkin 1987, 8)

---

[1] See Lydia Goehr: *The Imaginary Museum of Musical Works: An Essay in the Philosophy of Music*, Oxford University Press, 1992.

Continuing this reflection, we quote two so-called "organicist" definitions of musical form that were specific to the 19th and early 20th centuries. One comes from the internationally renowned dictionary of music, the *Oxford Companion to Music*:

> Form can be said to be the way in which the various elements in a piece of music – its pitches, rhythms, dynamics, and timbre – are organised in order to make it coherent to the listener. The definition of the word 'form' has been the subject of aesthetic debate for centuries, and in a musical context, 'form' cannot be separated from content.
> (Arnold, Latham and Dunsby 2016)

The 19th-century theorist, Hugo Riemann, also emphasised the unity of the work: form as a homogenous whole achieves its completeness when it is the result of oppositions, contrasts, conflicts (Cf. Riemann in A. Souris 1976: 248).

In 1957, the renowned composer and teacher, Arnold Schoenberg, defined musical form as follows:

> Used in the aesthetic sense, form means that a piece is *organised*, i.e. that it consists of elements functioning like those of a living *organism*. [. . .] The chief requirements for the creation of a comprehensible form are *logic* and *coherence*. (Schoenberg [1957] 1987: 15)

In spite of the reference to organicism and recalling without actually mentioning Goethe and his theories of plant morphogenesis,[2] the description of formal musical frameworks has been confined, until now, to the so-called *mechanicistic* scientific category.[3] The main categories of musical forms from the past are based on the juxtaposition of sections. V. Karbusický, the Peircian semiotician of music, presented the five formal archetypes that cover Western musical history (and sometimes even the forms recently discovered in zoomusicology):

A/ *Enumerative forms* [or *Reihenform*]:
1/ A A' A''' etc.;
2/ Rondo forms: ABACAD etc.;
3/ "Endless production": ABCD, etc.);
B/ The *so-called balanced forms* [or *Gleichgewichtsform*]: 4/ Palindromic forms ABA'; ABCB'A', etc.;
C/ *The various so-called "evolutionary" forms* [or *Entfaltungsform*]: 5/ The complex drama in four acts: superimposed sonata form and cyclic form.
(See Figure 1 below.)

---

[2] J. W. von Goethe: *The Metamorphosis of Plants*. MIT Press, Cambridge MA, 2009 [1970].
[3] See the entries on 'form' in major dictionaries such as *The Oxford Companion to Music, Grove Music Online*, Dictionary "*Die Musik in Geschichte und Gegenwart*", etc.

In the 1940s and 50s, the Belgian music form theorist, André Souris, criticised this mechanistic conception of musical form, taking inspiration from Gestalt theory. He drew on the ideas proposed in France by Paul Guillaume (1937) and considered *the totality of form* to be a primary consideration. In the history of music, this theory corresponds to the emergence of the new macrostructure in late Beethoven and in the music of Liszt, a form that would essentially be determined by its goal, its aim, and which we will call "teleological" form (see archetypal form N°5 below).

Sometime later, building on the work of Raymond Ruyer (2019 [1958]: *The Genesis of Living Forms*) and G. Bachelard, Souris called for a dynamic vision of the approach to musical forms, one that was also derived from discoveries in biology and physics but that went well beyond Gestaltism. He spoke of the relativisation of the strong and weak factors that define the distinctive features of form. He anticipated René Thom's ideas on catastrophe theory by speaking of processes and the sudden and unexpected transformation of qualities triggered by the change in quantity:

> Phenomena comparable to those of the physical world occur in music. An increase or decrease in quantity can, at a certain point, trigger a sudden transformation in quality. The standard example is water temperature. (Souris 1958:33)

In his 1971 lecture on "The General Problems of Semiotics", Greimas also announced that in the human sciences, two contradictory and complementary concepts can be found, namely system and process. "Every system is loaded with meaning and can only be considered to exist if it manifests itself by means of *processes, actions, real concrete acts, concrete production*" (Greimas 2017: 40–41, emphasis added). His following sentences explain that the human sciences should have the same approach as those used in biology or physics.

We know that theory always lags behind art and practice. When Souris and Greimas proposed a "creative" approach to the theory of forms, they could not have known that the 1970s saw the emergence of new musical forms inspired by the analysis of sound and natural phenomena (see the sonic naturalism of F. B. Mâche dating from 1969 and spectral music after 1975). Other composers such as T. Murail, C. Miereanu, H. Dufourt, M. Lindberg, P. Manoury, P. Dusapin, etc. showed a keen interest in the contemporary scientific literature from various fields. Murail and Dusapin had long been interested in the fractal geometry of Benoît Mandelbrot and James Gleick; Costin Miereanu drew on catastrophe theory to generate semionarrative structures as defined by Jean Petitot and Greimas;[4]

---

[4] C. Miereanu completed his PhD thesis at EHESS (School of Advanced Studies in the Social Sciences) under the supervision of Greimas in 1979. His book entitled *Fuite et conquête du champ*

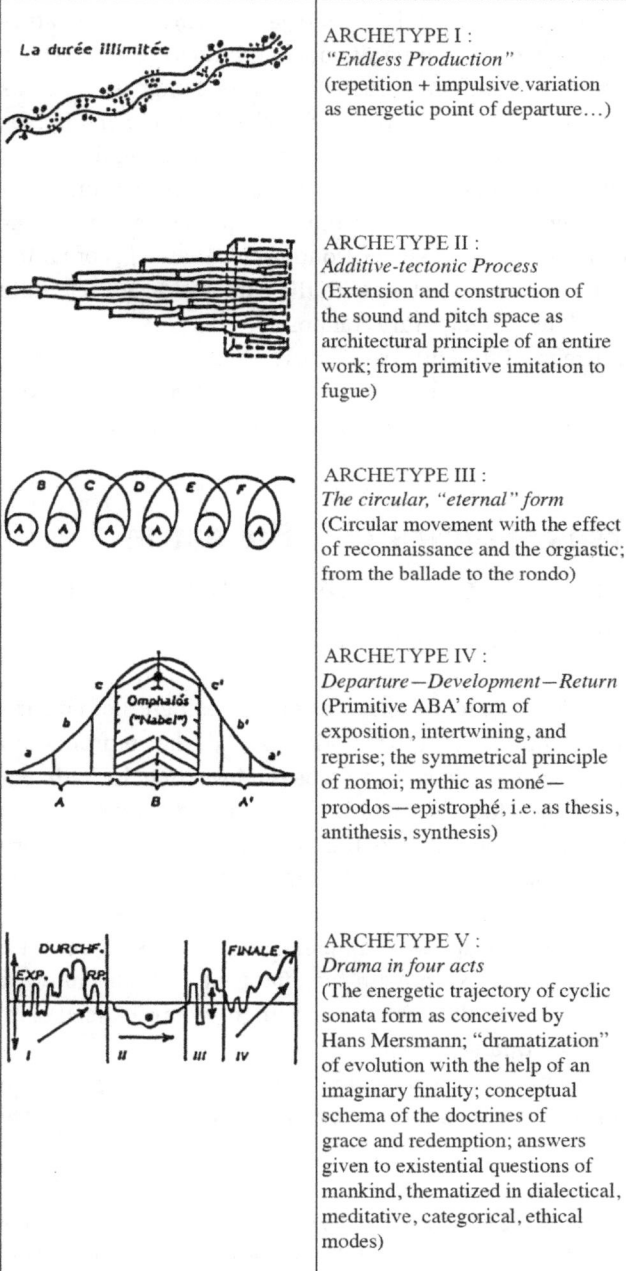

Figure 1: The five archetypal forms proposed by V. Karbuský (1990: 195).

F. B. Mâche explored the archetypes (phenotypes and genotypes) found in nature and in zoomusicology; most recently Philippe Manoury and Alberto Posadas have made use of the L-system in their musical structures;[5] other composers such as Dhomont, Dusapin, Mantovani, Hersant, Pesson, Schoeller, Saariaho and Eötvös have explored the narrative style and the study of myths in greater depth.[6]

Lately, within the publications of the Paris School semiotics, important works have appeared on visual semiotics and philosophical approaches to images (Beyaert-Geslin, A. and M. G. Dondero. 2014; Dondero M.G. and J. Fontanille 2012). This research is surprisingly consistent with the explorations of scientific and visual models practiced by contemporary composers.

It is in this sense that Greimas' structural semiotics have been closely linked – since the 1970s and 1980s – to musical compositions and creative process driven by the renewal and innovation of sound forms and content.

3 Structure versus signification: The battle between formalism (or "aesthetic nihilism") and the aesthetics of musical content

The quarrel between formalists and representatives of the aesthetics of musical content has existed since antiquity. In every historical period, the confrontation has taken on new guises, as for example at the very beginning when the Pythagoreans clashed with Aristotle and Plato. In the 18th century, this dualism deprived of mediation corresponded to the separation of the two movements in the history of philosophy: namely positivism and transcendental or subjective idealism (its equivalent in music would be the conflict between Rameau and Rousseau). In the middle of the 19th century, the cleavage was complete and the scission between the two approaches reached its paroxysm with the emergence of "absolute" or "autonomous" music (see E. Hanslick) and that of "program music" (see Liszt and Berlioz). (See Fubini 2000; Ujfalussy 1980).

Nowadays, with the advent of musical semiotics, we can still recognize the confrontation or antagonism between these two approaches: on the one hand, we

---

musical (Klincksieck, Paris, 1995), dedicated to Greimas, shows the influence of his teacher (the semiotic-musical interface: deep structures, surface structures of musical utterance; sound events and labyrinths, etc.).
5 The mathematical modelling of plant growth, developed by Aristid Lindenmayer.
6 In Beckett, Kafka, Heiner Müller, Faust, Homer, detective novels, etc.

observe semiosis or musical semiotics referred to as "immanent" (terms used by N. Meeùs and J. J. Nattiez in the context of formalist semiotics [!]), and on the other, we acknowledge musical semiotics built on the concept of "musical signification" since the creation (founding) of the international ICMS project (*International Conference on Musical Signification*) in 1984 in Paris, under the influence of Daniel Charles and Eero Tarasti and other students of Greimas such as Costin Miereanu, Ivanka Stoianova, Marcello Castellana, and later Márta Grabócz, Bernard Vecchione, Gino Stefani, Christine Esclapez, Jean-Marie Jacono, Christian Hauer, etc.

Musical semiotics, which I would describe as formalistic, emerged under the influence of Jean Molino, whose tripartition was applied to music by Nattiez (Nattiez 1975). Ole Kühl formulates the problem inherent in this *semiology of music without signs* in an interesting way: "I regard Nattiez's attempt to build a semiology without signs as primarily a way of legitimizing old-fashioned musical hermeneutics, and accordingly unable to contribute much towards a cognitive musicology. Nattiez's theories remain ungrounded in cognitive and neurobiological empirical studies." (Kühl, 2007:228) And the author adds as a footnote: "Nattiez explicitly states that 'semiology is not the science of communication'".[7]

During the years 1980–1990, music semiotics gained ground in the United States as well (Agawu, Allenbrook, Lidov). One of the starting points of R. Hatten's semiotic approach, for example, was M. Shapiro's theory of markedness. The interest of this approach is that it introduces a binary approach to the generation of meaning in the analysis of a musical form or discourse. Greimas' methods used in music by European semioticians (isotopy, seme, binarity, semiotic square [with contrariety, negation, etc.], narrative trajectory or programme along a euphoric or dysphoric axis, etc.) achieve the same results as those of English-speaking musicologists, starting with the theory of markedness and ending with "narrative strategies" or "strategies of expressive genres".

Also in the 1990s, the British semiotician and music aesthetician, R. Monelle, presented the Greimassian method at length (Monelle 1992: 220–274). But he also introduced criticism of and commentary on some dangerous positivist musical semiotics. "Even music semiotics – in the Molino-Nattiez version – began as an attempt to dismiss semantics" (2000:9). Monelle offers a caricature, under the name of Dr Strabismus, of a musicologist who is trying to scaffold a general theory, an encyclopaedic summation, and who only ends up with a collection of drafts.

---

7 Kühl 2007: 228, note 131.

> Finally, Strabismus was forced to declare his work as a collection of sketches. No comprehensive theory was possible for him. Only an overmastering stress on the *sense* of music, rather than its form or its syntax, united his random thoughts. He found himself in what has been called the *postmodern condition*. (Monelle 2000:4)

Currently, in the French-speaking countries, there are still two musical semiotics which fight on an everyday basis:[8] the formalistic semiotics based on J. J. Nattiez, N. Meeùs[9] and Sémir Badir, and Greimassian musical semiotics, which is concerned with the articulation of meaning, signifieds, and narrative programmes as an additional layer of analysis that completes and refines the examination of forms and structures in music. This second group of music semioticians currently rallies around Eero Tarasti and his ICMS project (after the death of Daniel Charles who supported and collaborated with him until 2008). Since 1984, this international research programme involves the organisation of biennial international conferences throughout Europe,[10] and is called the International Project on Musical Signification; the congresses are accompanied by publications of the conference proceedings.[11]

---

8 See, for example, the presentation of the theories of formalistic semiotics and those of Greimasian semiotics at the 9th European Music Analysis Conference, [9th EUROMAC], held in Strasbourg on 28 June – 1 July 2017.
9 His article "L'Autonomie de la sémiotique" (2009) offers an in-depth critique of certain Greimassian notions used in music (such as isotopy and the semiotic square). His text on "Le statut sémiologique de l'analyse musicale" (2001) states that "the signifier ... cannot itself be a material object. (. . .) The first opinion that a material signifier refers to a conceptual signified must be rejected for reasons of simple logic (. . .). But the second idea which situates both the signifier and the signified at the mental – and therefore individual – level, does not shed any light on semiosis as a social phenomenon." (Meeùs 2001: 554).
10 The city and the university change every two years, depending on the candidates applying from among the major European music centres (e.g. Helsinki, Imatra, Edinburgh, Paris, Bologna, Aix-en-Provence, Rome, London, Canterbury, Krakow, Leuven, Brussels, etc.).
11 The 15th ICMS congress was held in Barcelona in June 2022.

4 The question of meaning and signification in musique: The contribution of structural semantics, of semiotics, and Greimas' narrative grammar to the apprehension and deeper appreciation of musical works

The author of this essay was involved with Greimasian methods from 1985–1990, while constantly expanding the range of the master's semiotic methods as applied to music. This commitment can also be explained by the fact that the leading Hungarian and Eastern European musicologists of the 1960s – 1980s,[12] like Greimas, considered art as a social phenomenon; they saw artistic discourse, narrative or musical discourse as the embodiment of values within a society, and that *the "discourses" of the great composers* (as with the great writers or storytellers) were often read and listened to by these musicologists *as messages addressed to members of the cultural community or society,* while at the same time prompting them to reflect on questions relating to values.

Speaking of narratives (of all kinds) and their surface forms of expression, each of which conceals a deeper meaning, Greimas writes:

> It is the deciphering of these narratives (literary works of individual or collective creation, folklore) that enables us to discover the value systems hidden within them and the summaries of behaviour according to these value systems and ideologies. (Greimas 1971/2017: 44)

In the same article, referring to Bernanos, Greimas also talks about models or logical operations that can be used to detect or "resolve changes in the content of the work. (. . .). There is a certain dialectic, a logical dialectic that makes it possible to understand the transformations of the ideology behind the work, the transformations of the work (. . .)". (Greimas 1971/2017: 51)

Taking into account and making an inventory of all the contributions of Greimasian semiotics to musicology is beyond the scope of this contribution. I will restrict my discussion to the following: 1/ the items that correspond to the signified; 2/ a few models chosen to explain Greimas' contribution to the understanding of narrative strategies (or strategies for the organisation of the signified) in the musical works from various periods.

---

12 Musicologists who still had an almost encyclopaedic knowledge of the history of music, such as Szabolcsi, B; Ujfalussy, J., Asafiev, B., Karbusický V., then those of the following generation: Maróthy J., Jiránek J., J., Kroó, Gy., Somfai L., Tallián T., etc.

4.1 Terminology related to musical signifiers

From the Baroque period (when treatises identified musical rhetorical figures, followed by "madrigalisms"), there was a conscious shift towards signifying musical entities in the years 1930–1940 during the main period of activities of Boris Asafiev (a contemporary and companion of V. Propp and J. Tynianov). It was Asafiev who introduced the term "intonation" (following Jean-Jacques Rousseau) to refer to characteristic musical formulas (from the point of view of their musical parameters) having a specific expression that transmit a human or social meaning, and which can represent determined characters within a musical piece (see Ujfalussy, cited in Grabócz 2009: 45–46). The category of intonation also touches on *"the typical"* in the sense that the patterns of a style are recognized by all the members of a community, as elements belonging to a reservoir or collective memory. (See also Tarasti 2006:81–82; Monelle 1992: 274–303). From the 1980s onwards, Eero Tarasti and other musicologists [Stoianova, Miereanu, Grabócz, Cassar, Desquilbé, Ellis, etc.] have used the categories of "seme", "classeme" and isotopy as units corresponding to the signifieds in music (see the definitions of these terms in Grabócz 1996). In 1980, L. Ratner published the first work in the United States in which the concept of "musical topics" was introduced as a typical element with a universally recognised meaning in the classical period.[13] This concept corresponds to that of Asafiev's intonation, but also to that of the classeme (the length or duration covering a musical theme, i.e. about eight or sixteen bars). From the years 2000–2010, the term "topic" dominates the analysis of signification in music, to the detriment of other concepts (although the term "musical isotopy" still maintains its value as a longer signifying unit of form or a combination of other units). Today, it is the *Oxford Handbook of Topic Theory*, published in 2014 under the direction of D. Mirka, which has compiled the most complete repertoire of musical topics, with about 150 items from the Baroque to the 20th-century.[14]

4.2 Articulation of meaning and signifieds within musical forms

The second question of a semiotic nature implied by the analysis of forms in music concerns the strategy for organising the signifieds. Musicologists have

---

[13] The term is used in the sense of "commonplace".
[14] Examples of 18th-century topics are the pastoral; the solemn; the tragic, the grotesque; hunting; dance styles with a meaning such as the galliard, polonaise; siciliana, etc.

used several models of Greimas: most commonly the *semiotic square* is used to present the complex articulation of musical signifiers within a piece (Tarasti, Grabócz, Poirot, Mirka, Sivuoja-Gunaratnam, Uno Everett, Stepien, Jankauskienè, Pawlowska, etc.). Some applications of the Greimas square are "static" diagrams, others introduce temporality, evolution and transformation into the representation of forms using the elementary structure of signification.

Here is a "dynamic" example of the square (Figure 2).

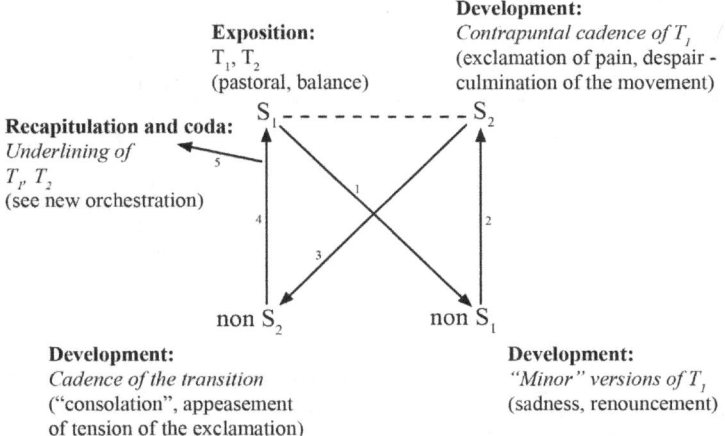

Figure 2: General diagram of the articulation of the semes (or affects, topics) in the Andante of Mozart's "Prague" Symphony K. 504 (the numbers on the lines correspond to the evolution and the stages in the unfolding of the sonata form).

Another model often used by musicologists is Greimas' *generative path* with its two main levels [surface level and deep level] and its discursive syntax (actorialisation, temporalisation, spatialisation). Eero Tarasti's exemplary overarching analysis of the first movement of Beethoven's Waldstein Sonata op. 53 explores all aspects of this syntax (Tarasti 1996: 76–103).

The formula of Greimas' *narrative programme* was also often used, with its subject of being, subject of doing, statement of doing, statement of being, and subject-related or not related to an object of value, etc. (See Figure 3.)

This first movement of the Waldstein sonata by Beethoven uses four narrative programmes, and it is *only the last one* (NP 4, i.e. Narrative Programme n°4) that offers the euphoric succession of S1-S2, followed by a completed and unnegated arrival (as in the previous NPs). The S1 corresponds to the restless and agitated gestures of birth or preparation; in contrast, the S2 – a solemn choral theme – corresponds to the rhetorical and solemn words of the poet himself. It is therefore

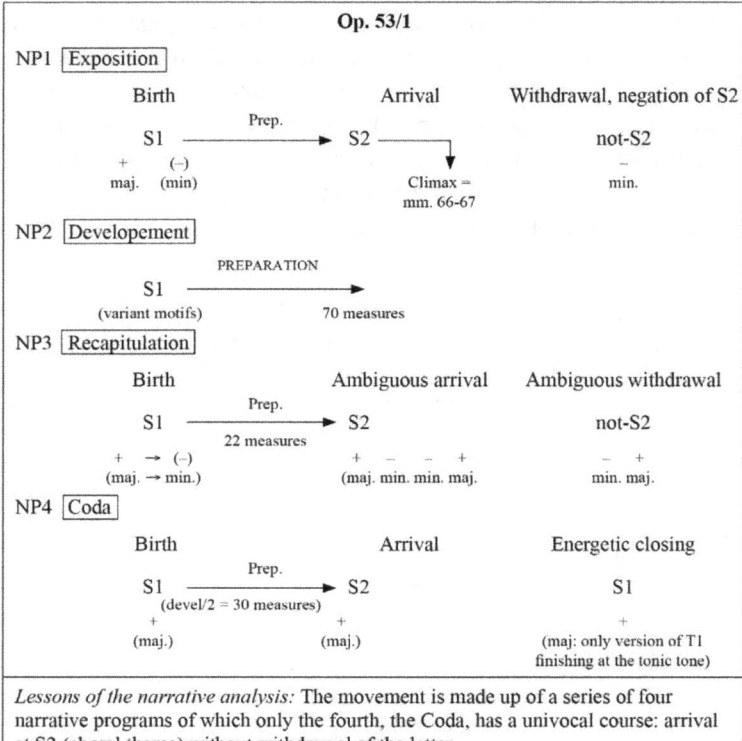

Figure 3: Diagram of the evolution of the signifieds in the first movement of Beethoven's Waldstein Sonata op.53 divided into four narrative programmes (Grabócz 2009: 188).

only the coda of the movement (NP4) that unambiguously renders the solemn and celebratory declamation of the choral theme in the style of the "speaking poet" [*Der Dichter spricht*], after a long preparation offered by the S1 and the entire movement. The idea of the joint value object (obtained or not) at the end of the actions between S1 and S2, explains very clearly what is at stake in the movement. (In previous NPs, as a result of the statements of doing, the object of value represented by S2 was constantly negated or withdrawn).

Another early and truly revolutionary use for musical analysis was the introduction of the concept of *narrative programme series* in the analysis of content in Chopin's *Polonaise-Fantaisie* Op.61 by Eero Tarasti (Tarasti 1987/1996: 195–216).

Another model of Greimasian theory that has often been used by musicologists is *modal theory* (Tarasti in Chopin, Stoianova, Pankhurst, Heimonen in Liszt, etc.) (Tarasti 1996: 217–254). See Figure 4.

In the future, it would be important to fully develop the rich potential of using Greimas' models in musical analysis. With this in mind, I will mention only what seems to me to be the most important in this first overview, without making any claim to exhaustiveness.

NP 1	Descent/ Rising, Elevation (mes. 1–8)	- +
NP 2	Birth of the main theme ([Polonaise]: mes. 9–21)	-
NP 3	Polonaise /version 1 (mes. 22–66)	+
NP 4	Modulations or topological interruptions, stoppages (mes. 67–91)	-
NP 5	Polonaise/version 2: extreme thymic (affective) states (mes. 92–115)	+ -
NP 6	Mazurka/version 1 (mes. 116–147)	+
NP 7	Nocturne/ version 1 (mes. 153–180)	-
NP 8	Mazurka/version 2 (mes. 181–198)	+
NP 9	Removal (distance) and return (mes. 199–240) Nocturne / 2 (mes. 201) B major Varied introduction (mes. 205–214) D major, C major Mazurka / 3 (mes. 215) F minor —Transition: (mes. 225) "a tempo primo" F minor	- -
NP 10	Fulfilment (mes. 241–288) Polonaise / 3: (mes. 242) A flat major Transition (variation of Mazurka) (mes. 248) B major Nocturne / 3 (mes. 253) —Superposition of Polonaise + Mazurka + Nocturne (mes. 267ff.): accelerando, sempre ff, A flat major	++

Figure 4: Diagram by M. Grabócz, after Eero Tarasti's analysis of Chopin's Polonaise-Fantaisie (Op. 61) divided into 10 narrative programmes (Tarasti 1987/1996). This chart was completed by M. Grabócz with regard to the marks of dysphoria or euphoria, thus pointing out the pathemic evolutions of the piece (+ or – signs).

*

5 Conclusion

As I have tried to point out above, traditional musicology is almost handicapped in terms of the understanding and complex analysis of dramatic (cathartic) instrumental pieces of the Classical period, of a large number of Romantic symphonic works, and of the elaborated or sophisticated musical dramaturgies of the twentieth and twenty-first centuries. The composers themselves most often focus on the content first, while the form, the surface expression adapts itself to the requirements of the subject matter or message.[15]

Apart from the fact that the search for semes, classemes and isotopes (or topics and intonations) provides a link to the cultural units of society, and of the period in which the work was produced, the large form of a musical piece often conceals a binary type evolution of pathemes and affects.

Where topics and affects do not emphasise contrast and contradiction (negation, etc.) in the evolution, the musical form remains consistent with the static frameworks described in treatises on composition and structure (such as ABA forms; palindromic forms; sonata form with its symmetry; rondo forms, etc.). But in the case of the dramatic instrumental works of Mozart and Beethoven (the exceptional sonatas or symphonies of Mozart; the late sonatas and quartets of Beethoven; the dramatic piano pieces of Chopin, Liszt and Schumann, etc.), traditional musicology is powerless: attempts to analyse the past acknowledge the lack of tools to describe everything that happens in a complex musical form.

Greimas' methods of textual semiotic analysis have shed light on the cathartic forms of both Mozart and Beethoven because by pointing out the relations of contrariness or contradiction and the relation of complementarity within the topics, we can see the transformation, even the creation of "new objects of value" within musical discourse, and these new objects of value, these new musical ideas, drive the form out of its usual boundaries. In terms of the analysis of musical styles, this means that these pieces from the classical period contain in themselves the essence of the Romantic structure: the "teleological form", which creates new values throughout the musical discourse (see, for example, the analyses of certain dramatic works, which became "teleological" in Mozart and Beethoven in Grabócz 2009: 111–130; 131–165; the analysis of the *Fantasy in D minor K. 397* presented in expressive narrative programmes by Tarasti 2016: 65–81).

In analysing the works of Chopin, Schumann or Liszt, the identification of topics and their evolution according to a binary sequence (i.e. variations in character through the dysphoric or euphoric alternation of the same themes) shows that it is the change – or even the profound transformation of the expressive genre – of the topic that guides the form, unlike the predetermined frameworks of the past (see Tarasti's analysis of Schumann's *Fantasy in C major* op.17, 2016:156–194).

---

[15] See, one of the first attempts to identify the influence of recent scientific theories on the innovation of contemporary musical forms, in Grabócz 2016 (proceedings of the 12th ICMS congress), and see Grabocz 2019.

In contemporary music, we are witnessing a revival of the concept of nineteenth-century program music, in the sense that composers consciously choose narrative, visual, scientific, astrophysical, psychological or other models to "communicate" with today's audiences. If the musicologist has no inclination to structurally analyse these "new semiotic objects", the understanding of new music will most certainly remain beyond their grasp.

Greimas' methods have also proved their worth in interdisciplinary analysis, particularly at the interface between music and literature, since the structuring of meaning is not strictly determined by the type of artistic expression. Examples include the comparison of myths with nineteenth-century symphonic poems by E. Tarasti (2003); the four-stage analysis of the Liszt canonical form (the succession of four obligatory isotopies) and the four-section structural analysis of Goethe's Faust produced by scholars of literature and philosophy (Grabócz 2009: 249–260; 221–248).

One can only hope that, in the future, the younger generation will evaluate the total contribution of Greimasian semiotics to musicology, by studying the forty-fifty key works that have marked the history of musical semiotics from 1980 to the present day.

References

Agawu, Kofi. 1991. *Playing with Signs. A Semiotic Interpretation of Classic Music*. Princeton: Princeton UP.
Agawu, Kofi. 2007. *Music as discourse*. Oxford: Oxford University Press.
Arnold, D. [n.d.]. Entry on "form", in Oxford Music Online, The Oxford Companion to Music. http://www.oxfordmusiconline.com (accessed 2012)
Bent, Ian & William Drabkin. 1987. *Analysis*, with a Glossary by William Drabkin. London : MacMillan Press.
Beyaert-Geslin, Anne & Maria Giulia Dondero (ed). 2014. *Arts et sciences. Approches sémiotiques et philosophiques des images*. Lièges: Presses universitaires de Liège.
Changeux, Jean-Pierre. 2012. *La Vie des formes et les formes de la vie*. Paris: Odile Jacob.
Cook, Nicholas. 2000. *Music: A Very Short Introduction*. Oxford: Oxford University Press.
Danuser, Hermann (ed.). 1982. *Gattungen der Musik und ihre Klassiker*. Regensburg: Laaber-Verlag.
Dondero, Maria Giulia & Jacques Fontanille. 2012. *Des images à problèmes. Le sens du visuel à l'épreuve de l'image scientifique*. Limoges : PULIM.
Formosa, Marcel et al. 1996. *Les Unités sémiotiques temporelles. Eléments nouveaux d'analyse musicale*, 18. Paris: Ed. ESKA.
Fubini, Enrico. 2000 [1983]. *Les philosophes et la musique*. Paris: Slatkine Reprints.
Goehr, Lydia. 2007. *The Imaginary Museum of Musical Works: An Essay in the Philosophy of Music*. Oxford: Oxford University Press.

Grabócz, Márta. 1996. The Role of Semiotic Terminology in Musical Analysis. In Eeero Tarasti (ed), *Musical Semiotics in Growth*, 195–218. Bloomington: Indiana University Press.
Grabócz, Márta. (ed). 2007. *Sens et signification en musique*. Paris: Hermann.
Grabócz, Márta. 2009. *Musique, Narrativité, Signification*. Paris: L'Harmattan.
Grabócz, Márta. 2016. Formes musicales sous influence des théories scientifiques dans les œuvres contemporaines. In Constantino Maeder & Mark Reybrouck (eds.), *Sémiotique et vécu musicale. Du sens à l'expérience, de l'expérience au sens*, 113–134. (Proceedings of the 12th ICMS conference). Leuven: Leuven University Press.
Grabócz, Márta. 2020. The Influence of Scientific Theories on Musical Form in Contemporary Instrumental and Electroacoustic Works (Dhomont, Mâche, Miereanu, Murail, Posadas). *Studia Musicologica*, Budapest, 60(1–4), 2019. 129–146.
Greimas, Algirdas Julien. 1971. Les problèmes généraux de la sémiotique (1971 lecture given in Vilnius). In Greimas: *Du sens en exil*. Limoges: Lambert-Lucas, 2017.
Greimas Algirdas Julien & Joseph Courtés. 1979 & 1983. *Sémiotique. Dictionnaire raisonné de la théorie du langage*, 2 volumes. Paris: Hachette.
Greimas Algirdas Julien & Joseph Courtes. 1982. *Semiotics and Language. An Analytical Dictionary*. Bloomington: Indiana University Press.
Greimas, Algirdas Julien. 1986. *Sémantique structurale*. Paris: PUF. (Structural Semantics: An Attempt at a Method ,1984, Lincoln, University of Nebraska Press).
Greimas, Algirdas Julien. 2017. *Du sens en exil. Chroniques lithuaniennes*. Ed. by Denis Bertrand, Ivan Darrault-Harris, Nastopka Kestutis & Žukas Saulius. Limoges: Editions Lambert-Lucas.
Guillaume, Paul. 1937. La Psychologie de la forme. Paris: Flammarion.
Hatten, Robert. 1994. *Musical Meaning in Beethoven. Markedness, Correlation, Interpretation*. Bloomington: Indiana University Press.
Hatten Rrobert. 2004. *Interpreting Musical Gestures, Topics and Tropes*. Bloomington: Indiana University Press.
Karbusický, Vladimír. 1990. *Kosmos-Mensch-Musik. Strukturalistische Anthropologie des Musikalischen*. Hamburg: Verlag Dr. R. Krämer.
Maeder, Constantino & Mark Reybrouck. 2016. *Sémiotique et vécu musical. Du sens à l'expérience, de l'expérience au sens*. Leuven: Leuven University Press.
McKay, Nicholas. 2007. On Topics Today. In *Zeitschrift der Gesellschaft für Musiktheorie*, n° 4 (January 2008), Gesellschaft für Musiktheorie. http://www.gmth.de/zeitschrift/artikel/251.aspx
Meeùs, Nicolas. 2009. L'Autonomie de la Sémiotique. In Christian Hauer & Bernard Vecchione (eds.), *Le sens langagier du musical : Sémiosis et hermenéia*, 187–196. Paris: L'Harmattan. Also see his website: http://nicolas.meeus.free.fr (consulted in December 2017).
Meeùs, Nicolas. 2001. Le statut sémiologique de l'analyse musicale. In Jean-Marc Chouvel & alia (eds.), Analyse et création musicales, 549–562. Paris: L'Harmattan, (also on his website http://nicolas.Meeus.free.fr (consulted in December 2017).
Miereanu, Costin. 1995. *Fuite et conquête du temps musical*. Paris: Klincksieck.
Mirka, Danuta. (ed). 2014. *The Oxford Handbook of Topic Theory*. Oxford: Oxford University Press.
Monelle, Raymond. 1992. *Linguistics and Semiotics in Music*. Chur: Harwood Academic Publishers.
Monelle, Raymond. 2000. *The Sense of Music*. New Jersey: Princeton University Press.
Nattiez, Jean-Jacques. 1975. *Fondements d'une sémiologie de la musique*. Paris: UGE 10/18.

Nattiez, Jean-Jacques. 2007. *Profession musicologue*. Montréal: Presses de l'Université de Montréal.

Ratner, Leonard. 1980. *Classic Music: Expression, Form and Style*. New York: Schirmer.

Rix, Eemmanuelle & Marcel Formosa (eds.) 2008. *Vers une sémiotique générale du temps dans les arts*. Sampzon, Editions Delatour/MIM/IRCAM/IDEAT.

Riemann, Hugo. 1961. *Le Dictionnaire de Musique de H. Riemann*, cited by A. Souris (1961), "Sur quelques termes fondamentaux du vocabulaire musical – Forme". In A. Souris (1976 [1961]) *Conditions de la musique et autres écrits*, 248–253. Bruxelles-Paris: Université de Bruxelles-CNRS.

Ruyer, Raymond. 2019. *The Genesis of Living Forms*. Lanham, MD, United States: Rowman & Littlefield.

Schoenberg, Arnold. 1967. *Fundamentals of Musical Composition*. London: Faber & Faber.

Sheinberg, Esti (ed.). 2012. *Music Semiotics: A Network of Significations: In Honour and Memory of Raymond Monelle*. Ashgate: Aldershot.

Souris, André. 1976 [1961]. *Conditions de la musique et autres écrits*. Bruxelles-Paris: Université de Bruxelles-CNRS. In particular: Souris A. (1961), Sur quelques termes fondamentaux du vocabulaire musical – Forme, 248–253 and Souris A. (1946), Conditions de la musique. Chapitre I. La 'forme' sonore, 23–35.

Tarasti, Eero. 2003 [1978]. *Mythe et musique: Wagner, Sibelius, Stravinsky*. Trans. by D. Pousset. Paris: Michel de Maule.

Tarasti, Eero (ed.). 1995. *Musical Signification. Essays in the Semiotic Theory and Analysis of Music*. Berlin/New York: Mouton de Gruyter [ICMS 1].

Tarasti, Eero (ed). 1996. *Musical Semiotics in Growth*. Bloomington: Indiana University Press.

Tarasti, Eero. 1996 [1994]. *Sémiotique musicale*. Trans. by B. Dublanche. Limoges: PULIM.

Tarasti, Eero. 2006. *La musique et les signes. Précis de sémiotique musicale*. Paris: L'Harmattan.

Tarasti, Eero. 2016. *Sémiotique de la musique classique: Comment Mozart, Brahms et Wagner nous parlent*. Trans. by L. Csinidis and M. Rousselot. Aix-en-Provence: Publications de l'Université de Provence.

Ujfalussy József. 1968. *Az esztétika alapjai és a zene*. [Les Fondements de l'esthétique et la musique]. Budapest: Tankönyvkiadô.

Ujfalussy József. 1980. Zene és valósàg [Music and reality], in Ujfalussy J., *Zenéröl, Esztétiklárôl* [On music, on esthetics], 150–179. Budapest: Zenemükiadó.

Bernard Vecchione
Existential semiotics and musical hermeneutics: On musical sense advention

Abstract: In this paper I consider the relation between existential semiotics (ES) and musical hermeneutics (MH) particularly on the issue of musical sense advention. As existential, ES roots the becoming sign of sign in Heidegger's hermeneutic circle, the *Dasein*'s structure of pre-understanding. But, as a semiotics, it aims to return from existence to sign, appealing, as Charles (2007) said, to Gadamer's or Ricœur's philosophical hermeneutics to enlarge the problem in direction of what Ricœur (1986) calls "the need for experience to become sign or text."

I take the problem where Charles has left it. – Broadening the subject from general philosophical hermeneutics to regional MH, I pose that, as a musical semiotics this time, ES is concerned with the MH's thesis (Vecchione 2009, 2013) that (1) *Musiklichkeit* (musicianity) – the musical hermeneutic experience embedded in Dasein – is a specification of Gadamer's *Sprachlichkeit* (the linguistic constitution of hermeneutic experience of the world) enlarged from linguisticity to *languagiarity* of musical experience; and (2) that musicianity (Musiklichkeit) is constitutive of an experience (Lebenswelt) that includes both *musical experience of life* and *musical experience of music*. – This problem I called "musication of existence" (Vecchione 2009: 267), shows that, such as MH, ES is concerned (1) with the *Dasein*'s necessity to be questioned on its own non-verbal (and therefore musical) part of hermeneutic experience (the fact that Being also needs to become meaningful musical signs or works); (2) but also with the dialectic between *musical veritas* – musical enunciating of Being (included musical Being) – and *musical alethéia* – musical annunciating of Being (including musical Being) to the breaking of musical enunciating; (3) and, by this means, with the MH's conjunction between an OB (. . .of Being) philosophy (musical enunciating of Being, musical annunciating of Being to the breaking of musical enunciating) and a BO (Being of. . .) philosophy (Being of musical enunciating, Being of musical annunciating to the breaking of musical enunciating). – By that way, ES appears as, not only related to the author's, the performer's, or the receiver's, the music reader's acting; but also to music which participates in its own history, its own traditions of writing and meaning; and to the changing advention of music, the musical Being adventure through cultures, history and societies, the becoming of musical Being (Vecchione 2013) that is the need for Being to become new meaningful musical signs and works and to deploy music into innovative possibilities for music to be music (Vecchione 2008).

Keywords: Existential Semiotics (ES), Musical Hermeneutics (MH), Existence becoming musical sign or work, OB Philosophy vs BO Philosophy, Musiklichkeit (*Dasein* Musical languagiarity constitution), Musicianity (Musician Experience), Musical enunciating / annunciating of Being vs Being of musical enunciating / annunciating, Musical Being deployment.

> Un trésor ténébreux fait l'éclat de vos jours:
> Un silence est la source étrange des poèmes.
> (A dark treasure makes the shine of your days:
> A silence is the strange source of poems.)
> Paul Valéry, *Le philosophe et «La Jeune Parque»*, in *Poésies*, Paris, 1929.

Eero Tarasti's *Existential Semiotics* (1998, 2000, 2003, 2004, 2009, 2011, for instance) (hereafter ES) is a new (though already twenty years old) and much-documented research project in semiotics. – As existential, ES roots the becoming sign of sign in Heidegger's *Dasein* structure of pre-understanding. – But, as semiotics, it returns from existence to sign, appealing, as Charles (2007: 142–146) said, to Ricœur's or Gadamer's philosophical hermeneutics to enlarge Heidegger's hermeneutical circle. – Here, I would like to take the problem where Charles had left it and show how, as musical semiotics this time, ES forces us to enlarge hermeneutical philosophy. Returning from existence to sign, ES appeals to an overtaking of, what we can call, the Heidegger's OB ("...of Being") philosophy: an opposition between *veritas* (enunciating of Being) and *aletheia* (annunciating of Being to the breaking of enunciating). Indeed, to question the need for *Dasein* to become meaningful musical signs or texts (Vecchione 1997), musical hermeneutics considers *Musiklichkeit* (musicianity) – the musical hermeneutical experience embedded in *Dasein* (Vecchione 2009; 2013) – as a part of Gadamer's *Sprachlichkeit* (the linguistic constitution of hermeneutical experience of the world), enlarging the understanding of *Dasein* hermeneutical constitution, from linguisticity to languagiarity, in order to include in *Dasein* any non-verbal (and therefore musical) hermeneutical experience. Thus, the issue of musical enunciating of Being (musication) is turned into that of the Being of musical enunciating. Finally, ES appears as participating to the current reconciliation movement of the two slopes of the broken hermeneutics inherited from Heidegger: the methodological one (that deals with the reading of difficult texts), and the philosophical one (that deals with the annunciating of Being to the breaking of enunciating). The OB ("... of Being") philosophy is turned into a BO (Being of...") philosophy. Reading is enlarged, from the deciphering of musical spoken to that of the forms of musical speaking, and that of the annunciating of Being to the breaking of musical enunciating (questioning, by the way, the breaking modalities of musical enunciating). Enunciating is not entirely transparent to itself, and annunciating of Being is seen as also concerned by the Being of musical enunciating.

1 Understanding *existential semiotics* in the light of musical hermeneutics

As existential, ES goes to Heidegger's philosophy; but, at the same time, as semiotics, it forces us to go beyond. With Heidegger, ES goes from sign to existence. But Heidegger's opposition (1959, for instance) between enunciating (*veritas*) and annunciating of Being to the breaking of any enunciating (*aletheia*) forces ES, with Ricœur's or Gadamer's post-Heideggerian hermeneutical philosophy, to return from existence to text: Ricœur's (1986) need for existence to become text.

1.1. From *Heidegger's Sein und Zeit* (1927) ES borrows the notion of *Dasein*, understood as existence, sense source of signs, sign rooting in existence, coming meaning to sign, presence of existence underlying the sign to inscribe, read, understand, interpret, and even redeploy itself differently. Very judiciously, Tarasti sees in *Dasein* the becoming sign of a sign, the source of its meaning: "*I have outlined a model based upon the concept of* Dasein – existence – which constitutes the world in which our 'semiotic subject' lives, acts and reacts." (Tarasti 2000: 18). ES theory of sign is in the framework of Pierce's infinite semiosis, Tarasti (2000, "*A semiotic sign and pre-sign*": 32–35) reconsiders in the dynamic unit of the whole life of a sign: as act-signs in works (in which we can include the process of invention-sign and the sign already constituted, acting in works), pre-signs or *enunciant* (in *Dasein*) (which I would gladly interpret as the source of Heidegger's annunciating of Being by the breaking of any enunciating), and post-signs or *interpretant*, their later spread into societies and cultures. The strong and most original point of ES is the pre-signity. For Tarasti, (2000: 19) pre-signs are: "*signs in the process of forming and shaping themselves*". A sign that unfolds in pre-sign, act-sign, and post-sign: what Tarasti reports through the transcendence of Heidegger's *Dasein*, a *Dasein* that, while presenting himself each time differently, never ceases to remain the same. Rooting sign in *Dasein* tells the silent origin of meaning. But what is exactly a pre-sign? Is a pre-sign already a sign, already a part of enunciating? Or is it the potential of languagiarity of the existence, what Gadamer calls *Sprachlichkeit* (1986a: 411), the need for *Dasein* to become language and to deploy later in works, in utterances as act-signs and post-signs? From an explicitly Heideggerian perspective, Tarasti considers that, if "*the subject relates to Dasein and its universal character* (*advention* Weltlichkeit)" (1998: 53), as *Dasein* is advention (*Geschehen*), "*interpretation is possible only by remaining within* Dasein – *but at the same time transcending it"* (1998: 52). As *Dasein* is the one among all the beings to have this ability to transcend itself, transcending *Dasein* does not mean to surpass, to leave it on its own, to detach or to annihilate it, but it means *Dasein* unfolding itself differently, by bringing in presentations (*Darstellungen*) what reveals it more and better. In other words, *Dasein* unfolds in other appearances, while remaining present in each as a potential of Being, a *posse*, a power-to-be, or more precisely a power to always be otherwise. This revelation of *Dasein*, which simultaneously is advention, fulfilment, is made by its coming to the sign (or the configuration of signs that forms a text). But what comes to the sign, what becomes a sign, what forms a sign as a sign, happens, not by deploying as categories of the beings, but from our existence. To be there is above all to exist. And the analytical of Being to be developed is not an analytic of the appearances of the beings but rather an analytic of its existence. This Tarasti (2000: 19) explains as: *"When the subject for a second time returns to his/her world of Dasein and recreates signs, these are existential, in the sense that they reflect the subject's journey through transcendence"*.

Thus, the ES project stems from a hermeneutic of existentiality, with this peculiarity, however, that it remains semiotics and therefore that what matters most is to understand and describe how the sign to mean must come from *Dasein*. To be sign, to be meaningful, to have this character of a sign, this signity which is the owner of a sign, to recognize it as a sign, to be both necessarily welled up *Dasein* in a state before its invention-sign and unfolded in *Dasein* by the very fact of becoming-sign, *Dasein* is, indeed, this Being that has the quality of being potentially silent and to form utterances meaningful signs or texts (including musical) potentially silent. Thus, a radical shift occurs, particularly in musical semiotics, which roots into hermeneutic foundations, and does not see hermeneutics solely as reading after the fact of music given as an object to perceive, in front of a subject listener or analyst (methodical hermeneutics), but also as reading before any given act-sign already functioning as such, and overall (philosophical hermeneutics) as a reading of the becoming sign process, the need for existence to become enunciating. For Tarasti, pre-sign is this fore-sign that tends towards its later establishment as a sign, this not-yet-sign, whose proper constitution of not-yet already orients it towards its advention-sign. In pre-sign, the prefix means the inscription of pre-sign in this *Dasein* potential of advention. Better: this power of *Dasein*, not only to understand and to announce itself to the breaking of any enunciating but also to promote enunciating (and particularly musical enunciating). In other words: the pre-signitive constitution of *Dasein*, its essence of advention-sign, orientation-sign, vection to sign, which indicates the inscription of pre-signity in what Gadamer (1996a: 411) calls *Sprachlichkeit*, the linguisticity constitution of the hermeneutical experience of the world.

Existential semiotics, thus, definitively leaves the limited perspectives of a 1960s pure semiotic theory of signs closed on themselves. Also, while encompassing the objectives of post-classical musical semiotics, which aimed to describe the complexity of the signs at work (even in the musical, the figurative or textual devices of the works) and the sign rooting in production-sign or reception-sign (situational or eco-textual roots), ES reintroduces the sign in its native site, which is not its original promoting or producing situation (circumstances), but the original hermeneutic world of *Dasein* and its preorientation signs (or texts) and more generally works enunciating. While the original signity of the sign only occurs in act-signs and at the stage of what I have called the invention-sign, the original signity of *Dasein* derives from its nature constitutively hermeneutic, the pre-understanding constitution of *Dasein*, already bent pre-sign, already a potential vector of signs. With this transcendence of *Dasein*, seen both as this potential vectoring of the sign (pre-sign), the coming of the sign to sign (the invention of act-signs), and the spreading of an act-sign (post-sign) through cultures and societies, semiotics now takes root in hermeneutics, hermeneutically rooted in the existential nature of the Heideggerian *Dasein* and the essence of *Sprachlichkeit* from all hermeneutic experience, the need for experience to become enunciating. In music, not only the spoken of utterances but also their forms of speaking are silent. So, musical hermeneutics has three fields of investigation: the silent spoken of musical enunciating, the silent forms of speaking of musical utterances (Vecchione 1997), and the *Dasein* silent annunciating to the breaking of musical enunciating (Vecchione 2013 for instance). The origin of a meaningful musical sign or enunciating is in this specific silent *hermeneia* of musical (Vecchione 2009), which originates in *Dasein* and makes it come true.

Referring to *Sein und Zeit*, Tarasti situates this origin of the sense of sign in the coming of *Dasein* (existence) in sign. *Dasein* is defined as its pre-understanding structure of a Being able to self-understanding. *Dasein* is this being which has the power to understand himself, i.e. to anticipate, by its constitutive structure of understanding being, what can later be formed sense in an act-sign, but also is derived from an act-sign in its multiple rewritings in post-signs. *Dasein* is present at any stage of the life of a sign: in the need of pre-sign to become an act-sign; in the coming of meaning to act-sign, and the possibility for an act-sign to turn into and spread in other post-signs in cultures and societies. How do pre-signs turn into act-signs? How are act-signs shaped for carrying meaning? How do act-sign re-configure themselves in other enunciative circumstances? Overall *Dasein* is this being endowed of pre-understanding, allowing us to make possible the sign producing and reading. Referring to *Dasein*, ES roots the becoming sign in Heidegger's hermeneutical circle, the *Dasein* temporal structure of anticipation. ES is animated by this back and forth movement: from sign to existence (explaining the becoming sign, the coming of meaning to an act-sign by involving existence, the power of act-signs to reconfigure themselves in post-signs); and in return from existence to sign (the need for existence to become signs or texts). ES appears as a study of the dynamic unit of signs, having this power not only to become meaning (transition from pre-sign to sign) but also (deploying an act-sign in post-signs) to become a sign always different than it has already been. *Dasein* property of transcendence confers to ES a very plastic conception of a sign. And, as Daniel Charles (2007) said, joining Carlo Sini's (1978) semiotic philosophy, Tarasti can connect in his sign theory the infinite semiosis inspired by Peirce to Heidegger's hermeneutic circle.

Another *Dasein* property is its non-subjectivity. What Tarasti draws from *Gelassenheit* (Heidegger 1952) allows us to consider existence as the situation in which we are, before posing ourselves up as subjects and opposing as objects, a situation from which we participate, and, therefore, that is not viewed through exacerbated feelings, for instance of anguish or absurd. Referring to *Dasein*, ES defends a non-subjective conception of existence, away from existential pathos. – For this reading of a sign, in its three dimensions, of pre-sign, act-sign, and post-sign, Tarasti appeals to the Heideggerian principle of letting-things-be: *"In the analysis, the principle of 'letting-things-be' (the Heideggerian Gelassenheit) is essential."* (Tarasti 2000: 11). Not only because this principle allows ES to respect the sign and what is said by the sign: *"How can we be sure that our interpretation, our analysis, does not violate the object? The analysis must not damage the phenomenon or change it by force"* (Tarasti 2000:11). Also, because it is the only way to access what is said by the sign and against it: letting the Being saying, annunciating itself to the breaking of enunciating, as well as annunciating its power of enunciating. –The problem is much more important than we think since it opens up to the very enunciation scene musical productions, ritual situations, ceremonial, commemorative, festive, but just as much concert, radio broadcasting, television or disc, scattering also in digital form through the Web. These circumstances, which have been addressed by musical semiorhetoric (Vecchione 2007), are various, as we see for instance in the diverse corpus of circumstance pieces from the 14th and 15th centuries: inductions of popes or doges in Venice, coronations of kings or Germanic emperors, consecrations of churches, fresco cycles, altar fronts or carved tombs, marriage ceremonies, incentives to take up arms or ratifications of peace treaties. . . All having motivated both the composition of works and the writing devices in which they were configured. But if one can include the social circumstances in existence, it is precisely because existence is no longer just designed as the only expression of heightened feelings, but as a situation, including anthropological or even historical and social circumstances, in which the work is expressed, the composer puts it into shape, the musician performs, the listener receives, or the reader that we are understanding it. In this way, ES is quite compatible, not only with historical musical anthropology (Vecchione 1985), musical hermeneutics (Vecchione 1997), but also with semiorhetoric (Vecchione 2007), whose goal is the reintegration of musical works into their native contexts of enunciation, to better study the dimensions that bind them to the audiences on which they aim to affect: not only the phatic (seductive) dimension of catching the attention of an audience by the work, but also their argumentative configuration, for some of them; their power for the trope to happen, this figure of rhetoric, to signify something states everything else, and thus at the double meaning; stylistic dimension, optimizing their musical formulation to increase their impact on audiences; and, more, a plural discursive enunciating (narrative, declarative, figurative, descriptive, argumentative etc.) combining all these aspects. So, all is said for signs is also said for texts (and particularly for meaningful musical signs and texts).

1.2. Going from the sign into existence, ES roots semiotics in hermeneutics, but does not dilute semiotics in hermeneutics. ES remains a semiotics, implying an opposite question: how is existence called to form a sign (or text)? In other words: what is the becoming sign (or text) of existence? What is this need for existence to express itself in utterances (signs or texts)? To the opposition between enunciating of Being and Being of enunciating, ES, as a science of enunciating, introduces another dimension. By rooting signs in Heidegger's Dasein, Tarasti not only poses that, to signify a sign anchors itself in existence, but he also wonders how existence, and therefore meaning, are coming to sign. This circle between sign and existence is not the Heideggerian hermeneutics circle between understanding and pre-understanding, but a circle between semiotics and hermeneutics, that asks a back-and-forth path: coming from sign to existence (going from semiotics to hermeneutics) and, in return, from existence to sign (returning from hermeneutics to semiotics). Thus, ES is animated by this double movement of questioning semiotics by hermeneutics on the meaning conditions of sign or text, and hermeneutics by semiotics on the sign conditions of meaning. How is it possible to go back from sign to existence? But also: how is it possible to return from existence to sign? How do we understand the need for existence to become sign or text enunciating?

ES is general semiotics, but also a specific musical one. The problem is the same for music, at the difference that in music not only the spoken of an utterance, the sign of text, generally remains silent, but also the works forms of speaking (figurative, narrative, rhetoric etc.) (Vecchione 1997). What is musical sense advention? How sense is coming to musical sign or musical works as texts? How musical sign (work) can be constantly reconfigured (in its interpretations by musicians-performers, re-readings, rewritings) in its later life of sign? Musical hermeneutics has shown the need, on the behalf of music, to question *Dasein* on its vection to enunciating and especially to produce meaningful musical (signs or texts) utterances (Vecchione 2009, 2013, for instance). Here, I extend Charles' (2007) article to the point as Charles has left it. If ES, as existential, goes to Heidegger's philosophy, and, as general semiotics, needs to overcome it by a call to Gadamer's hermeneutics, as musical semiotics, it must question Gadamer's philosophy on its own hermeneuticity of *Dasein*. How may *Dasein* explain the production of meaningful musical signs and texts? I propose here to inverse the OB ("...of Being") Heidegger's philosophy (enunciating of Being vs annunciating of Being at the breaking of any enunciating) in a BO ("Being of...") philosophy (Being of annunciating / Being of enunciating), and to question this Being of musical enunciating which integrates the *Dasein* vection to produce musical meaningful (signs or texts) utterances. The question is how understanding Gadamer's concept of *Sprachlichkeit*, Gadamer interprets himself as the linguisticity of the hermeneutical experience of the world ("*Weltlisches hermeneutische Erfahrung*") (1996a: 411), and I (Vecchione 2009: 263–265) as a more general languagiarity including non-verbal and especially musical arts hermeneutical experiences. In MH, the question is not only that of the silent musical spoken and the silent musical speaking, which deals with musical methodical hermeneutics (Vecchione 1997), but also that of the silent saying of Being to the breaking of any musical enunciating, which deals with post-Heideggerian musical philosophical hermeneutics (Vecchione 2009, 2013) – a triple dimension that I have called the silent *hermeneia* of music, and which needs to reconciliate in a dynamic unit the two broken hermeneutics inherited from Heidegger's philosophy.

In *Sein und Zeit*, Heidegger opposed the saying (*Reden*) of Being and the speaking (*Sprechen*) of utterances. For a long time, he was wary of the utterance. Hence, its distinction between the truth of an utterance (*veritas*) and the unveiling of Being to the breaking of enunciating (*aletheia*). In *Unterwegs zur Sprache* (1959), he specifies how utterance obscures Being, and how Being can only announce itself at the breaking of any enunciating. An utterance is seen as what falsifies Being, and against which Being had to work to reveal itself. If utterances speak, *Dasein* says, but it appears not by enunciating itself, rather at the breaking of enunciating. Vattimo comments: "*The* Zerbrechen, *the breaking of speaking* [...] *only can give an 'is'.*" (Vattimo 1987: 75). Being is not said but as-signed by the breaking of any enunciating; an ad-signatum that constitutes the language in its weakness, these misses of language, these accidents, these failures which the language skilfully orchestrates itself against itself. Tropes, as we easily see in catachresis, seem to already invite us to this fail of language. But for Heidegger, this failure is no less than that of a specific utterance than that of any form of language. More specifically, the act of problematizing what a text states are less than for the language the act of problematizing its own languagiarity. This self-problematizing of language is not that to which Michel Meyer's problematology (2008, 2010, for instance) refers us, it is not only the self-problematizing of the utterances to make see its hidden or troped dimension, but it is also, and above all, the self-problematizing of language that shadows itself, sinks, to its limit; the self-problematizing of language, as language, in its practice of language, its being of language as such; the showing of the limits of language in which any language has difficulty to give access to Being. In other words, the self-problematizing of its languagiarity. It is the language itself that organizes its problematization, which shows its problematic relationship to Being. That is why, as Vattimo (1987: 75) says, there is truly a *"shipwreck of language"* and a game for language to be wrecked if it wants to elicit Being, his relationship to Being. This shipwreck of language, this language wrecking in which the saying of Being is revealed, sinking all expression, these limits in which language is damaged, are the place where *Dasein* is experienced, extended in its unveiling, and understood. – Hence, says Gadamer (1995: 157–158), the distance between the *apophainesthai* of language (the "showing-itself-of-the-spoken") and the essence of the hermeneutic experience of *Dasein*. Enunciating only against its spoken reveals Being (*Dasein*) and, for Gadamer, the languagiarity constitution of human experience: *"The concept of utterance [. . .] lies in the most extreme opposition with the essence of the hermeneutic experience and with the Sprachlichkeit of the human experience of the world"* (Gadamer 1996a: 494). So, for Gadamer (1996b), the essence of hermeneutical experience *"is less that of language than that of the limits of language."* (Grondin 1993: 264).

A consequence of this Heideggerian suspicion towards the enunciating is the hermeneutics broken in two incompatible slopes: a methodological one (that aims reading difficult meaningful texts) and a philosophical one (based on Heidegger's hermeneutic circle temporal structure of anticipation and the Being annunciating to the breaking of enunciating). – It was the task of the post-Heideggerian philosophical hermeneutics, essentially that of Gadamer and Ricœur, to try to correct this difficulty. Returning to Heidegger's annunciating philosophical hermeneutics gives it a more extensive meaning than it had had in Heidegger. This need to return from existence to enunciating is well formulated by Ricœur (1986). But it is Gadamer (2002), going to Heidegger against himself, who applies annunciating of Heideggerian Being also to the Being of enunciating itself, so problematizing enunciating, beyond the true or false on Being fact-based scientific statements until the fictional literary texts. Ricœur, for his part, proposes a more complex theory of reference in fictional texts, making the "as if" one of the powers of Being. A vection to enunciating is also included in *Dasein* that is now seen as a need to become text, of any kind, scientific or fictional, they are. Therefore, *Dasein* constitution is seen, not only as the pre-understanding of Being and as the annunciating of Being to the breaking of any enunciating, but also in its need to become factual or fictional texts, if we can refer to this Genette's distinction (1986), and beyond works of all art forms. There is the same *Dasein* that announces itself to the breaking of enunciating as the Being itself of enunciating. Enunciating is not so transparent to itself as one might think. It is partly obscure to itself, as says Gadamer (2002: 125): *"Being is not determined in a fair way in its being if it's simply understood as the object of a possible representation. It's that it's also part of its Being to be able to refuse itself"*. Being of enunciating also manifests itself at the breaking of itself to let appear the rooting of enunciating in *Dasein* hermeneutic constitution. In epistemological terms, opening up another dynamic unit of semiotics and hermeneutics, ES calls to Heidegger's philosophy enlarging its hermeneutic circle temporal structure of anticipation to the whole life of signs, and above all, against Heidegger but in line with Gadamer, to a return on enunciating in order to question it on the Being itself of enunciating. In other words, ES roots in Heidegger's philosophy and overcomes it questioning Being on the need for existence to become signs, texts or artistic works, and on the Being itself of signs or texts enunciating.

1.3. ES is entirely in line with the current hermeneutical philosophy going both in the direction of Heidegger's existence philosophy and beyond Heidegger's opposition between enunciating and annunciating. But, as musical semiotics, ES has to question how *Dasein* possesses this vector property to become meaningful musical utterances (signs or texts), and forces us, going this time to Gadamer but against him, to question *Dasein* on its constitutive nature of musical hermeneutical experience. Back from annunciating to enunciating musical hermeneutics, indeed, questions *Dasein* on its power to becoming musical meaningful (signs or texts) utterances. It incorporates the OB (". . .of Being") Heidegger's philosophy (a path from enunciating of Being to annunciating of Being) but prolongs it by reversing it in a BO ("Being of. . .") philosophy that incorporates to *Dasein* the Being of enunciating (more particularly the Being of musical enunciating one), as we see in the diagram: (Figure 1)

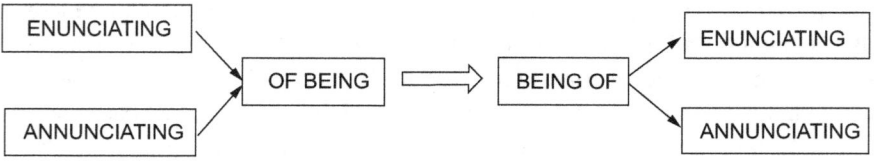

Figure 1: From a OB philosophy to a BO philosophy.

We can report to the first issue (musical enunciating of Being) through Merleau-Ponty's (1964: 13–14) judgment: "*To the writer, to the philosopher, one asks for advice and judgment, one does not accept that they hold the world in suspense, one wants them to take a stand, they can't decline the responsibilities of the talking man. Music, on the other hand, is too far from the world and the designated to appear anything other than the purities of the Being, its flow and ebb, its growth, its bursts, its whirls.*" It is also what we read in the scepticism of Molino's and Nattiez's musical semiology (a semiology of meaningless musical signs), as well as of their resulting protonarrativism (Nattiez 2011) (supposed incapacity of musical works to narrate). – The second issue (annunciating of Being to the breaking of enunciating) is Heidegger's philosophical theme imported in philosophical (even musical) hermeneutics. – In the third issue (Being of enunciating, and, notably, musical enunciating), we recognize the main theme of methodical musical hermeneutics (Vecchione 1997, for instance), a hermeneutics that questions the Being of musical enunciating on its power to form itself in signs, symbols or musical works understood in their various kinds of textuality (narrative or rhetorical texts like seduction, trope, argumentation etc.). – The fourth issue (Being of diverse types of annunciating, enlarging the understanding of *Dasein* and its annunciating to the annunciating of enunciating, and more specifically to musical enunciating) aims to incorporate into musical hermeneutics questioning on *Dasein* annunciating power. The inversion from an OB ("...of Being") philosophy to a BO ("Being of...") philosophy allows ES to leave the musical enunciating scepticism for a questioning on the real non-naive power of music to manifest Being. This is what ES, among the other musical languagiarity sciences (musical narratology, musical semantics, musical rhetoric etc.), aims to participate in.

Questioning musical enunciating is questioning musical works on their spoken but also on their forms of speaking (Vecchione 1997). Not only the silent spoken of musical utterances but the musical silent forms of speaking are to be interpreted, deciphered, and understood as such. It is a systematic refusal to investigate the musical spoken and the musical speaking that animates formalistic musical semiology and protonarrativism assumptions, as if the answer to the question of the nature of musical enunciating was to be decreed in advance, naively relying on appearances, and was not to be questioned. Sense of musical works (conceived as musical utterances, signs or texts in their spoken and forms of speaking) demands to be read, creating another opposition, within musical enunciating between SPOKEN and SPEAKING, the musical hermeneutics, aiming to reunify the two broken hermeneutical fields inherit Heidegger (the methodical and the philosophical one), is searching to articulate in a single dynamic unit the Heideggerian difference (ENUNCIATING vs ANNUNCIATING of Being) with the methodical enunciating difference (SPOKEN vs SPEAKING).

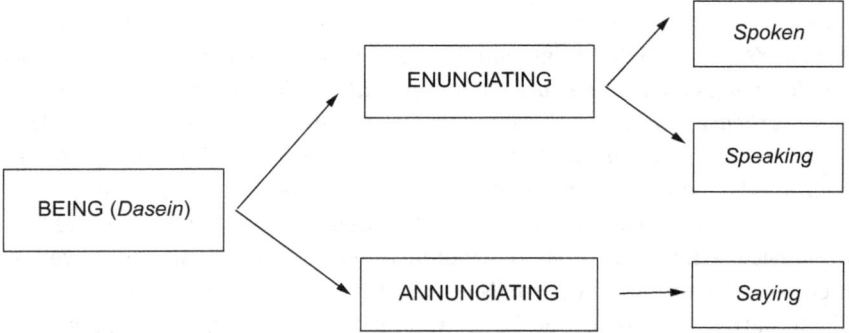

Figure 2: BO philosophy of enunciating / annunciating.

Like other musical languagiarity sciences, ES questions *Dasein* on its musical hermeneuticity: *Musiklichkeit*, this part of Gadamer's *Sprachlichkeit* that is the constitutive hermeneutical experience is deploying itself in various kinds of meaningful musical signs or texts. Finally, questioning this *Dasein* vection to musical enunciating, this need for existence to produce musical meaningful utterances, ES must go to Gadamer against Gadamer, overcoming Heidegger by hermeneutical philosophy, then enlarging this later by musical hermeneutics questioning *Dasein* on its *Musiklichkeit*: the involvement of music in the construction of our hermeneutical experience of the world.

2 ES Gadamer's hermeneutics enlargement: Questioning *Dasein* on musicianity

2.1. The movement towards Heidegger's *Dasein* is not enough. We must also question it on its power to deploy itself in a musical enunciating. Or better: in a musical *hermeneia*, which brings together the silent annunciating of Being to the breaking of musical enunciating (musical philosophical hermeneutics) and the musical enunciating (musical methodical hermeneutics) divided, in the case of music, in a silent spoken and a silent speaking. Ricœur's question of the becoming text of existence includes, as a singular case, that of the becoming meaningful musical signs and texts enunciating, and allows us not only to question musical enunciating on its true nature but also on the musical hermeneutical nature of *Dasein* that allows it to deploy in meaningful signs or texts musical utterances. The problem, I called *musication* of existence (Vecchione 2009: 267), roots in this part of *Dasein* hermeneuticity we can characterize as kneaded with musician experience that I called (Vecchione 2009: 267) *Musiklichkeit* or *musicianity*.

Gadamer's philosophy defines existence as an experience of life: the experience we gain from our insertion-world, from which participates the experience of oneself, of the other, and of the relationship we have to others, the constitutive nature of doing together – which, let us note it, is particularly present in the musical making. Gadamer relates the experience to the *Dasein* structure of anticipation of understanding and poses experience as a constitutively hermeneutical one (*Sprachlichkeit*) that would allow us to understand, not only how meaning comes to the sign, the symbol or the text, but also how existence can be expressed in enunciating. How can *Dasein* be intended to be expressed in utterances of various kinds, linguistic (literary, philosophic, scientific), but also artistic (plastic, musical, choreographic), and even polysemiotic (opera, movie, media, digital hypertext of the web etc.)? The problem is particularly complex with regard to the question of musical fictional enunciating and its rooting in *Dasein*. Gadamer (1996a: 411) links the hermeneutic experience to *"the essence of language of the experience of the world"* (*das Wesen der Sprachlichkeit der Weltlicher Erfahrung*), and considers that, if the meaning of discourse is to be sought *"upstream"* of the utterance, it is that *"this upstream of the utterance is still language, or more accurately* [. . .] Sprachlichkeit" (Grondin 1993: 263). It is in this concept of *Sprachlichkeit* that, as Ricœur says (1986: 351), philosophical hermeneutics "culminates". But what does Gadamer mean by *Sprachlichkeit*? For Ricœur (1986: 351), it is *"the linguistic dimension of any experience"* (*"la dimension langagière de toute experience"*). But, specifically, says Grondin (1993: 265), *"for Gadamer* Sprachlichkeit [. . .] *does not refer only to the 'linguistic' character of our experience of the world* [. . .], *but rather to the language virtuality, the search for meaning, the need for, what seeks to be understood, to become language."* The coming to expression is thus an essential condition of this virtual language constitution of experience. Thus, not only the general theme of *Dasein* is concerned by hermeneutics, but also the specific one of music towards *Dasein*, music in *Dasein*, how *Dasein* is musical, or how musical is *Dasein*, more specifically how *Dasein* is shaped as an experience of music by the musician. What I called *Musiklichkeit* or musicianity is this part of *Sprachlichkeit*, which, to recognize the inscription of musical experience in *Dasein*, I have called, not linguisticity but languagiarity of existence, a form of languagiarity that encompasses its linguistic forms as much as all its non-verbal one.

On behalf of music, the ES question is: how is Tarasti's musical pre-signity in *Dasein*? To solve it, we must go to an enlargement of Gadamer's hermeneutical philosophy. Something exists as a *Musiklichkeit*, understood as *Sprachlichkeit* of the musical experience, which also forms *Dasein* and in what reading of music (as spoken, speaking, and saying of Being to the breaking of musical enunciating) is made possible. Understanding ES is to understand both how, as existential, ES roots in Heidegger's philosophy, and how, as semiotic, as a science of musical enunciating, ES forces us to overcome Heidegger's philosophy, going to post-hermeneutical philosophy to understand how returning from *Dasein* to enunciating (signs, and more generally, texts, including non-verbal ones); and, then, how anchoring in *Dasein* the languagiarity of the musician hermeneutics experience of the world. Thus, we enlarge philosophical hermeneutics to a musical one, and more largely to a hermeneutics of non-verbal human activities. Musical hermeneutics is a post-Heideggerian philosophical hermeneutics that must go to Gadamer's hermeneutics and enlarge it to the questioning of *Dasein* on its musicianity. Hence, the issues: how are the ES involvements in post-Heideggerian philosophical hermeneutics? And how are, to transcend it, its involvements for adapting it, with musical hermeneutics, to specific musical enunciating? ES can be understood as this double movement of going to Heidegger and returning from Heidegger to philosophical hermeneutics, questioning it on the essence of *Dasein* endowed with hermeneutical musician experience. Going to Heidegger's philosophy is going from musical utterance to existence (ES as existential), but, in line with Heidegger's philosophy, returning from existence to musical enunciating is only possible by reaching *Dasein* annunciating to the breaking of musical enunciating and not by reaching musical enunciating itself. Going from existence to musical enunciating (ES as semiotics) needs then to overcome Heidegger's philosophy by going to Gadamer's philosophical hermeneutics, and going to philosophical hermeneutics needs to enlarge it to a musical (and more generally a non-verbal) one. Hence, the questions: What is musical enunciating? What is it this becoming sign or meaningful musical text that *Dasein* calls? What does this *Dasein* need to become signs or meaningful musical texts? By this double movement of rooting in Heidegger's philosophy, then overcoming it, as Charles (2007) says, an enlargement of Heidegger's hermeneutical circle, we find in Gadamer's hermeneutics enlarged to musical hermeneutics questioning *Dasein* on its musical (and more largely non-verbal) hermeneutical experience of the world and on the Being of musical enunciating as resulting from the *Dasein* need of becoming meaningful musical signs or texts, ES shows all its importance and its innovative character.

At this point, we must return to Gadamer's concept of *Sprachlichkeit* to question it on the understanding of the *Sprachlich* at what it refers. For Gadamer, language is the *"medium of hermeneutical experience"* (1996a: 405), and *Sprachlichkeit* the constitutive linguisticity of any experience of the world, the determination not only of the *"hermeneutical object"* (1996a: 411) but also of the *"hermeneutical operation"* even in its completion (*Vollzug*) (1996a: 418). How do we understand "language" in Gadamer's hermeneutical philosophy? We can stick to the *strict* sense given by Gadamer, namely as *"the original linguisticity of our hermeneutical experience of the world."* But semiotics has expanded "sign empire" beyond verbal signs, and ES and musical languagiarity sciences also to specific meaningful musical signs and texts. So, we must give to the term of language its most extensive meaning, by considering verbal language (linguisticity) only as a form of languagiarity among others. The field of *sprachlich* must be extended to all that *"infuses and transits all experience"* (Ricœur 1986: 59). That is why, I prefer in musical hermeneutics to give to the Gadamer's concept of *Sprachlichkeit* a more extensive meaning than its strictly Gadamerian one and consider it more as a principle of languagiarity, without reducing it to linguistic languagiarity (linguisticity), but extending it to any form of languagiarity, even non-verbal (iconic, musical, choreographic, and so on). *Sprachlichkeit* is at work in every languagial tradition. A languagiarity of principle at work in all fields of languagiarity, non-verbality as well – a non-verbality envisaged from the practice (the poïetic field), which one would understand as, from the beginning, constitutively languagiarity but of its own languagiarity, and, by its own means, a vector of languagiarity. (Vecchione 2009: 263–271). From this point of view, the non-verbal field has a languagiarity of principle in the same way as the verbal languagiarity, but, although it participates in the same legitimacy as if to say what the essence of the constitutive languagiarity is of any experience; the *Sprachlich* in it wears its brand. So if we question *Dasein* on its musical experience constitution (its *Musiklichkeit* or musicianity), we must recognize that this coming to sense through the musical (this coming from our experience of the world to its *musication*) does not escape the rule of any meaningful utterance. For the musician, its musicianity is this *Dasein source* of meaningful musical signs or texts, or, more precisely, the *Dasein* rooting of its musicianity, a *Dasein* partly made up of musicianity. A *Musiklichkeit* exists, which participates in the determination and extent of the *Sprachlichkeit*. *Musiklichkeit* is *Sprachlichkeit* revealed by the musicated enunciation of the world; by the *Musiklichkeit* virtues of its musicated expression, its musication of experience refers to what the music enunciating is talking about *Dasein*. This constitutive relationship of music to *Dasein* (this rallying of music to *Dasein* and the musication of existence we find in meaningful musical utterances) forms the sense of languagiarity of the musical, a sense of languagiarity that the musical itself has, that it is, and which defines the original hermeneuticity of music, the constitution of *hermeneia* of the musical. It is because music in itself has a sense of languagiarity, the sense of its silent constitutive languagiarity, that it is hermeneutical – or, more precisely, *hermeneia*. If one wonders what our musicianity has to do with *Dasein*, and if or what *Dasein* has to do with our musician experience of the world, the musician experience that we are, the answer is: our *Musiklichkeit*, the *Sprachlichkeit* of our musicianity, also forms *Dasein*. Unless it is *Dasein* who, by its constitution of existence, its constitution of experience, proves to be musicianity; and *Musiklichkeit, Sprachlichkeit* of our musicianity. Daniel Charles (1978: 220) says it explicitly: "*Sein und Zeit asked, about the "voice of consciousness": where does the call come from? who calls Dasein? And the answer was: the voice speaks of nowhere, of nowhere other than where "It" speaks, nowhere other than inside Dasein.*" If music speaks, it can only be from within the *Dasein* that this power of speaking comes, and not only to let Being say to the breaking of music enunciating but by this power of *Dasein* to form itself in utterances, its power of enunciating. So, not only *Dasein* says the Being of music, the Being of our musician experience, our insertion-world and insertion-music, but also *Dasein* is originally and constitutively musicianity, *Musiklichkeit, Sprachlichkeit* of our musicianity. *Dasein* says itself in annunciating, but it also speaks musician. Also, it is because it is, among other things, constitutively musicianity (*Sprachlichkeit* of our musicianity, and musicianity of our *Sprachlichkeit*), that it allows us to produce meaningful musical signs and texts, and to read a meaningful musical utterance, to interpret it (both as performance and as understanding, as an analytical reading of this meaningful enunciating). *Dasein* is this potential for languagiarity of our musical experience, our insertion-world, our insertion-music, but also of our musication of this potential of languagiarity, that it is, from the outset, formed of what Tarasti calls pre-signity, and that it has, by its *Dasein* transcendence property, the power to deploy itself in later musical act-sign and in a spread of musical post-signs by revisitation, rereading, rewriting, re(con) figuration through cultures and societies. The musical experience is active as an understanding of the world, and, through the music it produces, of our world-insertion, world situation, i.e. of our existence and our existentiality (existential character of our existence). It is not only an expression of our existence, but also the existence of our expression; to say our existence, at the door of our expression, to refer to Heidegger, but also to say the Being of our expression. Music is existence and existentiality. Through it, silently, our existence speaks. Daniel Charles (1978: 270) says: "*We have [. . .] to return to the indispensability for Being to be said by man.*" Not only as annunciating itself but also as the Being of enunciating (musical enunciating).

2.2. As far as music is concerned, hermeneutics will have to understand how musicianity participates in *Dasein* hermeneutic experience of the world and its constitution of languagiarity. How does the musical fit into a hermeneutic experience? As any human experience, musicianity is endowed with *Sprachlichkeit*. If I ask what *Sprachlichkeit* is for musicianity, I answer that it is the *Sprachlichkeit* of musicianity (*Musiklichkeit*). Hence, for ES and the other musical languagiarity sciences, questioning the musical enunciating on its spoken and on its forms of speaking: narrative forms (Tarasti 2004, Graböcz 2007, 2009, Vecchione 2008a, 2014, for example) and rhetorical forms (Vecchione 2007), under its varied properties of phaticity (listener attention capture), seduction, persuasion, argumentation (Vecchione 1997b, 1998), stylistic optimizations, trope figures (Vecchione 1999, 2001, 2008b), and so on. Where does this skill to read it, that is ours, come from? The problem is that of the musical sign or text sense advention; it is different from that of mere invention-sign, to which semiotics, in its post-classical state, had attached itself. Musical hermeneutics situates this skill in the experience that not only we have of music (musicality) but that also we are (musicianity), knowing that it is included in the more general experience we have of the world (existence) and that it participates in it as the specific musician experience of life.

It should be noted that Heideggerian Being theory applied to the relationship between music and musicology leads us to the same conclusions. Phenomenology of music is going to the music itself, regardless not only of what the music is or has been so far but also of what new musics will be in future (Being in perpetual advention). But phenomenology of music is also moving what has so far been said on music, as well as in musicological theory than in vernacular discourses, the discourses of daily life on music and the musical. We are thus led to distinguish, within the musical phenomenon, not only between music and musicology but also between the de facto musics (the being of this or that music) and the musical itself (the Being of the musical, the Be-musical). What is it to be music? It is certainly not to be music solely in this or that way but to be it both in every way and simultaneously to be like music until now has never been. Hence, the methodological importance of considering the new in music (Vecchione 2008b); also the importance to distinguish between the finite character of such musics and the infinite character of the musical has never completed in a de facto music (a factual music), because it is always revealing itself only by aspects, and always requiring other new musics to reveal itself in other aspects. A musical, thus, in perpetual deployment from one musics to another, and in a process of fundamental incompletion (since other music will emerge in the future, of which now we cannot imagine how they will be, but of which we are already sure that will deploy in new manners to be music, new aspects of the musical Being, this plastic power to be music in this or that way always otherwise). – What is valid here for the musical in its entirety is also true, in ES, for the implication of *Dasein* transcendence in the entire life of a sign, and especially for the post-sign musical semiotics, where one cannot know how an act-sign will unfold in later post-signs. In the process of post-sign, for an act-sign, some post-signs are already known to us (factual post-signs), but others are still solely in power (potential post-signs). The phenomenon of post-signity belongs to the advention of the being-deployed of an act-sign in post-signs, and so to the transcendence property of *Dasein*. Being of the musical is always unfinished. It is the being power of the musical (*posse*) to always become music otherwise. Also, being of post-signity (the power of an act-sign, by reading, rereading, rewriting, re(con)figurating, unfolding post-signs always otherwise) is always unfinished. Hence, the ES insertion into the infinite (for this reason, Charles (2007: 137–142) says "in(de)finite") Pierce's semiosis is quite compatible with the reference to Heidegger's philosophy. This is what the hermeneutical approach derived from Heidegger's philosophy, thus, recognizes to the Being, not only its Being (*esse*) but in addition its power-being (*posse*), which is its power to deploy itself in any field, always and everywhere, otherwise (Vecchione 2008b, 2013). – Thus, our distinction between the de facto musics and the musical, that is a matter of *Dasein* transcendence, of what Heidegger calls the adventure of Being, and on the behalf of music the adventure of Being-musical. Being in the making requires advention; and Being of the future requires incompletion, un-knowledge, surprise, openness, availability at reception, astonishment. For the musical, power to be in constitutively in(de)finite.

The power music has to perform meaning and the skills we have to read it as well, post-Heideggerian existential semiotics and musical hermeneutics situate them in this precondition, *Dasein*, our constitution of being there always understanding, formed of a hermeneutic experience constitutively *Sprachlichkeit*, and that would require, less to deploy itself in implementation (pro-duction), than to announce, on the occasion of implementation, to the breaking of any (and thus musical) enunciating. Beyond Heidegger, however, musical hermeneutics brings us back to the musical utterances (the spoken and the speaking of music), that is to say, it brings us back from the Being-musical to the de facto musics being, to the being of this or that singular music, singular work, and singular utterance of music. However, the reference to Heidegger plays here against this return from existence to the music enunciating. No longer a presentation of the work, or even a presentation of Being by the work; but an underlying presence, joint, adjacent, silent, absent from the utterance. What I described as the silent *hermeneia* of the musical (Vecchione 2009, 2013): behind its constitution of musical utterance (a construction always historically marked, and which orients reading towards the Being of enunciating rather than the Being annunciating itself to the breaking of annunciating), behind what musical utterance constructs, what musical work for speaking makes come as a musical utterance, a presence of Being, which remains, in the background, always constitutively (albeit always silently) saying. Music is silent on this annunciating of Being, but also on the spoken and the forms of speaking of its enunciating, and less on the power-being of the musical than in the experience that always it is (musicality) and that always we are (musicianity), and that allows us, not only to be but also to write, read, apprehend, interpret, understand, and alter, rewrite, review, revise. We can say that it is this experience that we are and that kneads not only the musical utterances than our competence to understand, live it, that ES is interested in.

2.3. Understanding ES is, then, to overcome Heideggerian philosophy by post-Heideggerian hermeneutics, specifically enlarged to the fictional musical enunciation of experience. But how do we overcome Heidegger's difficulty? How is existence appealed to becoming musical meaningful enunciating? *Dasein* must be understood as Being in a larger sense: as a Being that also includes the itself Being of enunciating as well as the itself Being of annunciating – and, notably, the itself Being of musical enunciating or annunciating. Under Heidegger's thesis, as Being announces itself only to the breaking of enunciating, enunciating would seem to be placed by Heidegger out of the Being itself. But, if Being is the Being that includes all beings, it must also include this *Dasein* property, not only annunciating itself to the breaking of enunciating, but also of the understanding of enunciating itself. Hence, the importance of musical languagiarity sciences, including ES, disciplines wider than literary, juridical or biblical hermeneutical studies. It is understanding how *Dasein* pre-understands musical meaningful signs and texts utterances, as a manner of saying musics *Dasein* can be, and needs to expand our understanding of Heidegger's *Dasein*, and notably includes in it further musications as possible musical meaningful enunciating developments. Gadamer's hermeneutics enlargement to musical enunciating contains this questioning of *Dasein* on the becoming meaningful musical signs and texts enunciating; and thus, on what Tarasti calls pre-signs. How does musicianity participate in *Dasein* constitution? What are the needs of musicianity to develop itself in meaningful musical enunciating? We can include in musicianity this need to overcome itself in such an enunciating, and, since *Dasein*, as partially woven of musicianity, conceive musicianity as endowed like *Dasein* with transcendence. Musicianity is pre-signity, and more generally need to become meaningful musical signs or texts enunciating. For musical hermeneutics (Vecchione 2009 for example), this need of musical enunciating, of musication of our experience, this becoming meaningful musical signs and texts, come from this inscription in *Dasein* of the musical hermeneutical experience – that is to say: a *Musiklichkeit*, the silent herménéia of experience, constitutively *Sprachlichkeit*, languagiarity of musical experience silently present in any musical advention enunciating as act-sign or post-sign.

Where does the musical sign come from? What does, from our experience, come to form a musical sign? What is this pre-signitive nature of pre-sign that vectors its later constitution as a sign? How is understanding pre-sign as *Musiklichkeit Dasein* constitution? The answer is to be sought in the Heideggerian thesis of a constitutively pre-ontological nature, the pre-understanding constitution of *Dasein*, adopted in Tarasti's ES while being wary of what exactly this term pre-ontological would mean in Heidegger's definition. If we want to understand how musicianity, the *Musiklichkeit* of any experience, is that what every musical experience constitutes, we must understand how *Dasein* and ontology are, from the Heideggerian origins, linked in hermeneutic, and how, from the beginning, they stand out. *"The understanding of Being is itself a determination of Dasein to be."* (Heidegger [1927] 1986: 36). But Heidegger (1986: 36) adds: *"What distinguishes Dasein [from all other ontic beings] is that it's ontological".* However, for the Dasein, *"being-ontological does not yet mean here: to set up an ontology"* (1986: 36). *"If we reserve the use of the term ontology to the theoretical questioning of the being of Being,* Dasein's *being-ontologicalness to which we think is characterized as pre-ontological. But this does not mean something as simple as being ontic: pre-ontological means instead that it enters into the way of being of Dasein to be an understanding of Being."* (1986: 36). It is precisely concerning this definition of the understanding of Being that a hermeneutics of the non-verbal can take a path that generalizes the Heideggerian thesis. In what forms does this understanding of Being that enters into the way of being of *Dasein* unfold? For Heidegger, the philosopher, it would seem mainly in the form of what, from experience, can come to the poetic, literary or philosophical text. But can *Dasein* become sign or text in another way? Like in music for example, or any other non-verbal language activity? Certainly, Heidegger calls existence *"the very being in relation to which Dasein can behave in this or that way and towards which it always has a certain attitude."* But, as we see, the question is less to understand what is in itself this signity which is that of the sign and makes be sign the sign, than to understand the originatedness of this process of setting-in-sign, what this becoming-sign imports, by forming it, by "refiguration of experience" would say Paul Ricœur, of what Heidegger calls our own constitution of being-connected: *"Dasein, as soon as it's, has each time already woven a privilege with a 'world' of encounter; by definition, to its being belongs this being-connected"* (Heidegger 1986: 125). The musical also defines in its own way this belonging, "reliance", "conjointureness" of the sign, of any sign (Heidegger 1986: 121). The question is also to understand how musical is originally pre-signed, pre-ontological. Or more precisely – because an ontology of the musical, in the sense Heidegger defines ontology, *"theoretical questioning of the being of the Being"* is rather to be a matter for musicology, theoretical questioning of the Being of the musical being – the question is to understand how this pre-signitive musical is constitutively and originally already triple-oriented: pre-ontological (towards a possibility to deploy later in an explanation of the musical by the words of musicological discourses), but also pre-ontopraxic and pre-ontoesthesic. Except to give the term pre-ontological a broader sense than that it strictly has in the Heidegger's text. For, from the outset, and especially in the musical, the further advention of a sign is made by the combined powers of producing and receiving, and the understanding of the musical as reading

(*Auslegung*) unfolds not only in the explanation of the musical by words (musicological discourse), but also in the explanation of the musical by its own deployment (the power of the musical to always be music otherwise), and its auditory reception itself (where the being of listening can always deploy itself in other forms of listening and always differently). Pre-ontopraxic opens us to the musician experience that comes to produce and perform musical works; pre-ontoesthesic opens us to the listener, the experience of listening to music that comes to perform in the auditory relationship to music (another form of understanding of being-listening, which originates in three types of listening, as I introduced (Vecchione 2008a): psychological (listening to music by a listener), poetical (the perspective of listening embedded in work, and that it proposes to its recipient to be better understood), and hermeneutical (listening to work, the availability in which we confront it, not only to seize its utterance but also the listening perspective it offers its audience). In performing, it is music that itself thinks of itself through its productions. But silently.

Thus, the problem of advention musical sign or text cannot be confused with that of the invention musical sign or text (figurative, narrative, rhetoric). Semiotics to come will combine textual enunciating with their situational source, but also with their existential source. A hermeneutics will determine it, which will include existential semiotics in the general problem of musical saying: a problem not limited to that of music enunciating (the signitive nature of music cannot be limited to the manifest, the musical appearances) nor to that of "keeping-traces" (the problem of meaning is not limited to the question of its productive causes; the meaning as meaning is out of causality) (Vecchione 2007: 276–281). What is indeed saying under the musical sign and text enunciating, against its spoken and against the intent to speak of its enunciator? Advention-sign cannot be confused with invention-sign, because inventing a sign is above all answering, and knowingly. Responding with a singular enunciating device, more or less intentionally produced, to a problem of communication, of negotiation with others that consciously or not, arises to its inventor. Invention-sign is a response, and enunciating response. But advention-sign is a question, it is questioning by the musical, and against it, what is saying against it, unbeknownst to it and its enunciator. Levels of enunciating – spoken, and musical forms of speaking – reveal levels of inscription. In invention-sign, the inscribed sign is only considered in its sign appearance, only at its shaping or configurating level: the level of its stating. To make a sign, to produce a sign, to invent a sign, is a transaction that takes saying into account only at this level of statement initiated by an enunciator. However, annunciating at work by the means of a musical work – or more precisely against it –, precisely because it is the saying of a "that" (Heidegger's "Es" that is *Dasein*, existence) manifesting itself to the breaking of enunciating, defines another level. As we have seen, not the levels of the spoken of enunciating and of the speaking of enunciating, but Heidegger's level of the saying of annunciating. Certainly, the speaking of the enunciator is "pro-moted" (in its meaning and its very being of musical speaking), only by an annunciating (a break, a laceration, an obscuration of the musical enunciating). But annunciating concerns both the annunciating of Being at the door of musical enunciating and the Being of musical enunciating (or annunciating). This is a darkening of enunciating itself which is not just about the annunciating of Being but also about the annunciating of its own nature of enunciating (a questioning of its own musical forms of speaking culminating in its own spoken). The enunciating order is overcome by the annunciating order that makes the enunciation disappear in order to the *Dasein* comes to say. The place where the saying lives cannot be confused with that of the appearance shown of the invented sign. The transcension sign of *Dasein*, the coming of *Dasein* to the sign in its dimension of enunciating forces us to question the very presignity and significance of this invented sign, its characters of presign, sign, and post-sign. But what is this character of a sign that makes it sign? What is its power to signifying? This character, which Heidegger calls significance, comes from the very intense nature of *Dasein*: *"This significance, with which Dasein is always already familiar, preserves in it the ontological condition of possibility so that the understanding Dasein can, while it explains it, discover something such as 'meanings'; and these, on the other hand, are in turn establishing the possible being of speech and language."* (1986: 125–126). The ontological condition, extended to the ontopraxic and ontoesthesic conditions, allows us to add: and any *poïesis*. The possible being of speech is also deployed against music and through the musician, and the possible being of music it leaves appear against and through the musician is to seek in the very nature of *Dasein* to be constitutively understanding, and while it happens, to let something of the sense of the experience shine through. The musical, thus, can bring about understanding. Also, to make an understanding, not only through the words and constructions of the verbal language – that is, to theorize, about music, on *Dasein*, languagiarity, experience, musicianity, or presignity into the musical – but to make happen, from itself, simply because of its production, understanding. It is a real-world power of the musical to be constitutively and by its means of understanding, and to make happen, by its own means, understanding. Understanding itself, its nature of *hermeneia*; the saying that manifests itself against the musical enunciating, thereby revealing the very hermeneutic being of the musical; and a deeper understanding of what speech is as what experience is, *poiesis*, hermeneuticity. The music included in its silent *hermeneia* being means this intense essence of the musical, its efficiency, its effectiveness in implementing, by its own means, understanding: understanding what is the *Dasein* saying, but understanding also what is musical enunciating, its spoken, its speaking and its saying also, the saying of *Dasein* on enunciating itself, this part of enunciating not transparent to itself. Hearing the musical is also to get along with oneself and hearing each other through it. The musical is inherently languagiarity. Also, if it is not in the sense that something similar to the functioning of verbal language (assertoric, narrative, rhetorical, phatic, seductive, persuasive, argumentative, figurative, troped etc.), that would make us qualify as such, it is in the sense of its nature to deploy the pre-understanding *Dasein*. If *Musiklichkeit* is constitutively *Sprachlichkeit*, then what hermeneutics must bring to the question is: what is understanding, what is languagiarity, what is the pre-understanding nature of *Dasein*, apart from their deployment by words? In what music participates in *Dasein*, not only to bring existence to musical enunciating but also to bring to musical enunciating not only the annunciating of *Dasein* but also the *Dasein* of enunciating.

This shift of musical hermeneutics takes the XXth philosophical hermeneutics out of its altogether narrow field of application. If it is universal, it is only within the linguistic sector, within the field of *Dasein* calling to verbal expression and it thus shows itself embarrassed to report on the *Sprachlich* of non-verbal activities. The model of the poem from which Heidegger drew his reflection on the languagiarity; the models of philosophical or of everyday dialogue, the understanding by the verbal exchange, which serves Gadamer's *Truth and Method* to bring to the philosophical text his questioning on the *Sprachlichkeit*; deserves to be extended to the expressive fields of the non-verbal, which form other functions of world understanding and offer us other possibilities for explaining than the *Dasein* only at work in its advent of verbal texts. *Dasein* also deploys itself out of the strict verbality: in works of art in particular, and specifically in musical productions, where the musical is being able to be music always otherwise. The entirety of *Dasein*, moreover, makes the weave of the musical itself with the verbal, or the plastic. Each signitive specificity is likely woven, although in varying proportions, from all the pre-signitive sources that constitute *Dasein*. Perhaps every dimension of experience remains, in a more or less explicit form, in more or less silent or more or less readable way, under dazzling deployment of other activities. Also, above all, the need for *Dasein* to come to musical enunciating, by saying itself to its breaking that manifesting Being manifests at the same time this part of Being that is the Being of musical enunciating.

The great novelty of ES is to look for the origin of the sign, rooting it in Heidegger's *Dasein*. But as ES is both existential and semiotics, it does not just go from sign to existence and hopes to be able to return from existence to meaningful musical signs or texts enunciating, thus overcoming Heidegger's philosophy by a call to philosophical hermeneutics. Existence, expanded to the existing situation in which every musical act in society unfolds, is now subject to a new expansion of understanding: to the call for *Dasein* to musical enunciating. Existence inscription, in meaningful musical signs or texts, is to question. First, on the spoken of musical utterances; then, on musical enunciating specificities (forms of speaking); and finally, on the possibilities for musication to let existence saying to its breaking. The saying of existence is thus questioned about its intentional shaping and its unintentional coming to appear; and musical work, in its anchoring in insertion-world, belonging to pre-existing enunciative style, traditions of music writing or performing, enunciative situations (that Gadamer called *Sitz-im-Leben*, the native site of a musical production). Thus, we leave the domain of musical work intentional expression for that of the musical insertion-world, musical enunciating inscription in traditions of shaping music to speak (or not, as in the case of music intentionally unspeaking and/or formalistic musical aesthetics refusing any musical ability to express), relationship to pre-existing practices (stylistic traditions), insertion of a musical utterance in a given moment, place, society, cultural circles seeking to negotiate, by this utterance thus shaped, something with other social groups, in a circumstance and for reasons. So joining the classic questioning of methodical hermeneutics: who speaks, to whom, of what, by what musical devices of writing (or rewriting), in what circumstances, and for what reasons? But adding to it another question: what is saying to us, intentionally in its will to speak, as unintentionally, by its insertion-world, musical-world, and to the breaking of musical enunciating? Also, what are the forms that take this musical breaking?

Finally, touching on the field of the new project of reunifying hermeneutics (including musical one), ES forces us to question *Dasein* on its exact nature of the musical (and more generally non-verbal) experience. What is musicianity as an experience of the world? What is *Musiklichkeit*, the constitutive languagiarity of musicianity, the hermeneutical dimension of musical experience of the world? Also, what is this call for *Dasein* to deploy itself in musical enunciating? How does the annunciating touch both the Being revelation annunciating itself to the breaking of musical enunciating, and the Being itself of musical enunciating (musical enunciating of Being and Being of musical enunciating) – anchoring enunciating in the annunciating this time of the Being of enunciating, and specifically *Dasein* annunciating in the Being of musical enunciating, the power of musical enunciating to express itself always differently? Thus, one leaves Heidegger and his theory of the incompatibility between annunciating and enunciating, for a hermeneutic theory of annunciating enlarged to annunciating of enunciating, including in the field of breaking the silent presence of the musical forms of speaking to decipher, and finally to the musical power to speak on itself. Annunciating is, thus, to see as the general annunciating of Being, including annunciating of the Being of musical enunciating, which leads us to wonder about what is given with musication. About its silent spoken and its silent speaking (methodical hermeneutics) (Vecchione 1997a): as we have seen, narrative, figurative, rhetorical, phatic, seductive, argumentative, persuasive, stylistic etc. discursive modalities of musical works, and about the saying of existence to the breaking of musical enunciating (Charles 2007, Vecchione 2009, 2013). Thus, what I called the silent hermeneia of musical (Vecchione 2009) touches three fields: musical silent spoken, musical silent forms of speaking, and silent existence saying to the breaking of musical enunciating. Even if for Heidegger, the hermeneutic circle was not a vicious circle, it is enough to know how to enter into it, post-Heideggerian philosophical hermeneutic, to which musical hermeneutic and ES force us to refer, gives hope to know how to get out. . . if *Dasein* transcendence allows us to get out.

References

Charles, Daniel. 1978. *Gloses sur John Cage*. Paris: UGE.
Charles, Daniel. 2007. De Heidegger à Tarasti: herméneutique musicale et sémiotique de l'existence. In Márta Grabòcz (ed.), *Sens et signification en Musique*, 133–154. Paris: Hermann.
Gadamer, Hans-Georg. 1995. *Langage et vérité*. Paris: Gallimard.
Gadamer, Hans-Georg. 1996a. *Vérité et méthode. Les grandes lignes d'une herméneutique philosophique*. Paris: Seuil. (Ed. orig. 1960. *Wahrheit und Methode. Grundzüge einer philosophischen Hermeneutik*, Tübingen, Mohr).
Gadamer, Hans-Georg. 1996b. Les limites du langage. In *La philosophie herméneutique*, 169–184. Paris: PUF.
Gadamer, Hans-Georg. 2002. *Chemins de Heidegger*. Paris: Vrin.
Genette, Gérard. 1986. *Fiction et diction*. Paris: Seuil.
Grabòcz, Márta. 2007. La narratologie générale et les trois modes d'existence de la narrativité en musique. In Márta Grabòcz (ed.), *Sens et signification en musique*, 231–252. Paris: Hermann.
Grabòcz, Márta. 2009. *Musique, sémantique, narrativité*. Paris: L'Harmattan.
Grondin, Jean. 1993. L'intelligence herméneutique du langage. In *L'horizon herméneutique de la pensée contemporaine*, 253–264. Paris: Vrin.
Heidegger, Martin. 1986 [1927]. *Être et temps* [Sein und Zeit]. Paris: Gallimard.
Heidegger, Martin. 1952. *Gelassenheit*. Pfüllingen: Neske.
Heidegger, Martin. 1976 [1959] . *Acheminement vers la parole* [Unterwegs zur Sprache]. Paris: Gallimard.
Merleau-Ponty, Maurice. 1964. *L'œil et l'esprit*. Paris: Gallimard.
Meyer, Michel. 2008. *De la problématologie: Philosophie, science et langage*. Paris: PUF.
Meyer, Michel. 2010. *La problématologie*. Paris: PUF.
Nattiez, Jean-Jacques. 2011. La Narrativisation de la musique. *Cahiers de Narratologie* 21|2011. http://journals.openedition.org/narratologie/6467.

Ricœur, Paul. 1986. *Du texte à l'action. Essai d'herméneutique*, II. Paris: Seuil.
Sini, Carlo. 1978. *Semiotica e filosofia. Segno e linguaggio in Peirce, Nietzsche, Heidegger e Foucault*. Bologna: Il Mulino.
Tarasti, Eero. 1998. Sur les pas de la sémiotique existentielle. In Costin Miereanu & Xavier Hascher (eds.), *Les universaux de la musique*, 43–57. Paris: Publications de la Sorbonne.
Tarasti, Eero. 2000. *Existential Semiotics*. Bloomington: Indiana University Press.
Tarasti, Eero. 2003. *Understanding/Misunderstanding. Contributions to the Study of the Hermeneutics of Signs*. Acta Semiotica Fennica XVI. Helsinki: International Semiotics Institute.
Tarasti, Eero. 2004. Music as Narrative Art. In Marie-Laure Ryan (ed.) *Narrative Across Medias. The Languages of Story Telling*, 283–304. Lincoln – London: University of Nebraska Press.
Tarasti, Eero. 2009. What is Existential Semiotics? From theory to application". In Eero Tarasti (ed.), *Communication: Understanding / Misunderstanding*, Proceedings of the 9th Congress of the IASS/AIS (Helsinki-Imatra: 2007, June 11–17), 1755–1772. Acta Semiotica Fennica XXXIV. Imatra: International Semiotics Institute.
Tarasti, Eero, 2011. Existential Semiotics and Cultural Psychology. In Jaan Valsiner (ed.), *The Oxford Handbook of Culture and Psychology*, III, 15, 316–343. Oxford – New York, Oxford University Press.
Vattimo, Gianni. 1987. Le bris de la parole poétique. In *La fin de la modernité. Nihilisme et herméneutique dans la culture post-moderne*, 69–81. Paris: Seuil.
Vecchione, Bernard. 1997a. Musique, herméneutique, rhétorique, anthropologie: une lecture de l'œuvre musicale en situation festive. In Françoise Escal & Michel Imberty (eds.), *La musique au regard des sciences humaines et des sciences sociales*, Vol. 1, 97–176. Paris: L'Harmattan.
Vecchione, Bernard. 1997b. Modélisation et heuristique dans les études sur la poésie et la musique comme argumentation. In Márta Grabòcz (ed.) *Les modèles dans l'art: musique, peinture, cinéma*, 21–65. Strasbourg: Presses Universitaires.
Vecchione, Bernard. 1998. Entre rhétorique et pragmatique : l'innovation sémantique dans les œuvres musicale de nature argumentative. In Gino Stefani, Eero Tarasti & Luca Marconi (eds.), *La significazione musicale: tra retorica e pragmatica / Musical signification: between rhetoric and pragmatics*, 341–390. Bologne: CLUEB.
Vecchione, Bernard. 1999. Tropes de catachrèse et tropes d'ironie dans le motet *Nuper rosarum flores / Terribilis est locus iste* de Guillaume Du Fay. In Jacques Viret (ed.), Communication to the Colloquium *Approches hermeneutiques de la musique*. Strasbourg: Université de Sciences Humaines.
Vecchione, Bernard. 2001. Dix leçons de silence. Essai sur la manière-trope de lire le sens musical. In Eero Tarasti (ed.), Communication to the ICSM 7. Imatra.
Vecchione, Bernard. 2007. Une approche sémiorhétorique du musical. In Márta Grabòcz, (ed.), *Sens et signification en musique*, 273–292. Paris: Hermann.
Vecchione, Bernard. 2008a. Entre poétique et herméneutique: Énonciateurs fictifs polymorphes, signes condensés, écoute multivoque. In Daniele Barbieri, Luca Marconi & Francesco Spampinato (eds.), *L'ascolto musicale. Condotte, pratiche, grammatiche*, 267–292. Lucca: LIM.
Vecchione, Bernard. 2008b. Dolce Stil Novo, Ars Nova, Nova Musica : L'idée de 'raison musicale trope' dans le motet de circonstance du Moyen Âge tardif. In Rossana Dalmonte & Francesco Spampinato (eds.), *Il Nuovo in Musica: Estetiche, tecnologie, linguaggi*, 105–122. Lucca: LIM.

Vecchione, Bernard. 2009. L'hermenéia silencieuse du musical. In Bernard Vecchione & Christian Hauer (eds.), *Le sens langagier du musical: sémiosis et hermenéia*, 351–384. Paris: L'Harmattan.

Vecchione, Bernard. 2013. Un (dé – bris de) silence de Daniel : d'un silence oublié ou d'un texte tu des Gloses sur Cage. In Márta Graböcz & Geneviève Mathon (eds.), *Daniel Charles In memoriam : des temporalités multiples aux bruissements du silence*, 259–309. Paris: Hermann.

Vecchione, Bernard. 2014. Une poétique du motet médiéval: Textes, hypotextes et niveaux de discours dans l'Ave regina celorum / *Tenor* [Joseph] / *Mater innocencie* de Marchetto da Padova. In Marco Gozzi, Francesco Zimei & Agostino Ziino, (eds.), *L'Ars Nova Italiana del Trecento. VIII. Beyond Fifty Years of Studies at Certaldo (1959–2009)*, 354–416. Lucca: LIM.

Mathias Rousselot
Lohengrin by Wagner. Existential narrative-analysis of the Prelude to act I

Abstract: A *magic formula* (Liszt, 1854: 48) inaugurates Richard Wagner's sixth opera. Lohengrin's Prelude to Act I – an emblem of romanticism – is magical, almost supernatural. Its radiance opens the imagination to an "immensity with no other setting than itself (Baudelaire, 1994: 13–14)". This Baudelaire's *reverie* was also experienced by Proust. Felt as a mystical emotion by Paul Valéry (1944: 708), close to somnambulistic ecstasy for Nietzsche, the Prelude transports us to the world of dreams.

In this paper, we'll highlight the narrative strategies deployed by Wagner in his work, thanks to the existential semiotics of Eero Tarasti (2000; 2009; 2015; 2016). We will show how conventional narrativity, organic narrativity and existential narrativity interact within the Prelude.

Keywords: Narrativity, narrative strategies, existential semiotics, Wagner, Lohengrin

*

A *magic formula* (Liszt, 1854: 48) inaugurates Richard Wagner's sixth opera. Lohengrin's Prelude to Act I – an emblem of romanticism – is magical, almost supernatural. Its radiance opens the imagination to an "immensity with no other setting than itself (Beaudelaire, 1994: 13–14)". This Baudelaire's *reverie* was also experienced by Proust. Felt as a mystical emotion by Paul Valéry (1944: 708), close to somnambulistic ecstasy for Nietzsche, the Prelude transports us to the world of dreams.

This work sometimes bewitched romantic musicians. Berlioz saw it as a masterpiece; Liszt devoted magnificent pages to it. Fascinated by the "Lord of the Ring", the Hungarian virtuoso wanted to paraphrase the Prelude, to describe his visions and his dreams.

> Wagner nous montre d'abord la beauté ineffable du sanctuaire, habité par un Dieu qui venge les opprimés, et ne demande qu'amour et foi à ses fidèles. Il nous initie au St Graal ; il fait miroiter à nos yeux ce temple de bois incorruptible, aux murs odorans, aux portes d'or, aux solives d'asbeste, aux colonnes d'opales, aux ogives d'onyx, aux parvis de cymophane, dont les splendides portiques ne sont approchés, que de ceux qui ont le cœur élevé, et les mains pures. (1854: 48–49)

Celestial, divine, the Prelude deploys its ethereal tones, densifies its timbre, intensifies the drama until the epiphanic appearance of the Grail, descends into an elegiac *unendliche Melodie*, tender and sad, then dies out gently, in a "harmonious and almost imperceptible murmur (Berlioz, 1872: 309)". Its "drawing" recalls the contours of the Sainte-Victoire seen from Bellevue, painted a hundred times by Cézanne, with its gently sloping north slope, its two small peaks, and its steeper south slope. Wagner wanted to show us a mountain, the mountain of the holy knights, where the Grail returns in the midst of a troop of angels. They appear before the theme of the Grail and disappear after a long diatonic and chromatic digression "in the depths of space".

*

For the German composer, a prelude must pose the means of execution and the musical *idea* of the opera, the constitutive principles of the drama, without revealing anything of the fate of the characters and nothing about the details of the plot. It must reveal only "the higher and philosophical question of the work, and immediately express the feeling which spreads there (1841: 34)". It should, in Lohengrin in particular (transition to the Wagnerian lyrical drama), quickly prepare the spectator for the drama, without summarizing the intrigue, at the very least, without providing precise details on the plot. If Wagner is to be believed, Lohengrin's Prelude to Act I is intended to be programmatic in this sense only. The musical ideas it contains would not narrate Elsa's condemnation, the revenge of Ortrud and Telramund, the appearance of the Knight, his marriage, etc. In addition, Wagner's commentary on his Prelude supports his correspondence and musicological writings: no character name from the libretto appears in this text. Only the Holy Grail – a metaphorical and symbolic character of the drama – figures there. The "knight" is mentioned, consecrated by the Grail, but without any particular mention on his identity, his psychology, his feelings, his destiny.

In accordance with the program commentary, only the Grail theme appears when listening to the Prelude. Heard three times in full and a fourth time truncated, it spans eight full bars.

Figure 1: Grail theme. bars 5 to 12, violin 5.

Played by two of the 8 violins during its first exhibition, it consists of two sentences, the first of which ends with a D (bars 9), 7th of the E7 chord. The second ends on the E, fundamental of the dominant chord of the main key (A major). Passionate, the theme develops in a weak ambitus (one octave). Simple, romantic as possible, it constitutes the essential of the thematic material of the Prelude. He also reappears within the opera, in bits and pieces, but also in full, especially in scene 3 of Act III. During the *Gralserzählung*, Lohengrin reveals the power of the Holy Grail with which he is invested (as well as his name), on the aria *In fernem Land*. We then hear the instrumental theme supporting the tenor aria.

The link between the composer's program commentary (*Revue wagnérienne*, 1888: 166), his Prelude, and his musicological writings seems to be confirmed. However, a meticulous analysis of the Prelude, which we propose to carry out in this article, attests that it perfectly sums up the opera. In addition to having structural similarities to the whole opera plot (music + libretto), it also condenses the most essential moments of the plot. It is therefore narrative and programmatic, at least for two reasons. And this is hardly surprising. Because we can bet, without taking the slightest risk, that Wagner had already anticipated this narrativity – although it is not really explicit in his program commentary. When he began his musical composition, from the spring of 1846, the libretto was already written (November 1845). He composed his opera in reverse, starting with Act III, and ending with the Prelude, which he wrote in one day, August 28, 1847 – before starting the orchestration. Thus, the German composer (and librettist) knows in advance the intrigue of his romantic opera: he knows its narrative content; he also knows "the superior and philosophical question" which governs him, as well as "the feeling which spreads there". It is therefore hardly surprising that – consciously – Wagner composed the Prelude in close relation to the libretto, and that both are reciprocal at some level.

Here our first question will be built: we need to reveal this classic or conventional narrative of the Prelude, and its fundamentally programmatic aspect.

But is there not in the Prelude a narrativity not anticipated by Wagner? In the light of modern narratological theories, is it possible to re-envision the narrativity of the Prelude, without being limited to the analogy between the textuality of the opera (the libretto) and the music form of the Prelude? Is the work narrative only in a conventional sense, or can we detect a non-programmatic narrativity, an existential narrativity (Tarasti 2009)?

What does the Prelude tell us? What is his secret plot?

1 Conventional narrativity

The Diguer's narrative scheme (1993) can offer a way to understand the Prelude, because it makes it possible to establish an obvious correspondence between its form and that of the plot, by showing that the points of attraction of both are similar.

The sound contour of the Prelude (figure 2) is narrative in the conventional sense: a stable initial state (Ricoeur 1980: 38), very airy, with an almost inert harmony in A major, then a densification of the harmony and its disturbance by modulations, an increase intensity and density (orchestral mass), to a climax – triumphal – then a long dramatic descent initiated in the key of F# minor), until a new stable state, with a very airy harmony in the initial key (A major). This responds to the "classic" narrative scheme, which semioticians and linguists (such as Greimas and the Paris School) have been able to characterize in the past century, but which artists have used since antiquity, long before its theorization.

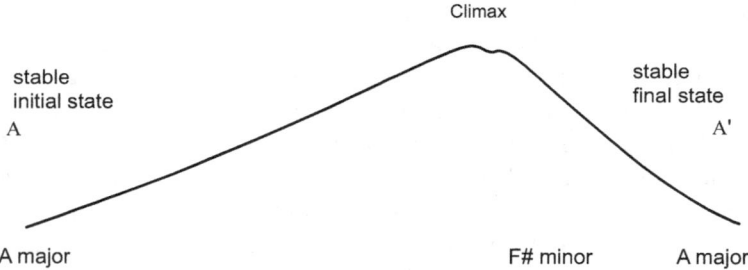

Figure 2: Prelude's «shape».

The prelude's shape, its "outline" is analogous to the sequence of events mentioned in the Wagner's program commentary. But eloquently, it is also analogous to the intrigue of the opera. The most salient aspect of the plot, of course, is the relationship between Elsa de Brabant and the Unnamed Knight. At the start of Act I, Elsa is charged with the murder of her brother; a knight is the protagonist of his dream. When King Heinrich der Vogler decides to invoke the judgment of God, the knight approaches Elsa in a basket pulled by a swan. So, the decor is set. This initial state, represented by the knight's approach to Elsa, is stable. He is disturbed when Lohengrin meets Elsa, and proposes to fight Telramund in order to defend her. This meeting evolves with the adventures, having for climax the revelation of the identity of Lohengrin, definitively sealing the fate of their union. This meeting ends at the time of the knight's farewell, when he has to break the link with Elsa, since he has revealed his line and his name: Lohengrin. When the knight retires, order is restored. Thus, we can consider that the opera develops its intrigue around a tripartite scheme: Lohengrin's approach towards Elsa, his meeting with Elsa (with the revelation, at its peak), then his farewell. The shape of the plot (figure 3) is analogous to the Prelude outline.

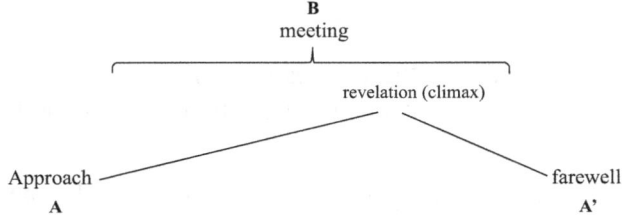

Figure 3: Plot «shape».

The tripartite division of the plot and of the Prelude, can be refined, subdivided, in order to show what are the points of attraction of the work and the narrative programs (NP) developed by Wagner within it. Louis Diguer's quinary scheme will be helpful for that task.

1) **"balance"** – initial state (figure 4), bars 1–12. (PN1) The initial state uses the key of A major, violins, flutes and oboe on the chord of A major, then F # minor, with ethereal keys, giving a feeling of weightlessness. Subsequently, the theme of the Grail (PN2) is exposed to the first and fifth violins (see Figure 1).

Figure 4: Initial state, bars 1 à 4.

2) **"Provocation"**, bars 13–50. Several phases of "provocation" (figure 5) are used, with an overall tendency to increase in intensity, to densify the harmony (first modulations). The two most salient phases are:
– phase 1. (PN3) Arpeggio of F# – (bar 13) and arrival on the leading-note (E #).

Figure 5: Bar 13.

– phase 2. (PN4) Arrival of the winds bar 20; densification of harmony, increase in intensity and densification of the timbre, resumption of the Grail motif with brass instruments.

3) **"Action"**, bars 50–56. Triumphant moment of the Prelude, in particular the fortissimo tutti (bar 54) and the Grail motif.
– (PN5) crescendo of the whole orchestra (figure 6) and timpani trill / fortissimo of the whole orchestra.

Figure 6: Crescendo of the whole orchestra, bars 50–51.

– (PN5) Arpeggio of D major (figure 7) on violins bringing us to a new fortissimo, on A7 chord.

Figure 7: Arpeggio of D major, bar 53.

– (PN6) last climax, bar. 56, corresponding to the last fortissimo, but this time without the string quartet, on G#-7^{b5} chord

4) **"Sanction"**, meas. 57–67. (PN7) The sanction is a slow dramatic descent using *unendlische melodie* (figure 8). This replaces the Grail theme: there is no longer any theme or even *motiv* development.

Figure 8: Slow dramatic descent bars 57–67.

5) **"balance"** [final state], bars. 68–75. (PN8) Balance is again reached after the perfect cadence of bars 66–67, thanks to the *stasis* in A major (figure 9), very airy, very ethereal.

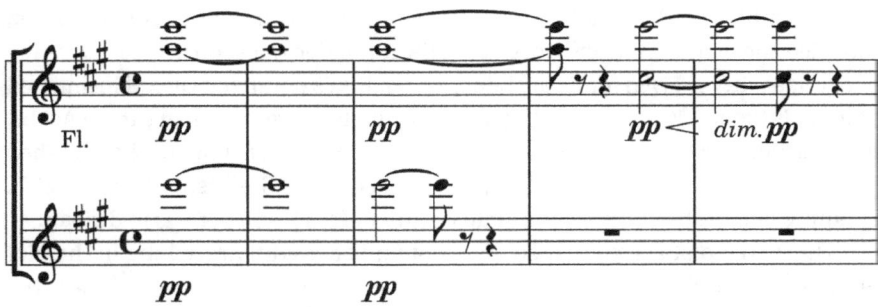

Figure 9: Final state, *stasis* in A major, mesure 68–72.

The instrumental Prelude is organized according to a classic narrative scheme, and shows a conventional narrativity: a codification specific to the narrative genre in general. It should also be noted that this codification, this standard, is eminently cultural, and therefore collectively internalized by romantic artists. Including Wagner. Thus, the opera as a whole reveals a conventional narrativity. As proof, the opera responds to what Márta Grabócz calls an elementary narrative program of the deep structure (Grabócz 2009: 59): the quinary model of Louis Diguer. We could have shown that it coincides with other classic narrative formalisms ... like the mythical actantial model of Greimas (1966: 177), or that of Etienne Souriau (1950) or that of Vladimir Propp (1928).

2 Organic narrativity

The organic level of the Prelude's narrativity refers to its specifically gestural and kinesic content, and therefore to the physical impression it leaves to the listener. But organic narrativity is not limited to the consecution of sensitive states imprinted by the work. It should be more favorably conceived as the "principle" of gestural and kinesic self-generation in the form of the Prelude.

How is a Prelude conceived by Wagner? It must establish the higher idea of the work and immediately express the feeling which spreads therein. And it is precisely this idea and this feeling that we must consider as principles, if we want to reveal an organic narrativity in the Prelude. What are these principles? And what are the compositional means – kinesic, gestural – used in the Prelude to express them?

In Eero Tarasti's theory (2009), organic narrativity is connected to conventional narrativity. So, let's turn for a moment to the plot. In Act I, Elsa is charged with the murder of her brother; the nameless knight will fight Friedrich for her, provided she marries him and doesn't ask the forbidden question. At the beginning of Act II, a party is given for Elsa. Then it was in Elsa's mind that Ortrud insinuated doubt. It's then. . . Elsa who must fight doubt with her love for Lohengrin. In Act III, now married, it is Elsa, anxious, who questions the identity of her husband. When Lohengrin finally reveals his identity, he reveals that the Grail sent him to . . . Elsa. Finally, when the Swan transforms into Gottfried, Elsa – still her – is in despair.

The whole plot is centered on Elsa, not on Lohengrin. Everything in the plot revolves around her. Contrary to what the title of the opera suggests, Elsa is the leading character in the drama. And according to Richard Wagner, "the whole point of this drama lies in what is going on in Elsa's heart." What is going on in Elsa's heart? Here it is: the principle of organic narrativity! Let us reformulate our problematic: what feeling drives Elsa deep within herself? And what idea governs this feeling? The most basic – existential – idea going through the opera is that of negation. Elsa's guilt then its negation, Elsa's hope in her savior then its negation, the disappearance of Elsa's brother then its negation (reappearance), the appearance of Elsa's savior and at the end of the opera his disappearance, Elsa's confidence in her savior and husband, then its negation, etc. In this opera, everything that directly or indirectly affects Elsa is affirmed and then denied. And on a sentimental level, this negation can be understood as a transition from faith to doubt, or from hope to doubt: a transition between her unconditional faith in her savior – object of her dream and hero coming to rescue her – to doubt in her savior, insinuated in her mind by Ortrud and Telramund. Now, this transition, this negation is quite perceptible in the form of the Prelude, on the physical level of listening. All the authors and composers cited in our analysis identified it in their own terms. After a long ascent of hope, up to the fortissimo and the intervention of percussions, timpani and cymbals (bars 51, 54, 56) – climax of the work – follows a large descending melodic line introducing doubt, despair, a negative emotional value (Rousselot 2016a) : the Wagnerian notion of "absolute pessimism ([1852] 2013)".

Let's take a closer look at the kinetic processes used by Wagner in the Prelude, allowing him to represent the ascent of faith, the climax articulating the transition from hope to despair, and the negation of faith.

2.1 Rise of faith / hope

The first part of the piece uses a typically romantic process of densification and accentuation, extended to all sound parameters: intensity, register and timbre. Music deploys this elementary kinetic power – bodily and, in fact, emotionally – like a *crescendo rossiniano* languid and spread out. It symbolizes the ascent of faith as well as the ascent to the Grail, and gives the general feeling of a growing bliss, for which harmony is also responsible. Besides, the key chosen by Wagner is not trivial. According to Mattheson, the key of A major would express happiness – Charpentier also describes it as a cheerful and rustic key (1682). But in the Prélude, the A major is above all a brilliant and lenitive key, which lends itself very well to the high registers. It is used for two exhibitions of the theme as well as for the very airy and soothing sounds of the beginning and the end. The main key quickly gives way to modulations in related keys and sometimes in remote keys, as in bar 29 where the harmonic course quickly passes through the key of the Neapolitan second degree (F major) of the key of the dominant (E major). Besides, let's allow ourselves a little digression. We hardly understand how the finesse of the harmonic sequences left Adorno with "an impression of inarticulate" and the feeling of a "lack of technical rigor", crossed by the poetic idea of "blur" (1966: 65).

The widening of the harmonic spectrum supports the rise in intensity of the dramaturgy. This "rise", felt bodily, draws on the horizon of the listener an inevitable peak. He now expects a climax, an apotheosis. This is his expectation, this is his hope.

But this hope (or expectation) remains aimless, if the object of hope does not appear on the horizon. It is the role of the theme and its three occurrences (bars 5–12, bars 20–27, bars 36–43). This is why in this part of the Prelude, Wagner closely connects organic narrativity and conventional narrativity: the physical sensation of ascent and the hope which results from it are oriented by the theme-actor towards an object: the Grail – object of the hope, and metaphorical actor symbolizing the most important male character of the opera: Lohengrin.

The treatment of thematic material is the perfect expression of Wagnerian knowledge. The theme reappears at regular intervals (or almost), with an intensification of the timbre and the sound density at each occurrence, until its apotheosis. It then sounds to the listener like an increasingly virulent reminder: "The Grail is the object of your hope!" It is during the fourth appearance of the theme that the object is finally unveiled, when the triumphant fortissimo sounded. But just before reaching this culminating summit – this luminous appearance of the Grail – Wagner makes us hear (figure 10) on the cello and the viola arpeggios (1st and 5th degrees) sounding like big breaths filled with celestial bliss, referring to the romantic theme of the ecstatic and contemplative man – which one can admire for example in the fascinating Caspar David Friedrich's Traveler. We breathe deeply, at a slow rate (*Langsam*), to the rhythm of the soul of the world (Tarasti 2009: 24), motionless, gazing with exaltation at the triumphant arrival of the object of our hope.

Figure 10: Bars 46–49.

The orchestral crescendo (bar 50) is a last breath before the vehement chord of D major (bar 51), and the luminous appearance of bar 54, corresponding to the fourth occurrence of the theme – this time truncated.

2.2 Bright appearance

Again, during this climax (of which the ascent of faith is the pre-sign), the organic, bodily, kinesic, primary narrativity (in the sense of Peircian primacy), is closely connected to conventional narrativity, of which we have said, following Wagner, that its main idea was "what is happening in the heart of Elsa". Hence our question: what does the luminous appearance in Elsa's heart correspond to? Of course, this is the appearance of Lohengrin, her savior and husband. Here we can reconnect the intrigue of the opera with this ardent and passionate moment of the Prelude: Lohengrin is clearly symbolized by bars 51 to 56 of the luminous appearance. But "appearance" can be conceived in two ways. a) The first appearance of Lohengrin is his transformation from metaphysical character to physical character, when he appears on a nacelle pulled by a swan. b) His second appearance, that is to say his transformation from knight *without name* to knight *with the name of Lohengrin*, when he reveals to Elsa his true identity. These two appearances are experienced as thunderbolts in Elsa's sentimental horizon, and it is precisely these "blows" that bars 51 to 56 can symbolize.

The aesthetic issue of the luminous appearance does not lie in the exploitation of harmony. Wagner uses the main key and the related keys, as well as secondary dominants (weak degrees, in general).
– bars 51–54 in A major,
– bars 54–56 in F # minor (with the secondary dominants of weak degrees and a very short transient modulation in E major).

The issue lies more likely in the tension created by the intensity and gravity modulations, that is to say "the sensation of gravity or weightlessness of sound: its weight on our body (Rousselot 2016a: 81)". The composer adopts a percussive, keraunic style, involving timpani and cymbals. The orchestra itself is used as a gigantic percussion on the fortissimo of bars 54 and 56. These bars are the most intense of the Prelude. Orchestral gravity strikes our body, as the appearance of Lohengrin and the revelation of her identity strike Elsa's heart. Therein lies the "organic" narrativity of the luminous appearance.

2.3 Elegiac descent

The accuracy and finesse with which harmony is displayed in the elegiac descent of bars 57 to 67 are extraordinary. The sequences of dominant seventh and ninth chords, with or without root note (diminished seventh chords), as well as the enharmonies allow the long chromatic and diatonic descents that Wagner likes, structuring his *unendliche Melodie* – which is just as much an unendliche Harmony – in which the composer saw almost a metaphysical dimension.

Why use continuous melody as a descending elegiac gesture? The continuous melody likes to descend, because the 7th (minor or diminished) and the ninth (major or minor) sound better when they follow their natural movement of resolution, when they are used as suspensions or appoggiaturas. Thus, the unendliche Melodie lends itself very well to great melancholic or elegiac romantic descents, such as that of the Prelude. Berlioz was also fascinated by this technique: "we notice there [. . .] a bass always ascending diatonically while the other parts descend: this idea is very ingenious", he said.

The constant avoidance of the cadence and the *suspension* of harmony prevent the listener from finding the comfort of the affirmation of the key, and the comfort of the tonic chord (another negation). And even when the first degree is reached (F# -), as at the very beginning of the descent with the chords F# -, DM, C#7, F#- (bars 58–59), the chord dissipates immediately in a second degree (G#) and the dominant (C#7), to reach the chromatic descent.

After the fortissimo of bar 56 – climax of the Prelude – Wagner deploys his *unendlische melodie*, until the romantic gesture (gruppetto), reminiscent of the first theme of Rienzi, announcing the perfect cadence with the ineffable C # minor chord (which we'll talk about later) then a *classical* cadence: I (sixth and fourth), V (7+), I (5)

Thanks to all these Wagnerian skills, we feel this sad and slow descent bodily, which symbolizes, if we connect this sensation to conventional narrativity, the distancing of Lohengrin in the heart of Elsa. Conventional narrativity and organic narrativity collide again.

In the work, the organic narrativity is gradually deployed. Discreet at the beginning of the Prelude, it is amplified in the thematic treatment, increase itself with the orchestral power of the luminous appearance, and increase again in the elegiac unendliche Melody.

On these three major gestures of the Prelude, oriented by negation, is anchored an existential narrative content...

3 Existential content and transcendence

3.1 Transcendence "Erscheinung" (coming out)

In Eero Tarasti's theory (2009), existential situations take place when the subject encounters Nothingness or Fullness. But we believe that transcendence can manifest itself in a third way. A third existential situation manifests when the subject is confronted with another *Dasein* than his own, more precisely when he is projected into the strangeness of this *Dasein*, into the strangeness of this otherness. The otherness is always a transcendental situation for each of us. We will see a little later how this "otherness" (heideggerian *Unheimlichkeit*) emerges in the Prelude.

We will therefore retain three existential situations: that of Nothingness, that of Fullness, and that of Otherness – three manifestations of transcendence. But how exactly do you spot these existential moments? Eero Tarasti (2009, 2016) does not provide any method. He simply advocates "watching things happen" (2009: 21), using the very phenomenological Heideggerian Gelassenheit (let – [things] -be), that is to say a posture where the subject (here, the analyst) does not expect anything predetermined. We are therefore simply confronted with the Prelude, and we let ourselves be guided by listening, without expecting that listening will conform to any *a priori* representation.

3.2 Some transcendent situations of the Prelude

The celestial light at the beginning (and end) of the Prelude is one of those existential moments. Baudelaire, Nietzsche, Proust, Liszt have experienced it. Wagner too. For him, it evokes the soul of Lohengrin (this is the transcendent aspect of the firsts bars of the Prelude). In the opera, the light flickers when Lohengrin is about to arrive on stage (the appearance of the swan in Act I), as if the spectator should be subjugated by the metaphysical hero who personifies and incarnates (Wagner 1851).

From an existential point of view, the etheric sound produced by the succession of chords on violins, flutes and oboe is clearly experienced in turn as Nothingness and Fullness: at the beginning of the Prelude, it gives the sensation of weightlessness described by Baudelaire – the vaporous ether described by Liszt; in the end, it brings soothing and comfort. This existential "travel" – characterized by the communication between *Dasein* and transcendence (2009) – is made possible by Wagner's "existential style", this style so well described by Eero Tarasti in his analyzes.

Another existential moment (figure 11) comes out on the C#- chord (bar 65) with the appoggiatura (F#), that create an empty "stack" of two perfect fifths (C#, G# / F#, C #), quickly transforming into a C#- chord, and then a C#Ø chord with the G ♮ (viola, bassoons and clarinets).

Figure 11: Bar 65, reduction of the orchestral score.

On the first beat of the measure, the chord can be interpreted as a suspended chord (sus4), infinitely empty because of the omission of the third. This void is experienced emotionally as an abandonment, a pathological despair: a situation of existential anxiety experienced as a leap into the void. In short, a musical catabasis, a dizzying fall, a plunge into the abyss, conceptually close to what Jean

Wahl calls *trans-descendance*. The entire sequence of bars 57 to 67 is a catabasis, except the *gruppetto* (the turn).

We should moreover be interested in this romantic gesture, cutting really with the rest of the melodic development of the elegiac catabasis, but also with the whole Prelude. From an aesthetic point of view, this rhetorical gesture establishes a certain elegance or virtuosity of which the work is almost completely devoid. Admittedly, Wagner uses the gruppetto as the central thematic element of the superb theme of the opening of Rienzi (bars 19 and 23), but not in the Prelude. Thus, this melodic ornament is felt when listening as strange, and from the point of view of the work, as otherness. This otherness is also a manifestation of transcendence, regarding the *Dasein* of the work and that of the listener. But here remains a question: who is this "other"? We could make a cautious suggestion here: Lohengrin is the only "other" coming from "elsewhere". This "other" could be Lohengrin. Lohengrin is the only transcendent (metaphysical) being in the work: protagonist of Elsa's dream, he "appears" (*Erscheinen*) in the work, sent by the Grail.

This intuition is reinforced by the presence of the gruppetto at various key moments in the opera. Within it, it is used only on rare occasions. It does not refer to existential moments, because it is connected to conventional narrativity (because of the libretto). It almost always celebrates or consecrates the union of Elsa and Lohengrin. For example, this melodic ornament occurs when Elsa and Lohengrin take their hands (Act II, scene 5, number 60). We also see this gruppetto in act III, scene 3, number 62, bar 47, on the words "Entbrennt mein Aug, entbrennt mein Aug" (My eyes burn, my eyes burn), while Elsa knows the identity of the Knight, finally united with "Lohengrin": the knight sent by the Grail having finally revealed his identity.

Other existential situations or moments can be experienced, such as the "breathing" of bars 46–49 (fullness), the luminous appearance of the following bars, or the elegiac descent. The listener's subjectivity and freedom makes possible many existential moments, referring to his experience and his imagination. According to Tarasti, the existential narrativity cuts us off from the conventional narrativity and the organic narrativity, to give us that freedom. But on closer inspection, existential narrativity is – like organic narrativity – connected to conventional narrativity, once the entire work is brought to our attention. There is congruence between the various types of narrativities . . . thus, the highlights of the three instances of the Prelude's narrativity coincide in fact. Moreover, it is interesting to note that the organic – bodily – narrativity of the Prelude refers to Elsa's body and heart in the libretto, carnal and emotional character of the opera, while the existential narrativity of the Prelude, refers in the libretto to the soul and spirit of Lohengrin, a metaphysical – transcendent – character of opera. This reciprocity between the organic and the physical body on the one hand, and between the existential and the metaphysical ether on the other, is probably the greatest achievement of the Prelude – beyond its sublime aesthetics. We also affirm that this reciprocity is always achieved by great works of the narrative genre. Whether literary, cinematographic, or musical, they have in common to bring characters to life and to develop situations impacting our physical body, echoing our experience and rebounding in our imagination (Rousselot 2016). They don't just narrate: through the characters and the drama, they inscribe conventional narrativity in our flesh and in our existence. We only identify with an opera or novel character through the image of ourselves (physical and psychic) that we project onto him; we only relive a romantic situation because we feel the movement of our own existence in it.

The Prelude is capable of this fabulous prowess.

References

Adorno, Theodor W. 1966. *Essai sur Wagner*. Paris: Gallimard.
Baudelaire, Charles. 1994. *Sur Richard Wagner*. Paris: Les Belles Lettres.
Berlioz, Hector. 1872. *À travers chants*. Paris: Michel Lévy frères.
Chrissochoidis, Ilias & Steffen Huck. 2010. Elsa's reason: On beliefs and motives in Wagner's Lohengrin. *Cambridge Opera Journal* 22. 65–91.
Dahlhaus, Carl. 1994. *Les drames musicaux de Richard Wagner*. Liège: Mardaga.
Diguer, Louis. 1993. *Schéma narratif et individualité*. Paris: PUF.
Dufetel, Nicolas. 2013. La Signification esthétique des harmonies non fonctionnelles chez Wagner d'après Liszt et Schoenberg: le Prélude de "Lohengrin". *Analyse Musicale, Société française d'analyse musicale*, Anniversaires Wagner – Verdi. 34–43.
Grabócz, Márta. 2007. *Sens et signification en musique*. Paris: Hermann,
Grabócz, Márta. 2009. *Musique, narrativité, signification*. Paris: L'Harmattan.
Grabócz, Márta. New Musicology. Perspectives critiques. In Makis Solomos & Márta Grabócz (eds.), *New Musicology. Perspectives critiques*, Filigrane, n° 11.
Greimas, J.-A. 1966. *Sémantique structurale*. Paris: Seuil.
Hatten, Robert. 2004. *Interpreting Musical Gestures, Topics, and Tropes: Mozart, Beethoven, Schubert*. Bloomington, IN: Indiana University Press.
Kramer, Lawrence. 2001–2002. Contesting Wagner : The Lohengrin Prelude and Anti-anti-Semitism. *19th-Century Music* 25(2–3). 190–211.
Kramer, Lawrence. 2004. *Opera and Modern Culture : Wagner and Strauss*. University of California Press.
Lacoue-Labarthe, Philippe. 1981. Baudelaire contra Wagner. *Études françaises*, Presses de l'université de Montréal, 17(3–4). 23–52.
Lavignac, Albert. 2016. *Le voyage artistique à Bayreuth*. Pari: Hachette, BNF.
Liszt, Franz. 1854. *Lohengrin et Tannhäuser de Richard Wagner*. F.A. Brockhaus.
Lohengrin, *Livret*, Lyon, Opéra national de Lyon, 2006.
Lohengrin, *Livret*, Paris, Premières loges, 2013.
Miner, Margaret. 1993. Putting the Emphasis on Music: Baudelaire and the "Lohengrin" Prelude. *Nineteenth-Century French Studies* 21(3/4). 384–401.

Nietzsche, Friedrich. 1991. *Le Cas Wagner* suivi de *Nietzsche contre Wagner*. Trans. by Jean-Claude Hémery, ed. by Giorgio Colli & Mazzino Montinari. Paris: Gallimard (Folio essais.

Pazdro, Michel (ed.). 1998. *Guide des opéras de Wagner*. Paris: Fayard.

Revue wagnérienne, 1885–1888 (tomes I, II, III), Paris [réimprimé Slatkine Reprints, 1993]. disponible via: www.gallica.bnf.fr

Ricœur, Paul. 1980. Le récit de fiction. In D. Tiffeneau (ed.), *La narrativité*. Ed. CNRS.

Rousselot, Mathias. 2016a. *Le sens de la musique. Ontologie et téléologie musicales*. Paris: l'Harmattan.

Rousselot, Mathias. 2016b. L'incontournabilité du préjugé, du sens à l'expérience. In Costantino Maeder & Mark Reybrouck (eds.), *Sémiotique et vécu musical*, Actes du colloque XIIth International Congress on Musical Signification (ICMS12), 95–107. Louvain la Neuve: Presses Universitaires de Louvain.

Strobel, Otto. 1937. Die Urgestalt des "Lohengrin": Wagners erster dichterischer Entwurf. In *Bayreuther Festspielführer*, G. Niehrenheim, 158–167.

Tarasti, Eero. 1996. *Sémiotique musicale*. Limoges: Pulim, 1996.

Tarasti, Eero. 2006. *La musique et les signes: précis de sémiotique musicale*. Paris: l'Harmattan.

Tarasti, Eero. 2009. *Fondements de la sémiotique existentielle*. Paris: L'Harmattan.

Tarasti, Eero. 2010. Daniel Charles ou le principe du non-vouloir. *Nouvelle revue d'esthétique* 5(1). 85–93.

Tarasti, Eero. 2012. *Semiotics of Classical Music: How Mozart, Brahms and Wagner Talk to Us*. Berlin: Walter de Gruyter.

Tarasti, Eero. 2015. *Sein und Schein: Explorations in Existential Semiotics*. Berlin: Walter de Gruyter.

Tarasti, Eero. 2016. *Sémiotique de la musique classique. Comment Mozart, Brahms et Wagner nous parlent*. Trans. by J.-L. Csinidis & M. Rousselot, C. Esclapez & M. Rousselot (eds.). Aix-en-Provence: Presses Universitaires de Provence.

Valéry, Paul. 1944. *Cahiers*, Pléiade II.

Wagner, Richard. 1992. *Lohengrin*. Paris: Éditions Premières Loges.

Wagner, Richard. 1841. De l'ouverture. *Revue et Gazette Musicale de Paris*, n° 5. Version numérique dudit ouvrage.

Wagner, Richard. 2013. écrits sur la musique. Paris: Gallimard.

Wagner, Richard. 1982. *Opéra et drame*. Plan de la tour, éd. d'Aujourd'hui.

Wagner, Richard. 2013. *Ma vie*. Paris: Gallimard (Folio).

Wagner, Richard, & Franz Liszt. 2013. *Correspondance*. Paris: Gallimard (coll. Blanche).

Wahl, Jean. 1937. Subjectivité et transcendance. *Bulletin de la Société française de Philosophie* 37(5).

Videography

Lohengrin DVD. Chœur et orchestre du Wiener Staatsoper, Claudio Abbado (chef d'orchestre), RM arts, 1990.

Tarasti, Eero. Entretien avec Eero Tarasti, *Retour sur la sémiotique*, accessible via http://www.archivesaudiovisuelles.fr/FR/_video.asp?id=37& ress=306& video=90306&format=68#226

Paolo Rosato
The emergence of individual subjects in Western music

Abstract: Thanks to the Homeostasis —the principle which regulates tensional-relaxation energetic processes in music as well as in living organisms— musical texts can be regarded as organic entities, and as individual subjects too, endowed of a proper inner intentionality —despite they are produced by empirical authors. Tarasti's Existential Semiotics offers theoretical tools useful in describing the combined action of different forces operating in the production of each individual musical text. By combining transcendental (Kant and Fichte), semiotic (Eco), and linguistic (Genette) approaches, this article firstly investigates the *a priori* conditions of interaction between the Subjectivity (the *Being-in-Myself*, or the *Moi*) and the Otherness (the *Being-in-Itself*, or the *Soi*) within the artistic text. Secondly, music in its concrete and historical being is analyzed with respect to the communal and individual structures which coexist in any text. By reflecting on the transformations within the ancient Plainchant, I assume a progressive passage from the slavery of the individual difference, subjected to the social identity, to its release, as in the Hegelian dialectic between bondsman and master. In such a process, the music itself discovers its potential autonomy from the word, and its own specific nature. The role of modalities (will, can, know, and must) changes alternatively, according to different perspective and points of view in the processes of individual distinction. In the Western culture the spontaneous idea of distinction has been transformed in that of a forced artistic originality at all costs, but we must not forget that *Soi* needs *Moi* in order to actually exist, but *Moi* comes out only by *Soi*.

Keywords: Homeostasis, existential semiotics, transtextuality, subjectivity, transcendence, Ich-ton, being-in-self, being-for-self

As in other complex natural phenomena, music may be comprised of organic and/or inorganic parts, and regarded as a complex system endowed with living properties (Rosato 2013).[1] Homeostasis – the principle which regulates tensional-

---

[1] Published originally in 2013 Paolo Rosato: *The Organic Principle in Music Analysis. A Semiotic Approach.* Acta Semiotica Fennica XLII. Approaches to Musical Semiotics. Helsinki: International Semiotics Institute of Imatra/The Semiotic Society of Finland.

https://doi.org/10.1515/9783110789164-049

relaxation energetic processes in music as well as in living organisms – plays a fundamental role in regarding musical texts as organic entities, and, consequently, as individual subjects endowed of proper inner intentionality, or "intention of the text" in Eco's terms (Eco 1992: 25). If musical texts are produced by empirical authors, nevertheless texts show inner strategies that are not reducible to the conscious will of such human subjects (cf. Eco 1992: 73). I have seen for myself that Tarasti's Existential Semiotics offers theoretical tools useful in describing the combined action of different forces operating in the production of each individual musical text.[2] In this article, I am applying such concepts diachronically to the hypothetical description of the first appearance and development of musical subjects in the Western tradition.

1 The notion of transcendence in music in the light of Tarasti's existential semiotics

Strictly related to the coming out of the subject – at any level of analysis – is the matter of transcendence. We can hypothesize that our process starts when a new organism comes to life. At the very beginning, we are in front of a new *Umwelt* —the inner environment— as opposed to a certain *Umgebung* – the external environment (see Tarasti 2000: 38).[3] The latter is the pure Otherness with respect to the former, which is the pure Subjectivity. But this new subject is not entirely pure: as an organism, he will possess, by means of genetic transmission, some characteristics which will condition its development and growth.

Some of these features, before any distinction between psychological and physical aspects (we can speak of psychobiological aspects), are transcendental, *a priori*, conditions of its life. That is to say, if our organism is a man, it necessarily has a brain and a connected intelligent activity *a priori*, although we can only know of which level it will be, and how it will be used *a posteriori*.[4]

---

2 See some analytical application of Tarasti's concepts to Beethoven's, Wagner's, and Chopin's works in Rosato 2013.
3 *Umwelt* depends on the interaction between inner (genetic and morphologic) and external (Umgebung) conditions; *Umgebung* depends on time-space conditions, which take shapes as acts and events.
4 On the distinction between *a priori* and *a posteriori* knowledge see Kant 2007, especially 17–21 and 37–40. Here, *a priori* is used in a non-literal meaning, as according to Kant "pure intuitions and pure concepts alone are possible *a priori*, empirical intuitions and empirical concepts only *a posteriori* (Kant 2007: 85). My sentence has to be intended as an analytic or elucidatory judgment because "nothing is added through the predicate to the concept of the subject [man endowed of

So, I want to consider the notion of transcendence in this ideal starting condition. My analysis will be always of a transcendental kind, although I do not want (yet I also cannot exclude) some 'cultural features' which were possibly transmitted genetically. These features will be considered as a possibility in our model. By following Tarasti's interpretation of Jacob von Uexküll (1992), we can call *Ich-Ton* what we called earlier Subjectivity. What is interesting in this case is that von Uexküll's theory "is based on the idea that every organism functions according to pre-established 'score' which determines the nature of its *Umwelt*" (Tarasti 2002: 98).

But how does this *Ich-Ton* act as a filter? Tarasti writes that "every organism [...] possesses its codes or something like a score, which determines which signs it accepts from *Umwelt* [here used instead of *Umgebung*],[5] and which it rejects" (Tarasti 2005: 227). The first model that shows this process is very simple: the sphere of the Subject is surrounded by that of the Otherness, i.e. transcendence (Figure 1). As there is not a Subject without a proper *Ich-Ton*, we can use the latter term as a synonym of the former.

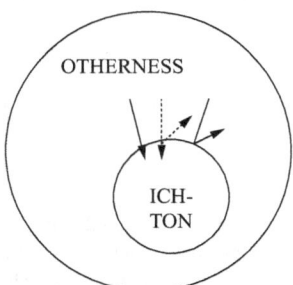

Figure 1: Ich-ton and Otherness.

In this model, we have three possible sign-relationships: signs totally accepted by the *Ich-Ton* (the first arrow from left), signs totally rejected (the third arrow), and signs partially accepted and rejected (the middle arrow).

Following Tarasti's perspective, every *Ich-Ton* presents two aspects: *Moi* and *Soi*. This articulation is internal to *Ich-Ton* in a structural way. That is to say, within each organism there is always a struggle between *Moi* and *Soi*, and also

---

brain], and the concept is only analyzed and broken up into its constituent concepts [a kind of semantic analysis] which had all along been thought in it" (Kant 2007: 43).
5 It seems to be clear that opposition between *Umwelt* and *Umgebung* does not correspond to the common use of German, but it is functional in Tarasti's discourse.

where one of them is clearly prevailing over the other one, this latter cannot ever be reduced to zero.

It is the same as in Fichte's structure of the Ego: to eliminate the Non-Ego would mean to eliminate at the same time the Ego itself.[6] Moreover, to admit the existence of the sole *Soi* would mean that organisms were totally identical with each other: to confute this idea, we can refer to Leibniz's identity of indiscernibles, according to which if two things have not got at least one difference, as small as possible, they are just the same thing.[7] The *Moi* is what Schopenhauer calls *principium individuationis*, thanks to which the absolute Will appears as individual willing subjects, determined in space and time.[8]

On the other hand, to admit the existence of the sole *Moi*, the absolute subjectivity, would imply not only the absolute incommunicability but also the absolute solipsism, because each Ego could not recognize anything but itself.[9] The elimination of one of the two aspects of *Ich-Ton* results in the elimination of the Otherness, although in two different manners. It means that no transcendence would be possible. It seems that the basic condition of our *Ich-Ton* is the presence of both the identity (*Soi*) and the difference (*Moi*), in many variable proportions (Figure 2).

---

[6] "In so far as the Non-Ego is posited, the Ego also must be posited; for both are posited as divisible in regard to their reality. And only now can you say of either, it is *something*. For the absolute Ego of the first fundamental principle is not *something*, (has no predicate and can have none;) it is simply *what* it is. But now *all* reality is in consciousness, and of this reality the part is to be ascribed to the Non-Ego which is not to be ascribed to the Ego, and *vice versa*. Both are something. The Non-Ego is what the Ego is *not*, and *vice versa*" (Fichte 1868: 83).

[7] "Definitio 1. Eadem sunt quorum unum potest substitui alteri salva veritate. Si sint A et B, et A ingrediatur aliquam propositionem veram, et ibi in aliquo loco ipsius A pro ipso substituendo B fiat nova proposito aeque itidem vera, idque semper succedat in quaecumque tali propositione, A et B dicuntur esse eadem; et contra, si edam sint A et B, procede substitution quad dixi" (Leibniz 1840: 94).

[8] "The eyes of the crude individual are clouded, as the Indians say, by the veil of *māyā*: it is not the thing in itself that shows itself to the individual, but only appearances in time and space, in the *principium individuationis* and in the rest of the forms of the principle of sufficient reason" (Schopenhauer 2010: 378–379).

[9] On the matter of artistic incommunicability, when speaking of artistic convention, Nietzsche says that "As a rule what is original is admired, sometimes idolized, but rarely understood; obstinately to avoid convention means wanting not to be understood. To what, then, does the modern rage point?" (Nietzsche 1996: 339). Such a sentence is the conclusion of the text quoted in footnote 25, the last of this article.

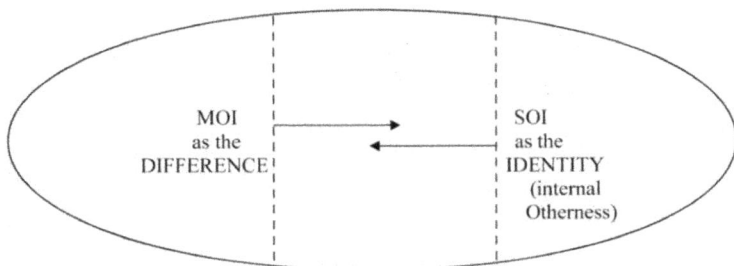

Figure 2: *Moi* as the Difference, *Soi* as the Identity.

This scheme shows *Ich-Ton* in its transcendental or *a priori* state before it interacts with an Otherness coming from outside. Opposed arrows represent the structural effort that each of the two parts makes for prevailing over the other. This is the inner transcendence of the *Moi*, with respect to which the *Soi* is the internal Otherness.[10]

But we have to analyze in which way Otherness interacts with *Ich-Ton* considered as internally articulated in being-in-myself, being-for-myself, being-in-itself, and being-for-itself. Let us see the following scheme, where a first model appears (Figure 3). In this scheme, the subject, or the *Ich-Ton*, formed by both *Soi* and *Moi* (cf. Tarasti 2005: 240), receives potential signs from outside, or the Otherness. These signs are actualized in the being-for-itself which assumes its proper (never fixed) form just in the struggle with the being-for-myself. Similarly, on the other side, where all potentialities of the being-in-myself are actualized in the being-for-myself while struggling with the being-for-itself. I remark that potentialities, of both *Soi* and *Moi*, can be studied exclusively on the basis of their actualizations in being-for-itself and being-for-myself.

---

10 The presence of such an internal Otherness can be compared with what Genette calls "*transtextuality*, or the textual transcendence of the text, which I have already defined roughly as 'all that sets the text in a relationship, whether obvious or concealed, with other texts'" (Genette 1997: 1). He had stated shortly before: "The subject of poetics, as I was saying more or less, is not the text considered in its singularity (that is more appropriately the task of criticism), but rather the *architext* or, if one prefers, the architextuality of the text (much as one would speak of 'the literariness of literature'). By architextuality, I mean the entire set of general or transcendent categories – types of discourse, modes of enunciation, literary genres – from which emerges each singular text" (Genette 1997: 1). In some lectures held at the University of Poznan and Austin, in 2016, I have adopted in a combined way both Tarasti's and Genette's categories to explain the generation processes of musical texts.

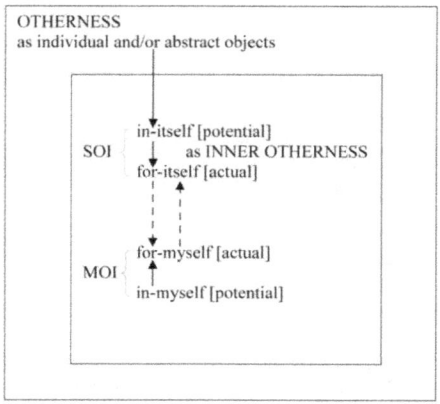

Figure 3: Otherness as individuals and/or abstract objects.

In the following scheme (Figure 4), I try to represent in which way *Moi* co-operates with *Soi* in filtering external Otherness. Sign 1 enters the *Umwelt* of *Ich-Ton* as being-in-itself. Then it is introduced in the area of the struggle between for-itself and my-self, where it is indirectly contrasted by the being-in-myself. This case exemplifies Tarasti's Diagram 5 on external and inner transcendence (see Tarasti 2005: 244).

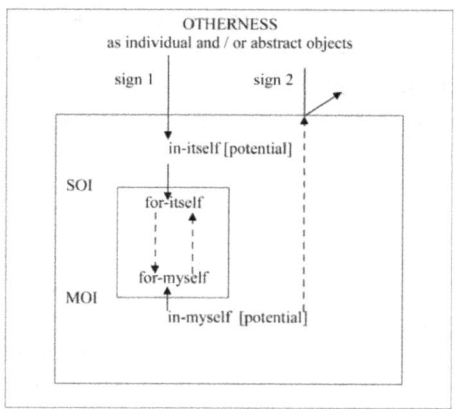

Figure 4: Co-operation between *Moi* and *Soi* in filtering external Otherness.

On the contrary, sign 2 is rejected before it can enter the *Umwelt*, because of the direct action of the being-in-myself. We can interpret this rejection in two different ways:

1) as a **physical opposition** to that sign in the perception (body as chair refutes it);[11]
2) or as a **psychical opposition** due to the unconscious action of the being-in-myself, maybe in the form of a para-praxis, i.e. a failed act.

Let us try to see in a more detailed way the possible processes of sign 1, that is a sign which can enter the *Umwelt*. In the next scheme (Figure 5), I better define two areas: that of the being-in-itself, and that of the actual subject (i.e., the surface level in which itself and myself are actualized as a result of their fight).

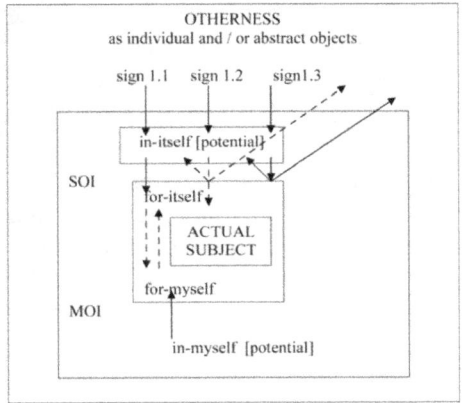

Figure 5: Being-in-itself and the actual subject.

Sign 1.1 is totally accepted in the actual subject. But what does it mean to be totally accepted? As we said, it is neither possible to reduce to zero to the *Soi* nor the *Moi*. Then, it means that a sign is accepted just as a part of a more general set of signs so that the struggle is only placed at another level. A unique sign is always a synthesis of *Soi* and *Moi*. A real piece of music – seen as a unique sign – cannot ever be a pure fugue (only *Soi*) or a pure set of sounds without any forms (only *Moi*).

Sign 1.2 enters only partially the actual subject. It means that after the fight between *Soi* and *Moi*, the subject accepts something and rejects something else. What is rejected can be put in the being-in-itself area, and used in a next situation (it goes to enrich the proper encyclopedia of the subject), or drawn out of the *Umwelt* towards the *Umgebung* and the external Otherness.

---

11 See also Eco's problems about noise, for instance in his 'elementary communicational model', 1976: 31–36.

At last, sign 1.3 is totally rejected from the actual subject, but it can remain in the *Umwelt*, in the being-in-itself area. As in the previous case, it can be also placed in the Otherness.

But what is the difference between this last case, in which a sign is rejected after the struggle between *Soi* and *Moi*, and the case in which a sign cannot enter the *Umwelt* at all because of the direct action of being-in-myself? In the latter case, we have to speak of an action not depending on the consciousness of the subject: possible causes are the body or the unconscious itself. In the former, the action is proper of the subject: in fact, is its *Ich-Ton* that rejects a sign from the actual subject. So, we can know that a composer learned something named X in the time Y. If X never appears in their work, it means that it was rejected to the external Otherness; if X appears in Y + n, it means that before it was employed, it had been rejected in the internal Otherness (being-in-itself). By the way, it is also clear that being-in-itself is not the same as absolute Otherness here, which according to Kant is not knowable.[12]

The result of the struggle between *Soi* and *Moi* is the **inner intentionality**, which is different from the pure will of the *Moi*. It results from the interaction of all the four modalities, as described by Tarasti, in their opposed directions (Figure 6).

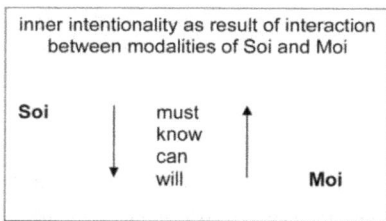

Figure 6: Inner intentionality.

External Otherness – which appears firstly by means of individual and secondly of general (abstract) Otherness-objects – converges in the **being-in-itself**, an area which incorporates the abstract forms (types) drawn from the individual ones (tokens). This process of abstraction —made of acts of acceptance/rejecting of external features – depends both on *Soi* and *Moi*, as shown by Tarasti apropos of Beethoven (Tarasti 2005: 244). However, I think that they operate in a joint filtering action, and not in a sequential way. Let us consider, for

---

[12] The Otherness is under certain respects comparable with Kant's *Dinge an sich*, i.e. things in themselves.

example, "the part of the intonation store which was taught to Beethoven", i.e. what he has heard and learned from different composers (Tarasti 2005: 244): this 'part' – which is of an environmental kind – could be almost the same for other human subjects contemporary to Beethoven. But to hear is not the same as to listen to, and to learn is again a more different thing, depending on the 'difference' of *Moi* just at the very beginning. In fact, if *Soi* is always a part of subjectivity, as Tarasti says, then *Soi*, as a part of *Ich-Ton*, becomes increasingly more individual also. At this point, we have to wonder if something that is really social does exist, or better if any subject can know the social in itself. We know that also the encyclopedia, in Eco's terms, is the result of the interaction of many subjects.[13] Each encyclopedia develops and transforms itself in space and time. In other words also the being-in-itself is always filtered by subject(s). But the matter is not that of idealistic risk: by reducing all reality to the Absolute Subject, idealism claims that the object is produced by the subject and then it would be totally knowable. The matter is that of incommunicable risk: by reducing all reality to the filtering action of individual subjects, no knowledge can have the certainty of objectivity.

We will adopt a pragmatical solution: an infinite dialectic between empirical subjects allows satisfying needs of both objectivity and subjectivity. Today, we are not terrified by the idea that absolute knowledge is not possible, at least for human subjects. So, we can well speak of a being-in-itself which changes through time, and that is historically, socially, and culturally determined.[14] As a result of this dialectic, we can identify, recognize, and understand outside reality. Such a dialectic is founded on the described interaction of *Soi* and *Moi* within each actual *Ich-Ton*.

---

13 "Eco's semiotics studies the signification of signs and their modes of interpretation and production inside the communicative activities. For Eco, the meaning of signs is not an individual or psychological phenomenon, but the result of a process mediated by shared knowledge: the production and the interpretation of signs involve a wide set of norms and information that belong to a multidimensional system of knowledge, which interpreters and producers share and renew in the communicative practice. Because of its heterogeneity, Eco calls this system of knowledge encyclopedia" (Desogus 2012: 501).
14 For a musical application of such a principle, see the chapter *Traditions, variants, and treasons in performing arts. Towards a dynamic notion of authenticity and re-definition of sense. Examples from and remarks on Rossini's* Barbiere (Rosato 2013: 486–504).

2 A diachronic approach to the being-for-self: Towards an individual musical subject

2.1 Analysis of being-for-self

This section explores music in its concrete, historical being. According to Tarasti's reformulation of terms, 'being-for-self' means here an 'actual' being. But our approach is still *a priori*, as we are analyzing the general conditions by which musical organisms reveal themselves to human subjects.

By surveying the Western musical tradition, we can hypothesize a movement from communal to an individual being. It does not mean that there is just one direction in musical history. If we take into account music from different social contexts, we can find both communal and individual pieces, in the same space and time.[15] So, in our analysis, we are considering the two opposite structures of musical being-for-self, the one within which *Soi* is stronger than *Moi*, the other within which *Moi* prevails over *Soi*. In the former, being-for-itself cooperates with what I call homeostasis1 (H1): that is to say homeostasis which has some of its proper historical features, and which has been culturally determined.[16] In the latter, being-for-myself fights in order to prevail over H1.

---

[15] By analyzing different kinds of musical repetition, and namely, the musematic one, related to the 'collective variative' form typical of pre-capitalist societies, in which individualization comes about through a continuous approach to the typical; and the discursive repetition, "strongly linked with the rise of the 'bourgeois solo song', appearing in the Middle Ages and reaching its maturity in the eighteenth and nineteenth centuries" [Middleton states that] these two types are historically not *entirely* mutually exclusive; indeed, they interact to form a variety of sub-types – hence the emergence of the 'narrative-lyric' and 'epic-lyric' types" (Middleton 1990: 270).

[16] "What I here call homeostasis is an universal, transcendental concept, consequent to the human substance (in Kantian terms). In a different way, when I speak of homeostasis in analyzing western music, I think to a specific, certain way to convey musical energy (melodic, harmonic, rhythmic, agogic, and so on), that is the result of historical and social processes. In this sense, I assume that there is also a kind of less universal homeostasis, at the same time transcendental (as an *a priori* condition of listening to) and historical (a condition limited in space and time). We can call the latter **homeostasis1 (H1)**, and the former **homeostasis0 (H0)**" (Rosato 2013: 404).

2.1.1 A community subject

"The primus motor of the music history is the becoming of the *Moi* from *Soi* or rather the constant rebellion of the *Moi* against the community, the conventional world of the *Soi*" (Tarasti 2005: 241). Here the problem of individualism in Western culture does emerge entirely. It reaches its apex in Romanticism, and our time is imbued with the idea of authentic art as the product of geniuses. But what does 'art' mean? Is not it an idea that we considered in the past, where art meant only technique?[17] Moreover, if we suppose the existence of art music, we have to wonder how non-art music runs: does it involve different linguistic structures and processes?[18] Yet there are also contrasting voices in Western culture, mainly influenced by oriental perspectives, as in the case of John Cage – with the idea that sounds have to be free from a composer's will – and Martin Heidegger, when he claims that Language is the only authentic Subject of any communications.[19]

But here I want to adhere to a purely descriptive level. So, let us consider ancient plainchant as a starting point for our analysis. Here, we are in front of only vocal music, without any instruments, so that we have to address the pure melody, which I refer to the Greek word 'melos'. Moreover, music works for the sacred word, and its aim is just to reinforce it. Musical individuality depends on the differences of sacred texts, but differences are entirely within social identity, and they only act in order to distinguish between general types. *Moi* is at its minimal level, and it consists as the mere duplication of model-organism. Individual transformations between organisms of the same type depending on external factors, like texts,[20] linguistic contexts, and social situations or enunciative circumstances.

We can, therefore, state that, in the beginning, a musical organism is entirely a 'subject' to the external Otherness. In such an organism, *Moi* is – as first – the musical difference to the word, and only then it becomes the difference in the

---

17 Cf. Walter Benjamin and his classic publication, *The Work of Art in the Age of Mechanical Reproduction*, dated 1936 (Benjamin 2008).
18 Recent developments in popular music studies have shown both the affinities and the differences between pop and art music as to the adopted musical systems, forms, and structures. See, among the others, Tagg (2013) and Moore (2016).
19 "The encountering saying of mortals is answering. Every spoken word is already an answer: counter-saying, coming to the encounter, listening Saying" (Heidegger 1982: 129).
20 Let us think of psalmody, where lines are of different lengths. In such a case, the relation between text and music relies on a diagrammatic iconicity, as melodic spans strictly depend on the structure of the verses. Cf. the application of iconic strategies in the opera by Costantino Maeder (2013).

music itself. Common words have usually a proper intonation depending, for example, on the interrogative, exclamatory, dubitative (and so on) characters of each statement. In such cases, intonation is not just a facultative variant, but a distinctive trait needed for a correct meaning. We can say that the musical subject is subjugated to the mastery of the word.[21]

It is interesting to remark that the word 'subject', to which we give an active role, comes from the Latin 'subiectum', past participle from the verb 'subicere' (to overpower, to conquer): 'sub' means under, below; 'iacere' means to throw, to fling. That means that the active role of the subject develops itself from a passive starting situation. 'Iacere' means also to lie, to stay, which are consequents of 'to have been flung, overpowered'. The term 'subject' is close to such terms as subjugated, enslaved or conquered. But to be subjugated means, at least, to be existent as a difference within the social identity. As in the Hegelian dialectic between bondsman and master, where the former – although subjected from the latter – discovers himself and becomes increasingly a free subject as a result of his own formative activity.[22]

In the first phase (Figure 7), modalities are coupled in an unusual way with respect to *Moi* and *Soi* [dotted arrows represent the order of priority according to Tarasti's model (Tarasti 2005: 242–243)]. In fact, music as a difference (or transcendence to the word) can develop, increase, and amplify the social identity of sacred texts due to the fact that it knows both linguistic rules and strategies of distinction within them. As stated previously, such a musical activity – a first appearance of the *Moi* – is internal to the word service. The latter, that we can also identify as the *Soi*, defines the boundaries of the action of the *Moi*: here, both must and will are of collective origin.

---

[21] We could speak of a progressive liberation from the slavery of the 'imagic iconicity'. According to Maeder, the recitative of both opera and oratorio mainly relies on imagic iconicity, where the "music mimes the prosody of human speech (rhythm, stress, and intonation)" (Maeder 2013: 275), as in our case.

[22] See the chapter "Independence and Dependence of Self-Consciousness: Lordship and Bondage" (Hegel 2009: 86–92).

The emergence of individual subjects in Western music — 875

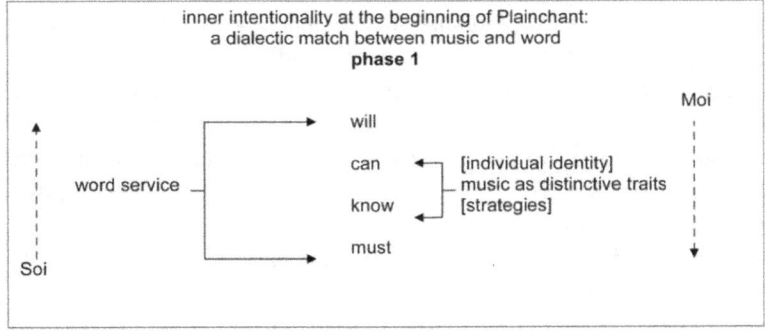

Figure 7: Inner intentionality at the beginning of Plainchant.

Now, we can represent all such relationships in a scheme (Figure 8). This time, something changed with respect to the other representations of *Ich-Ton*. In fact, we have now three, and not only two, systems. A new organism stays between the external Otherness and *Ich-Ton* itself: it is a social system which determines and regulates all contexts, enunciative circumstances, and situations wherein our *Ich-Ton* has to operate. As its aim is the preservation of the Sacred word and Jesus's message, it wants only to repeat the same things through time. Its goal is the common identity of Christians, not individual and singular identity.

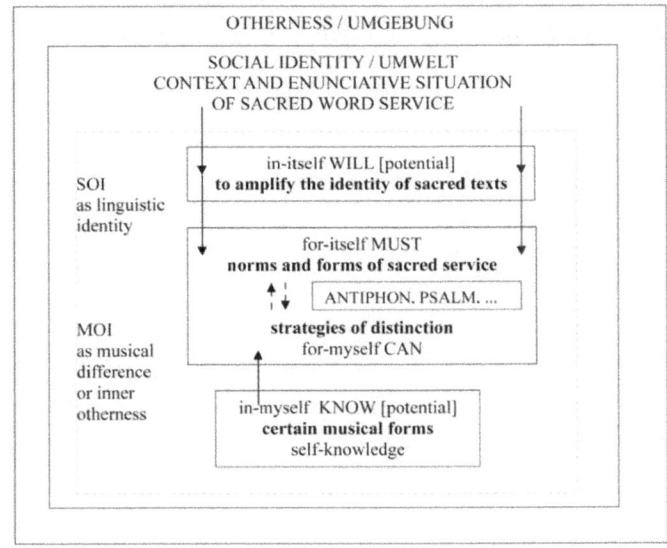

Figure 8: Scheme of relationships.

For this reason, the boundaries of *Ich-Ton*'s system are dashed. In fact, there is not a real difference between individual and social identity. The arrows which bring signs from context and enunciation almost directly flow in the area of the actual subject (an antiphon, a psalm, or other), and there such signs fight with those of *Soi*. That means that the being-in-itself of the *Ich-Ton*, its will, absolutely corresponds to the social will. This time, *Moi* has the role of the inner Otherness, as opposition to social identity.

We can notice that modalities attain a different placement with respect to the being categories. As seen above, being-in-itself appears not as a must, but as a will, because each individual recognizes itself as a member of the same and only social class. Being-for-itself acts as must, and not as know, as there are no spaces for individual solutions, but only for repetitions of social identity: there is no difference between abstract forms, norms and their actualization. It is not a case that the original sin was a sin due to the will of know!

As said, *Moi* has the role of the opposition to the common identity, in favour of an individual difference. So, being-in-myself appears as knowledge of certain musical forms, which are the possibility to know itself as different from linguistic Otherness. In short, being-for-myself is the only one that operates in the same way within *Ich-Ton*: it seems that it can have the power to apply to the sacred word some musical strategies which actualize the self-knowledge of *Moi*.

As a consequence, we have to change our semiotic square, as shown in Figure 9. Relationships between categories of being and modalities are of a variable kind. As Tarasti showed apropos of *Soi* and *Moi*, where will, can, know, and

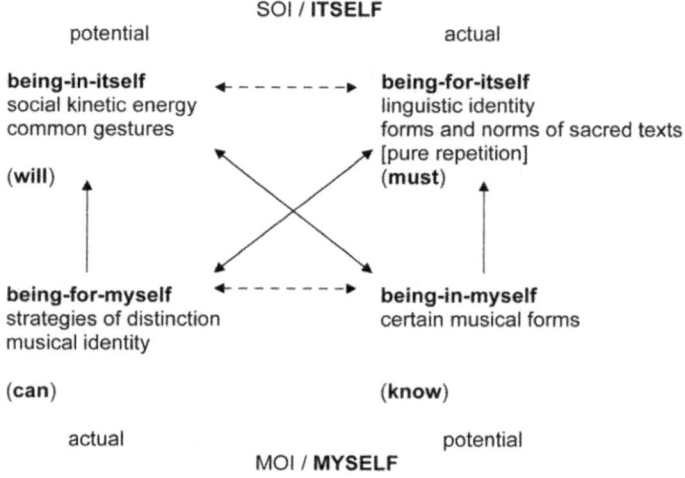

Figure 9: Relationships between categories.

must are all present although, with different roles (Tarasti 2005: 242), we can find for each of the four categories of being the proper action of each one of the four modalities.

Being-for-myself, as an actual musical identity, expresses the power (can) to give a certain form to the potential being-in-myself. But when struggling against being-for-itself, it has to 'know' its own identity, in order to contrast the 'must' of the being-in-itself. Both a will and a must, which pertain to the certain forms that being-for-myself is going to take on, are in existence. Obviously, four modalities act in specific and different ways within the four categories of being. Scholars will clarify the relationships each time more relevant according to their analytical perspectives.

In my square, an unusual relation comes out among the four modalities in themselves (Figure 10). Their order has been changed with respect to Greimas and Tarasti's models. The strongest oppositions, those on the axis of contradiction, are between 'will' and 'know' on the side of potentiality, and 'must' and 'can' on the side of the actualization. It depends on the fact that we are looking for a contrast between two different entities operating in the same subject or *Ich-Ton*. In fact, *Soi* is of a linguistic kind, while *Moi* is of a musical one. In particular, 'will' and 'must' have here a relation of reciprocal presupposition, as they stay on the axis of the contraries at this point. Greimas says that, in semiotics, it is very hard to apply the logical principle, according to which contrary terms can be together true or together untrue. But in some philosophical thoughts, such as those by Giordano Bruno, Baruch Spinoza, Nietzsche, and similarly Schopenhauer, we have a perfect

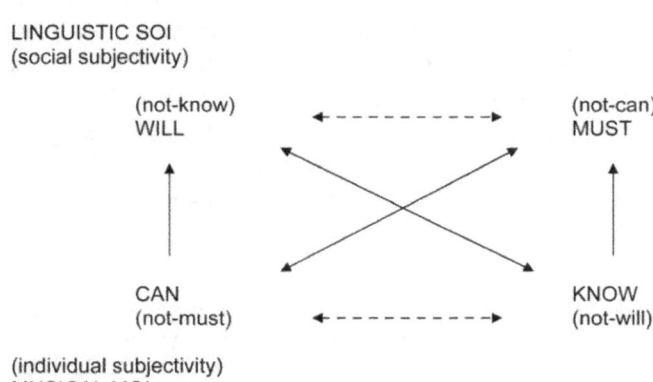

Figure 10: Musical and linguistic *Soi*.

correspondence between 'will' and 'must' in a more general metaphysical perspective, where man is only free of willing just what he must.[23]

The musical 'know', contained in a sacred word, is a potential musical self-consciousness, which will emerge through time by its opposition to linguistic will. The latter is of a collective kind (see Tarasti 2005: 242). It is potential because it acts as social energy, a common way to gesticulate, which can be actualized only in the forms of 'must.' This latter actually fights against the musical 'can.' As soon as music is increasingly more prevalent over linguistics, the former will appear as a new kind of subject, which will assume its own, inner modalities.

2.1.1.1 Towards an autonomous musical *Ich-Ton*

Let us consider now our musical subject as independent from any linguistic requirements, although it does not mean that it was unconnected from sacred words. I mean the subject which recognizes itself as endowed of a specific musical nature.

Music, or better, 'melos' discovers its own rules. As first, the musical 'will' – both potential and kinetic energy – expresses itself as H1, a potential common gesture which actualizes itself in certain modal forms, as studied in Jean Claire's theory of mother-chords.[24] These forms, as they are normative models, represent the musical 'must'. Both will and must are here again on the side of *Soi*, but *Soi* is now of a purely musical nature.

We can wonder what happens on the side of *Moi*, as, since this moment, it is operating within an entire musical *Ich-Ton*. Being-in-myself and being-for-myself are not acting against linguistic requirements any more, but they are now fighting to affirm an individual musical subject (as it will be in the next phase). So, as music is still cooperating with linguistics to amplify the sacred word, *Soi* is now imposing musical specificity, a reversal of roles is needed in this phase. *Moi* has to satisfy the requests of the sacred text. This is possible and not contradictory with the essence of *Moi* itself because musical *Moi* forms an alliance with the lin-

---

[23] I want to recall here Seneca's sentence – "Ducunt volentem fata, nolentem trahunt" which synthesizes the Stoic idea of human freedom. The human being can only choose whether to be dragged by destiny or to love him: "My formula for greatness is *amor fati* [love of the fate]: the fact that a man wishes nothing to be different, either in front of him or behind him, or for all eternity. Not only must the necessary be borne, and on no account concealed, – all idealism is falsehood in the face of necessity, – but it must also be *loved*" (Nietzsche 2012: 12).

[24] Claire published four articles in the *Revue Grégorienne* between 1962 and 1963. They were partially translated from French by Rosato and presented in his book (Rosato 2013: 248–256). Here the dialectical relation between melodic gestures and modal space is also studied.

guistic *Moi*. This way, a kind of individuality initially emerges, although limited in a strong social and common space. Being-in-myself and being-for-myself consist of certain musical forms and strategies of distinction respectively, both depending on the specificity of the sacred texts (Figure 11).

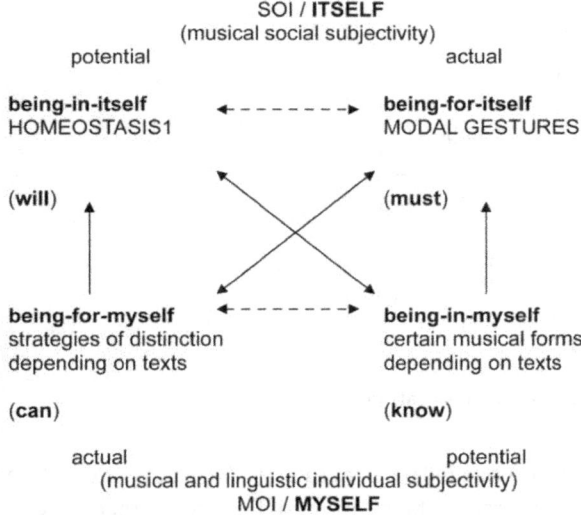

Figure 11: Musical *Moi* and *Soi*.

2.1.2 An individual musical subject

To conclude, we are considering the phase in which *Moi* becomes conscious of its own musical individuality. As mentioned at the beginning of this chapter, being-for-myself starts to fight against H1 but also against modal gestures and the inner-space that those gestures have been creating. The aim is to affirm its own diversity, its difference, within the musical social identity. Let us consider relationships between categories of being in this new phase (Figure 12).

It seems arduous to explain being-in-myself in purely musical terms. In fact, musical force and energy are *a priori* circumscribed in homeostasis and the oriented field.[25] If musical force would operate out of social or intersubjective

---

[25] See "Levels of modalization in existential and transcendental analysis" (Rosato 2013: 395–409), where the matter of Being-in-self is considered in the light of Tarasti's analysis of Beethoven's Op. 7.

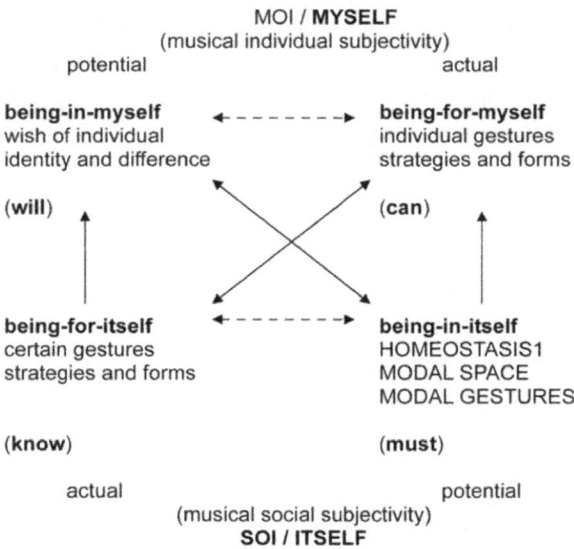

Figure 12: *Moi* becomes conscious of its own musical individuality.

relations (at least two subjects are needed) – as defined in *Soi* – it would not be recognizable as a musical fact. Therefore, being-in-myself can be defined only as a wish of distinction within the being-in-itself, a potentiality which operates in order to find individual gestures, strategies, and forms in opposition with certain forms, strategies, and gestures which are the actualization (being-for-itself) of historical structural (transcendental in the Kantian sense) conditions and possibilities of musical being-in-itself. The analytical aim is reconstructing, by hypothesis, this individual wish and will, and also clarifying its relationships with the inner intentionality of *Ich-Ton*. In fact, inner intentionality seems to result from all four categories of musical being.

Since this moment, 'will' becomes the most important modality of *Moi*, but we have not to forget that all modalities pertain both to *Moi* and *Soi*, although in different manners (cf. Tarasti 2005: 242). To express this situation of fact, let us consider how modalities actualize themselves with respect to *Soi* and *Moi* in this phase (Figure 13).

In this respect, coming out of *Moi*, or the will to be distinct from *Soi*, seems to be a natural process due to life itself: life is the reproduction of types – or ideas – possible only by *principium individuationis*, as remarked by Schopenhauer. We could say that Platonic ideas really exist only in actual tokens, but the reproduction into tokens implies differentiation at least in space, time, and a minimal causality. It could seem paradoxical, but being distinct is not a voluntary need of any

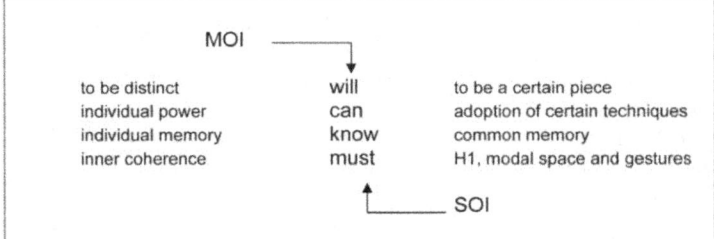

Figure 13: Modalities with respect to *Soi* and *Moi*.

subject. *Soi* needs *Moi* in order to exist, and *Moi* comes out only by *Soi*. As seen above, the will of 'being a certain piece' is proper of *Soi*, and distinction of *Moi* is founded in such a will. The distinction is naturally founded in the life of *Soi* itself, which in turn comes to life only as a result of *Moi*. It will be a historical, social, cultural process which will achieve —in Western culture – an exasperated and strong 'will' of *Moi*, which has been transforming the spontaneous idea of distinction in that of forced artistic originality at all costs.[26] In principle, *Moi* and *Soi* can cohabit in less stressful ways.

References

Benjamin, Walter. 2008 [1936]. *The Work of Art in the Age of Mechanical Reproduction*. London: Penguin Group.
Desogus, Paolo. 2012. The encyclopedia in Umberto Eco's semiotics. *Semiotica* 192. 501–521.
Eco, Umberto. 1976. *A Theory of Semiotics*. Bloomington: Indiana University Press.
Eco, Umberto. 1992. *Interpretation and overinterpretation*. With Richard Rorty, Jonathan Culler & Christine Brooke-Rose. Edited by Stephan Collini. Cambridge, UK: Cambridge University Press.
Fichte, Johann Gottlieb. 1868 [1794]. *The Science of Knowledge*. Trans. from the German by Adolph Ernst Kroeger. Philadelphia: J. B. Lippincott & Co.
Genette, Gérard. 1997. *Palimpsests: Literature in the Second Degree*. Trans. by Channa Newman & Claude Doubinsky. Lincoln and London: University of Nebraska Press.

---

26 "Three-quarters of Homer is convention; and the same is true of all Greek artists, who had no reason to fall prey to the modern rage for originality. They lacked all fear of convention; it was through this, indeed, that they were united with their public. For conventions are the *achieved* artistic means, the toilsomely acquired common language, through which the artist can truly communicate himself to the understanding of his audience [. . .] That which the artist invents that goes beyond convention he adds of his own volition and put himself at risk with it, the most favorable outcome being that he *creates* a new convention" (Nietzsche 1996: 339).

Hegel, Georg W. F. 2009 [1807]. *The Phenomenology of Spirit (The Phenomenology of Mind)*. Trans. by J. B. Baillie. Overland Park, KS: A digireads.com Book.
Heidegger, Martin. 1982 [1959]. *On the Way to Language*. Trans. by Peter D. Hertz. San Francisco: Harper.
Kant, Immanuel. 2007 [1781]. *Critique of Pure Reason*. Trans., edited and with an Introduction by Marcus Weigelt. London: Penguin Group.
Leibniz, Gottfried Wilhelm. 1840. *Opera Philosophica Omnia. Pars Prior*. Edited by Joannes Eduardus Erdmann. Berlin.
Maeder, Costantino. 2013. Opera, oratorio, and iconic strategies. In Lars Ellestrôm, Olga Fischer, Christina Ljungberg (eds.), *Iconic Investigations*, 275–294. Amsterdam: John Benjamins Publishing Company.
Middleton, Richard. 1990. *Studying Popular Music*. Philadelphia, PA: Open University Press.
Moore, Allan F. 2016. *Song Means: Analysing and Interpreting Recorded Popular Song*. London and New York: Routledge.
Nietzsche, Friedrich. 1996 [1878]. *Human, All Too Human*. Trans. by R. J. Hollingdale. Cambridge: Cambridge University Press.
Nietzsche, Friedrich. 2012 [1908]. *Ecce Homo*. Trans. by Anthony M. Ludovici. Mineola, New York: Dover Publications, Inc.
Rosato, Paolo. 2013. *The Organic Principle in Music Analysis. A Semiotic Approach*. Helsinki and Imatra: ISI.
Schopenhauer, Arthur. 2010 [1819]. *The World as Will and Representation*. Trans. and edited by Judith Norman, Alistair Welchman & Christopher Janaway. Vol. I. Cambridge: Cambridge University Press.
Tagg, Philip. 2013. *Music's Meanings. A modern musicology for non-musos*. New York and Huddersfield: The Mass Media Scholar's Press.
Tarasti, Eero. 2000. *Existential Semiotics*. Bloomington and Indianapolis: Indiana University Press.
Tarasti, Eero. 2002. *Signs of Music. A guide to Musical Semiotics*. Berlin and New York: Mouton de Gruyter.
Tarasti, Eero. 2005. Existential and Transcendental Analysis of Music. *Studi Musicali* XXXIV(2). 223–266.
Uexküll, Jakob von. 1992 [1934]. A stroll through the worlds of animals and men: A picture book of invisible worlds. Trans. by Claire H. Schiller. *Semiotica* 89(4). 319–391.

Július Fujak
Existential semiotics and correla(c)tivity of (non-conventional) music (Personal retrospection)

Abstract: The author developed the musical theory of correla(c)tivity in the range of existential semiotics based on thoughts of following remarkable scientists. František Miko (1920–2010), one of the main representatives of Nitra semiotic school in Slovakia, invented the system/network of expression categories and the existential conceptual framework of reception being of art, what influenced author´s understanding of creative dimension of music perception. Eero Tarasti (1948) in his substantial works, e. g. since *Existential Semiotics* (2000) till *Sein und Schein. Explorations in existential semiotics* (2015) deals with the justification as well as with many important issues how interdisciplinary semiotic research can be useful (no only) for the study of contemporary music art. He investigates also the peculiarities of "ontological-transcendental" questions of existential semiotics within a wide scope of subjects of musical aesthetics. Peter Faltin (1939–1981) founded the source for the appropriate semiotic reflection of music in the philosophy of Ludwig Wittgenstein, especially in his last work *Bedeutung ästhetischer Zeichen – Musik und Sprache* (1981). He questioned the very prerequisites and rules of musical syntax: how it is ever possible that musical tones or sounds create relations with resultant meanings. Jozef Cseres (1961) developed post-structuralistic philosophy of contemporary art in the intermedia context and the phenomena of postmodern, non-convential experimental music.

All theories above inspired the author to invent the alternative model of the three dimensional communication model of musical semiosis, which is based on existential theory of *musical correla(c)tivity* – focused on music semiosis as interactive existential symbiosis: an author's intention is embodied and articulated by sonant sounds – its accurate comprehension is a matter of listener's consciousness generating music meanings in the frame of his/her unique being.

Keywords: musical correla(c)tivity, semiosis of music, postmodern philosophy of art

My view on the significance of existential semiotic research of contemporary (mostly but not only) non-conventional music is conditioned by the circumstances of my personal story as an alternative musician and experimental composer who started to deal with the theories of semiotics seriously since the middle and second half of 1990s, when I met those right people in a right time. . . I was employed then as a teacher and researcher at the Institute of literary and artistic communication in Nitra (1996–2007), the centre of s. c. Nitra Semiotic School – the main representatives are František Miko, Anton Popovič, Ján Kopál, Tibor Žilka, Ľubomír Plesník, Zoltán Rédey, among others). I was occupied then – beside my continual musical and intermedia artistic activities – by PhD. thesis *The Creativity of Listening to Musical Shape* (graduated in 2004) and my co-supervisor[1] was legendary linguist and semiotician František Miko (1920–2010), the main figure of the expressive-reception aesthetics in Slovakia, so no wonder that alternative musical-aesthetic research could spread from of his theories. It was kind of the proverbial "U-turn", my first real encountering with the existential aesthetic approach to phenomena of art and music.

In an essential simplification of Miko's expressive-semiotic view, it can be stated that the meaning of the mutually interrelated (musical) forms/shapes is defined by (their) expression. Each expressional category of Miko's expressional framework is a kind of phenomenological "substratum" of certain uniqueness in the work of art in its suchness – it is the verbal expression of the existential touch with it. The range of expressive categories (e. g. expression of contrast, expression of detailness, expression of authenticity, expression of iconicity, etc.) basically confirms Miko's paradigmatically decisive concept of reception being/ existence of the work of art, i.e. the real existence and accomplishment of the work of art, i.e. generating its meanings in the dialogic process of its conscious creative reception and/or the perception of the work of art in terms of its existential experiencing. Miko's various models of the expressional framework resound strongly in the context of language and literature, however, they also in principle relate to the expressionality of musical art and the creativity of its perception, i.e. the space with the otherwise uncommunicated expressive nuances, which are understood from the inside in other levels than ("only") the rational and verbal one. In the spirit of Miko's view, one could conclude that the expressive culture of musical work of art relies on own imaginative intelligence and emotional empathy of the listener, because it stems from them. According to František Miko, the constantly implicit interpretation and the creative generation of meaning from the expression of correla(c)tive musical processes transpose our perception into the dialogic musical contemplation, in essence, to a different mode of consciousness.

In Miko's view, the neoscientism in musicology – with its tendency to axiomatisation, its dependence on natural science exactness and mostly because of

---

[1] Another supervisor of my dissertation was Miko's scholar Ľubomír Plesník, director of the Institute of literary and artistic communication in Nitra (1993–2003).

its artificial isolation of the object of its research from the essential existential relations and circumstances – is becoming inadequate when is exposed "vis-à-vis" to the actual problems of music-artistic communication. Limited by its positivism-based nature, it is not capable to accept (thus even harder to reflect on) the meaning of the spontaneous creativity of perception which is closely linked to the expressiveness and is present in the entire human life in all its areas important for survival (ways of obtaining and assessing information, ability to orientate oneself, awareness of one's being in the world, etc.).

Miko guided me to discovery that the state of finding oneself in "the being-otherwise" – while listening to music – hangs together with the overcoming of the impression of one's inner isolation, the impression of being imprisoned in oneself, that means with the experience of interconnection and a "mutual resonance" with the multidimensional flow of music happening. As if everything is made really present via creative musical perception.[2] It is because it makes relative our time-space conventions – the infinitely unwinding future-oriented time linearity just as the purely physical definition of time & space. This receptiveness synchronizes and overlays several time-space dimensions. It realizes the *hic et nunc* ("here and now") and thus can evokes in humans existential homeostasis inciting and holistic experience of "other-time" reality. To draw adequate consequences from the previous statements means to view the organism of musical work and its listener as a mutually interrelated system.

In 2001 during 7th International Congress on Musical Signification (ICMS) in Imatra, I met for the first time Eero Tarasti (1948), one of the most important semioticians ever, just one year after publishing his crucial book *Existential Semiotics* (2000), where he gives reasons for the re-evaluation of pragmatics philosophy and semiotics for the reflection of an existential experiencing of the world and the

---

[2] Creativity understood as a conditional factor of (not only) music reception stands against the stiff understanding the work of art as the finalised objective artefact, the object of our subjective "observations". Edwin Prévost, an experimental composer, musician and aesthetician interprets this degradation of art into art-object as a consequence of the (presently dominant) ideology of ownership individualism, which in its implications transforms the work of art into a commodity of market exchange. In his suggestive enunciation *Meta-Music and the Mutating Monster of Possessive Individualism – an Epic Struggle* (1990) he argues in favour of a radically different view of the purpose and nature of artistic creativeness. Without the creative participation of its recipient, this creativeness would lose its sense. He emphasizes that sound has no meaning when it is not heard and sound understood as art without any human thought-full reaction does not exist. According to him meaning exists in music only as far as the listener is in a disposition of a conscious and growing sense of being. Prévost in a direct allusion to L. Feuerbach thinks that the creativity of perception as well as the following action make the being of our species and to act differently means to deny our humanity (Prévost 1990).

ability to cope with it, and with ourselves in it as well. I remember there his lecture with significative title *Metaphors of Nature and Organic Unity (An Introduction to the Biosemiotic Analysis of Symphonic Music)* referring also to the *Umwelt* theory rooted in the conception of of Jakob von Uexküll and fully realised in Thomas Sebeok's philosophy. Tarasti explicates biosemiotics as a scientific paradigm, which opens new possibilities for a deeper understanding of existential modus in semiotic exploration. The aim of this new semiotics cannot be "only" the analysis of text structure but also of its life "factors", "circumstances" and experienced *Umwelt*. Such an analysis takes into account all processes of becoming the sign-text in its uniqueness, singularity and suchness, movement and variableness, expression quality, all of which are always existentially experienced.

He interpreted the musical-artistic communication as a process of mutual dynamic adaptation of both its "participants" – the work and the listener. I realized then that the relationship of the two is not a one-way and a one-level highway, it is rather a two-way and maybe even multilevel chain of communication. Inspired by his discoveries I became the member of Musical Signification Project, led by Tarasti as the president of International Association of Semiotic Studies (2004–2014), and six years later I have organised the international symposium *Convergences and Divergences of Existential Semiotics* in Nitra at the Faculty of Arts, Constantine the Philosopher University, where he was invited as the key lecturer.[3] He presented there lecture *On the Appearance or the Present Structure and Existential Digressions of the Subject*, where the category of appearance (Schein) – discussed in the classical semiotics (e. g. A. J. Greimas) in the 'vertical' direction – was conceive in the horizontal manner, *"as a temporal unfolding, as 'Erscheinung'(. . .) it will mean a radically new and more profound approach to such a notion as communication, so crucial in semiotics"*. (Tarasti 2007: 11)

We met often on different occasions mostly at another ICMS events and other semiotic congresses (in Lyon, Rome, Krakow, Brussels/Louvain-la-Neuve) exchanging the thoughts in very interesting dialogues. He has supported a still supports my activities – accordingly as F. Miko long time ago – in improvement of my theory based also on some of his ideas.

There were another "U turns" in my reasoning on (intermedia non-conventional) music caused of the confrontations with musical semiotics of Peter Faltin and postmodern aesthetics of Jozef Cseres, the both influenced me markedly in many ways. Musicologist, critic and semiotician Peter Faltin (1937–1981), key personality of Slovak avant-garde musical culture in 1960s (he invented and co-

---

[3] See more: Július Fujak (ed.). 2007. *Convergences and Divergences of Existential Semiotics*. Nitra: Faculty of Arts, Constantine the Philosopher.

organised Slovakian "Darmstadt courses", the legendary international Smolenice Seminars in 1968–1969) was one of the few scholars of his time, in the 1970s, who did not rely on the two fundamental semiotic lines – inspired by structural linguistics of Ferdinand de Saussure and logical pragmatism of Charles Sanders Peirce –, but primarily on the philosophy of Ludwig Wittgenstein (especially, from the period of his *Philosophical Investigations*), what was elaborated and finalized in last Faltin's pivotal work *Bedeutung ästhetischer Zeichen. Musik und Sprache* (1981).[4] Let us mention (along the lines of refuting the denotative fetishism) the principle of generating the meaning of the word in the so-called "language in use" by "living human being", which Faltin specifies in relation to music: in terms of creating the meanings of musical signs, he talks about their manifestative nature and replaces the term "use" with the term "listening".[5]

Faltin also exposes musical syntax to semiotic reflection, which he describes as the process of "attributing spiritual meaning", which is finalized exclusively in the human consciousness in the process of listening to the "sounding logic of musical relations". This is governed by certain categories of musical thinking, which are common to both the author and the listener. Faltin justifies the unsustainability of semiotic-linguistic instrumentalisation of the musical phenomena

---

4 The translation of the second part of Faltin's work we quoted above was published in the Slovak musicological magazine Slovenská hudba 3/1992. The work was originally published after Faltin's death with title *Bedeutung ästhetischer Zeichen – Musik und Sprache* (Ed. by Christa Nauch-Börner, Aechener Studien zur Semiotik und Kommunikationsforschung, Band 1, Rader Verlag. Aachen 1985). In the first part *Problem of Meaning*, the author focuses on several problems of aesthetics, semiotics of the aesthetic phenomena, meaning in semiotics and the specificity of the aesthetic sign. The third part *Language and Utterance* deals with the aesthetic and philosophical lectures of Ludwig Wittgenstein and analyses the aesthetic-semiotic question whether music is a special kind of language.

5 In the 1970's, Peter Faltin simultaneously devoted his research to the insufficiency of explanation of the musical-aesthetic semiosis interpreted solely through its communicative dimension. In his opinion, there is an important type of communication, musical communication, which is not an announcement or statement. According to him, nothing is "announced" or "mediated" in musical communication – first of all it is a kind of "utterance". This is why he replaces the notion of "message" with the notion of "utterance" in the "sender – message – receiver" pattern. The utterance is not a vehicle, mediator or a message of something else, but a self-expression, which articulates musical thoughts, images and ideas, which cannot be translated to any other code. Faltin finds the justification of this substitution in Husserl's typology of signs, in which he differentiates "expression", which does not double anything, but itself is the thought and the meaning of the sign. He also points also to Russell's notion of "ostentension", or Wittgenstein's "hint explanations" (Faltin 1992a: 311). In music, we deal with a different case of communication – it cannot be reduced to interaction only; it can take a form of (we could say existential) contemplation or sharing the spiritual musical ideas and their meaning generated in our consciousness (Faltin 1992a: 317).

that require a different semiotic and comprehensive approach equally involving the complementary of hermeneutics, reception aesthetics and analysis of musical and aesthetic structures and signs. In this sense, one of the key assumptions in my reflections on the specificities of musical and artistic semiosis is Faltin's conviction that the meaning of musical sign cannot be generated solely by their materiality or "use", but it resides in their mutual correlation, i.e. relation of the structural character of the musical sign (morphology, syntax) and the pragmatic (existential) context of its perception (Žabka 2004: 147).[6]

As an experimental musician, I was always interested in the theories of arts and music in the context postmodern ways of thinking – Faltin payed his theoretical attention also to this topic. In 1969, he wrote the remarkable text titled *Ontologické transformácie v hudbe šesťdesiatych rokov* (Ontological Transformations in the Music of the 1960s) which, despite the gap of more than five decades, can still provide us with productive tools for the understanding of paradigmatic otherness and uniqueness of (sometimes extremely) non-conventional music. It is noteworthy that after the analytical reflections of the function/proportion of shape/form and sonicity in music – from the time of the Renaissance to Impressionism and evidence of prevalence and/or full emancipation-autonomy of the importance of sonic structures in the musical Avant-garde of the 20th century until E. Varèse –, Faltin knowledgeably devoted himself to the non-conventional music of the 1960s, including the so-called improvised music. Note that the very title of the article clearly articulates that this time it is not "only" the deep transformations of the aesthetically transposed parameters of the musical forms, or the transformation of "composition techniques", or an extensive "enrichment of the sonic material", but a transformation of the *ontological status* of music! According to him, an important change occurred in the said period: "*the very concept has changed, and so did the meaning and function of music*" (Faltin 1992b: 175). After differentiating the solidified conservativism from the living tradition, he formulates the stances used for evaluating the vital "transgressive" shift in the non-conventional music of the 1960s, bridging the gap between the music work of art and the world, and/or the being, in an attempt to identify with them: "*The music wants to be – just like any human being – part of the world, and not just the testimony thereof*" (Faltin 1992b: 176). A tangible example of this identification is the freely improvised music (Faltin referring that time to the progressive pieces of

---

[6] As an employee of Department of Cultural Studies at the Faculty of Arts, Constantine the Philosopher University in Nitra (since 2007), I organized there in 2009 scientific symposium *The Questions of Musical Semiotics and Aesthetics* dedicated to Peter Faltin, commemorating 70th anniversary of his birth.

Cornelius Cardrew or Vinko Globokar) which, paraphrasing Faltin, replaces the hitherto "distance from the material" with a kind of merger with it:

> Improvised music is different from standard music not in its arbitrary nature, but because it is made fundamentally differently; the absence of music stands is not determinant – what matters is the fundamental change in musical thinking. Even the categories referred to as "natural", seemingly "innate" and "unchangeable", such as the form, time and shape, are subject to change. (Faltin 1992b: 176)

Faltin directly writes about "the conversion of the work of art as a depiction into the work of art as a totem"(!) – it is no longer the traditionally understood and interpreted sign system, but the demonstration of a being and "only" a utterance about it (Faltin 1992b: 177). If this is an indirect reference to the interpretation of the C. Lévi-Strauss' totem as a materialization of a specific form of thinking and understanding of the world, and analogically, with E. Cassirrer, as the indistinctness of the signifying and signified, i.e. the sign materiality and its spiritual meaning, then this confirms the onthological overlap of the new unconventional music and being, which was Faltin's focus in his theoretical treatises. This totemic *"total identification with the sonic material"* was inter alia possible thanks to the acquired new soundness (with its source in the 20th century in the singled-out uniqueness of timbre as an acoustic parameter, in its aesthetic transposition read: new music sonicity), as well as the radically different concept of processual nature and temporality, which are based on the principle of "hear and now". This also changes the role and position of the listener, who directly participates in this "sublimation" and identification with the being:

> The work of art used to be a statement of man to the world, however, these days it becomes a statement of the world to man. It does not aspire at beauty – it does not want to adapt the world to man – and it does not want to be the "message" – that is, man's adaptation to the world, but rather the creation of man and the world. (Faltin 1992b: 179)

If we do not consider today the variety of unconventional musical and artistic (inter)media – neofluxus, conceptual art, sound art, audial art, intermedia comprovisations and musical events – from a different paradigm, from the perspective of a non-matching ontological status and disregard their principal "transgression" of this model (applicable only to certain kinds of music), then they may seem incomprehensible to us. However, if we understand the decisive shift and significant transformations of ontological foundation, than we can perceive and accept their reducible-to-nothing otherness.

Jozef Cseres (1961), aesthetician, curator and intermedia art philosopher of poststructuralist paradigm – known also as conceptual artist $HE^{ye}RME^{ar}S$ – became another important person on my way of understanding the contemporary art and postmodern music since the second half of 1990s. I have recognized him due to organising many artistic events, festivals, scientific and seminars in Slovakia (Sound Off, Hermes' Ear in Nitra, PostmutArt, etc.) and central Europe. Cseres has examined structural relations between music and myth and the problem of artistic representation in the arts, especially in the taxonomically problematic space of contemporary, non-conventional artistic media. He also writes – e. g. in his monograph *Hudobné Simulakrá* (Musical Simulacra; 2001) – about changing textualities of different works of postmodern art: according to him, contemporary artists attack the ontological substance of media, their spatial-temporal coordination and limitations. He claims that the musical works of art are no longer restricted by the temporal frame of repetitions of live performances or mechanical-electronic reproductions anymore (Cseres 2004: 46). He points to very important role that music plays in the (post)structuralistic discourse: he aptly interconnects the theoretical thought of C. Lévi-Strauss, J. Attali, R. Barthes or G. Deleuze & F. Guattari (concepts of music, silence, noise, rhythm, refrain, language, code, and meaning). Cseres describes the features of remarkable qualitative shifts in the postmodern contemporaneity:

> In current music and sound poetry, everything (the sounds) happens (becomes) multi-linearly and transversally. The sounds are not isolated expressions, operations and events. They are 'sound blocks' without stable and well identifiable starting points, planes and coordinates, occurring in the space of in-between – in-between more decisions, in-between more sounds situations, in-between more acoustic orbits. Between the flash of mind and a sound reaction to it, a lot can happen, and so voices do not have the ambition to tell or memorize a story, rather they are trying to articulate the interactions between the sound events.
> (Cseres 2011: 3)

Cseres writes on multi-linear and transversal nature of current music, audio and sonic art in the spaces of "in-between" – while he resigns on telling the story or having some "meta-message" –, he, however, develops his thoughts even further on:

> They are simply intermezzi and it was not a poet or musician who named them "intermezzi", but a philosopher: 'The sound block is the intermezzo. It is a body without organs, an anti-memory pervading musical organization, and is all the sonorous' (Deleuze & Guattari). These voices do not declaim the messages for potential interpretations but they have the ambition to open the alternative spaces of perception. They are more interested in flexible matter from which a particular work of art (or a text) is woven. These are more than 'words-in-freedom', these are the interactive rules of new, unrepeatable grammar and syntax.
> (Cseres 2011: 3)

Convergent and correla(c)tive interference of (non-covential) music and other artistic media implicitly follows also from the fact that no artistic media is "sterilely pure". We are rarely aware of the fact that a sound is basically an energic motion of acoustic wave, kinetic movement of non-static resonant entities in concrete space and time. The movement, the process are fundamental characteristics of any artistic media. Jozef Cseres conclusively argues also in favour of mixmedia interpretation of arts. In his article *Zvuk a tón, hlas a hláska, jazyk a prehovor, text a dielo, . . .skrátka hudba* (Sound and Tone, Voice and Speech-Sound, Language and Speech, Text and Work of Art,. . . Shortly the Music) he writes that the expressive quality of "pure" painting is the result of process of laying colours, gestures, motion of artist´s thoughts etc. I think, it can be applied to the music as well:

> All of arts are composite and all of media are mixed because they combine different codes, discursive conventions, channels, manners of perception and the observation. Derrida points out that the writing not only makes language visible but first of all it de-constructs the possibility of pure picture or text. (Cseres 1999: 88)

Transmedia metamorphism of alternative, "bizarre" contemporary music tests the boundaries and new ways of our perception and makes the move of Derrida´s *diferänce* audible. It makes even the temporal-spatial "frames" of musical media relativistic. The contemporary (not only) non-conventional music manifests the pervasion of non-accidentally corresponding changes of every artistic media, which were actually never separated by any fence.

Inspired and influenced by above-mentioned epochal thoughts of all these original thinkers, I invented since the first decade of 21st century my theoretical concept of *musical correla(c)tivity*. It concludes the existence of a multi-level nature of human consciousness, in which unconsciousness can be spontaneously activated, stimulated and substantialized through experiencing the multi-dimensional musical work of art. Following the findings of Jung's psychoanalysis, transpersonal psychology, Buddhist wisdom, we can conclude that consciousness is not an undifferentiated totality, reducible to the mere rational functions of the brain,[7] but one can distinguish several cooperating levels in it: sensory contact, emotional, discursively and intuitively distinctive, creative volitional, mentally intellectual and spiritual, which includes and coordinates all previous levels (L. A. Góvinda). (When discussing the sensory level and the awareness of it, one cannot exclude corporality from the concept of consciousness, that is, the awareness of bodily sensations, which is apparent in the case of physiological and sensory effects of music). However, in the second pole, the multi-level understanding of consciousness also includes (except the substantial presence of intuition in the background) the oscillating "leakage" of the levels of personal

---

[7] These relations have for long been accentuated in Slovakia by composer Roman Berger, one of the main representatives of Slovakian music avant-garde in 1960s.

and collective unconsciousness – therefore, I resort to using the neologism *(un)consciousness* (or sometimes in last years *(supra)consciousness*). In intentional listening to the musical processes, the listener finds himself/herself in the changing modus and regime of the (un)consciousness. In a way, the listener falls into the space-time of a multi-dimensional musical "unraveling" of complementary functional melodic and harmonic, metro-rhythmic, dynamic and sonoristic processes. While listening to them, the often unpredictable and meta-sign associations of the different levels of (un)consciousness are activated – sometimes in very subtle way, but also in confrontation with extreme otherness of the musical work in sudden ruptures.

I understand the correla(c)tions of (un)consciousness and the musical work of art in musical semiosis as a unique dialog between the phenomenality of multi-level (un)consciousness of human being(ness) and the multidimensional organism of the music piece with the simultaneous, more than three- or four-dimensional processes in richly structured compositions (I. Xenakis). This is the encounter and a dialogic confrontation of the beings: the multi-level, specific and existentially unique human being(ness) – conditioned and determined by the environment of specific cultural and social circumstances of certain discourse practices (M. Foucault) – and a uniquely other being of multidimensional reality embodied in the passing musical processes, whose meanings are generated and interpreted by this human being.

In 2015, I finished the final version of alternative communication model of the music-artistic semiosis[8] which clarifies its dialogic nature in the spirit of musical correla(c)tivity, i.e. the mutual correlation of musical thinking in the multilevel (un)consciousness of the creator – incarnated in the multidimensional organism of the musical work of art – and multilevel, meaning-generating (un)consciousness of the percipient/listener (Figure 1):

The (un)consciousness of the creator "$C_{(un)c}$" and the percipient "$P_{(un)c}$" in this model are represented by two multilevel globes whose core symbolizes the levels of personal and collective (un)consciousness. The three-dimensional "lens" in the overlapping section symbolizes the multidimensional sign system of musical work of art ("MW"). In addition to generating musical meanings in the bipolar interaction of these multi-level entities, metasign associations can be formed in unexpected moments, which, being an integral part of the existential experience of art, emerge from the deeper levels of (un)consciousness[9]. As each other model,

---

[8] I presented the model of the musical semiosis in the very early stages of research at the 11th International Congress on Musical Signification in Akademia Muzyczna in Krakow (2010).
[9] Louise L. Anderson points to sedimentation of prior perception experiences, which allows each experience stored in the memory of the body, or (un)consciousness be part of the next one

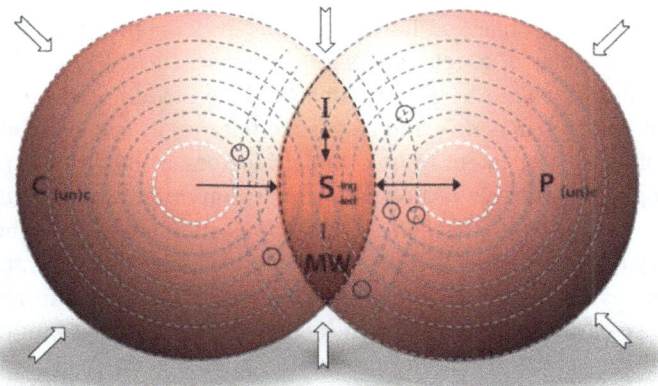

MW – music work of art
S_{-ing} – signifying
S_{-ied} – signified
I – interpretant
$C_{(un)c}$ – (un)consciousness of the creator
$P_{(un)c}$ – (un)consciousness of the percipient
I – listening
○ – meta-sign associations
⇒ – social influences and determinants

Figure 1: Alternative model of the musical semiosis.

even this iconic-symbolic one – accentuates only certain aspects of modeled the reality – is simplistic and incomplete. It is an expression of efforts to clarify the mutually determining together-being of the multidimensional nature of a musical organism and the listening multi-level human (un)consciousness.

These ideas I have presented on different occasions, including international congresses at some academic institutions in Europe, but something special for me was the possibility to introduce them in Eero Tarasti's metatus, University of Helsinki with his presence in May 2019.[10] I invited him to visit Nitra again, and it happened a couple months later the same year in November at Constantine the Philosopher Hall of our university. He had the lecture there titled *From Postcolonial Analysis to a Theory of Resistance – Social Aspects of Existential Semiotics*.[11]

(Anderson 2008: 293). Thus, the listener does not only perceive the events in the musical structures, but also everything encircling and surrounding him/her in the existential environment.

10 I had a series of the lectures then for the scholars of Department of Philosophy/History and Art Studies/Musicology, University of Helsinki with the topics 1. *The Existential Phenomenality of A Music (Alternative Model of the Music Semiosis)*, 2. *The Topicality of Peter Faltin´s Semiotics of Music*, 3. *Slovak Musical Alternatives*, and 4. *Influence of music semiotics and aesthetics on my music-intermedia arts*.

11 Tarasti lectured this time in the frame of series *Interdisciplinary Dialogues* of Faculty of Arts, Constantine the Philosopher in Nitra, November 13th 2019.

Tarasti presented in it three phases of latter semiotic development since 1960s, but mostly his own theories e. g. relation *Dasein – transcendence*, s. c. Zemic model of human mind (inspired by A. J. Greimas' square model), and he also questioned contemporary semiocrisis and resistance referring to indefensibility and malignance of explicit or latent (post)colonial ideology in humanistic discourse(!). These topics were deeply related with his very important work *Sein und Schein. Explorations in Existential Semiotics* (2015), opus magnum in the sphere of interdisciplinary (meta)semiotics, which involves philosophy, sociology, cultural studies, theories of art and the biosemiotics of organic systems. In resonant tension of the central categories *sein* and *schein*, he explores the "ontological-transcendental" questions of existential semiotics on a large thematic scale, and finds in original Zemic model many impulses to contemplate, to consider and reflect upon the questions of the subject (of its being as well as of its becoming) and the many consequences of our varieties of subjectivity. According to Tarasti, semiotic forces in the universe act in two opposite directions: from the body to values, from the concrete to the abstract, and from values and norms to the principle "khora". He deals also with issues such as transformations of the subject's being modus to other one, their dialogical relationship, the relation of the notion "schein" to reality, etc.[12]

For me there is another very important issue of Tarasti´s contemporary research: semio-crisis. . . According to him, semio-crisis lies in the fact that the observable signs of life and society do not correspond to their immanent structures anymore. They lose their isotopes, or connections, with real meanings. Mass media exploit, support and co-create this crisis state of things, while faking the exact opposite in a simulacrum way (coronacrisis/coronamatrix since 2020, please shows myriad sad and tragic examples and of this phenomenon). He questions the legitimacy of contemporary semiotics, this scientific discipline in today's radically different times of the internet and the voyeuristic, narcissistic, manipulating communication instigated by virtual social media and nets. He claims that (existential) semiotics is needed now much more than ever before, in this world

---

[12] Tarasti emphasizes that the real (together-)being of the text „in me/for me" is enacted between two poles of the world, where there is no sharp border line: between the *Dasein* and its transcendence. The transcendence is situated outside of reality (in absentia), but it is present (via *Dasein*) in our consciousness, i. e. not only in mine but in the consciousness of "the Other" as well. In these coordinates the author interprets also the term *mimesis* as the realization of transcendental meaning by the dialogical modelling of a certain new artistic reality *sui generis*, which affects the being of "the Other" in his/her irreducible and unknown otherness. (Tarasti 2015: 3–38).

of information smog and cultural slavery, especially when most of people do not know they live in it (S. Marcus).

I have to admit as an artist, musician and aesthetic scholar that existential semiotics plays very important role in my understanding the world, art, music and last but not least the meaning/the sense of uniqueness of human beingness. I can see a certain parallel between the experiences of art and semiotics despite of their disparities – I mean the richness of knowledge in *kairos*, in that "right moment". Meredith Monk, American woman composer, singer, director/choreographic artist, author of extraordinary specific type of opera, music theatre or "interdisciplinary performances" sees the usefulness of her whole artistic gesture (of music, poetry, detail choreography of motions) in the facts that it:

> affirms the imagination, mental freedom, creativity, and following your own path. . . . (What) art can do is to slow you down enough so that you really become more aware of reality. So that you actually wake up to look at the moment, what's going on in the moment. In that sense, art becomes a prototype or template for the richness of experience in the world that we're living in. And I think emotionally, because of the overload of speed and the kind of fragmentation that we live with and the density of information, I think that our nervous systems start numbing out. (Monk 2002: 5)

You must not agree with me, but I have sometimes co-equal experience while considering and contemplating the existential semiotic thoughts and ideas (not only about non-conventional music and art), which influenced my life more than I presumed.

References

Anderson, Louise L. 2008. The Musical Gesture: Does The Field Of Musical Semiotics Describe Our Phenomenal Experience With music? In *Music, Senses, Body*. Proceedings from the 9th International Congress on Musical Semiotics, Roma 19-23/09/2006. Imatra: UnwebPublications / Rome: Universtita of Roma Tor Vergata.

Cseres, Jozef. 1999. *Zvuk a tón, hlas a hláska, jazyk a prehovor, text a dielo, . . .skrátka hudba..* [Noise and tone, voice and speech-sound, language and talk, text and work of art. . . in short the music]. In *OS – Fórum občianskej spoločnosti 11*. Bratislava: Kalligram.

Cseres, Jozef. 2001. *Hudobné simulakrá* [Musical simulacra]. Bratislava: Hudobné centrum.

Cseres, Jozef. 2004. *Site & Room*. In: *Era21*. Brno.

Cseres, Jozef. 2010. Hudba, Etnológ, Ekonóm, Semiológ a Pojmotvorci (z cyklu *metaxu*) [Music, ethnologist, economist, semiologist, and conceptmakers (From the series *Metaxu*). In Július Fujak (ed.), *Otáz(ni)ky hudobnej semiotiky a estetiky*. Nitra: Univerzita Konštantína Filozofa.

Cseres, Jozef. 2011. *In the beginning was breath, not the word!* Text in booklet of CD Jean-Michel Van Schouwburg & Lawrence Casserley: *MountWind*. Nové Zámky: Kassák Cenre for Intermedia Creativity.

Faltin, Peter. 1985. *Bedeutung ästhetischer Zeichen. Musik und Sprache*. (Aechener Studien zur Semiotik und Kommunikationsforschung 1, ed. by Christa Nauch-Börner). Aachen: Rader Verlag.

Faltin, Peter. 1992a. *Význam v hudbe* [The Meaning in Music]. In *Slovenská hudba* [Slovak Music]. Bratislava: Slovenská muzikologická asociácia.

Faltin 1992b. *Ontologické transformácie v hudbe šesťdesiatych rokov* [Ontological transformations in music of 1960s]. *Slovenská hudba* 18(2). 175–179.

Fujak, Július. 2005. *Musical Correla(c)tivity. Notes on Unconventional Music Aesthetics*. Nitra: Faculty of Arts, Constantine the Philosopher University.

Fujak, Július (ed.). 2007. *Convergences and Divergences of Existential Semiotics*. Proceedings from symposium at Constantine the Philosopher University, April 12th 2007. Nitra: Faculty of Arts, Constantine the Philosopher University.

Fujak, Július. 2015. *Various Comprovisations. Texts on Music (and) Semiotics*. (Acta Semiotica Fennica XLVII, Approaches to Musical Semiotics 20). Helsinki: University of Helsinki, Semiotic Society of Finland.

Miko, František. 1989. *Aspekty literárneho textu* [The Aspect of Literary Text]. Nitra: Pedagogická fakulta.

Miko, František. 1995. *Význam, jazyk, semióza* [Meaning, Language, Semiosis]. Nitra : Vysoká škola pedagogická.

Monk, Meredith. 2002. *Frequently Asked Questions*. https://www.meredithmonk.org/

Morpurgo-Tagliabue, Guido. 1985. *Současná estetika* [Contemporary Aesthetics]. Praha: Odeon.

Prévost, Edwin. 1990. *Meta-Music and the Mutating Monster of Possessive Individualism – An Epic Struggle*. In *Marin d'Art*. Valencia.

Tarasti, Eero. 2000. *Existential semiotics*. Bloomington: Indiana University Press.

Tarasti, Eero. 2007. *On the Appearance or the Present Structure and Existential Digressions of the Subject*. In Július Fujak (ed.), *Convergences and Divergences of Existential Semiotics*. Proceedings from symposium at Constantine the Philosopher University, April 12th 2007. Nitra: Faculty of Arts, Constantine the Philosopher University.

Tarasti, Eero. 2015. *Sein und Schein. Explorations in Existential Semiotics*. Berlin/Boston: De Gruyter Mouton.

Žabka, Marek. 2004. *Avantgarda (autonomizácia hudobného materiálu)* [Avant-garde / Autonomisation of Musical Material]. In *Slovenská hudba* [Slovak Music]. Bratislava: Slovenská muzikologická asociácia.

Quotations from the texts written in Slovak language trans. by the author.

VEGA 1/0282/18 "The Nature and Development of the Independent Culture and Art in Slovakia after 1989" by this formulation, please: KEGA 041UKF-4/2022 "Preparation of Teaching Texts for Core Subjects of the Cultural Studies Program.

Lina Navickaitė-Martinelli
When a few Me-Tones meet: Beethoven *à la russe*

Abstract: When theorizing the phenomena related to the art of music performance, the question arises as to what extent those theoretical reflections, as well as historical, cultural, ideological issues and circumstances, influence the performers' interpretations. The main assumption of the present research is that no art is born ex-nihilo, even if an artist has no conscious interest in scientific studies or political proclamations. Artistic identity, interpretative choices, mental and physical selfhood of a performer are determined by various circumstances, including personal background, corporeal identity, stylistic requirements of a musical work, constraints of a particular tradition, etc. Employing Eero Tarasti's theory of the performer's subjectivity and his four logical cases in the light of Hegel and Fontanille (see Tarasti 2005) in order to produce a model of performance standards and individual performers' subjectivity, this article discusses interpretations of piano music by Ludwig van Beethoven as played by the twentieth-century Russian performers.

An important assumption in this article is that many stylistic qualities and semantic features of musical performance have their roots in schools of interpretation. Having acknowledged the existence of a "collective identity", and assumed that it affects performative signification, a further step is an empirical phase of research, which relates mostly to "subjective identity", that of the individual performer. Thus, of particular interest in the case of the "Russian Beethoven" is the conjunction of musical, personal and existential qualities necessary for communication to become possible between the endogenic (as well as exogenic) aspects of the several semiotic selves. The premise is that such an artistic encounter presupposes the interrelation of three *Me-Tones*: the composer himself, the specific Russian piano school with the standards and requirements it has set to its practitioners, and that of the individual pianists.

Keywords: Ludwig van Beethoven, Me-Tone, performer's subjectivity, music and ideology, Russian piano school

1 Introduction

My aim here is to apply existential semiotic theory to the field of musical performance, so as to show that many socio-musicological issues can be significantly expanded and enriched by approaching them from that perspective. Such issues as the artistic *Umwelt*, authenticity,[1] and the semiotic subject well apply to performance-related musicological research. Particularly with the notion of the semiotic subject, my hope is to enrich discourse about performance practices and the new meanings they create.

The semiotic subject, or self, consists of two essential aspects; namely, an inward and an outward side. This duality has been expressed in different ways by different scholars. We have, for instance, the "I" (self as such) and "Me" ("I" in the social context), as theorized by George Herbert Mead; *Moi* and *Soi* by French authors (Ricoeur, Sartre, Fontanille); the Controlling, deeper self versus the Critical self (Charles S. Peirce); and the Bergsonian differentiation between "superficial" and "deep" ego. Naomi Cumming, who has reflected deeply upon the performer's identity, speaks of "an outward and an inward face".

To the concept of semiotic self we add the code, or principle, of *Me-Tone* (*Ich-Ton*), borrowed from Jakob von Uexküll. By determining the characteristics—identity and individuality—of a particular organism, the concept of *Me-Tone* suggests further revelations about the performer's art. Each interpreter of music possesses one or several characteristic features, a kind of "semantic gesture",[2] which dominates his or her interpretation and distinguishes it from others. In addition to these immanent personal qualities, social and cultural background form the external identity of an artist, who may accept only some environmental norms while refusing others. Thus, a continual dialogue is established between the inner and outward sides of identity, the performer's *Moi* and *Soi*, the individual and collective subjectivities.

Eero Tarasti's (2005) theory of the performer's subjectivity and his four logical cases are applied here to twentieth-century Russian performers of Beethoven's piano music. It is proposed that three *Me-Tones* meet in this artistic encounter: the composer himself, the Russian piano school (with the standards

---

[1] The term "authenticity" is meant here not in its sense related to the early music revival and the authenticity movement in the field of music performance, but rather as a philosophical-semiotic term as used by Eero Tarasti and Dario Martinelli, among others, mostly in relation to ethical choices in culture.

[2] This broad and miscellaneous concept is used here rather freely. The term of a 'semantic gesture' belongs to the main figure of the Prague structuralism, Jan Mukařovský, and denotes (in the analysis of the individual aspects of a literary work) the uniqueness and entity of a literary sign.

and requirements it has set for its practitioners), and the individual pianists. We begin with the inner identity, or *Moi*, of Beethoven's music, and how it was perceived in Soviet Russia.

2 The composer

From today's perspective, Beethoven appears to stand, more or less, at a symbolic center of European music history; that is to say, between composers whose works and performing styles were discovered by historians and representatives of the early music movement, and those of slightly later generations, whose creative output, types of instruments and orchestras have remained consistent and almost the same as in their lifetimes. In a sense, Beethoven can be considered a "contemporary composer", in view of how his music still prevails in concert repertories. His masterpieces were not appreciated then left behind; rather, the tradition of listening to and performing Beethoven's works has continued from generation to generation. Thus, the history of Beethoven performances can be regarded as crucial to the general development of Western musical performance practices.

However, Beethoven's music, if constantly performed with conviction and delight, has yet remained something of an enigma. The reception of his music—especially the re-evaluation of it as a historical phenomenon—has led to ambiguity rather than certainty. Of course a significant factor in this paradox is that Beethoven's music can be attributed to two musical epochs at the same time, Classical and Romantic. And yet, when his works started being romanticized, everything that linked him with the Age of Enlightenment was forgotten with incredible ease.

As writings by his earliest critics attest, Beethoven's music enjoyed an almost immediate appeal, and its popularity has never waned. As a result of a propitious contiguity between the evocativeness of his music and events in his life, the mythicization of Beethoven proceeded steadily and unobstructed into the twentieth century. The myth was augmented by posthumous discoveries. The Heiligenstadt Testament, written in 1802 and revealing the composer's despair over his increasing deafness, proved the ideal combination of tragedy and genius. And there is his famous letter to the "Immortal Beloved", with its quintessential—almost stereotypical—features of the "true Romantic": the artist who feels marginalized and alienated from society; his strong desire for an idealized love; and his supreme gift for shaping such privations into unparalleled music.

All the pieces fell into place—and not necessarily posthumously. In the Biedermeier period, the then-emergent Romantic literary tradition had already started to frame Beethoven into fashionable conceptions of the creative artist, often coupled with metaphors of sanctity or martyrdom. Bettina Brentano compared Beethoven's creativity to the marvels of electricity, which the likes of Galvani and Volta were experimenting with in those days; E.T.A. Hoffmann would locate Beethoven in the "infinite realm of the spirit", the embodiment of the artist as suffering outsider and brave hero (quoted in Burnham 2001: 110–111).

The undisputed universality of Beethoven's music became so unique, in his and in following times, precisely because it was combined with eminently human elements: it was not the kind of universality that bears no face because it *transcends* individuality. On the contrary, it was a *sum* of individualities, the kind of universality that encompasses them all. As Richard Wagner wrote in 1851: "If by 'hero' we understand the complete, whole Man, to whom belong all the purely human feelings—of love, pain, and power—in their highest fullness and strength, we then grasp the correct subject that [Beethoven] shares with us in the gripping musical speech of his work" (quoted in Burnham 1995: xv). Humankind, indeed, came to be seen as the basic "matter" of his creation, as if Beethoven's music had to be a direct manifestation of human values.

2.1 Beethoven in Russia

The reception of art, and the discourses surrounding it, are inevitably woven into political and ideological contexts, at least to some extent. Yet, socio-political appropriation is not compulsory. It thus remains a charming experience to witness how the history of Beethoven reception abounds in episodes of this nature, related to both his music and his figure as a spiritual hero.

Beethoven's life surely was affected by the crucial and powerful changes of his society and his time, and all evidence suggests that he was far from indifferent to them. But that is a far cry from the numerous propagandist rewritings of his life and myth, naming Beethoven as their precursor and virtual supporter. German leaders, regardless of their political sympathies, have systematically exploited Beethoven's figure to support their actions and ideas. And, in principle, Beethoven's life itself has been constructed as that of a "political man" who would often compose "political music". David B. Dennis observes that in 1870 a unique confluence of events—the defeat of France, the founding of the Second Reich, and the one-hundredth anniversary of Beethoven's birth[3]—inspired apotheoses of the

---

3 Celebrating Beethoven's birthday was of no less importance also in Russia. The fact that these, as in the years 1927 or 1970, were even celebrated by the coining of several medals serves to il-

composer that welded the symbolic connection between his works and German politics (Dennis 1996: 5).

In this respect, many similarities might be observed in twentieth-century Russia, where art and politics were so intertwined and ideological viewpoints so dominant that to separate them was almost impossible. In addition to the overwhelming romanticizing of his music, another interesting paradox concerning Beethoven-reception came about. If political leaders of other times and contexts related Beethoven to their political discourses, the Soviet ideologues claimed that only they could truly appreciate the values of this composer. Revealing is a passage from the year 1927, which appeared in Moscow's main newspaper, *Pravda*:

> For the generation of the 20s and 30s of the last century, Beethoven was entirely too powerful. Only now, in the epoch of gigantic social changes, has the heroic voice of Beethoven received its due valuation. In commemorating him we emphasize how much he has to say to us in these days: the great musician and singer of heroism and civil achievements.
> (Braudo 1927: 4)

How did Beethoven, the representative of, first, German nationalism and, second, the bourgeois era, function in a country that had just experienced such an enormous cultural and political shock? Why was this composer allowed to remain in the repertories of Soviet musicians, and so much admired in this country?

In revolutionary Russia, it seemed at first inevitable that a workers' and peasants' government would be hostile to art institutions characteristic of the aristocracy and the *bourgeoisie*. And indeed, the relation of both revolutionary and Soviet Russia to any tradition (including their own) was complex and manifold.

Fortunately for the classics, Lenin proclaimed himself a philistine with respect to modern art movements. In an oft-quoted conversation with the German communist Klara Zetkin, he said, "We must preserve the beautiful, take it as a model, use it as starting point, even if it's 'old'. Why must we turn away from the truly beautiful just because it is 'old'? Why must we bow low in front of the new, as if it were God, only because it's 'new'?" (quoted in Schwarz 1972: 42). Moreover, the new so-called People's Commissar of Education, Anatoly Lunacharsky, was a highly educated and cultured man, who played a crucial role in mediating between a mistrustful intelligentsia and Bolshevik leaders. Both Lunacharsky

---

lustrate how admiring and possessive the Russian approach to Beethoven was. In 1927 the fourth volume of the History of Russian Music in Research and Materials was published by the Moscow Institute, and was called The Russian Book on Beethoven. Another important publication of that year was the so-called "Moscow Sketchbook" of Beethoven, which contains pencilled sketches for the String Quartets Op. 130 and Op. 132, commissioned by Prince Galitzin (see Schwarz 1972: 93).

and Lenin acknowledged the need for cultural continuity and for preserving old, "elitist" repertoires as firm foundations for a new, revolutionary art.

Fortunately for Beethoven, Russia's attitude toward him had been highly favorable ever since the nineteenth century, when Russian musicians immersed themselves in Beethoven studies. After the Revolution, a new element was added: the identification of Beethoven's personality and music with revolutionary ideals. Boris Schwarz (1972: 42) observes the following in his key study of musical life in Soviet Russia: "The idolization of Beethoven as a revolutionary hero became a Soviet obsession, stimulated by Lunacharsky, Asafiev, and many other authors". And we can see from Lunacharsky's manifesto to working youth, that Beethoven found a place at the core of the cultural heritage that the Soviets accepted.

> Above all music is adopted to be the language of the revolution, for revolution as was said by the poet [Aleksandr] Blok is in its very essence musical. It is dissolving [. . .] world-wide dissonance into harmony, into that which is acceptable to humanity, something definite about which can be said: there, it is attained. [. . .]

> History [gave] humanity at the beginning of the nineteenth century a great order—to reveal all storms of democracy organized for struggle. And humanity answered: "I have such an instrument. There is Ludwig von Beethoven." And it played [through] him [. . .] a gigantic prelude to the coming revolutionary music, when the Great French Revolution [was] replaced by the Great Russian—and with it also the World—Revolution. This is why Beethoven is akin to us.[4]

There is no need to discuss here all the subtle changes in political circumstances during the Soviet era. It is perhaps enough to mention the most important aesthetic doctrine in the country after 1934: *Socialist realism*. Espousing revolutionary aims in the socio-political sphere, and yet adopting a conservative canon of aesthetic values, in musical terms this doctrine resulted in the favoring of such forms as the program symphony, the dramatic cantata, and similar "narrative" genres, whose topics ranged from private suffering to the reaffirmation of social values. Naturally, there arose a connection with the Promethean works of Beethoven's middle period. "Naturally", because for a long time, and not only in Russia, the dispute over meaning in Beethoven's instrumental music had centered on a single issue: whether or not it has any "extra-musical" significance. In the course of time, as Scott Burnham argues, the original teller of a heroic story (Beethoven himself) became the *protagonist* of a similar story: "the romantic hero". Beethoven-reception treated him as the subject of his heroic-style works, bringing him through a

---

4 Address by the People's Commissar of Education at meeting of the working youth in Moscow. *Weekly News Bulletin* Vol. 4, No. 11–12 (March 25, 1927): 7–8.

similar trajectory of struggle and renewal to a point of apotheosis. The perceived meanings of the *Eroica* and the act of its creation merged, establishing a symbolic conjunction of work and artist (see Burnham 1995). Thus, it is no wonder that the meaning conferred on Beethoven's personality and his music in Soviet Russia was that of a revolutionary hero. In semiotic terms, the features of Beethoven's music accepted by Russian music theorists and practitioners were entirely taken from what they imagined to be his *Moi*, overwhelmingly dominated by the Greimassian modality of Will, and scornful of anything related to societal norms, the *Soi*, that is to say, all the Know and Must that Beethoven had mastered so well.[5]

In the works of the most influential music critic and theorist of the post-revolutionary period, Boris Asafiev, another interesting point emerges, something particularly suitable for Bolshevik ideology. In one of his many articles, Asafiev argues that Beethoven was perhaps the first composer-individualist, composer-citizen, i.e., a composer who no longer depended on church or aristocratic patronage. Asafiev emphasizes that only the composer's individualism was able to elevate music to such "heights of its possibilities", to bring out such "psycho-realistic tone" and "engaging-pictorial potentials"—all terms that Asafiev used in reference to Beethoven's works. In other articles, he found the sense of "collectivism" and "patriotism" in music—especially in collective song, one of the most important genres at that time—to have its roots in Beethoven. He further claimed that the sources of inspiration for Beethoven's "masculine rhythmic images" and melodies were the songs and theatrical life of a revolutionary Paris (see Asafiev 1957).

The importance of the existential values of Beethoven's music within the most diverse ideologies is unmistakably demonstrated by the use of his works (symphonies, above all) in countless political events and celebrations,[6] always with the implication, or open explanation, that such works carry distinctive, "elevated", moral qualities—surely, the same as those which the event in question intends to convey. In such cases, it is no surprise that mostly his "heroic" works were performed: the Third, Fifth, and Ninth Symphonies, in particular, became representative of monumentality and the Sublime, often as opposed to "mere" lyrical beauty. Paradoxically, for nineteenth-century Germans this

---

[5] While talking about the composer's work, Tarasti explains the modality of 'Will' as follows: the Greimassian *vouloir* appears in, say, Beethoven's sonata in those episodes where the composer is particularly heroic, that is, the way he wants to be (from Tarasti's Musical Semiotics seminars at the University of Helsinki, year 2005).

[6] Beethoven also wrote occasional music for political purposes; the best known are *Wellingtons Sieg oder Die Schlacht bei Vittoria*, Op. 91 (1813) and *Der glorreiche Augenblick*, Op. 136 (1814), both performed at the Congress of Vienna in 1814.

meant the difference between the German and the French or Italian traditions; then the Russians emphasized their own revolutionary values by relying on the very same musical works. Beethoven has also been exploited by modern politics: at a concert on 12 November 1989, commemorating the fall of the Berlin Wall, the Berlin Philharmonic performed the First Piano Concerto and the Seventh Symphony. It seems natural that the Finale of the Ninth Symphony, *An die Freude*, was approved as the anthem of the European Union. In Russia, such important events as Lenin's and Stalin's funerals featured Beethoven's music. As late as 2002, a concert in memory of the September 11 tragedy was held in the Grand Hall of Moscow Conservatory, at which event Beethoven's Ninth Symphony was performed. The press announcements proclaimed, "Beethoven to battle terrorists".

Two phenomena resulted from this passionately ideological atmosphere: the undying Russian political and theoretical admiration for Beethoven, and formation of the Russian piano school during the course of the twentieth century. Of particular interest from a semiotic point of view, is the impact of the strong ideological-aesthetic-pedagogical environment on the interpreter and on their individuality.

3 The school

The notion and influence of the school, or tradition, and its impact on the individual have changed over the course of time and are vanishing today, due to increasing standardization and cultural globalization. Can we still make any reasonable distinctions between individual or even collective styles in this context, where national and cultural diversities tend to interrelate and overlap? Especially relevant here is the gradual assimilation of individual styles and identities in musical performance, which started with the invention of the gramophone. It is certainly more difficult to talk about the notion of "school" when access to every kind of information has so significantly increased, compared with the times when the only means of absorbing someone else's knowledge, or getting acquainted with a certain tradition, was through live interaction. Several factors contributed to the increased standardization of performance practices, one of the most important being the significant penetration of the media into musical life, which helps create stereotypes in the minds of listeners and performers. Nowadays, favorable conditions for the unification of musical performance art are provided by the unprecedented access to any sort of information, from sound recordings to online masterclasses.

Hence, the validity of the notion of national school in the twentieth and twenty-first centuries is a controversial topic. Terms such as "global", "international", or "transnational", nowadays permeate political, economical, and cultural discourses.[7] In the field of musical performance, the pressing questions are, Can we still observe differences between performance styles and traditions? And, in particular, What tools can be used to analyze them? Finally, Is it reasonable to categorize artists according to the national or cultural heritage that they supposedly represent?

The concept of "school"[8] roughly denotes a type of standardization related to the style and type of playing technique and the gaining of experience. In this way it becomes a somewhat unifying factor in the pluralistic panorama of the several past ages of performance art. Moreover, in view of the increasing globalization of culture, the concept of school becomes not only a unifying factor, but one that helps preserve the cultural identity of a certain country or community. In any case, affiliation with a certain school embraces the *Soi*, the socially determined identity of an artist, which among other things consists of pre-established social codes and stereotypes of a given performance tradition (school). Below, I try to define the performance clichés or unifying features that allow for some generalizations in analyzing the art of Russian pianists.

3.1 Russian tradition of piano artistry

However vague the question of a national school might be nowadays, the idea of "the Russian piano school" was not coined merely for the sake of this article. Admittedly, the notion of the "school" has changed over the course of time, as has its influence on individual pianists; still, this term, especially in case of the Russian tradition, is widely used both among practicing musicians and music historians. Due to the country's comparative isolation for more than half of the last century, Russian pianists were following a tradition with roots in the Romantic era, thus forming a highly specific school as compared with Western pianism

---

7 For an excellent essay on issues of cultural globalization see DeVereaux and Griffin (2006).
8 According to Lithuanian violist and musicologist Donatas Katkus, the first constituent of a school is "a master, a concrete person possessing his or her knowledge and abilities, taste and aesthetic views as a certain whole which continues to repeat teaching every individual student"; the second constituent is "a school as a system where not one but many people draw on the similar principles, standards, aesthetic norms, tastes and fashions"; and the third constituent would define "tastes or aesthetic norms of the period, or, speaking in terms of the current practices, it would be a commercial image of music-making, i.e., a popular cliché" (Katkus 1997: 176).

of the same time. Moreover, in Russia, for a variety of reasons, the student-teacher bonds are much stronger than anywhere else. Unlike American piano students, for example, who are encouraged to add the names of as many teachers as possible to their resumés, Russians rarely have more than two teachers, and sometimes only one. Of course, the concept of the "Russian school" still serves perfectly as a commercial label, for instance, in the series of CDs issued by the Russian company *Melodiya*.

Institutionally, the bases for the Russian musical performance tradition were laid down in two conservatories: in St. Petersburg, founded by Anton Rubinstein in 1862, and in Moscow, placed under the directorship of Nikolai Rubinstein in 1866. The most prominent among the two conservatories' piano professors were Anton Rubinstein and Annette Yesipova; soon after, the first generation of graduates, such as Siloti, Safonov, Rachmaninov, and Goldenweiser, started their pianistic and teaching activities. Apart from the State conservatories, many private schools had been established in the two cities; some of them survived the post-Revolutionary exodus and the nationalization process, such as the school of the Gnesin sisters, which continued to produce many important virtuosos throughout the Soviet era.[9] An important note should be made on the distinction between the "Russian school on Soviet territory" and a "Russian school in Western Europe". As Schwarz (1972: 20) notes, for a time in the mid-1920s, so many Russian composers worked abroad that professional critics distinguished between these two manifestations of the Russian musical tradition. The same applies to the Russian school of musical performance, both of those times and in our day, with the necessary extension of this definition from Western Europe to the United States.

---

[9] In order to imagine better which personalities stand at the roots of the Russian piano performance tradition, some "genealogical trees" are rather helpful. Regarding Beethoven-interpretation, one can distinguish at least four lines of descent. (1) The rise of the Russian piano tradition stemming from its pioneer Anton Rubinstein, a distinctive propagator of Beethoven's music. The influence of Rubinstein's piano school is prominent in the art of Russian pianist Heinrich Neuhaus, who is considered a father of modern Russian piano performance school ("modern" in the sense that some of its representatives are still active pianists or teachers). (2) The line that derives directly from Franz Liszt: Konstantin Igumnov, a student of Liszt's pupil Paul Pabst, taught such influential Beethoven-specialists as Mariya Grinberg, Alexander Goldenweiser and Yakov Flier. (4) As an important branch of Igumnov's influence, we must mention the school of Goldenweiser, another important pillar of the Russian tradition. (4) Finally, less complex but equally important, is that branch in the line of Vassily Safonov's teaching, himself a pupil of Teodor Leszetycki and a director of the Moscow Conservatory. Names such as Scriabin and Medtner represent this school, as also Leonid Nicolaiev, who in turn taught Vladimir Sofronitsky, Maria Yudina, and Dmitry Shostakovich, among others. For more details on the "genealogical trees", see Navickaitė 2014.

So many pedagogues belonging to the Russian school are working abroad nowadays that in some Western conservatories it becomes impossible to talk about any influential local tradition.

To define the *Me-Tone* of a certain school might be the most dubious undertaking of this research, and for several reasons. Most of all, because it is difficult to name fundamental features of an "organism" that is quite heterogeneous and undergoing constant changes and development. Does the *Moi* of a "school" depend on the mentality of people living in a certain geographical space, under certain specific social or cultural circumstances? Or is it located in their immanent physical qualities? If the answer to these questions is Yes, we may assume the existence of several, specifically "Russian" features that are immanently characteristic of pianists born or trained in that part of the world.

What, then, are the specific features of Russian piano art? The subjective penetration into the inner world of music, beauty of timbre, extraordinary melodiousness and extension of piano sound, a wide range of emotional and dynamic contrasts—all these features distinguish the Russian piano school. Even if this somewhat mysterious "Russian technique" is only partly true, the artistic image, way of hearing and intoning, and embodiment of a certain idea in one's performance have always been more important to Russian performers than to others. From a purely technical point of view, some elements of piano teaching, such as how to use the natural weight of the arms and body in a relaxed state so as to create the phrase, are extremely important in the Russian pedagogical system. And this is again perhaps something that makes Russian pianists sound unique.

What is the *Soi* of this school? Is it the surrounding ideology? Particular training? The traditional training of young Russian players has proved to be highly beneficial and successful. The fact that each virtuoso there was expected, in turn, to devote part of their time to teaching insured the continuance of tradition. (Until very recently, the phenomenon of a "posting" to a certain job was in practice in the former Soviet territory.) In addition to technical aspects, cultural context is extremely important for Russian teachers. Many examples from literature, art, and cinema are used in their lessons, which undoubtedly contributes to creating imaginative minds in future virtuosos. We also should not forget the impact of prominent theorists on the art of performers. Boris Asafiev's writings on "intonation" come to mind. Indeed, a very precise intoning, attention to every phrase, and singing, "vocal-expressive" style are among the features of the Russian school. Just as evident is the reception of Beethoven as "powerful", "enthusiastic", "massive", "gigantic", "flying onwards", "stormy", "passionate", "revolutionary" —all terms used by Asafiev (1957) to describe Beethoven's music.

A certain semiotic framework would allow us see how the concepts borrowed from existential semiotics can contribute to the analysis of the art of musical performance. The third *Me-Tone*, that of the individual performer, is discussed below through a semiotic approach to the performer's subjectivity.

4 The performer

Musical semiosis, like all sign activity, is affected by many cultural, social and psychological factors. Artistic identity, interpretative choices, mental and physical selfhood of a performer are determined by various circumstances, including personal background, corporeal identity, stylistic requirements of a musical work, constraints of a particular tradition, etc. As stated above, every performer possesses a certain "semantic gesture" that distinguishes their interpretations from other performances. On the basis of this distinctive selfhood—the performer's *Me-Tone*—we can speak of two kinds of signs: endo-signs and exo-signs, inner and outer characteristics that dominate one's interpretative choices and that constitute the semiotic identity of a performer.

Revealing are Naomi Cumming's considerations concerning the performer's self. According to her, it may be considered as "having an outward and an inward face" (Cumming 2000: 10). On the outward side, Cumming (2000: 10) sees the perceptible result of an individual's patterned choices within a social domain, those characteristic manners of forming sound or gesture that distinguish him or her from the "crowd"—a personal "style". Perceiving selfhood as an intrinsically social, interactive, and mobile experience, Cumming writes:

> It is when I become aware of the "outward" face of my musical identity, as a pattern of actions, that I can begin to question how I am constrained in my performance. What is the ideology that governs me? What is the domain of my choice? How free am I? These are musical questions, and yet they are an allegory of broader questions about the expressivity of social life. Noticing those sounds I "cannot" make, I begin to gain awareness of those scarcely articulate "beliefs" that present themselves as inhibitions to a convincing performance of a work. I see that my musical inhibitions and social ones are not entirely unconnected. The "outward" identity, of choices audible in sound, reflects a pattern of belief, desire, and inhibition that constitutes an "inner self"—what it is to be "me".
>
> (Cumming 2000: 11)

To give these reflections a more structured shape, a semiotic model is employed here, to illustrate the inner and outer influences, individuality, and standards underlying the creative work of a performer. The scheme in Figure 1 is elaborated from Eero Tarasti's semiotic square of a performer's subjectivity, based on four logical cases.[10] The *Moi* side of the performer's self is related here to the Greimassian internal (endogenic) modalities Will and Can, while the *Soi* part of one's identity is reflected by the external (exogenic) modalities Know and Must; thus, encompassed are all spheres and categories through which the performer's art is communicated.

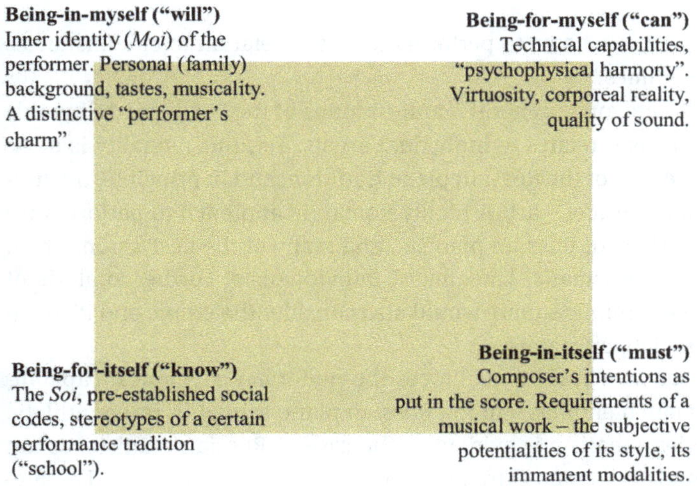

Being-in-myself ("will")
Inner identity (*Moi*) of the performer. Personal (family) background, tastes, musicality. A distinctive "performer's charm".

Being-for-myself ("can")
Technical capabilities, "psychophysical harmony". Virtuosity, corporeal reality, quality of sound.

Being-for-itself ("know")
The *Soi*, pre-established social codes, stereotypes of a certain performance tradition ("school").

Being-in-itself ("must")
Composer's intentions as put in the score. Requirements of a musical work – the subjective potentialities of its style, its immanent modalities.

Figure 1: Individuality and standards in the art of a performer (after Eero Tarasti's theory of subjectivity).

- *Being-in-myself* (Greimassian modality of "will") means the inner identity (*Moi*) of a performer. This may include personal (family) background, tastes, or spiritual beliefs. It also encompasses the person's musicality, together with a distinctive "performer's charm", or charisma.
- *Being-for-myself* ("can") embraces the performer's technical capabilities, "psychophysical harmony". Also included here are virtuosity, corporeal reality, and sound quality as realized in performance.
- *Being-for-itself* ("know"), or the *Soi* of a performer, consists of pre-established social codes, stereotypes of a given performance tradition (school);

---

10 Tarasti's theory of a subject is developed in the light of Hegelian logic, namely his categories of an-sich-sein (being-in-itself) and für-sich-sein (being-for-itself), which (as well as their expansion in Tarasti's work – 'being-in-myself' and 'being-for-myself') are altogether renounced in this study due to a different theoretical emphasis. For a broader explanation of these philosophical and semiotic concepts cf. Tarasti 2000, 2005, and 2012.

usually, according to certain standards, some manners of playing are rated higher than others.
- *Being-in-itself* ("must") means the composer's intentions as put in the score, the work's immanent modalities. It is something called for by the requirements of a musical work: the subjective potentialities of its style, without which the work could not "live".

How can one apply this scheme to performance art in relation to circumstances and tastes of Soviet times?

It is difficult to categorize general manifestations of the "will" modality; this seems possible only as it relates to individual artists. Yet, this modality is often considered to be the core of the Russian piano tradition, and in principle, the fundamental *Moi* of a performer's art. A highly Romantic approach to performance practice is characteristic of Russian pianists, and many of the best among them may be considered charismatic, "magnetic" individualists. Further analysis of the first angle of the semiotic square would also consider the ethnic and ideological identities of Soviet performers.

The modality of "can", which embraces the performer's technical capabilities, also receives much emphasis in the Russian piano school. A rather athletic conception of professionalism is evident in the case of Russian pianists, as are the big, broad sound and tempo extremes that mark their performances. The specific features of an instrument also belong to this modality, and are important to the Russian performance tradition, especially concerning the desired cantabile quality of the piano.

This brings us to the third modality, "know". Despite the wide variety of individual pianists of this school, most tend to follow the Romantic piano tradition. Consequently, they concentrate on tone and timbre, especially on deep, robust sound and as mentioned, on cantabile. Conveying extra-musical meaning is important, and in trying to achieve that goal, many ways of exuding a Romantic mystique are chosen, depending on the artist: from powerful emotionalism to meditative contemplation, from profound reflection to extravertive brilliance. The "know" modality represents also the idea of the institutional school, since in Russia even the bonds of the student-teacher relationship lean toward exaggeration.

Finally, we reach the modality of "must", where the composer's identity comes to the fore. Analysis of this semiotic aspect of performance surely has to take into account musical structures, through detailed examination of particular pieces and their various interpretations. Ideological content is also important here, and we have already mentioned Russians' admiration for Beethoven's persona and for the values reflected in his art. Both this ideological and theoretical idolization has undoubtedly contributed to the highlighting of Romantic and heroic values in Russian performances of his works.

Certain difficulties arise when deciding to which modality— "know" or "must"—one ought to ascribe the extremely strong censorship carried out by *Glavrepertkom*,[11] which regulated musical repertories and granted permission for concert trips during the Soviet era. Programs, announcements, posters, even concert bills were subject to advance approval. This was something that artists not only "knew" but also "had to" obey, in order to maintain at least their artistic careers, if not something more vital. One assumes that the same constraints apply to musicians working under similar totalitarian or fascist regimes.[12]

There is one modality absent from our scheme, namely, that of "believe", the importance of which should not be underrated. It is precisely the epistemic values of Beethoven's music that give it credibility. Its persuasiveness in reception, the implicit extramusical meanings that it holds for its performers and listeners— these are vitally important in its interpretations by Russian musicians. At least since the days of Asafiev, Beethoven's has been considered the "truest speech".

4.1 When the *Me-Tones* meet: Beethoven as played by Russian pianists

Some detailed accounts are relevant to the art of exponents of the Russian piano school, as gathered from their interpretations of Beethoven's piano sonatas. If the essence of Russian piano art is the prevalence of strong *Moi*, i.e., the breaking of common rules, eschewing of norms and interpretive clichés, then we may look at a few of the so-called eccentric, extravagant, and unpredictable artists who belong to the Russian piano tradition.

One of these was Vladimir Sofronitsky (1901–1961), an emotional and erratic artist, always intriguing, although his performance of the Classics may have been considered as lacking balance. Another equally unstable musician was the legendary Vladimir Horowitz (1903–1989), who, though ethnically Ukrainian, became an ardent disciple of the Russian piano school. Just after emigrating to

---

11 *Glavnaya repertuarnaya kommissia* (The Main Repertoire Committee) was a special section of *Narkompros* (*Narodnyj komissariat prosveschenija* (People's Commissariat for Enlightening), which approved of performers' repertoires.
12 Musicians, unlike, say, theatre artists or the literati, were often less harassed by regimes of all kinds, perhaps mostly due to music's non-referential nature; for more on this issue, see my interviews with representatives of the (Soviet) Russian piano school in Navickaitė-Martinelli 2010.

the West, Horowitz became known as the "Wild Russian", due to the spontaneous virtuosity and nervous strain of his performances.

In addition to the stylistic devices mentioned above, such as primacy of subjectivity and expressivity, fluctuations of tempo and dynamics are very typical of the Russian Romantic tradition. Analysis of tempo in musical enunciations shows alternations of general tempos among interpretations by different performers. I also have in mind such temporal strategies as retardations and accelerations within a basic tempo, as well as changes among dynamic levels. Dynamic, rhythmic, and tempo changes create a certain sense of disorder, which is rather characteristic of Horowitz's interpretations of the Classics. These features, together with emphasis on virtuosity, a broad dynamic spectrum, and much pedaling, well represent the Russian style. Horowitz did not play much Beethoven, but those works that do appear in his discography are worth study as representing this Romanticist tendency of interpretation.[13]

Especially in post-Revolutionary and post-War times, "healthy" emotions were greatly appreciated by the government and the people. Art was supposed to move masses of new listeners, to be natural and easily comprehensible. In this light, academic concepts predominated in performances. One such "normal", academically oriented player was Lev Oborin (1907–1974), winner of the first Chopin Competition in Warsaw in 1927, the first in what was to become a series of remarkable triumphs by Soviet-trained *virtuosi* at international competitions. Another player of similar orientation was Mariya Grinberg (1908–1978), the first female pianist to record the whole cycle of Beethoven sonatas. Her style of interpreting Beethoven is very romantic and somewhat "earthy" at the same time: impulsive and technically strong, with emphasis on the "meaning" or narrative in a piece. Even the first bars of the *Moonlight* Sonata, as she plays it, seem to "tell" (not just contemplate) something. There is always a yearning or going forward to be sensed in Grinberg's playing, with its deep sound, much pedaling, and consistently dramatic and passionate *fortes*.

The international success of the Russian piano school has strong connections with the name of Heinrich Neuhaus (1888–1964). A great teacher, Neuhaus created his own highly intellectual and at the same time very romantically oriented school of pianism. Having preferred a kind of "oral" pedagogical tradition,

---

[13] Performances of various sonatas by Beethoven as played by the Russian performers mentioned in this article were analyzed before any conclusions were drawn. The only ones referred to above are the Sonata Op. 27 No. 2 in C sharp minor, *Moonlight* as played by Maria Grinberg (rec. 1961) and Heinrich Neuhaus's interpretation of the Sonata Op. 31 No. 2 in D minor, *The Tempest* (rec. 1946).

Neuhaus's classes were always open for anyone from the Conservatory to attend. This undoubtedly can be considered a real, conscious creation of a "school".

We might study the requirements of the Neuhaus's school by examining his performance of Beethoven's Sonata Op. 31 No. 2, *The Tempest*. What first strikes one is the incredibly fast tempos and sudden tempo changes, many *ritardandi*, uneven rhythmic patterns, and numerous arpeggiations. Neuhaus's interpretation may be seen as indeed projecting images of a tempest: impulsive, chaotic, and romanticized, with dynamic and other contrasts markedly emphasized. What fascinates one about Neuhaus's interpretation is the subtle figurations of phrases and free manner of playing, which often evokes associations with a pianist of a younger generation, Vladimir Horowitz. Neuhaus's own preferences come to light where he writes about how Beethoven was performed by a famous pianist of the German school, Egon Petri: "Petri is a little formalist in Beethoven. He emphasizes first of all the intellectual, constructive sides of Beethoven's works. The natural, heroic pathos of Beethoven, his deep spiritual tension, incredible passion, his 'boiling' play of imagination – all this finds no adequate expression in the performance of Petri" (Neuhaus 1975: 157). Needless to say, all the aforementioned features find a place in Neuhaus's interpretations.

Among Neuhaus's students, two were rated as superb concert pianists: Sviatoslav Richter (1915–1997) and Emil Gilels (1916–1985). Richter's interpretations are widely known, thus requiring little discussion. Still, there is something to be said about the place that Beethoven's works occupied both in Richter's repertory and in his teacher-student relationship with Neuhaus.

Richter has played twenty-two sonatas by Beethoven. Yet Neuhaus only made him play Opus 110, which Richter did not want to do; but it was precisely in this work where Neuhaus taught him to obtain a singing tone, the one that Richter had always sought. Since then, and after several other important encounters with Beethoven's music, the composer's sonatas became highly significant of Richter's pianism. The style in which Richter preferred to play and to hear Beethoven differs greatly from the Romantic interpretations of his famous teacher. But as concerns a somewhat nationalist approach, it is suitable to quote Richter's notes after the Brandis Quartet performed Beethoven's Quartets Nos. 12 and 13: "A massive program solidly and ponderously played by large fat Germans. Not bad, but very German. After a concert like this, what better than to go to a restaurant and order sausages, sauerkraut *und so weiter*?" (quoted in Monsaingeon 2001: 302).

Another pupil of Neuhaus, Emil Gilels, serves as one of the most canonical examples of an earthy yet broadly passionate type of playing. As his teacher wrote in 1936, "treating Beethoven a little dry-scholastically still recently, now he [Gilels] has sort of 'revealed' him. And all these boundless treasures of the emotional and intellectual world of this greatest composer and human have confronted him" (Neuhaus 1975: 142). Gilels recorded the complete Beethoven concertos three times, but unfortunately died in 1985, while in the midst of recording the Beethoven sonatas for Deutsche Grammophon. Gilels's tone in Beethoven is especially robust; quite frequently his presentations sound over-pedalled and thick, falling sometimes into a tantrum of extremely loud chords. As David Dubal writes, "[. . .] in essence Gilels's Beethoven is not Germanic, but has been transformed into a Byronic Beethoven—or perhaps even 'Pushkinian' would be apt" (Dubal 1990: 104). One distinctive feature of Gilels's interpretations is the intense level of intimacy. This is not a quiet intimacy, but rather a complete removal of the distance between subject and object in the process of musical signification. His passionate, deep sound creates a sense of "nearness", indicating the importance of the interpreter's energy for the process of musical performance. Such are the main attributes of Gilels's musical communication.

4.2 Trends of the late 20th century

Compared with the times when prominent professors—Neuhaus, Igumnov, or Yakov Zak—were working at the Russian conservatories, one finds that much has been reduced to the average toward the end of the 20th century. What used to be piece-production has been put on a conveyer belt. As a result, many maintain the performer's individuality has been lost and that upon hearing contemporary young Russian pianists, even the strongest ones, we would hardly remember their names.[14] Still, some names, such as Mikhail Pletnev, Andrey Gavrilov, Arcady Volodos, or Denis Matsuyev, are undoubtedly steady carriers of the label "Russian Piano School" into the 21st century, where the youngest generation comes into the scene.[15]

A highly interesting pianist still active on the concert stage is Grigory Sokolov (b. 1950). Richter was already heading in this kind of "mystical" direction. But Sokolov's performances go even further in their deviation from a romanticist aes-

---

[14] Telling, however, is the case of the Chopin competition in Warsaw in autumn 2010. Five pianists representing Russia (one of them, the second-prize winner Lukas Geniušas, represented Russia/Lithuania) advanced to the final phase of the competition – a quite notable achievement even for a country with such a solid piano-performance tradition. Is Russian pianism making a "comeback"? Or does this simply prove once again the Russian school's particular strength in interpreting Romantic music?
[15] Playing of such original pianists as Daniil Trifonov (b. 1991), Evgeny Starodubtsev (b. 1981), Pavel Kolesnikov (b. 1989) or Alexander Kashpurin (b. 1996) allows making an assumption that this school's merging with other contemporary tendencies produces the best results, and yet the intrinsically *Russian* flavor is the most distinct in this recipe.

thetics. His appearance onstage is very ascetic, and his playing grabs the listener, almost inducing a kind of hypnosis. He can become a thinker or a wild, extremely intense player, according to whatever image is needed to interpret a particular piece of music. Extremes of tempo, dynamics, and inner tension are specific features of his art.

I would distinguish one more name, Evgeny Kissin (b. 1971), who is sometimes labeled as "the last" of the great Russian tradition. However, he is mentioned here not so much because of his marvelous qualities as a pianist, but mainly for his almost mysterious connection with his late teacher, Anna Kantor. Even after Kissin had achieved celebrity, Kantor remained his teacher, often offering advice and making suggestions—much as Alexander Goldenweiser did with Grigory Ginzburg, and Lazar Berman, or Heinrich Neuhaus with Richter, long after all three had become celebrated pianists. Kissin repeatedly states that the reason Kantor has been his teacher for so long, is simply because she knew him as an artist better than anyone else, which made her advice invaluable. Kantor's impact on Kissin might be compared with the influence that Alicia Keseradze had on Ivo Pogorelich, another remarkable representative of the eccentric branch of the Russian tradition.

5 Concluding remarks: "Beethoven à la russe"

As stated above, the process of musical semiosis is continuously affected by various cultural, social, and psychological factors. Thus, all compositional or interpretative insights and innovations are directly influenced not only by the subjective identities of composers or performers, but also by traditions and contexts, cultural constraints and circumstances, styles and trends. As regards musical performance, it might seem that interpretations of music should directly stem from structural and semantic depths, that is, from the narrative logic of the musical work. (Indeed, in most musicological circles, the composer's idea seems to be taken as a kind of absolute, and the performer is supposed to remain as "transparent" as possible.) What happens, though, is that we constantly face many different interpretations of the same work, the discursive figures and modal characteristics of which are significantly different from or even contrary to each other. And still, the performer is not absolutely free to make their interpretative decisions. What, then, are the conditions that govern the art of the interpreter?

An important assumption in this article, is that many stylistic qualities and semantic features of musical performance have their roots in schools of interpretation. Despite the fact that the ideals and influences of a school on the individual have changed over time, the longstanding, quasi-national approaches to music historiography still contribute to the persistence of different approaches to performance. One may ask, If differences in music theory in different countries are still quite distinctive, why should the matter be different in the field of musical performance? Even amid the general trend toward uniformity of style, the term "school" still enjoys wide usage, especially in the case of old, prominent traditions, such as the Russian, the French, the German, or Italian. Performers who can situate themselves in a certain distinctive professional genealogy are usually very eager to emphasize the importance of this aspect of their artistic practice.

Having acknowledged the existence of a "collective identity", and assumed that it affects performative signification, a further step is to enter an empirical phase of research, which relates mostly to "subjective identity", that of the individual performer. To do so requires the careful registering of subtle differences among various interpretations, determining the modalizations employed by each interpreter, and trying to find connections between those and the internal semiotic paradigm of certain musical works. In this way we may examine how "Beethoven *à la russe*", the uncompromising Beethovenian *Moi*, interacts with both the subjective and collective identities of a given performer.

Of particular interest in the case of the "Russian Beethoven" is the conjunction of musical, personal and existential qualities necessary for communication to become possible between the endogenic (as well as exogenic) aspects of the several *Me-Tones*. Thrown into the flow of passionately romanticized interpretations, the *Moi* of this composer, viewed as belonging to a certain cultural and ideological context, has gained remarkable universality. The doctrines or beliefs that shape our imaginings about this artist have continued to evolve from his lifetime up to the present day. This has enabled interpreters—of various ideological and aesthetic persuasions and trends, and from different cultural epochs and performing styles—to claim Beethoven's music and the extra-musical meanings surrounding it as being *theirs*.

References

Asafiev, Boris. 1957. *Izbrannyje trudy* [Selected Writings]. Vol. 5. Moskva: Izdatelstvo akademii nauk SSSR.
Bone, Jonathan. 2000. Militancy on the Cultural Front: 1920s Avant-Gardism and Cultural Revolution. http://www.uwm.edu/Course/448-343/index3.html (retrieved 30.3.2007)
Braudo, Eugene. 1927. Beethoven festivals in the USSR. *Weekly News Bulletin* 4 (15–16), April 22.
Burnham, Scott G. 1995. *Beethoven: Hero*. Princeton, NJ: Princeton University Press.

Burnham, Scott G. 2001. Beethoven, Ludwig van. In Stanley Sadie (ed.), *The New Grove Dictionary of Music and Musicians*, 2nd edition, Volume 3, 73–140. London: Macmillan.
Cumming, Naomi. 2000. *The Sonic Self: Musical Subjectivity and Signification*. Bloomington and Indianapolis, IN: Indiana University Press.
Dennis, David B. 1996. *Beethoven and German Politics, 1870–1989*. New Haven, CT and London: Yale University Press.
DeVereaux, Constance & Martin Griffin. 2006. International, global, transnational: Just a matter of words? Paper presented at the 4th International Conference on Cultural Policy Research. 12–16 July. Available at: www.eurozine.com
Dubal, David. 1990. *The Art of the Piano: An Encyclopaedia of Performers, Literature and Recordings*. London: I. B. Tauris.
Katkus, Donatas. 1997. Atlikimo stilius ir klišės [Styles and Clichés of Performance]. In Rūta Goštautienė (ed.), *Baltos lankos 9*. 164–182. Vilnius: Baltos lankos.
Monsaingeon, Bruno. 2001. *Sviatoslav Richter: Notebooks and Conversations*. Trans. by Stewart Spencer. London: Faber and Faber.
Navickaitė-Martinelli, Lina. 2010. *Pokalbių siuita. 32 interviu ir interliudijos apie muzikos atlikimo meną* [A Suite of Conversations: 32 Interviews and Interludes on Music Performance Art]. Vilnius: Versus aureus.
Navickaitė-Martinelli, Lina. 2014. *Piano Performance in a Semiotic Key: Society, Musical Canon and Novel Discourses*. Helsinki: Semiotic Society of Finland.
Neuhaus, Heinrich. 1975. *Razmyshlenija, vospominanija, dnevniki: Izbrannyje statji* [*Thoughts, Memories, Diaries: Selected Articles*]. Moscow: [n.p.].
Schwarz, Boris. 1972. *Music and Musical Life in Soviet Russia 1917–1970*. London: Barrie & Jenkins.
Tarasti, Eero. 2000. *Existential Semiotics*. Bloomington and Indianapolis: Indiana University Press.
Tarasti, Eero. 2005. Existential and Transcendental Analysis of Music. *Studi musicali* 2. 223–266.
Tarasti, Eero. 2012. Existential semiotics and cultural psychology. In Jaan Valsiner (ed.), *The Oxford Handbook of Culture and Psychology*, 316–341. Oxford, New York: Oxford University press.

Rodrigo Felicissmo
In the quest of compositional matrices for music themes concerning landscape: Exploring senses as a means for creative processes. Villa-Lobos and his existential signs

Abstract: This essay comprises the dialog between visual art and music. Since 2015, Elisa Bracher and Rodrigo Felicissimo have established new frontier in the discussion and production of a creative process known as the compositional technique "Melody of the Mountain", originally developed by the Brazilian composer Heitor Villa-Lobos (1887–1959). The aim of the artwork project is to bring out the experience acquired from this creative technique study over a series of art expeditions settled on the Artic mountains, Andes mountains the South American highlands of *Condoriri* in Bolivia, *Cuzco* in Peru and along the mountain range of Serra dos *Órgãos*, Rio de Janeiro, Brazil. In these expeditions Elisa Bracher has taken a range of landmark photographs with a pinhole camera. Back in her studio, she developed an array of artwork such as paintings, drawings, and sculpture.

Subsequently, Rodrigo Felicissimo registered these images in order to develop them, through Villa-Lobos compositional technique, in a set of graphics relating to the melodic themes. The obtained melodies finally were harmonized and composed for chamber music ensembles.

This ongoing research has taken ground into the field of music signification studies, based on the subject statement assign on Eero Tarasti's "Metaphors of nature and organicism, (2015).

The work in progress has so far produced a first series of paintings, photographs, poems, music composition in a suite form and a set of songs, one of them, *Vuoristoilmaa* ("mountain air") with the participation of the Finnish soprano Laura Pyrrö, that translated it into Finnish and sang the composition, during Rodrigo's presentation session in the Symposium Sources of Creativity: from Local to Universal, in Mikkeli, Finland, 2018. This essay present discussions, achievements and contributions obtained to this point and introduces new argument on the development of this technique focused on the mountains of Riverside County, California State mountains and the Grand Canyon National Park, under the guidance of Professor Paulo C. Chagas at the University of California – Riverside.

https://doi.org/10.1515/9783110789164-052

Keywords: creative processes, composition technique, melody of the mountains technique, photography and music, watercolor paintings, drawings

Figure 1: The "Melody of the Mountains" composition technique. The photo by Elisa Bracher represents a music transcription by Rodrigo Felicissimo's artistic sketch work from *Condoriri La derecha* at Andes mountains in Bolivia. The "Mirror of the Mountains Project" – **Bienalsur**, 2016.

The "Mirror of the Mountains Project" is an artwork in progress that gather pinhole photography, paintings, music sketches and composition regarding landscape setting.

This project comprises the dialog between visual art and music. Since 2015, Elisa Bracher and Rodrigo Felicissimo have established new frontier in the discussion and production of a creative process known as the compositional technique "Melody of the Mountain", originally developed by the Brazilian composer Heitor Villa-Lobos (1887–1959). The aim of the artwork project is to bring out the experience acquired by this creative technique study over a series of art expeditions settled on the Artic mountains, Andes mountains the South American highlands of *Condoriri* in Bolivia (as shown in figure 1), *Cuzco* in Peru and along the mountain range of *Serra dos Órgãos*, Rio de Janeiro, Brazil. In these expeditions Elisa Bracher has taken a range of landmark photographs with a pinhole camera. Back in her studio, she developed an array of artwork such as paintings, drawings, and sculpture.

Next, Rodrigo Felicissimo registered these images in order to develop them, through Villa-Lobos compositional technique, in a set of graphics relating to the melodic themes. The obtained melodies finally were harmonized and composed for chamber music ensembles.

The work in progress so far has produced a first series of paintings, photographs, poems, music composition in a suite form and a set of songs, one of them, *Vuoristoilmaa* ("mountain air") with the participation of the Finnish soprano Laura Pyrrö, that translated it into Finnish and sang the composition, during Rodrigo's presentation session in the Symposium Sources of Creativity: from Local to Universal, in Mikkeli, Finland, 2018. The intent of this essay is to present discussions, achievements and contributions obtained so far and to introduce new argument on the development of this technique focused on the mountains of Riverside County, California State mountains and the Grand Canyon National Park, with the collaboration of Professor Paulo C. Chagas from the University of California – Riverside.

Figure 2: In Elisa Bracher's exhibition, *Field of Bells (dedicated in memory of the educator Sonia Maria Sawaya Botelho Bracher)* was a musical poem installation that traces musical correspondence with the photograph taken by the artist in the Arctic. The piece was created using the method developed by Heitor Villa-Lobos, to musically transpose the sinuosity of the mountains. *Luctus Lutum Exhibition*, **Gallery Raquel Arnaud,** 2015.
Field of Bells – an artistic expedition toward landscape, sketches, and music composition: exploring geographical landmarks for creative purposes.

Field of Bells is the title of a musical composition by Rodrigo Felicissimo based on the images captured by Elisa Bracher in her journey in the Artic, part of their previous work together at an earlier date (as shown in figure 2). The music results from the application of a technique for reading images researched and studied by the author. It is a composition technique known as "Graph for Plotting the Melody of the Mountains of Brazil", used by Heitor Villa-Lobos (1887–1959) in his *Symphony No. 6 – "On the Outlines of the Mountains of Brazil"* (1944), *New York Sky-Line Melody* (1939) and *Pico do Itabira* (1943).

Therefore, our proposed approach involves the concepts of reading and understanding the signs of landscape phenomena as an important instrument for multidisciplinary research on composition creative processes and the epistemology of musical signification studies.

The research is focused in environmental ecology as an introduction to the subject related to phenomenology and the strategy for understanding the multiple perspectives of nature, landscape, and the continuing dynamics of transforming space through the behavior of men and nature itself. Sound sensations change as you cross valleys, climb mountains, enter deserted plains, pass through damp plateaus, sail to the islands, cross a glacier, stay overnight under the top of the rainforest, among others. That should partially reflect the idea of studying a specific region by maps, photograph camera, audio recorder, video camera, etc. As well, feel the scent must be taken as a way of perceiving the space, thus gathering the senses on multiple scale and forms to understand landscape and its symbolic illustration identities. It is truly a procedure of considering local culture traditions and their relationship with the natural habitat that surrounds them. Photographs as well, gives us a registered statement of landscape, an image of a context region, by observing, reveals a certain stage of development from social practices over nature. Furthermore, it reveals religious principles, identifying imagery into symbolic geographical landmarks.

This project was introduced during the 3rd Seminar and Symposium of the Academy of Cultural Heritages at Hermoupolis, Syros island (Cyclades), Greece 1.–8.08.2019; where was presented our research regarding landscape and music. This research has taken ground into the field of music signification studies, based on the subject statement assign on Eero Tarasti's 13th chapter – *"Metaphors of nature and organicism,"* book *Sein und Schein* (2015). It was also recognized therefore the proposition approach concerned of Johannes Gabriel Granö's book *Pure Geography* (1997) in the original Finnish translation of *Puhdas Maantiede* (1927). The idea of bringing up the contributions of the Finnish geographer Johannes Gabriel Granö (1882–1956) a pioneer in the research of landscape is due to his vision in attributing art and the auditory senses as an apparatus for observation, analyzes and understanding of landscape phenomena.

Francis Younghusband made the following statement in one of his speeches as president of the Geographical Society of London: "I hope therefore that the Geographical Society will finally realize that the tasks of geography include seeing the beauty of natural forms and events and comparing the special attractions of the various features with each other. This will even become the principal task of geography. . . We have formed a society in order to spread geographical knowledge and I hope and I wish that in the future we shall look upon a knowledge of the beauty of the earth as the most important kind of knowledge to be disseminated" (Younghusband, 1923: 209–210; in Granö, (1929) 1997: 7).

The significance of art for geographical description is undeniable, and we are convinced that if we were artists, we could give much more characteristic portrayal of our objects of study instead of the present destructive and distorting description which arises from our clumsy approach and even our total disregard for the facts. But the fallibility of our approach is to be found in our own limitations, of course, not in those of science. As surely as there is an environment, it will continue to constitute an object of scientific investigation, and sooner or later geography will learn to treat it as such a correct and scientific manner Granö, (1929) 1997: 7).

1 Finnish and Brazilian song cycle: Drawings, poetry, and music in cultural contemporary correspondences

In association to this ongoing creative process research, it is expected to initiate a path for a song cycle composition. The research is developed as an aesthetic and cultural dialogue between Finnish and Brazilian cultural forms of combining and understanding music and poetry. From this perspective, the song cycle creates a cultural exchange, approaching different meanings from distant cultural backgrounds.

Figure 3: Elisa Bracher, from the "Mirror of the Mountains" series, 2017. Painting on rice paper, 61 x 80 cm.

This project has produced a few songs based on paintings (as shown in figure 3), photographs, poems, and music composition. The first, *Vuoristoilmaa*, had part of the melodic theme derived from Elisa's abstract drawing and the poem, in Portuguese, has been translated by Laura Pyrrö into Finnish then made its first presentation in Rodrigo Felicissimo session at the "Symposium Sources of Creativity: from Local to Universal", in Mikkeli, Finland, 2018.

> Não é difícil alcançar as montanhas.
> No alto nevado do monte a suave falta de ar,
> Silêncio de vento
> Assobiam os passos
> As pedras cantam pelos pássaros
> Que sobrevoam as altas montanhas
> Onde encontro imagens antigas do tempo na planície.
>
> It is not challenging to reach the mountains.
> In the snowy top of the cliff the pleasant lack of air, Wind of silence
> Whistle the steps
> The stones sing for the birds
> That are flying over the high mountains
> Where I find old images from the time of the flat land.
>
> Elisa Bracher

The second song is entitled *Meadow Sky ("Chácara do Céu")*. It refers to a place up the hill in Rio de Janeiro. The lyric brings topics such as beauty, mystery, chant, and birds. It refers to a woman that can sing better than birds and with that plot she can seduce anyone.

The third song *Kaksi Merta* ("Two Seas") had the poetry written originally in Finnish by the lyricist Laura Pyrrö, insinuating the idea of two seas as a subjective metaphor for tranquility and tempest as one navigate in an ocean of thoughts, ideas and perspectives hovering over contemporary life. Also, this song gives the understanding that in the new age there is no more boundaries neither real time expectation. This perspective must be seen and understood as the new time related to technology and global network that brings up together the idea from cultures and nations that recently use to be distant concerning time and space.

2 The creation of a manual for searching the "Melody of the Mountains"

As a first objective in this discussion the purpose is to create an "educational manual" for students and teachers, focused on the study of the landscape in a

multidisciplinary approach, recording and analyzing geographical landmarks. This manual guides the field practices of observing and reading the multiple perspectives of a given landscape. Then, the idea is to advance in the studio work, considering the different perspectives of the re-signification of visual and sound phenomena through the perspectives of the landscape, emphasizing critical and aesthetic meanings for the analysis and awakening the senses for the practice of creative processes in music and visual arts. Likewise, the visual artist co-author Elisa Bracher, at the end of this project, will be able to develop and produce visual and sound installation exhibitions, as a result of the compilation of the collected materials. In addition, under the guidance of Professor Paulo C. Chagas there will be an art expedition to California, USA, when it is proposed to unravel and develop an artistic series concerning the sights to be studied during the research chronogram at the Experimental Acoustic Research Studio (EARS) and at the University of California – Riverside. In reference to the edition of a manual, in advance, it is proposed possible locations to be visited and noted throughout this research. Initially, emphasis should be drawn in local, regional, and national geographical landmarks, as follows:
- for local scale research it is important to point some locations on Riverside County Mountains, such as the Box Springs Mountain, the Sycamore Canyon Wilderness Park, the Moreno Valley, Santa Ana Mountains, and the San Bernardino National Forest.
- on a regional basis one should include some locations on the Mountains of California, Sierra Nevada range, such as, Monte Whitney.
- at national level, it is important to highlight the Grand Canyon – Parashant National Monument.

It is intended during the period of research, to be part at the interdisciplinary group studies at "EARS" and at the Music Department of UC-R, on course Sound Studies and Sound Art. The course and group study will be an important acquisition for the project research acknowledgement on *"cultural, social, political and philosophical issues of sound listening, auditory media and contemporary practices of sound production including experimental field of sound art"*, conferring to Professor Paulo C. Chagas (2020). Another important aspect as a Visiting Scholar member at UC-R is to be participant on *"lectures and discussions on a vast body of scholarship on sound studies, which raise significant intellectual and political questions of our time"*. That certainly, will provide critical endorsement for the research and bibliographical fulfilment on contemporary discussions basis, related to Sound Studies and Sound Art Studies.

3 The art expedition proposal: From local to regional and across national identities

The landmarks would take place first of all on the Orange County to the Grand Canyon sights. This study would put it into context the geographical landmarks of a region by establishing a series of audio, photographs, videos, paintings, and music composition. The observation of rereading of landscape by tracking the mountains of the Orange County, the Sierra Nevada Mountains, and the Grand Canyon. Registering photographs, recording sound, and putting into practice the "Melody of the Mountains Technique" on contemporary basis.

The idea is to establish an aesthetic sonic and visual exhibition of the landscape by means of organizing an installation for discussions related to the appointed environments in this proposal.

The edition of a manual for students and scholars could be an experiment for external expedition, gathering students to experience an outdoor artwork field. The second part of this process should be at the Experiment Acoustics Research Studio (EARS) with a learning activity on studio immersion by bringing this to the studio environment and experiencing this process among colleagues and with the guidance of composer and director Paulo C. Chagas. A bibliography would be provided associated to the context of this creational composition study. The idea is to promote a wider discussion on landscape and men production in the space of their studies registered areas.

An installation for visual and sonic art forms could be combined as a final proposal and may well be presented as a result from the research period on creative process method. This contribution should be shown in form of an art exhibition gathering the discussion and analysis of the expedition on geographical landmarks of the Californian Orange County across the Grand Canyon.

This study introduces the composition technique known as "Graphic for Plotting the Melody of the Mountains" and the orchestral treatment developed by the Brazilian composer Heitor Villa-Lobos (1887–1959), in the orchestral theme extracted from the second movement of the *Symphony* No. 6. This work demonstrates the inter-relationship throughout the aural and the visual arts as it relates the inventive thinking to the creational composition process. The turning point of this process is the use of graphics, to establish transpositions from drawings to music.

This creative music composition process requires two axes to convert drawings into music, demonstrating the organization between pitch (frequency) and time (rhythmic duration). The use of photographs and drawings as matrix to the

Figure 4: The "God's Finger" Mountain Range, from *Serra dos Órgãos*, Teresópolis, Rio de Janeiro, Brazil. Photograph by Eric Hess, extracted from (ALMEIDA, [no date]: p.153). Library collection of the Institute of Brazilian Studies from University of São Paulo. Discussion presented at the symposium Sources of Creativity: from Local to Universal. International symposium around Eero Tarasti's work in the eve of his 70th birthday at the Academy of Cultural Heritages and the Semiotic Society of Finland. Mikkeli, 8 – 10 August 2018.

composition process, generates graphics towards music making. It also establishes new ground on the perspective of music signifiers, once introduced in the creational process as image, memory, and cultural identity heritage. This creation process establishes a direct dialogue throughout visual arts and music, bringing musical signifiers to the melodic themes and so forth, to the composition process. It brings a bridge for new discoveries, once associated among the structural outlines of monumental geographic mountains forms, expressions of nature, here stated as photograph (as shown in figure 4) set to drawing, graphic establish as melody.

Next, it will be shown Villa-Lobos drawing of the outlines of the "God's finger" peak ("Dedo de Deus"), in Serra dos Órgãos and the Sugar Loaf mountains range, found at the Villa-Lobos Museum, as an important document for the understanding of his music composition technique utilized in the first and second movement of Symphony No. 6.

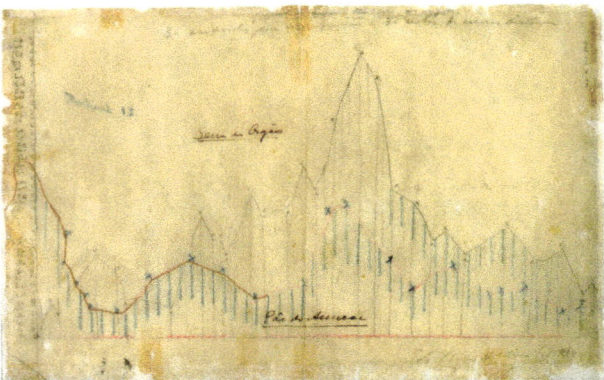

Figure 5: Silk paper, Villa-Lobos drawing graphic. Note the design of the melodic drawings written by the composer with detail the use of the chromatic scale, located to the left of the drawing. (VILLA-LOBOS, [no date], MVL-HVL millimeter scale 13- FE 833). Collection Villa-Lobos Museum.

Introduced by Eero Tarasti (1994: 209) on music and visual arts, it is opportune to emphasize the concept of "existential transcendence", as an important semiotic tool in the analysis of the theme of the second movement of Villa-Lobos *Symphony No. 6 – "On the Outline of the mountains of Brazil"*. It is intended to expose the "signifier" and its "sign systems" by launching the Villa-Lobos composition technique as an important creative process of transporting images to music. It also reveals the interesting exchange of parameters, between visual and sound art, passage to new meanings and interaction, expanding the systems of sign correspondence in the transdisciplinary territories of Fine Arts.

As introduction for the analysis, it should start by presenting some categories of "signifiers" related to the music theme structured by the Brazilian composer: 1) topographical landmark; 2) symbolic image that infers connection with God (the divine); and 3) transformation of iconic symbol into music structured theme. These categories of "signifiers", shows us the metaphor of nature and "organicism" in the epistemology of music, concerning to "musically organic" as refers the concept of Eero Tarasti (2015: 291).

The drawing and the melodic theme, (as shown in figure 5), illustrate, in a concise version, the exchange process established by Villa-Lobos to transform image into music. Therefore, it is intended to emerge the structures of the chain of signs, developed by Villa-Lobos during his musical creation process, using semantic values as a beacon, re-signified by the *Serra dos Órgãos* morphology representing time-space in the musical discourse.

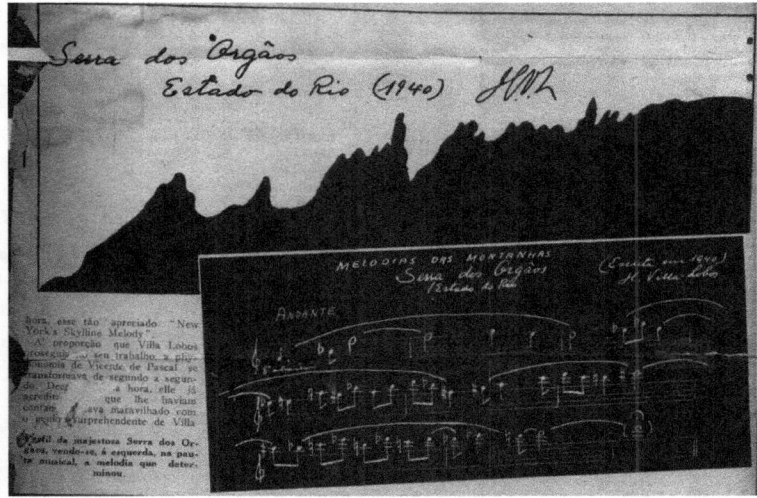

Figure 6: The "God's finger" melodic theme. Extracted from the *Cruzeiro* magazine (Pires, 1940). Collection Villa-Lobos Museum.

Figure 7: Transcription of the melody portrayed in the magazine *O Cruzeiro* (Pires, 1940). Villa-Lobos wrote this melody under a drawing of the rock formation of the *Serra dos Órgãos* mountain range.

Then, viola in solo contrasts a canon collection with reduced variation of the original theme presented by the clarinet in solo (as shown in figures 6 & 7).

Accordingly, by studying the structure of this mountain (object), one can presume the process generated as the result of the composer (subject) ideal of music "transcendence". The recreation of landscape image into music theme

Figure 8: The solo played by the clarinet cites the theme of the *Serra dos Órgãos* mountains range. Villa-Lobos, *Symphony No. 6* (measures 35–58). Handwritten copy by H. Villa-Lobos, p. 40.

Figure 9: The introduction of the second solo played by the viola, then the third solo is presented by the horns III, IV. Collection of Villa-Lobos Museum.

brings external influences, towards the recreation process of semantical identity gaining music meaning. It discovers the composer (subject) concerns towards its *Serra dos Órgãos* (object). Through the analysis of this chart it is possible to identify the process and the technique developed in the first section of the second movement, revealing the main theme and the atmosphere created along the harmony and counterpoint dialogs established by the composer in music discourse.

In this Symphony Villa-Lobos has elaborated five geographical Brazilian landmark symbols into musical structured discourse themes and sections. Those were identified in the first and second movements of the work. In the second episode of the first movement, it is presented the theme originated from the outline of the Sugar Loaf mountain on bar measure 43. On bar measure 108, the thematic section of *Corcovado* mountain begins. The orchestral section that refers to the melodic material where is mentioned the outline of *Tijuca* mountain is initially presented in bar measure 160. On the second movement the first section is associated with the *Serra dos Órgãos* range and the "God's Finger" peak, located in *Teresópolis* district (as shown in figures 8 & 9). The last mountain presented is *Serra da Piedade*, ("Mercy Range"), starting on musical section, bar measure 76, played by the flute, oboe, and bass clarinet. In this essay it will not be possible to detail all of these sections with due accuracy, however these sections have already been researched and published previously with the right attention.

Therefore, we return to the topic in question highlighted for this essay, next: the *Serra dos Órgãos* with the "God's Finger" peak or music theme.

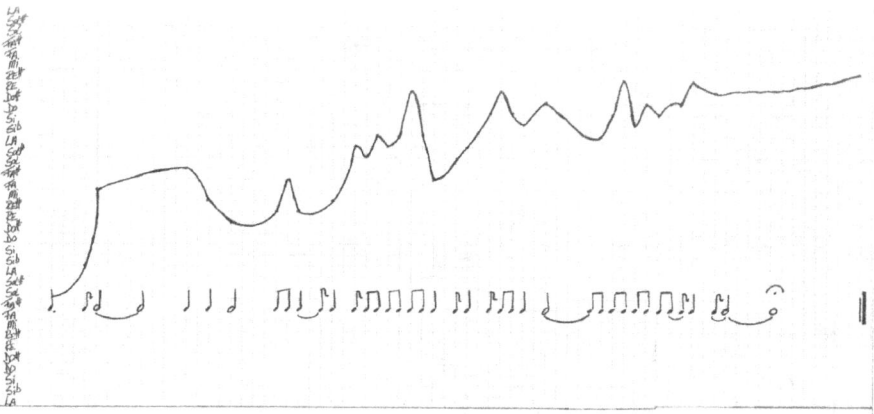

Figure 10: The chart above was carried out by fixing the points according to the melody notes obtained by Villa-Lobos. Our version is a retrograded version of the composer process.

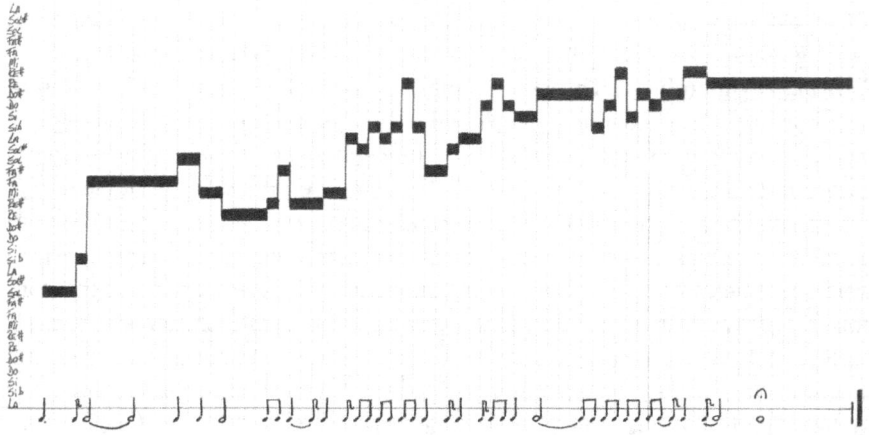

Figure 11: Graphic made from the melody notes obtained by Villa-Lobos manuscript of the *Serra dos Órgãos*. Our version shows the resulting design of the simple association of the notes.

From this section, one should grasp the music *"signifier"* that Villa-Lobos was trying to express in this music section. The Brazil landmark *Serra dos Órgãos*, characterize a deep chain of signs, which carry several important meanings of cultural heritage, such as: identity, religion, iconic sight, time and space. From this perspective, Villa-Lobos reveals its musical signification (as shown in figures 10 & 11).

In *Sein und Schein*, 11th chapter, Eero Tarasti (2015: 222) present "a proposal for the semiotic theory of performing arts":

> Insofar what is performed is a text, i.e. the performance has a certain preestablish model or starting point, what is involved is how this entity changes into some other mode of existence, a kind of transformation. Those meanings which dwelled as implicit in a text already can now burst into life and assumed quite new properties. Some art forms are based upon this i.e. they are not yet what they should be, before this process. That is also called interpretation, if one wants to underline the fact that the performing subject adds there something. In the theory of semiotics this could be called "modalisation" of a message or text.
>
> (A. J. Greimas)

That is just a general observation for the introduction of semiotic *"zemic"* model concept proposed by Eero Tarasti (2015) and what could be stated from Villa-Lobos symbolic representation on a music synthesis performance related to this composition technique. In relation to this model Eero Tarasti (2020) comment on Villa-Lobos and Jean Sibelius symbolic national representations, as follows next just the resume on Villa-Lobos discussion related to the *"zemic"* model:

> The Brazilian Villa-Lobos and the Finnish Jean Sibelius (1865–1957) are musical symbols of their countries: they constituted their national identities, just as Carl Dahlhaus has stated that national style never emerges iconically and organically from the cultural and natural roots; neither does it stem from the folklore; the most common misunderstanding of both composers is to consider them pure folklorists which neither of them was. Yet, the comparison of these two composers may reveal interesting analogies in the global music history, particularly in their relations to Europe. What unites them and make them unique, is the overwhelming, und foreseen and unconventional **creativity** in respect to everything they aspired as composers.
>
> In the analysis, I shall use the so called *"zemic"* model, which I have recently developed in my theories of existential semiotics. It articulates into four modes of "being" which are $Moi1$ = body = in music: the kinetic, sensual energy, $Moi2$ = person = musical actors, themes, $Soi2$ = social practices = musical forms, genres, $Soi1$ = values = musical aesthetics.
>
> $Moi1$: kinetic energy, "power" of primal elements in music: Villa-Lobos: extreme cases of sound, rhythm, and sensual physic nature of music.
>
> $Moi2$: "actors": Villa-Lobos: musical themes with different characters of Iberian, Indian, African, and European origin, but often as transformed, even to "grotesque" like in *Macunaima* by Mario de Andrade. (*Rudepoema*); yet no direct contact with Indians, all themes from secondary sources.
>
> $Soi2$: "practices": Villa-Lobos invented totally new genres like *Choros* and *Bachianas*; followed the social practice of Vargas government in education and promoter of nationalism.

Soi1: values: Villa-Lobos – non-European aesthetics, one cannot apply to the author the traditional manifest categories of European aesthetics like the tragic, the sublime, the gracious, the comic etc.; Villa-Lobos aesthetics goes into extreme and exaggerated expressions compared to the composers of the Old World; yet, similarities with avantgarde aesthetic ideas of his time (Stravinsky, Varèse); not aesthetically accepted by Mario de Andrade, the leading Brazilian intellectual. Excerpts extracted from *"Villa-Lobos, Sibelius and the deconstruction of the musical Europe"* (non-published abstract) Tarasti (2020) (Figure 12).

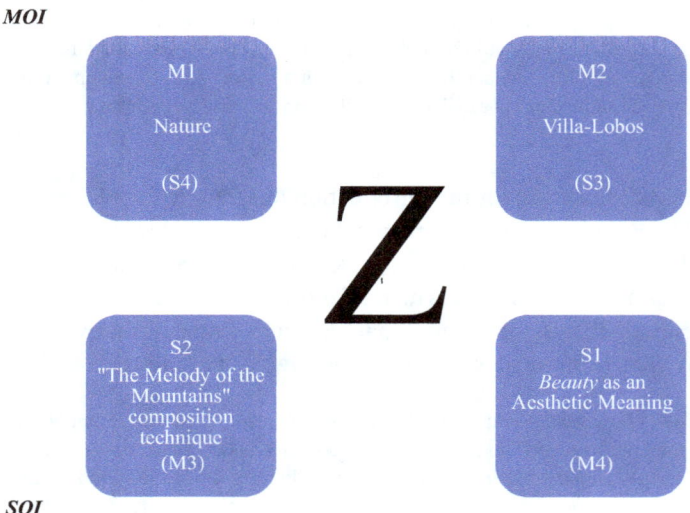

Figure 12: The *"zemic model"*[1] into Villa-Lobos compositional technique.

When assuming beauty as an aesthetic meaning, one could predict that this technique enlarge sensibility to a new modality of musical semiotics studies concern-

---

1 In this avenue towards renewal of already existing 'classical' approaches to semiotics, my theory is growing from the roots of European semiotics, and particularly the so-called Paris school of semiotics, once created by A. J. Greimas. In this path, a.o., the semiotic square became a 'Zmodel', and likewise many elements were changed. However, in this situation of 'neosemiotics' as I have called it, one canal so continues to be Greimassian, Lotmanian, Peircean without worries – the classical theories do not lose their validity in the study of our *Dasein*. However, the new theory offers perhaps a broader context, or it is like Greimas put it 'englobant', surrounding.

On the other hand, existential semiotics stems from the continental philosophy of the line from Kant, Hegel, and Kierkegaard, to Heidegger, Jaspers, Arendt, Sartre, Marcel, and Wahl. We never go back, we are in 2013 now, and the theory written now has to reflect its particularly conditions. Understand basic issues of contemporary world, its ethical and axiological problems. It brings both a synthesis of semiotic and philosophical traditions (Tarasti 2015: v).

ing research of the musical space field. Lenn E. Goodman (2010: 720), in Review of Metaphysics, in a critique to Roger Scruton, referring to the book *Beauty*, emphasizes that:

> Beauty, like some other aesthetic values, beckons toward transcendence. So, reductionists may debunk the category, date stamp or mark it counterfeit. Alienated artists at times reject the claims of beauty or deface its icons. . . . But beauty is resilient. Nature, art, and craft reaffirm its claims in every age and culture, responding to deep, distinctively human needs but also informing and enlarging the sensibilities that awaken us to its presence.
> (Goodman 2010: 720)

As Lenn E. Goodman (2010: 719) refers to "Thomas Aquinas's suggestion that beauty – like truth, unity, and goodness – is a transcendental, allowing finite things, each in its own way, to point beyond themselves, toward a higher reality that no one alone can encompass". The *Melody of the Mountains* technique developed by Villa-Lobos brings to semiotics studies of musical space, the enlargement of sensibilities towards music iconic images.

Eero Tarasti (1996: 113) introduced us to the studies of musical space in the third chapter of his book *A Theory of Musical Semiotics*:

> Certainly, it has to be understood in a somewhat metaphorical sense. For isn't music primarily something to be *heard* and not seen? If so, then musical space is a fictional "Third World" entity (in the sense of Karl Popper), and if any spatiality exists in music, it can be only imaginary nature. This view of musical space has had the support of various aesthetic experiences throughout the history of our culture. For example, Benoist-Méchin says in *La musique et l'immortalité dans l'oeuvre de Marcel Proust:* Each musician of genius receives as an innate gift a kind of inner realm which is constantly recognizable, and whose rapidly or slowness opens up to him a universe of form marked by what can properly be called "his originality" (1926: 94). In this case, spatiality in music would always be of an internal nature.
>
> At the same time, entire studies have focused on musical space, not as inner and metaphorical but geometrical, with properties similar to those of any visual spatial text. Cogan and Scot (1976) and Boulez (1971) have produced such studies. Conversely, space has often been interpreted in musical terms. These two views of musical space, the metaphorical and the geometrical, give us some hints about which direction to take. (Tarasti 1994: 77)

The inner spatial, abstract music is a metaphor of significance towards the "internal world" of the composer; it extends the aesthetics ideals of beauty through music. As well, a concrete practice established by the composer, represents music throughout sketches, diagram, graphics, and geometry. In this sense, we can assume, both categories are represented in Villa-Lobos method.

The imaginary boundaries of the mountains outline bring Villa-Lobos composition technique to western musical traditions by reporting the beauty of landscapes in *insights* through music discourse. We can gladly associate such work with Richard Strauss (1864–1949) *Alpine Symphony,* and Ludwig van Beethoven (1770–1827) *Symphony No. 6 – Pastoral*; nevertheless, we cannot assume that these compositions were developed under similar method and process. In these terms, this could be a good opportunity to extend the recognition of Villa-Lobos's achievements, but also to the research for those methods developed by Strauss and Beethoven.

On this dialogue between landscape and music, it enrolls other perspectives on a contemporary level of interpretation related to creative process discussions. For that matter it is crucial to be grounded on contemporary literature. The sound and image combined in dialogue, as stated by Paulo Chagas (2013: 2), next:

> The invention of photography was a revolution that transformed our thinking. The gesture of photographing is a philosophical gesture. As philosophy generates concepts, photography generates situations. The invention of the technical image – the image produced by technical apparatuses – reintroduced the power of imagination into the world. In the old societies, man communicated by means of traditional images and myths and so developed a power of imagination. The invention of writing weakened the power of imagination and developed conceptual, historical, and linear thinking. The invention of technical images – photography, film, video, etc. – introduced a new power of imagination that is taking over the function of the linear codes of letters and numbers. In other words, we've started to think through images and are abandoning texts. The power of the imagination, as suggested by Vilém Flusser (1994), unfolds a double meaning: it defines both the capacity to create images and the capacity to think by means of images.

According to Paulo C. Chagas (2013) article *"Musical Imagination: Sound and Image in Telematic Dialogue"*, it is reasonable to consider the great contribution on a critic actualization that could be stated in the discussions on the method "Melody of the Mountains", in terms of orientation through appointments and critics. Aspects of cultural, social, political, and philosophical program of studies are addressed to sound, listening, auditory media and contemporary practices of sound production including experimental field of sound art. That should be considered as an enforcement on contemporary literature as a result of this discussion.

Márta Grabócz, throughout the studies on semiotic of music in the fields of musical signification, narrativity and contemporary music has been another important reference to be highlighted for this study, as well as sound environment and synthesis in real time focusing on images and expressive forms in contemporary music in associations with the sound universe of composers such as François-Bernard Mâche. The literature of those topics presented by Márta Grabócz should be led in dialogue with this ongoing research.

In conclusion for this essay – we evoke the path taken on observing, analyzing, and understanding the musical meanings throughout Villa-Lobos "Melody of the Mountains" compositional technique, as an inventive way form of bringing meaning to musical discourse, and creative process. It was also explored the multidisciplinary knowledge exchange between music and visual art fields.

It has been here stated the contemporary art entrepreneurship "Mirror of the Mountains Project" among Elisa Bracher's creative process, a proposal of a manual for scholars and students to get along with this compositional method, a Finnish and Brazilian song-cycle in course, and to come a Californian expedition on geographical landmarks, based on EARS studio and at UC-R.

On the other hand, it was presented a theoretical interpretation of this method under the contributions of reading Villa-Lobos cultural heritage signs to western music society through Eero Tarasti's *Zemic* model theory and the categories of signifiers in the *"metaphors of nature and the organicism in the epistemology of music"*. We look forward in opening new discussions on this fertile ground to the Musical Signification Society with the benefit of exploring our senses through landscape since Villa-Lobos existential signs legacy.

References

Research primary sources Heitor Villa-Lobos Museum

Almeida, Guilherme. *Cidade e arredores do Rio de Janeiro* – a joia do Brasil. Rio de Janeiro: Livraria Kosmos, [s.d.]. Exemplar 99 de 321 cópias publicadas. Instituto de
Estudos Brasileiros da Universidade de São Paulo, IEB-USP.
MVL-HVL. Documento: **Obras Anotações/ Melodia das Montanhas**. Escala Milimetrada 13- FE 833. Rio de Janeiro: Museu Villa-Lobos.
Heitor Villa-Lobos. **Sinfonia No. 6**: sobre as linhas das montanhas. Rio de Janeiro, 1944. Cópia manuscrita de H. Villa-Lobos. Catálogo MVL 1990-21-0147 Rio de Janeiro: Museu Villa-Lobos. 1 partitura (120 p.) para orquestra.

Published sources

Bracher, Elisa. 1998. *Wood on Wood*. Sculptures Elisa Bracher, text Rodrigo Naves, photographs João Musa. São Paulo: Cosac & Naify Edições.
Bracher, Elisa. 2006. *Maneira Branca* – Gravuras de Elisa Bracher. São Paulo: Cosac Naify. Pinacoteca do Estado de São Paulo.
Bracher, Elisa. 2015. *Luctus Lutum Elisa Bracher;* [text and curator Elisa Byington]. São Paulo: Galeria Raquel Arnaud.

Chagas, Paulo C. 2013. Musical Imagination: Sound and Image in Telematic Dialogue. *Art Review* 24. http://www.revista-art.com/musical-imagination-sound-and-image-in-telematic-dialogue.

Chagas, Paulo C. 2014. *Unsayable Music: Six Reflections on Musical Semiotics, Electroacoustic and Digital Music*. Leuven: University Press.

Chagas, Paulo C.. 2018. Som espaço e afeto – conferência. *14º Encontro Internacional de Música e Mídia. Compassos Passos, espaços: os lugares da música*. EM&T Escola de Música e Tecnologia, São Paulo 11 a 13 de setembro de 2018. Musimid – Centro de Estudos em Música e Mídia. Freiburg im Bersgau, Germany (12 September 2018). https://youtu.be/FbnOwvp95c4 (accessed in 5th February 2020)

Duarte, Roberto. 2009. *Villa-Lobos errou?* (subsídios para uma revisão musicológica em Villa-Lobos). São Paulo: Algol Editora.

Felicissimo, Rodrigo Passos. 2017. *Estudo Interpretativo da Técnica Composicional Melodia das Montanhas: utilizadas nas peças orquestrais: New York Sky-Line Melody e Sinfonia No. 6 de Heitor Villa-Lobos*. Beau Bassin: Novas Edições Acadêmicas (OmniScriptum Publishing Group).

Grabócz, Márta. 2009. *Musique, Narrativité, Signification*. Collection Arts & Sciences de l'art. Paris: L'Harmattan.

Grabócz, Márta. 2013. *Entre Naturalisme Sonore Et Synthèse en Temps Réel*. Images Et Formes Expressives Dans La Musique Contemporaine. Paris: Editions des Archives Contemporaines.

Grabócz, Márta & Geneviève Mathon (eds.). 2018. *François-Bernard Mâche, Le Compositeur Et Le Savant Face À L'Univers Sonore*. Collections du GREAM/ Création contemporaine, dirigée par Pierre Michel. Paris: Hermann Éditeurs.

Granö, Johannes Gabriel. 1997. *Pure Geography*. Baltimore & London: The Johns Hopkins University Press.

Greimas, Algirdas Julius & Joseph Courtés. 1982. *Sémiotique: Dictionnaire raisonné de la théorie du langage*, tome 2. Paris: Hachette.

Scruton, Roger. 2009. *The Aesthetics of Music*. New York: Oxford University Press.

Tarasti, Eero. 1977. *Myth and Music*. A Semiotic Approach to the Aesthetics of Myth in Music, especially that of Wagner, Sibelius and Stravinsky. Mouton Publishers – The Hague – Paris – New York.

Tarasti, Eero. 1995. *Heitor Villa-Lobos. Life and Work*, North Carolina: McFarland (in Finnish 1987 *Heitor Villa-Lobos ja Brasilian sielu*, Helsinki: Gaudeamus)

Tarasti, Eero. 1994. *A Theory of Musical Semiotics*. Bloomington: Indiana University Press.

Tarasti, Eero. 2013. *Semiotics of Classical Music. How Mozart, Wagner and Brahms Talk to Us*. Berlin: Mouton de Gruyter.

Tarasti, Eero. 2015. *Sein und Schein – Explorations in Existential Semiotics*. Berlin: Walter de Gruyter.

Tarasti, Eero. 2016. *The Semiotics of A. J. Greimas – a European intellectual heritage, seen from inside and outside* (manus.). Helsinki. (Now published in Sign System Studies 45(1/2), 2017. 33–53).

Tarasti, Eero. 2020. Villa-Lobos, Sibelius and the deconstruction of the musical Europe (non-published abstract).

Younghusband, Francis. 1923. *Das Herz der Natur*. Leipzig.

CDs

Heitor Villa-Lobos. Sinfonia No. 6 [CD]. Orquestra da Rádio de Stuttgart (SWR) sob a regência de Carl St. Clair. Editora/ selo CPO, 2009.
Heitor Villa-Lobos. Sinfonia No. 6 – sobre a linha das montanhas [CD]. **Orquestra Sinfônica do Estado de São Paulo** sob a regência de **Isaac Karabtchevsky. Gravadora/ selo** Naxos. São Paulo, 2012.
Heitor Villa-Lobos. New York Skyline Melody [CD]. Orquestra da Rádio de Stuttgart (SWR) sob a regência de Carl St. Clair. Selo/ Editora CPO, 2010.

Malgorzata Grajter
Musical arrangement and literary translation as signs: Preserving and renewing cultural heritages

Abstract: Before the birth of Translation Studies as academic discipline in the 1970's, translation had been considered as 'subsidiary art', thus deprived of the dignity of an original work. Until very recently, the status of musical transcriptions and arrangements has been quite similar: considered as 'diminutive expression froms of the bourgeois culture' (Maciej Gołąb), they have been only randomly researched, with few exceptions, such as, for instance, the comprehensive book by Jonathan Kregor: *Liszt as Transcriber*.

Notwithstanding their secondary character, both literary translation and musical arrangement plays an important role in transmitting cultural heritages: in terms of Peirceian semiotics, they could be seen as signs which represent, 'pretend to be', or stand for original works (objects) in the eyes of a certain group of recipients. In other words, they serve the purpose of dissemination or preservation of a given masterpiece, making it available to a greater audience. Both translations and arrangements share the element of rendering the piece as a whole, and are subject to various transformations, depending on the target language or medium (musical style), or geographical and temporal factors affecting their creation. Oftentimes, a good translation, arrangement or cover version may even overshadow the original and surpass its quality. Hence, the importance of musical arrangement as a vehicle of cultural transfer cannot be overlooked and this phenomenon in itself deserves a firm place in the discourse on existential semiotics, next to the linguistic translation.

Keywords: Musical Arrangement, Translation Theory, Existential Semiotics, Triadic Model of Sign, Cultural Heritages

1 Introduction: Translation and arrangements as subject of research

Before the birth of Translation Studies as an academic discipline in the 1970's, due to its secondary character, translation had often been considered as subsidiary art, deprived of the dignity of an original work[1]. As an ultimate example of what Gérard Genette (1982) called *littérature au second degré*, it seems to have more to do with copying someone else, than creating an independent piece of art. The negativity, which grew around translations (especially bad ones) over the centuries was so strong at times, that it was even viewed as betrayal:

> *Mais que dirai-je d'aucuns, vraiment mieux dignes d'être appelés traditeurs, que traducteurs ? vu qu'ils trahissent ceux qu'ils entreprennent exposer, les frustrant de leur gloire, et par même moyen séduisent les lecteurs ignorants, leur montrant le blanc pour le noir.*
>
> But what shall I say of those, who are really more worthy of being called traitors, than translators? Since they betray those who they undertake to expose, depriving them of their glory, and by the same means seducing the ignorant readers, by showing them white as black.
>
> (du Bellay 2013, § 6; translation mine)

The other thing is that many translations are seen as results of merely reproductive, even automatic activity. Whether we are aware of it, or not, we translate all sorts of things on a daily basis. It is becoming more and more a mechanical process, often replaced by translation machines, e.g. Google Translate. Consequently, all too often we fail to acknowledge the human creative force needed for – and used in the translation process. Definitely, not all translations are worthy of the status of art, but certainly literary translation, or, poetic translation in particular, would not be possible without the highest level of artistic competences of a translator.

All these common opinions have taken their toll on how translation has been viewed, and dealt with, as a subject of academic research over the centuries. Until very recently, the status of musical transcriptions and arrangements has been quite similar: considered as "stunted forms of expression of the bourgeois culture" (Gołąb 2012: 85), they have received little scholarly attention, with few exceptions only. Nowadays, the kinship between translation and arrangement as resulting from similar processes has already been acknowledged by certain musicians and scholars,[2] but methodological solutions developed by translation theory has only recently started to slowly permeate the research on musical transcriptions and arrangements. The main focus of the present study is to lay foundations for the new methodology of research on musical transcriptions and arrangements, based on the adaptation of translation theories, and studying exemplary cases from Western art music as well as popular and ethnic music.

---

[1] The present text is an updated and broadened version of the paper given by the author at the Academy of Cultural Heritages in Syros, Greece, October 2019.

[2] See for example: Umberto Eco, *Experiences in translation*, Toronto: Toronto University Press 2001, Luciano Berio, *Remembering the future [Il ricordo del futuro]*, Cambridge MA: HUP 2006; Jonathan Kregor: *Liszt as Transcriber*, Cambridge: CUP 2010, Gabrielle Kaufman, *Gaspar Cassadó. Cellist, Composer and Transcriber*, New York: Routledge 2017.

2 Translation and arrangement as signs: Models of interaction

Several authors, dealing with translation theories, drew their methods of research from semiotics, both structuralist and interpretive. The basis for semiotic approach to translation is the interpretation of it as a sign. Definitely, translation as a whole "unit" can be considered as *aliquid stat pro aliquo* in the eyes of a certain group of readers. In order to examine possible interactions between the original work, its translation/translator, and recipients, Ubaldo Stecconi (1999) adapted Charles Peirce's triadic model of sign. He elaborates this simplified model of interaction by explaining stepwise the whole chain of such triads, including all the virtual and real stages of semiosis. The abstract idea of the work in the mind of its original creator, described by Eero Tarasti as *Pre-Sign* is the first virtual object of semiosis, which is then transformed into the real work – *Act-Sign*, and interpreted, again virtually, by the translator as a *Post-Sign* (Tarasti 2000: 33). This concept of *Pre-Sign* as an intentional essence corresponds with the observation on transcribing a musical work made by Ferruccio Busoni, namely that "every notation is, in itself, the transcription of an abstract idea" (Busoni 1962: 85). Next, in the process of translational semiosis, the virtual translator's interpretants (as new *Pre-Signs*) materialize as an actual translation (*Act-Sign*), which is then interpreted again by its the readers (*Post-Sign*) (Figure 1).

As a matter of fact, it can be said that translation determines its readers to refer to an original, to which the translation itself refers *in the same way* (Stecconi 1999: 254), i.e. the way the original is perceived by its recipients, is inevitably conditioned by the way it was previously interpreted by its translator. The same concept applies to musical arrangement: the dynamics of interaction between sign (arrangement), object (musical piece) and interpretant (listeners) are determined by the influence of transcriber, who was the interpreter of the work in the first place (Figure 2).

This concept is not, in fact, a new one: already in the nineteenth century a German theologian and philosopher Friedrich Schleiermacher saw the role of a translator as a mediator between writer and readers. According to his essay *Über die verschiedenen Methoden des Übersetzens* [On different methods of translation] based on a lecture given in Berlin in 1813, the dynamics of translation are basically twofold: "either the translator leaves the writer alone as much as possible and moves the reader towards the writer, or the translator leaves the reader alone as much as possible and moves the writer towards the reader" (Kregor 2010: 16). This concept seems to have withstood the test of time, since it was appropriated

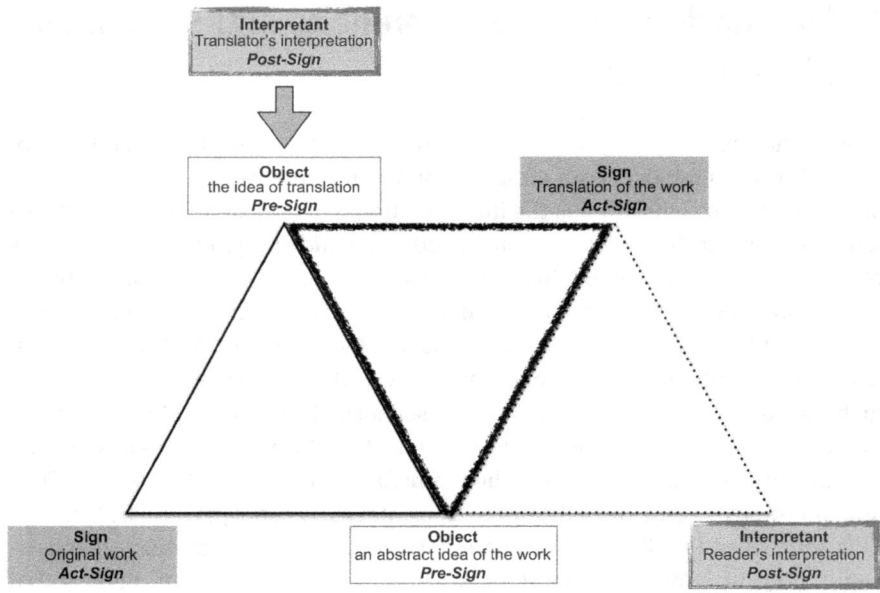

Figure 1: An object-oriented model of interactions between sign, interpretant and object (Stecconi 1999: 255; cf. Tarasti 2000: 33).

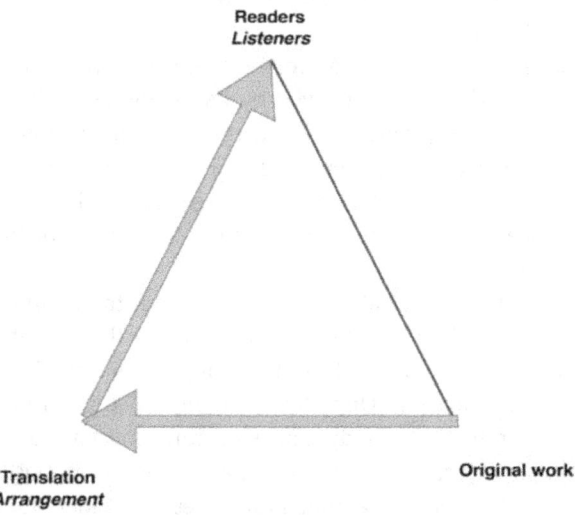

Figure 2: Triadic concept of a sign in reference to translation and its adaptation to musical arrangement.

by Lawrence Venuti in order to formulate modern terms: *domestication* and *foreignization* (Figure 3), towards the end of the past century (Venuti 1995: 19–20).

Similar observations can be made about nineteenth-century methods of musical transcriptions, especially piano reduction. In his piano version of Mozart's *Lacrimosa*, Carl Czerny, for example, chooses the domesticating method: his purpose is to write the piece anew as if it were meant for piano, leaving out the most problematic parts in favor of textural transparency and performer's convenience. In Jonathan Kregor's words, "he does not bend the language of the keyboard's technical vocabulary to accommodate and maintain the foreign" (Kregor 2010: 25); he rather brings the author towards the reader instead.

Liszt, on the other hand, in his *partitions* of Berlioz's *Symphonie fantastique*, Beethoven's symphonies or excerpts from Mozart's works, applied himself as scrupulously as if he were translating Holy Scriptures, paraphrasing his own words;[3] he bended his knee before the masters, trying to transfer all possible orchestral effects to the piano, thus producing almost unplayable piano versions of symphonic or vocal scores. For him, the Romantic idealism and worship towards the great composers overshadowed pragmatic aspect of performance.

This Utopian vision of piano as an instrument with limitless possibilities started to decline in the twentieth century: Arnold Schoenberg was certainly an advocate of the domesticating method of musical "translation". In his aphoristic essay *The Modern Piano Reduction* he wrote: "to write orchestrally for the piano is just as bad as to write pianistically for orchestra" (Schoenberg 1984: 349). He would have probably valued Czerny's method of piano transcription more than that of Liszt.

3 Equivalence

One of the key – but still controversial – terms in translation studies, is called *equivalence*, most generally defined as a "relationship between two texts: a source text (ST) and a target text (TT) [. . .] which allows the TT to be considered a translation of the ST in the first place" (Kenny 2009: 96). According to the Slovak translation theorist, Anton Popovič, equivalence in translation could also be defined as "correspondence of the means of expression between the original and the translation [. . .]" (Špirk 2009: 12). From the perspective of Charles Peirce's semiotic categories, equivalence in translation comprises three components: syntactic, semantic and pragmatic. In linguistic translation "these components

---

[3] "I have applied myself as scrupulously as if I were translating a sacred text". Quoted in: Kregor 2010: 28.

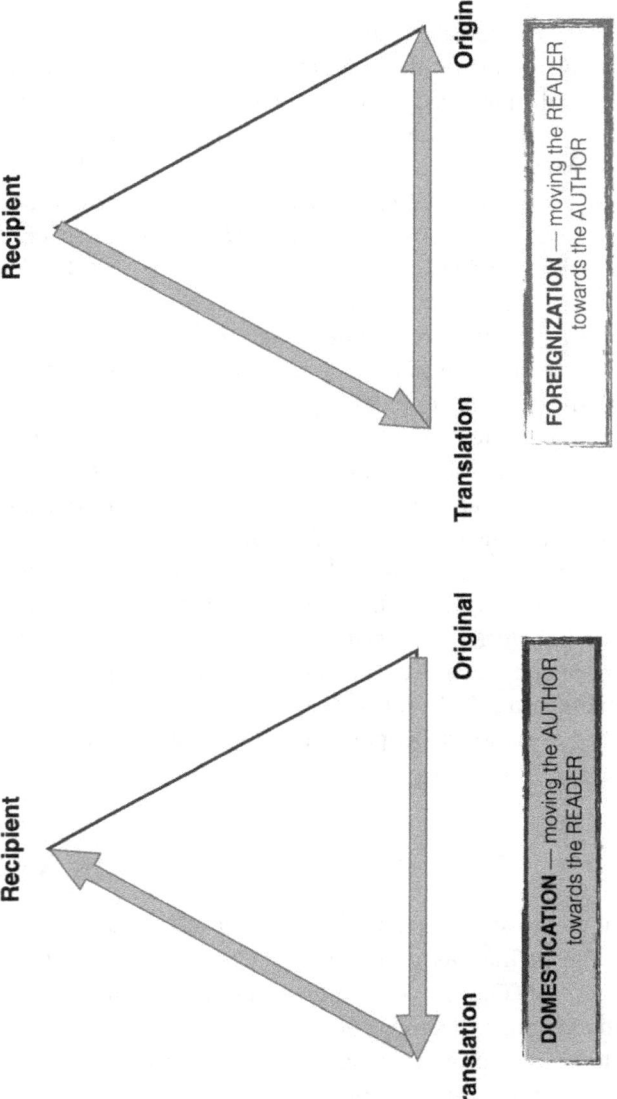

Figure 3: Domestication and foreignization as basic translational strategies described by Friedrich Schleiermacher and Lawrence Venuti.

are arranged in a hierarchical relationship, where semantic equivalence takes priority over syntactic equivalence, and pragmatic equivalence conditions and modifies both the other elements" (Bassnett 2002: 35). Here, a major difference between music and language can be observed. To quote Jonathan Kregor, "in a literary translation it is the word – that is the chief placeholder of meaning – that undergoes the greatest change. But in music, many of a composition's most foundational features – melody, harmony, form – ostensibly remain unaffected during the transferal from one medium to another" (Kregor 2010: 19). In other words, in musical translation it is syntactic equivalence that takes priority over semantic equivalence. In language, for example, we can easily change word order or even use different grammatical constructions to convey the same meanings in the target language and the translation will still serve its purpose. If the same is done with musical structures, this may result in getting an entirely different piece. This essential difference needs to be taken into account in the attempts to create viable methods of research into musical arrangement.

4 Invariance: The core of the work

In order to estimate, to what extent the relationship of equivalence between two texts is maintained and allows us to recognize TT as a translation of source text, one also needs consider another relationship, namely that existing between the invariant and variable elements in ST and TT. If translation is considered as a sign which represents another piece of art, then it seems obvious that it should transmit the core identity of the object (ST). It is therefore necessary to determine, which features of the work are its essence and need to remain unaltered. In Translation Studies a term *invariance* was coined for what stays constant during the translation process. Invariance can be understood in two ways: either as a requirement before translation, or as a concept that becomes relevant after translation (Munday 2009: 201). The first case concerns, in particular, the translator's work and his reading of what constitutes the essence of the text (a translational *Pre-Sign*). To quote Yuri Lotman: "The artistic reality is graspable when we proceed to separate the essential, without which the work would not be itself, from those features which are in some cases important, and nevertheless can be eliminated insofar as by replacing them the essence of the work is maintained and the work remains itself" (Lotman 1990: 33–34).[4]

---

[4] English translation after: Monticelli 2009, p. 329.

The attempt to use invariance as a musicological tool involves posing a question, which musical elements should remain intact so that the new version of the musical piece is relatively equivalent to the original? In the 19th century, following the explosion of piano reductions by Carl Czerny and others, François-Joseph Fétis in his *Treatise on the Accompaniment from Score by Piano or Organ* considered basic elements that should determine the work of a transcriber; Jonathan Kregor summarized them in the following hierarchical order: melody, harmony, articulation and texture (Kregor 2010: 25). It seems, therefore, that melody prevails over all the other features of the work, since it enables the listener to identify the piece easily.

In the second case the term is used *post factum* (as a *Post-Sign*) to compare and describe already existing translations of the same work. At the same time, a comparative study of a number of translations or arrangements may serve as a means of determining the *core* of the work. As Susan Bassnett writes:

> It is an established fact [. . .] that if a dozen translators tackle the same poem, they will produce a dozen different versions. And yet somewhere in those dozen versions there will be what [Anton] Popovič calls the 'invariant core' of the original poem. This invariant core, he claims, is represented by stable, basic and constant semantic elements in the text [. . .] In short, the invariant can be defined as that which exists in common between all existing translations of a single work. (Bassnett 2002: 35)

The extraction of invariant features of the work has the advantage of showing us the basic elements of its identity, which remains unaltered through the process of multiple, usually independent rearrangement. The collation of new versions gets us immediately to the core of the work, which shines through the outer, transformed layers (Figure 4).

Figure 4: Invariant core: Stanisław Moniuszko – *Znasz-li ten kraj* op. 73 nr 2, mm. 3–6 [1–4], extracted from transcriptions by: Bernhard Wolff, Henryk Melcer-Szczawiński, Władysław Krogulski, Jan Adam Maklakiewicz, Feliks Grąbczewski and Ignacy Rzepecki (editors), and jazz version by Włodek Pawlik. Author's elaboration.

The results of the above extraction of the invariant confirm Fétis' recommendations by and large, with the prevalence of melody, bass and harmonic scheme as the core of the musical work, at least with reference to the music of the so-called common practice period. Yet the idea of that which is invariant in music may differ according to various factors, e.g. the group of the works analyzed, the musical period, style etc. In modern arrangements, there is much more freedom regarding rhythm, melody and form: a borderline case example is provided in Brazilian song *Baião de quatro toques*.[5] In this radical form of a musical translation, the invariant core was intentionally and consciously reduced to the repeated four-note 'Fate' motif – as the lyrics explain, "É uma *Quinta Sinfonia de Beethoven que decantou e só ficou a raiz*" [It is Beethoven's *Fifth Symphony*, which decanted, and only the root is left].[6] The question remains open, of course, whether this new interpretation of Beethoven's *Fifth Symphony* still counts as translation; that is, whether the prerequisite of equivalence is met here.

In music, invariance may be understood not only in the *vertical* textural dimension, but also on the *horizontal*, syntactic level: an equivalent arrangement is expected to transmit all the formal and syntactic content of a musical narrative. Yet, many musical arrangements leave out certain parts of the musical text, while others may add *cadenzas*, extensions or improvisational sections. In these musical inscriptions or "translator's footnotes", the individual style of the translator-arranger is often revealed, making him, or her, more visible.

5 Variable elements – expressional changes

Variable elements, individual to each language, style and translator, also defined as expressional changes or shifts, need to be considered: Anton Popovič discussed this issue in his two books on artistic translation.[7] On macro-stylistic level, these changes or shifts are largely conditioned by the temporal, local and utilitarian aspects of translation, as well as an individual style of the translator's writing. In musical translations, the target *language* is replaced by the new instrumentation, *style* or musical genre – jazz, ethnic music etc. For better clarity

---

5 See, for example, the version performed by Andera Motis from the album *Do outro lado do azul* (2019) https://www.youtube.com/watch?v=oPW_vgWYzYw (retrieved 14.05.2020).
6 The song was written by Luiz Tatit, professor of Musical Semiotics at the University of São Paulo in collaboration with Miguel Wisnik – a musician and professor of Brazilian literature at the same University. I owe this remark to Daniel Röhe (University of Brasília)
7 Popovič 1971, p. 82; cf. idem, 1975, p. 130.

in reference to music, Popovič's notions of composition, language and style have been replaced here with the terms coined by Leonard B. Meyer (1996): *language* – music in general, *style* – a set of patternings, replicated in a group of works in particular culture, period, musical genre etc. and *idiom* – selection of stylistic patterns by an individual composer.

Macro-stylistics (musical language → musical style)

Adaptation → *Sachbezug*

Out of all types of expressive changes, *adaptation* seems to be the most pragmatically motivated one; its purpose is to adjust the piece so that it becomes available to some interpreters who would not be able to access of perform it otherwise; for example, a choir version of a song originally written for voice and piano, or a simplified version of a masterpiece made playable for a young adept.

Modernization → *Zeitbezug*

Modernization is an example of musical or literary translation, which is affected by conditions and demands of the contemporary market. It definitely calls for creative thinking in combining old with the new. Such is the recording of Bach's *Christmas Oratorio* by King's Singers and the WDR Big Band. In the opening choir, the initial motif of timpani is played on a drum and subject to rhythmic transformations; the whole piece undergoes a thorough reharmonization to dissonant jazz harmonies, involving parallel intervals. What remains of Bach is melody (understood as a set of pitches) and the initial concept of a dialogue between percussionist and the rest of the band. This example shows that the idea of what constitutes the invariant core of the piece, can be understood differently in each particular case. The German term *Zeitbezug* originally used by Popovič has a broader meaning than its English translation; it could also embrace stylistic changes, such as rewriting a poem in an old language or arranging a piece in an old style, i.e. **archaization.** Let us think, for example, about a song by The Beatles played on Medieval instruments by the Belarussian folk group Stary Olsa.[8]

---

[8] For example, *Ob-la-di, Ob-la-da* and *Yellow Submarine* (https://www.youtube.com/watch?v=ehFRmQ9G_r0), retrieved 14.05.2020.

Localization → *Ortsbezug*

Localization involves stylistic changes, depending on a specific geographical region or culture of the recipient. The arranger or translator's task aims at bringing foreign music or a piece of a literature closer to their own (domestication) or, conversely, transforming a piece originating from his, or her own culture so that it acquires some exotic features, and thus sending the author abroad (foreignization). For example, there are a lot of rearrangements of Western Classical music in the styles of African music,[9] flamenco,[10] Brazilian folklore[11] or salsa.[12]

Micro-stylistics (musical style → musical idiom)

To achieve the goals determined by the type of translation on its macro-stylistic level, individual decisions are made in order to fit the work into the new *entourage*. These are called micro-stylistic changes (below):
a. **Intensification of expression:**
    i. stylistic standardization – translating by stylistic means typical of the transcriber's idiom and style;
    ii. stylistic individualization – translating by stylistic means untypical of the transcriber's idiom and style.
b. **Correspondence of expression:**
    i. stylistic substitution – replacement of the original expressional features by domestic ones;
    ii. stylistic transformation – change in the expressional values of the model (source);
c. **Attenuation of expression:**
    i. stylistic leveling – simplification of the expressional qualities of the original (model);
    ii. loss of expression.

---

9 See, among others, the crossover project *Lambarena: Bach to Africa* (1993) – whole album available at: https://www.youtube.com/watch?v=EyNTCyPFFJA, retrieved 14.05.2020.
10 Maria Pomianowska, *Chopin in Andalusia* from the album *Chopin on Five Continents* (2010), https://www.youtube.com/watch?v=LJbol78ITdQ, retrieved 14.05.2020.
11 For example, Bach's works recorded by Camerata Brasil (https://www.youtube.com/watch?v=lAjfeFE4uD0), retrieved 14.05.2020.
12 See: S. I. Joner: *Cinco Salsa* https://www.youtube.com/watch?v=jafWlyfUabw, retrieved 14.05.2020.

These individual strategies adapted by the translator or arranger on micro-stylistic (idiomatic) level largely depend on the "target" style or potential recipient of the new version. For example, an **adaptation** for children will often require stylistic leveling, i.e. simplification of the expressional qualities of the work. In the case of **localization**, on the other hand, stylistic standardization and stylistic transformation may be employed, while **modernization** – as in the aforementioned example of jazz version of Bach's oratorio – may involve elements of stylistic standardization, stylistic substitution, and transformation.

Finally, the sum total of all these individual decisions regarding expressive means in translation allows us to determine the overall level of correspondence between ST and TT: from partial, through adequate, to oversaturated (Popovič 1971). It is not always possible to use these categories in reference to a translated or rearranged work in an indisputable way, though; since there are many dimensions of the musical, or literary work, which undergo transformations in different directions: e.g., an arrangement may enrich the sound or texture of the piece, while reducing some of its syntactic elements etc. In reference to music, Barbara Literska explained this phenomenon in detail, describing such inconsistent tendencies in musical arrangement as a "diffusion of ideal types" (Literska 2004: 217–219).

The theory of expressional changes, introduced by Popovič in the 1970's of the past century, which also involves the local aspect of a given translation, seems particularly innovative in the perspective of a more recent phenomenon observed in Translation Studies at the end of the 20th century, namely the "cultural turn" (see: Munday 2009: 179). As Doris Bachmann-Medick explains:

> In the process, the familiar categories of text-related translation, such as original, equivalence or faithfulness, were increasingly supplemented by new key categories of cultural translation such as cultural representation and transformation, alterity, displacement, discontinuity, cultural difference and power." (Bachmann-Medick 2009: 5)

6 Sociocultural function of musical arrangements

To conclude: both musical and literary works belong to the realm of *Cultural Heritages*, which Eero Tarasti defined from the point of view of as "foregrounded, linguistically marked, cultural Zetic units", or in other words, external signs of cultural identity, "which have to be remembered, preserved, maintained, fostered, in some cases even renewed" (Tarasti 2015: 207). Musical arrangement or literary translation play an important role in the process of transmission and protection of these cultural heritages in several areas, which are indicated below:

Preservation → protection of the cultural heritages

If we consider the – apparently negative – perception of translation as 'copy', then there is no doubt that each copy of the work increases the chances of its survival both in individual and collective consciousness of its recipients. Some examples from the musical field show that many works are better known in their new versions than in original, e.g. Modest Mussorgsky's *Pictures at the Exhibition* in Maurice Ravel's instrumentation (Mawer 2000). Nowadays, we can hardly imagine not being able to hear an orchestral performance of Beethoven's symphonies, but in the days of Liszt this was still very much the case; hence the piano arrangements, which helped broader audience get acquainted with these works. As a consequence, the second function is:

Dissemination → reaching potential audience

The abundancy of transcriptions in the 19th century, seen on the example of a variety of works by such composers as Beethoven, Chopin or Moniuszko, testifies to huge popularity of these pieces among amateurs. Transcriptions and arrangements seem to have played a significant role in home music making: this role was subsequently taken on by the radio, vinyl record, magnetic tape, CD, MP3 or Internet. Such massive dissemination of musical arrangement in the 19th century can be interpreted as the initial phase of the development of mass culture.

Education → creating abridged versions of literature and music, available to children / students

Creating abridged version for children or students (for example the so-called *editio purificata ad usum delphini* of Latin classics for the use of Louis, *le Grand Dauphin* of France, or Penguin series of abridged stories for new learners of the English language) is a form of translation, which can be employed in education. These adaptations have their equivalents in musical abridgements of the famous works, which serve the same purpose of building cultural awareness in young adepts through an implementation of canonic masterpieces in more accessible forms.

Cultural dialogue → exchange of cultural experience, building intercultural connections

In the age of globalization and post-colonialism, more and more often the cultural exchange takes place on terms of democratic equality and dialogue, through finding common grounds and celebrating differences at the same time. As the connection between translation studies and cultural studies became stronger towards the end of the past century, translation is "no longer perceived merely as a transaction between two languages, but rather as a more complex process of negotiation between two cultures" (Munday 2009: 179). This tendency is reflected in musical projects, bringing different musical cultures together through common musicianship, e.g. the music of Johann Sebastian Bach played on African instruments.

Renewing → adapting cultural heritages to modern circumstances.

An uninformed modern reader or listener might find it difficult to understand a piece of art, which is two or more centuries old. Just as the modern Polish language is different from that of Mickiewicz, the music which is played and listened to by young people (especially outside conservatories) is different from that of Chopin or Moniuszko. Therefore, the modernizing aspect of translation is crucial to maintain continuity between the past and the present.

The importance of musical arrangement as a vehicle of cultural transfer should inspire further studies. Undoubtedly, the development of Translation Studies and Existential Semiotics opens up new perspectives for the research into this phenomenon, thus far underexplored.

References

Bachmann-Medick, Doris. 2009. Introduction: The Translational Turn. *Translation Studies* 2(1). 2–16.
Bassnett, Susan. 2002. *Translation studies*. London: Routledge.
du Bellay, Joachim. 2013 [1549]. *Défense et illustration de la langue française*. Paris: Presses Électroniques de France.
Busoni, Ferruccio. 1962 [1911]. *Sketch of a New Aesthetic of Music*. Trans. by Theodor Baker. In *Three Classics in the Aesthetic of Music*, 73–96. New York: Dover.
Eco, Umberto. 2001. *Experiences in translation*. Trans. by Alastair McEwen. Toronto: Toronto University Press.
Genette, Gérard. 1982. *Palimpsestes. La littérature au second degré*. Paris: Éditions du Seuil.

Gołąb, Maciej. 2012. *Spór o granice poznania dzieła muzycznego* [The Controversy Around the Limits of Cogniton of a Musical Work]. Toruń: Wydawnictwo Naukowe Uniwersytetu Mikołaja Kopernika.
Kaufman, Gabrielle. 2017. *Gaspar Cassadó. Cellist, composer and transcriber.* London/New York: Routledge.
Kenny, Dorothy. 2009. Equivalence. In Mona Baker & Gabriela Saldanha (eds.), *Routledge encyclopaedia of translation studies*, 96–99. New York: Routledge.
Kregor, Jonathan. 2010. *Liszt as transcriber.* Cambridge: CUP.
Literska, Barbara. 2004. *Dziewiętnastowieczne transkrypcje utworów Fryderyka Chopina* [Nineteenth-century transcriptions of the works of Frederic Chopin]. Kraków: Musica Iagellonica.
Lotman, Juri. 1990. *Kultuurisemiootika: Tekst – Kirjandus – Kultuur* [Culture semiotics: text – literature – culture]. Tallin: Olion.
Mawer, Deborah (ed.). 2000. The Cambridge Companion to Ravel. Cambridge: CUP.
Meyer, Leonard Bunce. 1996. *Style and Music: Theory, History, and Ideology.* Chicago: Chicago University Press.
Monticelli, Daniele. 2009. Crossing boundaries. Translation of the untranslatable and (poetic) indeterminacy in Juri Lotman and Giacomo Leopardi. *Interlitteraria* 14. 327–348.
Munday, Jeremy (ed.). 2009. *The Routledge companion to translation studies.* New York: Routledge.
Popovič, Anton. 1971. *Poetika Umeleckého Prekladu. Proces a text* [Poetics of artistic translation. Process and text]. Bratislava: Tartan.
Popovič, Anton. 1975. *Teória Umeleckého Prekladu: Aspekty Textu a Literárnej Metakomunikácie* [Theory of artistic translation: Aspects of text and literary metacommunication]. Bratislava: Tartan.
Schoenberg, Arnold. 1984 [1923]. *Modern piano reduction*, reprinted in Leonard Stein (ed.), Leo Black (trans.) *Style and Idea, Selected Writings of Arnold Schoenberg*, 348–349. Berkeley-Los Angeles: University of California Press.
Špirk, Jaroslav. 2009. Anton Popovič's contribution to translation studies. *Target* 21 (1). 3–29.
Stecconi, Ubaldo. 1999. Peirce's semiotics for translation. In Paul Soukup and Robert Hodgson (eds.), *Fidelity and Translation*, 249–261. Franklin, WI: Sheed & Ward; New York: American Bible Society.
Tarasti, Eero. 2000. *Existential semiotics.* Bloomington: Indiana University Press.
Tarasti, Eero. 2015. *Sein und Schein: Explorations in existential semiotics.* Berlin/Boston: Walter de Gruyter.
Venuti, Lawrence. 1995. *Translator's invisibility. A history of translation.* London/New York: Routledge.

Joan Grimalt
Gustav Mahler's Wunderhorn orchestral songs: A topical analysis and a semiotic square

Abstract: This chapter presents a new way to interpret and classify Gustav Mahler's orchestral songs based on *Des Knaben Wunderhorn*. It is a condensed version of the doctoral thesis the author presented at the Universitat Autònoma de Barcelona in 2010. Mahler's *Wunderhorn* songs and his four first symphonies belong to one and the same part of his work, corresponding to the years 1888–1901. The starting point were the author's own analyses of the songs, including both syntax and semantics, i.e. integrating formal and hermeneutic analysis. Methodologically, the analyses follow the music semiotics school of Julius A. Greimas, as it is manifest in the research of Eero Tarasti, Márta Grabócz, Robert Hatten and Raymond Monelle. The latter supervised this thesis until his decease in March 2010. As for the contents, Grimalt followed and tried to continue Constantin Floros's path-breaking research on the semantic aspect of music, and of Mahler's music in particular.

The analyses' results were organized according to a Semiotic Square that Greimas redesigned from Ancient sources, in the 1960s. This structural representation, however, was not a starting point, but a result of this study: the Square seemed to suggest itself at the final classification of the analytical findings. At first, musical meanings –especially topoi and references– were distributed in drawers and cupboards, or rather, into different collective categories called isotopies. Later on, a classificatory system based on hermeneutic procedures revealed its capacity not only to classify and gather every single musical meaning found in the analyses, but also to graphically express the interrelations between those isotopies. The whole picture configures a structural map that might stand for the world evoked by Mahler's *Wunderhorn* music.

Among new topoi found, the 'Musical Laughter' and the 'Pastoral March' stand out. They can both be traced down in a long tradition before Mahler. The latter can be considered an idiomatic trait of his style, an emblem of his music.

Keywords: Gustav Mahler, Des Knaben Wunderhorn, Topical Analysis, Musical Signification, Semiotics

Αφιερωμένο στον Κωνσταντίνο Φλώρο

Il divertimento a sperimentare un metodo di pensiero
come un gadget che pone regole esigenti e complicate
può coesistere con un agnosticismo ed empirismo di fondo;
il pensiero dei poeti e degli artisti credo funzioni quasi sempre a questo modo.

Italo CALVINO[1]

1 Presentation

In Summer 1997 I was invited to conduct Mahler's First symphony at the Torroella de Montgrí Music Festival, in Catalonia. That concert was the start of my studies on Mahler and on Musical Signification. Fourteen years later, I presented a doctoral thesis on Mahler's *Wunderhorn* music at the Universitat Autònoma de Barcelona, under the supervision of the late Raymond Monelle. It was evaluated generously and unanimously as "excellent *cum laude*" by the thesis committee. I remember back then studying the score and trying to figure out what a story the music might be telling, and who were their main actors. I knew there was some story. Mahler had written some programme notes to the symphony, and I could sense that every element in the music was asking to be interpreted, or deciphered.

That sense and those questions were the impetus to many passionate readings about the elusive world of musical signification and about Gustav Mahler's music and life. In the middle of this learning process, parallel to my work as a performer and teacher, I had the privilege to read and meet some of the main representatives of the field: Constantin Floros, Márta Grabócz, Robert Hatten, Eero Tarasti. They all welcomed and encouraged this performer with musicological interests. A special mention deserves Raymond Monelle, that appeared as a model of musical integration between performance practice and theoretical reflection. He found the time to determine my thesis' structure, supervise its main issues, correct many mistakes. During many years, alongside all other occupations of his and mine, Monelle patiently transmitted to me his exacting standards and his enthusiasm in a respectful and demanding way and guided me to the completion of my PhD.

Gustav Mahler's *Wunderhorn* music is a richly rewarding work of art to study. It can also be seen as an entrance to the rest of Mahler's work, and therefore as a key to interpret its meanings. Among the innumerable Mahlerian bibliography, there was no global analysis of the music of this period and its significations. Many insightful contributions had been published pointing to manifold links

---

[1] Intervista di Maria Corti, in: CALVINO, Eremita a Parigi 1994: p. 254.

between the songs and the symphonies, and on the meaning o various moments in these works, but a general overview of the world they evoke, in this unique combination of pseudo-folk poetry and richly ambiguous music, was missing. My thesis intended to integrate the results of a topical analysis of these songs into a coherent whole that could be applied both to the so-called *Wunderhorn* symphonies and, to a certain degree, to the rest of Mahler's output.

Most of the topoi were recognised with the help of previous studies, above all those by Theodor W. Adorno, Constantin Floros, Julian Johnson, Raymond Knapp and Raymond Monelle. Some others were described for the first time. Using topical analysis by adapting the methods of Márta Grabócz, Robert Hatten, Raymond Monelle, Kofi Agawu or Eero Tarasti seemed a good first step to reveal what the music conveys to its listeners. On the other hand, the need to classify the findings of the analyses led to a four-part diagram, where large sections or meaning fields stand in a structural relationship to each other. For these larger meaning fields, we adopted and adapted the term isotopies. The coincidence of this scheme with the old semiotic square that Algirdas J. Greimas presented and used in the 1960s reinforced the sense that some valid, coherent whole had been achieved.

2 Methodology

The thesis intended to study the musical topoi and isotopies around which Gustav Mahler's early music revolves. The starting point was a thorough analysis of his orchestral songs based on the collection of folk poetry *Des Knaben Wunderhorn*. Special attention was devoted to the relationships between lyrics and music. The thesis' first part, 'Methodology and scope', offered a brief survey of the theory of musical topics and its semiotic ground. It also made explicit the methodological tools that had been used, both to analyse and to classify musical meanings. The second part, called 'Results', presented the description of some of Mahler's emblematic topoi and a Semiotic square that organised them in their interrelationships. Finally, the third part showed the analyses of each of the nineteen *Wunderhorn* orchestral songs that had served as a base for the whole study.

The limits of this dissertation are manifold. The intention was not –could not be– to uncover all musical meanings of the works analysed. Moreover, the narrative aspect, one of the main issues in the study of Mahler's music, especially on instrumental movements, had to remain mostly untouched on this occasion. However, its results changed my way to listen not only to Mahler's music, but also to that of his predecessors, and of some of his successors.

Back then, Mahler studies were already an extremely rich field. In the meantime, the bibliography has grown to be incommensurable. However, within the many monographies about Mahler's music, no attempt had been made to sustain a systematic topical analysis of any specific period in his œuvre, in a similar way as Grabócz Márta did it on Liszt's music.[2] Thanks to the lyrics and to the traditional topics, could it be possible to decipher the main musical meanings in the songs? Later on, every one of those topoi could be ascribed to a broader semantic field. The structural map resulting of these larger groups would amount to a graphic representation of the musical world to which those pieces refer to.

I decided to focus on what I knew best, both as a performer and as a listener. The so-called Wunderhorn years produced no doubt much more than youthful works. The composer sensed that and considered them among his greatest creations. In fact, insight into the meanings of this period's music opens the door to the rest of Mahler's work and, to a certain extent, to that of his contemporaries.

2.1 Musical topoi

Using topical analysis on Mahler's music seemed and seems the very right thing to do. The composer himself appears showing us listeners and analysts the way, when he says, for instance,

> Composing is like playing with building blocks, where new buildings are created again and again, using the same blocks. Indeed, these blocks have been there, ready to be used, since childhood.[3]

The theory of musical topoi originates in the research of Leonard Ratner (1980) and of his former students Wye Jamison Allanbrook (1983, 1998, 2014) and Kofi Agawu (1991, 2009). In the meantime, the concept of musical topos has developed into a whole "Topic Theory", arguably one of the most important contributions to analysis and to a musicology of signification in general. All major scholars in the field have contributed to the theory, that had a first culmination in The Oxford Handbook of Topic Theory, edited by Danuta Mirka (2014).

---

2 Grabócz 1996 (1987).
3 To Natalie Bauer-Lechner, in Summer 1899 (Revelge, Third Symphony.) Killian 1980: p. 138. *Das Komponieren ist wie ein Spielen mit Bausteinen, wobei aus denselben Steinen immer ein neues Gebäude entsteht. Die Steine aber liegen von der Jugend an, die allein zum Sammeln und Aufnehmen bestimmt ist, alle schon fix und fertig da.*

Musical topoi can be defined as *recurring references to cultural units imported and stylized from one medium to another*.[4] The correlation between signifier and signified –between a musical fragment and its cultural reference–, is the result of convention: a social agreement in a historical moment. That includes any human activities susceptible to having a musical correlate[5]. In this chapter, you will find references and topoi in simple quotation marks, to distinguish a represented 'minuet' –a topical reference to it– from the actual dance.

In Ancient Greece, a τόπος (topos) was a subject about which to debate, and also one of the categories into which any knowledge could be subdivided, e.g. according to genre, similarity or contrast, the whole and its parts, etcetera.[6] The term goes back to Aristotle and especially to Cicero's adaptation of it to build a basic methodology to study anything at all. In Rhetoric treatises of the 17th and 18th centuries, *loci topici* had a constant presence. Heinichen and Mattheson adapted many of them to music, in an effort to equate the art of sound with Rhetoric and its high prestige, admitting *they* do not need such 'crutches', but for somebody lacking *inventio* they might be useful. Without further explanation, however, they both provide some examples that sound constrained, unconvincing.[7]

The distinguished literature scholar Ernst R. Curtius (1886–1956) adopted topos in his theory in the sense of 'common place', to show how certain subjects – or topics– were recurrent in literature of all ages and territories. Curtius finds in medieval Latin literature sources for topoi such as 'affected modesty', 'the world upside down', or the *locus amœnus* that has been often described as the ideal place for Pastoral poetry and music. He also describes topoi in their tendency to increasing abstraction and stylization.[8] Leonard Ratner took his topoi from Rhetoric and from Curtius, possibly also inspired by his professor Manfred Bukofzer studying the 20th-century myth of *Affektenlehre*.[9] For Ratner, topoi are not so much abstract categories, but "characteristic figures" in musical discourse, or "random accumulations of musical commonplaces".[10]

---

4 Our definition of Musical Topos, or Topic, is based on Ratner 1980: 9; Allanbrook 1983: 2f.; Grabócz 2009: 22f.; Mirka 2014: 2.
5 Umberto Eco defined 'cultural or semantic unit' as 'simply anything that is culturally defined and distinguished as an entity'. Cf. Eco 1979, A Theory of Semiotics, p. 67. Quoted by Spitzer 2012: 211.
6 We follow here Allanbrook 2014: 91–111.
7 Allanbrook 2014: 93–96.
8 Curtius 2013 (1948): 193f.
9 For a criticism of the so-called Doctrine of Affects and of the Theory of Rhetorical Figures, see Zoppelli 1988, or Civra 1991. From a more global perspective, see also Gadamer 2010 (1960), Cook 1990, Kramer 1995, Cook & Everist 1999/2001, or Monelle 2008.
10 Allanbrook 2014: 96.

Musical topoi were perceived by contemporary listeners in their complexity; many are still recognizable today, especially with the help of some contextualising information. Viennese Classic music, the style where topic theory was first applied, seems to have something for every kind of listener, from the least refined amateur to the most sophisticated professional musician. This ability is more patent in genres addressed to a wider audience, dependant on pleasing publishers and costumers – especially the symphony, where references to comic opera predominate.[11] This trend to address a majority grows as the symphonic genre becomes a cultural emblem of the more and more powerful 19th-century bourgeoisie. The original, Aristotelian concept of *topos* is tightly linked to that of *doxa*, i.e. the set of beliefs, moral convictions, images shared by a community at a given moment.[12] Moreover, musical phrases rise to a climax and yield to a resolution in a similar way as spontaneous speech does. That is why it is possible to grasp most affects associated with topoi or even structural consequences derived from them by instinct, even without a great musical culture.[13]

Intuition and our audio-visual culture, trained in associating soundtracks with images and stories, make contemporary audiences fairly competent in deciphering the codes of most art music of the common-practice period, especially the late Romantic repertoire dealt with here. That might explain part of Mahler's popularity, a century after his time. On the other hand, getting to know about how his contemporary listeners might have perceived their musical topoi notably enhances the pleasure of the musical experience. This seems to match Johann K.F. Triest's emphasis on an imaginative response to new instrumental music, in a text from 1801. Triest distinguishes three hierarchically ordered listening attitudes: (1) 'Sensual tickle' (*Sinnenkitzel*), a most superficial background listening. (2) 'Understanding' (*Verstand*), where the rational element allows the listener to connect diverse elements and to orient her- or himself structurally. (3) 'Imagination' (*Einbildungskraft*), where the listener is able to supply him- or herself with images connected to the music, even when it is following no text.[14] The same intent to favour this imaginative listening might be the reason why Haydn, Brahms, Mahler from 1900 on, or so many others chose not to give any interpreting clues to their audience, nor to reveal the topical references they were using.

---

[11] Cf. Sisman 2014, Hunter 2014.
[12] Cf. Grabócz 2018: 5.
[13] Carol L. Krumhansl led and published in 1998 an experiment with Californian music students to investigate the psychological measurability of musical topoi. According to her results, professional musicians do not identify musical meanings any better than the rest of the population: Cf. Tagg & Clarida 2003. Agawu instead (1991) argues that a knowledge of the style is a prerequisite to understand the messages of classical music.
[14] Quoted by SISMAN 2014: 105f.

Besides topical analysis, the concept of **isotopy** was very useful when classifying the topoi that had been found. Adapting Algirdas J. Greimas' terminology, we call *isotopy* a series of related musical meanings that becomes representative of a composer's style.

2.2 Classifying topoi

Classifying elementary topics or musical *sèmes* into larger units, however, poses a difficult question. Every topos often seems to have two quite different meanings; one obvious, the other one accessible only through relationships to other meanings, be it affinity, contiguity or similarity.

For instance, a reference to a 'Military March' is easy to recognise. Its ultimate, latent meaning, however, depends greatly on its place among a composer's idiom. In Robert Schumann's musical world, it is normally linked to Florestan's troop of sunny idealists in war against the dull Philistines of his time.[15] In Mahler's music, instead, the 'March' reference plays a central role. Among its many variants, some dysphoric, brutal or carnivalesque 'marches' predominate. They seem to represent the blind forces of the collective which prevent the individual to fulfil their lives in satisfaction. Adorno called this image, quoting two places in Mahler's lyrics, the 'Worldly Tumult'. In Shostakovich's case, the meaning of the 'Military March' reference is also dysphoric, no matter whether his represented 'trampling monsters' are the Nazis (as he claimed to the Communist Party) or the Bolsheviks, as contemporary Westerners immediately felt. These debates, that were very heated around Shostakovich's time, are less and less significative to later audiences. For them –for us–, these topoi keep their affective flavour, whereas actual historical correlates blur progressively into abstraction.

Algirdas J. Greimas addresses the issue of different levels of meaning in his chapter about "*Le discours plurivoque*". He mentions Sigmund Freud's discoveries about a manifest and a latent meaning of any dream and enlarges it to any human manifestation. Greimas prefers the terms *text* and *metatext*. In both cases, to unveil the ultimate from the primary meaning, **interpretation** is required. That implies, according to Greimas, to integrate every single meaning in an abstract system that would represent the entire world conveyed by the text as a whole. He uses the example of crosswords and calls this "*une grille omnisciente, construite a priori*".[16]

---

[15] Florestan is the composer's impulsive alter ego. The other half is the dreamy Eusebius.
[16] Greimas 1986: p. 90.

This interpretive act is something we constantly do, in our daily attempts to fill in missing elements in any discourse. However, there is no possibility that this procedure could ever be completed mechanically – that would require a universal reference of every meaning in the world. That impossibility disturbs the structuralist. He feels the urge to reach definitive, exhaustive and absolute results – something impossible to gain, by definition, using interpretive tools.

> La nécessité d'une *grille culturelle* pour résoudre les difficultés relatives à la recherche de l'isotopie du discours, [...] remet en question la possibilité même de l'analyse sémantique objective. Car le fait qu'une telle grille est, dans l'état actuel de nos connaissances, difficile à imaginer pour les besoins de l'analyse mécanique signifie que la description elle-même dépend encore, dans une large mesure, de l'appréciation subjective de l'analyseur. Certains spécialistes, et des plus éminents –nous pensons notamment à Bar-Hillel –, vont jusqu'à affirmer que, faute de pouvoir enregistrer dans les mémoires électroniques la totalité des propos sur le monde, on n'arrivera jamais à obtenir une traduction mécanique de haute fidélité.[17]

Nowadays, interpretation is seen in a much more positive light. In fact, interpreting does not imply arbitrariness, provided it is supported by sustainable, intersubjective observations. Greimas himself provides, some pages away, a solution to this apparent problem. Commenting on a study about the epithets determining the lexeme *Death* in George Bernanos's literary work, he describes the usual act of interpretation, given a stable context where every meaning can be inscribed in:

> Pour peu que les mêmes épithètes apparaissent comme redondantes à d'autres endroits du texte et qu'elles tendent à s'y substituer les unes aux autres, elles permettent de découvrir, grâce à cet environnement contextuel stable, de nouvelles dénominations de *mort*, telles que *boue, ennui* ou *solitude*. Des procédures de l'établissement de l'isotopie de plus en plus sûres pourront donc être élaborées progressivement.[18]

That is precisely what the present thesis did, after having discerned topical units. Recognising redundant or akin (isotopic) elements allowed to "progressively establish more and more secure isotopies". Interpreting topoi means thus selecting among the information and the sheer amount of possibilities that a given music offers to the listener and to the analyst. That, in Kofi Agawu's words, includes some creative (or recreative) fantasy:

> Identifying topics, however, is only the first stage of analysis; interpretation must follow. [...] In practice, identifying topics can produce relatively stable results; interpreting topics, by contrast, often turns up diverse plots. Whereas identification entails a discovery of famil-

---

[17] Greimas 1986: 90.
[18] Greimas 1986: 93.

iar or relatively objective configurations, interpretation is the exercise of an imaginative will – a fantasy fuelled by the analyst's capacity for speculation.[19]

The same valuation of interpretation is found in Raymond Monelle, who has shown how decisive the context is to identify a topic. Examining some of the different musical topics involving 'horses', he writes:

> Hence, the perception of the musical topos depends on critical judgement, not on mechanical connections. If the music is vocal, reference in the text to a horse or to some other part of the cultural unit may make this easier. Without a text or evocative title, the topos may be eminently present, but naming it requires a more exuberant critical spirit.[20]

Kofi Agawu insists on that point and states the necessity of a broader view to broach an interpretation of the topics found.[21] The analyst needs a given context to elucidate whether their results yield a narrative or not, are absorbed in a larger structure, a vaster genre, or not.

As for the signifieds, correlates to musical topoi are so diverse they can be classified in a multiplicity of ways. There is one kind of topoi that can be called more specifically **references**. The advantage of saying a *'march' reference* is twofold: first, we are using a term that, unlike *topos* or *topic*, does not require any explanation, even with non-initiated. Second, we specify that within the whole cosmos of musical topoi, we are making reference to a particular genre. Topoi like the 'Hunt' or the 'Tragic Style' are in a certain sense also a reference, but in a more indirect, constructed sense. References to dance or vocal genres have an immediacy that deserves being stressed by the use of a specific term.

Based on the genres they refer to, references can be divided into **vocal** and **related to movement**. Vocal references are connected to the affects of their text, whether real or virtual: anger, sorrow, lyricism, humour. References implying movement invoke those genres connected with the body: dances and marches. This shapes an opposition within musical genres between motionlessness and in movement, between **Spirit** and **Body** (see Figure 1). European Christianity traditionally sought for spirituality at the expense of the body. This mystical longing has had a deep impact in the whole of Western culture. In European music, it found in a purely vocal music its preferent vehicle. A whole tradition of 'pure singing' lines ensues – it is music with no perceptible rhythmical pulse. Whether consciously or not, its roots lie in liturgical, Gregorian chant. Such ecstatic music

---

[19] Agawu 2009: 50.
[20] Monelle 2000: 65.
[21] Agawu 2009: 50.

sounds as if trying to leave the earth behind –and the legs and the movement that binds us to this world–, to encourage a spiritual quest for the highest goals.

The same opposition Body/Spirit seems to preside over another pair of expressive meanings, that opposing **pictorialism** and **symbolism**. The first one relates to definite, palpable realities of life, whereas the symbolic opens the listener's mind to associations of more ineffable nature. To interpret 'birdsong' as such is a simple procedure that exhausts itself in its recognition. To question further about the symbolic meanings such a musical sign might evoke –springtime, erotic love, pastoral setting and so forth– widens the listening experience towards the properly human. Music's descriptive abilities have been widely explored, but always with apprehension and under a poor evaluation. The symbolic instead has been acknowledged generally as the gate to artistic quality and prestige. The difference between a cut-short, simple, one-dimensional sign and a symbol produces a second axis, one dividing **intra-musical** meanings –derived from generic divisions– and **extra-musical**, which relate to the world outside of music.

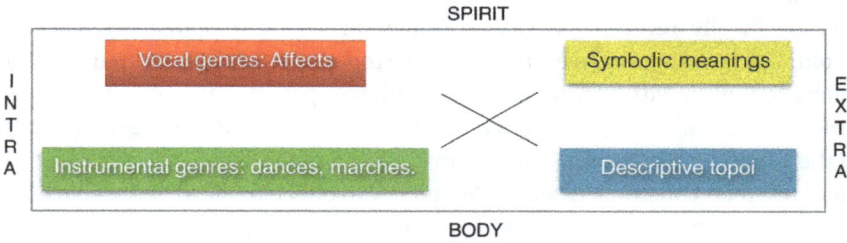

Figure 1: A semiotic square to classify musical meaning.

The four-part division represented in Figure 1 can be useful to classify musical meanings in a way that relates every one of the four corners to each other in what is called a Semiotic Square: more about it further. To be sure, real music does not present such naked categories, but combinations of them: a lyrical melody on a dance accompaniment; a polyphonic texture with descriptive features, and so on. Descriptive topoi – 'Laughter', 'Birdcall', the 'Gallop' – at first seem to exhaust themselves in a direct, univocal meaning. However, they usually carry with them a great deal of symbolic meaning as well. In fact, real musical meaning is never as 'pure' as it appears on Figure 1. It rather fluctuates between those four regions. The two axes and the four sides of the semiotic square are so closely interrelated that they tend to appear simultaneously. An affect such as 'anger', for example, is represented in the subgenre of the *aria di vendetta*, on the upper left side of the square, but this finds often bodily manifestations, such as 'Blows' and 'Shouts', the imitation through a *tirata* of the sound of unsheathing a sword, or the threatening tremolos of the 'Storm' topos. These signifiers all belong to the bottom part of our square. Moreover, all dance and bodily genres carry affective meanings with them: a 'March' can be triumphant, pastoral, dysphoric in character. Finally, any genre and the references to them can be subject of a symbolic use by any composer at a given time. The *Prometheus* 'Contredanse' towards which Beethoven directs his whole *Eroica* symphony, for instance, is a reference to a dance genre, which corresponds to the bottom left corner of the square. However, the way the contredanse was performed in ballrooms of the time favoured an intermingling of the social classes. This led to a symbolic understanding of the 'Contredanse' and its topical reference as a modern, egalitarian genre, akin to the Prometheus myth and also to the 'Hero of the people' that is being represented in Beethoven's 3rd symphony.[22]

3 Results

3.1 Two new, old topoi

Within the results of these analyses, two topoi deserve special attention: the 'Musical Laughter' and the 'Pastoral March'. The signified of the 'Musical Laughter' topos in vocal and instrumental music is a descriptive imitation of 'giggles' or 'laughs', usually in a feminine register.[23] Its signifier tends to take the form of downward scales of rhythmically equal, *staccato* notes: see example 1. In Mahl-

Example 1: W.A. Mozart, *Le nozze di figaro* II, n° 12, mm. 13–15.

---

22 About the expressive meaning of the 'Contredanse' reference in Beethoven, see Floros 2008 (1st ed. 1978) and Grimalt 2018a, 2018b.
23 See more about the 'Musical Laughter' topos in GRIMALT 2014b.

er's early music, the topos has a remarkable presence within the isotopy of 'False Appearances', where most of his humorous music takes place.

As for the 'Pastoral March', it is a Romantic topos with Classic roots that Mahler shares with the previous generation. In spite of its crucial role within Mahler's vocabulary, not only during the *Wunderhorn* years, it has never been studied or described in its deep, original meaning: the longing for the 'Subject's Fulfilment'. Most of the time, Mahler's music marches on its way, but only sometimes it does in a leisurely pace that corresponds to a 'Wayfarer March', i.e. that adaptation of the military march that hikers or student associations use, often related to patriotic issues.[24] *Wandern* in the mountains was one of Mahler's personal passions. The descending fourths that accompany such wayfarer marches, as an emblematic attribute, go along with most of the lyric utterances of his music – the rare occasions where the musical persona leaves its ironic mask aside.

The song in example 2, quoted by Brahms in his *Academic Overture* as one of many student songs of the 19th century, is the main thematic material of Mahler's Third symphony. Notice its characteristic accompaniment.

Example 2: *Ich hab' mich ergeben mit Herz und mit Hand.*

A variant of this accompaniment in fourths and fifths is found also in our next example. However, the 'steps' are interrupted occasionally, as if the represented musical persona would arrest her pace: see ex. 3. Is there a more beautiful correlate of a lost-in-thought, meditative, leisurely walk?

---

[24] Or maybe the other way around: patriotic activities with a hiking background.

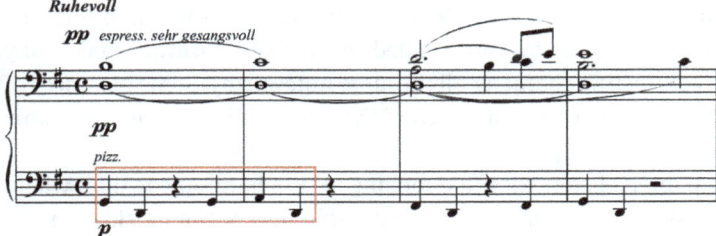

Example 3: Fourth Symphony III, begin.

3.2 Isotopies, semiotic square

The musical meanings found in the analysed *Wunderhorn* orchestral songs could be primarily divided into five categories, attending only to their obvious, in Freudian terms "manifest" meanings, i.e.
1. Nature,
2. Death,
3. World,
4. Love,
5. Music and Art.

These five areas configure a coherent net of interrelations, and also an expressive correlate to human existence. It is current to attest this quality to Romantic literature; music of the nineteenth century, including its Postromantic continuation, does that as well. However, going deeper into analysis showed how these categories did not correspond to the highest possible level. Thanks to the interpretive act described in the preceding paragraph, each one of the categories could be fitted into some more extensive concept. Nature, for instance, has two opposite meanings in Mahler's *Wunderhorn* world: one is akin to the traditional pastoral, whereas in other contexts, it can be related to the grim prospects of god Pan and to panic, and thus to a dysphoric meaning field.

Death, second in the list, is a broad terrain in Mahler's music, but there are many items that can be related to it. For instance, the 'Military March', or the 'Storm and Stress' topic. I found these can all be subsumed into the isotopy of the 'Worldly Tumult', i.e. a hostile collective image, responsible for the subject's non fulfilment

Looking with some perspective to the topoi that can be found in Mahler's *Wunderhorn* music makes apparent a remarkable amount of disharmony, the music showing most of the time discontinuity or dissonance, suggesting violence, fear, sadness and many other dysphoric meanings. This sombre main tonality, that may be associated to what Adorno called the **Worldly Tumult**, makes any appearance of a contrasting character all the more noteworthy. Some instances of Pan's march in the first movement of the Third Symphony might serve as example of this main isotopy.

Thus, what Mahler's listener is often longing for is a harmonic region, where all the struggle may find some truce, if not a durable peace. The music seems to achieve that appeasement only in a **Transcendent** region, beyond this chaotic world "under the sky". For instance, by the close of the Second, or the Third Symphonies. Now according to Greimas, these two poles, contradicting each other, could be called respectively, **S1** and **S2**. They constitute together what the music invokes as *existent*.

> S1 Worldly Tumult.. S2 Transcendent

But there is another corresponding pair of musical meanings to which existence is not granted: they belong to the Inauthentic (*Uneigentlich*). The **False Appearances**, with the famous Mahlerian Irony as a main weapon, complement the 'Worldly Tumult' –they point to it– and negate Transcendence. For instance, the bells at the beginning of the Fourth Symphony, of which Adorno wrote:

> They really are fool's bells, which, without saying it, say: none of what you now hear is true.[25]

By doing so, 'False Appearances' place themselves as the opposite of a **Subject's Fulfilment** that can only be sensed by intuition, but not achieved, except for some moments. These rare moments are what Adorno calls "spaces of lasting present", referring to a passage "following the exposition of the first movement" and to the beginning of the Adagio of the Fourth Symphony, both in G-Major.[26] Apart from these scarce exceptions, fulfilment is basically what is *longed for* in Mahler's music: it appears mostly as its hope, or its negation.

Erwin RATZ had already pointed out how much meaning is set in what Mahler *does not say*. It is what is missing that gives all its poignance to what is stated. Adorno quotes this, showing how useful it can be to take account of the opposites of any meaning value:

> In flagrant contradiction to everything familiar from absolute, program-less music, his [Mahler's] symphonies do not exist in a simple positive sense, as something granted to the

---

[25] Adorno 1960: Jephcott p. 56. German p. 106: Wirklich ist es eine Narrenschelle, die, ohne es zu sagen, sagt: Was ihr nun vernehmt, ist alles nicht wahr.
[26] Adorno 1960: Jephcott p. 44. German p. 193: Flächen der dauernden Gegenwart.

participants as a reward: on the contrary, whole complexes want to be taken negatively – one should listen, as it were, against them. "We see an alternation of positive and negative situations."[27]

Thus all lyric utterances, frequently interrupting or being interrupted in Mahler's discourse, are to be understood as the subject's longing for fulfilment, or mourning elegiacally for its impossibility. This is the very negation (contradiction) of the 'Worldly Tumult'. To the vertical, veridictional axis [Existence – NonExistence] a horizontal one can now be added, based on Greimas' *thymic* categories: [Euphoria – Dysphoria]. **"Thymic"** is a term borrowed from psychology that comes from the Greek θυμός, which is usually translated as 'passion'. For Plato, the *thymic* meant the animalistic in human sensorial perception, as opposed to rationality.[28] This bodily aspect of affections was incorporated into semiotic theory by the French school. According to Greimas and Courtès, *thymos* "articulates signification by immediately linking it to the personal perception of one's own body".[29] The distinction between euphoric and dysphoric belongs to perception, and thus to Psychology. In musical signification, it signals two of the most basic affects, namely 'joy' and 'sorrow', or 'wellness' and 'unwellness', with all their nuances. Grabócz (1993) and Tarasti (1994) were the first to adapt these terms from Algirdas Julien Greimas (1966), who used them in literary analysis.[30]

At this point, a structural map has been achieved, composed of four winds. They are related to each other in a way which corresponds with Greimas's semiotic square: see Figure 2.

---

27 Erwin Ratz, "Zum Formproblem bei Gustav Mahler. Eine Analyse des Finales der VI. Symphonie", in: Die Musikforschung, 9th year, № 2, p. 166. Included in: Gustav Mahler, Rainer Wunderlich Verlag: Tübingen 1966, pp. 90–122. Quoted by Adorno 1960: Jephcott p. 125. German p. 269: In eklatantem Widerspruch zu allem an absoluter, programmloser Musik Gewohntem sind seine Symphonien nicht einfach positiv da, als etwas, was den Mitvollziehenden belohnte, indem es ihm zuteil wird, sondern ganze Komplexe wollen negativ genommen, es soll gleichsam gegen sie gehört werden.
28 Tarasti 1994: 303.
29 Greimas & Courtés 1986: 396.
30 According to Greimas, a subject is euphoric when he is in conjunction with an object, when he possesses it, and dysphoric when he is in disjunction with that object. Greimas Du Sens II, 1983: 225–246. Quoted by Caux 2018: 200.

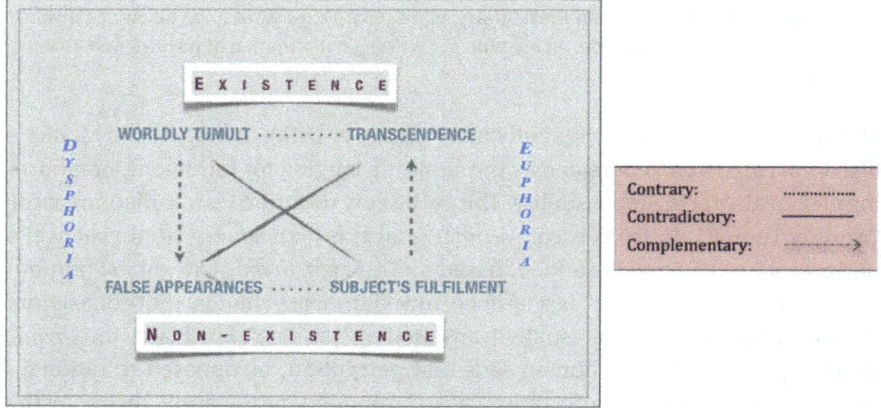

Figure 2: Semiotic Square with four isotopies in Mahler's *Wunderhorn* music.

The square can be read like this: Mahler's *Wunderhorn* music asserts the existence of a world that is hostile to the subject; a stupid, vulgar and cruel world, and the impossibility, therefore, of a fulfilled life for the individual. To that situation, as for example in the first movement of the Third Symphony, only two alternatives seem plausible: Irony, to unmask False Appearances, and a Transcendent reality, albeit as a promise, as in the Finale of the Second Symphony.

The results of our analyses relate Mahler's music to the literary Western tradition, expressed in musical terms: Lyric and Epic, on one hand, and Humour versus Sublime, on the other. On the heroic side, different versions of 'Marches' or 'Hunting' music can be subsumed into the isotopy of the 'Worldly Tumult'. Lyricism, one of Mahler's most idiomatic features, stands as the longing or mourning for a fulfilment that does not appear as a real possibility on earth. The category of the Sublime, an expression of transcendental ideals and yearnings, finds an expression in over-worldly matters. Finally, humour, and particularly irony, has often been regarded as one of the keys of Mahlerian language. In particular, we could discern the emblematic topos of 'Fallacious Beauty', where Mahler's music seems –and in fact is– too beautiful to be true.

This study came to the Semiotic Square by first deciphering some of these (topical) means, and by later interrelating them, taking account of the permeability of both Mahlerian genres, song and symphony, and between topical analysis and interpretation.[31] The graphic makes clear what has been worrying many Mahler scholars, from Adorno to Julian Johnson: the issue of **artistic truth**, one

---

31 Cf. Hatten 1994: 269.

of the main subjects of Romantic aesthetics. According to the idealist philosophy of Hegel, art is not an embellishment, but has to be true. What is real or genuine, both in life and in art, is often shown negatively, as what is fake, or non-existent. That explains the main role that all forms of ambiguity play in Mahler's music under the command of the omnipresent irony. In his recent study about *Mahler's voices* (2009), Julian Johnson concludes that

> In Mahler's music, the *what* lies entirely in the *how*, because in Mahler the problem with speaking *as such* is precisely the content of the music.[32]

It is, in other words, a quest for realism that informs many artistic productions of late Romanticism, and especially the French and Russian novel Mahler admired so much. In Deryck Cooke's words:

> What affronts the idealist –the cruelty, vulgarity, triviality and apparent meaninglessness of life– he stared boldly in the face: he neither escaped from it into a private paradise like the late romantics, nor ignored it altogether as a non-artistic element like the classics, but acknowledged it and fought against it. . . If half of him was romantic, the other half was that characteristic twentieth-century figure: the restless seeker for the naked truth (whether "beautiful" or "ugly"), ridden with doubt and perplexity, ill-at-ease in an unfriendly cosmos.[33]

Eventually, a quote by the composer himself, where he classified the different styles of his music in quite similar terms, confirmed both our findings and their classification. Shortly after sketching the present semiotic square on the *Wunderhorn* music, I came across a passage in Natalie Bauer-Lechner *Memoirs* that I had not been attentive to before. To my astonishment, it confirms some of the assumptions which the square implies, from the composer's mouth:

> We probably pick up all primeval rhythms and motifs from Nature, as it offers them already at its clearest in every animal sound. Man, and especially the artist, take also any material and any form from the world surrounding them, albeit in quite a different, enlarged sense. Whether he finds himself in a harmonic, contented accord with Nature, or whether he confronts it in a painful suffering or hostile negation; or whether he tries to deal with it from a superior look out position, with humour and irony: these result in the bases to the Beautiful-Sublime; to the Sentimental and Tragical; and to the Humorous-Ironic styles in the proper sense.[34]

---

32 Johnson 2009: p. 3.
33 Cooke 1980 (1959): p. 10.
34 Killian: p. 95. From Tyrol (Kitzbühel, Steinach and Gries am Brenner), in the summer of 1897. *Wahrscheinlich empfangen wir die Urrhythmen und –Themen alle aus der Natur, die sie schon in jedem Tierlaut in großer Prägnanz uns bietet. Wie ja der Mensch und der Künstler im Besonderen jeden Stoff und jede Form der Welt, die ihn umgibt, entnimmt, freilich in ganz anderem, erweitertem Sinne. Sei es nun, daß er sich in harmonisch-glücklichem Einklange mit der Natur befindet oder*

Mahler himself distinguishes in this revealing passage four different human attitudes regarding the outer world, which he calls *Nature*. First, harmony governs their relationship: it is what this thesis calls the 'Subject's Fulfilment'. Mahler links it to the Beautiful-Sublime. Second, nature is seen as hostile and causing pain: this corresponds to our isotopy of the 'Worldly Tumult'; the composer relates it to "the Sentimental and Tragical". Finally, he accords a third possibility, i.e. to adopt "a superior look-out position, with humour and irony". Mahler derives logically "the Humorous-Ironic styles" from this attitude, and omits only the 'Transcendent', admittedly the least represented in his work quantitatively, albeit a very important one qualitatively.

3.3 Mahler's vision

Both as listener and interpreter, however, one often senses that Mahler's instrumental music is telling things that transcend the purely musical to embrace what might be called today a multimedia language. Some authentic instructions on the scores do sound like stage directions: in the Second Symphony, e.g., the four offstage trumpets calling the dead to the Last Judgement should come from four different regions.[35]

Some scholars have vindicated Mahler's narrative qualities at a time when this was seen as problematic. Constantin Floros and Hans Heinrich Eggebrecht encouraged many of us to follow the pursuit of Mahlerian meanings, and even Adorno cannot help referring to some dramatic and semantic aspects in Mahler's work.

It should not surprise that a composer who spent most of his life in a theatre, caring a lot about the staging of the operas he conducted, composes in a dramaturgic way.[36] Mahler's conception of his own work –what he significantly calls his **vision**, *Anschauung*– could have been close to cinematography, or indeed to

---

sich zu ihr in schmerzvoll-leidenden oder feindlich-verneinenden Gegensatz stellt, sei es, daß er von überlegener Warte aus in Humor oder Ironie mit ihr fertig zu werden sucht: womit die Grundlagen zu dem schön-erhabenen, sentimentalen und tragischen und humoristisch-ironischen Kunststil im engsten Sinne gegeben sind.
35 Second Symphony V, n° 29.
36 Cf. Floros 2005.

the Wagnerian *Gesamtkunstwerk* aesthetics, to which he felt attached. Here is a statement of Justi's, Gustav's sister, on the Second Symphony:

> The triumph grew greater with every movement. Such enthusiasm is seen only once in a lifetime. I saw weeping men and youths eventually flinging their arms around each other's necks. And at the passage where the Bird of Death, hovering above the graves, utters its last, long, drawn-out call, there reigned such a dead silence, that the whole audience seemed to hold their breath.[37]

Justi refers to the moment just before the hymn *Aufersteh'n*, in the last movement of the Second Symphony (n° 30–31). It sounds like the description of a movie, rather than a symphony. In an interview he gave some years ago, the neurologist Patrik Nils JUSLIN describes a process called *Associated Mechanism of Visual Imagery*, through which music has the real power to create images in our mind:

> And when I say 'image' it is no metaphor, I don't mean auditive images, but visual images on our cerebral cortex.[38]

On the other hand, Mahler's songs and symphonies are much more than a visual spectacle. As Constantin Floros has clearly shown, Mahler the composer wants to communicate his thoughts through music. Natalie Bauer-Lechner reports in her *Memoirs* once and again about the intimate connection between his music and his life. Here, Natalie quotes Mahler's own words:

> And if one should know how to read, my life should appear to him transparent indeed. In my case work and experience are so interrelated that if my existence should henceforth flow as peaceful as a brook on a meadow, it seems to me I could not make anything more worth it.[39]

---

[37] Killian, p. 43: *Der Erfolg wuchs noch mit jedem Satze. Eine solche Art von Begeisterung kann man kaum wieder erleben. Ich [Justi] sah, dass Männer weinten und Jünglinge zum Schluß einander um den Hals fielen. Und bei der Stelle, da der Totenvogel auf den Gräbern seine letzten langgezogenen Töne schwirrt, da herrschte eine solche Totenstille, dass keine Wimper zu zucken schien.* Unless marked it is my translation.

[38] Cf. Justin 2008.

[39] Killian p. 26: *Und wenn einer gut zu lesen verstünde, müßte ihm in der Tat mein Leben darin durchsichtig erscheinen. So sehr ist bei mir Schaffen und Erleben verknüpft, daß, wenn mir mein Dasein fortan ruhig wie ein Wiesenbach dahinflösse, ich – dünkt mich– nichts Rechtes mehr machen könnte.*

Mahler saw the meaning of his symphonies summarized in the expression *Wahrheit und Dichtung in Tönen*, i.e. "Truth and Poetry in Sound".[40] It is an unconscious creation, one its creator himself cannot comprehend. He calls it a *mystical* activity: it is the Romantic aesthetics of a creation in a state of trance, such as Brahms and other contemporaries have described it. In Mahler's own words:

> Today I went through the whole Scherzo of my Second Symphony, that I hadn't looked at anymore since I made it and was quite surprised about it. It is a curious, dreadfully great piece! I didn't take it as such while I composed it. The creation and generation of a work are mystical, from the beginning to the end, for one has to do something, without the conscience of it, as if it were someone else's idea. And afterwards you can hardly comprehend how it fell into place.[41]

The relationship between Mahler's life and work, however, is a topic that should be approached with caution. The composer's tormented biography appears as an invitation to speculation, but already Adorno warned against this. Adorno's words sound as vivid as if they were written now. After dealing contemptuously with those who, in a "cheap" way, "chat around" (*schwatzen*) about Mahler as a psychological subject, he admonishes:

> It is as evident that Mahler, like all new music, is completely penetrated by the soul, as evident that it does not limit itself to the designs of the sounding forms in movement, as the fact that his symphonies, in their urge to renouncement and to totality, are not attached to any private person, which in fact became an instrument to produce them.[42]

The "sounding forms in movement" are an allusion to Eduard Hanslick's book *Vom Musikalisch-Schönen* (Leipzig 1854) – the formula Hanslick uses to emphasize the formal aspect of (classical) music, as a reaction to the *Neudeutsche Schule*. Raymond Monelle devoted a chapter, in *The Sense of Music* (2000), to *Mahler and Gustav*, where the distinction between œuvre and subject is made on non-formalist premises. According to Monelle, in Mahler's music there is an "abdication" of the composer's voice for the sake of nature – or the "folk", as the Romantic former generation would put it:

---

[40] Cf. Floros 1998, from p. 147 on, about the composer as an *untergeordneter Vollzugsorgan*, i.e., secondary executor of a transcendent command.

[41] Killian p. 26.

[42] Adorno 1960: p. 172. *So selbstverständlich Mahler, wie alle neuere Musik, Durchseelung voraussetzt; so wenig er bei den Tapetenmustern tönend bewegten Spiels sich bescheidet, so wenig sind seine Symphonien, in ihrem Zug zur Entäußerung, zur Totalität, an eine Privatperson gekettet, die in Wahrheit sich zum Instrument machte, um sie zu produzieren.*

> The composer's voice is absent from this music. The author is dead. Instead of strongly individualized themes, there are shreds of musical flotsam, echoes of the parade ground, the hunting field and the dance hall, of nursery songs and children's games. [...] Early listeners to Mahler were distressed to find no such signature in his music; [...]⁴³

Mahler's is thus an artistic vision, in its most immediate sense: the composer's own term underlines the three dimensional aspect of his music. Sometimes, Natalie Bauer-Lechner reports, Mahler sees the musical scene right in front of him, and this makes him laugh:

> And if one would not see that process in the most immediate way in front of his eyes [meaning the dumb face of the fish listening to St. Anthony's sermon, in the *Fischpredigt*], I do not think one could ever succeed; for in any art the main concern is the vision.⁴⁴

Or, in a letter to Max Marschalk, where the composer seems to optimistically evaluate his listeners able to "grasp" his visions,

> At several particular passages I can often see, later on, a real action in front of my eyes, in a dramatic development so to speak: this is easy to grasp from the essence of the music itself.⁴⁵

However, all these synesthetic connections take place through the Word, through literature. Mahler's starting point is literary-philosophical, and it takes a musical form only in a second stage, even if the process modifies the initial conception. As he explained to Natalie Bauer-Lechner in 1893, the link between sound and word is comparable to that between Antaeus and his mother Earth. She gives him "giant forces", and that is what the texts on which the music is founded do.⁴⁶

4 Conclusions

The first aim in this thesis consisted in identifying as many of the topics in the Mahlerian palette as possible, and then inscribing each one of them into a cat-

---

43 Monelle 2000: p. 176.
44 Killian p. 28: *Und schwebte einem ein solcher Vorgang nicht in der allerunmittelbarsten Anschauung vor, er könnte, glaube ich, nie gelingen; denn in jeder Kunst kommt es vor allem auf die Anschauung an.*
45 Hamburg, 17.XII.95, Gustav Mahler: *Briefe*, ed. by Herta Blaukopf 1996, p. 163: *Daß ich hinterher oft bei verschiedenen einzelnen Partien einen realen Vorgang vor mir sich –sozusagen- dramatisch abspielen sehe, ist aus dem Wesen der Musik leicht zu begreifen.*
46 Killian p. 34, summer 1893.

egory that helps to explain Mahler's musical world as a whole. The task of classifying multifarious topoi into four isotopies implied to interpret them in their final meaning, which often does not coincide with the first impression they give. I remember this interpretation as the most arduous yet rewarding task. Interpreting does not imply arbitrariness, provided it is supported by accountable, intersubjective observations and the ability to relate apparently unrelated information.

The final picture, the interrelated semiotic square gathering all the topoi revealed, should be useful in identifying other musical meanings in Mahler's music, or in applying and adapting it to the work of some other composers. They seem to offer an "idiomatic" musical language, i.e., idiosyncratic and consistent. This foursquare diagram, to be sure, is not the only one possible, but it might be a suitable image of Mahler's *Weltanschauung*, or rather of how his music in this period envisages two central issues of western modernity (and postmodernity): (1) the troubled relationship between the individual and the collective, and (2) the question of artistic truth and false appearances.

Topical analysis, based on the study of the traditional (classical) meanings and their etymological value, has proved its capacity to transcend isolated analytical findings by unveiling through interpretation a whole net of interrelationships, which in turn can be represented in a coherent structural map. This map could be a first solid step in tackling the task of interpreting Mahler's symphonies in a narrative sense, continuing Constantin Floros's pioneer work. The present investigation on these fascinating pieces should be continued, and its output applied to the symphonies, in greater depth than was possible here, as well as to the rest of Mahler's work.

References

Adorno, Theodor Wiesengrund. 2003 [1960]. Mahler. Eine musikalische Physiognomik. In Die musikalischen Monographien. Gesammelte Schriften, Vol. XIII. Frankfurt am Main: Suhrkamp; English trans. by Edmund Jephcott, Chicago and London: The University of Chicago Press 1992.
Agawu, Kofi. 1991. *Playing with Signs. A Semiotic Interpretation of Classic Music*. Princeton: Princeton University Press.
Agawu, Kofi. 2009. *Music as discourse*. Oxford: Oxford University Press.
Allanbrook, Wye Jamison. 1983. *Rhythmic Gesture in Mozart: Le nozze di Figaro and Don Giovanni*. Chicago: University of Chicago Press.
Allanbrook, Wye Jamison (ed.). 1998. *The Late Eighteenth Century*. Strunk's Source Readings in Music History, Vol. 5. New York: Norton and co.
Allanbrook, Wye Jamison. 2010. Is the Sublime a musical topos? *Eighteenth-Century Music* 7/2: 263–279.

Allanbrook, Wye Jamison. 2014. *The Secular Commedia: Comic Mimesis in Late Eighteenth-Century Music*. Oakland: University of California Press.
von Arnim, Achim and Clemens Brentano. 2003. *Des Knaben Wunderhorn. Alte deutsche Lieder.* Düsseldorf: Artemis & Winkler.
Calvino, Italo. 2009 [1994]. *Eremita a Parigi*. Milan: Mondadori.
Civra, Ferruccio. 1991. *Musica poetica. Introduzione alla retorica musicale.* Turin: UTET Libreria.
Cook, Nicholas. 1990. *Music, Imagination and Culture.* Oxford University Press.
Cook, Nicholas and Mark Everist (eds.). 2001 [1999]. *Rethinking Music.* Oxford University Press.
Cooke, Derick. 1959. *The Language of Music.* London: Clarendon Paperbacks.
Curtius, Ernst Robert. 2013 [1948]. *European Literature and the Latin Middle Ages.* Trans. by W. R. Trask. Princeton and Oxford: Princeton University Press.
Eco, Umberto. 1979. *A Theory of Semiotics.* Bloomington: Indiana University Press.
Floros, Constantin. *Gustav Mahler*, Breitkopf & Härtel. 3 volumes:
I. Die geistige Welt Gustav Mahlers in systematischer Darstellung. Wiesbaden 1977.
II. Mahler und die Symphonik des 19. Jahrhunderts in neuer Deutung. Zur Grundlegung einer zeitgemäßen musikalischen Exegetik. Wiesbaden 1977, 2nd ed. 1987.
III. Die Symphonien. Wiesbaden 1985. English *Gustav Mahler. The Symphonies*. Oregon: Amadeus Press 1993.
Floros, Constantin. 1998. *Gustav Mahler. Visionär und Despot. Porträt einer Persönlichkeit.* Zürich & Hamburg: Arche Verlag.
Floros, Constantin. 2008 [1978]. *Beethovens Eroica und Prometheus-Musik*, 2nd, enlarged edn. Florian Wilhelmshaven: Noetzel Verlag.
Floros, Constantin. 2016 [1989]. *Music as Message. An Introduction to Musical Semantics.* Trans. by E. Bernhardt-Kabisch. Frankfurt: Peter Lang 2016. (Original German Musik als Botschaft. Wiesbaden: Breitkopf 1989).
Floros, Constantin 2018. Über Liszts musikalische Symbolsprache. In Márta Grabócz (ed.), *Les grands topoï du xixe siècle et la musiq de Franz Liszt*. Paris: Hermann Éditeurs.
Gadamer, Hans-Georg. 2010 [1960]. *Wahrheit und Methode. Grundzüge einer philosophischen Hermeneutik*. Tübingen: Mohr Siebeck.
Grabócz, Márta. 1996. *Morphologie des œuvres pour piano de F. Liszt.* Paris: Ed. Kimé 1996. (Original Hungarian version: Budapest 1987).
Grabócz, Márta (ed.). 2007. *Sens et signification en musique.* Paris: Hermann Musique.
Grabócz, Márta. 2009. *Musique, narrativité, signification.* Paris: L'Harmattan 2009.
Grabócz, Márta (ed.). 2018. *Les grands topoï du xixe siècle et la musique de Franz Liszt*. Paris: Hermann Éditeurs.
Greimas, Algirdas Julien & Joseph Courtés. 2003 [1979 & 1986]. *Sémiotique. Dictionnaire raisonné de la théorie du langage*. Paris: Hachette; English version Semiotics and Language: an Analytical Dictionary. Bloomington: Indiana University Press 1982.
Greimas, Algirdas Julien. 2002 [1966]. *Sémantique structurale. Recherche de méthode*. (reed. 1986). Paris: Presses Universitaires de France.
Grimalt, Joan. 2011. Gustav Mahler's Wunderhorn orchestral songs: a topical analysis and a semiotic square. Unpublished PhD: Universitat Autònoma de Barcelona 2011.
Grimalt, Joan. 2012. *La música de Gustav Mahler. Una guia d'audició.* Barcelona: Ed. Duxelm.
Grimalt, Joan. 2013a. Mahler's Wunderhorn music and its world of meanings. In Nearchos Panos, Peter Nelson, Vangelis Lympouridis & George Athanasopoulos, *Proceedings of the International Conference on Music Semiotics In memory of Raymond Monelle*. (Edinburgh, October 2012). University of Edinburgh.

Grimalt, Joan. 2013b. "Spaces of lasting present" in Mahler's Wunderhorn music. In Teresa Malecka & Małgorzata Pawłowska (eds.). *Music: Function and Value*. Proceedings of the 11th International Congress on Musical Signification, (Kraków (Poland) 2010), Vol. 2, 29–40. Kraków: Akademia Muzyczna w Krakowie i Musica Iagellonica.

Grimalt, Joan. 2014a. *Música i sentits. Introducció a la significació musical*. Barcelona: Duxelm.

Grimalt, Joan. 2014b. Is Musical Laughter a Topic?. In Dario Martinelli, Eeero Tarasti and Juha Torvinen (eds.), *Philosophies of Performance*, 225–240. Helsinki: The Finnish Semiotic Society.

Grimalt, Joan. 2018a. Beethoven and Goya: Between Modernity and Ancien Régime. In Magdalena Chrenkoff (ed.), *Beethoven 7. Studien und Interpretationen*, 453–470. Kraków: Akademia Muzyczna w Krakowie.

Grimalt, Joan. 2018b. A humorous narrative archetype in the music of the Viennese classics as a subversive device. Unpublished paper presented at ICMS #14 in Cluj (Romania).

Grimalt, Joan. 2020. *Mapping Musical Signification*. Berlin, Heidelberg: Springer Verlag.

Hatten, Robert S. 1994. *Musical Meaning in Beethoven: Markedness, Correlation, and Interpretation*. Bloomington & Indianapolis: Indiana University Press 1994.

Hatten, Robert S. 2004. *Interpreting Musical Gestures, Topics, and Tropes. Mozart, Beethoven, Schubert*. Bloomington & Indianapolis: Indiana University Press.

Hébert, Louis. 2006. Thymic Analysis. In Louis Hébert (ed.), *Signo* [online], Rimouski (Quebec), 2006. http://www.signosemio.com (accessed March 2010)

Hunter, Mary. 2014. Topics and Opera Buffa. Chapter 1 in The Oxford Handbook of Topic Theory, ed. by Danuta Mirka.

Johnson, Julian. 2009. Mahler's Voices. Expression and Irony in the Songs and Symphonies. Oxford University Press.

Justin, Patrik Nils. 2008. Interviewed by Lluís Amiguet in: "la contra", **La vanguardia**: Barcelona January 14th, 2008.

Killian, Herbert (ed.). 1984. *Gustav Mahler in den Erinnerungen von Natalie Bauer-Lechner*. Hamburg: Wagner. (English trans. *Recollections of Gustav Mahler*, by Karl D. Faber & Faber, 1980.)

Kramer, Lawrence. 1995. *Classical Music and Postmodern Knowledge*. Berkeley, Los Angeles, London: University of California Press.

Mahler, Gustav. 1996. *Briefe*. Edited by Herta Blaukopf. Vienna: Szolnay.

Mahler, Gustav. 2005. *Liebste Justi! Briefe an die Familie*. Edited by Stephen McClatchie. Bonn: Weidle Verlag.

Mirka, Danuta (ed.). 2014. *The Oxford Handbook of Topic Theory*. Oxford: Oxford University Press (US).

Monelle, Raymond. 1992. *Linguistic and Semiotics in Music*. London: Routledge.

Monelle, Raymond. 2000. *The Sense of Music: Semiotic Essays*. Princeton University Press.

Monelle, Raymond. 2006. *The musical topic*. Bloomington: Indiana University Press.

Ratner, Leonard G. 1985 [1980]. *Classic Music. Expression, Form and Style*. California: Wadsworth Publishing.

Sisman, Elaine. 2014. Symphonies and the Public Display of Topics. In Danuta Mirka (ed.), *The Oxford Handbook of Topic Theory*, 90–117. Oxford University Press.

Spitzer, Michael. 2012. The Topic of Emotion. In Sheinberg (ed.), *Music Semiotics: a Network of Significations*. Farnham (GB) and Burlington VT (US): Ashgate.

Tagg, Philip and Bob Clarida. 2003. *Ten Little Title Tunes. Towards a musicology of the mass media*. New York & Montreal: The Mass Media Music Scholars' Press.

Tarasti, Eero. 1994. A Theory of Musical Semiotics. Bloomington: Indiana University Press.
Tarasti, Eero Signs of Music. 2002. A Guide to Musical Semiotics. Berlin and New York: Mouton de Gruyter.
Tarasti, Eero. 2012. Semiotics of Classical Music. How Mozart, Brahms and Wagner talk to us. Berlin and New York: Mouton de Gruyter.
Zoppelli, Luca. 1988. "Ut prudens et artifex orator": sulla consistenza di una "dottrina" retorico-musicale fra Controriforma e Illuminismo. *Rivista Italiana di Musicologia* XXIII. 132–156.

Małgorzata Gamrat
Beyond the signs: Art and an artist's life in Hector Berlioz's Opus 14

Abstract: Eero Tarasti's existential semiotics opens up new cognitive perspectives and leads to a deeper understanding of the products of human culture, including music, which is of special importance if we study a work so profoundly embroiled in relations with the subject's internal and surrounding world as Hector Berlioz's Opus 14. It is a composition which combines music with literature, and whose subject transcends the boundary between the real and the supernatural worlds, lingering for a moment in the borderland before the composer comes back to life. Berlioz makes it possible to understand his great project of creating a new type of music that would be close to the artist's own life and capable of conveying extra-musical concepts. His idea of combining such two vast and very different musical works into one whole still strikes us as innovative in our times (and is still frequently misunderstood). Opus 14 features a great wealth of meaning. It is replete with signs, codes, *topoi*, and intertexts, each of which separately and all of them variously interrelated open up virtually countless possibilities of interpretation. The meaning and understanding of this music have been sought and explored in many ways. It is, however, only by applying semiotic tools, especially those derived from existential semiotics, that we can gain profound and daring insights into the work, the person behind the work, and the culture that shaped that person.

Keywords: Hector Berlioz, *Symphonie fantastique*, *Lélio*, existential semiotics, musical semiotis, signs in music

1 Prelude

Eero Tarasti's existential semiotics opens up new cognitive perspectives and leads to a deeper understanding of the products of human culture, including music, which is of special importance if we study a work so profoundly embroiled in relations with the subject's internal and surrounding world as Hector Berlioz's Opus 14. It is a composition which combines music with literature, and whose

---

Note: This paper has been written as part of a project financed by the National Science Centre in Poland, entitled: "Philosophy of music. Metaphysical, phenomenological and deconstructivist directions in the study of music, its theory and practice, No. 2016/23/B/HS1/02325."

subject transcends the boundary between the real and the supernatural worlds, lingering for a moment in the borderland before the composer comes back to life. This makes him discover new meanings in the old content, and he is metaphorically reborn, a process described by Eero Tarasti (2000: 11) in his general principles of existential semiotics.

Let us, therefore, examine Berlioz's Opus 14, where all the compositional tools result from the actions of the subject and are motivated by his *désir*, which becomes an obsession, transformed into a musical concept that unifies the whole composition. Let us also attempt to find out how the composer makes use of the existing codes and signs, and how he transcends them in order to form a unique representation of an artist's work and life in a music work which became one of the most important manifestos of Romantic art.

In its final version,[1] Hector Berlioz's Op. 14 consists of two parts: Op. 14a that is the programmatic five-movement *Symphonie fantastique. Épisode de la vie d'un artiste*, and Op. 14b, a monodrama (or melologue) for speaker, tenor, baritone, choir, piano, and orchestra, entitled *Lélio, ou Le retour à la vie*. What both these works have in common is the literary narrative, the musical motifs, numerous quotations, the composition techniques applied, as well as Berlioz's idea of uniting life and art in music, in the form of a portrait of a Romantic artist. Berlioz constructs this portrait out of references to his own biography and works, as well as elements typical of the French Romanticism, combining all this with innovative orchestration.

The two parts of Op. 14 ought to be performed together, as the composer explains both in the *Symphonie* and in *Lélio*: "The following programme should be distributed to the audience every time the *Symphonie fantastique* is performed dramatically and thus followed by the monodrama of *Lélio*, which concludes and completes the episode in the life of an artist" (1855a); and, furthermore: "This work should be performed immediately after the *Fantastic Symphony*, which indeed it supplements and concludes" (1855b: 1). Notably, such an integral connection between great verbal-musical forms (belonging to different genres) on the level of both text and music precedes Wagner's tetralogy by many years. As a whole, the structure of Op. 14 is as follows:

---

[1] The first version of the *Symphonie* to have been performed publicly is dated back to 1830; the later revisions – to 1845 and 1855. *Lélio* was composed in 1831 and was likewise revised in 1855 (Berlioz 2017).

Movement	Symphonie fantastique	Lélio
1	Daydreams, passions	Monologue 1 – *The fisherman* – Monologue 2
2	A ball	*Chorus of the shades* – Monologue 3
3	Scene in the countryside	*Song of brigands* – Monologue 4
4	March to the scaffold	*Song of bliss* – Monologue 5
5	Dream of a witches' Sabbath	*Aeolian harp. Recollections* – Monologue 6
6	---	*Fantasia on Shakespeare's "Tempest"* – Monologue 7

2 The literary elements of the music work

Berlioz's symphonic innovations consisted not only in his treatment of the orchestra, and in the way he developed the classical form, but also in the addition of extensive literary-type commentary, in which he reflects on the life of an artist, the emotions that he is torn between, inspirations important for the subject, and on contemporary music criticism. Berlioz himself explained in the programme written for the symphony's first performance: "The composer's intention has been to develop various episodes in the life of an artist, in so far as they lend themselves to musical treatment" (1845). The literary text directly influences the expression and character of the music, as well as the artistic tools applied in it. Several years after the premiere of Op. 14, Berlioz wrote in his *De l'Imitation musicale* (1837) that he attached the greatest importance to conveying emotions and mental states by musical means.

In the first version of the programme, the composer wrote about the powerful feelings experienced by the subject, for which he is indebted to Chateaubriand's novel *René*, introducing the type of a hypersensitive and overly emotional character who cannot cope with his own feelings and frequently escapes into the world of his dreams. It was this kind of character that was adopted by Romantic literature as one of its key models. Berlioz wrote: "The author imagines [. . .] a young musician, afflicted by the sickness of spirit which a famous writer has called the vagueness of passions (*le vague des passions*)" (1845); and in a later version: "A young musician of morbid sensitivity and ardent imagination poisons himself with opium in a moment of despair caused by frustrated love" (1855a). Berlioz's romantic artist-hero is emotionally unstable and madly in love with a woman who becomes his obsession, which gives the whole composition its direction and momentum. He sees the world differently from ordinary people and is capable of insane, extreme emotions, such as euphoria, despair, and melancholy. Feeling lonely and cut off from the world by his own mental constitution, this young man pursues his love ideal, which brings him to many places and situations important for the Romantics (such as a ball, the countryside, and a witches' Sabbath), associated in literary tradition with definite emotional states. His ideal also leads him to depression and a suicide attempt (an opium overdose) which results in delirious visions – likewise one of the Romantics' artistic means of expression. In those visions, the artist turns into a murderer (killing his beloved in a fit of passion), is brought to the place of execution, and witnesses his own death and funeral, accompanied by a witches' Sabbath and by devilish orgies.

Later in the course of the piece, after crossing the boundary between the real and supernatural worlds, the artist returns to live as a different person, having gone through a rite of passage, and is given a new name – Lélio.[2] Jacqueline Bellas explains: "l'artiste éperdu abandonne littéralement sa dépouille maudite pour se muer en pèlerin orphique, selon une métamorphose qui est une renaissance" (1976: 120). Such a development of the subject, from obsession and delirium to creative maturity, has interestingly been interpreted by Bellas as a kind of "psychodrama", or a "voyage psychique", which perfectly fits in with the tenets of existential semiotics. This mental journey can be viewed as "la psychothérapie par le rêve éveillé, la forme de traitement la plus élaborée qui soit" (1976: 130). We should remember that the programme includes autobiographical elements, pointed out by the composer in his memories and by the majority of modern researchers (Bloom 1977: 89; Bartoli 1995: 45–46; Rushton 2000: 48; Langford 2000: 53; Catteau 2002: 175).

The subject, who speaks in *Lélio* in the first person singular rather than as a third-person narrator, makes it clear that his return to life was made possible by literature and music – which shifts the focus of discourse from the young artist's personal and emotional life to the *topos* of art. This is another of the key Romantic *topoi*, and the programme stresses the interconnection between different arts, which was crucial to Romanticism, as Tarasti points out: "In Romanticism [. . .] the relationship between music and the other arts intensified, and the impact of literature and painting could be felt more and more deeply in musical texts" (Tarasti 2002: 32–33). The music itself appears as an entity that can replace the woman as an object of admiration; but, rather than pushing the subject to self-destruction, it can provide support: "Oh, Music, Mistress so pure, so true, so faithful, alike esteemed and adored, thy friend, thy lover calls thee to his aid" (1855b: 62). The author also introduces a figure that serves as an alternative to the mad

---

[2] By the way, the name of the artist is far from accidental. It may be a reference to George Sand's novelette *La Marquise*, in which an actor by the name of Lélio is madly in love with the Marquise, or else – to a figure from the *commedia dell'arte*. (Bloom 1978: 361; Moore 2009: 34).

young artist. Lélio's imagined friend was taken from Shakespeare's play, the poet Horatio, "untouched by cruel passions" (1855b: 2), innocent like the fisherman from the Goethe fragment quoted at this point, who is a simple man tempted by forces which he cannot understand. Berlioz's artist decodes him as a supernatural being, a mermaid, related by the *idée fixe* to the object of his fatal obsession (1855b: 6). On his return to life, Lélio changes his attitude to this melody and to the female figure; she becomes a seductress and an element of life.

The subject directly points to his major inspirations and sources of artistic transformation: "Shakespeare has wrought a change in me, has revolutionized my inmost being to its deepest depths. Moore, with his dolorous melodies has completed thy work, thou creator of *Hamlet*" (1855b: 8).[3] Cécile Reynaud adds: "L''artiste' du *Retour à la vie*, comme Berlioz, s'identifie aux personnages de Shakespeare" (2003, 15). Jacqueline Bellas notes that by inspiring aesthetic explorations and new compositional solutions, Shakespeare becomes, in a way, Berlioz's spiritual father (1976: 124), and is eventually elevated to the status of the artist's god, when, in religious exaltation, he cries out: "oh great Shakespeare be thou my stay!" (1855b: 63).

Opus 14 is unique in Berlioz's output; in no other work did he expound his aesthetic views so clearly and in a manner so typical of Romantic literary texts (such as Balzac's *Massimilla Doni* and *Duchesse de Langeais* or Gautier's *Les Jeunes-France*). As a natural development of comments concerning sources of creative inspirations, Berlioz presents a vision of ideal music born out of specific literary works. In the first sections of *Lélio*, the subject finds inspiration in *Hamlet*, which cures him of the "writer's block" and activates his musical imagination: "What ideal orchestra is that playing within me?. . . [. . .] Sombre instrumentation. . . broad, sinister harmonies. . . a plaintive melody. . . a chorus in unisons and octaves. . . like one great voice uttering a threatening lament through the solemn, mysterious stillness of night" (1855b: 8). These thoughts are accompanied by distant music in the background. The listener gets involved in the narration, and, in front of his eyes, the music which the subject has only imagined becomes real; the *Chorus of the shades* begins. In his sixth and last monologue, Lélio presents the ideal of modern music which can express the poetic text and of its performance. This music can cause that "the voices of my sylphs shall be carried on light Clouds of harmony, aglow and brilliant with the magic splendour of their dazzling wings. . ." (1855b: 62). This time the commentary concerns a scene from Shakespeare's *The Tempest*, but with a text in Italian – the language

---

[3] A similar description of the impression that Shakespeare made on Berlioz can be found in his memoirs in chapter XVIII (Berlioz 2005).

of the opera (switching to a different language code is a very important semantic device). The ideal behaviour of the musicians who are to perform the work Lélio is now completing during the spectacle consists in: looking at the conductor as frequently as possible (which is a fail-safe way to avoid falling behind), playing with an expressive sense, melodious singing, as well as precise execution of the dynamic indications and performance guidelines contained in the score. (These demands reveal what kind of deficiencies troubled the orchestras of that time, and what difficulties Berlioz may have encountered in his efforts to ensure proper performance of his composition) (1855b: 63). However, the ideal interpretation ought to be tender, precise, and delicate (1855b: 149; Brittan 2017).

Finally, I would like to comment on the third monologue, in which the subject deals with the problem of contemporary music criticism, which, in his view, hinders the development of art with its conservatism and short-sightedness. Lélio accuses critics of a hostile attitude toward novelty and progress. He denounces critics as

> the inhabitants of the temple of joggtrotting, easy-going Tradition, fanatic priests, who would sacrifice to their idiotic divinity all the most sublime ideas of our time, if they had ever been endowed with any. Those young theorists of eighty, who wallow in a sea of prejudice, and believe that the world ceases with the shores of their islands; those old libertins of all ages, who expect music to charm, flatter, divert and carress[sic] them; denying the chaste muse all possibility of aspiring to a higher, a nobler mission. But still worse are those who dare to lay their desecrating hands of corruption upon our master-pieces, and to call their horrible mutilations by the name of improvements, for which, as they say, good taste is required. . . Curse upon them! They degrade Art to a miserable farce; they commit an outrage upon her. (1855b: 23)

Such attitudes make the Romantic artist feel rejected and lonely and make him isolate himself from society. Here we begin to explore more topics and themes typical of Romantic literature, such as the loneliness of the artist, misunderstood by the world, who chooses a voluntary solitude in order to be able to create and transcend boundaries in ways which the contemporary society fails to grasp, of which Berlioz tells us in metaphorical terms in the *Song of brigands* which follows this monologue (Gamrat 2019). One can hardly disagree with Frances Moore in her summary of Berlioz's literary affiliations: "Berlioz is using literary ideas to expand the horizon of what is possible within dramatic musical forms and trying to find ways of going beyond opera and drama to create something new" (Moore 2009, 32). This is also a very important and effective component of communication between the artist and society, as Márta Grabócz points out (with reference to the findings of Josef Ujfalussy): "les arts qui communiquent par les moyens objectifs et concrets (par des images, des mots, etc.) peuvent être médiateurs entre l'art musical et la société, c'est-à-dire que les autres arts (la littérature, la peinture, etc.) peuvent aider la musique a maintenir ses liens avec l'univers d'idées de la société, avec la vie quotidienne de son public" (2009: 89). Importantly, Lélio's third monologue reveals the third element which makes it possible to represent the "zemic" model inherent in Berlioz's Op. 14. The model may be represented as follows: *Moi1* – the body (the subject), *Moi2* – the artist's personality, *Soi2* – social practice (critics and artists), and *Soi1* – the value of new music in the eyes of the subject and the society.

3 The musical elements of literary narration

Musically Berlioz makes use of elements inherited from previous generations, such as musical rhetoric, the symbolism of keys and individual instruments, *topoi*, forms and genres. He also refers to elements introduced by most recent art, such as, in Romanticism, the inclusion of fantastical elements in artistic works, and, most importantly, attributing a central role to symbols, which from the semiotic perspective can be interpreted as signs. Most interesting among this great wealth of ideas applied by Berlioz are those which he creates himself, and those in which he combines known elements with others that were only taking root in tradition at that time. We can observe how he transcends these structures and thus builds new tools of communication and ways of exerting impact on the audience.

Musical rhetoric belongs to concepts most frequently applied by Berlioz. In his rhetorical solutions, he draws on traditional models, as in the case of the dialogue of instruments that opens the 3rd movement of the *Symphonie*, or creates his own ones, as in Lélio's 2nd monologue concerning music that can reflect in sound the ephemeral world of spirits by means of a figure based on an ascending D-flat-major chord performed *con sordino* by the strings. A similar approach can be observed in the composer's use of key and instrument symbolism, which he gradually developed in the course of his work as a composer, and defined in the *Traité d'Instrumentation et d'Orchestration* (1844). In the 3rd movement of the *Symphonie*, Berlioz applies instruments associated for many decades with the peace and quiet of the countryside (the oboe, the English horn), while in the 5th movement he introduces bells, which announce death. The harps, which are present throughout the piece, and would begin to be frequently employed by 19th-century composers, symbolise not only the fleeting, ethereal nature of the represented figures but also the glamour and opulence of events such as a ball (in movement II). Another instrument singled out by Berlioz, more imagined than real (a quality that attracted poets) was the Aeolian harp (movement V of

Lélio). These elements are associated with specific *topoi*: classical ones, such as a storm, an idyll, sacred or funeral music, and Romantic ones, including frenetic and oneiric moods, chaos, fantastical or demonic elements.

Throughout Opus 14 we can observe interesting use of musical forms and genres, which can be considered as a kind of code established in European culture by the traditional circumstances of their application. In movement I of the *Symphonie*, the composer makes use of a freely transformed (Romantic-style) sonata form in order to introduce the main musical motifs (including the *idée fixe*) and his forms of motivic development. The same motifs are present in both parts of Op. 14. In movement V Berlioz composes a 4-part fugue and a rondo (for the witches' Sabbath), as well as a chorale (in which we hear the sequence *Dies irae*). The ABA form, highly valued by the Romantics, appears e.g. in movement II of the *Symphonie*, based on the waltz (an element of German culture) and in some sections on the contredanse (imported from the British Isles). In this way, the composer bridges these two cultures with the French one and with salon dances popular in various generations. Another important genre and *topos* appearing in the *Symphonie* is the march, which had for centuries accompanied funeral processions and the advance of armies, driving them on with its (mostly rhythmic) force.

Berlioz commented: "*C'est la force du rythme qui, dans le pas de charge, entraîne des milliers d'hommes au-devant de la mort*" (1830: 111). The second part of Opus 14 features a wealth of musical genres, each of which contributes its own connotations related to the circumstances of its use and the culture it is derived from. The most important of these is, first, the mélange of the German Lied and the ballad, which opens the musical component of *Lélio* – a piece for voice and piano setting a French version of Goethe's text, enriched by rhythm and by the characteristic barcarole-like imitation of the flow of water. In *Chanson de brigands*, on the other hand, we find references to the *chanson à boire* and the Italian siciliana, as the subject fantasises about becoming the leader of a band of robbers in Calabria (local colour). The whole ends with the *par excellence* Romantic fantasy from Shakespeare's *The Tempest*.

As a whole, the composition seems to represent the ABA_1 form, where sections A and A1 belong to the real world and the subject's associations with that realm (movements I–III of the *Symphonie* and the whole of *Lélio*), while section B reflects the fantastical world (*Symphonie* movements. IV–V). This form could also be represented as ABA_B, where A is the real world of the artist on the verge of madness (movements. 1–3 of the *Symphonie*), B – his narcotic visions (movements. IV–V of the *Symphonie*), and A_B (*Lélio*) – the real world, but informed by some unreal elements, such as memories of visions, imagined friends, and fantasies of a happy life in some faraway place. Such a division also reveals the points of transition from earthly life to the transcendent reality. Opus 14 is a unique world, not only transcending the boundaries of musical forms and genres but also impossible to classify even by contemporary standards; the only composition of its kind, which revolutionised the history of the genre. Present-day researchers call it "one of the most revolutionary works in the entire history of the genre" (Langford 2000: 57), and "a touchstone for later composers" (Rodgers 2009: 3). Importantly, *Lélio* introduces the innovative concept of the "theatre of the imagination" (Moore 2009: 215). Opus 14 reflects Berlioz's idea of Romantic art, which depends on a perfect knowledge of the rules, but transcends them since it originates in "une inspiration libre" (1830: 110).

While the *Symphonie* has its separate programme and a symphony orchestra whose line-up changes in accordance with that programme, in *Lélio* the text and the music interact. This is related to the threefold manner of presenting verbal text: as recitation, a solo song with piano, and as solo and ensemble singing with orchestral accompaniment. The technique varies from that typicality of songs to operatic to cantata-like, which translates into the impact of the message. As concerns the language of Opus 14, the *Symphonie* is commented upon in French, while *Lélio* uses French as well as Italian (the latter – for the last section, the fantasy from Shakespeare's *The Tempest*, which comes the closest to the opera). In the first version of *Lélio*, Berlioz notably used a language he invented himself, which could be interpreted as another type of transcendence, on the level of language (movement II). I do not need to convince semioticians that language is one of the most important codes of communication.

Berlioz's great achievement, the *idée fixe*, is an extraordinary concept for the unification of a symphonic cycle (Abromont 2016) and of linking two great works by, first and foremost, assigning melodies to specific persons (as the composer explains in the programme of his *Symphonie*), and, furthermore, by transforming the theme so that it can match the emotions and mental states of the subject, represented in the programme or in the recited text. Such an *idée fixe* is a variant of Rousseau's *signe mémoratif* (1768), a term applied by this philosopher to designate a melody capable of stirring up strong emotions by bringing back memories, which in turn influences the behaviour of the listener. Senancour (1804) added that music can paint pictures, while Balzac (1832, 1837) popularised this idea in 19th-century literature. Berlioz implemented it brilliantly in his music, adding the element of obsession, which is the driving force behind much of Opus 14. The main theme, the all-integrating *idée fixe*, changes depending on the place, circumstance, and the subject's emotional state. Transformations are based, among others, on the change of musical *topoi*. The composer explains: "This melodic image and its model keep haunting him ceaselessly [. . .]. This explains the constant recurrence in all the movements of the symphony" (1845). In a later version of the piece, he continues to emphasise the link between the person (important for the subject) and the melody which symbolises that person: "His beloved becomes for him a melody and like an *idée fixe* which he meets and hears everywhere" (1855a). Jeffrey Langford observes that the emotions explored by the composer jointly constitute "a review of the composer's emotional response to particular dramatic situations" (2000: 54). As I mentioned above, relating the melodic *idée fixe* to a specific person also had a biographical aspect in Berlioz's work, as Eero Tarasti emphatically states: "[. . .] in musical communication melodies had an emotive function [. . .]. They forced one to pay attention to the experiences of the sender of the message, the composer himself. Some biographical studies have revealed connections between the creation of melodies and events in the lives of composers, such as the *idée fixe* of Berlioz alluding to his love" (2002: 40).

Notably, the transformations of the subject's mental states and of the *idée fixe* are an excellent illustration of the principles of existential semiotics. Tarasti writes: "The existential style in the arts reflects this transcendence, of either the world of Nothingness or of Fullness" (2000: 13). Berlioz's subject is thus thrown from the real world nearly into the limbo of Nothingness. This experience lets him overcome his own obsessions and limitations, return to life and look at it in a different manner. He also reinterprets the melody which once symbolised his obsession. In *Lélio* it becomes a recollection of the seductive force, and a sign of the subject's consent to the feminine principle being perpetually present in his life: "Once more – and for ever!" (1855b: 149). In this way, the old content is endowed with a new meaning (Tarasti 2000: 13). The table below represents the transformations of the *idée fixe* in its first appearances in each of the movements of Op. 14a as well as sections 1 and 6 of Op. 14b, and their relation to the musical *topoi*, the choice of key and instrument, and their symbolism according to Berlioz. He analysed the latter only *post factum* in the *Traité d'instrumentation* (1844). Still, it seems legitimate to look at the problem from the perspective of that late analysis, since it shows how the composer thought in the categories of signs-symbols which facilitate communication with the audience.

Mov.	Topos	Instruments	Instrument symbolism	Keys and their symbolism
1 SF	melancholic, love	violins + flutes	violins: power, grace, lightness, darkness, passion Flute: sad song, resignation, modesty	C major – serious, but hollow-sounding and mellow

Allegro sgitato e appassionato assai ♩= 120

2 SF	dance (waltz, contredanse), elegance	flutes + oboes	flute: sad song, resignation, modesty oboe: naïvety and innocence	F major – energetic and vigorous
	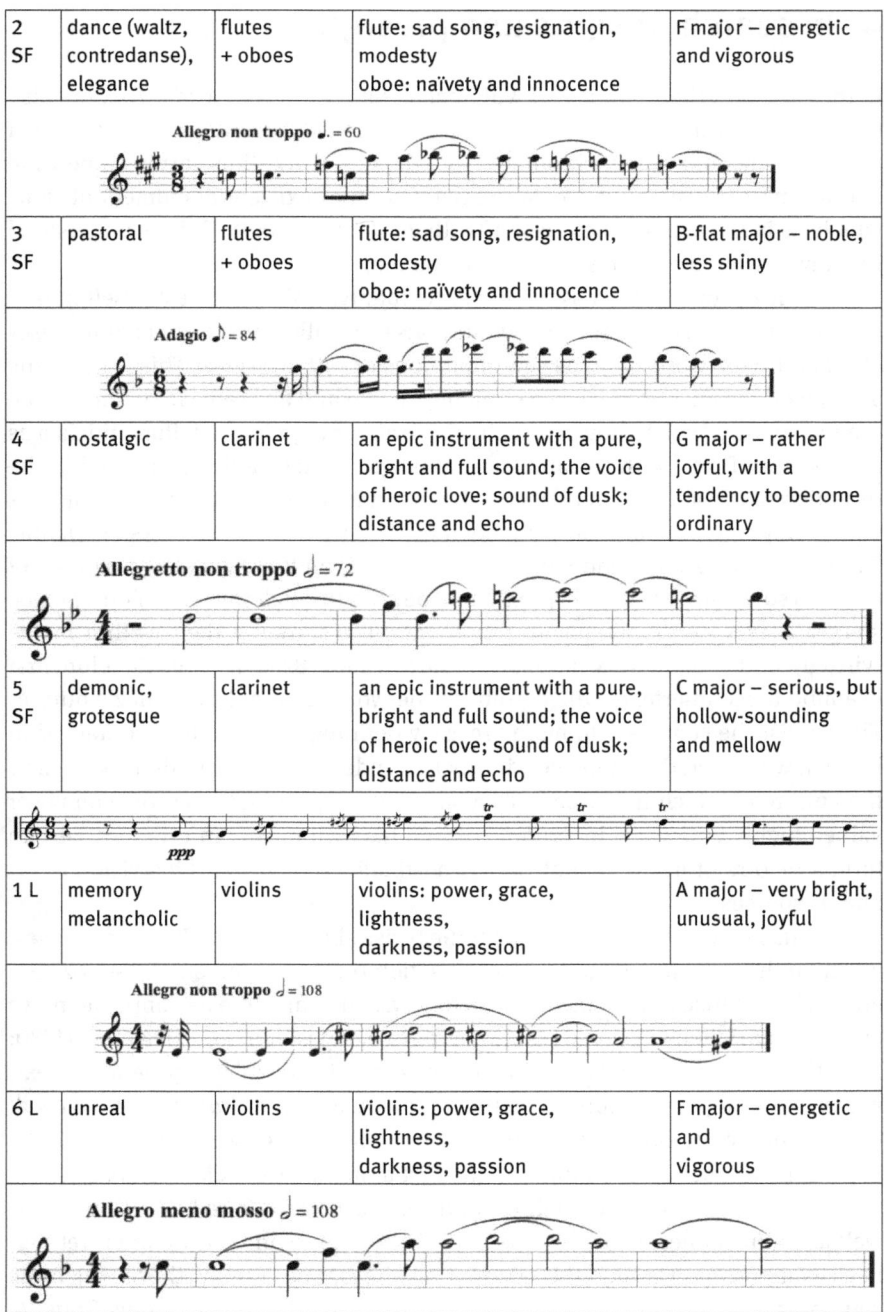 Allegro non troppo ♩. = 60			
3 SF	pastoral	flutes + oboes	flute: sad song, resignation, modesty oboe: naïvety and innocence	B-flat major – noble, less shiny
	Adagio ♪ = 84			
4 SF	nostalgic	clarinet	an epic instrument with a pure, bright and full sound; the voice of heroic love; sound of dusk; distance and echo	G major – rather joyful, with a tendency to become ordinary
	Allegretto non troppo ♩ = 72			
5 SF	demonic, grotesque	clarinet	an epic instrument with a pure, bright and full sound; the voice of heroic love; sound of dusk; distance and echo	C major – serious, but hollow-sounding and mellow
	ppp			
1 L	memory melancholic	violins	violins: power, grace, lightness, darkness, passion	A major – very bright, unusual, joyful
	Allegro non troppo ♩ = 108			
6 L	unreal	violins	violins: power, grace, lightness, darkness, passion	F major – energetic and vigorous
	Allegro meno mosso ♩ = 108			

4 In search of signs and presigns

In the case of Berlioz's Opus 14, I will treat as signs not only the *idée fixe*, but also the other major melodies, and as presigns – the same melodies in case they had existed before and were incorporated into the new work, thus earning a new life and meaning. Such an interpretation points to the "existential moment of sign" which "is in the moment before or after them" (Tarasti 2000: 7), here understood literally as what the given sign had been before.

This leads us to a discussion of intertextuality, which manifests itself in Berlioz's composition in two ways: as quotations from, allusions to, and paraphrases of other artists' works, and as self-quotations or self-allusions. This is naturally a very well-recognised musical technique, known and applied a long time before the 19th century, which, however, gained enormous popularity in Romanticism as an element of play with the audience, making listeners actively involved in the reception of the music. Intertexts can be found in many places, even in contexts where they were not originally intended by the artist, since, as Tarasti explains: "Almost all narration is more or less intertextual, and every text or part thereof refers to some other text. Every text must be read through the lens of other texts, since all texts inevitably absorb other texts, transforming them within in the (virtual) totality of intertextual space." (Tarasti 2002: 82–83). Let us therefore first examine those intertexts which point to the world external to Berlioz's output. They assist the composer in more precisely defining the meanings contained in his own work, and the audience – in a better understanding of both the work and the culture of which it is a part. They also help us find out what the composer valued highly enough to incorporate it into his own music. In this way, we can form a picture of his system of values, aesthetic opinions, and his vision of art and its sources.

Let us begin with two quotations: the Swiss shepherd tune *Ranz des vaches*, which in this case points to the place of action (in the countryside). Berlioz generally characterised Swiss melodies as follows: "un caractère de simplicité naïve et tendre parfaitement analogue aux mœurs des pasteurs de l'Helvétie" (1830: 110). The other quotation is a Latin sequence associated with the funeral context, present in European culture since the Middle Ages – *Dies irae*, which comes at the moment of the subject's demonic funeral, and symbolises the sanctity of the church, mentioned by the subject in the first monologue of *Lélio* (1855b: 2).

Next, there is a number of direct allusions to works referred to in Opus 14, as well as indirect ones, which can be "read between the lines" if we interpret Berlioz's composition through the prism of his times, and, finally, those which the composer discusses *post factum* in his memoirs in order to explain his Opus 14. The direct allusions include: Chateaubriand's novel *René* (1805) mentioned in the opening of the *Symphonie*'s programme; *La Ronde du sabbat* from Hugo's *Odes et Ballades* (1826)[4] in movement V of the *Symphonie*; as well as Shakespeare's works drawn upon in *Lélio*: *Hamlet* and *Tempest*. Indirect allusions are: Beethoven's cyclic technique from his *Symphony No. 5*; the structure and the programmatic character of his *Symphony No. 6*; Weber's *Der Freischütz* and the atmosphere of the Wolf's Glen scene reflected in movement V of the *Symphonie*. There is also a notable similarity between the theme of the 1st movement introduction from Berlioz's *Symphonie* and a melody from de Florian's *mélodrame pastoral* entitled *Estelle et Némorin*, with music by Henri-Joseph Rigel (1788), which in the latter play accompanies the song of the protagonist praising his beloved and his love for her (cf. ex. 1).

Example 1: Berlioz *Romanse d'Estelle* and Rigel *Romance* (beginning).

Concerning self-quotes and self-allusions, there is an abundance of them in the entire Opus 14. They allow the composer not only to preserve and "recycle" very well-formed melodies from earlier, unpublished works (Cairns 1989: 431) but also to present a kind of musical autobiography, made up of those works which played a role in his life. Berlioz turns these self-references into new signs, which pose a challenge for the audience and provide it with more tools for decoding the message contained in the piece. They can also be viewed as elements of "Berlioz's own artistic and personal return to life". (Moore 2009: 24). We will interpret them as presigns which from a different perspective (that of the earlier works) become an existential moment of the "after"-signs.

The *Symphonie* includes several quotations and paraphrases from Berlioz's earlier themes. In the opening movement I *Largo* (mm. 3–10) we hear *Romance d'Estelle* (1820) setting the text of *Estelle* by Jean-Pierre Claris de Florian (1788): "Je

---

4 Arnaud Laster points out similarities between the programme of the *Symphonie* (movements IV and V) and Hugo's poem *Dernier jour d'un condamné* (1976: 29). Vera Micznik claims that the experiment related to the structure and artistic tools applied in this work is an implementation of Hugo's postulates for Romantic art (2007: 196).

vais donc quitter pour jamais / Mon doux pays, ma douce amie" (Florian 1788: 46), associated with young Berlioz's unhappy love which he idealised till the end of his life. The *idée fixe* is a theme from his *scène lyrique* entitled *Hermine* (1828), to a text by Pierre-Ange Vieillard, composed for the Prix de Rome competition, where it won the 2nd prize. Combining these two different visions of love: youthful and mature, resulting first from the literary text, and then from the vicissitudes of the composer's own life, shows that "l'ideal feminine (. . .) remplace Estelle en son cœur" (Abromont 2016: 197). The 3rd movement comprises a paraphrase of the *Romance de Marguerite* from *Huit scènes de Faust* (1828–29) to a text by Goethe/Nerval, as well as the theme from movement III of *Messe Solennelle* (1824–25), *Gratias*, introducing an element of sacred peace as well as the memory of difficulties which the composer encountered before the premiere of this composition in a Parisian church (cf. ex. 2). Movement IV is a paraphrase of *March des gardes* from Berlioz's early operatic sketch *Les Francs Juges* (1829) to a libretto by Humbert Ferrand, which takes the audience to medieval Germany.

Example 2: Berlioz *Symphonie fantastique* part 3, theme from *Messe solennelle* part 3 *Gratias*.

Lélio is principally all made up of recollections of Berlioz's earlier works. Movements I and VI feature the *idée fixe* of the *Symphonie*, which takes on a new meaning here, as I have already explained. What follows are not paraphrases or quotations of some individual melodies, but complete pieces incorporated as a whole into the new work, with some modifications, a procedure which situates this composition somewhere between a palimpsest and a collection of musical ideas from various stages of the composer's artistic life. Thus, movement I is a romance for voice and piano, *Le pêcheur*, composed in 1826–1827 to a French paraphrase of Goethe's text, which becomes combined with the *idée fixe* in the melologue. Movement II is borrowed from the lyric scene *La mort de Cléopâtre* (1829) to a text by Pierre-Ange Vieillard, which likewise failed to earn Berlioz the 1st place in the Prix de Rome. Movement III paraphrases his earlier song *Chant du Brigand* to a text by Humbert Ferrand, as well as a brief motif from movement V of the *Symphonie fantastique*. Movements IV and V are rewritten sections (*Ode* and *Larghetto*) from the cantata *La mort d'Orphée* (1827), rejected in the same competition as unperformable. Movement VI is a remake of the *Ouverture dramatique sur La Tempête* (1830), which Peter Bloom links to the figure of "Camille Moke and her virtuosic piano playing" (1978: 357). Looking at the intertexts alone, one cannot help agreeing with Cécile Reynaud that "La *Symphonie fantastique* et *Le retour à la vie* (...) constituent les deux parties du récit de la vie d'un artiste imaginaire, [...] qu'il était son [de Berlioz – MG] propre double" (2003: 15).

A close look at the entire array of the musical and literary means applied by Berlioz, makes it possible to understand his great project of creating a new type of music that would be close to the artist's own life and capable of conveying extramusical concepts. His idea of combining two such vast and very different musical works into one whole still strikes us as innovative in our times (and is still frequently misunderstood). Opus 14 features a great wealth of meaning. It is replete with signs, codes, *topoi*, and intertexts, each of which separately and all of them variously interrelated open up virtually countless possibilities of interpretation. The meaning and understanding of this music have been sought and explored in many ways. It is, however, only by applying semiotic tools, and especially those derived from existential semiotics, that we can gain profound and daring insights into the work, the person behind the work, and the culture that shaped that person.

References

Berlioz, Hector:
1845, *Symphonie Fantastique. Épisode de la vie d'un artiste*, version 1 [1830], programme: http://www.hberlioz.com/Scores/fantas.htm
1855a *Symphonie fantastique en cinq parties*, last version, programme: http://www.hberlioz.com/Scores/fantas.htm
1831 *Le Retour à la vie*, programme: http://www.hberlioz.com/Libretti/Lelio.htm
1855b *Lélio, ou le retour à la vie*, last version, trans. by John Bernhoff; ed. Felix Weingartner, Breitkopf& Hartel, Leipzig, n.d.
1830 Beaux-Arts. Aperçu sur la musique classique et la musique romantique. *Le Correspondant*, 22 octobre, pp. 110–112.
1844 *Traité d'Instrumentation et d'Orchestration*. Paris / Bruxelles: Lemoine & Cie. 1837 De l'Imitation musicale. *Revue et Gazette Musicale de Paris*, No. 1, 9–11. 2005 Mémoires (eng.) http://www.hberlioz.com/Writings/HBM18.htm
Berlioz – documents:
2017 Catalogue: http://www.hberlioz.com/Works/Catalogue.htm
Abromont, Claude. 2016. *La Symphonie fantastique. Enquête autour d'une idée fixe*. Paris: Philharmonie de Paris.
Balzac, Honoré de. 1832. *La Duchesse de Langeais*. Paris: Charles Gosselin.
Balzac, Honoré de. 1839. *Massimilla Doni*. Paris: Souverain.
Bartoli, Jean-Pierre. 1955. Forme narrative et principes du developpement musical dans la Symphonie fantastique de Berlioz. *Musurgia* II(1). 25–50.

Bellas Jacqueline. 1976. La preuve par Hamlet. Essai d'interprétation du *Lélio* d'Hector Berlioz. *Littératures* 23. 117–145.
Bloom, Peter A. 1977. Une lecture de Lélio ou Le Retour à la vie. *Revue de Musicologie*, 63(1/2). 89–106.
Bloom, Peter A. 1978. A Return to Berlioz's *Retour à la Vie*. *The Musical Quarterly* 64(3). 354–385.
Brittan, Francesca. 2017. Le Retour à la vie: Natural Magic and the Ideal Orchestra. In Francesca Brittan, *Music and Fantasy in the Age of Berlioz*, 89–135. Cambridge: Cambridge University Press.
Catteau, Dominique. 2002. *Hector Berlioz, ou, La philosophie artiste*, vol. 1, Paris: Publibook.
Cairns, David. 1989 *Berlioz: The Making of an Artist 1803–1832*. London: Andr. Deutsch Limited.
Florian, Jean-Pierre Claris de. 1788. *Estelle et Némorin, mélodrame pastoral en deux actes, en prose. Tiré du roman de M. le chevalier de Florian. Représenté pour la première fois à Paris, sur le Théâtre de l'Ambigu-Comique, le 25 juin 1788. Paroles de M. Gabiot, musique de M. Rigel*. Paris: chez Cailleau Imprimeur-Libraire.
Florian, Jean-Pierre Claris de. 1838 [1788]. *Estelle*. Paris : chez Ménard Libraire-Éditeur.
Gamrat, Małgorzata. 2019. "Lélio" de Hector Berlioz et "Le contrebandier" de George Sand, ou une solitude d'un artiste (héros) romantique portant le masque du bandit. *Literaport. Revue annuelle de la littérature francophone* 6. 73–86.
Grabócz, Márta. 2009. *Musique, narrativité, signification*. Paris: L'Harmattan.
Langford, Jeffrey. 2000. The Symphonies. In Peter Bloom (ed.), *Cambridge Companion to Berlioz*, 53–68. Cambridge: Cambridge University Press.
Laster, Arnaud. 1976 Berlioz et Victor Hugo. *Romantisme* 12. 27–34.
Micznik, Vera. 2007. The Musico-Dramatic Narrative of Berlioz's *Lélio*. In David Charlton and Katharine Ellis (eds.), *The Musical Voyager: Berlioz in Europe*. 184–207. Frankfurt am Main: Peter Lang.
Moore, Frances Claire. 2009. *A Night at the (Imaginary) Opera: The visual dimension in Hector Berlioz's Lélio, Roméo et Juliette and La damnation de Faust*, A Master-of-Music thesis in musicology. Wellington: New Zealand School of Music.
Reynaud, Cécile. 2003. Un héros romantique. In Cécile Reynaud & Catherine Massip (eds), *La voix du romantisme: Berlioz*, 11–23. Paris: Fayard.
Rodgers, Stephen. 2009. *Form, Program, and Metaphor in the Music of Berlioz*. Cambridge: Cambridge University Press.
Rousseau, Jean-Jacques. 1768. *Dictionnaire de Musique*. Paris: chez la veuve Duchesne, Paris.
Julian Rushton. 2000. Genre in Berlioz, In Peter Bloom (ed.), *Cambridge Companion to Berlioz*, 41–52. Cambridge: Cambridge University Press.
Senancour Étienne Pivert de. 1804. *Obermann*. Paris: chez Cérioux, Libraire.
Tarasti, Eero. 2000 *Existential semiotics*. Bloomington & Indianapolis: Indiana University Press.
Tarasti, Eero. 2002 *Sings of Music. A Guide to Musical Semiotics*. Berlin & New York: Mouton De Gruyter

Aurèlia Pessarrodona
The singing body in a zemic approach: The case of Miguel Garrido

Abstract: The aim of this article is to do a *zemic* approach to the *singing body*, that is, the body of the singer as a creator of meanings onstage, in a performative sense (vocal, gestural) as well as a configurator of identities (roles, gender, charisma, etc.), and how it could influence the music of the past. The chosen object of study has been Miguel Garrido, one of the most popular *graciosos* (comic actor) of the last third of the eighteenth-century Spain, specialized in short theatre, that is, sainetes and their sung equivalent, *tonadillas*. In fact, the selected repertoire has been the six solo *tonadillas* (for one voice) composed for him, housed in the Municipal Historical Library of Madrid. The reason of this choice is twofold. On one hand, Garrido's success as a comic actor (gracioso) was so important that these *tonadillas* allow to study how such a specific singing body could influence the composition of his repertory. And, on the other hand, these six pieces for Garrido represent a rare exception in a subgenre like the solo *tonadillas*, which was principally performed by women. Fontanille's semiotics of the body and, especially, Tarasti's zemic theory have been revealed as excellent methodological frameworks to study at what extend the characteristics of Garrido as a singing body (his body and physical presence onstage, his charisma as a comic actor, his singing skills and his incarnation of roles, even women) influenced the composition of these pieces, made specifically for him.

Keywords: *tonadilla*, Miguel Garrido, singing body, Eero Tarasti, zemic theory, existential semiotics

1 Introduction

As singers we sing with the body: it is our instrument and our way of communicating with the world. Upon singing we project much more than an abstract voice, which has been especially problematic over the course of history. Listening to the voice permits us to empathize with its emitter from the body, since it does not merely consist of perceiving a mere disembodied sound, rather what Roland Barthes denominated the "grain of the voice" (1986): when we hear a voice, we are perceiving –feeling– also the body that emits it, its "grain", and all that which it entails.

This manner of understanding the role of the singer departing from the body I term the *singing body:* the singer implies his body, as emitter of the voice sung, as presence on the stage, as actor playing such and such character and, in general, as creator of meanings. I have arrived at this concept by means of a two-pronged approach: my own experience as a singer and my studies on eighteenth century Hispanic musical theatre, above all the *tonadilla*, a type of sung intermezzo, extremely popular across Spain during the second half of the eighteenth century. It consisted of a series of sung numbers, usually with very entertaining plots, drawn from everyday life. Throughout my research I have been able to observe that all the dramaturgic-musical elements of the tonadilla revolve around the body of the actor, understood principally in a double way: their individual body and the abstract bodies of the different roles that they would represent, normally caricatured social stereotypes[1].

The objective of this article is, thus, to study how the traces of the singing bodies were able to impregnate these works. This will be carried out based on a very special repertoire: the six solo tonadillas —for a solo singer, who goes onstage to expose something to the audience – composed for the most popular and charismatic comic actor of the last third of the eighteenth century: Miguel Garrido (Madrid, 1745 – Madrid, 1807). These six tonadillas are found in the Biblioteca Histórica Muncipal de Madrid [Municipal History Library of Madrid] and are the following (with anonymous librettos):

- *El vizcaíno* ["The Man from Biscay"], with music by Antonio Rosales (1777–1778, Mus 168-11);[2]
- *El hidalgo admirado* ["The Astonished Nobleman"] (1779, Mus 88-19), *La humorada de Garrido* ["Garrido's Joke"] (1786, Mus 92-1) and *Los celos de Garrido* ["Garrido's Jealousy"] (s. a., Mus 183-11, Tea 219-183), with music by Pablo Esteve;

---

[1] I presented a few first ideas on the singing body in this Spanish repertoire, still roughly sketched in my article "Cuerpo tonadillesco, cuerpo cantante" (2015), where I already distinguished between individual bodies (concrete actors) and abstract bodies (those of the characters incarnated, stereotyped and caricatured belonging to Madrid society, like *majos*, abbés, *petimetres*, etc.). In the same volume Miguel Ángel Aguilar-Rancel (2015) and I coincided in using the same concept of the *singing body* for something very similar; however, his perspective is quite removed from mine in that he focuses on current staging of operas of the past, while my approximation addresses the intrinsic corporality of the works, that is to say, the traces of the singing bodies present in the musical documents themselves. I have continued in this line in my article "El cuerpo cantante en las tonadillas a solo para Miguel Garrido" (Pessarrodona 2019), winner of the 2nd prize of the Otto Mayer-Serra Award (2018) and the departure point of current work, although there it drew above all from the semiotics of the body of Fontanille, and here it deepens in the application of the Zemic model.

[2] A published transcription exists (Lolo and Labrador 2005) and a recording on CD (Garrido, 2003).

- *Yo soy un majito* ["I am a Little Majo"], with music by José Castel (s. a., Mus 110-7);
 - *Las quejas* ["The Complaints"], with anonymous music and text possibly by Garrido (s. d., Mus 91-14, Tea 219-76 bis).

In dealing with works composed expressly for this actor, they allow an analysis of how a singing body so specific as his own could influence the composition of his repertoire.

2 Theoretical framework: Bodily dialectics and the Zemic model

Another objective of this work is to find an adequate theoretical framework to study the singing body that allows us to analyse the dialectic between different bodily identities depicted onstage. Just as Erika Fischer-Lichte expounds (2011: 159–162; original ed. 2004), the bodily presence of the actor onstage has historically been understood through the contrast between the *phenomenal body* of the actor (their physical body as being-in-the-world) and the *idealized body* of the character, created by the language of the work. Said very succinctly, it would correspond to the materialism / idealism duality, and as extreme examples of each one we would have *performance* and literary theatre. The dialectic between both types of body is fundamental to this work; however, between the real body of Garrido and that of the characters he could incarnate different degrees are found: one thing is the concrete physical body, another is how that body is constructed in its interpretations in relation with what the audience expected of him —in the majority of these works Garrido played himself— and another the physical concrete body incarnated in an idealized character. Likewise, Garrido belonged to a concrete typology of actor, the *gracioso* [the comic], a role belonging to Spanish theatre companies of the time specializing in comic roles, which also implied having to respond to certain conventions and expectations.

In my previous work on the subject (Pessarrodona 2019) I applied above all the semiotics of the body developed by Jacques Fontanille in *Soma et séma* (2004). However, here I would like to delve into the Zemic model of Tarasti, an extention of Fontanille's theory applied to his existential semiotics. In both cases, theoretical frameworks that allow "greys" to be established between the phenomenal body and the idealized body are addressed. Said in a very succinct way, Fontanille distinguishes between the *chair* [flesh] as enunciative instance when material *principle of resistance/impulse*, but also when *position of reference* and, likewise, the headquarters of the sensory-motor nucleus of the semiotic experience; and *le corps propre* [the body proper], that is the carrier of identity in construction and in becoming. Both entities together comprise the two faces of the *ego*: its physical bodily reality and its created image, constituted in and by the discursive activity, or as Fontanille says, the *Moi* [Me] and the *Soi* [Self].: *"la chair est le substrat du* Moi *de l'actant, et le* corps proper *est le support de son* Soi" ["The flesh is the substrate of the *Moi* of the actant, and the body is the support of its *Soi*"] (Fontanille, 2004: 23). The *Soi* is that part of ourselves in which the *Moi* projects in order to create itself through its own activity. But Fontanille differentiates two modes of construction of corporal identity "in *Soi*": *"d'un côté, une construction par repetition, par recouvrement continu des identités transitoires, et par similitude (le* Soi-idem*), et, de l'autre côté, une construction par maintien et permanence d'une même direction (le* Soi-ipse*)"* ["on one hand, a construction by repetition, by continuous covering of transitory identities, and by similitude (the *Soi-idem*), and on the other hand, a construction by maintenance and permanence of the same direction (the *Soi-ipse*)" (Fontanille, 2004: 23).

Eero Tarasti has broadened this theory within his existential semiotics passing it through the sieve of Greimas and the logic of Hegel. Said very succinctly, in the theory of Tarasti the relationship between the *Moi* and the *Soi* is articulated in four intertwining levels through the four modalities of being, easily comprehensible with the use of English modal verbs. Tarasti, following the semiotic "x" of Greimas, gives form to *z* in this dialectic between *Moi* and *Soi* (simplified as M and S) in what has been called the *Zemic model* (Figure 1).

M1-S4, *an-mir-sein*: our primary body, kinetic energy, desire, gestuality, our chaotic and fleshly physical existence. Primary kinetic energy, "khora" (*"will"*)	**M2-S3**, *für-mich-sein*: via habit, education and dialogue with others, our subjectivity reaches more stability and a identity. Musical identity, certain kinetic forms (*"can"*)
M3-S2, *für-sich-sein*: *Moi* reduced and subordinated to the *Soi*, to social practices and institutions. Individual solutions, applications, strategies (*"know"*)	**M4-S1**, *an-sich-sein*: abstractly normative aspect of our society, community and culture. Topics, norms, virtual categories, styles (*"must"*)

Figure 1: Tarasti's Zemic model (source: Tarasti 2012: 135–138).

This proposal of Tarasti helps to understand the dialectic between that which belongs to Garrido, his most carnal *Moi*, and the diverse degrees of stereotypes and conventionalisms until arriving at the incarnation of an abstract or ideal character (S1). If we consider the modal verbs that Tarasti uses, we could establish the following:

- M1-S4: what Garrido *would do* from his body (in an instinctive manner).
- M2-S3: what only Garrido *could do*, his bodily identity.
- M3-S2: that which Garrido *knew to do* in that situation (as much his own as that of the character), his theatrical identity, Garrido as comic.
- M4-S1: that which *had to be done* in that situation, whether Garrido or any actor.

The principal difference between Fontanille and Tarasti is that the first understands his categories as bodily identities, while the second conceives them as modes of being within existential semiotics. In any case, as much the *Soi-idem* of Fontanille, as the intermediate levels of M and S (2 and 3) of Tarasti offer us the possibility of categorizing degrees between the carnal body of Garrido and his interpretive incarnations. In fact, Tarasti himself has proposed this Zemic model to analyse performative practice (Tarasti 2015: 213–248). This theoretical proposal is articulated precisely around the complex dialectic between the individuality of the actor and abstract norms, that arise in the two directions of the z – "from a concrete, sensual body towards abstract norms and values, or from these intelligible categories towards their gradual exemplification and corporealisation" (Tarasti 2015: 227) – through the four modes mentioned, simplified as M1, M2, S2 and S1: body, person (identity), social practice, and values and norms. Tarasti observes, as well, that in scenic interpretation signs do not necessarily have to ascribe to a concrete mode, but they can fluctuate according to the interpretive plane of the performance (what he calls "three worlds of performance": natural world, narration or performance) and even change modes: for example, a performer's spontaneous gesture belonging to his M1 can end up changing into a genre sign in some social practice (Tarasti 2015: 230).

This paper aims to take a step further: not so much to analyse the concrete performative practice of an actor, rather how it influenced the music composed for him. We will consider this following three axes: that of the creation of bodily identities through the different modes, that of the gestuality of theatrical action, and that of vocality.

3 Bodily identities of Garrido on stage

Miguel Garrido developed his successful career principally in the theatres of Madrid, which he joined in 1773 after various years working in cities like Murcia and Seville (Cotarelo 1899: 520; Pessarrodona 2019: 5). There he remained until his retirement in 1804, after a successful career of thirty-one years testified by the great quantity of works created for him that remain with us today, such as the *sainetes* [short farcical skits] of Ramón de la Cruz *La competencia de graciosos*,

Garrido celoso and *¡Válgame Dios por Garrido!* (Cotarelo, 1899: 520), as well as numerous scenic-musical works such as zarzuelas and, above all, tonadillas. His success was resounding, but it also had its downside, since they obligated him to work more than he would have desired. As Le Guin has confirmed (2014: 86) regarding this: "the players were little more than slaves to the public taste".

The construction of the theatrical identity of Garrido drew on his physical image, which conditioned his *presence* onstage. In *Los celos de Garrido* Garrido begins by self-defining as "*arrebollado*", a deformation of "*arrepollado*", that is to say, having the shape of a cabbage. Indeed, Garrido was short and fat, as is mentioned in a multitude of the works of his own repertoire (Cotarelo 1899: 520 and Le Guin 2014: 86); in fact, further on in this same tonadilla he calls himself "pygmy" and "*almoldiguilla*", a deformation of "*albóndiga*" [meatball]. These comic descriptions coincide with the portrait *Garrido en traje de gitano* by Manuel de la Cruz and engraved by Juan de la Cruz, for the *Cuaderno de trajes de teatro* (Figure 2, left).

Figure 2: Comparision between the portrait of Miguel Garrido and that of José Espejo[3] (source: supplement by Cruz 1777).

---

[3] Museo de Historia de Madrid, Inv. 2505 and Inv. 3098, available online: <http://www.memoriademadrid.es> [consulted: February 20, 2017].

This physique corresponded to the theatrical stereotype of the comics in the eighteenth century, that in general were short and plump (Angulo 2005: 409). In Figure 2 we see that the portrait of Garrido is very similar to that of the other celebrated comic of the eighteenth century, José Espejo, from the same collection. In the context of Spain of the 1700s the body of the comic was unlike the social model of masculinity, represented onstage by the leading man, normally qualified as having "good figure". An excellent example would be the actor Isidoro Máiquez, portrayed by Goya. Therefore, the very *Moi* of Garrido, his most carnal M_1, coincided with the stereotype (S_1) of the comic and it defined him as an actor. In fact, many works of the repertoire of Garrido show their capacity to comically take advantage of his carnal image (Pessarrodona, 2012: 324–326).

This presentation of our protagonist in *Los celos de Garrido* manifests as a two-part number in G major with two lyrics. The first part appears written according to the conventions of the genre: measures of 3/8 time with amphibrachic- and iambic-like rhythms that tend to accentuate the second beat of each measure, giving as a result rhythmic patterns similar to those of *zarabandas*, *tangos* and *habaneras* (Pessarrodona 2015c). The majority of tonadillas as one-off songs — previous to the consolidation of the tonadilla as an autonomous scenic-musical genre — found in the archives of Madrid's public theatres housed in Biblioteca Histórica Muncipal de Madrid, present these same rhythmic characteristics. Thus, it is possible that they stayed as remnants in the solo tonadillas to indicate the opening of the tonadilla (Pessarrodona 2015c). In fact, similar rhythms appear at the beginning of other tonadillas that are the focus of this study, such as *La humorada de Garrido, Las quejas* and *El vizcaíno*.

What is interesting with regard to the case we are currently occupied with is the end of this section, where a short transition in *Allegro* appears bringing us to the second section, and an *Andante* with the air of a seguidilla in 3/4 (Ex. 1). In these four measures Garrido expressly asks the audience that they look at him, with a deictic text in which he demands that their attention be directed toward his own body: *"ya se ve, / eche usted, / mire usted, / ya se ve"*. The insistence on this simple motive with which he sings this text —embellished, furthermore, with trills of the violins— suggests a comic interpretation where Garrido would show his physique, maybe with different postures for each one of his pleas. These measures flow out into the air of a seguidilla beginning with the text *"mire usted qué gracejo"* ["You look my grace"], a maximum expression of self-awareness of his charisma onstage. As a matter of fact, this charisma is the principal power of seduction of Garrido, which makes him worth being *"el amo del gallinero"* ["the king of the roost"], a type of "alpha male" amongst women. Esteve especially specifies the word *"gallinero"* [roost or henhouse], a reference to women, accentuating the syllables with *staccati* and breaking with a silence the syllable *"ne"*, which suggests a particularly entertaining interpretation on behalf of Garrido. In this case the most carnal M1 of Garrido rapidly changes into his personal and physical charisma identity onstage, that is manifested through self-awareness of his charisma, his principal weapon of scenic seduction.

Something similar occurs with the tonadilla *Yo soy un majito*, although in a somewhat different modal plane. This tonadilla also begins showing the self-confidence of Garrido:

Yo soy un majito,	I am a little *majo*,
como ustedes ven,	as you can see,
hijo de Madrid,	son of Madrid,
me llamo Miguel.	my name is Miguel.
Sé galantear	I have known how to flirt
Desde mi niñez	since my childhood
a cuantas muchachas	whichever women
me parece bien.	I want.
Tejo mis cabriolas,	I weave my cabrioles,
bailo a lo francés,	I dance in French style,
canto tonadillas	I sing tonadillas
de gusto y placer,	with taste and pleasure,
y en muchos asuntos	and in many issues
hago mi papel.	I play my role.

Within the universe of tonadillas a presentation so self-indulging is significant. Habitually solo tonadillas began with a salutation to the audience, which normally included a *captatio benevolentiae* to regale them and earn their favour (Pessarrodona 2018: 30–31). Instead, in these tonadillas Garrido, aware of his success before the public, does not feel the necessity to earn their benevolence. He only does it in No. 3 of this same tonadilla, before singing a few *seguidillas* in a serious style.

These initial lines of *Yo soy un majito* are a perfect catalogue of the acting and personal talents of Garrido. He presents as a *majo*, that is to say, as a Madrilean very proud of his origins (Haidt, 2011: chp. 6 and 7). After he comments on his talent for conquering women, a power of seduction based more on his personal and physical charisma (his M2, as we have seen) than on his carnal physique, his M1.[4] What is most interesting in this passage is how Garrido shows his theatrical identity: he knows

---

[4] Nor in his real life, since according to the commissioners of the Theatre Council in 1788, Garrido lived "with his wife and in good conduct" (Cotarelo 1899: 520).

Musical example 1: Pablo Esteve, *Los celos de Garrido*, No. 1, mm. 66–75.[5]

how to dance, he knows how to sing tonadillas and play very different roles. We are, then, standing before the construction of Garrido's theatrical identity that is created by similitude and repetition through his acts upon the stage (his *Soi-idem*

---

[5] In these examples the French horns have been transcribed as they appear in the originals. Translation of the first lyrics: "As can be seen, / you see, / you look, / as can be seen. / You look my grace, / if it is worthy of being the lord / of the henhouse". Second lyrics: "You look if this panache / must be the lord / of that livestock".

according to Fontanille) and that would correspond to what people expected of him as an actor and a comic: his S2 according to the Zemic model of Tarasti.

Here the body of Garrido becomes present, once again, through small musical gestures. These lines are sung with an air very similar to that of the first number of *Los celos de Garrido*, this time in *Andantino*, 6/8 and a general D minor that alternates with its relative F major. Within this convention the *Moi* of Garrido is made between much blurting out and comic expressions, like the "*a la lilala*" with Phrygian major tones —to which perhaps he would dance— and in the diverse repetitions of the expression "*pipanfué*", that insist on the rhythmic declaration of the initial syllable "*pi*", giving the absurd word an onomatopoeic air.

Until now we have seen how Garrido incarnates himself on the stage and how his bodily identity would be constructed at least on the M1, M2 and S2 levels. By contrast, in *El hidalgo admirado* Garrido performs another character: a country nobleman who arrives to the city. The initial scene is frankly entertaining: the nobleman appears running onto the stage exclaiming the Latin expression "*exiforas, maleficium / exiforas, tentación*" as exorcism to avoid the temptations of the capital. Each lyric ends with the aside "*corre y se santigua*" ["he runs and makes the sign of the cross"], characterizing the extreme sanctimony of the character.

Esteve musically illustrates this appearance of the character in a style very unlike that which we have seen in other initial numbers of the solo tonadillas for Garrido: in *Allegro* in B flat major and a binary measure with a profusion of dotted rhythms.[6] In this case, this style proves to be an effective measure to represent the ridiculously solemn, sententious and moralist character of the nobleman. Hence, this music does not present the flesh (*Moi*) of Garrido, nor his body constructed as a comic, rather that of an external character, an S1, metaphorically representing an abstract body that is caricaturized and standardized. The music is used here as an element of characterisation, as if it were the costume or the makeup.

This musical representation contrasts with the attitude of the character onstage: running from one side to the other and making the sign of the cross repeatedly. The contrast between both gestures —auditory and visual— accentuates the comicalness of the scene.

Despite being a fictional, stereotyped and caricaturized character, in the musical representation of the nobleman the *Moi* of Garrido is present also in small gestures included in the musical discourse in a way that is more or less evident. For example, in mm. 125–129 of this No. 1 (Ex. 2) Esteve adds *staccati* to

---

[6] In many tonadillas there is a style normally associated with Frenchness (Pessarrodona 2016b: 167–196).

accentuate the concepts that the nobleman criticizes, just like the entertaining repetition of various syllables with *acciacature*.

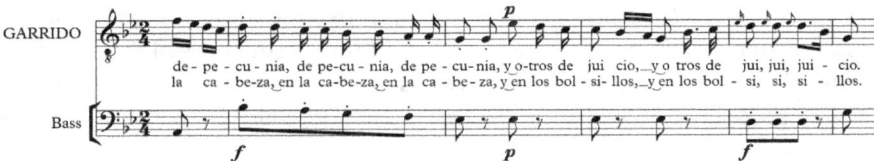

Musical example 2: Pablo Esteve, *El hidalgo admirado*, No. 1, mm. 125–129 (voice and bass).[7]

We find something similar in *El vizcaíno* by Antonio Rosales, where Garrido parodies a Basque. But in this case the character of the Basque (which would be in principle an S1) is subsumed by the *Moi* of Garrido, found dealing with a mere pretext to deploy his comic recourses. For example, the fast time of the central couplets (*Presto*) and its incomprehensible text provides the passage with an air of a tongue-twister with clear comic intention (Ex. 3).

Musical example 3: Antonio Rosales, *El vizcaíno*, No. 2, mm. 15–19.[8]

Therefore, we have observed that a dialectic is established between the standards and conventions of the solo tonadilla and the different bodily identities of Garrido, since in any moment of the theatrical-musical discourse small gestures referring as much to the gestual interpretation of Garrido as to his carnal and bodily presence can appear, above all in the scope of the *Moi*. They are gestures normally with comic intention that belong to what Tarasti (2015: 234) denominated the "performer's mannerism, part of his personality" which is situated in the realm of the M2. However, although everything seems to point to gestures identifiable with

---

7 Translation of the first lyrics: "[some are empty] of money, money, money / and others of sense". Second lyrics: "[they have too much wind in] the head, in the head, in the head / and in the pockets".

8 Translation of the first lyrics: "Pandos, pindos, pendos, / all were granddaughters / of Pandos Pirandas, / mothers, aunts, grandmothers." Second lyrics: "Pindos, the other ones / were single / because, pandos, pindos / were already married."

Garrido, it would remain to be investigated until what point they are his own characteristics, individual and subjective, or if they form part of the habitual codes of the comics, contrasting them with the repertory of other contemporaries such as José Espejo, or Mariano Querol. In any case, these gestures bring to light the "essential tension of the ontological *semiotics*" that occur between the extremes of the *z* (Tarasti 2015: 227), used here as a comic recourse related to the very scenic omnipresence of Garrido, that tinges these works with *Moi*.

4 The sexualized body and gender identities

Within the carnal and bodily representation of Garrido onstage gender identity is also included. We have seen how in these tonadillas he boasts of his masculinity and powers of seduction, but not so much of his carnal *Moi*, his M1, but rather for his physical identity constructed upon the stage, his M2.

In this sense, *La humorada de Garrido* is especially interesting. It was surely one of the most successful interpretations by Garrido, given it was advertised in the *Diario Curioso, Erudito, Económico y Comercial* at least from November 6th to 15th, 1786, an especially long time for a tonadilla. The story in the press, obviously, does not reveal what is most important: Garrido appears dressed as a woman. This surprising appearance gives way with music in 6/8 and A major with a pastoral air —emphasized by the use of flutes in place of oboes— that might try to represent a femininity of a bucolic or idealized cut, that would contrast with the real aspect — comic, caricaturized— of Garrido dressed as a woman. Thus, the habitual rhythms, iambic- and amphibrachic-like, in the first numbers sung, are transformed into others that are more pastoral, like the trochaic ones: with a simple change of the rhythmic accent Esteve manages to *subvert* the *genre/gender* in this work.

This work plays with the fact the Garrido has meddled in a basically female realm: the solo tonadilla. Indeed, the six solo tonadillas for Garrido that are the focus of this work represent a rare exception, since the immense majority of solo tonadillas conserved were written for women. The reason is clear: these works take advantage of the powers of attraction of those charismatic actresses onstage through their words, voices, gestures. . . ultimately, their body (Pessarrodona, 2016a). Therefore, in *La humorada de Garrido* we find an entertaining tension between the masculine M1 of Garrido and the S1 of the solo tonadilla, the female body, that would coincide with the bodily M1 of the singers of tonadillas. It is, then, the Zemic model of Tarasti brought to its final consequences.

The tonadilla ends with a reverse of the initial femininity: while it began with a bucolic and idealized image of women, in the final seguidillas we see its most "harsh" and urban version: la maja. As Garrido tells at the beginning of the number: "*En jarras plantadita / puesta en batalla / la que quiera camorra / salga a campaña*" ("Standing with my arms akimbo / ready for battle / the one who wants to fight / comes to the battleground"). The female *majismo* that it intends to portray — better said, caricaturize — is, then, highly aggressive, as we often find in this theatrical repertoire (Pessarrodona 2015a: 110). This aggressively majo temperament appears emphasized in the mm. 22–25 thanks to a passage with the air of a fandango, typical of the *seguidillas majas*. It was not the vain that the word *fandango* was a synonym for uproar and racket (Pessarrodona and Ruiz Mayordomo, 2016: 94).

5 Mimesis of theatrical action and the expression of feelings

The body of Garrido is also present in the theatrical actions represented by the music. It is, then, a body that develops the action through its movements, a *Moi* that becomes *Soi-idem* in its acts, but we will see that these gestures can be more or less spontaneous and individual, or stereotyped and stylized.

We have an excellent example in No. 3 of *Los celos de Garrido*, where Garrido imagines a fight with two rival actors of his, Antonio Robles and Sebastián Briñoli. Garrido explains the respective battles in such a vivid manner that he recreates them: the diegesis or *telling* turns into mimesis or *showing*, something very habitual in the solo tonadillas (Pessarrodona 2015b: 116–117). This number has two lyrics with parallel structure where each one serves to illustrate the corresponding battles (Ex. 4). The narration of each entrance of the enemy takes place in the relative B minor, where Garrido deictically indicates where his enemies would enter, and hereafter a very brief instrumental passage in *staccato* (mm. 16–18) takes place that makes us imagine the steps of the rivals almost in *mickey-mousing*. Second act, Garrido describes the military armament of the virtual rivals in nine measures with a tense harmonic development that increases the suspense. After a very brief musical bridge also in *staccati*, Garrido describes the beginning of the battle with various verses in which each one explains an action, as if it were a game of chess: first Garrido stands his ground, then he draws close to the enemy, etc. These actions are narrated/represented in a new harmonic progression, in this case from G major to A major, which adds tension to each action enumerated. Its melodic construction, individualized for each verse, would facilitate the gestural interpretation of each described movement. In fact, the word "*ansina*" (a colloquial deformation of "así", like that) makes reference to the very posture Garrido would adopt upon the stage.

Musical example 4: Pablo Esteve, *Los celos de Garrido*, No. 3, mm. 13–38 (without winds).[9]

---

[9] Translation of the first lyrics: "That Robles will come / from that side / carrying round / riffles and swords. / I stand in this way, / he will be approaching me, / I will slant the cape, / and he will want to cut me." Second lyrics: "That Briñoli will come / from the other side / with helmet and lance / and shield on his arm."

This passage manifests the capacity of scenic eighteenth-century music to imitate the gestuality of the action, which came to develop what is known as "comic realism", present in the Italian *intermezzi* since the beginning of the century (Troy, 1979: 91–94). According to Wye Allanbrook (2014: 15), in the opera buffa of the eighteenth century, comic mimesis reigns, which is summarized by the motto "*enargeia is energeia*", that is to say: "in opera buffa, vivid character depiction —energeia— is accomplished by energeia, or by showing us glimpses of men and women 'at work'". The characters are represented musically through the movement of their external acts, which unfolds "in constant gestural contrast – in the 'dialogued style', the 'tone of nature'" within a steady musical flow (Allanbrook 2014: 16). Comic mimesis is present in the tonadillas since their beginning, and it could even be said that it was decisive in the construction of the genre as an autonomous musical drama (Pessarrodona, 2015b). It connects, in fact, with the general tendency of the 18th century Hispanic toward shows and theatrical humour more visual than literary or textual. In the case of the comics, this visual comicity had a great dose of gestuality, surely very influenced by the *Commedia dell'Arte* (Doménech, 2005).

In any case, the music of Esteve manifests the theatrical body of Garrido in relation to the action that is narrated. But Esteve coordinates the music not only with the theatrical gestuality of Garrido, but also with the imaginary bodies of Robles and Briñoli. Indeed, the musical mimesis of Esteve reaches a point of such efficiency that, with few notes, he succeeds in making the absent bodies present. They are not small spontaneous gestures close to the most carnal and personal *Moi* of Garrido, rather musical gestures associated, in a way more literal or more metaphorical, to a real gestuality onstage transmitted in a manner that is stereotyped by the music. Although the music draws near to the carnality of Garrido, it is situated on a more stereotyped theatrical plane that is closer to the S2. We could say, then, that it is not the body of Garrido that directs Esteve, rather the hand of Esteve that guides it.

Something similar although much more visceral occurs in those moments in which the music seeks to represent emotions. In this case a gestuality that is more kinaesthetic and facial than proxemic is dealt with. According to the treatises of the time, it is not so much about the mimesis of an external action, but rather the exterior expression of an interior emotion (Doménech et al, 2012: 43–44); although in the case of the comics and of a genre as comic as the tonadilla, this always must be understood as susceptible to exaggeration and caricature.

An especially interesting example is *Las quejas*, sequel of *La humorada de Garrido*, where he laments the women of the audience have ignored him since he appeared dressed as a woman. In its No.1 Garrido manifests his rage singing the expression "*hecho un veneno*" ["made a poison"] with an ascending *glissando* that shows his agitation (Ex. 5). Here we have the angry *Moi* of Garrido, exposed in such a spontaneous manner that it seems an expression of his M1. This sensation of spontaneity comes highlighted by the contrast with what Garrido has sung (and perhaps what he has also danced) previously: the happy asemantic expression *"alajé"*.

Musical example 5: *Las quejas*, No. 1, mm. 56–77 (only voice and bass).

Further ahead, in the No. 3, is where Garrido expresses more clearly the feeling of sadness that jealousy provokes in him. As we see in Ex. 6, the words *"morir"* ["to die"], *"penar"* ["to lament"], *"sentir"* ["to feel"] and *"rabiar"* ["to rage"] appear accentuated with weepy apoggiaturas reinforced by the flutes. Afterwards Garrido laments in a passage in A Phrygian with raised third, typical of this repertoire, taking advantage of the harmonic instability of a music that does not resolve within the general environment of D minor. But the *Moi* de Garrido becomes patent in this music in two more concrete ways. On one hand, this passage appears written upon a pedal of A in the form of a *Trommelbass* of eighths, with which the anonymous composer (Esteve?) seems to want to embody the anguished beats of Garrido's heart. Here, then, the *Moi* of Garrido would be represented through a type of iconic *hypotyposis* that permits us to hear the interior of his flesh, in a similar way – although considerably more subtle— as the representation of beats in the Italian comic melodrama.[10] And, on the other hand, the painful *Moi* of Garrido is more palpable as he laments "ah" upon the semitone D and C#, accentuated by that of the bass B and A, that harmonically correspond to two Phrygian cadences in A major, divided by pauses to create an effect of *suspiratio*. In this case, although the composer would be that who directs the expression of Garrido's feelings, it supposes a stylized plane closer to that of the S2 —the stereotyped beats of the heart— with gestures clearly destined for the gestural, exaggerated and comic expression of Garrido, his M2.

---

[10] For example, the *"tippiti"* and the *"tappata"* with which Pergolesi reproduces the heart beats in *La serva padrona*.

Musical example 6: *Las quejas*, No. 3, mm. 39–65.[11]

---

11 Translation: "That is to die, / that is to lament, / that is to feel, / that is to rage. / Ah, my women of the gallery, / how bad you treat me! / You have been capable / of forgetting me! / Ah, ah! / But I don't care at all".

The vocality of Garrido

Many of Garrido's comic recourses were related to the voice, which should have been flexible enough as to approach them with solvency and comicity. In fact, the main verbal vehicle of expression of the singing body is its voice, which almost always takes place in a sung manner. In this case of these tonadillas, Garrido had to be able to easily alternate between the sung and the spoken voice: although the *parolas* [spoken parts] were not consubstantial to the genre of the tonadilla, many of the most personal gestures of Garrido referred to the declaimed use of the voice within a sung discourse. This could go from spontaneous exclamations —like the "eh" of Ex. 5— to spoken interpolations to other members of the show, as occurs in the No. 2 of *Las quejas* where Garrido interrupts his sung discourse addressing the orchestra or the prompter in especially humorous moments.

In spite of the ambiguity with which the masculine voices in the tonadillas are written – almost always in the same key as women, C in the first line – , from these six tonadillas we can deduce that Garrido was a tenor: his habitual tessitura, according to the Franco-Belgic index, was written from F4 to G5, that sung in his voice would be an octave lower. It would not be strange that Garrido sing in his deeper tessitura in works of greater magnitude to help vocally differentiate roles.[12] In any case, Garrido would not be the equivalent of a buffo bass (Le Guin, 2014: 87). On the contrary, he would belong to the Hispanic tradition of comic male roles with high-pitched voices, like the comic tenor of the posterior zarzuelas.

In this sense the final seguidillas of *Yo soy un majito* and *Los celos de Garrido* become very interesting, since they offer two sung vocalities of Garrido that are absolutely different. In the first case, Garrido tries to demonstrate his vocal capacities singing a few virtuosistic seguidillas in *"Cantabille"* [sic].[13] At the beginning of the sung part Garrido shows his "serious style" of singing with a passage full of fast ornaments that could indicate certain knowledge of the technique of *belcanto*. However, the vocal range only covers an octave between G3 (with an exceptional F#) and G4, his habitual tessitura. Therefore, the vocal virtuosity of these seguidillas (S1) would be adapted to the tessitura more comfortable for Garrido (his M1), helped moreover by the almost constant doubling of the first violins.

In contrast, the final seguidillas of *Los celos de Garrido* are consciously made for his vocal *Moi*. The whole central part of these seguidillas (mm. 35–127), where

---

12 In fact, in the zarzuela *La fontana del placer* by José Castel (1776) the role that Garrido plays is written entirely in a tenor key, C in forth line, contrary to the other male voices —in C in first line – , and in the concertants he is in charge of the lowest vocal line (Castel, 2016).

13 The error appears in all parts, as caricature-like hyperitalianization.

Garrido explains/represents a musical function that he saw in Fuencarral, is a masterpiece by Esteve created for the overall skill of Garrido. Although the whole passage is worthy of commentary, we will center on the first subsection, where Garrido (mm. 35–64) praises the virtues of the village with a parody of religious music. In these measures the music presents a pastoral air in *Allegretto*, 6/8 and D minor (accompanied by the relative F major) to create the rural environment of the village. In this musical context, Garrido sings imitating the two extreme voices, the tiple and the bass, of an imaginary polyphonic work (Ex. 7). For this purpose Esteve deliberately plays with the extremes of the vocal M1 of Garrido: A4 is his highest note and C3 his lowest. Furthermore, the instrumentalization helps the vocal contrast: the tiple appears doubled only by the first violins in *piano* and *staccato*, while the bass is accompanied by all the instruments in a resounding *forte* in *staccato* (presumibly *marcato*, since in original notation there was no distinguishing between these articulations). In addition, Garrido could use falsetto in the tiple, not only to more easily reach the A4 —a note that would already belong to his head register – , but also as a parody of high-pitched children's voices.[14]

Musical example 7: Esteve, *Los celos de Garrido*, No. 4, mm. 41–45.[15]

---

14 Other works for Garrido also suggest his ability to use falsetto, like la tonadilla *Las lecciones*, second part (1780), also by Esteve (Biblioteca Histórica Municipal de Madrid 114-10), where he parodies a female singing teacher intoning a few seguidillas majas in macaronic Italian and, literally, "in a woman's tone".
15 Translation: 'Hail, distinguished place of Foncarral".

Conclusions: Toward a *bodily turn*

Over the course of these pages we have seen how the singing body is given in a carnal way and is corporally constructed onstage through vocal and gestural interpretation, according to what is expected of each concrete singer and the role they are playing. However, we have seen a very concrete and especially complex singing body, that of Garrido, in a repetoire made for him in which he normally plays himself. This music incarnates the singing body of Garrido through an interesting dialectic between, on one hand, the conventions of the compositional practice of the genre, and, on the other hand, the flesh and the body of the actor, his M1 and M2, with musical gestures that the corresponding author knew to put in the correct place to facilitate the comic brilliance the audience expected of Garrido. These gestures are, then, the "grain" of Garrido present in the scores. As well, we have observed that the visual humoristic conception of this music can carry out the materialisation of absent bodies, as well as the bodily representation of stereotyped characters, for example through choreomusical topics such as march airs or seguidillas majas.

What is most interesting of the Zemic model of Tarasti is that is has served to bring to light the existing tension precisely between the various scenic identities of Garrido and the norms and conventions of the genre and allows, moreover, understanding that there are gestures that can fluctuate between different modes according to which interpretive plane we situate ourselves on. This is because in the commented cases the initial z of Tarasti is complicated with the implication of diverse *Soi*, "confronted" with the *Moi* of Garrido: the incarnated characters, the dramatic-musical embodiment of the action on behalf of the composer, the possible humoristic stereotypes of the genre and the comics, a school of singing learned, etc. The dialogue between these *Soi* and the *Moi* of Garrido is constant, since it is always present being works created expressly for him.

The most radical conclusion of the work would be that only a new Garrido could return to interpret these tonadillas in their fullness. This study on the *Moi* of Garrido would give as a result a new S1: a new ideal construct about how to interpret this repertoire based on the concrete corporality of Garrido. However, although it would be tempting to recreate a new Garrido, it is absurd to intend to dilute our bodily identity in that of a Garrido impossible to reconstruct. The purpose should be that us interpreters, would understand these works empathising with these bodies of the past from our bodily individuality, our *Moi*, to achieve an interpretation understood from the bodily dialectic. This type of analysis has to serve as incentive so that interpreters (singers and instrumentalists) and investigators between to understand this repertoire *from the body* and not only as mere notes written on the page. From here, it proposes then, a *bodily turn* for the study and the interpretation of this repertoire.

References

Aguilar-Rancel, Migual Ángel. 2015. Corpografías de Tolomeo: cuerpo cantante y género en puestas en escena recientes de la ópera *Giulio Cesare*. In T. Cascudo (ed.). *Música y cuerpo*: 83–107.
Allanbrook, Wye Jamison. 2014. *The Secular Commedia. Comic Mimesis in Late Eighteenth-Century Music*. Oakland: University of California Press.
Angulo, María. 2005. El gracioso en el teatro del siglo XVIII. In Luciano García Lorenzo (ed.), *La construcción de un personaje: el gracioso*, 383–424. Madrid: Fundamentos.
Cascudo, Teresa (ed.). 2015. *Música y cuerpo. Estudios musicológicos*. Logroño: Calanda.
Castel, José. 2016. *La fontana del placer*. Study and edition by J. P. Fernández-Cortés. (Monumentos de la Música Española, 82.) Madrid: CSIC.
Cotarelo, Emilio. 1899. *Don Ramón de la Cruz y sus obras*. Madrid: José Perales y Martínez.
Cruz, Juan de la. 1777. *Colección de trajes de España*. Madrid: Casa de M. Copin.
Doménech, Fernando. 2005. Trufaldines y Cobielos (La influencia de la *Commedia dell'Arte* en el gracioso del siglo XVIII). In Luciano García Lorenzo (ed.), *La construcción de un personaje: el gracioso*, 413–424. Madrid: Fundamentos.
Doménech, Fernando, David Conte Imbert, Francisco de Paula Martí, Duagelupe Soria Tomás & Fermín Eduardo Zeglirscosac. 2012. *La expresión de las pasiones en el teatro del siglo XVIII*. Madrid: Fundamentos.
Fischer-Lichte, Erika. 2011. *Estética de lo performativo*. Madrid: Abada.
Fontanille, Jacques. 2004. *Soma et séma. Figures du corps*. Paris: Maisonneuve et Larose.
Haidt, Rebecca. 2011. *Women, Work and Clothing in Eighteenth-Century Spain*. Oxford: Voltaire Foundation.
Laserna, Blas de. 1970. *El majo y la italiana fingida*. Arrangement for voice and piano by José Subirá, Madrid: Unión Musical Española.
Le Guin, Elisabeth. 2014. *The Tonadilla in Performance. Lyric Comedy in Enlightenment Spain*. Berkeley / Los Ángeles / Londres: University of California Press.
Lolo, Begoña and Labrador, Germán. 2005. *La música en los teatros de Madrid: Antonio Rosales y la tonadilla escénica*. Madrid: Alpuerto.
Garrido, Gabriel (ed.). 2003. *El maestro de baile y otras tonadillas*. Ensemble Elyma, K617, Harmonia Mundi.
Pessarrodona, Aurèlia. 2012. Desmontando a Malbrú. La dramaturgia musical de la tonadilla dieciochesca a partir de *La cantada vida y muerte del general Malbrú* (1785) de Jacinto Valledor. *Dieciocho* 35(2). 301–332.
Pessarrodona, Aurèlia. 2015a. Concertantes, finales y acción en las tonadillas de Jacinto Valledor. *Nassarre* 31. 101–137.
Pessarrodona, Aurèlia. 2015b. Cuerpo tonadillesco, cuerpo cantante: una aproximación al teatro musical breve de la segunda mitad del siglo XVIII. In Teresa Cascudo (ed.), *Música y cuerpo*, 109–142.
Pessarrodona, Aurèlia. 2015c. Ritmos de tonadilla. Algunas consideraciones a partir de la obra conservada de Jacinto Valledor. *Cuadernos de Música Iberoamericana* 25. 80–116.
Pessarrodona, Aurèlia. 2016a. La mujer como mujer en la tonadilla a solo dieciochesca. *Bulletin of Spanish Studies*, 93(2). 211–238.
Pessarrodona, Aurèlia. 2016b. Representaciones musicales de lo francés en tonadillas dieciochescas. *Mélanges de la Casa de Velázquez*, 46(1). 167–196.

Pessarrodona, Aurèlia. 2018. *Jacinto Valledor y la tonadilla*. Sant Cugat del Vallès: Arpegio.
Pessarrodona, Aurèlia and María José Ruiz Mayordomo. 2016. El fandango en la dramaturgia musical tonadillesca: el gesto en su contexto. *Música Oral del Sur* 13. 75–104.
Tarasti, Eero. 2012. *Semiotics of Classical Music: How Mozart, Brahms and Wagner Talk To Us*. Berlin/Boston: De Gruyter.
Tarasti, Eero. 2015. *Sein und Schein*. Berlin/Boston: De Gruyter.
Troy, Charles. 1979. *The Comic Intermezzo. A Study in the History of Eighteenth-Century Italian Opera*. Ann Arbor: UMI.

Notes on contributors

Pertti Ahonen, D.Soc.Sc. in Political Science, M.Sc. Econ. in Business Accounting, is Professor of Political Science on an emeritus contract at the University of Helsinki. He is also Adjunct Professor (Docent) at the Universities of Tampere, Vaasa, and Jyväskylä, all in Finland. He has publications, for instance, in *Semiotica*, *Sage Open*, *Big Data & Society*, *Management and Organizational History*, *Administration & Society*, *Party Politics*, *International Journal of Public Administration*, and *Religion, State & Society*. His recent studies witness of research interest in, for instance, the use of methods with artificial intelligence in examining texts with special reference to texts with a political science interest, organization theory and organization research, the history of political science, government regulation, its assessment, and its reform, and government ownership in companies.

Kristian Bankov is a professor of semiotics at New Bulgarian University and Department Chair of the Southeast European Center for Semiotic Studies. His interest in semiotics dates back to the early 90s when, as a student in Bologna he attended the courses of Prof. Ugo Volli and Prof. Umberto Eco. Bankov graduated in 1995 and has since taught semiotics at NBU. In 2000 he defended a doctoral thesis at Helsinki University under the guidance of Prof. Eero Tarasti. In March 2006 he was awarded the academic title "associate professor in semiotics" and in 2011 he became full professor of semiotics. Currently Professor Bankov is the Secretary General of the International Association for Semiotic Studies, elected at the 12th Congress of the Association held at NBU, Sofia in 2014.

The scientific interests of Prof. Bankov were initially in the field of continental philosophy of language, philosophy of Bergson and existential semiotics. He then focused his research on sociosemiotics and issues of identity. Since 2005 he has been exploring consumer culture, while recently his interest has been directed to the new media and digital culture.

Kristian Bankov is the author of five books and numerous articles in Bulgarian, English and Italian.

Merja Bauters is a research professor in digital transformation and lifelong learning at the School of Digital Technologies, Tallinn University and a docent of semiotics at the University of Helsinki. Bauters has been involved and executed research, planned and guided co-design, participatory and design thinking processes in multiple EU- and national projects on learning and technology-enhanced learning. She was a president, UMWEB International association of semiotics and publishing house 2003–2010 Bauters has been lecturing in over 30 different courses on semiotic, design, design methods and project communication. She received her PhD from the Department of Philosophy, History, Culture and Art Studies, University of Helsinki 2007, discussing Charles Peirce thoughts on interpretation. She has directed PhDs, over 100 bachelor thesis and acted as an opponent to PhD on teachers learning in Socio-Technical System.

Massimo Berruti has been teaching Semiotics of Narration and Semiotics of Interpretation at Helsinki University, Finland. He is the author of the first monographic study on the literature of American poet and writer Robert H. Barlow, and of many articles on H. P. Lovecraft, William H. Hodgson and other writers of the fantastic genre that have appeared in anthologies, and journals such as Lovecraft Studies, Studies in Fantasy Literature, Studi Lovecraftiani, and

Semiotica. In addition to teaching and conducting research, he has translated into Italian language fictional and non-fictional works by Lovecraft, Algernon Blackwood, Ambrose Bierce, and has edited volumes of literary criticism in the fantastic genre. Currently he resides in Helsinki, Finland.

Daniel Charles (1935–2008) was a legendary French music philosopher and scholar, known by his writings on many diverse topics from Heidegger and zen-buddhism to John Cage and avangarde of our time. He was pupil of Olivier Messiaen in his famous class at *Conservatoire National Supérieur de Musique de Paris*, where he got his diploma in 1956. Since 1969 he founded and directed Department of Music at the University of Paris VIII, but he also taught aesthetics in Paris IV; then he served as professor of philosophy nine years at the university of Nice Sophia Antipolis. He has published hundreds of articles and tens of works among which *Le Temps de la voix* (1978), *Gloses sur John Cage* (1976), *Pour les oiseaux. Entretiens avec John Cage* (1976, in English *For the Birds* 1981), *Musik und Vergessen* (1984), *Zeitspielräume* (1989), *La fiction de la postmodernité selon l'esprit de la musique* (1999), *Musiques nomades* (1998). He was also one of the carrying forces in the international music semiotical research project Musical Signification since its foundation in 1984.

Ricardo Nogueira de Castro Monteiro serves as professor of Composition, Conducting and Semiotics at the Federal University of Cariri (UFCA) in Brazil, where he also conducts the university orchestra and is its resident composer. His professional activities include his academic career, various works as a composer, playwright and music director and a consulting portfolio on applied semiotics including major brands such as Johnson&Johnson and Unilever, among others. He is a member of the "Semiotics of Cultural Heritage" research group led by Prof. Eero Tarasti, havng his branch of the project supported from 2014 to 2016 by São Paulo Research Foundation (FAPESP), and presently directing a research group dedicated to the verbal and musical transcription and semiotic analysis of the still vigorous corpus of traditional musical dramas orally transmitted throughout centuries in the Brazilian Northeast. His recent activities include two scientific presentations as a guest of the Université Aix-Marseille and the Université de Lyon (France), and a series of conferences about the history of Brazilian music invited by the Karol Lipinski Academy of Music (Poland).

Aurel Codoban is Professor of Philosophy at Babes-Bolyai University, at University of Art and Design Cluj-Napoca, and at „Dimitrie Cantemir" Christian University, Bucharest. He has a PhD in philosophy since 1984 with the thesis French Structuralism and Cultural Problems at Babeș-Bolyai University in Cluj-Napoca and teaches courses on Semiotics and Hermeneutics, Communication Theories and Philosophy of Religions. He has published: Philosophy as a Literary Genre (2006, Cluj-Napoca: Idea Design & Print); The Decline of Love. From Love as Passion to Corporal Communication (2003, 2004, Cluj-Napoca: Idea Design & Print, Prize of Babes-Bolyai University); Sign and Interpretation. A postmodern introduction to semiotics and hermeneutics ("Dacia" Publishing House, Cluj-Napoca 2001 Dacia Cultural Foundation Prize for The Philosophy Book of the Year); The Sacred and Ontophany. For a New Philosophy of Religions (1998, Iasi: Polirom, Prize of Romanian Academy, 2000); Introduction to Philosophy (Argonaut Publishing House, Cluj-Napoca 1995; 1996), Philosophy as a literary genre (Dacia Publishing House, Cluj-Napoca, 1992 second revised and supplemented edition 2005, Cluj-Napoca: Idea Design & Print), Semiotic Structure of Structuralism (Dacia Publishing House, Cluj-Napoca, 1984) Coordinates and

Prefiguration Essays on the history and epistemology of the sociology of art (Dacia Publishing House, Cluj-Napoca, 1982 National Prize for Essay, awarded by SLAST Journal1983).

Tristian Evans, PhD., is a freelance pianist and musicologist. He graduated with a Doctorate from Bangor University, Wales in 2010, and later published a monograph entitled *Shared Meanings in the Film Music of Philip Glass: Music, Postminimalism and Multimedia* (Routledge, 2015). More recent publications include an entry on Glass for *The Grove Music Guide to American Film Music* (OUP, 2019). He serves as an examiner for Trinity College London, and in 2016 he was awarded a Fellowship of the Royal Schools of Music. As a pianist, he performs regularly as a solo recitalist, in addition to working as a composer, particularly within a multimedia setting.

Rodrigo Felicissimo is a conductor, post-doc researcher at University of São Paulo (USP) and was a visiting researcher at the Faculty of Arts of the University of Helsinki. He is a PhD in music creation processes, from the School of Communications and Arts of USP; Master's in human Geography from the Faculty of Philosophy, Letters and Human Sciences of USP. He is Bachelor in conducting at Santa Marcelina College and Bachelor in Geography from USP. Born in São Paulo, Brazil, he began his musical education at Waldorf School. He has experience in the field of research, choir and orchestra, with activities concerned to music education at *Acaia* Institute (NGO) and the Youth Symphony Orchestra of East São Paulo. Since 2016 Rodrigo is improving his studies in conducting, under the guidance of maestro Roberto Duarte. He is author of the book *Estudo Interpretativo da Técnica Composicional Melodia das Montanhas*. Since 2020 Rodrigo is a member of the advisory board of the Çarê Institute and artist with an artistic production scholarship.

Július Fujak Aesthetic scholar, a semiotician of music, experimental composer, multi-instrumentalist, organiser of unconventional intermedia events. He graduated at Faculty of Arts, Comenium University, Bratislava (aesthetics and musical science in1990) and became researcher in Institute of Literary and Artistic Communication in Nitra (1996–2007). Currently, he lectures at Department of Cultural Studies at faculty of Arts, Constantine the Philosopher in Nitra (since 2007).

His compositions and intermedia projects were performed and broadcasted in many countries of Europe, USA, and China. He is also curator and organiser of international series of contemporary unconventional music *Hermes' Ear in Nitra* (1999–2007), and international festival of intermedia arts *PostmutArt (sound/image – gesture/text)* (since 2008).

Małgorzata Gamrat is an assistant professor at John Paul II Catholic University of Lublin (Poland) and Academy of Art in Szczecin (Poland). Her research interests include the European culture of the 18th-, 19th-, 20th- and 21st-Century, including history of music, literature, music aesthetics, music criticism, music philosophy, history of music education, music analysis, musical semiotics, composers' migrations, reception of music, music in culture and social practice, working on musical sources, interactions of music with other fields of art, new musicology methods, and the methodology of interdisciplinary research as well as comparative studiep. Most particular subjects of her research are music of Franz Liszt, Hector Berlioz, and Alexander Tansman, as well as literary work by Honoré de Balzac. She also translates from French into Polish the texts about music by Aleksander Tansmana and Vladimir Jankélévitch. Her publications include: two books on Franz Liszt's music and essays, ig,: "*Lélio* de Hector Berlioz et *Le contrebandier* de George Sand, ou une solitude d'un artiste (héros) romantique portant le masque du bandit" (2019), "Musique et vie intérieure chez Balzac" (2019), "Jankélévitch: freedom, music and unfinished project" (2018), "Between the sound and the word – methodological challenges in the analysis of Liszt's piano transcriptions of his own Lieder" (2017).

Rahilya Geybullayeva is the head of the Azerbaijani Literature Department, Baku Slavic University, founder and head of Azerbaijan Comparative literature Association (in 2005), a member of the Executive Committee for International Semiotics Association (since 2009). She received her Ph.D. from Lomonosov Moscow State University (1989, Moscow).

As a recipient of *UNESCO*, Carnegie, and Fulbright Fellowship, Prof. Geybullayeva served as a visiting scholar at SOAS, London University (Intercultural Dialogue Regular Programme -*for project "Unity in Diversity: Dialog between Cultures"*); at the Comparative Literature Department, University of Wisconsin -Madison, USA (for project *"Conception of National Literature"*); the University of California, Berkeley (Field Development project on "Cross-disciplinary social sciences and methodology and theory"; for syllabus and field studies on *Comparative Literature and Azerbaijani Literature*). Dr. Geybullayeva's last research was *Past in the future: rules to follow in the mirror of the past* (October 2019–2020) was at the Anthropology Department, Harvard University. Her last project was *Nizami in modern interpretations'* international conference (2018) (author of the workshop concept) and co-editor for the following book published in 2020.

Among her elective courses taught in recent years:
- Comparative Literature: Starting points and criteria of national literature and culture;*(based on the experience of Postcolonial Studies)*
- Comparative Culture: Semiotics and Cultural Matrix;
- Social Anthropology: Historiography of Contemporary Traditions (based on Azerbaijani identity)
- Literary Anthropology: woman and marriage
- Audio-Visual Semiotics and Cognitive Anthropology: Contemporary Traditions in the mirror of the past (based on Azerbaijani identity),

Marta Grabócz Professor at the University of Strasbourg (France) and honorary member of Academic Institute of France (IUF). Between 1977–1990 she was scientific researcher at the Institute for Musicology of the Hungarian Academy of Sciences where she established the first Hungarian Computer Music Studio for research, creation and education. Since 1991: assistant professor, and since 1995: professor of musicology at Strasbourg University. Between 2009 and 2010 she is member of the Academic Institute of France (IUF). Between 1997 and 2010 she was one of the organizers and the responsible for the research group of 'Arts' ('Contemporary approaches in the artistic creations and reflections') at Strasbourg University. Since 1986 –until this day – she has been a member of the international research group on Musical Signification (ICMS), and between 1999 and 2007 she was a member of the executive committee of the International Association of Semiotic Studies (IASS).

Her main publications concern musical signification and narrativity in eighteenth- and nineteenth- twentieth-century instrumental music on the one hand, and contemporary (mostly electroacoustic and computer) music on the other hand. Her monographs: *Musique, narrativité, signification* (L'Harmattan, Paris 2009); *Morphologie des œuvres pour piano de*

F. Liszt (2nd edition, Kimé, Paris 1996); *Entre naturalisme sonore et synthèse en temps réel. Images et formes expressives dans la musique contemporaine* (EAC, Paris 2013). Her books as editor (a selection) : *Méthodes nouvelles, musiques nouvelles. Musicologie et création* (PUS, Strasbourg 1999); *Sens et signification en musique* (Editions Hermann, Paris 2007); *Gestes, fragments, timbres: la musique de György Kurtág* (co-ed.: Jean-Paul Olive; L'Harmattan, Paris 2009); *Les opéras de Peter Eötvös entre Orient et Occident* (EAC, Paris 2013) ; *Des temporalités multiples aux bruissements du silence. Daniel Charles in memoriam.* Sous la direction de Márta Grabócz et Geneviève Mathon, Hermann, 2013 ; *Festschrift à la mémoire de József Ujfalussy* ; dirigés par M. Berlàsz et M. Grabócz, Budapest, L'Harmattan, Hongrie, février 2014, 500 pages ; *Les grands topoï du XIXe siècle et la musique de F. Liszt.* Hermann, Paris, 2018 (430 pages in large format) ; *François-Bernard Mâche : Le compositeur et le savant face à l'univers sonore.* Codirection avec G. Mathon, 2018, Hermann (430 pages avec DVD) ; *Modèles naturels et scénarios imaginaires dans les œuvres de Peter Eötvös, F.-B. Mâche et J.-C. Risset,* Hermann, Paris, 2020. Forthcoming : *La Narratologie musicale. Topiques, théories et stratégies analytiques,* (an anthology) Hermann, june 2021 (600 pages). She also edited five books containing the writings of contemporary composers (Mâche, Risset, etc.)

Małgorzata Grajter Music theorist and pianist, Master of Arts and PhD graduate of The Grażyna and Kiejstut Bacewicz University of Music in Łódź, Poland, currently Assistant Professor in the Department of the Music Theory at her Alma Mater and guest researcher at the University of Łódź, Faculty of Letters. She took part in a number of international seminars and conferences, such as: Beethoven-Studienkolleg (Bonn), XI and XIV International Congress on Musical Signification (Kraków and Cluj), International Beethoven Symposium (Warsaw), International Beethoven Conference in Manchester, Academy of Cultural Heritages (Ermoupolis), Beethoven-Perspektiven (Bonn).

Since her master thesis about Beethoven's oratorio *Christus am Ölberge* she was devoted to the topic of Beethoven's vocal music. Her doctoral thesis, *Das Wort-Ton-Verhältnis im Werk von Ludwig van Beethoven,* which had previously been granted a prestigious Reverend Hieronim Feicht Award in Poland, was published in the German language by Peter Lang Verlag (2019). She is also an author of a number of articles in Polish, English, German and Portuguese.

Joan Grimalt Orchestra conductor (Vienna University), philologist (Barcelona University), PhD in musicology (Universitat autònoma de Barcelona) with a thesis on Gustav Mahler, which the late Raymond Monelle supervised until his decease. After a decade devoted exclusively to interpretation, conducting above all opera in Central Europe, he combines since his going back to Catalonia practical musicianship with teaching and research at the *Escola Superior de Música de Catalunya.*

Joan's main field of research is Musical Signification, especially those regions on the edge to literature and language: hermeneutic, rhetoric, poetic metres. The intersection between musicological reflection and performance has also been a constant point of interest. As a conductor, his former involvement with the Vienna *Volksoper* (1995–1997) stands out.

Grimalt is a member of the international research group on Musical Signification around the figures of Eero Tarasti, Robert Hatten and Grabócz Márta. He has presented and published most of his research at the periodical international conferences of this group. In September 2021, he is the local organizer of the last of these meetings, the International Congress on Musical Signification n. XV, in Barcelona. In his last book, *Mapping Musical Signification*

(Springer), Joan gathers his colleagues' and his own research on musical meaning in a systematic textbook.

Aleksi Haukka is a doctoral student at the University of Helsinki. His thesis deals with political and patriotic music from the 19th century from the existential semiotic point of view. He has published multiple articles on different topics from the existential semiotic point of view in the Finnish journal *Synteesi*. His main interest is applying and developing the existential semiotic point of view as a holistic framework for human sciences.

Guido Ipsen studied English and German philology, history, philosophy and history of the arts (Kassel, Germany) and information systems engineering (Wolverhampton; MA (UK) 1995). He became research assistant at the semiotics division at Kassel and worked there as an assistant professor until 2003, when he became Professor for Scientific Communication at the TU Dortmund. From 2010 to 2012, he taught as Docent for Media and Communication at the University of Applied Sciences Münster. Between 2004 and 2009, he was guest professor at the Finnish Network University for Semiotics, Helsinki.

His works include his PhD thesis on *HybridHyperSigns* (2001), his Habilitation on *Cultural Communication* (University Witten-Herdecke; 2011), and numerous articles on linguistic and semiotic theory, cultural and media studies as well as editions on general and media semiotics in collaboration with several journals.

Currently, Ipsen is involved in the teacher training programme at the Department of History of the University of Kassel and teaches there and at local high schools. His current research interests include the cognitive theory of didactics, the critical review of semiotic theory, and effects of digitalization on society and culture.

Sari Helkala-Koivisto, PhD, is a scholar of musicology and existential semiotics. She holds a doctorate from the University of Helsinki. She has been a researcher of the International Musical Signification project and participated also in the project of Cultural Heritages. Her semiotic study focuses on Julia Kristeva's psychoanalysis, and Eero Tarasti's existential semiotics, applied to musical signification between autism- and non-autism cultures and individuals. Her scientific interests are musical semiotics and prosody in the arts, globality of languages, and epistemological question between evidence-based and experience-based idea of human conception. In addition to the Semiotics of Disability, her current research deals with the semiotics of childhood – Childhood/ Children's Semiotics and art education in the European cultural heritage.

Dr. Jean-Marie Jacono is assistant professor in musicology at Aix-Marseille Université (Aix-en-Provence, France). He mainly deals with sociology of the musical work in the fields of Russian music (19th century) and Popular music (Rap and French song). He also deals with semiotics and musical signification. He has been member of the International research network on musical signification for a long time and was the co-organizer of ICMS 6 in Aix (1998). He was also several times co-director of the International Doctoral and Postodoctoral of musical Semiotics founded by prof. Eero Tarasti. He edited a major volume about the composer Henri Tomasi with Lionel Pons (*Henri Tomasi : du lyrisme méditerranéen à la conscience révoltée*, PUP, 2015) He currently works on Musorgsky's musical works.

Katriina Kajannes (b. Haapasalo), born and living at Jyväskylä, Finland. Appointed docent of Finnish Literature, Department of Art and Culture Studies, Faculty of Humanities, University of Jyväskylä. Docent, University of Jyväskylä. 1979 M.A., 1987 Ph.Lic., 1997 Ph.D. Studies in Italy, Institutum Romanum Finlandiae, 1978. Studies in Finnish Literature, University of Helsinki.

Circa 30 years as teacher and researcher at university. Main fields of research: Cognitive Analysis of Literature, Semiotics, Modernism, Postmodernism, Contemporary Literature, Finnish Culture and Literature, Comparative Literature, Medieval Latin Drama. Dissertation entitled *"Maisema ulkona ja sisällä on sama" – kognitioanalyyttinen tutkimus Lassi Nummen proosasta"* (SKS 1997) [*"The Landscape outside and inside is the same" – A cognitive-analytical study on Lassi Nummi's prose works*]. Monographies, edited books, scientific articles. Many activities in registered literature associations.

Terri Kupiainen is researcher of consume behaviour and strategic marketing management. Her research focuses mainly on consumer values, marketing of food products and the semiotics of marketing objects and experiences.

Altti Kuusamo is a professor emeritus in Art History at the University of Turku. Kuusamo has been known in Finland mainly of his contribution to semiotic studies, especially in the visual field. The main areas of Kuusamo's scholarly work are the methodology of Art History, theories of art, Post-Renaissance art, contemporary Finnish art, the relationship between the arts, semiotics of visual culture, the research of perception and theories of art criticism. Numerous publications comprise also critique and other generally comprehensible writings within the field of art and culture. Lately he has been making research on Modern and Early Modern melancholy in the arts.

Altti Kuusamo has published over 400 scientific and professional articles – including eight books. Kuusamo is the member of the executive committee in the International Association for Semiotic Studies (IASS), since 1999. He is also adjunct professor in Art History at the University of Helsinki, and adjunct professor in Mediasemiotics at the University of Lapland.

Eric Landowski Semiotician. Research director until 2014 (CNRS, Paris). Visiting professor at the university of São Paulo (PUC-SP) since 1992; co-founder and director of the Centre for Sociosemiotic Research (PUC- São Paulo). Visiting professor at the university of Vilnius since 2002. Editor (1979–1987 and 2012–2020) of the journal *Actes Sémiotiques* (co-founded with A.J. Greimas in 1979). Co-founder and former editor of the *International Journal for the Semiotics of Law*. Founder of the online journal *Acta Semiotica* (2021). Main topic of research: the elaboration of a semiotic theory of meaning-construction in social interactions. Main books published: *La Société réfléchie. Essais de socio-sémiotique*, Paris, Seuil, 1989; *Présences de l'autre*, Paris, PUF, 1997; *Passions sans nom*, Paris, PUF, 2004; *Les interacions risquées*, Limoges, PULIM, 2005.

Otto Lehto is a philosopher and political economist with a master's degree in Social and Moral Philosophy from the University of Helsinki. He is a PhD student at King's College London. He specializes in the study of complexity, evolutionary theory, naturalism, evolutionary political economy, the philosophy of law, and political philosophy. Find out more at his website: www.ottolehto.com

Massimo Leone is Tenured Full Professor ("Professore Ordinario") of Philosophy of Communication, Cultural Semiotics, and Visual Semiotics at the Department of Philosophy and Educational Sciences, University of Turin, Italy, Vice-Director for research at the same University, and part-time Professor of Semiotics in the Department of Chinese Language and Literature, University of Shanghai, China. He has been visiting professor at several universities in the five continents. He has single-authored fifteen books, edited more than forty collective volumes, and published more than five hundred articles in semiotics, religious studies, and visual studies. He is the winner of a 2018 ERC Consolidator Grant, the most prestigious research grant in Europe. He is the chief editor of *Lexia*, the Semiotic Journal of the Center for Interdisciplinary Research on Communication, University of Turin, Italy, of *Semiotica* (De Gruyter; the most important globally in the field), and editor of the book series "I Saggi di Lexia" (Rome: Aracne), "Semiotics of Religion" (Berlin and Boston: Walter de Gruyter), and "Interdisciplinary Face Studies" (London and New York: Routledge). He directed the MA Program in Communication Studies at the University of Turin, Italy (2015–2018) and is currently vice-director for research at the Department of Philosophy and Educational Sciences, University of Turin, Italy.

Yuan Liu, male, from Huixian, Henan province. PhD student in Comparative Literature and World Literature at Capital Normal University. His research interest includes the relationship between Chinese and foreign literature. Email address: 1184521007@qq.com.

Solomon Marcus (1925–2016) was born in Bacău, Romania. He graduated from Ferdinand I High School in 1944, and completed his studies at the University of Bucharest's Faculty of Science, Department of Mathematics, in 1949. Marcus obtained his PhD in Mathematics in 1956, with a thesis on the *Monotonic functions of two variables*. He was appointed Lecturer in 1955, Associate Professor in 1964, and became a Professor in 1966 (Emeritus in 1991).

Marcus was one of the leading semioticians in the world and his output is extremely interdisciplinary having contributed to the following areas: Mathematical Analysis, Set Theory, Measure and Integration Theory, and Topology, Theoretical Computer Science, Linguistics, Poetics and Theory of Literature, Semiotics, Cultural Anthropology, History and Philosophy of Science, Education. He taught in many continents and was permanent visitor at the ISI congresses in Imatra. His approach to semiotics was deeply epistemological, and he could deal even with such notions as transcendence in his reflections. He was founder of mathematical linguistics and poetics.

Marcus published about 50 books, and 400 articles in most varied languages. Among his honours are Order of the Star of Romania and Knight of the Royal Decoration of *Nihil Sine Deo* by Romanian Royal Family.

Dario Martinelli, musicologist and semiotician, is Full Professor of History and Theory of Arts at Kaunas University of Technology, and is also affiliated to the University of Helsinki, as Adjunct Professor in Semiotics and Musicology, and to the University of Lapland, as Adjunct Professor in Methodologies of Semiotics and Communication Studies. He is also Editor-in-chief of the series "Numanities – Arts and Humanities in Progress", published by Springer.

As of 2021, he has published fourteen monographs and nearly 200 among edited collections, studies and scientific articles. His most recent monographs include *What You See Is What You Hear* (Springer, 2020), *Give Peace a Chant* (Springer, 2017), *Arts and Humanities in Progress: A Manifesto of Numanities* (Springer 2016), and the forthcoming *The Intertextual Knot: An Analysis of Alfred Hitchcock's* Rope (Springer 2021).

He has been recipient of several prizes, including, in 2006, a knighthood from the Italian Republic for his contribution to Italian culture.

Roberto Mastroianni is a philosopher, art critic and curator.

Independent researcher at C.I.R.Ce – Interdepartmental Research Centre on Communication and Direction Committee member the Unesco Chair in Sustainable Development and Territory Management at the University of Turin.

President of the Museo Diffuso della Resistenza, della Deportazione, della Guerra, dei Diritti e della Libertà of Turin and scientific and artistic advisor on Graffiti-Writing, Street Art, Urban Art, Urban Designand Youth Creativity for the "Creative Turin" Department of the City of Turin and curator for public art, urban creativityand Urban Art for the "Contrada Torino"-Onlus Foundation, and the open-air museum "To Shape-Urban Art District" of Turin.

After graduating in Theoretical Philosophy, under the supervision of Gianni Vattimo and Roberto Salizzoni, and obtaining a Ph. D. in Philosophy and Communication, under the supervision of Ugo Volli he focused his research mainly on Philosophical Aesthetics, General Theory of Politics, Anthropology, Semiotics, Urban Studies, Communication and Cultural Studies, Urban Innovation and Cultural Heritage, Sustainable Development and Political Ecology, Contemporary and Irregular Art and Philosophical Criticism.

He is the author, co-author and curator of several books, articles and essays on political theory, philosophy and art criticism. He has also curated numerous exhibitions and shows in public and private spaces and national and international museums as well as public artand street artprojects.

He currently teaches Theory and Techniques of Contemporary Arts at the Albertina Academy of Fine Arts in Turin.

Cleisson Melo, better known as Son Melo, is a master and doctor in music. Researcher linked to the research group PAMVILLA (Analytical Perspectives for the Music of Villa-Lobos) coordinated by Dr. Paulo de Tarso Salles; NEMUS (Nucleus of Music Studies) [UFBA] coordinated by Dr. Pablo Sotuyo; The Semiotics of Cultural Heritage [UH] and collaborates with ACH (Academy of Cultural Heritage), both coordinated by Dr. Eero Tarasti. Member of IASS-AIS (International Association for Semiotic Studies) and TEMA (Brazilian Association of Music Theory and Analysis). His publications include articles and chapters in the area of musicology and musical analysis with an emphasis on the work of Brazilian composer Heitor Villa-Lobos and musical semiotics in general. He develops research about Saudade and its socio-cultural, musical and philosophical unfolding as part of the research group entitled *Cultural Heritage: memory, identity and representation*, coordinated by him.

As a bassist, composer and music producer, he has participated in more than 40 works (CDs, DVDs, EPs, Singles, etc.), including producing some of them. Among the many artists we can highlight Manuela Rodrigues, André Bernard, Jeff Decker, Sérgio Otanazetra, Elpídio Bastos and Val Macambira. As a composer he has had some of his works premiered and performed by Federal University of Bahia Orchestra (OSUFBA) and ensembles.

Currently a professor of Music Department at the Federal University of Campina Grande (UFCG), coordinator of the Studio and Audio Laboratory (LEA) and assistant editor of the ICTUS periodical of the post-graduation program on music of Federal University of Bahia (UFBA).

Ramunas Motiekaitis studied composition at Lithuanian and Norwegian academies of music. He pursued and completed his doctoral studies at the University of Helsinki (2011). During 2008–2010 with support of Japanese ministry of education, Motiekaitis worked as a researcher in Tokyo Musashino Academy of Music. During 2013–2014 with support of Canon foundation in Europe he continued postdoctoral research at Nanzan Institute for Religion and Culture in Nagoya, Japan. Motiekaitis lectured on Japanese intellectual history at the Vilnius University, on East Asian Buddhism and Arts at Vytautas Magnus University. Currently he lectures on aesthetics, XX century philosophy and East Asian Art in Lithuanian Academy of Music and Theatre. Research interests: semiotic theories, metaphysics of Buddhism, philosophy of the twentieth century, Japanese culture.

Leena Muotio (formerly known as Mäkelä-Marttinen) graduated (M.A.) from the University of Helsinki in 1995. Her major was comparative literature and large minor theoretical philosophy (philosophy of language). She also studied semiotics, aesthetics and theatre research. Her licentiate dissertation took place in 1999. Her two children were born in 1999 and in 2000. In 2008, she defended her doctorate dissertation: *Olen maa, johon tahdot. Timo K. Mukan maailmankuvan poetiikkaa*. (*I am the Land Beckoning you: A Poetics of Timo K. Mukka's World View*).

Muotio has been researching literature widely, from the American popular literature and Russian 19th century literature to the modern Finnish novel. She has been interested in semiotics of literature. For example, she has studied Mario Puzo's novel *The Godfather* from the narratological point of view. Her master degree study concerned the glasnost writers Vladimir Duduntsev's novel *White Robes*. As a licentiate thesis, she wrote a comparative study about William Faulkner's novel *As I Lay Dying*, Graham Swift´s novel *Last Orders* and Jari Tervo's novel *Pyhiesi yhteyteen* (*Among the Saints*). She has written several academic articles about semiotics of literature, and she has presented semiotics of literature in many point of views at several conferences both at home and abroad.

In literary studies, her main methodological interests have been Mikhail Bakhtin's theory of novel, his ideas about dialogical relationship between characters of the story, and also the dialogue between genres in the novelistic form of literature and the idea about chronotope. She is also interested in the wide conversation about Bakhtin´s studies that is going on in the academic world. One of her main interest is Sigmund Freud´s and his followers' thoughts about concepts of melancholy, narcissism and tabu.

Since the year, 2002 Muotio has been working at the South-Eastern University of Applied Sciences as a principal lecturer of Culture Department. During her career she has been published several articles concerning design research, design methodology, culture studies and development of higher education. She also works as a project expert in culture and creative industry projects.

Reijo Mälkiä has an education in architecture and a master's degree in philosophy. He is currently doing his dissertation at the Faculty of Theology of the University of Helsinki. He has presented an essay on the topic e.g. At the 2nd Symposium of the Academy of Cultural Heritage in Syros, Greece. In his work at Senate Properties, he has been responsible for the buildings of state cultural institutions.

Lina Navickaitė-Martinelli, PhD, is Professor and Senior Researcher at the Lithuanian Academy of Music and Theatre, as well as Chair of the Musicologists' Section at the Lithuanian Composers' Union. She has presented numerous conference papers, keynote and guest lectures, edited academic collections and published scientific articles in international journals and article collections. Her books *A Suite of Conversations: 32 Interviews and Essays on the Art of Music Performance* (2010) and *Piano Performance in a Semiotic Key: Society, Musical Canon and Novel Discourses* (2014) have been awarded as the best Lithuanian musicological works of the respective years for innovative research of music performance. Navickaitė-Martinelli is the founder and coordinator of the LMTA Hub of Artistic Research and Performance Studies (HARPS). Her research deals with various phenomena within the art of music performance, with a specific focus on semiotic and sociological aspects as well as practice-led research. More information at linamartinelli.wordpress.com.

Juha Ojala, Ph.D. (musicology), M.M. (piano; composition; electronic and computer music), is professor of music performance research at the DocMus doctoral school, Sibelius Academy of the University of the Arts Helsinki, Finland. He is also the vice dean of research and doctoral education at the Sibelius Academy, and docent of musicology (University of Helsinki) and music education research (University of Oulu, Finland). He has published widely across musicological fields, such as semiotics, education, technology, philosophy, and psychology. The variety of scholarly work is often drawn together by a framework in pragmatism and semiotics, established e.g. in *Space in musical semiosis*, his dissertation at the University of Helsinki, published by the International Semiotics Institute. His main research interests are in semiotics and signification in music, performance, composition, learning and education of music.

Aurèlia Pessarrodona Licensed in Humanities (UPF, 2000), PhD in Musicology (UAB, 2010), Postgraduate in Archivistics (UNED, 2018) and with training in the field of digital edition (UOC, 2018, Univ. of Paderborn, 2020). She began her research career with a grant for young researchers of the Joan Maragall Foundation (2001) to study contemporary religious music; but her further research has been focused particularly on 18th-century Spanish musical theatre, above all the *tonadilla*. After obtaining the PhD in 2010 with a thesis on the *tonadillas* by the composer Jacinto Valledor, her research was developed mainly through four postdoctoral fellowships: at the Universität des Saarlandes (2011) with a DAAD fellowship: at the Dipartimento delle Arti of the Univ. Bologna with a postdoctoral fellowship of the Spanish Government (2011–2013); at the Dipartimento di Lingue, Letterature e Culture Moderne of the same university with a postdoctoral contract (2013–2015); and at the Department of Art and Musicology of the Autonomous University of Barcelona with a "Juan de la Cierva incorporación" fellowship. Since 2017 she is a teacher of the History of Music, Aesthetics and Research Methods at the Higher Conservatory of Music of the Liceu (Barcelona). She also collaborates with the Bachelor's degree in Musicology at the University Alfonso X el Sabio and she is thesis supervisor of the official Master's Degree in Musical Interpretation and Research at the International University of Valencia.

Her approach to 18th-century Spanish musical theatre has been really wide and varied, from the edition of musical sources to the study of meaning constructions, particularly those related to the impact of the body in musical dramaturgy (dance, gestures, voice, dance topics, etc.). In fact, she has linked her research to her practice as a singer in some of her spectacles. The results of these researches have been presented also in many international conferences and published in high-impact journals and prestigious publishers as monographies or book chapters. In 2018 her article "El cuerpo cantante en las tonadillas a solo para Miguel Garrido" won the second prize of the Otto Mayer-Serra Award, of the University of California-Riverside.

Susan Petrilli is Professor of Philosophy and Theory of Languages, Bari University, Visiting Research Fellow, Adelaide University, Vice-President of International Association for Semiotic Studies, 7th Sebeok Fellow of the Semiotic Society of America. She has authored, translated and edited numerous essays, book chapters and volumes. Her publications in philosophy of language, semiotics and translation theory include: *Signifying and Understanding* (2009), *Sign Crossroads in Global Perspective* (2010), *Sign Studies and Semioethics* (2014), *The Global World and Its Manifold Faces* (2016), *Signs, Language and Listening* (2019); and recent essays in *Semiotica* (IASS), *International Journal for the Semiotics of Law*, *Philology*, and *Calumet*.

Sami Pihlström is (since 2014) Professor of Philosophy of Religion at the University of Helsinki, Finland. He has previously served, e.g., as Professor of Practical Philosophy at the University of Jyväskylä (2006–2014) and as the Director of the Helsinki Collegium for Advanced Studies (2009–2015). He is currently also, e.g., the Chair of the Research Council for Culture and Society at the Academy of Finland (2019–21) and (since 2016) the President of the Philosophical Society of Finland. He has published widely on transcendental philosophy, pragmatism, philosophical anthropology, ethics, metaphysics, and philosophy of religion. His recent books include *Death and Finitude: Toward a Pragmatic Transcendental Anthropology of Human Limits and Mortality* (Lexington, 2016), *Kantian Antitheodicy: Philosophical and Literary Varieties* (with Sari Kivistö, Palgrave Macmillan, 2016), *Why Solipsism Matters* (Bloomsbury, 2020), *Pragmatic Realism, Religious Truth, and Antitheodicy: On Viewing the World by Acknowledging the Other* (Helsinki University Press, 2020), and *Pragmatist Truth in the Post-Truth Age: Sincerity, Normativity, and Humanism* (forthcoming with Cambridge University Press). He is a member of the Finnish Academy of Sciences and Letters, the Finnish Society of Sciences and Letters, Academia Europaea, as well as Institut International de Philosophie (I.I.P.).

Vesa Matteo Piludu is a postdoctoral grant researcher and a scholar of Study of religions at the University of Helsinki. His main research interests are related to Finnish mythology and folk beliefs and to the representation and interpretation of Finnish myths in visual arts, music and dance. His PhD dissertation *The Forestland's Guests: Mythical Landscapes, Personhood, and Gender in The Finno-Karelian Bear Ceremonialism* deals with the traditional Finnish rituals of the bear hunt and the relations between hunters and forest spirits. Piludu has worked as a coordinator of the study unit of semiotics at the University of Helsinki and as a teacher of Semiotic of Arts and Semiotic of Cultures, giving the following courses on Finnish mythology and arts and music: *Myths and Music* (2010), *Kalevala Suite: Finnish Myths in Music* (2011), *Kalevala and the Muses* (2014 ja 2015). He obtained the membership of the prestigious *Kalevala Society* for scientific merits, and in 2011, he organized an international seminar celebrating the centenary of the Society in Italy, editing with Frog, the publication of the proceedings in Italian and English: *Kalevala: Epica, Magia, Arte e Musica Epic, Magic, Art and Music*. In 2018, he has been accepted as member of the Helsinki Institute for Sustainability Sciences (HELSUS) of the University of Helsinki and he participated in the University of Helsinki's Future Development Fund international Project, *The Materiality of Indigenous Languages: Co-Creating Landscapes*.

Augusto Ponzio, Professor Emeritus of Philosophy and Theory of Languages, Bari University, is a renown philosopher of language and semiotician. He directs several book series including from 1990 "Athanor". As editor of scholarly publications, translator, author he has disseminated ideas of Petrus Hispanus, Mikhail Bakhtin, Emmanuel Levinas, Karl Marx, Ferruccio Rossi-Landi, Adam Schaff, Thomas Sebeok, Roland Barthes. With Susan Petrilli he has co-authored *Semiotics Unbounded* (2005), *Fundamentos da Filosofia da linguagem* (2007), *Dizionario, Enciclopedia, Traduzione* (2019), *Identità e alterità* (2019). Recent books: *Rencontres de parole* (2010), *Semiotica e letteratura* (2015); *La coda dell'occhio* (2016), *Emmanuel Levinas* (2019), *A Ligereiza da palavra* (2019).

Paolo Rosato composer, musicologist, and writer, holds degrees in Choral Music (Florence), Composition (Pescara), Philosophy (Chieti) and PhD in Musicology (University of Helsinki). He studied music analysis with Fulvio Delli Pizzi. He teaches at the Conservatory of Fermo.

He was co-editor (1986–1999) with Michele Ignelzi of *Eunomio*, an Italian journal for theory, analysis, and semiotics of music. Member of the International Project on Musical Signification, directed by Eero Tarasti, he has been presenting papers in international congresses (Edinburgh, Paris, Helsinki, Rome, Wien, Dresden, Krakow, among the others). His writings are published in many books and reviews. He is the author of *The Organic Principle in Music Analysis. A Semiotic Approach* (Helsinki 2013). His original approach to the study of the tonal models was presented at the University of Austin (2016) and published on the *Indiana Theory Review* (2018).

Member of the *SIMC* (the Italian Society for Contemporary Music) and *Nuova Consonanza* (Rome), his music (more than 200 compositions) is performed in various festivals and Countries. Author of three operas: *Il ritratto* (from James's "The tone of time", Pescara 2003); *Lars Cleen* (from Pirandello's "Lontano", Helsinki 2015); and *Didone* (from Marlowe, Pescara 2009). Some of his compositions were recently premiered at *La Biennale Musica* in Venice, *Mozarteum* in Salzburg, and the *Hungarian Institute* in Paris.

Mathias Rousselot is an Associate professor at the University of Toulouse (France). His research mainly concerns musical semiotics, musical narrativity, as well as musical philosophy. He participated in ICMS XII in Louvain-la-Neuve and ICMS XIII in Canterbury. Author of a book on musical improvisation (2012) and a book on the sense of music (2016), he wrote the preface of the French translation of Semiotics of Classical Music: How Mozart, Brahms and Wagner talk to us by Eero Tarasti.

Daniel Röhe, Ph.D., is a psychotherapist with private practice in Brazil. His Master's and Doctoral researches focused on the intersection between Musicology, Psychoanalysis, and Semiotics. He is the author along with Francisco Martins and Inês Gandolfo of *Oedipus goes to the opera: Psychoanalytic inquiry in Enescu's Œdipe and Stravinsky's Oedipus Rex*, published by the International Forum of Psychoanalysis/Routledge. He is also the author/contributor to works published in Portuguese. In 2017, he performed clarinet chôros at the Apollo Theatre (Syros Island). He is the International Communication Advisor for the Academy of Cultural Heritages (special area Latin America).

Antonio Santangelo is a researcher in semiotics at the University of Turin, where he teaches Semiotics and Semiotics of Digital Cultures. His main interests are in the field of structuralist semiotics of Saussurian and Lévi-Straussian derivation, as well as in narrative theory, audiovisual studies and internet studies. He is the author of several books and articles, including "Sociosemiotica dell'audiovisivo" (Santangelo, 2013) and, together with Guido Ferraro, "Uno sguardo più attento" (2013), "I sensi del testo" (2017) and "Narrazione e realtà" (2017).

Hamid Reza Shairi is a specialist in semiotics and text sciences. He is a University Professor in the French Department at Tarbiat Modares University in Iran. In collaboration with the University of Limoges and its scientific representative Jacques Fontanille, the University of Isfahan and the Scac, he founded a Summer University (1998–2000), where seminars and workshops in text didactics and Semiotics of discourse were taught by French (J. Fontanille, Denis Bertrand, Michel Arrivé, JF Jeandillou) and Iranian professors for three consecutive years.

Hamid Reza Shairi was also one of the founders of the Semiotics Team at the Academy of Arts in Tehran (2002–2008). He is part of the founding committee of the Association of French teachers in Tehran. He is one of the founders of the Semiotic Circle of Tehran (2009) which he currently directs. He is a representative of his country within the International and World Association of Semiotics as well as within the French Semiotic Association.

He is also the Editor-in-Chief of two scientific journals: Linguistic Related Research and Narrative Studies at the Faculty of Human Sciences of Tarbiat Modares University.

Hamid Reza Shairi is the director of several French plays which have been performed in theaters in Tehran.

He is also the author of numerous articles and several semiotic works written in Persian (The prerequisites of New Semiotics, Samt, 2002; Semiotic analysis of discourse, samt, 2007; Pour une semiotique du sensible, Editions Elmi va Farhangui, 2009 ; Visual semiotics, Editions Sokhan, 2012; Semiotics of literature, University of Tarbiat Modares, 2016).

Hamid Reza Shairi has been twice medalist by the High Research Council of his University: first time elected as best director of the French Department and a second time elected as best professor-researcher, by the High Scientific Council of Tarbiat Modares University.

He was also awarded a medal by the Farabi International Festival for the Scientific Review, of which he is editor-in-chief.

He was also named Chevalier in December 2014 in the order of academic palms of the French Republic.

Francesco Spampinato obtained a Ph.D. in Musicology at the University of Aix-en-Provence in 2006, under the supervision of Professor Bernard Vecchione on "Debussy and the imagination of Elements. Metaphorization and corporeality in musical experience". From 2002 to 2008, he was a temporary lecturer for Musical Philosophy and Musical Psychology at the University of Aix-en-Provence. Between 2007 and 2010, he taught History of Music at the Music Conservatories in Italy. Since 2016 he is researcher at the University of Strasbourg: CREAA (Centre de Recherches et d'Expérimentation sur l'Acte Artistique) and ACCRA (Approches Contemporaines de la Création et de la Réflexion Artistiques). Since 2008, he has published several books on the bodily foundations of music imaginary: *Les Métamorphoses du son. Matérialité imaginative de l'écoute musicale* (2008), *Debussy, poète des eaux. Métaphorisation et corporéité dans l'expérience musicale* (2011), *Les incarnations du son. Les métaphores du geste dans l'écoute musicale* (2015), *Musica a pelle. Immaginario tattile e Globalità dei Linguaggi* (2019), *Claude Debussy e l'immaginario pittorico* (2020).

Eero Tarasti, professor of musicology at the University of Helsinki (chair) in 1984–2016. He was President of the IASS/AIS (International Association for Semiotic Studies), 2004–2014 and is now its Honorary President. He was the founder and President of the International Semiotics Institute (ISI) in Imatra, Finland, in 1986–2013. In 2016 he has founded the Academy of Cultural Heritages.

He studied music in Sibelius Academy, Helsinki, and then in Vienna, Paris, Rio de Janeiro and Bloomington. He got his PhD from Helsinki University (1978) after studies in Paris with Claude Lévi-Strauss and A.J. Greimas. He is one of the founders and the director of the international research group Musical Signification since 1984.Tarasti has become Honorary Doctor at Estonian Music Academy, New Bulgarian University (Sofia), Indiana University (Bloomington), University of Aix-Marseille and Georghe Dima Music Academy in Cluj-Napoca, Rumania. He has published about 400 articles, edited 50 anthologies, and written 30 monographs; among them one finds: *Myth and Music* (1979), *A Theory of Musical Semiotics* (1994), *Heitor Villa-Lobos* (1996), *Existential Semiotics* (2000), *Signs of Music* (2003), *Fondéments de la sémiotique existentielle* (2009), *Fondamenti di semiotica esistenziale* (2010), *Semiotics of Classical Music* (2012, in French 2016),and *Sein und Schein, Explorations in Existential Semiotics* (2015); two novels: *Le secret du professeur Amfortas* (2002) and *Retour à la Villa Nevski* (2014, in Italian *L'heredità di Villa Nevski*, 2014 in Finnish *Eurooppa/Ehkä* 2017). He has supervised 150 PhD:s in Finland and abroad.

Mattia Thibault is Assistant Professor at Tampere University. He is a member of the Gamification Group and Affiliated Senior Researcher at the Centre of Excellence in Game Culture Studies. His research projects "LudoSpace" (CoE GAMECULT) and "ReClaim" (EU MSCA-IF 793835) focus on urban gamification and the relationship between play and the built environment. In 2017 he earned a PhD in Semiotics and Media at Turin University, where he subsequently worked as research fellow in 2018. Thibault has been visiting researcher at Tartu University (Estonia), The Strong Museum of Play (Rochester, NY, US), Helsinki University (Finland), Amsterdam University of Applied Sciences (Nederland) and Waag (Nederland).

Jaan Valsiner I was born in Tallinn, Estonia in 1951. Currently I consider myself a cultural psychologist with a consistently developmental axiomatic base that is brought to analyses of any psychological or social phenomena. I find contemporary psychology's empiricism deeply uninteresting and concentrate upon theoretical innovation through transdisciplinary scholarship. After working for over three decades in USA at University of North Carolina at Chapel Hill and Clark University, I accepted in 2013 the position of Niels Bohr Professor of Cultural Psychology at Aalborg University, Denmark. in combination with collaboration with University of Luxembourg and Sigmund Freud Privatuniversität Wien in Austria and in Berlin. My main contributions are monographs The guided mind (Cambridge, Ma.: Harvard University Press, 1998), Culture in minds and societies (New Delhi: Sage, 2007), Ornamented Lives (Charlotte, NC: Information Age Publishers, 2018) and Sensuality in Human Living (Springer, 2020). Currently I am working on a major theoretical treatise New General Psychology (to appear in 2021 by Springer) that would synthesize William Stern's personology with my theory of Cultural Psychology of Semiotic Dynamics that builds on the theoretical heritage of James Mark Baldwin, Karl Bühler and Lev Vygotsky. I am a member of the Estonian Academy of Sciences. Prior to being awarded this Prize by APA I have been awarded major research prizes in Europe-- the Alexander von Humboldt Prize of 1995 in Germany, and the Hans-Kilian-Preis of 2017 in Europe for interdisciplinary synthesis.

Morten Tønnessen is a Norwegian philosopher and semiotician. He is currently Professor of philosophy and Head of department at Department of social studies, Faculty of social sciences, University of Stavanger. Tønnessen has been President of the Nordic Association for Semiotic Studies (NASS) since 2017, and has previously served as co-Editor-in-Chief of *Biosemiotics* 2013–2018 and lead Editor-in-Chief 2018–2020. His ph.d. dissertation is titled "Umwelt Transition and Uexküllian Phenomenology – An Ecosemiotic Analysis of Norwegian Wolf Management" and was defended at University of Tartu, Estonia, in 2011. His publications include "Outline of an Uexkullian Bio-Ontology" (article in *Sign Systems Studies*, 2001), "Steps to a Semiotics of Being" (article in *Biosemiotics*, 2010), "I, Wolf: The Ecology of Existence" (book chapter, 2011), "Semiotics of Being and Uexküllian Phenomenology" (book chapter, 2011), and "Phenomenology and biosemiotics" (editorial in Biosemiotics, 2018, with Alexei Sharov and Timo Maran). The book *Semiotic Agency: Science beyond Mechanism* (written with Alexei Sharov, to be published by Springer Nature) is forthcoming in 2021.

Bernard Vecchione. Triple training in music, humanities and philosophy. Music: composition studies with Pierre Schaeffer (Paris 1969), Iannis Xenakis (Acanthes International Center, 1978), Pierre Boulez, Luciano Berio (Accademia Musicale Internazionale Chigiana, Siena 1980), and André Boucourechliev, of which he was a research assistant at Aix-en-Provence University (1978–1984). Humanities: university certificates in sociology / ethnology (Jean Poirier, Nice 1972), linguistics / semiotics (Georges Mounin, Jean Molino, Aix-en-Provence 1974), Master's degree in Experimental Psychology of Music Perception (Aix-en-Provence 1975), PhD in Music and Musicology (André Boucourechliev dir., Aix-en-Provence 1984). Philosophy: State Doctorate in Æsthetic Philosophy (Daniel Charles dir., Paris 1985). Co-founder and scientific director of MIM (Music and Computer Lab, Marseilles Conservatory of Music, 1983–1990), and MSRC (Music Sciences Research Center, 1983–1997) become MLS (Musical Languagiarity Sciences) International Project in 1997. Lecturer (1983–1988) then Professor (1988–2017) at Aix-Marseilles University. Joined Eero Tarasti's ICMS in 1991. Member of IDEAT (Institute of Aesthetics, Arts and Technology, University of Paris I-Panthéon Sorbonne (dir. Costin Miereanu) (2005–2011). Adviser of the French Minister of Universities (2007–2011). Numerous publications in different areas (epistemology of Musicology, Computational Musicology, Music and Humanities, Musical Semiotics, Rhetoric and Stylistic, Musical Hermeneutics, Medieval Motet Discourse Studies. . .). Retired form academic life in 2017. Lives now in Tuscany.

Vilmos Voigt Studied in Budapest (Eötvös Loránd University). Major fields of research: Finno-Ugric studies, comparative religion, folklore. Initiator of semiotics in Hungary, also in Finno-Ugric confine. He was the first person who taught semiotics in Helsinki. University. Honorary Doctor of the Tartu University, honorary professor of Bucuresti University. Founder of Hungarian Society of Semiotics. His introduction of international semiotics: Bevezetés a szemiotikába (2008, updated edition). Member of several organs of semiotics. Professor emeritus of Eötvös Loránd University.

Elżbieta Magdalena Wąsik is University Professor in the Faculty of English at the Adam Mickiewicz University in Poznan. The domains of her specialty includes Frisian, Germanic

Languages, Human Linguistics, Semiotics of Culture and Communication Theory. Her basic education, she obtained from the University of Wrocław, with MA in German and Dutch (1986), and Ph.D. in General Linguistics (1995). Subsequently, she completed her D.Litt. at the School of English of AMU in Poznań in 2008. Being the author of four books and numerous articles on minority languages and ecological grammar of human linkages, linguistic functionalism, existential semiotics and phenomenology of speech, she has marked her presence at international conferences as a participant of thematic sessions and as convener of workshops as well as co-organizer of panels in Poland, Germany, Czechia, Slovakia, Slovenia, Belgium, Finland, Latvia, Estonia, Greece, United States of America, and Iran. For her scientific achievements, she has been elected Fellow of the International Communicology Institute, Washington, DC.

Professor Zdzisław Wąsik specializes in linguistic semiotics and semiotic phenomenology. At present he is employed as professor at the Wrocław School of Banking, where he also acts as president of Academic Council & coordinator of linguistics in The Research Federation of WSB–DSW Universities, Gdańsk. His didactic experience has been enriched through a long-lasting cooperation with the universities in Wrocław, Opole, Poznań and Toruń as well as with the vocational schools of higher education in Wałbrzych, Jelenia Góra, and Wrocław. In recognition of his leading role in the activity of professional societies, as of January 2, 2018, he has been nominated the fifth "Laureate Fellow" of the International Communicology Institute. Two years ago in the Autumn of 2019, he has been distinguished by the Republic of Poland Prime Minister's Award among six persons with outstanding scientific and artistic achievements for his contributions to the knowledge of language as a system of signs functioning in discursive environments. He has delivered conference papers and given guest lectures, inter alia, in the USA, Yugoslavia (Kosovo), Brazil, Norway, the Netherlands, Bulgaria, Germany, Finland, Sweden Slovenia and Belgium.

Xiaofang Yang, female, from Yongzhou, Hunan province. Associate professor of the Faculty of Literature, Nanning Normal University, Visiting scholar of the University of Helsinki, Beijing Normal University and Peking University. Her research interests focus on semiotics theory, film criticism, and cultural criticism. Email address: 67514129@qq.com.

Person index

Abel, Jacob Friedrich von 31
Abram, David 330–331, 334, 337, 340–341, 402, 544
Adorno, Theodor 93, 160–161, 604–605, 855, 861, 959, 963, 970–972, 974, 976, 978
Aeneas 559
Agawu, Kofi 163, 807, 815, 959–960, 962, 964–965, 978
Ahlqvist, August 631
Aho, Juhani 757, 759–760, 762–766, 768, 770–771
Aho, Kalevi 96, 631–632, 640, 643–644, 655
Alasuutari, Pertti 409, 421
Alberti, Leon Battista 589, 595, 597
Alexander, Hubert G. 206–207, 221
Allanbrook, Wye 960–961, 978–979, 1013, 1019
Almeida Junior, José Ferraz de XVII, 533–535
Andrade, Mario de XVI, 507–508, 510, 513, 519, 933–934
Andrew, Michael 659–661, 677
Ans, André-Marcel 179
Aquinas, Thomas 10, 85, 540, 726, 729, 738, 935
Archer, Margaret 413, 422
Arendt, Hannah 257, 462, 542, 565, 744, 754, 934
Aristotle 25, 77, 79–83, 93, 96, 101, 105, 173, 200–201, 205–206, 221, 498, 708, 806, 961
Asafiev, Boris 809–810, 902–903, 907, 911, 916
Augustine 8, 10, 12, 738
Austin, John Langshaw 22, 33, 44, 246, 309, 410, 422, 683, 738, 770, 798, 867, 1033

Bach, J. S. 91, 605, 950–952, 954
Bachelard, Gaston 18, 804
Badiou, Alain 7–8, 11–12
Badir, Semir 622, 808
Baker, D. P. 53–54, 56–58, 60–61, 74, 217, 581, 591, 736, 738, 954–955

Bakhtin, Mikhail XIX, 40–45, 258, 302, 309, 311, 757–759, 768–770, 798, 1030, 1033
Balakirev, Mili 158, 484
Barthes, Roland 7, 35, 38–40, 44, 249–250, 371, 570, 576, 615, 617, 622, 674–675, 699, 890, 999, 1033
Bateson, Gregory 19–20, 33, 241, 244, 247
Bauman, Zygmunt 460, 465, 471–473, 477
Beaumont, Mark 666–667, 682
Beckett, Samuel 668–670, 682–683, 806
Beethoven, Ludwig van XIX, 172, 632, 749, 804, 811–812, 814, 816, 861, 864, 870–871, 879, 897–907, 909–917, 936, 945, 949, 953, 967, 979–980, 995, 1025
Bekker, Immanuel 502, 519
Benjamin, Walter 34, 45, 126, 128, 221, 435, 457, 604, 873, 881–882
Benveniste, Emile 182, 196
Berg, Alban 172, 396–397, 422
Berger, Peter Ludwig 243–244, 406–407, 409, 419, 421–422, 686, 688, 697, 891
Bergman, Ingmar 296, 301, 306, 309, 707
Bergson, Henri 80, 99, 107–108, 111, 117, 127, 166, 182–183, 187, 196, 201, 203, 221, 303, 1021
Berkeley, George 120, 155, 402–403, 427, 682, 709, 799, 955, 980, 1019, 1024
Berlioz, Hector 172, 806, 847–848, 857, 861, 945, 983–985, 987–998, 1023–1024
Berman, Lazar 915
Bernanos, Georges 701–702, 706, 809, 964
Berruti, Massimo 35, 46, 258, 773, 798–799, 1021
Bertalanffy, L. von 20
Bertrand, Joseph 27–28, 79, 92, 96, 422, 816, 1034
Bilac, Olavo 523, 537
Blomstedt, Väinö 634
Blumenberg, Hans 167–169, 177–178, 180
Bocchi, Francesco 595, 597

Bohm, David 277, 287
Bohr, Niels 15, 17–18, 33, 1035
Boiles, Charles 179–180
Boltzmann, Ludwig 377
Bonnet, Charles 335–337, 341
Bourdieu, Pierre 290, 298, 309–310, 410, 412, 422, 765
Bourgeois, Louise 391, 393, 402, 872, 901, 941–942
Bracher, Elias XX, 919–921, 923–925, 937
Brahms, Johannes 85, 97, 172, 214, 223, 520, 537, 817, 862, 938, 962, 968, 976, 981, 1020, 1033
Bresson, Robert 699, 707–709
Broad, C. D. 8, 79, 93, 96, 111, 115, 121, 133, 253, 255, 275, 280, 367, 534, 742, 898, 910, 912, 969, 987
Broms, Henri 246, 742–743, 754
Buddha 10, 543, 553
Busoni, Ferruccio 178, 943, 954
Butor, Michel 169

Cage, John 165, 423, 843, 845, 873, 1022
Caillois, Roger 568, 570, 576
Calabrese, Omar 150, 154, 585
Cameron, James 685, 689–690, 692–693, 696
Cardrew, Cornelius 889
Cassirer, Ernst 19, 232–234, 244, 246
Cassone, Idone 570–571, 575–576
Castellana, Marcello 807
Chagas, Paulo C. 97, 919, 921, 925–926, 936, 938
Chateaubriand, François-René de 985, 994
Chesterman, Andrew 743, 754
Chipman, Abram 395–396, 401–402
Chomsky, Noam 21, 33
Chopin, Fryderyk XIX, 812–814, 864, 912, 914, 951, 953–955
Clapp, Mortimer 583, 597
Clifford, James 145, 154
Clouzot, Henri-Georges 394, 402
Cobley, Paul 44, 245, 541, 564–565, 600, 605
Coetzee, J. M. XVIII, 711, 713–718, 720–723

Cohen, Leonard 659, 668, 673–679, 682–683
Colapietro, Vincent 44, 293, 298, 309
Commoner, Barry 22
Connolly, William E. 408, 422
Cooren, François 407, 422
Costamagna, Philippe 585, 591, 593, 597
Courtés, Joseph 96, 154, 598, 816, 938, 979
Cseres, Jozef 883, 886, 889–891, 895–896
Cummings, Naomi 221
Curtius, Ernst R. 961, 979
Cygnaeus, Fredrik 624, 627–631, 638, 642, 653
Czarniawska, Barbara 407, 420, 422
Czerny, Carl 945, 948

D'Annunzio, Gabriele 743, 745, 748
d'Olivet, Antoine Fabre 158
Dahlhaus, Carl 167–168, 861, 933
Damasio, Antonio 289–296, 298, 302, 304–305, 307–310
Danesi, Marcel 44, 235, 246
Danto, Arthur C. 7
Danuser, Hermann 801, 815
Darwin, Charles 273–281, 283, 285, 287, 485
Debreu, Gérard 30
Debussy, Claude 157–158, 162, 349–351, 1034
Deleuze, Gilles 82, 182, 196, 313, 318–320, 325, 547, 564, 593, 596–597, 663, 682–683, 700, 890
Derrida, Jacques 7, 40, 120, 125, 128, 157, 160, 408, 423, 462, 571, 891
Descartes, René 54, 75, 87, 165, 182, 201, 221, 280, 309, 328, 332, 375, 667
Détienne, Marcel 145
Dewey, John 262, 264, 270
Dilthey, Wilhelm 11, 99, 103–105, 117, 412
DiMaggio, Paul 417, 423
Dinis, Dom 522
Dondero, Maria Guilia 610, 622, 806, 815
Dostoevsky, Fyodor 40–41, 43, 644, 714
Dreyer, Carl 707, 709
Dufourt, Hugues 804
Dunsby, Jonathan 803

Durand, Gilbert 15, 18–19, 33, 523, 537
Durant, Will 206, 221
Dürer, Albrecht 585

Eagleton, Terry 430–431
Eco, Umberto 11, 45, 83, 99–107, 109,
    117–118, 250, 257–258, 265, 270, 329,
    390, 402, 433, 456, 486, 489, 540,
    562–564, 654, 656, 694, 697, 700,
    742–743, 823, 863–864, 869, 871, 881,
    942, 954, 961, 979, 1021
Ehrat, Johannes 700, 709
Elias, Norbert 483, 489, 625, 657
Emmeche, Claus 20, 33, 341
Empedocles 81
Ende, Michael 432–433
Erdös, Paul 28
Erkko, J. H. 178, 631
Escoubas, Eliane 177
Espejo, José XXII, 1005, 1010

Faltin, Peter 883, 886–889, 893, 896
Fauré, Gabriel 157
Favareau, Donald 328, 341
Ferdinand II of Spain 517
Fermi, Enrico 337
Ferraro, Guido 505, 519, 692, 694,
    696–697, 1034
Fétis, François-Joseph 948–949
Fichte, Johann Gottlieb 182, 863, 866, 881
Filho, Mello Moraes 504, 506, 508, 511, 519
Fischer-Lichte, Erika 1001, 1019
Floros, Constantin 957–959, 967, 974–976,
    978–979
Flusser, Vilem 126, 128, 936
Fontanille, Jacques 140, 154, 238–240, 244,
    299, 511–512, 519, 571–572, 576, 600,
    610–612, 615–616, 619, 622, 725, 738,
    806, 815, 897–898, 999–1003, 1008,
    1019, 1034
Forsblom, Harri 742
Forster, Kurt 581–582, 584, 586, 597
Friedrich, Caspar David XXI, 96, 221–222,
    225, 237, 244–245, 341, 425, 624, 660,
    752, 854, 856, 862, 882, 943, 946
Fromm, Erich 468, 473, 478

Frye, Northrop 778, 799
Fubini, Enrico 806, 815

Gadamer, Georg 8, 11, 201, 204, 221,
    257–258, 744, 754, 819–822, 826–828,
    830–833, 837, 841–843, 961, 979
Gadegård, Nils H. 726, 729, 738
Gale, Richard M. 59, 74
Galilei, Galileo 15, 17
Gallen-Kallela, Akseli 178, 624, 634–639,
    642, 653–654, 656–657
Gamow, Georg 18, 33
Gandhi 449–450
Gardner, Howard 293, 309
Garfinkel, Harold 406, 409, 411–414,
    420–421, 423, 426
Garrido, Miguel XXII, 999–1019, 1032
Gauguin, Paul 603
Gavrilov, Andrey 914
Genette, Gérard 715, 828, 843, 863, 867,
    881, 942, 954
Geninasca, Jacques 132, 135, 154
Gennep, Arnold van 696–697
Giddens, Anthony 413, 423, 469, 472, 478
Gilels, Emil 913–914
Ginsberg, Allen 668, 683
Ginzburg, Grigory 915
Giorgione 719
Glass, Philip 576, 659, 661–662, 666,
    668–684, 784, 1023
Globokar, Vinko 889
Gödel, Kurt 32
Goehr, Lydia 802, 815
Goethe, J. W. von 726, 743, 745, 803, 815,
    987, 990, 996
Goffman, Ervin 408–409, 416, 424, 426
Gogh, Vincent van 603, 605
Goldenweiser, Alexander 906, 915
Goodman, Lenn E. 935
Gołąb, Maciej 941–942, 955
Granger, Gilles-Gaston 173
Granö, Gabriel 922–923, 938
Great, Gregory the 726, 732, 738
Greimas, A. J. 1, 4, 7, 28, 77–79, 84, 96,
    128, 131–135, 139–141, 143, 149, 154,
    160–162, 164–165, 167, 172–174, 179,

181–182, 187, 189, 195–196, 238–240, 244, 246, 249–250, 260, 278, 407, 420–421, 462, 482, 504, 511–512, 519, 571–572, 576, 591, 597–598, 621–622, 685, 687, 689–691, 694–697, 699, 701–703, 709, 712, 716, 719–720, 773, 788, 801–807, 809, 811, 813–817, 850, 853, 861, 877, 886, 894, 909, 933–934, 938, 957, 959, 963–964, 970–971, 979, 1002, 1027, 1035
Greisch, Jean 175
Grinberg, Maria 906, 912
Gronow, Pekka 407, 424
Grout, Donald Jay 167
Grzybek, Peter 234, 244
Guattari, Felix 182, 196, 313, 318–319, 325, 547, 564, 593, 596–597, 890
Guillaume, Paul 804, 816, 844

Haavikko, Paavo 631, 641, 656–657
Hadamard, Jacques 15, 26, 28, 33
Halbwach, Maurice 745
Hartmann, Viktor 481, 485–486, 488
Hatten, Robert S. 456, 807, 816, 861, 957–959, 972, 980, 1025
Hauer, Christian 351, 807, 816, 845
Hegel, G. Fr. W. 2, 5, 65–66, 77, 79, 86, 96, 123, 167, 170, 177–178, 182, 192, 201–203, 221–222, 225, 237–239, 244, 281, 299, 313, 316, 321–322, 325, 338–339, 341, 462, 498, 540, 676, 683, 703, 874, 882, 897, 934, 973, 1002
Heidegger, Martin 8, 11, 15, 17, 77, 93, 99, 103–104, 107–109, 118–119, 123, 158–160, 164, 169, 181–183, 185–187, 189–194, 196, 201, 204, 222, 226, 229–230, 236–237, 239, 244–245, 252–253, 256, 258, 268–269, 273–277, 279–283, 285, 287, 338–339, 341, 353, 462, 527, 536–537, 541–542, 565, 602, 668, 687, 701, 819–821, 823–830, 832, 834, 836–844, 873, 882, 934, 1022
Heisenberg, Werner 15, 17–18
Heiskala, Risto 407, 424
Hermite, Charles 27–28
Hesse, Hermann 124, 128, 743
Hewitt, John P. 213, 222

Hintikka, Jaakko 93
Hjelmslev, Louis 7, 19, 102–103, 260
Hobbes, Thomas 96
Hoffmann, E. T. A. 900
Hoffmeyer, Jesper 20, 33, 341
Hofstadter, Douglas 19
Holbrook, Morris B. 460, 462–463, 469, 478
Holmberg, Kalle 640
Homer 31, 561, 565, 629, 806, 881
Horowitz, Vladimir 911–913
Hotakainen, Kari 757–759, 762–763, 766, 769–770
Hugo, Victor 755, 803, 817, 995, 998
Huizinga, Johan 568, 570, 573, 576
Hume, David 56, 201–202, 222
Husserl, Edmund 11, 50–51, 74, 112, 122, 182–183, 187–188, 196, 201, 203–204, 222, 226–228, 230, 232, 245, 258, 406, 420, 600, 887

Igumnov, Konstantin 906, 914
Ingold, Tim 145, 154
Ivanov, Vyacheslav V. 234, 245, 248

Jacquette, Dale 68–70, 72, 75
Jakobson, Roman 37, 46, 173, 250, 260, 265, 270
James, William 53, 59, 64, 68, 73–76, 96, 145, 154, 182–183, 201, 203, 221–222, 244, 270, 280, 290, 292–293, 298, 302, 309–311, 380, 383–384, 387, 425, 427, 478, 685, 689–690, 693, 696, 738, 790–791, 800, 804, 1033, 1035
Jankélévitch, Vladimir 157–166, 1023–1024
Jaspers, Karl 77, 237, 245, 252, 258, 282, 659, 668, 670–673, 682, 701, 708, 731, 934
Jaulin, Robert 167, 171, 173–174, 179
Jeremiah 491, 494–500
Jiránek, Jaroslav 809
Johansen, Jørgen Dines 243–245, 799
Jolles, André 19, 173
Joyce, James 78, 96, 408, 424
Jullien, François 145, 154

Kafka, Franz 139, 169, 663, 806
Kaipainen, Mauri 259, 261, 263–264, 266, 269–270

Kajanus, Robert 172, 632
Kant, Immanuel 2, 47–50, 53–56, 58–61,
    65–66, 71, 74–75, 77, 88, 100–103,
    105–107, 118–120, 123, 125, 182,
    201–202, 217, 222, 225, 237, 245, 277,
    281, 299, 313–315, 321, 325, 456, 462,
    498, 540, 863–865, 870, 882, 934
Karbusický, Vladímir XIX, 803, 805,
    809, 816
Katkus, Donatas 905, 917
Kaufman, Gabrielle 942, 955
Kaurismäki, Aki 707
Kazantzakis, Nikos 716
Kelly, Richard 424, 663, 682
Kerenyi, Karl 179
Keršytė, Nijolė 135, 154
Keynes, John Maynard 340–341
Kierkegaard, Søren 2, 7–8, 87–88, 123, 167,
    201–203, 222, 237, 245, 252, 282, 299,
    313, 316–318, 325, 338–339, 342, 462,
    483, 527, 601, 603, 726, 794–795, 934
Kilpinen, Erkki 290, 296–301, 310
Kissin, Evgeny 915
Kivi, Aleksis 623–624, 630–631, 640–643,
    645, 649, 651–652, 654–658, 744
Kivinen, S. Albert 79
Klinkenberg, Jean-Marie 608–609, 622
Koster, Henry 503, 519
Kramer, Jonathan 666, 683, 861, 961, 980
Kregor, Jonathan 941–943, 945,
    947–948, 955
Kreutzwald, Friedrich Reinhold 624
Kristeva, Julia 7, 39–40, 44, 250, 363, 369,
    390, 403, 462, 571, 596–597, 611, 622,
    743, 1026
Kriszat, Georg 227, 247
Kroeber, Alfred 686, 694, 697
Kull, Kalevi 226, 245, 279, 341

Lacan, Jacques 313, 322, 324–325, 390,
    403, 703
Laclau, Ernesto 410, 424
Lamartine, Alphonse de 27
Landowski, Eric 131–132, 134–136, 138–142,
    144–146, 148, 150, 152, 154–155, 407,
    424, 504, 519, 614–615, 622, 1027
Langer, Susanne 234, 246, 366, 371

Launis, Armas 172, 631, 640
Leech, Geoffrey 242, 245
Lehto, Leevi 78
Lehto, Otto 273, 277, 287
Leibniz, Gottfried Wilhelm von 29, 33, 77,
    83–85, 88, 93, 96, 866, 882
Leino, Eino 178, 640
Lenin, Vladimir 422, 901–902, 904
Leonardo da Vinci 392
Leopardi, Giacomo 139, 955
Lermontov, Mikhail 158
Lessing, Gotthold Ephraim 169
Lévi-Strauss, Claude 150, 155, 167–168,
    170–176, 179, 282, 889–890, 1035
Levinas, Emmanuel 39, 44–46, 251–254,
    258, 1033
Lévy-Bruhl, Lucien 167
Leyden, Lukas van 201, 585–586
Li, You zheng 699
Lidov, David 807
Lipps, Theodor 6
Liszt, Franz 157–158, 167, 172, 804, 806,
    812, 814–815, 847, 859, 861–862, 906,
    941–942, 945, 953, 955, 960, 979,
    1023–1025
Littlefield, Richard 163, 370, 537, 817
Lock, Grahame 171, 437–438
Locke, John 201–202, 212, 222, 260
Lönnrot, Elias 625–628, 631, 639, 642,
    653, 657
Lotman, Yury 7, 162, 176, 232, 234–235,
    245–246, 273, 280, 569–571, 574–577,
    623–624, 652, 657, 701, 947, 955
Lovecraft, H. P. 773–800, 1021–1022
Luckmann, Thomas 243–244, 406–407, 409,
    419, 421–422, 686, 688, 697
Luhmann, Niklas 209, 222
Lukacs, György 19
Lyotard, Jean-François 167–168, 178–180,
    468, 479, 671

MacCormac, Earl R. 34
Macdonel, Grisell 537
Mâche, François-Bernard 804, 806, 816,
    936, 938, 1025
Maeder, Costantin 816, 862, 873–874, 882
Magnússon, Ágúst 676, 678, 683

Mahler, Gustav XXI, 93, 957–963, 965, 967–981, 1025
Mairet, Philip 672–673, 683
Majava, Heikki 641, 643, 657
Malpas, Jeff 65, 75
Malraux, André 175
Man, Paul de 7
Mandelbrot, B. 19, 804
Manen, Max van 226, 231–232, 247
Mann, Thomas 378, 387, 743, 752
Mannheim, Karl 412, 421, 425
Marcel, Gabriel 77, 327–328, 341
Marcus, Solomon 15–16, 18–20, 22, 24, 26, 28, 30, 32, 34, 341, 753, 882, 895, 1028
Maritain, Jean 252
Martini, Simone 635
Martins, Francisco 390, 537, 1033
Marx, Karl 122, 275, 314–315, 339, 419, 425, 439, 1033
Matsuev, Denis 914
Mattheson, Johann 855, 961
Maturana, U. 19, 209, 222
Maupassant, Guy de 712, 716
Mauss, Marcel 412
McLuhan, Marshall 22, 34, 126, 128
McTaggart, J. M. E. 77–79, 82, 86, 88–93, 96
Mead, Georg Herbert 293, 296–302, 308, 310, 406, 414–415, 425, 427, 898
Meeus, Nicolas 816
Memling, Hans 586
Mendel, Gregor 274
Mendeleev, Dmitry 173–174
Merleau-Ponty, Maurice 8, 11, 13, 37–38, 44, 138–139, 141, 155, 174, 181–193, 196–197, 201, 205, 222, 226, 230–231, 246, 252, 341–342, 600, 602, 606, 617, 622, 829, 843
Merrell, Floyd 33, 44, 292–293, 298, 310, 601, 606
Metz, Christian 699–700
Meyer, Michel 406, 411, 419–421, 425–426, 827, 843, 950, 955
Michelangelo 595–596, 598
Mickūnas, Algis 186, 197
Miereanu, Costin 804, 807, 810, 816, 844, 1036

Miko, František 883–886, 896
Milhaud, Darius 172
Mill, John Stuart 84, 221, 411, 419, 425, 439
Milner, Marion 391, 403
Mirka, Danuta 810–811, 816, 960–961, 980
Mizoguchi, Kenji 707
Mohr, John W. 221, 407, 425, 754, 843, 979
Monelle, Raymond 262, 270, 481, 490, 807–808, 810, 816–817, 957–959, 961, 965, 976–977, 979–980, 1025
Monet, Claude 350
Moniuszko, Stanisław XXI, 948, 953–954
Monk, Meredith 37, 895–896
Moore, A. W. 50, 75
Moore, G. E. 78, 97
Moore, Henry 401
Moore, Allan 873, 882
Moore, F. C. 986, 988, 991, 995, 998
Morgan, Michael L. 53, 427
Morris, Charles 7, 120–121, 128, 310, 478–479, 659, 667
Morse, Marston 31
Mozart, W. A. XIX, 15, 26, 97, 214, 223, 483, 489, 520, 537, 811, 814, 817, 861–862, 938, 945, 967, 978, 980–981, 1020, 1033
Musil, Robert 139
Mussorgsky, Modest XVI, 157, 162, 481–490, 953, 1026

Napoleon 168
Nattiez, Jean-Jacques 807–808, 816–817, 829, 843
Neuhaus, Heinrich 906, 912–915, 917
Newton, Isaac 15, 17, 29, 45, 83, 275
Nicomachus 200
Nietzsche, Friedrich 82, 92, 122, 158, 163, 279, 281, 410, 425, 660, 668, 681, 752, 844, 847, 859, 862, 866, 877–878, 881–882
Nishida, Kitaro 181–189, 191–193, 197
Nöth, Winfrid 9–10, 13, 34, 260, 270, 296, 328, 341, 384, 387
Nummi, Jyrki 629–630, 657, 759–760, 771, 1027

Oborin, Lev 912
Ortega y Gasset, José 94, 670, 683
Ozu, Yasujirō 707, 709

Pallasmaa, Juhani 602, 605–606
Palonen, Kari 411, 416, 425
Pankhurst, Tom 96, 812
Panofsky, Erwin 412, 425, 588, 598
Papanek, Viktor 451, 457
Papst, Josephine 92
Paraske, Larin 632
Parret, Hermann 132, 155, 157, 160, 172
Parvizi, Josef 290–292, 302, 310
Pascoaes, Teixeira de 522, 537
Pasolini, Pier Paolo 700
Peirce, Charles Sanders XV, 3, 7–8, 20, 28, 59, 75, 92–93, 99, 103–107, 111, 118, 120–121, 127–129, 132, 157, 160, 250, 260, 270, 273–281, 283, 285–287, 289–301, 303–304, 306–311, 373–377, 379–382, 384, 387–388, 406, 411–412, 415, 420, 426, 527, 562, 564, 600, 605, 700–701, 708–709, 762, 824, 844, 887, 898, 943, 945, 955, 1021
Perec, Georges 661, 683
Perron, Paul 79
Pessoa, Fernando 522, 537
Petitimbert, Jean Paul 144, 155
Petitot, Jean 804
Petri, Egon 96, 913
Petrus Hispanus (Peter of Spain) 36, 44, 1033
Picasso, Pablo 394, 402
Pike, Kenneth 240, 246, 704
Pinelli, Antonio 581–582, 586, 598
Planck, Max 377, 387
Pletnev, Mikhail 914
Poe, Edgard Allan 38, 45, 557, 565, 794, 800
Pogorelich, Ivo 915
Poincaré, Henri 15, 27–28, 374–375, 387
Poinsot, John 10, 12
Pontormo, Jacopo XVII, 579–589, 591–593, 595–598
Ponzio, Augusto 8, 35–38, 40–46, 304, 311, 1033
Popper, Karl 242, 246, 935

Poulenc, Francis 172
Poutanen, Samuli XVIII, 645, 648–650
Powell, Anna 663, 683
Powell, William W. 406, 409–410, 412–413, 417, 421, 423, 426
Prévost, Edwin 885, 896
Propp, Vladimir 19, 83, 173, 179, 700, 773, 788, 810, 853
Proust, Marcel 5, 78, 139, 600, 606, 743, 747, 755, 847, 859, 935
Pyrrö, Laura 919, 921, 924
Pythagoras 25, 29, 31

Rabinow, Paul 145, 155
Rachmaninov, Sergei 906
Ratner, Leonard 810, 817, 960–961, 980
Ratz, Erwin 970–971
Reggio, Godfrey 659, 668, 670–673, 679–680, 683–684
Reich, Steve 176, 659–660, 666–670, 681, 683, 900
Reinotti, Francesco 695
Richter, Sviatoslav 913–915, 917
Ricoeur, Paul 7, 28, 122, 128, 364, 371, 850, 898
Riemann, B. 28, 803, 817
Rigel, Henri-Joseph 995, 998
Rimsky-Korsakov, Nikolai 158, 172, 484
Robinson, A. 29, 32, 222, 244, 341, 537, 689, 713
Romero, Silvio 503–507, 520
Rorty, Richard 7, 114–115, 118, 249, 258, 262, 270, 276, 881
Rosset, Clement 174
Rousseau, Jean-Jacques 81, 570, 806, 810, 991, 998
Rovati, Pier Aldo 103
Rubinstein, Anton 906
Rubinstein, Nikolai 906
Russell, Bertrand 19, 28, 79, 92, 96, 477, 887
Ruyer, Raymond 804, 817

Saarikoski, Pentti 78
Saarinen, Tero XVIII, 623–624, 630, 644–651, 653–657

Safonov, Vassily 906
Sallinen, Aulis 623–624, 630–631, 638, 640–644, 649, 653–654, 656–657
Salmenhaara, Erkki 172
Santaella, Maria Lucia 8, 384, 388
Sapir, E. 21, 34, 550
Sarto, Andrea del XVII, 581, 589–590, 598
Sartre, Jean-Paul 2, 7–8, 50, 77, 119, 123–124, 139, 141, 155, 201, 204–205, 215, 223, 237, 239, 246, 252–254, 279, 282, 299, 330, 338, 355, 407, 415–416, 421, 425–426, 433, 462, 479, 483, 527, 601, 603, 668–669, 672–673, 676, 683, 686–687, 697, 777, 795, 898, 934
Sassatelli, Roberta 459
Satie, Erik 165, 172, 662
Saussure, Ferdinand de 6–7, 19, 37, 77, 120–121, 129, 169, 250, 260, 278, 686, 688, 692, 694, 697, 700–701, 706–707, 887
Schantz, Johan Filip von 631
Scheler, Max 19
Schelling, F. W. J. 5, 77, 82, 86–87, 93, 96, 178, 793
Schleiermacher, Friedrich 943
Schmidt, Benjamin
Schmidt, Raymund
Schmidt, Siegfried
Schönberg, Arnold 165, 172
Schrodinger, Erwin 20
Schubert, Franz 172, 674, 677, 683, 861, 980
Schumacher, Ernst 449–451, 457
Schütz, Alfred 406–408, 419–420, 424, 427
Schwartz, Shalom 459–460, 462, 465, 472, 479–480
Schwarz, Boris 901–902, 906, 917
Seailles, Gabriel 26
Searle, John 22, 34
Sebeok, Thomas A. 7, 9, 13, 20, 44, 46, 209, 223, 233–235, 242, 245–246, 250, 270, 280, 299, 689, 701, 886, 1032–1033
Seneca 878
Serres, Michel 167, 174, 175
Shannon, Claude 19–20, 265, 270, 378, 388
Shapiro, Michael 807
Shelley, Percy Bysshe 430, 674
Shostakovich, Dmitry 906, 963

Sibelius, Jean 164, 167, 172, 176, 178, 249, 271, 389, 395, 399–403, 623–624, 631–635, 638, 640–641, 644–645, 647, 650, 653–656, 658, 759, 817, 933–934, 938, 1031, 1035
Siloti, Alexander 906
Sini, Carlo 160, 763, 769, 824, 844
Sjöstrand, Carl Eneas XVII, 624, 628–629, 639, 658
Skinner, Burrhus Frederic 410–411, 425, 427
Sloterdijk, Peter 254, 258
Snyder, Jack 528, 537, 679
Söderblom, Ulf 640
Sofronitsky, Vladimir 906, 911
Sokolov, Grigory 914
Somfai, László 809
Sontag, Susan 708
Soulez, Antonie 92–93, 96
Souris, André 803–804, 817
Sparre, Louis 632
Spinoza, Baruch 77, 85–86, 93, 96, 877
Stalin, Josif 750, 904
Stasov, Vladimir 484
Stendhal 151–152
Stern, Robert 53, 55–56, 58, 61, 75, 97, 244, 346, 351, 460, 480, 1035
Sterne, Laurence 139
Stjernfelt, Frederik 233, 246, 335, 341
Stoianova, Ivanka 807, 810, 812
Stokhof, Martin 70–72, 75
Stonier, Tom 20, 34
Stout, Rowland 54, 75
Stravinsky, Igor 164, 172, 249, 271, 403, 657–658, 817, 934, 938, 1033
Strawson, P. F. 55, 76
Svevo, Italo 139

Tanalı, Ziya 601–604, 606
Tarasti, Eero passim
Tarkovsky, Andrey 707
Tawaststjerna, Erik 401–403, 632–633, 658
Taylor, Charles 52–54, 56–62, 72–76, 222, 246, 310, 405, 424, 518, 520, 594, 598
Tazartes, Maurizia 585, 590–591, 593, 595, 598
Thales 31
Theodotion 728

Tilghman, B. R. 61, 63–64, 76
Tolbert, Pamela S. 415, 417, 421, 427
Tolkien, John Ronald 624, 653, 658
Topelius, Zachris 178, 627–628, 631, 653
Toporov, Vladimir N. 234, 248
Townsend, Patricia 391, 393, 401, 403
Toynbee, Arnold 22
Trifonov, Daniil 914
Troyat, Henri 726, 739
Tully, James 53, 76, 427
Turner, Victor 145, 155

Ujfalussy, József 801–802, 806, 809–810, 817
Umiker-Sebeok, Jean 37, 46

Valéry, Paul 27, 820, 847, 862
Välimäki, Susanna 363, 371
Valsiner, Jaan XV, 1–2, 4, 6, 118, 223, 271, 302–305, 308, 311, 500, 771, 844, 917, 1035
Varela, F. 19, 209, 222
Vasari, Giorgio 579–581, 585, 587–588, 593, 595–596, 598
Vattimo, Gianni 100–101, 103, 106, 118, 120, 125, 129, 252, 697, 826–827, 844, 1029
Vecchione, Bernard XIX, 348, 351, 807, 816, 819–820, 822–826, 828–840, 842–845, 1034, 1036
Vermeylen, Jacques 726, 728–729, 731, 735, 739
Vernant, Jean-Pierre 145, 154
Villa-Lobos, Heitor XX–XXI, 172, 530–531, 919–921, 926–939, 1029, 1035
Volli, Ugo 257–258, 573, 577, 1021, 1029
Volodos, Arcadi 914
Voloshinov, Valentin 43
Vygotsky, Lev 110, 118, 297–299, 302, 308, 311, 1035

Wagner, Richard 1, 3, 87, 91, 97, 117, 157–158, 161, 164, 172, 214, 223, 249, 271, 350, 403, 520, 537, 658, 743, 753, 755, 817, 847–851, 853–862, 864, 900, 938, 980–981, 984, 1020, 1033
Wahl, Jean 77, 158–159, 462, 792–793, 860, 862, 934
Wallace, Robert M. 168, 479

Warburg, Aby 597–598
Warren, Austin 700
Wąsik, Elżbieta Magdalena 199, 212–213, 220, 223, 371
Wąsik, Zdzisław 225–226, 228, 236, 242, 247–248, 371
Watzka, Heinrich 69
Weaver, Richard 265
Weber, Carl Maria von 995
Weber, Max 407, 412, 420, 427, 439
Wegelius, Martin 178
Weierstrass, K. 27–28
Weissmann, Augustus 19
Welby, Victoria Lady 8, 44, 311
Wheeler, Wendy 328, 337, 342, 800
Whitehead, A. N. 19
Whorf, Benjamin Lee 21, 34, 550
Wiener, Norbert 20, 402, 862
Wischnitzer, Rachel 583–584, 598
Wittgenstein, Ludwig 47, 51, 53, 63–64, 67–72, 74–79, 86, 92–97, 250, 258, 568, 577, 668, 883, 887
Wölfflin, Heinrich 612, 622
Woltjer, Jan 335–337, 341
Woolf, Virginia 139
Wright, Georg Henrik von 68, 76, 78–79, 92–93, 97, 265, 267–268, 271, 401, 425

Xenakis, Iannis 892, 1036

Yesipova, Annette (Anna) 906
Younghusband, Francis 922–923, 938
Yudina, Maria 906

Zak, Yakov 914
Zaliznyak, Andrey A. 234, 248
Zapffe, Peter Vessel 329, 334, 336, 338–339, 342
Zerubavel, Eviatar 408, 411, 420, 428
Zhao, Henry 703, 709
Žižek, Slavoj 593, 598
Zlatev, Jordan 208, 210–211, 223
Zoonen, Lisbeth van 115, 118
Zucker, Lynne G. 411, 415, 417, 421, 427–428
Zweig, Stefan 743

Subject index

act-Signs 2, 122, 346, 701, 780, 784–785, 787, 792, 796–797, 821, 823–824
Advertising 453, 478–479, 659–661, 663, 667, 671
Affect 39, 65, 67, 84, 110, 128, 137–138, 140–141, 153, 185, 279, 295–297, 302, 304, 308, 346, 349, 358, 395, 440, 526, 582, 593–596, 646, 686–687, 690, 696, 775, 811, 814, 825, 854, 894, 897, 916, 961–962, 965–966, 971
Affirmation 16, 85, 158, 190, 193, 215, 218, 348–349, 379, 382–383, 460, 462–463, 466, 471–472, 476, 488, 491, 511, 527, 532, 541, 607, 611–612, 616, 618–619, 621, 641, 659–660, 664–665, 676, 679, 687–689, 708, 753, 774–776, 778, 785, 857
Agency 57, 60, 62, 144, 328, 407, 410, 412–415, 418–419, 422–423, 425, 1036
Alienation 126–127, 218, 279, 281, 284, 327, 329, 338–339, 402, 416, 471, 593, 751
Angst 279, 338, 461
Animals 9–10, 12, 20, 108, 200, 207, 211, 225–229, 233, 235, 241–243, 246–247, 277, 279, 281, 283–284, 286–287, 294, 329, 331, 334, 336, 338, 396, 630, 882
Architecture 5, 148, 349, 357, 389, 402, 582, 599–600, 605–606, 1030
Arrangement 32, 137, 207, 378, 442, 450, 784, 941–945, 947–949, 951–955, 1019
Autism 127, 353–355, 359–360, 362–364, 368–371, 719, 1026
Autobiographical self 290–294, 302, 306

Beauty 5, 217, 356, 531, 551, 579–580, 595–596, 604, 613, 643, 676, 678, 695, 726–727, 731, 760, 780, 889, 903, 907, 922–924, 934–935, 972
Behaviorism 433
Being-for-myself 2, 217–218, 238, 240, 463, 482–483, 488, 527–528, 600–601, 762, 867, 872, 876–879, 909

Being-in-myself 2, 217–218, 238, 240, 360, 463, 482, 527–528, 600, 762, 863, 867–868, 870, 876–880, 909
Belief 28, 52, 54–56, 58–61, 63, 67, 76, 79, 88, 104, 117, 128, 132, 165, 202, 219, 241, 260, 275, 280, 287, 294–296, 301, 304, 307–308, 334, 373, 375–377, 379, 383, 385, 460, 463, 516, 543, 552–553, 705–709, 750, 763, 766, 780, 793, 861, 908–909, 916, 962, 1032
Bible 158, 222, 491, 493, 496, 500, 553, 703, 713, 738, 955
Bildungsroman 759, 770
Biology 16, 19–20, 37, 222, 233, 243, 245–247, 273–274, 276, 278, 280, 285, 328, 334, 341, 548, 804
Body 32–33, 37–38, 41, 84, 88–89, 110, 113, 141, 153, 175, 183–186, 188, 197, 201, 205, 208–210, 212, 214, 218, 221, 230–232, 238–240, 260, 262–263, 266, 270, 277, 280, 282, 285–286, 290, 292–293, 302, 309, 318–319, 322, 328, 336, 338, 340, 343–347, 349–351, 354, 360, 362–363, 366, 371, 384–385, 398, 400, 470, 492, 498–499, 525–527, 543–544, 554, 571, 589, 600, 607, 610, 615–616, 618–619, 627, 643, 647, 650, 652, 657, 679–680, 683, 693, 696, 703–706, 718, 732, 747, 754, 760–762, 766, 779–780, 782, 787–788, 798–799, 857, 860–861, 869–870, 890, 892, 894–895, 907, 925, 933, 965–966, 971, 989, 999–1003, 1005, 1007–1011, 1013, 1015–1019, 1031
Brasil 503, 519–520, 937, 951
Buddhism 181, 183, 186, 546, 1022, 1030
Bureaucratization 429–435, 437, 439, 441, 443, 445, 447, 449, 451, 453, 455, 457

Calligraphy 607–613, 615–621
Capitalism 319, 325, 427, 547, 564, 668, 751
Chinese 186, 327, 707, 709, 1028
Chora 363, 571

1050 — Subject index

Choreography 350, 623, 630, 644–651, 654–655, 895
Christianity 85, 127, 492–493, 554, 716, 965
Chronotope 757–758, 1030
Cognitive 20, 24, 40–41, 47, 53, 56, 100, 106, 110–111, 137, 145, 147, 182, 199, 202, 208, 210, 212, 223, 225, 232, 259–264, 266–267, 269–271, 277, 279, 287, 293, 297, 309, 315, 330, 350, 355, 357, 359, 361–362, 365–366, 375, 417–418, 504, 534, 539–540, 544, 549–550, 562, 600, 621, 714, 754, 807, 983, 1024, 1026–1027
Colonialism 450, 954
Commercial 99, 659–667, 671, 676–677, 681–682, 690, 712, 714, 750, 905–906
Communication 3–4, 9–10, 15, 20, 22–23, 37–39, 44–46, 114, 117–121, 123–129, 136–137, 139, 176, 199, 203, 205–206, 208–213, 215–216, 220–223, 228, 232, 235, 242–247, 254, 256, 258, 261–263, 265, 267, 270, 279, 293, 300, 309, 343, 353–356, 358–359, 361–364, 366–368, 370–371, 384–385, 388, 401, 422, 434, 436–437, 448, 468, 475–476, 479–480, 482, 527, 535, 537, 539–540, 558, 569, 574, 599–600, 608, 617–620, 650, 686–687, 703, 705, 709, 741, 750–752, 754, 777–778, 784, 789, 807, 839, 844, 859, 873, 883–887, 892, 894, 897, 914, 916, 988–989, 991–992, 1021–1023, 1026, 1028–1029, 1033, 1037
Composer 157, 162, 169, 172, 175–176, 265, 349–350, 359, 362, 394, 481–487, 489, 530, 619, 631, 633–634, 640, 644, 660–661, 670, 677, 752, 803–804, 806, 809, 814–815, 824, 848–849, 854, 857, 870–871, 873, 885, 891, 895, 897–899, 901, 903, 906, 910, 913, 915–916, 919–920, 926, 928–929, 931–936, 942, 945, 950, 953, 955, 960, 963, 967, 973–978, 983–986, 989–992, 994–996, 1014, 1018, 1022–1023, 1025–1026, 1029, 1031, 1033
Computation 18, 576
Condition humaine 432–434
Connectionism 266–267

Consumer 6, 430, 459–463, 465–472, 476–480, 661–662, 1021, 1027
Core self 291–294, 302, 306–307
Counterfactuality 574
Creativity 15–16, 26–28, 30–32, 106, 169, 178, 218, 292–293, 310, 353, 389–391, 393–399, 401–403, 435, 601, 746, 752, 884–885, 895–896, 900, 919, 921, 924, 927, 933, 1029
Cultural heritage 249, 257, 353, 364, 389–390, 399, 401, 403, 491, 493, 495, 497, 499, 501–502, 751, 902, 905, 922, 927, 937, 941–942, 952–954, 1022, 1025–1026, 1029–1030, 1033, 1035
Cybernetics 19, 209, 279

Deconstruction 101, 125, 197, 225, 242, 253, 281, 438, 533, 934, 938
Desire 33, 35–36, 83–84, 105–106, 110, 125, 128, 141, 144, 177, 215, 218, 255, 262, 313–314, 322–324, 460–463, 467, 469–470, 476–480, 498, 511, 523, 525, 527, 529–531, 533, 535–536, 543, 545, 549, 554, 595, 600, 602, 661, 671, 682, 693, 701, 704–705, 725, 761–763, 777, 899, 908
Dialogical self 2, 6, 356–357
Dialogism 35, 40–42, 258, 753
Duration 96, 107–108, 166, 336, 610, 667, 810, 926
Dynamic object 107, 109, 112, 114–117
dysphoria 512–513, 579, 582, 591–594, 813, 971

Eco-philosophy 329
Education 37, 81, 217, 231, 247, 291, 293, 310, 343, 356, 358, 422, 429–430, 433, 435, 447, 455–457, 467, 545, 565, 568, 570, 588, 597, 625, 627, 631, 642, 653, 663, 676, 683, 691, 709, 719, 749, 762–764, 901–902, 933, 953, 1023–1024, 1026, 1028, 1030–1031, 1037
Embodiment 40–41, 43, 77, 80–81, 84–85, 87, 89, 100, 110, 176, 210, 232, 240, 809, 900, 907, 1018

Emotions 20, 105, 124, 138, 208–210, 212, 215, 233, 289–293, 295, 297–305, 307–309, 311, 346–347, 356, 361, 463, 593, 605, 660, 676, 702, 709, 731, 745, 751, 767, 789, 912, 985, 991–992, 1013
Entropy 20, 373–375, 377–379, 381, 383–387, 776, 787
Enunciation 364, 519, 608–612, 615, 618–620, 718, 824–825, 833, 837, 840, 867, 876, 885, 912
Environment 3, 101, 106, 110, 127, 135–136, 141, 151, 154, 187, 200–201, 208, 210, 214, 219–220, 225–227, 230, 240–241, 243, 260, 262–263, 266, 269, 278, 281, 283, 289, 293–294, 296, 301, 303, 308, 333–334, 337, 353, 357, 369, 382, 390–391, 403, 445, 450, 470, 476, 481–483, 488, 499, 524, 527, 529, 562, 627, 638–639, 664, 674, 681, 707, 709, 864, 892–893, 904, 923, 926, 936, 1014, 1017, 1035, 1037
Estonian 235, 341, 488, 624, 747, 1035
Ethics 60, 63, 67–72, 74–76, 85, 90, 96, 200, 221, 275, 281, 287, 293, 341–342, 380, 460–461, 464, 467, 469–474, 477–479, 608, 618–619, 1032
Ethnomethodology 405–406, 409, 414, 420, 423
Euphoria 512–513, 579, 582, 588, 591–594, 813, 971, 985
Europe 161, 402, 432, 434–435, 519, 548, 669, 704, 741–747, 749–756, 808, 890, 893, 906, 933–934, 938, 998, 1023, 1025, 1028, 1030, 1036
Europeanity 741, 753
Exact sciences 15, 17, 19, 21, 23, 25, 27, 29, 31–33, 802
Existential 1–13, 15–16, 23, 25, 28, 32, 34–36, 39, 46, 51, 76–79, 81–83, 85, 87–89, 91–93, 95, 97, 99–100, 112, 116–117, 119, 121–129, 131–133, 135, 137, 139–143, 145, 147, 149–153, 155, 157, 160–161, 164, 166, 172, 181–182, 184, 186, 195, 199–200, 203, 214–220, 223, 225–227, 229–232, 236–241, 246, 249–259, 261–271, 273–283, 285–287, 289, 291, 293, 295–297, 299, 301, 303, 305–309, 311, 313–325, 327, 329–331, 333–337, 339–344, 346–348, 350–351, 353–359, 361–363, 365–367, 369–371, 373, 379–384, 388–391, 393, 395, 397, 399, 401, 403, 405–407, 409, 414, 420, 424–425, 427, 433, 457, 459–463, 465–478, 480–483, 485–492, 495, 498–501, 510, 513, 521, 523, 526, 528, 533, 537, 540–542, 553, 556, 563, 567–568, 571, 573–576, 599–603, 605–621, 623–624, 654–655, 658–661, 663–665, 667–671, 673–677, 679–681, 683, 685–689, 691, 693–697, 699, 701–703, 705, 707–709, 716, 725–728, 731–732, 737, 739, 741–745, 751–753, 755–758, 771, 773–781, 783–785, 787–789, 791–797, 799–800, 819–827, 829, 831–837, 839, 841, 843–845, 847, 849, 854, 858–860, 862–864, 879, 882–889, 891–898, 903, 908, 916–917, 919, 928, 933–934, 937–938, 941, 954–955, 983–984, 986, 992, 994–995, 997–999, 1001–1003, 1021, 1026, 1035, 1037
Existentialism 1, 7, 11, 119, 123–124, 203, 214, 237, 249, 251–254, 256, 273, 276, 279–280, 327, 329, 338, 340, 355, 461, 465, 479, 567, 569, 571, 573, 575, 577, 605, 659–661, 663, 667–669, 672–673, 676, 679, 682–683, 687, 690, 706
Exosemiotics 208
Exosigns 216, 599, 796

Fallibilism 277
Feminine 158, 397, 550–551, 595, 632, 967, 992, 996
Firstness 103, 162, 275, 277, 291, 293–294, 300–301, 304–307, 379, 382, 527, 600–601, 708, 762

Gelassenheit 191, 824, 843, 858
Gesamtkunstwerk 162, 176, 975
Gestaltpsychologie 179
Globality 335, 343, 345, 354, 363, 369–370, 750, 1026
God 9–10, 12, 47, 49–50, 52–56, 58–59, 61–66, 70–72, 74–75, 79, 85–86, 144,

158, 169, 186, 194, 279, 284, 314–317, 336, 377, 403, 491–495, 503, 507–508, 511–512, 522, 543–544, 546, 548–551, 553–557, 559, 563–564, 590, 607–608, 628, 641, 677, 693, 705–706, 727, 729–730, 732–737, 781, 850, 901, 927–929, 931–932, 969, 987
Grace 21, 33, 53, 57–58, 84–86, 676, 678, 708, 992–993, 1005, 1007
Ground 1, 55, 120, 133, 144, 168, 170, 176, 179, 191–192, 194–195, 210, 229, 245, 252, 275, 301, 340, 343–344, 375, 381, 383, 385, 401, 423, 454, 465, 472, 546, 554, 563–564, 573, 581, 589, 595, 608, 631, 639, 647, 716, 763, 775, 778, 790, 807, 919, 922, 927, 937, 954, 959, 977, 1011
Growth 81, 212, 214, 286, 340, 342, 356, 360, 369, 373–375, 377, 379, 381–383, 385, 387, 430–431, 442, 647, 705, 741, 752, 759, 794, 806, 816–817, 829, 864

Hedonism 460, 466–467, 469–471, 473–475, 478
Helsinki 51, 76, 79, 96–97, 99, 117, 161, 181, 197, 236, 246, 270–271, 286, 309–310, 327, 370–371, 401, 456, 500, 537, 605–606, 623, 629, 635–637, 644, 655–658, 738–739, 750, 753–756, 758, 760, 768, 770–771, 808, 844, 863, 882, 893, 896, 903, 917, 938, 980, 1021–1023, 1026–1028, 1030–1033, 1035–1037
Heteroglossia 757–758
Homeostasis 863, 872, 879, 885
Humanism 473, 660, 672, 683, 741, 755–756, 1032
Humor 974

Iberian 501, 516–517, 933
Ich-Ton 227, 282, 299, 361, 481–482, 488, 863, 865–868, 870–871, 875–878, 880, 898
Idée fixe 987, 990–992, 994, 996–997
Identity 9, 26, 32–33, 35–37, 39, 46, 53, 76, 89, 111, 115, 117, 142, 152–153, 177, 181, 186, 190, 192, 195, 199, 206, 211–214, 216–219, 238–239, 253, 292, 298, 309, 322, 328, 338–339, 345, 354, 363, 365, 367–368, 403, 408–410, 420, 422–424, 427–428, 443, 459, 461, 463, 467, 471, 475–476, 478, 483–485, 501–505, 507, 509, 511–515, 517–519, 525, 527–528, 530, 533, 536, 542, 558, 576, 582, 601, 603, 645, 651, 656–657, 660, 664, 667, 681–682, 685, 688–696, 704, 744, 746, 749–750, 753, 757, 761–764, 767–768, 770, 777, 782, 802, 848, 850, 854, 857, 860, 863, 866–867, 873–877, 879, 897–899, 904–905, 908–910, 915–916, 922, 926–927, 931, 933, 947–948, 952, 999, 1001–1004, 1006–1010, 1018, 1021, 1024, 1029
Illumination 15–16, 26–27, 32, 534, 708, 731, 753, 787, 795
Imperfection 111, 141, 154, 169, 273, 284, 621–622, 685, 687, 689, 691, 694–695, 697
Information 19–20, 30, 34, 85, 108–109, 128, 171, 202, 208–209, 212, 218, 243, 253–254, 258, 264, 292, 303, 356, 364, 378, 383, 387, 424, 437, 444, 457, 468, 470, 475, 493, 609, 645, 703, 716, 727, 750–751, 871, 885, 895, 904, 962, 964, 978, 1026, 1031, 1035
Intentionality 36–37, 144, 146, 150, 183–184, 187–188, 190, 195, 199, 204–205, 220, 283, 332, 525, 529, 614, 713, 719, 776, 863–864, 870, 875, 880
interactionism 405–406, 409, 412, 414, 422–423
Intonation 37–41, 43, 527, 600, 762, 801, 810, 814, 871, 874, 907
Irrationality 15, 24, 28, 31–32, 419, 742
Islamic 502, 516, 539–540, 542, 546, 554, 556

Japan 181, 183, 185, 187, 189, 191, 193, 195, 197, 551, 1030

Kalevala 167, 176, 178, 623–630, 632–635, 637–638, 640, 642–643, 647, 649, 652, 655–657, 1032

Langue 36–38, 120, 244, 519, 692, 696, 801, 954
Lebenswelt 204, 211, 225–231, 233, 235–237, 239, 241, 243, 245, 247–248, 296, 332, 406, 412, 420, 819
Lifeworld 56, 112, 204, 211, 216, 225, 227–228, 230–232, 237, 357–358, 363, 370–371, 461, 465, 797
Local 19, 31, 173, 178, 286, 336, 390, 441, 450, 460–461, 466, 472–473, 475–476, 525, 529, 536, 583, 624, 626, 705, 750, 907, 919, 921–922, 924–927, 949, 952, 990, 1025–1026
ludification 567–571, 573–577

Mannerism 579–580, 582, 1009
Marxism 43, 46, 315, 489
Masculine 397, 534, 550–551, 632, 757, 759–765, 767–769, 771, 903, 1010, 1016
Mass media 3, 128, 882, 894, 980
Mathematics 15–16, 26, 28–31, 111, 171, 233, 279, 1028
Melancholy 398, 521, 530–531, 579, 582, 587–589, 591–594, 596–598, 674, 681, 760, 985, 1027, 1030
Melody 1, 26, 93, 158, 165, 171, 176, 290, 379, 484–485, 487, 532, 632, 640, 662, 665, 675, 681, 857–858, 873, 903, 919–921, 924, 926–927, 929, 932, 934–936, 938–939, 947–950, 966, 987, 991–992, 994–996
Memory 79, 85, 96, 108, 117–118, 160, 177, 203, 212, 218, 221, 230, 239, 250, 283, 291–293, 295–296, 304, 306–307, 343–351, 384, 395, 427, 457, 508, 522, 525, 527–537, 600, 608, 694, 713, 717, 741–755, 810, 817, 890, 892, 904, 917, 921, 927, 979, 986, 990–991, 993, 996, 1029
Metaphor 12, 15, 23–25, 33–34, 65, 85–86, 164, 173, 178, 190–191, 194, 254, 260, 278, 292, 345, 395, 401, 431–432, 438, 463, 473, 478, 491–493, 510, 512–513, 516, 523–524, 528, 541, 569, 571, 573, 623, 628, 631, 638, 654, 677, 685, 688, 692, 694–696, 712, 720, 723, 747, 751, 753, 760, 768, 886, 900, 919, 922, 924, 928, 935, 937, 975, 998

Metaphysics 48–49, 55, 67, 71, 75–76, 79, 82, 94, 96, 158, 160, 187, 190, 196, 203, 229–230, 245, 275, 281–282, 287, 464, 708, 935, 1030, 1032
Mimesis 44–46, 215, 425, 894, 979, 1011, 1013, 1019
Mind 6, 20, 26, 33, 71, 79, 81, 86, 99, 106, 108–109, 112–114, 116, 132–133, 164, 182, 184–186, 197, 199, 201–203, 206–210, 212, 215, 217, 219–221, 237, 240, 243–244, 259–263, 265–267, 269–271, 273, 275, 280, 290, 292–294, 296, 298–301, 306–311, 313–316, 318, 324, 329, 331, 333, 337, 350, 354, 356–363, 365–366, 368–369, 373, 377, 381–382, 384–385, 388, 391–392, 425, 431, 434, 441, 443, 446, 451, 460, 463, 486, 491, 499, 522–523, 526–529, 535, 554, 576, 588, 595–596, 602–605, 623–624, 630, 641, 647, 651, 654–655, 657, 664, 668, 672, 691, 699, 703, 708, 721, 731, 742–743, 745–747, 758, 760, 762, 765, 768, 780, 784, 787, 800, 813, 854, 882, 890, 894, 904, 907, 912, 943, 966, 975, 1035
Minimalism 162, 659–662, 666, 671, 682
Modelling 107, 143, 233–236, 246, 279, 331, 567–568, 570–571, 576, 806, 894
Moi/Soi 10, 77, 299, 306, 527
Monadology 83
Monde naturel 663
Moor 501–502, 504, 506–508, 510–514, 516–517, 520
Music 1, 5–7, 9, 15, 27, 39, 44, 78, 82–83, 91–94, 97, 137, 157–161, 163–181, 197, 214, 217, 223, 249, 257, 259–271, 325, 343–347, 349–351, 353–367, 369–371, 390, 394, 398, 403, 436, 456, 481, 483–487, 489–490, 504, 520–522, 530–532, 537, 618, 623–624, 631–633, 635, 637–638, 640–641, 644, 647, 651, 655–671, 673–683, 726, 731, 739, 742, 744, 747, 749, 752–753, 755, 771, 801–811, 813, 815–817, 819, 822–823, 825–826, 829–831, 833–842, 844, 849, 855, 861–865, 867, 869, 871–875, 877–879, 881–893, 895–907, 911,

1054 — Subject index

913–917, 919–929, 931–933, 935–939, 942, 947, 949–955, 957–970, 972–981, 983–991, 994–995, 997–1001, 1003, 1008, 1010–1011, 1013–1014, 1017–1020, 1022–1026, 1029–1036
Music criticism 985, 988, 1023
Musical semiotics 160–161, 163, 166, 179, 181, 260–262, 269–270, 351, 371, 683, 771, 801, 806–808, 815–817, 819–820, 822–823, 826, 828, 835, 863, 882, 886, 888, 895–896, 903, 934–935, 938, 949, 981, 998, 1023, 1026, 1029, 1033, 1035–1036
Musical topoi 959–962, 965, 991–992
Musicology 92, 161, 249, 257, 259–263, 267, 271, 371, 656, 742, 801, 807, 809, 813–815, 835, 838, 861, 882, 884, 893, 960, 980, 998, 1023–1026, 1028–1029, 1031, 1033–1036
Musiklichkeit 819–820, 830–831, 833–834, 837–838, 841–842
Muslims 502, 506, 511, 516, 544, 546, 549, 553
Myth 31, 34, 157–159, 164, 166–182, 233–234, 249, 268, 271, 341, 403, 409, 419–421, 425–426, 432, 495, 522–523, 525, 529, 549, 555–556, 559, 568, 575, 586, 623–626, 629–631, 635, 638, 640, 646, 652–653, 656–658, 742, 748, 753, 766, 779, 788, 806, 815, 890, 899–900, 936, 938, 961, 967, 1032, 1035

Naming 107, 409–411, 420, 424, 603, 720, 900, 965
Narrative grammar 125, 134, 137, 140, 143, 809
Narrative program 503, 851, 853
Nationalism 117, 471, 751, 754, 901, 933
Negation 4, 8, 16, 85, 95, 193, 195, 215, 217–218, 237, 239, 318, 321–322, 324, 330, 348–349, 364, 369, 379, 382, 415–416, 449, 454, 456, 462, 471, 483, 485–486, 488, 491, 499, 527, 541, 574, 601, 607, 611–613, 616, 618–619, 621, 659–660, 664–665, 676, 687, 706–707, 727, 733, 737, 753, 766, 774–775, 777–778, 786–787, 807, 814, 854–855, 857–858, 970–971, 973

Neosemiotics 214, 239, 526, 934
Neurophysiology 260
Nothingness 28–29, 139, 158, 185, 191–195, 197, 204, 223, 237, 246, 275, 283, 330, 379, 382–383, 415, 426, 432–433, 664–665, 676–677, 685–686, 706, 773–777, 785–787, 798, 858–859, 992

Ontogenetic 219, 343, 347–350
Ontology 8, 49, 70–72, 75, 101–102, 206, 223, 237, 246, 274, 281, 335, 341–342, 459–461, 464, 466–467, 469–470, 472–477, 479, 838, 1036
Opera 157, 161–164, 169, 257–258, 389, 396, 484–485, 487, 604, 630–631, 640–645, 648–651, 654, 665, 670, 743, 752–753, 831, 847–850, 853–856, 859–861, 873–874, 882, 895, 962, 974, 980, 988, 991, 998, 1000, 1013, 1020, 1025, 1033
Otherness 35, 37, 39, 41, 43, 45, 81, 113, 251, 253–254, 256, 258, 298, 408, 501, 512–513, 541, 585–586, 755, 778, 858, 860, 863–870, 873, 875–876, 888–889, 892, 894

Paris 7, 12–13, 33, 44–46, 77, 81, 84, 96, 128–129, 154–155, 166–167, 180, 221–223, 238, 244, 246, 258, 271, 325, 350–351, 387, 399, 402–403, 485, 489–490, 519, 576, 591, 593, 597–598, 622, 668–669, 682–683, 697, 702, 723, 738–739, 742, 745–746, 751, 755, 759–760, 768, 771, 806–808, 815–817, 820, 843–845, 850, 861–862, 903, 934, 938, 954, 979, 997–998, 1019, 1022, 1024–1025, 1027, 1033, 1035–1036
Paris school of semiotics 84, 238, 702, 934
Parole 36–38, 46, 120, 154, 843–844, 998, 1033
Passion 131, 138, 140, 149, 154, 231, 238, 244, 274, 318, 402, 462, 503–504, 511–512, 519, 523, 543, 556, 568, 572, 576, 586, 596, 617, 637, 648, 651, 767, 913, 968, 971, 985–987, 992–993, 1022, 1027
Performance 5–6, 93, 134, 155, 162–163, 184, 199, 216, 297, 356, 358–359, 361,

367, 407, 417, 420–421, 438, 448, 477, 481, 484, 487, 489, 510, 513, 537, 574, 633–634, 645, 666–667, 669, 674, 683, 785, 834, 890, 895, 897–899, 904–917, 933, 945, 953, 958, 980, 985, 987–988, 1001, 1003, 1019, 1025, 1031
Performatives 410
Persian 79, 552, 607–611, 613, 615, 617–619, 621, 1034
Phenomenology 7, 11–13, 50–51, 58, 74, 97, 112, 119, 123, 153, 182–183, 192, 196–197, 202–205, 221–222, 225–228, 230–232, 236–238, 241, 243–247, 281, 316, 325, 329–330, 341, 343, 348, 350, 406, 424, 473, 686, 708, 835, 882, 922, 1036–1037
Phenosemiotics 208
Phenosigns 216, 599
Photography 128, 616, 715, 920, 936
Phylogenetic 219, 343, 347, 349–350
Play 43, 61, 64, 66–67, 73, 93, 106, 137, 142, 150, 153, 159, 162, 165, 169, 176, 189, 250, 264, 289–291, 293, 298, 305, 307, 314, 322–324, 327, 329, 345, 377, 379, 391, 394, 414, 437, 453, 483, 567–577, 631–632, 650–651, 655–656, 663, 669–670, 676, 678, 705, 741–742, 744, 752–753, 773, 785, 787, 836, 864, 890, 895, 912–913, 941, 952, 963, 973, 987, 994–995, 1006–1007, 1010, 1016–1018, 1034–1035
Pluralism 53, 74, 76, 460, 466–469, 473–475, 478
Polyphonic novel 40–41, 43
Positivism 112, 373–374, 376, 387, 806, 885
post-Signs 2, 216, 346, 701, 780, 785, 821, 823–824, 834–836
Postmodernism 7, 122, 125–126, 467, 472, 683, 741–742, 745, 1027
Poststructuralism 490
Practice 5, 9, 39, 53, 59–61, 63, 66, 69, 73, 97, 112, 115, 120, 126, 128, 132–133, 135, 138, 146–147, 152, 162–163, 217, 222, 225, 231–232, 240, 247, 250, 253, 257, 274–277, 281, 287, 307, 310, 354, 357–361, 370, 376, 383, 390–391, 403, 406, 409, 413, 418, 422, 424–425, 428,

437, 440, 447, 464, 466–467, 469, 471–472, 475, 479, 481–482, 495–496, 498–499, 514, 525, 527–529, 539, 572, 612, 619, 621, 662, 682, 703–704, 711, 723, 749, 761, 765, 804, 827, 833, 842, 871, 892, 898–899, 904–905, 907, 910, 916, 922, 925–926, 933, 935–936, 949, 958, 962, 964, 983, 989, 1003, 1018, 1023, 1031, 1033
Pragmatic 31, 51–53, 56, 58–61, 67, 72–75, 119–120, 122–125, 160, 220, 242, 245, 264, 271, 274, 302, 406, 449, 468, 493, 504, 506, 574, 778, 799, 844, 885, 888, 945, 947, 1032
Praxis 86, 88–89, 127–128, 226, 249–251, 253–258, 275, 341–342, 416, 607, 619, 869
pre-Signs 2, 121–122, 216, 254, 271, 304, 344, 346–347, 371, 701, 775, 780, 784, 787, 792–793, 796, 821, 823, 837, 943
Primary modelling system 234–235, 246
Prosody 353–355, 363–365, 874, 1026
Psychoanalysis 18, 106, 139, 325, 369, 371, 389–393, 395, 397, 399, 401, 403, 594, 596–598, 746, 891, 1026, 1033
Psychology 1–2, 6, 15, 26, 33, 48, 78, 97, 116, 121, 135, 143, 182, 203, 213–214, 222–223, 228, 231, 245, 270–271, 279, 309–311, 313, 348, 403, 422, 427, 439, 478–480, 500, 606, 641, 651, 653, 771, 844, 848, 891, 917, 971, 1031, 1034–1036
Psychopathology 237, 245, 394, 398

Quantum physics 17–18

Realism 56, 59–61, 72, 75, 94, 460, 466, 468–469, 472, 474–475, 484, 637, 665, 770, 784, 790–791, 793, 902, 973, 1013, 1032
Reality 2, 18, 30, 33–36, 62, 64–65, 71, 73, 75, 79, 87–88, 94, 99, 101–106, 109, 112–114, 116–117, 124, 126–128, 136, 138, 141, 145, 147, 149, 165, 169, 182, 188, 190, 199, 202–203, 207–208, 213, 218, 221, 225, 233–237, 239, 241, 243–244, 248, 250–251, 255–257,

266–268, 270, 275, 278–280, 282–284, 286–287, 323, 337–338, 340, 355, 358, 363–364, 369, 371, 374, 383, 391–392, 396, 400, 422, 431, 433, 439–440, 444, 463, 468–469, 475, 483, 489, 493, 529–531, 533–535, 539, 575–576, 594, 599, 609–610, 612–613, 615, 620, 626, 641, 654, 673, 675, 685–686, 697, 699–701, 703–707, 709, 727, 741, 743–744, 746, 750–752, 759, 765, 774, 776–777, 779, 785–786, 789, 791–793, 817, 866, 871, 885, 892–895, 909, 935, 947, 966, 972, 990, 1002
renaissance 281, 427, 586, 588, 594–595, 597–598, 630, 634, 640, 888, 986, 1027
Resistance 4, 36, 81, 89, 99–118, 127, 151, 238, 289, 292–295, 305–307, 311, 381, 391, 419, 427, 432–433, 441, 449, 454, 456–457, 478, 511–513, 567–568, 573–575, 600, 635, 706, 708, 712–713, 741, 743, 746, 755–756, 776–778, 785, 893–894, 1001
Russian 10, 19, 43, 46, 234, 244–245, 282, 481–482, 484–488, 544–548, 550–551, 554, 556, 625, 628, 634, 745, 747, 897–898, 901–907, 910–912, 914–916, 973, 1026, 1030
Russian piano school 897–898, 904–905, 907, 910–912, 914

Saudade 521–537, 1029
Schizophrenia 319, 325, 396–398, 403, 547, 564
Secondness 103, 105, 162, 275, 277, 291, 294, 301, 304, 306–307, 382, 600–601, 708
Self 2, 6, 8, 15–16, 19–22, 25, 33–34, 40, 44–45, 50, 53, 56–59, 74, 76, 83, 90–92, 105, 115, 127, 140, 142, 144, 150, 182–186, 189, 191–194, 197, 199–200, 202–203, 205–206, 208–213, 215–220, 222–223, 231–232, 235, 238–240, 242–243, 246, 257, 278–279, 281–287, 289–304, 306–310, 316, 327–331, 334, 338–339, 341, 354–358, 360–366, 368–369, 380–381, 384, 386, 395, 400, 408–409, 414–417, 421, 425, 427, 434, 437, 448, 450, 452, 459, 461–463, 465, 469, 471–472, 476–478, 482, 504–505, 511, 526–527, 530, 548, 571, 588, 594, 599, 601–605, 627, 631, 652–653, 667–668, 672, 675, 681, 706, 708, 761, 774, 778, 783, 787–789, 791–793, 795, 800, 823, 827, 854, 863, 868, 872, 874, 876, 878–879, 887, 897–898, 908–909, 917, 986, 994–995, 1002, 1004–1006
Semiocrisis 3–4, 429, 431–434, 440, 449, 567–568, 573, 575, 741–742, 749–750, 754, 894
Semiosis 1–2, 6, 28–29, 35, 77, 99, 101, 106–110, 112, 117, 119, 123, 125, 209, 215, 221, 250–251, 253, 264, 266, 270, 275–279, 281–283, 289, 291, 293–295, 297–309, 311, 327–329, 331, 333, 335, 337, 339, 341, 344–346, 351, 355, 361, 365, 367, 369, 373–375, 377, 379–387, 391, 398, 456, 574, 599, 604–605, 663, 754–755, 787–789, 792, 807–808, 821, 824, 836, 883, 887–888, 892–893, 896, 908, 915, 943, 1031
Semiosphere 4, 162, 232, 234–235, 245, 282, 328, 517, 567–568, 570–571, 573, 623–624, 741, 746, 752
Semiotic square 1, 7–8, 172, 181, 194–195, 239–240, 278, 463, 501, 528, 571, 600, 701–703, 706, 807–808, 811, 876, 908, 910, 934, 957, 959, 966, 969, 971–973, 978–979
Sexuality 395, 430, 573, 721, 757, 761–762, 767
Situation 3, 8, 18–19, 21–22, 24–25, 36, 62, 71, 78, 86, 90–91, 107, 111–113, 115, 117, 122–123, 127, 131–137, 140, 143–144, 152, 169, 184, 188, 191, 203–204, 212–213, 216, 228, 231, 249–254, 256–259, 261–269, 271, 274–275, 291, 293, 295, 304–305, 337, 339, 351, 355, 358, 360, 364–366, 368–369, 380, 383–384, 395, 398–400, 406–407, 411, 413, 429–432, 434, 436, 444, 446–447, 459–460, 462, 467–468, 475, 483–486, 491, 516, 525, 583–584, 590–591, 593, 600, 605, 627, 650, 689, 696, 702, 708, 718, 727, 731–732, 736–737, 741–742,

Subject index — **1057**

745, 749, 762–763, 765–766, 768–769, 774, 778, 785, 797, 823–824, 834, 841–842, 844, 858–861, 869, 873–875, 880, 890, 934, 936, 971–972, 986, 992, 1003
Sociology 249, 273, 310, 378, 410, 412, 421–427, 471, 479, 481–483, 485–487, 489, 541, 576, 658, 894, 1023, 1026, 1036
Solipsism 69, 74–75, 124, 127, 263, 266–267, 270, 866, 1032
Sonata 91, 632, 803, 811–812, 814, 903, 912–913, 990
Soul 26, 33, 47–49, 54, 84–85, 124, 175, 201, 339, 491, 499, 521–523, 530, 543–544, 638, 642–643, 654, 708, 732, 750, 760, 770, 774, 776, 780, 782, 793, 856, 859–860, 976
Soundtrack 659, 661, 663, 665, 667–669, 671, 673, 675, 677–679, 681, 683, 962
Spain 36–37, 44, 502, 517, 520, 999–1000, 1005, 1019
Speech act 15, 21–22, 34, 220, 410
Sublimation 38, 77, 80–81, 83, 85, 87, 89, 189, 240, 334, 389, 394–395, 398–399, 889
Sublime 68, 593, 598, 608, 612, 617, 619–621, 861, 903, 934, 972–974, 978, 988
Substance 55, 77, 80–86, 88–91, 93–94, 185, 201, 280, 284, 361, 779, 790, 872, 890
Symphony 93, 172, 178–179, 389–390, 395, 400, 402–403, 656, 749, 811, 814, 902–904, 921, 926–928, 930–931, 936, 945, 949, 953, 957–960, 962, 967–970, 972, 974–976, 978–980, 984–985, 991, 995, 998, 1023
Synesthesia 344–345, 348

Taoism 186, 190
Theater 234, 484, 569, 1034
Theology 10, 54–55, 60, 499, 1030
Therapy 343, 353–354, 356, 358–359, 369, 371, 392, 401, 758
Thermodynamics 19–20, 377–378

Thirdness 162, 275, 277, 291, 293–294, 298, 300–302, 304, 306–307, 376, 378–379, 382, 386, 601, 708
Thymic 182, 591, 813, 971, 980
Topics 9, 12, 162, 206, 266, 324, 443, 514, 528, 568, 608, 714, 752, 810–811, 814, 816, 861, 893–894, 902, 924, 936, 959–961, 963–965, 977, 980, 988, 1018, 1022, 1026, 1031
Topos 185, 191, 510, 513, 585–587, 960–963, 965, 967–968, 972, 978, 986, 990, 992
Traditionalism 460, 466–467, 471–472, 474, 476, 479
Tragical 518, 973–974
Transcendent 27, 35–36, 40, 47–75, 95, 144–145, 166, 194, 241, 313–314, 347, 380–381, 386, 462–464, 475, 491, 493, 497, 541–542, 550, 552, 563–564, 572, 603, 699, 707–709, 711, 713, 715, 717, 719, 721, 723, 746, 786, 859–860, 867, 970, 972, 974, 976, 990
Transcendental 1, 4, 47–77, 85–86, 96, 174, 183, 202–205, 214–216, 222, 226–227, 230, 236, 245, 251, 256, 300, 308, 317, 348, 357–358, 360, 362, 364, 366–367, 371, 380–384, 386, 391–392, 462–465, 488–489, 491, 493, 523, 527, 535, 540–541, 545, 563, 599, 602–603, 608, 613, 615, 652–654, 686, 688–689, 694, 707, 709, 727, 731, 773–780, 782, 784–788, 792–793, 796–798, 806, 858, 863–865, 867, 872, 879–880, 882–883, 894, 917, 935, 972, 1032
Transcription 40, 179, 505, 508–509, 551, 920, 929, 941–943, 945, 948, 953, 955, 1000, 1022, 1024
Trauma 646, 651, 654, 742, 748–751, 754
Triangle 107, 284, 346–347
Truth 5, 9, 54, 56, 58–59, 62, 77, 88, 95, 99–101, 103, 105, 107, 109, 111–115, 117–118, 124, 158, 165, 189–191, 193–194, 202–204, 212, 218, 221, 280–281, 286, 314–317, 322, 373–375, 377, 379–381, 383–384, 386, 402, 468–469, 477, 531, 545, 565, 670, 699, 702, 706–707, 729, 731, 753, 766, 774,

780, 782, 786, 790, 792, 794, 826, 841, 935, 972–973, 976, 978, 1032
Tychism 276–278, 280

Umwelt 9, 210–211, 225–227, 229–231, 233, 235–237, 239, 241, 243, 245, 247–248, 278–280, 282–285, 289, 293–294, 296–297, 299–305, 307–308, 330, 332, 342, 481, 488–489, 864–865, 868–870, 886, 898, 1036
Understanding 1, 6, 10–12, 20, 24, 30, 38–39, 44, 47–48, 50, 56, 59, 63, 75, 78, 85, 93, 116, 119, 122, 124, 143, 145, 147, 192, 201–202, 204, 206, 209, 212, 220, 222, 225–226, 228, 232, 237, 246, 260, 267–269, 279, 283, 287, 289, 298–299, 309–310, 313, 315–316, 318, 320–322, 325, 327, 329, 353, 360, 362–363, 366–367, 370, 378, 386, 414, 423, 443, 449, 453, 459, 472, 475, 477, 480, 528, 536–537, 541, 545–546, 601, 605, 642, 653, 672, 700, 705–706, 726, 738, 741–742, 744, 746–747, 752–755, 773, 777, 784–785, 789, 792–793, 795, 801, 809, 813, 815, 819–821, 823, 825–826, 828–829, 831–832, 834, 836–842, 844, 881, 883, 885–886, 888–889, 891, 895, 922–924, 927, 936, 962, 967, 983, 994, 997, 999, 1018, 1032

unendliche Melodie 848, 857
Universals 81, 102, 327, 329–337, 339, 341, 480

Violence 433, 497, 499, 545, 623–629, 631, 633, 635, 637–639, 641–647, 649, 651–655, 657, 712, 722–723, 969
Vocality 1003, 1016
Voice 6, 35–43, 45–46, 64, 67, 138, 147, 158, 175, 255, 311, 341, 359, 367, 376, 393, 480, 511, 518, 545, 594, 598, 627, 638, 653, 671–675, 678, 681–682, 721, 736, 745, 748, 753, 763, 766, 792, 834, 873, 890–891, 895, 901, 950, 973, 976–977, 980, 987, 990, 993, 996, 999, 1009–1010, 1014, 1016–1017, 1019, 1031

Z-graph 8–11
Zemic 77–97, 240, 313, 315–316, 318–324, 389–390, 397, 481–482, 491, 493, 495–498, 500, 513, 519, 527, 541, 571–573, 623, 627–628, 631, 652, 658, 703–704, 725, 737, 739, 757–759, 761–762, 768, 770, 894, 933–934, 937, 989, 999–1003, 1005, 1007–1011, 1013, 1015, 1017–1019
Zoosemiotics 7, 9–10, 13, 327, 330

www.ingramcontent.com/pod-product-compliance
Lightning Source LLC
Chambersburg PA
CBHW051548020526
44115CB00041B/2520